The Cambridge Dictionary of Sociology

Providing an authoritative and comprehensive overview of the classical and the contemporary, this volume is an indispensable guide to the vibrant and expanding field of sociology. Featuring over 600 entries, from concise definitions to discursive essays, written by leading international academics, the *Dictionary* offers a truly global perspective, examining both American and European traditions and approaches. Entries cover schools, theories, theorists, and debates, with substantial articles on all key topics in the field. While recognizing the richness of historical sociological traditions, the *Dictionary* also looks forward to new and evolving influences such as cultural change, genetics, globalization, information technologies, new wars, and terrorism. Most entries incorporate references for further reading, and a cross-referencing system enables easy access to related areas. This *Dictionary* is an invaluable reference work for students and academics alike and will help to define the field of sociology in years to come.

BRYAN S. TURNER is Professor of Sociology in the Asia Research Institute at the National University of Singapore, where he leads the research team for the Religion and Globalisation cluster. Prior to this, he was Professor of Sociology in the Faculty of Social and Political Sciences at the University of Cambridge. Professor Turner is the author of *The New Medical Sociology* (2004) and *Society and Culture: Principles of Scarcity and Solidarity* (with Chris Rojek, 2001), and is the founding editor of the *Journal of Classical Sociology* (with John O'Neill), *Body & Society* (with Mike Featherstone), and *Citizenship Studies*. He is currently writing a three-volume study on the sociology of religion for Cambridge University Press.

The
Cambridge Dictionary of
SOCIOLOGY

General Editor

BRYAN S. TURNER

CAMBRIDGE
UNIVERSITY PRESS

CAMBRIDGE UNIVERSITY PRESS

Cambridge, New York, Melbourne, Madrid, Cape Town, Singapore, São Paulo

Cambridge University Press
The Edinburgh Building, Cambridge CB2 2RU, UK

Published in the United States of America by Cambridge University Press, New York

www.cambridge.org
Information on this title: www.cambridge.org/9780521540469

First published 2006

Printed in the United Kingdom at the University Press, Cambridge

A catalogue record for this book is available from the British Library

ISBN-13 978-0-521-83290-8 hardback
ISBN-10 0-521-83290-X hardback
ISBN-13 978-0-521-54046-9 paperback
ISBN-10 0-521-54046-1 paperback

To the memory of my parents Sophia Turner (née Brookes) and
Stanley W. Turner

Contents

THE DICTIONARY

List of contributors

Gabriel Abend, *Northwestern University*
Gary L. Albrecht, *University of Illinois, Chicago*
Jeffrey Alexander, *Yale University*
Tomas Almaguer, *San Francisco State University*
Patrick Baert, *University of Cambridge*
Jack Barbalet, *University of Leicester*
James Beckford, *University of Warwick*
Stephen Benard, *Cornell University*
Michael Billig, *Loughborough University*
Mildred Blaxter, *University of Bristol*
Mick Bloor, *University of Glasgow*
William A. Brown, *University of Cambridge*
Brendan J. Burchell, *University of Cambridge*
Stewart Clegg, *University of Technology, Sydney*
Elizabeth F. Cohen, *Syracuse University*
Ira Cohen, *Rutgers University*
Oonagh Corrigan, *University of Plymouth*
Rosemary Crompton, *City University, London*
Sean Cubitt, *The University of Waikato, New Zealand*
Tom Cushman, *Wellesley College*
Tia DeNora, *University of Exeter*
Peter Dickens, *University of Cambridge*
Michele Dillon, *University of New Hampshire*
S. N. Eisenstadt, *The Jerusalem Van Leer Institute*
Tony Elger, *University of Warwick*
Anthony Elliott, *Flinders University of South Australia*
Amitai Etzioni, *The Communitarian Network, Washington*
Mary Evans, *University of Kent*
Ron Eyerman, *Yale University*
James D. Faubion, *Rice University*
Janie Filoteo, *Texas A & M University*
Gary Alan Fine, *Northwestern University*
David Frisby, *London School of Economics*
Loraine Gelsthorpe, *University of Cambridge*
Julian Go, *Boston University*
David Good, *University of Cambridge*
Philip Goodman, *University of California, Irvine*
Susan Hansen, *Murdoch University*

Bernadette Hayes, *University of Aberdeen*
Chris Haywood, *University of Newcastle upon Tyne*
John Heritage, *University of California, Los Angeles*
John Hoffman, *University of Leicester*
John Holmwood, *University of Sussex*
Robert Holton, *Trinity College, Dublin*
Darnell Hunt, *University of California, Los Angeles*
Geoffrey Ingham, *University of Cambridge*
Engin Isin, *York University, Canada*
Andrew Jamison, *Aalborg University*
Valerie Jenness, *University of California, Irvine*
Bob Jessop, *Lancaster University*
James E. Katz, *Rutgers University*
Douglas Kellner, *University of California, Los Angeles*
Krishan Kumar, *University of Virginia*
John Law, *Lancaster University*
Charles Lemert, *Wesleyan University*
Donald N. Levine, *University of Chicago*
Ruth Lister, *Loughborough University*
Steven Loyal, *University College, Dublin*
Mairtin Mac-an-Ghaill, *University of Birmingham*
Michael Macy, *Cornell University*
Jeff Manza, *Northwestern University*
Robert Miller, *Queen's University, Belfast*
Jan Pakulski, *University of Tasmania*
Edward Park, *Loyola Marymount University*
Frank Pearce, *Queen's University, Canada*
Emile Perreau-Saussine, *University of Cambridge*
Chris Phillipson, *Keele University*
Gianfranco Poggi, *Università di Trento, Italy*
Dudley L. Poston,[*] *Texas A & M University*
Stephen Quilley, *University College, Dublin*
Mark Rapley, *Edith Cowan University*
Larry Ray, *University of Kent at Canterbury*
Isaac Reed, *Yale University*
Thomas Reifer, *University of San Diego*
Derek Robbins, *University of East London*
Chris Rojek, *Nottingham Trent University*
Mercedes Rubio, *American Sociological Association*

*Dudley Poston wishes to thank the following graduate students for their assistance: Mary Ann Davis, Chris Lewinski, Hua Luo, Heather Terrell and Li Zhang.

Rogelio Saenz, *Texas A & M University*
Kent Sandstrom, *University of Northern Iowa*
Cornel Sandvoss, *University of Surrey*
Jacqueline Schneider, *University of Leicester*
Jackie Scott, *University of Cambridge*
Martin Shaw, *University of Sussex*
Mark Sherry, *The University of Toledo*
Birte Siim, *Aalborg University, Denmark*
Susan Silbey, *Massachusetts Institute of Technology*
Carol Smart, *University of Manchester*
Vicki Smith, *University of California, Davis*
Nick Stevenson, *University of Nottingham*
Rob Stones, *University of Essex*
Richard Swedberg, *Cornell University*

Piotr Sztompka, *Jagiellonian University, Poland*
Edward Tiryakian, *Duke University*
Kenneth H. Tucker, Jr., *Mount Holyoke College, MA*
Bryan S. Turner, *National University of Singapore*
Jonathan Turner, *University of California, Riverside*
Stephen P. Turner, *University of South Florida*
Arnout van de Rijt, *Cornell University*
Ann Vogel, *University of Exeter*
Frederic Volpi, *University of St. Andrews*
Alan Warde, *University of Manchester*
Darin Weinberg, *University of Cambridge*
Andrew Wernick, *Trent University, Canada*
Kevin White, *The Australian National University*
Fiona Wood, *Cardiff University*

Acknowledgments

I would like to thank Sarah Caro, formerly Senior Commissioning Editor in Social Sciences at Cambridge University Press, for her tireless and cheerful commitment to this *Dictionary*, and her enthusiasm for the project of sociology as a whole. Her quiet determination to get the job done provided me with an enduring role model. More recently, John Haslam has effectively seen this project to a conclusion. Juliet Davis-Berry of the Press worked unstintingly to get lists, entries, and authors organized. Carrie Cheek has provided generous and careful secretarial and editorial support in collecting entries, corresponding with authors, overseeing corrections, and dealing with my mistakes. Without her ongoing support, the *Dictionary* would not have been completed. Leigh Mueller worked with extraordinary vigilance to correct the proofs of the *Dictionary* and to impose some standard of excellence on often wayward English.

The editorial board members – Ira Cohen, Jeff Manza, Gianfranco Poggi, Beth Schneider, Susan Silbey, and Carol Smart – contributed to the development of the list of entries, read and re-read draft entries, and made substantial contributions of their own. Ira Cohen, in particular, wrote major entries, advised authors, and recruited his daughter as a contributor. The authors kindly responded to criticism and correction of their draft submissions with considerable tolerance. Many authors struggled with major illness, family breakdown, and the sheer cussedness of everyday life to complete entries on time. The following authors wrote many additional and extensive essays, often at the last minute to fill in gaps caused by entries that were missing for a variety of reasons, and I am especially grateful to them: Stewart Clegg, Tony Elgar, Mary Evans, Susan Hansen, John Hoffman, John Holmwood, Charles Lemert, Steven Loyal, Stephen Quilley, Mark Rapley, Larry Ray, Darin Weinberg, and Kevin White. The *Dictionary* is, in short, a genuinely collective effort. However, any remaining errors and omissions are my responsibility.

Introduction

At one level, sociology is easy to define. It is the study of social institutions – the family, religion, sport, community, and so on. We can study institutions at the micro-level by looking at interactions between family members, for example, or we can examine macro-relations such as the family and kinship system of a society as a whole. Below this level of minimal agreement, there is considerable dispute as to what sociology really is, and during the twentieth century and into this century many critics of sociology have periodically pronounced it to be in crisis or to be moribund. It is said to be prone to jargon, or it is claimed by its critics to be merely common sense. A natural scientist at my former Cambridge college, on hearing that I was editing a dictionary of sociology, inquired in all seriousness whether there would be enough concepts and terms for a whole dictionary. My problem as editor has by contrast been the question of what to leave out. In this context of lay skepticism, a dictionary of sociology is in part a defense of the discipline from its detractors, and in part a statement of its achievements and prospects. It aims to give a precise, informative, and objective account of the discipline, including both its successes and failures, and in this sense dictionaries are inherently conservative. A dictionary seeks to give an informed guide to a particular field such that both the expert and the student can benefit intellectually.

In many respects, part of the problem for sociology as an academic discipline lies in its very success. An outsider to the academy at the end of the nineteenth century, sociology is now influential in archaeology, the arts, the history and philosophy of science, science and technology studies, religious studies, organizational theory, and in the teaching of general practice and community medicine in medical faculties, where the social dimension of everyday reality is now taken for granted. The study of contemporary epidemics in public health, especially the AIDS/HIV epidemic, has employed sociological insights into networks and risk taking. The management of any future pandemic will draw upon sociological research on social networks, compliance behavior, and the impact of such factors as social class, gender, and age on prevalence rates. Other areas such as art history and aesthetics often draw implicitly on sociological notions of audiences, art careers, art markets, and cultural capital. Science and technology studies more explicitly depend on the sociology of knowledge. Dance studies frequently adopt insights and perspectives from the sociology of the body. It is often difficult to distinguish between historical sociology, social history and world-systems theory. Cultural studies, women's studies, and disability studies have drawn extensively on debates of social construction in sociology. Activists

in social movements in support of disability groups have directly adopted sociological ideas about how disability as a social construct involves the curtailment
of social rights. Ethnomethodology – the study of the methods or practices that
are important in accomplishing tasks in the everyday world – has contributed to
research on how people use complex machinery in workplace settings. Conversational analysis has been important in understanding how conversations
take place, for example between doctor and patient. The emerging area of
terrorism studies will no doubt have a substantial input from sociologists on
recruitment patterns, beliefs, and social background. In short, there has been
a great dispersion and proliferation of the sociological paradigm into adjacent
fields and disciplines. Much of this intellectual dispersion or seepage has
practical consequences.

The danger is, however, that the sociological perspective will, as a result of
this intellectual leakage, simply dissolve into cultural studies, film studies,
media studies, and so forth. Sociological insights and approaches have been
successfully dispersed through the humanities and science curricula, but the
intellectual connections with sociology are not always recognized or indeed
understood. The contemporary enthusiasm for multidisciplinarity and interdisciplinarity often obscures the need to preserve basic disciplines. Although
this dispersal of sociology into various areas within the humanities and social
science curricula is satisfying in some respects, it is important to defend a
sociological core, if sociology is to survive as a coherent and valid discipline.
The idea of defending a "canon" has become somewhat unfashionable. In
literary studies, the problem of the canonical authority of the received great
texts has been a crucial issue in English literature since the publication of, for
example, F. R. Leavis's *The Great Tradition* in 1948. The idea of a sociological
canon has been attacked by feminism and postmodernism for being too
exclusive and narrow, but a canonical tradition does not have to be unduly
narrow or parochial, and students need to understand how sociology developed, who contributed to its growth, and where contemporary concepts
emerged historically. I would contend further that classical sociology, when
generously defined, remains relevant to understanding the contemporary
world. The study of "the social" remains the basis of the discipline, where
the social is constituted by institutions. Where the intellectual roots of
the discipline are ignored, the strong program of sociology as an autonomous
discipline is eroded. A dictionary of sociology is an attempt to (re)state the
principal theories and findings of the discipline, and thereby inevitably contributes to the definition of a canon. Sociology remains, however, a critical
discipline, which constantly questions its origins and its evolution.

Of course, in many respects, sociology is not a homogeneous or seamless
discipline. It has always been somewhat fragmented by different traditions,
epistemologies, values, and methodologies. Sociological theories and ideas are
perhaps more open to contestation and dispute, precisely because their social
and political implications are radical. A dictionary of sociology has to articulate the coherence of the subject, and at the same time fully to recognize its

diversity. For example, one major division in sociology has been between the American and the European traditions. The basic difference is that sociology in America became thoroughly professionalized with a strong association (the American Sociological Association), a variety of professional journals, a clear apprenticeship process prior to tenure, and a reward system of prizes and honors. In Europe, professional associations have not been able to establish an agreed core of theory, methods, and substantive topics. While European sociology defines its roots in the classical tradition of Marx, Durkheim, Weber, and Simmel, American sociology more often sees its origins in the applied sociology of the Chicago School, in pragmatism, and in symbolic interactionism. American sociology has favored empiricism, pragmatism, and social psychology over European sociology, which has its foundations in the Enlightenment, the humanism of Auguste Comte, the political economy of Marx, and the critical theory of Adorno and Horkheimer. We should not overstate this division. There have been important figures in sociology, who, to some extent, have bridged the gap between the two traditions – C. Wright Mills, Talcott Parsons, Peter Berger, Neil Smelser, and more recently Jeffrey Alexander and Anthony Giddens. W. E. B. Du Bois was trained in both American and European traditions. Nevertheless the divisions are real and these historical differences have been, if anything, reinforced in recent years by the fact that European sociology has been more exposed to postmodernism, deconstruction, and poststructuralism than has the American tradition. In negative terms, European sociology has been more subject to rapid changes in fashions in social theory. Pragmatism, social reform, and applied sociology in America have been seen as an alternative to the excessive theoretical nature of European thought. While Adorno and Horkheimer saw American empiricism as the worst form of traditional theory, the Marxist revival in the 1960s and 1970s in Europe had little lasting impact in America. Talcott Parsons's sociology in fact never gained dominance in American sociology, partly because *The Structure of Social Action* was too European. More recently the pragmatist revival in America – for example in the social philosophy of Richard Rorty – has attempted to show once more that American social theory does not need any European inspiration. Recent European debates have not had much impact on mainstream American sociology. Two illustrations are important. The development of cultural studies that has been influential in British sociology, around the work of Richard Hoggart, Raymond Williams, Stuart Hall, and the Birmingham School, has had relatively little consequence in mainstream American sociology. The debate around Ulrich Beck's notion of risk society and the theory of individualization has not extended much beyond Europe.

In this new *Cambridge Dictionary of Sociology*, I have attempted to cover both American and European traditions by ensuring that the editorial board and the authors reflect these different approaches, and that the entries have afforded ample recognition of the richness of these different perspectives. Entries therefore attempt to provide a more global coverage of sociology by attending to these differences rather than obscuring or denying them. The

Dictionary examines key intellectual figures in both European and American sociology, and also reflects different substantive, theoretical, and methodological perspectives. Although there are important differences that are the product of separate historical developments, the *Dictionary* also looks forward to new influences that are the common concerns of sociologists everywhere.

What are these new developments in sociology that the *Cambridge Dictionary* attempts to address? First, there is the debate about globalization itself. Sociologists have been concerned with two significant aspects of this process, namely the globalization of trade and finance following the collapse of the Bretton Woods agreements and the rise of the Washington consensus, and the development of technology and software that made possible global communication in an expanding economy. Sociologists have examined a variety of substantial changes relating to globalization, such as diasporic communities, global migration, fundamentalism, and the rise of the global city. Various theoretical responses to these changes are also fairly obvious. The analysis of risk society itself can be seen as a sociological response to the uncertain social consequences of economic globalization. Another development is the use of social capital theory to look at the social impact of global disorganization and economic inequality on individual health and illness. While the original foundations of globalization theory were explored in economics and politics (for example the global governance debate), sociologists have become to some extent more interested in cultural globalization in terms of mass media and cultural imperialism. As a result of globalization, sociologists have been exercised by the possibility of new forms of cosmopolitanism, and whether a cosmopolitan ethic can transform the character of sociology. These debates and concepts are fully represented in this *Dictionary*.

One important aspect of globalization has been a revival of the sociological study of religion. In the 1960s the sociology of religion was especially dominant, partly through the influence of sociologists such as Peter Berger, Thomas Luckmann, Bryan Wilson, and David Martin. However, as the secularization thesis became dominant, the intellectual fortunes of the sociology of religion declined. In American sociology, the study of cults and new religious movements was important, but the sociology of religion was no longer influential in sociology as a whole, and it was not at the cutting edge of sociological theory. The globalization process has given rise to a revival of the sociology of religion, especially in the study of fundamentalism. In this respect, the work of Roland Robertson on (cultural and religious) globalization has been particularly influential. Here again, however, there are important differences between America and Europe, because American sociology has been much more influenced by the applications of rational choice theory to religious behavior, giving rise to the notion of a "spiritual marketplace." Whereas European societies have experienced a history of religious decline in terms of church attendance and membership, religion in America has remained an influential aspect of public life. The "new paradigm" in American sociology of religion has taken notice of the "supply side" of religion, where competition in the religious market has expanded religious choice and fostered a buoyant spiritual marketplace.

It is obvious that 9/11, and the subsequent "war on terrorism," have had and will continue to have a large impact on sociology. This political and military crisis demonstrated that the largely positive views of global society that were characteristic of the early stages of the study of globalization, for example on world democracy and governance, were somewhat one-sided, premature, and indeed utopian. The brave new world order had come to a sudden end. Global uncertainty was reinforced by the Afghan war, the war in Iraq, and the more general war on Al-Qaeda; and these world events have opened a new chapter in the history of sociological thought – the sociology of global terrorism. The bombings in Bali, Madrid, and London demonstrated the global nature of modern terrorism. We might argue that the sociology of globalization has, as it were, taken a dark turn. There is growing awareness of the need to study the global sex industry, including pornography, child sex abuse, sexual tourism, and the wider issues of slavery and the trade in women. The war on terrorism has made the sociology of the media even more prominent, but it has also demonstrated that sociology has until recently ignored such prominent social phenomena as war, terrorism and violence, money and exchange, and religion, human rights and law. There is also greater awareness of the need for a new type of medical sociology that will examine the globalization of epidemics of which HIV/AIDS, SARS and avian flu are dramatic examples. Critics have argued that the "cultural turn" in sociology that gave rise to a new interest in cultural phenomena in everyday life and to new interpretative methods, from discourse analysis to deconstruction as a method of textual analysis, has resulted in the neglect of traditional but important social phenomena – social class, poverty, inequality, power, and racial conflict. One further consequence of 9/11 and 7/7 (the bombings in London) has been a growing disillusionment with multiculturalism, and many social scientists have proclaimed "the end of multiculturalism" and have identified the rise of the "new xenophobia" in western societies. Future research on race, ethnicity, and identity will be colored by the despairing, bleak mood of the first decade of the new millennium.

While sociologists have been interested in the social causes of fundamentalism in general, research on political Islam has been especially prominent in current sociological research. These recent developments have resulted in various re-evaluations of Max Weber's comparative sociology of religion. The debate about the relevance of the Protestant Ethic Thesis to Islam continues to interest sociologists, and there has also been much interest in the revival of Confucianism in Asia. There is, however, also recognition of the fact that we need new ways of thinking about modernization, secularization, and fundamentalism. The work of S. N. Eisenstadt in developing ideas about "multiple modernities" offers innovative theoretical strategies for sociological research. Globalization is therefore stimulating a rich arena of research in modern sociology, such as George Ritzer's work on McDonaldization, Manuel

Castells on the media, Martin Shaw on global military conflict, Thomas Cushman on global human rights, and David Martin on global Pentecostalism. This *Dictionary* provides substantial coverage of these issues, theories, and authors.

One major dimension of globalization is of course the expansion and transformation of media technology and information. Marshall McLuhan in the 1960s invented a variety of expressions to describe the arrival of a new age – in particular the idea of a global village. Every aspect of modern society has been revolutionized by these developments in communication and information – from "cybersex" and "telesurgery" to smart bombs. To understand the social changes that made possible the information society, there has been a revival of interest in technology. What had been rejected by Marxist sociology as "technological determinism" has become increasingly central to the sociological understanding of how the world is changing. Research on the impact of technology on spatial relationships, speed, and social networks can be seen in the growing interest in the idea of mobilities, social flows, and networks in the work of John Urry. The concern to understand technology has forced sociologists to think more creatively about how we interact with objects and networks between objects. The development of actor network theory has brought together spatial, technological, and science studies to understand the interactional relations between human beings and the world of objects. Many sociologists believe that these changes are so profound that a new type of sociology is required to analyze speed, mobility, and the compression of space. The "cultural turn" (a new emphasis on culture in modern society) was followed by the "spatial turn" (a new preoccupation with space, the global city, and urban design). In order to encompass these developments, the *Dictionary* has included many entries on information, communications, and mass media.

Technological change in modern society often involves a combination of information, genetics, computerization, and biomedicine. These developments in society have transformed the old debate about nature and nurture, and raised new issues about surveillance, individual freedoms, eugenics, and governmentality. The relationship between the human body, technology, and society has become increasingly complex, and the emergence of the sociology of the body can be regarded as one response to these intellectual, social, and legal developments. The ownership of the human body has become a major issue in legal conflicts over patients, patents, and profits. The early stages in the evolution of the sociology of the body were closely associated with feminism, the anthropology of Mary Douglas, and the work of Maurice Merleau-Ponty and Michel Foucault, but developments in micro-biology and information sciences are beginning to change these concerns with the body "as organism" to the body as "genetic map." These new challenges arising from the implications of genetics for human aging and reproduction have given rise to the possibility of what Francis Fukuyama has called "our posthuman future." This new intellectual confrontation between biology, informatics, and sociology has also produced a considerable re-assessment of the legacy of Charles Darwin, social Darwinism, and evolutionary thought. The social problems associated with the application of genetics have stimulated a renewed interest in the changing nature of reproduction, gender, and the family. Stem-cell research, therapeutic cloning, and regenerative medicine are changing the intellectual horizons of medical sociology, and are raising new questions (for example, can we live forever?) – for which we have no satisfactory answers.

A reassessment of the relationships between sociology and biology is recasting the old debate between education and endowment, and in turn forcing us to rethink sex, sexuality, and gender. In the 1960s and 1970s mainstream sociology often neglected feminist theory and gender. The debate about how to measure social class, for example, often failed to take into account the class position of women by concentrating exclusively on the class position of men in the formal labor market. In the 1970s and 1980s, feminist analysis flourished and the work of Juliet Mitchell, Kate Millett, Germaine Greer, Ann Oakley, and Shulamith Firestone had a comprehensive impact on sociological research. Although feminist thought was often fragmented into materialist, socialist, and postmodern versions, feminism gave rise to a rich legacy of social theory and empirical work. Sociology has also been influenced by sexual politics, debates about identity, and queer theory. These debates over gender, sex, and sexuality were heavily influenced by the debate around social construction, perhaps first clearly enunciated by Simone de Beauvoir's claim that women are created by society rather than by biology. Medical technology has transformed the conditions under which people reproduce and has produced new methods of reproduction that do not require sexual intercourse between men and women. These new reproductive technologies are forcing sociologists to re-think the social relations of biological reproduction.

The emergence of gender studies, women's studies, and gay and lesbian studies has often meant that traditional areas such as sociology of the family and marriage have been overshadowed by new questions and new foci of research. While contemporary sociologists explore gay and lesbian cultures, an older, perhaps more socially conservative, tradition, represented by the work of Peter Laslett, Peter Willmott, Michael Young, and Elizabeth Bott in Britain and by W. J. Goode in America, went into decline. This relative decline of the family as a key topic of research is ironic – given the alleged ideological dominance of heterosexuality ("heteronormativity") in mainstream society and in conventional sociology. We can imagine, however, that current sociological views of what constitutes gender and sexuality will have to change radically with changes in how humans reproduce through new reproductive technologies, surrogacy, same-sex marriages, "designer babies," and cloning. These developments constitute a considerable component of this *Dictionary*.

Alongside the sociology of the body, there has been an important development of the sociology of the emotions, where the work of Jack Barbalet has been particularly innovative. By drawing on the legacy of William James, Barbalet pushed the debate about emotions away from social psychology towards seeing emotions as the link between social structure and the social actor. His work reminds us of the connection between contemporary theories of emotion and the work of classical economists such as Adam Smith in *The Theory of Moral Sentiments* of 1759. The contemporary analysis of emotions needs to be understood as part of a legacy of classical sociology and the Enlightenment.

Another way of approaching these critical debates is through the influence of postmodernism. Because conventional sociology has been associated with the Enlightenment tradition and modernity, postmodern theory was seen as an attack on classical sociology. Thinkers such as Durkheim and Weber were held up to be the epitome of modern as opposed to postmodern social theory. There are at least two problems associated with these critical evaluations of classical sociology. They often fail to distinguish between postmodernity as a state of society (for example, as illustrated by flexibility in employment, the dominance of service industries, the growth of information technologies, the rise of consumerism, and the general decline of a post-Fordist economy) and postmodernism as a type of theory (which employs textual analysis, irony, bathos, essay form, and aphorism). We can therefore understand postmodernity without difficulty via sociological concepts (that are related to the theory of postindustrial society) without having to accept postmodern theory. Postmodern theory in Europe is still influential in the sociological analysis of culture and identity, and it was influential in the expansion of new methodologies that questioned the legacies of positivism and behaviorism. In the postwar period there was initially a dominant focus on survey data and quantitative analysis, but there has been a growing interest in qualitative methodologies, ethnographies, biographical research, oral history, and discourse analysis. There is also an emerging interest in the use of electronic communication as a method of conducting research. These movements in social theory – constructionism, postmodernism, poststructuralism, and queer theory – have been somewhat eclipsed by the growing interest in globalization theory and awareness of the negative aspects of globalization such as new wars, terrorism, slavery, and crime. With the impact of globalization, new debates will emerge in sociology around the question of cosmopolitanism and global sociology.

The Cambridge Dictionary of Sociology attempts therefore to cover these new, important and controversial developments in sociology, but it is also concerned not to become disconnected from the sociological tradition. In developing this modern *Dictionary*, I have been at pains to retain a lively and committed relationship to the diverse traditions and legacies of classical sociology, which have shaped the sociological imagination in the last century. Maintaining the core of sociology preserves a basis for further innovation and creativity. The *Dictionary* has been developed to recognize the continuities between classical sociology and the work of such sociologists as Ulrich Beck, Raymond Boudon, Pierre Bourdieu, James Coleman, Anthony Giddens, and Neil Smelser. The *Dictionary* attempts to be relevant to modern social theory and changes in contemporary society, while describing these developments in the context of the legacy of classical sociology.

How to use this *Dictionary*

Sociology is a critical discipline, and its concepts are typically contested. There is no consensus over the meaning of globalization, risk, information, culture, and society. The aim of this *Dictionary* has therefore been discursive. Its entries are designed to illustrate and debate concepts, showing their diverse origins and contested meanings. Some entries – on culture, family, gender, genetics, globalization, health, information, mass media and communications, power, race and ethnicity, religion, science and technology studies, social movements, and work and employment – are very long (around 5,000 words). These major entries allow authors to explore these critical issues in depth. The variable length of entries is intended to reflect the complexity and importance of different topics and fields in sociology. These large entries on key aspects of society are intended to be, as it were, the intellectual backbone of the *Dictionary*.

The *Dictionary* also contains a large number of entries on sociologists, both classical and contemporary. While the selection of these entries will always be somewhat arbitrary, they are intended to illustrate current debates as reflected in the work of living sociologists. This selection of contemporary sociologists will cause some degree of annoyance to those living sociologists who are not included. I hope they will accept my apologies for their absence, but these choices are unavoidably eccentric to some degree. I have if anything been overly inclusive rather than exclusive.

There is no list of bibliographical references at the end of the entries. Because references are included in the text, the reader can get an immediate grasp of the key bibliographical sources. The entries also contain many cross references in bold print that allow the reader to make immediate connections to other related entries. With foreign works, the first date in round brackets refers to its original publication, while dates in square brackets refer to publication dates of titles in English translation. Where possible I have referred to the English titles of translated works rather than to the original language of the publication. There are no footnotes or endnotes. The aim throughout has been to achieve simplicity rather than clutter entries with scholarly conventions that are not necessarily helpful to the reader.

Finally, the authors have been drawn from many countries in a bid to reflect the contemporary richness and cosmopolitanism of sociology. The entries are written in a simple, discursive, and accessible language that strives to avoid jargon or excessive dependence on a technical and arid vocabulary. I have encouraged authors to write in business-like, clear English. There are relatively few diagrams, charts, or figures.

It is intended that the *Dictionary* will offer a lively defense of sociology as a vibrant and expanding field of study. The more complex and difficult modern society becomes, the more we need a relevant, critical, and energetic sociological understanding of society. This *Dictionary* is intended to assist that understanding.

Bryan S. Turner
National University of Singapore

A

accounts

The term account – along with the related terms accountable and accountability – is a term of art largely associated with **ethnomethodology**. However, it has come into wider usage as various broadly ethnomethodological insights and sensibilities have drifted into mainstream sociology. Following Marvin Scott's and Stanford Lyman's article "Accounts" (1968) in the *American Sociological Review*, some users of the term have dwelt primarily on accounts as linguistic devices used to neutralize the disapproval caused by seemingly untoward behavior. Thus, the term has been distinguished as a particular subset of the category **explanation**. According to this line of argument, accounts may be divided into two sub-types: excuses and justifications. The first device acknowledges an act to have been "bad, wrong, or inappropriate" but denies the apparently culpable party is fully responsible for what has occurred. The second device denies the act was bad, wrong, or inappropriate in the first place. Insofar as these devices rely for their efficacy on invoking what **C. Wright Mills** once called certain shared "vocabularies of motive" (1940) in the *American Journal of Sociology*, they may be used as empirical windows on the wider world of moral sensibilities shared by a studied social **group**.

Ethnomethodologists use the terms accounts, accountable, and accountability in a rather more inclusive and fundamental way. Indeed, they argue that it is only by virtue of its accountability that any kind of collaborative **social action** is at all possible. In its specifically ethnomethodological sense, the accountability of social action is more than just a matter of linguistically excusing or justifying untoward conduct. It entails exhibiting and coordinating the orderliness and reasonability of social action in the widest sense. Hence, the terms account, accountable, and accountability are used to capture various constituent features of social action as such. Social action is accountable in this sense to the extent that its witnesses find it non-random, coherent, meaningful, and oriented to the accomplishment of practical goals.

Moreover, for ethnomethodologists, the accountability of social action is much more than just a theoretical matter or one of disinterested interpretation. As social actors, we are not just accountable to one another in the sense that we can linguistically describe each other's actions. Rather, the very fact that social action is describable in this way, or that it can be accounted for, is linked to another sense of its accountability. As social actors, we are also accountable in the sense that we may be held to account if our behavior fails to exhibit orderliness and reasonability to those with whom we find ourselves engaged. Social actors need not linguistically describe conduct in order to find it accountable in these senses.

Ethnomethodologists also stress that sociologists can make use of the fact that social action is manifestly accountable to social actors themselves as a resource for making sociological sense of what is going on in social action. In principle, all of the various linguistic and non-linguistic devices through which social actors make their actions accountable to one another should also be recoverable for use as resources in the empirical sociological analysis of their actions.

DARIN WEINBERG

act

– see **action theory**.

action research

– see **action theory**.

action theory

"Did he jump or was he pushed?" Jumping is an action. Being pushed is an event. Action theory is an approach to the study of social life that is based on the ontological premise that people jump. For example, the flow of traffic on a busy street differs from the flow of electrons on a copper wire. Electrons are pushed, drivers are not. From a structural perspective, we can learn a great deal about the flow of traffic by focusing on exogenous determinants, without ever knowing much about what drives human behavior. While few action theorists

1

would disagree with the value of structural analysis, they also see the need to look beyond the constraints on action, to the intentions, purposes, and goals that motivate efforts to push back.

Action theory has roots in **Max Weber**'s interpretative method and in **Talcott Parsons**'s effort to integrate this with **Émile Durkheim**'s macrosocial approach. In "The Place of Ultimate Values in Sociological Theory," Parsons insisted that "man is essentially an active, creative, evaluating creature" whose behavior must be understood in terms of the ends of action, and not "in terms of 'causes' and 'conditions'" (1935). His "voluntaristic theory of action" opposed the deterministic account of human behavior as "pushed," whether by **Sigmund Freud**'s "unconscious" or Pavlov's bell.

Action theory informs a diverse range of contemporary sociological theorizing, including rational action, **symbolic interactionism**, conflict theory, and **hermeneutics**. Conceptually, there are two main branches – one based on interests, the other on identity. Rational-action theory posits instrumental pursuit of self-interest, which can include an interest in public as well as private goods and an interest in social approval and avoidance of sanctions. Using mathematical formalism, the theory can generate testable predictions from a relatively small number of assumptions. However, the scope of the theory is limited by heroic assumptions about perfect information and unlimited calculating ability. Even versions based on "bounded rationality" are limited to actions intended to maximize utility, which excludes expressive and enthusiastic behavior and actions motivated by normative obligation and moral righteousness.

That void has been addressed by theories of action based on identity rather than interest. For identity theorists, "interests are only the surface of things. What is beneath the surface is a strong emotion, a feeling of a group of people that they are alike and belong together," according to Randall Collins in *Sociological Insight* (1992: 28). Individuals order the social world by carving out cognitive categories through interaction with others, leading to stereotyping, in-group favoritism, and out-group **prejudice**. Social and moral boundaries are defined and affirmed by punishing deviants. Punishment is not calibrated to deter **deviance**; rather, it is unleashed as an expression of indignation at the violation of normative boundaries, even when this may excite opposition rather than suppress it.

Interest and identity theories of action both emphasize the dynamics of interaction among autonomous but interdependent agents. However, they differ in how this interdependence is understood. Interest theory posits *strategic* interdependence, in which the consequences of individual choices depend in part on the choices of others. Game theorists (see **game theory**) model this interdependence as a payoff matrix defined by the intersection of all possible choices of the players, with individual payoffs assigned to each cell. For example, the payoff for providing favors depends on whether the partner reciprocates. Peer pressure is also an example of strategic interdependence created by the application of sanctions conditional upon compliance with expected behavior.

Identity theorists point instead to the *cognitive* interdependence of agents who influence one another in response to the influences they receive, through processes like communication, persuasion, instruction, and imitation. Action theory poses three related and perplexing puzzles: the problem of social order, the tension between structure and action, and the problem of free will and determinism. Contemporary research on complex dynamical systems has enriched action theory by providing plausible solutions to each of these puzzles, based, in turn, on the principles of self-organization, emergence, and deterministic chaos.

Macrosocial theories of social order posit a structured system of institutions and norms that shape individual behavior from the top down. In contrast, action theories assume that much of social life emerges from the bottom up, more like improvisational jazz than a symphony orchestra. People do not simply play roles written by elites and directed by managers. We each chart our own course, on the fly. How then is social order possible? If every musician is free to play as they choose, why do we not end up with a nasty and brutish cacophony, a noisy war of all against all?

Parsons addressed the "Hobbesian problem of order" by positing a set of shared **norms** and **values** that secure the cultural consensus necessary for social systems to function. Yet this is not a satisfactory solution. In effect, society remains a symphony orchestra in which the musicians must still learn their parts, except that now the Leviathan needs to carry only a thin baton, and not a lethal weapon.

An alternative solution was anticipated by Parsons's student, **Niklas Luhmann**. Luhmann bridged the gap between action theory and systems theory by placing individual actors in a web of communicative interaction with others. His rather abstruse ideas on autopoietic systems of interaction find clearer expression in **complexity theory**. The emergence of order out of local interaction in complex systems has come to be known as "self-organization" according to S. Kaufman in *Origins of Order* (1993). The archetype is biological evolution, but there are parallels across the sciences, cases in which surprising (and often quite exquisite) global patterns emerge from interactions among relatively simple but interdependent processes, in the absence of central coordination, direction, or planning. These include flocks of birds, traffic jams, fads, forest fires, riots, and residential segregation. There is no leader bird who choreographs the dance-like movement of a flock of geese. There is no supervisor in charge of a riot. There is no conspiracy of banks and realtors who are assigning people to ethnically homogeneous neighborhoods. These processes are examples of complex systems in which global order emerges spontaneously out of a web of local interactions among large numbers of autonomous yet interdependent agents. Emergence is a defining feature of complex systems and is ultimately responsible for the self-organization we find beneath the apparent chaos of nature (Coveney and Highfield, *Frontiers of Complexity*, 1995).

Emergent properties are not reducible to the properties of the individual agents. The idea of emergence was anticipated by one of the founders of sociology, who established this as a fundamental rule of the sociological method. "The hardness of bronze is not in the copper, the tin, or the lead, which are its ingredients and which are soft and malleable bodies," Émile Durkheim wrote in *The Rules of the Sociological Method*, "it is in their mixture." "Let us apply this principle to sociology," he continued; "[Social facts] reside exclusively in the very society itself which produces them, and not in its parts, i.e., its members" (1986: xlvii).

Structuralists have reified Durkheim's theory of social facts as emergent properties, leaving individual actors as little more than the incumbents of social locations and the carriers of structural imperatives. Heterogeneity in preferences and beliefs affects only which individuals will fill which "empty slots," the origin of which lies in processes that operate at the societal level.

In *The Structure of Social Action* (1937), Parsons also argued for the emergent properties of social systems, but believed Durkheim went too far in concluding that these "social facts" are entirely independent of individual consciousness. Parsons corrects the hyperstructuralist interpretation of Durkheim by incorporating an essential insight of **Joseph Schumpeter**'s "**methodological individualism**," the idea that societal patterns emerge from motivated choices and not from social facts external to individuals. Methodological individualism can be taken to imply that social facts are but the aggregated expression of individual goals and intentions. For example, residential segregation reflects the preferences of individuals for living among people similar to themselves. In contrast, structuralists assume that individual differences in ethnic identity affect who will live where in segregated neighborhoods but are not the cause of neighborhood segregation, which emanates from societal processes like red-lining and patterns of urban development.

Action theory is often most effective when it steers between these extremes. A classic example is Thomas Schelling's model of neighborhood segregation in his "Dynamic Model of Segregation" in the *Journal of Mathematical Sociology* 1971 (1). Schelling challenged the macrosocial assumption that segregation is imposed from the top down, through institutional means like "red-lining." At the same time, his famous experiment also challenged the microsocial assumption that segregation floats from the bottom up, through the aggregation of individual prejudices against ethnic minorities and outsiders. Schelling randomly distributed red and green chips on a large checkerboard and moved individual chips to empty locations if the number of in-group neighbors fell below an individual's threshold of tolerance. He discovered that extreme segregation can emerge even in a population that tolerates diversity, as agents relocate to avoid being in the minority. This surprisingly strong tendency towards neighborhood segregation is an emergent property of the population, generated by local interactions among large numbers of interdependent but autonomous agents, even when every individual is tolerant of diversity.

Action theory explains social life by identifying the *reasons* for action (whether instrumental interests or symbolic meanings). As **Anthony Giddens** put it in *The Constitution of Society*, "I propose simply to declare that reasons are causes" (1984: 345). Yet most people now accept that everything in the universe is physically determined. How can this determinism be reconciled with a voluntaristic theory of action? Consider a sunbather who moves his/her towel to fend off a late afternoon shadow. Meanwhile, next to the towel, a heliotropic plant turns to follow the sun's trajectory, thereby maximizing its access to an essential resource. Even the most dedicated Cartesian would not suggest that a sunflower is a purposive agent whose actions can be explained by the plant's need for photosynthesis. How do we know that the sunbather is any different? One answer is that the sunbather could have chosen to remain in the shadow, while the sunflower could not. However, it is trivial to construct a stochastic sunflower that "chooses" to move, based on a probability distribution given by the location of the sun. A better answer is that the sunbather can tell you that the desire for sunlight is the *reason* for the action, while the sunflower will tell you nothing of the kind. Plants cannot provide reasons for their behavior, humans can. But does this mean that the sunbather is right? Is it possible that the sunbather, like the sunflower, is simply responding to physical stimuli that induce heliotropic movement, and, unlike for the sunflower, this movement is accompanied by the epiphenomenal feeling of choosing?

There is mounting evidence from neuroscientists and experimental psychologists that supports that possibility. In 1983, Benjamin Libet found that "cerebral neural activity ('readiness potential') precedes the subject's awareness of his/her intention or wish to act by at least 350 msec" ("Commentary on 'Free Will in the Light of Neuropsychiatry,'" 1996). More recently, in *The Illusion of Conscious Will* (2002), Daniel Wegner reported substantial evidence to support the hypothesis that "conscious will" is largely an illusion, useful to help us remember our authorship of actions whose causes lie elsewhere. These and other studies point to the possibility that our intentions are formed in the course of initiating action, but in a separate cognitive subsystem that assigns authorship after the fact. If so, then perhaps humans are unique in the ability to provide rational accounts for our actions, but we have no more free will than does a sunflower.

The theory of complex systems suggests an alternative possibility – that free will is compatible with determinism. Even relatively simple dynamical systems can require exponential amounts of computing power for every additional input into the system, until the number of bits required to predict system behavior, even in the near term, can exceed the number of particles in the universe. Thus, a highly nonlinear deterministic system like the brain can be indeterminable, which leaves open a window for intentional choice that is not reducible to system determinants (James P. Crutchfield, "Complexity: Order Contra Chaos," 1989).

Meanwhile, a growing interest in complex adaptive systems has opened up action theory to "backward-looking" approaches in which intentionality is empirically variable rather than presupposed. In backward-looking models, the ends of action attract the behaviors that produce them, whether or not the agent intended the outcome or is even aware of its existence. From a forward-looking perspective, this idea appears hopelessly teleological since the ends of action are located in the future and cannot reach back through time to attract the choices needed to bring them about. Models of complex adaptive systems avoid this problem by pointing backward, not forward – attributing action to outcomes that have already occurred. In agent-based evolutionary models, outcomes of a given action alter the population distribution of agents who engage in that action. In learning models, outcomes of a given action alter the probability distribution of actions within the repertoire of any given agent. Either way, the link between action and outcome is a set of experiences, not intentions. Agents look forward by holding a mirror to the past. They jump when they are pushed.   MICHAEL W. MACY

actor network theory

Actor network theory (ANT) is a family of approaches to social analysis that rests on six core assumptions. First, it treats **institutions**, practices, and actors as materially heterogeneous, composed not only of people but also of technologies and other materials. Second, it assumes that the elements making up practices are *relational*, achieving their shape and attributes only in interaction with other elements. Nothing is intrinsically fixed or has reality outside the web of interactions. Third, it assumes that the network of heterogeneous relations and practices is a process. If structures, institutions, or realities are not continuously enacted then they disappear. Fourth, it therefore assumes that realities and structures are precarious in principle, if not in practice. Fifth, this implies that the world might be different, a suggestion that opens up interesting political possibilities. And sixth, it explores *how* rather than *why* realities are generated and maintained. This is because even the most obvious social causes are relational effects and therefore themselves subject to change.

ANT developed initially in the 1980s in Paris with the work of such authors as Michel Callon, **Bruno Latour** (*Science in Action*, 1987), and John Law (*Organizing Modernity*, 1994). It grew (and grows) through empirical studies of technologies, science practices, **organizations**, **markets**, health care, spatial practices, and the natural world. Indeed it is not possible to appreciate ANT without exploring such case studies. Philosophically, it owes much to Michel Serres (1930–5) and is generally poststructuralist in inspiration. It thus shares with the writing of **Michel Foucault** an empirical concern with material–semiotic patterns of relations, though the patterns that it discerns are smaller in scope than those identified by Foucault.

The approach is controversial. First, since it is non-humanist it analytically privileges neither people nor the social, which sets it apart from much English-language sociology. Second, since it offers accounts of how rather than why institutions take shape, it is sometimes accused of explanatory weakness. Third, political critics have suggested that it is insensitive to the "invisible work" of low-status actors. Fourth, it has been accused in some of its earlier versions of a **bias** towards centering, ordering, or even managerialism. And fifth, feminists have observed that it has shown little sensitivity to embodiment (see **body**).

Whether these complaints are now justified is a matter for debate. Indeed, ANT is probably better seen as a toolkit and a set of methodological sensibilities rather than as a single theory. Recently there has been much interchange between ANT, feminist material-semiotics (**Donna J. Haraway**) and **postcolonial theory,** and there is newer "after-ANT" work that is much more sensitive to the politics of domination, to embodiment, to "othering," and to the possible multiplicity and non-coherence of relations. A key issue remains politics. Such "after-ANT" writers as Annemarie Mol (*The Body Multiple*, 2002) and Helen Verran argue that relations are non-coherent and enact overlapping but different versions of reality, so there is space for "ontics," or an "ontological politics" about what can and should be made real. This means that alternative and preferable realities might be enacted into being or made stronger: reality is not destiny.   JOHN LAW

adaptation

– see **evolutionary theory**.

addiction

In its original usage, addiction meant simply to be given over to someone or something. It was a term used widely to describe passionate investments in various sorts of activities, as can be seen in Shakespeare's *Othello* where we read "Each man to what sport and revel his addiction leads him." Well into the nineteenth century the concept of addiction was used to describe a diverse assortment of human fixations. But as Temperance movements grew in the mid nineteenth century, the term was increasingly considered as a medical or quasi-medical term of art and its scope was delimited to describing an individual's seeming enslavement to alcohol or drugs. A multitude of efforts have been made to provide biological **explanations** for some people's apparently pathological attachment to alcohol or drug use but each has met with rather serious conceptual obstacles. In response to these difficulties, most medical lexicons have now dispensed with the term addiction in favor of the presumably less conceptually troubling concept dependence. However, the term addiction continues to be found in both clinical and popular discourse regarding alcohol and drug problems and has indeed been extended to new forms of apparently compulsive behavior including over-eating, gambling, compulsive sexual behavior, and others.

In sociology, addiction has been approached from several distinct theoretical vantage points. Regrettably, the term has often been used interchangeably with other terms including deviant drug use, drug misuse, and drug abuse. Such imprecision results in a confusion of questions concerning the social approval of various sorts of alcohol or drug use with questions concerning whether this use is voluntary. Much of the history of **social policy** concerning alcohol and psychoactive drugs has been predicated, at least ostensibly, on the claim that these substances possess unusual powers over people and must be regulated to protect citizens from their own personal proclivities to succumb to addictive use. If we are not able to distinguish claims regarding the putative **morality** of alcohol or drug use from claims regarding people's ability to control their use, we are poorly equipped to evaluate effectively the history of policies predicated on the notion that people need protection from putatively addictive substances. We are also poorly equipped to evaluate social research which either endorses or rejects this idea. If it is to have any meaning at all, the term addiction cannot be considered as synonymous with terms denoting voluntary substance use.

The earliest sociological research concerned specifically with addiction was conducted by Alfred Lindesmith under the tutelage of **Herbert Blumer** at the University of Chicago. Lindesmith noted that, whereas users who acquired heroin on the street were often vulnerable to addictive patterns of use, those who had been administered opiates in hospital settings were not so vulnerable. He explained this by suggesting that, whereas both hospital and street users experience physiological withdrawal symptoms upon cessation of use, only street users are consciously aware of the fact that the source of their distress lies in their heroin deprivation. Lindesmith argued that, by using drugs specifically to alleviate withdrawal, mere drug users were transformed into genuine drug addicts. This theory was attractive to sociologists in the twentieth century because it insisted the symbolic meanings actors found in their drug experiences were essential elements of the addiction process. While Lindesmith's theory remains the classic canonical benchmark for contemporary sociological theorizing on addiction, it has been subject to several rather serious critiques. Most fundamentally, his theory presumes that physiological withdrawal distress is a necessary prerequisite for the onset of addictive patterns of behavior. In the wake of the so-called crack cocaine "epidemic," theories of addiction predicated on the experience of physiological withdrawal distress have been undermined. Because they do not involve gross physiological withdrawal symptoms, crack cocaine addiction, along with nicotine addiction and behavioral addictions like those to eating, gambling, and sex, have cast doubt on the generalizability of Lindesmith's theory and have even put in question its validity with respect to opiates themselves.

During the mid twentieth century, structural functionalists offered a variety of theoretical accounts for apparently addictive behavior that departed in important ways from Lindesmith's seminal work. Seeking wholly social structural explanations, these theories shared in common a departure from Lindesmith's presumption of a necessary physiological component to addiction. In his famous essay "Social Structure and Anomie" (1938, *American Sociological Review*), **Robert K. Merton** suggested that chronic drunkards and drug addicts might exemplify the retreatist adaptation, one of his five modes of adjustment whereby social actors adopt ostensibly deviant patterns of action. According to Merton, the addict could be understood as an individual who believes in the propriety of both cultural goals and the institutionalized procedures society affords for achieving those goals but who cannot produce the desired results by socially sanctioned means. The result of this failure is a retreat from social life into "defeatism, quietism, and resignation." This proposition was developed by Richard Cloward and Lloyd Ohlin in their book *Delinquency and Opportunity* (1960) in what became their fairly influential "Double Failure" hypothesis regarding addictive behavior. In contrast to Merton, Cloward and Ohlin suggested addicts were not opposed to adopting illegitimate means of achieving legitimate

cultural goals, but rather were incapable of using even these means for securing social rewards. Hence, addicts were double failures in the sense that they failed to achieve by either legitimate or criminal procedures. Heavy drug use was held to alienate the putative addict from both mainstream and delinquent **subcultures**, thus further minimizing their opportunities for social success. Some structural functionalists moved beyond **explanations** of the distribution of addicts across social structural positions to consider the social psychological processes that motivated addictive patterns of alcohol or drug use. The best-known of these was normative ambivalence theory, according to which dysfunctional substance use will arise when agents are bombarded with competing normative orientations to their use. According to functionalists, apparently addictive behavior patterns were to be regarded as eminently rational, if painful and socially notorious, adaptations to social structural deprivation. The functionalist approach tended to stereotype addicts as necessarily socially disadvantaged and sometimes to confuse the trappings of **poverty** with the trappings of addiction. But it had the virtue of freeing sociological research from the presumption of a brute biological basis for addiction and of allowing sociologists to entertain the possibility that people might experience alcohol or drug problems simply as a result of the ways they had learned to use these substances to cope with the social structural circumstances of their lives.

Structural functionalist approaches were rivaled by approaches to addiction (and deviant substance use more generally) proffered by ethnographers broadly allied with **symbolic interactionism**. As part of a more general critical turn against structural **functionalism** in the second half of the twentieth century, many of these sociologists distanced themselves from what David Matza, in his book *Becoming Deviant* (1969) dubbed the "correctional" perspective found in structural functionalist theories of addiction and deviant substance use, and moved towards what he called an "appreciative" analytic stance towards such putatively deviant behavior. Noting that modern **societies** were a good deal more pluralistic and conflicted than structural functionalists had generally allowed, these researchers advocated an agnostic moral regard for putatively dysfunctional or deviant behavior and an effort to empathize with putatively deviant individuals and subcultures. No longer was it assumed that behavior reviled in mainstream **culture** was necessarily viewed negatively by those who themselves engaged in the behavior. Nor was it any longer assumed that the social mechanisms according to which these behaviors were produced and sustained need reflect a functional breakdown of either the individual or his or her society. Indeed, many of these studies highlighted the existence of subcultural prestige hierarchies, wherein the use and sale of illicit substances was valued as a mark of adventurousness and other subculturally valued characteristics. Substance use was depicted as a source of meaning in the lives of users. Hence studies focused on such matters as drug slang or argot, the settings of drug-related activity, the **norms** and practices characteristic of drug and alcohol using subcultures, and the **careers** through which drug users passed as they moved from initiates to seasoned veterans of drug- or alcohol-using social worlds. The concept of career has also been used by researchers to emphasize the important **influence** exercised by labeling on putatively addictive behavior patterns.

More recently, the topic of addiction has been taken up by leaders in **rational choice theory** who have properly recognized it as an apparent counterexample to the axiomatic proposition that **social action** is necessarily rational action. Some of these theorists have sought to reconcile empirical instances of addictive patterns of behavior with core propositions of rational choice theory. Others have concluded that addiction is essentially irrational and more thoroughly rooted in neurological dysfunction than micro-economic decision-making mechanisms. While these efforts have produced some interesting technical refinements of rational choice theory itself, they have done less to shed new sociological light on why some people seem to experience rather severe levels of difficulty refraining from the use of alcohol or drugs, even after repeated negative experiences with them. Another more recent line of theoretical work on addiction hails from attribution theory. Attribution theorists turn their attention away from why certain people fall into apparently addictive behavior patterns and instead consider social and psychological explanations for why people attribute behavior to addictions. Attribution theory properly highlights the fact that objective characteristics of social behavior and efforts to explain that behavior are intimately linked to one another. In addition to research that considers why certain activities are so addictive for certain people, fruitful insights can come from the study of why the concept of addiction is itself so compelling for certain people acting in certain social contexts.

To date, sociologists have illuminated various important dimensions of problematic substance use but have recurrently found it almost impossible to validate the concept of addiction without recourse to biological accounts of physiological dysfunction. Those who have taken the idea of involuntary substance use seriously have overwhelmingly incorporated reference to biological mechanisms as indispensable elements of their own sociological theories. In contrast, the vast majority of those who have not drawn from biology have found it difficult to account for the apparently involuntary aspects of addiction. In his book *The Alcoholic Society* (1993), Norman Denzin develops a theory of "the alcoholic self" which takes important theoretical strides towards a more thoroughly sociological explanation by incorporating his more general approach to the sociology of **emotions** into his theory of addiction. While an undeniably important contribution, Denzin's research on the emotionality of addiction exhibits consequential ambiguities that make it difficult to square fully with the claim that addictive patterns of behavior are genuinely involuntary. In a series of essays including "The Embodiment of Addiction" (2002, *Body and Society*), Darin Weinberg has drawn upon the growing literature on the sociology of embodiment to reconcile the **phenomenology** of addiction as involuntary affliction with the longstanding sociological claim that people might acquire problematic patterns of substance use simply by virtue of the ways they have learned to use these substances to cope with the social structural circumstances of their lives. He argues that the sociology of embodiment allows us to appreciate more fully that not all meaningful, or socially structured, behavior is behavior that we deliberately choose or with which we self-identify. This work suggests a fruitful interface between the sociology of embodiment, the sociology of moral inclusion, and sociological work on the boundaries of human agency.

Rather predictably, most contemporary sociological research on drugs and alcohol focuses on questions pertaining to the various **social problems** that arise from either substance use itself or the **social policies** in place to control substance use. No doubt these questions will, and should, continue to occupy the attentions of social scientists, whether or not they require use of a concept of addiction. But the sociology of addiction as such also holds promise as a valuable empirical test case for **social theories** concerned with the relationship between much more general sociological themes, including nature/culture, structure/agency, **rationality**, emotion, embodiment, and **social exclusion**. This type of research will certainly require a vigilant enforcement of the conceptual distinction highlighted earlier – that between addiction per se and voluntary activity that is merely deviant.   DARIN WEINBERG

Adorno, Theodor Wiesengrund (1903–1969)

Born in Frankfurt, Germany, on September 11, 1903, into an upper-class bourgeois family, the son of a German Jewish father and Italian Catholic mother, Adorno studied philosophy, psychology, and musicology at the University of Frankfurt where he received his PhD in 1924. With the rise to power of Hitler's **fascism**, Adorno first emigrated to England and then joined the Institute for Social Research in exile at Columbia University in New York.

During the 1930s, he became closely connected with the Institute's attempt to develop a **critical theory** of society. This involved Adorno in one of the first attempts to develop a Marxian critique of mass culture, which Adorno and the Institute discerned was becoming ever more significant as an instrument of ideological manipulation and social control in democratic **capitalist**, fascist, and **communist** societies. Working with the "father of mass communications," **Paul Lazarsfeld**, at the Princeton Radio Project and then at Columbia University, Adorno participated in one of the first sustained research projects on the effects of popular music. Later, Adorno was also to work on one of the first attempts to develop a critical analysis of television, producing an article on "How to Look at Television" in 1954.

Adorno was a key member of the interdisciplinary social research projects at the Institute and worked on their studies of fascism and anti-Semitism. Adorno and Institute director **Max Horkheimer** went to California in the early 1940s, where they worked closely on the book that became *Dialectic of Enlightenment* (1948 [trans. 1972]). In *Minima Moralia* (1974) and other essays of the period, Adorno continued the Institute's studies of the growing hegemony of capitalism and the integration of the working class as a conservative force of the capitalist system. In such a situation, deeply influenced by his sojourn in New York and California, Adorno only saw the possibility of individual revolt. He also feared, however, the resurgence of **authoritarianism** in the United States and collaborated on a groundbreaking collective study of *The Authoritarian Personality* (1950) with a group of Berkeley researchers. The project embodied the Institute's desire to merge theoretical construction with empirical research and produced a portrait of a disturbing authoritarian potential in the United States. Adorno was responsible for elaborating the theoretical implications and helped design the research apparatus.

In the early 1950s, Adorno returned with Horkheimer to Germany to reestablish the institute in Frankfurt. Here, Adorno continued his studies in sociology and culture, though he turned primarily to philosophy in the last years of his life. During the 1950s, he participated in the Institute's sociological studies of education, students, workers, and the potential for democracy. Adorno wrote many sociological essays at this time and participated in the debates published in *The Positivist Dispute in German Sociology* (1976). In these debates, Adorno defended the Institute's conception of dialectical social theory against positivism and the "critical rationalism" defended by **Karl Popper** and other neopositivists.

Increasingly critical of communism and skeptical of Marxism, Adorno primarily engaged in cultural criticism and studies of philosophy and aesthetics during his last decade. As he died suddenly of a heart attack in 1969, his magnum opus, *Aesthetic Theory*, was published posthumously (1984).   DOUGLAS KELLNER

aesthetics

A notion invented in the eighteenth century in the German-speaking world, the term aesthetics was bequeathed to the history of ideas with philosopher Alexander Gottlieb Baumgarten's *Aesthetica* (1750–8). As developed by Baumgarten, aesthetics was the study of the beautiful. He conceived of this project as a science of "sensuous cognition," and from its inception aesthetics was concerned with the effects of art works on their recipients, perhaps most famously illustrated in Immanuel Kant's (1724–1804) concept of the sublime and the idea of purposeless, transcendental art works. In the English-speaking world, aesthetics was subsumed under a concern with the philosophy of taste and is represented in the work of John Locke (1632–1704) and David Hume (1711–76).

As the century waned, British and continental theories of aesthetics were increasingly preoccupied with notions of beauty and unity in the arts, pointing to structural correlates between music and the plastic arts in terms of their effects, and fueling more general notions of unity in the arts and sciences, notions that would continue to develop in the following century. As part of the general rise of interest in aesthetics, Aristotle's *Poetics* was translated into English in 1789. During the second half of the eighteenth century, an acquaintance with the science of aesthetics was often considered to be part of an individual's equipment for social life, and it is here that the initial conception of aesthetics as the science of beauty and its effects began to provide seeds for subsequent critical considerations of the role of the arts in relation to social classification. Concurrently in the late eighteenth century, the arts flourished, stimulated by burgeoning publics, **urbanization**, and the status-seeking strategies of increasingly professionalized artistic workers in London, Paris, Vienna, and other European cities. During these years, new aesthetic hierarchies were articulated by artistic workers and appropriated by arts consumers as a resource for status creation and maintenance.

Many sociologists of the arts have described how aesthetics (understood as beauty and value) and taste in the arts have been resources for social boundary work. **Pierre Bourdieu**, for example, sought to turn Kant on his head in *Distinction* (1979 [trans. 1984]), by arguing that aesthetics could never be disinterested but was rather linked to **lifestyle** and position in social space. More recently, scholarship in environmental and **social psychology**, arts sociology, and cultural geography has returned to the original focus of aesthetics, albeit from an empirical and pragmatically oriented perspective, highlighting the concept of aesthetic ecology and aesthetic agency, and developing theories of what may be afforded by art works and aesthetic materials broadly construed.

TIA DENORA

affirmative action

Affirmative action, or positive **discrimination** as it is known in the United Kingdom, entails the provision of various types of advantages to members of **groups** who have been systematically oppressed for their membership in that group. The term stems from the legal understanding of affirmative or positive remedies which compel wrong-doers to do something in addition to merely refraining from the wrong-doing itself. Affirmative action policies can be found throughout the world. Though they can focus on any group that has suffered systematic discrimination, affirmative action policies tend most often to concern ethnic groups historically oppressed within a given society, and women. They tend to provide advantages in the domains of **education**, employment, **health**, and social welfare.

Affirmative action first became a topic of serious debate in the wake of the civil rights movements of the 1960s when it was discovered that legal proscriptions against historical wrong-doings were not wholly successful in creating equal opportunities for members of historically oppressed groups. Activists began suggesting that, in addition to the negative remedies proscribing discrimination against historically oppressed groups, it would be necessary to implement affirmative or positive strategies to correct past wrongs. Various approaches have been taken to distributing affirmative action advantages. Some societies have favored quota systems that require the ratio of recipients of certain scarce resources, like state building contracts or university admissions, to resemble the ratio found in the larger society between majority and minority groups. Others have favored a less restrictive entitlement to consider issues of **ethnicity** and **gender** in deciding how best to distribute scarce resources. But, regardless of approach, affirmative action policies have very often met with rather fierce resistance, primarily from members of historically privileged groups who resent what they call reverse discrimination. Much more rarely, resistance has come from members of the groups presumed to benefit from affirmative action on the grounds that affirmative action policies sustain racial, ethnic, or gender antagonisms and/or prove demoralizing to their beneficiaries.

Sometimes, particular affirmative action policies have been critiqued on the grounds that they tend to benefit only the most privileged among historically oppressed groups and fail to remedy the much more devastating hardships and **inequalities** suffered by what **William Julius Williams** (*The Truly Disadvantaged: The Inner City, the Underclass, and Public Policy*, 1987) has called the "truly disadvantaged." In addition to failing to help the most disadvantaged segments of historically oppressed groups, it has been suggested that such policies discredit affirmative action as such by giving benefits to people who neither deserve nor need them. In place of ethnicity- and gender-based affirmative action policies that are insensitive to the comparative hardships suffered by their recipients, some have suggested policies more explicitly pegged to actual disadvantage. These kinds of arguments have met with vigorous counterarguments suggesting that race- and gender-based affirmative action remain crucial to the project of institutionalizing a more egalitarian society. Many high-profile former recipients of affirmative-action advantages, including former American Secretary of State Colin Powell, have come out in favor of such policies despite political pressures not to do so.

DARIN WEINBERG

affluent society

The Affluent Society is the title of an influential book originally published by the American economist, John Kenneth Galbraith (1908–2006) in 1958 (there have been numerous subsequent editions). As a work of **political economy**, it begins with a critique of classical political economists (such as Adam Smith [1723–90] and David Ricardo [1771–1823]) who had emphasized above all the primacy of increasing production and the requirement for a minimum of public consumption (that is, low taxes) if this was to be achieved. This he labeled as "conventional wisdom," better adapted to historic conditions than to the realities of the contemporary United States, which had become, after World War II, an "affluent society," one whose productive capacities could easily meet the needs of its citizens. Indeed, under conditions of affluence, production could be increased only through the creation of new desires and needs via advertising and marketing, which succeeds because of the development of a "culture of emulation." Moreover, the lack of investment in public goods (schools, parks, roads and refuse disposal) had created a world of "private affluence and public squalor," in which, for example, increasingly elaborate private cars clog increasingly inadequate public roads. Galbraith argues for increased expenditure on public goods, and that the "social balance" between the allocation of resources to private and public goods must be created by political organizations. He also identifies the emergence of a new class (see **social class**) of educated labor, for whom work itself is considered to be a source of recreation, and for whom the maximization of income is not a primary goal. The expansion of this class will also contribute to an improved social balance.

ROSEMARY CROMPTON

affluent worker

The argument that sections of the working class had experienced embourgeoisement became popular in the 1950s and 1960s, to explain changing **values** and political allegiances among manual workers. Increasing affluence was seen to underpin a move from working-class to middle-class **lifestyles** and values, so that such workers *became* middle-class. This argument was challenged, both theoretically and empirically, by **J. Goldthorpe** and colleagues, in *The Affluent Worker in the Class Structure* (1969). They agreed that important changes had occurred in the market and work experience of affluent manual workers, but argued that related changes in lifestyles (privatism) and political attitudes (instrumentalism) remained

distinctively working-class. Partial convergence with white-collar workers should not be conflated with assimilation to the middle class.

This neo-Weberian analysis challenged presumptions about the necessary decline of **trade unions** and the United Kingdom Labour Party, just as union membership was growing and the Labour Party regained electoral success. Instead, these authors portrayed a movement from a "traditional **solidarity**" working class to an increasingly "instrumental collectivist" working class. In turn, however, the adequacy of this contrast and projection was widely challenged, as shifts in forms of working-class class consciousness and organization were found to be more varied, uncertain, and contested, for example by F. Devine in *Affluent Workers Revisited* (1992). This encouraged more complex accounts of the relationships between working-class experience, forms of consciousness, and **politics**, undermining strong claims for links between specific class locations and forms of consciousness and action, which had been shared by many currents in British studies of **social class**.

TONY ELGER

African-American studies

This field of interdisciplinary studies charts the experiences of people of African descent in black Atlantic societies including the United States, the Caribbean, and Latin America. It studies the social structures and cultures that African people in the **diaspora** have created. More specifically, it studies the social, cultural, and political processes that have shaped the experience of people of African ancestry. There are a large number of study centers and research institutes providing interdisciplinary programs in higher education in the United States. Many of these centers, such as the University of California Los Angeles Center for African American Studies (1969), date from the 1960s. The National Association of African American Studies was founded by Dr. Lemuel Berry Jr. at the Virginia State University at Ettrick, Virginia, in 1992 and it held its first annual conference in 1993. African-American studies draws some of its intellectual inspiration from the work of black American **intellectuals** such as **W. E. B. Du Bois**, and the Institute for Afro-American Studies at Harvard University (1975) is named after him.

There are several academic journals that cater to this interdisciplinary field, including the *Journal of Black Studies* (1970), *The Black Scholar* (1969), the *Western Journal of Black Studies* (1977), and *Womanist Theory and Research* (1994) from the Womanist Studies Consortium at the University of Georgia.

African-American studies is part of a significant expansion of interdisciplinary studies since the 1960s dealing with **justice** issues, such as **Latino studies** and **women's studies**.

While African-American studies is not confined to sociology, sociologists have made important contributions to the field, including **Paul Gilroy** whose *Black Atlantic* (1993) has been influential. African-American studies has not had a significant impact on the study of **race and ethnicity** and **racism** in the United Kingdom or Europe. In sociology, the study of "race relations" in the United Kingdom has been critically discussed by scholars influenced by **feminism** or **Marxism** for its failure to analyze **politics** and **power**. African-American studies has not flourished in the United Kingdom for the obvious reason that black British citizens are also from India, Pakistan, and Bangladesh, as well as the Caribbean and Africa. For similar reasons, **critical race theory** has not been a dominant paradigm in British sociology. British radical sociologists have been influenced more by **Franz Fanon** than by DuBois, more by **Stuart Hall** and Paul Gilroy than by African-American academics, and have in recent years drawn more from **Pierre Bourdieu**'s studies of Algeria, **migration**, and **poverty** in *The Algerians* (1958) [trans. 1962] and *The Weight of the World* (1993) [trans. 2000] than from American social science. While racism is a common problem in the United States and Europe, the sociological study of race has taken rather different directions.   BRYAN S. TURNER

age

The study of age in sociology covers influences affecting individuals across all phases of the life-course, as well as the specific period known as old age. In practice, although findings on the long-term impact of changes in early and middle age have begun to emerge, most research focuses still on "older" or "elderly" people. **Matilda White Riley**, an influential figure in American sociological research, refers to the *interdependence* of aging on the one side and society on the other. She argues in *On the Significance of Age in Society* (1987) that, in studying age, we not only bring people back into society, but recognize that *both* people and society undergo process and change: "The aim is to understand each of the two dynamisms: (1) the *aging of people* in successive cohorts who grow up, grow old, die, and are replaced by other people; and (2) the *changes in society* as people of different ages pass through the social institutions that are organized by age."

Sociological perspectives on age adopt a contrasting approach to other social science disciplines. The sociologist starts from the view that old age is interesting because – although it is an enduring human phenomenon handled differently by different societies – it is at the same time changing and influencing human behavior. The sociologist is concerned to explore the processes involved and how they are being interpreted by men and women, from different social classes, ethnic groups, and cultural settings. This approach contrasts with **social policy** and government interests in old age. In these contexts, old age is often regarded as a problem (for the economy or the health service, to take two examples), hence the need for some analysis and collection of data. This approach has its own validity and justification but may lead to a distorted view of social aging, together with a limited selection of topics to be analyzed and discussed.

The experience of aging has been influenced by shifts in the patterning of the life-course over the past 100 years. Changes in the **demography** of aging and in patterns of work and retirement have been especially important in shaping contemporary aspects of later life. On the first of these, improvements in life expectancy have been crucial in creating "middle" and "old" age as significant phases in the life-course. In 1901, life expectancy at birth was around forty-five years (for men) and forty-nine years (for women), with many people (especially those from working-class backgrounds) dying before they reached what would now be recognized as old age. With life expectancy at birth in the United Kingdom (in 2001) seventy-six years for men and eighty-one years for women, survival past middle age is normal, even if frequently accompanied by heightened awareness of the aging process and of future mortality.

Changes in the organization of work and employment have also been consequential in re-shaping the life-course. In general terms, the period from 1945 to the mid-1970s confirmed the emergence of a "standardized" life-course built around initial education, work, and leisure. This period is associated with the creation of **retirement** as a major social institution, with the growth of entitlements to pensions and the gradual acceptance of an extended period of **leisure** following the ending of full-time work. In fact this model of the life-course lasted a relatively short span of time in historical terms, with the period from 1945 to 1975 defining its outer limits.

From the late 1970s a number of changes can be identified, arising from the development of more flexible patterns of work and the impact of high levels of unemployment. These produced what may be termed the reconstruction of middle and old age, with the identification of a "third age" in between the period of work and employment ("the second age") and a period of mental and physical decline ("the fourth age"). An aspect of these new features of social aging is the ambiguity and flexibility of the boundaries of the third age, at both its lower and upper ends. Both of these now involve complex periods of transition, with the move away from employment, and with the blurring of dependence and independence in late old age.

Age is a marker of a number of changes affecting older people – these reflecting a mix of physiological, social, and biographical factors. First, changes associated with poor health are highly significant for many older people. For example, it is estimated that, among those people aged eighty-five and over, one in five will have dementia and three in five a limiting longstanding illness such as osteoarthritis or osteoporosis. Second, changes in social relationships are also substantial, with the loss of close friends and relations a striking feature of later life. Third, age may exacerbate rather than reduce inequalities experienced earlier in the life-course. **Social class** remains a stronger predictor of **lifestyle** than age, and older people are likely to have more in common with younger people of their own class than they will with older people from other classes.

As well as social class, age is also affected by social divisions associated with **gender** and **race and ethnicity**. The gender imbalances of later life are now well established. Because women outlive men by an average of five years, there are around 50 percent more women than men among those sixty-five and over. The gender imbalance is even more marked in late old age: among those aged eighty-five and over, women outnumber men by three to one. Sara Arber and Jay Ginn in *Connecting Gender and Aging* (1995) conclude that: "The fact that over half of older women are widowed, whereas three-quarters of older men are married, has consequences for gender, identity, relationships, and roles in later life."

Race and ethnicity are another important division running through age-based relationships. In the early part of the twenty-first century, there will be a significant aging of the black community as the cohorts of migrants of the late 1950s and 1960s reach retirement age. Older people from minority ethnic groups are likely to have distinctive experiences in old age, these including: first, increased susceptibility to physical ill-health because of past experiences, such as heavy manual work and poor housing; second, great vulnerability to mental health problems, a product of **racism** and cultural pressures; third, acute financial problems, with evidence of elderly Asians being at a particular disadvantage. The problems faced by ethnic elders have been defined as a form of "triple jeopardy." This refers to the fact that ethnic elders not only face discrimination because they are old; in addition, many of them live in disadvantaged physical and economic circumstances; finally, they may also face discrimination because of their culture, language, skin color, or religious affiliation.

The above divisions have led Joe Hendricks in *Structure and Identity* (2003) to conclude that: "People do not become more alike with age; in fact the opposite may well be the case . . . Their heterogeneity is entrenched in disparate master status characteristics, including membership groups and socioeconomic circumstances, race, ethnicity, gender, subcultural, or structural conditions on the one hand, and personal attributes on the other."

Research on social aspects of age focus on the **norms**, **values**, and **social roles** associated with a particular chronological age. Sociologists emphasize the way in which ideas about different phases in the life-course – such as childhood, mid-life, and old age – change over time and across cultures. John Vincent in *Old Age* (2003) suggests that even if the experience of a life-cycle in which an individual feels a sense of loss when they have passed their "prime" is a universal, it says nothing about the timing, meaning, and cultural content of the social category of old age: "The variety of ways of being 'old' are as different as the ways of being in one's 'prime'. A re-evaluation of old age in the West requires an appreciation of the variety of ways it is possible to live one's 'old age' and an escape from culturally bound stereotypes."

From a social perspective, age may be viewed as constructed around various social practices and institutions. It is associated in particular with the regulation of movement through the life-course. Western societies standardize many aspects of public life on the basis of chronological age. Social institutions control access and prescribe and proscribe certain behaviors by age. In consequence, birthdays have social as well as individual significance. Legal rights and duties are commonly associated with particular ages, with access to a range of institutions moderated through age-based criteria. The various responsibilities associated with citizenship are strongly associated with age, notable examples including the right to vote, military service, and duty to serve on a jury.

Age is also constructed through the phases associated with pre-work, work, and post-work. Western societies have come to define old age as starting at sixty or sixty-five, ages associated with receipt of a pension following retirement. This development can be seen as a twentieth-century invention, consolidated with the rise of the **welfare state**. Other markers of old age are, however, possible and increasingly likely, given further extensions in life expectancy. With pressures to extend working life, retirement at seventy would, for example, present a new boundary at which "old age" would begin.

Social relationships built around family and friends remain crucial for understanding many aspects of the lives of older people. Most older people are connected to family-based networks, which provide (and receive from the older person) different types of support. Relationships with peers, and friendship in particular, has also been shown to be central to well-being in later life, with research pointing to the value of a "special relationship" or confidant in adjusting to the stresses and strains of later life. Overall, the research evidence would point to an increase in the importance of friends in the lives of older people. In the early phase of retirement, and even (or especially) into late old age, friends will be significant in maintaining morale and self-identity. For many older people, faced with reduced income and poor health, the loss of close friends may pose acute problems of adjustment and threats to the integrity of the **self**.

Processes and experiences associated with age have been examined in a number of sociological theories drawing on functionalist, symbolic interactionist, and neo-Marxist perspectives. Functionalist approaches to the study of age such as role theory (formulated in the early 1950s) focused on the impact of losing work-based ties – this producing, it was argued, a crisis of adjustment following retirement. Advocates of this view, such as Ruth Cavan and Robert Havighurst, took the position that morale in old age was enhanced through involvement in new roles and activities, notably in relation to work and leisure. "Disengagement theory" (as developed by Elaine Cumming and William Henry) was another functionalist perspective (developed in the late 1950s) that took an opposing view, suggesting that withdrawal from mainstream social responsibilities was a natural correlate of growing old. Old age was viewed as a period in which the aging individual and society both simultaneously engage in mutual separation, with retirement in the case of men and widowhood in respect of women.

Through the 1960s, and for a period in the 1970s, activity and disengagement theory set the parameters of debates within social gerontology. "Activity theory" stimulated the development of several social psychological theories of aging, including "continuity theory" (by Robert Atchley) and theories of "successful aging" (by Rowe and Kahn). Drawn from "developmental" or "life-cycle theory," continuity theory asserts that aging persons have the need and the tendency to maintain the same personalities, habits, and perspectives that they developed over their life-course. An individual who is successfully aging maintains a mature integrated personality, which also is the basis of life satisfaction. As such, decreases in activity or social interaction are viewed as related more to changes in health and physical function than to an inherent need for a shift in or relinquishment of previous roles.

Increasingly, however, through the 1970s, concern came to be expressed about the individual-level focus of theories of aging and their failure to address the impact of social and economic factors on the lives of older people. Riley's "age stratification theory" was an early example, exploring the role and influence of social structures on the process of individual aging and the stratification of age in society. One dimension of this theory is the concept of "structural lag," which denotes that social structures (for example policies of retirement at age sixty-five) do not keep pace with changes in population dynamic and individual lives (such as increasing life expectancy). The implications of the theory are that human resources in the oldest – and also the youngest – age strata are underutilized, and that excess burdens of care and other responsibilities are placed upon groups in the middle years.

Another important approach which moved beyond individual adjustment to aging, and which was also influenced by the age stratification model, has been the life-course approach (as initially developed by Glen Elder). Here, aging individuals and cohorts are examined as one phase of the entire lifetime and seen as shaped by historical, social, economic, and environmental factors that occur at earlier ages. Life-course theory bridges macro–micro levels of analysis by considering the relationships among **social structure**, social processes, and social psychological states.

Passuth and Bengston in *Sociological Theories of Aging* (1996) suggest that the key elements of the approach are that: "(1) aging occurs from birth to death (thereby distinguishing this theory from those that focus exclusively on the elderly); (2) aging involves social, psychological and biological processes; and (3) aging experiences are shaped by cohort-historical factors."

From the early 1980s, neo-Marxist perspectives such as political economy theory became influential within studies of aging. Beginning in the late 1970s and early 1980s with the work of Carroll Estes and Alan Walker, these theorists initiated the task of describing the respective roles of **capitalism** and the **state** in contributing to systems of domination and marginalization of older people. The political economy perspective is distinguished from the dominant liberal-pluralist theory in political science and sociology in that political economists focus on the role of economic and political systems and other social structures and social forces in shaping and reproducing the prevailing power arrangements and inequalities in society. In the political economy perspective, social policies pertaining to retirement income, health, and social service benefits and entitlements are examined as products of economic, political, and socio-cultural processes and institutional and individual forces that coalesce in any given socio-historical period. Social policy is an outcome of the social struggles, the conflicts, and the dominant power relations of the period. Policy reflects the structure and culture of advantage and disadvantage as enacted through class, race/ethnicity, gender, and age relations. Social policy is itself a powerful determinant of the **life chances** and conditions of individuals and population groups such as older people.

Another important approach is that of cultural and humanistic gerontology, sometimes referred to as moral economy or more broadly as cultural gerontology. This perspective, first developed by Thomas Cole and Harry Moody, has gained popularity, as the classical theoretical opposition of structure versus agency and culture versus structure has given way to an appreciation of the interplay and "recursive" relationships of culture, and agency and structure. Cultural gerontology is part of the trend towards theories that reject the sole determinacy of economics in explaining social institutions such as the state and old age policy. The approach provides a re-formulation of the unidirectional causality implied in the classical base/superstructure (see **ideology**) model of **Marxism**. What has followed is an intensified focus on

addressing issues relating to meaning and experience in later life, with critical questions raised about the efficacy of western culture in providing adequate moral resources to sustain the lives of older people.

Biographical perspectives have also emerged as a significant stream of work within gerontology. Biographical or "life history" research has an extensive pedigree in the social sciences (building on the work of **W. I. Thomas** and Florian Znaniecki, *The Polish Peasant in Europe and America*, 1918–20). Some of the key researchers in the field of aging using biographical and life history techniques have included James Birren, Joanna Bornat, Peter Coleman, Paul Thompson, and Gary Kenyon. Birren's influential edited collection *Aging and Biography* (1996) took the view that biographical approaches could contribute towards understanding both individual and shared aspects of aging over the life-course. Examining reactions to personal crises and turning points could, it was argued, provide researchers with unique insights into the way individuals construct their lives. Equally, however, studying lives provides a perspective on the influence of social institutions such as **work and the employment** and the **family**. Biographical data thus help in understanding what Ruth and Kenyon (*Biography in Adult Development and Aging*, 1996) refer to as the possibilities and limits set by the historical period in which people live.

Finally, theories of aging drawn around issues relating to **identity** and the self have also gained in importance. Mike Hepworth and Mike Featherstone in *The Body* (1991) have developed the view that aging can be best explained as a mask. Here, physical processes of aging, as reflected in outward appearance, are contrasted to a real self that remains young. This theory, which has come to be known as the "mask of aging," holds that over time the aging body becomes a cage from which a younger self-identity cannot escape. The body, while it is malleable, can still provide access to a variety of consumer identities. However, as aging gathers pace, it becomes increasingly difficult to "re-cycle" the failing body, which simultaneously denies access to that world of choice. Simon Biggs in *The Mature Imagination* (1999) suggests that the struggle between inner and external worlds may result in older people being at war with themselves, in a battle between a desire for youthful expression and the frailties generated by an aging body.

Globalization is another significant issue affecting both theories of aging and the daily lives of older people. An important development at a macro-level arises from the interplay between demographic change (notably longer life expectancy) and the trends associated with political and cultural globalization. Awareness of living in an interconnected world brings to the fore questions of cultural diversity, different understandings about what it means to grow old, and the issue of who we take to be an older person.

The tendency in studies of aging has been to use western models of development to define old age, these taking sixty or sixty-five as the boundary set by conventional retirement and pension systems. But in some continents (notably sub-Saharan Africa), old age may be more meaningfully defined as starting from fifty (or even earlier). Access to pension systems to mark the onset of old age is itself a culturally specific process. Relevant to western contexts (though changing even here with privatization), it has little resonance in countries such as China where, out of 90 million people aged sixty-five plus, just one-quarter have entitlement to a pension. In a number of senses the traditional formulation of "aging societies" is unhelpful, given global inequalities. Global society contains numerous demographic realities – aging Europe, to take one example, as compared with increasingly youthful United States, and falling life expectancy in Russia and sub-Saharan Africa. Such contrasts create significant variations in the construction of growing old – national, transnational, subcultural – producing, as a result, new questions and perspectives for research in the field of aging.   CHRIS PHILLIPSON

age differentiation
– see **age**.

age group
– see **age**.

ageism
– see **age**.

agency and structure

Beginning in the 1970s, the expression "agency and structure" has been employed to thematize the relationship between the enactment of social practices on the one hand and large-scale and historically enduring social phenomena on the other. **Language** is often used to illustrate several important issues in agency–structure relations. On the one hand, language exists as an observable reality only when actors use language (converse, read, or write) in specific ways at particular moments in local settings. On the other hand, from a structural point of view, a given language exhibits general patterns (for example, syntax, semantics, grammar) that are never fully realized in any single conversation or piece of writing, although they are presupposed by all of them. In the case of language, the problem of agency and structure focuses on the relationship between the enactment of linguistic practices on the one hand and the large-scale structure of language on the other.

In terms of the agency–structure problem, agency implies enactment rather than autonomy or empowerment, which in other contexts the term sometimes implies. The term structure is used in several different ways. Language is only one example of cultural structures, a category that also comprises culinary cultures, religious cultures, cultures of dominant and subaltern groups, and so on. Material structures are relevant as well. For example, a capitalist **market**, no matter how extensive and dynamic it may be, exists only so long as traders engage in acts of exchange of material resources. If acts of exchange were to cease, say following the collapse of the value of instruments of credit, then even the most massive and structured market would come to a halt and ultimately cease to exist. Fields of the distribution of scarce resources can be framed in terms of the agency–structure problem as well. For example, the practice of continuous reinvestment of profits, about which **Max Weber** wrote, enables entrepreneurs and investors to accumulate large quantities of capital. Skillful reinvestment can ultimately concentrate large amounts of capital under the control of a very small group while the majority of a population is not very prosperous. But if profits are not skillfully reinvested in practice, then the structure of **inequality** may change. Finally, social **networks** and other patterns of articulated social relationships may be understood in terms of the agency–structure problem as well. For example, the networks of weak ties at the center of **Mark Granovetter**'s well-known research may be understood as a set of casual, intermittent interactions among acquaintances, during which useful information is discussed and thus transmitted. Each link in the network is an enacted set of conversational practices, and the form of the network is produced one link at a time as these conversations occur.

To appreciate the specificity of the agency–structure problem, it must be understood in contrast to the problem of the relationship between the individual and the collectivity. This second problem, which is one of the oldest and most intractable dilemmas in **social theory**, restates in sociological terms the philosophical conundrum of free will versus **determinism**. Are individuals so constituted and constrained by their structural circumstances that they have little or no free will at all, as **Émile Durkheim**, for example, maintained? Or are **social structures** merely the epiphenomenal consequences of what actors do as they each pursue their personal interests and desires, as can be inferred, for example, from the writings of Adam Smith (1723–90)? The dilemma here is that the sociologist is virtually compelled to assume a reductionist position. Either individuals are epiphenomenal to structures or structures are epiphenomenal to individuals. The agency–structure problem does not compel the sociologist to reduce one phenomenon to another. This is because, from an agency–structure point of view, the individual is no longer a counterpoint to structure. Instead, the counterpoint to structure is social praxis, that is, the enactment of forms of social conduct or behavior. Enacted forms of behavior generate (that is, construct or produce) the realities of social life, whether they be cultural, economic, distributional, or network patterns. The same cannot be said of individuals. Individuals may want to act in certain ways in order to achieve their interests or wants, but they may lack the competence or resources to do so. In other words, individuals in a given setting may not be able to enact certain practices, even if motivated to do so. Conversely, actors may generate aspects of social reality (for example, cultural domination as **Pierre Bourdieu** suggests) though they are unaware they exercise agency in this regard.

How is the agency–structure problem amenable to non-reductive solutions? To begin, consider not a single locally enacted practice, but rather a single form of practice, which is to say a form of practice that may be enacted each day by numerous actors in different settings and may be enacted as well by successive generations of actors. Now we can introduce the idea of social reproduction, which is to say the recurrent reenactment of similar forms of practice. Of course, no two instances of enactment are entirely the same: for example, when conversing, people make grammatical and syntactical mistakes, or engage in creative wordplay rather than speaking in conventional forms. Nonetheless, over many instances, people use language in broadly similar ways, and this is what it means to say that forms of linguistic practice are reproduced. But, as previously mentioned, no single form of practice can generate a large-scale structure such as an entire language or market. Large-scale structures are generated when many different forms of practice are reproduced. Since this reproduction takes place over some duration of time in a variety of different locales, sociologists can analyze structures best by abstracting structural properties of praxis they find to be associated with one another. Indeed, the same set of interactions may help to generate a number of different structures. For example, a capitalist market is generated in ongoing sequences of commercial practices and economic exchange. But the same practices generate a network of business acquaintances. Practices may also result from the use of a common language or dialect, and so on. Which of these structures is of interest is an analytical choice on the part of the sociologist.

We now can see how structured practices (practices that are reproduced in broadly similar forms) can sustain large-scale structures, but what part do these structures play in the enactment of practices? The issue here turns on social competencies. Babies and newcomers to a culture or society do not arrive knowing how to speak a given language or how to execute a market trade. Individuals gain agency (the ability to enact given practices) as they learn how to perform the forms of conduct that are a matter of routine in a given group. From this point of view, the structured form of social practices precedes and shapes how that practice is performed. Looked at from a broader perspective, the set of practices that form a language or a capitalist market or a network of weak ties precedes any given round of social reproduction. In the end what we have is what **Anthony Giddens** terms in *The Constitution of Society* (1984) a "duality of structure." That is to say, there is an ongoing reciprocal relationship between structure and agency. Structural circumstances provide the means to reproduce social practices, but when social practices are reproduced they perpetuate the structure, making it a social reality in a new historical moment. In very stable social groups, for example tradition-bound villages, this reciprocal relation between structure and agency in social reproduction may go on for generations.

Reductionism may not be inevitable when social life is conceived in terms of the connection between agency and structure, but it is still a potential pitfall. Symbolic interactionists, for example, sometimes reduce structures of all kinds to the practices through which they are produced without regard for the structural properties of practices that have been reproduced many times over in the past. Structure, in effect, is reduced to enactment. It is symptomatic of this problem that **symbolic interactionism** stresses the prospect of creativity in interaction and other social processes. In a more balanced view, the structural conditions of praxis, including all necessary competencies and resources needed to engage in social conduct, both enable actors to perform actions in certain ways and thereby also limit actors to performing according to their competencies. However, creativity and resistance to established ways of doing things are not thereby ruled out. Indeed, many practices, especially those found in the modern era, permit and sometimes require some degree of innovation. This is vividly illustrated in the fine arts, where structured practices (for example, techniques for painting, musical composition, dancing, and so forth) are employed to produce novel works, or, more radically, new artistic genres. Similar possibilities exist in many walks of life, including, of course, **politics**, where resistors and rebels may resist oppressive practices to oppose and replace the powers that be.

It is also possible to reduce agency to structure. This happens when practices are conceived as so completely derived from structural conditions that their social reproduction is inevitable. This form of reductionism can be observed in the works of Bourdieu. Bourdieu often investigated how it happens that groups of actors who are disadvantaged and subordinated to others somehow participate in the reproduction of their own disadvantages and subordination. He conceives the practices in which they engage (key elements of their habitus; see **habitus and field**) as unselfconsciously reproducing a field of inequality. It is symptomatic of Bourdieu's structural reductionism that he conceives very few opportunities for actors to resist or rebel or, for that matter, even to recognize the ways in which they reproduce the structural conditions of their own inequality. While agency only denotes the enactment of practices in the agency–structure duality, it leaves open the possibility, given the proper situation, that actors may seize the moment to devise new practices that improve the conditions in which they live.

Giddens's **structuration** theory as expressed in *The Constitution of Society* (1984) and discussed in Ira Cohen's *Structuration Theory* (1989) is widely regarded as the most thoroughly developed set of sociological concepts that pivots on the relationship between agency and structure. Giddens's work has influenced numerous empirical works, and new, substantively oriented innovations in structuration theory are currently under development

by the British sociologist, Rob Stones. Giddens's structuration theory has also attracted a great deal of criticism, most extensively from another British sociologist, **Margaret Archer**. She argues, *inter alia*, that Giddens is guilty of a peculiar form of reductionism in which structure and praxis are inextricably linked. She believes that structure and practices must be distinct objects of sociological analysis. However, in her main criticisms, in *Realist Social Theory* (1995), Archer appears to misconstrue the level of analysis on which Giddens addresses the agency–structure link. Giddens writes in ontological terms, that is, in terms of how the duality of structure and agency generates social life at large. Archer seems to make an epistemological argument in which she calls for separate sociological analyses on the structural and praxiological levels. If this is taken into account, Archer's position may differ from those of Giddens's less than may at first appear.

A more difficult problem, for Giddens and others who theorize in terms of agency and structure, is what to do about the individual's wants and interests that they originally set aside. Giddens and Bourdieu, along with most others who theorize along these lines, rely on tacit and unconscious motives to account for social reproduction. But it is empirically demonstrable that at least some segments of **social actions** are consciously driven by actors' interests, desires, and attachments to others. Where do these motives come from? Are they freely chosen or are desires and interests socially derived and reproduced? Here the problem of individual versus collectivity reemerges. In the future, theorists may feel challenged to find a way to address the problem of agency and structure and the problem of individualism and collectivism from an integrated point of view.

IRA COHEN

aging
– see **age**.

alienation
The process whereby people become estranged from the world in which they are living, the concept is associated with **Karl Marx**'s early works, especially *Economic and Philosophical Manuscripts* (1844) and his critique of **W. G. F. Hegel** and Ludwig Feuerbach (1804–72). For Hegel, people created a culture, which then confronted them as an alien, objectified force. Human activity was the expression of Spirit, of *Geist*, whose creations were not self-transparent to their creators,

although they would become so at the end of history. The work of Feuerbach, a "Young Hegelian" was also significant. Ludwig Feuerbach (1804–72) criticized what he called Hegel's reduction of Man's Essence to Self-consciousness, and developed a critique of **religion** as "self-alienation." Rejecting Hegel's idealistic philosophy and advocating materialism, Feuerbach emphasized the individual, purely "biological" nature of humans, in which thought was a purely reflective, contemplative process. But in religion, the human potential for love, creativity, and **power** were alienated into the mythical deities to which such powers were attributed. In *The Essence of Christianity* (1843), Feuerbach claimed that God is the manifestation of human inner nature; religion is the "solemn unveiling" of human hidden treasures, the avowal of innermost thoughts, the open confession of the secrets of human love. But this image of perfection becomes the source of rules that are reimposed on people's lives as regulations and self-denial.

Both the Hegelian and Feuerbachian use of alienation were important for Marx. He accepted much of Feuerbach's critique, but took issue with the notion of a human essence projected onto God. Human self-alienation is not psychological, but social and historical, and specifically arises from the system of production. Marx's use of the concept was critical and in some ways ironic, in that he was taking a term that was widely used by Hegelian philosophers and subjecting it to parody (a point generally missed in debates about whether the concept continues to inform Marx's later works). Marx insisted that it was human **labor** that created culture and history but that Hegel had substituted a mystical substance – Mind – for the real subject of history. For Marx it was practice rather than thought that changes the material world and practice is a process of objectification, whereby the products of labor are manifest in material forms. This process is part of human "species being," that is, a potential creativity essential to being human. This enables people to affirm themselves by objectifying their individuality in objects and enabling others to enjoy the products of their labor. It is thus a social and affirmative process. However, in conditions of commodity production, this becomes distorted – no longer a free affirmation of life but, on the contrary, an alienation of life, since workers must work in order to live. What could be the basis of creative human self-expression is reduced in bourgeois society to the most profound form of alienation in wage labor. Wage-workers sell their labor (in *Capital* this is refined to *labor power,* the

capacity to work for a determinate period) to satisfy basic needs for food, shelter, and clothing, while capitalists own the labor process and dispose of the products of labor for profit.

In *The Economic and Philosophical Manuscripts*, Marx discussed four types of alienation. The first was alienation from the product, where the means of production are owned by capitalists who appropriate and exchange the products of labor. These then take on a life of their own, separate from the needs and wishes of the producers; thus, workers "build palaces but live in hovels." Second was alienation from productive activity, where work becomes external to the lives of workers, who "feel freely active" only when eating, drinking, and procreating – activities that humans share with animals. Third was alienation from "species-being", such that creativity, an essentially human capacity for objectifying ourselves through work, is degraded in systems of production that are exploitative and where work becomes drudgery. Finally, there was alienation of "man from man" where community is dislocated, all social relations are dominated by economics, and hostile classes are formed. The fundamental injustice of **capitalism** is that it targets for exploitation precisely what differentiates humans from other animals, namely our capacity for productive creativity, which will be fulfilled in a future, emancipated society.

In later works the concept of alienation appears less often, although similar ideas are found in Marx's theory of commodity fetishism. The domination of commodities in our society is so pervasive that it seems to be an inevitable, natural state of affairs. All our achievements, everything we produce, appear as commodities. Capitalism is the first system of generalized commodity production, in which the commodity has become a universal category of society as a whole. Yet the commodity is "mysterious" in that value and price appear to be properties arising from the process of circulation on the market (as relationships between things rather than people). Commodities acquire social characteristics because individuals enter the productive process only as the owners of commodities. It appears as if the market itself causes the rise and fall of prices, and pushes workers into one branch of production or out of another, independent of human agency. The impact of society on the individual is mediated through the social form of things. However, Marxist analysis attempts to show that these apparent relations between things are really social relations of production in which value is created through the exploitation of wage laborers.

Marx's theory seems to assume a relatively time-less "human nature," although this was a concept he elsewhere rejected. He did, however, assume that people would be most fulfilled when engaging freely in creative labor, famously depicting in *The German Ideology* (1845) non-alienated exist-ence in a future communist society as one "where nobody has one exclusive sphere of activity but each can become accomplished in any branch he wishes, . . . to hunt in the morning, fish in the afternoon, rear cattle in the evening, criticise after dinner, . . . without ever becoming hunter, fisherman, herdsman or critic." But this does raise the question of whether alienation *can* be elimin-ated in modern societies characterized by com-plex divisions of labor and inequalities. In later works, Marx was more circumspect, suggesting that the co-ordination and division of labor prob-ably cannot be eliminated. Similarly, there is the question of the extent to which social processes in complex societies can be self-transparent or whether opacity is inevitable. With the decline of interest in Marxist theory since the collapse of Soviet Communism, interest in the concept of alienation has waned too.　　　　LARRY RAY

Althusser, Louis (1918–1990)

Althusser was one of the best-known Communist Party theoreticians of the twentieth century, who latterly became associated with Eurocommunism. Three influential works were *For Marx* (1965 [trans. 1969]), *Lenin and Philosophy* (1965), and *Reading Cap-ital* (1967 [trans. 1970]). Key concepts associated with his philosophy are "the problematic" (texts were understood as effects of an underlying matrix of concepts that could be revealed through "symptom-atic reading"), "epistemological break" (between hu-manism and science), "overdetermination" of a "conjuncture" in which revolutionary change might occur, and **interpellation**. He attempted to reconcile **Marxism** with **structuralism**, an intellec-tual fashion with which Althusser and his student **Michel Foucault** were associated. This theory stressed the persistence of "deep structures" that underlie all human cultures, leaving little room for either historical change or human initiative. Althusser rejected the positive content of empirical knowledge entirely. Althusser asserted that Essence is not to be found in Appearance, but must be discovered through "theoretical practice," in which objects appear not as real-concrete objects but as abstract-conceptual objects. Althusser further rejec-ted the concept of contradiction in **Karl Marx** and **Georg Wilhelm Friedrich Hegel**, which he saw in structuralist terms as "over-determination" – where

outcomes have multiple simultaneous causes that together create a "conjuncture", the resolution of which is unpredictable. This is part of a wider rejec-tion of much of Marx's work, which had to be read critically and rigorously to separate the "human-ism" from scientific theorization of capitalist soci-ety. "Humanism" in this context referred to belief in the self-realization of the human species through creative agency.

In 1980 Althusser murdered his wife and was confined to a psychiatric unit until his death.

　　　　　　　　　　　　　　　　　　LARRY RAY

ancient society

This term has a broader and a more restrictive denotation, the two of which are analytically dis-tinct, though deployed so much together and so much in the same context that they are often confused. The former is almost as old as Christian reflection on the Old Testament, but it has its first official social scientific usage as the nineteenth-century register of an anthropological and evolu-tionist distinction between human **society** from its primitive beginnings forward to the advent of industrialism and human society as it had come to be in the aftermath of industrialization. In just such a usage, it can serve as the title of the com-pendious treatment (*Ancient Society*, 1877) by Henry Lewis Morgan (1818–81) of material cultural evo-lution from the foraging band to the alphabetic-ally literate city-states of pre-Christian Greece and Rome. The crucial divide that lay for Morgan be-tween ancient society and its counterpart – the "modern society" – was the divide between a pre-industrial and an industrial **economy**. **Karl Marx** and **Friedrich Engels** were the most notable of classical social theorists explicitly to engage Mor-gan's theorization of the "savage," "barbaric," and "civilized" stages of social evolution, but **Spencer**, **Weber**, and **Durkheim** could agree that the great divide between the ancient and the modern was as Morgan would have it be. The lexical and theor-etical tradition of a distinction between "ancient preindustrial" and "modern industrial" society survives today, but, like the distinction between the "primitive" and the "modern," is vulnerable to Johannes Fabian's critique of the "denial of coevalness" in *Time and The Other* (1983).

In its more restrictive usage, the term is a philological-historical category. Its exemplary denotata are precisely the city-states of pre-Chris-tian Greece and Rome. It is the fulcrum of a debate dating from the Renaissance over the extent to which the ancient past is culturally continuous with the modern present (and, if not continuous, the extent to which it is more or less virtuous than the modern present). Since the later nineteenth century, social theorists have consistently emphasized the discontinuities between the two, if to incompatible critical ends. Champions of **progress** such as Spencer, for example, construe the gap as that between a form of society whose survival and growth depend essentially on **war** and a higher form whose survival and growth can at last rest in cooperation and the increasingly universal pursuit of enlightened self-interest. Such occasional Romantics as Weber, in contrast, might construe the gap instead as that between a form of society still capable of sustaining a **public sphere** unified in its commitment to a common store of transcendent **values** and a depleted form in which the gods themselves are perpetually at war and *Homo economicus* reigns in their stead. The spirit, if not the letter, of Spencer's position has more contemporary representatives in both **Jürgen Habermas** and **Niklas Luhmann**. Echoes of the Weberian position continued in the twentieth century in the anti-populist republicanism of such political theorists as **Hannah Arendt**.

JAMES D. FAUBION

Annales School

A movement of French historians founded by Lucien Febvre (1878–1956) and Marc Bloch (1886–1944) with their journal, *Annales: Economies, Societies, Civilizations*, the school reacted to the prevailing narrative method of history and its concentration on political and diplomatic events – whose exemplary exponent was Leopold von Ranke (1795–1886) – by broadening both the content and the methodological approach of history. This included: (1) extending the historian's purview to broad areas of human behavior and activity generally neglected by traditional historians, by drawing on a variety of other disciplines including sociology, anthropology, psychology, linguistics, and geography; (2) the use and development of new methods of historical investigation, including qualitative and quantitative methodological approaches in addition to standard archival resources; (3) examining the *longue durée* or broad long-term persistence of structures within history.

The Annales approach was in no way unified and included a number of divergent standpoints within the group. According to Peter Burke in *The French Historical Revolution* (1990), the school can be divided into three phases covering three successive generations of historians. The first generation, which existed from the 1920s to 1945, included Bloch and Febvre. Heavily influenced by

Émile Durkheim's sociology, Bloch examined the prevalence of the medieval belief that the king could cure scrofula by touching people afflicted by this skin disease in *The Royal Touch* (1924). However, his most influential work is undoubtedly his two-volume study *Feudal Society* (1939–40), which dealt not only with the juridical and political dynamics of medieval society, but with its whole worldview and culture. These books showed Bloch's concern with characteristic features of the Annales movement: collective representations, the history of mentalities, and long-term problem-based comparative historical analysis. In contrast to the influence of sociology on Bloch, Febvre was heavily influenced by the historical geographical approach of Paul Vidal de la Blanche (1845–1918), but he also focused on collective mentalities. In his major work, *The Problem of Unbelief in the Sixteenth Century: The Religion of Rabelais* (1939), he argued for the impossibility of atheism in the sixteenth century.

The emphasis on geographical factors continued in the work of the second generation of writers, whose most prominent representative, and perhaps the most influential of all the Annales scholars, was Fernand Braudel (1902–85). In his doctoral dissertation, later published as *The Mediterranean and the Mediterranean World, in the Age of Philip II* (1949), Braudel pursues a "total history" in which he examined the geography and economic, social, and political structures of the Mediterranean world, as well as outlining its political, diplomatic, and military history. He stressed the important effect that geohistorical structural constraints had on shaping states and economies, as well as events and individuals.

Emmanuel Le Roy Ladurie (1929–), whose most noted work is *Montaillou* (1975 [trans. 1979]), and Jacques Le Goff (1924–), who has written widely on the Middle Ages, most acutely in *Medieval Civilization 400–1500* (1988), were the most prominent of the third generation of historians who emerged after 1968.

The writings of the Annales movement provided an important intellectual resource for many Marxist historians, as well as having a bearing on the work of **Michel Foucault**. Its work continues in the Fernand Braudel Center at Binghampton, which was founded in 1976 and whose director is **Immanuel Wallerstein**.   STEVEN LOYAL

anomie

From the Greek *a-nomos*, meaning without laws, mores, and **traditions**, in sociology, the concept refers to absence of **norms** and of the constraints these provide. In *The Division of Labor in Society* (1893 [trans. 1960]) **Émile Durkheim** describes how the division of **labor** fails to produce **solidarity** or social cohesion through an absence of proper regulation of relations or a type of regulation not in keeping with the development of the division of labor. He calls this condition the anomic division of labor. In *Suicide* (1897 [trans. 1951]), anomic **suicide** results from inappropriately low levels of social regulation. Economic crises, both depression and excessive growth, are held to be a source of anomie. Curiously, the regulation of **marriage** has contrasting consequences for men and women, according to Durkheim: unmarried men are susceptible to anomic suicide, whereas the regulation of marriage has the reverse effect on women (married women are more likely to commit suicide than unmarried ones). For Durkheim, anomie is a feature of social structure not of individual persons. **David Riesman** in *The Lonely Crowd* (1950), on the other hand, regards anomie as a psychological feature of individuals. **Robert K. Merton**, though, distinguishes in *Social Theory and Social Structure* (1968) between the source and the experience of anomie, acknowledging the psychological impact of anomie but denying it has a psychological source. Merton advances Durkheim's account in two ways: he sees the conflict of norms and not merely their absence as a source of anomie, and he recognizes the creative potential of anomie as well as its destructive side.   JACK BARBALET

antiglobalization movements
– see **globalization**.

Archer, Margaret (1943–)
Professor of Sociology at the University of Warwick and Co-director of the Centre for Critical Realism, Archer is best known for her contributions to sociological theory. She was President of the International Sociological Association (1986–90). Her early work was on the development of educational systems in *Social Origins of Educational Systems* (1974). She developed the analysis of human agency through a study in cultural sociology in *Culture and Agency: The Place of Culture in Social Theory* (1988), in which she defends the separate causal importance of **culture** and **social structure**. Her work is closely associated with a realist **epistemology** which she has explored in *Realist Social Theory: The Morphogenetic Approach* (1995). She has therefore contributed to the analysis of **agency and structure**, where she has been critical of the absence of any causal account of

structure in the work of **Anthony Giddens**. There are broadly two versions of the notion of "structure." The first, favored by Giddens, treats structure as generative rules and resources, and emphasizes the voluntary nature of **social action**. The second version defines structure as organized patterns of social relationships that are causally efficacious. Archer supports this second interpretation, which incorporates the idea of the causal priority of structure over agency, but she defends the importance of the reflexivity of social actors in *Structure, Agency and the Internal Conversation* (2003). She has, with Jonathan Tritter, also brought her perspective into the debate about rational choice in *Rational Choice Theory* (2000).   BRYAN S. TURNER

Arendt, Hannah (1906–1975)
Born in Hanover, Germany, Arendt was, from 1967 until her death, a university professor of the Graduate School at the New School for Social Research in New York, and editor of Schocken Books (1946–48). Arendt was one of the leading political philosophers of her time and a critic of the **social sciences**, whose language she found pretentious and obfuscating. In an important debate with **David Riesman**, starting in 1947, she argued that **sociology** had failed to explain the unprecedented rise of **totalitarianism**. Riesman countered that Arendt exaggerated the capacities and competencies of totalitarian leaders and their **bureaucracies**, and that no adequate political theory could be developed without an adequate sociological theory of society. This debate was seminal in defining the relationship between the concepts of the social and the political.

Having completed her thesis on *Love and St Augustine* (1929 [trans. 1996]) under the supervision of Karl Jaspers (1883–1969), she escaped from Germany to work with Zionist organizations in France and eventually settled in the United States, becoming a citizen in 1951. She became famous initially for her work on *The Origins of Totalitarianism* (1951). Although this work is clearly a contribution to political theory, it has important implications for sociologists, because she argued that people in modern society are forced out of a shared public life into a lonely, isolated, and interior existence. In their isolation, there are pressures towards uniformity that undermine their autonomy, and as a result they are psychologically exposed to the totalitarian social forces of a **mass society**. The clear distinction between private and public life in the classical world has been confused in modern times by the emergence of "the social." In contemporary society, people are connected together, but these common threads are, paradoxically, their private consumer desires. In a mass society, the social becomes the basis of mass conformity and the ethical calling of the political sinks into mundane petty politics.

Her most influential philosophical work was *The Human Condition* (1958) in which she divided human activities into labor, work, and action. She argued that human life can only be meaningful if people can engage effectively in the public sphere. This view of politics and her critique of the social were further expanded in *On Revolution* (1963), *Between Past and Future* (1961), and *Men in Dark Times* (1970). In her report on the trial of Adolf Eichmann in 1961 in *Eichmann in Jerusalem* (1963), she coined the expression "banality of evil" to describe the impact of bureaucratic **norms** on personal responsibility for the Holocaust. Her essays on personal morality and collective responsibility were edited as *Responsibility and Judgement* (2003).   BRYAN S. TURNER

Aron, Raymond (1905–1983)

A French journalist, political philosopher, and sociologist, Raymond Aron studied at the École Normale Supérieure and spent some time in Cologne and Berlin. He was Professor in Sociology at the Sorbonne from 1954 until 1968. In 1970 he was elected to a Chair at the Collège de France. Amongst his many publications are *German Sociology* (1935 [trans. 1957], *Introduction to the Philosophy of History* (1938 [trans. 1961]), and two volumes of *Main Currents in Sociological Thought* (1960, 1962 [trans. 1965, 1967]). He contributed to the study of **industrial society** in *Eighteen Lectures on Industrial Society* (1963), and to the sociology of **war** in *Peace and War; A Theory of International Relations* (1961), *The Century of Total War* (1951), and *Clausewitz; Philosopher of War* (1976). He positioned himself in the French liberal **tradition**, stretching back to **Baron Charles de Montesquieu** and **Alexis de Tocqueville**. Aron introduced **Max Weber** to French sociology and political science. He was particularly sympathetic towards Weber's political stance and his **methodology** of history. Aron insisted that the positivist view was inapplicable to the analysis of social phenomena. He took issue with the tendency of **Émile Durkheim** and some Marxists to embrace holism and to explain social processes by a "prime mover." For Aron, the search for a single primary cause, whether it is economic or cultural, does not do justice to the complexity of social life. An opponent to **Marxism**, Aron insisted that we should never abandon our aim for objectivity in the **social sciences**, even if it can never be

obtained. He was highly critical of **utopianism** and regarded Marxism as a dangerous route to **totalitarianism**. These views made him unpopular amongst the **generation** of May, 1968, but he has since been rehabilitated. Jon Elster and **Raymond Boudon** worked under his supervision.

PATRICK BAERT

arts

The field of (the sociology of the arts) deals with art works, forms, and genres in social, political, and historical context. It has shifted, over the past five decades, from a concern with the arts and society, to a concern with the social shaping of the arts, to, more recently, a focus on how the arts may provide conditions for action and organization in various social milieux. In all of these projects, notions of the autonomy of the arts, of absolute artistic worth, and of the isolated genius creator are replaced by considerations of arts **occupations**, **organizations**, and **institutions**, by a focus on material and technical resources, and by studies of reception and use of the arts.

This empirical focus has distinguished arts sociology since the mid-1970s from earlier theoretical and philosophical approaches (most notably the perspective of **Theodor Wiesengrund Adorno**) that adopt an evaluative stance in relation to styles, genres, or epochs within the arts. It is also different from semiotic readings of art works characteristic of scholarly research on the arts within literature, and from art and music history, in that it tends either to evade the question of meaning or to explore that question through the responses and actions of artistic consumers. Various **surveys** of the field have detailed this shift, such as Vera L. Zolberg's *Constructing a Sociology of the Arts* (1990) and, more recently, Victoria Alexander's *Sociology of the Arts* (2003).

During the 1980s, arts sociology centered on three main foci – the production of **culture** or art worlds perspective, a focus on taste-as-classification, and the study of individual and collective arts **consumption**.

Within the first area, Howard Becker's *Art Worlds* (1982), Janet Wolff's *Production of Art* (1981), and Richard A. Peterson's edited collection *The Production of Culture* helped set the agenda. These works described perspectives for grounding arts sociology, albeit at different levels, in empirical research and drew it away from earlier models of arts sociology, most prevalent in the classical canon (for example, **Max Weber**'s essay on *The Rational Foundations of Music*, 1958, or **Pitrim Sorokin**'s study of *Social and Cultural Dynamics*, 1937, in which he contrasted the vision of ideational with sensate cultures). These contributions emphasized abstract parallels between form or structure in art works and **social structures** writ large. While the concept of the art world drew upon Howard Becker's classic *American Sociological Review* article "Art as Collective Action" (1974), and conceptualized the arts in terms of **networks** and conventions, the approach associated with the term production of culture brings into relief institutional arrangements and contextual factors that shape individual art works, styles, and patterns of distribution/reception.

The focus on the connection between taste in and for the arts and **social status** has been most closely associated with the work of **Pierre Bourdieu**, such as *Distinction* (1979 [trans. 1984]). In Bourdieu's vision, the arts function as signs of social location and, owing to the various codes of artistic appropriation associated with arts consumption, as boundary tools. This perspective has been developed through various studies of arts patronage and cultural **entrepreneurship**, for example by William Weber (*Music and the Middle Class*, 1974) and Paul DiMaggio ("Cultural Entrepreneurship in Nineteenth-Century Boston," 1982, in *Media, Culture and Society*), and criticized through comparative and empirical studies of geographical regions outside France, most notably in the United States, where high socioeconomic status has been associated with broad cultural and artistic consumption (the "omnivore" concept) as opposed to a concern for exclusive distinction, as in Richard A. Peterson and Albert Simkus's work on taste and social status ("How Musical Tastes Mark Occupational Status," 1992, in *Cultivating Differences*).

Beginning in the late 1970s with, most notably, work by members or associates of the **Birmingham Centre for Contemporary Cultural Studies**, focus on the arts was used as a means for understanding the social mechanisms of group membership and identity formation. Here was one of the first explicit attempts to focus on the links between the arts, the meanings that the arts hold for their recipients (here conceived as consumers), and social formation. Equally significantly, the focus on artistic works or products dispensed with the high/popular distinction in favor of eclectic, user-driven classification systems, via, for example, the concept of articulation first developed by **Stuart Hall**. This perspective, illustrated in work by Paul Willis and Simon Frith, and by Dick Hebdige's *Subculture and the Meaning of Style* (1979), bound together anthropological attention to collective

representation, identity formation, and arts sociology, whether focused on **fashion**, decoration, or music consumption, in ways that have bequeathed important methodological tools to more recent work in arts sociology.

In the early 1990s, the call for a "return to meaning" in arts sociology began, taking various forms, from a concern with cultural structures, cognition, repertoires, and new institutionalism, to a focus on situated contentions of artistic meaning and **value**.

More recently, work in sociology of the arts, once somewhat marginal to the discipline of sociology as a whole, has been linked to a range of areas. In the work of Tia DeNora (*After Adorno*, 2003) and Antoine Hennion ("Taste as Performance," 2001, in *Theory, Culture and Society*), music has been explored as an exemplar for various forms of identification work, from self-identity to emotional work. It has also been explored by Ron Eyerman and Andrew Jamieson (*Music and Social Movements*, 1998) as a social movement activity. Depictions of the **body** in the plastic arts have been examined in connection with gender **politics** and sculpture, in particular high-profile public works, and have been considered in relation to the formation and stabilization of collective memory and from the perspective of "technologies of memory" (Robin Wagner-Pacifici, "Memories in the Making," 1996, in *Qualitative Sociology*). New work, at the interstices of sociology and **social psychology**, is emerging on aesthetic agency and environmental **aesthetics**, in organizational contexts and in the public sphere; and studies of arts production and arts distribution **technologies** have been linked to the historical and situated formation of subjectivity. Boundaries between "arts sociology," other sociologies, and work in cultural geography, community music therapy, social psychology, philosophy, and work in the arts and performing arts are continuing to blur, in ways that decant the once specialist concern with the arts into the realm of **everyday life** and social **institutions** and bring to the fore a concern with the aesthetic dimension in areas seemingly far removed from the arts, traditionally conceived.

TIA DENORA

Asian-American studies

From their historical roots as one of the smallest and most geographically concentrated racial groups, massive international **migration** since the passage of the Immigration Act of 1965 has made Asian Americans the fastest-growing segment of the United States population. According to the US Census (2000), from 1960 to 2000 the population of Asian Americans grew from fewer than 1 million to over 10 million, raising their share of the US population from less than 1 percent to over 4 percent. While Chinese, Japanese, and Filipinos made up the overwhelming share of the Asian-American population before the 1960s, the Asian-American population today is characterized by tremendous ethnic diversity, resulting from massive migration from nearly all parts of Asia. The ethnic diversity of Asian Americans has been matched by their class diversity. While laborers dominated the earliest waves of Asian immigration before the 1920s, contemporary Asian immigration has been characterized by significant class diversity, including large numbers of highly trained and educated professionals as well as unskilled workers, political refugees, and undocumented immigrants who face severe economic disadvantage and social marginalization. For the Asian-American poor and the working class, the prevailing "model minority" image that depicts all Asian-Americans as economically successful and highly educated functions to mask their plight.

In addition to these social characteristics, Asian Americans, as a racial term, represents one of the most important and instructive lessons on American race relations and racial categorization. On the one hand, as Michael Omi and Howard Winant show in *Racial Formations in the United States* (1994), the term Asian American highlights the dominant role of the state in the creation of racial categories. Most notably, through successive federal legislations and court decisions, the term Asian American found its most politically powerful meaning as an externally imposed legal category to deny Asians from South and East Asia the right to become citizens under the Naturalization Act of 1790 that originally limited naturalized **citizenship** only to "free whites." The denial of naturalized citizenship was joined through various state laws to exclude Asian Americans from ownership of land, to subject them to anti-miscegenation laws, and to justify exclusion from immigration. This *de jure* discrimination did not end until the civil rights movement of the 1960s. On the other hand, the term Asian American has served to organiz internally the political activities and social life of this group in powerful ways. In electoral politics, as Yen Le Espiritu demonstrates in *Asian American Panethnicity* (1992), the Asian-American banner creates a much more potent political presence than can be achieved through ethnic-specific organizing. In this sense, Asian American has

become a category of empowerment. In addition to strategic deployment in **politics**, Asian American is increasingly becoming an important term for explaining a wide range of social behaviors and cultural formations, ranging from residential and marriage patterns to literary and cultural productions that shape collective action and personal identity. Perhaps the most important sociological lesson of Asian American is to show that all racial categories are socially constructed and their significance and meaning are constantly undergoing change and transformation.   EDWARD PARK

Asiatic mode of production
– see **Karl Marx**.

assimilation
Originally developed by the **Chicago School**, assimilation refers to the process by which outsiders (especially migrants) give up their distinctive culture and adopt the cultural **norms** of the host society. This was typically thought to occur among second-generation migrants. There is no single model of assimilation but the concept was closely related to the "melting pot" metaphor used by **Robert Park** in relation to the United States, an anticipated result of which was a diminution of ethnic and racial divisions. Although often regarded as a "one-way" process, assimilation actually attempted to understand how heterogeneous societies develop though the reciprocal cultural interpenetration and adaptation of many different groups. The end result would then be a society in which a uniform cultural identity (for example "the American") would reflect the merging of diverse cultural and religious ingredients. Modern forms of organization, including **urbanization**, the **market**, mass culture, and universal **education**, were driving assimilation. Later theories in the 1960s developed more nuanced models. **Gunnar Myrdal** emphasized the contrast between American ideals of **equality** and the practice of racial discrimination, which he hoped would be overcome through the democratic political process. Milton Gordon developed a model of seven types of assimilation (cultural, structural, marital, identificational, attitudinal, behavioral, and civic) that need not always coincide. More recently the theory has been criticized on many grounds. These include failing to address structural racism, a deterministic and unilinear evolutionary logic, the persistence of religious and ethnic differences in modern societies, and existence of globalized transnational communities.

                                                                    LARRY RAY

associative democracy

The relationship between **voluntary associations** and **democracy** is one of the most enduring issues in **social theory**. While **modernity** is often defined as the process which eliminates all intermediate associations and affiliations between the individual and **state** or society, the actual unfolding of **modernization** has been much more complicated than this image implies. Rather, voluntary associations were the fundamental elements of the vitality of democratic life without which modern democratic states could not function. That this is the case is the starting point of theories of "associative democracy," especially as put forward by Paul Q. Hirst in *Associative Democracy: New Forms of Economic and Social Governance* (1994) and *Can Secondary Associations Enhance Democratic Governance?* (1995). Hirst argued that an associative democracy model would address the recurring dilemmas of social democratic models that rely on the state, which create forms of dependency and pluralist democratic models that rely on voluntary initiatives, which create **individualism**. That such theories were put forward clearly indicates that those social theorists in the nineteenth century, notably **Émile Durkheim** in *The Division of Labor in Society* (1894 [trans. 1984]), who had foreseen the increased polarization of democratic life between the individual and the state, were indeed prescient. Throughout the twentieth century, the rise of the social **welfare state** and then its rapid retrenchment and withdrawal have illustrated these intractable dilemmas of the right measure of balance between individual and social responsibility. Those who argued for associative forms of democracy highlighted the importance of voluntary associations and social groups in democratic life, fostering both individual and social responsibility. Others have argued more generally that, without fostering an associative culture, democratic states would become increasingly dominated by **politics** as professional expertise and the society as professional administration. The possibilities of associative democracy remain one of the most vital and lively questions of social and political theory.   ENGIN ISIN

attitude

This concept has a long, if sometimes controversial, history in sociological research. An attitude is generally defined as a learned disposition or belief that allows us to predict behavior. If, for example, we discover that an individual holds a positive attitude (learned disposition or belief) towards a presidential candidate we should, all other things

being equal, be entitled to predict s/he will vote (behavior) for that candidate. Research based on assessments of people's attitudes is sometimes held in higher scientific esteem than other types of survey research on the grounds that well-established attitude **scales** are said to have a higher level of validity and reliability than other types of survey research instruments. Attitudes are usually understood to occur on several different measurement continua, including those moving from highly favorable to highly unfavorable; stronger to weaker levels of intensity; and higher to lower levels of resolution or stability. Hence, we may hold a highly favorable attitude towards a presidential candidate, more or less intensely. If our attitude is less intense we may be less likely to act on it than if it is more intense. Likewise we may hold a highly favorable attitude towards a presidential candidate, more or less resolutely. This means that our attitude might be both highly favorable and highly intense but also highly subject to change based on new evidence. Attitudes that are held with high levels of intensity and high levels of stability are said to be those that offer the best grounds for predicting behavior.

DARIN WEINBERG

attitude scales
– see **scales**.

audience

While earlier forms of **cultural studies** focused on textual analysis and the production of **culture**, beginning in the 1960s a variety of individuals associated with the **Birmingham Centre for Contemporary Cultural Studies** began paying close attention to audience use of media, and the concept of audience studies became a key part of Cultural studies. The Birmingham group argued for an active audience that was able to dissect critically and make use of media material, arguing against the media manipulation perspective. Rooted in a classic article by **Stuart Hall** entitled "Encoding/Decoding" (1980), British Cultural studies began studying how different groups read television news and magazines, engaged in consumption, and made use of a broad range of media. In *Everyday Television: Nationwide* (1978), Charlotte Brunsdon and David Morley studied how different audiences consumed TV news; Ien Ang (*Watching Dallas*, 1985) and Tamar Liebes and Elihu Katz (*A World Connected*, 1990) investigated how varying audiences in the Netherlands, Israel, and elsewhere consumed and made use of the US TV series *Dallas*; and John Fiske (*Understanding Popular*

Culture, 1989; *Power Plays, Power Works*, 1993) wrote a series of books celebrating the active audience and consumer in a wide range of domains.

Some critics believed that audience studies went too far in valorizing an active audience and called for mediation between theories like those of the Frankfurt School that posited that the media were all-powerful instruments of manipulation, and theories like those of Fiske that emphasized the autonomy of audiences and their power of resistance. Since the mid-1980s, there has been a proliferation of how different audiences in various parts of the world use media according to their **gender**, **race and ethnicity**, **social class**, and ideology. In addition, media industries have always been interested in audience studies, and so the audience has entered the center of a wide range of communication, cultural, and **social theories** in the contemporary moment.

DOUGLAS KELLNER

audience research
– see **audience**.

Austro-Marxism
The term Austro-Marxism was coined before World War I to describe a group of young Marxist theorists in Vienna – the most prominent being Max Adler, Otto Bauer, Rudolf Hilferding, and Karl Renner. They expounded a form of **Marxism** that was rigorous yet undogmatic and that (unlike the revisionism of the German Social Democratic Party) remained revolutionary. Most had been involved in the Austrian socialist student movement and remained politically active in the Austrian Social Democratic Party. Their influence declined after the annexation of Austria to Nazi Germany in 1934, although neglect of their ideas underestimates their significance for Marxist theory. Austro-Marxists were interested in the development of Marxism as an empirical **social science** and were influenced by other intellectual currents in Vienna at the time, notably logical **positivism** and neo-Kantianism. The specific ideas of the Austro-Marxists are illustrated by the four major studies undertaken by Adler on the philosophy of science, Bauer on nationality and **nationalism**, Hilferding on finance **capitalism**, and Renner on social functions of law (see **law and society**). Much of Adler's work was devoted to the clarification of the theoretical foundations of Marxism and to its re-presentation as an empirical social science. He drew on both neo-Kantian and positivist philosophies to claim that the Marxist concept of "socialized humanity" was a conceptual a priori that made

the investigation of causal regularity possible. Adler's view of Marxism as a sociological theory was broadly shared by other Austro-Marxists and in turn influenced the development of **sociology** in Austria up to 1934. Over three decades Austro-Marxists analyzed the profound changes in capitalism the most significant of which is characterized by Hilferding as *Finance Capital* (1910). This work was concerned with problems of circulation and capitalist production and addressed the theory of **money**, growth of joint-stock companies, monopoly capital, economic crises, and **imperialism**. Hilferding argued that there had been a structural change in capitalism with the separation of ownership from control in the joint-stock company. This enabled small numbers of people to acquire control over a large number of companies in which a central role was played by the credit system and banks ("finance capital"). But technological progress makes ever-larger quantities of capital necessary, so the volume of fixed assets increases, the rate of profit falls and competition is curtailed through the formation of cartels and monopolies. This in turn changes the role of the **state**, which increasingly engages in conscious rational organization of society. The aim of socialist politics is, then, not the abolition of the state but the seizing of state **power** in order to bring this rationalization and direction of social life to fruition. However, a further aspect of this closer relationship between state and cartels is the emergence of imperialist politics, involving a struggle over world **markets** and raw materials. In this context, **socialism** will not arise from any inevitable breakdown of capitalism but through the political organization of working-class **political parties** creating a rational economic system. These ideas are reflected in Renner's theory of the relative autonomy of law and Bauer's theory of nationalism as the **ideology** of imperialism.

LARRY RAY

authoritarian personality
World War II was followed by the rapid development of social scientific analyses of **prejudice** and **racism**. One of the most influential but controversial of these was *The Authoritarian Personality* (1950), the result of research undertaken by **Theodor Adorno**, Else Frenkel-Brunswick, Daniel Levinson, and R. Nevitt Sanford as part of the Berkeley Public Opinion Study and for the Institute of Social Research, also known as the **Frankfurt School**. *The Authoritarian Personality* used two psychodynamic tests, the A (**authoritarianism**) and F (**fascism**) scales, and was based on interviews with

émigré Germans in the postwar United States. It examined the connection between deep-rooted personality traits and prejudice, and analyzed the formation of the "potentially fascistic individual." This authoritarian personality type displayed characteristics of "authoritarian submission" – disliked giving orders but had an uncritical attitude towards idealized moral authorities of the in-group; "authoritarian aggression" – a tendency to seek out and condemn people who violate conventional attitudes; anti-intraception – opposition to imagination and creativity; superstition and stereotyping – would believe in superstition and think in rigid categories; **power** and toughness – identification with powerful figures; cynicism – generalized hostility and belief in conspiracies; projectivity – projecting onto stigmatized groups unconscious emotional impulses; and preoccupation with sex and concern with "goings-on." This personality type will become anxious and insecure when events upset their previously existing worldview. The personality type was associated particularly with (what the authors saw as) the highly sexually repressed lower middle class, a group that felt threatened by both large corporations and **socialism** and was predisposed to support authoritarian politics.

LARRY RAY

authoritarianism

The term authoritarianism indicates a political regime in which government is distinguished by high-level state power without legitimate, routine intervention by the populace governed, for example through binding procedures and practices of popular consent-formation, public opinion, free speech, and government accountability. Citizens' appeal against the decisions of the ruler is discouraged and, eventually, repressed by coercive means. A wide array of nation-state societies have historically been governed by such regimes. Although authoritarian rule is usually deployed as a shorthand for oppressive measures, it can also (but not wholly without coercion at some point) feature as paternalistic benevolence. Authoritarian rulers hold themselves responsible (but not accountable) for the ruled subjects' well-being and may enforce strict conformity "for the subjects' own good."

In the political sociology of **Max Weber**, the term also occurs in the characterization of the transition between authority systems in the West. Traditional differs from modern (that is rational-legal) authority in that, by character, law in the authoritarian regime is particularistic, both formal and substantive **inequality** before the law exist, and the ultimate purpose of law as coherent body is not well elaborated. According to Weber's differentiation of ideal-typical regime-type activity, non-authoritarian regimes are characterized by adjudication (highly rationalized law) rather than administration. They emphasize **rights**, including social rights, and political **authority** is impersonal and impartial, with sovereigns serving citizens to maintain and develop their rights.

In comparative-historical method and macro-sociology, the authoritarian regime-type is commonly differentiated from totalitarian and democratic systems. Whereas there is wide consensus over the general distinction between democratic regimes on one hand and authoritarian and totalitarian on the other, there is much disagreement over the difference between authoritarian and totalitarian regimes in history. There are two camps, one arguing that **totalitarianism** is a more extreme form of authoritarianism, and a second arguing a categorical difference between the two. The regime-type distinction became particularly important in a practical sense to international relations during and following the Cold War period, because it allowed governments to argue it would be ethically unproblematic for them to interact with authoritarian nations charged with human-rights violations, because these nation-states would be capable of political reform and therefore should not be isolated – unlike totalitarian ones. Authoritarian and totalitarian regimes are usually compared with regard to their degree of subordination of their political subjects' lives. The full control of the citizenry and the enforcement by terror under both **fascism** and Stalinism are two well-documented examples of totalitarian regimes in the twentieth century. One outstanding analysis of the parallels of these two regimes was delivered by **Hannah Arendt** in *The Origins of Totalitarianism* (1951), in which she emphasized that totalitarian ideologies are marked by the purposeful, radical liquidation of any freedom, thereby denying any space for action and thought, as well as aiming at changing human nature. Another defining criterion is the extent to which regimes are revolutionary or conservative – authoritarian regimes are argued to be the latter, while totalitarian regimes are said to transform the basic structure of society.   ANN VOGEL

authority

The concept of authority has a long and rich history within western political philosophy, where it has been often coupled and contrasted with liberty and other significant concepts. It has not had the same resonance within sociology, where it often appears in the same context as the **power** concept. The relationship between the two concepts, however, is construed in rather different ways.

Sometimes authority is categorically contrasted with power. For instance, **Robert Nisbet**, in his influential work *The Sociological Tradition* (1967), has argued that, with the advent of **modernity**, the power phenomenon has displaced authority. This displacement has happened in a particularly dramatic manner in the course of the second of the "twin revolutions" – the industrial one with its main site in England, and the political one breaking through in France. Much in the sociological tradition, he suggests, constitutes a critical reflection on the power phenomenon, and compares it unfavorably with "authority." The latter was a very significant aspect of pre-modern European **society**, where it was enmeshed in, and structured, magnified, justified, and bounded by, such forces as **religion**, the **family**, law, and **tradition**. Power, instead, de-coupled itself from these phenomena, and sought to control and modify society through sheer, factual force, first and most signally exhibited in all its brutality in the "terror" phase of the French Revolution.

The nostalgia for the premodern order which Nisbet considers intrinsic to the whole sociological tradition expressed itself also in its reverence for authority. This is much in evidence in the response of Edmund Burke (1729–97) to the revolutionary events themselves, in the proto-sociology of French Restoration thinkers, and later in **Alexis de Tocqueville**'s worried reflections on the penchant of democratic societies for a new form of despotism. Among later social theorists, Nisbet emphasized **Émile Durkheim**'s hankering for authority, especially in the form of laws and other public arrangements which would restrain the ruthless greed of the over-individualized, atomized members of modern society.

In these conceptualizations, authority is characterized by the sense that it speaks from above individuals, with a voice at the same time forbidding and benevolent, whose commands evoke respect and create in their addressees a sense of obligation. But if here authority is contrasted with power, other sociological renderings of the concept juxtapose it to power. For instance, in the context of recurrent arguments about the respective conceptual provinces of power, force, coercion, **influence**, manipulation, and authority,

the latter is sometimes seen as exemplified by the phenomenon banally characterized as "doctor's orders." Here, authority typically seeks to induce subjects to actions they would not engage in on their own, but does so because it is grounded on another subject's superior knowledge of the circumstances and expresses its concern with the interests of the former subjects. The benevolence component of the first understanding is strongly stressed. To simplify these complex conceptual relations, we might say that a further use of "authority" subordinates it conceptually to "power."

This variant needs closer reflection, because it has lent itself to much elaboration by social theorists. Let us begin with **Max Weber**'s concept of power (*Macht*) which sees power present, within a social relationship, if and to the extent that one party to it is in a position to realize its own interests, even against the (actual or virtual) opposition of the other party. Weber himself remarks on certain liabilities of this understanding of power, such as the fact that it can be applied to relations of no great significance, and that within a given relation "power" so understood may easily shift from one party to the other, and then vice versa, as the issues vary. Given this difficulty, it is preferable, in sociological discourse, to make use chiefly of a concept narrower than power, characterizing situations where power asymmetries are particularly marked, and affect and structure larger and relatively durable contexts of interaction. This may happen, in particular, when power is "legitimate."

For legitimate power, Weber proposes the concept *Herrschaft*. This term means literally "lordship," but it has seemed appropriate, to the English translators of Weber, to employ a different expression. One of the alternative translations proposed, besides "rule," "rulership," and "domination," is "authority." In *this* capacity, that is in its conceptualization as "legitimate power," authority has acquired much currency in English sociological discourse. It was put forward in 1947 as *the* translation of *Herrschaft* by **Talcott Parsons** and A. M. Henderson in *The Theory of Social and Economic Organization*, their edition in English of the first part of Weber's *Economy and Society* (1922 [trans. 1968]), which for about two decades held sway in the English-speaking world. Furthermore, even the later, complete, and much better edition of *Economy and Society* by Guenther Roth and Claus Wittich (1968), while making some use of an alternative version of *Herrschaft* (domination) continued to use "authority" in rendering Weber's final statement of his typology of *Herrschaft* – widely recognized as one of his most significant contributions to sociology and political science. What follows refers chiefly to that typology.

First, what does "legitimacy" mean? According to Weber, it constitutes a significant qualification of a relationship where commands are routinely issued which evoke obedience. They can do so, however, on rather different grounds: because the addressees of commands are totally accustomed to automatic, unreflected submission; as a result of those addressees' calculation of the respective probabilities and effects of obedience versus non-obedience; finally, because the addressees sense that, as moral beings, they *owe* obedience to those commands, that these *ought* to be obeyed because they have been duly issued by people entitled to issue them.

In this last case, commands can be said to be legitimate. This entails that they are more willingly and reliably obeyed, that sanctions (see **norm[s]**) for disobedience are less likely to be called for, that the whole relationship – while remaining, at bottom, a relationship of power – is rendered more stable, durable, wide-ranging, and effective.

These advantages of authority, that is of power endowed with legitimacy, have long been recognized – for instance, in a statement from Jean-Jacques Rousseau (1712–78) in his *Social Contract* (1762): "the strongest person is never sufficiently strong to be always master unless he converts his strength into right, and obedience into duty." Weber imparts an original twist to this generalization. If a power relationship turns into one of authority insofar as it is grounded on an argument, however implicit, to the effect that those in power are entitled to issue commands, and those receiving commands are duty-bound to obey, then one may differentiate the various types of authority by referring to the contents of that implicit argument.

Weber then argues that, at a high level of abstraction, where the whole range of historical reality can be encompassed conceptually by few ideal-typical constructs, that argument has always had one or the other of *three* contents, each characterizing a distinctive kind of authority.

Traditional authority. This rests on reverence for the past, on the assumption that what has always been the case is sacred and deserves to persist. Thus, what makes a command rightful is the extent to which it echoes previous, time-hallowed commands; the rightful power holder is the descendant of a former power holder (typically, a patriarch); the appropriate sentiment towards him of those subject to his power is that of filial devotion; and so on.

Charismatic authority. Here, the commands are issued by a person to whom transcendent forces have imparted a "gift of grace," enabling that person to perform extraordinary feats that bear witness to the power of those forces and benefit those who follow the person in question. These feats may be victories obtained through unprecedented military action and leading to wide-ranging conquest and much booty; or the proclamation of new beliefs and values, opening up novel understandings of the meaning of existence and avenues to after-worldly salvation. Accordingly, those commands are intrinsically innovative, break with tradition instead of reasserting it, and are to be obeyed because they express the unchallengeable will of the person in question.

Legal authority. Here, single commands constitute correct instantiations of rules of lesser or greater generality, valid in turn because they have been formed and enacted according to certain procedural rules. These establish which individuals are entitled to issue which commands in which circumstances, and thus constrain the impact of the personal interests of those individuals on the content of the commands. In turn, obedience does not express the personal subjection of those practicing it to those issuing the commands, but constitutes, however implicitly, the dutiful observance of an entire system of rules which justifies and orients those commands.

What Weber thus typifies are at bottom cultural realities, sets of understandings, and justifications which can be, and sometimes actually are, advanced in the context of discourses. On this account, his typology has sometimes been interpreted idealistically, as if in Weber's mind the nature of its legitimacy determined all significant features of an authority relation.

This is not an acceptable interpretation. As we have seen, the reference to legitimacy serves to differentiate conceptually a phenomenon which presents aspects of a very material nature, in particular those relating to the exercise or the threat of violence as the ultimate sanction of commands, or the arrangements made to provide those in command with material resources. Furthermore, legitimacy itself often emerges, in one configuration or another, only over time, as a by-product of those or other material aspects of the authority relationship. Figuratively, one might say that authority develops as naked power, over time, clothes itself in legitimacy – a development that in turn has considerable consequences for the nature and the effects of those very aspects.

For instance, the extraction from the **economy** of resources to be made available to those in a position of power, can be facilitated by the emergence and the consolidation of a feeling, within the collectivity, that the commands through which such extraction is carried out appeal to the dutiful submission of subordinates to their legitimate superiors. Furthermore, the extraction process will vary in its forms, tempo, intensity, predictability, according to the nature of the legitimacy vested in those superiors. Those features of it will in turn have distinctive effects on other aspects, both of the authority relation and of social life in general.

In fact, Weber's typology of authority, while privileging the varying nature of the legitimacy as a way of partitioning conceptually that phenomenon, subsumes under the resulting partitions a whole range of further components, such as the arrangements for the judicial settlement of disputes and punishment of crime, the typical ways in which those in authority present and represent themselves and those subject to their commands, and above all the arrangements made for administration.

In other terms, some of the most significant concepts produced by Weber's thinking about **politics**, such as those of patriarchalism, **patrimonialism**, **feudalism**, administration by notables, or **bureaucracy**, are framed within his typology of authority, and are among his most important legacies. They convey the expressly sociological nature of that thinking, for in his judgment other approaches to the concept of authority, particularly philosophical and juridical ones, had not paid sufficient attention to the day-to-day aspect of authority, such as administration itself. It seemed very important, to him, to create typologies of the ways in which administrators are recruited, trained, instructed, deployed, monitored, controlled, or rewarded, as well as the "strategies of independence" vis-à-vis the rest of the polity which these very arrangements made possible for the administrators themselves. In this manner

Weber's treatment of authority and its variants opens itself to a consideration of the dynamics of the whole authority phenomenon.

GIANFRANCO POGGI

automation

This concept indicates machinery-driven processes of production in which human intervention is intentionally minimized to ensure predictable and standardized outcomes. Automation can refer to linkages between different machine devices (robot machine tools) to produce a continuous intervention-free flow of production, to automatic control over production, or to the full computerization of production.

Historically, automation has been associated with assembly-line production and **Taylorism** but it is not exclusive to the economies of scale and mass production connected to **Fordism** (see **post-Fordism**). The post-Fordist era of **capitalism** is characterized by a refinement of automated processes in the area of assembly-line and off-line assembly production. Automation can be part of the integration, via the computerization of the total production chain, that also reaches into areas of distribution. As a result of the historical development of the automobile industry, and later of a broad range of consumer goods industries, automation is mainly associated with manufacturing, but in the service sector of the **economy** it can also be observed in the form of **technologies** and **ideologies** that are deployed to minimize human intervention.

Automation is a key phenomenon in industrial sociology because it not only affects relations between workers and their production tools, and thus the intrinsic meaning of human work, but also influences social relations in work organizations and thus participation in the production process. Automation has been an empirical referent in **sociological theory** with respect to such prominent themes as **alienation**, **deskilling**, and the **labor process**.   ANN VOGEL

autopoiesis
– see **Niklas Luhmann**.

B

Bales, Robert Freed (1916–2004)

An important figure in the growth of the study of **group dynamics**, Bales received his PhD from Harvard University, becoming Harvard Professor of Social Relations (1945–86). He spent the entirety of his academic career at that institution.

During the 1950s and 1960s when the study of small groups was at its height, Bales was a major figure in exploring the dynamics of group life. His 1950 book, *Interaction Process Analysis: A Method for the Study of Small Groups*, is considered a classic work, particularly in its development of a twelve-category coding scheme for direct observation and coding of verbal statements and nonverbal acts in both natural and laboratory groups. This method permitted social psychologists to explore systematically behavior in collective settings.

Bales was a close associate of the Harvard social theorist **Talcott Parsons**, and was one of the contributors to Parsons's project for the development of a general theory of social action. Consistent with the interests of many of his Harvard colleagues, Bales maintained a lively involvement in **psychoanalysis**, a theory that affected both his research and his teaching.

Later in Bales's career, he extended the model of interaction process analysis into a three-dimensional coding system, eventually termed SYMLOG (SYstem for the Multiple Level Observation of Groups). Towards the end of his career, Bales became more involved in consulting, applying his models of group life to social problems, and eventually created a consulting group for his SYMLOG system.

Bales may have been particularly well known for the self-analytic group course that he ran at Harvard for over a quarter-century, which became a model for similar courses throughout the United States. In these courses, students were trained to analyze their own group communication, while simultaneously learning theories of group dynamics. These groups also served as a training tool for graduate students under Bales's direction.

GARY ALAN FINE AND KENT SANDSTROM

Barthes, Roland (1915–1980)

Widely hailed as one of the most important French **intellectuals** of the postwar years, Roland Barthes's semiological approach to the study of society sought to demonstrate how cultural production reproduces itself through the signs it creates (see **cultural reproduction**). We live in a world pulsating with signs; and each sign in the system of cultural production has meaning, according to Barthes, only by virtue of its difference from other signs. In elaborating this semiological vision of society, Barthes drew from an eclectic range of theorists, including **Ferdinand de Saussure**, Roman Jakobson, Émile Benveniste, Mikhail Bakhtin, and **Jacques Lacan**. His entire theoretical edifice (less a coherent system than a kind of ongoing conceptual crossreferencing) sought to decode the signs our society generates.

Barthes made two principal contributions to sociological categories of analysis. First, in *Writing Degree Zero* (1953), he inverted Saussure's claim that linguistics is part of the broader discipline of **semiotics**, through demonstrating that the field of signs is, in fact, part of the more general domain of linguistics; the language of signs, says Barthes, always overflows with meaning, exhausts itself. Second, in *Mythologies* (1957), he demonstrated how cultural production is always veiled by its signifiers, through penetrating readings of, for instance, wrestling, the Tour de France, as well as a celebrated cover of *Paris-Match*.

Among his other works are *Elements of Semiology* (1965), *The Fashion System* (1967), *Roland Barthes by Roland Barthes* (1977), *Empire of Signs* (1983), and *The Pleasure of the Text* (1990).   ANTHONY ELLIOTT

base/superstructure
– see **ideology**.

Baudrillard, Jean (1929–)

Currently Professor of the Philosophy of Culture and Media, European Graduate School, Saas-Fée, Switzerland, Baudrillard taught at the University of Nanterre, Paris, between 1966 and 1987. He is closely associated with **postmodernism**. He moved from an early political involvement with **Marxism** and the **situationists** to focus on symbolic forms of exchange in *The Object System* (1968). His work on simulation argued that consumer culture is dominated by hyperreality and the cultural elevation of irony and fatality in *The Mirror of Production* (1973), *Simulacra and Simulation* (1994), and *America* (1989). The notion of intrinsic value that was the inspiration of radicalism was portrayed as defunct and the conventional distinction between reality and illusion was compromised. He held that there are no historical agents capable of transforming history. **Consumption** and sign value were portrayed as replacing production and use value. Baudrillard's fascination with the United States reflected his assessment of it as the most fully developed consumer culture in the world in *America*.

Reception of his work was assisted by **globalization**, the internet, and deregulation. Each provided metaphors for the virtual universe that Baudrillard's theoretical work postulated. His theory of simulation renewed the specter of Ad-Mass world produced by **mass society** theory in the 1950s and 1960s. But it dehumanized the notions of control and manipulation by proposing that no social formation is capable of authoritative engagement with simulation.

His work was important for exposing the dogma of many fossilized positions in **social theory** between the 1970s and 1990s. However, his epigrammatic style and provocative theses are subject to the law of diminishing returns. Analytically, his thought is best seen as a colorful contribution to the renewal of the sociology of fate.   CHRIS ROJEK

Bauman, Zygmunt (1925–)

Born in Poland and educated in the Soviet Union, Bauman held academic posts in various countries (including Poland, Israel, and Australia) before taking up the chair of **sociology** at the University of Leeds – where he is now Emeritus Professor. A leader of the cultural turn in sociology as far back as the 1970s, his first book in English, *Between Class and Elite* (1972), took the British **labor movement** as its field of investigation. In following years, in books such as *Culture as Praxis* (1973), *Socialism: The Active Utopia* (1976), and *Memories of Class* (1982), he established himself as an erudite analyst of the connections between **social class** and **culture**. His master work, *Modernity and the Holocaust* (1989), is a dark, dramatic study of **Enlightenment** reason and its possible deathly consequences. Auschwitz, in Bauman's view, was a

result of the "civilizing" mission of **modernity**; the Final Solution was not a dysfunction of Enlightenment rationality but its shocking product.

Various intellectual spinoffs followed, including *Modernity and Ambivalence* (1991), *Life in Fragments* (1995), *Liquid Modernity* (2000), and *Wasted Lives* (2004). In these books, Bauman moved from a concern with the historical fortunes of the Jews in conditions of modernity to an analysis of the complex ways in which postmodern culture increasingly cultivates us all as outsiders, others, or strangers. As a result of this provocative critique, Bauman's sociology on the traumas of contemporary life has become renowned.

                                   ANTHONY ELLIOTT

de Beauvoir, Simone (1908–1986)

Born in Paris, the elder of two daughters of bourgeois parents, de Beauvoir's intellectual abilities were apparent from an early age; the loss of her family's secure economic status allowed her to follow a career as a secondary-school teacher of philosophy. This radical departure from bourgeois convention was accompanied by de Beauvoir's long partnership with Jean-Paul Sartre, documented in the four volumes of de Beauvoir's autobiography (*Memoirs of a Dutiful Daughter*, 1958; *The Prime of Life*, 1960; *Force of Circumstance*, 1963; and *All Said and Done*, 1972). De Beauvoir worked with Sartre on the articulation of the philosophical movement which was to become known as existentialism; de Beauvoir, in her essays *Pyrrhus and Cineas* (1944) and *The Ethics of Ambiguity* (1948), discussed the implications for individuals of existential tenets. The same theme informed de Beauvoir's first published novel (*She Came to Stay*, 1943).

These works, in which philosophical ideas are illustrated through literature, were overshadowed by the publication, in 1949, of *The Second Sex*, the work for which de Beauvoir became world-famous. The study developed out of de Beauvoir's previous preoccupations, in particular the status of the other in human relationships. For de Beauvoir, women are the other in all aspects of social life; men are the norm of human existence and women are judged in terms of how they are not men. The most famous dictum of *The Second Sex* is "women are made and not born." This comment opened numerous theoretical possibilities for the study of gender differences, from ideas about sexual **socialization** to the thesis of Judith Butler about the "performance" of **gender**. But this specifically feminist interest in de Beauvoir's work was to emerge some years after the initial publication of *The Second Sex*; it was second-wave **feminism** that encouraged a rethinking of de Beauvoir's work. Throughout the decades following the publication of *The Second Sex*, de Beauvoir continued to publish novels (the best-known of which, *The Mandarins*, won the Prix Goncourt in 1955), volumes of autobiography, and a lengthy study of old age.

From the end of World War II, de Beauvoir had taken a prominent part in left-wing politics in France and was a vehement critic of French policy in Algeria and that of the United States in Vietnam. In the last two decades of her life, as a younger generation of readers discovered her work, she became closely associated with feminist campaigns (especially around issues of reproductive rights) but consistently rejected the position of other French feminists on the essential difference of male and female thinking and language. Although the concept of the binary difference of male and female was central to de Beauvoir's work, she remained consistent in the view that the process of the accumulation of knowledge was not gendered. Nevertheless, a recurrent theme in her work is that of loss, a theme she elaborated in her account of the death of her mother (*A Very Easy Death*) and the short stories published under the collective title *A Woman Destroyed*. De Beauvoir increasingly identified with feminism in the last years of her life, and she retains iconic stature as a person who chose, entirely self-consciously, to devote herself to intellectual life and, in so doing, helped to shape our understanding, and the politics, of gender difference.   MARY EVANS

Beck, Ulrich (1944–)

Professor of Sociology at the University of Munich, Beck is famous for developing the notion of **risk society** and reflexive **modernization** in his *Risk Society. Towards a New Modernity* (1986 [trans. 1992]). His argument is that late **modernity** increases uncertainty, hazard, and risk. The result is a new type of society involving reflection, expert opinion, knowledge systems, and internal critique. Beck has criticized mainstream **sociology** for retaining an implicitly utopian or at least optimistic view of **modernization** without examining its unintended, negative consequences. In his *Ecological Politics in an Age of Risk* (1995), he applied this approach to the problems of environmental pollution and green politics. In his more recent work, he has more closely associated his analysis of risk to theories of **globalization** in *The Reinvention of Politics. Rethinking Modernity in the Age*

of *Global Social Order* (1997) and *World Risk Society* (1999). Although Beck is now specifically identified with the debate about risk and environmental **politics**, his theory of individualization examines the breakdown and fragmentation of the institutions that were integral to industrial **capitalism**, such as the **family** and love, in *The Normal Chaos of Love* (Beck and Elisabeth Beck-Gernsheim, 1990 [trans. 1995]). Individualization should not be confused with neo-liberal **individualism** but with the "disembedding" of individuals from **social structures**. Individual identities are no longer defined by the secure structures of **social class**, **social status**, family, and **neighborhood**. This perspective is applied to a variety of social phenomena in Beck and Beck-Gernsheim, *Individualization* (2002). In his most recent work, he has considered the possibility of **cosmopolitanism** in relation to globalization.   BRYAN S. TURNER

Becker, Howard S. (1928–)

Becker's work has spanned **symbolic interactionism**, **deviance**, sociology of the arts, **occupations**, **education**, medical work, and the techniques of writing. Perhaps most popularly known for his work on deviance in *Outsiders* (1963), Becker's studies were conducted at the University of Chicago where, taught by Everett Hughes (1897–1983), he was part of the second generation of the **Chicago School**. Taking inspiration from **Georg Simmel**, as well as **Robert E. Park** and Hughes, Becker's perspective treats social life as the result of the work people do. This focus deals with learning, cooperation, and convention.

In his article "On Becoming a Marijuana User" (1953, *American Journal of Sociology*), Becker pushed this approach into the study of embodied perception, emphasizing the role that learning plays in structuring the psychosomatic experience of a drug's effects and perceived value. His 1982 work, *Art Worlds*, tapped his own experience as a jazz pianist and applied the focus on collective action to the making and valuing of artistic products, proposing artworks and their reputations as the outcome of **networks** of personnel, conventions, organizational patterns of distribution, funding and **consumption**, materials and technologies. In emphasizing this middle level of social organization – networks – *Art Worlds* inaugurated a new mode of inquiry in arts sociology and simultaneously provided a model for how to investigate creative work in other areas such as science. In these respects Becker's work has affinities with **Bruno Latour**'s work on science, such as *Science in Action* (1987).   TIA DENORA

behaviorism

An explanation of behavior, this perspective goes back at least to René Descartes (1596–1650), for whom animals were machines responding automatically to pleasurable or painful stimuli. Similarly, David Hartley (1705–57) noted, in *Observations on Man* (1749), that "the fingers of young children bend upon almost every impression made upon the palm of the hand, this performing the act of grasping, in the original automatic manner." In the modern era, behaviorism is classically associated with Ivan Pavlov's (1849–1936) dogs salivating at the sound of a bell. They are responding, machine-like, to a stimulus associated with food.

This view of behaviorism has been challenged. Burrhus Frederic Skinner (1904–90), the psychologist most associated with behaviorism, argued that the study of observed behavior needed to penetrate beyond mere reflexes. A person is a "locus," a point at which biological and environmental conditions combine to produce a behavioral effect. Factors within the organism (including, most importantly, learning processes) combine with environmental stimuli to generate behavior.

George Herbert Mead (1863–1931) is usually considered the prime *social* behaviorist. He insisted on recognizing social **interactions** and the distinctive mental and linguistic capacities of humans. **Language** and gestures within a social **group** intervene between stimulus and response, interaction making human identity.

Behaviorism has therefore moved beyond a simple stimulus–response model to include learning behaviors, interaction, and internal behavioral propensities. It remains, however, an example of **empiricism**, resisting theories seen as speculative and insufficiently based on evidence. For these reasons, it resists theories of the **self** (for example, those of **Sigmund Freud**) which argue for underlying, but not directly experienced, structures to human nature. Similarly, behaviorism underplays the influence of **social structure** and **power** on individual behavior.   PETER DICKENS

Bell, Daniel (1919–)

Bell's extensive body of work has made a major contribution to many areas of sociological inquiry, including **social change** and **modernity**, the evolution of **capitalism**, and the dynamics and conflicts within western culture. Born in New York, he is a graduate of City College, and became a prominent Harvard academic and social commentator. He is probably best known as a theorist of **postindustrial society**, and as someone who anticipated many contemporary economic and cultural trends associated with **postmodernism.** His best-known works are *The End of Ideology* (1960), *The Coming of Post-Industrial Society* (1973), and *The Cultural Contradictions of Capitalism* (1976).

The End of Ideology advanced the notion that a historical epoch dominated by grand ideological conflict had come to an end as a result of the successes of western democratic **politics** and capitalism. This reflected an epoch of optimistic confidence that seemingly intractable conflicts that had dominated the nineteenth and much of the twentieth century could and had been overcome. Neither **Karl Marx**'s prognosis of endemic class conflict (see **social class**) nor **Max Weber**'s discussion of the iron cage of rationalized bureaucratic domination had come about.

Criticized for complacency and exclusion of Third World perspectives, Bell responded to the social changes and upheavals of the late 1960s and early 1970s with two more critical contributions to sociological analysis. In *The Coming of Post-Industrial Society*, subtitled *A Venture in Social Forecasting*, he diagnosed a shift from an industrially based to an information-driven, service-oriented postindustrial society. This elevated the role of knowledge and knowledge-holders as new and dominant elements within structures of **power** and **social stratification**. Professionals rather than entrepreneurs occupied the key positions in the new social order. This argument marked an early and influential statement of what became known as new class theory. Bell did not invent the idea of postindustrial society, which had been around throughout the twentieth century; rather he gave this concept a greater focus and analytical rigor. Similarly, his emphasis on knowledge and **social structure**, while drawing on earlier thinkers like **C.-H. Saint-Simon** and Weber, was less speculative and better grounded in empirical complexities than that of his predecessors.

The newly emerging postindustrial structure, investigated further by Bell in *The Cultural Contradictions of Capitalism*, pursued the theme of the evolving social structure and cultural formations of western nations. A key idea here was that of a profound cultural cleavage between the realms of production and **consumption**. While the former depended on the work ethic and deferred gratification, the latter elevated hedonism and personal fulfillment as the overriding **values**. This argument disputed the contention, associated with **Talcott Parsons,** that western social systems could be integrated around a relatively stable set of normative frameworks. For Bell, by contrast, the moral foundations of capitalism would remain shaky and uncertain. In this way, Bell anticipated certain postmodern arguments against the unitary nature of social order.   ROBERT HOLTON

bell curve
– see **intelligence**.

Bellah, Robert N. (1927–)

Elliott Professor of Sociology Emeritus at the University of California, Berkeley, and born in Los Angeles, Bellah attended undergraduate and graduate school at Harvard University, receiving his PhD in Sociology in 1955. He taught at Harvard in 1957–67, moving thereafter to his position at Berkeley.

Bellah's work has centered on the sociology of **religion** and cultural sociology. His earliest book, *Tokugawa Religion* (1955), explored Japanese religion in a comparative framework. In *Beyond Belief* (1970), he wrote on a variety of religious traditions, viewing religion not as an objective set of timeless truths, but as an attempt to find meaning in the modern world. In *The Broken Covenant* (1975), a very controversial work, Bellah discussed the idea of **civic religion** in the United States. He argued that abstract but shared religious values give American ideas such as the republic and liberty a sacred dimension. Critics accused him of collapsing the distinction between religion and **politics**, a criticism rejected by Bellah.

Bellah has continued his concern with the moral life of Americans in his recent works, *Habits of the Heart* (1985) and *The Good Society* (1991), both written with Richard Madsen, William Sullivan, Ann Swidler, and Steven Tipton. Bellah finds that American democratic **institutions** are threatened by a powerful and widespread belief that self-interest and self-expression are the essence of freedom. He thinks that Americans have difficulty grasping the interdependency of the contemporary world and the complexity of many of their basic **values**, including the meaning of success, freedom, and justice. Bellah states that many Americans have trouble conceptualizing and acting on these issues because they assume that individuals are isolated from their social and cultural contexts. For Bellah, this is a fiction. Most Americans are profoundly involved in social relationships that entail **community** and caring, yet they lack a language that articulates the richness of their commitments to one another.

Bellah states that Americans lack such insight into their communal obligations and experience because they have privileged their individualistic cultural beliefs over other aspects of their cultural life and **traditions**. Yet these communal themes run deep in American history. He labels these communal traditions republicanism – which advocates a society based on political equality and participatory self-government – and the biblical tradition – which posits a good society as a community in which a genuinely ethical and spiritual life can be lived. Bellah calls for a resurrection and rethinking of the biblical and republican traditions, which he sees manifested in Americans' desire for meaningful work, their wish to make a difference in the world, and their devotion to **family** and friends which often overshadows their commitments to work. For Bellah, these traditions represent an ideal of a community of participatory individuals who have strong ethical bonds with one another. American institutions, from work to government, must change so that people do not view them as hindrances to self-development. Individuals must be able to grasp the interconnection of personal and public welfare, so that they can actively participate in shaping their lives.

KENNETH H. TUCKER

Bendix, Reinhard (1916–1991)

A German-born sociologist who emigrated to the United States in 1938, Bendix taught at the University of Chicago from 1943 to 1946, and then, following a short stint at Colorado, at Berkeley.

Bendix's work on political theory and historical and comparative sociology fused theoretical depth with expansive empirical detail. He wrote three major historical-comparative books: *Work and Authority in Industry* (1956), which examined the role of **bureaucracy**; *Nation Building and Citizenship* (1964), which followed **T. H. Marshall**'s arguments concerning working-class incorporation into modern society; and *Kings and People* (1978), which expanded on Weber's famous distinction between feudal and patrimonial **authority**. He was, however, most well known for his penetrating intellectual biography of **Max Weber** (1960), which provided an alternative reading to the then dominant Parsonian interpretation of the German thinker.

In *Social Science and the Distrust of Reason* (1951) and later works such as the two-volume *Embattled Reason* (1988–9) and *From Berlin to Berkeley* (1986), he advocated responsible partisanship which balanced scientific scholarship with humanistic ideals. He also edited two influential books with

Seymour M. Lipset: *Class, Status and Power* (1953) and *Social Mobility in Industrial Society* (1959).

STEVEN LOYAL

Benjamin, Walter (1892–1940)

Although not a sociologist and initially recognized more as literary critic and philosopher, the German theorist Walter Benjamin has had a significant impact upon aspects of sociology in recent decades. Perhaps most widespread has been the debate upon and extension of his reflections on "the work of art in the age of its mechanical reproducibility." In his essay of that title (1969; 2002) [1936] and elsewhere, Benjamin argued that, whereas the traditional work of art possessed auratic qualities, the result of its uniqueness and authenticity, mechanical reproduction of images and art works removed their auratic qualities and potentially opened up democratic possibilities. Benjamin's interest in the technologies of image and art work reproduction led him to explore the media of film, photography, radio, and new modes of operating with existing media such as modern drama and the press. This interest in images accords with his assertion that an important feature of **modernity** is the huge proliferation of images.

More recently, the translation of his massive, unfinished prehistory of modernity, the *Arcades Project* (1999), on which he worked for over a decade collecting images, descriptions and evidence, has been influential. This project focused in a radical manner upon Paris as capital of the nineteenth century and was intended as an excavation of modernity that would be crucially relevant to our contemporary experience. Defining modernity as a world dominated by illusion and fantasy ("phantasmagorias"), and especially the illusion of the "new," Benjamin maintained that the origins of modernity lay embedded in the nineteenth century. Their excavation was to be approached methodologically through attention to the fragments, the refuse of the past in our present, through the construction of dialectical images that would force the past into our present, through a critique of the dream-world of historicism, and through awakening from the illusions of modernity. The investigation of the origins of modernity were to be undertaken by the partly metaphorical figures of the archaeologist / critical allegorist, the collector/ragpicker, and the *flâneur*/ detective. The new reading of the **city** as text revealed the transformations in experience of modernity through a rich construction of the city, commencing with its arcades, and moving through to its streets, the bourgeois interior, the masses, the phenomenal life of the commodity, and the transformations in perception of things.

DAVID FRISBY

Berger, Peter L. (1929–)

Born in Vienna, Berger moved to the United States after World War II and is currently a professor at Boston University. Berger's contribution to sociology is prolific and extensive but he is most renowned for his writings on **religion** and **secularization**, and for the phenomenological understanding of social life articulated in *The Social Construction of Reality* (1966), coauthored with **Thomas Luckmann**. In this highly influential book, Berger emphasized what today might seem an obvious point – that society is a product of human design – but which in the 1960s, a time when sociologists primarily emphasized the determining power of large-scale impersonal **social structures** (for example, **capitalism**) and processes (for example, **modernization**), was highly innovative. Berger's focus on **everyday life** and the pragmatic constraints of living in the "here and now" was quite radical. It made scholars and students alike pay attention to the small but potent ways in which ordinary people get on with, make sense of, organize, and find meaning in the everyday reality that confronts them. Berger's emphasis on the thoroughly social foundation of **institutions**, and the possibility that institutional and **social change** emerges when the taken-for-granted institutional routines no longer make sense in a particular social context, opened up an emancipatory view of human (social) agency, but one, clearly, that recognized that humans as social beings – the products too of **society** – are always in **interaction** with socially institutionalized ways of organizing collective life, for example, **language**. The dialectic by which humans engage the objective, socially created external world, and in turn internalize and act on that external reality provides a highly dynamic model of the interactive power of institutional structures and individual consciousness and meaning in the construction of social life.

One of Berger's core interests has been how the religious domain, itself the product of human design rather than divine blueprint, allows individuals to impose order on the chaos of everyday reality. Religion provides like-minded individuals who interact together within a symbolic universe of shared beliefs, **symbols**, and meanings with an overarching *Sacred Canopy* (1967), which facilitates the plausibility of their sense-making and thus enhances their **social integration**. But, as Berger noted, in modern society – with its rationally differentiated institutional spheres and cultural processes – religion is but one of many competing universes of meaning; science and art, for example, are other (often conflicting) sources of shared meaning in society. Within the religious sphere, moreover, Berger argued, the plurality of **denominations** and choices available reduces the plausibility or the certainty of any one individual's beliefs (or choices).

Berger was a leading proponent of secularization, seeing it as an inevitable and global phenomenon of **modernization** and the necessary loss of domination of religious institutions and symbols over social institutions, **culture**, and individual consciousness. Although he acknowledged that secularization did not proceed uniformly across all societies or across all sectors of society, he nonetheless argued that any continuing symbolic power of churches would necessarily rest on churches becoming more secularized themselves. In recent years, however, Berger has revised his earlier thesis in *Christian Century* (1997), stating that most of the world today is not secular but very religious. Berger's *Invitation to Sociology* (1963) remains an influential and accessible introduction to sociology.   MICHELE DILLON

Bernstein, Basil (1924–2000)

Within the British tradition of empirical sociology, Bernstein was unusual in being open to the philosophical currents in "continental" thought. His early reading of Ernst Cassirer (1874–1945), Benjamin Whorf (1877–1957), Lev Vygotsky (1896–1934), and Alexander Luria (1902–77), and his knowledge of the work of **Émile Durkheim**, caused him to become primarily concerned with how cultural and linguistic frames of thinking mold our experience of the world. Before and after studying at the London School of Economics after World War II, Bernstein had experience of working and teaching in socially deprived parts of east London. His combination of theoretical interest with concrete experience of non-traditional or non-academic contexts fostered the research which he undertook and inspired at the Sociological Research Unit at the Institute of Education of the University of London from 1963 until his death. During this period he was responsible for the production of a series of studies under the general title of *Class, Codes and Control* (1971, 1973, 1975). Both the first and the third volumes of this series reprinted his seminal article entitled: "On the Classification and Framing of Educational Knowledge." Bernstein was responsible for drawing attention to the correlation between class difference and the capacity of people to draw upon "restricted" or "extended" linguistic codes. He was necessarily interested in **pedagogical practices**, and it is significant that his research provided a basis for examining sociologically the function of schooling, at a time when thinking about **education** was still dominated in the United Kingdom by philosophers, and when opposition to schooling was expressed in the **de-schooling** movement.

DEREK ROBBINS

bias

Bias refers to those aspects of the social research process that may skew the findings in some way. The main identified sources of bias concern the researcher or informant, the **measurement** instruments or methods, and the **sampling** procedures. Biased measures fail to do a good job of measuring the things they are purported to measure and therefore lack validity. Biased samples are not representative of the relevant population or set of cases they are meant to reflect.

The issue of whether or not one can eliminate bias is contested. Some argue that to eliminate all sources of bias is to purge research of human life. From this viewpoint, the task of the researcher is not to eliminate bias but to be reflexive about potential distortions of accounts. Others disagree and stress that it is the researcher's duty to make every effort to eliminate or minimize distortion in the research process.

The dispute arises because the meaning of bias is ambiguous. The notion that bias is a systematic deviation from a true score is problematic because concepts such as "truth" or "**objectivity**" sit uneasily with the study of the social world, where "truths" differ across time and place. It is less problematic to define bias as systematic errors that distort the research process. The main safeguard against such systematic distortions is that others in the community of scholars will challenge biased research. For example, feminist scholars have played an invaluable role in challenging pervasive **sexism** in sociological concepts and measures.   JACKIE SCOTT

biological reductionism
– see **biologism**.

biologism

In its strongest form, this perspective suggests that the social position of **social classes** or ethnic groups (see **ethnicity**) largely stems from genetically inherited levels of **intelligence**. Similarly, the high levels of child-care or domestic work conducted by women are an expression of their innate caring capacities. As with **social Darwinism**, such arguments clearly suggest that **power** and **inequality** are mainly a product of an inherent human nature. Criminality too is sometimes seen as a product of biological inheritance.

Biologism, in its crudest forms, is a thinly veiled **ideology** in which white males have exercised power over women, nonwhites, and others. Such pseudoscience is clearly unacceptable. On the other hand, blank rejection of the natural sciences by sociologists runs the risk of throwing out the biological baby with the bathwater. Humans, like all animals, remain a natural datum. Their biological structures and potentials must be related, however loosely and distantly, to their behaviors, social positions, and identities. Biological and psychic mechanisms are certainly overlaid with, or "overdetermined" by, social relations, but this cannot mean that biological mechanisms can never offer explanatory purchase. Social **institutions** and **social structures** may be realizing or suppressing biologically based structures and capacities in complex and varied ways which are not well understood.

Sociologists are therefore right to criticize extreme forms of biologism. But they must also guard against charges of "sociologism," a denial of biological or psychic bases to human behavior and/or crude assumptions about the plasticity of the human body and human nature. Neither sociology nor biology can offer total explanations, and dogmatic charges of "biologism" could result in the premature closure of transdisciplinary analysis. Despite a legacy of suspicion, sociology must remain open to contributions from the natural sciences.   PETER DICKENS

biopolitics

A general term referring to the way biology intersects with **politics**, commerce, the **law**, and **morality**; more specifically, the term refers to the contentious politics and conflicts concerned with nature and the **environment**. Environmentalism and animal rights are two **social movements** whose cognitive and political praxis can be characterized as forms of biopolitics.

The term has a more specified meaning in what is called the "transhumanist movement." The phrase was first coined by James Hughes, an American professor, to refer to a pro-technological outlook which takes the Luddites as its polar opposite. As a form of biopolitics, transhumanism is a movement towards a posthuman or cyborg society. Leading social theorists associated with the

concept are **Michel Foucault**, **Donna Haraway**, and Peter Singer.   RON EYERMAN

biotechnology

This term is used to describe a process through which biological materials are modified. Specifically, it refers to the use or development of techniques employing living organisms, such as cells and bacteria, in industrial or commercial processes.

The field of biotechnology not only integrates a number of disciplines, drawing on molecular biology, biochemistry, cell biology, microbiology, **genetics**, immunology, and bioinformatics, it also employs a range of different techniques and technologies including, among others, DNA sequencing, the polymerase chain reaction, and micro- and macro-injection. Although interventions such as the selective breeding of plants and animals and the use of yeast to make bread have been taking place for centuries, the term biotechnology is associated with more recent developments, such as the late twentieth-century breakthroughs in molecular biology, genetic engineering, and the current convergence of science and technology aided by bioinformatics.

The birth of modern biotechnology is generally dated to the early 1970s when American scientists developed recombinant DNA techniques. This is a method for transferring genes from one organism to another unrelated organism. Since then, a number of other technologies have been developed leading to innovations such as genetically modified foods, stem cell research, and gene therapy.

A new industry sector has been built up around biotechnology. This sector is playing a critical role in knowledge transfer, where knowledge from universities is transferred into commercial applications, and contributing to the emerging, global knowledge-based economy. Biotechnology companies tend to be recent start-ups established by researchers from universities or research institutes, funded by venture capitalists, and having extensive **networks** of research alliances and collaborators. They are usually built up around a single idea backed up by patents, with few, if any, products on the market. Biotech **firms** often initiate drug development, selling their products to large pharmaceutical companies which continue with the process of bringing the drug to market. In drug development, biotech firms commonly rely on continual investments from venture capitalists and bankers for an eight- to ten-year period before the products are realized or larger pharmaceutical companies acquire the firm.

Since the first biotech firms were established in the late 1970s, the industry has expanded rapidly. The subsequent successful production of cloned genes for producing proteins that enabled the production of new pharmaceutical drugs and agricultural applications prompted massive governmental investments in the United States, Europe, and emerging **markets** around the world.

As with recent developments in genetics, biotechnology has been heralded by scientists, policymakers, and the business world as having the potential to bring about new and revolutionary changes for both society and the global economy. A system of intellectual property rights, and global regimes to protect them, has been deployed in relation to biotech discoveries. A number of sociologists have drawn attention to both the ever-increasing blurring of boundaries between the private and public sectors, and the propensity for biotechnological development to be subject to excessive hyperbole. Notions of a biotechnology revolution underpinned by scientific, governmental, and regional policy initiatives designed to bring about the twin objectives of wealth and health creation have generated widespread expectations about the rapid impact of biotechnology. Sociologists highlight the ways in which promoters of new technologies build expectations through the creation and citation of technological visions. Social scientists Paul Nightingale and Paul Martin demonstrate in their article "The Myth of the Biotech Revolution" (2004, *Trends in Biotechnology*), that, counter to expectations of a revolutionary model of innovation, biotechnology innovation is instead following a historically well-established process of slow and incremental change. These commentators note that most research fields can be seen to move through various cycles of hype and disappointment, expressing tensions between generative visions on the one hand and the material "messiness" of innovation on the other.

While governments worldwide are pursuing ambitious and competitive programs to foster bioscience-based industries, the prominence of biotechnological processes and innovation has prompted sociologists to grapple with the associated myriad social, political, and ethical issues. Issues such as the impact of biotechnologies on individuals and society, the altering of boundaries between nature and **culture**, and questions about human nature have all captured sociologists' attention. **Risk** in the form of the consequences of genetic engineering or genetic modification of human and other living organisms has also been a subject of substantial debate for scholars. The concept of a risk society, as argued by **Ulrich Beck**, has been drawn on by some sociologists analyzing such risks.

There is also concern that genetic engineering of humans in the form of gene therapy, where faulty genes are either repaired or replaced, might alter the germline cells (those cells that have genetic material that may be passed on via reproduction to a child) and irreversibly change the genetic make-up of future generations. In *The Future of Human Nature* (2001), **Jürgen Habermas**, for example, argues that genetic engineering, along with other forms of genetic enhancements, should be forbidden, as such alterations undermine what it is to be human. Other scholars have argued that decisions about whether or not to pursue such developments should be premised on democratically accountable mechanisms. Others again have been more optimistic about the potential biotechnology provides to move beyond a nature/culture opposition and develop life-enhancing reconfigurations that provide the means to overcome our biological, neurological, and psychological limitations.

Controversies over genetically modified foods, cloning, and stem cell research have become major flashpoints in the political and public arenas. Sociologists, particularly those specializing in **science and technology studies**, have drawn attention to the contested and uncertain nature of science. Public opposition to genetically modified foods has furthered debates on public understanding of science, the role of **democracy**, and the necessity for governance and regulation. While policymakers and scientists frequently suggest such opposition is based on a public deficit of scientific knowledge, social scientists refute this. For example, Brian Wynne in his article "Public Uptake of Science: A Case for Institutional Reflexivity" (1993, *Public Understanding of Science*), claims that the public understands only too well the provisional nature of scientific knowledge and are aware that problems can emerge in the future that are in the present unknown. More recently, in response to a perceived breakdown in the public's **trust** in science, attempts have been made by science-funding agencies, policymakers, and governmental bodies to adopt public engagement strategies. These strategies are often presented as part of a more inclusive democratic process of government and entail such activities as setting up citizens' juries and carrying out surveys and public consultation exercises. Such work is often undertaken by sociologists and other social scientists. Some scholars suggest that this is evidence of the emergence of new forms of biological or scientific **citizenship** and represents a more participatory or deliberative form of democracy. Others are more skeptical and claim that such exercises are designed to stave off the kind of public opposition that has thwarted the deployment of genetically modified foodstuffs in Europe and other western countries.   OONAGH CORRIGAN

Birmingham Centre for Contemporary Cultural Studies

Opened in 1964, the Centre for Contemporary Cultural Studies (CCCS) was founded at the University of Birmingham by **Richard Hoggart**. **Stuart Hall** was recruited as Hoggart's partner to manage the day-to-day affairs of the Centre. His contribution rapidly made the climate of work in the Centre more theoretical and political. CCCS was an anti-elitist, postgraduate teaching and research institution. Initially, it was organized intellectually around a tripartite division between literary, historical-philosophical, and sociological research. However, the historical–philosophical and sociological elements soon took precedence, especially after 1970 when Hoggart left to take up a post in UNESCO.

Under Hall's leadership, work gravitated towards the central issue of the articulation of **power**. This was chiefly examined at the cultural level by the attempt to fuse native traditions of "culturalism" with continental "**structuralism.**" Culturalism was a version of cultural materialism committed to examining "the whole way of life" of a **social class**. In contrast to elitist approaches, it emphasized the "ordinary" character of culture. Politically, it was a variant of left-wing humanism. During the Birmingham heyday, while their work differed in many important particulars, the chief representatives of this tradition were recognized as **Raymond Williams**, Edward Thompson, and Richard Hoggart. Hall's reservations about culturalism centered on its tendency to privilege agency over structure, its neglect of questions of reflexivity, its under-developed interest in the positioning of agency, and its general anti-theoreticism. The most ambitious and defining project in Birmingham lay in the attempt to graft continental structuralism, embodied above all in the work of **Antonio Gramsci**, **Louis Althusser**, and **Karl Marx**, on to the native tradition of culturalism. Structuralism was held to offer theoretical determinacy, an emphasis on totality, and a recurring interest in the articulation of **ideology** through praxis.

This project was developed along several fronts. Arguably, the work on British **state** formation, the formation of ideology, schooling as cultural resistance, policing and the drift to the law and order society, encoding and decoding in mass communications, and the politics of **hegemony** was of most enduring influence.

In 1979 Hall left to become Professor of Sociology at the Open University. Although the Centre continued, it never regained the public profile or intellectual prominence that it achieved under his leadership. Despite maintaining a sound record of student recruitment, it was closed by the University in 2002, allegedly in response to a disappointing performance in the national Research Assessment Exercise.

The principal achievements of the Centre are threefold. At the theoretical level, it synthesized a rich range of native and continental traditions to examine cultural articulations of power. In doing so, it broke decisively with elitist perspectives on culture and related the question of articulation to divisions of class, **gender**, and **race and ethnicity**. The sophisticated use of culture to elucidate praxis was seminal in the emergence of cultural studies.

At the political level, it twinned culture with **politics**. Hall's model of intellectual labor was borrowed from Gramsci's concept of the organic intellectual, that is, an individual who set out to operate as a switch-point between cutting-edge ideas and political activism. Following Althusser, the state was identified as the pre-eminent **institution** of normative coercion. The analysis of the historical role of the British state in managing dissent and the consistent analytic relation of the state's "war of maneuver" to ordinary cultural forms and practice was compelling and mold-breaking. This work was crucial in developing the model of authoritarian **populism** that Hall developed in the 1980s to explain working-class support for Thatcherism.

At the pedagogic level, the emphasis on collaborative research between staff and postgraduates, and the self-image of developing the curriculum of Cultural studies, provided a compelling non-hierarchical, dialogic model of teaching and research. The Centre was one of the major training grounds for the study of culture in the twentieth century and has some claim to be regarded as pivotal in the development of Cultural studies and the cultural turn in **sociology**. Among its alumni are Charlotte Brundson, **Paul Gilroy**, Lawrence Grossberg, Dick Hebdige, Gregor McLennan, Angela McRobbie, David Morley, and Paul Willis.

The major figures in the Birmingham diaspora retain a powerful global influence in protecting and enhancing the heritage and perspectives developed in the 1960s and 1970s.

The weaknesses of the Birmingham tradition inversely reflect its achievements. Conceived as a series of projects located at the periphery of the academy and elite culture, the work of the Centre gradually migrated to the core. It set agendas of discourse and research rather than critically responding to them. This exposed underlying faults in the project.

First, in opening up the subjects of culture and articulation to serious academic enquiry, the Centre progressively surrendered a tenable political focus. Tensions with feminist students in the late 1970s raised awkward questions about the limitations of reflexivity and persistence of ideology in the Centre's ordinary activities. The reaction was to be more responsive to feminist and psychoanalytic traditions. This invited criticism that the Centre was over-willing to embrace intellectual fashion and added to the confusion about the practical political objectives of the Birmingham project.

Second, the engagement with popular culture became so entwined with questions of theoretical relevance that the analysis became forbiddingly abstract. Key concepts, such as articulation, conjuncture, enunciation, hegemony, and ideology, were often used inconsistently and with different inflections. The Centre's work became vulnerable to the charge of conceptual slippage and intellectual incoherence. These criticisms were intensified by Hall's work after the 1980s, in which the notion of unity in difference became prominent. Many commentators have found this to be elusive and obscure.

Third, the balance of cultural articulation was heavily skewed to the roles of the state and social divisions of class, race, and gender. The Centre evinced a remarkable failure to investigate the culture of the corporation, and its analysis of the mass media never extended beyond encoding, decoding, and media amplification. Although Hall and his associates accurately predicted the rise of the New Right in Britain, they failed to anticipate the significance of **globalization** for critical analysis.   CHRIS ROJEK

black economy

– see **informal economy**.

black studies

– see **African-American Studies**.

Blau, Peter M. (1918–2002)

A prolific sociological theorist and researcher, Blau made important contributions to **exchange theory**, and to the study of complex **organizations** and **social stratification**. Born in Vienna, he narrowly escaped Nazi Europe on the last civilian boat to leave France, arriving penniless in New York in 1939. Blau studied for a doctorate at Columbia University with **Robert Merton**. He was professor at the University of Chicago from 1953 to 1970, then at Columbia University from 1970 to 1988. He held numerous distinguished visiting positions and was President of the American Sociological Association in 1974.

Blau's *Dynamics of Bureaucracy* (1955) developed Merton's approach to **functionalism**, showing how innovation occurred in the enactment of rules of formal organizations. This was followed by a major work in the comparative theory of organizations, coauthored with Richard Scott, *Formal Organizations* (1963). With functionalism under criticism for its neglect of concrete individual actors, Blau turned to the micro-foundations of structural analyses in *Exchange and Power in Social Life* (1964). He acknowledged the criticism that exchange theory was frequently narrowly utilitarian, elaborating normative principles of reciprocity and **justice** alongside **rationality** and marginal utility in order to understand both conflict and integration within social relationships. Together with **Otis Dudley Duncan**, he produced a landmark study of stratification, *American Occupational Structure* (1967). This combined a sophisticated theoretical model of **social status** attainment with innovative techniques of **data** analysis to study trends in **social mobility**; it is a classic of American empirical sociology. He continued to work on **micro–macro theory** in the later part of his career, publishing *Structural Contexts of Opportunities* (1994), in which he reformulated exchange theory to allow emergent properties of social structures that constrained opportunities.

JOHN HOLMWOOD

Blumer, Herbert (1900–1987)

Though Blumer was theoretically a symbolic interactionist, his major writings were in the areas of race relations (see **race and ethnicity**), **labor** and management conflict, **urbanization**, and **popular culture**, represented in his *Selected Works* (2000), which were appropriately subtitled *A Public Philosophy for Mass Society*. Empirically, he remained true to the Chicago style of ethnographic study (see **Chicago School**): his forte was the detailed empirical observation of the ways in which whatever subjects were under scrutiny went about sustaining and negotiating meaning. For Blumer, people act on the basis of the meanings that they impute to situations, which they build up over time by the use of **language** in social **interaction** with others. In this way, they develop a sense both of their **self** and the other, often through the process of seeing themselves as the other might – taking the role of the other. Just as social inter-action is processual, the sense of the self that one has is also built and changed processually: there is no inherent **identity** – only that which the self makes up in interactions with others. Blumer did not see the meaning of any act as inherent in the act itself but as socially constructed by the responses that such acts elicit and the flow of interaction in anticipation of future acts. Thus, while meaning may attach to quite tangible phenomena, such as a building or a river, or to something quite intangible, such as **justice** or **discrimination**, what that meaning is constituted as being is always an effect of the meanings that society sustains, contests, and frames over time.

STEWART CLEGG

body

From the 1980s, there has been growing interest in the sociology of the body as illustrated by B. Turner in *The Body and Society* (1984), M. Featherstone, M. Hepworth, and B. Turner in *The Body. Social Process and Cultural Theory* (1991), and C. Shilling in *The Body and Social Theory* (1993). Over a longer period, there was an erratic interest in the body among sociologists such as **Erving Goffman** in *Stigma* (1964), and **Norbert Elias** in *The Civilizing Process* (1939 [trans. 1978]) in which Elias explored the regulation of bodily practices. However, con-temporary interest appears to be driven by signifi-cant changes in society relating to **consumption**, cultural representations, medical science, and **health**. Scientific and technological advances, par-ticularly the new reproductive technologies (see **reproduction**), cloning techniques, and stem-cell research have given the human body a problem-atic legal and social status. The social world is being transformed by genetic and medical tech-nologies that reconstruct social, especially **kin-ship**, relationships, and create the possibility of genetically modified bodies and "designer babies." In particular, assisted reproduction is changing the generative connections between parents and children, and reconstructing the **family** as an **in-stitution** of reproduction. In addition, aging (see **age**), disease, and **death and dying** no longer appear to be immutable facts about the human

condition, but contingent possibilities that are constantly transformed by medical sciences. The development of regenerative medicine and the use of stem cell research to offset the negative side-effects of aging and chronic disease hold out the utopian promise of living forever, or at least extending life expectancy considerably.

The emergence of the body as a research topic in the humanities and social sciences is a response to these technological and scientific changes, and to the diverse **social movements** that are associated with them, such as gay and lesbian movements, environmentalism, and anti-globalism on the one side, and religious **fundamentalism**, pro-life move-ments, and conservative cultural **politics** on the other. More importantly, the human body, or more specifically its genetic code, is now a key factor in economic growth in a wide range of biotech industries. In a paradoxical manner, the pathology of the human body is itself a productive factor in the new economy. Disease is no longer simply a constraint on the productivity of labor, but an actual factor of production. The body is increasingly a code or system of **information** from which economic profits can be extracted through patents, rather than merely a natural organism. In his *Our Posthuman Future*, Francis Fukuyama (2002) has claimed that the biotechnol-ogy revolution will transform the nature of politics by changing human life.

Different philosophical and sociological trad-itions have shaped contemporary approaches to the body. Firstly, the body is often discussed as a cultural representation of social organization. For example, the head is often used as a metaphor of government, and the word "corporation" to describe the modern company has its origins in such bodily metaphors. In this sociological trad-ition, research on the body is concerned to under-stand how the body enters into political discourse as a representation of **power**, and how power is exercised over the body. This approach to the body is associated with **Michel Foucault**, whose work on the discipline of the body in *Discipline and Punish. The Birth of the Prison* (1975 [trans. 1977]) gave rise to research on the government of the body in schools, prisons, and factories. This approach to the body was therefore concerned with questions of representation and regulation in which diet, for example, is a method used in Turner's *Regulating Bodies* (1992). The Foucauldian perspective is not concerned with understanding our experiences of embodiment; it is not concerned with grasping the lived experience of the body in terms of a **phenomenology** of the body. The starting point for the study of the "lived body" has been the research of the French philosopher **Maurice Merleau-Ponty** in *Phenomenology of Perception* (1945 [trans. 1982]), which examined how the perception of reality always occurs from the particular location of our body. Merleau-Ponty showed how our cognition of the world is always an embodied perception. In short, phenomenology was a critique of the dualism of the mind and body, in which the body is passive and inert. Research inspired by this idea of the lived body has been important in showing the intimate connections between body, experience and **identity**.

In addition, there is an influential anthropological tradition, which examines the body as a symbolic system. The dominant figure in this tradition is the British anthropologist **Mary Douglas**, whose *Purity and Danger: An Analysis of Concepts of Pollution and Taboo* (1966) shaped subsequent research. Douglas showed how notions of pollution were associated with uncertainty and danger. The body provides human society with metaphors of social stability and order by defining areas of ambiguity. In this sense, we use the body as a method of thinking about society. In anthropology, there is another tradition, however, that has examined how human beings are embodied and how they acquire a variety of cultural practices that are necessary for walking, sitting, dancing, and so forth. The study of embodiment has been the concern of anthropologists who have been influenced, in particular, by the work of **Marcel Mauss**, who invented the concept of "body techniques" in the *Journal de Psychologie Normale et Pathologique* (1935). This anthropological legacy encourages us to think about the body as a multitude of performances. These anthropological assumptions have been developed in contemporary sociology by **Pierre Bourdieu** in terms of the concepts of hexis and **habitus**, by which our dispositions and tastes are organized. For example, within the everyday habitus of **social classes**, Bourdieu showed in *Distinction: A Social Critique of the Judgement of Taste* (1979 [trans. 1984]) that the body is invested with symbolic capital (see **social capital**) whereby the body is an expression of the hierarchies of social power. The body is cultivated within the particular habitus of social classes, and it thus expresses the aesthetic preferences of different class positions. This form of distinction is illustrated by the different types of **sport** which are supported by different social classes, and which require different types of embodiment. Obviously bodies that are developed for rugby may be inappropriate for tennis, and these bodies express

the taste (the organization of preferences in a habitus) of different social strata.

This development of interest in the body has also involved a recovery of philosophical anthropology, especially the work of Arnold Gehlen (1904–76). In *Man: His Nature and Place in the World*, Gehlen (1940 [trans. 1988]) argued that human beings are "not yet finished animals." By this notion, he meant that human beings are biologically poorly equipped to cope with the world into which they are involuntarily born. They have no finite or specific instinctual equipment for a given environment, and therefore require a long period of **socialization** in order to adapt themselves to their social world. Human incompleteness provides an anthropological explanation for the human origins of social **institutions**. Gehlen's work has been important in the development of contemporary sociology, especially in, for example, **Peter Berger** and **Thomas Luckmann**'s *The Social Construction of Reality: A Treatise in the Sociology of Knowledge* (1966).

The contemporary sociology of the body has been further influenced by twentieth-century **feminism**. **Simone de Beauvoir**'s *The Second Sex* (1949 [trans. 1972]) was indirectly a major contribution to the study of the body, and in particular to the patriarchal regulation of the female body. She argued that women are not born, but become women through social and psychological processes that construct them as essentially female. Her research on human aging in *Old Age* (1970 [trans. 1977]) drew attention to the social invisibility and powerlessness of older women. Her work inaugurated a tradition of research on the social production of differences in **gender** and **sexuality**. Feminist theories of the body have been associated with **social constructionism**, which posits that the differences between male and female (bodies), that we take for granted as if they were facts of nature, are socially produced. Germaine Greer's *The Female Eunuch* (1971), Kate Millett's *Sexual Politics* (1971), and Ann Oakley's *Sex, Gender and Society* (1972) were important in demonstrating the difference between biologically determined sex and the social construction of gender roles and sexual identities. The underlying theory of gender **inequalities** was the idea of **patriarchy**, and much empirical research in sociology has subsequently explored how the social and political subordination of women is expressed somatically in psychological depression and physical illness. Much of the creative work in this field went into research on anorexia nervosa, obesity, and eating disorders, such as Susan Bordo's *Unbearable Weight: Feminism, Western*

Culture and the Body (1993). The popular literature on this issue was influenced by Susan Orbach's *Fat is a Feminist Issue* (1984). More recently, there has been increasing interest in the question of men's bodies and **masculinity**, for example in R. W. Connell's *Masculinities* (1995).

Critics argue that one paradoxical consequence of this feminist legacy has been that the emphasis on the social construction of women's bodies has led to the absence of any concern with the lived body and embodiment. For example, Judith Butler, drawing on the work of the Marxist philosopher **Louis Althusser**, has argued in *Bodies That Matter* (1993) that, in a social world dominated by heterosexuality, bodies that matter are ones that materialize in terms of this regulatory **norm**. She argues that we must pay attention then to the dominant discourses that interpellate men and women into hierarchical positions in society. In this approach, the body becomes merely an element in the rhetorical construction of gender relations in which the lived experience of embodiment in daily practices is neglected.

The basic notion that the "naturalness" of the human body is a social product has been applied to an increasingly large array of topics. For example, the sociological analysis of the body has played a major role in the development of the "social model" in disability studies in order to make a distinction between **disability and impairment** in W. Seymour, *Remaking the Body* (1998) and C. Barnes, G. Mercer, and T. Shakespeare, *Exploring Disability* (1999). The sociological focus on the body has also begun to transform the sociology of aging, in, for example, C. A. Faircloth, *Aging Bodies: Images and Everyday Experience* (2003). The sociology of the body has also influenced dance studies, theories of **popular culture**, and the study of **sport**, where ethnographic studies have produced a rich collection of empirical studies of the body in society in, for example, H. Thomas and J. Ahmed, *Cultural Bodies: Ethnography and Theory* (2004).

By treating the body as a representation, discourse, or text, it becomes difficult to develop an adequate sociology of performance. For example, where dance studies have been influenced by **postmodernism** and by the French philosopher Gilles Deleuze (1925–95), there is little interest in the ethnographic study of movement and performance, despite Deleuze's emphasis on movement and event. From the perspective of postmodern theory, bodily practice and action become irrelevant to the understanding of the body as cultural sign. For example, if sociologists wanted to study ballet as performance rather than as representation, they would need to pay attention to the performing body. Richard Shusterman in *Performing Live* (2000), drawing on the work of Bourdieu and developing a pragmatist aesthetics (see **pragmatism** and **aesthetics**) has argued that an aesthetic understanding of performance such as hip hop cannot neglect the embodied features of artistic activity. The need for an understanding of embodiment and lived experience is crucial in understanding performing arts, but also for the study of the body in sport. While choreography is in one sense the text of the dance, performance takes place outside the strict directions of the choreographic work, and has an immediacy, which cannot be captured by the idea of the body as text. It is important to re-capture the intellectual contribution of the phenomenology of human embodiment in order to avoid the reduction of bodies to cultural texts. The social differences between men and women are consequences of culture, but understanding two people doing the tango requires some attention to bodily performances.

We might conclude therefore that there are two dominant but separate traditions in the anthropology and sociological study of the body. There is either the cultural decoding of the body as a system of meaning that has a definite structure existing separately from the intentions and conceptions of social actors, or there is the phenomenological study of embodiment that attempts to understand human practices, and is concerned to understand the body in relation to the **life-course** (of birth, maturation, **reproduction**, and death). Bourdieu's theory of practice offers a possible solution to this persistent tension between meaning and experience, or between representation and practice. Bourdieu's notions of habitus and practice in *Outline of a Theory of Practice* (1972 [trans. 1977]) and *Logic of Practice* (1980 [trans. 1990]) provide robust research strategies for looking simultaneously at how **social status** differences are inscribed on the body and how we experience the world through our bodies that are ranked in terms of their cultural capital. The analytical reconciliation of these traditions can be assisted by distinguishing between, first, the idea of the body as representation, and, second, embodiment as practice and experience.   BRYAN S. TURNER

Bogardus scale

– see **scales**.

Boudon, Raymond (1934–)

A professor at the University of Paris, with François Bourricaud, Boudon edited the *Critical*

Dictionary of Sociology (1982 [trans. 1989]), and made important contributions to **rational choice theory** in *The Logic of Social Action* (1979 [trans. 1981]) and (with Tom Burns) *The Logic of Sociological Explanation* (1974). He worked with **Paul Lazarsfeld** and they edited a collection of essays on the empirical problem of causal mechanisms in sociological **explanations** in *L'analyse empirique de la causalité* (1966). One of his key interests is the exploration of *The Unintended Consequences of Action* (1977 [trans. 1982]). He has written extensively on the classical tradition in sociology (with Mohamed Cherkaoui) in *The Classical Tradition in Sociology* (1997). He has also examined **inequality**, **social mobility**, and educational opportunity in *Mathematical Structures of Social Mobility* (1973) and *Education, Opportunity and Social Inequality* (1974). He has consistently addressed the question of **social change**, for example in *Theories of Social Change* (1984 [trans. 1986]). He has been a critic of **cultural relativism** in *The Origin of Values* (2000) and *The Poverty of Relativism* (2005). His study of **Alexis de Tocqueville** has appeared as *Tocqueville for Today* (2006).

BRYAN S. TURNER

Bourdieu, Pierre (1930–2002)

Bourdieu's work was always concerned with the relationship between the ordinary behavior of people in **everyday life** and the discourses constructed by social scientists to explain that behavior. Bourdieu made important contributions to the **philosophy of the social sciences**, but he insisted that these were meant to be practically useful rather than abstract. Methodologically, he argued for a dialectic between theory and practice, claiming that, too often, **social theory** was divorced from social enquiry and, equally, that too much empirical research proceeded as if it were possible to operate a-theoretically. The titles of some of his texts are indicative of this orientation: *The Craft of Sociology* with J.-C. Passeron and J.-C. Chamboredon (1968 [trans. 1991]), *Outline of a Theory of Practice* (1972 [trans. 1977]), *The Logic of Practice* (1980 [trans. 1990]), and *Practical Reason. On the Theory of Action* (1994 [trans. 1998]).

Born in southwestern France, Bourdieu studied in 1950–4 at the Ecole Normale Supérieure, Paris. His early social trajectory embodied a tension between the indigenous cultural influences of his family (what he was to call **habitus**) and the culture which he needed to acquire (what he was to call cultural capital, allied to **social capital**) in order to communicate successfully in the field of Parisian intellectual exchange. As a student, he was influenced by **phenomenology**, historians

and philosophers of science, and **Maurice Merleau-Ponty**. He served as a conscript in the French Army in Algeria in the early years of the Algerian War of Independence (1956–8) before gaining a post as an assistant at the University of Algiers. He wrote three books in which he presented the findings of research carried out in Algeria. These showed evidence of the influence of **Claude Lévi-Strauss** but, on returning to France in 1961, he became secretary to the research group that had been established by **Raymond Aron**. He ceased to present himself as a social anthropologist and became initiated as a "sociologist" in the 1960s, but he always retained the sense that scientific explanation, offered in whichever discourses, ran the risk of being conceptually colonialist in a way which was analogous with the French presence in North Africa. During the 1960s, he carried out research in relation to education and university life. Working with J.-C. Passeron, this led to the publication of *The Inheritors* (1964 [trans. 1979]) and *Reproduction in Education, Society and Culture* (1970 [trans. 1977]). In the same decade, he also carried out research on cultural production and reception, leading to the publication of *Photography: A Middle-Brow Art* (1965 [trans. 1990]) and *The Love of Art: European Art Museums and their Public* (1966 [trans. 1990]). As a result of the translations into English of his educational research, he was at first primarily associated with the sociology of **education**, but the analyses of photography and art museums were the prelude to work on **aesthetics** and taste which was most clearly presented in his *Distinction: A Social Critique of the Judgement of Taste* (1979 [trans. 1986]).

It was in the early 1970s that Bourdieu began to define his intellectual position most clearly. He revisited his Algerian fieldwork and reinterpreted it in *Outline of a Theory of Practice* (1972 [trans. 1977]). The original French text offered a critique of the **structuralism** of his earliest articles, whilst the English "translation" modified the original in order to point towards the benefits of **poststructuralism**. Bourdieu outlined a working **epistemology** by suggesting that there should be three forms of theoretical knowledge. The primary form corresponds with the knowledge of their situations held unreflectingly by social agents. It could be said to be pre-logical or pre-predicative knowledge. This category is explicable in terms of the **ontology** of Martin Heidegger (1889–1976), as well as of the phenomenology of Edmund Husserl (1859–1938). It is the kind of taken-for-granted knowledge which **ethnomethodology** endeavored to elicit. Following the historical epistemology of

Gaston Bachelard (1884–1962), Bourdieu argued that scientific knowledge has to be deliberately differentiated from such primary knowledge. If primary knowledge is subjective, scientific knowledge is a form of constructed objectivism. It operates in accordance with rules of explanation which are socially and historically contingent. So that contingent explanations should not be taken to be absolutely true, Bourdieu contended that there had to be a second "epistemological break," whereby the conditions of production of objectivist structuralism should be subjected to a second-level sociological analysis. This was the origin of Bourdieu's commitment to "reflexive sociology," outlined in *An Invitation to Reflexive Sociology* (1992 [trans. 1992]). For Bourdieu, poststructuralism was not anti-structuralism. Poststructuralism was able to derive benefit systematically from the insights of both ethnomethodology and structuralism.

Bourdieu did not advocate an armchair reflexivity. By encouraging everyone to reflect on their own situations and to analyze the provenance of the conceptual framework within which they undertook that reflection, Bourdieu believed that he was encouraging a form of "socio-analytic encounter" which would enable people to become equal, participating members of social democracies. After publishing his *Homo Academicus* (1984 [trans. 1988]) in which he analyzed the social conditions of production of the field of Parisian higher education and of his own work within that field, Bourdieu began to deploy his accumulated "cultural capital" within the political sphere. Responding tacitly to the work of **Louis Althusser**, Bourdieu analyzed sociologically the construction of a "state apparatus" in his *The State Nobility* (1989 [trans. 1996]) so as to encourage, in contrast, the emergence of new sources of political **power**, located in **social movements**. From the mid-1990s until his death, Bourdieu was an influential public figure in France, and his disposition to favor the cause of the underprivileged gained for him a following in an international political context as well as in the field of international social science. His socio-analytical method and his political engagement were both demonstrated in the project which he directed that was published as *The Weight of the World: Social Suffering in Contemporary Society* (1993 [trans. 1999]). To these last years belong engaged texts such as *Acts of Resistance* (1998 [trans. 1998]), but it was his last course of lectures as professor at the Collège de France, *Science de la science et réflexivité* (2003), which best represents the balance of his intellectual and

social project. His work has been influential across a variety of sociological subjects, irrespective of the canonical status of areas of research enquiry. His *Pascalian Meditations* (1997 [trans. 2000]), for example, contributed importantly to the sociology of the **body**.   DEREK ROBBINS

British Marxist historians

This label refers to a diverse cohort of Marxist writers who, from the 1930s onwards, individually and collectively contributed to the development of social history and **historical materialism**. There are a number of disparate members within the group, working in a number of distinct fields of historical inquiry – ancient, medieval, and from the sixteenth to the nineteenth century. The core of the group includes: Maurice Dobb, whose *Studies in the Development of Capitalism* (1946) began a protracted debate on the transition from **feudalism** to **capitalism**; Rodney Hilton, whose analysis of feudalism in *The Decline of Serfdom in Medieval England* (1969) focused on the English experience of the **peasantry**; Christopher Hill, who, in *The World Turned Upside Down* (1972), examined the English Revolution and the ideas which arose from it; E. P. Thompson, whose *The Making of the English Working Class* (1963) outlines the historical importance of working-class agency (see **social class**), experience, and the processual nature of class; and Eric Hobsbawm, who, in a monumental four-volume study, the *Age of Revolution* (1962), the *Age of Industry* (1968), the *Age of Capital* (1975), and the *Age of Empire* (2000), provided an expansive survey of social and political changes throughout the world. Other, more peripheral figures within the category include John Saville, V. G. Kiernan, Geoffrey Ste. de Croix, George Rudé, and Perry Anderson.

Many of these thinkers developed their political commitments during the rise of **fascism** and after the onset of World War II. Their related intellectual perspective arose in response to Whig and non-Marxist interpretations, including those of **Max Weber**, **R. H. Tawney**, and **Werner Sombart**, as well as against Soviet-sanctioned readings of **Marxism**. With reference to the latter, they maintained an ambiguous and tense relationship with the British Communist Party, especially after the Soviet invasion of Hungary in 1956.

Despite their internal differences, as a collective entity their work, as Harvey Kaye in *The British Marxist Historians* (1984) shows, shares a number of characteristics. First, there is a rejection of economic and technological determinism: all these scholars, though to different degrees, have seen the Marxist explanatory use of the theory of base/superstructure (see **ideology**) as highly restrictive and problematic. Instead, they argued for the important and irreducible role that culture, ideas, and beliefs played in shaping the historical process without, however, relapsing into idealism. Second, a number of them were concerned with the transition from feudalism to capitalism. Third, drawing on a tradition of people's history, they consistently emphasized the actions, struggles, and point of view of the lower classes; that is, they wrote from a "history-from-below" perspective. Finally, they reasserted the importance of class struggle, experience, and consciousness as crucial factors in understanding the historical process.

Both individually and collectively, their work has had an important influence on the interpretation of historical materialism, of the political implications of history, and how history is taught and understood. It also had a bearing on the development of **cultural studies**. A number of the group's theoretical and empirical contributions to history are contained in the journal *Past & Present*, which they founded.   STEVEN LOYAL

burden of dependency

– see **age**.

bureaucracy

While bureaucracy as a practice stretches back into antiquity (especially the Confucian bureaucracy of the Han dynasty), and while **Max Weber** in *Economy and Society* (1922 [trans. 1978]) explored its traditional origins (see **tradition**), the modern rational-legal conception of bureaucracy emerged in France in the eighteenth century. Indeed, the word is French in origin: it compounds the French word for an office – a *bureau* – with the Greek word for rule. In the nineteenth century, Germany provided the clearest examples of its success. Weber realized that the modern German state's success had been possible only because of the development of a disciplined bureaucracy and standing army – inventions that became the envy of Europe. In the military, nothing exhibited bureaucratic discipline better than goose-stepping, which the Prussians invented in the seventeenth century. The body language of goose-stepping transmitted a clear set of messages. For the generals, it demonstrated the absolute obedience of their recruits to orders, no matter how painful or ludicrous these might be. For civilians, the message was that men drilled as a collective machine would ruthlessly crush insubordination and eliminate **individualism**. Not surprisingly,

nineteenth-century German industrial **organizations** incorporated some of the forms of rule whose success was everywhere around them. While the workers did not goose-step into the factory, they were drilled in obedience to rules.

Bureaucratic organization depended, above all else, on the application of what Weber termed "rational" means for the achievement of specific ends. Techniques would be most rational where they were designed purely from the point of view of fitness for purpose. Weber's conception of **rationality** was not purely instrumental: relating a set of means as mechanisms to achieve a given end was only one version of rationality, albeit one which Weber believed would become dominant in the twentieth century.

Weber defined bureaucracy in terms of fifteen major characteristics: (1) **power** belongs to an office and not the officeholder; (2) **authority** is specified by the rules of the organization; (3) organizational action is impersonal, involving the execution of official policies; (4) disciplinary systems of knowledge frame organizational action; (5) rules are formally codified; (6) precedent and abstract rule serve as standards for organizational action; (7) there is a tendency towards specialization; (8) a sharp boundary between bureaucratic and particularistic action defines the limits of **legitimacy**; (9) the functional separation of tasks is accompanied by a formal authority structure; (10) powers are precisely delegated in a hierarchy; (11) the delegation of powers is expressed in terms of duties, rights, obligations, and responsibilities, specified in contracts; (12) qualities required for organizational positions are increasingly measured in terms of formal credentials; (13) there is a career structure with promotion by either seniority or merit; (14) different positions in the hierarchy are differentially paid and otherwise stratified; and, finally, (15) communication, coordination, and control are centralized in the organization.

Weber identified authority, based on rational-legal precepts, as the heart of bureaucratic organizations. Members of an organization will obey its rules as general principles that can be applied to particular cases, and that apply to those exercising authority as much as to others. People will obey not the person but the officeholder. Members of the organization should "bracket" the personal characteristics of the officeholder and respond purely to the demands of office. Weber's view of bureaucracy in *From Max Weber* was that "Precision, speed and unambiguity, knowledge of the files, continuity, discretion, unity, strict subordination, reduction of friction, and of material and personal cost ... are raised to the optimum point in the strictly bureaucratic administration" (1948).

Weber saw modern bureaucratic organizations as resting on a number of "rational" foundations. These include the existence of a "formally free" labor force; the appropriation and concentration of the physical means of production as disposable private property; the representation of share rights in organizations and property ownership; and the **rationalization** of various institutional areas such as the **market**, **technology**, and the law. The outcome of processes of rationalization will be the production of a new type of person: the specialist or technical expert. Such experts will master reality by means of increasingly precise and abstract concepts. **Statistics**, for example, began in the nineteenth century as a form of expert codified knowledge of everyday life and death, which could inform public policy. The statistician became a paradigm of the new kind of expert, dealing with everyday things but in a way that was far removed from everyday understandings. Weber sometimes referred to the results of this process as disenchantment, meaning the process whereby all forms of magical, mystical, traditional explanation are stripped from the world, open and amenable to the calculations of technical reason.

Bureaucracy is an organizational form consisting of differentiated knowledge and many different forms of expertise, with their rules and disciplines arranged not only hierarchically in regard to each other, but also in parallel. If you moved through one track, in theory, you need not know anything about how things were done in the other tracks. Whether the bureaucracy was a public- or private-sector organization would be largely immaterial. Private ownership might enable you to control the revenue stream but day-to-day control would, however, be maintained through the intermediation of experts. And expertise is always fragmented. This enables the bureaucracy to be captured by expert administrators, however democratic its mandate might be, as **Roberto Michels** argued in *Political Parties* in his famous "iron law of **oligarchy**" (1911 [trans. 1962]).   STEWART CLEGG

bureaucratization
– see **bureaucracy**.

Burgess, Ernest W. (1886–1966)
A member of the **Chicago School** of sociology, urban sociologist, and sponsor of community action programs, Burgess was born in Tilbury, Ontario, Canada. He received his PhD from the University of Chicago in 1913, where the Department of Sociology under **Albion Small** had pioneered the idea of social research in pursuit of reform. He returned to the department in 1916, where he spent the rest of his academic career, becoming its chair in 1946. He was elected president of the American Sociological Society (the forerunner of the American Sociological Association) in 1934.

Cautious and meticulous, he came under the influence of the charismatic **Robert Park**, with whom he wrote *An Introduction to the Science of Society* (1921).

His early research focused on the **urban ecology** of Chicago. Together with Park, he developed the **concentric zone theory** of spatial organization in *The City* (1925). They pioneered research into **race and ethnicity**, supporting a large number of doctoral students in this area. Burgess's research interests included the spatial distribution of **social problems** and led to his involvement with a number of community programs, especially those concerned with the **family** and young people. His papers have been collected in Donald Bogue (ed.), *Basic Writings of E. W. Burgess* (1974).

JOHN HOLMWOOD

C

Canguilhem, Georges (1904–1995)

He is known mainly as the intellectual *éminence grise* lurking behind some of the most influential post-World War II French social theorists, notably **Michel Foucault** and **Pierre Bourdieu**. Although he was an influential teacher and thinker, he published few major texts and, to date, these are not readily accessible in English translation. Born in southwest France, he was taught in Paris by the philosopher Émile Cartier (1868–1951), otherwise known as Alain, before entering the École Normale Supérieure in the same year, 1924, as **Raymond Aron**, Jean-Paul Sartre (1905–80), and Paul Nizan (1905–40). He wrote a postgraduate thesis on **Auguste Comte** under the supervision of Célestin Bouglé (1870–1940) and taught philosophy at Toulouse from 1936 to 1940 while commencing medical studies. He was active in the Resistance in the Auvergne during the Vichy regime and resumed teaching at Strasbourg in 1944. He submitted his doctoral dissertation in medicine in 1943. This was published in 1950, and republished many times after 1966 as *On the Normal and the Pathological* – famously, in 1978, with an introduction by Foucault (whose dissertation on madness and unreason had been examined by Canguilhem in 1960). He succeeded Gaston Bachelard (1884–1962) as Professor of Philosophy at the Sorbonne in 1955 and retired in 1971. He specialized in the history and philosophy of science, with particular reference to the life sciences, publishing *Ideology and Rationality in the History of the Life Sciences* (1977 [trans. 1988]). He made important contributions to **epistemology** and his discussions of **health** and disease relate as pertinently to the societal as to the individual condition.   DEREK ROBBINS

capitalism

The study of capitalism represents a classical topic in **sociology**. Both **Karl Marx** and **Max Weber** were, for example, deeply interested in capitalism and made it their main focus of research. During much of the twentieth century, on the other hand, sociologists have tended to take capitalism for granted, often neglecting to discuss it in their analyses of **society**. Exceptions exist, and there are also some signs that capitalism is currently enjoying a comeback as a central topic in sociology. We are, for example, witnessing an increasing number of studies on the theme of "varieties of capitalism."

This revival of the study of capitalism will be reviewed later on in this entry. First, however, the question "What is capitalism?" needs to be addressed. There will also be a presentation of what the classics have to say about capitalism (Marx, Weber, and **Joseph Alois Schumpeter**). Their works are still unsurpassed, and they also constitute the foundation for much of the current discussion.

In order for human beings and societies to survive, the economy has to be organized in a special manner, of which capitalism is only one. There has to be production; what is produced has to be distributed; and what has been distributed has to be consumed. There exist different ways of organizing these three processes of production, distribution, and **consumption**. According to a well-known argument, the key distinction when it comes to economic organization is between "housekeeping" (*Haushalten*) and "profit-making" (*Erwerben*). As Weber argued in his *General Economic History* (1922 [trans. 1978]), you either produce for consumption or for profit. Marx in *Capital* (1867 [trans. 1996]) referred to the same distinction when he spoke of "use value" versus "exchange value," and so did Aristotle when he contrasted *oekonomia* (household management) to *chrematistika* (money making).

Karl Polanyi in *Trade and Market in the Early Empires* (1957) further elaborated the distinction between housekeeping and profit-making when he introduced his well-known typology of the three different ways in which an economy can acquire unity and stability: reciprocity, redistribution, and exchange. Each of these three terms, Polanyi explains, expresses a form of **social action**, but also answers to an **institution**. For exchange, the equivalent institution is the **market**; for redistribution, it may be the **state**

A. The economic process in general

B. The economic process where redistribution (Polanyi) is predominant

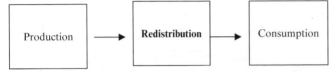

C. The economic process where reciprocity (Polanyi) is predominant

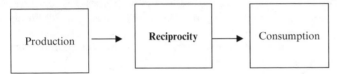

D. The economic process where exchange (Polanyi) is predominant

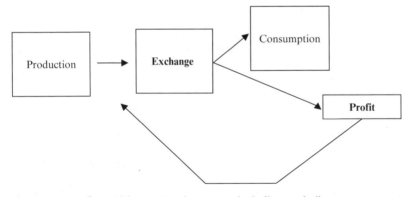

Figure 1 Ways of organizing economic process, including capitalism

or a political ruler; and for reciprocity, the tribe, the kin group, or the **family**.

While exchange and the market answer to the category of profit-making, it should be noted that Polanyi's real innovation was to introduce *two* categories for housekeeping: reciprocity, and re-distribution. Based on this idea by Polanyi, we see that the process of the **economy** can actually be organized in primarily three different ways. First of all, we have the kind of economies where *redistribution* is central; and where what is produced is distributed via, for example, the state, before it is consumed. Second, there are economies where *reciprocity* constitutes the social mechanism through which production is distributed for

consumption. Here we may think of the way that the economy of a modern family is organized. Last – and this is where we come to capitalism – there is the situation which is characterized by the fact that what is being produced is distributed via the market. Here, however, all does not go to consumption; and what drives the process just as much as consumption, is the search for profit (see Fig. 1).

Capitalism, in brief, can be defined as an economy which is organized in such a way that what is being produced for consumption is distributed via exchange in the market *and* where some portion of what is being produced also goes to profit. The more of the economy that gets drawn into this type of **organization**, the more the economic system can be characterized as capitalistic. There also has to be a constant reinvestment of the profit into production, for the capitalist process to become permanent.

From this model, we also understand why it is valuable not only to study middle-range phenomena in sociology, as mainstream sociology tends to do today, but also to look at the macro level. In a capitalist economy, the three processes of production, distribution, and consumption are all closely linked to one another. What is being produced has to be sold, which means that production and consumption are deeply influenced by the market. Consumption and production, to phrase it differently, cannot be studied in isolation from the profit motive and its organization.

We may also take a concept such as production and further subdivide it into, say, factors of production (land, **labor**, capital, **technology**, organization). If we do this, we soon see how these are all oriented to the market and the necessity to produce profit. Labor, for example, needs to be socialized and educated in order to survive on the **labor market**. Technology cannot simply be developed according to the criteria of what is the most efficient, but has to be produced in such a way that it can be sold on the market, and so on.

While such important institutions in modern society as law (see **law and society**), **politics**, and **culture** are not included in the model of capitalism that has just been presented, it can be suggested that each of them will either speed up, slow down, or block the process of accumulation in the capitalist economy. One may, for example, argue that certain types of legislation (say bankruptcy law, corporate law, and contractual law) are important for an advanced capitalist system to exist. The same is true for certain types of political institutions, such as the rational state. That a country's general culture can be important for its development was something that **Charles-Louis Montesquieu** and **Alexis de Tocqueville** had already commented on.

Polanyi's categories of reciprocity, redistribution, and exchange also allow us to capture the phenomenon that all real economies consist of *a mixture* of different sectors. A modern capitalist economy, for example, usually has a considerable state sector that operates via redistribution (pensions, subsidies, welfare, and so on). Households are often organized according to the principle of reciprocity (even if we also know that this reciprocity is closely influenced by stratification (see **social stratification**) according to **gender** and **age**).

We may therefore speak of three main economic sectors in modern capitalist society: *the market economy, the state economy,* and *the household economy.* Some countries also have a developed *non-profit economy* (foundations, private universities, **voluntary associations**, and so on). This sector operates according to a mixture of Polanyi's three types of distribution.

While sociologists hold that the notion of a single inventor is something of a myth and that all discoveries tend to be "multiple discoveries," it is nonetheless possible to single out Marx as the one who invented the theory of capitalism. In *Capital* and related writings, Marx was also the first to theorize capitalism in analytical terms as a distinct system of its own. This system is socioeconomic as well as dynamic in nature.

What characterizes capitalism as a distinct socioeconomic system, according to Marx, is that **money** is used as capital and not simply as money. In the latter case, we have the situation where an individual sells a commodity (C) in order to buy some other commodity with the money (M). This process Marx writes as C-M-C. The capitalist, in contrast, uses money to produce commodities that are sold for profit; and here we have instead M-C-M1 (where M1 equals M plus some fraction of M).

According to Marx, it is crucial to understand how money can become something more than itself (M1), and instead of ascribing this process to the successful selling of some commodity on the market (as economists tend to do), Marx suggests that there exists one very special commodity that has the capacity to produce *more* value than it costs. This is human labor, and the extra value that it creates Marx terms surplus value. Marx's theory of surplus value consequently stands at the very center of his theory of capitalism as well as his theory of exploitation. To Marx, in other words, what happens in production (where surplus value is created) is more important than what happens in the market (where surplus value is just given a monetary form). The market, Marx specifies, is indeed central to capitalism – but its key role in capitalist society is primarily one of *mystification* since it is precisely the fact that commodities are bought and sold on the market, *at what seems to be their "right" price*, that makes it so hard for those who are exploited in capitalism to understand that labor is *always* underpaid in capitalism.

While Marx presented an analytical model of the capitalist process and, on the basis of this model, theorized how the economy would develop in the future, he also pioneered a deeply historical and empirical study of capitalism. Few readers of *Capital* will fail to have noticed this, and one may cite Marx's powerful descriptions of life in the factories or the process of enclosures that set off capitalism in England.

Capitalism, as Marx sees it, is not restricted to some special area or sphere of society, as economists see it today, but constitutes its very foundation. The economy, as a result, influences not only what goes on in the workplace but also a host of other phenomena, such as law, politics, literature, philosophy, the household, and the relations between the sexes. There is, in brief, no separate economic sector, according to Marx.

It may finally be mentioned that Marx also criticizes past and present economists for their view of capitalism. They often do not mention the existence of classes (see **social class**), and, if they do, they do not see exploitation. Most importantly, however, according to Marx, economists simply take capitalism for granted and think that categories such as "capital," "labor," "profit," and so on are universal and given, once and for all. They fail, in brief, to understand that capitalism is a deeply historical phenomenon. And as a result, they produce **ideology** rather than a scientific theory about capitalism.

There exist many critiques of Marx's theory of capitalism and little needs to be added to these. It is, for example, clear that capitalism does not operate according to "Natural Laws" which "work with iron necessity towards inevitable results," to cite the preface to *Capital*. There is much controversy over what is alive and dead in Marx's analysis, for example, in Jon Elster's *An Introduction to Karl Marx* (1986). It deserves nonetheless to be emphasized, when one discusses Marx's view of capitalism, that Marx has relatively little to say about corporations and other key capitalist institutions, such as the market, the stock exchange, and so on. For Marx, capitalism was grounded in production, and since production typically takes place inside the modern factory, this is also where it primarily should be studied.

Weber was deeply influenced by Marx and his analysis of capitalism. Like Marx, Weber, for example, saw capitalism as the defining feature of contemporary society and also as an ominous force for humanity. While Weber was well aware of capitalism's capacity to advance the material aspects of **civilization**, he also – like Marx – felt that there was something deeply non-ethical and inhuman about the system. The reader may recall Weber's famous metaphor of "the iron cage"

(*stalwarts Ghettoes*), which has taken on a life of its own in contemporary social science. Weber himself, however, used this metaphor to indicate that life in modern capitalist society is unbearably harsh. One reason for this has to do with the unrelenting demand that everybody works all the time; there is also the fact that life in modern capitalist society lacks a deeper meaning.

But even if there exist parallels between the views of Marx and Weber on capitalism, they also differ on several important points. One may single out five such points of profound difference. First of all, while Marx saw capitalism as centered around production, Weber saw it as centered around the market. Second, while Marx argued that there only exists one type of capitalism, Weber disagreed and suggested that there are several such types. Third, Marx and Weber differed in the way that they conceptualized the role that law, politics, and culture play in modern capitalism. Fourth, Weber's theory of the origin of capitalism differed from that of Marx. And finally, Weber introduced the concept of *meaning* into the analysis of capitalism – a concept that does not exist in Marx.

That Weber saw capitalism as centered on the market, as opposed to production, comes out very clearly in his general view of capitalism. From Weber's *The Agrarian Sociology of Ancient Civilizations* (1909 [trans. 1976]), one may cite what is probably the most succinct definition of capitalism that can be found in his work: "where we find that property is an object of trade and is utilized by individuals for profit-making enterprise in a market economy, there we have capitalism."

Second, while Marx argued that there was no capitalism in Antiquity and that capitalism could only be found in the West, Weber sharply disagreed. As opposed to Marx, Weber in *Economy and Society* (1921–2 [trans. 1978]) suggested that there are three major types of capitalism: *political capitalism*, *rational capitalism*, and *traditional-commercial capitalism*. Political capitalism can be found where profit-making is directly dependent on politics, say where merchants operate under the direct protection of an imperialist power or where business contracts can only be secured through the mediation of state officials. Political capitalism, according to Weber, existed in Antiquity, in the West, and elsewhere, and can also be found in modern society. Rational capitalism, in contrast, is a uniquely western product, and first came into full being from the time of the Reformation and onwards. It is characterized by a strongly methodical approach to all economic matters and by the use of institutions such as the modern **firm**, rational technology, and capital accounting. Traditional-commercial capitalism can be found in all societies, far back in history as well as today, and it consists of small trade in goods and currencies.

Third, while Marx conceptualized the role of law, politics, and culture in capitalism as all being influenced by economic forces in a decisive manner, Weber had a different approach. In principle, the causality can go both ways. He also argued that, as society develops, so do its various spheres – such as the economic sphere, the political sphere, the religious sphere, and so on. Each of these spheres has its own internal dynamic and autonomy vis-à-vis society as a whole (*Eigengesetzlichkeit*). How clashes between spheres will be solved is an empirical question and cannot be predicted in advance. Basically, however, politics and law need to be predictable and reliable for rational capitalism to thrive.

Fourth, Weber and Marx differed on the historical origin of western capitalism. Both saw capitalism as the result of a long evolutionary history and not as the result of one critical event or factor (for Marx on this point, see *Capital*; for Weber, *General Economic History*). Still, while Marx singled out the enclosures in England as extra important in this development, Weber did the same with the creation of "the spirit of capitalism" during the Reformation and onwards. Whether Weber was correct or not in his thesis that certain Protestant ideas (especially the notion of work as a vocation), helped to jumpstart modern capitalism is still a much-debated question as Gordon Marshall demonstrates in his *In Search of the Spirit of Capitalism* (1982).

The last point on which Marx's and Weber's analyses of capitalism differ importantly from one another has to do with the concept of meaning (*Sinn*). While Marx was very interested in understanding the relationship between capitalism and culture, he nonetheless never addressed the issue of the meaning that the actor attaches to his or her actions. By explicitly including this aspect, Weber can be said to have opened up the analysis of capitalism in many directions that remained closed to Marx.

Schumpeter was deeply influenced by the works of Marx and Weber, including their analyses of capitalism. While he admired both authors, he also regarded *Capital*, as well as *The Protestant Ethic and the Spirit of Capitalism* (1905 [trans. 2002]), as having serious flaws. He was not impressed by Weber's argument that a qualitative change had

somehow taken place in the mentality of western capitalists at the time of the Reformation, and he disapproved of most of the economics that Marx had used in his argument. Schumpeter in his *Essays* (1961) saw capitalism as gradually evolving from Antiquity or "early capitalism" to contemporary times or "the modern phase," that is, "1898 and today," traversing in the process "mercantile capitalism," from the sixteenth century till the end of the eighteenth century, and "intact capitalism," during the nineteenth century. He emphasized continuity, and he saw no reason to refer to primitive accumulation or Luther's ideas about *Beruf* (vocation).

Schumpeter nonetheless deeply admired Marx's idea that the economy is not something that only responds to influences from the outside, as in conventional equilibrium analysis. He also tried to construct his own theory of capitalism on this insight by Marx, although he picked a different central actor: the entrepreneur rather than the capitalist. The entrepreneur, Schumpeter argues, can be defined as an economic actor who, by piecing together a new combination of already existing factors, creates innovations and economic change. Stimulated by the huge profit that an entrepreneur makes, a number of imitators will appear, till there is no more room for making a profit, and the economy starts to slide downwards. The business cycles that always accompany capitalism are, according to Schumpeter, basically caused by the entrepreneur and the wave of imitators that follows in his or her footsteps.

Something must also be said about *Capitalism, Socialism and Democracy* (1942) when it comes to Schumpeter's analysis of capitalism. He here comments on a period of the history of capitalism when Marx and Weber were not alive, namely the interwar period. Like Weber, however, Schumpeter singles out the giant corporations with their huge bureaucracies as the key actors – and also as being deeply problematic. Indeed, Schumpeter was so fearful of these giant corporations that he saw them as a major reason why capitalism was bound to go under and be replaced by **socialism**. Like Marx, Schumpeter was convinced that capitalism one day would disappear, but in contrast to Marx he thought that this would be caused by its success and not by its failure. Many factors were involved in this process, including the quality of the capitalists. With the success of capitalism, he argued, capitalists would eventually turn complacent and lose their desire to counter the attacks of socialists and **intellectuals** – and this failure to respond would slowly undo "the capitalist civilization," including its otherwise well-functioning economic system.

Socialists more or less monopolized the use of the term capitalism from around 1900 – when Werner Sombart (1863–1941) popularized it in *Der moderne Kapitalismus* (1903) – till something like the 1970s. From this point on, however, it has been as much embraced by economists, liberals, and the right wing as by social democrats and the left wing. The theory of capitalism that can be found among economists today is also no longer restricted to theories of how prices are set through the interplay of demand and supply; it also includes reflections on the institutions that give structure to capitalism, including the state.

To discuss the various models of capitalism that can be found among twentieth-century economists would demand a longer essay than this, and the reader is referred to the works of people from **J. M. Keynes** to Milton Friedman (1912–), and John Kenneth Galbraith (1908–2006). A few words must nonetheless be said about the economists' creation of what may be termed the neo-liberal theory of capitalism, since it is this way of looking at capitalism that has come to dominate the current discourse on this subject.

The neo-liberal theory of capitalism has deep roots in the nineteenth century and was given an early and theoretically sophisticated expression in the works of Austrian economists Ludwig von Mises (1881–1973) and Friedrich von Hayek (1899–1992). These two thinkers insisted on the decentralized, spontaneous nature of capitalism and that the state must stay out of the economy – for example, Friedrich von Hayek, *Individualism and Economic Order* (1948), and Ludwig von Mises, *The Anti-Capitalistic Mentality* (1956). Prices carry enough information for the entrepreneur to know what to do; and while legal and political institutions are necessary for the market to work properly, they must under no circumstances be allowed to interfere with its workings or to counter its results through welfare measures. The market will produce liberty and wealth if it is left alone; and this is what matters.

Since the 1980s, when Margaret Thatcher and Ronald Reagan came to power, this vision of neoliberal capitalism has become the official economic ideology of the West, and it is still as strong, if not stronger. As applied to the situation of the economy in developing countries, neoliberalism is known as "the Washington consensus" and has come to expression in official statements by the International Monetary Fund, the US president, and so on.

Other academics besides liberal economists have produced important scholarship on capitalism during the post-World War II period. Leaving aside Andrew Shonfield's pioneering *Modern Capitalism* (1965) in order to continue with the theme of the neo-liberal vision, a mention should be made of the idea of *disorganized capitalism* which emerged in the 1980s. It is here argued that the attempt to organize capitalism at the top (via cartels, monopolies, and the like) and at the bottom (via **trade unions**, cooperatives, and so on) is about to come to an end – for example in Scott Lash and John Urry, *The End of Organized Capitalism* (1987). The result of this process will be strife and disorganization, and will work out differently depending on the country in question.

During the 1990s a novel approach to the study of capitalism emerged, which also is opposed to neoliberalism. This is the school of *varieties of capitalism*, which is close in spirit to the French regulation school (see **regulation theory**) and the so-called economics of conventions. All of these approaches work in the tradition of political economy and draw on a mixture of heterodox economics and political science. Their focus is on capitalism in individual countries, and comparisons are often made between various countries, as well as between groups of countries. A central task that the varieties-of-capitalism approach has set for itself is to show that non-liberal and heavily regulated economies work just as well as neoliberal and de-regulated economies. Sweden and Germany, for example, have capitalist economies that are as efficient as, say, the United Kingdom and the United States (see, for example, Colin Crouch and Wolfgang Streeck, *Political Economy of Modern Capitalism*, (1997) or Peter Hall and David Soskice, *Varieties of Capitalism*, (2001). In analyzing the way that capitalism is organized in different countries, much emphasis in this type of literature is also laid on the mode of governance. And in doing so, many more actors are usually taken into account than in conventional economics, including chambers of commerce and other business associations. Much attention is finally also paid to different types of regulations, from legal systems to the many rules that are produced in modern society.

An attempt has also recently been made to draw on the tradition of economic sociology in analyzing capitalism (for example Victor Nee and Richard Swedberg, *The Economic Sociology of Capitalism*, 2005). This approach is heavily indebted to Weber and Schumpeter and primarily attempts to outline the social structure of the various economic institutions that are at the core of capitalism, from firms and markets to entrepreneurship more generally. Proponents of this approach are closer to New Institutional Economics than to the tradition of political economy. They also center their analyses around the notion of *interest*, and view institutions as embodying interests or as channeling interests rather than as a set of rules – for example, in Richard Swedberg, *The Concept of Interest* (2005).

It may finally be noted that, according to Marx, capitalism is always revolutionizing itself in its attempts to seek new profits. This means that the analysts of capitalism are looking at a target that is moving very rapidly, something that tends to cast them in the unhappy role of the famous owl of Minerva, always arriving too late. Nonetheless, since capitalism is at the center of modern society, and since it constitutes "the most fateful force in our modern life" (Weber), it is absolutely crucial that it also remains at the center of social science.

RICHARD SWEDBERG

capitalist mode of production
– see **Karl Marx**.

carceral society
– see **Michel Foucault**.

care
The social implications of care have been highlighted by sociologists whose work has emphasized the often unseen work that is performed (largely in the household). The study of care has been responsible for the "denaturalization" of those responsibilities (looking after children, the ill, the infirm, and the elderly) which were once, if not assumed to fall to, then at least assigned to, women. A generation of sociologists (including Hilary Graham, Miriam David, Clare Ungerson, and Hilary Land) asked questions about who cared for those not able to function as independent and autonomous adults and found that the answer was largely, although not exclusively, women. As a result of these studies, "caring work" has been recognized in much of Europe as work that merits economic payment.

There is another sense, however, in which the extension of the understanding of the term work has enlarged our perception of care. It lies in the development of what has become known as the "ethic of care." In 1982, Carol Gilligan (1936–) argued, in *A Different Voice*, that women approached moral choices in terms of the implications of their actions for others. Gilligan – and

other later writers – have defined this attitude as that of an ethic of care which prioritizes the needs of others, rather than abstract and ideal moral systems, in making moral and ethical choices. The recognition of the giving of care has also created the social recognition of "carers," those millions of people (largely female) whose lives are ruled by the dependence of others. For aging societies, the issue of care and carers has become central to welfare policies, since for many people the traditional expectations surrounding care have become unacceptable, not least in the assumption that caring for others will always be willingly, and voluntarily, accepted.   MARY EVANS

career
In commonsense usage, this is the progression of an individual through an **occupation** via a series of predefined institutional gateways which secure standing in the **community**, increasing levels of seniority within the occupation, and increasing levels of pay. The hierarchal structure of a university career provides a good example: from tutor, to lecturer, senior lecturer, associate professor, and, finally, professor. **Max Weber** argued in *The Protestant Ethic and the Spirit of Capitalism* (1905 [trans. 2002]) that the development of the career as a calling or vocation was a secular solution to the problem of salvation in Protestantism, providing a secular form of salvation through service to the community. Sociologists, particularly those in the symbolic interactionist tradition, have focused on the temporal sequencing of a career and particularly the problems that arise for organizations when individuals become blocked in their career aspirations. More broadly then, the concept of career can be applied to any ongoing sequences of changes of **social status** over time. Thus, the sequencing of the events that go to make a **family** can be conceptualized as a career. While careers are usually taken to be positive life experiences, as in a career in the **professions**, they can also be negatively evaluated. **Erving Goffman** drew attention to the negatively evaluated "moral career" of the mentally ill patient, who through a series of degradation ceremonies – the loss of an autonomous adult identity, the replacement of street clothing with institutional garments, and boundaries around their ability to interact with others – experienced a stigmatizing career. In **criminology**, there is also the notion of a "criminal career" in which an offender passes through a series of stages towards full-time criminal activities.

Contemporary sociologists have focused on the changing nature of work in **postindustrial society**, which makes the possibility of a life-long career increasingly unlikely as work becomes more fragmented and discontinuous, because companies downsize and outsource functions previously undertaken by long-term employees: such as, for example, IBM outsourcing its computing functions to India. Under the impact of neoliberalism in the **state** sector, the idea of a career in the public or civil service is also on the wane as the state out-sources many of its functions to the private market. **Richard Sennett** has, in *The Corrosion of Character* (1998) and *Respect* (2003), claimed that, with the decline of career in the modern **economy**, there is a corresponding transformation of **personality**, namely an erosion of character.   KEVIN WHITE

case study

The term case study refers both to methodological strategy and subject of study. Social scientists use the case-study approach as a methodological strategy when they wish to provide rich descriptions and analyses of a single case, or a small number of cases. This approach allows researchers to develop a detailed view of processes, interactions, and meaning systems in a way they would find difficult if they were examining dozens or hundreds of cases. A case-study research project is limited in its capacity to support universalizing sociological generalizations but its advantage is that it can reveal more meaningful data about a case. Case-study data can yield specific insights that form the bases for hypothesis testing (see **hypothetico-deductive method**) in studies that use large datasets. Many researchers in this tradition use the **comparative method**, wherein close examination of two or three targeted cases allows them to isolate the causes and consequences of particular case features and dynamics. Qualitative field researchers, and historical, comparative, and quantitative methodologists all use the case study approach.

A case-study project might take as its subject work organizations, **social movements**, communities, political regimes, schools, and myriad other case types. The particular population from which a researcher draws his or her case follows from the theoretical and substantive goal. For example, if a sociologist wishes to know whether and why social **inequality** persists in organizations that are committed to democratic, progressive **social change**, she or he might study worker-owned cooperatives or feminist, peace, and other social movement organizations.   VICKI SMITH

Castells, Manuel (1942–)

A Spanish-born sociologist, Castells has roots in urban sociology and the sociology of **social movements**, which are examined in his *The Urban Question* (1977), *City, Class and Power* (1978), and *The City and the Grassroots* (1983). Between 1967 and 1979 he taught at the University of Paris, first on the Nanterre campus and, after 1970, at the École des Études en Sciences Sociales. In 1979 he was appointed Professor of Sociology and Professor of City and Regional Planning at the University of California, Berkeley. In 2001 he became a research professor at the Universitat Oberta de Catalunya, Barcelona. In 2003 he joined the University of Southern California, Anneberg School of Communication as Professor of Communication and Technology. Castells's work climaxed with a number of cross-cultural studies on the information age and global (see **globalization**) **network** society that **Anthony Giddens** compared in significance to **Max Weber**'s *Economy and Society*. These were *The Rise of Network Society* (1996), *The Power of Identity* (1997), and *The End of the Millennium* (2000). A more telling comparison might have been with **Karl Marx**'s *Capital* (1867). For Castells operates in the neo-Marxist tradition to explore the theme of the perpetual revolutions under **capitalism, technology**, production, **power**, and experience. He ultimately links the purpose of sociology to the goal of human liberation. Employing powerful comparative and historical methods of analysis (see **comparative method**), he demonstrates how a new type of production has emerged in the West (based around **information**), with a new type of society (network society) and a new form of identity politics (critical pluralist/virtual).

Castells demonstrates how "replaceable generic labor" has been repositioned through the casualization of employment, with considerable discontinuity in **careers** and personal crises, illnesses, drug/alcohol **addiction**, loss of assets, and negation of distinction. He posits three fateful cleavages in network society: (1) *skills-based divisions* between information and communication workers and deskilled **labor**; (2) *obsolescent citizens*, divided between laborers who are defined as surplus to the requirements of the system and what might be called the "stakeholders" in **civil society**; and (3) *intensified alienated labor*, divided from stakeholders. His work constitutes a magisterial account of the many-sided restructuring of capitalism in the twenty-first century.

CHRIS ROJEK

causal explanation

– see **explanation**.

causal inference

– see **explanation**.

causal modeling

– see **modeling**.

causality

In **sociology**, disputes over the notion of "causality" reflect deep divisions in the discipline. With the success of eighteenth-century Newtonian science – and the postulation that there are laws of nature which can be discovered through empirical research – came the ideal of a science of **society** with its own laws. This was the inspiration for **Auguste Comte** to propose a wholly secular explanation of social life, through what he called the positive method (hence **positivism**) that restricted **explanation** to observable facts. Combined with the development of evolutionism – of the idea of the development of complex social forms from preceding primitive ones, and the idea of **social structure** (developing out of the analysis of the **state** in the work of Thomas Hobbes [1588–1679], John Locke [1632–1704], and Jean-Jacques Rousseau [1712–78]) – the scene was set for postulating the lawful progression of societal types based on empirically observable facts. **Émile Durkheim** defined the subject of sociology as the study of social facts. These are objective, existing independently of any individual's consciousness of them, are external to the individual, and coerce the individual to behave in specific ways. As Durkheim puts it, social facts such as the **family**, the legal system, or **marriage**, for example, "will be felt to be real, living active forces, which because of the way they determine the individual, prove their independence of him" (*Suicide*, 1897 [trans. 1951]). Thus in Durkheim's approach society is a causal factor in determining how individuals act. Durkheim's approach, which claims that the **social sciences** are pursuing general knowledge of society, is, nomothetic, in seeking to produce causal-explanatory knowledge. However, the position that there are causal relationships in social life was hotly disputed in the **Methodenstreit** – the debate over whether the methods of the natural sciences were useful in the social sciences – in German history at the end of the nineteenth century. Wilhelm Dilthey (1833–1911) and Wilhelm Windelband (1848–1915) both argued that because the subject matter of the social sciences was the conscious subject – unlike the inert nature studied in the natural sciences – the social sciences had to develop their own unique methods of study in which the goal was interpretation and understanding rather than explanation and prediction. Furthermore, the social sciences are idiographic, because they could only ever provide knowledge of the specific situation. To achieve this, the social science researcher had to be able to understand empathically the subjective meanings attributed by social agents to their actions. This method was called **Verstehen**, or interpretive sociology. However, it was also a form of intuitionism, and according to **Max Weber** we could never be secure in our knowledge of whether we had got our subject's position "right." He proposed to resolve the antimony between the objective search for the laws of society and the subjectively driven origins of **social action** in the individual actor.

As Weber put it in *Economy and Society* (1922 [trans. 1968]), "sociology is a science concerning itself with the interpretive understanding of social action and thereby with a causal explanation of its course and consequences." He (in *Roscher and Knies: The Logical Problems of Historical Economics*, 1903–6 [trans. 1975]) defines causality in the same way as David Hume (1711–76): "the idea of an effect, the idea of a dynamic bond . . . between phenomena qualitatively different from each other . . . [and] the idea of subordination to rules." Like Hume he rejects empirical correlation as evidence of causal relationships. A causal claim is that an event x, coming first, will cause an outcome y on every occasion. According to Hume, in his famous critique of causality, a causal link cannot be demonstrated between x and y. Rather, the most that can be said is that x and y are a succession of occurrences which, because they always follow each other, we come to expect to be together. However, in Hume's argument, we cannot prove that they cause each other. Unlike Hume, Weber argues that a form of causal explanation is achievable in the social sciences, that is, to establish the elective affinity between events. This causal explanation is to be produced not by empathy (as in Dilthey) but through understanding why it is that an actor gives meaning to what they do in the context of a culturally specific situation. Thus, in his account of the *Protestant Ethic and the Spirit of Capitalism* (1905 [trans. 2002]), Weber does not seek to "enter" the mind of his subjects, but, through constructing an **ideal type** of how someone faced with the metaphysical impact of Protestantism would make sense of their situation and act, provides a causal account of their attempts to establish for themselves that they were saved (to save **wealth** as a sign of salvation) and an explanation of the empirical correlation with the development of **capitalism** (the accumulation of capital) in Protestant countries.

Later debates in the social sciences about causality have been rendered under the rubric of the agency and structure debate, that is the relationship between intentional action and **social structures**. In the works of Roy Bhaskar, *A Realist Theory of Science* (1975), Rom Harré and E. Madden, *Causal Powers* (1975), and **Anthony Giddens**, *The Constitution of Society* (1984), the task is to examine how enduring social structures, which predate the individual, and in which s/he has no choice but to participate, can at the same time be transformed in social practices.

While these debates have had echoes in American sociology, particularly in the European-originated works of **Alfred Schutz** and his development of phenomenological sociology, in general it has been dominated by a simple integration of Durkheimian ontology (social facts exist and have the force to make individuals act in specific ways) with a naive positivistic **empiricism** (that these social facts are demonstrated by probabilistic **statistics** and evidenced in correlations). KEVIN WHITE

cause

– see **causality**.

census

The process of collecting demographic, social, and economic **data** from all members of a population, censuses are distinct from **surveys**, which are focused on data from a subset, or sample, of a population. Censuses have a long history, and were first used in ancient Rome. In their modern form, censuses are used to justify the allocation of resources by the **state**. Thus, the ways in which censuses categorize and count ethnic and other minority groups, including transient and indigent populations, has become a matter of some concern and debate – as these may have a direct bearing on the resources available to members of these groups. This controversy has been the catalyst for the introduction of **sampling** methods in order to achieve a more accurate census of the true numbers of such systematically undercounted groups.

Samples of anonymized records (SARs) are samples of de-identified individual-level data extracted from censuses. SARs are distinct from commonly available census outputs in that they have not been aggregated into pre-determined tables. In fact, SARs more closely resemble survey data, in that they contain a separate record for each individual. The very large sample sizes of SARs distinguish them from most surveys, as SARs allow for the analysis of data by sub-groups and by regional areas.

As microdata sets, SARs permit multivariate statistical analysis at the individual level. SARs may be used in the investigation of a broad range of social issues including the composition of households, ethnicity, **health**, **education**, and employment. MARK RAPLEY AND SUSAN HANSEN

charisma

For **Max Weber** charisma is first a matter of **authority** and its **legitimacy**. A charismatic leader is not, as he explains in *Economy and Society* (1921 [trans. 1968]), merely forceful and strong but one whose authority is based on supporters' "devotion to the exceptional sanctity, heroism or exemplary character of an individual person, and on the normative patterns or order revealed or ordained by him." This Weber contrasts with rational and also traditional grounds of authority, in which obedience is respectively owed to the impersonal order and to the person occupying a traditionally sanctioned position. Charismatic authority, then, unlike rational and traditional authority, is particularly vulnerable to attack: a challenge to the incumbent of charismatic authority necessarily brings the legitimacy of the authority of the social order into doubt. This situation does not arise with either rational or traditional authority.

An additional element of charismatic authority contributes further to its instability. What is decisive for the validity of charisma, according to Weber, is recognition from those subject to it that the charismatic individual possesses exceptional **powers** or qualities. Such extraordinary powers can be revealed to followers or disciples only by their demonstrable exercise. Thus, in the necessarily emotional relationship between authority incumbent and followers, it is necessary that the leader constantly prove that his divine, magical, or heroic powers have not deserted him. The charismatic leader is thus compelled constantly to reaffirm the legitimacy of his authority in order that he may continue to hold it. One consequence of this noted by Weber is the incompatibility of charismatic authority and continuous economic activity devoted to regular **income** and economizing. Plunder and extortion, Weber says, are typical means of provision under charismatic rule.

Because it is based on the personal qualities of the individual incumbent, charismatic authority is contrary to routine and offers no solutions to the problem of succession or the movement from one leader to another. Within charismatic communities that persist there is therefore a tendency towards routinization of charisma. Weber treats routinization in terms of the development of both succession mechanisms and means to appropriate or select charismatic staff. Mechanisms of succession include: (1) search for a new leader possessing certain qualities; (2) revelation by oracle or priestly technique; (3) *designation* by prior charismatic leader or by his administrative staff; (4) hereditary; and (5) ritual transmission of charisma from one person to another. The transformation of the charismatic mission into an office, by routinizing charismatic staff, is also achieved through a number of possibilities associated with different bases of selection and remuneration.

Elements of charismatic authority may be found with other forms of rule. Weber mentions plebiscitary presidential regimes and cabinet government as two instances in which charisma and legal rational authority may coexist.

Edward Shils in *The Constitution of Society* (1982) developed a non-Weberian account of charisma. Charismatic properties of central **institutions** satisfy a need for order, and roles that are associated with such institutions enjoy derivative charisma, leading to relations of deference, even in egalitarian societies.   JACK BARBALET

Chicago School of Sociology

The Chicago School of Sociology was a body of social research associated with a group of professors and their students affiliated with the Sociology Department of the University of Chicago. The School emerged around 1915, and lasted until about 1935. Its most prominent members included **Robert Park** and **W. I. Thomas**, alongside such figures as **Ernest Burgess** and Ellsworth Faris. In the later period of the School, the sociologists **Herbert Blumer** and **Louis Wirth** continued its research tradition. The School was the first group of sociologists to practice a systematic research agenda in the United States. It influenced the development of the **symbolic interactionist** tradition, and the emphasis on **social psychology**, **qualitative research**, **participant observation**, and **ethnography** associated with this theoretical orientation.

The Chicago School focused on a wide variety of social processes, such as social organization and disorganization, urban sociology, **social change**, immigration, **deviance**, **race relations**, and **social movements**. It often analyzed these processes in the context of the city of Chicago, developing a lasting influence in urban sociology through such concepts as ecology and succession. Its researchers helped establish the importance of empirical investigation into social issues through analyzing documents and conducting interviews, as well as engaging in first-hand observation of various groups. Two of its most important studies include *The City* (1925), a selection of essays by Park, Burgess, and R. D. McKenzie, and *The Polish Peasant in Europe and America* (1918–20), a five-volume work by Thomas and Florian Znaniecki. Other works include Nel Anderson's *The Hobo* (1923), Wirth's *The Ghetto* (1928), Harvey Zorbaugh's *The Gold Coast and the Slum* (1929), E. Franklin Frazier's *The Negro Family in Chicago* (1931), and Paul Cressy's *The Taxi-Dance Hall* (1932). Park and Burgess also wrote an introductory text, *Introduction to the Science of Sociology* (1921), which helped popularize the School's approach.

The Chicago School linked thought and action, positing that ideas and attitudes are tied to the social and historical conditions in which they arise and are situated. The School's focus on social issues such as **crime** and deviance was tied to the reformist impulse of many of its researchers, who were concerned with solving **social problems** in the pre-World War I Progressive era in the United States. Its reformist orientation was strengthened by the ties to journalism of one of its members, Robert Park. Yet the Chicago School advocated an objective and scientific study of society, and its members attempted to implement a disinterested sociology.

The Chicago School supported the use of the ethnographic methods of anthropologists, arguing that the same methods could be employed to investigate social processes within the United States as were used to study non-western cultures. But the School was much more diverse than this characterization. Its researchers did assume that individuals could not be studied in isolation from one another and were influenced by the **groups** that encompassed them, and that **social change** developed through the **interaction** of individuals and groups with one another. Yet many of the School's scholars, such as **William Ogburn**, embraced versions of **quantitative analysis**, such as **survey** research. Researchers did not engage in mindless **empiricism**, however. They always approached their data with a theoretical interest in mind.

The Chicago School emphasized that the social and historical context in which one lived dramatically influenced social processes. But individuals were not passive products of their environment. **Social structure** and individual agency could not be separated from one another. People could change the social structures in which they lived, but these economic, social, and cultural conditions influenced their attitudes and actions. Indeed, the actions of individuals often had unintended consequences. Social structure and geographic location accounted for much of social behavior. Researchers often wrote of natural, relatively predictable processes of history and geography, shaped by the similar social location and **traditions** that groups shared, and the arrangement of commercial establishments and residential housing in a particular area. Such concerns led to the study of social organization and disorganization, the latter considered to be the main cause of social problems.

Much of their work focused on Chicago. In Park, Burgess, and McKenzie's *The City*, Park encouraged his students to engage the denizens of the city, "become acquainted with people," to "nose around" those groups that they were interested in studying. For Park, one could only be impartial by understanding the point of view, the subjective experience, of other people. Thus, the social life of the **city** could be understood through intense **fieldwork** in particular **neighborhoods**. The study of urban life should investigate a city's **culture**, occupational structure, and physical organization. The social profile of the city was conditioned by structural factors such as its economic and geographical conditions, including its location on transportation and trade routes. The sociological imagination must combine these two dimensions, the structural and the subjective, into a coherent study.

For Park, integrated city neighborhoods progressively broke down as secondary, impersonal relationships increasingly based on the **market** and law (see **law and society**) replaced the primary relationships of **family** and ethnicity. Cities created more contacts for individuals, and offered them an array of different **lifestyles**, but these contacts tended to be transitory. The city also allowed deviant individuals, from the genius to the criminal, to flourish in its heterogeneous environment.

Burgess took a somewhat different approach to the study of urban life. He too saw cities as characterized by heterogeneous, diverse **occupations**, employing a large percentage of young and middle-aged individuals, and occupied by a high percentage of foreign-born immigrants. Burgess focused on processes of growth and expansion in the cities, viewing them as natural adaptations to new types of social organization. He analyzed urban expansion through his theory of concentric zones. An inner industrial zone was surrounded by zones consisting of the ghetto, working-men's homes, and at the outmost region more suburban residential areas. Each inner zone expands as it invades an outer zone, a process Burgess labeled succession. This expansion involves simultaneous processes of decentralization and concentration of people and industries. Burgess also utilized the notion of **urban ecology** to study the social life of cities. Drawn from biology, the concept of ecology emphasizes the interdependence of urban life, and how an individual relates to his or her environment. Processes of competition and accommodation influence the development of the urban milieu, as a **community** expands or declines as economic development waxes or wanes. The differentiation and segmentation of urban populations accompany such social changes.

Park and Burgess contended that the American city could not be understood apart from immigration. The major work on immigration produced by this School, and the study that contributed most prominently to its research reputation, was Thomas and Znaniecki's *The Polish Peasant in Europe and America*. *The Polish Peasant* examined Polish immigrant adaptation to the United States, focusing on their experiences in Chicago. Thomas and Znaniecki's study encompassed much more than an examination of Polish immigrants. They explored immigration within the context of **modernization**, utilizing systematic qualitative methods (see **qualitative research**). Their research emphasized the social psychological needs of the **peasant** immigrant, how his attitudes and **values** interacted with those of the larger society, and the ways in which the ethnic community helped shape the immigrant experience. They placed immigrant experiences with social change at the center of their analysis.

Thomas and Znaniecki focused on the formation of the Polish ethnic community rather than on individual **assimilation**. They viewed the Polish community as tightly integrated and insular, its economic and social life characterized more by shared, reciprocal values than the profit motive. The ethnic community was a novel American creation, and it was a positive development which encouraged adaptation to American society. The ethnic community emerged in a particular geographical environment, its development influenced by processes of **segregation** and integration within the city. The immigrant community inherited from Europe could not survive intact in its new American context, however. Over time, the ethnic community began slowly to disintegrate, and its resulting social disorganization diminished the influence of shared social rules on individuals. More contacts with the world outside of the community and increases in individual decisionmaking and freedom overshadowed the importance of family and traditional ethnic ties in shaping individual **identity**.

There were clear limitations on the Polish peasant studies as an exemplar for the study of immigrant communities. The authors concentrated on the urban experience of immigrants, and did not examine how immigrants fared outside of cities. They also downplayed the roles of **religion** and **discrimination** in the formation of the ethnic community. Workplace issues and questions of political **power** also did not occupy a central place in the study.

The Polish Peasant helped popularize the assimilation thesis that, over time, immigrant ethnic groups became incorporated into the Anglo mainstream. Yet the study demonstrated the problems associated with assimilation, including the difficulties that an ethnic community faces in adapting to American mores, the complex process of the loss of immigrant ethnic **solidarity** and its reconstitution in the American context, and the continued importance of the family and other primary groups as ethnic groups assimilated into the American mainstream. In criticizing any simple assimilationist model, *The Polish Peasant* posited that distinctive ethnic communities contribute to the **pluralism** of the United States.

The Polish Peasant was influential in the subsequent history of the sociology of immigration. Early American research on immigration had an assimilationist bias, interpreting *The Polish Peasant* as an argument for assimilation to an Anglo community. This was a misinterpretation, as Thomas and Znaniecki's study emphasized the reshaping of the mainstream as new ethnic communities became part of American society. Moreover, Thomas and Znaniecki studied the perceptions of the United States developed by the immigrant, stressing an active view of the immigrant experience. They also emphasized that both material and cultural factors were important in the formation and maintenance of ethnic communities.

Contemporary pluralist studies which celebrate ethnic communities have returned to Thomas and Znaniecki's emphasis on immigrant agency, but with a greater awareness of the power of, and constraints on, immigrant communities. The most recent and influential book on US immigration, *Remaking the American Mainstream: Assimilation and Contemporary Immigration* (2003), by Richard Alba and Victor Nee, returns to *The Polish Peasant*'s emphasis on the active immigrant who seeks a better life in the United States. Alba and Nee see assimilation resulting from the interaction of different ethnic groups, which transforms and blurs any simple notion of a mainstream culture. They also argue that geographic context is central to processes of immigration and assimilation, which are also constrained by the power of existing **institutions**.

By the 1930s, the influence of the Chicago School was in decline, replaced by the new fascination with statistical methods associated with **Paul Lazarsfeld** of Columbia University, who engaged in opinion polling and market research. His concern with predicting consumer and **voting** behavior left little room for theory and the vagaries of history and social interaction. Yet after World War II a "second Chicago School" emerged, as researchers such as **Howard Becker** and **Erving Goffman** continued the qualitative and theoretical orientation of the School, examining issues from deviance to the rituals of **everyday life** from complex ethnographic angles.

The Chicago School remains an important influence on sociology. Contemporary sociologists and studies influenced by this tradition include **Herbert Gans**, *The Urban Villagers* (1962), Gary Alan Fine, *Gifted Tongues: High School Debate and Adolescent Culture* (2001), and *Kitchens: The Culture of Restaurant Work* (1996), and more theoretical works by authors such as Andrew Abbott, in his *Time Matters: On Theory and Method* (2001), among many others. Though its researchers are known primarily as ethnographically inclined, its proponents advocated a variety of research methods, depending on the particular problem under study. The School also offers a distinctive interactionist theoretical alternative to the quantitative research position that views people as isolated individuals whose ideas and attitudes can be captured through statistical instruments such as surveys. For the Chicago School, social interaction shapes group and individual identity. Researchers must immerse themselves in the group that they are studying in order to grasp how perceptions of **self** and society arise within these complex social relations, and in turn are impacted by social structure.   KENNETH H. TUCKER

Chicano studies

These studies had their origins in the student activism, identity politics, and intellectual foment of the civil rights movement of the 1960s. Like the other nationalist movements of the era, it emerged as a field of scholarly inquiry that placed special emphasis on linking academic research with the **politics** of social **justice**. It made explicit that link between activism and scholarship through terms like action research and consciously sought to improve the educational, social, and political status of the Mexican-origin population in the United States.

The founding moment of Chicano studies occurred in spring 1969 when a group of Chicano/Chicana activists and educators met at the University of California, Santa Barbara, to draft *El Plan de Santa Barbara*. This foundation document called for the creation of Chicano studies departments devoted to a curriculum and scholarship that addressed the unique historical experiences and contemporary condition of people of Mexican descent. It recognized the central role of knowledge in the reproduction of social **inequality** within our communities but also in producing meaningful strategies of **social change** and community empowerment.

The initial focus of the emerging field was on recovering the historical experience of the Chicano population in the southwestern United States and contesting previous interpretations of that history. Special emphasis was placed on the legacy of community organizing and labor activism in various industries in which the Mexican American population had toiled under onerous working conditions. Rodolfo Acuna's *Occupied American: The Chicano's Struggle Toward Liberation* (1972) and Mario Barerra's *Race and Class in the Southwest: A Theory of Racial Inequality* (1979) were emblematic of this early historical recovery project. Both works drew upon various theoretical perspectives – **Marxism**, **political economy**, internal **colonialism**, and labor market segmentation – to advance a revisionist Chicano history in the American southwest. Professional associations such as the National Association for Chicano and Chicana Studies, founded in 1972, further advanced the explicit connection between scholarship and activism and the importance of ideological struggle in the academy.

From the very beginning, Chicana activists and scholars ensured that the experience of women of Mexican descent was central to both the scholarship and activism in Chicano studies. The male-centered, masculinist, and "heteronormative" underpinnings of early works in the field were rapidly accompanied by a more complex rendering of those experiences and the multiplicity of social **identities** within the Chicano population. Cherrie Moraga's *Loving in the War Years* (1983) and Gloria Anzaldua's *Borderlands / La Frontera: The New Mestiza* (1987) were emblematic of this de-centering of the Chicano male subject and the move towards a more complex and nuanced construction of the Chicana subject. While revisionist histories continued in importance, works such as these were more interdisciplinary and literary in approach and drew upon **feminism**, **postmodernism**, **poststructuralism**, and **cultural studies** in reframing the Chicana subject and other marginalized identities. They challenged not only the masculinist production of knowledge in the field, but also the paradigms, methodologies, and pedagogy inherited from traditional academic disciplines and area studies.

More recently, issues pertaining to the social construction of **gender**, **sexuality**, gay/lesbian subjectivities through literature and **popular culture**, as well as **globalization**, transnationalization, and migration processes, have reached center stage in Chicano studies. The field is increasingly constructing a more complex and situated rendering of the Chicano/Chicana subject and, in the process, exploring the multiplicity of identities in all their myriad and hybrid forms.

At the present time, there are over 35 million Latinos in the United States (65 percent of whom are Chicano or of Mexican descent). Latinos have now surpassed African Americans as the largest minority group in the United States and play an increasing and undeniably important role. For example, one-third of California's population is of Mexican descent and nearly one-half of the school-age children in the state are from this background. For these demographic reasons alone, Chicano studies will increasingly become an important area of academic inquiry for anyone interested in race relations and the diversity of modern life in the United States. As in its inception, political activism and the ongoing struggle for social justice will continue to play a central role in the evolution of Chicano studies in the future.   TOMAS ALMAGUER

childhood/children

Sociology as a discipline did not display much interest in children until the end of the twentieth century (A. James and A. Prout, *Constructing and Reconstructing Childhood*, 1990). Childhood was perceived as being mainly in the domain of psychology, **education**, or perhaps history, and children themselves rarely appeared as sociological actors who could influence events or who might matter particularly. Traditionally, the sociological interest in children was embedded in the notion of **socialization**. Thus, one of the main functions of the **family** was seen to be the socialization of children into the next **generation** of workers, or parents, or even criminals. The experience of being a child was not an issue of sociological enquiry, although the question of what children might become when they reached adolescence or adulthood was important. Thus children were important in terms of their future as adults, not in terms of what they might "be" or "do" as children.

It is perhaps accurate to suggest that, while sociology had little interest in children per se, it did have more of an interest in childhood because, like parenthood, or the family, or the education system, childhood was conceptualized as a social **institution** rather than a naturally occurring phenomenon. The work of the social historian Philippe Ariès in his *Centuries of Childhood* (1962) was highly significant in challenging any naturalistic assumptions about childhood by showing how the institution changed at different moments in history, and by revealing how our ideas of what a child might be (including what a child could and should do) have changed dramatically according to time and place. Other historical studies which have compared nineteenth-century childhood with contemporary childhood, or working-class childhood with middle-class childhood, have managed to show that there can be a huge variation in cultural expectations of children (for example Eric Hopkins, *Childhood Transformed*, 1994). Even defining what a child is, or when childhood starts and finishes, is open to contestation. The boundaries between the infant, the toddler, the child, the adolescent, the teenager, and the young adult blur as cultural **norms** and material circumstances change. For example, it was traditionally assumed that a child became an adult on reaching puberty (for girls in nineteenth-century England this might have been as late as sixteen or eighteen). However, modern **lifestyles** and diets (in the West at least) have affected physical rates of growth so that puberty comes earlier (for example ten or eleven years for girls). This means that traditional indicators of maturity become less relevant and it is less sensible to rely on the body to act as the visible marker of transition from childhood to adulthood.

Ariès pointed to the lack of differentiation between "the adult" and "the child" under the *ancien régime*, and the very strict differentiation between the generations that grew up in the Victorian era – especially for middle-class children. For Ariès childhood is a modern invention. This challenge to the idea of childhood as a natural state has given rise to sociological debates about whether contemporary **cultures** are now molding childhood in problematic ways. For example, some recent work on childhood has started to document the end of childhood, and to argue that modern society is truncating childhood. The end-of-childhood thesis points to such factors as the premature sexualization of children, the growth of children's fashions and styles of dress which are similar to adult styles, the rise of the child as a consumer in capitalist societies, and of course the impact on children of the media, which are seen to introduce them to adult realities such as **violence** long before it is necessary. Ranged against the end-of-childhood thesis is an alternative perspective which points to the way in which developed **welfare states** now almost refuse to let children become adults. This is achieved through policies which enforce prolonged economic dependence on parents, extend full-time **education** to eighteen or even twenty-one years, and apply restrictions on access to such things as paid employment, birth control, abortion, or alcohol. These policies which keep young adults in a state of dependency are, it is argued, exacerbated by an over-protectiveness in parents which means that children are escorted by an adult wherever they go (for example school, friends' houses, playgrounds, and so on). Modern children, it is argued, are kept in a state of emotional and economic dependency for longer than previous generations.

These analyses of childhood are, of course, derived mainly from wealthy industrialized societies. They do not reflect the material realities, nor social meanings, of childhood as it may be experienced in countries such as Thailand, China, or Japan, or in African countries. Moreover, they may not even reflect all childhoods found in western societies because of the tendency to overlook the different forms that childhood might take in minority ethnic or religious communities, or among refugees, or among traveler families. For this reason, it has become increasingly important to think in terms of the diversity of childhoods which may co-exist locally and globally.

Alongside this expansion in sociological understandings of childhood(s) (for example Chris Jencks, *Childhood*, 1996) we have witnessed the growth of what is increasingly referred to as the "standpoint" of children (Berry Mayall, *Towards a Sociology for Childhood*, 2002). There is an interest in the experience of being a child and a parallel concern to try to appreciate social reality from the point of view of children themselves. This has given rise to many empirical projects which allow children to express their own understandings of the social world – rather than relying on teachers or parents to convey what children might think or feel. This shift towards including the standpoint of children has started to produce a conceptual change in the discipline, comparable to the way in which the introduction of the standpoint of women transformed sociology in the 1980s. As a discipline, sociology is starting to appreciate how "adultist" it has been and, just as it has had to come to terms with other neglected aspects of power relations, such as **racism**, **sexism**, **ageism**, and heteronormativity, so it has started to analyze more systematically power that is exercised between the generations.   CAROL SMART

Chodorow, Nancy (1944–)

Obtaining her BA from Radcliffe College and then, in 1975, her PhD from Brandeis University, Nancy Chodorow is currently Professor of Sociology at the University of California, Berkeley.

Chodorow's *The Reproduction of Mothering* (1978), was a feminist rethinking of **Sigmund Freud**'s version of childhood development. Because of his patriarchal environment, Freud did not understand how females develop a **gender** identity. Chodorow reformulates Freud's theory of female **socialization**. She argues that the infant's relationship to the mother, rather than the father, is the crucial bond in an infant's life. Gender identity is rooted in the infant's relationship to the mother because in most families mothers have responsibility for child rearing. Girls have a more continuous relationship with their mother than do boys. Accordingly, they develop a more complex gender identity in which nurturing, caring, and sensitivity are more important than the rigid ego boundaries and competition important to males. Chodorow contends that most societies value these male traits more than female values, so

that women's distinctive psychology and **culture** are undervalued.

Chodorow's work has influenced the work of many feminist thinkers, from Lillian Rubin's *Intimate Strangers* (1983) to Carol Gilligan's *In a Different Voice* (1982). Chodorow has been criticized for generalizing the experience of middle-class white women to all women, and neglecting cultural factors in psychological development. In her most recent work, *Femininities, Masculinities, Sexualities* (1994) and *The Power of Feelings* (1999), she addresses these criticisms, arguing that culture intersects with psychological development in complex ways, and that researchers should be wary of universal generalizations about gender differences.   KENNETH H. TUCKER, JR.

church–sect typology

This typology derives from **Max Weber** and was also popularized by the Christian theologian, **Ernst Troeltsch**, who was interested in elaborating different types of religious experiences. Weber's ideal-typical distinction in *Economy and Society* (1922 [trans. 1978]) between church and sect was part of his theoretical analysis of the **rationalization** of different forms of legitimation and **authority**. Weber identified four characteristics of a church: (1) a professional priesthood; (2) claims to universal domination, such as the elimination of ethnic or national barriers; (3) the rationalization of doctrine and rites; and (4) compulsory membership by birth, all of whom (whether believers or not) are subject to the church's **charisma** and discipline. Distinctive to a church is the separation of charisma from the person and its linkage instead to the institutional office (hierocracy), an office charisma (or grace) of which the church is the universal expression and trustee.

By contrast, a sect is a **voluntary association** or **community** of personally charismatic individuals whose charisma or qualification must be publicly demonstrated (for example through rebaptism for Baptists). In Weber's definition, a sect is a select group whose associational claims in essence preclude universality and require the free consent of its qualified members; it is not a group that splits off from another because of persecution or condemnation. Sects typically reject office charisma, adhering instead to a democratic model whereby authority lies in the congregation, who, through daily knowledge of the individuals in the community, are qualified to determine who among them is visibly deserving of sect membership. Although sect membership is voluntary, based on individual choice rather than ascribed by birth, admission and continued participation is contingent on the individual's consistent adherence in everyday life to the sect's religious beliefs and moral standards.

The sect community functions as a selection apparatus for separating the qualified from the unqualified, and for ensuring that qualified members interact with each other rather than with nonmembers. Although a negative consequence of this boundary maintenance is that it encourages withdrawal from, rather than engagement or accommodation with, the nonqualified, a positive function is the **solidarity** and **social integration** that sects provide their members, especially necessary for blunting the **anomie** and **alienation** found in highly mobile **modern** societies and among diasporic religions (such as Judaism). Moreover, Weber argued, the high moral and ascetic standards typically associated with sects means that their business interests thrive, because members and nonmembers alike **trust** their economic security to them. Although the small congregation is best suited to monitoring sect members' behavior, Weber emphasized that a sect is not a small group; as he noted, the Baptists are one of the most typical sects and also one of the largest Protestant **denominations** in the world.

The contrasting universal and compulsory claims of a church against the selective and voluntary nature of a sect are particularly useful in understanding how different emphases on freedom and especially on freedom of conscience filter into public debates and assumptions about the relation between church and **state**. Whereas a church would typically argue for the universal applicability of its moral teachings to human society, a sect would typically argue in favor of a differentiation between religious and political matters.   MICHELE DILLON

Cicourel, Aaron Victor (1928–)

An American sociologist, who contributed seminal work to cognitive **sociology** and **ethnomethodology**, Cicourel received his BA and MA from the University of California, Los Angeles, in 1951 and 1953 respectively, and his PhD from Cornell University in 1957. Cicourel has taught all over the world but primarily within the University of California system, and is currently Research Professor of Cognitive Science, Pediatrics, and Sociology at the University of California, San Diego. Cicourel has made important contributions to the sociology of **education**, **law and**

society, medical sociology, **methodology**, and **sociological theory**. The bulk of his research has focused on the nature and function of tacit knowledge in social **interaction**, particularly in institutional settings. His fundamental interest has been to reveal the internalized interpretive schema that govern how social actors assign meaning and relevance to objects in their environments and how they discern the relevance of social **norms** and **social roles** in specific practical situations. More specifically, his research explored how tacit knowledge and tacit social competences underlie and inform language use, practical inference, and the application of standardized procedures in different social organizational contexts. Cicourel is particularly well known for a series of groundbreaking articles and books including "The Use of Official Statistics" (1963, *Social Problems*, with John Kitsuse), *Method and Measurement in Sociology* (1964), and *Cognitive Sociology* (1974), wherein he articulates a foundational critique of sociological research methodologies that fail to attend adequately to the tacit presuppositions and social competences that underlie their application in actual instances of empirical research.   DARIN WEINBERG

citizenship

The notion of citizenship can be traced back to the Greek *polis* that tied rights to membership of the **city**, excluding women and slaves. The modern version of citizenship is connected to the twin processes of nation building and industrialization following the American and French Revolutions. Freedom of contract and protection of **property** rights were important elements, and the growth of markets contributed to breaking down traditional hierarchies and to fostering **equality** and opportunity.

Citizenship has become a key concept at the center of policy debates within and across national borders. **T. H. Marshall**, in *Citizenship and Social Class* (1950), first developed a modern framework for the notion of citizenship based upon principles of freedom, equality, and solidarity. Since then citizenship has had a double focus: as a vision of equal **rights** and respect, and as a tool to analyze the social and political development of modern societies.

In social science, citizenship has become a key concept, and studies have focused both on social rights (in sociology) and on participation (in political science). Citizenship has different meanings, institutional designs, and patterns cross-nationally. The definition includes three different dimensions: (1) individual rights and obligations; (2) political participation including the right to vote; and (3) belonging to a nation-state. Modern citizenship has proved to be Janus-faced: it can express both exclusionary and inclusionary state practices and be a basis for discipline as well as resistance.

Today immigration, **globalization**, and Europeanization have challenged the meaning and practice of citizenship and new forms of claims-making by minority groups have widened the content of citizenship. This has raised questions about what a good citizen is, whether citizenship can be transferred from the nation-state to the transnational level, and whether it is possible to combine citizenship rights tied to the nation-state to global citizenship and human rights?

In Marshall's seminal work, citizenship was defined as "a status bestowed on those who are full members of a community." All citizens should have the same rights and duties. Marshall's work was based on a vision of equal rights for the working class in capitalist society inspired by the evolution of civil, political, and social rights in Britain from the eighteenth to the twentieth century.

Citizenship is part of the two major political traditions of civic republicanism and **liberalism**. Liberalism has been preoccupied with the defense of the freedom of individuals and civil rights vis-à-vis the state, and has given priority to the private virtues of individuals over public virtues. This understanding has been criticized, because it tends to underestimate the need for an active state to defend political liberty and for a political community that can defend individual freedom.

Civic republicanism has been preoccupied with the creation of a just society, and it has given priority to the creation of solidarity between citizens tied together in a political community. This understanding has been criticized because it underestimates civil rights and tends to subsume individuals under the needs of the political community. **Communitarianism** has a strong emphasis on belonging to the political community and can be understood either as a form of civic republicanism or as a separate tradition.

Marshall's framework has become a key reference for analysis of contemporary citizenship from a cross-national context and has also been taken up by marginalized social groups. It has been criticized for its Anglo- and Eurocentric bias as well as for its male bias, because it was premised upon the reality and vision of a British model and on the second-class citizenship of women and minorities.

A number of scholars have tried to rethink the framework of citizenship from a historical and comparative perspective. One example is Bryan Turner who, in his article "Outline of a Theory of Citizenship" in *Sociology* (1990), introduced a model that aims to identify political dynamics as well as variations in citizenship regimes: (1) an active/passive dimension that expresses how citizenship rights became institutionalized in modern **democracies** "from above" by the involvement of the monarchy or "from below" through revolutionary movements; (2) a public/private dimension that expresses whether citizenship rights and **norm(s)** are associated with the public or private arena.

The first differentiates between an active, participatory republican model and a model with institutionalization "from above." The second differentiates between a liberal model – with an emphasis on private, individual rights and a passive state – and a model that emphasizes public virtues and an active state.

Another example is Richard Bellamy, Dario Castiglione and Emilio Santoro's recent study, *Lineages of Citizenship: Rights, Belonging and Participation in Eleven Nation States* (2004). It gives an overview of the different legal traditions and historical contexts which have contributed to creating various liberalisms and republicanisms. This study differentiates between a "polity" dimension, which specifies the territorial and functional spheres – seeing the subjects either as passive or active – and a "regime" dimension, which refers to the political arrangements and styles of governance, the scope of intervention in private life.

The three main European traditions – the German, the French, and the British – correspond to some extent to the three legal citizenship traditions: the ethno-cultural definition of nationality (*jus sanguinis*), the romantic definition of nationality (*jus soli*) and the English common law. Since the 1990s, political developments in relation to immigration and asylum have moved the three closer together.

Marshall's focus was on the social and political inclusion of the working class in society, while post-Marshallian frameworks raise new issues and debates. **Gender** and marginalized social groups represent a major challenge for the universal framework of citizenship to respect diversity. This tension between equality and difference/diversity has inspired alternative frameworks, models, and designs.

Carole Pateman, in *The Sexual Contract* (1988), presented one of the first feminist approaches to citizenship. She analyzed the dilemma of Mary Wollstonecraft (1759–97) that illustrates that women in modern societies are caught between a strategy focusing on equality and inclusion of women as equal citizens that tends to deny their particularity "as women," and a strategy focusing on inclusion of their difference and particularity that tends to reproduce inequality. Ruth Lister, in *Citizenship: Feminist Perspectives* (1997), has noticed that the tension between the universalistic ethic of **justice** and the particularistic ethic of **care** that gives equal status to women and men in their diversity is a creative tension that can be overcome by a "differentiated universalism."

Another influential approach has introduced models that link the inclusion of women with marginal social groups. One example is Iris Young, who, in *Justice and the Political Difference* (1990), emphasizes inclusion and empowerment "from below." Another example is Anne Phillips, who, in *The Politics of Presence* (1995), emphasizes inclusion "from above" through a change of the institutional design.

In the development towards multicultural societies, **ethnicity** tends to become an independent factor explaining differentiation in citizenship rights. Ruud Koopman and Paul Statham, editors of *Challenging Immigration and Ethnic Relations Politics. Comparative European Perspectives* (2000), have introduced an institutional model with two dimensions that is used in comparisons between different ethnicity regimes. One is the formal and legal basis for citizenship – the vertical dimension – that places a regime between an ethno-cultural – *jus sanguinis* – and a territorial – *jus soli* – pole. The other is a political-cultural – horizontal – dimension, that places a regime between cultural monism (assimilation) and cultural pluralism.

Multiculturalism has also inspired normative models that stress minority rights. One example is in Will Kymlicka's *Multicultural Citizenship* (1995), which introduced the notion of multicultural citizenship based on group rights of minorities. He differentiates between rights of autonomy for national minorities, for example aboriginals; poly-ethnic rights such as financial support and legal protection of ethnic and religious groups; and rights of representation involving, for instance, guaranteed seats to ethnic and national minorities. The multicultural approach has initiated a debate about multiculturalism and gender equality, and, in a famous article, Susan Moller Okin (1999), in the volume edited by J. Cohen,

M. Howard and M. C. Neusbaum on *Is Multiculturalism Bad for Women?*, considers whether multiculturalism is incompatible with gender equality.

Sexual and ecological citizenship are examples of new meanings of citizenship. In *Citizenship: Feminist Perspectives*, Lister defines sexual citizenship as the claims for sexual autonomy by women, lesbians, and gays. The politics of citizenship thus promotes the citizenship status of sexual minorities and articulates new claims to "sexual rights," understood as "a set of rights to sexual expression and consumption." Ecological citizenship refers both to rights and responsibilities of citizens and to their relationship to nature and the wider **environment**, for example green activism.

Finally, globalization and European integration have inspired a notion of post-national citizenship. Marshall's framework was tied to the nation-state, but membership of a community allows for a broader discourse about local and global levels of citizenship. It is contested whether the vision of a global citizenship can become a reality and what kind of model of global citizen should indeed prevail. Skeptics argue that the state has the power to exclude outsiders through the policing of the boundaries of citizenship and residence. Optimists (such as Derek Heater in *World Citizenship*, 2003) have argued that globalization could become the basis for a multi-layered conceptualization of citizenships that would embrace the notion of global citizenship and the use of international human rights law.

One key issue in the current debate about **cosmopolitanism** is whether it is possible to transform the values of responsibility, individual rights, and democracy associated with nation-state citizenship to the international level? The globalization of rights and responsibilities can be seen as the essence of a globalization of citizenship. David Held and Anthony McGrew in *Globalization/Anti-globalization* (2002) differentiate between a strategy for cosmopolitan democracy aiming to develop a set of democratic institutions at the global level and a strategy for radical democracy aimed at forming a global **civil society** "from below," through which **social movements** and nongovernmental organizations can pursue their goals across national borders.

Global governance has created both problems and opportunities for democracy. **Markets** are hard to control, but political globalization may be used to expand democracy and human rights through the "human rights regime" – that is, an international framework for the protection of human rights. The international movement for women's rights as human rights is one example of an expansion of the scope of human rights to protect women.

It is contested whether the discourse of human rights is more appropriate once we live outside the confines of the nation-state? Bryan Turner in his "Outline of a Theory of Human Rights" in *Sociology* (1993) has argued that there is a need for a sociological theory of human rights as a supplement to the theory of citizenship. There is also a need for a global concept of citizenship that can contribute to focusing the responsibilities of the more affluent nation-states vis-à-vis those societies in the "developing world" that lack the resources to translate the development of human rights, as defined in the UN Covenant, into effective citizenship rights.

Another main issue is the dilemma connected to EU citizenship. The European Union has given citizens new rights, for example attached to paid work, but many scholars find that the European Union is an elitist project of nation-building where rights are the entitlements of subjects rather than citizens. On the one hand, the European Parliament has obtained more **power**, but on the other hand there is a democratic deficit, and political identities are still tied to local, regional, and national communities rather than to transnational politics. There have been developments in EU citizenship, and the anti-discrimination doctrine of the Amsterdam Treaty that incorporates **race**, **ethnicity**, and sexual preference in anti-discrimination law may suggest a more inclusive definition of rights and protection in the European Union.

Globalization and **migration** have made new claims from minorities for recognition and respect for diversity into a contested question for nation-states and the global community. At the analytical level, it is a challenge to develop institutions that may help to bridge the tension between equality and respect for diversity. At the normative level, it is a challenge to develop a vision for an inclusionary and multi-layered citizenship that is able to reconcile national belongings with a transnational notion of citizenship.   BIRTE SIIM

city

Given the dramatic increase in **urbanization** in the nineteenth century and the claim of much **social theory** and **sociology** to be an analysis of contemporary societies, it is surprising that the nature of contemporary cities was not deemed worthy of wider study. **F. Engels**'s 1844 study of the urban

working class in Manchester and elsewhere and his writings on the housing question must be set against **Karl Marx**'s neglect of cities in his analysis of **capitalism**, despite his statement that the division between town and country is one of great historical importance. Of the major sociologists around 1900, only **Max Weber** provided a historical analysis of the rise of towns and cities. Although many of the analyses of dimensions of contemporary society by Weber, **Émile Durkheim**, **Ferdinand Tönnies**, **Werner Sombart**, and others clearly presupposed a metropolitan **modernity**, this was seldom reflected upon in any detail. Only **Georg Simmel** made the modern metropolis one of the sites of modernity.

Beyond the confines of sociology, there was an increasing interest in the nature of the modern city and its populations. This concern took the form of early **ethnographies** such as the studies of London by Henry Mayhew (1812–87), and, later, the London **survey** by Charles Booth (1840–1916), and **W. E. B. Du Bois**'s study of **segregation** in Philadelphia. Both the state and local city authorities also increasingly devoted attention to their populations, as evidenced in population surveys and other statistical compilations and modes of governance. By the late nineteenth century in Germany, for example, which experienced one of the greatest urban expansions since its unification in 1870, the issue had arisen as to what constituted a city. The statistically expedient but by no means unproblematic solution was to declare an urban concentration with 100,000 or more inhabitants as a city, while a world city or metropolis had a population of 1 million (in 1900, only Berlin achieved this status).

In part influenced by Simmel's concern with modes of "sociation" in the city, the **Chicago School** of the early twentieth century had a major impact upon the study of the city. Yet its key figures **Robert Park, Ernest Burgess**, and **Louis Wirth** did not have a unified research program. Rather, their focus upon the city was diverse, ranging from studies of land use and social segregation, through the city as a social laboratory, programs of social reform, the ecology of the city, and urban ethnographies, to the urban way of life in modernity. It could be argued that the ethnographic tradition is what has remained significant for later study of the city.

In more recent decades, the turn to the **political economy** of cities has been in evidence, whether it be as sites of collective **consumption** and the local state (**Manuel Castells**, *The Urban Question*, 1977), the production and reproduction of urban capital (David Harvey, *Social Justice and the City*, 1973, and *Consciousness and the Urban Experience*, 1985), or, more recently, global cities and their **networks** (Saskia Sassen, *Global Cities*, 2001). The city has also been examined in a more differentiated manner, somewhat belatedly exploring gendered urban spaces. This has been accompanied since the mid-1980s by explorations of new dimensions of the modern/postmodern city (David Harvey, *The Postmodern Condition*, 1989; Michael J. Dear, *The Postmodern Urban Condition*, 2000; Nan Ellin, *Postmodern Urbanism*, 1999); the space of flows in the information economy and the emergence of the dual city and changes in the occupational structure (Manuel Castells, *The Informational City*, 1989); postcolonial cities in the world **economy**; the uneven development between and within cities, including gentrification and economies of **consumption**; transformations of the **public sphere** within cities; cybercities (Christine M. Boyer, *Cybercities*, 1996); and the disjunction between suburbanization and the metropolis.

Many of these transformations have been associated with the supercession of place by space as the focus of analysis. In part, this coincided with a focus upon urban space, prompted by Henri Lefebvre (1901–91) and others. Modifying Lefebvre's tripartite conceptualization in *The Production of Space* (1991) into the production of urban space, the representations of urban space and spatial practices also drew attention to the representations, images, and imaginaries of the city, as well as how the city is negotiated and contested in everyday practices (as in Michel de Certeau's analysis of taking a walk [*The Practice of Everyday Life*, 1984]).

The study of representations of the city is indicative of wider interest in images of the city that were already present, if often only implicitly in earlier characterizations of the city. The city has been variously viewed, for instance, as a moral and political order, as a social and medical problem, as an aesthetic object, as a work of art, as ensemble of communities, as absent **community**, as utopian site, as dystopia, as apocalyptic site. The significance of cultural dimensions of economic aspects of the city and the problems of reading the city have been given fresh impetus in the reception of writers such as **Walter Benjamin**, whose work seems at some distance from urban sociology. His treatments of the city as text, as narrative, as dream-world, as site of collective memory / collective forgetting, as

spectacle, as visual regime, recognize the city as not merely an agglomeration of silent built structures, as a concentration of producers and consumers, but also as imaginary, as aspiration. The often fragmentary experiences of the city, the shaping of everyday life in the city, everyday practices and the constitution of images of the city, contested spaces and boundaries, and modes of resistance are also consistent elements in understanding the contemporary city.   DAVID FRISBY

civic culture

Also referred to as political culture, this is the **culture**, beliefs, and **values** that direct a political system, but the study of such cultures also involves attending to the **institutions** that bring about political **socialization**. The term became influential in political sociology following the publication of Gabriel Almond and Sydney Verba's *The Civic Culture* (1963) in which they argued that the success of stable **democracy** was the result of civic institutions promoting democratic participation and creating opportunities for commitment and **trust**. The idea of political culture is thus closely connected with the idea of **civil society**. Almond and Verba undertook a comparative study of five countries – the United States, Italy, United Kingdom, Mexico, and West Germany. For various historical and structural reasons, the United States and the United Kingdom have vibrant civic cultures because these societies have many local and national channels whereby ordinary individuals can participate in political processes such as **voting**, registering opinions, selecting political leaders, and influencing political opinion. Their research has been criticized in methodological terms by Robert Dowse and John Hughes in *Political Sociology* (1986) on the grounds that **surveys** and **questionnaires** cannot easily tap into political cultures. Another criticism is that each **social class** will have its own political culture and therefore, where social class divisions are significant, it would be misleading to presuppose a unified civic culture. In other words, Almond and Verba did not take into account the issue of internal variations in political cultures. Another critical response, which was developed by Michael Mann in *Consciousness and Action among the western Working Class* (1973), has been to argue that liberal democracies survive because the working class have a "pragmatic acceptance" of their place in **capitalism** and because there is a general lack of any consistent commitment to values in the society.   BRYAN S. TURNER

civil religion

This is a term initially used by Jean-Jacques Rousseau (1712–78) and reintroduced to **sociology** by **Robert N. Bellah** in a highly influential essay published in the mid-1960s, "Civil Religion in America" (1967). Extending **Émile Durkheim**'s understanding that all things in society can be classified as either sacred or profane, Bellah developed the idea that, quite apart from institutionalized church **religion**, American society also has a publicly articulated and institutionalized civil or civic religion that anchors the **civic culture**. In the United States, Bellah argued, the "American way of life," the core founding **values** and ideals of the republic, are given a sacred meaning in and of themselves, and are given an added religious dimension by their intertwining with specifically religious motifs, most usually drawn from biblical archetypes. In pluralistic societies wherein religious **denominational** beliefs may have a sectarian function, the affirmation of the nation's civil religion serves **social integration** rather than fragmentation. A civil religion blends sacred cultural ideas and **symbols** with religious affirmations and is invoked to unify the **nation** and strengthen the shared communality of its people, to provide an **"imagined community"** out of diversity. A society's civil religion is most evident during highly ceremonial public **rituals** – presidential inaugurations, parliamentary convocations, and other symbolically rich public events (assemblies, protests) that take place at the country's sacred (civic) places. The complexity of a civil religion lies in the tension between appealing to sufficiently broad (nonsectarian) religious symbols and to the society's high ideals (for example **equality**), while simultaneously not being appropriated in a sectarian manner to legitimate public policies that in practice may threaten rather than enrich social **solidarity**.   MICHELE DILLON

civil rights

– see **rights**.

civil rights movement

– see **social movements**.

civil society

An expression that became influential in eighteenth-century theories about the individual, **social contract**, and the **state**, this denotes an area of social consensus based on agreements about **norms** and **values**. Whereas the state requires some level of force, civil society implies a degree of freedom. The concept was used by Adam

Ferguson (1723–1816) in his *An Essay on the History of Civil Society* (1767) to make a contrast between the **civilization** of western Europe and the despotism of the East. The connection between "civil society" and "civility" and "civilization" was made clear in **Georg Wilhelm Friedrich Hegel**'s *The Philosophy of Right* (1821 [trans. 1942]), where the German term is *bürgerliche Gesellschaft*. He recognized civil society as a specific area of ethical life, which exists or mediates between the **family** and the state. The word family was originally associated with *oikos* or "household," and the word **economy** originally referred to the running of a household. In short, Hegel saw civil society as existing between the state (a coercive **institution**) and the economy (an institution based on self-interest). The freedom of the individual and the enjoyment of **rights** were made possible by the historical evolution of civil society as a manifestation of bourgeois civilization.

The adjective *bürgerlich* means "civil, civic" and also "middle-class, bourgeois." Civil society is thus an area of social life that contrasts the world of the bourgeoisie from those of the nobility and clergy. These notions are also closely connected with the idea of **citizenship**.

Gesellschaft or "society" derives from *Geselle* or "companion." Sociology is the scientific study of society or *Gesellschaftwissenschaft*. It became commonplace in sociology to distinguish between affective social ties and more abstract social relations. Thus **Ferdinand Tönnies** made an important distinction between organic **communities** (*Gemeinschaft*) and mechanical association (*Gesellschaft*) in his *Community and Association* (1887 [trans. 1957]).

The concept of civil society was shared by both **liberalism** and **socialism**, albeit with different significance. For John Locke (1632–1704) in the *Two Treatises of Government* (1690) the social contract was necessary to protect the individual and property rights, and it was this contract that created civil society in contrast to the "state of nature." Liberal civil society requires limited government, the separation of **powers**, the rule of law, and rule by representative government. These political institutions are important for securing civil society, but Locke argued that a primary responsibility of government was the protection of **property**. Locke has been attacked by, for example, C. B. Macpherson, *The Political Theory of Possessive Individualism* (1962), for providing a crass defence of **capitalism**. In contrast, John Dunn, *Western Political Theory in the Face of the Future* (1979: 39), argues that, in the language of his day, Locke treated "property" and "right" synonymously, and hence Macpherson's criticism represents a translation error.

Karl Marx was critical of Hegel's understanding of civil society and, in his *Economic and Philosophical Manuscripts* (1844 [trans. 1964]), he argued that bourgeois society was characterized by economic self-interest and the struggle between **social classes**. Civil society was not an arena of civilized co-operation, but the epitome of bourgeois **culture** which merely masked the objective struggle between irreconcilable classes.

The idea of civil society was revived in the twentieth century by the work of the Italian Marxist revolutionary **Antonio Gramsci**, who argued that the state was a mixture of force plus consent, or **hegemony** with coercion. While political society organizes force, civil society is that set of social institutions that provides consent. The **leadership** of the working class by **intellectuals** requires the transformation of civil society by political **education** if the dominant hegemony is to be challenged. Gramsci recognized that, because the Roman Catholic Church was influential in providing moral leadership in Italy, it was necessary to provide a moral alternative at the local level. This tradition of analysis of civil society has been continued, for example, by Norberto Bobbio, *Democracy and Dictatorship* (1980 [trans. 1989]).

The notion of "civil society" continues to be important in contemporary sociology because the vitality of civic institutions is seen to be essential for sustaining **democracy**. Civil society is also the **public sphere** within which opinions are formed, developed, and exchanged. This arena of debate is important in the minimal sense that it permits lively criticism of government policies and ministers. One function of bourgeois society was that it created social spaces in which conversation, debate, and criticism could take place. The idea that the transformation of **mass media and communications** by the monopolistic ownership of newspapers, radio, TV, and film has seriously curtailed the possibility of critical dialog and argument was put forward by **Jürgen Habermas** in his *The Structural Transformation of the Public Sphere* (1962 [trans. 1989]).

Habermas's pessimistic view of modern society has in turn been challenged by sociologists, partly influenced by the idea of network society in **Manuel Castells**, who claim that modern electronic **technology** – such as cell phones and computers – has created new opportunities for debate and dialogue. These technologies make possible a new global civil society which cannot be easily controlled by the state, and they allow rapid, cheap means of political discussion. If the coffee house was the principal site of Habermas's traditional bourgeois public sphere, where newspapers could be read and debated over coffee, the cyber café is the location of the new forms of information exchange.   BRYAN S. TURNER

civilization

A concept referring to an advanced stage or condition of organized social life and social development, often used in distinction to **primitive societies**, the most important contribution to an understanding of civilization comes from **Norbert Elias**. In *The Civilizing Process* (1939 [trans. 2000]), Elias examines the sociogenesis and the social function of the concept. He argues that the term was formed in the second half of the eighteenth century, replacing the concepts of *politesse* or *civilité* which, before its arrival, had formed the same function: to express the self-image and specific kind of behavior of the European upper class, in relation to others whom its members considered simpler or more primitive. One of its earliest usages is found in the work of the Comte de Mirabeau, Honoré-Gasriel Riqueti (1749–91), who reformulated the concept of *Homme civilisé* while simultaneously drawing on the progressivism and reformism prevalent in the Parisian circles of court society. Like the Physiocrats, he believed that social events followed laws, and that a knowledge and understanding of these laws could be used as a progressive force by kings in their rule. Civilization stood between barbarism and a false "decadent" civilization engendered by a superabundance of money.

Mirabeau's approach was extended by Enlightenment thinkers, such as Anne-Robert Jacques Turgot, Baron de l'Aulne (1727–81), and P. H. T., Baron d'Holbach (1723–89), who also called for the improvement of **institutions**, **education**, and law, equally within a reformist framework. Though society had reached a stage on the road to civilization, it remained partial and incomplete since the masses remained uncivilized. This essentially middle-class idea for reform and the liberation of the broader sections of the population from all that was irrational in existing conditions, including class restrictions on the bourgeoisie, became fused with the aristocratic belief, which was pervasive in court society, that all others outside this sphere were uncivilized or barbaric with reference to morals, manners, and **lifestyle**.

Though it did not play a considerable role in the French Revolution, following the revolution it was used to justify French national expansion and colonization. Whole nations henceforth began to consider the process of civilization as completed within their own societies – while forgetting the social conditions of its emergence – and came to see themselves as superior standard-bearers of an expanding civilization and architects of colonial conquest. Elias argues that civilization came to express the self-consciousness of the West: "It sums up everything in which western society of the last two or three centuries believes itself superior to earlier societies or 'more primitive' contemporary ones" (2000: 5). This pride could be related to its level of **technology**, its type of manners, its development of scientific knowledge, or to its religious ideas and customs.

However, the term did not mean the same thing to different nations. The French and English use of the concept could be contrasted with the German term, *Zivilisation*, which, although referring to something useful, only had a secondary value. It was the concept of *Kultur* which expressed the self-image of the Germans in their own achievements. While the French and English use of civilization was expansionary, outward-looking, and emphasized what was common to all human beings, the German concept of *Kultur* accentuated national differences and group **identity**, and was inward-looking. The conceptual antithesis between **culture** and civilization reflected the two different worldviews and the marked social division between a relatively powerless middle-class German intelligentsia, which emphasized genuineness, **personality**, sincerity, and intellectual development, on the one hand, and a French-speaking, politically powerful, German court nobility, which championed outward appearance and manners on the other. This conceptual and social contraposition in turn reflected the political fragmentation of Germany as compared with the unified "good society" found in France, in which the rising middle classes, as already noted, readily adopted aristocratic traditions and behavioral models, and only showed a moderate reformist opposition to aristocratic world-views. For Elias, the implications of this were crucial in the different paths of development of England, France, and Germany and their subsequent use of the term.

The contrast between civilization and culture also formed a crucial conceptual opposition in a number of books which influenced Elias's work: Thomas Mann's *Reflections on a Life* (1924), which, as part of his revolutionary conservative world-view, affirmed inward culture against moralistic civilization; **Sigmund Freud**'s *Civilization and Its Discontents* (1930), which examined the conflict between sexual desires and social mores as the basis for aggression and **violence** in modern civilization; and Oswald Spengler's *Decline of the West* (1918 [trans. 1926 and 1928]), which employed biological metaphors to argue that cultures pass through cycles in which they rise, mature, and decline. For Spengler, civilization was the inevitable destiny of culture, and an expression of its decline: "Civilizations are the most external and artificial states of which a species of developed humanity is capable. They are the conclusion, the thing-become succeeding the thing-becoming, death following life, rigidity following expansion" (31).

Equally, the British historian Arnold Toynbee, in his comparative study of civilizations in *The Study of History* (1934–61), attempted to analyze the rise and decline of twenty-six civilizations, while placing an emphasis on **religion** as a regenerative force. More recently, Samuel Huntington, in *The Clash of Civilizations* (1998), has taken the concept of religion further by understanding civilizations largely as synonyms for it in a conflict-ridden world.

However, because the concept refers to a variety of contradictory facts, it has been notoriously difficult to define and use. **Émile Durkheim** and **Marcel Mauss** in "Note on the Notion of Civilization" (1913 [trans. 1971, *Social Research* 38]) defined civilizations as referring to phenomena which pass beyond political and national frontiers: these are "interdependent systems, which without being limited to a determinate political organism are however, localizable in time and space . . . systems of facts that have their own unity . . . and form of existence a kind of moral milieu encompassing a certain number of nations." More recent writers, by contrast, have classified civilizations according to the relationship between humans and their **environment** (Felipe Fernandez-Armesto, *Civilizations, Culture, Ambition*, 2000). Moreover, the connotations of collective self-approbation, especially by Europeans and Americans, which have become attached to the word have made many **social sciences** reluctant to use the concept as an analytical category.   STEVEN LOYAL

civilizing process
– see **Norbert Elias**.

class conflict
– see **social class**.

class consciousness
– see **social class**.

class interest
– see **social class**.

cluster analysis
A multivariate statistical technique, used in the **social sciences** to divide a heterogeneous sample into a number of smaller, more homogeneous clusters, based on their similarity on a number of variables, there are a number of different ways of performing a cluster analysis. Small samples (tens of cases) can be clustered by building the clusters one link at a time, by joining cases with their nearest "neighbor" in terms of their similarity on the variables. For larger numbers of cases, algorithms exist to determine an appropriate number of clusters, and iteratively allocate each case to a cluster.

Cluster analysis was developed to deal with biological **data** (for instance, determining the family structure of species of plants from the dimensions of their various components). It rarely gives such conclusive solutions in the social sciences (where cluster membership is more complex, and there can be many cases that do not easily fit into any of the clusters). But it can be a very useful exploratory technique, to determine the viability and usefulness of treating a sample as one whole or as several sub-samples.

For instance, Brendan Burchell and Jill Rubery in "An Empirical Investigation into the Segmentation of the Labour Supply" (1990, *Work, Employment and Society*) used cluster analyses on a sample of 600 employees to divide them up into their different positions and trajectories in the **labor market** and to examine the ways in which advantaged and disadvantaged **groups** of employees are composed. They described five main clusters, for which the labor market operated in very different ways. They interpreted their results as supporting segmented labor market theories, whereby the labor market is better characterized as a number of non-competing groups for whom the relationship between productivity and rewards are very different. Each of the five clusters was assumed to represent one segment in the labor market. The results of this analysis partly supported previous theoretical accounts of labor markets, but also revealed new insights into the very different sorts of labor market disadvantage suffered by males and females in declining labor markets.

BRENDAN J. BURCHELL

coding
The coding, categorizing, or classification of social phenomena – an activity described by Robert Edgerton in "Quality of Life from a Longitudinal Research Perspective," featured in *Quality of Life: Perspectives and Issues* (1990), as "the American passion for reducing complex qualitative concepts to simple scalar instruments" – is an essential part of sociological research methodology under **positivism**. Coding, in theory, transforms otherwise unwieldy masses of disorderly phenomena, research participant reports or **participant observations**, into tractable **data**. The process of coding, essentially an exercise in the disaggregation of higher-order social phenomena and the assigning of numerical codes to theoretically important, and operationally defined, sub-phenomena (for example identifying a specific **suicide** as anomic, egotistical, or altruistic), is a core component of the **experimental method**, essential for the statistical manipulation of data, and the employment of inferential statistics to make population-based claims about the generality of sociological issues employing the logic of the **hypothetico-deductive method**.

Coding operates on a number of levels, may take place either before, during ("field-coding"), or after data collection, and may index very different practices for different research methods. For example, what is meant by coding for a study influenced by **grounded theory** – with the important methodological and epistemological distinction in such work between the procedures of latent and of manifest coding of textual material – differs dramatically from the meaning of coding to the designer of a study using **scales** to assess the intensity of racial **prejudice**, or **questionnaires** to measure quality of life. In the former case, as with the very limited use of coding in **discourse analysis** (where in practice the term often means little more than the identification of like interpretative repertoires, in much the way one might "code" one's socks by their color), the coding of emergent themes is a posteriori: categories/codes arise from inspection of the data. In the latter cases, coding refers to the assignment of a priori (numerical/value) codes to broad categories of expressed attitudes, beliefs, values, etc., by researchers. An example of an extremely simple coding scheme is illustrated in R. Schalock and K. Keith's *Quality of Life Questionnaire* (1993). Their semi-structured measure of quality of life is presented in Table 1. As is evident, coding the potentially infinite possible interviewee responses to the item "How much fun and enjoyment do you get out of life?" as 1 (not much), 2 (some), or 3 (lots), is not only massively to attenuate the substantive content of *all* possible responses, but also, of necessity, to engage in an impossibly unreliable exercise (by the standards of the experimental method) in on-the-spot interpretation.

Table 1. Field coding scheme for prescribed response alternatives

Item:	How successful do you think you are, compared with others?	Code
Response (a)	Probably more successful than the average person	1
Response (b)	About as successful as the average person	2
Response (c)	Less successful than the average person	3
Item:	How much fun and enjoyment do you get out of life?	Code
Response (a)	Lots	1
Response (b)	Some	2
Response (c)	Not much	3

In this regard it is crucial that we recognize the potential shortcomings inherent in any account of sociological phenomena we derive from analyst-imposed classification.

MARK RAPLEY AND SUSAN HANSEN

cognitive dissonance

A theory developed by Leon Festinger (1919–90) in his *Theory of Cognitive Dissonance* (1957); he proposed that anyone holding two contradictory cognitions experiences an aversive motivational state. This leads the individual to reduce the dissonance by changing one of the cognitions, or by including some justification into their thinking which would reconcile the difference.

An example of this is provided by one of the original tests of the claim. Subjects completed an exceptionally dull task, and were then asked to misrepresent it as very interesting to the next subject in the study. In one condition, subjects received $20 ($135 in 2004 prices) for their duplicity, but only $1 in the other. Subsequently, subjects rated how interesting the task was. The $20 subjects gave it significantly lower ratings than the $1 ones.

The explanation in cognitive dissonance terms was that the $20 subjects witnessed a conflict between their experience of the task and their description of it to the next subject, but had a justification for their behavior in the size of the reward, so did not experience dissonance. The $1 subjects did not have this, and so, as a result of the experienced conflict, were motivated to revise their belief as to the inherent interest of the task.

In essence it was a theory of why **attitudes** and beliefs change. Subsequent work has elaborated on what a cognition is, whether or not the aversive motivational state is essential, and the role played by an individual's sense of **self** and **identity** in motivating or constraining a change.

DAVID GOOD

cohorts

– see **generation(s)**.

Coleman, James S. (1926–1995)

Professor of Sociology at the University of Chicago, Coleman's career covered work in various areas of social science, **methodology** and theory, but his main contribution was to the theory of **social action** and structure (see **agency and structure**). His early work was concerned with conflict and power which he explored in *Community Conflict* (1957), *Power and the Structure of Society* (1974), and *The Asymmetric Society* (1982). He was a prolific writer of books and journal articles over his long career, and he focused on areas such as mathematical sociology in his *Introduction to Mathematical Sociology* (1964); the sociology of **education** in *The Adolescent Society: The Social Life of the Teenager and its Impact on Education* (1961), *Equality and Achievement in Education* (1990), and (with David Court) in *University Development in the Third World* (1993); and the analysis of **social change**. In the area of the sociology of education, his research on the positive effects of integrated schooling for underprivileged black children, the Coleman Report (*Equality of Educational Opportunity*, 1966), was most influential. He won many awards for his work including the Paul Lazarsfeld Award for Research in 1983, the Educational Freedom Award in 1989, and the American Distinguished Sociological Publication Award in 1992 for his book *Foundations of Social Theory* (1990), which contained some of his contributions to the theory of **social capital.** His later research focused on **rational choice theory**, for example in *Individual Interests and Collective Action: Selected Essays* (1986) and (with Thomas J. Fararo), *Rational Choice Theory: Advocacy and Critique* (1992). He founded the journal *Rationality and Society* in 1989. His most influential contribution was to the development of the theory of social capital.

BRYAN S. TURNER

collective action

This concept refers to the process by which interest groups produce a public good. Pure public goods have two properties: non-excludability (anyone can consume it, including noncontributors) and jointness of supply (an increase in consumption does not reduce the amount available to others). Collective action can also take the form of mutual restraint in depleting shared resources, a problem known as the tragedy of the common good.

Collective action differs from **collective behavior** such as rioting or "groupthink," in which people in **groups** suppress critical faculties. However, collective action is not necessarily motivated by rational self-interest. In *The Logic of Collective Action* (1965), Mancur Olson (1932–98) argued that rational actors will not contribute to public goods if: (1) they can enjoy the public good even if they do not contribute (the free-rider problem), and (2) they cannot substantially increase the public good even if they do contribute (the efficacy problem). Thus, rational actors will participate in collective action in large groups only if selective incentives reward contributors and punish noncontributors.

Olson's work was criticized by sociologists who countered that the provision of incentives is itself a public good that presumes collective action rather than explaining it. However, Douglas Heckathorn showed that it can be rational to contribute to sanctions even when it is not rational to contribute to public goods in the absence of **social control**.

Gerald Marwell and Pamela Oliver also challenged Olson's argument. In *The Critical Mass in Collective Action* (1993), they showed how, with high jointness of supply, collective action without selective incentives is more likely in large than in small groups. Large groups are more likely to contain a critical mass of highly interested and resourceful members. These statistical outliers may be willing to provide the public goods for everyone, no matter how many others benefit for free.

Formal models of collective action have also examined the role of social **networks**. It is often easier to mobilize a critical mass of contributors locally, which can then spread from cluster to cluster until the entire population is involved. Local **interaction** also facilitates informal social control, such as the spread of reputation.

While much research on collective action uses formal theory, researchers have also used experimental laboratory research to study social dilemmas. An important branch of research attributes collective action to the cohesive effects of social identity rather than shared interests in a public good. Henri Tajfel, *Social Identity and Intergroup Relations* (1982), shows how individuals are more likely to contribute to public goods when a group identity is salient. However, in "The Group as the Container of Generalized Reciprocity" (*Social Psychology Quarterly*), Toshio Yamagishi and Toko Kiyonari argue that these studies may have confounded the effects of identity with a self-interested expectation of generalized reciprocity. These and other experimental studies are reviewed by Peter Kollock in the 1998 *Annual Review of Sociology*.

Another branch of collective-action research focuses on the mobilization of participation in **social movements**. Key approaches include resource mobilization, which considers the strategic attitudes and actions of participants, the political process model, which examines the intersection of political opportunities, social movements sectors, and cycles of protest, and the new social movements perspective, which explores structural determinants and outcomes of movements.

MICHAEL MACY AND STEPHEN BENARD

collective behavior

Treated generically, this term refers to behavior that is carried out by some sort of collective rather than by an individual. While there are classic accounts of concerted action in the writings of **Karl Marx** and of **Max Weber**, there have been a variety of recent, more focused, approaches to the mobilization of such behavior. The specific "collective behavior" approach developed in the United States is associated with two otherwise quite different theorists, **Herbert Blumer** and **Neil Smelser**. Blumer's symbolic interactionist emphasis on elementary forms of collective behavior, in which there is a lowering of the self-consciousness that barricades the individual against the influence of others, has much in common with **Émile Durkheim**'s stress on collective sentiments, **rituals**, and **symbols**. Blumer distinguishes between three elementary groupings in which individualism and privatism are transcended. These are: (1) a crowd, in which physical proximity and density are important, and which may range from the casual and passive to the expressively intense and active; (2) a mass, such as the audience for **mass media** events, in which similar action can be provoked in spatially disparate individuals by a common point of reference; and (3) a public, in which there is an interactional coming together of previously disparate individuals in order to debate issues of common concern. Blumer analyzes how these nascent and spontaneous forms of collective behavior can be transformed into more enduring and durable forms when the response to conditions of unrest involves the active creation of **social movements** with an esprit de corps, clear ideological values, and an organizational structure.

The so-called "value-added" approach of Smelser's *Theory of Collective Behavior* (1962), drawing its inspiration from **functionalism**, emphasizes the structural over the agency side of collective behavior. He identifies the response of groups to what they see as "structural strain" in their environment as central amongst several factors that affect whether, and to what extent, collective behavior will occur. The other factors include: the specific configuration of opportunities and constraints confronting the **group**; the growth and spread of generalized beliefs about what is wrong and what should be done; the "trigger" of concrete events that act as a focus for mobilization; communication **networks** that aid the coordination and organization of the mobilization; and the response of social control agencies such as the police or the media.

Employing the prisoner's dilemma from **game theory**, Mancur Olson's influential *The Logic of Collective Action* (1965) highlighted a specific problem in mobilizing collective action, that of the "free rider." The problem is that self-interested individuals will prefer to free-ride on the activities of others, gaining the benefits of collective actions but avoiding the costs of personal commitment. According to Olson, it is rational to defect from such actions unless individual incentives are provided. Such an individualistic and rationalistic approach sits uneasily with Blumer's and Smelser's more sociological emphasis on extra-individual **values**, beliefs, and collective sentiments. More recent work has refined and complemented earlier insights. The resource mobilization school has demonstrated the significance for collective actors of resources gained from external **organizations** and networks, while innovative works such as Doug McAdam, Sydney Tarrow, and Charles Tilly's *Dynamics of Contention* (2001) have developed historically specific and grounded analyses of "cycles" and "repertoires of contention."   ROB STONES

collective goods
– see **social capital**.

collective rights
– see **rights**.

Collège de Sociologie

The powerful intellectual presence in France of **Émile Durkheim,** prior to his death in 1917, was due to the intellectual and organizational coherence of his school and to its elective affinity with a politically significant reformist socialist republican movement. Their collective work produced some positive responses from prominent members of other disciplines, but it equally provoked hostility, which helps explain its subsequent limited role in higher education. After World War I, few chairs in sociology were created and many Durkheimians gravitated to specialized research institutes. True, the Durkheimians influenced secondary education, but at the cost of a subsequent increasingly abstract, nationalistic and technocratic development of its precepts.

In the 1930s, intellectual ferment was linked with Surrealist subversions of conventional art and literature, an interest in more "primitive cultures," and a renewed interest in the ideas of German thinkers, such as **Georg Wilhelm Friedrich Hegel**, **Karl Marx**, Friedrich Nietzsche (1844–1900), **Sigmund Freud**, and also Martin Heidegger (1889–1976). The work of the Durkheimians became increasingly marginalized: Paul Nizan even blamed them for the authoritarian nationalistic cast of education. Surprisingly, in 1937, the dissident Surrealists and anti-fascist activists Georges Bataille (1897–1962), Michel Leiris (1901–90), and Roger Caillois (1913–78) organized a Collège de Sociologie which met in a Parisian bookshop between November 1937 and July 1939. First announced in Bataille's journal *Acéphale*, the Collège aimed to create a contagious "Sacred Sociology." Unaffiliated with any academic institution, the reputations, connections, and **networks** of the Collège's organizers and the promise of the "note" in *Acéphale* brought to its sessions many European literary figures, Surrealist and otherwise, historians, social theorists, and philosophers, including Alexandre Kojève (1902–68), Pierre Klossowksi (1905–2001), Denis de Rougemont (1906–85), Hans Mayer (1907–2001), **Jacques Lacan**, Georges Dumézil (1898–1986), Jean-Paul Sartre (1905–80), **Claude Lévi-Strauss**, and **Walter Benjamin**. Its major focus was the study of the problems of **power**, the sacred, and **myths**. This required forms of inquiry which would embrace a person's total activity and would entail working in common with others, seriously, selflessly, and with critical severity. To understand manifestations of the sacred, or their absence, historical and comparative anthropological materials and theories were needed and these were to be found in the work of Durkheim, Robert Hertz (1881–1915), Henri Hubert (1872–1927), and **Marcel Mauss**. The lectures at the College and many associated writings have been brought together in Denis Hollier (ed.), *The College of Sociology 1937–39* (1988).

In their joint presentation in 1937 on the "Sacred Sociology and the Relationships Between 'Society,' 'Organism,' and 'Being,'" Bataille and Caillois endorse Durkheim's view that **society** was an emergent *sui generis* reality, society being something other than the sum of its individual members, and while these naively represent themselves to themselves as indivisible unities they are transformed by their subjection to the "communifying movements" of society, which is a "compound being." Such movements create a feeling of being a society, but this may be precarious, since one society can produce a number of different collectivities at the same time. Both Caillois and Bataille drew on Durkheim's analysis of the **sacred and profane dichotomy**.

For Caillois, as he made clear in his lecture "Festival," the sacred is a key element both in ordinary life and in the festivals found in **primitive societies**, and to a much attenuated degree in contemporary societies. Ordinary life tends to be regular, busy, and safe; insofar as it is part of a cosmos ruled by a universal order, the sacred only manifests itself against potential disturbances of this order or as expiations for any such disturbances. The very passage of time may be wearing and exhausting and individual human beings and social **institutions** get used up and every socially conscious act leads to the accumulation of potentially toxic wastes. Regeneration may depend upon the person who is its agent becoming polluted, for what is unclean may contain within itself a positive active principle. The popular frenzy of the festival may also be regenerative in that it can release an active sacred energy, which reverses the normal course of time and the forms of social order, encouraging sacrilegious words and deeds including sexual excesses. The festival helps rediscover the creative chaos associated with cosmic time and space and it may not only purify and renew the established social order but change it in fundamental ways.

Modern carnivals, however, are but dying echoes of earlier festivals – for example, the joyful destruction of a cardboard representation of a buffoon-like king has little sacral relevance because, when an effigy replaces an actual human victim, expiation or fertility are not a likely consequence.

Caillois was a rigorous Durkheimian and his analysis is in accord with Durkheim's belief that all forms of social phenomena that keep recurring within societies of a particular species — whether the phenomena superficially seem conformist or deviant — are either themselves functional for society as a whole or a necessary concomitant of something that is functional.

Bataille significantly modified Durkheim's distinction between the profane and the sacred. Durkheim distinguishes between phenomena or categorizations, homogeneous internally but heterogeneous each to the other, but Bataille reinterprets the distinction as one between the "homogeneous" and the "heterogeneous." The profane involves homogenization: deferred gratification, analysis and calculation, planning and utility, production and the controlled **consumption** necessary for the reproduction and conservation of economically productive human life, conformist individuals experiencing themselves as separate self-sufficient subjects, the possession and consumption of objects.

The sacred is associated with heterogeneity: socially useless activity, unlimited expenditure, orgiastic impulses, sexual activity, defecation, urination, ritual cannibalism, with extreme emotions, tabooed objects and their transgression — for example corpses and menstrual blood. The sacred evokes feelings of both attraction and repulsion and is linked with **violence** and its violent containment; with the cruelty of sacrificing others and with the subsumption of individuals within totalizing group processes when they fearlessly confront death and are willing to sacrifice themselves. It is potentially dangerous and destabilizing. More generally, while in contemporary societies sacral processes have become more obscure and suppressed, less obviously religious, they are still present, as can be seen in the way that men are attracted to sacrificial ceremonies and festivals. This discussion is to be found in "The Use-Value of D. A. F. de Sade: An Open Letter to My Current Comrades" in "Attraction and Repulsion" (Hollier, 1988: 106–22): "The Structure and Function of the Army" (1988: 139–44), "Joy in the Face of Death" (1988: 325–28), and "The College of Sociology" (1988: 333–41).

In fact, historically, the sacred has been generated by taboo-violating rituals, and sacrifices have been key elements in festivals which both regenerate the sacred and corral it. The activities that both Caillois and Bataille describe are renewing and transforming cosmological social meanings and interpersonal and social relations, but Bataille provides a model which presumes a much lower level of integration, and which assumes less "societally functional" outcomes, than does the model found in the discourses of Durkheim (and Caillois). It is more marked by contradictions and tensions and, hence, possibly also subject to imperative elements.

The meetings of the Collège de Sociologie consisted of lectures followed by a discussion. Something less traditional is hinted at in Bataille's final lecture at the Collège. Bataille argues that the sacred is produced when human beings communicate in such a naked way that they form new beings. When humans unite with each other, for example through love, this always involves a mutual tearing and wounding. But lovers fear that sustaining their relationship for its own sake may subvert their ability to love to the point of losing themselves in love. Thus, to sustain the intensity of their feelings they must give themselves to turbulent passions and be with each other in a state of heightened drama, even to the point of being willing to embrace death. This may involve just the two, but they may seek to increase the intensity of their experience by incorporating another person into their erotic domain, leading to an even more annihilating expenditure. It is not hard to see why Bataille would conclude his lecture by claiming that eroticism slips easily into orgy, but it is not as self-evident why he links this, as he does, with sacrifice becoming an end in itself and a universal value.

At that time, Bataille hoped, by the ritual execution of a consenting victim, to release sacred energies. This was to have been a ritual enacted by the members of the second Acéphale, the anti-Christian and Nietzschean secret society Bataille formed in 1936 and for which the Collège represented an outside activity. Much has been revealed in the recent volume edited by Marina Galletti, *L'Apprenti Sorcier du cercle communiste démocratique à Acéphale: Textes, lettres et documents (1917–1962); rassemblés, présentés et annotés par Marina Galletti* (1999). From this it is evident that Acéphale's goals — "to change the torture that exists in the world into joy within us; the Crucified into happy laughter; our old immense weakness into will to power" – were meant to be "communifying." They

found a willing victim, probably Leiris, and it is believed that Caillois was offered the role of the sacrificer, the actual executioner. Immediately after the sacrifice, the sacrificer was also expected to kill himself – for Bataille, the executioner's desire was to be a victim. Caillois did not accept the offer. Further, according to French sacrificial theory, each sacrifice involves not only a victim and a sacrificer but also a sacrifier (the source of the desire for the sacrifice), and in this case each member of the group was a sacrifier, and presumably each of them – through "contagion" – could have been both sacrificer and victim. The human sacrifice never took place.

Now, in his sole lecture at the Collège, "The Sacred in Everyday Life," Leiris's emphasis was psychological and personal. He was concerned with the variety of things – objects, places, or occasions – that awaken the mixture of fear and attachment taken as indicating the sacred. Much of his lecture was devoted to the symbolic meanings and associations of the sacred things that he was familiar with in his own early years, but this style of engagement had few resonances with other lectures at the Collège. In fact, Leiris soon distanced himself from its activities. One might speculate that this was associated with the failure of Acéphale's sacrificial promise, but, overtly at least, he did so, from another place, as a professional ethnologist. In a letter to Bataille he suggested three major objections to the way the activities of the Collège had developed. It tended to work from ideas that were ill-defined, thus comparisons were often carelessly made with societies which were very different from each other; it was in danger of becoming a mere clique; and, finally, it overemphasized the sacred, thereby subverting Mauss's idea of a total social fact. Caillois had made clear that the quality of the collective work should be such that its results could be substantiated and that the research would command respect. He had become increasingly uneasy about the extent to which this was being achieved. Indeed, his lecture "The Sociology of the Executioner" could be seen as a critique of Bataille's overly voluntaristic and socially decontextualized understanding of sacrificial ritual, an understanding which also, it might be added, underestimates the necessary role that *alea* or chance plays in producing the sacred. Eventually, Caillois also distanced himself from the Collège. Bataille, alone of the three, in July 1939, attended the last session. In September of the same year, all of its members withdrew from Acéphale.   FRANK PEARCE

Collins, Randall (1941–)

Professor of Sociology at the University of Pennsylvania, Collins has made important contributions to historical sociology, the study of **networks**, and **sociological theory**. His work in **macrosociology** has been influenced by **Max Weber**, and he has developed a distinctive interpretation of Weber in *Conflict Sociology: Towards an Explanatory Science* (1975), *The Credential Society. An Historical Sociology of Education and Stratification* (1979), *Weberian Sociological Theory* (1986), and *Max Weber. A Skeleton Key* (1986). From a Weberian perspective, Collins has analyzed the rise and fall of major civilizations and empires, and studied the conditions for capitalist growth in *Macro History. Essays in Sociology of the Long Run* (1999). His most ambitious and influential study was on the global consequences of networks for the development of philosophy in his *The Sociology of Philosophies. A Global Theory of Intellectual Change* (1998). He has also used the work of **Erving Goffman** to develop a theory of "interaction chains" to study such phenomena as **violence** and sexual interaction in *Interaction Ritual Chains* (2004).   BRYAN S. TURNER

colonialism

Often treated as synonymous with **imperialism,** it seems helpful to distinguish between them. Imperialism refers to rule by a superior power over subordinate territories, but it is consistent, as with the Roman Empire, with the extension of **citizenship** to members of the conquered territories. The early forms of colonialism, as with the ancient Greeks, could also give rise to more or less equal, self-governing colonies; but modern colonialism, which has given the term its dominant meaning, usually refers to a fundamental inequality between metropole and colony, often codified in **law**, and resulting in a basic dependence of the colony on the metropolitan power.

There have been two main forms of modern colonialism. In the first, inhabitants of one country establish colonies in another country, often in the process displacing or even exterminating the indigenous inhabitants of that country. This was the case, for instance, with the British colonies in North America, Australia, and New Zealand; though originally unintended, this also turned out to be essentially the condition of the Spanish and Portuguese colonies in the New World. Even though it is clear that the colony is an off-shoot of the parent body and remains tied to it in many ways, the similarity of sentiment, habits, and political attitudes between metropole and colony tends to mean that the colonies eventually aim at independence and self-rule – even if, as in the case of some of the American colonies, this has to be accomplished by force. We can – cautiously – call this the Greek model, as it follows the basic pattern of Greek colonization in the ancient world.

The other form of modern colonialism is closer to the old Roman model. Here a superior power incorporates, usually by conquest, peoples of different ethnicities and levels of development. Examples of this form would include the European colonization of much of Asia, Africa, and the Pacific in the eighteenth and nineteenth centuries. In this form, colonialism shades over into imperialism. There is usually an official **ideology** of "the civilizing mission," whereby the colonizing power aims to bring up the colonies to the levels of **culture** and material standards of its own society. There is no expectation, in principle at least, that the colonies will eventually achieve independence, though their people may well, as in the case of certain French colonies, achieve degrees of citizenship. Though the civilizing mission is offered as justification to the world at large, to their own peoples colonial powers usually justify colonial possessions in terms of their benefit to the mother country. They are expected to be a source of wealth and **power**, and to provide raw materials and **markets** for the goods of the colonial powers, together with opportunities for investment. The fact that in very few actual cases have things turned out as the colonizers hoped has not prevented many people from continuing to believe in the benefits of colonies – the Nazis, for instance, attempted a form of colonialism in Eastern Europe, as did the Italian fascists in North Africa.

In the best-known instances of colonialism, the colonies are overseas, separated from the metropole by large distances. But there can also be "internal colonialism," in which what are effectively colonies exist on the doorstep of the metropole. Such, argued Michael Hechter in an influential book *Internal Colonialism* (1975), is the case of the United Kingdom, with the English the dominant "colonial" power in relation to the "colonized" Welsh, Scottish, and Irish. A similar argument has been made about Russia in relation to its eastward expansion, especially as regards regions such as Siberia. There is an obvious degree of truth in this conception, but the limitations of the internal colonialism model become apparent in the cases of Spain and Canada, where the regions of

Catalonia or Quebec do not at all fit the idea of exploited "colonies," whatever the protestations of the inhabitants.

Colonialism gave rise in due course to **decolonization**, especially in the period following World War II, when most European empires shed their colonies, with varying degrees of **violence** and usually under the pressure of nationalist movements. Decolonization was generally hailed as a victory for the principles of democracy and national self-determination, and in some senses therefore could be held to be the fulfillment of the western mission, since the principles clearly derived from western thought and practice. But to many observers the triumph was hollow, since what took the place of formal colonialism was informal neo-colonialism. In this view, the colonies achieve formal independence and national sovereignty, but remain in many essential respects as dependent on the former colonial powers as when they were colonies. This is shown in such matters as a narrow economic specialization, geared to the requirements of the economies of the advanced nations, and a culture that is equally dependent on foreign, mostly western, sources. Neo-colonial theorists point, as a telling parallel, to the situation in Latin America, whose countries were never formally colonized but whose pattern of development was in important respects dictated by the needs and interests of dominant foreign powers, notably Britain and the United States.

One should mention, finally, post-colonialism. Unlike the other terms, this refers mainly to a school of cultural criticism and analysis concerned with the conditions of societies that have achieved independence, following a period of dependence and subordination as a part of colonial empires. Its most thriving branch to date has been on the Indian sub-continent, especially in the work of the Subaltern Studies group; but it is normal also to refer, for the founding texts, to such works as **Franz Fanon**'s *The Wretched of the Earth* (1961) and **Edward Said**'s *Orientalism* (1978). Post-colonial studies cover a wide variety of fields, but are especially marked by their exploration of the complex and often contradictory effects of the interaction between the colonized and the colonizers in imperial settings, and of the lasting legacy of this experience in the post-colonial period.   KRISHAN KUMAR

color blind

– see **prejudice**.

commodity Fetishism

– see **alienation**.

communism

As a form of social organization and ideas about it, the term indicates societies in which **property** is commonly and fully owned and shared. In this sense, the only societies to which this definition is empirically applicable have been pre-agrarian (hunter and gatherer societies) or early agrarian stateless societies. This so-called primitive communism is said to have disappeared with sedentary living, economic surplus, and **social status** differentiation related to material wealth. In **Karl Marx**'s stage-theory, history began with primitive communism. Within modern state societies, forms of communal living with shared property have occurred, but for sociological purposes are not treated as examples of communism. Likewise, contemporary hunter–gatherer societies have escaped this label in sociological theorizing, partially as an outcome of disciplinary struggles with anthropology. In contemporary usage in the **social sciences**, communism is often used as a shorthand for the political regimes of the twentieth century that were based on a diverse range of interpretations of Marxist theory and doctrine. China, Cuba, and North Korea are contemporary examples of societies explicitly led by communist doctrine.

Where it is used as regime-type label, however, the connotation deviates sharply from the original theorizing of communism by Marx and **Friedrich Engels**, where it did not signify a future and desirable ultimate type of society (as interpreted by the Young Hegelians), but a "real movement" to transcend contemporary society grounded in the present – for example in the *German Ideology* (1845 [trans. 1965]) of Marx and Engels. Therefore in Marx's system of thought, communism was no **utopia**. Marx's concept of communism is deeply rooted in philosophical debates, specifically the Hegelian concept of **time**. Disagreeing with **Hegel**'s conception of the Spirit and its role in history, Marx understood the transcendence of time and history as resulting from human action. Seeing humans as expressing themselves and their purposes, rather than merely reproducing themselves, when engaging in economic activities, Marx came to define the workers as the agents of such transcendence. This proposition introduced a much-debated paradox into Marx's theorizing, because he had to argue that, at the same time as the material conditions of capitalist production brought drudgery and misery to the workers, work itself was also the source of human creativity and self-fulfillment for the laboring class. The crux of the matter for Marx was that labor time, not labor as such, was commodified in the capitalist mode of production, thus leaving a residual for the self-actualization of labor. As he argued, with what now appears as great foresight, taking control of labor time becomes a paramount concern in class struggle, **industrial relations**, and **management** in capitalism.

Within this paradox, Marx – decisively for future generations of Marxian faith-based political systems – had carved out a charismatic role for labor, in the form of collective proletarian revolutionary action. This vision contradicted his evolutionary understanding of history, according to which gradual progress within existing bourgeois institutions (the fulfillment of particular objective material factors) would eventually bring about ultimate human freedom. Marx took the concept of communism to mean the **social movement** uniting all revolutionary proletarians, but it remains unresolved as to how proletarian autonomy and consciousness, necessary to transcend the current conditions, can be achieved against the historical-materialist axiom of the theory that social existence determines consciousness and not vice versa.

Marx's writings show incoherence in terms of his assessment of the possibilities lying in the empirically existent working class during his lifetime. On one hand, he argued, the totality of the relations of production, constituting the economic structure, is the foundation of the legal–political superstructure, corresponding to definite forms of social consciousness. The working class thus was locked into structures provided by the laws of history (see **social structures**). On the other, as he and Engels argued in *The Communist Manifesto* (1848) and observed in reality, he saw some societies at the eve of a revolution, and hoped this would carry enough critical mass to overthrow the ruling classes and deliver a wholesome transformation.

Marx himself, after many years as a commentator on labor's **collective action**, became the leader of the first International, which was founded in 1863 by labor leaders as a nation-spanning alliance of workers in pursuit of the replacement of the current economic system with one of collective ownership of the means of production. The International became an active political threat to those in fear of the "specter of communism" the *Manifesto* had promised, and although it

dissolved in 1876 it was followed by two more Internationals. The political movement behind the International featured both agreement and disagreement about the overthrow of capitalism from diverse progressive forces.

The history of social organization based on communist **ideology** cannot be understood without reference to **socialism**. While all forms of socialism are critical of capitalist organization and the resulting social **inequality**, not all variants agree over a centralized role for the state and the elimination of private property as preconditions for a better society. Eduard Bernstein (1850–1932), for example, embraced Marx's scientific theory but found it at odds with the real development of industrial capitalism that showed an improved standard of living and class inequalities far less polarized than anticipated by Marx. He found a pacification of class protests and institutionalization of socialist and communist parties. Bernstein emphasized the role of **democracy** and advocated social reform. A departure from Marx in another direction was made by **V. I. Lenin**, who forged the idea of the necessity of a vanguard party that would translate the interests of the workers into revolutionary action. Lenin's version of Marxian theory stressed socialism as more than a transitional phase: the bourgeois state would be eliminated while the proletarian state would be built. Marx had anticipated, on the contrary, that the state would wither away. He did not use in his writings the term "dictatorship of the proletariat," but subsequent ideologies and regimes, and commentators on them, used the term to establish or express the supreme role of the communist party in state leadership.   ANN VOGEL

communitarianism

A social philosophy that favors social formulations of the good, communitarianism is often contrasted with **liberalism**, which assumes that the good should be determined by each individual. To the extent that social **institutions** and policies are required, these should be based on voluntary agreements among the individuals involved, expressing their preferences. In contrast, communitarians view institutions and policies as reflecting in part **values** passed from **generation** to generation. These values become part of the self through internalization, and are modified by persuasion, religious or political indoctrination, leadership, and moral dialogues.

In the 1980s communitarianism was largely advanced by Charles Taylor, Michael Sandel, and Michael Walzer. They criticized liberalism for its failure to realize that people are socially "embedded," overlooking that people can have a strong attachment to their societies. They lamented liberalism's focus on the individualistic concept of self-interest.

Asian communitarians argue that, to maintain social harmony, individual **rights** and political liberties must be curtailed. Some seek to rely heavily on the **state** to maintain social order (for instance, leaders and champions of the regimes in Singapore and Malaysia), and some on strong social bonds and moral culture (as does Japan). Asian communitarians also hold that the West's notion of liberty actually amounts to "anarchy"; that strong economic growth requires limiting freedoms; and that the West uses its idea of legal and political rights to chastise other cultures that have inherent values of their own.

In 1990, a new school of communitarianism was founded. Among its leading scholars are William A. Galston (political theory), Mary Ann Glendon (law), Thomas Spragens, Jr. (political science), Alan Ehrenhalt (writer), and sociologists **Philip Selznick**, **Robert Bellah** and his associates, and **Amitai Etzioni** who wrote books that, in 1990, laid the foundations for responsive (democratic) communitarianism. Key communitarian texts include *Habits of the Heart* (1985) by Robert Bellah and colleagues, *The Spirit of Community* (1993) and *The New Golden Rule* (1996) by Amitai Etzioni, *Communitarianism and Its Critics* (1993) by **Daniel Bell**, and *The Communitarian Persuasion* by Philip Selznick (2002).

Responsive communitarians, a group founded by Amitai Etzioni, assume that societies have multiple and not wholly compatible needs, in contrast to philosophies built on one core principle, such as liberty for libertarianism. Responsive communitarianism assumes that a good society is based on a balance between liberty and social order, and between particularistic (communal) and society-wide values and bonds. This school stresses responsibilities people have for their families, kin, **communities**, and societies – above and beyond the universal rights all individuals command, the focus of liberalism.

While a carefully crafted balance between liberty and social order defines a generic concept of the good society, communitarians point out that the historical–social conditions of specific societies determine the rather *different* ways a given society in a given era may need to change to attain the *same* balance. Thus, contemporary Japan requires much greater tolerance for individual rights, while in the American society excessive **individualism** needs to be curbed.

Communitarians pay special attention to social **institutions**. Several of these form the moral infrastructure of society: families, schools, communities, and the community of communities. Infants are born into families whose societal role is to introduce values and begin the development of the moral self. The role of schools is to develop the moral self and to remedy moral development if it was neglected or distorted by the **family**.

Communitarians emphasize that children reared in well-functioning families and schools will still not be sufficiently equipped for membership in a good, communitarian society. This is a point ignored by those social philosophers who assume that, once people have acquired virtue and are habituated, they will be adequately guided by their inner moral compass. In contrast, communitarians assume that commitments to moral values tend to deteriorate, unless these are continuously reinforced. A major societal role of communities is to reinforce these commitments in their members. This is achieved by the community's "moral voice," the informal sanctioning of others, built into a web of informal affect-laden relationships, that communities provide.

Within this context, responsive communitarians point out that, if a society has communities whose social webs are intact, who share a moral **culture**, and whose members are willing to raise their moral voice, such a society can rest its social order largely on moral commitments rather than on the coercive state. That is, the moral voice can reduce the inevitable tension between liberty and social order and enhance both.

In the same vein, communitarians argue that, while everyone's right to free speech should be respected, some speech – seen from the community's viewpoint – is morally highly offensive and, when children are exposed, damaging. For instance, the (legal) right to speak does not render verbal expressions of hate (morally) right.

While sociologists made numerous contributions to altered communitarian thinking, this philosophy challenged sociology to face issues raised by cross-cultural moral judgments. Sociologists tend to treat all values as conceptually equal; thus sociologists refer to racist Nazi beliefs and those of free societies by the same "neutral" term, calling both "values." Communitarians use the term "virtue" to indicate that some values have a high moral standing because they are compatible with the good society, while other values are not and hence are "aberrant" rather than virtuous.

In the same vein, communitarians reject the claim of **cultural relativism** that all cultures command basically the same moral standing, and do not shy away from passing cross-cultural moral judgments. Thus, they view female circumcision, sex slaves, and traditional *hudud* laws (such as chopping off the right hand of thieves) as violations of liberty and individual rights, and abandoning children, violating implicit contracts building into communal mutuality, or neglecting the environment as evidence of a lack of commitment to social order and neglect of social responsibilities.

Communitarian terms became part of the public vocabulary in the 1990s, especially references to assuming social responsibilities to match individual rights, while the term communitarianism itself is used much less often. The number of articles about communitarian thinking in the popular press increased during the last decade of the twentieth century.

AMITAI ETZIONI

community

Critics argue that the concept of the community is of questionable value because it is so ill defined. In Colin Bell and Howard Newby's edited *The Myth of Community Studies* (1974), Margaret Stacey argued that the solution to this problem is to avoid the term altogether. Bell and Newby similarly pointed out, "There has never been a theory of community, nor even a satisfactory definition of what community is" (1974: xliii).

Amitai Etzioni (*New Golden Rule*, 1996) points out that community can be defined with reasonable precision. Community has two characteristics: (1) a web of affect-laden relationships among a group of individuals, relationships that often crisscross and reinforce one another (as opposed to one-on-one relationships); and (2) a measure of commitment to a set of shared histories and identities – in short, a particular **culture**. David E. Pearson states:

> To earn the appellation "community," it seems to me, groups must be able to exert moral suasion and extract a measure of compliance from their members. That is, communities are necessarily, indeed by definition, coercive as well as moral, threatening their members with the stick of sanctions if they stray, offering them the carrot of certainty and stability if they don't. ("Community and Sociology," 1995, *Society*)

Critics generally suggest that those who long for communities ignore the darker side of traditional communities. "In the new communitarian appeal to **tradition**, communities of 'mutual aid and memory,'" writes Linda McClain in "Rights and Irresponsibility" (1994: 1029) in the *Duke Law Journal*, "there is a problematic inattention to the less attractive, unjust features of tradition." Amy Gutmann ("Communitarian Critics of Liberalism," 1985, *Philosophy and Public Affairs*) pointedly remarks that communitarians "want us to live in Salem," a community of strong shared values that went so far as to accuse nonconformist members of witchcraft during the seventeenth century.

Communitarians counter that behind many of these criticisms lies an image of old, or total, communities, which are neither typical of modern **society** nor necessary for, or even compatible with, a communitarian society. Old communities (traditional villages) were geographically bounded and the only communities of which people were members. In effect, other than escaping into no-man's-land, often bandit territories, individuals had few opportunities for choosing their social attachments. In short, old communities had monopolistic **power** over their members.

New communities are often limited in scope and reach. Members of one residential community are often also members of other communities, for example, work, ethnic, or religious ones (see **work and employment**, **ethnicity**, and **religion**). As a result, community members have multiple sources of attachments; and if one threatens to become overwhelming, individuals will tend to pull back and turn to another community for their attachments. Thus, for example, if a person finds herself under high moral pressure at work to contribute to the United Way, to give blood, or to serve at a soup kitchen for the homeless, and these are lines of action she is not keen to follow, she may end up investing more of her energy in other communities – her writers' group, for instance, or her church. This multicommunity membership protects the individual from both moral oppression and ostracism.   AMITAI ETZIONI

community enterprise
– see **social economy**.

community studies
These studies are concerned with interrelationships of social **institutions** in a locality. Some studies encompass all such relations, while others (for example **Michael Young** and Peter Willmott's *Family and Kinship in East London*, 1957) focus on particular relations. Community studies traditionally understand "community" as a space defined by multiple contiguous social **networks**. Studies often share a number of characteristics. They often use **participant observation** with the researchers living in the locale, sharing some of

the experiences of the inhabitants, for whom they consequently display sympathy. They tend to offer detailed and lively descriptions of community life but may not be extensively theorized. Robert and Helen Lynd's classical *Middletown: A Study in American Culture* (1929) charted cultural change and strain in a "typical" American town, organized around six themes – "getting a living," "making a home," "training the young," "using **leisure**," "religious practices," and "community activities." Many studies followed, one of the most famous being W. F. Whyte's *Street Corner Society* (1943), a study of gang life in Boston's East End. Community studies remained popular through the 1950s and there were several classical British studies including N. Dennis, F. M. Henriques, and C. Slaughter, *Coal is Our Life* (1956), but the method was increasingly criticized as a-historical, having an implicit model of functional equilibrium and difficulty analyzing change. Ray Pahl's six-year study of the Isle of Sheppey (1978–83), later published as *Divisions of Labour* (1984), addresses these criticisms by exploring changes in household divisions of **labor** over time in relation to broader social structural processes. But in a period of high **social mobility**, internet communications, and transnational networks, the notion of spatially defined communities has become less central to sociology.   LARRY RAY

companionate marriage
– see **marriage and divorce**.

comparative method
It is rather paradoxical to write about comparative method. All sociological method is intrinsically comparative in the sense that it either involves explicit and direct comparison of time and/or space differentials or involves concepts that were developed through such comparisons. **Émile Durkheim** was well aware of this paradox already when he argued that "comparative sociology is not a particular branch of sociology; it is sociology itself, in so far as it ceases to be purely descriptive and aspires to account for facts," in *The Rules of Sociological Method* (1895 [trans. 1982]). But what exactly did comparison mean? Did it mean simply to compare and contrast across time and space? Did it mean to search for analogies and parallels across cultures and societies? **Max Weber** certainly opposed such simplistic comparisons. In a note on method hastily added to his *The Agrarian Sociology of Ancient Civilizations* (1909 [trans. 1976]), almost as an afterthought, Weber suggested that

[a] genuinely analytic study comparing the stages of development of the ancient polis with those of the medieval city would be welcome and productive . . . Of course . . . such a comparative study would not aim at finding "analogies" and "parallels," as is done by those engrossed in the currently fashionable enterprise of constructing general schemes of development. The aim should, rather, be precisely the opposite: to identify and define the individuality of each development, the characteristics which made the one conclude in a manner so different from that of the other. This done, one can then determine the causes which led to these differences. (1976: 385)

For Weber, then, comparison did not consist in drawing parallels and analogies but in exploring the trajectories of social **institutions** in their irreducible differences and singularities (for example, Stephen Kalberg, *Max Weber's Comparative-Historical Sociology*, 1994). Here, as elsewhere, Weber's debt to Nietzsche's conception of genealogy is unmistakable and perhaps remains one of Weber's lasting legacies for empirically grounded theorizing (for example, David Owen, *Maturity and Modernity: Nietzsche, Weber, Foucault and the Ambivalence of Reason*, 1994).   ENGIN ISIN

complexity theory
A recent development in **social theory**, gaining currency through the last decade of the twentieth century, this has been described as an amalgam or "rhetorical hybrid" of a range of insights drawn from a variety of different fields, mainly in the natural sciences, and applied to social relations. Complexity theory is closely associated with the foundation of the Santa Fe Institute in 1984, an interdisciplinary research institute comprising physicists, mathematicians, computer programmers, and systems analysts. It was also championed by world-systems sociologist **Immanuel Wallerstein** and Nobel-prize-winning scientist Ilya Prigogine (1917–) in the Gulbenkian Commission's influential 1996 report on the restructuring of the **social sciences**, *Open the Social Sciences*. The theory is essentially concerned with issues of order, adaptation, and feedback emerging from interactions between the different elements or parts of complex systems, from weather systems to business **organizations**. While it has produced compelling insights in economics it is probably too soon to say how fruitful it will prove to be in sociology.

An essential point for complexity theory, as it is for **realism**, is that the properties, powers, and effects of the system or entity that emerges from the combination of parts can be both greater than and different from the parts themselves. In *Global Complexity* (2003), John Urry explains this, using the taste of sugar as an example. This taste is simply not present in the prior carbon, hydrogen, and oxygen atoms that need to combine to produce sugar. The flavor of sugar is thus an "emergent" property that results from the relational inter-action between the parts. It is a "nonlinear" conse-quence (one that differs from a "linear," billiard ball, conception of cause and effect, in which nei-ther the ball that is hit nor the ball that hits alters its essential properties) that arises from a transfig-uring combination of individual components.

Complexity theory embraces insights from chaos theory, sharing the latter's emphasis on nonlinear laws, but its focus is ultimately on order rather than anarchy. Chaos theory concentrates on the disruption of order, on turbulent behavior in complex systems in instances where nonlinear laws amplify the smallest of changes in initial conditions, as in the classic example of the flap-ping of a butterfly's wings producing large weather effects on the other side of the world. Complexity theory is more interested in the *com-bination* of order and disorder that is produced by such emergent interactions, stretching away, as they do, across space and time in open and inter-dependent **networks**. Institutionalized social pro-cesses, from households to large international organizations, are in fact conceptualized as islands of order within a sea of disorder. However, even these forms of order themselves, manifested as they are in billions of repeated social actions, are seen to be constantly changing and transmu-ting, as the tiniest of local changes in these repeated, iterated, actions generate "unexpected, unpredictable, and chaotic outcomes, sometimes the opposite of what agents thought they were trying to bring about." Thus there are "pockets" of relative order existing within an overall pat-terning of disorder, and the relations between the two are complex. The effects of any particular localized action within this context is said to be highly contingent; they can be microscopic or global. Relatively ordered systems that appeared robust can turn out to be vulnerable, and the reverse can equally be the case. Metaphors, from attractors and fractals, through implicate orders and self-organization, to autopoeisis and emer-gent orders, have been liberally imported from many natural and social science **paradigms** and combined in an attempt to theorize this sense of "order on the edge of chaos" and guidance without a guide.   ROB STONES

Comte, Auguste (1798–1857)

A grand philosophical synthesizer who coined the term **sociology**, he was the first to attempt its establishment as a science. For Comte, **society** was a rule-governed order of reality, irreducible to the individuals who comprised it, and sociology was a fundamental branch of knowledge which, together with mathematics, astronomy, physics/chemistry, and biology, made up knowledge as a whole. Comte's approach to sociology was com-parative and historical, aiming to understand how each type of society was institutionally con-stituted, and by what logic of development human society passed from one form to another. Comte divided his sociology into a "statics" (laws of order) and a "dynamics" (laws of **progress**). The first stressed the fragile relations between individual and society, and the importance of **family** and **religion** in securing the social tie. The second was organized around a "law of stages" according to which collective mental development, like that of an individual, passed from an infantile "theistic" stage, marked by imaginary causes and anthropo-morphic projection, to a hybrid and abstractly idealizing – "metaphysical" – stage of adolescence, to a maturely "positive" stage where knowledge, understood to be limited, became soundly based on the evidence of the senses.

The rebellious son of a Catholic-royalist family, Comte studied mathematics at the École Polytech-nique in Paris and later transferred to the École du Médecine at Montpellier to study biology. After moving back to Paris he became **Claude Henri de Rouvroy, comte de Saint-Simon**'s private secretary from 1817 until their acrimonious parting in 1824, and then supported himself through writing, private teaching, and a part-time post as a secondary school mathematics examiner. Comte's overall project was to provide the science-based (*positiviste*) intellectual and religious synthesis he saw as needed to complete the work of the French Revolution by establishing a new industrial form of society. He founded the Positiv-ist Society as his main organizational vehicle which, following his conversion in 1854 (associ-ated with the death of his beloved Clothilde de Vaux), assumed the explicit character of a church, with *l'Humanité* as its god and Comte as its *grand-prêtre*.

At the center of Comte's attention was the post-1789 crisis of **industrial society**, with its unre-solved class and ideological warfare between, as he saw it, one-sided partisans of order and **pro-gress**. Comte diagnosed the ongoing turmoil of

French society as a crisis of transition, which he tried to understand and resolve by seeking to synthesize the secular-progressivist viewpoint of Étienne Condillac (1715–80) with the integralist social theorizing of Catholic counter-revolutionaries like Joseph de Maistre (1753–1821). In all this, Comte followed Saint-Simon, but before advocating a specific program of social reform he insisted on the need for preparatory intellectual work, beginning with the establishment of sociology. Sociology would not only provide **politics** with a scientific basis, but was itself an essential element of the new synthesis of scientific knowledge without which the moral order appropriate to industrial society could not be constructed. Comte's six-volume *Système de philosophie positive* (1830–42) carried out both aims. His later work – including *Système de politique positive* (1851–4) as well as his unfinished *Synthèse subjective* – was taken up with further developing his system, now centrally organized around **positivism** as a religious and not just theoretical project, and expanded to include feelings (with altruistic love as the highest), as well as knowledge and action, as organizing categories. Sociology, in this revision, was the theology of Humanism, doctrinally anchoring an elaborate and grandiose plan for the unification of *l'Humanité* through planetary federalism and the establishment of a new post-theistic world religion.

Comte is a relatively unexamined founding figure of modern sociology. Ignored because of his eccentricities, passion for systems, and sectarianism, his thought, nevertheless, has strongly influenced classical and post-classical French sociology, as well as many philosophers and social theorists from **John Stuart Mill** and Friedrich Nietzsche to **Karl Mannheim**, Gaston Bachelard, and **Louis Althusser**.   ANDREW WERNICK

concentric zone theory

– see **urban ecology**.

conjugal roles

This term belongs to those sociological traditions that assumed heterosexual marriage to be the normal status of adult human beings. Despite the fact that this pattern never accorded with all known individuals in any society, it was nevertheless assumed that women and men would internalize sets of social **norms** about the behavior appropriate to **marriage**. Each party was expected to acquire an understanding of both the rights and the responsibilities of their role (for example, the husband to "provide" for his wife and the wife

to agree to sexual relations with her husband) and this understanding could be expected of all married individuals. The theory did not allow for differences in **power** in marriage (for example, the control of husbands over money) nor conflicts that might arise from distinct and conflicting interpretations of a particular conjugal role.

The very concept of a conjugal role, with its implicit fusion of husband and wife (and its equally implicit expectation of the greater power within marriage of the husband – a power reflected in much western law until the 1970s), disappeared when **feminism** challenged the masculinist assumptions of certain aspects of sociology and – with gay and **queer theory** – problematized previously held understandings about **sexuality** and marriage. Empirical studies of the household suggest that many traditional expectations about male and female behavior in marriage/cohabitation persist but that these no longer have the social or legal **legitimacy** which the idea of conjugal roles once enjoyed.

                                                    MARY EVANS

conservatism

This is a political movement – an **ideology** with a set of principles that relate to human nature, **rationality**, and the role of the **state** and nation. It arises historically as a reaction to **liberalism** and a fear that the logic of liberalism points to notions of universal emancipation that conservatives consider unrealistic and utopian.

Conservatism is not, then, a disposition or **attitude** to life. This makes the notion far too broad. It is often said that being a conservative involves a pragmatic view that if things are "not broken, don't fix them." While a conservative disposition may involve an unwillingness to accept change, conservatism as a social and political movement is much more precise than this (see **social movements**).

It is argued – particularly by conservatives who follow the ideas of Edmund Burke (1729–97) – that conservatism is too flexible to be an ideology or an "-ism." But if we use the term ideology to denote merely a system of thought (and not an argument that is inherently dogmatic and authoritarian), then conservatism is an ideology since it has a set of principles, and these principles become clear when the doctrine is challenged.

Conservatism sees people as naturally unequal, and therefore holds that people do not have rights that are universal. Why are they unequal? People have differing innate abilities; they are brought up in differing circumstances; some are more rational than others; they are influenced by the particular nation in which they live; and so forth. It is revealing that, although Margaret Thatcher is often seen as a "neoliberal" and a Whig, rather than a true Tory, she argues that people are inherently unequal. In this, she is impeccably conservative. It is true that "libertarian" conservatives of the New Right pushed further away from traditional conservatism by extolling the virtues of the "pure" **market**. They are better described as anarchists – anarcho-capitalists – rather than conservatives as such.

The notion of difference for conservatives expresses itself in the form of natural hierarchies. Conservatives have interpreted the notion of "nature" to indicate a **differentiation** in roles – between men and women, "civilized" and "uncivilized" – and conservatives, for this reason, have at times opposed **democracy**, sexual (that is, relations between gays and straights) and gender **equality**, the rights of all nations to determine their own destiny, and so on. Nature is an eternal force that promotes hierarchy and differentiation rather than equality and sameness.

Conservatism is not just a philosophy of "**realism**." Conservatives may advocate radical change in egalitarian societies that they deem "unnatural." The status quo deserves to be conserved only if it is conservative!

Although ancient conservatism (as among the Greeks) opposed democracy and the rule of the "free" poor, in its modern form conservatism takes its identity from opposition to the French Revolution. Conservatives were particularly scandalized by the French Revolution because of its beliefs in natural rights and universalistic notions of freedom and equality. These were seen as abstract – that is, propositions that ignored circumstance and context. Notions of emancipation and "perfectibility" are anathema since these concepts ride roughshod over hierarchy and hierarchical differentiation.

Conservatives favor the concepts of **family**, state, **religion**, and **nation**. It is revealing that in the statement so often cited by Margaret Thatcher – "there is no such thing as society" – she does speak of individuals and their families. The family as a patriarchal and hierarchical construct is favored by conservatism since it deemphasizes individual choice and stresses differentiation and **inequality**. This accounts for the fact that there is invariably a tension between conservatism and the market, since market forces are seen as eroding hierarchical communities and traditional relationships. Indeed, **Marxism** draws upon

conservative critiques of the industrial revolution, while demurring at the aristocratic "solutions" to the problem. Charity is preferred to welfare rights since the former relies upon the benevolence of the few rather than the entitlements of the many. Support for private **property** must fit into a hierarchical view of society.

The state is favored as an **institution** (although of course conservatives may disagree on the extent of state intervention) on the grounds that people cannot govern their own lives, but need leaders and authorities to tell them what to do and think. The need to use force as a weapon of last resort accords well with the conservative argument that order cannot rest simply upon rationality or persuasion. Some conservatives do not reject reason so much as a view of reason that is deemed abstract and liberal. Humans are imperfect, and will harm others or themselves unless social pressures including force are brought to bear upon them. Rulers are like parents who have, from time to time, to chastise wayward children.

Religion is important for conservatives, since they are skeptical that people can act in an orderly way without an element of **prejudice** and mysticism. God is conceived as a patriarchal creator, a lord and master whom we should obey instinctively (as we do our parents). National and local sentiments that differentiate insiders from outsiders, are seen as natural and inevitable. Historically, conservatism supported empire and, in the case of Benjamin Disraeli (1804–81), conservatives regarded it as the key to "safely" expanding the vote, and the creation of working-class conservatives. Conservatives are nationalists since they believe that certain nations are "naturally" more preeminent than others and regard any attempt to replace the nation-state with international institutions as dangerous and misguided. Altruism, whether collective or individual, is something that extends only to family, neighbors, and friends. Of course, the conservatives of one nation will differ from those of another nation, even though, ironically, the mutual antagonism arises from broadly shared principles.

It is important to differentiate conservatism from doctrines of the radical right, like **fascism**, even though conservatives often supported fascist regimes on the grounds that they were the only force capable of crushing **socialism** and **trade unions**. Fascism is counterrevolutionary – creating a society that is quite new – whereas conservatism seeks to restore traditional regimes and **values**.

JOHN HOFFMAN

consumer society

This is an ill-defined, but nonetheless popular, concept gesturing towards the enhanced societal importance of the purchase of commodities and their cultural meanings and significance, it implies a comparatively greater role for **consumption** – in contrast with **work and employment**, **religion**, **family**, investment, or **politics** – in determining economic organization, cultural **institutions**, and personal motivations and experience. In general it is a term with negative connotations, appearing mostly in the course of critiques of the misuse of affluence in postwar western countries. It is less frequently used than the term consumerism, which is often considered one of its associated properties. It has received much less systematic scholarly attention than the concept of consumer culture, a term with more ambivalent and polysemic moral connotations and which has produced its own distinctive tradition of research.

John Benson, in *The Rise of Consumer Society in Britain* (1994), summarizes the historians' depictions of consumer societies as those "in which choice and credit are readily available, in which social value is defined in terms of purchasing power and material possessions, and in which there is a desire, above all, for that which is new, modern, exciting and fashionable." But there is no consensus on the defining empirical features of a consumer society. There is also much disagreement about when such a society might have first come into existence, its origins having been dated variously from the seventeenth century to the 1980s.

In **social theory**, the term was promulgated partly in reaction to economistic explanations of **social structure** and **social change** prominent during the period of the revival of neo-Marxism in Europe in the 1960s and 1970s. In 1970, **Jean Baudrillard** published the French version of *The Consumer Society: Myths and Structures* (1970 [trans. 1998]), a reflection on the contemporary role of consumption. Arguing that the productivist concepts of **Marxism** – use-value and exchange-value – were inadequate to capture consumerist tendencies, he directed attention to sign-values. Commodities are given meaning through a logic of signs. The system of consumption was like a symbolic code or language, a basis for communication rather than for the satisfaction of needs. Baudrillard's writing soon after took a postmodernist turn: indeed, consumer society is now considered by some as coterminous with postmodern society. His personal legacy is found more in **cultural studies** of consumption.

Zygmunt Bauman, also a principal theorist of **postmodernity**, is the most eminent recent theorist of consumer society. He maintains that consumption has superseded production as the dominant organizing principle of society. Whereas industrial society engaged with its members in their capacity as workers, the consumer society "engages its members – primarily – in their capacity as consumers. The way present day society shapes up its members is dictated first and foremost by the need to play the role of the consumer" (*Work Consumerism and the New Poor*, 1998). The consumer attitude becomes pervasive; that is to say, people expect that their problems will find a solution, and their needs satisfaction, through their capacity to purchase goods and services. Consumption then becomes the principal means of achieving social integration as a majority of the population are seduced by the promises of consumer freedom.   ALAN WARDE

consumption

A somewhat nebulous concept which has only recently been used extensively by sociologists, it remains primarily a topic of interdisciplinary attention, with the related concept "consumer" more widely deployed, especially in economics, psychology, and marketing. Its growing importance arose from observation that, in a context of material abundance, in **consumer societies**, focal interests in much of **everyday life** had been reoriented towards the possession and use of an increasingly wide range of goods and services, most purchased through the **market**, but also many provided by the **state**.

The concept has two separate historic meanings. The first, and earlier, one had a negative connotation – to destroy, to waste, to use up. In political economy in the eighteenth century, a neutral sense emerged to describe market relationships, hence distinctions between consumer and producer, consumption and production. This second meaning signaled concern with the changing values of items exchanged in market economies, rather than the purposes to which goods and services might be put. These two meanings persist in analytic and normative tension.

Negative attitudes to consumption long prevailed, Puritan and Protestant cultures in particular displaying suspicion of luxury and waste. **T. Veblen** coined the term conspicuous consumption in his *Theory of the Leisure Class* (1899) to describe the competitive pursuit of **social status** through display of possessions by a section of the

American middle class. The **Frankfurt School** were critical of mass consumption for its uniformity, cultural mediocrity, and tendency to induce passivity. Modern modes of consumption were said, variously, to engender narcissistic and hedonistic personalities, to reduce public participation, to be indifferent to the labor conditions under which goods are produced, and to cause environmental damage. Such critiques were often associated with a more general critique of **capitalism**, especially the fundamental process of commodification.

Empirical research about consumption was rare until recently, the main exception being the tradition of research on **poverty** and **inequality** whose roots lie in the nineteenth century. Access to food, drinking water, and adequate health care, still critical issues from the perspective of global inequality, were tackled through state welfare provision in Europe and North America throughout the twentieth century. In recognition, studies of the material circumstances of private households were complemented in the 1970s by analyses of collective consumption, examining the extended role of the state in delivering income, goods, and public services to citizens. If the modern postwar **welfare state** resulted in some overall de-commodification, as provision through the market was replaced or supplemented, the policies of the New Right from the 1980s gradually reversed this. One consequence was described as the creation of consumption cleavages. Some people depend on public provision – for transport, health care, housing, and pensions – while others purchase these services through the market. To the extent that state provision is of poorer quality, which it may be because raising taxation to pay for expensive services for everyone is politically contentious, a new social division (arguably, superseding class) emerges. Those entirely or mostly dependent upon public provision are comparatively disadvantaged, with some demonstrated effect on their voting behavior and political attitudes.

Differential consumption of goods and services became of increasing interest in studies of **social stratification** and cultural sociology in the later twentieth century. **Pierre Bourdieu**'s classic study *Distinction: A Social Critique of the Judgement of Taste* (1979 [trans. 1984]) demonstrated a strong association between class position and cultural taste in France. He showed differences in taste between the commercial and professional bourgeoisie, the intellectual fraction of the middle classes, and the working class. They differed in their preferences, for example for food, interior decoration, and music. Taste was shown to be a weapon in **social conflicts**, as groups and classes towards the top of the social hierarchy used their economic and cultural capital (see **social capital**) to establish and legitimate their privilege.

Another source of inequality is access to positional goods. A positional good is one which delivers value to its user for only so long as not too many others also have it. Thus, the use-value of an automobile decreases the more roads become congested with other motorists. The distinguishing symbolic value of a prestigious, novel, or fashionable product declines as others acquire them.

Symbolically significant items attracting the attention of sociologists of consumption include possessions, cultural knowledge, and cultural participation, as well as preferences. As part of the "cultural turn" in the 1970s, attention was increasingly shifted from the instrumental aspects of consumption, from use-values, to the symbolic dimension of the process, to sign-values. Increasingly, consumption came to be seen as a means by which individuals and **groups** expressed their identities. When combined with diagnoses of postmodern culture, which stressed the fluidity and malleability of identity, consumption came to be understood as a key element in a process of continually renewed self-constitution or self-assembly. The slogan that "there is no choice but to choose," now frequently applied to consumer behavior, captures the sense in which individuals are attributed with an autonomy previously denied both by lack of resources and by the weight of group or community conventions.

In tandem came a reorientation in the ethical evaluation of consumption. Beginning in the 1980s in European sociology and **cultural studies**, the moral condemnation of consumer behavior was increasingly contested. (The USA had earlier, from the late nineteenth century but particularly from the 1930s, a much more optimistic understanding of the cycle of economic growth and increased consumption.) The view of the consumer as a passive victim of processes associated with mass production, of which advertising was the epitome, was countered by demonstrations of how people actively and creatively engaged with goods, appropriating them for their own purposes. The importance of consumer **social movements** and associations, mobilizing in the name of "the consumer" was also increasingly appreciated. And as they flourish, governments claim more frequently to speak and act on behalf of "consumers," rather than of, say, classes, the nation, or citizens, and political discussion increasingly refers to consumer sovereignty, consumer choice, and consumer rights. The discourse of neo-classical economics takes prominence in contemporary practical and ideological understanding of consumption.   ALAN WARDE

consumption cleavages

– see **consumption**.

consumption function

Rarely used in sociology, this term was central to the macro-economics of **J. M. Keynes**, who was concerned with the relationship between expenditure for **consumption** and saving (and thus capital investment) in fluctuations in capitalist economic growth. The consumption function describes the relationship between consumption and **income**, proposing that, all things being equal, consumption increases in proportion to income, though not necessarily instantaneously. Indeed, many conditions must be met for this relationship to hold; stability of prices, rate of replacement of durables, availability of credit, and level of inflation all affect the decision about when and whether to consume. The proportion of income devoted to saving also increases with rise in income; the poor being less able to afford to save, and poor countries therefore having less resources for investment. Subsequent work modifies the Keynesian account. One alternative argues that the relationship holds only in relation to permanent income: if income fluctuates from year to year, expenditure levels will be set in anticipation of long-run and predictable levels of income. This is the permanent income hypothesis associated with Milton Friedman (1912–). Another alternative, the life-cycle hypothesis, maintains that the age of consumers affects their expenditure, with the young and the old spending a larger part of their income on consumption, less on saving, than those in middle age. Such accounts aim to estimate aggregate levels of expenditure and the savings ratio, indicators important to national macro-level economic management but of limited relevance to understanding the social and cultural dimensions of consumption.   ALAN WARDE

control group

This term relates to classic experimental design, such as the pretest–posttest control group design, which may be diagrammed like this:

Group		Pretest	Stimulus	Posttest
Experimental	R	$O_1 \longrightarrow$	$X \longrightarrow$	O_2
Control	R	$O_3 \longrightarrow$		O_4

For a somewhat facetious example, let's say that a researcher suspects that cigarette smoking causes health problems. She or he recruits 10,000 young children, and randomly divides them into 2 groups of 5,000 each. The experimental group is required gradually to take up smoking in childhood, with the amount of cigarettes gradually rising to between 15 and 35 per day. The other 5,000, the control group, are never allowed to smoke. The researcher then monitors the health of the two groups over the decades. If the experimental group tends to develop more medical conditions such as emphysema, lung and throat cancer, and heart disease than the control group, the researcher can conclude that smoking *causes* disease and lowered life expectancy. The experimental and control groups are the same beforehand, during the course of the experiment the only difference is that the experimental group is exposed to the "experimental stimulus" (in this case, smoking), so that any difference in the end must be due to (caused by) the experimental stimulus.

The control group is the group in an experimental design that does not receive the experimental stimulus and hence provides the essential comparator for the experimental group.

The essence of the true experiment is control – the researcher controls everything except the experimental stimulus so that any difference between the experimental and control groups must arise from the experimental stimulus. The main advantage of the randomized experiment is that, if it is carried out correctly, the researcher can infer causality.

     BERNADETTE HAYES AND ROBERT MILLER

convergence

Identifying a tendency for societies to become more alike, in principle on any institutional dimension, the term "convergence" has most usually been applied to macro-economic and political trends, most notably in the work of Clark Kerr, John T. Dunlop, Frederick Harbison, and Charles Myers in *Industrialism and Industrial Man* (1960). Their convergence thesis, an account of social development much debated in the 1960s and 1970s, maintained that there was a tendency for industrializing countries to develop similar institutional arrangements. They argued that "industrial systems, regardless of the cultural background out of which they emerge and the path they originally follow, tend to become more alike over an extended period of time" and that they move towards a "pluralistic industrialism" where **power** is shared between **state**, **firms**, and individuals. Consciously in opposition to Marxist and conflict theoretical accounts of **social structure**, the convergence thesis envisaged greater harmony and consensus as industrialization progressed (see **industrial society**). Driven by the so-called "logic of Industrial Society industrialism," causal priority was given to **technology** and the requirements of the industrial system. It was anticipated that industrialization would produce similar patterns of division of **labor** and **industrial relations**, the separation of households from work, **urbanization**, with **rationalization** spreading from the economic sphere into other realms of social life. Hence, the social and cultural differences between pre-industrial societies would reduce. In many ways, this amounted to a prediction that all countries would eventually converge on a pattern established by the modern societies of the western world. This quasi-evolutionary account has not stood the test of time. It has been criticized for inadequacies of theoretical explanation; for its propensity to economic and technological determinism; for the implication that there is only one possible direction for the path to economic development, that taken in Europe and North America; and for lack of clarity as to whether it is industrialism rather than **capitalism** that has the effects detected. Empirically, while industrial societies do have features in common, they still exhibit very considerable variation in their economic, social, and political arrangements. It is currently more common to consider instead varieties of capitalism, seeing the prior institutional arrangements of countries as laying down different paths of development. Nor does it appear that material **inequalities** between countries are diminishing, another condition which would have to be met in order to achieve convergence. Though the convergence thesis is no longer invoked, some accounts of the effects of **globalization** make similar projections regarding the homogenization of culture, based on the worldwide diffusion of the production activities of large corporations.   ALAN WARDE

conversation analysis

A field of study concerned with the **norms**, practices, and competences underlying the organiza-tion of social **interaction**, conversation analysis (CA), notwithstanding the name, is concerned with all forms of spoken interaction, including not only everyday conversations between friends and acquaintances, but also interactions in medical, educational, mass media, and sociolegal contexts, "monologic" interactions such as lecturing or speech-making, and technologically complex interactions such as web-based multiparty communication. Originating within sociology in the 1960s and then developing with the privately circulated lectures of **Harvey Sacks** in 1992, CA has grown into a field of research that is practiced worldwide.

CA emerged from two intellectual streams in sociology. The first is based on **Émile Durkheim** and derives most proximately from the work of **Erving Goffman**, who argued that social interaction constitutes a distinct institutional order comprising normative rights and obligations that regulate interaction, and that function in broad independence from the social, psychological, and motivational characteristics of persons. The second is **Harold Garfinkel**'s **ethnomethodology**. This stresses the contingent and socially constructed nature both of action and of the understanding of action, and the role of shared methods in the production, recognition, and shared understanding of joint activities. The CA perspective was formed from a fusion of these two perspectives by H. Sacks and Emmanuel Schegloff, who were in direct contact with their originators. Within CA, the Goffmanian interaction order structures the production, recognition, and analysis of action as it unfolds in real time, through the use of shared methods or practices. This process (and its analysis) are possible because participants reflexively display their analyses of one another's conduct in each successive contribution to interaction. Correlative to this, CA starts from the perspective that (contra both Noam Chomsky and **Talcott Parsons**) the details of conduct in interaction are highly organized and orderly and, indeed, that the specificity of meaning and understanding in interaction would be impossible without this orderliness.

CA research centers on the analysis of audio- or video-recorded naturally occurring interaction. Recording is essential because no other form of data retrieval is sufficiently detailed and accurate. Naturally occurring interaction is essential because other forms of interaction – for example, scripted theatre, role playing, or interaction in experimental contexts – are designed in terms of the designer's beliefs about interaction which bear an unknown relationship to the interaction order itself. Accordingly, CA practitioners regard naturally occurring interaction as the basic data for the analysis of interactional structure and process.

CA proceeds at several analytic levels. At the most basic level, CA looks for patterns in social interaction for evidence of practices of conduct that evidence systematic design. To be identified as a practice, particular elements of conduct must be recurrent, specifically situated, and attract responses that discriminate them from related or similar practices. A central feature of this procedure is that the analysis of the practices used to perform a social action (for example, prefacing an answer to a question with "oh," or identifying a co-interactant by name in the course of a turn) can be validated through the examination of others' responses.

Second, CA focuses on sequences of actions. In performing some current action, participants normally project (empirically) and require (normatively) the production of a "next" action, or range of possible "next" actions, to be done by another participant. Moreover, in constructing a turn at talk, they normally address themselves to immediately preceding talk, and design their contributions in ways that exploit this basic positioning. By the production of next actions, participants show an understanding of a prior action and do so at a multiplicity of levels – for example, by an "acceptance," an actor can show an understanding that the prior turn was possibly complete, that it was addressed to them, that it was an action of a particular type (e.g. an invitation), and so on. Within this framework, the grasp of a "next" action within a stream of interactional projects, the production of that action, and its interpretation by the previous speaker are the products of a common set of socially shared practices. CA analyses are thus simultaneously analyses of action, context management, and intersubjectivity, because all three of these features are simultaneously, if tacitly, the objects of the actors' actions.

At a third level, practices cohere at various levels of systemic organization. For example, the turn-taking system for conversation is composed of sets of practices for turn construction and turn allocation. The question–answer pair is organized by a large number of practices that structure the timing and internal organization of responses to maximize social solidarity. Evaluations of states of affairs are structured by a range of practices through which people manage the relative priority of their rights to evaluate them, and so on.

Based on this framework, CA has developed as an empirical discipline focused on a range of domains of interactional conduct, including turn-taking (the allocation of opportunities to speak among participants), the organization of conversational sequences, the internal structuring of turns at talk and the formation of actions, the organization of repair (dealing with difficulties in speaking, hearing, and understanding talk), story-telling and narrative, prosody, and body behavior.

Implicit in CA's sequential perspective is the idea that social action is both context-shaped and context-renewing, and that social context is not a simple "container" of social interaction, but rather something that is dynamically created, sustained, and altered across an interaction's course. Similar conclusions hold for the relevant social identities of the participants, which are also activated, sustained, or adjusted on a temporally contingent basis. This perspective has generated a growing CA research presence in the analysis of social **institutions**. Some of this research has investigated practices, sequences, and organizations that are earmarks of particular institutions or their tasks. Much of this work has been descriptive and naturalistic, but it has also been used in explanatory or predictive multivariate models. Because these analyses are internally valid in an "emic" sense, they have proved to be robust predictors of conduct, attitudes, and social outcomes, and this use of CA is likely to grow in the future.

JOHN HERITAGE

Cooley, Charles Horton (1864–1929)

Rooted near his birthplace by the University of Michigan campus, Cooley led an uneventful life as an eccentric, renowned professor. A student of John Dewey, he helped introduce **pragmatist** ideas into American sociology.

Cooley's *Human Nature and the Social Order* (1902) set forth his famous notion of the "looking-glass self" – that the individual's sense of **self** is "mirrored" through others. He propounded this against prevailing utilitarian assumptions of the self as a natural given. His view of the self as a social product – that individual and society are not separable, but different aspects of the same thing – became a key stimulus, along with ideas of **George Herbert Mead**, to **symbolic interactionism**. Relatedly, Cooley called on sociologists to employ an empirical method he called sympathetic introspection – investigating the consciousness of actors by putting oneself in their place. This formulation anticipated by generations the late psychoanalytic catchword of "empathic introspection."

In *Social Organization: A Study of the Larger Mind* (1909), Cooley elaborated another key concept, the primary **group**, a core process at the heart of institutions where close, intimate, face-to-face interactions establish common **symbols** and meanings. His *Social Process* (1918) emphasized how human plasticity leads to **social change** as a never-ending but fragile process of reciprocal change in self, primary group, and social definitions. His pragmatist conception of the creative potential of social disorganization held that social dissolution of traditions generates virtues as well as vices.

Other works include *Life and the Student: Roadside Notes on Human Nature, Society, and Letters* (1927) and posthumous papers, *Sociological Theory and Social Research* (1930). A volume of selected writings, *On Self and Social Organization* (1998), was edited by Hans-Joachim Schubert, who wrote an authoritative intellectual biography.   DONALD LEVINE

corporate crime

– see **crime**.

correlation

Used in a number of more or less precisely defined senses in sociology, in its loosest sense, this means that two variables are related. So, if we state that longevity is positively correlated with **social status**, then we are saying that higher-status people in any society live longer than lower-status individuals. A negative or inverse correlation would mean that as one variable increases, the other decreases. So, cigarette smoking and longevity are negatively correlated.

In its stricter sense, correlation is defined as a statistical test to determine whether two variables are related. There are a number of different classes of **statistic**, and the choice of the appropriate type of correlation to calculate is determined by the nature of the **data**, and whether it is parametric or non-parametric.

Knowing that two things are correlated is itself interesting, but usually social scientists want to go beyond simple correlation and investigate cause before they can really state that they have started to understand the relationship between two variables. Just the fact that two variables are correlated tells us little about the causal relationships between them. For instance, there is a correlation between the affluence of a country and the proportion of lawyers in the population. Is this because people like the services of lawyers, so as

they get richer they can afford more of the good things in life like ice cream and lawyers? Or is it because lawyers make an **economy** operate more efficiently, so that countries with more lawyers become richer? Or is the relationship spurious, and both lawyers and affluence are by-products of a certain type of **capitalism**? We would need some more complex form of analysis than simply calculating the correlation to be able to understand that one!   BRENDAN J. BURCHELL

Coser, Lewis A. (1913–2003)

Born Ludwig Cohen in Berlin, Coser left for Paris in 1913, where he studied comparative literature and sociology. He was arrested by the French government in 1940, but eventually escaped, emigrating to the United States in 1941, where he changed his family name to Coser. Under the guidance of **Robert Merton** and **Paul Lazarsfeld**, he obtained his doctorate from Columbia University. In the postwar period, he became a member of the circle of New York **intellectuals** and published critical articles in *Partisan Review, Commentary*, and the *Nation*, and with Irving Howe and others he founded *Dissent*, for which he served as co-editor. He founded the sociology department at Brandeis University and taught there for fifteen years, before moving to the University of New York – Stony Brook, where he remained until his retirement. He was the President of the Society for the Study of Social Problems in 1967–8. He was President of the American Sociological Association in 1975. Coser received an honorary degree from the Humboldt University in Berlin in 1994.

Coser is well known for his contributions to the history of sociological theory, including *Men of Ideas* (1970) and *Masters of Sociological Thought. Ideas in Historical and Social Context* (1971). He edited, with Bernard Rosenberg, *Sociological Theory* (1957). He contributed to the study of **social conflict** in *The Functions of Social Conflict* (1956). The principal influences behind Coser's sociology were **Max Weber** and **Georg Simmel** who inspired his approach to classical sociological theory, but it was Simmel in particular who shaped his study of social conflict. Coser was concerned by the process of professionalization in American sociology, which had to some extent undermined the importance of sociology as social criticism. He feared that the dominance of **empiricism** and methods would erode the substance and significance of sociological investigation. Coser was an influential teacher of sociology, as illustrated in his *Sociology Through Literature* (1963).

BRYAN S. TURNER

cosmopolitan sociology

With the development of **globalization**, critics of traditional **sociology** have argued that it was implicitly concerned with studying societies that were nation **states**, and hence, to become more relevant to a global world, sociology would have to change direction and become more cosmopolitan. The conventional methodologies that employed, for example, comparative and historical research could not understand global flows of goods and communication where national boundaries are of declining relevance. **Ulrich Beck** (2000) in *Want is Globalization?* has spoken of the emergence of a cosmopolitan vision in the evolution of transnational society, calling for sociology to embrace a global understanding of an open world horizon. A similar stance has been taken by **Anthony Giddens** in *The Consequences of Modernity* (1990) where he argued that classical sociology had been too much focused on the **social structures** of the nation-state, which was implicitly but inadequately equated to the universalistic study of society.

There are at least three issues which the notion of cosmopolitan society raises. The first is possibly trivial, namely, did traditional sociology make an unwarranted equation of society with nation-state? For example, while anthropological research had the consequence of promoting the idea of human diversity, nineteenth-century sociology as a product of the **Enlightenment** embraced the idea of a unified science of society. **Claude Saint-Simon** and **Auguste Comte** (1798–1857) shared a common evolutionary view of society in which the new industrialism would bring about the destruction of Christian **religion**, but Comte saw sociology as a new science – a new "religion of humanity." Positivist sociology promoted the idea of **socialism** to transcend both the **social class** divisions of **capitalism** and the Darwinian struggle of the races. **Émile Durkheim**, as the heir of Saint-Simon and Comte, saw the moral dimension of socialism as a solution to the **individualism** and **anomie** of modern society. For Durkheim, the role of the **state** was to provide some moral guidance to society to compensate for the instability that was engendered by the **market** in a capitalist environment. Because Durkheim belonged to the Enlightenment tradition, his view of history was universalistic, and, while he was influenced by British anthropology in *The Elementary Forms of the Religious Life* (1912 [trans. 1954]), his thought did not incline towards **cultural relativism**. In *Professional Ethics and Civic Morals* (1992) he defended the

idea of "world patriotism" against the narrow **nationalism** of his day. It can also be argued that the political economy of **Karl Marx** sought to understand the global economic process of capitalism, and through **communism** developed a socialist version of cosmopolitanism.

Second, the globalization thesis may often underestimate the resilience of the sovereignty of the nation-state, and hence sociologists may be justified in concentrating on the United States or United Kingdom or France rather than on global **networks**. There is little evidence that the growth of global networks of interaction and communication have seriously undermined the political sovereignty of states, or that there is any prospect of global governance.

Finally, it raises methodological problems about how exactly sociologists might study global society. While sociology has developed a **methodology** that is relevant, for example, to the study of social **groups**, **cities**, and societies, we have yet to develop adequate methodologies relevant to global society. The study of the internet is, of course, one promising area of research, and sociologists – for example, in Chris Mann and Fiona Stewart's *Internet Communication and Qualitative Research* (2000) – have started to develop the opportunities made possible by electronic communication systems.

Despite these criticisms, cosmopolitanism will become an important research topic in sociology, and the moral implications of cosmopolitan duties will have important consequences for the evolution of sociology, which to some extent remains bound within its national frameworks, despite the emergence, for example, of the International Sociological Association and the International Institute of Sociology. While globalization is influencing the intellectual development of sociology, the American Sociological Association remains the dominant national institution, and publishing houses still focus on the publication of work that is relevant to the English-speaking, western world.

BRYAN S. TURNER

cosmopolitanism

Historically cosmopolitanism has two related meanings. Firstly, a cosmopolitan is someone who embraces plurality and difference. In this respect, modern cities are often seen as providing the backdrop for the development of cosmopolitan sensibilities in that they house a number of distinctive **cultures**, **ethnic groups**, and **lifestyles**. A cosmopolitan is a polyglot who is able to move comfortably within multiple and diverse communities, while resisting the temptation to search for a purer and less complex identity. Cosmopolitan selves and communities, in this understanding, will thrive when the right to be different is respected. Second, a cosmopolitan is literally a citizen of the world. This refers to a set of perspectives that have sought to jettison viewpoints that are solely determined by the **nation**, or their geographical standing within the world.

The political philosophy of Immanuel Kant (1724–1804) argued that a cosmopolitan **democracy** should be developed to replace the law of nations with a genuinely morally binding international law. For Kant the spread of commerce and principles of republicanism could help foster cosmopolitan sentiments. Kant's vision of a peaceful cosmopolitan order based upon the obligation on states to settle their differences through the court of law has gained a new legitimacy in the twentieth century with the founding of the United Nations and the European Union.

More recently a number of political philosophers have argued that Kant's earlier vision can be revised to provide a new critical politics for an increasingly global age. A cosmopolitan political response is required where national politics has lost much of its power but little of its influence. **Globalization** has undermined the operation of national democracies as they are increasingly unable to control the flow of **money**, refugees, and asylum seekers, viruses, media images, and ideas and perspectives. Many have argued that to begin to address these problems requires the construction of overlapping forms of political community connecting citizens into local, national, regional, and global forms of government. The development of cosmopolitan perspectives is fostered by the growing acceptance that many of the problems that face the world's citizens cannot be resolved by individual states and are shared problems. The cosmopolitan project seeks to revive democracy in an age where it is increasingly under threat.

There are three main criticisms of these arguments. (1) Such proposals are part of the liberal enterprise of state building and fail to appreciate the power of strategic interests apparent on the global stage. In this understanding, many have been concerned that the United States (the world's last remaining super power) will refuse, and even try to subvert, cosmopolitan institutions. (2) Cosmopolitan politics is an elite top-down version of politics that will inevitably come to represent the interests of the powerful rather than more "ordinary" or excluded populations. In this respect, some have suggested that we focus upon the emergence of cosmopolitanism from below in respect of nongovernmental organizations (NGOs). (3) Finally, some have been concerned that the two meanings of cosmopolitanism are not compatible with one another. Despite the acceptance of universal **human rights**, the rule of law, and democracy, many communities remain excluded from participatory forms of democracy. Here there is a concern that universal rules fail to appreciate the difference in people's identities.

NICK STEVENSON

counterfactual

– see **explanation**.

credentialism

"Credentials" are the key factors at the interface between systems of **education** and systems of employment. **Randall Collins**'s *The Credential Society* (1979) was an extension of his doctoral thesis on "*Education and Employment*" which coincided closely with the publication in 1967 by **Peter M. Blau** and O. D. Duncan of *The American Occupational Structure*. Belief in the acquisition of credentials – educationally tested and graded capacities to perform occupationally in commensurately graded employment tasks – is a by-product of a technocratic model of the social function of **education**. As Collins succinctly represented it, the model assumes that "Education prepares students in the skills necessary for work, and skills are the main determinant of occupational success . . . Hence education determines success." Collins perceived that the **de-schooling** movement was an attempt to liberate education from credentialism, and that the early work of **Pierre Bourdieu** on social reproduction (which he linked with that of **Louis Althusser** on the reproduction of the class relations of capitalism) was also an attempt to discredit the claims of technocratic and meritocratic thinking. Nevertheless, neither critique sufficiently emphasized the importance of cultural markets in distorting the transmission of occupational opportunities. Collins argued that even the civil rights movement in the United States failed to destroy the supposed legitimacy of an a-cultural model of educational and occupational allocation. Disadvantaged groups sought to work the system of credentialism, generating an inflation of grades dubiously related to levels of educational achievement.

Collins argued that in the 1960s the credential system went into a state of "explicit crisis." He suggested that the credential system was caught between opposing forces. On one side the system had become central to sustaining an **economy** of excess productive capacity. On the other side, it had become very expensive and relatively unrewarding for many individual investors. A balance remained possible but there was a potential crisis on either side. In the first instance, too much growth in the credential market generates disillusion and withdrawal of material investment, while, in the second, too little investment produces economic depression.

He suggested that different ideological positions had been adopted about credentialism. The basic opposition was between what he called "credential **capitalism**" and "credential **socialism**," but pressure from ethnic groups stimulated "ethnic-patrimonial" or "patronage" credentialism which, in turn, provoked "credential **fascism**" in reaction. He characterized "de-schooling" as a form of "credential radicalism" but his view was that there were only two "honest and realistic" positions: either "credential Keynesianism" which would recognize that education "creates an artificial credential currency" which does not assume any precise occupational purchasing power, or, preferably, "credential abolitionism" which would force education to re-emphasize its intrinsic, rather than instrumental, value.   DEREK ROBBINS

crime

Societies have been concerned about behavioral expectations, disruptions to social order, and the protection of the natural flow of life since ancient times. Ancient Babylon's Code of Hammurabi is the earliest evidence of a society that clearly identified a set of rules governing social life. King Hammurabi (1795–1750 BC) established a historical precedent for other societies to follow. By drawing notice to his subjects of what he saw as acceptable behavior, he laid the foundation for a more organized, purposeful, and civilized social order. With varying degrees of formalization and success, rulers have endeavored to protect their kingdoms, albeit the **wealth** and **power** of monarchs have frequently superseded the interests and protection of their citizens. The key issue here is that rules governing social life have been part of the social order of human communities since recorded time. Violations of these codes of conduct have also been part of the social fabric and social experience since humans began living in social **groups**.

Hammurabi was no doubt a prescient ruler. There was a lengthy period between his rule and the eventual codification of conduct into formal criminal and procedural laws. Before the development of such formalized codes, wrongs were dealt with on an individual level. The **norm** was for aggrieved parties to settle disputes or to right wrongs between themselves. However, as societies became more densely populated, urbanized, and organized, behaviors that violated the sensitivities of the collective were handled more formally and eventually judiciously. Codification of unacceptable behavior became necessary. This formalization of expectations established the boundaries of acceptable behavior by which citizens were to abide. These violations of the social order have evolved into what is today referred to as "crime."

Jay Albanese in *Criminal Justice* (2002: 13) asserts that "[c]rime is a natural phenomenon, because people have different levels of attachments, motivation, and virtue." He was, no doubt, building on the notion first put forward by **Émile Durkheim**. Crime, Durkheim observed, is present in all societies and is seen as an integral part of "healthy" communities. In the chapter on "The Normal and the Pathological" in *The Rules of Sociological Method* (1895 [trans. 1958]), Durkheim asserted that "what is normal, simply, is the existence of criminality, provided that it attains and does not exceed, for each social type, a certain level." He further defined crime as being actions that offend certain very strongly held "collective sentiments" (1958: 67). What makes crime "normal" for Durkheim and Albanese is society's inability to be exempt from it. In other words, all societies experience transgressions, albeit in varying forms and varying levels of severity. The mere presence of crime across time and place makes it a normal and expected part of group living.

Interestingly, once a society can identify tangibly those actions that are disruptive, the presence of crime can play a unifying role. For example, if particular behaviors are seen as offensive or threatening the greater social order, those behaviors will be barred, thus strengthening what a group believes to be important defining characteristics of its culture. Violations that offend core values and beliefs of a collectivity become the foundations for the formalization of codes of conduct at a given point in time and place. The critical issue here is that the behavior must offend collective sentiments rather than the sentiments of an individual, thus differentiating between civil and criminal wrongs.

While violations of social norms are a constant in all societies, the term "crime" is stubbornly recalcitrant to precise definition. It is a complex concept that has been the focus of criminological and juridical research for many centuries. Crime is a concept whose definition varies across time and place. The definition is dependent upon perspective, viewpoint, and perception. Within **criminology**, there exist several competing theoretical foundations, all of which construct different and distinctive definitions of crime.

As with any element of social science, context, perspective, and **ideology** play a significant part in the formulation of concepts, variables, and their operational definition. Crime is a social construct that reflects normative **values**, customs, mores, and **tradition** of a given society at a given point in time. Definitions of crime are also reflected in the political values and historical foundations of a social system. For example, the medieval church played an important and instrumental role in shaping and monitoring the **morality** of society, which in turn shaped what was defined as criminal. For example, in seventeenth-century Europe, the criminality of witchcraft was constructed by political leaders who were profoundly influenced by the religious community. The practices of witchcraft and sorcery were feared and regarded as a serious crime against the community, and as a result punishments were ultimately severe. Most jurisdictions have since abolished their statutes and laws pertaining to witchcraft with the development of **secularization**.

Another example of how community values shape the definition of crime is the specific crime of theft. In western societies, theft is commonly included in criminal statutes. However, in some indigenous communities, there is no recognizable crime of theft owing to a longstanding tradition of community ownership. Because there is no legal tradition of private property, there is no corresponding formulation of a crime of theft. Finally, religious doctrine also influences criminological and juridical perspectives on what is acceptable behavior and what constitutes a crime. For example, the holy law of Islam, the Shari'a, is deeply rooted in the religious practices and institutions of Muslim societies, and the basic assumptions of the various schools of religious law are reflected in the criminal codes of many Middle Eastern and Asian societies today. However, in the United States and other western societies, there exists a philosophical and juridical doctrine that mandates the separation of church and state. The result is that many beliefs and activities that are offensive to religious groups are not necessarily criminalized.

Three perspectives have been prominent in the definition of crime, namely the legalistic approach, conduct norm, and conflict perspectives. While there are other perspectives – as described, for example, in John Hagan, *Modern Criminology: Crime, Criminal Behavior and Its Control* (1987) – these three approaches have been at the intellectual core of the definitional debate for some decades. Undoubtedly, criminologists and others who study crime will never come to any firm agreement or lasting consensus as to what exactly constitutes a criminal act. Nevertheless, these perspectives or approaches do yield some important starting points.

Somewhat naively, crime has been taken for granted as simply being acts that violate criminal law, the basis for the legalistic perspective. William L. Marshall and William L. Clark in their essay on "The Legal Definition of Crime and Criminals," in Marvin E. Wolfgang, Leonard Savitz, and Norman Johnston (eds.), *The Sociology of Crime and Delinquency* (1962: 14), state very clearly that "crime is an act or omission prohibited by public law for the protection of the public, and made punishable by the state in a judicial proceeding in its own name." Inherent in this perspective is the fact that laws are based on consensus. There is general agreement as to what behaviors are repugnant and unacceptable. These are then reflected in substantive criminal law. Crime is, therefore, a function of beliefs and morality. Those actions which violate morality and general social mores become crimes and are constrained by law. In theory these laws are to be applicable to all members of society, regardless of **social class** and the personal attributes of individuals.

Marshall and Clark clarify the argument that crimes are public wrongs in contrast to civil injuries, which involve individual victimization. These authors' views on the legal framework of crime are not uncommon. In fact, from the Classical School through to the 1970s the legalistic approach has existed somewhat in isolation, and has gone without systematic challenge. More simply put, crime, according to the legal approach, is any behavior prohibited by criminal law. Elements that constitute criminal behavior and that are codified in the law change over time. This problem of **social change** emerges from the fact that norms, values, and beliefs evolve in a given social context. Interestingly, at various points in time, the norms and values of a given society may well conflict with legal statutes. For example, in the United States during the 1920s, national and local laws prohibited the sale, distribution, and manufacture of alcoholic beverages. However, the existing laws did not quench the public demand for alcohol. Public demand for alcoholic drinks is believed to have contributed to the emergence and proliferation of organized criminal **gangs**. In the 1930s, social pressure forced the US government to reconsider its stance, which led to the decriminalization of laws pertaining to the sale, transportation, and manufacture of alcohol.

Two principles of law are associated with the legalistic approach. Under common law, the basis for many western legal systems, crimes are classified as either *mala in se* (evil in and of itself) or *mala prohibita* (proscribed by law). Additionally, under the legalistic approach, for a crime to occur, it must have three elements. The first feature of any crime is that of a guilty act (*actus reus*). The second feature is that of a guilty mind (*mens rea*). Finally, both of these must concur – the criminal act must converge with a culpable mental state.

Crimes are generally categorized as felonies, misdemeanors, and acts of treason. Felonies are the more serious transgressions and are usually punishable by imprisonment for over a year. Misdemeanors are considered less serious and punishments range from community-based sanctions through to jail time for less than one year. Treason is an act against the **state**, thus reflected in Federal Law, although some state constitutions and statutes do contain treason definitions and provisions.

While seemingly accurate, the legalistic perspective does not address the complexities and intricacies of the conceptual problems surrounding crime. Therefore the reliance on the legalistic aspect only tells a partial story.

The conduct norm model for defining crime is perhaps best described in Thorsten Sellin's *Culture Conflict and Crime* (1938). He postulated that the norms and values of the dominant social class are reflected in criminal law. There is, as a result, a built-in opportunity for disagreement and conflict between the dominant group and subordinate sections of society. Frequently, splinter groups emerge that are based on racial or ethnic criteria of membership, and as a result they formulate their own **subcultures**. From this situation, a set of conduct norms evolve based on their own values, beliefs, and interests. Therefore, society can be regarded as a collection of diverse groups that compete for scarce resources because they possess conflicting interests and politics. The perspective is built around a division between the conflicting interests and resources of dominant elites and those of marginalized social groups, thus setting the stage for constant conflict.

Closely aligned to the conflict school of criminology, definitions of crime within the conduct norm perspective are constructed in the interests of the dominant class. In other words, the group exercises power in such a manner as to construct criminal laws to reflect their economic and social position and interests. Furthermore, laws are unevenly applied in society. The poor and the underclass are most susceptible to unequal and unfair practices and treatment before the law. Examples of this inequality are the harsh treatment and punishments handed down for street crime, traditionally attributed to offenders from the poor and the underclass segments of society. White-collar offences, such as embezzlement and insider trading, have far-reaching fiduciary losses and long-term implications for their victims, but they carry with them relatively minor penalties in comparison to street crimes. However, the treatment of professional and business leaders in the Enron accounting scandals in the United States may suggest a change in legal attitudes towards such business crimes.

According to the conduct norm perspective, definitions of crime are controlled by the wealthy and powerful people of position, not from the broad consensus of society. Therefore, crime is a political concept designed to protect the powerful members of the ruling class. According to this perspective, "real" crimes include economic and political domination, poor and inadequate working conditions, violations of human rights as reflected by **racism**, **sexism**, and **imperialism**, and inadequate opportunities for education, housing, and health care, and unequal participation in the political process.

Along with the conflict and conduct norm perspectives, the symbolic interactionist perspective began to challenge the legalistic perspective from the 1970s. The interactionist perspective in defining crime has its roots in the works of **George Herbert Mead**, **Charles Horton Cooley**, and **William I. Thomas**. The tenets of this intellectual tradition hold that people act in accordance to their subjective interpretation of social reality, through which they assign meaning to things and events. Individuals learn the meaning of reality based on the ways in which others react, either negatively or positively, towards those social definitions. From this reaction, a person re-evaluates and interprets his or her own behavior in accordance with the meaning and symbols they have learned from others.

The definition of crime reflects the preferences and opinions of people who hold social power in a given area. These individuals use their influence to impose definitions of "right" and "wrong," "acceptable" or "unacceptable," on the rest of the population. As a result, criminals are those whom society labels as undesirable or as outcasts. The reason for this label is that they have behaved in a manner counter to the norms and values of the rest of the group. Crimes are outlawed because society or the group defines them as such, not necessarily because they are evil in and of themselves.

The interactionist perspective is similar to the conflict tradition in that people of influence determine the boundaries of acceptable conduct. However, unlike the conflict school, the interactionists in criminology do not assume that the exploitative relations of capitalist society are the chief determinant of the disparity. By contrast, interactionists argue that the boundaries of behavior are determined by moral crusaders, and when morality shifts, so too do the criminal laws. Larry Siegel sums up the interactionists' definition of crime in *Criminology* (2000: 20) by concluding that "[c]rime is a violation of society rules of behavior as interpreted and expressed by a criminal legal code created by people holding social and political power."

Hagan in *Modern Criminology* (1987) identifies several additional ways in which the term crime can be defined. These definitions include: the formal legal; social harm; cross-cultural universal norm; labeling; human rights; and human diversity. In line with the legalistic perspective, the formal legal definition holds that whatever the state defines as being criminal constitutes a crime. Social harm, according to Hagan, includes both civil wrongs (disputes between individuals) and criminal actions (disputes between the state and the individual). The universalistic interpretation of crime assumes that there is no variation in different societies. For example, the crime of murder is a universal violation in all societies. A crime can only exist when a society reacts to the repulsiveness of its consequences. The foundation of the labeling perspective therefore regards social reaction to the offensive action as the most critical issue. The most comprehensive way to define crime is Hagan's human rights perspective, in which any action that violates an individual's human rights would constitute a crime. This would include acts of oppression, sexism, and racism. Finally, Hagan defines crime via a human diversity approach. Related to the human rights perspective, an action is a crime as a consequence of the social deprivations that arise from oppressive and discriminatory situations.

The determination of what exactly constitutes a crime has far-reaching consequences. It is not just the philosophical considerations that are taken into account when trying to set the boundaries for acceptable and unacceptable social behavior. The process of defining a behavior as criminal is left to the legal scholars and criminologists to determine. However, the practical ramifications are important for policymakers. How a society decides to respond to and enforce the laws is somewhat dependent on the perceived **legitimacy** of the existing law. For example, laws that prohibit the personal use of marijuana have not been enforced to the full extent that law permits. Rather, the law enforcement community, in some areas, has been implicitly tolerant of the infraction, thus giving it a degree of legitimacy.

The study of crime has captured the attention of many different academic fields. Many schools of criminology have emerged over the past decades, and in the social sciences the study of crime is multidisciplinary, including sociology, psychology, biology, economics, ecology, and law. In historical terms, criminology is a new member of the social sciences. Within these **social sciences**, countless research programs have been conducted over the decades in order to understand the process of criminality, and how and why crime occurs. The search for causal answers to the existence of crime has covered free-will arguments, biological and genetic causes, psychological and sociological variables, and more recently environmental influences.

Eugene McLaughlin, John Muncie, and Gordon Hughes in *Criminological Perspectives* (2005: 8–9) claim that crime is a "social fact." Crime is a product of free will, meaning that offenders make rational choices when deciding to engage in specific criminal behaviors. This viewpoint is compatible with the classical school of criminology's founding fathers. Cesare Beccaria (1738–94), a utilitarian philosopher, believed that people exercise free will when they choose to engage in any form of behavior, including criminal actions. He also argued that people's choices could be influenced by the level of the corresponding punishment, which should be proportionate, swift, severe, and certain. Another juridical philosopher, Jeremy Bentham (1748–1832) postulated that humans considered several factors before engaging in a particular behavior. Specifically, the hedonistic or "felicific calculus" measured various aspects of pleasure and pain, thus providing a framework for decisionmaking. Simply stated, if the pleasure gained from engaging in the activity outweighs the pain associated with it, the person will engage in the crime. Derek Cornish and Ronald V. Clarke in *The Reasoning Criminal: Rational Choice Perspectives on Offending* (1986) further developed the idea of a rational criminal by exploring the decisionmaking process of contemporary offenders. Deciding on whether or not to engage in crime, the person considers personal circumstances and motivations, such as the need for money, revenge, in relation to situational constraints or opportunities, for example the degree to which a target is protected, secure, or monitored. The decision to commit the crime will take into account the risks of apprehension and the threat of punishment against the benefits of partaking in the activity. It is a matter of personal choice, given the availability of attendant information.

Since the earliest foundations of criminology, biological causes of crime have also been assessed, especially in the debate about "criminal types." Cesare Lombroso (1836–1909) studied physical attributes of offenders in Italian prisons and concluded that there were indeed "born criminals." Other biologically related studies included works by Enrico Ferri (1856–1929) and William Sheldon (1898–1977). In contemporary criminology, there is a renewed interest in turning to genetics in the explanation of crime. In particular, studies have focused on chromosomal abnormalities, chemical imbalances, and nutritional deficiencies among offenders. The research results of this approach are mixed and inconclusive in their findings, but the resurgence in biological theories has been significant in modern criminology. The search for a "criminal gene" is perhaps the most prominent feature of this resurgence.

Psychological approaches to the study of crime examine how and why the mind operates and therefore influences individuals to commit crime. Historically, the ideas of **Sigmund Freud** were influential in suggesting a variety of conditions, such as the weakened ego or superego structures, that fail to contain the urges of the id, in the explanation of criminal behavior. In addition to the psychoanalytical approach, cognitive theories approach crime slightly differently. Cognitive theorists believe that crime occurs as a result of a particular pattern of thinking, which often includes short-term, self-indulgent, and self-gratifying actions in the absence of thoughts about how the behavior may affect others.

The sociological approach to crime is by far the most common and popular among those available. These sociological approaches evolved out of the weakness of biological and psychological theories in their ability to describe and explain fully the occurrence of crime. Jay Albanese in *Criminal Justice* (2002) categorizes the sociological approaches to crime into four types: learning theories; blocked opportunity theories; social bond theories; and choice-based theories, which have been discussed previously. Edwin H. Sutherland in *Principles of Criminology* (1934) first posited that, along with all other forms of behavior, crime is learned. Individuals learn how to behave by watching others or through role modeling. In essence, those who commit crime have interacted with others who have committed crime, thus learning the process of committing the particular offense, including ways of eluding police, or improving their criminal technique. Theories highlighting blocked opportunities developed during the 1940s–1950s, resulting eventually in the classic work of Richard A. Cloward and Lloyd E. Ohlin in *Delinquency and Opportunity* (1960). Crime, according to these theories, occurs as a result of individuals encountering structural barriers that prohibit them from achieving culturally acceptable goals through legitimate means. Travis Hirschi in his seminal research on the social bond in *Causes of Delinquency* (1969) found that the degree to which a person is "tied" to society directly reflects the probability of committing crime. In other words, someone who has a great deal of attachment to a community, including feelings of commitment to others, to conventional activities, and to a sense of moral values, is less likely to commit a crime.

A final approach to the study of crime is the environmental perspectives. According to Jacqueline Schneider in *The Blackwell Encyclopedia of Sociology* (2006), environmental criminology is a theoretical tradition that examines crime in relation to its physical setting. Anthony Bottoms and Paul Wiles in "Environmental Criminology," in the *Oxford Handbook of Criminology* (2002), also claim that environmental criminology, rooted theoretically in human and social ecology, studies crime, criminality, and victimization in relation to place, space, and the interaction between the two. Of particular concern to environmental criminologists is the manner in which criminal opportunities are generated by the characteristics and attributes of the physical setting. The overall aim is to identify methods by which to alter these spatial characteristics in order to reduce criminal opportunities at various points in time. Although environmental criminology has been historically under-utilized within mainstream criminology, the perspective has been gaining prominence since the 1970s.

Pat Brantingham and Paul Brantingham in *Environmental Criminology* (1991) observe that crime has four determinants: law; offenders; targets; and places. Classical criminology has focused on the legal aspects, while the positivists have concentrated their work on the offenders and their motivations. Environmental criminology addresses the last two determinants, targets and places.   JACQUELINE SCHNEIDER

criminal justice system

This refers to a set of legal and social **institutions** established to enforce the criminal law in accordance with defined procedural rules and limitations in any one country, **society**, or subdivision of a society.

There are generally four key elements in a criminal justice system: (1) law enforcement – involving the police, prosecution, and defense, which deal with offenders from the stage of reporting of a crime and arrest to prosecution in court; (2) the courts – which normally make decisions about pre-trial detention, adjudicate on the guilt of offenders, and decide on sentences for those convicted; (3) the penal system (or department of corrections) – which involves fine enforcement through the courts, and the delivery of penalties through community-based penalties and intermediate sanctions such as supervision, probation, and prisons, jails, or reformatories. In addition, parole agencies or boards determine whether or not offenders might be released from custody early and under what conditions; (4) the fourth element of criminal justice concerns crime prevention – which, in addition to the agencies already mentioned, often involves a local or regional unit of government and a wider group of agencies which address broad social and structural conditions that may lead to crime (for example, drug **addiction** help sources and housing advisory services). In addition, there are numerous other agencies whose work involves criminal law enforcement: vehicle licensing agencies, tax authorities, and transport authorities, for example.

The criminal justice system in each jurisdiction undergoes periodic change, most often following a change in government and ideological direction, or following media attention to a miscarriage of justice or a **moral panic** regarding particular crimes. The shape of the criminal justice system may also be influenced by business and public-employee organizations, which have a major stake in criminal justice issues. Although legislators and other elected officials are not involved in individual cases, they are involved in the formulation of criminal laws and criminal justice policy, and this necessarily has a major impact on the way in which a system functions.

Other institutions may also affect the operations and policy of criminal justice. In Europe, for example, the European Court of Human Rights serves to protect the rights and liberties of individuals within Europe. In this sense, the European Court serves as a final appeal court for those dealt with within European criminal justice systems.

There have been longstanding debates about how far agencies of the criminal justice system cooperate, how far they have a shared vision, and how far they might be said to serve as a smooth-functioning system rather than as a series of loosely connected agencies. In this sense, we may distinguish between agency-specific functions and the goals of the system as a whole. Existing systems include some ancient components (for example, jury trials) and some which are of recent origin (for example, specialized drug courts).

There are many variations in criminal justice systems around the world. Crime, guilt, and punishment are conceived and dealt with very differently according to the laws and cultures of different countries. The operation of any one criminal justice system inevitably raises issues of fairness and **equality**, **rights**, and responsibilities. Crime control (with a focus on repressing criminal conduct) and due process (with a focus on the inviolability of legal rules and procedures so as to protect the offender and victim from the arbitrary exercise of **power**) have been presented as alternative models of criminal justice by Herbert Packer in *The Limits of the Criminal Sanction* (1968) as if systems are one or the other, but often criminal justice systems are a mixture of these values or completely different.

In Australia and New Zealand, for example, crimes are perceived as community conflicts and resolved outside the formal criminal justice system via local restorative justice mechanisms which involve local families and communities meeting to resolve the conflicts and find informal ways of repairing the harm done. Such approaches (sometimes known as family-group conferencing) are commonly used by indigenous populations. Increasingly, criminal justice systems across the world are expressing interest in the possibility of adopting and adapting elements of this approach as an adjunct to the formal system.

LORAINE GELSTHORPE

criminal statistics

– see **crime**.

criminology

The study of **crime** has a longstanding and rich history. In its earliest days, criminology was thought to encompass any study that pertained to the problem of crime. This simple description was born out of a fundamental desire to know more about deviant behavior, those actions that violated social norms and mores. Today, criminology is an advanced theoretical field of study pertaining to crime, criminal events, the actors – offenders, victims, and those who respond to crime – the etiology of crime, legal foundations and parameters, and societal reactions to crime. However, the definition, while accurate, is somewhat misleading and seemingly uncomplicated. Reality tells us another story. Criminology is not simply a science left to criminologists. There are a number of related disciplines, with varied interests and perspectives, associated with this particular social science. Criminology is firmly rooted in **sociology**, but is also studied by anthropologists, biologists, psychologists, economists, political scientists, and legal scholars, among others. Criminology has been described by Eugene McLaughlin, John Muncie, and Gordon Hughes in their edited volume *Criminological Perspectives* (2003) as "a 'site' of contested meaning where competing theoretical perspectives meet." Owing to the diverse nature of those involved in the study of crime, the literature is often rich with discussion, debate, and interpretation.

Modern criminology is faced with multiple areas of focus, thus making it a truly multidisciplinary field of study. The particular focus of criminology is dependent on the perspective taken. Generally speaking, criminology: describes and analyzes the extent, nature, and distribution of the various forms of crime, offenders, and victims; analyzes causes of crime with the aim of forwarding theoretical constructs; studies formulation of criminal law; studies the processes of justice, including police, adjudication, and punishment; evaluates policy responses and initiatives; and evaluates social reactions to crime. Given the large undertaking, the great task of all criminology, according to John Tierney in his book *Criminology: Theory and Context* (1996), regardless of which underlying perspective is utilized, is to "unravel, or deconstruct, the concept of crime."

The study of crime could be said to have originated with theologians, who equated criminal behavior with sin, demonic influences, or witchcraft. Transgressions were investigated and found to have causes firmly rooted in the dark workings of the netherworld. Clergy were the obvious choice to turn to for intervention, becoming responsible for purging society from evil doings (that is crime) by way of very harsh methods, such as exorcisms and trials by fire. After this period of religious influence, came two defining periods that shaped today's criminology: the Classical School and the Positivist School.

Foundations for modern criminological thought were laid down during the eighteenth century with the seminal works of Cesare Beccaria (1738–94) and Jeremy Bentham (1748–1832), thus creating the Classical School of Criminology. Developed during a time where individual rights and interests were competing against those of the states, most of Beccaria's and Bentham's writing revolved around the need for reformation of the **criminal justice system**. In other words, they were advocates for structural changes that ended the arbitrary application of laws and severe punishments. Instead, Beccaria and Bentham called for the universal application of laws to all society's citizens, thus providing equal protection before the law. Following this, they called for proportionate punishment. The utilitarian ideal of proportionality meant that punishment was determined by the severity of the crime committed, not on the individual characteristics of the offender. This idea provides the foundation for most criminal justice systems worldwide, thus leaving the classical school's ideological mark on modern society.

Prevention was another guiding principle of the Classical School. Feeling that prevention is far preferable to punishment, the philosophers put forth the idea that social systems of control must take into account the rationality of people. Beccaria and Bentham believed that free will guided behavior and that decisions to violate laws were calculated in accordance to hedonistic tendencies. People wanted to experience pleasure and avoid pain; therefore individual decisions were based on the probability of detection, and of being punished, set against the pleasure gained by partaking in the offending activity.

The classical school ended a system of arbitrarily applied justice and punishment. It also provided a new way of examining theories of criminality that acknowledge the free will of participants. However, this school falls short in its undertakings by failing to acknowledge external forces that may well influence criminal behavior, for example, **social stratification** and **inequality,** thus providing a foundation for a new paradigm to evolve.

The origin of the positivist tradition in criminology in the late nineteenth century is often associated with the work of Cesare Lombroso (1835–1909), whose main contribution to the field was the measurement of physical characteristics of Italian prisoners. It is important to note that, while the Positivist School rejected the free will philosophies of the Classical School in favor of determinism, the most important contribution of the new school was the step-change in **ideology** that was characterized by the drive to measure empirically those phenomena associated with crime. While Lombroso's work is largely acknowledged as the starting point, the quest to measure social phenomena can be traced to the work of French and Belgian statisticians in the 1820s. For example, Adolphe Quetelet (1796–1874) found predictability in the distribution of crime and crime rates within French society. Therefore, the key aim of the Positivist School was to quantify observations. Measuring phenomena provided data upon which investigators could make inferences about causal relationships. Empirical evidence obtained via methods used in the natural sciences not only provided an avenue for theorists to advance their work, but also gave to the field of inquiry scientific respectability.

The work of Lombroso, Enrico Ferri (1856–1929), and William Sheldon (1898–1977) into physical characteristics and body types highlighted the Positivist School's contributions to criminology. Lombroso, referred to as the father of criminology, was a physician employed by the Italian penal system, who noted the physical characteristics of those imprisoned, thus putting forth the idea of a criminal type. Running parallel with the work of **Charles Darwin**, Lombroso's scientific observations of the physical characteristics of prisoners made generalizations about criminality possible.

Going beyond the examination of body types and their connection to criminality, the Positivist School also focused on isolating the differences between criminals and non-criminals in terms of psychological, social, and economic factors. Positivists disregard the notion of free will, as forwarded by the classical criminologists, in favor of the idea that an array of social factors impacted behavior. In other words, a range of social factors caused or determined the course of action an individual took.

The legacy of the positivists is the use of scientific methodology to frame criminological enquiry. However, this school is not without its shortcomings. While the utilization of scientific method is preferable to conjecture, there exists the possibility of the misapplication of technique and misinterpretation, thus resulting in misleading conclusions.

Other criticisms of the Positivists relate to the definition of the term "crime." Conflict criminology emerged in response to positivists' claim that an underlying consensus existed regarding the nature and meaning of the concept of "crime." Rather, conflict criminologists believe that state interests and the interests of the powerful determine the definitional parameters of the concept. This skewed viewpoint puts those already at the margins of society at risk for further disadvantage.

Additionally, critics believe that, all too often, positivists ignore the relevance of cultural differences, as well as varying value systems that underpin the concept of crime. The power of criminology is in its ability to "travel." In other words, theories, strategies, and criminological and criminal justice policy generated in one country are increasingly exported to other countries. The influence is not just in the empirical research, but also in the language and conceptual framework. These can have a profound impact on politicians, policymakers, and government officials, not to mention those who are afflicted by crime, as well as the general citizenry. However, it is ultimately important to gain a firm understanding about the values, culture, and social expectations within a given society before setting forth to seek causal explanations for crime.   JACQUELINE SCHNEIDER

critical race theory

Critical of liberal theories of **rights**, especially in the area of **race and ethnicity**, this theory evolved initially in legal theory in the post-civil-rights era. Critical race theory (CRT) attacked the color-blind approaches to **justice** that were typical of the early days of reform. In fact, lack of significant progress in social reform for black Americans was the main force behind critical race theory. Many leading black American intellectuals, such as Cornel West in *Race Matters* (1993), criticized the hollow promises of liberal reform and argued that there was a cynical if implicit acceptance of racial hierarchy and **inequality** in the distribution of economic **wealth** and **power** in the United States.

In an influential article, D. A. Bell in "Remembrance of Racism Past. The Civil Rights Decline," in J. Hill and J. E. Jones (eds.), *Race in America. The Struggle for Equality* (1993: 73–82), outlined three shortcomings of existing liberal philosophies of race. First, the Constitution rewarded property over claims for justice. Second, whites support racial reform only when it is in their self interest; and finally, whites will not support reform if it is a challenge to their **social status**. CRT had its origins in jurisprudential debates about justice, but it has also had an impact on educational theory and practice, where it is argued – for example by W. F. Tate in "Critical Race Theory" (1996: 201–47), and by J. A. Banks in "The Historical Reconstruction of Knowledge about Race" (1995: 4–17) – that a restrictive interpretation of anti-discrimination laws limits the progress and educational attainment of African-Americans. CRT has also begun to influence theories of **multiculturalism**, where the liberal agenda does not appear to have been successful from the perspective of black America.

CRT has a number of distinguishing features. It has been critical of the traditional binary division between "black" and "white," especially where blacks have "race" as a biological category and whites have "ethnicity" as a social category. It has welcomed sociological studies of the law because conventional jurisprudence has often neglected the social conditions that determine injustice. It has taken a more positive view of victims in giving recognition to the personal narratives of the oppressed. For example, M. Matsuda, R. Delgado, and K. Crenshaw, in *Words That Wound* (1993), explored victims' narratives to understand the connections between hate speech, the law, and racial **violence**. Like **African-American Studies**, CRT has encouraged interdisciplinary and comparative studies of racial oppression, such as Howard Winant's *The World Is a Ghetto* (2001).

There are several valuable introductions to CRT, such as Richard Delgado and Jean Stefancic's *Critical Race Theory. The Cutting Edge* (2nd edn., 2000) and K. Crenshaw, N. Gotanda, G. Peller, and K. Thomas (eds.), *Critical Race Theory. The Key Writings that Formed the Moment* (1995). Although CRT has been influential in law and pedagogy, it has been less prominent in the sociology of race and ethnicity. It appears to have had relatively little impact outside the United States, possibly because

racism in European societies has had a somewhat different history.   BRYAN S. TURNER

critical theory

This phrase operates implicitly as a code for the quasi-Marxist theory of society of a group of interdisciplinary social theorists collectively known as the **Frankfurt School**. The term Frankfurt School refers to the work of members of the Institut für Sozialforschung (Institute for Social Research) that was established in Frankfurt, Germany, in 1923 as the first Marxist-oriented research center affiliated with a major German university. Under its director, Carl Grünberg (1861–1940), the Institute's work in the 1920s tended to be empirical, historical, and oriented towards problems of the European working-class movement.

Max Horkheimer became director of the Institute in 1930, and gathered around him many talented theorists, including **Erich Fromm**, Franz Neumann (1900–54), **Herbert Marcuse**, and **Theodor Wiesengrund Adorno**. Under Horkheimer, the Institute sought to develop an interdisciplinary social theory that could serve as an instrument of social transformation. The work of this era was a synthesis of philosophy and social theory, combining sociology, psychology, Cultural studies, and political economy.

The first major Institute project in the Horkheimer period was a systematic study of authority, an investigation into individuals who submitted to irrational authority in authoritarian regimes. This culminated in a two-volume work, *Studien über Autorität und Familie* (1936), and a series of studies of **fascism**, including Adorno, Else Frenkel-Brunswik, and Daniel J. Levinson, *The Authoritarian Personality* (1950). Most members were both Jews and Marxist radicals and were forced to flee Germany after Hitler's ascendancy to power. The majority emigrated to the United States and the Institute became affiliated with Columbia University from 1931 until 1949, when it returned to Frankfurt.

From 1936 to the present, the Institute has referred to its work as the "critical theory of society." For many years, "critical theory" was distinguished by its attempt to found a radical interdisciplinary social theory rooted in Hegelian–Marxian dialectics, **historical materialism**, and the critique of political economy. Members argued that Marx's concepts of the commodity, **money, value, exchange**, and fetishism characterize not only the capitalist economy but also social relations under **capitalism**, where human relations and all forms of life are governed by commodity and exchange relations and values.

Critical theory produced theoretical analysis of the transformation of competitive capitalism into monopoly capitalism and fascism, and hoped to be part of a historical process through which capitalism would be replaced by **socialism**. Horkheimer claimed that: "The categories which have arisen under its [traditional theory's] influence criticize the present. The Marxist categories of class, exploitation, surplus value, profit, impoverishment, and collapse are moments of a conceptual whole whose meaning is to be sought, not in the reproduction of the present society, but in its transformation to a correct society" ("Traditional and Critical Theory," 1972: 218). Critical theory is thus motivated by an interest in emancipation and is a philosophy of social practice engaged in "the struggle for the future." Critical theory must remain loyal to the "idea of a future society as the community of free human beings, in so far as such a society is possible, given the present technical means" (230).

In a series of studies carried out in the 1930s, the Institute for Social Research developed theories of monopoly capitalism, the new industrial state, the role of **technology** and giant corporations in monopoly capitalism, the key roles of mass culture and communication in reproducing contemporary societies, and the decline of **democracy** and of the individual. Critical theory drew alike on Hegelian dialectics, Marxian theory, Friedrich Nietzsche (1844–1900), **Sigmund Freud**, **Max Weber**, and other trends of contemporary thought. It articulated theories that were to occupy the center of social theory for the next several decades. Rarely, if ever, has such a talented group of interdisciplinary intellectuals come together under the auspices of one institute. They managed to keep alive radical social theory during a difficult historical era, and provided aspects of a neo-Marxian theory of the changed social reality and new historical situation in the transition from competitive capitalism to monopoly capitalism.

During World War II, the Institute split up due to pressures of the war. Adorno and Horkheimer moved to California, while Leo Lowenthal (1900–93), Marcuse, Neumann, and others worked for the United States government as their contribution to the fight against fascism. Horkheimer and Adorno worked on their joint book *Dialectic of Enlightenment* (1947 [trans. 1972]), which discussed how reason and enlightenment in the contemporary era turned into their opposites, transforming what promised to be instruments of truth and liberation into tools of domination. In their scenario, science and technology had created horrific tools of destruction and death, culture was commodified into products of a mass-produced culture industry, and **democracy** terminated in fascism, in which masses chose despotic and demagogic rulers. Moreover, in their extremely pessimistic vision, individuals were oppressing their own bodies and renouncing their own desires as they assimilated and made their own repressive beliefs and allowed themselves to be instruments of labor and war.

Sharply criticizing enlightenment scientism and rationalism, as well as systems of social domination, Adorno and Horkheimer implicated, however implicitly, Marxism within the "dialectic of enlightenment" since it too affirmed the primacy of labor, instrumentalized reason in its scientism and celebration of "socialist production," and shared in western modernity and the domination of nature. After World War II, Adorno, Horkheimer, and Frederik Pollock returned to Frankfurt to reestablish the Institute in Germany, while Lowenthal, Marcuse, and others remained in the United States.

In Germany, Adorno, Horkheimer, and their associates published a series of books and became a dominant intellectual current. At this time, the term Frankfurt School became widespread as a characterization of their version of interdisciplinary social research and of the particular social theory developed by Adorno, Horkheimer, and their associates. They engaged in frequent methodological and substantive debates with other social theories, most notably "the positivism dispute," where they criticized more empirical and quantitative approaches to social theory and defended their own more speculative and critical brand of social theory. The German group around Adorno and Horkheimer was also increasingly hostile towards orthodox **Marxism** and were in turn criticized by a variety of types of "Marxists–Leninists" and "scientific Marxists" for their alleged surrender of revolutionary and scientific Marxian perspectives.

The Frankfurt School eventually became best known for their theories of "the totally administered society," or "one-dimensional society," which analyzed the increasing power of capitalism over all aspects of social life and the development of new forms of **social control**. During the 1950s, however, there were divergences between the work of the Institute relocated in Frankfurt and the developing theories of Fromm,

Lowenthal, Marcuse, and others who did not return to Germany, which were often at odds with both the current and earlier work of Adorno and Horkheimer. Thus it is misleading to consider the work of various critical theorists during the postwar period as being produced by members of a monolithic Frankfurt School. Whereas there were both a shared sense of purpose and collective work on interdisciplinary social theory from 1930 to the early 1940s, thereafter critical theorists frequently diverge, and during the 1950s and 1960s the term the Frankfurt School can really be applied only to the work of the Institute in Germany.   DOUGLAS KELLNER

cross-sectional design data

One of the most common forms of **data** used in sociological analysis, this is the sort of data gathered by a simple **survey**. It can be collected relatively quickly and (dependent on how the **questionnaire** is administered) cheaply. For instance, if a researcher wanted to determine the **attitudes** of employees to their jobs, then a simple cross-sectional design research project could be completed by sending questionnaires to a sample of, say, several hundred or thousand employees. If care was taken, and the employees were selected to be representative of a larger population (say, all employees in the United Kingdom) then the results could be generalized to that larger population through the use of inferential **statistics**. Averages could be calculated to describe the typical British employee, or **correlations** or **regressions** could be calculated to investigate the relationships between the variables, and find answers to questions such as "what sorts of employees are most satisfied with their jobs?"

However, cross-sectional designs have a number of limitations that restrict their usefulness for serious sociological enquiry. They provide a "snapshot" of how things are at one particular point in time, but do not provide **information** on the dynamics of a system; for example how things develop over time, how **inequality** is perpetuated, or how **institutions** reproduce themselves. They are also poor at determining the causal nature of the relationships that are detected.

Because of these limitations, much effort has been expended on gathering large datasets that provide more insight into how things change over time, for instance the British Household Panel Survey (BHPS) that re-interviews the same individuals and households each year (see **panel studies**), or birth cohort studies such as the National Child Development Study that follows an entire cohort born in one week in March, 1958, across the United Kingdom, to investigate the relationship between childhood environments and experiences and outcomes in adult life or old age.

         BRENDAN J. BURCHELL

cult(s)

The word cult is often used interchangeably with **new religious movements** and, in everyday language, tends to have a strong negative connotation (for example James Beckford, *Cult Controversies: The Societal Response to New Religious Movements*, 1989). Cults are generally seen as evolving around individuals and/or beliefs that are outside the mainstream. Specifically, the term is used to denote the group **solidarity** attendant on an excessive degree of attachment and ceding of influence to a particular person or to a particular set of ideas and beliefs. The imposing **leadership** qualities displayed by founders of new religious movements, such as Jim Jones (the People's Temple) or David Koresh (Branch Davidians), or specific ideas about Unidentified Flying Objects (UFOs) or paganism can variously produce a tightly bound cult following among their respective associates and believers. Cult-like behavior, however, is not confined to religious movements; paralleling **charisma**, of which it is an accentuated expression, leadership or personality cults are found across politics (for example the cult of the emperor) and pop culture (for example Princess Diana), and in economic corporations, among other spheres. Within the religious domain, moreover, there is a long history of cultic adoration – the cult of the saints and of devotion to the Virgin Mary represent strong traditional forms of popular religion. Such cults play a large role today in religious **tourism** and the popularity of religious festivals, devotional **rituals**, local apparition sites, and pilgrimages (see W. Swatos and L. Tomasi (eds.), *From Medieval Pilgrimage to Religious Tourism*, 2002). Cults promote religious engagement, but also stimulate concerns among church officials that the cultic status of a particular saint may undercut the routinized and institutionalized **authority** of church (see **church–sect typology**) officials to demarcate sacred beliefs, practices, and places.   MICHELE DILLON

cultural capital

– see **social capital**.

cultural deprivation

This phrase refers to the idea that some racial and/ or working-class cultures are deficient because they hinder school and social success. Cultural deprivation theory was influential during the 1960s and 1970s. It was linked to ideas about the culture of **poverty**, the underclass (see **social class**), and to the idea of a cycle of poverty in which the values associated with being poor (such as fatalism and an antipathy to individually accumulated wealth) and the practices associated with poor communities prevented marginalized groups from social and economic advancement. Within the purview of cultural deprivation theory, the concept of **subculture** took on its earlier derogatory (and now discredited) definition as a deviant or otherwise marginal milieu.

From within the sociology of **culture**, the idea of cultural deprivation drew upon work by **Basil Bernstein** and **Pierre Bourdieu**. While Bernstein's focus was on **language** – in particular, the notion that working-class speakers employed a "restricted" (versus "elaborated") communicative code – Bourdieu's emphasis was on the idea that the dominated class were unable to appropriate "legitimate" forms of culture and thus were deprived of opportunities for advancement. Work in the sociology of **education** buttressed these ideas by showing how children from backgrounds lacking in cultural capital or "home advantages" were destined to fail because of a mismatch between the cultures of home and school. This argument was explored in Annette Lareau's *Home Advantage* (2000). The idea of cultural deprivation has inspired various policy initiatives, such as Headstart, from the 1960s onward, with the aim of providing working-class and minority **children** with the cultural tools they otherwise lack. It has also been subject to considerable critique on a variety of fronts, most notably ethnographic and sociolinguistic.

On the linguistic critical front, William Labov's many studies – such as *Language in the Inner City* (1972) – of nonstandard English described how depictions of the inferiority of black communicative styles were simply ignorant of the meanings associated with that speech community, therefore also showing how the idea of cultural deprivation illustrated the white middle-class bias of both social institutions and social science. In her study of a black and economically disadvantaged community in Chicago, Carole Stack in *All Our Kin* (1978) demonstrated how community members posed alternative values and meanings, ones that were, given the structural disadvantages and routine contingencies they faced, highly logical and deeply practical. In Britain, Paul Willis's *Learning to Labour* (1977) showed also how the "lads" (as

the schoolboys came to be known in his study) were seen to be actively engaged in processes of resisting the meanings and values of mainstream life. While the versions of cultural deprivation theory developed by Bourdieu and Bernstein were extremely useful in illuminating some of the cultural mechanisms through which stratification systems are reproduced, the idea of cultural deprivation can be understood as, ultimately, conservative, insofar as it implied that marginalized groups needed to abandon their initial logics and practices in favor of "legitimate" forms, to gain access to economic and expressive opportunities. In this respect, cultural deprivation perpetuates what **Richard Sennett** and Jonathan Cobb once famously referred to as *The Hidden Injuries of Class* (1972).   TIA DENORA

cultural imperialism

Though the impact or imposition of foreign cultural **values** on subject peoples can be routinely regarded as part of the general phenomenon of **imperialism,** the term cultural imperialism has come to be used more widely in discussions of the influence of the values and beliefs of the dominant global powers on the poorer and weaker societies of the world, whether or not these are or have been subject colonies. Specifically the term refers to the use of superior economic and political **power** to export or impose values and attitudes at the expense of native **cultures.**

At the most general level, this imposition can be considered as a cultural or ideological offshoot of the more general spread of a whole economic system, such as that of capitalism (communism in its heyday was also accused of cultural imperialism). In that sense, cultural imperialism takes the form of the promotion of capitalist values of individualism, competition, and materialism, at the expense of alternative or more traditional values, such as communalism and cooperation. More discretely, cultural imperialism can be seen simply as the expression of the influence and popularity of the culture industries of the great powers – the reach and influence of their television, film, music, publishing, and advertising products.

While certain non-western and non-capitalist powers – such as China in Tibet or the Soviet Union in eastern Europe – have been accused of cultural imperialism, it is generally laid at the door of the major western capitalist societies, the European and, especially, the American. In many ways, indeed, cultural imperialism has become synonymous with Americanization, since even some European societies, notably that of France, have protested at the degree of American influence on their culture. What is normally meant by this is the steady spread of such things as American eating habits, as symbolized by the McDonald's chain, and the dominant position in the world of the American film and television industries, as symbolized by Hollywood. Another common concern is the worldwide spread of large leisure and entertainment complexes, such as the Disney Corporation with its Disneylands and Disneyworlds, and the dominant position assumed by large news corporations such as CNN.

But "Americanization" is something of a misnomer, as is clear from the power of the Australian media magnate Rupert Murdoch and his company News International – even though this has large American operations, and Murdoch himself became an American citizen in 1985. Moreover, it has been shown by many studies that the idea of cultural imperialism exaggerates the one-way flow of values and ideas. The claim for the **McDonaldization** or "Disneyfication" of the world ignores the extent to which local cultures mediate and reinterpret the influences from outside, large as these may be. The ambience and use of, say, a McDonald's restaurant can be very different depending on whether it is in Dallas, Delhi, or Beijing. In general one might say that cultural imperialism is bound up with **globalization,** and while, as with all processes of globalization, there is a general tendency towards standardization and uniformity, this is by no means uncontested or ever complete.   KRISHAN KUMAR

cultural lag
– see **William F. Ogburn.**

cultural logic of late capitalism
– see **Fredric Jameson.**

cultural materialism
Materialists have traditionally seen **culture** as a representation of an external reality. Culture is deemed truthful to the extent that it "reflects" the material world in an accurate way.

Cultural materialism breaks from this notion in two ways. The first is that it argues that culture itself is part of the material world. Culture is defined much more broadly as human activity – the way we organize our lives – rather than an aesthetic representation of the world through music, literature, and art. For example, the houses we build, the way we relate to others, the leisure

activities we pursue, should be deemed cultural since they are part of (rather than reflect) material reality. Whereas a traditional materialist view of society examines the difference between social reality and our cultural perceptions of it, a cultural materialist view of society sees this social reality as itself culturally constituted.

Culture, then, is a force that actually creates (rather than reflects or expresses) the material world. Even conventionally conceived culture – literature, music, and art – is seen as practical and not merely theoretical, since it constitutes the world as "discourse." To put the matter philosophically, culture ceases to be simply "epistemological" – that is, concerned with accuracy, truthfulness, etc. – and becomes "ontological" – that is, it constitutes the real world.

Cultural materialism is vulnerable to the argument that it makes critique impossible, since to criticize a culture it is necessary to refer it to a world that is external to it.   JOHN HOFFMAN

cultural relativism
This doctrine has two prevailing variants. One of these is a version of moral conventionalism positing that the validity of **norms** and **values** is culturally specific and transcends cultural boundaries only coincidentally. Less rigorously but more familiarly, this is a version of moral **liberalism** that acknowledges that values vary both cross-culturally and interpersonally, and prescribes the accommodation of as great a plurality of them as is procedurally possible. It has partial precedents in the celebration by Johann Gottfried von Herder (1744–1803) of the special "genius" of each **"nation"**; in Giambattista Vico's liberation of the history of the "gentiles" from the preordained destiny of the elect; even in the legal contextualism of such Renaissance humanists as Desiderius Erasmus. Narrowed to a principle of method, it emerges in the German humanistic academy in the later nineteenth century, hand in hand with the development of **hermeneutics** and the principles of the *Geisteswissenschaften* (see **human sciences**). Thus narrowed, it is an intrinsic aspect of **Max Weber**'s interpretive sociology – in principle if not always in Weber's own practice. It has a more expansive – and, in Europe at least, even more influential – analogue in **Émile Durkheim**'s early insistence on the analytical precedence of the intersocietal variety of normative prescriptions and proscriptions over the normatively universal. As Elvin Hatch points out in *Culture and Morality* (1983), it has its first advocates in the United States in the anti-racialists and anti-evolutionists

of the end of the nineteenth and early twentieth centuries, none of them of greater academic importance than the founder of American cultural anthropology, Franz Boas. It remains the signature of that anthropology from Boas at least until the 1970s, when it begins to weaken with the weakening of the conceits of cultural insularity and of ethnographic neutrality themselves.

The other variant of the doctrine is one version or another of epistemological conventionalism, positing at its most radical that what constitutes knowledge is culturally specific and culturally bounded. It has its most immediate ancestor and most enduring complement in the linguistically inflected conventionalism that emerges among such German Romantic philosophers as Friedrich von Schlegel (1772–1829) in the late eighteenth and early nineteenth century, and acquires increasing temper and refinement in the work of linguist Benjamin Sapir, anthropologist Melville Herskovits, philosophers Williard Quine and Nelson Goodman, and historians **Thomas Kuhn** and **Michel Foucault** in the twentieth. Lucien Lévy-Bruhl argues more directly for the incommensurability of primitive and modern scientific thought in *How Natives Think* (1922 [trans. 1926]) and several other works of the same period. The issue of the cultural relativity of both reason and conceptualization engages the contributors to Bryan Wilson's important collection, *Rationality* (1970). If there is a single manifesto of the several versions of epistemological conventionalism circulating in the contemporary disciplines of cultural analysis, however, it is most likely **Peter Berger** and **Thomas Luckmann**'s *The Social Construction of Reality* (1966). The "cultural relativism" of only a few decades past seems to have been largely displaced by the "**social constructionism**" of the present.   JAMES D. FAUBION

cultural reproduction

This refers to the transmission of cultural capital through inheritance; the cultivation of order through normative coercion. The concept is most closely associated with the sociology of **Pierre Bourdieu**, who developed it in relation to the analysis of **habitus** and "symbolic repression" in *Outline of a Theory of Practice* (1972 [trans. 1977]) and *Distinction* (1979 [trans. 1984]). He proposed that every individual interiorizes symbolic master-patterns of thought and values as a condition of the socialization process. These constitute a distinctive social and cultural perspective that facilitates orientation and acts as a marker of social belonging. These symbolic master-patterns are reinforced through interaction with others. Each carries distinctive social status within the social order and constitutes the basis for economic resource allocation and the distribution of **prestige**.

Alternative uses can be found in the work of **Louis Althusser** (*Lenin, Philosophy and Other Essays*, 1971) in relation to the functions of the Repressive State Apparatus, the Ideological State Apparatus, and the **interpellation** of subjects; in **Antonio Gramsci** (*Selections From Prison Notebooks*, 1971) in relation to **hegemony**, complex unity, and cultural resistance; and in **Basil Bernstein**'s *Class, Codes and Control*, 1971–7), an analysis of schooling, **power**, and elaborated and restricted **codes**.

The concept is often criticized for dissolving agency, knowledge, and reflexivity into social mechanics. On this account, cultural reproduction is a substitute for social determinism. However, in Bourdieu's sociology, the concept is generally attached to the notion of an intellectual or symbolic field which allows for the reflexivity of the agent. Moreover, it is difficult to envisage how questions of social order and change can be addressed without utilizing a version of the concept.   CHRIS ROJEK

cultural rights
– see **rights**.

cultural studies

This is an interdisciplinary field that arose in the late twentieth century, and that focuses on the study of modern and postmodern **culture**, culture being broadly understood as meanings, representations, **symbols**, and **identities**, together with related sites and practices. Cultural studies draws on many disciplines and discourses, including **semiotics**, communications studies, literary theory, **psychoanalysis**, **feminism**, **Marxism** of various kinds, **sociology**, cultural anthropology, continental philosophy, **(post)structuralism**, and **critical theory**. Media and **popular culture** are prominent topics, but it encompasses high as well as popular arts, literature and speech as well as newer media, and extends to the examination of advanced industrial culture as a whole. The methods and perspectives of Cultural studies have also been applied to early and pre-capitalist phenomena. While there have been tendencies to institutionalize Cultural studies as a new trans- or quasi-discipline, it is not unitary, and the lines between it and neighboring areas like sociology and literary studies have remained blurred. In larger compass, Cultural studies is the site of a more general, and contested, renovation of the humanities and **social sciences**, as shaped by the explosive post-1960s growth of various forms of critical theory.

The emergence of Cultural studies as a distinct (and distinctly named) area of study has been mainly a development of the English-speaking world. In the United Kingdom, a formative role was played by the **Centre for Contemporary Cultural studies** (CCCS) at Birmingham University established in 1964 under the directorship of **Richard Hoggart**. His *Uses of Literacy* (1958) traced the impact of commercialized media (especially print) on the formation of working-class culture. Another early influence was **Raymond Williams**, whose *Culture and Society* (1958) traced the history of, and broadened, the category of culture itself, and whose later writings on literature, **politics**, and **mass media** connected these interests with the 1960s and 1970s revival of European **Marxism**, especially with regard to the non-mechanistic understanding of **ideology** and consciousness.

Under Hoggart and his successor (in 1968) Stuart Hall, the CCCS did groundbreaking work on urban youth **subcultures**, consumerism, and the cultural side of Thatcherism and post-Fordist restructuring. As against the **Frankfurt School** critique of "mass culture," the Birmingham School tended to emphasize the active and creative side of popular culture, its differential elements of class, **race**, and **gender**, and the political ambiguity of, for example, punk. Its theoretical inspiration was Marxist and neo-Marxist (**Antonio Gramsci, Georg Lukács, Walter Benjamin, Theodor Wiesengrund Adorno, Lucien Goldmann**), but this was accompanied by the assimilation of semiology via **Roland Barthes** and Mikhail Bakhtin; poststructuralism via **Louis Althusser**, **Michel Foucault**, and Jacques Derrida; **Sigmund Freud** through **Jacques Lacan**; as well as of feminist theory and much else. The conceptual strains introduced by this mixture led to controversies about agency, the status of the human subject, and the social **power** of discourse, as well as to a noteworthy polemic, in E. P. Thomson's *Poverty of Theory* (1978), against the elevation of theory as such. Following the CCCS lead, other centers for Cultural studies were established in the United Kingdom, Australia, Canada, and elsewhere. From the 1980s onwards a prominent role was also played by (the journal and center) *Theory Culture & Society (TCS)* led by Mike Featherstone. The *TCS* current was more closely linked to sociology, and has pursued themes such as the **body, technology**, and virtuality, the cultural **economy** of media, and **globalization**.

American Cultural studies has followed the same general course. Here too a turn to culture within literary studies and **social theory** combined, in the context of post-1960s intellectual radicalism, with a turn to (European) theory. This is exemplified in the work of **Fredric Jameson**, who moved from a Lukacsian examination of modernist literature to a multi-dimensional (though still Marxist) interest in **language**, painting, and architecture. The work of Jameson and others was also important in fashioning an analysis of **postmodernism** (as an aesthetic and intellectual style) in relation to "the cultural logic of capital." Cultural studies in the United States, however, was less social-science oriented than in Britain, and more an outgrowth of developments in literary studies, philosophy, and art history. Hence an emphasis on reading cultural phenomena, as in the title of the influential journal *Social Text*. It was in the United States too that there first developed a characteristic emphasis on the social construction of race and gender, and on the marginalization and silencing of various types of oppressed other. While some work in this vein has been linked to identity **politics** and has tended to be experiential and anti-theoretical, an interest in otherness has also connected to high theory through the ethical **phenomenology** of Levinas and through the linguistically and philosophically self-conscious spirit of Derridean **deconstruction**. Judith Butler's *Gender Troubles* (1989) drew anti-essentialist implications for understanding gendered bodies and helped to initiate **queer theory**. **Donna J. Haraway**'s "Manifesto for Cyborgs," in *Simians, Cyborgs and Women* (1991), developed and celebrated a general notion of **hybridity**. Also related has been the development of postcolonial studies, with **Edward W. Said**'s *Orientalism* (1978) as a **paradigm**, to which are linked such further developments as subaltern studies in India (spearheaded by Gayatri Spivak) and the growth of aboriginal studies in Australasia, Canada, and Latin America.

A further ingredient in the formation of Cultural studies has been the rise of media theory, especially as influenced by the Toronto School of communications, with its sensory grammar of media and its civilizationally attuned interest in media, culture, and **technology**. This **influence** has been felt mainly through **Marshall McLuhan**, though the Cultural studies mainstream has been largely dismissive of McLuhan's work both because of its apparent technological **reductionism** and because of its crypto-theology (the "global village" of "the electric age" has echoes of Teilhard de Chardin's "noosphere"). Chardin (1881–1955) defined "noosphere" as the stage of evolutionary development characterized by the emergence of consciousness, the mind, and interpersonal relationships. In Canada, the work of McLuhan's mentor, Harold Innis, has also received renewed attention, while a more Baudrillardian version of the culture and technology approach is evident in the work of Arthur Kroker and the journal *C-Theory*.   ANDREW WERNICK

culture

Traditionally the province of either anthropology or the humanities, culture has become increasingly central to **sociology**, both as a subject of study, and as a theoretical challenge to sociology's self-conception. The sociological definition of and approach to culture, which refers to the form, content, and effects of the symbolic aspect of social life, has emerged out of a critical encounter with the two more traditional definitions.

In the definition of the humanities, culture refers to intellectual and artistic activity and the artifacts produced thereby, to what Matthew Arnold (1822–88) called "the best that has been thought and said." Culture is taken as the highest moral and aesthetic achievements of civilization. The sociology of culture has always provided critical distance from the pretensions of culture so understood and its ensuing enshrinement in the literary, dramatic, and musical canon. By showing the links between social status maintenance and taste, but also by carefully examining the aesthetics of both popular cultural artifacts, and the creative cultural activities of **social classes**, races, and **genders** traditionally excluded from the realm of high arts production, the sociology of culture has been essential to the deconstruction of the high/middle/lowbrow culture typology. In approaching culture as a social object of study, the sociology of culture forms a subfield alongside the sociology of religion and the sociology of science, and takes within its purview both high literature and pulp fiction, Fellini films and Hollywood schlock, art music and rock 'n' roll. With the advent of the production of culture perspective in the 1970s, centered around the work of Richard Peterson, and the concepts of field and cultural capital, drawn from the work of **Pierre Bourdieu**, this subfield has gained both empirical purchase and theoretical sophistication.

In the anthropological definition, culture is expected to do the comparative work of differentiating the peoples of the world, and thus also to unify their study; it forms the counterpoint to physical anthropology's theories of human nature. Historical sociology, however, has shown the connections between the anthropological imagination and various nationalist and colonialist projects of nineteenth-century Europe, whereby the totalizing concept of culture was complicit in the exoticization and simultaneous subordination and colonization (and sometimes extermination) of native populations. Extensive debates about the political valences and historical guilt of the concept of culture have ensued. But perhaps more importantly for ongoing empirical research, sociologists have found the anthropological concept of culture to be underspecified; for sociology, differentiating culture from nature is not enough. Rather, culture must be defined in relation to society, history, and individual psychology, and, furthermore, the differentiation between culture and nature must itself be examined historically with an eye towards its varying social effects (many anthropologists have also come to this conclusion). Thus, while sociology has drawn extensively on symbolic, structuralist, and linguistic anthropology for its own studies of culture, it has resisted the temptation to conflate culture directly with the social as such, and the culture/society distinction has been a productively unstable one. And it would be fair to say that social constructionist forms of cultural research have distanced themselves significantly from the "essentializing" concepts of an earlier era.

However, both the sociology of culture and the critique of culture inside and outside of anthropology beg fundamental questions. Why are social actors so interested in cultural artifacts in the first place, as opposed to other, functionally equivalent, status markers? If cultural difference cannot be grasped inside scientific anthropological theory, does that mean that it cannot be grasped at all? What is the role of meaning and symbolic structures in modern and late capitalist societies? To answer these questions outside of the confines of the humanist tradition and postcolonial anthropology has been the central task for cultural sociologists, who since the 1960s have developed a set of increasingly subtle and nuanced approaches to this contested term of culture.

For sociology, then, culture refers to the symbolic element of social life, which has been variously conceptualized, identified, and studied: signifiers and their signifieds, gestures and their interpretation, intended and unintended meanings, written discourse and effective speech, situational framing and scientific paradigms, and moral and political ideals. Concretely, culture refers to those social objects and activities which are primarily or exclusively symbolic in their intent or social function, such as art, music, and sports. Analytically, culture refers to the symbolic and ideational element of any social action, social relationship, or historical pattern. In modern and postmodern societies, these two senses of culture are increasingly intertwined in ways that must be studied empirically: people may learn how to conduct intimate relationships from poetry or romantic movies, and rock stars may endorse politicians.

The methodologies for studying culture so conceived range widely, and include surveys of attitudes and beliefs, **participant observation**, **ethnography**, structured and unstructured interviews, textual analysis of written and visual media, and **conversational analysis**. Ultimately, however, all of these methods involve the interpretation of meaning, and thus cannot be mapped directly from the methods of the natural sciences, though the extent to which scientific methods can be adapted to the study of culture is a matter of significant dispute. Furthermore, culture not only requires interpretation, but the meanings of symbols have to be understood in a holistic manner, which is to say that any given sign or symbol takes its meaning in relation to those with which it is contrasted and figuratively related. The meaning of the term culture is not an exception to this, and as culture has become central to sociology, its meaning has emerged in relation to three central concepts, namely **social structure**, **action theory**, and **critical theory**. After discussing these, we will briefly discuss the ways in which the consideration of culture has affected other aspects of the sociological field.

The distinction between culture and society is, like culture itself, contested and controversial, and, since it often conflates the analytic and concrete dimensions of culture, it is perhaps better to discuss the relationship of culture to social structure. **Talcott Parsons** distinguished the cultural from the social system in a strictly analytic fashion (his student **Niklas Luhmann** would later claim that this should in fact be a concrete distinction). And Parsons suggested that the study of culture in all its symbolic elaborations could be left to anthropology, and that sociology could focus on the place where culture and social structure met, namely, on the institutionalization of **values** and **norms**. Structural-functionalism

suggested that culture, through the normative interpenetration of society, could perform an integrative function in the service of social equilibrium, and thus that social change came with a breakdown in value consensus (as in Chalmers Johnson's (1931–) theory of social revolution).

These assertions were then subjected to relentless ideological attack for suppressing the role of strife and domination in society (and in the use of culture). However, it is perhaps more instructive, now, to notice a deeper problem with structural-functionalism, namely its interpretive deafness. By approaching culture as "norms and values," structural-functionalism not only projected certain liberal ideals onto its model of society, but more significantly, evacuated meaning from culture, robbing its analysis of nuance and empirical specificity. For an engagement with the multiple layers of the symbolic immediately reveals that culture in modern societies is neither homogenous nor consensual. Rather, the size and makeup of collectivities that share certain symbolic articulations vary significantly (from small religious **cults** to large voting populations), and these symbolic articulations are contested both within and without collectivities.

Mid-century **Marxism** and post-1960s conflict theory insisted that culture was more of a guarantor of hierarchy, exploitation, and inequality, and thus saw culture as **ideology**. And though the political commitments and theoretical presuppositions of conflict theory were fundamentally at odds with those of Parsonian functionalism, one can discern in the studies of the objective basis of systematically distorted communication, and in references to the political and economic functions of ideology, very similar problems to those that plagued the structural-functional approach. Here too, culture is assumed to be relatively uniform, at least in its social effects, and its study is guided by theoretical intuitions about the workings of the social system, in particular the exploitation of labor, and for a contemporary example see David Harvey's *The Condition of Postmodernity* (1989). Thus Marxist repudiations of culture as ideology also suffered from a lack of musicality, and inattention to the empirical details of culture's varied production, performance, and reception.

In both cases, these problems were exacerbated by imagining social structures as hard, real, and external to the actor, in opposition to culture as a more pliable and less efficacious possession of individual minds. Furthermore, both structural-functionalism and Marxism were embedded in teleological philosophies of history and social evolution that enabled them to locate the appropriate relations between social structure and culture in an a priori theoretical manner. As these teleologies came to be seen as more the meaningful, ideational constructions of sociologists' own cultures than ontological certainties about actual societies, the strict scientific distinction between social structure and culture began to break down, as did the various conceptions of their relationship. This breakdown created an opening for sociology to develop the tools necessary for a more sensitive and empirically sophisticated approach to culture in its collective forms. This has been accomplished by studying culture as a structure in its own right, a theoretical development that has taken three main forms.

First, the study of symbolic boundaries, associated with the work of Michele Lamont (*Money, Morals and Manners*, 1994) and her students, has shown how actors construct and maintain meanings as a mode of ordering, including, and excluding their fellow humans, over and against the exigencies of social structure. Thus, the economic basis for class is overwritten by an attribution of certain moral qualities to certain humans, based on criteria (including religion, race, and so forth) that may crosscut the expectations of more reductively minded sociologists that would map class consciousness directly onto economic position, and so on.

Second, the study of discourse and its relationship to power, based on the pioneering work of **Michel Foucault**, has enabled sociologists to examine not only articulated boundaries, but also unstated exclusions, and more generally the cultural construction of certain taken-for-granted "positivities" of modern life. Thus one can examine from a reflexive historical perspective how certain kinds of human subjects (for example, insane people and medical patients) and **social problems** (for example, homosexuality) came to be of such great concern, and how their meaningful construction effected the way they were dealt with, inside and outside mainstream society. Though Foucault's work has been largely appropriated in the humanities as a set of theorems concerning power and knowledge more appropriate to critical theory than to empirical sociology, his early studies of madness, medicine, and the episteme of the classical and modern ages are in fact rich historical reconstructions of landscapes of meaning, and their essential role in the social processes of treatment, exclusion, and philosophical understanding. These issues are developed

in Foucault, *Madness and Civilization* (1961 [trans. 1971]) and Chandra Mukerji, *A Fragile Power: Scientists and the State* (1990).

Finally, the conception of culture as a structure in its own right has enabled the sociological transformation of a set of tools from literary theory and semiotics. Culture can be studied as a social text, replete with codes, narratives, genres, and metaphors. Then, culture can be examined in both its concrete and its analytic autonomy from social structure, which enables us to isolate and make clear its effects (and its varying political valences) from a sociological point of view. So, for example, the long struggle for women's rights in the United States can be seen as a discursive battle for civil inclusion, according to which a new set of actors came to be coded in a democratic and morally positive way (Jeffrey Alexander, "The Long and Winding Road: Civil Repair of Intimate Injustice," 2001). This conception of culture suggests, moreover, that social structures themselves are interpreted variably by social actors, and thus must be attended to hermeneutically by cultural sociologists, with an eye to their meaningful aspects, their locality, and their historical specificity (see Clifford Geertz, *The Interpretation of Cultures*, 1973, and Jeffrey Alexander, *The Meanings of Social Life*, 2003).

If culture was often contrasted to social structure, and furthermore associated with subjectivity, then it should not be surprising that it has often been erroneously conflated with action and its related terms: agency, reflexivity, and consciousness. However, as culture has become recognized as a structure in its own right, the relationship of culture to action has become a key component both of sociological action theory and of sociological research more generally. The ongoing debate about culture and action has its roots in two different sociological traditions, both of which contribute to the contemporary understanding of culture within sociology.

On the one hand, the analytic tradition, descending from Parsons's formalization of **Max Weber**'s means–ends approach to action, approached culture in terms of the ways culture sets the ends of action. Action is thus structured not only by interests, but by norms as well. Originally opposed to economistic accounts of social action, the strictly analytic approach to purposive action has been revived in contemporary sociological debates about agency and rationality. But a deeper understanding of the role of culture for action has been developed from within this tradition by recognizing culture as an internal environment for action, arguing thus that culture orients action by structuring subjectivity. Social actors respond to sets of internal typifications of the social world and thus are dependent upon meaningful symbolization in setting their goals, and in imagining how they can go about meeting them. By reintroducing the symbolic as an environment of action full of rich narratives and morally and emotionally loaded oppositions, this approach integrates the expanded approach to culture-as-structure elaborated above.

On the other hand, the pragmatic tradition, descending from **George Herbert Mead** and **Herbert Blumer**, rejects the means–ends characterization of action outright, and suggests instead that actors constantly negotiate situations in an improvisatory way, attempting to make sense of and solve both social and physical problems as they arise. Originally, because of its distance from the analytic abstractions of the Parsonian tradition, and its tendency towards **methodological individualism**, this tradition was not really oriented towards culture per se, though it had a conception of the use of symbols and framing on the micro level. Increasingly, however, the descendants of this tradition have developed a conception of culture-as-use that conceives of the knowledgeable agent as the link between culture and society. It is actors, in social situations, who draw on culture when institutional consistency breaks down.

Thus the contemporary debate is structured by two positions, that of culture-in-action which is illustrated by Ann Swidler in "Culture in Action: Symbols and Strategies" (1986), and that of culture as thick environment for action by Jeffrey Alexander in *Action and Its Environments: Toward a New Synthesis* (1988). Both approaches have significant insights to offer. The first emphasizes that actors continually work to render coherent and solvable discursive and institutional problems that arise in the flow of social life. The second emphasizes the way in which the social world is constructed for the actor by previous interpretations and collective languages. In either case, these approaches suggest the importance of culture for the study of social life. For example, we should perhaps discuss the discursive repertoires of politicians, and the resonance of these repertoires with the shared codes of their audience–electorates, as opposed to the "revealed preferences" of either. The contrasts between the two approaches have, however, produced significantly different forms of theory and research.

One important manifestation of the symbolic interactionist tradition has been Gary Fine's development of the concept of idiocultures, whereby small **groups** develop an idiosyncratic set of meanings (beliefs, knowledge, and customs) that forms the basis for mutual understanding and further interaction and action. Thus, cooks in various classes of restaurants develop an aesthetic language that enables them to communicate with each other concerning the manifestly practical problems of smell and taste.

Alternately, Robin Wagner-Pacifici, in *The Moro Morality Play* (1986) and *Theorizing the Standoff* (2000), has developed the concept of social drama within the more analytic tradition of action and its environments, so as to enable the study of social situations where symbolic and physical violence interact. In studying terrorist kidnappings, standoffs between government and its discontents, and surrenders, she develops a deep understanding of morally loaded environments for action. When the social fabric is breached, actors must work within certain dramatic frameworks, and with certain obtainable identities. Thus, in a standoff between the Freemen of Montana and the United States Government, it was a mediator who had fought in Vietnam and, like some of the leaders of the Freemen, had formed his core identity in the crucible of that experience and its subsequent narration who was able to bridge the symbolic gap between the antagonists. Action was deeply structured by the symbolic environments of traumatic memory and the enactment of **masculinity**.

The specificity of the kinds of meanings that are enacted, however, points both to the possible misinterpretations of the relationship between action and culture, and to the way forward in the theoretical debate. For the exclusive emphasis on culture as it is used by actors can support the naturalistic approach to social structure and thus an understanding of culture as unstructured and primarily the possession of individuals. In this conception, it is meaningless institutions that set the parameters of the action problem, and culture is merely the way actors make sense of things as they are solving it – perhaps important for filling out an explanation, but not essential to it. The environments to action approach is faced with a similar danger, for, insofar as it retains vestiges of Parsons's action frame of reference, it can be taken to indicate that sociology can produce, in theory alone, a mechanistic explanation of the interaction of norms and interests that will apply everywhere, regardless of cultural differences.

Perhaps most significantly, it is important that action theory be prevented from becoming a sort of existential meditation on the capacities (or incapacities) of human freedom, rather than a way to examine the social contingencies of actually existing meaning. If the knowledgeable agent becomes a sort of philosophical and methodological hero, whose reflexivity about her location in structure ultimately makes her the master of the cultural formations in her head, then the sociological purpose of examining cultural structures is vitiated, as collective meaning formations melt away in the face of agency and knowledge as developed by **Anthony Giddens** in *The Constitution of Society* (1984).

Thus, the way forward in the action–culture debates lies in the development of a meaningful account of action through a theorization of social performance, by linking action theory to **Erving Goffman**'s dramaturgical sociology and Kenneth Burke's literary theory, but also to Judith Butler's reconception of the poststructuralist tradition of social thought. By thinking of social situations of varying scope (from small-group interactions to media events watched by millions) as dramas being played out on a public stage, with certain actors and audiences, props and social powers, emergent scripts and cultural backgrounds, we can conceive of the exigencies of social action in a thoroughly cultural way that does not reduce meaning to social structure. Action, then, involves putting certain intended and unintended meanings into the social scene. This is to say that the theorization of action not only has to take into account cultural structures, but must further focus on how actions are themselves interpretations of these structures, and thus respond to logics of meaning and identity underneath the interests and norms that were once supposed to do the analytical work of explaining these actions; this argument is developed in Jeffrey Alexander, Bernhard Giesen, and Jason Mast (eds.), *The Cultural Pragmatics of Social Performance* (2006).

The sociological critique of culture used to be based almost entirely on references to the social as existing outside of culture itself. It was thus diametrically opposed to the sense of criticism associated with the detailed reading of the literary canon, and with humanistic studies more generally. The obvious exception was Marxist literary criticism, in particular that of **Georg Lukács** and **Raymond Williams**, which entered into literary texts themselves to find the logics of **ideology** in the content and form. While their work foreshadowed the development of Cultural studies, it remained nonetheless within the discourse of suspicion about culture, usually understood as *bourgeois* culture (and its discontents). Increasingly, however, sociology has brought its normative concerns with democracy, social inclusion, and the critique of **power** to the interpretation of culture, as well as to the debunking of ideology. This is to say that the project of hermeneutics, once associated with the conservative aesthetic hierarchies of the German philosophical tradition, can now be seen as a rich source of critique in a post-positivist and post-orthodox-Marxist age, as exemplified by the work of Michael Walzer, Luc Boltanksi, and Laurent Thevenot. The epistemological implication of their work is that sociological critique must abandon its pseudo-scientific assumption of an exterior stance or view from nowhere, and develop critical distance through extensive engagement, dialogue, and interpretation. They develop critical perspectives on contemporary societies that share some of the empirical purchase of cultural sociology, but have as their ultimate goal the articulation of new normative understandings of justice and equality. More generally, in so far as sociological critique is no longer beholden to scientific certainty, revolutionary upheaval, and the genre of debunking, its normative repertoire of critical tropes, subtle ironies, and imagined ideals can be expanded.

That culture has become a central theoretical term in sociology means that it has had significant effects on the sociological imagination as a whole, extending beyond the study of culture as a set of socially produced artifacts. "Culture," in sociology, indicates a perspective as well as an object of study, and as such has addressed itself to nearly all of the classic and varied problems of sociological research. We cannot do the wide variety of cultural research in sociology full justice here, rather we will point to a few particularly telling examples.

Sociology's ongoing occupation with **modernity**, and the history of **state** formation, has led to a focus on the constitution of nations as collective identities. In explaining economic takeoff in western Europe, the consolidation of the power of states, and the emergence and importance of democratic publics and the free press, sociologists have increasingly focused on the construction of nations as "imagined communities," or "discursive fields," and nationalism as "a unique form of social consciousness," for example in Benedict Anderson's *Imagined Communities* (1991), Lyn Spillman and Russell Faeges, "Nations," in Julia

Adams, Elisabeth S. Clemens, and Ann Shola Orl-off (eds.), *Remaking Modernity* (2005), and Liah Greenfeld's *Nationalism* (1992).

The sociology of sex and **gender** has likewise experienced a cultural overhaul. While feminist and **queer theory** have questioned the naturalness of the sex/gender distinction, sociological research has examined the effects of actually existing cultural schemas of gender and sex for social outcomes, including family structure, women's tendency to join or opt out of the workforce, and the ongoing existence of sexism in wage levels and status attainment. These studies examine both gender as a highly rigid structure of meaning, and its varying enactment by women and men who attempt to negotiate the political and economic contradictions of modern society, for instance in Judith Stacey, *Brave New Families* (1990); Sharon Hays, *The Cultural Contradictions of Motherhood* (1996); and Mary Blair-Loy, *Competing Devotions* (2003).

Finally, sociology's longstanding normative concern with **democracy** and its incipient populism has also taken a cultural turn. For example, analyses of American political participation and activism have investigated how certain meanings either enable or discourage civic participation. The results have often been counterintuitive: doctrines of individual empowerment encourage activity and public responsibility, while norms of civility and politeness discourage political conversation and involvement, a theme which is developed in Nina Eliasoph, *Avoiding Politics* (1998), and Paul Lichterman, *The Search for Political Community* (1996).

Culture has thus moved towards the center of sociological discourse, as both a topic of study and a perspective from which to view the social. As reinterpretation is a primary form of theoretical advance, the perhaps predictable result of this is that, simultaneously, the classics of social theory have come to be seen in a new light. New readings of **Karl Marx**, Weber, and **Émile Durkheim** have emerged.

While all twentieth-century Marxisms have given more importance to culture and ideology than did the crude economic Marxist orthodoxy that followed Marx's death, the turn to culture in the 1960s and 1970s is evident in the increasing attention given to Marx's analysis of commodity fetishism in *Capital*, as well as to the importance of the early, humanist, and perhaps even idealist-Hegelian Marx. Either way, Marx is read as attentive to the capacity of meaning as a social force. One important result of this has been the way

structuralist and poststructuralist theories of language have merged with Marxist historiography to produce a central thesis concerning postmodernism, namely that the postmodern age is one in which the workings of capitalism are increasingly dependent on signifiers as well as signifieds, that is, on the relational field of social symbolism. These approaches are illustrated by Frederic Jameson, *The Cultural Logic of Late Capitalism* (1992), and Jean Baudrillard, *For a Critique of the Political Economy of the Sign* (1972) [trans. 1981]).

Likewise, since the mid-1960s, we have seen a recovery of Weber's sociology of art, as well as continuing debate on the Protestant Ethic thesis. However, most significantly, the concern with culture has also entered into Weberian debates about the consolidation of state **power** and the institutionalization of rational **bureaucracy**. Here, sociologists have increasingly read Weber as a hermeneutic student of rationality as a cultural form specific to western history. In doing so, Weber's concerns are read as not so different from Foucault's, and bureaucracy as less a mechanism to be uncovered than a form of symbolic action to be interpreted. This interpretation is developed in Philip Gorski, *The Disciplinary Revolution* (2003).

Finally, the cultural turn in sociology has seen a renaissance and reconsideration of Durkheim's later works, and, in particular, of *The Elementary Forms of Religious Life* (1912 [trans. 2001]). This work has come to be seen as a key prolegomena to the symbolic study of society as a general project, as well as to the study of the role of culture in modern, industrial societies. Durkheim is thus read as uncomfortable with the materialist interpretations given to *The Division of Labor in Society* and as having made a key epistemic break in the years between the publication of *Suicide* (1897 [trans. 1951]) and that of *Elementary Forms*, an argument developed by Jeffrey Alexander in "Rethinking Durkheim's Intellectual Development II" (1986). As a result, Durkheim can be seen as a precursor to cultural structuralism in his emphasis on the autonomy of symbolic forms, and the importance of belief and ritual for the organization of society.

If culture has become central to sociology (though some may not hold this opinion, or at least be unhappy with this development), it has also remained a controversial subject. And as empirical research on culture has exploded, the theoretical presuppositions of this work, which often does not fit the model of positivist or scientific-realist sociology, have been left relatively unexplored. This is to say that, in the future, social theory must address not only culture, but its accompanying methodological and epistemological term: interpretation. This can be done by returning to the fundamental questions of the philosophy of social science, as well as by articulating the immanent epistemological self-consciousness of cultural research in sociology. There are two fundamental concerns central to the question of sociological interpretation, broadly understood.

The first regards the role of the investigator in social analysis. Though most cultural sociologists accept neither scientific norms nor postmodern normlessness as the parameters for their truth claims, what norms they do accept is an important issue to discuss in the abstract. In particular, it seems clear that sociologists want the meanings they reconstruct to be translatable, so that cultural comparison is possible, not so much so as to determine active and latent mechanisms, but so as to perceive more clearly the varied relationships of meaning in action. Thus, even single case studies or ethnographies implicitly contain a comparison, at least to the investigator's own meaningful social contexts, and this comparative consciousness forms an important basis for the development of theory and research in cultural sociology.

The second question concerns how much the methods and modes of explanation common to cultural sociology may apply outside the domain of what is analytically or concretely called culture. A lot of work within poststructuralist theory has examined the symbolic and discursive basis for what sociologists are more likely to call social structure, namely, institutional formations, social sanction and exclusion, and even violence, as argued in Judith Butler's *Gender Trouble* (1989). But the extent to which these aspects of social life can actually be explored empirically remains to be verified by an **epistemology** more comfortable with the possibility of truth claims that are relatively autonomous from power. Thus, for example, we need to ask how even the reconstruction of political strategies and economic exigencies involves the interpretation of highly reified and strictly executed meaning.

Ultimately, then, the advent of culture in sociology and the study of its subtleties and social contestations leads to fundamental questions about sociology itself. If culture is a perspective from which to examine society, it is also a perspective from which to examine the meaning-formation called sociology. As such, its most important effect will be to push the central concepts of sociology (structure, action, critique), empirical research topics, and the readings of sociological classics towards the interpretation of meaning.   ISAAC REED AND JEFFREY ALEXANDER

culture industry
– see **Theodor Wiesengrund Adorno**.

culture of poverty
– see **poverty**.

custom
– see **norm(s)**.

cybernetics
A field of scientific inquiry devoted to self-regulating information systems, cybernetics, derived from the Greek word meaning helmsman or governor. Developed alongside computing in the later years of World War II, the reference to governors attaches the term to the regulatory mechanisms first used on nineteenth-century steam engines. The first phase of cybernetic science was mathematical, an attempt to quantify the amount of **information** in a given system. A critical breakthrough came with the information theory proposed in *The Mathematical Theory of Information* (1949) by C. E. Shannon and W. Weaver, employees of Bell Labs, the leading commercial research laboratory of the time. Bell needed to find engineering solutions for massive increases in telephone use in the later 1940s. Shannon and Weaver proposed a probabilistic model in which the information content of a message could be calculated as the ratio of signal – meaningful communication – to noise. "Noise" they defined as anything insignificant, from static hiss to repetitions and redundancies. Mathematically, the highest probability was for randomness in communication. In the Cold War period, early cyberneticians identified randomness with entropy, the tendency of systems to cool down, to move to less ordered states. In complex systems such as living beings or social organizations, increasing entropy dissipates the information content or patterned relationships. The task of cybernetic technologies was to maintain homeostasis: the state of a system with a high degree of predictable structure, or order.

As the term suggests, however, homeostasis is negative entropy in the sense that it resists change. This was the tenet of two Chilean researchers, H. R. Maturana and F. J. Varela, in *Autopoesis and Cognition* (1980); they proposed the term that ushered in cybernetics' second phase: autopoesis. Consonant with the ambitions of the Macy conferences which, through the 1950s, extended the scope of cybernetics to embrace fields as diverse as economics and meteorology, the concept of autopoetic machines is a general model of any self-sustaining system: a unity composed of processes which produce components which in turn realize the processes and constitute, continually reconstituting, the machine or organization as a unity. This internal circuit depends, more explicitly than earlier models, on the interaction of the autopoetic machine – technological, organic, or human – with its environment. This variant of cybernetics provided **Niklas Luhmann** with the foundations for his influential conception of **society** as a network of discrete functional systems (law, **education**, science, and so on), each of which replicates itself according to its own processes, but does so by treating neighboring systems as environmental inputs. For Luhmann, society's internal differentiation debars it from acting as a single unified entity, a capacity restricted to its internal systems. It can and indeed must, however, embody the mutual feedback mechanisms between its distinct components.

The third phase of cybernetics abandoned the centrality of homeostasis in favor of theories capable of explaining change. Variously known as chaos or **complexity theory**, contemporary cybernetics uses dynamic models like hydrodynamics to model complex boundary states between order and chaos, with a special interest in the emergence of new ordered states from apparently chaotic forebears. Importantly, the term chaos does not signify randomness but rather a system whose subsequent states are not entirely predictable from its original state. The model is closely allied with the development of network communications, and may be related to **Ulrich Beck**'s concept of risk society, but is also widely used to justify free-market economics.   SEAN CUBITT

cyberspace

This term is used to refer to electronic communications **networks** and was first used by science-fiction author William Gibson in his 1986 novel *Neuromancer* to describe a fictional parallel universe created by computers and inhabited by **information** (including the "avatars" or data representations of human characters). With the arrival of the worldwide web in 1993, the term took on a practical application, describing the online world, the **interactions** and **networks** of persons, groups, and information connected electronically through the worldwide web. In some usages, for example that of the Electronic Frontier Foundation, the term describes an open terrain which may be occupied or homesteaded on the model of the westward expansion of the United States during the 1870s, and is in this conception a liberated and liberating geography, parallel to reality – physically copresent social transactions – but potentially far larger. The ambiguity of the term cyberspace and the juxtaposition to real, social life – does it describe an actual or a metaphorical geography? – derives from the unprecedented social relations which the worldwide web enabled.

For some, cyberspace denotes a field of open opportunities distinguished from the real world by its freedom from constraint. For others, it denotes a new **market** in information and services – one not substantially different from other markets, but different in the degree to which it has only begun to be tapped. For many social theorists, cyberspace is interesting both for its internal relationships – new forms of **socialization** such as bulletin boards (BBSs) and massively multiplayer game environments (MMPs) – and for its articulation with real, geographical material spaces.

The interconnection with reality takes several forms. Cyberspace is a source of news and opinions, many of them unsanctioned by traditional gatekeeping institutions, which may provide infrastructure for the development of new forms of public life. Cyberspace is also feared as a barely comprehensible jungle where pedophiles and con artists thrive. The greatest fear is that, through the powers of the internet, cyberspace may intervene in real, social space, for example in allowing a child molester to make a rendezvous with a potential victim, or con men to access real bank accounts. Since Amsterdam's, France's, and India's initial forays in the early 1990s, many city and some national governments have extended the provision of services to online environments, including in some cases **voting** and other forms of citizen participation in government. At the same time, the subversion of electronic systems ("hacking") has become a weapon of **war**, notably in the Middle East during the Second Intifada in the Israeli–Palestinian conflict. Identifying even such basic data as the number of participants in cyberspace has proved difficult. Describing its sociological characteristics is equally difficult, and a nascent scholarly field. Among significant contributions are A. R. Galloway's *Protocol* (2004),

S. Lash's *Critique of Information* (2002), C. May's *Information Society* (2002), and T. Terranova's *Network Culture* (2004).

The material infrastructure of cyberspace is composed of a large number of computers linked by electronic networks. A proportion of these computers act as servers, storage devices allowing open access from other computers. A smaller proportion are routers, responsible for conveying data across the network. A small number of globally agreed software packages (protocols) permit the traffic to be used on almost every personal or institutional computer. Some subnetworks (intranets) are closed to all but named users. The major languages employed are English, Mandarin, Spanish, and Korean. Many networks, routers, and servers are integrated with national and global telecommunication and entertainment corporations. But many are not, and the technology is cheaply available to individuals, groups, and companies who wish to communicate with the public. The most successful applications to date are e-mail, which allows person-to-person communication, and file-sharing, through which users can swap data, commonly music, images, and software. Cyberspace raises serious challenges for law (intellectual **property**), **justice** (online and international **crime**), the military (information warfare), and representational **democracy.**   SEAN CUBITT

D

Dahrendorf, Ralph (1929–)

The author of close to thirty books including *Class and Class Conflict in Industrial Society* (1959) and *Society and Democracy in Germany* (1967), Dahrendorf's most influential contributions to sociology include the conceptual elaboration of factors affecting the likelihood of group conflict (see **social conflict**), which are empirically variable across time and place; an attendant critique of **Karl Marx**'s universalizing of his historically narrow analysis of class conflict in nineteenth-century Europe; an insistence on the analytical differentiation of industrialism from **capitalism**; and a concern with formal variations in types of **organization** and association, in types of **authority** relations, in patterns of conflict regulation, and in relations of stratification along a number of axes.

Dahrendorf is popularly known as a "conflict theorist" but in fact has always refused to oversimplify reality through exaggerating tendencies of integration (as, for example, in **functionalism**) or of conflict (as, for example, in Marx). He is an anti-utopian who urges people to have the maturity to live with complexity. To emphasize this complexity, he has drawn attention throughout his work to the relatively independent nature of many aspects of social life, from those specific to international relations, **industrial society**, politics, and nuclear weapons, through divergent forms of ownership and control to, latterly, those related to the environment and to biological issues associated with genetic engineering, to name just some. His sociology is marked deeply by a political commitment to liberal values and to the **welfare state**, to both liberty and **citizenship** entitlements.

Dahrendorf has combined his intellectual work with a hugely impressive presence in the practical worlds of both politics and academic administration. At the end of the 1960s he was a Free Democrat (FDP) member of the German Bundestag and a parliamentary secretary of state at the Foreign Office, then a European Commissioner in Brussels in 1970–4, before becoming the Director of the London School of Economics in 1974–84. From 1987 to 1997 he was Warden of St. Anthony's College, Oxford. He was created a United Kingdom life peer in 1993.

ROB STONES

Darwin, Charles (1809–1882)

The theory of natural selection was developed independently by **Charles Darwin** and Alfred Wallace (1823–1913). It was first introduced by Darwin in 1859 in *Origin of the Species*. Both men developed the theory on the basis of intensive and substantial empirical work.

From 1831 to 1836 Darwin served as naturalist aboard the HMS *Beagle*, a mapping and scientific expedition sponsored by the British government. During this voyage he worked in the Galapagos Islands and elsewhere, studying new species and collecting them for later study. Wallace worked in the Amazon area and the East Indies in the 1840s. He also collected examples of species unknown to the western world.

Their studies led to the assertion that evolutionary change is gradual, stretching over thousands of millions of years. The main mechanism for evolution was a process called natural selection. And they argued that the millions of species alive in the modern era probably arose from a single original life form through a branching process called "specialization."

Biological laws, Darwin and Wallace argued, affect all living beings, including humans. Population growth within limited resources leads to a struggle for survival. Certain characteristics confer advantages and disadvantages upon individuals during this struggle. The selection of these traits, and their inheritance over time, leads to the emergence of new species and the elimination of others.

For many social scientists, the theory of natural selection should be seen as a product and reflection of its time. This was a point made in our contemporary era by, among others, **Michel Foucault**. Darwin is seen as a high Victorian, his ideas being little more than the struggle for existence in society being transferred to the natural world. Furthermore, even the distinction between scientific and nonscientific knowledge is seen by many contemporary sociologists as spurious. "Science" is obfuscation, a way of legitimating the **power** of **institutions** and dominant **social classes**.

The parallels between the theory of Darwin and Wallace and the society in which they worked were also pointed out by **Karl Marx**. The class struggle in Victorian England, he argued, was being transplanted by Darwin back onto the natural world. Similarly, the "specialization" of species was the division of labor in human society, again extended to the realm of nature. Marx, and to an even greater extent **Friedrich Engels**, nevertheless recognized that Darwin's theory was an exceptionally important piece of science. Darwin and Wallace had uncovered real causal mechanisms which were generating species. These issues regarding the social construction of Darwin and Wallace's scientific theory remain important and are developed and discussed in a number of texts concerned with the social construction of science. These include D. Amigoni and J. Wallace, *Charles Darwin's "The Origin of Species"* (1995).

Darwin's and Wallace's theories and ideas were certainly colored by the experience and predominant values of their day and they have since been developed by scientists such as S. Gould, *Ever Since Darwin* (1980). But the fact that Darwin's and Wallace's theory has survived largely intact for over 150 years suggests that it is much more than a social construction. It described, as Marx and Engels implied, real relationships and processes. All knowledge is inevitably "socially constructed," but this need not mean that knowledge is *only* socially constructed. It can refer to relationships, processes, and mechanisms which are real, if not necessarily observable. But, as discussed in **evolutionary psychology**, **social Darwinism**, and **Herbert Spencer**, the direct application of Darwin's and Wallace's ideas to human **society** remains full of difficulties and dangers. Human behavior cannot be simply attributed to our evolutionary history, evolutionary processes being always mediated in complex ways by social relations and social processes. Similarly, and despite the attempt by Spencer and others to transfer Darwin's work to human society, there are few useful parallels to be made between the structure of organisms and those of society.

Darwin himself was very cautious about making parallels between biological and social **evolutionary theory**. On the other hand, his 1901 book *The Descent of Man and Selection in Relation to Sex* did make some preliminary forays into these difficult connections. And his 1872 text, *The Expression of Emotions in Man and Animals*, suggested that human emotions and expressions could be traced back to "man's" evolutionary origins. It can be seen as an early version of evolutionary psychology.

PETER DICKENS

data

The term data (which is plural) comes from the Latin "things given." This notion is a misleading one because usually the gathering of evidence involves much painstaking endeavor on the part of the social scientist. Data come in all shapes and forms and include responses to **questionnaires** or **interviews**, observational materials, documentary records, statistical information, visual materials, oral histories, and so on. The key question for researchers is how the sources of knowledge (data) and the sources of understanding (theory) relate.

The data-design phase of research involves considering how best to collect data that will allow the investigator to answer the questions that he or she has posed. One of the frequent divisions drawn in data type is the distinction between quantitative and qualitative. These two approaches to data collection have often been pitted against each other as if quantitative and qualitative researchers had completely different understandings of how to gather knowledge of the social world. While there may be some difference in emphasis between those who work mainly with numeric or statistical data and those who work with more interpretative and phenomenological data, there is much overlap between the two. The importance of data design is in getting a "good fit" between research question and type of data. If you want to know the differences between men's and women's pay in the United Kingdom it is unlikely that you will get far without delving into **statistics**; but qualitative information on how men and women view their pay may also provide important insights into differences. If you want to know why women are under-represented in top managerial jobs, then you will require not only statistical knowledge about the relative success rate of job applicants but also highly contextualized information on men's and women's different life circumstances. Ideally, quantitative and qualitative data should complement each other.

Another distinction is between primary and secondary data. It is wrong to think of social research solely in terms of the first-hand collection of data by means of, say, observation or asking questions. A great deal of information is already available having been collected by others, and often for other reasons. A wide range of data sources is available to the social researchers. Here I will just deal with two: statistical data sources and documentary sources. Recent developments in information technology, such as the worldwide web, make data sources increasingly accessible and amenable.

There is a huge array of statistical data, commonly referred to as official statistics. These are collected by government agencies. But the degree to which the data are official varies enormously. Some data, such as vital statistics, are the by product of administrative processes like the statutory registration of births, marriages, and deaths. Others, like many of the **surveys** assembled by the Office of National Statistics, are based on collections of data by voluntary social surveys. The Census is the most extensive (in the sense of sample coverage) data that is available and, in Britain, the Office of National Statistics Longitudinal Study, based on just 1 percent of the total population, allows for the tracking of population change on a year by year basis.

The whole process of archiving and dissemination of large-scale survey data has been revolutionized because of the increasing availability of computing power. It is now possible for the researcher to select survey data for secondary analysis and to download the whole survey or particular sub-samples for further analysis. Secondary data analysis involves extracting new findings from existing data by reanalyzing the original data resource.

The important thing in using secondary data is to be mindful of the original purpose for which they were collected and the particular agendas that the collection of the data may have served. Many quantitative researchers are acutely aware that statistics are, to some extent, social constructions. In other words, the concepts and measures often reflect those that dominate official, political, and economic life (*Government Statisticians' Collective*, 1979). For example, employment surveys may use a definition of work that is at odds with the sociological interest in non-paid caring and leads to an under-valuing of women's contribution to the **economy**. This does not mean that data from employment surveys are not useful for sociological analysis, but it does mean that the researcher has to be fully aware of its limitations and strengths.

Written documentary sources also pose great opportunities and challenges for social scientists. Few researchers need reminding that documents can rarely be taken at face value. To assess the value of documentary sources as evidence, it is necessary to know why they were gathered in the first place. Documents differ in terms of their authorships – whether they are personal or official documents. They also differ in terms of access, which varies from closed through to openly published. John Scott, in his book *A Matter of Record* (1990), proposed that knowledge of authorship and access is important for answering questions about a document's authenticity (whether it is original and genuine), its credibility (whether it is accurate), its representativeness (whether it is representative of the totality of documents in its class), and its meaning (what it is intended to say).

Social-research data cannot be separated from ethical and political concerns. Most professional bodies have ethical guidelines that govern the collection of data and stipulate desirable practices, such as the obtaining of informed consent. However, arguably, some of the most serious instances of data abuse come at the analytical and writing-up stages. Research claims sometimes far exceed what the evidence or data warrant. This is a practice that W. G. Runciman in his book *The Social Animal* (1998) describes as an "abuse of social science." He cites several examples of where sociologists are espousing **ideology** or opinion which goes far beyond what the data can support. The importance of being wary of over-stretching data claims should apply, whether or not the conclusions drawn are deemed politically correct.

Data archives (both quantitative and qualitative) serve many important roles in modern social science. It is worth mentioning three. First, they allow for data to be widely accessed for secondary research. Second, they encourage the cumulative nature of social science by allowing researchers to build on and replicate (often in different contexts and times) what has gone before. Third, they help safeguard the highest professional standards by ensuring that social science evidence is available for further scrutiny and reanalysis. JACKIE SCOTT

data analysis
– see **data**.

data resources
– see **data**.

Davis and Moore debate
– see **functional theory of stratification**.

de-professionalization
– see **profession(s)**.

de-schooling

Ian Lister, in *Deschooling. A Reader* (1974), has claimed that the "de-schooling movement" was "a general drift of thinking" which flourished in the 1970s in advanced capitalist societies. A precursor of the movement was the American social critic, Paul Goodman, who published *Compulsory Miseducation* (1962). In the United Kingdom, John Holt, who had written *How Children Fail* (1964), *How Children Learn* (1967), and *The Underachieving School* (1971), considered himself a "de-schooler" from the early 1970s. This coincided with the publication of the work and author most identified with the movement, Ivan Illich's *De-Schooling Society* (1971), and also with Everett Reimer's *School is Dead* (1971). Reimer defined schools as "**institutions** which require full-time attendance of specific age **groups** in teacher-supervised classrooms for the study of graded curricula." The defining characteristics of de-schooling thinking are implicit in this definition. De-schoolers opposed the institutionalization of learning, arguing that state-controlled **socialization** inhibited the expression of individual freedom and creativity. Logically, they could have no time for **credentialism**. There was a nonconformist zeal about their views: schools should be disestablished and secularized. "To identify schools with education," wrote Illich, is "to confuse salvation with the church." While the movement might have seemed to be in alliance with the radical pedagogy of educationists in the Third World, such as Paulo Freire (1921–97), there was an ambivalence in that the resistance to state intervention might be interpreted as a conservative inclination to retain the social status quo and to resist the potential of state schooling to counteract **inequality**.   DEREK ROBBINS

death and dying

At its simplest, the cessation of life, death appears to be a biological rather than a sociological phenomenon. However, diagnosing death is not a simple process as conflicts around the status of patients in persistent vegetative states demonstrate. Within medicine, death can be defined in different ways: as the cessation of pulse and breathing; as the loss of the body's coordinating system, that is, lower brain stem, death; and cerebral cortex, that is higher brain stem, death. The current definition of death as the cessation of cerebral functioning is intimately tied to the harvesting of organs from people now dead, but whose vital physical functions – circulation and breathing – are intact and keeping their organs viable for transplantation.

While all individuals will die, how and when they die will reflect broader patterns of **inequality** in society, especially around socioeconomic status, **gender**, and **ethnicity**. Unskilled manual workers die earlier and sooner of known preventable diseases than their skilled and professional counterparts. While women experience more diagnoses of ill-health – based around the **medicalization** of their reproductive functions – they will outlive men by five years; and members of significantly disadvantaged ethnic minorities, particularly aboriginal people, will die from preventable conditions twenty-five years earlier than the affluent and educated members of higher **social classes**, who have much longer life expectancy. The greater the inequality in a society, the poorer the quality of life and the earlier the death for those at the bottom of the social system. Death is far from a straightforward biological event occurring to individuals as a consequence of fate.

The occurrence of death, particularly in hospitals, is a socially accomplished event. In *Time for Dying* (1961), Barney Glaser and **Anselm L. Strauss** demonstrated how dying was accounted for and made explicable and conformed to scripts that enabled patients, staff, and relatives to handle it. They identified "trajectories of dying"; the lingering death, which placed greatest strain on those around it; the expected quick death, which the staff could handle, but which took the relatives by surprise; and the unexpected quick death which challenged everyone's account of the situation. David Sudnow, in *Passing On: The Social Organisation of Dying* (1967), demonstrated the medicalization of dying in the hospital, where the doctor decides when death has taken place, certifies its occurrence and announces it, and coordinates the process so that those affected perform according to the rules. He also showed how the diagnosis of death would be delayed and heroic measures taken to save the life of an individual based on their perceived social standing: the young, the white, and the apparently well-off were all subjected to more medical interventions before they were finally "dead." Sociologists have also argued that social death can occur long before biological death. In this, individuals (for men as a consequence of **retirement** from **work** and for women as a consequence of widowhood) lose their social **networks**, become socially isolated, and lose the **social roles** that had provided their **identity**.

As a consequence of the demographic transition as a result of which more individuals now survive infancy and more women survive childbirth, social reactions to death have also changed. In the past, as Philip Ariés (1914–84) has shown (*Western Attitudes Towards Death From the Middle Ages to the Present*, 1974), the presence of death in **everyday life** was commonplace. As such it involved the whole **community**, with the dying person at the center of the event, presided over by a priest, with extensive public mourning. Modern death, under the control of the medical **profession**, is hidden away in the hospital, individualized and medicalized with little or no scope for public mourning. Death has become dirty and disgusting and an affront to modern medicine. The cultural highpoint of this attitude to death was reflected in the development of funeral parlors in the United States where morticians recreated the dead person as life-like, making them up and setting their hair.

Ariés's picture has in part been challenged by the rise of the hospice movement, established in England in 1967 by Dame Cicely Saunders (1918–2005). In a reaction to the prolongation of death as a consequence of medical interventions, Saunders sought to free death from medical control and its bureaucratization in the hospital, and to reassert its meaning in the context of a secular society. With the growth of hospices and the occupation of bereavement counselors we are now urged to talk about our death, to anticipate it as a serene and comfortable process, even to experience it as an opportunity for growth. Legislative changes around the **rights** of the terminally ill reflect this change: living wills allow us to stipulate do-not-resuscitate orders if we suffer neurological damage from accidents or medical misadventure; and lobbying for euthanasia – the right to a good death – is on the agenda of many European **political parties**. The assertion of the right to experience bereavement, too, has been legitimated by the popularity of the works of Elizabeth Kubler-Ross (*On Death and Dying*, 1969) and her argument that denial and anger were appropriate responses to death. As the population ages in the West, issues of rationing at end of life, definitions of death, euthanasia, and various forms of physician-assisted **suicide** will all become major social policy issues.   KEVIN WHITE

Debord, Guy (1931–1994)

Born in Paris, Debord committed suicide in 1994. He was a founding member of the revolutionary group Situationist International, whose journal of the same name he established and edited from 1958 to 1969. He was influenced by, and critical of, Dadaism and Surrealism, and more importantly a critical reading of **Karl Marx**'s work, Korl Korsch's *Marxism and Philosophy* (1923 [trans. 1973]) and **Georg Lukács**, *History and Class Consciousness* (1923 [trans. 1971]), as well as at crucial junctures works by Georges Bataille and especially Henri Lefebvre. Debord is best known for his writings for *Situationist International* but, above all, for his *Society of the Spectacle* (1967 [trans. 1970]). He is much less well known for his films, including *La Société du spectacle* (1973).

Set out in the form of theses, and lacking a specific definition of the spectacle, Debord outlines a critique of capitalist society as a whole as a society of the spectacle of the commodity. For him the spectacle should not be understood as a collection of images (and therefore is not confined to mass media technologies) but as a social relation between people that is mediated by images. The social relations in question are those of the dominant capitalist economic order, a world of appearances, of independent representations. The spectacle unites individuals as spectators only in their separation. Such reflections constitute Debord's attempt to think through Karl Marx's theory of commodity fetishism (see **alienation**) and Lukács's conception of reification in the context of contemporary capitalist societies, with an apparent abundance of commodities, such that the latter have totally colonized social life. The suggestive nature of the theory of the spectacle impacted upon later social theories of **consumption** and **consumer society**, and in the critique of modern urbanism and the notion of the **city** and its spaces as spectacle. The historical analyses of techniques for the creation of the spectacle have also been informed by Debord's work. As an intended revolutionary theory, it informed the student revolt of 1968 and beyond.

DAVID FRISBY

decarceration

This concerns a deliberate process of shifting attention away from prison towards the use of alternative measures in the **community**. While the search for alternatives to imprisonment has roots in the nineteenth century, the decarceration movement developed in the 1960s as part of a general critique of institutional responses to **crime** and deviancy and as part of what Stan Cohen in *Visions of Social Control* (1985) has termed the "destructuring impulse." Prisons and other total institutions (see **Erving Goffman**) attracted criticism for their degrading treatment of offenders, and their ineffectiveness in deterring and rehabilitating them.

The decarceration movement is closely associated with the radical penal lobby and abolitionist movement in Scandinavia, western Europe, and North America. Strong as these movements have been, there is seemingly little evidence to suggest effectiveness; on the contrary, prison rates soar on a worldwide basis. Thus "prison-centricity" continues to dominate political thinking about punishment. Critics have also indicated unintended consequences of decarceration. Andrew Scull, for example, in *Decarceration: Community Treatment and the Deviant – A Radical View* (1984), has pointed to the benign neglect of offenders within the community. Cohen has suggested that the extension of community treatment and punishment in place of prisons serves to reflect **Michel Foucault**'s notion of "dispersed discipline" in *Discipline and Punish* (1977). Thus, ever wider and stronger nets of **social control** are created rather than community measures displacing imprisonment. In recent years, the boundaries between liberty in the community and confinement in prison have been blurred through the development of home curfews and electronic monitoring, in particular.   LORAINE GELSTHORPE

decolonization

By the end of World War II, European conquest left some 750 million people, roughly one-third of the world's population, living under **colonialism**. Propelled by national liberation movements, decolonization proceeded relatively rapidly, albeit unevenly in time, space, and form, with experiences ranging from violent revolution via guerrilla warfare in Algeria – theorized by revolutionary **Franz Fanon** in *The Wretched of the Earth* (1961 [trans. 1965]) – to India's non-violent resistance led by Mahatma Gandhi (1869–1948). Uprisings were often brutally repressed, as Caroline Elkins, *Imperial Reckoning: The Untold Story of Britain's Gulag in Kenya* (2005), makes clear. Tragically, independence often ushered in new ruling **elites**, an "administrative bourgeoisie" as Gerard Chaliand argues in *Revolution in the Third World* (1989). In other instances, peoples elected to remain part of the metropolitan country as citizens, as in the Caribbean island of Martinique, in a move supported by leading figure of the African **diaspora** Aimé Césaire.

While Haiti and Latin America underwent decolonization during the revolutions establishing independent republics in the 1800s, in 1945 parts of the Middle East and much of Africa and Asia were still colonies. In the context of Cold War rivalry, postwar American **sociology** and western social science became engaged in the study of decolonization and newly independent Third World states, initially as part of the field of **modernization** studies. Yet the transformation of academic life during the turbulent 1960s opened up a variety of new approaches towards these questions, emphasizing **social conflict** over consensus. Among the new approaches seeking to understand the decolonization process were variants of what became know as **development theory**, including dependency and **world-systems analysis**. More recently, a host of other approaches to the question of decolonization have appeared, from **postcolonial theory** to the work of the subaltern school.

Recent work by sociologists emphasizes that colonization and decolonization come in waves, with the latter intimately related to hegemonic transitions and great power wars. So, for example, the global wars that characterized the period before the final emergence of British **hegemony** in the 1800s set off the Hispanic American revolutions. Likewise, World War II helped set off the period of formal decolonization of much of the rest of the world during the period of American hegemony. Peruvian sociologist Anibal Quijano coined the term "coloniality of **power**," to deal with the continuation of colonial-type relationships between core states and racial-ethnic, class, and gender groups even after formal decolonization. Mahmood Mamdani in *Citizen and Subject* (1996), and Crawford Young in "In Search of Civil Society," in J. Harbeson, D. Rothchild, and N. Chazan (eds.), *Civil Society and State in Africa* (1994: 33–50), have brilliantly analyzed **colonialism** and decolonization in Africa. There is now a dialogue taking place on these questions, with calls for a new, more radical, round of decolonization.

Imperialism, colonialism, and decolonization are key processes that have shaped the world, with reverberations right up to the present. The varieties of the colonial and postcolonial experiences, and perspectives on the aftermath of European, Japanese, or Soviet conquest, whether they be from the frameworks of neocolonialism, postcolonialism, or the coloniality of power, will continue to play an important part in debates regarding the past, present, and future of humanity.   THOMAS REIFER

deconstruction

This refers to a poststructuralist philosophy, associated with **structuralism**, much of whose impetus was provided by the writings of the French philosopher Jacques Derrida (1930–2004). Its early key texts were his *Of Grammatology* (1967 [trans. 1977]) and *Writing and Difference* (1967 [trans. 1978]). The contested nature of this philosophy, which has had a significant impact in literature, Cultural studies, architecture, gender theory, and some postmodern social theory, lies in its rejection of traditional philosophical groundings of knowledge and language. The latter assumes that the meaning of something is directly accessible to consciousness by its presence. Derrida, in contrast, argued that our understanding of an object necessitates grasping how it relates to other things and contexts, that is, to its difference. In particular, claims to universality would be challenged by this position. So too would be the binary oppositions found in structuralist analyses, in sociology (sacred/profane; **community/society**) and in wider discourse (man/woman).

The deconstruction of such oppositions or dualisms, which hierarchically privilege the first of the two oppositions in the dualism, also has a subversive intention. This is directed at what Derrida termed the "logocentrism" of western thought, which has been devoted to the search for an order of truth and a universal language. Derrida argued that there were no fixed orders of meaning. Deconstruction therefore challenges the legitimacy of such preestablished hierarchical dualisms, in order to remove their authoritative status. It therefore also aims to empower those marginalized by such discourse, and to encourage the proliferation of difference.

DAVID FRISBY

deduction
– see **explanation**.

deferential workers
These workers were identified by **David Lockwood** in *The Blackcoated Worker* (1958) while he was researching car workers in the British General Motors plant at Vauxhall. Many workers entered the automobile industry from other **occupations**, attracted by high postwar wages. Lockwood analyzed their images of **society**. Some had deferential attitudes to **authority**, which, as Howard Newby in *The Deferential Worker* (1977) explored, were ingrained in rural life and which translated into their attitudes to authority in the plant. Not everyone shared the same image of society and the differentiation was patterned. For Lockwood, the patterning was attributable to social origins and their social reproduction through extended **networks** of social **interaction**; it was through the latter that the former were reproduced or

transformed. Where the moral framework of the dominant value system promotes the endorsement of existing **inequality** in ways that the subordinated accept as legitimate, and this **legitimacy** is expressed through their deference both to those in positions of localized and immediate authority and to the **social status** order in general, which they exemplify through the types of **civil society** that they choose to construct through their networks, then deferential workers are reproduced. These deferential workers presume that the social order comprises an organic entity, with the rich man in his castle and the poor man at his gate. Thus, inequality is seen to be inevitable as well as just; the social order is seen as fixed and the individual's place within it is relatively unchangeable. The idea of the deferential worker has been widely used and generalized to address the overlay of both **gender** and ethnic relations on the basic **social class** model of society that Lockwood employed.

STEWART CLEGG

definition of the situation
– see **William I. Thomas**.

delinquency
– see **deviance**.

delinquent subculture
– see **deviance**.

demedicalization
– see **medicalization**.

democracy
Derived from the Greek terms *demos* (the people) and *kratos* (power), democracy usually describes a form of political rule that is justified and exercised by the people for the benefit of the people. Democracy is a model of government that can apply to different types of political communities and levels of political **organization**. In the contemporary context it is most commonly associated with the institutional framework of the nation-state. However, modern democratic states are representative democracies and therefore quite different from the democratic order that was initially proposed in the classical Greek model of direct democracy. This distinctiveness is probably best expressed in terms of different notions of freedom, as described by Benjamin Constant in *The Liberty of the Ancients Compared with that of the Moderns* (1819 [trans. 1988]). In the classical direct democracy system, each citizen had a fair chance of holding political office and, therefore,

of influencing the political choices of the **state**. In a modern representative democracy, in contrast, individual citizens can only influence the political decisionmaking process at the margins, and their involvement in democratic governance is generally limited to electing the political representatives who will speak in their name. It must be stressed, however, that early forms of democracy could only provide such political opportunities by restricting the political franchise to certain categories of citizens. In later democratic systems, the franchise slowly expanded to include the poor, women, slaves, and other ethnic/racial groups, but this greater inclusiveness unavoidably reduced the number of opportunities for direct political involvement available to any one citizen.

Early critics of representative forms of democratic government, like Jean-Jacques Rousseau (1712–78), argued that this model of democracy was so far removed from the original conception of this political process that it did not deserve its name. This criticism is also at the heart of many contemporary critiques of democratic **politics** (for example neo-**Marxism**, radical democracy, grassroots democracy), which argue that people experience a very limited form of democracy in the **institutions** of the modern nation-state. There are, however, powerful arguments that support the notion of representative democracy as the most appropriate form of modern governance. **Max Weber** presented the emergence of this representative model as a consequence of the rise of the bureaucratic state and the bureaucratization (see **bureaucracy**) of politics. In "Politics as a Vocation" (1919 [trans. 1994]), Weber argued that, because of the complexity of government and **society**, political parties staffed by professional politicians were needed to organize mass politics in a manageable and effective way. This process was conducive to a plebiscitarian type of democracy, in which people's ability to govern themselves was to be understood principally in terms of their being able to choose their leaders from amongst those professional politicians running for office. This empirical approach to understanding the functioning of modern democracy was reinterpreted by **Joseph Alois Schumpeter**, and it became popularly known as a "minimalist" model of democracy. In *Capitalism, Socialism, and Democracy* (1942), Schumpeter likened this approach to democratic politics to an analysis of the economic behavior of agents in free-market **capitalism**. To liken voters' behavior to consumers' choice is to say that the agents' freedom essentially consists in buying or not buying the products that are being offered by

competing parties/companies. Such an approach provided the impulse for the statistical study of electoral politics in terms of voters' behavior that dominates political life today.

The other important difference between modern and ancient democracy is the role of the liberal Constitution. Building on the tradition of **liberalism**, modern democratic states are constitutional orders that stress the importance of a rule of law (see **law and society**) that protects the **rights** of the individual. This constitutional model, which, in the tradition of **Baron Charles de Montesquieu**'s *The Spirit of the Laws* (1748 [1989]), usually involves a degree of formal separation between executive and legislative power, protects citizens not only from the despotism of unelected leaders, but also from the abuses of democratically elected governments. This latter concern is probably best presented in terms of the opposition between constitutional democracy and majoritarian democracy. Liberal constitution orders are designed to avoid the main drawback of majoritarian systems that **Alexis de Tocqueville** described in *Democracy in America* (1835–40 [trans. 2000]) as "the tyranny of the majority." While in a majoritarian democracy it is possible for the majority to vote in favor of the elimination of a minority, in a liberal democracy such a possibility can be countered by constitutional provisos. Although the people can change the Constitution, this process is a lengthy and complex one, which ensures that in the short term at least certain political options are not available to the elected political leaders – but as the example of the Weimar Republic (1919–33) illustrates, this system is never entirely foolproof.

At the end of the twentieth century the notion that democracy is most meaningfully embodied by a liberal democratic form of government has become widespread, particularly after waves of democratization swept across Latin America and southern and eastern Europe as far as Russia. However, the idea that democracy and liberalism necessarily go hand in hand has been challenged in east Asia and in the Muslim world by proponents of "Asian **values**" and "Islamic democracy." These actors argue that the "Western" liberal assumptions contained in this dominant discourse about democratic governance reflect a cultural bias. Today, despite the efforts of advocates of deliberative democracy, like **Jürgen Habermas**, who emphasize the possibility of a consensus reached through public deliberation, it seems that the only definition of democracy that can avoid these cultural dilemmas is one that is couched in negative terms. In other words, democracy is a form of government in which those wielding political **power** do so only by virtue of the popular mandate that they received from the citizens, and no other claim to **legitimacy** can trump this principle of democratic rule. As a political principle, the utilization of the notion of democracy has, therefore, important epistemological implications. It indicates that in this political order, as a matter of principle, no citizen can claim to know better than his or her neighbor what is politically desirable and achievable. Democracy as a form of government simply reflects this equality of judgment in political life and its institutionalization in a political system. And, as we enter the **information** age, changes in the way in which political opinion can be estimated and fed back into the decisionmaking process have the potential to redefine democratic politics at the level of both party politics and state politics.   FREDERIC VOLPI

democratization
– see **democracy**.

demographic transition
– see **demography**.

demography
The term demography comes from the Greek words for population (*demos*) and for description or writing (*graphia*). The term *démographie* is believed to have been first used in 1855 by the Belgian statistician Achille Guillard in his book *Elements of Human Statistics or Comparative Demography* (1855 [trans. 1985]).

Demography is concerned with how large (or small) populations are – that is, their size; how the populations are composed according to age, sex, race, marital status, and other characteristics – that is, their composition; and how populations are distributed in physical space, for example how urban and rural they are – that is, their spatial distribution. Of equal or greater importance, demography is interested in the changes over time in the size, composition, and distribution of populations, as these result from the processes of **fertility**, mortality, and **migration**.

Demography is also concerned with answering the question of why these variables operate and change in the way they do. That is, why do populations increase (or decrease) in numbers? Why do they become older or younger? Why do they become more urban or rural?

One paradigm in demography uses mainly demographic variables to answer the above questions,

and this is known as formal demography. Another paradigm uses mainly non-demographic variables drawn from sociology, economics, psychology, geography, biology, and so forth, to answer the questions, and this is known as social demography or population studies.

For instance, formal demographers might address population differences in birth rates or in death rates by examining their differences in age composition or in sex composition. Other things being equal, younger populations will have higher birth rates than older populations; and populations with an abundance of females over males will have lower death rates than populations with an abundance of males.

Alternately, social demographers might address the above differences in populations by examining differences in, say, their socioeconomic status. Other things being equal, populations with high socioeconomic status will have lower birth rates and death rates than populations with low socioeconomic status.

Demographic **data** will help illustrate the differences between these two approaches. Take the demographic question of why human populations have different levels of fertility. Countries differ with respect to their total fertility rates (roughly defined as the average number of children born to a woman during her childbearing years). In Spain and Italy in 2004, for instance, women were producing an average of 1.3 children each, whereas in Somalia the average number was 7.1 and in Niger, 8.0 (Population Reference Bureau, 2004). Why do these fertility differences exist? The social demographer would go beyond purely demographic concerns and might focus on the processes of industrialization and **modernization**, while the formal demographer would rely more on purely demographic kinds of explanations.

Another example focuses on rates of population growth. In 2004 the rates of population change due only to births and deaths in Hungary and Bulgaria were –0.4 percent and –0.6 percent respectively. In contrast, the rates in Malawi, and Saudi Arabia were 3.1 percent and 3.0 percent, respectively.

Why are these four countries growing at such drastically different rates? Why do two of the countries have negative growth rates and the other two positive rates? The formal demographer might develop an answer by considering the birth rates of these countries. The numbers of babies born per 1,000 population in 2004 in Hungary, Bulgaria, Malawi, and Saudi Arabia were 9, 9, 51 and 32, respectively. The latter two countries have higher rates of growth than the former two countries partly because their birth rates are higher. The social demographer would first consider the birth rate differentials, but would then go beyond this demographic consideration to an answer involving non-demographic factors which may be influencing the birth rates. Perhaps the economy has something to do with these differences, where countries with low per capita incomes and low literacy rates for women tend to have higher birth rates. Perhaps the level of industrialization of the country has an impact (the more industrialized countries generally have lower birth rates).

Social demography is broader in scope and orientation than formal demography. As S. H. Preston writes in "The Contours of Demography: Estimates and Projections," in *Demography* (1993: 593), it includes "research of any disciplinary stripe on the causes and consequences of population change." Demographers, however, do not always agree about the boundaries and restrictions of their field. J. Caldwell states the problem succinctly in "Demography and Social Science" (1996): "What demography is and what demographers should be confined to doing remains a difficult area in terms not only of the scope of professional interests, but also of the coverage aimed at in the syllabuses for students and in what is acceptable for journals in the field."

In the United States, most graduate training programs in demography are located in departments of sociology (although this is not the case in many other countries). Some American demographers thus argue that demography is best treated as a subdiscipline or specialization of sociology, owing to this organizational relationship. The late Kingsley Davis (1908–97), who served at different times as President of both the Population Association of America and the American Sociological Association, wrote in 1948 in his classic sociology textbook, *Human Society* (1948), that "the science of population, sometimes called demography, represents a fundamental approach to the understanding of human society." The relationship between sociology and demography is hence a fundamental one: "Society is both a necessary and sufficient cause of population trends."

Change in the size of a population over a certain period of time is due to changes in the same time period in the three demographic processes of fertility, mortality, and migration. A population may change its size over a given time interval by adding the number of persons born during the period, subtracting those dying during the interval, and adding the number of persons moving into the area and subtracting those moving out of the area.

The dynamics of population change may be represented in a form known as the population equation, also known as the balancing equation

$$P2 = P1 + B - D + / - M$$

where P2 is the size of the population at the end of the time interval; P1 is the size of the population at the beginning of the time interval; B is the number of births occurring in the population during the interval; D is the number of deaths occurring in the population during the interval; and M is the net number of migrants moving to, or away from, the population during the interval.

To illustrate, the following are data for the United States for the time interval of July 1, 2001 to June 30, 2002:

US population size, July 1, 2002: 288,368,698;

US population size, July 1, 2001: 285,317,559;

Births from July 1, 2001 through June 30, 2002: 4,047,642;

Deaths from July 1, 2001 through June 30, 2002: 2,445,837;

Immigrations from July 1, 2001 through June 30, 2002: 1,664,334;

Emigrations from July 1, 2001 through June 30, 2002: 215,000.

These data may be incorporated into the population equation as follows:

$$P2(288,368,698) = P1(285,317,559) + B(4,047,642)$$
$$-D(2,445,837) + M(1,664,334 - 215,000)$$

The population equation describes a closed and determinate model, provided its geographical area remains the same. This is so because population change can occur only through the operation of the three demographic processes. Stated in another way, a population changes in terms of two forms of entry (births and in-migration) and two forms of exit (deaths and out-migration); no other variables need be entertained. Of course, if one wishes to determine why fertility and mortality are at certain levels, or why in-migration and out-migration are different, other non-demographic variables need to be entertained. As discussed above, these are the concerns of social demography.

The word "population" derives from the Latin *populare* (to populate) and the Latin noun *populatio*. Geoffrey McNicoll, in the *Encyclopedia of Population* (2003), notes that, in ancient times, the verb *populare* meant to lay waste, plunder, or ravage and the noun *populatio* meant a plundering or despoliation. These usages became obsolete by the eighteenth century. The modern use of the word population first appeared in 1597 in an essay by Francis Bacon (1561–1626).

Strictly speaking, a population is a group or collection of items. But to a demographer a population is a group or collection of people. We may distinguish between a specific population or group of actual people alive at a given period of time – for example the population of the United States as of April 1, 2000 – and the population that persists over time even though its actual members may change, for example the population of China over the past 4,000 years, and even into its future. The more common use of the term population by demographers and in modern English usage is with reference to a delimited set, with unambiguous membership criteria, such as the population of the People's Republic of China as identified and enumerated in its 2000 census.

In a similar vein, N. B. Ryder, in "Notes on the Concept of a Population" (1964 *American Journal of Sociology* 69 (5): 447–63), defines a population as an aggregate of individuals defined in spatial and temporal terms. It is not necessarily a **group**, which in sociological terms requires some forms of interpersonal **interaction** and the development of a sense of **community**. The analysis of human populations is inherently dynamic because attention is focused on changes in the population over time. The population equation is a demonstration. Ryder also states that the population model is both microdynamic and macrodynamic in nature. This means that processes of change in fertility, mortality, and migration can be identified at both the individual and aggregate levels. This distinction lies at the very heart of the population model because it introduces Alfred J. Lotka's distinction between the persistence of the individual and the persistence of the aggregate, to be found in *Analytical Theory of Biological Populations* (1934 [trans. 1998]). All human beings are born, live for some period of time, and then die. But a population aggregate is not temporally limited, provided that enough individuals continue to enter the population to replace those exiting; the population in this sense is immortal.

Population aggregates, in terms both of the changes in numbers and of the characteristics of those entering and exiting, can experience changes not reducible to individuals who constitute the population. For instance, when individuals enter a population through birth or in-migration, they will "age" by becoming older. But the population aggregate cannot only become older, it can also become younger, provided that births exceed deaths and the in-migrants are younger than the out-migrants. The racial and sex composition of a population aggregate may also change if more members of one race (see **race and ethnicity**) or sex enter it than another. Typically, persons do not change their race or sex. Indeed, all human **institutions** and **organizations** may be conceived in these terms. One way that **social change** may be studied is by the monitoring of compositional change caused by entrances and exits.

Age is the key variable in the study of populations because it reflects the passage of time. It is subject to metric measurement and provides a precise statement of the time spent by individuals in a population. Demographers use two key concepts in studying age-related changes, namely, the life-cycle and the cohort. The former permits the charting of the **life-course** experiences of individuals, for example, age of entry into and exit from formal education, entry into full-time employment and subsequent **retirement**, first **marriage**, births of first and last **children**, and so forth.

The cohort is an aggregate of individuals who experience important events in their life-cycles at the same time. The defining event is often year of birth, but cohorts are also based on year of entry into or graduation from college, year of birth of first child, year of retirement, and so forth. In this context, age as the passage of time is the linkage between the history of the individual and population.

Cohorts (see **generations**) are valuable analytically because they are subpopulations intermediate between the behaviors of individuals and the population. In terms of birth cohorts, we can conceptualize the population at any given moment in time as a cross-section of cohorts which are arranged uniformly in a staggered manner, each one on top of its immediate predecessor in time.

In recent decades some of the most impressive and enduring accomplishments in demography have been made in formal demography. Features of the population model, some of which have just been discussed, have been developed, and the fruitfulness of the approach and its core concerns have been demonstrated.   DUDLEY L. POSTON

denomination

This term is used to differentiate among diverse religious traditions and to categorize diverse affiliations within a shared **tradition** (most usually within Protestantism and Judaism). Denominationalism emerged as a useful construct in describing and understanding American religious history because of the **pluralism** of its religious traditions and the notable diversity of the range of Protestant sects (see **church–sect typology**) that have characterized America since colonial times. Symbolically, denominationalism offers tacit acknowledgment that there is no "one true universal Church," but that diverse religious denominations, while founded in a belief in a common divine source, develop in particular ways and assume particular organizational characteristics because of the accretions of history and **culture**. Denominationalism is a dynamic process contingent on multiple contextual factors and in American society is seen as a critical component of cultural **identity** and belonging. Will Herberg argued that the tripartite options of *Protestant-Catholic-Jew* (1955) offered a socially acceptable way for Americans of diverse ethnic and religious backgrounds to maintain a distinct identity while affirming their shared commitment to **religion** and, by extension, to American **values** (its **civil religion**). Denominationalism is intertwined with other significant aspects of American religion, including the centrality of personal freedom and choice in regard to churches and doctrines.

The heuristic use of denomination rather than church or religion offers a nuanced way of thinking about the place of religion in a particular society; in the contemporary United States, for example, although Protestantism is the largest religious tradition (or church), Catholicism is the largest single denomination, and is followed by (Protestant) Southern Baptists. The comparative **social status** of different denominations (in terms of membership, institutional activities, political influence) over time is also a useful way of tracking, and theorizing about, changes in denominational membership and activities. Historically, denominational splitting occurred within Protestantism because of disputes over various theological and doctrinal questions (for example, requirements for salvation or the meanings of baptism and the eucharist) or forms of **authority** (hierarchical or congregational), differences in geographical region, ethnic/national origins (for example, Scotch Presbyterians), or **social class**, and in regard to political issues (such as **slavery**). Each denomination, therefore, has a discrete historical, cultural, and organizational identity whose worldview and practices distinguish it from other denominations.

In recent decades, there is increased evidence that denominational identity is weakening in the United States. Although it was never an all-encompassing identity – as indicated by the significant rates of intermarriage among Protestants of different denominations, and of church and denominational switching or mobility more generally – it has lost some of its salience both as an anchor of individual identity and in terms of demarcating sociocultural and political boundaries. There is some evidence that the conservative/liberal ideological division within denominations is more important in differentiating individuals and producing coalitions among individuals and groups independently of denomination (for example, **Robert Wuthnow**, *The Restructuring of American Religion*, 1988). Denominational affiliation still matters, however, and constrains or moderates individual attitudes and behavior (such as health and life-style practices). Strong denominational loyalties and commitments on the part of individuals can also constrain interorganizational relationships between denominations, and have an impact on specific issues (such as **welfare reforms** and gay marriages) in the formation of **public policy**.

One of the tensions confronting denominations today is to achieve a balance between articulating their own particular denominational identity and simultaneously engaging in interdenominational and interchurch discourse and cooperation across various theologically charged (for example, abortion or stem-cell research) and economic and political issues (such as **globalization**).

MICHELE DILLON

denominationalization
– see **denomination**.

dependency theory
– see **development theory**.

deprivation
– see **relative deprivation**.

descent
– see **kinship**.

descent groups
– see **kinship**.

desegregation
– see **segregation**.

deskilling
Philosophical anthropology sometimes conceives of the essence of humankind in terms of *homo faber* rather than *homo oeconomicus*. The former highlights people's capacity to acquire skills,

engage in creative **labor**, and derive pleasure from exercising these skills. In contrast, rational economic calculation could lead to deskilling to cut material and monetary costs. In general, deskilling reduces the skills needed for a given product or service and/or involves loss of skills due to failure to exercise them (for example, through long-term **unemployment**).

Classical **political economy** discussed deskilling. Adam Smith (1723–90) illustrated it through the division of labor in pin manufacture, and **Marx** showed how this was reinforced by the transition to machinofacture. Postindustrialism in turn deskills intellectual labor through smart machines and expert systems that integrate tacit knowledge and intellectual skills. Examples include automation of scientific tests, software for legal work, and work in call centers.

Labor economists and economic sociology continue to discuss whether modern economies require more or less skilled labor. This reflects two countervailing trends: while new labor processes and products may be more knowledge- and skill-intensive, the pressure to rationalize such processes and products may lead to deskilling. These contradictory tendencies were both emphasized in the work of Harry Braverman, the foremost proponent of the deskilling thesis in monopoly **capitalism**, in *Labor and Monopoly Capital: The Degradation of Work in the Twentieth Century* (1974). Some commentators also suggest that deskilling leads to worker **alienation**, disempowerment, and dehumanization, and may prompt resistance from manual and mental labor. Others emphasize that it can lead to cleaner and less physically demanding work.   BOB JESSOP

determinism

This is the view that, given certain prior conditions, there is an inevitability about the social processes, events, and happenings that will subsequently be brought about. These subsequent happenings are said to be entirely determined by the given prior conditions. Determinism can take many forms but perhaps the Marxist variant is the most well-known sociological example. Determinism here is associated with those interpretations of **Karl Marx**'s work in which the economic base is said to determine what happens at the level of law, **politics**, and **ideology**. The determining conditions here are the economic and class relations structured around the mode of production, whether this be feudal, capitalist, or some other. Politics, law, and ideology, the so-called superstructures, would be seen as merely the

surface manifestations, the epiphenomena, of the deeper economic and class structures that provide the real force and energy driving all of social reality. Determinism can also take a range of other forms in which, instead of the economic taking the role of the determining force, this role is given to the genetic, cultural, discursive, demographic, or militaristic dimensions of social life, to name but some. Thus, many racist and sexist arguments are based on forms of genetic determinism in which allegedly inferior genetic inheritances determine lower levels of capability. Or, in a military version, it may be assumed that the nation with the greatest firepower will inevitably come to dominate the world **economy**. It is the economy this time that plays the role of epiphenomenon.

While there can sometimes be some truth in deterministic arguments – such that the economic level does clearly have effects on other aspects of life, and that genetic inheritance will make some things broadly possible and other things impossible – the truths are often partial and overly simplified, and at other times they are simply wrong. Two salient weaknesses can typically be found in deterministic arguments. The first entails a crude view of the nature of the object or set of relations that are said to be doing the determining. Thus, to take the Marxist example, the economic level itself does in fact require certain legal, political, and ideological preconditions for it to exist in the first place, something stressed by many twentieth-century neo-Marxists. The economic level is itself a more complex and plural entity than a crude account suggests.

The second weakness is closely related, and entails an overly simple, or reductionist, view of the causal process by which the determining object is said to bring about the things it determines. In contrast to a laboratory experiment in which strict controls ensure that object X produces certain effects on object Y without any unwanted factors intervening, causality in social life is freighted with a plurality of complicating factors. Any effect that an object such as the economy has on another entity such as politics – even if it were possible to draw a ring around the two so neatly – would typically be mediated, tempered, and complicated by many other factors. These factors could include anything from constitutional statutes and party doctrines to media representations and nationalistic ideologies, not to mention the uncertainties and creativities of human **agency** within each of these spheres.

The typical stance of determinism has been a view that social events are pre-determined, and that they are pre-determined by a particular kind of entity to the exclusion of other entities. A more adequate view is that social happenings do have causal determinants which bring them about, but that these determinants tend to be both internally complex and plural, and that they combine to produce social events but without having been bound to do so.   ROB STONES

detraditionalization
– see **tradition**.

development theory
Coming to prominence in the context of United States **hegemony** and attendant Cold War superpower rivalry, development or **modernization** theory assumed the existence of national societies developing in parallel with each other in a natural and universal evolutionary process. There were strains, to be sure. The Russian Revolution, as Theodor Shanin argued in *Russia 1905–07. Revolution as a moment of Truth* (1986), can be seen as the outcome of some of the contradictions of "developing societies," and rapid industrialization (see **industrial society**) thereafter – though brutal – was held up as a model for Third World states seeking to overcome economic backwardness. Both the United States and the Soviet Union aimed to convince other states to ally with them in the Cold War in exchange for military and economic aid, each arguing for the superiority of their model of economic development.

Structural-functionalist theorists, notably **Talcott Parsons**, held up those industrialized capitalist societies that had achieved high levels of **wealth** and democratic political forms, notably western Europe, its settler offshoots – the United States, Australia, Canada, and New Zealand – and states such as Japan, as models of successful development. **Poverty** and underdevelopment were conceived of as reflecting the prevalence of traditional cultural **values** thwarting moves towards greater economic development and **differentiation**.

In the context of the wave of **decolonization** after World War II, and new international bodies like the United Nations (UN), new voices challenged this consensus. One early important critique was that developed by the UN Economic Commission on Latin America (ECLA), based in Santiago, Chile, and formed in 1948 despite the strong objections of the United States, and led by the Argentine Raúl Prebisch (1901–86). While Latin America had been independent since the Hispanic American revolutions of the 1800s, the

ECLA's economists emphasized the continued structural dependence of the region on advanced countries such as the United States. The ECLA analyzed how the formation of peripheral export economies served the needs of the powerful states at the center of the global capitalist economy throughout the colonial period and thereafter.

The ECLA's studies had a major impact on the emergence of a distinct Latin American perspective on development and underdevelopment, thus playing an important role in the emergence of dependency theory. The career of Celso Furtado (1920–2004), widely regarded as the most influential Brazilian economist of the twentieth century and a leader of the structural economists of the region, exemplifies this connection. Prebisch saw Furtado's ability early on and chose him as the first head of the newly created economic development division. In a 1956 book, Furtado became one of the earliest social scientists to use the term dependency, and went on to serve as Brazil's Minister of Planning in the populist government of João Goulart (1918–76), until the United States overthrew the democratically elected government in 1964.

The structural economists of ECLA advocated the importation and development of infant industries through import substitution industrialization (ISI) and Keynesian (see **John Maynard Keynes**) techniques of economic demand stimulus. Yet, aside from the relatively unique experience of East Asia, for all the gains made in economic growth and development, ISI failed to overcome economic dependency on foreign actors and thus gave way to the emergence of a radicalized dependency theory. In the context of the Cuban Revolution and the United States response to this in the region, including through support for the emergence of military regimes, many of the dependency theorists advocated anti-imperialist revolutions, often as part of a broader socialist or Marxist-inspired strategy for Third World development.

Marxist economist Paul Baran (1910–64) was an early precursor of the *dependentistas*, who included left-wing social scientists such as Samir Amin, Frederick Clairmonte, Alain de Janvry, Anibal Quijano, Cheryl Payer, Dudley Seers, Walter Rodney, and Theotonio dos Santos. Among the most prominent were Fernando Henrique Cardoso (later President of Brazil) and **André Gunder Frank**, both of them associated to varying degrees with ECLA. Frank coined the term "the development of underdevelopment," arguing the two dimensions were dialectically related. In contrast to the modernization school, dependency theorists argued that the poverty of the periphery and wealth of the core were a structural outcome of unequal power relations between different states and peoples, not cultural differences or **tradition**. Such so-called feudal remnants – the domination of landed classes and so forth – were seen instead as products of capitalist development in the Third World dictated by the center. While inspired by the arguments of **Karl Marx**, dependency theorists differed in that they argued **capitalism** brought not modernization but instead subordination and polarization through surplus extraction. The institutional structure of domination here included what Peter Evans, in *Dependent Development* (1979), called the "triple alliance" of multinational, **state**, and local capital. Associated critical actors, which Robin Broad, David Pion-Berlin, Michael McClintock, and others have analyzed, included the core states, US-dominated Bretton Woods **institutions** – the International Monetary Fund (IMF) and the World Bank (WB) – and associated core military intervention and support for repressive regimes.

Despite all the frustrations of postwar development, it is now seen by many as the golden age of postwar capitalism. Governance of market forces and related social programs led to high growth rates and a growing advantage in the 1960s and 1970s for Third World states in the area of trade and development. The 1980s, in contrast, saw such dramatic reversals in social gains that it was called "the lost decade of the South." The generalized economic crisis hit both the Second and Third Worlds, eventually leading to the collapse of the Soviet Empire in eastern Europe and the breakup of the Soviet Union, and the return of much of the region to its original Third World role. These epochal shifts of the 1980s were part of the "counterrevolution in development policy" associated with the hegemony of **neoliberalism**, **globalization**, and finance capital, propelled by the United States' move towards high interest rates and massive borrowing on the global capital markets. Yet among radical critics, such as those of **world-systems analysis**, what was signaled here was actually not the victory but instead the crisis of developmentalism, the shared belief among self-declared capitalist or communist states that the gains and benefits of the world economy were open to all those who put in the requisite effort. Here, the rise of liberation theology, Islamic **fundamentalism**, and other **social movements** were seen as part of the resistance to developmentalism and its failures.

The US economic boom of the 1990s, coming in the wake of the communist collapse, added to the revival of modernization **ideologies** and the neo-liberal Washington Consensus, seen as the endpoint of history by scholars such as Francis Fukuyama in his *The End of History and the Last Man* (1989). For a time, the Asian economic crisis of 1997 and concomitant dramatic plummeting of **incomes** in the region led to renewed discussion about the superiority of the United States model of capitalism. Yet soon afterwards mainstream **intellectuals** such as Jagdish Bhagwati, along with radical critics such as Walden Bello, and Peter Gowan in his *The Global Gamble* (1999), pointed towards the unleashing of speculative capital – from hedge funds to derivatives – called for by neo-liberal policymakers, as causing the crisis. In the wake of the collapse of the US speculative boom, the bursting of the bubble, the ensuing corporate scandals and economic meltdown of Argentina – the former darling of the IMF – more sober assessments, questioning both the modernization and neo-liberal approaches, thus gained ground.

Authors such as Alice Amsden, Bruce Cumings, Chalmers Johnson, Robert Wade, and former chief World Bank economist Joseph Stiglitz, highlighted the structural conditions allowing for East Asia's economic advance and the role of neoliberalism in the crisis. Particular attention was paid to the developmental state, as Meredith Woo-Cumings explores in her edited volume (*The Developmental State*, 1999), and Alexander Gershenkron's advantages of backwardness or late development, along with a host of unique conditions – land reform, US military aid for export-oriented industrialization in a productivist mold, limitations on foreign direct investment, and capital controls – that allowed for East Asia's ascent, now joined by China. In essence, contrary to ideologies of neoliberalism, in East Asia's export-oriented industrialization the **state** played a pronounced role in guiding market forces. More recently, Ha-Joon Chang in *Kicking Away the Ladder* (2002) has shown that virtually all the developed countries used infant industry promotion and protectionism before opening their **markets** to free competition, as Frederich List predicted, by telling the rest of the world – through organizations ranging from the IMF to the World Trade Organization – that they were not allowed to use such mechanisms. Indeed, advanced countries still interfere with market forces in numerous ways, from agricultural subsidies to military spending serving to prop up high-technology industry.

Development theory is today being radically reformulated by a host of iconoclastic scholars, from Mike Davis in *Late Victorian Holocausts: El Nino Famines and the Making of the Third World* (2001) to the efforts of the Nobel-prize-winning economist Amartya Sen. Though Sen generally stays away from the question of **power** in the global economy as a whole, his works nevertheless complement these perspectives. In books such as *India: Development and Participation* (2002), Jean Dreze and Amartya Sen redefined development as the process of enhancing human freedom, focusing on the quality of life and related social opportunities, seen as both the means and ends of development. By shifting focus from the question of income to human capabilities – with poverty redefined as capability deprivation – Sen and his colleagues redirected attention towards **inequalities** within states and regions. Though not denying the potentially positive relationship between economic growth, rising incomes, and livelihood, Sen demonstrates that various countries with a high Gross National Product have abysmal indicators in terms of the quality of life, while, through political action and **public policy** other societies have made tremendous achievements in terms of quality of life, even in the absence of significant economic performance. Moreover, in books such as *Development and Freedom* (1999), drawing on a wealth of empirical studies, Sen demonstrated the positive relationship between the improvement of people's freedom and capabilities – notably basic **education**, **health**, rights to **information**, and democratic participation, especially for women – for economic growth, development, and fertility reduction. Sen has furthermore highlighted success stories, from the Kerala region in India to East Asia, the latter of which, for all its problems, can be seen in relative terms as what Fernado Fajyzylber, in his important *Unavoidable Industrial Restructuring in Latin America* (1990), called the "Growth-with-equity-industrializing countries."

World-systems analysts have drawn on the work of Roy F. Harrod (1900–78) who, in a series of famous articles, created the modern theory of growth. In particular, Giovanni Arrighi in *The Long Twentieth Century* (1994) and Fred Hirsch in *The Social Limits of Growth* (1976) have shown that, while options for upward mobility are open to some, ultimately they rest on relational processes of exploitation and exclusion that reproduce the oligarchic structures of the world economy, within which income and resources are used disproportionately by the few at the expense of the many. Though many states of the South internalized aspects of the **social structures** of the core through industrialization, this failed to close the widening development gap. Recent *United Nations Human Development Reports* (1998, 1999) note that (1) the wealthiest 20 percent of the world's population accounts for some 86 percent of private consumption expenditures; and (2) income inequality between the world's poor and rich states has increased from roughly 3:1 in 1820, to 11:1 in 1913, before rising from 35:1 to 70:1 from 1950 to 1992. The *Forbes* (2004) most recent annual report on the nearly 600 billionaires in the world reveals their wealth to be close to US$1.9 trillion; this at a time when over a billion persons across the globe live on under a dollar a day, according to World Bank statistics, while the gap between high-, middle-, and low-income states continues to widen. In recent years these increasing inequalities have given rise to a global social **justice** and peace movement, replete with its own annual World Social Forum, bringing together concerned citizens and activists in non-governmental organizations, to build a better world. Thus, at the dawn of the twenty-first century, the questions of economic development and what model(s) might allow for truly universal values of greater global **democracy**, prosperity, and sustainable development remain one of the great unresolved questions of the present.   THOMAS REIFER

deviance

In simple terms, this can be defined as (real or purported) non-normative behavior that, if detected, can be subject to informal or formal sanctions. Deviant behavior is norm-violating conduct that is subject to **social control**. In their textbook *Social Deviance and Crime: An Organizational and Theoretical Approach* (2000), Charles Tittle and Raymond Paternoster summarize the predominant ways in which sociologists have defined deviance and offer their own definition: any type of behavior that the majority of a given group regards as unacceptable *or* that evokes a collective response of a negative type (13). Deviants are those who engage in behavior that deviates from **norms** in a disapproved direction in sufficient degree to exceed the tolerance limits of a discernible social **group**, such that the behavior is likely to elicit a negative sanction if detected.

Howard S. Becker, an influential scholar of deviance, pointed out in *Outsiders: Studies in the Sociology of Deviance* (1963) that deviance is not a *quality* of the act one commits, but rather a consequence of the *application* by others of rules and

135

sanctions to an "offender." Whether an act is deviant depends on how others who have social **power** and **influence** define the act. One could commit any act, but it is not deviant in its social consequence if no elements of society react to it. Becker called social acts "rule-breaking behavior," and actors violating norms of **society** "rule-breakers." As John I. Kitsuse (1923–2003), a well-known scholar of deviance best-known for furthering a "labeling approach" to understanding rule violation, made clear in his body of work spanning over three decades, forms of behavior per se do not differentiate deviants from nondeviants; conventional and conforming members of the society identify and interpret behavior as deviant, and then transform rule-breaking behavior into deviance and persons who break rules or norms into deviants.

Many theoretical frameworks, including strain, subculture, learning, and labeling, have been developed by sociologists to explain the occurrences, forms, consequences, and labeling of deviance. One way to make sense of these various frameworks is to organize them according to the degree to which they are designed to address one of two central questions in the study of deviance. First, normative theories ask "who violates norms and why?" Second, reactivist theories ask "why are certain types of norm violations by certain types of individuals (and not others) reacted to as deviant and result in the stigmatization of the rule-breaker?" Relatedly, theories of deviance can be classified as macro and micro. Macro-theories focus on societal and group structures, while micro-theorists focus on individuals and the interactional patterns in which they engage and to which they are subject. Classified along these dimensions, many – but not all – theories of deviance have been categorized by James Orcutt as "macro-normative," "micro-normative," "macro-reactionist," and "micro-reactionist" (*Analyzing Deviance*, 1983). In recent decades, however, sociologists have integrated theories of deviance so that elements of these four types of theories can be found in a single theory organized around a central causal mechanism.

The macro-normative approach to the study of deviance examines how societies and communities are organized, to determine why varying rates of deviant behavior appear across subgroups in the population, locations in a **community** or society, and at different points in history. For example, the French sociologist **Émile Durkheim,** perhaps the most frequently cited classical theorist of deviance, studied how **social structure** facilitates or impedes the production of deviance, by emphasizing that structural strain produces what he called "pathology" in the population. Based on empirical data on suicide rates across Europe in the latter part of the nineteenth century, Durkheim argued in *Suicide* (1897 [trans. 1964]) that changes in the rate of suicide are not adequately explained by individualistic approaches to deviance. Rather, fluctuations in the rates of suicide within and between societies were best explained by the way societies were structured, especially in light of three types of social conditions that produce strain: (1) **anomie,** a societal condition characterized by a state of normlessness in which individuals become disassociated from a collective moral **authority**; (2) egoism, a societal condition in which the normative order is too weak and individuals are not sufficiently integrated into society, and thus they are not bound by the norms of the society; and (3) altruism, a societal condition in which the normative order is too strong and individuals are overly integrated into society in ways that compel them to willfully take their own life.

From a Durkheimian point of view, an appropriate level of "pathology" is "normal" for society because it serves positive functions, including: a boundary-setting function that delineates the distinction between right and wrong; a group solidarity function for those united in collective opposition to the normative threats of nonconformity; an innovation function insofar as breaking norms often leads to healthy **social change**; and a tension-reduction function for those who "blow off a little steam" by engaging in low-level forms of deviance (Durkheim, 1895 [trans. 1938]).

Consistent with Durkheim's path-breaking approach to deviance, many contemporary deviance theorists explain varying rates of deviant behavior in terms of an array of structural features of society. **Robert K. Merton,** for example, extended Durkheim's work in *Social Theory and Social Structure* (1957). He sought to explain why people in the same environment behave differently, sometimes conforming and sometimes exhibiting deviant behavior. He borrowed Durkheim's key term – anomie – to conceptualize structural strain as an acute disjuncture between cultural norms and goals and the socially structured capacities of the members of the group to act in accord with them. In simple terms, Merton argued, when people are faced with blocked access to legitimate means to reach culturally acceptable goals, they will "adapt" to the situation by pursuing illegitimate means – deviant behavior – to achieve conventional goals. Because economic opportunity is not evenly distributed across society, rates of deviance, especially **crime** and delinquency, are also unevenly distributed. More recently, Steven Messner and Richard Rosenfeld in *Crime and the American Dream* (1994) reformulated Merton's theory by proposing that anomie fostered by economic **inequality** is most likely to produce crime and delinquency when economic and noneconomic **institutions** fail to offset the material success available to those engaging in deviance.

Versions of social ecological theories of deviance constitute another type of structural explanation of deviance. Social disorganization theory, which developed at the University of Chicago in the 1930s and continues to inspire volumes of research today, emphasizes the correlation between spatial location and rates of criminal and deviant behavior. The concept of social disorganization refers to both social and cultural conditions, such as value and norm conflicts, mobility, cultural change, and weak relationships. Social disorganization undermines internal and external social control, thereby promoting unconventional and deviant behavior.

Some spatial locations have so much social disorganization that a delinquent subculture arises. Albert Cohen argued in his book *Delinquent Boys: The Culture of the Gang* (1955) that youth become frustrated (a form of anomie) when they find themselves unable to perform in school on a par with their more privileged peers. Seeking solace with other lower-class peers, together they engage in deviant acts as a way to flaunt traditional norms. Richard Cloward and Lloyd Ohlin furthered subculture theory with their book *Delinquency and Opportunity: A Theory of Delinquent Gangs* (1960). They specified three types of delinquent gang subcultures: criminal, conflict, and retreatist. Criminal subcultures focus more on making money than being violent; conflict subcultures are violent towards law-abiding and criminal groups alike; and retreatist subcultures comprise individuals who cannot make it in either the legitimate or the criminal world – therefore, they resort to deviant (and illegal) activities such as the excessive or inappropriate use of drugs, alcohol, and so forth.

Other ecological theories of deviance include: routine activities theory, which posits that the convergence of a motivated offender, a suitable target, and the absence of a capable guardian produces crime and deviance (Lawrence Cohen and Marcus Felson in "Social Change and Crime Rate Trends: A Routine Activity Approach," *American Sociological Review*, 1979); gender and power-control theory (John Hagan, *Structural Criminology*, 1989), which points to the **family** as the primary source of varying **socialization** experiences for boys and girls, to explain gender differences in nonconforming behavior; classic control theory, such as Travis Hirschi, *Causes of Delinquency* (1969), which emphasizes sources of social bonding and attachments as key to understanding who deviates and why; and contemporary control theory, which emphasizes lack of self-control and directs attention to the social organization of the family as producing (and inhibiting) deviance (for example, Michael Gottfredson and Travis Hirschi, *A General Theory of Crime*, 1990).

Others have theorized about why some people in an environment (and not others) fail to conform to group norms and, instead, engage in deviant behavior. These theorists focus on the experiences and interpersonal **interactions** of those who learn to engage in deviant behavior. Orienting to deviance as a form of learned behavior, these theorists treat the underlying mechanisms that produce deviance as essentially no different from those that produce conformity. However, theorists disagree on what the precise mechanisms of learning entail.

The early roots of a learning perspective on deviance can be found in a French magistrate's work on imitation and suggestion as the "cause" of juvenile delinquency and crime. **Gabriel Tarde** argued in *The Laws of Imitation* (1890 [trans. 1912]) that the explanation of crime lay not in biology but in the social world and that crime is transmitted through intimate personal groups. In simple terms, he argued good boys associate with and imitate bad boys and, in the process, become bad boys themselves. Regardless of what characteristics one has at birth, Tarde argued, one must learn to become criminal by association with and imitation of others, just as one learns a trade or learns about and imitates the latest fads and fashions.

A far more systematic and consequential learning theory was presented in 1939 by the American criminologist Edwin H. Sutherland in *Principles of Criminology*, which is now in its eleventh edition and continues to be one of the best-selling criminology textbooks (see Sutherland, Cressey, and Luckenbill, [eds.] 2002). Sutherland argued that crime and other forms of deviance do not result from social disorganization; rather, some groups are organized for criminal activities and some are organized against these activities. Sutherland hypothesized that any person can be trained to adopt and follow any pattern of criminal behavior and any pattern of conforming behavior. Such patterns were developed through differential social organization and differential association. Sutherland, and later his co-authors Donald Cressey and David Luckenbill, argued that differential social organization could explain the crime rate (just as the macro-normative theorists would suggest), while differential association could explain the criminal behavior of a particular person. The differential association element of this approach posits that deviant behavior is a product of learning via communicative interaction. This type of learning involves defining certain situations as the appropriate occasions for deviant behavior; mastering the techniques of successful deviant activity; and acquiring the motives, drives, attitudes, and rationalizations that justify violations of norms and/or laws (see **law and society**).

One key to learning deviance is what Gresham Sykes and David Matza refer to as "techniques of neutralizations," which are justifications and excuses for committing deviant acts ("Techniques of Neutralization: A Theory of Delinquency," *American Sociological Review*, 1957). By denying responsibility, denying injury or harm, denying the victim, and appealing to higher loyalties, deviants are able to free themselves from the pressure to conform to social norms for a specific act. Techniques of neutralization play a key role in deviance disavowal – the deviant's rejection of the application of deviant labels – by enabling the deviant to distinguish himself from his deviance in an effort to maintain a conventional identity as a conventional member of society.

Techniques of neutralization also play a key role in deviancy drift theory as developed by Matza in *Delinquency and Drift* (1964). Matza's drift theory assumes that people live their lives on a continuum somewhere between total freedom and total constraint, and often people move between conforming and deviant behavior. This movement occurs because delinquents can maintain a commitment to the dominant norms while neutralizing their controlling effect on their deviant behavior. Indeed, the frequent deployment of techniques of neutralization shows that deviants generally hold **values** and beliefs very similar to those who conform.

More contemporary theoretical treatments of the role learning plays in producing deviance have examined other dynamics crucial to learning both deviant and conforming behavior. For example, Ronald Akers (*Social Learning and Social Structure*, 1998) looks beyond differential association to differential reinforcement. Reinforcement refers

to the process by which other people reward or punish a particular deviant act. Akers stresses that this process is complex and is built upon reciprocal feedback loops that precede the moment of engaging in deviance.

Moving away from the normative question of who engages in deviance and why, sociologists working within the "constructionist" or "reactionist" tradition analyze the origins and content of rules, norms, **traditions**, and laws in order to understand why certain types of behavior and people are constructed and categorized as deviant in the first place. Here the focus is on the social construction of deviance, a process whereby conduct, events, and people are constructed as abnormal, atypical, pathological, and ultimately stigmatizable. Rather than focusing on the causes and correlates of deviant behavior, this perspective devotes analytic attention to the processes whereby the boundaries between "normal" and "deviant" are demarcated at the societal level.

At the macroscopic level, sociologists have studied the formation of criminal law and other forms of **social policy** and rule-making as one empirical measure of a group, community, or society marking behavior as unacceptable and subject to **social control**. Over a half a century ago, Edwin Sutherland published one of the earliest and best-known sociological investigations of the origins of a specific type of criminal law. In "The Sexual Psychopath Laws" (*Journal of Criminal Law and Criminology*, 1950), Sutherland argued that the origins and the diffusion of sexual psychopath laws are largely the result of two things: the manipulation of public opinion by the press and the influence of experts on the legislative process. These factors invented what is now identifiable as the sexual psychopath, declaring certain people deviant and in need of social control.

Since the publication of Sutherland's classic study on the criminalization of sexual psychopathy, sociologists have pointed to a plethora of demographic, organizational, political, structural, and institutional conditions that shape when and how social behaviors and statuses become defined as deviant over time and across geopolitical boundaries. For example, taking a decidedly materialist approach to criminalization, William Chambliss detailed in his now-famous and often reprinted article "A Sociological Analysis of the Law of Vagrancy" (*Social Problems*, 1964) how changing demographic and economic conditions enabled vagrancy laws, which define people without a permanent residence as deviant, to emerge in the fourteenth century. A more recent work on the topic of homelessness by Gregg Barak (*Gimme Shelter: A Social History of Homelessness in Contemporary America*, 1991) demonstrates that gentrification and redevelopment in central cities, coupled with changing views of "the homeless," led to a plethora of laws that criminalize homelessness and, in the process, deviantize the homeless as misfits and vagabonds living outside the conventional moral order and threatening those who do not.

Similarly, Joseph R. Gusfield in *Symbolic Crusade* (1986) explains how the distribution and sale of alcoholic beverages was constitutionally defined as criminal in the United States in the early twentieth century. In the process, native groups effectively deviantized immigrants, Catholics, and urban dwellers, who consumed alcohol in more visible ways than natives, Protestants, and rural dwellers. In more recent work on status politics and law, Valerie Jenness and Ryken Grattet analyzed in their book *Making Hate a Crime* (2001) the crucial role grassroots activists and organized **social movements** have played in instigating and formulating hate-crime law in the United States that criminalizes bias-motivated **violence** across the nation; as a result, in the latter part of the twentieth century, age-old violent behavior deriving from bigotry became recognizable as hate crime. Similarly, Elizabeth Boyle's work *Female Genital Cutting: Cultural Conflict in the Global Community* (2003) shows how processes of **globalization** have redefined centuries-old normative behavior – female genital cutting – as unacceptable, deviant, and, in some cases, criminal behavior.

At the microscopic level of analysis, sociologists of deviance examine the **interactions** between deviants and "normals" and the consequences of such interactions for the production and management of **stigma**, the engine around which deviantization motors. The term stigma (or stigmata) dates back to the Greek word for "tattoo-mark" and references the mark made with a hot iron and impressed on people to show they were devoted to the service of the temple, or on the opposite spectrum of behavior, that they were criminals or runaway slaves. In its most literal usage, the term stigma refers to a mark or stain that ruins an individual's reputation. To understand the concept of stigma and its relevance to the social construction of deviance, **Erving Goffman**'s classic work *Stigma: Notes on the Management of a Spoiled Identity* (1963) emphasized a distinction between virtual social **identities** and actual social identities. Virtual social identities are normative expectations about how people should behave and characteristics people should possess; and actual social identities are the actual behavior of individuals and the characteristics individuals actually possess. Goffman argued that discrepancies between virtual and actual social identities often cause us to reclassify an individual from one socially anticipated category to another less desirable one. For example, coming to understand someone is homosexual, an ex con, or the carrier of a fatal disease, after presuming the individual was heterosexual, a law-abiding citizen, or generally healthy, can result in the reclassification of someone as a particular type of person. However, attributes do not, in and of themselves, cause stigmata; whether or not an attribute is stigmatizing depends upon the circumstance and the social audience. An attribute that stigmatizes one type of person can confirm the usualness of another and therefore is neither creditable nor discreditable as a thing in itself. Context matters because it is only within specific contexts that attributes get negatively labeled and reacted to as such. In short, deviance is necessarily relative.

The process of labeling, as anticipated by Frank Tannenbaum, conceived by Goffman, and elaborated by Howard S. Becker, Edwin Schur, Edwin Lemert, and Stephen Pfohl, has loomed large in empirical studies of deviance. Relying upon the basic tenets of **symbolic interactionism,** sociologists have documented many sources and consequences of stigma by empirically examining diverse types of people, situations, and judgments that spoil actual social identities in an array of institutional settings. For example, stigma attached to the presence of a criminal record reduces the perceived value of potential employees for potential employers. Moreover, specific sexual practices, health conditions, family histories, bodily forms, and religious practices can, if and when they become known, demote individuals in the eyes of what Goffman called "normals."

Finally, identities and subcultures can be organized around shared stigma, and deviance can be amplified as a result. In Lemert's classic formulation (*Human Deviance, Social Problems, and Social Control*, 1967), primary deviance is norm-violating behavior that does not result in consequential public labeling because it does not surpass a group, community, or society's tolerance threshold; therefore it is ignored or normalized. In contrast, secondary deviance occurs when norm-violating behavior passes the group, community, or society tolerance threshold, is subject to a "dramatization of evil" (Tannenbaum's terminology) and stigmatized, and results in a changed self-concept for the deviant(s). Unlike primary deviance, which derives from multiple causes and is sporadic, secondary deviance is role-based behavior and is more predictable. In other words, secondary deviation is a function of societal reaction and stigmatizing labels. Related, deviance amplification is the unintended consequence of formal and informal social control efforts, which often stimulate a spiral of deviance. The way people (for example teachers and parents) and **organizations** (for example the criminal justice system) react to relatively minor deviance can result in the formation of deviant subcultures and deviant **careers**. This is because stigmatization changes self-concepts, and changed self-concepts provide the principal link between the stigmatized labels and future deviant behavior. In simple terms, **labeling theory** posits that people take on deviant identities and play deviant roles because they are strongly influenced into doing so by the application of stigmatizing labels to them. This line of thinking has been applied most commonly to juvenile delinquents, as well as the mentally ill, rapists, nudists, homosexuals, ex-convicts, shoplifters, and people struggling to manage their weight.

Sociologists have also examined the ways stigmatized identities and groups organized around them have become the source of political consciousness and attendant social movement activity. For example, in the latter part of the twentieth century, those sustaining the gay and lesbian movement, the prostitutes' rights movement, the disabilities movement, the movement to advance fat acceptance, and the movement to normalize mental illness have sought to destigmatize the very attributes, identities, and behaviors that bind them together as a discernible social-political group. Kitsuse commented on this uniquely modern trend in a presidential address to the Society for the Study of Social Problems aptly titled "Deviance Coming Out All Over: Deviants and the Politics of Social Problems" (1980). A little over a decade later, United States senator Daniel Patrick Moynihan, a sociologist, reiterated the constructionist theme of the elasticity of social boundaries between conventional and deviant behavior and expressed concern about the degree to which what was once seen as deviant behavior is now seen as conventional behavior in an article entiled "Defining Deviancy Down" (1993).

More recently, Joel Best has pointed out in his history of deviance, *Deviance: Career of a Concept* (2004), that labeling theory came under fire from feminist critics who found labeling theorists too sympathetic towards those who victimized women, identity politics that sought to remove the stigma from certain activities and attributes, and mainstream sociologists who claimed that labeling theory was empirically wrong, which was probably the most damaging of the critiques. According to Best, as labeling theory became unpopular, scholars turned to more specialized studies – such as the study of **social problems** and social movements and deviant transactions – because they allowed the scholars the freedom to condemn some deviants while celebrating others.

Since the mid-1970s, a number of explanations for deviance have emerged that do not fit into the categories of theories described above, precisely because they are integrated theories. Integrated theories, by design, draw elements from normative and reactionist theories at both the macroscopic and microscopic levels, add new causal mechanisms to elements drawn from these theories, and present the synthesis as a new explanatory framework.

Developing integrated theories requires the scholar to recognize that the elements of one theory are compatible with another, even though the theories operate on different levels of abstraction. Ernest Burgess and Ronald Akers in their article "A Differential Association–Reinforcement Theory of Criminal Behavior" (*Social Problems*, 1966) successfully combined social learning theory and Sutherland's differential association theory. As Messner and Liska point out in their textbook *Perspectives on Crime and Deviance* (1999), Burgess and Akers did this by recognizing that youths "hanging out" with delinquent peers and learning from them (differential association) is merely one particular type of operant conditioning (learning theory). A second integrated theory is found in John Braithwaite's *Crime, Shame and Reintegration* (1989). Braithwaite draws upon elements of structural strain theory, learning theory, and societal reactionist theory to argue that the type of shaming to which rule-breakers are subject is crucial to producing deviance. Specifically, one type of shaming – disintegrative shaming – reproduces deviance; another type of shaming – reintegrative shaming – reduces the occurrence of subsequent deviance by providing the opportunity for individuals to recommit to conventional society. More recently, in *Control Balance: Toward A General Theory of Deviance* (1995), Charles Tittle relies upon elements from many different theories and the notion of "control-balance" to develop a new theoretical framework. In Tittle's theory, "control-balance," or the ratio of how much a person is able to control compared to how much the individual is controlled (itself a product of social structures, interaction patterns, and other ecological variables), explains both conforming and deviant behavior.

As integrated theories continue to be developed, so too do general assessments of the status of the sociological study of deviance. On the one hand, the sociology of deviance's book-length obituary has been written by Colin Sumner (*The Sociology of Deviance: An Obituary*, 1994), who accuses the field of no longer advancing a viable, coherent, and legitimate body of knowledge. This skepticism about the future of the field has been affirmed by others, including Anne Hendershott, who argues in her book *The Politics of Deviance* (2002) that scholars have romanticized deviant behavior; and by J. Mitchell Miller, Richard Wright, and David Dannels in their article "Is Deviance 'Dead?'" (2001). On the other hand, Erich Goode has pointed out in several articles and in his popular textbook *Deviant Behavior* (1994) that practitioners of the sociology of deviance continue to teach graduate and undergraduate courses on the topic across the United States and abroad.

Arguably, Alexander Liazos's strident critique in 1972 of the sociology of deviance as the impoverished study of "nuts, sluts, and perverts" has been overcome by what continues to be a vibrant and exciting field that remains intimately connected to larger sociological concerns. Influential scholars continue to write articles and books that offer new and improved approaches to the study of deviance. For example, Charles Tittle and Raymond Paternoster's book *Social Deviance and Crime: An Organizational and Theoretical Approach* (2000) calls for an organizational approach to deviance. In addition, others call for approaches to the sociology of deviance that integrate normative and reactionist frameworks and build more flexible and inclusive definitions of the term deviance (see Alex Heckert and Druann Maria Heckert's article "A New Typology of Deviance: Integrating Normative and Reactivist Definitions of Deviance," *Deviant Behavior*, 2002). Finally, leading scholars specializing in deviance, including Jack Katz and Christopher Williams, have encouraged colleagues to recognize that engaging in deviance and **crime** can be fun and exciting, perhaps even creative and artistic. As these calls for reform circulate, the sociological study of deviance continues to be integrated with other areas of sociology, most notably **criminology**, the study of **social stratification, community, queer theory, moral panics**, and **social movements**.

VALERIE JENNESS AND PHILIP GOODMAN

deviance disavowal
– see **deviance**.

deviancy
– see **deviance**.

deviancy amplification
– see **deviance**.

deviancy drift
– see **deviance**.

deviant behavior
– see **deviance**.

deviant case analysis
Perhaps one of the clearest instances of the differentiation of quantitative and qualitative approaches in sociology is the treatment of deviant cases in a dataset. Anomalous cases in the quantitative tradition are regarded as sources of error, **bias**, or "noise," tend to be termed "outliers" and are, if not deleted, "transformed" until they approach "normality" prior to statistical analysis. In contrast, in qualitative work, particularly in the sub-disciplines of **ethnomethodology** and **conversational analysis** (CA), deviant cases are actively cherished for their potentially crucial analytic import.

These qualitative approaches, which were originally inspired by **Harold Garfinkel**'s *Studies in Ethnomethodology* (1967), analyse "breaches" in the mundane social order in which the exception may illuminate an otherwise-taken-for-granted, and hence "invisible," rule. The analysis of cases/instances that seem to run counter to established patterns or theoretical claims has become a canonical methodological procedure in ethnomethodology and CA, and in variants of discursive psychology which draw upon this heritage. The analysis of deviant cases is designed, then, in order to get at, in Garfinkel's terms, the "seen-but-unnoticed background features" of everyday life.

Thus, given contemporary ethical constraints on real-life "breaching experiments," investigators will actively search for naturally occurring breaches of conventionally normative social conduct. An example can be taken from Alec McHoul and Mark Rapley's "Should we make a start then?: A Strange Case of a (Delayed) Client-Initiated Psychological Assessment" (2002, *Research on Language and Social Interaction*, 35). This case involved the study of the initiation of a psychological test by the *testee* rather than, as would normatively be expected, by the *tester*. Deviant case analysis may, alternatively, involve – for example – combing a dataset of telephone-call openings. Emmanuel A. Schegloff, in "Sequencing in Conversational Openings" (1968, *American Anthropologist* 70), looked for the single instance (that is deviant case) out of a collection of 500 in which a social actor ("member") broke the putative rule that "answerer speaks first," to develop a more sophisticated theoretical account. Thus, in Schegloff's research, the analysis of the deviant case showed that it did, in fact, lend support to a higher-order theoretical conception of "summons–answer" sequences. Similarly, the McHoul and Rapley study supported the work of **Harvey Sacks** in his two-volume *Lectures on Conversation* (1995). Through an analysis of the breach of the normative conventions of membership in asymmetric social categories, Sacks's account of the conditions under which an omni-relevant device for conversation may be theoretically inferred were, in fact, empirically demonstrable.

MARK RAPLEY AND SUSAN HANSEN

dialectical materialism
– see **Marxism**.

diaspora

A term originally applied to the experience of a people dispersed from their original homeland for long periods, yet who retain cultural memories and ties, diaspora has gained increasing currency to describe a host of such peoples in a world in which movement and flight are common. While the term was traditionally applied to the stateless Jewish people, among the most important diaspora communities today are, ironically, the Palestinians displaced from their homeland with the formation of the Jewish state of Israel, thus pitting two diasporic communities against each other.

The modern world has seen numerous large-scale **migrations**, forcible and voluntary, from the African slave trade, to the movement of the Irish during the potato famine and thereafter. Today, the experience of the African and Irish diasporas form important components of the blossoming field of diaspora studies. Sociologist Paul Gilroy coined the influential term *The Black Atlantic* (1995) to capture the African diaspora experience, while Irish scholars now use the term "The Green Atlantic." Increasingly, with **globalization**, there are transnational diaspora **communities** – including those fleeing **war** and **poverty** – of overseas migrants and citizens whose resources are critical to those left in their home countries.

Thus, diaspora communities, from the experience of Puerto Ricans, Salvadorans, or Latinos as a whole, are today proliferating. And with the ascent of East Asia and China in the contemporary global **economy**, there has also been increased attention paid to the (often wealthy) Chinese diaspora community in East Asian and Chinese development.

THOMAS REIFER

diasporic studies
– see **diaspora**.

differential association
– see **deviance**.

differentiation

The differentiation of tasks in **society** – or the division of **labor** – is a central focus of **sociology**. Sociologists have studied the effects of increasing specialization and complexity and have classified societies in terms of the nature and level of differentiation.

During the Scottish Enlightenment, writers like Adam Ferguson (1723–1816) and John Millar (1735–1801) distinguished four sociologically distinct stages of society: hunters and gatherers; shepherd or pastoral society; husbandmen or agricultural society; and commercial society. **Karl Marx**'s materialist theory of history represents social development in terms of successive modes of production. Marx introduces the idea that social differentiation is associated with **inequality** and that conflict among **social classes** is one of the principal motors of **social change**.

Functionalism provides an alternative account of differentiation, concerned with the problem of interdependence among the parts of a differentiated system. **Émile Durkheim** set out a model of types of societies from elementary to more complex types. The two poles of this continuum were respectively characterized by *mechanical* and *organic forms* of **solidarity**. **Talcott Parsons** expanded this scheme with a full theory of structural differentiation, where the four functional imperatives that all societies must meet allows a classification of societies in terms of the degree of institutional specialization around each of the functions these four functions were called the **pattern variables**, relating to the **economy**, polity, value system, and motivation that all societies must satisfy.

Many sociologists became suspicious of the emphasis on linear development and the teleological implications of both Marxian and functionalist approaches. Feminist theory criticized each approach for the neglect of the sexual division of labor and the role of gender inequalities in capitalist **modernity**. Postmodern sociologists have emphasized the possibility of dedifferentiation as well as forms of hyperdifferentiation.

JOHN HOLMWOOD

digital divide

As the internet has grown in scope and usefulness, so too has concern about equitable access to its services and benefits, especially to **information**. The term digital divide is a catch-all phrase to cover many perspectives addressing equity issues in terms of the way mediated electronic communication and information resources are available to, or used by, various **groups**. The emphasis is on disparities among groups.

An early digital-divide concern, which came to particular prominence in the late 1980s, was over computer access. Computer access was seen as being mal-distributed along gender lines. Some felt that, since males were by far the heaviest users, aggressive intervention programs were needed to boost female participation. Although varied programs were launched to interest girls in **careers** in computer science, little appear to have been accomplished. A similar concern regarding **gender** was expressed in the early era of the internet, when males were heavy adopters. However, over time, advancing ease of use and engaging content alone appear to have solved this "divide" as women have become as heavily involved in online activities as men. While there is some variation, such as women appearing to be more interested in online social **interaction** than are men, this dimension of concern over a possible digital divide has largely disappeared.

Yet gender is but one of a series of other possible digital divides reflecting various inequities. These would include mal-distributions along lines of geographic, racial/ethnic, economic, institutional, age, educational, religious, and handicapped status. In many ways, there appears to be little about these "divides" that is uniquely digital. The very factors that might create a digital divide have already acted to create other opportunity divides. For instance, digital-divide concerns along international dimensions is actually a subset of the already existing **inequality** between "rich nations" and "poor nations." Also, from a practical viewpoint, conceptual distinctions in access to digital resources are multiple and overlapping. At the same time, there are some interesting ways that the **politics** of the issue play out. While there is broad public concern over inequitable access to

internet resources, similar inequalities in access to mobile communication resources command little attention. This is true despite the fact that it may be that mobile communication resources are more important economically to those on the margins of the global system than to those at the core.

In terms of geographic digital divides, there are stubborn problems of unequal distribution of information and other resources, with rural and less densely populated areas not keeping up with their urban counterparts. In addition, poorer areas tend to be less well-served with information and other resources. Much has been made of perceived racial/ethnic inequalities, and these concerns are frequently accompanied by far-reaching program proposals. While it is true that certain racial/ethnic minorities are underrepresented in the online world, it is equally true that others are "overrepresented." Interestingly, when educational achievement is considered, it is generally the case that the racial/ethnic divide disappears. Put differently, people with low education are the ones who have low participation rates, rather than there being something unique or disinclining about their cultural characteristics that prevent members of that culture from using the internet. There are enormous differences internationally among usage levels of the internet. These also seem to be a result of international inequalities of **income** and productivity, as well as local telecommunication pricing policies. Although the internet was seen originally as a solution to the gap between the rich and poor countries, it now appears that many international aid bodies feel that efforts are no longer necessary to try to wire the less-developed countries. As J. Katz and R. Rice show in *Social Consequences of Internet Use* (2002), mobile communication, especially via cell phones, is seen as an avenue for economic progress in developing countries.

JAMES E. KATZ

diploma disease

– see **credentialism**.

disability and impairment

Both terms, which are culturally specific and contested, are used to designate a particular relationship of the individual to bodily **norms** and to **society** in general. Disability has different meanings in different **cultures**, and in many western countries legislative definitions of disability have become increasingly complex, because they result in the provision of rehabilitation services or welfare payments to disabled people. Indeed, the definitions adopted by western governments have changed so often that one can argue that disability is basically defined by **public policy**, and therefore disability is socially produced by policy decisions.

In the traditional medical literature, impairment is defined as the inability of a physiological or body system to perform the function for which it was designed. A functional loss occurs when an impairment limits a person's ability to perform basic functional activities like climbing stairs, running, or jumping. Disability is present when the functional loss limits a person's ability to ambulate, do daily self-care activities, perform the duties of a parent, work and function in society.

Scholars in the United States and United Kingdom objected to this "medicalized" view of disability because it focused on individual limitations and deficiencies, not on the larger environment. In the British version of the social model of disability, impairment is the term used to refer to medical conditions, or differences from normal bodily or cognitive functioning, and disability refers to the social reactions to impairment, particularly experiences of **discrimination**, oppression, **social exclusion**, and marginalization.

Today, it is evident that disability cannot be simply reduced to a medical or biological definition nor located entirely in the environment. From an ecological perspective, disability is defined not only by the biology of the injury or disease, but more significantly by the interaction between biology and an individual's physical, social, economic, and political environment, as well as by the demands of the person's physical, social, and occupational activities. Disability is a physical condition and social experience that is not necessarily permanent and can be modified, if its determinants can be altered.

Dealing with impairment can be a very difficult experience, because it often involves admitting vulnerabilities, revealing intimate or private bodily details, and dealing with unexpected biographical disruptions. Every impairment has its own unique features, but there are four important factors affecting the way an individual responds to their impairments: the age at which a person acquires impairment, the visibility of the impairment, the degree to which others comprehend the impairment, and the influence of illness. The social acceptability of the impairment is also important – some types of impairment are far more stigmatized than others.

This distinction between impairment and disability, which is at the heart of the social model of disability, is valuable because it emphasizes the need to remove the barriers, discrimination, negative images, and lack of opportunities which many disabled people experience. Access is fundamental to the construction (and contestation) of disability. There is a sense in which every discrimination can be seen as a problem about access: access to an equal, unhindered **social role**. Social restrictions and discrimination are a central part of the experience of disability for people with any sort of impairment. Regardless of whether these barriers stem from inaccessible built environments, proscriptive notions of **intelligence**, the inability of the public to communicate using sign language, a failure to provide resources in accessible formats, or the discrimination experienced by people with invisible impairments, these experiences have a negative social dimension which can be addressed in the creation of a more just and equitable society.

A medical model of disability might suggest that such problems with access are caused by an individual pathology, but the social model of disability which is favored by disability rights activists and by disability studies suggests that the unaccommodating nature of the environment is to blame. The politicization of access issues could therefore be seen as one of the great benefits of distinguishing between impairment and disability in this way. Understood through a social model, disability is not an individual trait, it is a social construction constantly made and remade through beliefs, practices, **institutions**, environments, and behavior. In this vein, disability is produced by the perception of physical, mental, and emotional variation. The implication is that non-disabling environments and patterns of behavior can be developed – if disabled people have rights, support, recognition, and self-determination.

A British group, the Union of Physically Impaired Against Segregation (UPIAS), was particularly influential in promoting the distinction between impairment and disability and in defining disability as a form of oppression. UPIAS has argued that it is **society** which disables physically impaired people. Disability is something which is imposed on top of existing impairments by the ways in which people with impairment are unnecessarily isolated and excluded from full social participation. Disabled people are consequently an oppressed social **group**. In order to understand this situation, it is necessary to recognize the distinction between physical impairment and the social situation called the "disability" of people with such impairments. Impairment is defined as lacking part of or all of a limb, or having a defective limb, organ, or mechanism of the body, while disability is the disadvantage or restriction of activity caused by contemporary social arrangements. Disability occurs when social institutions take little or no account of people who have physical impairments, thereby excluding them from participation in the mainstream social activities. Physical disability is a particular type of social oppression.

Although the initial definition of disability provided by UPIAS focused on people with physical impairments, it was subsequently broadened to include other impairments. The UPIAS definition of impairment and disability has become well known, partly due to the fact that a leading disabled academic, Mike Oliver, has consistently relied on them in his work, but also because other academics have accepted these definitions.

An important element of the UPIAS approach to disability was the promotion of self-determination. UPIAS has rejected the idea of experts and professionals holding forth on how people should accept disabilities, or providing academic lectures about the psychology of impairment. In contrast, UPIAS argues that they are interested in finding ways to change their own conditions of life, thereby overcoming the disabilities which are imposed over and above existing physical impairments.

This approach identifies disabled people as the experts on their own lives, and has given many disabled people the confidence to challenge the barriers and negative attitudes which they experience in their daily lives. Instead of the sense of powerlessness, dependency, and shame which may result from the medical model of disability, such an approach gives disabled people a sense of confidence, empowerment, and removes feelings of **shame**, **stigma**, and guilt from discussions of access requirements.

The central element of this approach to disability is its emphasis on the need to remove the barriers that prevent people with impairments from taking their rightful roles in society. The essential message is that, although disabled people may have significant bodily, cognitive, or psychological differences which distinguish them from non-disabled people, those differences do not justify **inequality** and should not result in the denial of citizenship **rights**. Society creates many of the problems that disabled people experience and society has a responsibility to address them. Thus it is suggested that it is impossible to

identify the number of disabled people in a society. From the perspective of the social model of disability, people are only disabled by an environment which does not meet their needs. There is no fixed number of disabled people, because people with impairments may not be disabled in every context.

MARK SHERRY AND GARY L. ALBRECHT

discourse
– see **discourse analysis**.

discourse analysis

An omnibus term to describe a wide range of socio-cultural analytic perspectives developed in the aftermath of the **linguistic turn** in the **social sciences** during the 1960s, at the broadest level, the domain of discourse analysis encompasses the study of language use beyond the level of the sentence or utterance, in relation to social or societal context. In this broad conception, discourse analysis embraces both speech and **interaction** and written texts as objects of study.

Much of Anglophone discourse analysis stems from the widespread influence of the "ordinary language philosophy" practiced by John L. Austin (1911–60) and John Searle (1932–). This perspective was elaborated in opposition to the notion that the primary function of **language** is representational. Austin in *How to Do Things with Words* (1962) at first argued that language use involves both "constative utterances" (that represent states of affairs) and "performatives" (for example, "I now pronounce you man and wife") which function to perform social actions and which only do so if certain normative conventions are satisfied. Subsequently Austin concluded that speech mingles the performance of actions with the predication of states of affairs, and this theme was given more formal expression in Searle's development of "speech act analysis" in *Speech Acts* (1979).

At the same time Anglophone discourse analysis has embraced the notion that language use embodies indexical properties which ensure that the meaning-making process will inevitably involve the use of the relationship between utterance and context to elaborate the meanings of social actions. These basic ideas have been developed in several distinctive intellectual and disciplinary contexts. In linguistics, H. Paul Grice (1913–88) created the theory of "conversational implicature" (implicit meaning derived from construing what is said explicitly in relation to social context). Based on the notion that cooperative conversation is organized in terms of a number of basic principles that license inferences about the communication of meaning, this theory has been highly important in the development of linguistic pragmatics which incorporates the analysis of speech acts, presupposition, "deixis," and related topics. In anthropology, Dell Hymes (1927–) built on the theory of speech acts to develop a broader model of the **ethnography** of speaking, based on sixteen dimensions of a speech event. This marks a departure from the traditional anthropological emphasis on documenting and preserving threatened indigenous languages, and towards a focus on the relationship between language, **culture**, and the use of speech acts within given communities and activities. Moreover, it does so with the provision of an anthropologically informed sense of the variety of **language games** that may be sustained within a given culture. In **sociology**, **Erving Goffman**'s conception of social interaction as driven by normatively mediated face wants was a proximate source both for the development of **conversational analysis**, and for the development of a theory of positive and negative face in Penelope Brown and Stephen Levinson's highly influential cross-linguistic analysis of face-threatening behavior and politeness.

In all the forms of discourse analysis described so far, the fundamental research effort is to isolate the endogenous **norms**, practices, and reasoning which inform the participants' construction and interpretation of social interaction. Other forms of discourse analysis, in particular critical discourse analysis, approach the analysis of text and interaction by examining them in relation to **power** and **ideology** and to the perpetuation of race-based, gender-based, and other forms of disadvantage and **social exclusion**. While this method has been applied to social interaction, some of its most successful manifestations have emerged in the analysis of written texts such as newspaper articles, political directives, and so on. This work has links to the broader poststructuralist discourse analysis associated with **Michel Foucault**, Fredric Jameson (1934–), **Stuart Hall**, and others. Moreover, in its focus on text and other forms of cultural production (including art, film, and television), this form of discourse analysis has clear affinities with broader trends in cultural and semiotic analysis.

The emergence of discourse analysis has coincided with a new emphasis on narrative as a vehicle for the communication of basic human understandings, as a basic form in which human knowledge is stored and represented, and as a means of **socialization**, memory, empathy, and

catharsis. Vladimir Propp's analysis of Russian fairy tales in his *Morphology of the Folk Tale* (1969) was among the first efforts to subject narrative to systematic description and it has been followed by many others which analyze narrative as a sociolinguistic, conversational, cultural, and artistic process. In this way **narrative analysis** has become a major site at which many forms of discourse analysis converge, ranging from the microanalytic study of story-telling as situated action, to macrocultural analyses of the narratives of political decisionmaking and warfare, and the historical narratives of imagined communities.

JOHN HERITAGE

discrimination

This is a social practice that organizes prejudicial **attitudes** into the formal or informal **segregation** of social **groups** or classes stigmatized by the collective **prejudice**. The earliest use of the word in the English language was in the sense of "to discriminate" as to cultural taste, for example in **Pierre Bourdieu**'s *Distinction* (1979 [trans. 1984]). Discrimination can therefore be defined, sociologically, as a practice whereby the cultural tastes of a dominant group or **social class** are projected negatively on groups or classes they consider inferior. Discrimination presents as a cultural attitude but is organized and sustained as a structural effect with legal, social, and economic consequences.

The term is commonly associated with racial discrimination, but discrimination has also come to be used as a general term to denote any discriminatory practice of sufficient structural durability to exclude classes of people from economic opportunities, political **rights**, or social freedoms; for example, the 1964 US Civil Rights Act, while directed primarily at racial discrimination, was broadly conceived to end discrimination with respect to **race**, color, **religion**, sex (**gender**), or national origin. Discriminatory beliefs and actions are rooted in everyday-life attitudes and social practices, usually ones backed by a long **tradition**. They are, therefore, so embedded in the local or regional **culture** that they are difficult to define legally and sociologically: for example, the distinction between racial and ethnic discrimination, the reluctance to take gender discrimination seriously, and the outright hostility to legislation aimed at eliminating discrimination on the basis of **sexualities**.

CHARLES LEMERT

disorganized capitalism

– see **capitalism**.

distribution

This refers to the nature of any variable that is collected as part of a quantitative research method. For instance, it could be measures of the **income** of individuals, the levels of **crimes** of **cities** or the health differences between nations. But a statistician's approach to examining a distribution of a variable is the same regardless of whether we are measuring **health** or **wealth**, or whether our units (or cases) are individuals or countries. When we examine any distribution, there are four key aspects that should be examined. If any of them are missed, the sociologist risks missing some important features of the **data**. These features are the central tendency, the spread, the shape, and outliers.

The expression "central tendency" is a summary of the average **value** in the data. Most commonly this is calculated with the mean, although in many cases the median gives a better typical value. The mean is calculated by summing all of the cases, and dividing by the number of cases. The median is obtained by rank-ordering the cases, and taking the value of the middle case. For categorical variables, the mode (the most commonly occurring category) is the most common measure of central tendency.

Although less obvious, sociologists are often more interested in how spread out, or heterogeneous, the cases are. For instance, amongst the richest few dozen countries in the world, the nature of the societies and the quality of life of the citizens seems to vary surprisingly little with the mean level of income. But the spread of incomes – that is the size of the gap between the richest and poorest, seems to have a greater effect on outcomes such as health and average life expectancy. Often sociologists and statisticians pay too much attention to averages, and neglect the spread of data. There are a number of measures of spread, the common ones being the standard deviation and the midspread (aka the interquartile range).

Many statistical tests assume that, when the data are plotted in a histogram, they will form a bell-shaped curve, also called the normal or the Gaussian distribution. In practice, few sociological variables actually form such a neat distribution – so to call it a normal curve is somewhat of a misnomer. For instance, the distribution of hourly income in most countries is very skewed, with a long upwards straggle towards the small number of employees with very high incomes, while most people's wages are slightly below the mean. And if one plots weekly hours of work, one obtains a "bimodal" graph, with one peak around full-time (36-40 hours) and the other peak around half-time (20 hours). In such cases the shape of the distribution tells one far more than the average value.

In many sociological measures, a small number of cases on "outliers" seem to be very different from all the others. For instance, if one counted the number of sexual partners that individuals had over the past twelve months, many people would score 0 or 1, but a small proportion would have had dozens or hundreds of sexual partners in that time – for instance, prostitutes. Pooling all of the cases to calculate an average would be misleading. For some analyses, it would be appropriate to exclude those extreme cases, called outliers. In other cases, the research might learn more from those cases that deviate from the **norm**, the exceptions that prove the rule. But beware, those extreme cases often arise because of some error in the research!

To summarize, it is good practice in sociological research to investigate all four of these aspects of any distribution. BRENDAN J. BURCHELL

division of labor
– see **labor**.

divorce
– see **marriage and divorce**.

domestic labor
– see **labor**.

domestic violence
– see **family**.

double consciousness

A theory of black consciousness in the United States that is associated with the sociology of **W. E. B. Du Bois**, who was influenced in his analysis of white–black relationships in America by **G. W. E. Hegel**'s description of the master–slave relationship. For Hegel, the master and the slave cannot enter into a relationship of mutual recognition and respect because they are separated by a relationship of absolute **power**. Du Bois argued in *The Souls of Black Folk* (1961: 16) that the black man always has consciousness of himself through the consciousness of the white man, and thus "[i]t is a peculiar sensation, this double-consciousness, this sense of always looking at one's self through the eyes of the others, of measuring one's soul by the tape of a world that looks on in amused contempt and pity." The black man's consciousness had been destroyed by the experience of **slavery**, and Du Bois proposed an educational reform that would begin to restore self-respect and hence self-consciousness.   BRYAN S. TURNER

double shift
– see **family**.

Douglas, Mary (1921–)
A former student at Oxford and biographer of E. E. Evans-Pritchard (1902–73), Douglas is the most widely influential British anthropologist of the second half of the twentieth century. She conducted her original fieldwork among the Lele of present-day Zaire, but from the 1960s onward her expertise in the **ethnography** of Africa has been put to broader comparative purposes. Two thematics dominate her mature work. The first is the social-organizational determination of perception, classification, and cosmology. The second is the dynamic tension between social order and self-interest. Both thematics come to her from **Émile Durkheim** through Evans-Pritchard's mediation. Analytically, she remains virtually the only Durkheimian purist writing in anthropology today. Critically, she tends to favor hierarchy more vigorously and to take greedy individualist self-interest to task more readily than even Durkheim was ever inclined to do. She is comparable in this respect to her British-trained contemporary, **Louis Dumont**. Her own biographer, Richard Fardon (*Mary Douglas: An Intellectual Biography*, 1999), attributes such "sociological conservatism" less, however, to her postsecondary training than to her continuing devotion to the Catholicism into which she was born.

Purity and Danger (1966) and *Natural Symbols: Explorations in Cosmology* are the double centerpiece of her theoretical program. In the earlier work, she argues that any given **society**'s collective preoccupations with purity and pollution are the more salient the more its moral system is ambiguous or paradoxical. In the later work, noticeably but not fundamentally revised from its first (1970) to its second (1973) edition, she postulates that the intersection of the variable intensities of the two general dimensions of **social control** that she names "grid" and "group" operate on the ever-ready semiotic vehicle of the human **body** to generate distinctive pairings of the expression of the **self** and the imagination of the cosmos. In tandem, these works join **Pierre Bourdieu**'s *Outline of a Theory of Practice* (1970 [trans. 1977]) as contemporary foundations of the anthropology

of the body and as productive challenges to the sociological insensitivity of many of the applications of phenomenological **hermeneutics** in cultural and in religious studies. They are also the point of departure for her own further research into such diverse topics as dietary prescriptions and proscriptions; the patterns and the teleologies of **consumption** (in *The World of Goods*, with Baron Isherwood, 1978) and the correlative definition of **lifestyles**; and the study of dietetics and dietary theology that are the focus of her last work to date, *Leviticus as Literature* (1999). Douglas has largely lived in and worked on the society of the United States since moving there in 1977. She subsequently collaborated with Aaron Wildavsky in writing *Risk and Culture* (1982), a somewhat unflattering portrait of the ecological anxieties and opportunistic activism of the American middle classes that, unsurprisingly, was not well received in the United States itself. After the 1970s and in the midst of several forays into the **epistemology** of the **social sciences** and the sociology of epistemology, her most systematic refinement of her theoretical commitments remains *How Institutions Think* (1986).   JAMES D. FAUBION

dramaturgical analysis
– see **Erving Goffman**.

drug abuse
– see **addiction**.

Du Bois, W. E. B. (1868–1963)
A historian, sociologist, race man, social theorist, poet, journalist, political and civil rights leader, in his time, William Edward Burghardt Du Bois was ignored by white-dominated official sociology in the United States. Yet, as the **segregation** of blacks subsided, Du Bois emerged as one of the most original academic sociologists of the twentieth century.

Du Bois was born in Great Barrington, Massachusetts, in 1868, in the years following the American Civil War. In this small New England town, he was accepted in the local schools and excelled as a pupil. His higher education began in 1885 at Fisk University in Nashville, where for the first time he encountered the vicious **racism** of the American South; he then studied at Harvard and in Germany (1892–4) before earning his PhD at Harvard. His doctoral thesis, *The Suppression of the African Slave-Trade to the United States of America, 1638–1870*, became the first of his published scholarly books in 1896. Du Bois began his academic career at Wilberforce University (1894–6) before accepting a research position at the University of Pennsylvania. There he did the exhaustive fieldwork on Philadelphia's Negro **community** which led to *The Philadelphia Negro* (1899), the first important urban **ethnography** in America by an American.

Shortly after, Du Bois published the book that established his reputation as a major social thinker and writer, and a fresh voice in American racial **politics**, *Souls of Black Folk* (1903). *Souls* is best known for its poetic description of the **double consciousness** (or "twoness") concept that appeared in its lead essay: "One ever feels his twoness, – an American, a Negro; two souls, two thoughts, two unreconciled strivings; two warring ideals in one dark body, whose dogged strength alone keeps it from being torn asunder." The double-consciousness idea exerted its influence late in the twentieth century as a model for postfeminist social theories of the **self** as comprising a number of conflicting **identities** shaped from a matrix of domination (for example Patricia Hill Collins, *Black Feminist Thought*, 1990). *Souls of Black Folk* also introduced the cultural and political theory of racial uplift as led by a **talented tenth** of highly educated black leaders. Du Bois's emphasis on cultural training set him at odds with the then-reigning race-leader in the United States, Booker T. Washington (1856–1910), founder of the Tuskegee Institute in Alabama. Washington's program for racial uplift was based on the agricultural and industrial education of poor blacks. From 1895, when Washington declared his Atlanta Compromise (that blacks would work with whites economically, but keep themselves socially separate), until his death in 1915, Booker T. Washington was anointed by whites as the spokesman for blacks in America. In "On Mr. Booker T. Washington and Others" (also in *Souls*), Du Bois directly challenged Washington's philosophy. Thus began a political feud that would last until Washington's influence began to wane after 1910, the year Du Bois joined in the founding of the NAACP (National Association for the Advancement of Colored People).

In 1910, Du Bois left his academic position at Atlanta University, which he had held since 1897, to work in New York City with the NAACP. He immediately founded *Crisis* magazine, which soon became, under his editorial leadership, the most widely read news and literary paper in black America. He continued in this work until 1934 when his authority as Washington's successor as the foremost Negro leader in the United States fell under attack.

Du Bois's 25-year association with the NAACP was always uneasy. He was temperamentally a man of firm ideas and methods. He did not suffer fools gladly, especially those who kowtowed (as Washington had) to powerful whites. Throughout these years in New York, Du Bois continued to write prolifically, to engage in political commentary and direct action, and to assert his lifelong commitment to the importance of **culture** (notably as a leader in the Harlem Renaissance of the 1920s).

Du Bois's career as an academic sociologist was split into two parts, both at Atlanta University. In the early years (1897–1910), he taught economics and history while engaged in empirical sociological research. In addition to *The Philadelphia Negro*, Du Bois conducted a series of field studies of rural Negro communities in the South. **Max Weber** attended one of the conferences on these studies during his 1904 visit to the United States. Du Bois's second academic career was as Chair of the Department of Sociology at Atlanta (1934–44). Though he was in his eighth decade of life, Du Bois returned to sociological scholarship with the vigor of a young man. It was in this period that he completed his most important work of historical sociology.

Black Reconstruction (1935) is increasingly recognized today as a brilliant structural sociology of **social change** in the United States after the Civil War. The book attacked the history profession's then current attitude that the failure of Reconstruction (1863–77) was a failure of the freed Negroes to make economic and social progress. Du Bois responded in sharply sociological terms that demonstrated that the freed people had made remarkable progress given the structural constraints. The three and a half million freed Negroes, as a class, were trapped in a structural conflict between the poor white workers and the planter class. Planters ultimately restored their economic dominance after 1877 by using the poor whites as political pawns to pressure the federal government to give up Reconstruction. The poor whites were, in effect, granted the higher racial status in compensation for their economic misery. This has been called the racial wage by David Roediger in *Wages of Whiteness* (1991). The genius of Du Bois's concept was that it was empirical, structural, and historical sociology that explained a local practice (segregation) as an element in the **social structures** of the post-Civil-War South.

Du Bois died in 1963, in Accra, Ghana, in exile from the United States he had sought to redeem in his youth. The civil rights movements of the 1960s brought Du Bois's ideas into currency. He earned a place in history as much for his political work as for his scholarship and writing.   CHARLES LEMERT

dual economy

Dual economy models were developed to challenge unilinear accounts of capitalist development, by emphasizing the persistent importance of areas of economic activity that do not involve large-scale corporations, mass production, or even formal market relations. One example, from development studies, concerned the coexistence of an informal subsistence **economy** with a formal plantation economy. Another addressed the persistence of small-scale enterprises and low-paid work alongside the business alliances and internal welfare regimes of corporate capitalism, as in R. T. Averitt's analysis of *The Dual Economy* (1968) in the United States, and N. Chalmers's analysis of *Industrial Relations in Japan* (1989). Here, dualism between types of firm was matched by **labor market** dualism, as large **firms** utilized primary, and small firms, secondary, labor markets.

The critical power of these analyses depends on explaining the survival of the subordinate economy in terms of its role for the dominant economy, by absorbing surplus labor or providing low-cost production capacity. However, such dependencies have been specified in quite varied ways, with different implications for the dynamics and persistence of dualism. For example, M. J. Piore and C. F. Sabel, in *The Second Industrial Divide* (1984), portray the erstwhile subordinate small-firm sector as a potential challenger to large-scale mass production. Dual economy models also rest on clear contrasts in the organization and dynamics of the two economies, but specifications of the interlinkages and dependencies between them often lead to more differentiated accounts of production chains and hierarchies of employment conditions. This moves away from a clear dualism, but still addresses the processes that may sustain **differentiation** and uneven development in capitalist economies over time.

                      TONY ELGER

Louis Dumont (1911–1998)

A student of **Marcel Mauss**, his early work was on French festivals, about which he published an ethnographic study of *La Tarasque* (1951). He made a major contribution to the analysis of Indian **social structure** in *Homo Hierarchicus. The Caste System and its Implications* (1972) and *Religion, Politics and History in India. Collected Papers in Indian Sociology*

(1970). He also wrote on **ideologies** of **equality** and **individualism** in western societies in *From Mandeville to Marx. The Genesis and Triumph of Economic Ideology* (1977) and *Essays on Individualism. Modern Ideology in Anthropological Perspective* (1986). He contrasted the hierarchical caste **society** of India, with its emphasis on the social whole over the individual, and western society where the social whole is subordinated to the individual. Following the tradition of French **structuralism**, Dumont wanted to uncover the underlying principle of caste, which he argued was the contrast between pure and impure. Caste hierarchy was founded on this dichotomous principle. By "hierarchy," Dumont did not mean **social stratification**. Rather, hierarchy explains a relation of opposites that can nevertheless cohere within a cultural unity. Dumont's contrast between holism and individualism has become an important aspect of the debate with **Orientalism**.   BRYAN S. TURNER

Duncan, Otis Dudley (1921–2004)

Completing his PhD at the University of Chicago in 1949, Duncan was a member of the Faculty at Penn State University, and the universities of Wisconsin, Chicago, Michigan, Arizona, and California, Santa Barbara. His most influential publication was with **Peter M. Blau** on *The American Occupational Structure* (1967) which received the American Sociological Association Sorokin Award for the most distinguished scholarly publication in 1968. Using the first large national **survey** of **social mobility** in the United States, Blau and Duncan showed how parents transmit their social standing to their children mainly by influencing their children's **education**. Their approach to social mobility showed that mobility takes the form of small rather than dramatic steps up the social ladder. In addition to its substantive findings, *The American Occupational Structure* showed how an important sociological topic could be analyzed rigorously with appropriate quantitative methods. Through his exploration of **path analysis**, Duncan contributed to the development and use of structural equation models in the **social sciences**. He invented a measure of social standing of **occupations** – the Duncan Socioeconomic Index. He also developed an index of residential **segregation** between blacks and whites in Chicago. He was President of the Population Association of America in 1968–9. He published *Notes on Social Measurement* (1984), *Statistical Geography: Problems in Analysing Areal Data* (1961), and with H. Pfautz he translated M. Halbwach's *Population and Society: Introduction to Social Morphology*. His general argument was that quantitative sociology summarized empirical patterns in between-group differences, while temporarily ignoring the pattern of within-group individual differences.

BRYAN S. TURNER

Durkheim, Émile (1858–1917)

Generally considered as one of the founding fathers of **sociology**, and by some as the sociologist *par excellence*, Durkheim labored to establish the intellectual distinctiveness and significance of the discipline and to charter it as a fully legitimate component of academia. The following account of his thought is focused on four books that are conventionally considered the most significant.

Born in 1858 to a Jewish family, in the French town Epinay (Lorraine), Durkheim witnessed as an adolescent the defeat of the Second Empire in the Franco-Prussian War and the subsequent tragedy of the Paris Commune. In 1879–82, at the École Normale Supérieure, in Paris, he studied chiefly philosophy and history. Subsequently he taught philosophy in a *lycée*, but five years later joined the faculty at the University of Bordeaux. His teaching subject was the philosophy of **education**, but early on he coupled it with "social science" and later with "sociology."

At the time, in France and in other parts of Europe, sociology was cultivated by **intellectuals** and scholars, but was not accepted as an academic discipline. Durkheim gave the first major demonstration of his own understanding of it, and of its entitlement to recognition and institutionalization, in his massive doctoral dissertation *The Division of Labour in Society* (1893 [trans. 1933]). Targeting a phenomenon which had been and was being thematized chiefly by economists, *Division* agreed with them that the division of **labor** was a most significant phenomenon, particularly so in modern society. He also agreed with the social Darwinist view of the division of labor (put forward principally by **Herbert Spencer**) as the human variant of a universal biological process, the progression from simple forms of life to differentiated, complex ones.

Durkheim, however, rejected what later came to be called the utilitarian interpretation of the causes and consequences of the division of labor. He believed that the causes could not lie, as Spencer had claimed, in the individual's pursuit of his own egoistic advantage through increasingly specialized, and thus increasingly efficient and competitive, activity. The division of labor had taken off originally in societies so simple and so cohesive that their members did not conceive of themselves as possessing interests of their own, to be pursued at their own behest and initiative.

That all early human societies were so constituted was indicated, according to Durkheim, by the way they typically responded to violations of their **norms**. That response took the form of punitive sanctions, of inflictions of pain on the violators by, or in the name of, the whole society, in order to reassert universally shared and strongly entertained understandings.

These early societies all embodied the following "morphological" pattern. A small population, with low demographic density, subsists in a relatively large territory, exploiting its resources extensively, through very simple practices, assisted only by the most primitive **technology**. Such societies are segmented into even smaller, very similar subunits, which subsist in the manner indicated, each embodying the same culture but interacting with the others chiefly on ritual occasions, which renew in everyone the awareness of and dedication to shared, sacred beliefs and practices. Under these conditions, the society hangs together *mechanically*, because it is highly homogenous, and presents no fissures to be mended.

Many times in the course of pre-history, the equilibrium of such a society, according to Durkheim, has been disturbed by a critical development of a distinctively social nature, not expressing the intentions and strategies of individual actors (who at this point exist only as separate biological entities). An increase in population occurs, and the increased demographic density puts the resources under growing competitive pressure. Either the society in question falls prey to strife and disorder, thus leaving no further trace on the pre-historic record, or it spontaneously embarks on a course of sustained change, chiefly by dividing labor.

This latter solution leads, over many **generations**, to a society with dramatically different traits from the previous one. Its population is large, and, although it operates over a large territory, is much denser. It now makes intensive use of the territory's resources, because distinct parts of that territory are as different as the countryside on one hand, towns on the other. Furthermore, a differentiation process has also penetrated those parts, for that intensive use requires the components of the population of even the same locality to develop different skills and different technologies.

Only a very small part of the society's cultural patrimony is shared by all parts and by all the components of each part. Increasingly diverse beliefs and norms now activate and guide individuals in their differentiated activities. They are less sharply formulated than those obtaining in the former kind of society. They authorize and broadly orient the individual's diverse activities rather than commandeering them and narrowly directing them. They allow for more variation in the ways they are understood and implemented. They also acknowledge, regulate, and protect the pursuit by individuals of interests which are private to themselves.

The violation of the greater part of the norms, in particular, does not evoke the wrath of the whole society. Rather, sanctions are typically not punitive but "restitutive," that is they seek to remedy the damage the violation has done to the interests of given individuals, and only if these request such remedy.

Thus the normative bonds underwritten by and addressed to the whole society are fewer, relative to the totality of sanctioned expectations, and somewhat looser. But this does not abandon the society to disorder and strife. It now hangs together primarily because its different parts interact with, and deliver goods and services to, one another. The *mechanical* solidarity of simple society with a minimal division of labor has been replaced by an *organic* one. This reminds one of the evolution of advanced biological species, which present organs which are diverse in structure and operation, but all subserve the needs of each other and of the whole.

This result was the main consequence of the division of labor, not the increased happiness of society as Spencer claimed. Spencer, furthermore, while correctly emphasizing the role that contracts play in establishing and managing the relations between individuals in modern societies, had not realized that "not everything in the contract is contractual." These individuals only avail themselves of the contracts as juridical instruments of their private pursuits because public authorities had created and sanctioned the **institution** of the contract. In fact, advanced societies required such authorities to work towards their integration, not to shrink into mere "night watchmen" as Spencer wanted them to.

The Rules of Sociological Method (1895 [trans. 1958]), which appeared two years after *Division*, was a manifesto for a positivistic conception of sociology's mission, for it considered the natural sciences as an appropriate methodological model for the development of sociology itself. Durkheim, however, did not like the expression "positivistic"

to be applied to him, for it was associated with a specific philosophical posture, and in spite of his philosophical training he was keen to lay a boundary between philosophy and sociology. His strategy was to commit sociology, by means of two chief arguments, to a self-conscious strategy of empirical reference. First, sociology had a distinctive realm of facts – *social* facts – to attend to. Second, it had to treat those facts *as things*, that is as phenomena which are external to those perceiving them (including those studying them) and which lay constraints on their activity.

A further boundary had to be established between sociology and psychology. The most significant social facts are collective ways of acting and thinking, that is *représentations*, or mental constructs, unavoidably lodged in the psyches of human individuals. Collective representations, however, are distinguished from those that are not collective – and which can be left for psychology to study – by one significant characteristic. They are sanctioned, that is society makes arrangements for the eventuality that they are not, in a given case, respected and complied with.

It is in the very nature of such representations that they can and indeed are occasionally violated. On this account, Durkheim shockingly declared, even **crime** itself is *normal*. Its occurrence and its modalities should be registered by sociologists, and its causes investigated, without indulging in philosophical moralizing.

The same empirical posture is implicit in various strategies of investigation Durkheim recommended to sociologists. For instance, they should, as early as possible, define clearly the phenomenon they study (and their definitions may well vary from the conventional ones). They should be aware of variations in that phenomenon, study them comparatively, and seek to establish their *causes*, and distinguish these from their consequences or *functions*. The more significant variations will probably be associated with different types of society. These types are to be constructed in the first instance by the morphological criteria already developed in *Division*, which emphasize the *complexity* (or lack thereof) of a given society or **group**.

Durkheim continued teaching at Bordeaux until 1902, when he was appointed to a chair of science of education at the Sorbonne, in Paris. However, he had already become identified as the most authoritative practitioner and promoter of sociology. He was committed to the discipline also on moral grounds, expecting it to attain valid scientific results regarding the conditions obtaining in his beloved France. Such results could in turn find practical and political use in the construction of new and more appropriate public **institutions** by the Second Republic. Durkheim sought to accomplish this, among other things, by acting as a consultant to ministerial authorities. He also worked hard at selecting and training young people who shared his own view of sociology's scope and method, and subsequently sought to have them appointed to the positions which were being created in that discipline and in neighboring ones.

Most of Durkheim's tireless energy, however, was expended in strictly scholarly tasks. In 1896 he began editing, in Paris, *L'Année Sociologique*, a journal devoted to reviewing, year by year, the most significant publications which had appeared in sociology and in neighboring disciplines, in several European languages, over the previous year or two. It also published original contributions, including essays by Durkheim himself and by his students.

In 1897 Durkheim published his third major sociological book – *Suicide: A Study in Sociology* (trans. 1951). The phenomenon the book addressed was, and remains, of considerable public significance. It was relatively well documented, and had already been discussed by many scholars from various European countries. Durkheim's treatment of it focused on a particular aspect. **Suicide** is, on the face of it, a most private act, a peculiarly individual undertaking. Yet the data concerning its occurrence, which Durkheim painstakingly assembled and analyzed over years of research, showed remarkable regularities in the suicide rate, that is the frequency of the occurrence of suicide relative to the size of the population.

The suicide rate varies, sometimes widely, from country to country, or from one to another subunit of a country's population, and does so consistently, year in, year out. Furthermore, the differences between subunits (for example, city dwellers versus country dwellers, women versus men) are remarkably similar from one country to another, and are stable over time. Finally, over longer periods of time, one may detect consistent trends in the suicide rate, the most significant trend being its increase in modern times.

These data, Durkheim argued, suggest unequivocally that a certain propensity to suicide is a significant collective property of a given population or population subunit. That property manifests itself through a number of suicidal occurrences, each the product – we may well assume – of the particular circumstances of the individual in question, the final episode in a unique biography. The attempts other students have made to account for the regularities in the suicide rates by referring, for instance, to the geographical environment of a national population, or its ethnic composition, are demonstrably inadequate. The reasons for such regularities must then be found in the "moral constitution" of a given population or subunit, in the varying nature and intensity of the "suicidal currents" associated with that constitution.

The prohibition or the strong disapproval of suicide is common to all such constitutions. In this perspective, the universality of the suicide phenomenon (for all its variation) suggests that it should be interpreted by reference to two aspects of all societies. These are, on the one hand, the extent to which in a given society individuals are induced to interact, to take each other into account, and to form more or less cohesive bonds with one another, and, on the other, the extent to which societies address individuals with rules, and with normative guidance about how they should conduct themselves and think. Each aspect, however, may impinge on the suicide rate (or on the occurrence of other forms of **deviance**) both when the moral constitution of a society emphasizes it excessively and when that emphasis is too weak.

According to Durkheim's analysis, many of these data point to high suicide rates that correspond with a low significance of one (or both) of those aspects, namely bonding or regulating. For instance, Protestants show much higher suicide rates than Catholics. He attributes this difference to the lower social cohesion the Protestant **denominations** generate by stressing the autonomy of the individual believer, by their less pronounced and authoritative hierarchical structure, and by the lower frequency and intensity of their ritual occasions. Alternatively, the suicide rate is lower among married than among unmarried adults, lower among those married and with **children** than among those without children.

This last instance shows the untenability of what could be called a utilitarian understanding of differential suicide rates, which would associate higher rates with situations more likely to put people under pressure, or to confront them with greater hardships. Memberships which impose demanding responsibilities upon those holding them, by the same token, put in place support structures which may support them if they find themselves in those desperate circumstances which tempt them to suicide.

Looser, less demanding, but by the same token, less cohesive memberships are less likely to offer such support. This, paradoxically, may take the form of reminding individuals of their responsibilities and obligations towards other members, for to fulfill such obligations requires them in the first instance to remain alive. Without such reminders, individuals who face a particularly harsh crisis may well succumb to that "suicidogenic current" Durkheim calls "egoistic," for it results from the supremacy in their own minds of considerations relating exclusively to their own well-being, which is now seriously threatened.

Lack of regulation, of morally authoritative criteria by which to judge one's circumstances and to orient one's conduct, exposes individuals instead to the threat of "anomic" suicide. **Anomie** may derive from the accelerated pace at which social and cultural change occurs, from the individuals' exposure to a multitude of diverse stimuli, inciting them to seek ever-new experiences, new horizons, or new occasions of pleasure. Insofar as they yield to such entreaties, individuals place themselves outside the reach of established, sanctioned expectations. By the same token, their continuous effort to respond to those stimuli, to challenge the current boundaries of their existence, becomes an end in itself. Supposing again that a serious crisis befalls them, they cannot overcome it by appealing to norms and **values** which confer significance on what they have and who they are. The conventional sources of meaning may no longer suffice, and have not been replaced by new ones.

The suicido-genic effect of anomie is proven according to Durkheim by the high suicide rates of such people as divorcees, especially male divorcees. The bounding of desire, the framing and shaping of conduct previously afforded them by marriage, is no longer available, leaving them at a loss. Also, variations of the suicide rate over time suggest this circumstance, for it rises during periods of accelerated economic change – and that not only, Durkheim claims, at times of bust, but also at times of boom. Economic booms engender a general feeling that one must improve one's position, devalue old possessions and associations, strive for continuous improvement. People who act upon that feeling are out on a limb; should any misfortune befall them, it may find them unable to attach to their identities and possessions, to whatever they had accomplished in the past, a value which may sustain them, justifying the effort to remain alive and the related burdens.

Egoism and anomie together, according to Durkheim, increasingly characterize the moral atmosphere of modern society, the one amounting to a deficit of cohesion, the other to a deficit of meaning. But *Suicide* also points to the suicidogenic effects of an excess of cohesion. Under certain conditions, people may have such a sense of their own dependence on society, of society's entitlement to their devotion and sacrifice, that they become prone to a third, "altruistic" type of suicide. In some cases, society positively expects them, in certain circumstances, to dispose of themselves. In others, it gives them such a diminished sense of their own significance, of the value of their own survival, that if (again) a deep crisis occurs in their existence they easily surrender to it.

This phenomenon is much more in evidence in Oriental societies than in western ones, but is echoed here, Durkheim claims, by the relatively high suicide rate characteristic of a specific constituency – the members of the military profession. The army teaches the individuals that compose it to attach much less significance to themselves, *qua* individuals, than they attach to the group of which they are part, be it the fatherland or a specific military unit. It thus predisposes them to a suicide flowing not (as with egoistic suicide) from their acute sense of their own importance, but from a heightened sense of their dispensability.

All three suicide types (egoistic, anomic, and altruistic) are connected with universal social norms – respectively, that enjoining the individual to take some responsibility for her/himself; that encouraging her/him, under certain circumstances, to seek experiences "unprogrammed" by conventional culture; finally, that urging the individual to consider and to place her/himself at society's disposal. It is the priority among these different, though equally significant, commandments that varies from society or group to society or group – and unavoidably so, because of their mutual incompatibilities.

There is, however, a certain affinity between egoism and anomie (Durkheim acknowledges the difficulty of clearly distinguishing them), which together, as we have seen, characterize modern society. This is largely because egoistic attitudes and anomic dispositions are intrinsically connected with that society's economic arrangements, currently dominated by industry and centered on the **market** and on technological innovation.

The growing hold of such phenomena on society at large increasingly worries Durkheim, who in *Suicide* (as in other writings) suggests how to moderate the damage it can do to the society's moral temper. Again, public action is called for – but not directly that of the **state**. This (as Durkheim conceives of it) is an organ for the formation of general norms and of broad, durable policies, incapable as such of attending competently to the highly diverse and dynamic processes of economic life. Rather, public action on economic phenomena should be entrusted to corporate bodies organizing all those who are professionally involved (as employers or employees) in the various branches of industry. Such bodies can identify the potentialities and needs of each branch, regulate its activities, moderate the conflict between employers and employees, and generate among their constituents both a feeling of fellowship towards one another and a sense of responsibility towards the broader public.

The concern over the current tendencies of modern society that motivates such proposals is to an extent sublimated away in Durkheim's last great book, *The Elementary Forms of Religious Life* (1912 [trans. 2001]). The theme of **religion** had attracted him before, possibly because of its close connection with **morality**. For Durkheim, it had long been axiomatic that society was at bottom a moral reality. Its continuing existence and welfare depended on the willingness of individuals to consider each other not as instruments, but as fellow beings equally entitled to respect and **solidarity**, and society itself as demanding not only obedience but devotion. Society, furthermore, was not just the addressee, as it were, of moral conduct, but the source itself of morality. Durkheim argued that morality, in all its forms, is only encountered in society, and only varies in relation to social conditions. Society imparts to its expectations a quality of moral obligation that its own sanctions are meant mainly to symbolize, rather than to engender, and that is the essence itself of morality.

Morality refracts itself, as it were, in a plurality of social institutions. For all the variety of the social interests they guard and they discipline, all institutions, at bottom, impart to their own commandments, more or less openly, that same quality of intrinsic dutifulness. (Although it has its own institutions, the sphere of economic life is least likely to orient to such considerations the conduct of those taking part in its activities – and *that* is what worries Durkheim about it). The relationship of the whole institutional realm to religion is revealed in the close affinity between the quality in question – the particular *prestige* moral facts enjoy in the mind of a society's

members – and the distinctive *sacredness* of religious beliefs, norms, and practices.

According to Durkheim, all institutions, mundane as their themes may be, have arisen as articulations and differentiations of a single, great institutional matrix – religion itself. For, as Durkheim sees it, religion, in all its varieties, rests on and affirms the very distinction between its own realm – that of the sacred – and the contrasting realm of the profane, which encompasses all that must be kept at a distance from the sacred, acknowledging its unique powerfulness, awesomeness, dangerousness. The *noli me tangere* of all social institutions – their projecting themselves as public realities which individuals must not tinker with in their private pursuits, but accept and continuously validate as legitimate constraints upon them – is a derivation, however remote, of the sacred so understood.

But the question becomes – what engenders the division itself between the sacred and the profane? Durkheim holds that such a primordial and universal distinction must be rooted on an equally primordial and universal experience, best conveyed by the most primitive form of religious life one can find, which he claims to find in the totemism of Australian aboriginal populations. Here multiple, diverse bodies of beliefs and ritual practices, different as they are, agree on two points. Each celebrates the unchallengeable sacredness and the unique significance of an object (generally a biological species). Each asserts the identity between that object – the totem – and the tribe itself, among other things by attaching to both the same name.

This assertion provides Durkheim with a critical cue. As it worships the totem, the tribe worships itself. Quite generally, in fact, it is the confrontation with the superiority, the powerfulness, the generosity of a group, that generates in its members the experience of the sacred itself – an experience which **myth** and **ritual** continuously revisit and reproduce. When religions attain an idea of God, that idea symbolically represents society itself. Other religions may convey a less distinctive notion of a sacred force. All of them, however, partition reality into a sacred and a profane realm, assert an asymmetry of significance between them, and design collective activities which celebrate that asymmetry and align the participants with the higher realm. As they do so, the participants draw new strength and assurance from that part, rededicate themselves to the myths and the rituals of the group, many of which affirm the intrinsic obligatoriness of its *manières* *d'agir et de penser.* At the same time (dialectically, one might say), the participation of the faithful in the worship of that superior force posits and reconstitutes its existence (and thus the unique validity of those *manières*).

All religions do this, though perhaps none as clearly as the totemic ones. Even these, of course, do so in varied and contrasting ways. Each tribe attributes sacredness to a different totemic being, and thus implicitly to itself. Each celebrates it through a different ensemble of myths and rituals. This very diversity may suggest to the observer that religion itself is at bottom an arbitrary exercise in self-delusion, a delirium.

Yes, Durkheim agrees – "but it is a well-grounded delirium." In all its forms, religion asserts symbolically a basic truth. The individual owes everything to the society. Reciprocally, only the individual's respect for and devotion to society itself, asserted more directly through religious practice, less directly by dutiful submission to varied institutional commands, confirms the very existence of society and the continuing validity of its institutions.

If this is the core argument of *Elementary Forms*, one may well see one problem it poses for Durkheim himself. If religion is the ultimate source of all morality, and if it is necessary to the very survival of society, what of modern society itself? Has **modernization** not displaced religion?

By the time he wrote *Elementary Forms*, Durkheim himself had recognized some validity to the secularization thesis, and had become less and less confident in the validity and sustainability of the modernization project. Yet in *Elementary Forms* and in other writings he tries hard, one senses, to be optimistic. Modern society, like all others, *needs* religion, for without religion society would face dissolution. And it has in fact, for all appearances to the contrary, a religion of its own,

compatible of course with other aspects of its nature, but not yet sufficiently conscious of itself and of its own distinctiveness.

Modern religion – the cult of the individual – sacralizes the human person, the human being as such. It surrounds with a halo of dignity each member of society, forbidding others to treat the individual as a morally neutral, merely factual component of society, as a means or as an obstacle. Its content is revealed, in particular, by political constitutions which attribute some rights to all citizens, irrespective of their social condition.

This recognition of a juridically significant capacity which belongs equally to everyone is a significant moral advance of **modernity**. That capacity is periodically celebrated by political rituals, and its scope is destined to grow in the future. Its moral significance is under threat from contemporary developments which encourage egoism instead of affirming the sacredness of the individual. But such developments can be countered by institutional innovations, in particular those that regulate and constrain competitive conduct on the market. Furthermore, it can be expected that more and more societies – beginning with European ones, which represented for Durkheim the front edge of modernity – will assert in their constitutions the equal moral significance of all their members. They will thus contribute to establishing a form of religion appropriate to modernity.

Durkheim's expectations of further moral advances from European societies were harshly negated by the advent of World War I. This conflict at first gave new impulse to his French patriotism; but at length its carnage brutally thinned out the ranks of his own students. When his own son perished during a military expedition in the Balkans, this personal tragedy broke Durkheim's heart and paralyzed his mind. He died in 1917.

GIANFRANCO POGGI

E

economism

This is a term for theories that regard economic activity as the primary focus of social life, in which political or cultural arrangements are, at best, secondary to, or derivative of, more fundamental economic forces. Examples of economism include theories (such as the economics of the **market**, and certain types of **Marxism**) and social activities (such as free trade or trade unionism) that are perceived as neglectful of interactions between economic and noneconomic aspects of social life.

The term is usually applied by critics rather than supporters of economism. To describe something or someone as economistic is usually to diagnose a one-dimensional approach to social analysis that is inadequate to the complex or multidimensional character of social phenomena. Few sociologists would identify with economism in an extreme form, even though many would regard the **economy** as a central (perhaps *the* central) aspect of **social structure**, **power**, and social **inequality**.

The idea of economism rests on the modern assumption of a social **differentiation**. This perspective sees **society** as becoming differentiated into distinct spheres – the economy, government, law, and **culture** – that are autonomous from one another and centered on specialized institutions – such as markets and factories, parliaments and law courts, and so forth. The idea of differentiation, however, raises questions as to the relationship between different spheres, in this case between the economy and the rest of society. While economistic thinking sees this in terms of the causal primacy of the economy over polity and culture, this assumption remains controversial. Sociologists generally prefer alternative accounts which emphasize the role of government and culture in the constitution and regulation of economic life.   ROBERT HOLTON

economy

In the most simple and general sense, the concept of the economy is used to refer to the social **organizations** and **institutions** that are involved in the production and distribution of goods and services in **society** – **firms**, **labor**, money-capital, and the **markets** and **networks** by which they are connected and articulated. The term is derived from the ancient Greek *oeconomicus* which referred to the practical activity of household (*oikos*) management. From the late Middle Ages onward, particularly in western Europe, the social organization of production and exchange became increasingly detached from the feudal and communal social relations of households, manors, and patrimonial estates. Home and work gradually became structurally separated. An early sociological analysis of this process is contained in **Max Weber**'s *General Economic History* (1927 [trans. 1981]).

Early nineteenth-century classical economics saw the resulting "economy," comprising the factors of production of land, capital, and labor, as a relatively autonomous subsystem of society that was governed by the economic laws of the market, conceptualized by Adam Smith (1723–90) as the "invisible hand." This approach identifies the "economy" with the "market." **Talcott Parson**'s **social theory** endorsed this distinction between "economy" and "society"; but there have also been two critical responses within sociology to this conceptualization. First, **Karl Polanyi**, following **Karl Marx** and Weber, contended that the modern market economy should be understood as a historically specific type of economy in which production and exchange had become separated, or "disembedded" from wider social relations and **norms**. Second, as **Mark Granovetter** has argued, economic relations in modern economies are also social relations.

In a critique of the postulate of natural **scarcity** in classical economics, Marx argued that it was a socially produced consequence of the unequal and exploitative relations in the economy. He classified different types of economy as historically located modes of production, distinguished by different technological "means" and "social relations" of production between owners and nonowners. Marx identified a sequence of development from primitive **communism** – through ancient, Asiatic, feudal, and capitalist – to communism or socialism.

The general Marxian approach to the analysis of economies is developed by the modern Parisian Regulation School, exemplified in Michel Aglietta's *The Theory of Capitalist Regulation* (1979). **Regulation theory** identifies three successive modes of regulation of capitalist economies from the middle of the nineteenth to the late twentieth century: (1) the nineteenth-century competitive mode of regulation; (2) twentieth-century "monopoly **capitalism**" and mass production or Fordism (see **Post-Fordism**); and (3) the 1970s crisis of Fordism and the subsequent partial disintegration of **flexible specialization**, and development of regional industrial districts, or disorganized capitalism.

In *The Long Twentieth Century* (1994), Giovanni Arrighi synthesized the Marxian and Weberian classical **sociology** with the economics of Adam Smith (1723–90) and with the history of Fernand Braudel (1902–85), to produce an analysis of the successive **hegemonies** of structurally different capitalist economies from the Renaissance Italian city-states, to the Netherlands, Britain, and the United States.

Modern sociology, for example in P. Hall and D. Soskice (eds.), *Varieties of Capitalism: The Institutional Foundations of Comparative Advantage* (2001), has been concerned with the question of the diversity of modern capitalist economies. In the first place, the success of East Asian capitalism and the rapid advance of the German and French economies after World War II led to a debate on whether there existed equally efficient and effective forms of capitalism to the Anglo-American liberal market system. In *Stock Market Capitalism: Welfare Capitalism, Japan and Germany Versus the Anglo-Saxons* (2000), Ronald Dore argued that Japan and Germany had been able to combine economic success with social welfare. The debate continues in the context of the relatively poor performance of these economies from the late twentieth century. Second, the transition from the central planning of communism in the former Soviet Union and the continued liberalization and growth of the Chinese economy have stimulated a debate on the type of capitalist economy that is likely to develop in the former state socialist economies.

A further important consideration, also discussed in Bruno Amable's *The Diversity of Modern Capitalism* (2003), is whether economic **globalization** will reduce the existing diversity of different types of capitalism in a process of convergence towards the Anglo-Saxon liberal market type of economy.   GEOFFREY INGHAM

education

A concern with education has been inseparably linked with the development of sociology, especially in the French tradition. In defining sociology, **Auguste Comte** argued that there had been a historical progression in the advancement of all science from deploying religious and metaphysical conceptual frameworks to adopting procedures of positivist analysis, based on observation. This intellectual progression was mirrored institutionally by corresponding forms of social organization – from feudal and aristocratic systems to that culminating form which would be the consequence of secular, social engineering. The emergence of positivist analysis of human and social relations would necessarily entail the construction of forms of social organization which, for the first time, would be founded on science rather than **prejudice** or **privilege**. Positivist scientists would become the legislators of mankind. Comte was aware that the prevalence of positivist principles in social practice in **mass society** would require some emotional underpinning, and he proposed the institutionalization of a positive **religion** which would generate a sense of ideological and social inclusion, operating as a secular, surrogate Catholic Church.

The third French Republic – of "**intellectuals**" – tried, from 1871, to introduce a system of state education which would perform the function that Comte had projected for an organized positivist religion. The function of the education system would be to generate social **solidarity** by initiating the whole population of the country into the secular values which informed its organization and operation. It was **Émile Durkheim** who tried to implement Comte's program in the 1890s by carrying out sociological research and by articulating rules which should govern the method of sociological enquiry, but it is important to remember that he taught pedagogy at the same time as sociology for the whole of his life. In his first post at the University of Bordeaux, from 1887 until 1902, he gave weekly lectures on pedagogy to teachers and, when he moved to Paris, it was to the Chair in the Science of Education at the Sorbonne. Durkheim's writings on education were assembled posthumously, notably *Education and Sociology* (1922 [trans. 1956]), *Moral Education: A Study in the Theory and Application of the Sociology of Education* (1925 [trans. 1961]), and *Pedagogical Evolution in France* (1938 [trans. 1977]). In his introduction to the first of these texts, Paul Fauconnet insisted that Durkheim's parallel attachment to sociological and educational analyses was not at all accidental, but, rather, that "it is in as much as it is a social fact that he approaches education: his doctrine of education is an essential element of his sociology." The two dimensions of Durkheim's thinking explain the traditional affinity between sociology and the study of education: on the one hand **pedagogical practices** within the educational system were necessary instruments for fulfilling the social mission which was the legacy of Comtist thinking. On the other hand, it was important that the study of education should exemplify sociological rigor. Typically, Durkheim began his discussion in *Education and Sociology* with a critical examination of the existing definitions of education. He argued that the word had been used too broadly to include the influence of nature on human will and **intelligence** and that, instead, it should be restricted to mean solely the action which adults exercise over the young. To define this education more closely would entail an analysis of educational practice in different times and places. In faithful positivist fashion, Durkheim concluded:

> We do not know *a priori* what is the function of the respiratory or circulatory systems for living beings. By what privilege should we be better informed concerning the educative function? ... Hence, must it not be the case that to constitute a preliminary notion of education, to determine the thing which is denominated in this way, historical observation appears to be indispensable.

His social history of pedagogy in France fulfilled just this function. For Durkheim, the sociology of education was to be pedagogically prescriptive by being methodologically exemplary.

The inaugurating concern of sociology with education was the product of a particular set of social and intellectual circumstances in France at the end of the nineteenth century. Consideration of the legacy of this concern raises broad questions about the transcultural and transtemporal applicability of the **social sciences**. In considering the "predisciplinary history of social science" in general, in his *The Rise of Social Theory* (1995), Johan Heilbron has argued that this rise was part of a progressive **secularization** of human societies. At first this involved a return to the works of classical antiquity, and to Aristotelian "practical philosophy" in particular, but this was the starting-point for the articulation of modern notions which characterized the predisciplinary history of social science. There followed stages of development which, in Heilbron's view, moved from primary interest in conceptions of **state** and law to concern with

economic theory until, in the eighteenth century, there emerged a secular approach to the concept of **society** which meant breaking with both theology and political theory.

There is a reciprocal relationship between developing social conditions which generate new social sciences and the contributions which social scientific analyses of these emergent developments make towards their realization. Durkheimian sociology of education was in a reciprocal relationship with those social and political forces which suggested that the introduction of a state-controlled national education system would actualize the concept of a *conscience collective* which would ensure social cohesion and foster a national identity. There was an affinity with the distrust of **individualism** manifested at the same time in Germany in the formulation of the notions of *Gemeinschaft* and *Gesellschaft* (see **Ferdinand Tönnies**).

In the United Kingdom in the same period, the response to similar forces arising from similar phenomena of industrialization (see **industrial society**) and democratization (see **democracy**) developed within a different conceptual framework – that of **liberalism**. In his contribution to *The Rise of the Modern Educational System: Structural Change and Social Reproduction, 1870–1920* (1987), the English Marxist social historian, Brian Simon, demonstrated that the consequence of the United Kingdom Elementary Education Act of 1870 was that three levels of schooling came into being in the period from 1860 to 1900: "public" schools for the upper middle class, elementary schooling for the working class, and a new set of schools aimed at accommodating the middle classes. The outcome, he contended, was "the establishment of a highly differentiated system in which each level served, in theory at least, a specific **social class** (or subsection of a class), with each having a specific function." In the early years of British sociology, the problem of education was much less central than in France precisely because education was not required to perform the same social function. There was little expectation that the educational system should contribute towards the development of a self-conscious social democracy and, rather, the enlargement of educational provision was a carefully regulated mechanism for legitimating the allocation of individuals to pre-established, stratified, social and professional positions.

In general terms, the liberal tradition led to research which focused on the performance of individuals and on the relationship between educational and occupational hierarchies. In part, the emphasis was on educational psychology and the measurement of intelligence. In so far as this tradition generated a sociology of education, it was a sociology which, particularly in the United States, responded to the given structure of relations between education and the economy. It was the impulse towards egalitarianism provided by World War II which, in the United Kingdom, stimulated an adoption of a Durkheimian orientation towards the sociological analysis of education. It is significant that it was in this period that Durkheim's texts on education were first translated into English, and sociological analysis began to operate reciprocally in tandem with the movement towards the comprehensivization of the schooling system.

The stimulus given to British sociology of education by the publication in 1971 of the collection of articles edited by M. F. D. Young, entitled *Knowledge and Control. New Directions for the Sociology of Education* – which first popularized early articles by **Basil Bernstein** and **Pierre Bourdieu** – came largely from a re-discovery of Durkheim's societal perspective. In France, however, Bourdieu's work was provoked by his sense that the official **ideology** of the French educational system masked social **differentiation** and that it was no longer possible, in any case, to assume that the achievement of equality within an educational system could guarantee social **equality**. Bourdieu problematized the systemic legacy of Third Republic educational ideology and also refused to limit the sociology of education to the analysis of pedagogical relations within schooling **institutions**. The shift in his thinking was accurately reflected in the English rendering of the title of his book on reproduction which, in France in 1970, was subtitled "Elements for a Theory of the Educational System", but, in English in 1977, was called *Reproduction in Education, Society and Culture*. Writing within the Durkheimian tradition, Bourdieu offered a framework for analyzing the function of schooling within a society which was conceived as being in a state of conflict or competition, where educational attainment, cultural taste, occupational position are mobilized in interacting ways to acquire and legitimize the acquisition of **power**. Without renouncing the ideal of the socialist tradition – of achieving social equality, solidarity, and inclusion – Bourdieu provided a conceptual apparatus which could accommodate the interests of the liberal tradition. It is significant that Bourdieu's work of the 1960s became available in translation in the United States at the end of the 1970s. The technocratic model of

education had become dominant in the United States. It operated on the assumption that the graded performance of students in education was a reliable indicator of eligibility for posts in a correlative hierarchy of **occupations**. Several challenges to this assumption emanated from the United States: the **de-schooling** movement; the articulation of the influence of a **hidden curriculum** in formal learning contexts; and the critiques of **credentialism**. In different ways, these were all attempts to rescue the sociology of education from subservience to the status quo of assumed relations between school and work and, therefore, between educational and economic opportunities. The refusal to accept the a-cultural assumptions of the technocratic model was strengthened by the association with the civil rights movement (see **social movements**) and the concomitant interest in **affirmative action** as a way of enabling educational opportunity to overcome cultural disadvantage.

If we accept, first, that the sociology of education at any time is in reciprocal relationship with educational policies; second, that it has emerged in the West in two, ideal-typical, philosophical traditions of **socialism** and **liberalism**; and, third, that its history in the West demonstrates the effects both of the internal reciprocity between theory and practice and of cross-cultural conceptual transfer between these competing traditions – then, two provocative questions arise, one local and the other global. If the **hegemony** of the conservative party in British **politics** from the 1970s to 1997 suppressed the resurgence of a socialist sociology of education, has the effect of the New Labour accommodation with Thatcherism, associated with the sociological work of **Anthony Giddens**, neutralized sociological critique and encouraged the development of a postmodern version of the technocratic model? Does the appropriation of cultural difference through the overriding force of economic performativity now mean that a sociology of international education is doomed to stand impotently by as the technocratic model begins to prevail globally?

                                                    DEREK ROBBINS

Eisenstadt, Shmuel Noah (1923–)

Emeritus Professor in the Department of Sociology and Anthropology at the Hebrew University of Jerusalem and a recipient of the Balzan Prize in 1988, Eisenstadt has made important contributions to comparative, historical and political sociology. In *The Political System of Empires* (1967), he examined pre-industrial societies to establish the conditions that contributed to their instability and ultimate transformations. He made a major contribution to the study of **generations** and **social change** in *From Generation to Generation: Age Groups and Social Structure* (1971). Eisenstadt was in general concerned to understand development in non-western societies in terms of the legacy of **Max Weber** in *The Protestant Ethic and Modernization* (1968). He has been fascinated by Japanese society in *Japanese Civilization* (1996), because Japan raises many acute questions about whether the western model of development is unique. Eistenstadt has therefore been influential in arguing that there are many forms of **modernity** rather than a single, uniform process of **modernization.** His idea of "multiple modernities" has been explored in *Patterns of Modernity* (1987) (with D. Sachsenmaier), and he edited *Reflections on Multiple Modernities: European, Chinese and other Interpretations* (2002) and *Comparative Civilizations and Multiple Modernities* (2003). He has also contributed to the sociological understanding of **fundamentalism** in *Fundamentalism, Sectarianism and Revolution* (1999), arguing that Islamic fundamentalism is not anti-modern or even traditional, but another type of modernity.

BRYAN S. TURNER

elective affinity
– see **Max Weber**.

Elias, Norbert (1897–1990)
Born in Breslau, German sociologist Elias studied medicine and philosophy before graduating with a doctorate in philosophy in 1922. He worked with Alfred Weber, before becoming academic assistant to **Karl Mannheim** in Frankfurt in 1929. After fleeing to Paris in 1933, following the rise of the Nazis, Elias settled in England in 1935, taking a research fellowship at the London School of Economics. In 1954, he was appointed to the subsequently influential Sociology Department at the University of Leicester. He also held university positions in Frankfurt, Ghana, Bielefeld, and Amsterdam.

Elias's approach has often been characterized as figurational sociology, though he came to prefer the term process sociology. This approach was designed to avoid reified accounts of social **institutions** and to emphasize the historical character of social life. His work is therefore often contrasted with the **functionalism** of **Talcott Parsons**.

The defining features of this approach hold that: (1) human beings are born into relations of interdependency so that the **social structures** that they form with each other engender emergent dynamics, which cannot be reduced to individual actions or motivations. Such emergent dynamics fundamentally shape processes of individual growth and development, and the trajectory of people's lives; (2) these figurations are in a constant state of flux and transformation; (3) longterm transformations of human social figurations are largely unplanned and unforeseen; and (4) the development of knowledge takes place within such figurations and forms one aspect of their overall development.

Elias's first work, though not published until 1969, was *The Court Society*, in which he examined the social pressures facing the "court nobility" under the reign of Louis XIV. According to Elias the court **rationality** of the nobility, in which rank and prestige determined expenditure, can be contrasted with the economic rationality of the bourgeoisie, where **consumption** is subordinated to **income**. Like economic rationality, court rationality involved forms of self-restraint which were expressed in literature, architecture, and philosophy. Elias's magnum opus, however, remains *The Civilizing Process* (1939 [trans. 2000]). Drawing on a variety of thinkers, including **Karl Marx**, Mannheim, **Max Weber**, and **Sigmund Freud**, Elias offers a bifocal investigation of psychological and behavioral transformations among the secular upper classes in the West, which, he shows, are integrally tied above all to processes of internal pacification and state formation. Because of the late and separate publication of volumes I and II in English, in 1978 and 1981, the study of long-term psychological changes, the history of manners, and the capacity for greater self-control in volume I has often, misleadingly, been read independently from the study of changes in social structure and state formation outlined in volume II.

Elias's other writings often develop ideas originally elaborated in *The Civilizing Process*. Together with *Involvement and Detachment* (1987), which outlines the social conditions for the possibility of a scientific sociology, Elias's other crucial work is *What is Sociology?* (1978), in which he outlines among other things a series of "game models." These demonstrate the regularity of social processes which generate emergent dynamics that cannot be reduced to individual actions. These constrain and mold the **habitus** and behavior of individuals.

Other important works by Elias include (with J. Scotson) *The Established and the Outsiders* (1965); and (with Eric Dunning) *Quest for Excitement* (1986); *The Society of Individuals* (1991); and *Time: An Essay* (1992).

STEVEN LOYAL

elite(s)

While in classic analyses the term elite carries a connotation of superiority ("the cream"), in contemporary social analysis it is used in a non-evaluative manner: it means a powerful minority affecting public and political outcomes in a systematic and significant way. Elite **influence** reflects control over "power resources" concentrated in large **organizations**, for example capital, **authority**, means of coercion, mass communication, knowledge, and **charisma**, as well as the capacity of elite **groups** to act in concert. Elites emerge in all organized **societies**, especially those with strong bureaucratic states. Therefore, the most visible parts of national elites are political elites (leaders). In democratic regimes, such elites operate electoral systems in which they compete for popular support. They also interact – collaborate, compete, and sometimes contend – with state-administrative, business, media, trade union, military, and religious elite groups. If this interaction is peaceful, and if elite groups achieve a high degree of consensus, stable democratic regimes may emerge. Elite warfare, by contrast, is a trademark of unstable and non-democratic polities.

While the empirical delineations of elites are arbitrary – **power** and **influence** are matters of degree – most elite researchers restrict their size to about 300–1,000 persons. Such elite persons are identified "positionally," as holders of the top power positions in the largest and most resource-rich organizations, or by involvement in making key decisions, or by reputation among their peers, or, finally, by a combination of the three methods. National elites are also seen as internally stratified, with political leaders typically placed at the apex of national power structures. At the other end of the power spectrum are the masses ("non-elites"). Between these two extremes, social scientists also distinguish "political classes" – the power strata from which elites are drawn, and on which elites rely in wielding power – and "influentials," those who can affect elite decisions.

Elites are sometimes conflated and sometimes contrasted with "ruling classes" (see **social class**). The latter are seen as much broader collectivities distinguished by ownership of capital. Class theorists typically see elites as "executive arms" of the ruling class(es). Elite theorists, by contrast, criticize class reductionism and point to the autonomy of political elites, as reflected in their capacity to expropriate ownership classes (for example in revolutions).

Classical elite theory was developed at the turn of the nineteenth and twentieth centuries by **Vilfredo Pareto**, **Gaetano Mosca**, and **Robert Michels**, under the strong influence of both positivism and the theories of **Max Weber**. It constituted a critique of democratic theory that predicted a radical dispersion of political power, and of Marxism that foresaw class conflicts and a triumph of egalitarian **socialism**. In contrast with both, the classic elite thinkers suggested persistent and inescapable power concentration in elites' hands. Revolutions (see **revolution, theory of**), including "socialist revolutions," claimed elite theorists, merely reconstituted elites, and they did not narrow down the elite–mass power gaps.

Both classic and contemporary elite theorists see the bases of elite power in certain psychological predispositions, organizational abilities (rare in general populations), small size, and internal cohesion. Elite cohesion does not preclude the possibility of temporary intra-elite conflicts and divisions on specific policy questions. However, when their power is threatened, elite members defend it in a solidary way. Their firm grip on power is strengthened by alliances with non-elite social forces – dominant strata, movements, classes, and organized groups – and by control over their succession exercised through exclusive schools, corporate hierarchies, and party machines. Contemporary elite theorists, such as **C. Wright Mills**, see the United States elite as firmly anchored in the core organizations: the national government, the military directorate, and the largest business corporations.

A comprehensive overview of modern elites is provided by Tom Bottomore in *Elites and Society* (1993) and by Robert Putnam in *Comparative Study of Political Elites* (1976). Bottomore highlights elite – ruling class connection. Putnam stresses elites' anchoring in social and institutional structures, and he sees elite conduct as heavily constrained by **ideologies** (revolutionary elites) and national legal frameworks (liberal elites). Other contemporary elite theorists, such as John Higley and Eva Etzioni-Halevi, elaborate the conceptions of elite unity and **democracy**. They focus on elite effectiveness, consensus, and competition. According to Higley and his collaborators, elites that "craft" and maintain stable democratic regimes are united in their support of peaceful electoral competition, broadly integrated, and well connected with the major mass constituencies, typically through party organizations and civic associations. Etzioni-Halevi sees effective "coupling" of elites with lower/working classes as a key condition of democracy, the latter seen as a regime of competing elites.

More recently, there has been a shift in elite researchers' attention, reflecting a change in the structure and composition of contemporary elites. It can be summarized in five points:

(1) The emergence of transnational power **networks** and elites. While nation-states remain the most important institutional loci of power, other power concentrations emerge in the process of **globalization** and the formation of such transnational bodies as the United Nations, the World Bank, the International Monetary Fund, Greenpeace, and Islamic movements. The increasingly transnational/global nature of the problems national elites face (for example **terrorism**, environmental degradation, the drugs trade, uncontrolled **migrations** and the spread of AIDS) forces them into supra-state and transnational domains.

(2) Widening elite autonomy. One of the key trends of the last decades seems to be a widening of non-elective elites capable of initiating, and sometimes directing, **social change**. Thus what are arguably the most momentous events of the twentieth century, such as the dissolution of the Soviet Union, the collapse of Soviet **communism** in eastern Europe, and the liberalization of the Chinese economy, have been engineered by elites.

(3) Emergence of pro-democratic elites. The recent wave of democratization (1989–95) has been championed mainly by elites "crafting" and consolidating democratic regimes, often with only weak support from mass populations. Pro-democratic elites have emerged in southern Europe, Russia, central and eastern Europe, and East Asia.

(4) Intense elite **differentiation** and circulation. Contemporary studies show that new elite groups emerge with the expansion of new industries, civic groups, **social movements**, and nongovernmental organizations.

(5) The declining impact of **ideologies** in advanced western societies. Western elites cultivate mass support in a pragmatic and ad hoc manner, often through media "spin" and campaigns focusing on personalities of leaders. This reflects the fact that the support constituencies of western elites are less anchored in specific classes, ethno-segments, or religious categories.   JAN PAKULSKI

embeddedness

This concept suggests that economic conduct is embedded within and influenced by wider **social structures**, **institutions**, and **cultures**, and represents a sociological critique of standard economic models that equate economic processes with atomistic market transactions between self-interested individuals. **Mark Granovetter** codified this critique in "Economic Action and Social Structure: The Problem of Embeddedness" (1985), in the *American Journal of Sociology*. He argued that trust, suspicion, and manipulation in market transactions cannot be explained by the calculations of autonomous (undersocialized) economic actors or by (oversocialized) cultural determinism. Rather, they are explicable in terms of the specific **networks** of social relations inhabited by such actors: a shared network may underpin trust rather than suspicion, but may also create more scope for abuse of trust.

This is not an argument for uniform embeddedness. First, in some societies economic processes are largely structured in terms of nonmarket relations, in which case formal market models are entirely inappropriate. Second, market processes in capitalist societies are not autonomous and self-sustaining, as much economic theory implies, but rather generate tensions and challenges that prompt efforts at institutional regulation. Third, market transactions are differently conditioned by specific institutional features: thus different liberal market and "alliance" **capitalisms** involve various levels and types of embeddedness. Finally, the greater embeddedness of economic processes in "alliance" capitalisms, through ties among enterprises and with the **state** (and sometimes organized **labor**), *may* generate trust and cooperation more readily than liberal market capitalisms.

However, the invocation of embeddedness only provides a starting point for such arguments. The consequences of different sorts of embeddedness, and their advantages and disadvantages for different economic actors, have to be addressed through more detailed specification and research.
TONY ELGER

embodiment
– see **body**.

emotional labor
– see **emotions**.

emotions

Although typically understood in terms of feelings and bodily sensations, which are components of any emotion, emotions are best regarded as experiences of involvement. Social circumstance, expressive communication, and actor intentions are crucial to the genesis of emotional experience and its quality. Thus, emotions can be seen to underscore **values**, interests, and meanings in social life. Emotions, then, are implicated in rational as well as irrational action and outlook. **Max Weber**'s distinction, for instance, between rational action and affective action, therefore loses its coherence when emotion is not confined to a particular type of action but seen to underlie all action. Similarly, while some emotions may rise and fall within a short time-frame, it is not a necessary characteristic of emotions that they are of short duration, though this applies to those emphasized by experimental work in psychology: here laboratory research studies chiefly reactive and highly visceral emotions, readily elicited from experimental subjects usually drawn from undergraduate student populations. Many important emotions, however, are not brief and episodic but enduring or ongoing. Another misunderstanding holds that those experiencing emotions are necessarily conscious of them. They need not be. Many emotions, including the most important for social processes, are experienced below the threshold of awareness. **Thomas J. Scheff**, for instance, has shown that much social conformity can be explained in terms of **shame** of which the subject is not consciously aware.

The relevance of emotions to sociological **explanation** is original to the discipline, central to the eighteenth-century precursors of sociology, including Adam Smith (1723–90) in *The Theory of Moral Sentiments* (1759) and Adam Ferguson (1723–1816) in *An Essay on the History of Civil Society* (1767), and to nineteenth- and early twentieth-century sociological pioneers, including **Alexis de Tocqueville**, **Émile Durkheim**, **Vilfredo Pareto**, **Ferdinand Tönnies**, and **Georg Simmel**. Since the 1970s, after at least half a century of neglect by sociologists, a sociology of emotions has emerged. An approach associated with these developments concerns emotion management and emotional labor as in **Arlie Russell Hochschild**'s *The Managed Heart* (1983). Emotion management is the broad process that matches face or emotional expression to circumstance, a process achieved by emotional labor. Emotional labor, like **labor** in general, refers to activities performed in an employment setting for a wage, in which the labor is to induce or suppress feelings in order to sustain an outward countenance or emotional expression intended to produce a particular state of mind in others. The affective parameters within which emotional labor is performed are the culturally defined feeling rules that prescribe the content of emotional expression and the circumstances in which particular expressions are appropriate.

Hochschild estimated that, in the early 1980s when she wrote her book, approximately one-third of American workers had jobs substantially involving emotional labor and that approximately half of all female workers had jobs involving such forms of emotional work. She argues that the costs of emotional labor to those engaged in it are high: it affects the capacity to feel and may lead to loss of the function of emotional display or expression. The deleterious consequence of performance of emotional labor postulated by Hochschild is supported in many of the documented cases of emotional labor. And yet **case studies** seldom control for other aspects of the work that may be responsible for negative emotional outcomes. In a comparative examination of occupations, Amy Wharton in *Work and Occupations* (1993) found that emotional laborers are no more likely than other workers to suffer emotional exhaustion and somewhat more likely to be satisfied with their job. What determines whether work leads to emotional exhaustion or a sense of emotional inauthenticity is the level of job autonomy and involvement. When these are low then the jobs involved tend to produce emotional exhaustion and low job satisfaction, whether emotional labor is a primary aspect of the job or not.

The sociology of emotion management and emotional labor predominantly understands emotions in terms of social and cultural manipulation, transformation, and restraint. While this aspect of emotions is important it does not exhaust the ways in which emotions may be sociologically considered. The way in which emotions spontaneously emerge in social processes and also the extent to which they constrain and orient social processes. A general theory of emotions developed by Theodore Kemper in *A Social Interactional Theory of Emotions* (1978) postulates three basic propositions. First, all social **interactions** can be characterized in terms of two formal dimensions of social relations, namely **power** and status, or involuntary and voluntary compliance, scaled in terms of whether they are in excess of what is required in the relationship, adequate for it, or insufficient. Agency – who might be responsible for too much or not enough power, say – can similarly be differentiated, as "self" or "other." Second, specific physiological processes are stimulated by specific experiences of power and status.

Finally, particular emotions are physiologically specific. Physiological processes are thus the mechanisms that translate the structure of inter-actions into the emotions of the actors and are therefore an intermediary variable. In summary, the particular emotions that people experience arise out of the structure of the relations of power and status in which they are implicated. Thus, insufficient power in a relationship is likely to lead to experience of fear, excess of power to guilt; excess status is likely to lead to **shame**, insufficient status to depression, and so on. According to this account, emotion is in the social relationship: the subject of relations of power and status experiences emotional change, and, in being so changed, is disposed to change the relationship itself. Thus emotion is a necessary link between **social structure** and social actor. The connection is never mechanical, though, because emotions normally do not compel but bias activity. Emotion is provoked by circumstance and is experienced as transformation of dispositions to act. It is through the subject's active exchange with others that emotional experience is both stimulated in the actor and orientating of their conduct. Emotion is directly implicated in the actors' transformation of their circumstances, as well as the circumstances' transformation of the actors' disposition to act. JACK BARBALET

empiricism

This is a position in **epistemology** which states that only that which is observable, that is, empirical, can be used in the generation of scientific knowledge. There can be no recourse to unseen forces, underlying causes, or claims that behind the appearance of reality there lies a more fundamental reality.

In contrast to theological accounts of how we gain knowledge of the world – through divine revelation, faith, and the teachings of the church fathers – empiricism was an epistemological position, evolved through the **Enlightenment**, arguing that knowledge of the world was a product of careful observation by the individual, the sorting of these observations, and the generation of laws governing them. As developed in Newtonian mechanics, the world was conceptualized as orderly and lawful. As developed by John Locke (1632–1704) in political philosophy, we are born into the world as a blank sheet and, through sensory experience and by induction (that is, by moving from the knowledge of the particular to the knowledge of the general), gradually build our

knowledge of the world. However, Immanuel Kant (1724–1804) argued that reality is too infinitely complex for us to know what to abstract out of it; that in our own lifetime we could never make sense of it; and hence the mind must come prepared to make sense of the empirical world. Thus he proposes that the categories of reason – of **causality**, mass, weight, **time**, and so on – are a-priori characteristics of the human mind. Alternatively, **Émile Durkheim** proposed that the categories of the mind are not individual achievements since we are born into already existing **explanations** of the world, and that knowledge, natural and social, is a social achievement, specific to each **culture** in its own time.

Applied in the **social sciences** by **Auguste Comte** and Durkheim, empiricism led to the claims that **society** could be studied in the same way as nature, and that, with the methods of the natural sciences (observation, classification, comparison, and experiment) and the use of **statistics**, the laws of social life could be demonstrated.

The critique of the empiricist position has continued in the history and philosophy of science in the twentieth century. On the one hand, historian of science **Thomas Samuel Kuhn** argued, in *The Structure of Scientific Revolutions* (1970), that scientific knowledge was not the product of nature, but of the scientific **communities** who constructed it. We come to have knowledge of the world through **socialization** into specific world-views, which give a definition of what reality is, how to investigate it, what questions to ask about it, and how to answer them – in short, **paradigms**. Kuhn demonstrated that paradigms rose and fell and that knowledge was not cumulative: for example, Newtonian mechanics and Albert Einstein's **relativism** are not cumulative and they cannot be reconciled. Put another way, our knowledge of the world is not built on any correspondence theory of truth. This point was made most importantly by W. V. Quine, in *Words and Objects* (1960), where he argued that there was nothing in reality or our sensory experience of it that led to the logical distinctions that we make about it. KEVIN WHITE

encoding/decoding
– see **Stuart Hall**.

end-of-ideology thesis
– see **ideology**.

endogamy
– see **kinship**.

Engels, Friedrich (1820–1895)

An interpreter, collaborator, and popularizer of **Karl Marx**. Born in Barmen, Germany, he went to Britain to manage the family factory in Manchester. He first met Marx in 1842 and his *Outlines for a Critique of Political Economy* was well received by the latter. The two agreed to work together in attacks on the Young Hegelians and in 1845 Engels published his *Condition of the Working Classes in England*, a study based on detailed empirical work on the plight of workers, particularly in Manchester.

Engels's strength was his clarity of argument. Critics have felt that he oversimplified Marx and extended Marx's theory into areas such as the natural sciences where it is not appropriate. His loyalty (and financial assistance) to Marx is not questionable, however. He wrote fascinating historical work on Germany after the crushing of the 1848 revolutions (see **revolution, theory of**), and his *Anti-Dühring* was a fierce critique of a German socialist. His *Socialism: Utopian and Scientific* appeared in English in 1892, a popularizing work that was widely read. In 1894 he wrote the *Origin of the Family, Private Property and the State*, a work that built sympathetically on the anthropology of Lewis Henry Morgan (1818–81). In 1888 his *Ludwig Feuerbach and the End of German Classical Philosophy* was published, and did much to expound Marxist theory as a dialectical and **historical materialism**. His *Dialectics of Nature* appeared posthumously in 1927. After Marx's death, Engels devoted the rest of his life to editing and translating Marx's writings.

JOHN HOFFMAN

Enlightenment

In the western tradition, Enlightenment (*éclaircissement*, *aufklärung*) refers to the process of becoming rational in thought and action. It can be individual or society-wide. Either way, reason is figured as a light that illuminates the understanding and dispels the darkness of ignorance and superstition. Enlightenment thus conceived has two sides. Positively, it entails the empowering discovery of well-founded knowledge; critically, it is a movement of demystification, skeptical towards anything that cannot give an adequate account of itself before the bar of reason or experience.

Historically, the term is associated with the eighteenth-century European intellectual movement that championed reason and **progress** against the enchainment of thought by, especially religious, **tradition** and belief. Hence "the Enlightenment" (capitalized) to designate that movement, and the broader shift towards secularism, republicanism, humanism, and science to which it was connected. Important centers of Enlightenment thought were Scotland (Hutchinson, Hume, Ferguson, Smith), France (Montesquieu, Diderot, Voltaire, D'Alembert), England (Shaftesbury, Paine, Bentham, Wollstonecraft), and the United States (Franklin, Jefferson), though its crowning philosopher was Immanuel Kant (1724–1804). For many Enlightenment thinkers, a model for reason (and intellectual progress) was provided by the natural sciences, with Francis Bacon taken as their prophet and Isaac Newton's "terrestrial" and "celestial" mechanics as their paradigm – whence a further ambition to extend the scientific model to the human realm. Just as the sciences of nature could lead to material progress, so knowledge of man as part of nature could lead to social and moral progress. Such thinking led to ambitious totalizations like that of the French *Encyclopédistes*, as well as to the more specialized development of what became the disciplines of psychology, economics, **sociology**, and anthropology. While Enlightenment thinking had a technocratic strain, it also linked reason with freedom and autonomy, as in Kant's 1794 definition of enlightenment as "man's leaving his self-caused immaturity" by "daring to think." Optimism about the emancipatory and civilizing potential of knowledge-based progress peaked in the nineteenth century, but waned in the disasters of the succeeding century. **Max Horkheimer** and **Theodor Adorno**'s *Dialectic of Enlightenment* (1948 [trans. 1972]) criticized the actual course of enlightenment in their own time as a totalitarian disaster in which enlightenment itself had regressed to **myth**. Against this, and also against postmodernists like **Jean-François Lyotard** and Jacques Derrida who deconstructed logocentric narratives of progress, **Jürgen Habermas** has defended enlightened **modernity** as "an unfinished project."

ANDREW WERNICK

entrepreneurship

This topic is discussed in several social-science disciplines, and therefore a sociological view of entrepreneurship has to include references to non-sociological works. This, for example, is decidedly the case with the work of the founder of the study of entrepreneurship, economist **Joseph Alois Schumpeter**.

Schumpeter presented the essentials of his theory of entrepreneurship in *The Theory of Economic Development* (1911 [trans. 1934]). The essence of entrepreneurship, it is here suggested, is a new combination of already existing elements in the **economy**. Schumpeter also emphasizes that one of the great difficulties for the entrepreneur is that he or she has to break with the past. There is typically a strong resistance to change that has to be overcome, if there is to be an innovation.

In a famous passage in *The Theory of Economic Development*, Schumpeter enumerates the main types of innovation: (1) the opening of a new **market**; (2) the introduction of a new merchandise; (3) the introduction of a new method of production; (4) a change in the organization of an industry; and (5) getting a new and cheaper source of raw materials or half-manufactured goods. Innovations, in other words, can happen anywhere in the economic process, from the assembly of material for production to the end product being marketed and presented to the prospective customer. What drives the entrepreneur is not so much money, Schumpeter also argues, as the joy of creating, the possibility of creating one's own kingdom, and to succeed for the sake of success. A successful innovation, Schumpeter adds, creates entrepreneurial profit – which tempts others to imitate the initial entrepreneur till a situation is reached when no more entrepreneurial profit is to be had. In *Capitalism, Socialism and Democracy* (1942) Schumpeter, finally, feared that huge corporations would kill the initiative of the individual to be an entrepreneur.

As Richard Swedberg shows in *Entrepreneurship* (2001), post-Schumpeterian research on entrepreneurship has, to repeat, been interdisciplinary in nature. There exists, for example, whole literatures on entrepreneurship by psychologists, economic historians, and economists.

Sociologists lack a sustained tradition of studying entrepreneurship but have nonetheless produced a number of interesting studies during the last few decades. One genre of such studies deals with so-called ethnic entrepreneurship or the role that entrepreneurship plays in various ethnic groups. One insight, for example in Roger Waldinger's *Ethnic Entrepreneurs* (1990), from this type of literature is that successful ethnic entrepreneurs have to find other customers than their co-ethnics ("the ethnic market") if they are to become truly successful. Sociologists also tend to emphasize the role of the **group** in entrepreneurship, as opposed to the single individual. Entrepreneurship in modern corporations, for example, often means the putting together of a group, in combination with an effort to stimulate its members to work on some task, as Rosabeth Moss Kanter shows in *The Change Masters* (1983). Finally, much contemporary sociological research looks at the earliest stages of entrepreneurship, so-called start-ups, but also what goes on before these exist – an issue which is discussed in Howard E. Aldrich's entry on "Entrepreneurship," in R. Swedberg and N. Smelser (eds.), *Handbook of Economic Sociology* (2004).   RICHARD SWEDBERG

environment

Since its emergence as a political and social issue during the 1960s, the environment has been a topic of sociological interest. Owing to its intrinsic complexity and its intimate connection to a nonsocial and nonhuman "natural" realm, the environment has shown itself to be difficult to subject to sociological scrutiny, however. The traditional demarcation between nature and **society** that is assumed by many, if not all, sociologists to be a defining characteristic of **modernity** has caused difficulties, which have been reinforced by institutional barriers which tend to separate sociologists from other environmental scientists, as well as from the users of their knowledge.

Nonetheless, in recent years sociologists interested in the environment have produced a variety of theoretical insights and empirical research findings, even though there is little agreement among them about how environmental issues are most appropriately to be comprehended and investigated. The sociology of the environment, or environmental sociology, as it is sometimes called, has suffered from many of the same processes of specialization and compartmentalization that have affected other sociological subfields.

In comparison to other areas of social life, and in relation to the discipline as a whole, the environment has remained a relatively marginal topic of explicit sociological interest. It can be suggested that other social scientific disciplines have been more successful in "appropriating" the environment as a topic for investigation. Particularly in regard to external research funding and programs in environmental science, sociologists have tended to be less active and less visible than political scientists, psychologists, economists, geographers, and policy scientists. This is not merely because of a lack of entrepreneurial skill or energy on the part of sociologists. There is also a structural or disciplinary basis for the relative lack of interest in the environment among sociologists.

For one thing, most of the classic sociological texts give short shrift to environmental problems, and have thus provided little intellectual guidance in helping latter-day interpreters to deal with them, either theoretically or empirically. Generally viewed as "side effects" or subplots in the main story-lines of **modernity** and **modernization**, environmental issues were, for the most part, bracketed out of the foundational narratives of the discipline. **Karl Marx**, **Max Weber**, **Émile Durkheim**, and **George Herbert Mead**, as well as **Herbert Spencer** and **Ferdinand Tönnies**, all expressed in varying degrees a positive attitude to the human exploitation of the natural environment, if they referred to it at all. They all shared a respect for, and indeed sought to emulate, the natural and engineering sciences, whose development is generally considered to be one of the root causes of environmental problems.

It can be suggested that this identification with science, and the attempt to make sociology itself into a science, has served to limit the seriousness with which sociologists have concerned themselves with the environment. Even though there were significant differences among them, the founding fathers of the discipline placed whatever criticisms they might have had about science and technology and the exploitation of nature in the margins, or footnotes, of their works. While Marx, for instance, praised the "civilizational role" of modern industry and of its science and **technology** in no uncertain terms, he only noted in passing that this **civilization** had negative implications for nonhuman nature. He never placed environmental issues in the foreground of his analyses of capitalist society, which was exclusively focused on the underlying dynamics, or laws of society. Similarly, Max Weber analyzed and, on occasion, bemoaned the **rationalization** processes of contemporary life, but the environmental implications of those processes were never examined explicitly. As such, the environment was marginal to the formation of a sociological identity, or imagination.

As sociology became institutionalized in the course of the twentieth century, the environment continued to be neglected as a topic of investigation. The kinds of environmental problems that became socially significant in the 1960s – industrial pollution, energy and resource limitations, consumer **risk** and safety – were issues that fell far outside the disciplinary mainstream. They had either been delegated to other social science disciplines (economics, geography, and political science, in particular) or they were seen as aspects, or secondary dimensions, of other sociological concerns, such as **urbanization**, **social conflict**, regional development, or science and technology. It might be suggested that the paradigms or

disciplinary matrices of sociology as a field had come to "frame" the sociological objects of study in such a way as to make environmental issues marginal at best and invisible at worst. The environment was seldom viewed as an independent variable or a social issue in its own right.

The environmental debate of the 1960s, associated with such popular writings as Rachel Carson's *Silent Spring* (1962) and Paul Ehrlich's *The Population Bomb* (1968), had only a minor impact on sociology. The key texts of the environmental "movement" were written by natural scientists or science writers, and received little interest from sociologists. For reasons of language and **education**, as well as inclination and interest, the new issues were considered of secondary importance for sociologists. It was not until the emergence of major environmental conflicts in the 1970s, particularly over energy policy, and nuclear energy in particular, that an environmental subfield began to develop with any intensity.

Subsequent sociological concern with the environment has been strongly divided into what **C. Wright Mills**, in *The Sociological Imagination* (1959), once called "grand theory" and "abstracted **empiricism**." While the theorists have sought to integrate environmental issues into broader conceptualizations and frameworks of interpretation, the more empirically minded have gradually added environmental issues to the growing number of **social problems** and **social movements** that they investigate. In this respect, a sociological interest in the environment has often been mixed with an interest in other social domains: the media, public administration, urban conflicts, and development. Little attempt has been made to "test" the rather abstract notions that the theorists have proposed with empirical research, and there has been little coordination of the various projects carried out by the empiricists in order to develop generalizations or systematic comparisons. As a result, the sociology of the environment has come to be fragmented into a number of approaches that are seldom combined in any meaningful way.

In theoretical terms, sociologists have generally tried to incorporate the environment into the received frameworks of interpretation that they have derived from the so-called classics. Many have been the attempts to apply the terminology of Marx, Weber, or Durkheim to the sociology of the environment. An early effort by Alan Schnaiberg (*The Environment: From Surplus to Scarcity*, 1980) proposed the concept of the "treadmill of production" to characterize the social basis of environmental problems, which was derived from the Marxian concept of capital accumulation. Schnaiberg and the many other Marxian theorists who have followed have generally sought to frame environmental problems in materialist or historical materialist language, and thereby to connect the environment to relations of production. As with environmental economists, these theorists have tended to see environmental problems as dependent on, or determined by, other more fundamental social processes.

The influential theory of **Ulrich Beck** has, on the other hand, drawn on the classical conceptions of Tönnies and Weber to develop a **social theory** in which environmental problems are given a more central or determinant place. In the 1980s, Beck proposed the concept of risk society as an all-encompassing term to reflect the underlying **social changes** that had brought environmental issues into social and political life. Like other theorists of **postindustrial society**, Beck's theory posits a fundamental shift in the overall logic, or **rationality**, of society, in his case from the production of goods to the manufacture of uncertainty, endemic risks, and dangers. Environmental problems are thus a structural characteristic of the contemporary age, a determinant factor in society. For Beck and many of the "risk" theorists who have been inspired by him, social processes and activities are no longer dominated by the conditions of modern industry – instead, we have entered the age of what Beck terms "reflexive modernization."

At a somewhat lower level of abstraction, and with a more explicitly political ambition, the risk-society thesis has been modified into a theory of "ecological modernization," which has exerted a wide influence over many European social scientists and policymakers. Ecological modernization has been developed both by sociologists and by political scientists for analyzing institutional arrangements and administrative procedures that have been devised, primarily in relation to the political and social programs of so-called sustainable development. As such, ecological modernization has served perhaps more as a political **ideology** or policy doctrine than as a theoretical framework for academic sociologists.

A distinction can be made between those theories that seek to link environmental issues explicitly to **sociology** and social theory and those that draw on concepts from the natural and environmental sciences, and are thus less directly disciplinary. This "ecological turn" has been facilitated by interdisciplinary research programs in global environmental change and human ecology, as well as by institutional linkages, or **networks** that have been established between sociologists and environmentally interested scientists in other fields. Some have distinguished between environmental sociology and ecological sociology. In the more ecological theories, social processes are depicted in terms of resource and energy flows, as theorists make use of concepts derived from systems theory, and, more recently, **complexity theory**.

The sociological interest in the environment has from the 1970s been fragmented into a number of empirically delineated specialty areas. Sociologists have investigated a wide range of environmental conflicts, movements, and forms of activism, as well as the myriad processes of institutionalization, professionalization, (see **profession(s)**) and organization of environmental concern. There has also been a continuous research activity, using quantitative and survey methods to explore public attitudes to environmental problems, shifts in media coverage of environmental issues, membership patterns in environmental organizations and campaigns, and aspects of environmental **lifestyles** and consumer preferences. In these more empirical areas, links have been established between environmental sociologists and sociologists of science and technology, as well as with organizational sociologists and scholars of social and political movements. In many cases, particularly in relation to local environmental conflicts, sociologists have combined an academic and an activist role in new forms of action, or action-oriented research.

In both theoretical and empirical terms, the sociology of the environment has provided fundamental contributions to what might be called the reinvention of the sociology of knowledge. Since the use of knowledge and expertise plays a central role in almost every significant environmental conflict, sociological analysis has helped elucidate some of the main processes involved. Depending on the terminology, these processes have been characterized as organizational learning, reflexive knowledge, citizen science, or cognitive praxis, to mention only some of the concepts that have been developed. In this respect, the sociology of the environment has contributed to the broader social understanding of knowledge production, and has, in many specific cases, combined environmental sociology with the sociology of science, or scientific knowledge. The way in which science has come to be used in environmental policy has been a major focal point of sociological investigation.

The sociology of the environment has also been central to the opening of sociology as a whole to interdisciplinary and cross-cultural interactions. An environmental focus or point of departure has proved valuable for initiating collaboration across disciplinary boundaries and for opening spaces for communication between the human and the nonhuman sciences. As a result, there has been a fertilization and "translation" of theoretical terms and concepts in both directions, and there has also been a variety of hybridizations of social scientists and natural scientists into transdisciplinary environmental scientists.

In the future it can be expected that the tension between environmental sociology as a distinct subfield within the discipline and as a part of a broader and less academically defined intellectual activity will continue. The value of sociological understanding for the resolution of environmental conflicts and the solution of environmental problems is significant, and it is to be hoped that sociologists will continue to contribute to the broader pursuit of a sustainable development or an ecological society.   ANDREW JAMISON

environmental movements
– see **social movements**.

environmental rights
– see **rights**.

epidemiology
Defined as the study of the patterning and determinants of the incidence and distribution of disease, the discipline of epidemiology is concerned with environmental factors – whether physical, biological, chemical, psychological, or social – that affect **health**, and also considers the course and outcomes of disease in individuals and in **groups**. Where social variables are emphasized – the distribution of disease by social circumstances and **social class**, for instance, rather than more strictly biological aspects of sex, **race**, or geographical **environment** – the term social epidemiology is often used.

The formal beginning of the discipline was in the nineteenth century with the work of the pioneers of **public health.** John Snow (1813–55), in his *Report on the Cholera Outbreak in the Parish of St. James, Westminster* (1854), famously demonstrated the transmission of cholera through contamination of the London water supply, "cured" by the removal of the handle of the Broad St. pump. The epidemiological approach, comparing rates of disease in subgroups of populations, became increasingly used in the late nineteenth and early twentieth century, applied at first mainly to the investigation and control of communicable disease.

Well-known examples of its nature and successes include assisting in the eradication of smallpox in the world by the 1970s. A classical triumph of epidemiology was the conclusive demonstration by Sir Richard Doll (1912–2005) in 1954 of the association between smoking and lung cancer. This classical follow-up study of the mortality of almost 35,000 male British doctors continued to offer results for over fifty years. In 2004 a new report in the *Lancet* celebrated this milestone in public health by showing that the risks of persistent cigarette smoking were actually greater than previously thought, and about one-half to two-thirds of all persistent smokers would eventually be killed by the habit. It was also shown, however, that quitting at any age, even up to the 60s, gains years of life expectancy.

Epidemiology is essentially a statistical discipline, dealing in rates of disease and mortality, but has always acknowledged multiple and interactive causes of ill-health. Behavior and **lifestyle** are increasingly held to be important in the causal analysis of population, and epidemiology studies their effects, and also how the control and prevention of problems in both can be more effective.

One of the most recent examples of the contribution of epidemiology has been to the study of the HIV/AIDS epidemic, where it has been vital to trace out the worldwide patterns of spread and control, rates of transmission, and changing outcomes. This health crisis has also been responsible for some coming-together of ethnographic and qualitative sociological methods of enquiry with the more statistical science represented by epidemiology, since unconventional methods were necessary to gain knowledge (of, for instance, drug use, prostitution, and intimate sexual behavior) essential for the **modeling** of epidemiological **statistics** and predictions.

Medical **sociology** in some respects grew out of social epidemiology, and still has close links with it. Some divergence between the disciplines, however, relates to the fact that epidemiological statistics are *population* statistics and so can say nothing about any individual. How doctors present this to patients, and how lay people interpret at a personal level the statistical facts of epidemiology in the form of rates and probabilities, is a topic of interest in medical sociology, particularly in the currently active fields of **genetics** and **risk**.

Environmental epidemiology, an important branch of the discipline, faces contemporary challenges of global change. The study of causal pathways at societal levels is sometimes called eco-epidemiology. **Globalization** is also relevant in relation to the necessity for global control of pandemic diseases.   MILDRED BLAXTER

epistemology

The theory of knowledge, epistemology is one of the core subjects within philosophy. It tries to answer questions about the nature, sources, scope, and justification of knowledge. In some languages, epistemology is often equated with the philosophy of science. However, in sociology, epistemology has also often been used in a broader sense. Epistemology of the **social sciences**, for instance, deals with issues of method. What, if any, methodological guidelines ought to be adopted? What, if any, are the differences between the social and the natural sciences? In this respect, two debates are worth mentioning. First, in the *Methodenstreit* in nineteenth-century Germany, **positivism** and **hermeneutics** were opposed to each other. Positivist authors postulated methodological unity between the social and the natural sciences; it assumed the existence of laws or law-like generalizations in the social realm; and it postulated the possibility of value-free social science. Hermeneutic authors argued that the study of historical and social phenomena aims to understand (not explain) specific instances (not general laws). They also argued that **sociology** and history could never obtain value-neutrality. **Max Weber** adopted an intermediate position in this debate. Second, in the 1950s the *Positivismusstreit* opposed the positivist school and **critical theory**. Positivist-inclined authors, like Hans Albert and **Karl Popper**, tried to establish the scientific foundations for sociology. For critical theorists, like **Theodor Adorno** and **Jürgen Habermas**, sociology should be preoccupied with self-emancipation and critique of society. For them, value-neutrality is impossible.

In philosophy the traditional notion of epistemology searches for the universal foundations which underpin an individual's knowledge and secure its validity and neutrality. This notion of epistemology has come under recent attack. First, influenced by American **pragmatism**, Richard Rorty (1931–) argues that we should substitute hermeneutics for epistemology. Whereas epistemology tries to establish a-temporal foundations for cognitive claims, hermeneutics is sensitive to the situated nature of knowledge. For Rorty, recent developments within analytical philosophy (for instance, the work of Donald Davidson [1917–2003] and Willard Quine [1908–2000]) have made epistemology (as the search for foundations of knowledge) untenable. Philosophy should aim at *Bildung* and self-edification. Second, social epistemology pays particular attention to the social aspects of the sources, justification, and diffusion of knowledge. Social epistemology draws on **Science and Technology Studies**. It can be an explanatory and descriptive endeavor (for instance, how did a particular theory become widely held?) or a normative enterprise (for instance, how can we organize academic **institutions** more effectively?). Third, feminist epistemologists emphasize the gendered nature of knowledge, the extent to which men and women develop different types of knowledge. Some forms of **feminism** challenge the assumption of neutrality and advocate standpoint theory. According to standpoint theory, women are in some respects better placed to obtain knowledge. This is by virtue of their specific position in society. Some theorists extend standpoint theory to refer to superior forms of knowledge linked to any marginal, subordinated, or oppressed category.

PATRICK BAERT

equality

The problem of equality has been a persistent topic of western philosophy and political theory. There is considerable debate about equal treatment of individuals in **society** as a normative principle ("people ought to be equal") and the claim "all human beings are equal" as a statement of fact. Before the **modernization** of society, human beings were thought to be equal ("in the eyes of God") in religious terms, or they were equal (in nature) under Natural Law. The contradiction between the normative view and the empirical condition of **inequality** produces conditions for radical **social change**. Secular theories of equality are associated with **Karl Marx** who argued that human beings were equal before the advent of private **property** and the development of class relations in **capitalism.** For Marx, **socialism** would restore the equality between men through a revolutionary change of society. In his study of *Equality* (1931), **R. H. Tawney** combined socialism and Christian theology to develop a normative theory of society. Tawney was critical of capitalist society that intensified inequality by stimulating human greed for commodities. His study of *Religion and the Rise of Capitalism* (1926) developed a critique of **individualism** as an alternative to **Max Weber** and *The Protestant Ethic and the Spirit of Capitalism* (1905 [trans. 2002]). In the post-war period, social reconstruction was often pursued through the Keynesian (see **Keynes, John Maynard**) **welfare state**, and by developing social **citizenship** many western governments committed themselves to **social policies** that were designed to reduce inequalities. However, in the 1970s and 1980s many western governments embraced neo-liberal social policies, associated with British Prime Minister Margaret Thatcher (1925–) and the American President Ronald Reagan (1911–2004), that emphasized **entrepreneurship**, individualism, profit, and self-reliance. The consequences of these policies, which involved, for example, cutting personal income tax, were to increase the efficiency of industry and the profitability of investment, but they also increased social inequality, as measured, for instance, by post-tax **income**. Some economists such as Partha Dasgupta in *An Inquiry into Well-Being and Destitution* (1993) argue that infant mortality rates, life expectancy at birth, and literacy rates provide better measures of resource allocation in society than measures of income inequality, such as the gini coefficient. These can be regarded as traditional measures of inequality, but with **globalization** and the revolution in **information** there are new aspects to inequality such as the **digital divide**. Access to electronic information via the internet is increasingly important as a measure of equality.

The principal theme in philosophical debate has been to determine to what extent differences between human beings can be derived from natural differences and from social evaluation. For example, as a matter of fact, men in the United States are on average taller than men in Japan, but should this natural difference lead to any difference in evaluation? **Ralph Dahrendorf**, in a famous essay "On the Origins of Social Inequality" (in P. Laslett and W. G. Runciman (eds.), *Philosophy, Politics and Society* 2nd series, 1962), distinguished four types of inequality. The first concerns natural differences of kind (such as the color of eyes). Second, there are natural differences of rank (between talents or **intelligence**). Third, there is the social **differentiation** of positions (such as the division of **labor**); and finally there is **social stratification**, involving a rank ordering of individuals (by **prestige** and **wealth**). Sociologists have typically concerned themselves with this fourth type of inequality, have sought to avoid normative judgements about the ontological equality of people as human beings, and have focused their empirical research on the various dimensions of inequality in studies of **poverty**, income distribution, and

wealth. As a result, equality has not been studied directly, because it is implicitly treated as the residue of inequality. The level of equality in society is implicitly measured by the extent of inequality.

There are broadly four types of equality. First, there are religious arguments in favor of an ontological equality of human beings, regardless of their de facto differences. This type of equality was supported by Natural Law philosophers, but it is now associated with human **rights**, because Article 1 of the United Nations *Universal Declaration of Human Rights* announced in 1945 that "All human beings are born free and equal in dignity and rights." Second, there is the liberal notion of equality of opportunity, which means that access to important social **institutions** such as higher **education** should be available to all on universalistic criteria. This principle emphasizes talent over inheritance and promotes the idea of meritocracy (see **credentialism**). The argument is that **social roles** should be open to achievement and competition, not ascription. Sociological research shows, however, that this form of equality is often limited as a result of racial **discrimination** or gender bias against women.

Equality of opportunity can never fully guarantee a "level playing field." For example, successful parents will tend to pass on their wealth and cultural capital (see **social capital**) to their children. Third, equality of condition involves various strategies to address limitations in equality of opportunity. For example, taxation (of personal income and the inheritance of property) can be used to reduce inter-generational inequalities. Affirmative action programs also attempt to ensure that equality of condition is not compromised by negative attitudes, for example towards the employment of mothers, the elderly, or minority groups. Affirmative action programs are also relevant to the fourth type of equality, namely equality of outcome. A university that decided to offer every student a degree regardless of their actual performance would have a policy of equality of outcome. However, to create an egalitarian society requires considerable state intervention into society, especially in the **market**, through taxation, **affirmative action**, and legislation. Liberals and anarchists believe that the state should not interfere with the right of individuals to dispose of their own assets. Liberals argue that the fundamental principle of freedom is the right to individual property. From the perspective of **functionalism**, individuals have to be motivated to fill positions in society that are dangerous, or demanding, or require extensive training. In the Davis and Moore debate (see **functional theory of stratification**), social inequality in terms of prestige and wealth is necessary to ensure that functionally necessary tasks are undertaken.

Although liberal democratic societies typically embrace the idea, expressed in the *Declaration of Human Rights*, that all human beings are equal, very few governments are willing or able to implement policies that would radically promote equality among their citizens. In a parliamentary **democracy**, the economic interests of the wealthy will always prevail over the interests of the poor. Since the early 1980s, governments adopting post-Keynesian strategies have cut personal taxation, reduced expenditure on welfare, and privatized social services. The consequence has been to increase inequality.   BRYAN S. TURNER

essentialism

This term has been, since the mid-1980s, at the heart of debates about the extent to which the human condition is formed by the natural characteristics of **gender** and **race**. The politics of essentialism have revolved around the double-sided possibilities of essentialism: asserting the importance of a category such as "woman" allows a politics organized around that term and yet at the same time contains female people within a concept which may be interpreted as naturalistic and potentially coercive. Similar arguments apply to the use of racially and ethnically specific terms; in all cases, the powerful arguments for political organization and mobilization around certain definable characteristics – which often underpin considerable similarities of circumstance and experience – are contested by those who argue that any form of "essential" **identity** is in itself an identity imposed, and maintained, by those who are more powerful.

For women, essentialism has been contested because it positions women within a binary opposition in which they can never be men and in which all forms of social negotiation have to be conducted through a "natural" condition. From the end of the twentieth century, considerable theoretical energy has been devoted to separating both **masculinity** and femininity from male and female; resistance to this idea remains considerable, particularly from psychoanalytically informed sociology which maintains that distinct biologies of male and female do exist and that the recognition of this fact (and consideration of its consequences) does not in itself constitute essentialism.

MARY EVANS

estates

A system of **social stratification** in which **rights** and duties were legally defined, estates were based on a common principle of the hierarchical organization of social strata in pre-industrial societies, such as **feudalism**. The analysis of the survival of estate systems has been an important aspect of the theory of **revolutions.** In *Economy and Society*, **Max Weber** (1922 [trans. 1978]) classified estates as a form of traditional **authority**, specifically patrimonial authority or "estate-type domination." Estates, which were typically divided into nobility, clergy, and commoners, flourished in France, Germany, and Russia before the rise of **capitalism**, when new forms of economic **power** confronted the traditional distribution of aristocratic titles and privileges. Estate domination in Weber's terms involved an authoritarian, militarized nobility surrounding a monarch or emperor. The heyday of the French system of estates corresponded with the rule of Louis XIV (1643–1715) and the consolidation of absolutism in the seventeenth century. Whereas in France the estate system remained an inflexible system of privilege, the English **social structure** permitted the entry of bourgeois capitalists into the nobility. Although the traditional authority of the English nobility was undermined by the English Civil War and the execution of Charles 1 in 1649, the division between the House of Lords and the House of Commons in the British parliamentary system represents the last vestiges of the "estates of the realm." The French system of estates was destroyed by the French Revolution (1789–98), but a militarized and conservative nobility (known as the Junkers) survived in Germany and was an important aspect of Weber's analysis of the political and cultural rigidity of Germany at the beginning of the twentieth century. The German nobility was shattered by the crisis of World War I, but the political system based on authoritarian "statism" survived much longer, according to G. Kvistad in *The Rise and Demise of German Statism* (1999). An estate system also existed in Russia until the Bolsheviks came to power after the October Revolution of 1917, when military defeats, food shortages, and revolutionary conflict brought an end to autocratic Tsardom. Given the strength of the Russian estate system, Weber remained pessimistic about the possibilities of **social change** in Russia in his *The Russian Revolutions* (1917 [trans. 1995]). In conclusion, the rigidity of the system of estates – the survival of the nobility and the peasantry into modern times – has often been seen as an obstacle to the development of **democracy**, for example in

Barrington Moore's *Social Origins of Dictatorship and Democracy* (1966).   BRYAN S. TURNER

ethnic group
– see **ethnicity**.

ethnic mosaic

This expression is a euphemism used by dominant ethnic **groups** to represent their political and economic intentions towards ethnic minorities as benign or, even, well-intentioned. Similar expressions include "melting pot," "salad bowl," and "**multiculturalism**." From the late twentieth century, terms like "melting pot," which convey the cultural ideal that ethnic differences will in time melt away, have been replaced by terms that serve to respect the differences as reconcilable if unbridgeable. Thus, after the 1960s in the European **diaspora**, popular groups tended to speak of the national **society** as a salad bowl, in which the differing vegetables contribute to the cultural taste of the whole without relinquishing their differences. Evidently multiculturalism is a somewhat more abstract version of the same well-intentioned theory that different ethnic groups can achieve a state of peaceful coexistence – as in fact they occasionally do, for example between the French and the English in Canada and the Walloons and Flemish in Belgium. Ethnic mosaic is a somewhat more scientific term used in the social sciences to lend an analytic legitimacy to what is otherwise a historical incongruity. The ethnic mosaic, like the metaphorical salad bowl, connotes the ideal that ethnic conflicts are aberrations limiting the social good which can be achieved when groups set aside differences to work together for the common good. In real history, the ethnic mosaic ideal strains against **ethnocentrism**, which seems to be a deeper structural feature of ethnic groups. The disposition to consider one's own group as superior aggravates, even in the most stable of ethnic mosaics, the potential for affirmation of differences that the dominant **culture** may be unable to suppress.

CHARLES LEMERT

ethnic nationalism
– see **nationalism**.

ethnicity and ethnic groups

These concepts are intended to define social differences associated with, but theoretically distinct from, racial ones. It is common, thereby, for social analysts to link **race and ethnicity** to suggest that ethnic differences go beyond, while including, racial ones. The distinction is not entirely arbitrary owing to the predominance of biological theories of race in late modern European diasporic cultures. Among the most notable modern examples of the confusion wrought by race and ethnicity is the United States, where **racism** has long been a structural feature of its status in the capitalist world-system. It is necessary to distinguish race from ethnicity when there is reason to justify a national or regional economy's reliance on **slavery** or other pre-modern forms of feudal or despotic production. West African people captured and transshipped to the Americas from the long sixteenth century until the nineteenth century, were defined as a race as opposed to an ethnic group for two reasons: one, they had lost their ties to their original ethnic **cultures** in Africa; two, the shame of economic reliance on slave labor called for a pseudo-scientific justification in the form of the racial attribution being offered as a sign of an inherent biological difference that stipulated the mental, even categorical, inferiority of blacks. Today, it is very well known that racial differences are biologically insignificant and that ethnicity must be considered quite apart from its assumed associations with race.

The word ethnic descends from the Greek noun *ethnos*, which has entered into modern languages, including English, variously as "people" and "nation." Yet, the somewhat awkward derivative "ethnicity" did not come into play until relatively late in the nineteenth century when **sociology** and other academic **social sciences**, still immature institutionally, were forced to account for the **social conflicts** arising from the presence of immigrant groups in European and North American cities. It was then that "heathen" or "barbarian," a third but already archaic sense of ethnic differences, may be detected in analytic usages. Ethnic differences are thus most severe in host societies when groups considered foreign come to live in close proximity. Their languages, customs, religions, cuisines, and other cultural practices appear strange to established citizens of the host nations — even when their own ancestries can be traced to groups whose social habits were once alien.

Simply put, ethnicities are of analytic importance when differing peoples are forced to live close by each other in an established region or political territory such as the modern nation-state. Ethnic differences are most acute when the prevailing nation-state is unable to manage the conflicts that inevitably ensue when established groups of the region depend on the aliens to satisfy their need for cheap and plentiful labor. In the United States, for example, in the nineteenth century, European groups were recruited to the eastern and middle states, as Asian groups had come to the western states, to relieve the acute shortage of workers for hard labor in industry, farming, and mining. In times of rapid economic expansion, industrializing areas necessarily suffer labor shortages. Whatever scruples the dominant **group** may have as to the cultural habits of foreigners, they must embrace them if the economic growth is to continue. The embrace is almost always false and short-lived. Very often, the foreign labor is recruited from among the most stigmatized groups in the host nation, as when, in the United States after 1914, World War I cut off access to European immigrant labor, forcing the northern industrial centers to recruit blacks from the rural South.

Usually, ethnic groups are invited as (in the European expression) "guest workers" to work in low-end service, manufacturing, or agriculture sectors. Yet, ethnic differences can also rise to perplexing visibility when immigrant workers are needed for highly skilled labor, as when, from the last quarter of the twentieth century, South Asian peoples came to play a major role in technological and financial sectors throughout the European diaspora.

Ethnicities, thus, are most salient when the host nations are unable to manage the conflicts that inevitably arise between the new ethnic groups and the assimilated dominant groups or among the ethnic groups themselves. Ethnic conflicts can break into open warfare and civil discord when the political sovereignty of the national or regional authorities weakens, as, after 1989, when the collapse of the Soviet Union led to ethnic **violence** in regions once under the control of the Warsaw Pact — Chechnya and the Balkans, among others. The extremes of ethnic violence are realized when ethnic conflicts occur in regions where there is little or no legitimate political **authority** — as in Rwanda, Burundi, Congo, and Uganda. Late in the twentieth century, ethnic conflict between the Hutu and Tutsi led to the slaughter of hundreds of thousands of innocents, and early in the twenty-first century ongoing **violence**, mainly against women and **children**, is laying waste to villages in the Darfur region of the Sudan. The fact that the global powers, notably the United States, largely ignored these ethnic wars while simultaneously seeking to manage

similar ones in Iraq among the Shi'a, Sunni, and Kurds illustrates the role of economic and geo-political interests in ethnic conflicts. A dominant ethnic group with the power to do so will intervene in conflicts among other groups only when its perceived interests are at stake. **Ethnocentrism** seems, therefore, to be a naturally occurring attribute of ethnic groups who will engage rival groups with unusual ferocity when their sense of ethnic privilege is threatened.

The artificiality of the analytic distinction between race and ethnicity is evident, thus, in the degree to which the ethnic differences interact with political realities. In the United States, for example, people of the African **diaspora** were recognized as a legitimate ethnic group, African-American, only after 1965 when the American Civil Rights Movement forced the dominant whites of European extraction to accept the civic (if not social) legitimacy of blacks who, to that point, had been defined narrowly as an excludable racial minority. After the Voting Rights Act of 1965 in the United States, descendants of slaves captured from West Africa as long as three centuries before increasingly claimed an African ethnic **identity** of which most were necessarily ignorant. Thus, ethnic practices can occasionally be latterday inventions intended to connect people to a lost ancient **tradition**, as in the case of the African-American Kwanzaa, a holiday introduced in 1966 to celebrate the ancient traditions of West Africa. At the same time, when the dominant ethnic group or groups are forced, in times of relative domestic or regional peace, to accept formerly obnoxious cultural differences, they will themselves invent cultural ideals celebrating their own civility, as in the case of expressions like **ethnic mosaic** or melting pot, which serve to cover their own history of incivility and cruelty towards ethnic minorities.

In short, ethnicity is a sociological concept meant to disentangle the complex historical ties between cultural differences and political and economic **power**.   CHARLES LEMERT

ethnocentrism

The seemingly universal cultural habit of considering one's own **ethnicity** unique, and thus in some sense – or several senses – special, the most striking instance of ethnocentrism in the modern world is that of the North American peoples in the United States who, over more than two centuries of history, thought of "America" as exceptional for the purity and goodness of its **values**. American "exceptionalism," like most forms of ethnocentrism, has shown itself to be a plastic cultural attitude equally capable of reference to religious **culture** (as in America as the New Israel in the seventeenth-century Puritan theory of divine providence) as to secular principles (as in the doctrine of manifest destiny, an expression used to justify the appropriation of lands from Mexico in the 1840s). More often, if less accurately, ethnocentrism is used to describe the evident unwillingness of foreign and domestic ethnic **groups** to yield their distinctive cultural practices in order to assimilate to those of the more powerful dominant groups in control of state or regional **power**.

Analytically, ethnocentrism describes the vicious cycle of inter-group relations by which differing ethnicities respond to contact with each other by claiming a natural superiority for their own cultural practice, hence for themselves as a people. CHARLES LEMERT

ethnography

Involving the first-hand exploration and immersive participation in a natural research setting to develop an empathic understanding (**Verstehen**) of the lives of persons in that setting, ethnography has its origins in the nearly simultaneous emergence in the early twentieth century of social anthropological studies of the **cultures** of native peoples and the social ecology studies of city dwellers by sociologists of the **Chicago School** (**Ernest W. Burgess**, **Robert Ezra Park**, and **William I. Thomas**). The Chicago School wedded Thomas's appreciation of the theoretical insights of **Charles Horton Cooley** and **George Herbert Mead** to Park's practical experience as a journalist. Once **symbolic interactionism** emerged from Chicago, it found a natural partner in ethnographic methods, adapted to the study of **organizations** and other settings as constituted by the **interactions** of the participants. Likewise, it is difficult to see how **Erving Goffman's** dramaturgical perspective could have been developed except in the explication of ethnographic data.

Ethnography as a method retains a commitment to naturalistic enquiry, that is, a commitment to richly contextualized, extended, participant-eyed description of the setting (alias the "thick description" recommended by **Clifford Geertz** in *The Interpretation of Culture*, 1973), with a minimum of pre-existing hypotheses and a determination to represent the phenomena at hand faithfully. Thick description is an outcome of the sustained immersion in the research field alongside the writing of detailed reflective fieldnotes, which enable the researcher to represent the culture in a multi-layered richness that is broader and more comprehensive than schematic grand narratives.

The ethnographic **tradition** does not commit itself to a specific data collection protocol, rather it comprises a number of different methods, the main components being **interviews**, **participant observation**, and documentary analysis. Indeed, some commentators distinguish ethnography, as the written report and interpretation of a culture, from **fieldwork**, as the modes of observing the culture. The importance of the written ethnography has led some to observe that the ethnographer's task is story-telling through personal narrative, alongside other tasks of theory or typology development. Participant observation is generally considered to be central to the ethnographic method. Participant observation involves collection of data by participating in the social world of those being studied, and interpreting and reflecting upon the actions, **interactions**, and **language** of individuals within that social **group**. Fieldnotes are used to record observations and fragments of remembered speech. The use of multiple methods within an ethnographic project enables different insights to emerge. For example, interviews provide access to subjects' descriptions, rationalizations, and reflections about their behavior, while observation provides insights, both into non-rational behaviors that may remain undisclosed in an interview, and into the mundane everyday activities of the **habitus,** frequently taken for granted and unarticulated within subjects' usual reportage.

The level to which ethnographers may choose to integrate themselves into cultures can vary considerably, from fully participating in the interaction to remaining on the periphery of the action as an observer. Participation of the ethnographer, and engagement in (or withdrawal from) some activities in the fieldwork setting, places the ethnographer within certain categories used by participants (friend, confidant, guest, and outsider). **Social distance** between the ethnographer and members of the culture being studied can result in lack of **trust**, a lack of understanding, or not knowing enough about the phenomena under study to ask the right questions.

Good fieldwork relations are crucial and ethnographers will need to consider how best to manage their personal **identity** accordingly (dress, speech, and behavior). Field relationships may also be facilitated by the skills, knowledge, and abilities of the ethnographer, which may range from giving advice on medical or legal problems to helping with daily chores. Maintaining a reflexive awareness will also enable the ethnographer to assess the impact of field relationships on the data collected.

Analysis of ethnographic data should start at the piloting stage, continuing throughout data collection where the purpose of the research is progressively focused, and into the process of writing. Indeed, the progressive focusing that occurs as a consequence of continual analysis and reflection often results in a significant shift of focus in terms of the original aims of the study. During this inductive process, the ethnographer will make analytic notes in which are recorded ideas about emerging features and patterns (whether they be surprising or mundane), along with ideas of how such patterns might be explained. While some ethnographies remain mainly as descriptions or accounts of the way of life in a particular setting, other ethnographies are more theorized accounts which focus on specific phenomena, or aspects of the culture.

Traditionally, ethnography has been criticized for its lack of **objectivity,** scientific rigor, and generalizability, and its relevance to social and political practice. Thus, there have been many insightful ethnographies of drug use, from **Howard S. Becker**'s *Becoming a Marihuana User* (1953) onward, but their contribution to the formation of national policies on drug misuse has been minimal. More recently, ethnography has been subject to more varied criticisms. Thus, ethnographers have experienced "the revolt of the subject," challenged as to whether s/he who is not a party can ever be a judge: persons with disabilities, for example, have questioned whether those without disabilities have the capacity to conduct disabilities research. Furthermore, doubts have been raised about realist claims of the author's **authority** to represent the truth about the social world. Geertz himself is among those who have condemned the production of "author-evacuated texts" as an implicit denial of the necessary dependence of all ethnographic writing on particular discursive practices for establishing their verisimilitude. These relativist challenges have allowed multiple interpretations of social phenomena and encouraged ethnographers to demonstrate a reflexive awareness of the researcher's constitutive contribution at all stages of the research – including ethnographic writing. The resulting tension between ethnographers' commitment to **realism** and their recognition of **relativism** has been addressed by Martyn Hammersley's advocacy of "subtle realism" in *What's Wrong with Ethnography?* (1992). Subtle realism acknowledges

that different and competing accounts of social worlds may be offered by ethnographers but requires that competing claims to knowing about social worlds must be assessed for their plausibility and credibility.   MICK BLOOR AND FIONA WOOD

ethnomethodology

Originally developed by **Harold Garfinkel** during the 1950s and 1960s in theory-laden empirical studies subsequently published in his *Studies in Ethnomethodology* (1967), ethnomethodology is an original approach to what Garfinkel terms the seen but unnoticed aspects of social practices. The term ethnomethodology also refers to the sociological **community** of scholars who have refined, extended, and, in one case, refashioned Garfinkel's theoretical position.

The ethnomethodological community came into being with the first generation of Garfinkel's students, notably including **Harvey Sacks**, who founded **conversational analysis** (commonly called CA) as a semiautonomous theoretical position. New centers of ethnomethodological research subsequently emerged in California, on the East Coast, and in the Midwest in the United States, and in England and Scotland as well. Ethnomethodologists tend to maintain deep loyalties to their position and they build their intellectual **networks** through ties that are stronger than is often the case in other intellectual communities in sociology. Though ethnomethodologists themselves often prefer to work within the boundaries of Garfinkel's and Sacks's founding principles, the ethnomethodological view of social practices has shaped a variety of other sociological projects and programs as well. This is especially true of the so-called strong program in the sociology of science, which analyzes the social construction of scientific knowledge and of **Anthony Giddens**'s **structuration** theory. Neither are ethnomethodological in the strict sense of the term, but neither would look quite the same in the absence of Garfinkel's original insights.

Ethnomethodology begins with an extremely prosaic insight: **social action** in context is an actively produced accomplishment. From a distance this may seem to put Garfinkel in the company of philosophers such as John Dewey (1859–1952), **George Herbert Mead**, **Ludwig Wittgenstein** (in his later works), John Austin (1911–60), and Garfinkel's fellow sociologist **Erving Goffman**. This is not entirely a false impression. All of these theorists reject the centrality of consciousness in any form as the pivot of social behavior (via such things as conscious motivation, existential meaning, rational interest, emotional reactions, or personal attitudes) and all make social practices in local contexts the center of their concern. All of them thus break with both longstanding utilitarian views of interest-driven action and Immanuel Kant's (1724–1804) views of meaning in action, such as those adopted by **Max Weber** and **Alfred Schutz**. Yet, on closer inspection, Garfinkel discovered a dimension of social action as an active human accomplishment that bears little resemblance to the moral dimension in Goffman's analyses of facework and other interaction rituals, Austin's performative analyses of speech acts, and Dewey's and Mead's efforts to decenter consciousness from social praxis without losing sight of consciousness altogether.

Garfinkel's distinction is to be the only leading sociologist to concentrate exclusively on how local action is accomplished or produced. One of his fundamental insights concerns the central role of reflexivity in the production of action. Reflexivity, a term that has several other sociological denotations that are irrelevant here, refers to the fact (demonstrated in many of Garfinkel's early studies) that every move in a social action or **interaction** takes its significance from the context that has been produced by previous moves, and, reflexively, each move sustains or alters the local context that shapes the significance of the next move. For example, if I open an interaction by saying "hello" in a friendly way, then this move creates a context in which whatever my interlocutor says will be regarded as a reply to my specific greeting. My interlocutor may say, for example, "I have been sick, but I am better now." The context has now changed and my next remark will be significant in light of my friend's response to my initial greeting. I could say, for example, that a mutual friend of ours has been sick as well, which changes the context of conversation once again. Even if I altogether omit the slightest allusion to my friend's illness, that very omission will be significant in the contextual light of the report of illness that preceded my remark. Each move in an action or interaction is thus constructed within the locally produced context, and every move advances that context so that the entire sequence unfolds as a reflexive series of contextualized and context-producing moves.

There is a sense in which Garfinkel's key insight into reflexivity and contextuality invites sociologists to give careful, fine-grained consideration to the minutiae of **everyday life**. For example, the timing of responses, as measured in fractions of a second, may make a big difference to the significance of a reply. If, to provide one illustration, I greet my friend with a rapidly enacted set of words and gestures and my friend pauses for, say, three seconds before responding to my rapid-fire greeting in any way, then this pause becomes part of the context just as surely as if my friend had responded instantaneously, but with a different effect on it. Ethnomethodologists typically investigate these minute yet significant aspects of social praxis by using video transcriptions of interaction, which they break down into small segments for purposes of analysis. There is now a standardized set of ethnomethodological symbols to record pauses, vocables (meaningless sounds uttered during conversations), episodes of people talking over one another, and more. Though not as central to current ethnomethodological studies, other aspects of locally produced conduct such as tone of voice, static and shifting body postures, and even changes in perspiration, respiration, and eye-blink rates are open to ethnomethodological investigation insofar as they add reflexive significance to a complex practice.

But if Garfinkel's basic insights into reflexivity and contextuality lead in one direction into the minutiae of everyday life, in another direction they lead to some of the most profound issues not only in the sociology of action, but in the philosophy of action as well. Consider the question of the nature of human reason, which has been at the top of the philosophical agenda since René Descartes (1596–1650) famously declared, "I think, therefore I am," and which **Talcott Parsons** used as the template for his analyses in *The Structure of Social Action* (1937). These and other views conceive reason as a logically structured form of thought, replete with tightly constructed models of means and ends in action, or axioms, deductions, and hypotheses in science. For Garfinkel, **rationality** does not arise in practice as an abstract and universally applicable form, which structures social action. Instead, rationality is produced locally as actors reflexively produce chains of reasoning that make sense only in and through the development of the local contexts. Can local interactions in context be logical in the more formal sense of the term? On occasion, perhaps, say, in the shop talk of mathematicians. But these instances in no way epitomize how other sorts of contextual reasoning proceed. One of Garfinkel's early studies demonstrates how local reasoning operates through the analysis of discussions of jurors deliberating about the case they are charged to decide. Though the judge has instructed jurors to reach a verdict by strict rules of reasoning based on a given set of legal principles, the jurors actually created a form of reasoning on their own that did not necessarily correspond to the legal statutes prescribing how jurors are supposed to reach a verdict.

The contextually constructed nature of reason is matched by a deeper understanding of how a theory-laden scientific fact is constructed. In 1981, Garfinkel was senior author on a study of conversations between scientists, taped on the evening when they pieced together for the first time the notion of an optical pulsar through conversations regarding observations made by telescopes and electronic data. Unlike others in the strong program in the sociology of science, Garfinkel and his junior colleagues specifically affirm that physical objects somehow are exhibited in the flow of observations. However, it is also essential to the construction of scientific discovery that scientists make sense of these facts in their conversations through the reflexively unfolding process whereby participants take turns in talking. In fact, the scientific article reporting the results of the observation of the optical pulsar is republished as an appendix to the ethnomethodological analysis, allowing readers to compare how the empirical scientific discovery was produced in conversation with the very different and far more logical way it was reported to the astronomical community. A second study of empirical discovery appears in Garfinkel's reconstruction of how Galileo constructed his inclined plane demonstration of the real motion of free-falling bodies. This study is published in Garfinkel's *Ethnomethodology's Program* (2002).

Garfinkel writes in a profoundly idiosyncratic narrative voice replete with etymologically obscure neologisms, technical usages of commonplace American English terms, and lengthy cascading lists of conceptual synonyms and variations in place of a single term. Whatever Garfinkel's motivation for writing in this way, his style has had two consequences for ethnomethodology. First, it has injected a certain gnostic quality into the ethnomethodological community, making many practitioners believe that they possess rare insights unavailable to the uninitiated. Second, it has confused outsiders who sometimes grotesquely misinterpret ethnomethodology's insights and often end up feeling estranged from not only Garfinkel's writings but his insights as well. It is therefore Garfinkel's good fortune to have had two fine exegetes, John Heritage and Anne Rawls, who have done much to clarify Garfinkel's work and build original bridges to other classical and contemporary theories.

In her perceptive and accessible introduction to Garfinkel's *Ethnomethodology's Program* and in her more technical theoretical essays elsewhere, Anne Rawls derives from well-known works by **Émile Durkheim** an emphasis on enacted social practices, and via this interpretation demonstrates that Garfinkel's basic ethnomethodological insights are not only consistent with Durkheim's thought, but expand upon some of Durkheim's classical themes. In *Garfinkel and Ethnomethodology* (1984), John Heritage grounds Garfinkel's insights in his reactions to Talcott Parsons, with whom Garfinkel trained, and Alfred Schutz, with whom he studied. Heritage also makes a significant independent contribution. In an early essay, Garfinkel reported a series of experiments in trust (technically not experiments), which demonstrated the intense attachment actors have to the enacted practices through which they collaboratively generate their contextually situated social reality. His strategy was to disrupt the normal course of enactment; his findings indicated that these disruptions produced profound reactions amounting to an implicit struggle to avoid **anomie**. Heritage observes that these studies point to a cognitive problem of order. This problem concerns not what constrains the behavior of actors outside the immediate context such that they produce social order in society, but rather how actors produce and sustain social order in everyday life. In developing this theme, Heritage indicates how Garfinkel both borrowed from and departed from Schutz's social **phenomenology**. However, though Heritage never explicates the point, Garfinkel's experiments in trust further demonstrate not only that Garfinkel discovers a cognitive problem of order but also that people will engage in sustained struggles against anomie when order is disrupted. This indicates a deep subconscious motivation to produce some sense of order at all times. This theme is further developed by Anthony Giddens in his conception of ontological security in structuration theory.

The branch of ethnomethodology known as conversational analysis takes the production of order in a new direction by stressing that the mechanisms for such conversational practices as turn-taking, opening, closing, and so on have formal properties (invariant across contexts) that constrain the production of order. In turn-taking, for example, a person may be unable to interject remarks into a conversation at a given point, no matter how significant their contributions may be, since they have no immediate access to a turn at talking.

Despite Garfinkel's brilliant insights, ethno-methodology often ends up in a sociological cul-de-sac. As it pushes ever deeper into the details of social praxis, it loses sight of institutional and psychological dimensions of social life. Anthony Giddens opens ethnomethodology to the structural conditions of social life in structuration theory. However, no one as yet has built theoretical bridges between the enacted production of local social order and actors' existential experience of meaning and emotion in social life. That bridge, when it is built, should make ethnomethodology's profound insights intuitively more interesting to wider audiences.   IRA COHEN

Etzioni, Amitai (1929–)

Professor at the George Washington University and Director of the Institute for Communitarian Policy Studies, and former White House adviser (1979–80), Etzioni is an American founder of **communitarianism**. He was Professor of Sociology at Columbia University for twenty years and guest scholar at the Brookings Institution in 1978. He served as President of the American Sociological Association in 1994–5, and in 1990 he founded the Communitarian Network. He was the editor of *The Responsive Community: Rights and Responsibilities* from 1991 to 2004. In 1997 Etzioni was awarded the Simon Wiesenthal Center Tolerance Book Award.

He has championed the cause of peace in a nuclear age in *The Hard Way to Peace* (1962), *Winning Without War* (1964), and *War and its Prevention* (Etzioni and Wenglinsky, 1970). His recent work has addressed the social problems of modern **democracies** and he has advocated communitarian solutions to excessive **individualism** in *The Spirit of Community. The Reinvention of American Society* (1993) and *New Communitarian Thinking* (1996). Etzioni has been concerned to facilitate **social movements** that can sustain a liberal democracy in *The Active Society. A Theory of Societal and Political Processes* (1968) and *A Responsive Society* (1991). He has been a critic of the erosion of **privacy** through modern surveillance **technologies** and threats to **identity** in *The Limits of Privacy* (1999). His most recent work was *From Empire to Community. A New Approach to International Relations* (2004).

Etzioni has also contributed significantly to the sociology of **organizations** in *Modern Organizations* (1964) and *A Comparative Analysis of Complex Organizations* (1961).   BRYAN S. TURNER

eugenics

– see **genetics**.

everyday life

The term everyday was in English usage as early as the seventeenth century to refer to ordinary or ongoing ways of life such as work routines and interpersonal demeanor, as well as to items of material **culture** such as clothing and décor. The synonymous term quotidian had appeared in English in the fourteenth century, with roots in earlier French and Latin usages. Though many of these usages imply contrasts with extraordinary situations (for example, holy days, days of mourning, **war**, disaster), in **sociological theory** the term is often used to refer to knowledge of ordinary and routine ways of life. The appropriate contrast here is with sociological knowledge that selectively abstracts and reorganizes elements of daily life based upon theoretical concepts or empirical methods of research. In this sense, the purest form of the sociology of everyday life is found in **ethnographies** that forgo second-order analysis for first-order verisimilitude. **Clifford Geertz** produces and advocates this way of studying everyday life.

A second denotation of the **sociology** of everyday life refers to the analysis of the interaction order. The latter term, as defined by **Erving Goffman**, refers to forms of activity where participants are either copresent or in immediate communication with one another. Everyday life here contrasts with more encompassing institutional orders (**bureaucracy**, **markets**, and **states**). Selective analyses of everyday life are possible in this sense of the term. Goffman was the master of sociological metaphors that depend upon sociological correspondences rather than literary resemblances. Ethnomethodologists also deal with the everyday production of ordinary social events, by focusing on carefully isolated, minute aspects of it.   IRA COHEN

evidence-based-policy

– see **social policy**.

evolution

– see **evolutionary theory**.

evolutionary psychology

A form of psychology, this claims to explain human behavior with reference to humanity's *phylogeny*, their evolutionary history. The brain, or mind, is seen as having evolved to help solve the adaptive problems encountered by our hunter–gatherer ancestors on the African savannah between 4 million and 100,000 years ago. It was during that era, according to Steven Pinker in *How the Mind Works* (1998), that modern humanity evolved with a collection of devices which influence behavior to this day.

The **lifestyle** enjoyed by our African ancestors was one of hunting and gathering. The prime requirement for such people was simply to reproduce into future **generations**. Mental "organs," or brains and minds, assisted towards that overriding goal. These early people developed a distinctive set of motives, conceptual frameworks, emotions, and even aesthetic preferences to use and adapt to their **environment.** These included, for example, a liking for particular types of physical landscapes in which they could see potential aggressors approaching.

Aesthetic predispositions are, however, seen as one of the less damaging results of humanity's evolutionary history. Our inherited mental apparatus is seen by evolutionary psychology as generating forms of behavior which are both self-destructive and damaging to the social order. A demand for **prestige**, **property**, and **wealth**, a male preference for young women as sexual partners, a division of **labor** by sex, hostility to other **groups**, conflict within groups, and a male predisposition towards **violence**, rape, and murder are all damaging results of inherited predispositions which are not easily shaken off. Similarly, stepparents are more likely to murder their stepchildren because they are not genetically related to them.

Evolutionary psychology therefore offers precise and seemingly scientific insights into contemporary **society** and its disorders. It is a close cousin to sociobiology, a form of biological analysis that was extended to the human condition in the mid-1970s. Two of its main advocates were E. O. Wilson, who wrote *Sociobiology: The New Synthesis* (1975), and R. Dawkins in *The Selfish Gene* (1976, 1989). The central claim of sociobiology was also that an organism such as an animal or human being has evolved to interact and compete for resources in such a way as to maximize its "success" in spreading genes to later generations. The prime explanatory unit in sociobiology was the gene. Individual animals, including people, were envisaged as "survival machines," beings programmed by their genes towards the expansion of "inclusive fitness." This latter concept referred to the sum of an individual's fitness plus that of other blood relatives. The concept is perhaps best summed up by the distinguished biologist J. B. S. Haldane who, when asked whether he would lay down his life for his brother, replied: "not for one brother. But I would for two brothers or eight cousins." Sociobiology was also seen as solving the puzzling problem of altruism. The reason why an individual should assist another, apparently selflessly, is that this is the best way of getting assistance back at a later date. It is another unconscious way in which the genes ensure they are reproduced. Sociobiology captured the spirit of thrusting **individualism** in the neoliberalist era of the 1970s and 1980s, though it finds little support today.

Evolutionary psychology claims, however, to have advanced beyond sociobiology. One of the many criticisms of sociobiology was that it told "just-so stories," implying that all traits and behaviors inherited during the evolutionary process necessarily result in a better adaptation of organism to environment. But there is a wide recognition among evolutionists that this is not the case. Certain traits and characteristics that are nonadaptive, for example, are passed on. Some "junk" genes are doing very little at all. Evolutionary psychology claims to circumvent these problems by focusing on what Pinker calls "reverse engineering." This entails identifying a goal and specifying in general terms the kind of design that would best meet it. The next stage is to examine how well an organ or organism under study actually does perform the demands made of it.

The question of "mind" is especially important to evolutionary psychology. Sociobiology was also often criticized for reading off "behavior" from genes, with unsatisfactory attention to complex mental processes. Evolutionary psychology, in contrast, focuses on "mental organs" which "generate" behavior. The mind is equated to a computer processing incoming **information**. But the human computer is "preprogrammed." It is meeting the adaptive needs of its owner; on the other hand, it contains assumptions about the nature of the physical world, such as the existence of material objects in three-dimensional space. Evolutionary psychology also seeks to avoid the universalism of sociobiology. It recognizes that behavioral propensities may well be dysfunctional to people and societies when they encounter new environmental and social circumstances.

The question arises, however, whether evolutionary psychology really does avoid the charge of biological reductionism leveled against sociobiology. H. Rose and S. Rose consider some of these criticisms in *Alas Poor Darwin* (2000). Explanations of social **power** and social relations remain blinkered, still focusing on the unchanged, biologically based predispositions. And, like sociobiology, evolutionary psychology systematically ignores forms of biology that give much less attention to genes (though considering them important in explaining the development and growth of the organism during its lifetime) and much more attention to the developing organism in its social and ecological context. P. Dickens outlines some of these alternative perspectives in *Social Darwinism* (2000).

Despite their continuing problems, evolutionary psychology and sociobiology have managed to shake **social theory** out of thinking it has a unique purchase on human behavior and that the biological world is of no explanatory importance. The focus of future research must be that of combining ideas from biology, psychology, and social theory in more nuanced ways, recognizing the complexity of their **interactions**. This would certainly entail recognizing the importance of genes and biology in affecting the overall growth and psychic propensities of human beings. But it would also recognize that households, educational systems, work hierarchies, and the like all deeply affect how these biologically based tendencies work out in practice. Similarly, the human mind is almost certainly less "hard-wired" and inflexible than the proponents of evolutionary psychology suggest. Different kinds of psychic structure come into play according to the social relations which the mind encounters and indeed contributes to.   PETER DICKENS

evolutionary theory

Evolution and learning are two principal mechanisms of adaptive self-organization in complex systems. Learning alters the probability distribution of behavioral traits within a given individual, through processes of reinforcement and observation of others. Evolution alters the frequency distribution of individual carriers of a trait within a given population, through differential chances of selection and replication. Selection depends on heterogeneity which is replenished by random mutation in the face of replication processes that tend to reduce it. Selection pressures influence the probability that particular traits will be replicated, in the course of competition for scarce resources (ecological selection) or competition for a mate (sexual selection).

Although evolution is often equated with ecological selection, sexual selection is at least as important. By building on partial solutions rather than discarding them, genetic crossover in sexual reproduction can exponentially increase the rate at which a species can explore an adaptive landscape, compared to reliance on trial and error

(random mutation) alone. Paradoxically, sexual selection also tends to inhibit ecological adaptation, especially among males. Gender differences in parental investment cause females to be choosier about mates and thus sexual selection to be more pronounced in males. An example is the peacock's large and cumbersome tail, which attracts the attention of peahens (who are relatively drab) as well as predators. Sexually selected traits tend to become exaggerated as males trap one another in an arms race to see who can have the largest antlers or be bravest in battle.

Selection pressures can operate at multiple levels in a nested hierarchy, from **groups** of individuals with similar traits, down to individual carriers of those traits, down to the traits themselves. *Evolution Through Group Selection* (1986) was advanced by V. C. Wynne-Edwards as a solution to one of evolution's persistent puzzles – the viability of altruism in the face of egoistic ecological counterpressures. Prosocial in-group behavior confers a collective advantage over rival groups of rugged individualists. However, the theory was later dismissed by George C. Williams in *Adaptation and Natural Selection* (1966) which showed that between-group variation gets swamped by within-group variation as group size increases. Moreover, group selection relies entirely on differential rates of extinction, with no plausible mechanism for the whole-cloth replication of successful groups.

Sexual selection suggests a more plausible explanation for the persistence of altruistic behaviors that reduce the chances of ecological selection. Contrary to **Herbert Spencer**'s infamous view of evolution, following **Charles Darwin**, as "survival of the fittest," generosity can flourish even when these traits are ecologically disadvantageous, by attracting females who have evolved a preference for "romantic" males who are ready to sacrifice for their partner. Traits that reduce the ecological fitness of an individual carrier can also flourish if the trait increases the selection chances of other individuals with that trait. Hamilton introduced this gene-centric theory of kin altruism in "The Genetic Evolution of Social Behaviour" (*Journal of Theoretical Biology*, 1964), later popularized by R. Dawkins in *The Selfish Gene* (1976, 1989).

In "The Cultural Evolution of Beneficent Norms" (*Social Forces*, 1992), Paul Allison extended the theory to benevolence based on cultural relatedness, such as geographical proximity or a shared cultural marker. This may explain why gene–culture coevolution seems to favor a tendency to associate with those who are similar, to differentiate from "outsiders," and to defend the in-group against social trespass with the emotional ferocity of parents defending their offspring. This model also shows how evolutionary principles initially developed to explain biological adaptation can be extended to explain social and cultural change (see **social change**). Prominent examples include the evolution of **languages**, **religions**, **laws**, **organizations**, and **institutions**. This approach has a long and checkered history. **Social Darwinism** is a discredited nineteenth-century theory that used biological principles as analogs for social processes such as market competition and colonial domination. Many sociologists still reject all theories of social or cultural evolution, along with biological explanations of human behavior, which they associate with racist and elitist theories of "survival of the fittest." Others, like the sociobiologist E. O. Wilson, believe "genes hold culture on a leash" (*On Human Nature*, 1988), leaving little room for cultural evolution to modify the products of natural selection. Similarly, evolutionary psychologists like Leda Cosmides and John Tooby search for the historical origins of human behavior as the product of ancestral natural selection rather than ongoing social or cultural evolution.

In contrast, a growing number of sociologists and economists are exploring the possibility that human behaviors and institutions may be heavily influenced by processes of social and cultural selection that are independent of biological imperatives. These include Paul DiMaggio and Walter Powell (the new institutional sociology), Richard Nelson and Sydney G. Winter (evolutionary economics), and Michael T. Hannan and John H. Freeman (organizational ecology). One particularly compelling application is the explanation of cultural diversity. In biological evolution, speciation occurs when geographic separation allows populations to evolve in different directions to the point that individuals from each group can no longer mate. Speciation implies that all life has evolved from a very small number of common ancestors, perhaps only one. The theory has been applied to the evolution of myriad Indo-European languages that are mutually incomprehensible despite having a common ancestor. In sociocultural models, speciation operates through homophily (attraction to those who are similar), xenophobia (aversion to those who are different), and **influence** (the tendency to become more similar to those to whom we are attracted and to differentiate from those we despise).

Critics counter that socio-cultural evolutionists have failed to identify any underlying replicative device equivalent to the gene. Dawkins has proposed the "meme" as the unit of cultural evolution but there is as yet no evidence that these exist. Yet Darwin developed the theory of natural selection without knowing that phenotypes are coded genetically in DNA. Perhaps the secrets of cultural evolution are waiting to be unlocked by impending breakthroughs in cognitive psychology.   MICHAEL MACY

exchange theory

The social division of **labor** is mediated by exchange. Exchange theory conceptualizes this as a bargaining process that reflects the relative dependence of the parties involved. Not all social **interactions** involve bargaining and exchange. **Peter M. Blau**, who developed the field in 1964 with *Exchange and Power in Social Life*, warned that "People do things for fear of other men or for fear of God or for fear of their conscience, and nothing is gained by trying to force such action into a conceptual framework of exchange" (1964: 88). Yet Blau did not regard most social relations as outside this framework. "Social exchange can be observed everywhere once we are sensitized by this conception to it, not only in market relations but also in friendship and even in love" (88). Social exchange differs from economic exchange in three important ways. First, the articles of exchange are not commodities but **gifts**. No money is involved, nor credit, nor contract. Giving a gift is a "selfish act of generosity" in that it creates in the recipient the need to reciprocate with something that is desired by the giver. Both parties to the exchange "are prone to supply more of their own services to provide incentives for the other to increase his supply" (89). Simply put, a gift is not an expression of altruism; it is a way to exercise **power** over another. Second, the terms of exchange are unspecified (91). One side offers something the other values, without knowing how or when the partner will return the favor. Third, the exchange is not instrumentally calculated. Without a quid pro quo and in the absence of explicit bargaining, one cannot know if the gift is optimal in a given transaction. Instead, optimization takes place through incremental adjustments to behavior in response to experience. These need not be conscious adjustments but could be experienced merely as feelings of satisfaction or dissatisfaction with the relationship, such that the terms of exchange emerge as a byproduct of a learning process. Each partner evaluates the outcomes from the exchange relative to a "comparison level" corresponding to what the actor expects to receive from their best alternative relationship. When the value falls below this standard, the individual is dissatisfied and seeks alternative partners whose offers are perceived as superior. On the other hand, according to Susan Sprecher in *Social Exchange Theories and Sexuality* (1998: 34), "if the outcomes they are receiving from their current relationship are better than what they expect to receive from their best alternative(s), they will feel dependent on the relationship and become committed to it."

These differences with economic exchange make social exchange applicable to emotionally charged behaviors where instrumental manipulation of the partner would ruin the experience for both. Social exchanges can be experienced as acts of generosity towards those we love and **trust**. In particular, trust is necessary because of the unspecified terms of exchange. Attraction and trust increase when the generosity is satisfactorily reciprocated and decrease when it is not.

Although social exchange lacks explicit terms of trade, enforceable contracts, or a monetary medium, it nevertheless follows the basic principles of economic bargaining over the price of commodities, such as the "principle of least interest," summarized by Karen Cook and Richard Emerson in "Power, Equity and Commitment in Exchange Networks" (*American Sociological Review*, 1978): "The party who is receiving the least comparative benefit from a trade has the greater bargaining power to improve upon that trade. If that power is used . . . then the terms of the trade will shift until power is balanced" (724).

This theory applies to the balancing of power in exchanges between workers, neighbors, friends, business associates, and marriage partners, as noted by Ed Lawler and Shane Thye in "Bringing Emotions into Social Exchange Theory" (*Annual Review of Sociology*, 1999): "Whether it is two lovers who share a warm and mutual affection, or two corporations who pool resources to generate a new product, the basic form of interaction remains the same . . . Two or more actors, each of whom has something of value to the other, decide whether to exchange and in what amounts" (217). One of the best-known examples of the general principles of exchange is Gary Becker's *Treatise on the Family* (1992) which models mate selection as a marriage market in which people exchange **status**, sex appeal, **wealth**, or **intelligence**.

Although numerous studies of the "law of attraction" have found strong tendencies towards homogamy based on **age**, **race and ethnicity**, **religion**, **education**, and occupational status, exchange theory provides an alternative explanation. Homogamy may reflect not a taste for similarity but rather constraints on the ability to attract a partner who has more valued resources. From an exchange-theoretic perspective, romantic relationships are formed through a matching process in which women and men look for the best "catch."

Exchange theory has also been applied to the exercise of power in the **family**. The principle of least interest predicts a positive effect of relative socioeconomic position on conjugal power in decisionmaking. For example, studies show that women in high-paying **occupations** are less dependent on their husbands and thus have more power in marital exchange than do women without such occupations.

Marital exchange is an example of dyadic exchange. In contrast, generalized exchange involves three or more actors who each provide valued resources to others with no expectation of direct reciprocity. In *Social Exchange Theory: The Two Traditions* (1974), Peter Ekeh distinguished between "group generalized exchange" in which resources are pooled and then redistributed, and "chain generalized exchange," which is illustrated by *kula*, a ceremonial exchange of wreaths of flowers for food or betel-nut, as described by **Bronislaw Malinowski** in his studies of the Trobriand Islanders. Although both these systems appear to depart from rationally self-interested behavior, exchange theorists have shown that this need not be the case, especially where reputation and status depend on exhibitions of generosity, or where gifts have far greater value to others than to the giver.

Social **networks** are of central importance in exchange systems. A variant of exchange theory, called "network exchange theory," predicts power from actors' locations in network structures. For example, in a "3-Line" network (B_1-A-B_2), A has power over B_1 and B_2 because A has access to multiple exchange partners, each of whom has access only to A. But if we simply add a link between B_1 and B_2, A loses its structural advantage. In this triangle network, all three actors now have equal power because all are excluded with the same probability. The predicted effects of network structure have been strongly supported in laboratory studies of bargaining behavior. In *Network Exchange Theory* (1999), David Willer reviews these studies and provides an overview and history of the field.

MICHAEL MACY AND ARNOUT VAN DE RIJT

experimental method

Experimental research constitutes a minority of all sociological research. The experimental method is a research paradigm borrowed from the physical and natural sciences. Experiments are studies employing the **hypothetico-deductive method** specifically designed to determine whether there is a cause and effect relationship between two or more phenomena. Other forms of sociological research have accordingly divergent goals. Thus, for instance, survey-based research is designed to provide descriptive information about a topic of interest, as it pertains to a specific sample of persons, and ethnomethodological studies are designed to provide formal descriptions that display the features of the cultural machinery assumed to have produced these features.

The experimental method entails the systematic variation in the levels of one or more independent variables, and then the measurement of the effects of this manipulation according to one or more dependent variables. The manipulation of the independent variable is achieved by altering the qualitative or quantitative levels of this variable. The levels of a qualitative independent variable are often established by the presence or absence of a particular variable (for example exposure to anti-racism training, or no exposure to anti-racism training); or by measuring the effects of various different kinds of training. In all such cases, the **groups** in question do not experience different amounts of the independent variable, but rather the presence or absence of a particular treatment or experimental condition. In contrast, the levels of a quantitative independent variable entail quantitatively different amounts of exposure to that variable. For example, Gordon Allport's contact hypothesis, expounded in *The Nature of Prejudice* (1954), would predict that the amount of time spent exposed to minority groups (given certain other necessary conditions) should systematically reduce the level of **prejudice** expressed towards that group. Thus, subjects may be divided into groups that spend one week, two weeks, and three weeks interacting with minority group members under such conditions. The dependent variable (expressed prejudice) would be measured before and after these quantitatively different amounts of exposure to the independent variable. These three levels of the independent variable are expressed according to a quantitative dimension, time.

However, as these examples perhaps make clear, it is only possible to infer a cause and effect relationship between variables if all other variables remain constant. If conditions are not held constant, an uncontrolled source of **influence** – or confound – may affect the dependent variable(s), and thus interfere with the expression of the independent variable(s) – either through offering an alternative account for its effects, or through masking the expression of an effect. In the social scientific community, attention to identifying the effects of potential confounds arguably reflects a positive level of skepticism towards too readily inferring causal relationships between variables.

In order to identify potential confounds, one should pay close attention to those other factors – besides the independent variable – that may systematically vary during the experiment (for example, students from a particular socioeconomic area may already have experienced different levels of exposure to **racism**, compared to students from a different socioeconomic area, thus potentially confounding the effects of anti-racism training).

Another major concern for experimental social scientists is that of ecological or external validity. This form of validity (see **sampling**) refers to the ability of the researcher, on the basis of the experimental results, to generalize from the experimental context to the equivalent real-world situation. Further, work on the sociology of scientific knowledge has demonstrated that, in practice, the experimental method is by no means culture-free and objective.

MARK RAPLEY AND SUSAN HANSEN

explanation

Most sociologists seek to explain. Explanations often draw on **counterfactual** thinking, trying to assess the impact of *x* by imagining what would have happened if *x* did not occur.

There are many types of explanation, and little consensus exists as to what kind of explanation is preferred. A common type of explanation is a causal one, but there are various types of causal explanation and causal inference. Some causal explanations are mechanistic. They explain a phenomenon by referring to the fact that it was caused by other social factors, but without a precise reference to the mechanisms or powers at stake. For example, a mechanistic explanation for the rise in suicide rates may refer to the rise in unemployment figures. Alternatively, people's dissatisfaction at **work** might be explained by reference to the **technology** involved in their employment. Some commentators argue that such mechanistic accounts are not explanations because they fail to answer why- and how-questions. Rather than providing answers, they seem to beg questions.

Other causal explanations are intentional. In intentional explanations, people's purposes or reasons are treated as causes for their actions. Sociologists subscribing to **methodological individualism** use intentional explanations. Methodological individualism is a research program that focuses on how individuals act purposefully while producing not just intended but also unintended and unanticipated effects. **Max Weber** and **Karl Popper** are amongst the main advocates of methodological individualism. They oppose holistic forms of explanation, which refer to systemic or societal needs. Some methodological individualists use rational explanations. These are intentional explanations but with the added assumption that people act rationally. People act rationally if they have a clear preference ordering and make choices consistent with that preference ordering. In addition, they have rational beliefs about how to get what they want and about the costs and benefits involved. **Rational choice theory** (or rational action theory as some prefer to call it) advocates rational explanations. Within this theory, there are differences as to the universality and applicability of rational explanations. There is also disagreement as to whether people make conscious calculations. Externalists like Gary Becker simply argue that people act as if they are rational. They do not assume that people necessarily go through a conscious decision process. Sometimes they might, sometimes they might not.

In opposition to methodological individualism, some sociologists are drawn to holistic forms of explanation. Most holistic explanations are functional. Functional explanations account for the persistence of certain social phenomena by referring to their (often unintended) effects for the cohesion and stability of the broader social system in which they are embedded. For example, some sociologists explain the persistence of religious rites by referring to the **solidarity** and cohesion they create. Most sociologists occasionally use functional explanations, but **functionalism** is a sociological school that primarily and self-consciously uses functional explanations. **Robert K. Merton** and **Talcott Parsons** are well-known self-proclaimed functionalists. Within this theoretical framework, there are many differences. Earlier functionalists, like A. R. Radcliffe-Brown (1881–1955) and **Bronislaw Malinowski**, assumed

that most, if not all, practices are functional and indispensable. Later functionalists relaxed this position.

Evolutionary explanations rest on a combination of **causality** and selection, and **evolutionary theory** is a school that promotes such explanations. There are two types of evolutionary explanation. First, sociobiology uses biological factors to explain social phenomena. For instance, it tries to demonstrate that biological differences between sexes manifest themselves in social differences. Second, some theorists account for social processes by drawing on analogies with biological evolution. For instance, it might be argued that, through time, **institutions** and even whole societies undergo evolutionary selection. Or it might be asserted that certain practices or ideas are eventually selected out, while others replicate more easily. Some sociologists combine evolutionary analogies with methodological individualism. This was the case for **Herbert Spencer**, one of the first sociologists to employ evolutionary reasoning. Others use evolutionary analogies in conjunction with a more holistic approach. **Émile Durkheim** was one of the first to do this. Since the publication of Richard Dawkins's *The Selfish Gene* (1976), evolutionary analogies have regained popularity in the **social sciences**. Examples are **Walter Garrison Runciman**'s two-volume *Treatise on Social Theory* (1983, 1989) and Rom Harré's *Social Being* (1993).

While there are many types of explanation, there is also disagreement as to how to evaluate explanations. Many philosophers argue that explanations need to have some empirical content. This led logical positivists to call for verifiability: explanations ought to be formulated so that it is possible to find empirical evidence that supports them. Popper suggested falsifiability: explanations ought to be stated so that they can be refuted on the basis of empirical evidence. Highly falsifiable explanations are preferred over cautious explanations: they are more informative and more precise. The school of critical realism focuses on the difference between explanations and descriptions. For a statement to be explanatory, it ought to include precise **information** about the mechanisms, structures, or powers at work. These mechanisms might not be immediately accessible to observation.

Finally, there are also different views as to how to arrive at explanations. The inductivist tradition insisted on the primacy of theory-independent empirical observations. It employs induction, whereby one generalizes from observational statements to arrive at universal statements. Deductivists like Popper and Carl Gustav Hempel (1905–97) insist on the value of deduction, whereby one starts with theoretical assumptions and initial conditions to infer empirical hypotheses. Hempel's view of science is known as the **hypothetico-deductive method**. Different again is the "retroduction" or "abduction" of Charles Peirce (1839–1914) referring to the process by which one makes sense of a new phenomenon through drawing analogies with something familiar.

PATRICK BAERT

expressive revolution
– see **Talcott Parsons**.

extended family
– see **family**.

F

face-to-face group
– see **group(s)**.

face work
– see **Erving Goffman**.

factor analysis
One of the most widely used, and misused, of the complex multivariate **statistics** that have become more accessible since the spread of computing power, this can reduce a larger number of measured variables into a smaller number of latent variables, or "factors." It is thus a "data reduction" technique, aimed at simplifying **data** while retaining its important features.

Factor analyses take as their input a number of different variables, usually all measuring similar related constructs (such as items in a standard personality **questionnaire**). The **correlations** between these measures are computed, and the number of dimensions (in a multi-dimensional space) that one needs to extract to describe the important variance, while screening out the error variance, is estimated. These factors are then constructed, and rotated to facilitate their interpretation. Finally, each case can be given a score on the newly created factors, for instance to describe respondents' **personality** along each dimension of the model.

Factor analysis was critical to the conceptualization and development of research into **intelligence** and personality in early and mid-twentieth-century psychology. For instance, R. B. Cattell, in *The Scientific Analysis of Personality* (1965), started by extracting all of the words in the English language to describe personality. Even after removing synonyms, there were still thousands of words. So Cattell used factor analysis to reduce this down to a list of fourteen personality scales, which became a standard model for many years in personnel selection and social research. H. J. Eysenck, in *The Scientific Study of Personality* (1982), went a stage further, and produced a model with just two dimensions, extraversion–introversion and neurotic–stable (and later a third dimension, psychoticism).

The initial appeal of factor analysis is that it would provide a scientific basis for answering some fundamental questions, such as how many dimensions there are to human personality or intelligence. Unfortunately, this promise to provide a scientific objectivity has not materialized, and in many cases different researchers, each using factor analyses, have arrived at very different conclusions. This is largely because there are a number of ways in which the computation of any particular model can be influenced by fairly arbitrary decisions by the researcher. At each stage, the number of factors extracted, the method of rotation, and the method of separating error from true variance are often matters of judgment by the researcher, rather than being given by the model. And, probably, the most contentious decision of all is how one chooses which variables to include in the factor analysis. For instance, if one is attempting to create a model of intelligence, we would all agree that we should include mathematical, logical, and linguistic skills, but what about musical ability, creativity, or coordination?

Two forms of factor analysis are currently employed by sociologists. Exploratory factor analysis is the more common variety, typically used (as the name suggests) to investigate the way in which variables can be simplified into their underlying dimensions. As long as no grand claims are made about determining the true nature of reality, researchers can avoid the controversy associated with the early uses of factor analysis, and can pragmatically simplify the analysis of complex datasets. The second form, confirmatory factor analysis, works to a different philosophy, and determines how well a set of data conforms to a theoretical model.

BRENDAN J. BURCHELL

falsification
What makes a theory scientific was a question that haunted **Karl Popper**, and, more particularly, how we could distinguish a scientific theory from a non-scientific one. He argued that traditional **explanations** of what made a scientific theory scientific – that it was based on careful observation

and then the formulation of laws regarding the relationships discovered, that is induction – were wrong. This is because, while events might regularly occur together, there is no way to establish that they cause each other: the problem of **causality.** The bigger question at hand for Popper was how to distinguish pseudo-science from science, and in particular to demonstrate why it was, as he thought, that **Marxism** and the works of **Sigmund Freud** were "pseudo-sciences." The answer was that no evidence could disconfirm either Marxism or **psychoanalysis**: if the proletariat did not rise up in rebellion today as predicted, then they would one day. The observation was modified to protect the hypothesis. If the patient did not resolve their anxiety neurosis, then it was not because their psychoanalysis failed, but because the patient was repressed. Thus the theories could explain everything that did (or did not happen) and appeared to be constantly verified. Given this, they could continue to claim to be scientific and no evidence could satisfactorily challenge them. Popper argued that it was too easy to search for verifications of theories and that a new way of putting the question had to be formulated. Rather than look for evidence to support it, a scientific theory had to pose questions that could prove it wrong, that is falsify it. So the criterion of a scientific theory for Popper is that it be falsifiable by empirical observations. The example that Popper uses is Albert Einstein's prediction that light would be attracted towards a heavy body, that is, that it could be seen to bend as it neared the gravitational pull of say, the sun. This was, as Popper put it, a risky hypothesis since, if it was not confirmed, then Einstein's theory would be falsified (which was not in itself a problem, since the hallmark of good science is that it can be falsified). However, Einstein's theory of gravitation was confirmed in 1919 by A. S. Eddington's observations of the transit of Venus. So Einstein's theory survived a challenge that could have falsified it. While we cannot conclude that it is true, we can now proceed to work with it as a scientific theory. Until Marxism or psychoanalysis, like science, makes predictions that are falsifiable by evidence, then we can conclude that, whether they are true or not, they are not scientific. However, Popper is still left with the problem of what is to count as an independent observation that could falsify a prediction. As work by later historians and philosophers of science was to show, particularly that of **Thomas Samuel Kuhn** (*The Structure of Scientific Revolutions*, 1970) on **paradigms**, scientific theories are self-contained, largely self-confirming,

sets of statements, sustained by specific scientific **communities**. They establish what questions can be asked, what will count as an observation, and disregard non-confirming evidence. On this ground, no theory can be scientific in Popper's sense.   KEVIN WHITE

families of choice
– see **Family**.

family
There are many sociological explanations and accounts of families, from those that concentrate on grand theories and relate family structure to **industrial society**, **capitalism**, and/or **patriarchy**, through to those that are derived from more ethnographic studies of everyday family **interactions** and negotiations. Families can be, and have been, studied at all levels of analysis. At times families have been seen as homogeneous unities of people who co-reside, often with a sole head of household, clearly defined **social roles**, and a distinct division of **labor**. At other times families are understood to be real or imagined **networks** based on obligations and affections of an interpersonal nature rather than being structurally determined. These differences reflect, to a large extent, changing fashions in sociological theorizing and enquiry. At certain times particular modes of **explanation** are seen as especially insightful (for example. functionalist approaches), while at others different issues seem more important, particularly if they have been previously ignored or rendered invisible (for example domestic **labor** in the household). In more recent times, the very prospect of a sociology of the family has been deemed to be uninteresting and theoretically arid, and the subject has been described as slipping into the doldrums. Indeed **Ulrich Beck** and Elisabeth Beck-Gernsheim, in *The Normal Chaos of Love* (1990 [trans. 1995]), suggest that it has only recently become interesting again: "Family research is only gradually waking up from its drowsy fixation on the nucleus of the family."

The core issue that all sociologies of family life and relationships have had in common, however, has been the problem of turning the sociological gaze onto areas of life which are routine, commonplace, and part of almost everyone's everyday experience. The family is a naturalized concept, by which it is meant that it is taken-for-granted as natural – notwithstanding how much families differ and change. The sociological task is therefore to de-naturalize the family in order that it may become the focus of social analysis. It is this project of de-naturalization that links otherwise disparate sociological approaches.

It is almost inevitable that any synopsis of sociological work on families should start with **Talcott Parsons** and **Robert Bales** (*Family, Socialization and Interaction Process* (1955). Not only did their functionalist approach set the tone of much work on families for generations in the United States and the United Kingdom, but it became the standard against which more critical work later pitted itself. Parsons and Bales broadly argued that a sociological approach to families should construe them, not simply as natural collectivities, but as a social system.

There arose the tendency among functionalists to speak of *the* family, because "it" was theorized as one **institution** amongst several core social institutions (such as the church and the **state**). The institution of the family was however, in this schema, a relatively junior player, because its structure and functioning was deemed to serve the needs of other (more significant) institutions. Indeed, Parsons and Bales argued that an indication of how "advanced" a **society** was lay in whether the family was in a subsidiary status when compared with other institutions. They saw the decline of the significance of kinship as indicating a cultural rise of merit over the **values** of familialism. Their approach tended to suggest that phenomena such as family size (two children rather than ten, for example) or segregated gender roles within the family were a result of the needs of the **economy** or of industrialization, rather than arising from the motivations or interests of the members of families. The family was therefore depicted as the handmaiden of larger social forces, and its core function was to produce socially appropriate (well socialized) citizens of the next **generation** to take their place in the economy and wider society. Men, women, and **children** were seen as having different roles and functions in the family, which had evolved to meet the needs of society. Thus women were inevitably unpaid housewives and child carers, while men were the breadwinners because this system produced the most stable outcomes for society. Moreover, men were deemed to be heads of the household, because the model of family living deployed by the functionalist approach presumed that **authority** and **leadership** could only come from one source. Parsons and Bales predicted (unwisely as it turns out) that this division of labor would remain unchanged in the future.

There are, of course, many criticisms that can be made of this early sociological work on *the* family, and some of these will be rehearsed below. However, it is useful to locate this work in its own time and intellectual moment in order to appreciate the way in which it can be given a certain amount of credit for developing the field. The task that Parsons and Bales set themselves was a complex one because they saw the family as a social system, but also as the site where individual **personality** was formed. They also saw the types of personalities that were formed there as contributing (in an iterative fashion) to the wider **culture** of a given society. They were therefore working with three main concepts. The first was the idea of the family as a system, the second was the idea of the personality as a system, and the third was the wider culture – a concept which is ultimately underdeveloped in their work. For the latter two concepts they drew heavily on **psychoanalysis** particularly the work of **Sigmund Freud**, and anthropology particularly the work of **Margaret Mead**), respectively. Their work brought together quite different disciplinary approaches which in turn gave rise to their insistence that the family was itself a site of production of personalities and that its workings could not be conceptually reduced to the impoverished idea that families were mere microcosms of wider society. Notwithstanding the fact that Parsons and Bales are largely remembered for their ideas about the way in which the family functioned to support other social institutions and the desirability of the gendered division of labor, they spent a great deal of time exploring the internal dynamics of families and even raising the issue of sexual relationships between spouses – something that later sociologists conspicuously avoided.

At virtually the same time that Parsons and Bales were producing their general theoretical analysis of the family, **Michael Young** and Peter Willmott (*Family and Kinship in East London*, 1957) published their micro-analysis of changing family life based on empirical research within working-class **communities**. Young and Willmott's study sought not only to analyze family change but also to allow the voices of the family members to be heard in the text through the liberal use of quotations from the interviews they conducted with couples. Their approach to research and their style of presentation was almost the complete antithesis of Parsons and Bales's formal and abstract interpretations. Where Parsons and Bales ignored the extended family, focusing almost exclusively on the ideal of the nuclear family,

Young and Willmott located families within kinship **networks** and talked about the importance of family members helping each other and sustaining (adult) intergenerational links. The latter did not conceptualize families as isolated from their communities (although they did note how things changed as **neighborhoods** were demolished in the postwar era). While Parsons and Bales's work can now be interpreted as a paean to the nuclear family, Young and Willmott might be described as a hagiography of the working-class family. Their work sought to re-write the working-class family as a site of warmth and mutual support between husband and wife, and to retrieve it from the widespread belief (generated by the writings of early feminists, philanthropists, and campaigners against **poverty**) that it was a wretched place, dominated by male **violence**, drunkenness, grime, and relentless childbirth. Their vision was optimistic too. They argued that there were far fewer broken homes in Britain in the 1950s than in previous decades, and they saw this as something continuing into the future because they understood the main cause of disruption as being the death of the male head of household (usually in wars) or of either parent (owing to disease). This optimistic framework carried forward into their later work, *The Symmetrical Family* (1973), in which they described the emergence of a new type of family. This family was described as home-centered or "privatized," as nuclear rather than part of an extended kinship network, and, most significantly, as having much less segregated roles for husbands and wives. In some ways this new vision was closer to that of Parsons and Bales, except that the latter did not predict any change to the rigid **segregation** of the male breadwinner and female housewife. By the time *The Symmetrical Family* was published, the sociology of the family (in both the United Kingdom and the United States) had become wedded to the idea of the nuclear, home-loving, monogamous, heterosexual family where other family forms were dismissed as aberrant or dysfunctional. It seemed as if there was little more to be said about families; theoretically the field was still predominantly functionalist in orientation, and empirical research was happily documenting progress towards an egalitarian, child-centered, companionate family form in which, although there might still be problems, progress was being made.

Beck and Beck-Gernsheim describe the sociology of the family as becoming a zombie category, still occupying a place in the sociological canon and yet holding to ideas and conceptualizations long dead in other fields of sociology and **social theory**. Yet this criticism is only accurate if one dismisses the significance of the new feminist work which began to dominate the field in the 1970s in both Britain and United States. This feminist work challenged the idea of the family as a companionate, egalitarian institution, and sought to understand the workings of families from the standpoint of the women who lived and worked in them. There were two particularly important strands of work that developed: the first was a re-interpretation of the meaning and significance of the gendered division of labor in the family, and the second was the re-discovery of domestic violence in families.

While Young and Willmott were identifying the rise of the symmetrical family, other studies were beginning to reveal that the movement of married women into the labor force seemed to be generating a double shift for women, rather than a sharing out of paid and unpaid labor. Empirical studies showed that husbands did not take on more housework or child-care responsibilities, but that wives would come back from paid work only to find that they remained responsible for all (or almost all) domestic duties. Men might have spoken of their willingness to "help" in Young and Willmott, but this was seen by later feminists as merely confirming that domestic work remained the responsibility of women. Research by feminists such as **Ann Oakley** (*The Sociology of Housework*, 1974) drew attention to the idea that housework was "real" work and that it was, moreover, never finished. She dismissed the idea that modern **technology** had lightened women's load because, although the physical labor associated with each task might have become less arduous, standards of cleanliness and child care rose exponentially. Following Oakley's attempt to force sociology to take "women's work" in the home seriously, there arose a more explicitly Marxist analysis which became known as the domestic labor debate. In this debate, the feminist position argued that a materialist analysis of **capitalism** should include consideration of women's unpaid labor, because housework and child care were part of the reproduction of labor power needed by capital to keep those in paid employment (see **work and employment**) fit and capable of working long hours in the process of producing profit. Without women's unpaid labor in the family, it was argued, capitalism could not survive, and women's labor indirectly contributed to the creation of profit.

Linked to this argument was the idea that women continued to give their labor freely because they subscribed to (or were brainwashed by) the **ideology** of familialism. It was argued that ideas that women's roles as mothers or as housewives were a natural component of women's being and psyche were a kind of false consciousness, which kept women willingly confined to economically dependent and subservient positions in their families. Rather than seeing women's economic and social vulnerability as either god-given or as functionally necessary, this approach saw it as exploitative and oppressive. Marxist feminist work became associated with a profound critique of the family, and this oppositional stance is exemplified in the work of Michelle Barrett and Mary McIntosh, *Anti-Social Family* (1982).

While the domestic labor debate was about housework, other feminists turned their attention to "care" work. This approach focused on two aspects of hidden work in families. The first was the work of caring for others, not only children, but also often elderly or infirm relatives. These activities had previously been treated as extensions of women's *natural* caring capacity, and so the process of redefining it as work was part of a process of making it more visible and understood as a social activity. The second approach centered more on emotional labor. This activity was identified as women's responsibility, and its focus was to keep the breadwinner happy, to attend to his emotional needs, and to provide an emotionally comforting and restorative environment. It is interesting that, in bringing these activities to the fore, feminists at this time used the terminology of work or labor to give a kind of concrete status to these otherwise apparently ephemeral activities. But, in so doing, both **care** and emotions were reduced to a form of labor which could be measured and assessed.

Throughout this period, work on the family therefore sought to deconstruct taken-for-granted ideas about the warmth, love, and support supposedly found in families. Instead it focused on power relations, something notably absent from earlier approaches. However, because emotions were seen as suspect, this feminist work banished a sphere of enquiry on love, care, and attentiveness for over a generation. Indeed, it was argued that the very term family should be avoided, and in its place the concept of the household used, because this was free from naturalistic assumptions about gender roles, affection, duties of care, and unequal, heterosexual relationships.

However, the attempt to remove the term family from the sociological lexicon ultimately failed.

The rediscovery of domestic violence (itself a contested term) was also linked to the focus on power relations in the family. The term was coined to counterpoise the idea of the domestic as an environment of harmony and safety, with concepts typically associated with the **public sphere**, namely danger and harm. It was later criticized because it obscured the fact that this violence was inflicted overwhelmingly by men, and so it was seen as disguising men's moral responsibility for their behavior. But whether the term wife beating or domestic violence or woman abuse was used, the focus on violence was a crucial part of the redefinition of the family as a universally "good thing." Feminist work sought to explain why women had little choice but to stay in violent relationships, and also argued that violent men gave rise to violent sons and intimidated daughters. Through this focus on violence it was also argued that heterosexual relationships were dangerous for women and that, even though not all men were violent, the cultural acceptance of male violence in the home served to empower all men in their relationships with women.

Research on domestic violence highlighted the core problem of women's economic dependence on men, especially when they had children and had left the **labor market**. It also revealed the extent to which both criminal and family law protected the privilege of husbands within the **privacy** of the family. Assaults, which would have led to criminal proceedings if carried out in public, were treated as a private matter between spouses, and there was little help an assaulted wife could call on. When combined with the recognition of women's double shift, emotional labor, and economic exploitation in families, there emerged an argument that the monogamous, heterosexual family was an arrangement which was highly detrimental to women, and which reproduced the privileged position of men in western societies. For at least a decade feminist work on family life was largely preoccupied with these questions of power and exploitation, and sought to challenge the idea that families had become more democratic and egalitarian institutions.

The feminist critique on the family is often (rather simplistically) seen to be the cause of the decline of the family. This is because the depiction of the family as a poor choice for women coincided (in western societies) with a rise in the divorce rate, a decline in marriage rates and the birth rate, a rise in cohabitation and lone motherhood, and also a rise in people living alone. However, it is important to recognize the extent to which concerns and predictions about the decline of the family are a historical phenomenon. It is hard to find a moment when someone was not expressing alarm that the family was no longer the decent, patriarchal household of the past, with obedient children and subservient wives. Even Parsons and Bales started their book on the family with reference to the worry that changes in family structure were causing in the postwar United States. Each new generation would appear to have identified slightly different reasons for the perceived decline or disorganization of the family. Some saw the shift from extended to nuclear families as a profound loss, other saw the loss of "functions" of the family (for example **education**) to the state as an indication of moral decline. Yet others saw (and still see) the rise in divorce (see **marriage and divorce**) as a clear indicator of decline, while opponents argue that the high rate of divorce is a sign that people set great store by the value of good personal relationships and so will no longer tolerate bad, or abusive, situations.

These concerns gave rise to the so-called Pro-Family Right, predominantly in the United States, but also to a lesser extent in the United Kingdom. In a kind of backlash against the perceived **hegemony** of feminist thinking, the Pro-Family Right depicted fatherless families as the cause of rises in delinquency, idleness, and poverty (David Popenoe, *Disturbing the Nest: Family Change and Decline in Modern Societies*, 1988). A dystopian vision of family life came to dominate much of this writing with each rise in the divorce statistics or rise in numbers of children born out of wedlock interpreted as a nail in the coffin of the family. As early as 1983 Brigitte and Peter Berger, in *The War over the Family*, were trying to find the middle ground between those promoting policies to re-establish the traditional family (by which it was meant the patriarchal breadwinner / dependent housewife model) and those who saw the family as the site of the reproduction of both gender and class oppressions. In the United States the "war" was highly charged because of the direct link with both policy and **politics**, which meant that studying the family had become less an academic pursuit than a politically fraught enterprise. This politically charged engagement suggests that the study of the family might not have been in the doldrums as Beck and Beck-Gernsheim

suggest, but in fact their point still stands because the interminable debate about family decline was ultimately intellectually reductive and circular. The claims and counterclaims became familiar territory, and it seemed to become impossible to move beyond this narrow conceptual straitjacket.

In fact, sociological work on families did manage to move forwards (although not completely) as new ways of thinking about family relationships started to emerge. A key re-conceptualization came from David Morgan in *Family Connections* (1996), where he succeeded in ultimately breaking with the functionalist tradition of seeing the family as an institution with its roles and core functions, and instead saw the family as something people "did." He coined the terminology of "family practices." He conceptualized the family as a web of relationships which was created and recreated by what people did and how they related to one another through their ordinary practices. This meant that the family was set loose from traditional ideas that it was fundamentally about the co-residence of a man and a woman and their children, who all occupied a given status in relation to one another. He grasped what is acknowledged in everyday experience, namely that those whom people feel to be family *are* family and that co-residence is not vital to form a family, but affective (and other emotional) bonds and everyday practices are. This conceptual shift provided a means to think differently about families and to start to include varieties of previously unrecognized families without constantly comparing them to the nuclear ideal. Morgan also rehabilitated the term family. He acknowledged that it is a problematic concept because of the ideology of familialism which idealizes a particular type or set of relationships. The term family is also apparently resolutely heterosexual in intonation; some would argue it is heteronormative, because of its focus on and privileging of marriage and opposite sex biological **reproduction**. But Morgan's work pointed to the flexibility of the concept of family in everyday usage and the ways in which it has been stretched and molded, notwithstanding sociology's attempts to fix a definition of the family as comprising two opposite sex parents and their children. Morgan also pointed out that the term family is deeply culturally significant, and, even though it may have many different meanings, it is still meaningful and so should not be discarded, since it encapsulates and reflects a range of cultural values which should be the focus of enquiry. The task for sociology, he suggested, was to explore more imaginatively how people "do" family life.

These ideas were simultaneously being reflected in a new body of empirical research on families. Of particular significance was the work of Janet Finch and Jennifer Mason, *Negotiating Family Responsibilities* (1993), who re-incorporated ideas about values and meaning into how people live their family lives. They used the term negotiating in order to express how, even in close kin relationships, people were not governed by a sense of handed-down rigid obligations, but were guided by their feelings about their relatives and by their own sense of ethics, or "the proper thing to do." Almost all family relationships were thus seen as negotiable and so variable. Yet they also found that there remained an important sense of obligation and commitment to kin. This micro-level analysis focused much more explicitly on the values that people live their family lives by; it looked at everyday workings and gave precedence to the meanings that family members themselves constructed in living their families. This focus on meanings and values in everyday living has also been reflected in other empirical studies which have attempted to capture the complexity of both relationships within families and those between generations. This greater attentiveness to the ways in which real, complex, and multilayered relationships are lived has finally ended the sociological tendency to speak about the family as if it was an entity of like-minded, homogeneous people who react in a uniform way to the "outside world" rather than themselves being (inter)active agents. An example of this development is found in *How Families Still Matter* by Vern Bengtson, Timothy J. Bibblaz, and Robert E. L. Roberts (2002). This is a longitudinal study of American families which focuses on intergenerational change and continuity across time. Four generations were included in the study, with the first generation born at the turn of the twentieth century, the second born around the 1920s, the third around the 1950s, and the fourth in the 1970s. The importance of this study is that, through its longitudinal methodology, it has been able to capture continuity and change across generations, while also mapping such changes onto the changing historical times through which the families lived and are still living. The study is also able to capture individual change, for example the authors can compare what people say now with what they said ten or twenty years ago. They can, moreover, compare what older people born in the 1950s actually

said and felt when they were in their twenties with what twenty-year-olds now say and feel. This move to qualitative and quantitative longitudinal research marks an important shift in the extent to which sociology can actually grasp family life and also the actual processes of family and **social change**. Most significantly, it is able to deal with the problem of "golden age" thinking in which family life of the past is always depicted as better, more moral, more loving, and generally superior to family life now.

Observations of the interiority of family life have also brought a new level of imaginative thinking to the field. John Gillis, in *A World of their Own Making* (1996), has distinguished between families we live "with" and families we live "by." The latter are the families in people's memories, hopes, and imaginations, the families people represent to themselves; while the former are the actual co-resident families who may be far from the ideal held in thoughts or longings. Gillis points to the constant iteration between these two levels of experiences of, and thinking about, families. His focus is on **myth** and **ritual** (for example family holidays or the ways in which ancestors influence lives lived in the present) in order to reveal the ways in which people live their families in their heads, not just in the material present. To some extent, Gillis has rehabilitated the older concept of the ideology of the family which, when deployed by feminist writers in the 1970s, was seen as a kind of imposed, malign influence which kept women in their place. In other words he has reintroduced the significance of hopes and feelings into an understanding of families, without the prior assumption that these are oppressive devices.

These shifts in conceptualizing families, namely seeing families as kinship networks which need not co-reside, focusing on negotiations, highlighting the importance of the representation of families both culturally and personally, and the idea that it is important to capture process and change, rather than taking a series of snapshots, have all produced a sociology of family life which is far more complex and subtle than the early functionalists were able to produce. But factors such as **gender**, **social class**, **ethnicity**, **religion**, and sexual orientation remain an important component of a sociological imagination about family life. Families remain one of the most significant means of the transmission of privilege, **wealth**, and cultural capital (see **social capital**) across generations. The personal nature of family life which is captured above is also part of the reason why abuses of power across genders and generations remain hidden and tolerated. Moreover, the fact that one is born into a family (usually) and that one's kin is identified in advance (through blood ties and lineage) still means that families, unlike friendships, are imposed rather than entered into voluntarily.

This idea that families are inevitably given, rather than chosen, has been challenged however. Kath Weston, in *Families We Choose: Lesbians, Gays, Kinship* (1991), has pointed to the growing creation and recognition of families of choice. The exclusion of gays and lesbians from supposedly proper (that is, heteronormative) families in conventional thinking has led to a reclaiming and remolding of the concept of family so that it can be used to signify people living together in close relationships notwithstanding the fact they are unable to marry and are not blood relatives. The increase in, and increasing visibility of, lesbian mothers and gay and lesbian adoption, has profoundly affected the taken-for-grantedness of the heterosexual family. The claim by lesbians and gays to form families has been controversial, precisely because the family has been seen inevitably to incorporate and promote heterosexual privilege; however, this move can also be seen as part of the redefinition of what families are in contemporary society and as a blurring of the boundaries between traditionally privileged relationships and those that were once ignored and denigrated.

It has been suggested above that sociological work on families operates on two levels, with macro-theoretical work progressing in a parallel fashion with more micro-level work. Of course there are conversations between the two, but there is also a tension between the more finely tuned, nuanced work of those engaged in more empirical work, and those who are seeking to develop broader theories about how family life is changing. There has been a revival in sociological interest in families at the macro level which has not been apparent since the decline of the functionalist perspective (if one treats the feminist interventions as slightly separate since they did not emerge from mainstream sociology). Social theorists who have typically dealt with traditionally conceived big themes (such as capitalism or modernity) have turned their interest towards families. Most notable here is the work of Beck and Beck-Gernsheim (*Individualisation*, 2002, *The Normal Chaos of Love*) who have returned to the perennial theme of social change and families. As part of their overall thesis on the rise of individualization in modern societies, they depict the family as a site of fragmentation and of constant (exhausting) balancing and negotiation. They argue, "Family life no longer happens in one place but is scattered between several different locations . . . The lives of individual family members, with their different rhythms, locations and demands, only rarely fit together naturally."

They depict a tension between individual life projects and the collective needs of families which are hard to resolve, and relate these trends to wider developments in a highly individualized society. They suggest that western societies are moving towards a post-familial family but, unlike others who have observed family change and seen alarming signs of decline, their analysis identifies a range of new family forms which do not conform to the nuclear ideal but which will take their place alongside the more traditional family structure. The theoretical scope of this work has brought families back into mainstream sociological thinking and reconnected the sociological understanding of family life with wider social changes. However, the tension with the more grounded empirical work remains, especially where evidence of the changes that Beck and Beck-Gernsheim impute to the interiority of family life is seen as tenuous or at least is disputed. Notwithstanding this, the sociological study of families has become reinvigorated and has returned to a more central place in the sociological canon.

CAROL SMART

Fanon, Franz (1925–1961)

Born in Martinique, a French overseas territory in the Caribbean, to a middle-class family of African origin, Fanon studied medicine and psychiatry in France in the late 1940s. He developed an anti-colonial political doctrine that became a main reference point for the Third World movement. Fanon became involved in **politics**, both as a writer and as an activist in the 1950s while directing a psychiatric ward in Algeria (another of France's overseas territories) during the country's **war** of **decolonization** (1954–62). Having joined the Algerian independence movement, the Front de Libération Nationale (FLN), he proposed a radical brand of political existentialism in which the realization of Algerian **identity** necessarily coincided with the destruction of the French presence in the country.

His Hegelian-inspired construction of the black/colonized **self** through the negation of the white/colonial presence was developed in two main works: *Black Skin, White Masks* (1952 [trans. 1967] and *The Wretched of the Earth* (1961 [trans. 1965]). Fanon showed how structures of domination, mediated by **culture** and discourse, consistently reminded the colonized of their fundamental inadequacy in a world created by white colonizers in their image. Hence, Fanon emphasized the therapeutic aspect of **violence** by the oppressed against their oppressor, which freed them from their inferiority complex and restored their self-respect. Influential in **postcolonial theory** despite its controversial apology for violence, Fanon's work has nonetheless been criticized for over–emphasizing the racial dimension of domination at the expense of aspects such as **gender** or **religion**. His political essays are collected in two further works: *Studies in a Dying Colonialism* (1959 [trans. 1965]) and *Toward the African Revolution* (1964 [trans. 1967]).   FREDERIC VOLPI

fascism

Sometimes used as a word of abuse to refer to movements or individuals who are intolerant or authoritarian, fascism is certainly intolerant and authoritarian, but it is more than this. It is a movement that seeks to establish a dictatorship of the "right" (that is an ultra-conservative position that rejects **liberalism** and anything associated with the "left"). It targets communists, socialists, trade unionists, and liberals through banning their parties and their members, so that these groups cannot exercise their political, legal, or social **rights**. It is anti-liberal, regarding liberal **values** as a form of "decadence" and seeing them as opening the floodgates to socialist, communist, and egalitarian movements.

As a movement, fascism extols action and practice over ideas and theory. It uses ideas with considerable opportunism, mixing socialist ideas, avant-garde positions, anti-capitalist rhetoric, ecological argument, and pseudo-scientific ideas to do with **race and ethnicity** in a veritable potpourri. Is it an **ideology** at all? Some have suggested that fascism is too jumbled and incoherent to be called an ideology, but, while fascism is peculiarly "flexible," there are particular features that characterize it, so that a general view of fascism can be created.

The term derives from the *fasces* – the bundle of rods carried by the consuls of ancient Rome; the word *fascio* was used in Italy in the 1890s to indicate a political **group** or band, usually of revolutionary socialists. But fascism is essentially a twentieth-century movement, although it draws upon **prejudices** and stereotypes that are rooted

in **tradition**. Italian fascism saw itself as resurrecting the glories of the Roman Empire, and Alfredo Rocco (1875–1935), an Italian fascist, saw Niccolo Machiavelli (1459–1517) as a founding father of fascist theory. Nazism (which is an extreme form of fascism) was regarded by its ideologues as rooted in the history of the Nordic peoples, and the movement embodied anti-Semitic views that go back to the Middle Ages.

Fascism appeals particularly to those who have some **property** but not very much, and are fearful that they might be plunged by market forces into the ranks of the working class. Fascism is particularly hostile to **Communism**, since it is opposed to the cosmopolitan contentions of Marxist theory, and its belief in a classless and stateless **society**. It is a movement that dislikes universal **identities** of any kind, although of course fascists may call for unity with kindred spirits in other countries. Nevertheless, it is intensely nationalistic, and takes the view that the people must be saved from enemies whose way of life is alien and threatening. Differences are deemed divisive and menacing, and **war** extolled as a way of demonstrating virtue and strength. The idea that people are divided by **social class** is rejected in favor of the unity of the nation or people, so that industry is to be organized in a way that expresses the common interest between business and **labor**. In practice, this did not happen, and it is arguable that fascism is anti-capitalist only in theory, not in practice.

Fascists vary in their attitude towards the church (extreme fascists may see religious **organizations** as a threat to the **state**), but they regard **religion** in a loose sense as being a useful way of instilling order and loyalty. Certainly, they use a religious style of language in invoking the need for sacrifice, redemption, and spiritual virtue, and fascists attack **materialism**, consumerism, and hedonism as decadent and unworthy. Although women can be fascists as well as men, fascism is a supremely patriarchal creed, by which I mean that women are seen as domestic creatures whose role in life is to service men, to have children, to be good mothers and wives, and to keep out of **politics**.

Fascism is hostile to the liberal tradition, and it dislikes the notion of reason. It regards the individual as subordinate to the collectivity in general, and the state in particular. Liberal freedoms are seen merely as entitlements that allow the enemies of the "nation" or the "people" to capture **power**. Fascist regimes are highly authoritarian, and use the state as the weapon of the dominant party to protect the nation, advance its interests, and destroy its enemies. They are strongly opposed to the idea of **democracy** (although fascists may use democratic rhetoric to justify their rule or use parliamentary **institutions** to win access to power), and regard the notion of self-government (the idea that people can control their lives in a rational way and without force) as a dangerous **myth**. As a movement based upon repressive hierarchy, fascism argues that all institutions should be controlled by "reliable" leaders, and the "leadership principle" comes to a climax with the supreme leader, seen as the embodiment of the nation and the people. Fascist leaders may be civilians, but they are closely identified with the army and police, since these institutions are crucial to rooting out opponents. Fascist movements extend beyond the **state**, but the **violence** of these movements is condoned and encouraged by the state; given tight control over the media, this violence is then justified in the light of fascist values.

Fascists see themselves as revolutionary in that they are concerned to "rejuvenate" a tired and decadent society, and some fascists speak of creating a "new man" in a new society. They are, therefore, anti-conservative as well as anti-liberal, although they may form tactical alliances with other sections of the right when they can establish momentary common ground. Many regimes, loosely called fascist, are in fact conservative and reactionary systems – Franco's Spain, Pétain's "Vichy" France (a regime that collaborated with the Nazis who occupied the country), Japan under Tojo, and so forth. They may have fascist elements within them, but they are not really anti-conservative in character.

Postwar fascism has generally sought to distance itself from intrawar ideologies in Germany and Italy, and has ranged from movements that see the European Community as containing the germ of a "United Europe" to movements hostile to the European Union. Some fascist movements claim democratic credentials, although these are not really plausible, given their intense chauvinism, anti-feminism, and hostility to liberalism and **socialism**.   JOHN HOFFMAN

fashion

The study of fashion in the sociological tradition has a long history. However, it is important to distinguish between two related approaches: (1) an emphasis on the study of fashion as a cultural phenomenon of **modernity**; and (2) fashion as the study of clothing and the **body** in specific cultural contexts. These features are often run together although we should recognize that they are analytically separate. The sociologist **Georg Simmel** argued that fashion emerges in a society that is built upon social and cultural change. For Simmel, fashion is built on the impulse to distinguish yourself from others, while also satisfying the need for social adaptation and imitation. Fashion is mainly structured by **social class** and is caught in constant cycles of innovation and emulation. As **elites** attempt to set themselves apart through observable social markers like dress, others seek to copy the new styles as they emerge from above. Consequently, elites respond by inventing further new styles and so on. Fashion in this analysis becomes a novelty mania, where collective tastes are being born and replaced at ever faster rates. Indeed, if fashion becomes routinized and formalized it can lose the charm it exercises over its consumers.

Simmel's arguments were further developed by **Thorstein Veblen** (1857–1929), who similarly argued that the cycles of fashion were structured by class. For Veblen what became fashionable was largely determined by what was in short supply and expensive. This was a way (as Simmel also suggested) of distinguishing classes, but also of displaying **wealth** and **power**. Fashion was a way of making wealth visible through "conspicuous consumption" so that it might be admired by others.

There are two main objections to such views: (1) the analysis tends to ignore other sociological features such as **age**, **race**, and **gender**, which are perhaps even more important than class in structuring fashion; and (2) elites are no longer, if indeed they ever were, the main purveyors of fashion. In modern societies, elites often find themselves "out of fashion" or even lagging behind current trends.

Other studies of fashion have tended to emphasize features other than social class. Gender is now seen as a key determinant in the study of fashion. In Elizabeth Wilson's *Adorned in Dreams* (1985), fashion is seen to represent the Romantic movement's critique of the culture of instrumentality that accompanied the industrial revolution. In this view fashion is explicitly concerned with sensuality, **aesthetics**, and **individualism**. Further, fashion values the life of the **city** by emphasizing the spirit of play, fluidity, and performance over authenticity. Fashion is a form of adult play made possible by the development of **modernity**. In this respect, Wilson criticizes some feminist authors for dismissing fashion as a form of masculine control, when it offers women, its main consumers, with the potential for aesthetic creativity.

Indeed many have argued that the "grand theorists" of fashion have mistakenly presumed it to be an explicit product of western society. Here the study of fashion has become the recognition of the acceptable codes of behavior that govern the presentation of the body. In particular these features have emphasized the role of gender and **youth** in the construction of fashion. Particularly important here has been the shift from equating fashion with the **lifestyles** of social **elites** and the rise of a mass fashion industry over the course of the twentieth century. If, in the 1920s, Hollywood helped democratize ideas of glamor and beauty, it was the 1960s that provided the first genuinely mass fashion. Further, the 1970s witnessed the emergence of supermodels, who were highly paid international figures who helped promote a certain look. Most of these developments sought to target women as the main consumers of a fashionable image, but this would change in the 1980s. Until this period heterosexual men's clothing was probably more conformist than that of women. This was a direct consequence of the fact that men risked being labeled effeminate for showing too much interest in fashion. Expressive fashions up until this point were mostly confined to gay men, ethnic groups, and popular entertainers. The shift in fashion occurred during the 1980s for three main reasons: (1) the arrival of high-street stores that explicitly offered affordable stylish clothes for men; (2) new visual representations of men (in particular the softer and more caring form of masculinity that was represented in the new man); and (3) the arrival of new style and fashion magazines.

Other sociologists have emphasized how fashion can become a site of cultural struggle. Dick Hebdige, in *Subculture* (1979), argues that the adoption of different styles on the part of young people can act as a form of defiance. Fashion and clothing can become a way of subverting dominant discourses and codes that seek to regulate acceptable behavior. Youth cultures and subcultures hold out the possibility of suggesting new and oppositional meanings in different social contexts. The rise of new youth lifestyles since the emergence of rock and roll in the 1950s offered opportunities to subvert the **values** and meanings of the dominant parent culture. However, whatever the role that fashion plays in the formation of **identity**, it continues to be linked to a wider culture of modernity in a way that was

recognized by earlier classical thinkers. In particular, fashion is a requirement of the economic system. Unless consumers are willing to buy new things, get into debt, and give up old tastes in preference for the new, then **capitalism**'s ability to expand would be severely curtailed. If fashion represents change and the formation of identity, it nevertheless continues to represent the cycles of profit maximization in an increasingly commercial world.   NICK STEVENSON

fatherhood/fathers

In patriarchal societies fathers are a source of both **authority** and **power** in the ordering of the lives and social experiences of family members. The role of fatherhood is an **identity** taken up outside the workplace in the private sphere. In **industrial society** the main role of the father was to be both a provider for, and protector of, the **family**. Many objected that such was the **authority** of the father that the nuclear family was actually a form of domination requiring the subordination of women and **children**. Further the image of the father proved to be a powerful one with many national leaders earning the title "father of the nation." In more recent times, the authority of individual fathers has been challenged by the development of democratic **norms** (women's and children's **rights**) and the development of the welfare functions of the modern **state**. In western industrialized societies, since the 1950s, the role of fatherhood has been the subject of transformation and change. The development of dual-labor households and new expectations in respect of **intimacy** have arguably changed the role of fathers. Further, the development of lesbian and gay **social movements**, **feminism**, and other features have all sought to increase the diversity of family types and has arguably unsettled previous patterns of male dominance.

The changing roles of men and women and the shaking of heterosexual norms have all taken their toll on the social privileges of the father. In *The Transformation of Intimacy* (1992), **Anthony Giddens** has argued that families have become more contingent social arrangements. Fatherhood is no longer defined by economic necessity, but has become an empty sign to be filled by the participants within the relationship. This does not mean that the family has become more harmonious. Indeed with the decline of overt class antagonisms, the family is the place where most individuals are likely to experience conflict. Yet if the role of fatherhood is being redefined, it is not clear that men themselves have kept pace with the new demands now being made of them. In the demand for new intimate and caring family ties, men have become "laggards" in the shift towards more egalitarian relationships. Such a situation has meant that traditional forms of **masculinity** (and fathering) continue to exist, as a backlash in the face of the demand for more equal relations, mainly coming from women.

Many feminists have criticized the idea that we are currently living through a transformation of this type. First, many radical critics argue that **patriarchy** has been intensified rather than diminished by current social transformations. Under the **hegemony** of the **market** and masculine values, **motherhood** has become a non-identity. The **care** of children and vulnerable adults is increasingly outsourced and is work of low **social status**. Here the small steps that some fathers have taken in respect of a more nurturing role should not be allowed to overshadow more disturbing transformations. Second, other critics have contested the view that the home has been democratized, pointing to the slow change of masculine values and the continued subordination of women, children, and other sexual identities.

NICK STEVENSON

fecundity

– see **fertility**.

feminism

Histories of feminism usually assume that feminism is a western, post-Enlightenment **social movement** which has contributed significantly to changes both in the social situation of women and in social perceptions of women. This assumption has frequently made feminism the subject of attacks from women in non-western **cultures** who have identified the movement as pre-occupied with western issues and unable to understand the gender relations of other **societies**. Thus it is first and foremost important to recognize the possible ethnocentricity of feminism, while at the same time acknowledging that feminism, in the broadest sense of the protest of women against a subordinate **social status**, is both global and takes different forms in different cultures. Where feminism stands universally united is on issues of the valid claim of women to **education**, to a public voice, and to **equality** with men in **law**.

The most usually recognized starting point of western feminism is in the eighteenth century and, in particular, the publication, in 1792, of Mary Wollstonecraft's A *Vindication of the Rights of Woman*. This book emerged out of a number of social and intellectual changes in the eighteenth century: the growing assumption of the equal rights of all individuals and what Thomas Laqueur has described as the invention of sex in his *Making Sex* (1990). From the beginning of the eighteenth century onwards, numerous writers (including Mary Wollstonecraft's husband, William Godwin) articulated what was to become the rallying cry of the French Revolution: "Liberty, Equality, and Fraternity." Mary Wollstonecraft (1759–97) entirely supported the first two of these propositions but took issue with the idea of "fraternity." Her argument suggested that no society should allow men to control the public space or to have no knowledge of, or responsibility for, the private, domestic sphere. Thus Wollstonecraft argued not just for the education and public emancipation of women, but also for the domestic education and participation of men.

Wollstonecraft died the death of thousands of eighteenth-century women when she gave birth to her daughter, Mary Shelley. But her book was recognized both before and after her death, and was influential in what became known as the domestication debates of the early nineteenth century. Although her **influence** on writers is often implicit rather than explicit, what Wollstonecraft had done was to identify the social making of **gender**: this made it possible for later writers to suggest (as **Simone de Beauvoir** was to do in the twentieth century) that women are "made and not born."

Throughout the nineteenth century, in both Europe and the United States, women (and occasionally men such as **John Stuart Mill**) questioned the **social role** of women and argued for their greater participation in the social world and equality of education. Perhaps inevitably, in the nineteenth quite as much as in the twentieth century, feminism and feminist demands were complicated by differences between women. In Britain these differences were generally differences of **social class**, while in the United States racial and ethnic differences were to have equal significance.

Throughout the nineteenth century, feminism, on both sides of the Atlantic, was to constitute an important part of social debates and the culture which informed literature and the visual arts. Classic **liberalism**, for example in Mill's *On the Subjection of Women* (1869), emphasized the importance of the education of women: this emphasis was hugely influential and made education, and access to education, a consistently important part of feminist campaigns in both the nineteenth and the twentieth centuries. (Indeed, in the late twentieth century this argument still continues: the economist Amartya Sen has suggested that the key to reducing the birth rate, and a greater degree of economic prosperity, lies in the education of women.) In both the United Kingdom and the United States, white, middle-class women campaigned for women to have access not just to schools – which had always been allowed, if less enthusiastically than for men – but to higher education. By the end of the nineteenth century, this objective had been achieved in both Britain and the United States and a very small number of women had begun to attend university.

Feminist campaigns for education were, however, only part of feminist history in the nineteenth century, and a part which was largely the concern of middle-class women. Of equal importance were the campaigns, often far more disruptive and socially contentious, for the right of women to own their own **property** and for a form of sexual **morality** which did not take for granted male sexual **rights** over women. Alongside these campaigns – fought throughout the West – were the struggles of working-class women to secure rights in paid **work**. One of the longest battles which has been fought by western feminists is that for equal pay: this battle continues into the twenty-first century. The arguments involved have changed considerably over the past 100 years and second-wave feminism in the West secured the greater recognition of the concept of "equal work of equal value," which did much to overturn the more traditional idea of the different (and deeply gendered) **value** of different kinds of work.

A second campaign fought by feminists has a similar historical length to battles over the rewards of paid work. This is the campaign by women for control over their **bodies**: a campaign which first arose in the nineteenth century over the question of the sexual double standard and has continued into the twentieth and twenty-first centuries in relation to issues related to new forms of **technology**, notably contraception and the new reproductive technology. In the nineteenth century, campaigners such as Josephine Butler succeeded in over-turning legislation which assumed male rights of sexual access to women. In the early twentieth century, women such as Marie Stopes argued for women's right to contraception and heterosexual fulfilment. All these debates, as much in the nineteenth century as in the twentieth, lie within the remit of feminism

(since they imply an explicit commitment to the rights of women), yet they are at the same time complicated by the different **politics** of the women involved. For example, Marie Stopes had views about **genetics** and the **reproduction** of "the race" which would nowadays be regarded with some suspicion; other women involved in campaigns around reproduction and **sexuality** were committed to normative heterosexuality and the social status quo.

It is thus that the history of feminism is complicated by the diverse politics which women (and very occasionally men) have held. In the twentieth century, there was a very general approximation of the coincidence of feminist and progressive views about women and women's emancipation with left-wing and radical politics. Thus the right-wing, fascist regimes of the twentieth century (Franco's Spain, Mussolini's Italy, and Hitler's Germany) have all supported traditional views of women and passed legislation designed to ensure the exclusion of women from the public world. At the same time, it is also the case that those equally radical, although left-wing, regimes such as that of Stalin's Russia, while fully integrating women into paid work (and putting in place a social infrastructure to make this possible) have minimized sexual difference and articulated a model of human beings as male. This eradication of gender difference has been widely questioned, and feminist writing of the late twentieth century has claimed that feminism should be about the recognition of the female/feminine rather than the equalization of the female/feminine with the male.

At the beginning of the twenty-first century, feminist writers have come to recognize that feminism is a broad church and that the interests of feminism cannot be easily summarized. The great work of twentieth-century feminism, de Beauvoir's *The Second Sex* (first published in 1949 [trans. 1972]) famously argued that women are made by society and the social world, and that the social world which "makes" women has a consistent **tradition** of misogyny. This social constructionist view of women has been widely influential and there was little significant challenge to the view until the publication, in 1974, of **Juliet Mitchell**'s *Psychoanalysis and Feminism*. In this discussion of **Sigmund Freud**, Mitchell argued that feminists should re-consider the impact of biological difference on behavior and our symbolic interpretation of the world. The work was extremely influential and opened up new developments which made feminism itself more reflective.

In large part this greater self-consciousness led feminists to re-consider the relationship of feminism to the social world and to consider, as Sheila Rowbotham (1943–) has done in *Hidden from History* (1973), the emergence and practice of western feminism as part of the politics of liberal **capitalism**. What this view does is to shift the claims of feminism from those of a movement of social transformation to those of a movement of social integration. Without for one moment denigrating the achievements of feminism (which in areas such as paid work, property and legal rights, and sexual **politics** have been of value to all women, regardless of class and **race and ethnicity**), this argument sees feminism in wider terms and as part of the transformation of western capitalism to a social system based on **consumption**.

The history of feminism is generally divided into the first-wave feminism which extends from the middle of the nineteenth to the early twentieth century, and second-wave feminism which developed from 1970 onwards. Feminism at the beginning of the twenty-first century is often described as part of the "mainstream" in that many institutional contexts demand gender equality and policies which recognize the claims of women and men to equal treatment. At the same time, while institutional contexts have achieved significant forms of recognition of the rights of women, there remain numerous aspects of social life where gender differences are still considerable. Throughout the West it is still the case that the birth of children impinges far more on the lives of women than on the lives of men, and women have far less involvement in political, public **power** than men. These gender differences are clearly resistant to **social change**, despite the fact that, in the United Kingdom, women over the age of thirty have had the vote since 1918, partly as a result of the political impact of the Suffragettes – a **social movement** associated with Mrs. Emmeline Pankhurst (1858–1928) who successfully campaigned for the enfranchisement of women.

These issues remain of consistent importance to individual women and to those feminist **groups** which campaign on specific issues related to the situation of women. In this sense, the contemporary history of feminism is similar to its history in the past: as a movement its concerns are rooted in a particular historical and social context, even though the thread which unites all feminist movements is that of the universal social subordination of women. But what has become a central part of contemporary feminism is the acknowledgment that claims such as the "universal subordination of women" are complicated by the differences between women and the part which women themselves play in determining their own situation. Thus feminism today recognizes the considerable degree of female agency, with the crucial implication that this may powerfully disrupt the idea of a single feminist agenda.   MARY EVANS

fertility

This term refers to the actual production of **children**. Demographers thus distinguish between the actual production of children and the ability to produce children, known as fecundity. Medical scientists do not make such a distinction, and use the term fertility to refer to reproductive ability. French-speaking and Spanish-speaking demographers (like their English-speaking counterparts) also distinguish between the potential and actual production of children, but they reverse the English usage of the terms. Thus French-speaking demographers use the term *fertilité*, and Spanish-speaking demographers the term *fertilidad*, to refer to reproductive ability, and *fécondité* and *fecundidad*, respectively, to refer to actual reproductive performance.

An easily understood and interpreted method for quantifying fertility is the crude birth rate (CBR), that is, the number of births in a population in a given year, per 1,000 members of the population. It may be expressed as follows:

$$CBR = \frac{\text{births in the year}}{\text{population at mid-year}} \times 1,000$$

Using data for China for 2004, the equation becomes:

$$CBR = \frac{15,600,000}{1,300,000,000} \times 1,000 = 12$$

This means that in China in 2004, there were 12 babies born for every 1,000 persons in the population. Crude birth rates among the countries of the world in 2004 ranged from lows of 9 in several countries, including Austria, Germany, Bulgaria, Poland, and Greece, to highs of 55 in Niger and 51 in Malawi. The range of crude birth rates is much greater than that for crude death rates, which in 2004 extended from a low of 2 to a high of 29.

Lay persons tend to employ the CBR more often than any other fertility measure, but it is not the most accurate of the measures. Its denominator does not really represent the population exposed to the risk of giving birth because males, pre-puberty females, and post-menopausal females are included. Because of this overly inclusive denominator, the CBR should be interpreted with caution.

Demographers use more refined fertility measures, including the general fertility rate (GFR), age-specific fertility rates (ASFR), the total fertility rate (TFR), the gross reproduction rate (GRR), and the net reproduction rate (NRR). The GFR, ASFR, and TFR are increasingly more accurate measures of the childbearing experiences of the population. The GRR and the NRR measure not fertility but actual **reproduction**.

Demographers have developed extensive theories of fertility. Prominent explanations include demographic transition theory, wealth flows theory, human ecological theory, political economic theory, feminist theory, proximate determinants theory, bio-social theory, relative income theory, and diffusion theory. The view of some that demography is void of theory is an incorrect one. Indeed there is more theory in demography than in most of the social sciences.

A major explanation of fertility change and dynamics has its origins in demographic transition theory (DTT), as first developed by Frank W. Notestein in "Population – The Long View," in T. W. Schultz (ed.), *Food for the World* (1945), and by W. S. Thompson in his article "Population" (1929, *American Journal of Sociology*). Current versions of DTT propose four stages of mortality and fertility decline that occur in the process of societal **modernization**. The first is the pre-industrialization era with high birth and death rates and stable population growth. With the onset of **industrialization** (see **industrial society**) and modernization, the society transitions to lower death rates, especially lower infant and maternal mortality, but maintains high birth rates, with the result of rapid population growth. The next stage is characterized by decreasing population growth due to lower birth and death rates, which lead then to the final stage of low and stable population growth.

DTT argues that the first stage hinges on population survival. High fertility is necessary because mortality is high. Thus societies tend to develop a variety of beliefs and practices that support high reproduction, and these are primarily centered on the **family** and kinship systems. The forces of modernization and industrialization alter this state of near-equilibrium, and the first effect is often a reduction in mortality. Indeed the beginnings of mortality decline in many European countries were stimulated not so much by medical and public health improvements as by a general improvement in levels of living. This intermediate stage resulted in rapid rates of population growth because fertility remained high after mortality had declined. In the next stage fertility declines also to lower levels. The causal linkages are complex. Underlying the global concepts of industrialization and modernization are such determinants of fertility as women's participation in the labor force and the changing role of the family. The normative, institutional, and economic supports for the large family become eroded, and the small family becomes predominant. The increasing importance of **urbanization** affects the family by altering its role in production. Also, urban families meet considerably higher demands for consumption from their children, especially for **education** and recreation.

J. C. Caldwell, in "Toward a Restatement of Demographic Transition Theory" (1976, *Population and Development Review*), has called for a restatement of demographic transition theory. His fertility theory of wealth flows is grounded in the assumption that the "emotional" nucleation of the family is crucial for lower fertility. This occurs when parents become less concerned with ancestors and extended family relatives than they are with their children, their children's future, and even the future of their children's children. He argues that ideally there are two types of **societies**; the first is where "the economically rational response is an indefinitely large number of children and the second where it is childless." But why from an economic view would couples want either an unlimited number of children or none at all? Caldwell explains that it depends on the direction of the intergenerational flows of **wealth** and services. If the flows run from children to their parents, it is entirely rational for parents to want to have large families. In modern societies where the flow is from parents to children, it is rational to want small families. To say that parents in the less developed countries are "irrational" because they continue to have large families is to misunderstand these societies. Caldwell states that fertility behavior is rational in virtually all societies irrespective of their levels of development.

Two other prominent fertility paradigms are based on human ecology and political economy. The human ecological theory of fertility is a macro-level explanation and argues that the level of sustenance-organization complexity of a society is negatively related with fertility. In the first place a high fertility pattern is dysfunctional for an increasingly complex sustenance organization because so much of the sustenance produced must be consumed directly by the population. High fertility should reduce the absolute amount of uncommitted sustenance resources thereby limiting the population's flexibility for adapting to environmental, technological, and other kinds of changes and fluctuations. Low fertility is more consonant with the needs and requirements of an expansive sustenance organization. More sustenance would be available for investment back into the system in a low-fertility population than in a population with high fertility. Large quantities of sustenance normally consumed by the familial and educational institutions in a high-fertility population would hence be available as mobile or fluid resources in a low-fertility population. Sustenance organization in this latter instance would thus have the investment resources available for increasing complexity, given requisite changes in the environment and **technology**. This leads to the hypothesis of a negative relation between organizational complexity and fertility.

The political economy of fertility is not really a theory of fertility per se, but an investigative framework or "analytic perspective" for the study of fertility, according to S. Greenhalgh in "Toward a Political Economy of Fertility: Anthropological Contributions" (1990, *Population and Development Review*). Diverse fields of knowledge are integrated into the political economy approach. It is a "multileveled" approach, combining both macro- and micro-level explanations of fertility patterns occurring in a given locale. This means that determinants are considered and measured at every level, including, for instance, global, international, and national forces; political, structural, and legal shifts; community factors; and characteristics of the individual couple. Central to this perspective is the appreciation of "**agency and structure**," or **structuration,** which refer to the structural elements and stages that delineate the existing choices people have, as well as the incentives and tactics that come into play as individual objectives are met. This framework entails both quantitative and qualitative approaches. A good example of a political economy approach to fertility is Dennis P. Hogan and David I. Kertzer, *Family, Political Economy and Demographic Change* (1989), a study of Casalecchio, Italy. They tracked one rural **community** over a few change-laden decades of the nineteenth and twentieth centuries, using individual-level **data** and directed by a life-course perspective. They touched on often ignored historical events, such as labor and marriage patterns, and found that fertility varies with the **social class** or **occupation** of the individual family.

DUDLEY L. POSTON

feudalism

This term is used to describe forms of political, economic, and social relationships found during the Middle Ages, principally in western Europe but also in Japan and sometimes China. It is derived from the Latin term *feodum* and the Germanic *fief*, but was not used until the seventeenth century. When defined narrowly as a legal relationship, it refers to a set of reciprocal legal and military obligations within the nobility between a lord and a vassal. In this hierarchical relationship, the lord granted land, or a fief, to a vassal through a commendation ceremony involving homage and an oath of fealty. In return for the land and, in addition, protection from the lord, the vassal was obliged, through the principle of *fidelitas*, to provide military service and to give "counsel" or aid to the overlord (suzerain). There was also often a process of subinfeudation in which a vassal would grant part of his fief to another vassal and become a lord himself. Although having some basis in Roman times, this system of allegiance is generally regarded as having emerged slowly during the ninth and tenth centuries as a means to reinstitute social order, and to protect against further incursion, following the Germanic incursions.

With reference to political rule, owing to poor communications and transport, and the localized character of the agricultural **economy** based essentially on a manorial system, feudalism was characterized by decentralized **institutions** of **power**. Although the king was generally regarded as the chief lord, in reality governmental **authority** was fragmented so that individual lords and barons had considerable autonomy and largely administered their own **estates**. Power was exercised by the lords predominantly through jurisdiction and the holding of courts to settle disputes. This was backed by the ideological power of the church which owned a considerable amount of land, as did many bishops and abbots. The church also emphasized the divinely created and hierarchical nature of a **society** divided into three major **social classes**: those who prayed (clergy), those who fought (nobility), and those who worked (**peasants**).

A second definition of feudalism gives prominence to economic rather than juridical relations. Here the hierarchical relationship between lord and vassal is extended to include the socioeconomic obligations of peasants and serfs. For

Karl Marx, feudalism was primarily a mode of production, which, unlike **slavery** and **capitalism**, permitted some control over the means of production to peasants, especially through customary **rights**. The dynamic underlying feudalism was sustained through the exploitation of peasant tenants by lords, vis-à-vis the extraction of feudal rent, usually through labor services on the demesne (home farm). The level of feudal rent was determined by the relative military or political strength of the lords as compared to the serfs, who, at minimum, had to maintain family subsistence. This antagonism was often expressed in peasant uprisings.

Rather than the etymological question of whether and to what extent feudalism existed, the crucial question for many Marxists has concerned the transition from feudalism to capitalism and the role played by internal relationships of feudalism as opposed to the external impact of the **market** in accounting for the transition.

There have, however, been other more general definitions of feudalism which have attempted to fuse these definitions by accentuating the social, political, and economic criteria existing in the Middle Ages. Writing from a sociological perspective, Marc Bloc in *Feudalism* (1939–40) has argued that feudalism includes: a subject peasantry; widespread use of the service tenement (that is, the fief) instead of a salary; the supremacy of a class of specialized warriors; ties of obedience and protection which bind man to man and, within the warrior class, assume the distinctive form called vassalage; fragmentation of authority, leading inevitably to disorder; and the survival of other forms of association.

However, given the diversity of practices, types of social relationship, and customs characterizing this period, as well as the diversity of national and geographical differences and inflections, medieval historians, such as Elizabeth Brown in her essay "The Tyranny of a Construct: Feudalism and the Historians of Medieval Europe" (1974, *American Historical Review*), have argued that the varied use of the term renders it meaningless, and that its application to the medieval world is confusing and inaccurate. Nevertheless, given the existence of key characteristics and concepts associated with the Middle Ages, the term is still widely used in history and sociology.

STEVEN LOYAL

Feyerabend, Paul (1924–1994)

Born in Austria, Feyerabend initially studied philosophy at the University of Vienna and then at the London School of Economics under **Karl Popper**. He made an important, albeit iconoclastic, contribution to the philosophy of science. He initially followed Popper's philosophical outlook, but soon deviated from it, embracing instead the historical approach of **Thomas Samuel Kuhn** in his *Structure of Scientific Revolutions* (1962). From the early 1960s onwards Feyerabend devoted himself to exploring the relevance of the history of science for the philosophy of science. Feyerabend was a prolific author; his main contribution remains *Against Method; Outline of an Anarchistic Theory of Knowledge* (1975). He contributed to the debate surrounding falsificationism. This debate is summarized in *Criticism and the Growth of Knowledge* (1970), edited by Alan Musgrave and Imre Lakatos.

At the time, many philosophers, like Popper, tried to uncover the method common to all scientific practices and which distinguishes them from non-scientific activities. Feyerabend questioned the validity of this philosophical enterprise. The history of science shows that there is no single method common to all sciences: a detailed historical outlook demonstrates that scientists operate in very different ways. The consequences for critical rationalism were devastating. Feyerabend argued that not only did scientists not operate in a Popperian fashion, but also, if they had followed Popper's prescriptions, they would not have progressed to the same extent.

PATRICK BAERT

fieldwork

This is a broad type of **qualitative research** also sometimes known as **ethnography** or as observation and **participant observation**. Regardless of the label, the research is based upon collecting information through observation of how people live "real life." Fieldwork is a qualitative technique because the researcher is striving to obtain richly detailed information about the social situation they are interested in and will be using inductive methods of analysis to generalize from the **data** in order to develop conceptual ideas.

Fieldwork can be grouped into three types, each with an increasing level of involvement and contact between researchers and their subjects.

The observation of some ongoing social situation but without direct contact or involvement by the researcher. For example, I am interested in barbecue culture in the southern United States and decide to observe the interactions between customers and staff in Dizzy's Bar-B-Q.

With observant participation, the researcher begins to observe and collect information about some ongoing social situation that s/he is already involved in during their normal everyday activities. That is, the researcher has to "step outside himself/herself" and begin to look at the everyday social environment from a new point of view – that of the researcher – and begin to apply techniques of observation, note-taking, and analysis. For example, I am a regular at Dizzy's Bar-B-Q and decide to carry out a systematic observation of the interactions between the manager, employees, and customers. The advantages of observant participation are that researchers already have access and are their own source of insider knowledge. The disadvantage is that, unlike the observer coming from outside, one may find it difficult to switch to the role of a researcher. Things that have always been taken for granted may be important and can easily be overlooked.

Where the researcher immerses him/herself in a social environment that is new to him/her: for example, getting a job in Dizzy's in order to do research on southern barbecue culture. This immersion starts to give the researcher the same level of access and opportunity to gain insider knowledge but participant observation is more than that. It is the process of gradual internalization by the novice researcher of the cultural mores of the observed group that is the key to true participant observation and that makes it truly qualitative. The researcher is immersed in a social environment that is new to him/her, and the presumption is that they can be aware of how their own reactions and feelings alter as they become socialized. In effect, the researcher's *own* feelings, and how they change, become data.

A crucial decision the researcher must make is whether to reveal to those being observed that they are being researched – to carry out overt research – or to keep the research subjects unaware – to adopt a covert role. The advantages of a covert role include: (1) it may be impossible to observe some types of behavior or **groups** unless it is done covertly – when this is the case and the topic of research is sufficiently important, this can be a justification for covert research; (2) access, getting permission to carry out research, is not a problem if the research is covert – if no one knows you are doing it, obviously there is no problem; (3) people may behave differently if they know they are being researched – if they don't know they are being observed, the problem of reactivity is avoided.

There are a number of disadvantages to covert fieldwork, such as the practical difficulties and psychological costs of maintaining a front, but the main disadvantage of covert research is its questionable ethics. The research subjects are being deceived and their **privacy** may be invaded. Specifically, they obviously do not have the opportunity to give informed consent.

ROBERT MILLER

figurational sociology
– see **Norbert Elias**.

firms
This is the organization of production of large-scale enterprises, employing wage **labor** and financed by bank-credit **money**, and is a typical element of **capitalism**. This superseded various forms of domestic and household production in which work and the household are integrated, and production is financed entirely from saved **income**. There are three general theories of this development: (1) new institutional economics; (2) Weberian theories of **bureaucracy**; and (3) Marxist theories of exploitation.

(1) New institutional economics is an attempt to explain social **institutions** as the result of rational economic maximization. If, as economic theory maintains, the **market** is the most efficient form of organization, why, the Nobel prize-winner Ronald Coase (1910–) asked in 1935, do firms exist? Why did the large vertically integrated firm replace the putting-out system in which independent domestic producers were connected and coordinated by contractual market relations? Coase answered that firms exist when there is a cost to using the market mechanism. In a series of publications beginning with *Markets and Hierarchies* (1975), Oliver Williamson has elaborated this insight and integrated it with Alfred Chandler's *The Visible Hand* (1977). Market relations incur "transactions costs." For example, there may be only a few acceptable suppliers of raw material ("small numbers bargaining" and "asset specificity") which may enable them to take advantage of a producer ("opportunism with guile"). These market relations can be controlled only by costly surveillance and legal contracts, which may be more efficient to replace by internalizing them into an integrated hierarchy. The firm replaces production chains and **networks**, as command and **authority** replace contract. Types of firm, varying by levels of backward or forward integration, may be placed on a continuum: from vertically integrated bureaucratic firms through looser structures such as franchising or dealerships. Transactions-cost economics is used to explain the transnational firm (see

transnational **corporations**); hierarchy is less costly than transnational contracts with spatially and culturally distant suppliers. Several problems persist with this analysis owing to an inadequate treatment of "hierarchy" as a structure of **power**, rather than as merely a rationally devised cost-reducing mechanism. Where does power to choose an organizational form come from? Large firms are not simply an alternative to costly market exchange, but a means of superseding the market to make monopoly profits, as argued in Giovanni Arrighi, *The Long Twentieth Century* (1994).

(2) An alternative sociological explanation of the firm's role in producing economic **rationality** is provided by **Max Weber**. In *General Economic History* (1927 [trans. 1981]), he contrasts the rationality of the capitalist firm with traditional workshop production and booty capitalism. Rationality is seen as the capacity to calculate and is linked to the use of double-entry bookkeeping to strike a balance (rational capital accounting). This capacity is structurally dependent on the bureaucratic firm. Like the modern **state**, the capitalist firm is a corporate body that becomes structurally differentiated from household and **family**, which enables the removal of arbitrary nonrational decisionmaking based on traditional **norms** and family ties. This is attributed in part to the use of external credit finance and the need for the precise calculation of returns due to nonfamily, as opposed to a share in the common family pot. This occurred most clearly in the West; for example, in trading associations – such as the ship's company and the spreading of risk in *commenda* finance. This analysis remains relevant for modern debates. Is oriental family capitalism a viable alternative to the western model, or is it crony capitalism that impedes economic rationality? Similarly, is the joint-stock corporation, owned by outsiders, the most efficient form of organization? Weber appears to concur with modern economic analysis that the firm's separation from family ownership creates a competitive market in which a firm's market value, based on performance, is a means of monitoring the managerial bureaucracy.

Formal rationality (calculation of profitability) has a substantive basis in the **power** and control that comes with the complete appropriation of nonhuman means of production and the formally free **labor market**. Capitalists and their managers can freely manipulate the production process, and hire and fire workers at will to maximize returns to capital (see Marxist theory below). The firm is an agency for calculation, not (as in economic theory) an aggregation of calculating agents. Therefore, in contrast to the view of new institutional economics, the bureaucratic firm is not an alternative to the market, but the complementary location of economic rationality. For Weber it is a question of markets *and* hierarchies, not markets or hierarchies.

(3) For **Karl Marx**, the capitalist firm exists in order to dominate and exploit wage labor. In his critique of classical economics, Marx made a distinction between labor and labor-power. The worker does not sell a fixed unit of labor input for a wage in an equal exchange. Rather, the worker sells, or alienates, labor power – or productive potential – to be organized by the capitalist. Labor not only exchanges effort for reward, but submits to domination in the **labor process** which enables the capitalist to extract surplus value through exploitation. Thus, the form taken by the capitalist firm is the means by which labor is transformed into capital. In "What Do Bosses Do? The Origins and Functions of Hierarchy in Capitalist Production," in Anthony Giddens and David Held (eds.), *Classes, Power and Conflict* (1982), Stephen Marglin argues that the division of labor and the centralized hierarchical organization of the firm are not determined by **technology**, but by the need to create and accumulate capital. The bourgeoisie play its historic role by exploiting the workers in order to gain a competitive advantage and, in doing so, advances the means of production. In *Labor and Monopoly Capital* (1974), Harry Braverman distinguishes two central features of the capitalist firm: the social division of labor (**occupations**) and task specialization; and the separation of hand and brain through the **deskilling** and appropriation of the knowledge function in a management hierarchy. Both are determined by the need to maintain power and control in the firm.

In *Chaos and Governance in the Modern World System* (2000), Giovanni Arrighi and Beverly Silver identify three dominant historical forms of capitalist firm. Each is associated with successive capitalist state **hegemonies**: (1) Dutch and English joint-stock chartered companies in the seventeenth and eighteenth centuries; (2) British family-enterprise capitalism in the nineteenth century; and (3) American multidivisional, multi/transnational corporations from the early twentieth century. Each attempted global monopolization of the most profitable activities; each was dependent to a significant degree on external financing; and, in the development of a contradiction, each comes to depend increasingly on, but is ultimately subversive of, hegemonic state power.

(1) Joint-stock chartered companies had their origins in *commenda*-trading ship finance in Italian city-states such as Venice and Genoa during the sixteenth and seventeenth centuries. The English East India Company (1600) and Dutch East Indies Company (1602) were granted monopoly charters by their respective **states**, which were not quite powerful enough to monopolize the trade themselves. These firms were a hybridization of capital and coercion. They internalized their protection costs with their own armies; but externalized transactions costs by organizing production in long chains of domestic production. That is to say, unlike earlier empires, these company states did not only exact tribute and taxes, or impose direct controls on an **economy**, but also financed and coordinated indigenous workshop/communal production into a chain, as in the European putting-out system. A dynamic Indian cotton industry exported to Europe. But there were two contradictions; the increasing coercion costs were borne by the Company, and its repatriated profits helped to transform the British textile industry which opposed the East India Company's monopoly, which was consequently abolished in 1813.

(2) Nineteenth-century British family-enterprise capitalism was based on the protection of global networks, undertaken by imperial powers, in which domestic production became linked to exploitation of empires' primary products. European domestic production was transformed by mechanization, which facilitated the reorganization of proto-capitalist putting-out chains into factories that reduced transactions costs, and the subordination of the workers to a calculable regime of rigorous exploitation. As Adam Smith (1723–90), and later Marx and Engels, observed, the intense competition, unchecked by state-controlled monopolies, and reduction of capital costs through mechanical innovation led to falling profits and a deflationary spiral, culminating in the sharp down-turn of the business cycle.

(3) Modern corporations emerged at the top level of capitalist economies, most clearly in the United States, in the last quarter of the nineteenth century. They were large oligopolies or monopolies with bureaucratic management, separated to some degree from owners. From their inception, the American enterprises were multidivisional and multi/transnational. Two factors were involved. First, as Marx observed, incapable of raising enough capital for large-scale mass production **technology**, family capitalism was replaced by joint-stock corporations. Second, vertical integration of production chains in large corporations and horizontal combination in cartels were means of avoiding the earlier competition that had reduced profits to intolerable levels. Different paths were taken in dominant economies.

In Germany, as part of a state-building process, there was horizontal and vertical integration in association with the big banks. Families retained some power via large banks and the state **elite**. This path was also characteristic of Japanese capitalism.

Britain moved more slowly towards monopoly capitalism. A looser and more fragmented family-based structure persisted until after World War II. The City of London remained cosmopolitan and concerned with commercial and financial activity of the world as explained in Geoffrey Ingham, *Capitalism Divided?* (1984).

In the United States, the bureaucratic, multi-divisional, multi/transnational corporations based on mass production created a "second industrial revolution" (Chandler, *The Visible Hand*, 1977). Bureaucratic management first appeared in railroads and the telegraph, based on West Point military hierarchical command and control. It quickly spread to mass retail and mail order; Sears Roebuck was processing 100,000 orders per day by 1905. This was accompanied by the creation of the mass consumer by advertising and the "democratization of luxury," according to Weber. A populist political backlash against banking "money trusts" produced a departure from the path taken in Germany to the joint-stock system of diffused mass stock/share ownership. The "roaring Twenties" culminated in the Wall Street Crash (1929) and were followed by the ideological relegitimization of capitalism, as occurred after the early 21st-century technology stock crash and the corporate frauds in Enron, Worldcom, and other corporations. In the 1930s, this involved the professionalization (see **profession[s]**) of management in **Taylorism** and **scientific management**. Managers were portrayed as the technically expert guardians of a "peoples' capitalism," in which dispersed shareholding separated ownership from (management) control.

These vertically integrated enterprises gained competitive advantage by greater control and calculation of speed of throughput, based on a further reduction of transactions costs and an extension of control over labor by assembly-line technology. They were multinational from the outset. By 1914, American direct investment abroad, at 7 percent of Gross National Product, was as high as in the 1960s; and, by the late 1920s, Ford and General Motors had firms in Britain and Europe.

However, this mode of capitalist **regulation**, based on monopoly mass production and mass consumption could be limited, as **John Maynard Keynes** realized, by a lack of "effective demand." The underconsumption/overproduction crises of the 1930s were overcome by the post World-War-II "warfare–welfare state," based upon state expenditure and the United States' bid for global dominance in order to capture foreign markets. For example, the United States government supported the European Common Market on condition that there was no discrimination against US multinationals.

As before, the successful capitalist organizational innovation was emulated with varying degrees of success by competitors with similar results. There was an intensification of competition; but innovators of earlier developments in industrial organization may become locked in to a path dependency that inhibits the adoption of the next innovation. The French were quick learners and, under state direction, systematically set about Americanizing its industry. In contrast, the fate of the British automobile industry is testimony to continued difficulties with the adoption of large-scale organization and mass production.

By the 1980s, it was argued, for example in Michael Piore and Charles Sabel, *The Second Industrial Divide* (1984), that the dominance of American "dinosaur" corporations was being overcome by new forms of organization: first, by flexible specialization and informal networks/alliances between small and medium-sized firms in local industrial districts; and, second, by the challenge of East Asian forms of industrial organization, especially Japanese "relational contracting" and "just-in-time" methods of vertically disintegrated production chains. American corporations responded to this competition by cutting costs with the "downsizing" and "delayering" of management and labor, in order to increase profitability and "stockholder value." By the late 1990s, the large multi/transnational American enterprise had survived as the dominant form of organization.

The modern capitalist enterprise is the site of a struggle for its economic surplus. Reliance on external finance from either banks or the stock market and the growth of managerial bureaucracy have rendered this conflict more complex than the conflict between capital and wage labor in the nineteenth-century family-owned firm, as outlined by Marx. This question of "ownership and control" or "corporate governance" was first addressed in the stock-market-based American economy by Adolf Berle and Gardner Means, in *The Modern Corporation and Private Property* (1932). They asserted that stock ownership in almost half the largest American nonfinancial corporations was so dispersed that no "dominant" ownership interest was evident and, therefore, they must be controlled by the managers. Coming after the American Senate's Pujo Committee's (1913) critical, populist "money-trust" interpretation of US capitalism, and the Wall Street Crash, *The Modern Corporation and Private Property* conveyed a clear ideological message. "Managerialism" maintained that managers were neutral technocratic guardians of "peoples' capitalism" in enterprises in which there was no inherent conflict of interest due to the widespread share ownership.

Marxist analyses of twentieth-century capitalism have been influenced by Rudolph Hilferding's *Finance Capital* (1910 [trans. 1981]), which analyzed the dominance of large banks in the German economy. Until recently, the "finance capital" interpretation was seen simply as an alternative to Berle and Means's "bourgeois managerialism." However, they are referring to two different patterns of corporate financing – bank lending and stock markets – and their effects on corporate governance.

Research in the 1970s lent support to the "managerialist" account of the American economy. Echoing Keynes's "euthanasia of the stockholder," John Kenneth Galbraith (1908–2006) argued in his *New Industrial State* (1967) that the modern corporation was controlled by a managerial "technostructure." Unlike owners with a direct financial stake – that is, families, stockholders, banks, and other financial interests – managers did not pursue profit maximization, but, rather, growth, sales, and **prestige** in order to consolidate their **power** and security.

During this period of American "managed" monopoly capitalism after World War II, financial and creditor interests were less powerful. During the 1970s, however, a combination of falling profits, **inflation**, global recession, and a collapse of the stock market led to a reassertion of financial interests and a rebalancing of power between creditors, stockholders, managers, and workers. A new coalition of corporate managers, investment-fund managers, and stockholders aimed to "unlock shareholder value." This new neoliberal settlement reestablished the dominance of financial interests as outlined in Geoffrey Ingham, *The Nature of Money* (2004), and Neil Fligstein, *The Architecture of Markets* (2001). In a wave of mergers, acquisitions, and hostile take-overs during the 1980s, managers' interests were aligned with those of the stockholders with the use of stock options as managerial remuneration. Unsatisfactory performance brought the threat of a hostile takeover or of a "leveraged buyout" (LBO) by a new class of financial entrepreneurs such as Kohlberg Kravis Roberts. The resulting private companies fell under the financial discipline of the new owners and, with its management holding stock options, they released the "free cash flow" to shareholders. According to Doug Henwood in *Wall Street* (1997), "An LBO is a form of class struggle."

In *The Political Determinants of Corporate Governance* (2003), Mark Roe has extended this analysis and argued that the Anglo-American type of large corporation based on the separation of diffuse stockholder ownership and management control is incompatible with social democratic political systems based on high levels of employment security and welfare. In these circumstances, management and workers both benefit from the maximization of growth and employment rather than profits. Unless the interests of shareholders and management can be aligned as they were in the United States and Britain in the 1980s, then, shareholders will find it difficult to impose the changes that might maximize "shareholder value." Strong social democracies, such as those of continental Europe, with high levels of welfare, job security, and takeover controls encourage management to define their interests in terms of security and the avoidance of **risk** and radical change. In order to resist this alliance of management and workers, ownership is more concentrated in the hands of banks and families – as in France, Germany, and Italy. On the basis of empirical evidence, Roe identifies two patterns of corporate governance and social democratic **politics** in the fifteen wealthiest nations during the post-World-War-II period: (1) diffuse ownership and low social democracy – for example, the United States, Britain; and (2) concentrated ownership and high social democracy – for example, Germany, Italy, France. **Globalization** appears to be changing the latter pattern. The deregulation of capital markets is leading to the erosion of concentrated bank and family ownership in national economies and stronger shareholder interests in the form of global investment funds. With the intensification of global competition, shareholder interests exert pressure to replace employment security and social welfare with economic "flexible" labor market policies.   GEOFFREY INGHAM

First Nations

These are peoples asserting a common cultural and linguistic heritage and descent from common ancestors who were the original and enduring inhabitants of circumscribed territories later absorbed into modern **states**. Most broadly conceived, they constitute what is often called the Fourth World and include all of the aboriginal populations of the Americas and of Australia; the Inuit and Aleut peoples of the American and Eurasian Arctic; the transhumant pastoralists of Scandinavia, Russia, and the Balkans; minority populations of the insular Pacific such as the Japanese Ainu and natives of Hawaii; the Hmong of China and Laos; peoples of Africa such as the Pygmies, the Nuer, and the San; and many others.

More narrowly conceived, they are those Native American peoples formerly referred to as "bands" that the government of Canada officially recognizes as being entitled in principle to self-government. The term First Nations emerged in Canada during the later 1970s and its use is still far more common there than elsewhere. Native American bands began to adopt it as a self-designation in the course of asserting their right to be recognized as one of the "founding nations" of Canada, together with the English and the French. They effectively established it as a self-designation at the First Nations' Constitutional Congress, convened by the now-defunct National Indian Brotherhood in 1980. There are currently more than 600 First Nations in Canada and their numbers are likely to grow as smaller and more scattered populations win governmental recognition in future decades. They do not, however, and probably will never include the Metis, a large population descending from unions between French colonists and Native Americans that is concentrated especially in the southeast of Canada and has episodically but enduringly cultivated a distinctive **nationalism** of its own. The situation of the Metis nevertheless points to one of the most controversial aspects of the very concept of "First Nations," whether broadly or narrowly conceived – that of what degree of cultural and genealogical "purity" is necessary, and what other criteria are sufficient, to establish membership.

JAMES D. FAUBION

flexible specialization

This term was introduced in the 1980s to redescribe a familiar type of **labor process** and to identify a new type of economic strategy in response to the crisis of Fordism. It refers to the use of flexible machinery by skilled or craft labor to produce a wide range of products to exploit economies of scope. It is contrasted with Fordist mass production, which involves the use of dedicated machinery and plant by semi-skilled labor to produce long runs of standardized products to exploit economies of scale. It would be wrong to see these as the only types of labor process. There are many other ways to organize this, depending both on the nature of the products and on the dominant social relations.

Michael Piore and Charles Sabel argued in *The Second Industrial Divide: Possibilities for Prosperity* (1984) that the growing displacement of craft production by mass production in the late nineteenth century was more the result of a paradigm shift produced by social and political struggles than to inherent technical superiority. They suggested that the crisis of Fordist mass production was an opportunity to revive craft production in the form of flexible specialization. And they also claimed that success in this regard would usher in a democratic republic of craft workers in control of their working lives, for flexible specialization reskills and empowers workers so that they were no longer simple appendages to the machine. This combination of advocacy and analysis has been a marked feature of the flexible-specialization literature and makes it vital to distinguish between: (1) the theoretical and historical claims made for flexible specialization as an **ideal type** of production **organization**; and (2) the normative-political claims made for it as an idealized type of production organization that should therefore be adopted.

Analysts and advocates of flexible specialization normally identify three variants: (1) a small-firm variant exemplified in the industrial districts characteristic of the Third Italy, an industrial region that was initially created in the 1950s and 1960s to foster co-operation between small, craft-based **firms**; (2) a West German model based on internal decentralization of large firms; and (3) the Japanese just-in-time production model based on large firms' sponsorship of complex, multi-layered subcontracting **networks.** In each case, productivity and innovation depend on collective efficiency and economies of scope in the use of flexible machinery and flexible labor. In the first variant, a key role is played by local authorities and consortia of small firms. The second and third variants, in contrast, involve the delegation of financial, marketing, and research services to a combination of semi-autonomous internal business units and cooperative external suppliers.

These examples all involve "offensive flexibility," that is, forms of flexibility that promote high-quality production and high productivity. There are also "defensive" forms that involve hire-and-fire labor markets, flexi-wages (including downward flexibility), and a focus on cost reductions. While offensive flexibility may prove sustainable in the medium term, defensive flexibility is more likely to be a short-term solution.

BOB JESSOP

focus group

This research method is designed to generate **data** on group beliefs and group **norms** by capturing intra-group **interaction** in specially composed **groups** (a range of differently composed groups is normally required), where the researcher seeks to facilitate and record that interaction. Although methods akin to focus groups were used by academic sociologists researching the persuasiveness of United States government World War II propaganda, focus group methods are a crossover method from commercial market research. However, as Michael Bloor, Jane Frankland, Michelle Thomas, and Kate Robson have pointed out in *Focus Groups in Social Research* (2001), there is now a divergence between market research and academic social research in their uses of focus groups. The former primarily uses focus groups as a locale for conducting group **interviews**. In the latter, rather than conduct a question-and-answer session with the group, the facilitator seeks to generate intra-group discussions which are illustrative of group norms. A focus group should also be distinguished from a delphi group, a panel of experts which may be repeatedly consulted or reconvened to derive authoritative consensus statements of group belief or policy.

Facilitators typically seek to generate a general discussion by asking the group to perform a set task, or focusing exercise. A common type of task is a ranking exercise, where the group will be asked to look at a series of statements and then rank them in order of correctness or importance. Fictitious vignettes may also be presented and the group may be asked to discuss what action the central character in the vignette should undertake next. Analysis of focus groups is normally based on the study of transcripts of audio-recordings. Email communication has permitted research using virtual focus groups, where the facilitator/moderator operates a closed email distribution list. Such groups can have many more participants than conventional focus groups and, of course, have no attendance and/or transcription costs.

Focus groups are used more frequently as an ancillary method than as the main research instrument. They are often used in **pilot studies** for larger projects to collect data on group norms and on everyday language use, in order to assist in planning the next phase of the investigation. Focus groups are also often used at the close of projects to collect feedback from respondents on preliminary research findings.

Whether or not it is preferable for focus group members to be known to each other has been a matter of controversy. It has been argued that, by recruiting from pre-existing friendship groups, work groups, and so on, focus group researchers may be able to tap into group interactions that approximate to naturally occurring data, which might otherwise be only slowly accumulated by an ethnographer. However, in research on sensitive topics there is a real danger of over-disclosure by animated participants.

The fashionableness of focus group methods had looked set to wane due to difficulties with recruitment and analysis. But the development of virtual focus groups has ensured their continuing popularity.   MICK BLOOR AND FIONA WOOD

folk religion
– see **religion**.

folkways
– see **norm(s)**.

food

The economic, social, and symbolic significance of food is a highly complex interdisciplinary topic of study which sociology, understandably, has addressed in only some aspects, and then unevenly. The diversity and complexity of the topic has resulted in its analysis through many different theoretical lenses – of **political economy, structuralism, feminism, poststructuralism, actor network theory**, conventions theory – and via historical, institutional, and developmental approaches.

For most people throughout history, food production has involved local, small-scale organization for household **consumption**, with the implication that what was eaten was seasonal and limited by geography and climate. **Industrialization** required, and supplied the means, to transform food production. Urban populations could not supply sufficient of their own raw materials, impelling changes in agricultural techniques and processes and new means of distribution. The

logic of industrial production also spread to food as a product. Now a substantial part of food production is organized on a global basis, by large corporations, operating internationally, to grow, process, and distribute foodstuffs. **Rationalization** of production results in less employment (see **work and employment**) in agriculture (a feature of all societies undergoing **modernization**), larger production units, and greater commodification of food provision.

Contemporary agro-food studies encompass issues associated with rural and economic sociology in western societal contexts. Interest in the organization of rural **communities** has declined with the reduced size of rural populations and their lesser dependence on employment in agriculture. Instead attention has focused on the organization of the food industries, particularly the feature of organization into a chain of successive, non co-located, commercial episodes of production and exchange, of farming, processing, and retailing, each with intermediating processes of transportation and storage. Explaining the restructuring of these connections, which themselves vary for different types of produce, has generated competing theoretical frameworks of various provenance, including world system theory, **regulation theory**, commodity system and commodity chain analysis, a systems-of-provision approach, and later hybrid accounts paying greater attention to the impact of local and cultural diversity on food production.

One consequence of the increasingly global span of the food chain is the greater visibility of the unevenly developed supply of adequate food. The highly secure, varied supply to the rich countries contrasts markedly with continued shortages and famines in other parts of the world. And even within the most **affluent societies**, though malnutrition as a consequence of **poverty** has mostly disappeared, there remain significant inequalities in access to diets of good-quality and nutritious foodstuffs.

Food provision and preparation remains a key activity of households even in the industrial and **post-industrial societies**, because most eating occurs within the home and requires much domestic **labor** of shopping, preparation, cooking, and cleaning. Most work of this kind is done everywhere by women, part of the unequal division of labor which defines gender **inequalities**. Such work is integral to the reproduction and maintenance of family relations and family life, symbolizing belonging and care, and a source of emotional attachment and conflict.

Eating is a fundamentally social activity; in general people have not preferred, and do not prefer, to eat alone. Households are defined for official purposes as those who eat together, and in societies where people live predominantly in elementary or nuclear **families**, the family meal has been seen as a central temporal and social organizing principle of **everyday life**. The extent to which it may be in decline has attracted much attention. Meals away from home, in restaurants, canteens, and other homes are also social events, ones which increase with industrialization and the growth of consumer services. The meal is a major social **institution**. All social **groups** have **norms** and conventions governing the social relations of commensality, concerning who should eat together and what foods are appropriate to which gatherings. These norms are partly definitive of relationships of intimate and distant **kinship**, **friendship**, and **interaction** with strangers. Norms of hospitality vary greatly between societies, ethnic groups, and **social classes**.

What is considered fit and appropriate to eat varies between **cultures** and many societies have complex culinary conventions which comprise cuisines to which nations, ethnic groups, and social classes have strong symbolic attachments. Also, more elaborate cuisines develop in places with particular hierarchical types of **social structure**. For example, the French royal court not only ate differently from the peasantry but also was central to the refinement of table manners which **Norbert Elias** in *The Civilizing Process* (1939 [trans. 2000]) considered a key element of the western civilizing process. Cuisine types are now marketing devices for restaurants and cookery books, and although isolating precisely the defining characteristics of French, Persian, or Chinese food may be difficult, national and regional ways of selecting and preparing preferred ingredients persist, and indeed are often increasingly valued. The symbolic aspects of food have been most powerfully analyzed by anthropologists, but cultural sociology and sociology of **consumption** has increasingly become involved. Food preferences are made to reflect and indicate differences in class distinction and aesthetic taste, to express ethnic group membership, and also personal **identity**.

Many eating events are now more informal than before. As foods become more highly processed and require less preparation – as with "fast food" and convenience foods – greater opportunities exist for people to adopt individualized habits of consumption. Meals are now less regular, uniform, and predictable. Also, it has become harder to justify what to eat and perhaps more necessary to do so in the face of unprecedented variety. This has gone along with perhaps some greater anxiety about food, symbolized, for example, by epidemics of anorexia and obesity. Anxieties are also apparent as a sense of **risk** arising from the technologies of food processing – additives, genetic modification, and so on. This has had an impact through food scares and crises of consumer **trust** which have in turn led to renewed effort being devoted by political authorities to legislation and regulation and restructuring of the activities of market actors. These are also increasingly prompted by **social movements** promoting new types of diet, for instance vegetarianism; new production standards as with organic foods; and styles of eating, for example the Slow Food Movement. People, either individually or through consumer associations, often with the collaboration of niche producers, attempt to modify and regulate their food consumption in accordance with their ethical and political principles, their attitudes towards body maintenance, and their aesthetic preferences.

ALAN WARDE

Fordism
– see **post-Fordism**.

formal organizations
– see **bureaucracy**.

Foucault, Michel (1926–1984)

Foucault was born in Poitiers, France, and died at the age of fifty-seven from an AIDS-related illness. He studied both psychology and philosophy at the École Normale Supérieure and went on to teach psychology in a department of philosophy while also working as a researcher in a hospital in Paris. The latter posting provided the inspiration for his first book, *Mental Illness and Psychology* (1954 [trans. 1976]). Foucault continued this practice of simultaneously teaching and holding practical postings throughout his career, which allowed him to write *Madness and Insanity in the Age of Reason* (1961 [trans. 1965]), *Birth of the Clinic: An Archaeology of Medical Perception* (1963 [trans. 1973]), *Discipline and Punish: The Birth of the Prison* (1975 [trans. 1977]), and the volumes that constituted *The History of Sexuality*, such as *The History of Sexuality Volume One: An Introduction* (1976 [trans. 1978]); volume II, *The Use of Pleasure* (1984 [trans. 1985]), and *The Care of the Self* (1984 [trans. 1986]).

Foucault's intellectual investigations originated with an inquiry into the ways in which scientific discourse shapes the boundaries between, and relationship of, good and evil, safety and danger, and **health** and illness. He observed that the development of microtechnologies of surveillance paved the way for **society** to act upon these ideas in order to control the behavior of individuals and diffuse **norms** among large **groups**. This creates what he termed an environment of panopticism, so titled after Jeremy Bentham's (1748–1832) eponymous prison in which inmates were subject to a regime of constant and complete surveillance. Ultimately, it was therefore not simply discourse, but the entire infrastructure of the rational, scientific face of governance, that was implicated in the dual processes of individuation and massing. In the twentieth century, these processes culminated in the installation of authoritarian regimes responsible for some of the most grievous atrocities humankind has visited upon itself.

Equally crucial to Foucault's thought was the tenet that science infuses social life with particularly powerful behavioral norms, therefore equipping individuals with technologies of the **self** that cause them to internalize social norms through which they become self-policing. Thus, even the most private acts become moments during which people reproduce cultural understandings of the normal or the decent, and the abnormal or the indecent. **Technology** permits those dangerous individuals who are not "self-disciplining" to be disciplined by social institutions and the **state**. Hospitals, prisons, and insane asylums therefore function both to reinforce norms for those who might stray and to discipline the recalcitrant. Their logic and impact extends beyond their own walls creating a carceral society in which discipline is imposed on all individuals privy to public spectacles of punishment.

Through his study of the natural and human sciences, Foucault was able to reveal the capillary nature of **power**. So, in his example, students submit willingly to examinations, disciplining themselves physically and mentally, even when they have no expectation of immediate, coercive punishment from a centralized **authority**. The implications of the capillary nature of **power** also allowed Foucault to reconceive the study of **politics**, and more specifically government, by indicating that it is the channels through which power flows, and the methods by which it is exercised, that ultimately constitute power. **Governmentality** is a set of successful techniques whose ultimate achievement is control and political coordination of specific populations. In this view, the state is only the most readily apparent articulation of the larger process of governmentalization.

Because Foucault was committed to demonstrating the manner in which the sciences are not abstracted academic pursuits, but rather important and unrecognized channels of power, his substantive and methodological projects are inextricably linked. Foucault's most significant methodological injunction is that meaning must be sought by examining evidence not simply *qua* evidence, but rather as composed of organic artifacts laden with meaning beyond that explicitly stated by their authors. In the case of historical knowledge, we must be cognizant that history is a product as much of the present in which it is unearthed as the past that buried it. Meaning is revealed via an intricate process of what he initially termed archeology but later came to be known as genealogy. The idea of a legitimate authority of truth is debunked insofar as knowledge and those who seek it are each simultaneously the objects and tools of power. This renders the concept of academic disciplines one in which scientists discipline and are in turn disciplined by the subjects of their inquiries.

Foucault himself rejected the claim that he was a structuralist, though many find his approach to show the influence of structuralist logic. Scholars of Foucault have also engaged in a heated debate about the intellectual coherence of his corpus. Some have argued that, contained within the entirety of his work, is an almost Rousseauian set of distinct and sometimes inconsistent strains of thought: one liberal and the other radical. The liberal Foucault views power more neutrally than does his more radically skeptical alter ego. To critics, this also indicates an important inconsistency in his understanding of power. Alternatively, the disaggregation of power from domination has the effect of redistributing the pejorative connotations others have associated with power. This makes room for a more normatively neutral and less fatalistic vision of human interaction, which both rescues Foucault from internal contradiction and opens avenues for the study of how individuals exercise power in ways that resist domination.

Foucault attributed to his own work influences that included Friedrich Nietzsche, **Max Weber**, **Theodor Adorno**, and **Max Horkheimer**. In turn his legacy has shaped the contributions of innumerable social scientists, notable among them

Pierre Bourdieu, Anthony Giddens, Nancy Fraser, and Edward Said. His intellectual presence is felt throughout the social sciences and remains both particularly strong and controversial in the fields of cultural geography, discourse analysis, criminology, and the sociology of medicine.

ELIZABETH F. COHEN

Frank, André Gunder (1929–2005)

Born in Berlin and educated at the University of Chicago where he obtained his PhD in Economics in 1957 for his dissertation on Soviet agriculture, Frank went to Latin America in 1962 where he taught at the University of Brasilia. In 1965 he moved to the National Autonomous University of Mexico, and in 1968 he was a professor of sociology at the University of Chile, where he became involved in the social reforms of the Salvador Allende administration, and, after the military coup in 1973, he escaped to Europe where he became Visiting Research Fellow at the Max-Planck Institute in Starnberg, Germany, from 1974 to 1978. In the years leading up to his retirement in 1994, he held many professorial appointments in Britain, Belgium, France, Germany, the Netherlands, and the United States.

Frank published extensively but his principal contribution was to the emergence of development theory in which he was a critic of modernization. He argued that development was not a unilinear or inevitable process from tradition to modernity, because the developed world caused the underdevelopment of peripheral economies and societies. These critical assessments of the impact of capitalism in Latin America appeared in Capitalism and Underdevelopment in Latin America (1969) and Dependent Accumulation and Underdevelopment (1978). He was critical of the western bias in economic history and historical sociology, and in ReOrient: Global Economy in the Asian Age (1998) he sought to re-assess the independent growth of Asian economies before the age of western imperialism.

BRYAN S. TURNER

Frankfurt School

Although there was no "School" in the sense of any agreed body of theory and research, the term Frankfurt School is associated with theorists of the Institut für Sozialforschung (Institute of Social Research), founded in Frankfurt in 1923 and at first directed by an orthodox Marxist, Carl Grünberg (1861–1940). In 1930 Max Horkheimer assumed control and promoted interdisciplinary research guided by a broadly Marxist social philosophy. The Institute attracted a diverse group of heterodox Marxist theorists, including Theodor Adorno, Walter Benjamin, Herbert Marcuse, Fredrick Pollock, Franz Neumann (1900–54), and Leo Lowenthal (1900–93), who, between the 1930s and 1960s, developed distinctive critical analysis of western capitalism and culture, drawing insights from many sources, including Georg Wilhelm Friedrich Hegel, Immanuel Kant (1724–1804), Friedrich Nietzsche (1844–1900), Max Weber, Georg Simmel, Sigmund Freud, and Jewish philosophy. In 1937 Horkheimer expounded the concept of critical theory, as a programmatic statement of his philosophy, which was to become one of the most influential social theories of the twentieth century. In opposition to "contemplative theory," or detached observation of the world, Critical Theory would seek engagement with radical sources of critique and emancipatory practice, building into its concepts the possibility of a better society.

However, by the 1930s the world had changed dramatically from that represented in the classical Marxist critique of capitalism. World War I had demonstrated the capacity for mass destruction created by technological warfare and unsettled belief in progress though the development of technology and science. The failure of revolutionary movements in western Europe and the success of the Russian Revolution created a new global polarization compounded by the consequent fission of the left into democratic socialist and communist parties, and the dominance of fascism over much of Europe. Further, the increasing complexity of capitalist economies, the emergence of new mass communications media (see mass media and communications), and the increasing role of the state in the economy meant that the Marxist notions of class formation and class-consciousness needed rethinking. In particular these developments made the possibility of successful proletarian revolution uncertain. However, the "death of the proletariat" motif in Critical Theory should not be exaggerated; in 1941 Horkheimer wrote the optimistic revolutionary essay "The Authoritarian State," invoking the "trailblazing" tradition of workers' councils going back to 1871, which was imminently to sweep aside the authoritarian state. Even so, in Dämmerung (1934), Horkheimer had suggested that there were "subtle apparatuses" (education and mass media) working to protect capitalism against revolutionary consciousness. Indeed, in a world dominated by totalitarianism (Stalinist and fascist) on the one hand, and the mass culture industry on the other, any belief in the redemptive potential of class struggle appeared naive.

Any revolutionary cultural or political impulse risked being incorporated and becoming itself an instrument of domination. Thus, according to Adorno, as the practical possibilities of emancipation are closed off, "philosophy returns to itself." **Karl Marx**'s early works such as *Hegel's Philosophy of Right* had talked about the utopian core of Hegelian philosophy being "realized," that is instantiated, through the real-life struggles of the working class. But by the 1940s the realization of this "moment" of history had been missed and the urgent task of Critical Theory was to keep alive the possibility of critical thought at all, by developing perspectives that critique the world from the standpoint of a future emancipated society. One such influential and controversial critique was that of the popular culture industry epitomized in big band jazz and the Hollywood cult of stardom. As **culture** was produced for a mass market, the commodity form entered the very process of creation or composition of works of art, thereby undermining their aesthetic form. This development created an uncritical and soporific culture reconciled to the status quo that lacked the glimpse offered by aesthetic experience into the possibility of a non-alienated existence.

Unlike orthodox Marxism, Critical Theory was receptive to Freudianism. A distinctive feature of Frankfurt research was the combination of class analysis with analysis of the psychodynamics of the **family** and **authority**. This theme came to the fore after 1933, when the Institute was forced to leave Nazi Germany, and functioned in exile in Geneva, then New York, and finally California. Marxism and **psychoanalysis** were combined with empirical **social psychology** to generate a new theory of authoritarianism (the **authoritarian personality**) and critical reflection on the fate and direction of western **modernity**. This combined several themes of Frankfurt thinking, in particular the economic and cultural logics of late capitalism, the psychosocial processes of authority and family, and their relationship to mass culture and **consumption**.

In *Dialectic of Enlightenment* (1944 [trans. 1973]), Horkheimer and Adorno located the origins of domination deep in human history, at the point at which scientific calculating reason was deployed to overcome the forces of nature, which were often symbolized in **myths**. In the process of enlightenment, on which cultural modernity is based, instrumental calculating reason (*Verstand*) gained dominance over objective reason (*Vernunft*), which could pose questions about the **rationality** of social **institutions**. The consequence of this was that ultimate questions about the worth of human societies were deemed "irrational," and all **values** (whether fascist or liberal, for example) became matters of personal decision rather than objective judgment. The Culture Industry contributes further to this degeneration of public life.

By 1953 the Institute was able to move back to the University of Frankfurt in Germany, where Adorno assumed a co-directorship with Horkheimer in 1955. He died in 1969 and Horkheimer in 1973. The Institute of Social Research continued but what was known as the "Frankfurt School" did not. Critical Theory has continued as an increasingly diverse body of theory with less direct connection with Frankfurt. The most significant figure in this phase was **Jürgen Habermas**, who studied philosophy and **sociology** at the Institute in the 1960s and returned to a chair at the University of Frankfurt in 1982. Over four decades of work, Habermas has drawn on virtually the whole corpus of **social theory** and philosophy to develop a comprehensive Critical Theory that remains critical of the commercial and technocratic colonization of the **public sphere** yet locates new sources of rational critique and emancipatory practice. In particular he has sought to defend aspects of the Enlightenment tradition associated with modernity that he considers to be constructive and emancipatory from what he sees as their premature rejection by an earlier Critical Theory.

LARRY RAY

Frazier, E. Franklin (1894–1962)

In 1948 Edward Franklin Frazier was elected President of the American Sociological Association, at a time when the United States had not begun to deal with its **racism**. The high regard in which academic sociology held this black man was founded on Frazier's broad learning and pathbreaking scholarship, which led to eight books, of which two are classics, *The Negro Family in the United States* (1939) and *Black Bourgeoisie* (1957). Both were years ahead of their time in sociology's attempt to understand the strengths of the black **family** and the weaknesses of the black bourgeoisie.

After attending Baltimore schools, Frazier was a student at Howard University (BA, 1916), after which he taught mathematics, history, English, and French at several schools, including Tuskegee Institute. His interest in sociology dates to graduate work at Clark University (MA, 1919), then to further study at the New York School of Social Work (1920–1) and the University of Copenhagen (1921–2). Frazier then taught at Morehouse College, Atlanta University, and the Atlanta School of Social Work. He was forced to flee Atlanta when white racists were provoked by his 1927 essay "The Pathology of Race Prejudice." He then pursued doctoral studies in sociology at the University of Chicago (PhD, 1931).

After teaching at Fisk University (1929–34), Frazier began his long tenure in sociology at Howard University, from which he retired in 1959. An academic at heart, Franklin always put his learning to use in public service and race **politics**.   CHARLES LEMERT

Freud, Sigmund (1856–1939)

The founder of **psychoanalysis**, Freud was born in Freiberg, a part of the Austro-Hungarian Empire. A studious child, he undertook medical training in 1881, and subsequently pursued his clinical interest in hysteria with a colleague, Josef Breuer (1842–1925). *Studies in Hysteria* (1895 [trans. 1957]), the book that emerged from the researches of Freud and Breuer, developed a path-breaking theory, one that underscored the central role of sexual memories in the formation of mental disturbance. The work laid a skeletal structure for the theoretical development of psychoanalysis, which emerged in 1900 with the publication of Freud's *The Interpretation of Dreams* (1900 [trans. 1958]).

Therapeutically, Freudian psychoanalysis is perhaps best known as the "talking cure" – a slogan used to describe the magical power of **language** to relieve mental suffering. Theoretically, psychoanalysis is rooted in a set of dynamic models relating to the human subject's articulations of desire. Freud's originality is to be found in his analysis of the unconscious as repressed. In his celebrated essay "The Unconscious" (1914) in *The Standard Edition of the Complete Works of Sigmund Freud*, vol. XIV, he argued that the individual's self-understanding is not immediately available to itself, that the human subject is itself split, torn between consciousness of **self** and repressed desire. In discussing human subjectivity, Freud divides the psyche into the unconscious, preconscious, and conscious. The preconscious can be thought of as a vast storehouse of memories, most of which may be recalled at will. In contrast, unconscious memories and desires are cut off, or buried, from consciousness.

We become the **identities** we are, in Freud's view, because we have inside us buried identifications with people we have previously loved (and also hated), most usually our parents – and particularly the mother. The breakup of our primary emotional tie to the maternal **body** is, for Freud, the founding moment not only of individuation and differentiation, but also of sexual and gender difference. Loss and gender affinity are directly linked in Freud's theory to the Oedipus complex, the psyche's entry into received social meanings. For Freud, the Oedipus complex is the nodal point of sexual development, the symbolic internalization of a lost, tabooed object of desire. In the act of internalizing the loss of the pre-Oedipal mother, the infant's relationship with the father (or, more accurately, symbolic representations of paternal **power**) becomes crucial for the consolidation of both selfhood and gender identity.

Freud's writings show the ego not to be master in its own home. The unconscious, repression, libido, **narcissism**: these are the core dimensions of Freud's psychoanalytic dislocation of the subject. Freud's dislocation of the subject reemerges in various guises in contemporary sociological theory. In the critical theory of the **Frankfurt School**, it is part of an attempt to rethink the powerlessness of identity in the face of the objectifying aspects of contemporary science, **technology**, and **bureaucracy**. For **Jürgen Habermas**, it is a series of claims about the nature of distorted intersubjective and public communication as a means of theorizing repressive **ideologies**. For **Jacques Lacan**, it is a means for tracing imaginary constructions of self-concealment, as linked to the idea that language is what founds the repressed unconscious.   ANTHONY ELLIOTT

friendship

This concept played an important role in ancient philosophy, where the virtues of loyalty and **trust** were seen to be pre-eminently displayed in relations between friends. Friendship designated a social relation that is neither instrumental nor selfish. In contemporary philosophy, there has been a renewed interest in the ethical nature of friendship, for example in L. Blum, *Friendship, Altruism and Morality* (1980).

In *The Care of the Self* (1984 [trans. 1986]), **Michel Foucault** examined the Roman conception of friendship between a man and a woman, and between men and boys. In this classical conception, a manly affection for a young boy could exist through life, and was not subject to the vagaries of aging. In Homeric Greek, according to E. Benveniste in *Indo-European Language and Society* (1969 [trans. 1973]), *philos* (friend) was closely connected with *aidos* (reverence or respect), indicating that a bond of friendship was defined by a strong sense of obligation. There was also an obligation of friendship towards a "guest-stranger" (*xenos*). Although in contemporary society, friendship implies an intimate, close, and private, but not sexual, relationship, in Greek society the word *philia* covered a range of relationships, including passionate and erotic ones. Aristotle distinguished between friends of utility, pleasure, and virtue, and, in the latter, friendship involved the whole person. In the *Nichomachean Ethics*, Aristotle claimed that friendship as a universal **emotion** forms the basis of the *polis*. Plato also saw friendship as the basis of harmony and consensus, and hence necessary to **politics**. Although friendship can therefore be treated as quintessentially ethical, political philosophy has been primarily interested in the relationship between friendship and government. In *Redeeming American Political Thought*, J. N. Shklar, in the chapter on "A Friendship" (1998), discussed the complex relations between politics and friendship, noting that there are obvious tensions between loyalty to a friend and to government.

With some important exceptions, such as Ray Pahl's *On Friendship* (2000), the topic has been somewhat neglected in sociology. When friendship is analyzed by sociologists, it is typically in the context of the study of **privacy** and **intimacy**. For example, **Barrington Moore**, in his study of *Privacy* (1984), examined the ambiguities of friendship in classical society. Aspects of friendship have also been analyzed in **exchange theory**, in, for example, George Homans's *Social Behavior: Its Elementary Forms* (1961) and **Peter M. Blau**'s *Exchange and Power in Social Life* (1964). In the perspective of exchange theory, people make and keep friends because they are useful or rewarding. These theories implicitly accepted Aristotle's definition of friendships of utility, thereby admitting that by the 1960s friendship had become a commodity. The corrosion of friendship in modern society is an implicit topic of recent research on **emotions**. In a **consumer society**, where emotional **work** (for example of air-hostesses) involves the production of fleeting intimacy for cash, friendliness is commercialized. For example, in *Postemotional Society* (1997), S. Mestrovic argues that synthetic, quasi-emotions become the basis for manipulation in public life. The commercialization of friendship represents a form of **alienation**.

In summary, friendship has been important in philosophy but not in **sociology**. This neglect is curious given the fact that sociology is literally the study (*logos*) of companionship or friendship (*socius*), pointing once more to the notion that friendship is the ultimate root of both the polity and the **community**. In Latin, the idea of *civis* is best translated as "fellow-citizen" or companion.

BRYAN S. TURNER

Fromm, Erich (1900–1980)

A psychoanalyst and philosopher, Fromm was for a time associated with the **Frankfurt School,** though they split acrimoniously in the early 1940s. Fromm developed a theory of the cultural roots of **personality**, organized around the ideas of freedom and autonomy. The scope of freedom in human **societies** emerges historically and appears most strongly with modern **individualism**, but living with freedom is difficult and people seek means of escape in ways that are set during **socialization**. These include, first, **authoritarianism**, of which the most extreme forms are masochism and sadism, although milder versions are widespread. Second, destructiveness, which can be outwardly directed through brutality or inwardly directed in, for example, drug **addiction**, alcoholism, and passive entertainment. Third, automaton conformity escapes from freedom through submission to social hierarchies or by following the dictates of mass cultural forms of **fashion** and style. This is the dominant form of personality in modern society. In these strategies for escaping freedom, people become alienated from themselves. Finally, there is potentially the productive and loving personality type in which freedom is accepted – this would be developed in a humanistic socialist society. In later work Fromm brought together psychoanalytical insight and evidence from physical anthropology to develop the concept of a "necrophilous personality" (such as Adolf Hitler [1889–1945] and Joseph Stalin [1879–1953]), passionate to transform life into death. Major works include *Escape from Freedom* (1941), *Man for Himself* (1947), *The Art of Loving* (1956), *The Sane Society* (1955), and *Anatomy of Human Destructiveness* (1973).   LARRY RAY

functional theory of stratification

At the heart of the functional theory of stratification is the argument that structured social **inequality**, that is the differential allocation of social rewards and facilities, enhances social efficacy and **social integration**. This is both its (seldom realized) "social purpose" and "social cause"; stratification, in turn, has become universal because it engenders "evolutionary advantage."

We owe the classical formulation of allocative functionalism to Kingsley Davis and Wilbert Moore. In "Some Principles of Stratification," in the *American Sociological Review* (1945), they argued that in all complex **societies** the functional importance of social positions and **social roles** vary. Some positions are more strategically important than others, and they require special and rare talents and skills. Because such talents and skills are scarce, and because they typically require long and costly training, there have to be incentives for their display and cultivation. Differential rewards inherent in stratification systems provide such incentives for cultivating knowledge, skills, and talents. Similarly, the optimal allocation of the best candidates to the most important jobs and continuous motivation of incumbents to perform well require differential rewards. Societies that fail to develop such a system of functional stratification lose efficacy, and they are in a position of disadvantage in developmental competition.

Thus there are a number of preconditions of socially functional stratification – and a number of criticisms directed at functional arguments:

(1) The reward structure has to reflect accurately the social consensus as to which roles and positions are more, and which less, strategically important. Critics point out that this assumption is unrealistic.

(2) Rewards should effectively attract the best incumbents and motivate them in their performance. According to critics, incompetent **elites** prove that this condition is seldom met.

(3) The recruitment process has to be open and merit-based. In functionally stratified systems there is no place for inheritance, ascription, and closure. This claim produced the most serious bone of contention between functionalists and their critics. While Davis and Moore recognized that inheritance and ascription persist, and it weakens the functionality of stratification, they nevertheless disagreed with those critics who argued that functional theory was unrealistic. The critics also question the functionalist explanation of the universality of stratification. Since functional principles are similar in most societies, one would expect to find similarities in stratification systems, at least among contemporary societies at a similar level of development. Yet one of the striking features of modern societies has been a broad diversity of social hierarchies – a fact that contradicts allocative functionalism.

These criticisms resulted in a gradual eclipse of allocative functionalism. In the 1960s–1970s a more sophisticated Parsonian version of integrative **functionalism** gained a currency among sociologists. **Talcott Parsons** suggested that functionality of stratification systems consisted in strengthening social integration around core **values**. Differential rewards, according to Parsons, contribute to such integration by rewarding commitments to central societal values. Stratification also contributes to effective value **socialization**, because it increases the transparency of the core value standards according to which social rewards are allocated. Thus the system of structured inequalities strengthens value integration and aids value socialization.   JAN PAKULSKI

functionalism

Functionalists argue that **society** should be understood as a system of interdependent parts. The different parts of social life depend on each other and fulfill functions contributing to social order and its **reproduction**.

Functionalism can be traced to **Émile Durkheim** and **Herbert Spencer**. The anthropologists **Bronislaw Malinowski** and Alfred Radcliffe-Brown (1881–1955) drew on Durkheim to develop a distinctive form of functionalist anthropology in the early twentieth century. Functionalism came to prominence as a school of **sociology** in the United States in the 1950s. It was associated with **Talcott Parsons** and **Robert Merton**, although they differed in approach. From the 1960s, functionalism was subjected to major criticism and few sociologists defended it until the 1980s when Jeffrey Alexander identified a convergence with functionalism by erstwhile critics such as **Jürgen Habermas**, **Anthony Giddens**, and **Margaret Archer**.

Functionalism departs from the traditional logic of causal argument where a cause should precede its consequences. Functionalists identify a causal loop or feedback linking cause and effect. When an anthropologist asks "why do the Hopi dance for rain?" a functionalist considers the consequence of the dance and notes that it maintains group **solidarity**. The functionalist concludes that if the rain dance did not have this positive function it would not be reproduced.

Functionalists are aware of illegitimate teleology, arguing that the explanation of the origins of a practice should be distinguished from that of its reproduction. Radcliffe-Brown distinguished sharply between diachronic and synchronic analysis, between the analysis of change in a system and the analysis of the interaction among parts of a system at a moment in time. The latter was the proper domain of functional analysis.

Malinowski argued that all societies have to meet some universal and interconnected requirements – as well as group solidarity, economic subsistence, **social control**, sexual reproduction, **socialization** and **education** of new **generations**, and the management of sickness and death – and that these can form the basis for comparison. Parsons was influenced by Malinowski, but believed his identification of functions to be ad hoc, arguing that functions must be theoretically specified in a general framework.

For Parsons, there are four different interconnected systems bearing upon human action: the human organism, the individual **personality**, the social system, and the cultural system. The behavioral organism is concerned with the human **body** as the primary vehicle for engaging the physical environment; that of personality corresponds to the individual actor viewed as a system. It includes conscious and unconscious **motivations** (or need dispositions). Actors respond not only to positive rewards, but also to internalized feelings of guilt, anxiety, and the need for approval. The social system is a system of positions and roles organized by expectations and maintained by sanctions; the culture system refers to the **symbols** and meanings that are drawn upon by actors in the pursuit of their personal projects.

Parsons's primary focus is the social system. He proposed four functional imperatives necessary to its constitution and operation (the A-G-I-L scheme). *Adaptation* is concerned with relationships to external **environments** and the utilization of resources in the pursuit of goals. *Goal attainment* is concerned with the direction of systems towards collective goals. *Integration* refers to the maintenance of coordinated relationships among the parts of the system, while *latency*, or pattern-maintenance, describes the symbolic order in terms of mutually reinforcing meanings and typifications.

The A-G-I-L scheme also allows the classification of societies in terms of the level of structural **differentiation** or institutional specialization around functions – for example, the extent to which political **institutions** are separated from economic institutions, or economic institutions separated from the household. The idea of the "superiority" of higher over lower stages of developmental complexity carries the implication of evolutionary change, where better-adapted forms are realized out of the deficiencies of "lesser" forms. **Modernity** – more substantively,

the United States, which Parsons called the new "lead" society – is the culminating stage of development. This seemed to critics to be an extreme form of teleology, one that revealed an ideological **bias** inherent in a scheme that Parsons had presented as the "indispensable logical framework in which we describe and think about the phenomena of action" (*The Structure of Social Action*, 1937: 733).

While Parsons regarded functionalism as part of a unified general theory, Merton saw it as an adjunct to the development of empirically grounded theories of the middle range. His argument, originally in 1949 in "Manifest and Latent Functions" and reprinted in *Social Theory and Social Structure* (1968), was taken to be a veiled criticism of Parsons, especially the latter's emphasis on integration. Merton identified three unsatisfactory postulates of functionalism: the *functional unity* (or integration) of a society, *universal functionalism*, and *indispensability*.

According to Merton, it may be that some nonliterate societies show a high degree of integration, but it is illegitimate to assume this would pertain to all societies. It is also possible that what is functional for society, considered as a whole, does not prove functional for individuals or for some **groups** within the society, and vice versa. This suggests that, alongside the concept of function, it is necessary to have a concept of *dysfunction* – that is, where the consequences of an item are negative for some individuals or groups. For Merton, persisting forms have a net balance of functional consequences, either for society considered as a whole or for sub-groups. Finally, it is necessary to distinguish between functional prerequisites – preconditions functionally necessary for a society – and the social forms that fulfill those prerequisites. While the former are indispensable, it is not required that particular forms meet those functions. There are always alternative ways of meeting any particular function. Each of Merton's qualifications was designed to transform the postulates into variables.

As a form of methodological holism, functionalism was criticized by methodological individualists, such as **George Caspar Homans** or **Peter M. Blau,** working within the exchange-theory perspective. Functionalism was also criticized by conflict theorists such as **John Rex** and **Ralph Dahrendorf,** for its neglect of **power**, though the criticism was more aptly applied to Parsons and his definition of functions in terms of the generalized collectivity. Merton's more empirical approach had asked "functional for whom?" **David**

Lockwood sought to reformulate functionalism in order to allow a concept of system contradiction. **Alvin Gouldner** argued that functionalism was an ideological expression of welfare **capitalism**.   JOHN HOLMWOOD

fundamentalism

Combining both political and religious radicalism, fundamentalism constitutes a distinct, specific, modern **social movement** and **ideology**, promulgating adherence to a strict and intense interpretation of a scripture or holy text. Although it is a reaction against the secular dimensions of **modernity**, it cannot be regarded as a traditional movement. It developed in the late nineteenth century, first in the United States, and then spread, especially in the last decade of the twentieth century, to a variety of Protestant, Jewish, and Muslim **communities** around the world.

Among such movements, it is important to consider the American Council of Christian Churches, founded in 1941, and the more recent Christian Coalition founded in 1989, the Gush Emunim (Block of the Faithful) and various ultra-orthodox movements (both non-Zionist and anti-Zionist) in Israel from the 1970s onwards, and many similar movements in the Muslim world which developed in the nineteenth century, blossoming in the last decades of the twentieth century. The most successful among these movements was the Iranian Revolution (1978–9) which was led by the Ayatollah Khomeini (1900–89).

With the exception of movements in the United States and more recently Europe, most of these fundamentalist movements developed in those states which were established, like the Kemalist government of Mustafa Kemal Ataturk (1881–1938) in Turkey, after World War I, or in the colonial-imperial states, which were constituted by the various national movements after World War II. Social **groups** which were dislocated from their respective traditional settings, and drawn into modern frameworks, formed a central component of these movements. These social groups often advanced within a modern context – for example, the experience of social **progress** among many Muslim women in Iran, Turkey, or Egypt – but they also felt culturally dislocated in these settings and often alienated from them. In the Islamic movements, the confrontation with secular modernity constituted a central component of these movements.

In all these societies and historical settings, the fundamentalist groups constitute what we may call "Jacobin movements," that is totalistic or totalitarian movements. These totalitarian tendencies were rooted in the Jacobin tradition that emerged in the French Revolution of 1789, which promulgated the total reconstitution of man. Jacobinism, named after the Jacobin club, was a society of deputies, which acted to concentrate **power** and which believed that the truth of its vision of society was sufficient to guarantee its **authority**. Jacobinism can also be seen in the high level of political mobilization in the period between the two world wars, which represented a major challenge to the pluralistic constitutional regimes of the **democracies**. The tendency towards Jacobinism can also be seen in various communist regimes.

Therefore, contrary to the widely accepted wisdom of many interpretations, these fundamentalist movements are not traditional or antimodern **religions** but distinctively sectarian-utopian, modern, Jacobin movements which promulgate an ideological and essentialist conception of **tradition**.

Fundamentalist ideologies, movements, and regimes share, with other Jacobin developments such as **Communism** and utopian sects, the tendency to promulgate a strong vision or gospel of salvation, which is combined with a total worldview, the implementation of which is to take place in this world and in the present.

The institutionalization of such totalitarian visions entails the establishment, through the powerful mobilization to political action of an existing social order, of collective and individual **symbols** of **identity**, and the constitution of sharp social boundaries between the pure inside and the polluted outside. Such political actions often involve the sanctification of **violence** and terror, oriented above all against both internal and external evil forces and enemies. From the fundamentalist perspective, the enemy is typically seen to be rooted in the secular dynamics of modern society, that is the West, the United States, or Israel.

This modern Jacobin mobilization of fundamentalist movements and regimes is often combined, paradoxically, with anti-modern, or at least an anti-liberal, ideology. This contradictory combination of the modern and the traditional is most clearly expressed in the fundamentalist attitude to women. On the one hand most of these movements promulgate a strong patriarchal, anti-feminist attitude, segregating women and men, and placing far-reaching restrictions on the former. At the same time, and in stark contrast to traditional regimes, these modern fundamentalist movements mobilize women in the **public sphere** through demonstrations, paramilitary organizations, and religious associations, and in the central political arena through elections to parliament.

Although they can often appear to be seemingly traditional, in fact, these movements are in some paradoxical ways anti-traditional. They negate the living traditions of popular and folk religions, with all their inevitable cultural complexity, changeability, and heterogeneity, in their respective societies. Instead they uphold a highly ideological and essentialist conception of tradition as an overarching ideological principle couched in a modern idiom, with a strong emphasis on mobilization, participation, and the organizational dimensions of modern political programs. These decidedly modern components of fundamentalist movements and regimes can also be seen in some aspects of their institutionalization as regimes, namely in the continuation, albeit with strong Jacobin components, of modern **institutions** such as political constitutions. The *majilis* parliament in Iran following the Revolution basically had no roots in traditional Islam, and the elections to the parliament are illustrations of this. Thus these fundamentalist movements do not overtly and consciously promulgate modernity, but rather attempt to appropriate modernity on their own terms.

The approach of these movements to tradition is also manifest in their **attitudes** to the more conservative religious leaders and establishments, as well as to the more popular manifestations of tradition. They also typically involve some degree of distance and separation beween young **generations** of fundamentalists and their traditionalist parents or grandparents, who come to be regarded as a cohort who are or were not pure enough in their **lifestyles** and **everyday life**.

Although these fundamentalist movements and regimes appear to have been politically successful in many respects, they have also faced some distinctively modern problems, which have attended their institutionalization. These problems are in fact manifestations of the basic tensions which are the legacy of their Jacobinism and their acceptance of the basic institutional frameworks of modernity.   s. n. eisenstadt

G

Gadamer, Hans-Georg (1900–2002)

Hans-Georg Gadamer made a substantial contribution to hermeneutic philosophy. Born in 1900 in Marburg, he studied under Martin Heidegger and also attended the lectures of Edmund Husserl. Gadamer's professional life was spent mainly in Germany, although after his retirement from his Chair in Philosophy at Heidelberg in 1968 he took up various visiting posts abroad. In the course of the 1970s sociologists became increasingly interested in **hermeneutics**, hence there was a growing interest in Gadamer's writings. Gadamer's main book is *Truth and Method* (1960 [trans. 1975]). In this book, Gadamer distanced himself from the emphasis on method in nineteenth-century hermeneutics; like Heidegger, Gadamer heralded the "ontological turn." He criticized philosophers of the **Enlightenment** for failing to appreciate the pivotal role of **tradition** in knowledge acquisition. He saw understanding as a dialogical process in which we draw on our presuppositions to make sense of other people, but these presuppositions are themselves affected by this encounter. Gadamer talked about a "fusion of horizons" to hint at the dialogical nature of the interaction between the reader and the text, or the observer and observed. Gadamer applied his hermeneutic approach to medicine and medical practice in *The Enigma of Health* (1996 [trans. 1993]).

In the late 1960s, **Jürgen Habermas** engaged in a debate with Gadamer. For Habermas, Gadamer was right to point out the limitations of **positivism**, but his plea for hermeneutic understanding lacks a critical edge. Gadamer's reply was that Habermas failed to acknowledge that his own critical standpoint is itself embedded in tradition. Later, Richard Rorty's argument for an edifying philosophy, beyond **epistemology**, drew on Gadamer's dialogical model. Gadamer also inspired Charles Taylor's philosophy of **social sciences**, in particular its reflexive component.

PATRICK BAERT

game theory

This is a mathematical tool for modeling **social conflict** and cooperation among two or more players, where payoffs for a given strategy depend in part on the strategies of other players. This strategic interdependence can be represented as a payoff matrix (the "normal form" for simultaneous moves by the players) or as a decision tree (the "extensive form" for sequential moves).

Strategic interdependence allows for two types of games. In zero-sum games, a gain for one player is always a loss for the partner, which precludes the possibility of cooperation for mutual gain. In positive-sum games, everyone can gain through cooperation, defined as a strategy combination that is Pareto-efficient (see **Vilfredo Pareto**) (any improvement for some would come at someone else's expense). Nevertheless, cooperation may fail for two reasons: the fear of being "suckered" by the partner and the temptation to cheat. These failures can be avoided in two ways, through enforceable contracts that preclude "cheating" ("cooperative games") and through collusion (in "non-cooperative games").

A cooperative game consists of a set of players and a value function that assigns a value to every possible coalition of players based on the total amount of transferable utility the players of that coalition can distribute. Sociologists such as F. J. Bienenstock and P. Bonacich have used the cooperative-game paradigm to study the effects of network structure on power **inequality** in social exchange ("The Core as a Solution to Negatively Connected Exchange Networks," 1992, *Social Networks*).

Non-cooperative games are played without the benefit of an enforceable contract, hence the opportunity for cheating. These games are generally more interesting to sociologists because they can be used to model social dilemmas – games in which rational self-interest can lead players into an outcome that is not Pareto-efficient. In a social dilemma, mutual cooperation is Pareto-efficient yet may be undermined by the temptation to cheat or by the fear of being cheated or by both. In the game of Stag Hunt, the problem is "fear," and in the game of Chicken the problem is "greed." The problem is most challenging when both fear and greed are present – as in the celebrated game of Prisoner's Dilemma.

Although the games vary widely, the theory of games provides a solution concept that can be universally applied. In *Non-Cooperative Games* (1950), John F. Nash showed that every game contains at least one Nash equilibrium – an outcome where every strategy is a "best reply" to the other strategies played; hence, no player has an incentive to change strategy unilaterally. The Nash equilibrium predicts mutual defection in Prisoner's Dilemma, unilateral defection in Chicken, and either mutual cooperation or mutual defection in Stag Hunt. Nash also identifies a Pareto-deficient mixed-strategy equilibrium in Chicken and Stag Hunt. A mixed strategy chooses randomly from all available behavioral choices following a particular probability distribution (for example, "cooperate .45, defect .55"). Knowing that a configuration is a Nash equilibrium means that if this state should obtain, the system will remain there forever, even in the absence of an enforceable contract. However, even when Nash can identify a unique equilibrium, this does not tell us whether this state will ever be reached, or with what probability, or what will happen if the equilibrium should be perturbed. Nor does Nash equilibrium explain social stability among interacting agents who are changing strategies individually, yet the population distribution remains constant, as in a homeostatic equilibrium.

Both Chicken and Stag Hunt have three equilibria, and game theory cannot tell us which one will obtain. Worse yet, if these games are repeated by players who care about future payoffs in an ongoing relation, the number of Nash equilibria becomes indefinitely large. When games have multiple equilibria, Nash cannot tell us which will obtain or with what relative probability. Nor can Nash tell us much about the dynamics by which a population of players can move from one equilibrium to another. Game theorists have responded to the problem of equilibrium selection by proposing procedures that can winnow the set of possible solutions to include only those that are risk-dominant (players follow a conservative strategy that earns the best payoff they can guarantee for themselves), payoff-dominant (every other equilibrium is less preferred by at least

one player), and subgame-perfect (all nodes along the equilibrium path can be reached in the extensive form). However, these equilibrium selection methods are theoretically arbitrary (for example, there is no a-priori basis for payoff-dominant or risk-dominant behavior) and they often disagree about which equilibrium should be selected (for example, in Stag Hunt, payoff dominance and subgame perfection identify mutual cooperation while risk dominance points to mutual defection).

These limitations, including concerns about the cognitive demands of forward-looking **rationality**, have led game theorists to explore backward-looking alternatives based on evolution and learning. Evolutionary game theory allows for the possibility that players rely on cognitive shortcuts such as imitation, heuristic decision making, stochastic learning, Bayesian updating, best reply with finite memory, and local optimization. Evolutionary models test the ability of conditionally cooperative strategies to survive and reproduce in competition with predators (John Maynard-Smith, *Evolution and the Theory of Games*, 1982). Biological models have also been extended to military and economic games in which losers are physically eliminated or bankrupted and to cultural games in which winners are more likely to be imitated (Robert Axelrod, *The Evolution of Cooperation*, 1984; Jürgen Weibull, *Evolutionary Game Theory*, 1995).

Evolutionary game theory is based on the consequentialist assumption that strategic choices can be explained by the associated payoffs. The payoffs that matter are those that have already occurred, not those that a forward-looking optimizer might expect to obtain in the future. Repetition, not calculation, brings the future to bear on the present, by recycling the lessons of the past. Through repeated exposure to a recurrent problem, the consequences of alternative courses of action can be iteratively explored, by the individual actor or by a population. Iterative search relaxes the highly restrictive cognitive assumptions in analytical game theory, thereby extending applications to social and cultural adaptation by highly routinized actors, such as bureaucratic **organizations** or boundedly rational individuals whose behavior is based on heuristics, habits, or **norms**. The game **paradigm** obtains its theoretical leverage by modeling the social fabric as a matrix of interconnected agents guided by outcomes of their **interaction** with others, where the actions of each depend on, as well as shape, the behavior of those with whom they are linked. Viewed with that lens, game theory appears to be especially relevant to sociology, the social science that has been most reluctant to embrace it.

MICHAEL MACY AND ARNOUT VAN DE RIJT

gangs

This term refers to a group of individuals collectively engaging in social activities that are often deviant or criminal. While the term has been used to label a wide range of criminal or deviant groups, **criminology** has more narrowly focused on gangs that reflect the findings of the first systematic study, *The Gang* (1927), by Frederic M. Thrasher. According to Thrasher, gangs, usually composed of male adolescents, form in urban areas and function as a primary group based on strong loyalty and a clear territorial focus.

Thrasher's colleagues at the **Chicago School** account for a number of theories aimed at explaining gang-based deviant behavior. **E. H. Sutherland** in his textbook *Principles of Criminology* (1939) developed the notion of "differential association" which explains criminal activity in the immediate social context of various **subcultures** in society. Criminal activities are thus peer-group-induced. Albert Cohen's *Delinquent Boys* (1955) describes gangs as working-class **subcultures** engaging in a deliberate rejection of middle-class **values**. Drawing on **Robert Merton**'s functionalist approach to **crime**, Cohen ascribed the formation of delinquent subcultures such as gangs to the frustration of working-class youths over their lack of **social status** and **mobility**.

The work of another sociologist associated with the Chicago School, **Howard S. Becker**, was instrumental in the foundation of **labeling theory**. According to Becker, in *Outsiders* (1963), **deviance** is a relational, socially constructed label through which powerful sections of **society** exercise control: "deviancy is *not* a quality of the act a person commits, but rather a consequence of the application by others of rules and sanctions to an 'offender.'"

The significance of **social class** in the formation of gangs is highlighted further by studies in New Criminology, closely associated with the **Birmingham Centre for Contemporary Cultural Studies**. New Criminology portrays deviant gang behavior as a deliberate act of resistance by working-class youths to the existing social and economic order. Ian Taylor in *Football Mad* (1972), for instance, explains the rise of hooligan gangs as a result of excessive **social control** and the **inequalities** of postwar **capitalism** in Britain. However, these approaches have been criticized for insufficiently accounting for the victims of gang-related activities, which, as in the case of inner-city street gangs and hooligans, are often found among other disadvantaged sections of society. Moreover, in light of the deterritorialization of social **identities** and subcultures, the strong emphasis on local working-class culture seems increasingly difficult to maintain.

The sociological study of gangs also raises important methodological questions. As gangs naturally shield at least part of their activities from the public gaze, **participant observation** is the only qualitative method promising detailed **data** on gangs. Such **qualitative research**, however, involves immediate dangers and ethical pitfalls for the researcher (by becoming a victim or complicit to criminal behavior) and the researched (through the exposure of their activities and possible legal repercussions). With their entry into the field, researchers are also forced to take sides in relation to the gang's struggle, a theme pursued by Becker in *Whose Side are we on?* (1967) and Ned Polsky in *Hustlers, Beats and Others* (1967).

CORNEL SANDVOSS

Gans, Herbert J. (1927–)

Born in Cologne, Germany, Gans migrated to the United States in 1940, and gained his MA in social science at the University of Chicago, and his PhD in city planning from the University of Pennsylvania. His research reflects interests in both sociology and urban planning. He was a professor of sociology at Columbia University, and 78th President of the American Sociological Association in 1988.

He has made significant contributions to sociological debates about **poverty** in *The War against the Poor. The Underclass and Antipoverty Policy* (1995). In *More Equality* (1973), he challenged the cynical view that the poor are valuable clients for professional groups such as social workers, family lawyers and doctors, and the owners of pawn shops and brothels. There is also an economic argument that the poor are useful in prolonging the life of certain commodities such as day-old bread or second-hand clothing. In arguing for more **equality**, Gans argued that much dirty work should be done by automation and that higher wages could be given to the poor for dirty but necessary work without damage to the **economy**.

Gans also contributed to the development of urban sociology in *The Urban Villagers. Group and Class in the Life of Italian-Americans* (1962) and *The Levittowners: Ways of Life and Politics in a New Suburban Community* (1982), and to the sociology of the media and **culture** in *Popular Culture and High Culture* (1974), *Deciding What's News* (1980), and *Democracy and the News* (2003). Gans's basic argument is that news is top-down, favoring high-ranking government officials over low-ranking officials, government agencies over opposition **groups**, and organized groups over unorganized individual citizens. The concentration of the ownership of the news and the pressure to increase profitability compromises the independence of journalism and corrodes audience confidence. Finally, Gans has been an important critical observer of American life in *Making Sense of America* (1999). Finally, he published a collection of essays in honor of **David Riesman** in *On the Making of Americans* (1979).

BRYAN S. TURNER

Garfinkel, Harold (1917–)

The originator of **ethnomethodology**, Harold Garfinkel has made original contributions to how sociologists understand the production of **social action**. Along with **George Herbert Mead**, John Dewey (1859–1952), and **Erving Goffman**, Garfinkel was one of the initiators of the shift from definitions of social action in terms of subjective consciousness and existential meaning to definitions in terms of enacted social practices. Ethnomethodology, a neologism Garfinkel coined, refers to the methods people use to produce conduct in local settings. As demonstrated by essays in his two major books, *Studies in Ethnomethodology* (1967) and *Ethnomethodology's Program* (2002), Garfinkel investigates the accomplishment of social action in minute and pains-taking detail. His investigations reveal a realm of what he terms seen but unnoticed practices that contribute to the constitution of local action. Garfinkel is also famous – many would say notorious – for his convoluted narrative voice. Once one masters his style, Garfinkel appears to be profoundly self-conscious about the precision of his prose. However, even his staunchest supporters admit to being daunted by their first encounters with his works. All stylistic matters notwithstanding, Garfinkel's contributions remain fertile ground for new developments, and his writings on ethnomethodology will influence **sociological theory** for many years to come.

Garfinkel was born in 1917 and raised in Newark, New Jersey, where his father owned a small furniture business. He graduated from the University of Newark (unaccredited then but now a large campus of Rutgers University) in 1939. He completed his master's thesis in sociology at the University of North Carolina in 1942. After serving

in the military for several years, Garfinkel enrolled at Harvard University from which he received his PhD under the nominal supervision of **Talcott Parsons** in 1952. Garfinkel, however, was already an original thinker and he was inclined to follow a non-Parsonian position from the start. His main influences were social phenomenologists, including two internationally well-known scholars, Aron Gurwitsch (1901–73) and **Alfred Schutz**, who provided Garfinkel with intellectual support. In 1954 Garfinkel took a position at the University of California, Los Angeles (UCLA), and this became his base for the rest of his career.

Garfinkel has never acted as a solitary, inimitable thinker in the manner of **Georg Simmel** or Goffman. At UCLA he has been blessed with successive cohorts of loyal, gifted graduate students, including many who are now senior scholars of distinction in their own right. This list includes **Aaron Cicourel**, **Harvey Sacks**, David Sudnow, and Emmanuel Schegloff. Sacks and Schegloff are well known for **conversational analysis**, which is a semiautonomous offshoot of Garfinkel's original program. Over the half-century since Garfinkel moved to UCLA, ethnomethodology has grown into an international movement with centers in Great Britain and elsewhere, as well as across many departments of sociology in the United States, including Boston University and the University of California, Santa Barbara. Garfinkel's writing style demands clarification and it has been Garfinkel's good fortune to have fine exegetes such as John Heritage in *Garfinkel and Ethnomethodology* (1984), and Anne Rawls.

IRA COHEN

gay rights movement

– see **social movements**.

gay studies

The study of the **culture**, history, and character of gay **sexuality** and gay **identity**, this is associated with the **social movement** for gay and lesbian liberation. The gay rights movement was influenced by the riots that followed the police raid on the Stonewall Inn in New York in 1969, when the New York Gay Liberation Front was formed. The Front rejected the conventional **social roles** and gender definitions of mainstream or "straight" **society**. The first Gay March took place in 1970 and was quickly imitated in other countries, from European capitals to Sydney, Australia. The self-recognition of homosexuality came to be known as "coming out," an expression taken from the American notion of "coming out of the closet" or rejecting the **stigma** of hidden or concealed sexual identity. This process of coming out was given its definitive expression in **Eve Kosofsky Sedgwick**'s *Epistemology of the Closet* (1990).

Gay studies eventually emerged in university curricula where they were modeled on **lesbian studies**, **gender studies**, and **women's studies**. There are many journals related to gay culture and experience, such as *GLQ – A Journal of Lesbian and Gay Studies* (1994–), *Sexualities* (1998–), and *Journal of Homosexuality*. The diversity and depth of journals, conferences, study programs, and **institutions** relating to gay studies were explored in Ken Plummer's *Modern Homosexualities* (1992). The development of gay **politics** in Britain from the nineteenth century to modern times was described by Jeffrey Weeks in *Coming Out* (1977). In 1991 the Center for Lesbian and Gay Studies was founded in the Graduate Center of the City University of New York to study the cultural and political issues that are important for lesbian, gay, bisexual, and transgender individuals.

Professional mainstream sociology has somewhat neglected the study of human sexuality. There are of course some classic illustrations of research on same-sex behavior and practice, such as Laud Humphrey's *Tearoom Trade* (1975). There has also been some research on sex re-assignment surgery, for example Frank Lewin's *Transsexualism in Society* (1995), but we know relatively little about the long-term health-care needs of transsexuals. Sociology became heavily involved in the study of the HIV/AIDS epidemic mainly through the study of **networks**. Because gay men often have friends and lovers who have predeceased them, they are often in a chronic state of grieving or "bereavement overload" and may experience "survivor guilt." These traumatic experiences have contributed to a variety of self-help movements and have generated a new gay consciousness, as documented in, for example, R. A. Isay's *Becoming Gay: The Journey of Self-acceptance* (1996) and E. Rofes's *Reviving the Tribe: Regenerating Gay Men's Sexuality and Culture in the Ongoing Epidemic* (1996).

In British sociology, the work of Ken Plummer on narratives such as *Telling Sexual Stories* (1995) has represented an innovative approach to human sexuality. The *Handbook of Lesbian & Gay Studies* (2002), edited by Diane Richardson and Steven Seidman, is a valuable guide to this diverse field of research. Jeffrey Weeks also produced a series of influential studies, such as *Coming Out*, *Sex Politics and Society* (1990), and *Against Nature* (1991).

Some gay activists have, however, come to the conclusion that gay studies was merely a strategy for co-opting a more radical aspect of gay politics, thereby making gayness a dimension of more conventional sexual identity. In addition, the gay movement came to be stigmatized once more by the HIV/AIDS epidemic in the 1980s. In response to these changing circumstances, **queer theory** emerged, in which a stable homosexual identity was rejected in favor of the notion that gay was really an epistemological critique of stable categorization, and hence queer theory adopted elements of **postmodernism** and **postcolonial theory**. One example of these developments is *Queer Theory / Sociology* edited by Steven Seidman (1996). The work of **Michel Foucault** played a major part in rethinking sexual identity as an aspect of the struggle over the relationships between **power** and knowledge in different historical settings. Foucault demonstrated that homosexuality was a building block of male **friendship** in classical Greece in *The Use of Pleasure* (1984 [trans. 1985]). Foucault, who died of an AIDS-related illness in 1984, became an icon of politics relating to men's **health** and his role has been defended and celebrated by David Halpern in *Saint Foucault. Towards a Gay Hagiography* (1995).

In **sociology**, queer theory and Gay Studies have influenced the ways in which **masculinity** as a sexual identity is conceptualized. In particular, **social constructionism** rejected **essentialism** and claimed that, while homosexual feelings or practices had always existed, "the homosexual" was a construct of a particular time and place. These approaches rejected the conventional psychological view that homosexuality was an illness or a form of social **deviance**. Gay studies are therefore concerned to reject these negative labels and to explore the complex historical manifestation of homosexual identity, culture, and institutions.

BRYAN S. TURNER

Geertz, Clifford (1926–)

Among the most eminent American anthropologists of the latter half of the twentieth century, Clifford Geertz has made many contributions to diverse areas of anthropology and to the **social sciences** more broadly. These contributions include the **ethnography** of Java, Bali, and Morocco, and, as much outside anthropology as within it, to the theorization of **religion**, of **politics**, and of **culture** itself. Though a student of **Talcott Parsons**, he gradually moved away from a merely functionalist treatment of culture and, by the middle 1960s, had begun to piece together, from the thought of **Max Weber**, Ruth Benedict, **Bronislaw Malinowski**, Gilbert Ryle, Suzanne Langer, and **Ludwig Wittgenstein**, among others, an "interpretive anthropology" of "the native's point of view" that cast culture as a loosely integrated totality of institutionally and perspectivally specific systems providing models of and models for the world and life within it, whose constituent **symbols** acquire their meanings from the contextually specific occasions of their use. Geertz followed many of his American predecessors in presuming the diverse expressions of culture to be sufficiently bounded for any one of them to be readily distinguished from the next. He shared their tendency to privilege the broadest collective themes of a culture over their more idiosyncratic refractions. He departed from them, however, in arguing that the key to human nature lay not in the cross-culturally universal but, instead, in cross-cultural diversity itself. His major works include *Peddlers and Princes* (1963), *Islam Observed* (1968), *Negara* (1980), and two volumes of essays, *The Interpretation of Cultures* (1973) and *Local Knowledge* (1983).

JAMES D. FAUBION

Gehlen, Arnold (1904–1976)

A member of the Nazi movement in Germany, Gehlen was a philosopher, anthropologist, and sociologist whose work was influenced by Hans Driesch, Nicolai Hartmann, and Max Scheler. He joined the Nazi party in 1933, and his career benefited from opportunities for advancement created by the removal of Jewish and anti-Nazi academics from universities in the Third Reich. His work during this time attempted to create a "National Socialist philosophy" (*Der Idealismus und die Gegenwart*, 1935). His major work was *Man: His Nature and Place in this World* (1940 [trans. 1980]) in which he developed a philosophical anthropology based on Nietzsche's idea that humans are "not yet finished animals": they are dependent on **society** and **culture** for a long period of maturation; they have "world-openness" because of a lack or deficit of instincts; thus modern life is precarious and humans require a secure political and social **environment** to provide discipline. Human dependence on social **institutions** and culture creates ontological frailty and existential precariousness. A meaningful life can be lived only through conformity to institutions; thus emancipatory efforts (such as those of Enlightenment critique) are risky because institutions are easily destroyed but difficult to establish. Gehlen was therefore highly critical of the radical **social movements** of 1968. The ideas of ontological frailty and precariousness have

been influential in sociology, for example in the work of **Peter Berger** and **Thomas Luckmann** (*Social Construction of Reality*, 1966).   LARRY RAY

Geisteswissenschaften
– see **human sciences**.

Gellner, Ernest (1925–1996)

Formerly Professor of Anthropology at Cambridge University, Gellner made significant contributions to the study of Islam and **nationalism**. In his *Saints of the Atlas* (1969), Gellner contrasted the puritanical **religion** of the towns, in which the authority of the Qur'an was paramount, and the mystical religion of the Sufi saints in the countryside, where their personal **charisma** (or *baraka*) was sought after by their disciples. While urban religiosity stressed the equality of believers, the Islam of the Sufi saints was hierarchical. Gellner employed this model of religion in his subsequent work on the political structure of North African **societies**. He developed a theory of elite circulation, which he adopted from **Ibn Khaldun**. The tribal **groups** of the countryside have greater social **solidarity** (*assabiya*) than the towns, and they periodically replace the urban **elites** that have become weak, fragmented, and corrupted. This circulation of elites explains the periodic intrusion of nomadic tribes into urban **civilization**. This pattern has, however, been transformed by modern **technology** which has allowed the towns to control the hinterland more effectively, and has also allowed the spread of puritanical, Quranic, egalitarian Islam into the interior. Gellner thus developed, in *Muslim Society* (1982), an early appreciation of the importance of **fundamentalism** in modern **politics**.

Gellner was also concerned, in *Thought and Change* (1964), to understand the force of nationalism in modern societies. He regarded nationalism as a product of modern societies, arguing that nations are invented. In modern **democracy**, there is a demand to be ruled by our own ethnic group (see **ethnicity and ethnic groups**), and hence national **identity** becomes a major issue of modern democratic politics.

Gellner was, in *Legitimation of Belief* (1974), a critic of trends in cultural anthropology, because he was hostile to **cultural relativism**. He defended the idea of rational criticism against relativism, which Gellner thought was self-defeating. He was consequently, in *Postmodernism, Reason and Religion* (1992), critical of the impact of **postmodernism** on modern anthropological theory, and defended traditional ethnographic methods against postmodern emphasis on narrative **deconstruction**. In *The Psychoanalytic Movement* (1985) he brought his critical perspective to bear on Freudian (see **Sigmund Freud**) therapy, which he dismissed as incoherent and ineffective.

BRYAN S. TURNER

Gemeinschaft and Gesellschaft
– see **Ferdinand Tönnies**.

gender
For many students of **society**, gender is the most important form of social division, far more important than **social class** or **race and ethnicity** in the impact that it makes on individual lives. Yet the history of the concept of gender is not a long one; unlike the concept of class, the idea of gender does not have roots in the nineteenth-century origins of **sociology**, and it is since the mid-1960s that the question of gender has come to be central to discussions of social life. In large part, the emergence of the concept of gender owes much to second-wave **feminism**, which drew attention to sexual divisions in society and to the patterns of social difference and **inequality** that arose. But what differentiated the concept of gender from the concept of sex was work by feminists in the 1970s that took issue with the idea of essentialist **explanations** of sexual difference. These interventions, for example by sociologists such as **Ann Oakley**, pointed out that biological sex differences did not in themselves lead to differences in behavior between the sexes. Oakley, in common with other sociologists and anthropologists, pointed out that across **cultures** and historical periods there were very considerable differences in the ways in which women and men were expected to behave. What persisted were biological differences of sex, but what differed were social constructions of **masculinity** and femininity, namely constructions of gender. Gender, it became accepted, was the articulation of social expectations about how a person of a particular biological sex should behave, but that performance of gender could differ significantly across time and space.

What this separation of gender and sex did was to establish the idea that there was no such thing as naturally male or female behavior. **Simone de Beauvoir** had famously written in *The Second Sex* (1949 [trans. 1972]) that women are "made and not born" and it is precisely this view which is at the heart of contemporary understandings of gender. De Beauvoir argued that feminine behavior has numerous aspects to it; there is no one condition

of femininity, but diverse conditions relevant to the particular situation of an individual woman. But in all cases, for de Beauvoir, the specific femininity which women display places them as the other in human society. The male, and masculinity, constitute the **norm** and it is from this that women deviate. De Beauvoir's view has been hugely influential because it challenges the assumption that the categories of women/femininity and men/ masculinity are fixed and static. Although much recent work on gender has been initiated by feminist debates and feminist writers, it is also the case that the challenge of the idea of gender has made a considerable impact on conventional assumptions about men and masculinity.

Although de Beauvoir was critical of much of **Sigmund Freud**'s work and was skeptical about his theories of sexual development, one similarity in the work of both these writers is the acknowledgment that sexual **identity** is not fixed but can be changed by circumstance and even, on occasion, by choice. But what both Freud and de Beauvoir are working with is the post-Enlightenment recognition of the difference between male and female biology. To modern students of gender, this is now a taken-for granted assumption, but a crucial part of the history of the idea of gender is the recognition that it was not until the eighteenth century that the physical differences between the sexes were fully recognized, and even then it was not until the twentieth century that the extent of hormonal differences between male and female were more fully investigated. Thomas Laqueur in *Making Sex* (1990) has pointed out that it is only recently that sex, as a stable biological attribute, has existed. Laqueur argues that human biology, that is the stable, ahistorical, and sexed **body**, has to be understood as the "epistemic foundation" for prescriptive rather than descriptive claims about the social order. Before this agreement about biology, the social identity of being a woman or a man depended on social factors and the division between male and female was not a binary division but one in which "maleness" and "femaleness" could be greater or lesser according to the particular situation of women.

But by the nineteenth century most of Europe had come to accept a division between male and female, a division which, in the majority of human beings, was visible at birth and which was then made the basis for social divisions. Women in the nineteenth century were expected, in order to meet middle-class **norms** of femininity, to show distinct patterns of behavior from those of men. The social reality of nineteenth-century

Europe was such that this norm was meaningless for the majority of women who spent their lives in agricultural and/or domestic work, but social expectations about biology had been established. It was those norms which women such as de Beauvoir challenged: forced by economic circumstance to provide for herself, de Beauvoir lived out the contradictions of gender and indeed protested against them.

In her own life, and in her writing, de Beauvoir demonstrated an iron determination to claim for herself the same **rights** to an intellectual life as those of men. In this sense, much of her work is not about claiming a different form of femininity but about being allowed to occupy the same space as men. This reaction to gender stereotyping implies an internalized sense of a division between male and female, a sense which is powerfully present in de Beauvoir's account of her childhood, *Memoirs of a Dutiful Daughter* (1958 [trans. 1959]). What de Beauvoir tells readers about in this, the first volume of her four-volume autobiography, is the process of becoming a girl, and the way in which the acquisition of that identity inhibits various kinds of activity. The book provides an excellent example of the complex way in which **children** acquire a sense of the social implications of their physical sex; it is not just for de Beauvoir that the passage to an adult sexual identity is riven with difficulties and contradictions. But what de Beauvoir encounters in her childhood and adolescence is a contradictory set of social expectations about her possible gender. As a bourgeois girl in France in the first half of the twentieth century, de Beauvoir, like others of her class, is not expected to entertain educational ambitions, still less to study a subject – philosophy – which is associated with anti-clericalism and often a critical attitude to social convention. But as a poor bourgeois girl, the only way out of penury is either to marry or to study. Lacking the personal inclination, or social attributes, that might have made possible an advantageous marriage, the option for de Beauvoir was to study and to learn to provide for herself. The expectations of gender had to be surrendered to those of class.

The autobiography of the author of *The Second Sex* – a woman always claimed as the greatest feminist writer of the twentieth century – provides an outstanding example of the way in which gender identity can be both subverted and changed, while also being maintained. The "bonds of femininity" were, for de Beauvoir, always bonds which could be broken, and much of her fiction is concerned with the stories of women who cannot

break those bonds or re-interpret femininity in other ways. At the same time, the case of de Beauvoir provides for us an example of the impact of social conditioning on a particular individual: the hurdles faced by de Beauvoir in her educational career were not fantasies of her own making, but real difficulties in the social world. Thus, the evident strength of social **mores** can be seen in the cases of de Beauvoir and of other women of her **generation**. We know, from this individual case and from all **information** about more general situations, that all societies organize social life on the basis of sex differences, and that constructed ideas of gender play a considerable part in the maintenance of these differences. It is now well known that, in the United Kingdom in the nineteenth and twentieth centuries, many people, including medical specialists, took the view that women should not be over-taxed by intellectual work, lest this damage their reproductive systems. This notion, hardly relevant to the majority of the female population who were engaged in arduous manual **work**, was just one of the many nineteenth-century views of femininity, albeit one which attracted both derision and support.

Since the late twentieth century, we have come to regard with some suspicion ideas about differences between male and female which support theories about distinctions between the male and female brain. In *Biological Politics and Sexual Divisions*, Janet Sayers (1982) has outlined much of the literature on the physiological differences between the sexes, particularly in terms of the differences, if any, in the brains of women and men. But the point of this literature, as Sayers argues, is not only the actual conclusions about differences in the brain, but the **social structures** which are built on them. From the eighteenth century onwards, a consensus developed about the existence of differences in physical strength between women and men; at the time, these differences had a relevance to the **labor market** and underpinned the sexual exclusivity of certain **occupations**. The changes in the European labor market of the late twentieth century have largely marginalized the potential impact of differences in physical strength, but what has become more important has been identified as the persistence of gender differences which persistently advantage men and disadvantage women.

It is at this point that academic debates about gender encounter the reality of the social world. Since the 1970s, and the impact of second-wave feminism on academic debates, the question of the construction of gender has become central to both the academy and the wider social world. Following the **tradition** (albeit a tradition with its own internal differences and contradictions) which included Freud and de Beauvoir, a consensus emerged in which it was generally agreed that gender was socially constructed out of biological sex differences. The emphasis (as suggested above) was initially on the social construction of femininity, but by the 1980s authors such as Victor Seidler and Jeffrey Weeks had demonstrated that, just as femininity was socially constructed, so the same was true of **masculinity**. In short, our social/sexual **selves** were as unstable as Freud had assumed and what could be demonstrated – and was demonstrated, for example by Ken Plummer in work on homosexuality – was the strength of social norms to create individual sexual persona. This academic work became part of more general social concerns about gender stereotyping.

Thus by the end of the 1980s there was, throughout the West, a general consensus that recognized the way in which all societies made, of sexual difference, differences of gender. Anthropologists demonstrated that qualities associated with men in some societies (for example competence in the economic **market**) were of little value in others, and that the meaning of masculinity and femininity in the twentieth and twenty-first centuries was as variable as it been in previous centuries. The view of "natural" attributes of male and female had little credence in academic circles. It was at this point that a book by Judith Butler, *Gender Trouble* (1990), was published, which pushed the debate on gender even further towards the conclusion that all gender attributes are constructed and, as Butler describes it, "performed." For Butler, gender is the defining division of the social world and debates on this issue with Nancy Fraser have involved numerous participants. But Butler's central case - since developed in *Bodies that Matter* (1993), *Excitable Speech: A Politics of the Performative* (1997), *The Psychic Life of Power* (1997), and *Antigone's Claim: Kinship between Life and Death* (2000) – has become a central part of the analysis of gender.

For Butler, gender is a strategy, a "corporeal style" which individuals pursue, because if they do not they are punished by society. For example, one of the reasons Joan of Arc was condemned was that she wore men's clothes. This is an extreme example, but in other cases social sanctions are still present and societies overwhelmingly police the correct "performance" of gender. But, so far, this idea of people being coerced into behaving in ways that are deemed to be appropriate for a member of their physical sex is not in itself

innovative or radically different from anything that has been said before. What makes Butler's argument different is the suggestion, in *Gender Trouble*, that people are not copying an original or correct model of gender behavior since no such original exists.

It is in this way that Butler's work differs from that of **Harold Garfinkel**, who, in the study of the young person named Agnes, had demonstrated that individuals could very convincingly do gender and thus make others believe in whichever gender was chosen. In her argument, Butler has recognized the existence of individuals such as Agnes in the history of gender (and indeed the history of – literally – the wardrobe of gender). But she has also insisted that each **generation**, in putting together a gender identity, is not using the original but only the various forms in which gender had so far been performed. One of the strengths of Butler's argument is her recognition of the way in which dress (for both sexes) has always had a rich vein of both parody and subversion. Equally, one of the problems with Butler's argument is the question of what becomes chosen as the norm at any place or time: there might well be a huge amount of choice in modes of dress, but there are always limits to social toleration and a point at which the welcome for the new turns to the condemnation of the bizarre.

Butler's work has been influential across a number of disciplines, in both the **social sciences** and the humanities, since what she offers is a way of seeing gender as always and inevitably radically unstable. She does not regard cross-dressing or drag as necessarily radical or subversive, for the very good reason that both these forms simply invoke and confirm gender stereotypes. Thus her work is less a celebration of popular forms of subverting fixed gender identities (these, in her view, merely re-inforce existing expectations of gender) but rather a method of studying the ways in which, in social life, literature, and the visual arts, gender is constantly being re-made. But the social world, which prefers the order of fixed gender identities, works against subversions of gender, because it is fixed distinctions of gender which, to Butler, maintain the social world. It is here that her work has led her to conflict with those critics (for example Martha Nussbaum and Nancy Fraser) who have argued that the social world of late **capitalism** can function perfectly well, whatever the **politics** of gender. The idea of a world without gender, Butler argues, would be a world in which there would be no expectation of "feminine" qualities of **care** or masculine attributes of "strength" but only the recognition of human qualities. Those industries related to the various forms of the manipulation of the body (**fashion**, health and beauty, and cosmetic surgery) and indeed the expected tensions of much popular entertainment (how the couple of either homosexual or heterosexual desire is going to be formed) would collapse, Butler suggests, if we did not have fixed gender identities to maintain.

For many sociologists, Butler's work, while recognized as important, is regarded as somewhat removed from social reality, in which sexual difference still plays a crucial role in the determination of social identity. Beverley Skeggs, in *Formations of Class and Gender* (1997), and Linda McDowell, in *Gender Identity and Place* (1999), have argued that both femininity and masculinity are not just attributes of a particular sex, they are also constructed in different contexts of class. Skeggs has shown how, for working-class women, maintaining that sense of femininity which prioritizes the care of others (both personally and professionally) is an essential part of what they see as their best hope of an advantageous marriage; McDowell has suggested that, for middle-class men, the demonstration of the supposedly female qualities of "caring" and co-operation with others is a highly positive attribute, whereas supposedly "masculine" characteristics in women do not receive the same approval. What both authors are able to show is that constructions of gender differ from social class to social class, but a model of behavior which accords with traditional expectations of femininity is of positive social **value** for middle-class men, but of negative social value for working-class women.

These possible differences in the social value of different gender identities open up a further question about the relationship of gender to the social world. Many writers have seen the **Enlightenment**, and **modernity** itself, as an inherently "masculine" project. Although there is considerable evidence to suggest that the question of gender was important to writers in the Enlightenment, and that the writers were both male and female, what has emerged as the dominant view of the Enlightenment is that of a way of looking at the world which values reason above feeling, the rational over instinct. That binary division (the association of women with nature and men with culture) has long been assumed to be at the heart of the Enlightenment. But if we can observe the increasing social value of the attributes of the feminine, we also have to remember that this greater social value is only gained by men rather than women.

Thus, although the postmodern might include the blurring of gender boundaries (and the concomitant furious resistance in some quarters to these newly apparent forms of **sexuality** and gender identity), what does not appear to be taking place is any realignment in the hierarchies either of class or of gender identity that is related to biological difference. Hence some men can, to their advantage, do femininity, but women cannot do masculinity.

For many writers on gender, however, shifts in the social construction of gender identity, apparent and important though they may be, break down when confronted by actual biological differences between the sexes and the impact that these differences have on individual lives. For biological determinists, there are (as there always have been in different ways) differences between women and men which are fixed and both transhistorical and transcultural. At the same time Freudian psychoanalysts would resist any attempt to eliminate biological sexual differences from either the study or the understanding of the human. Empirical sociological investigation has also demonstrated that, although men, particularly middle-class men, may be willing to do femininity in certain aspects of employment, their willingness – in common with that of working-class men – to take over female responsibilities in the household or in caring work is still extremely limited. In these circumstances, the gender politics of **everyday life** demonstrate a resistance to the re-thinking of gender which is very marked, as do various forms of social reaction to behavior in women (for example what is seen as the excessive drinking of alcohol) which is more generally associated with men. **Arlie Russell Hochschild** is among those sociologists who have investigated the present ordering of gender relations in the private space of the home and found that traditional patterns of gender persist.

This continuing **inequality** in gender relations (and the theories such as that of **Anthony Giddens** in *The Transformation of Intimacy* (1992) which argue that gender relations in the private sphere are shifting to a more egalitarian model) is explained by L. McNay, *Gender and Agency* (2000), following **Pierre Bourdieu**, in terms of a challenge to the cognitive, reflexive, and deliberate refashioning of gender identity which Giddens assumes. Bourdieu's concept of **habitus** is used to explain the indeterminacy of gender and embodiment. Social ideas and expectations about gender are enacted at a pre-reflexive level: what is being suggested here is that individuals have certain deeply held, often unconscious, investments in conventional patterns of masculinity and femininity, and these patterns are not easily over-turned, either by objective decisions or by social situations in which the rejection of these norms might appear to be the socially meaningful and rewarding choice. Thus, while gender identity is not an immutable or essential pattern of behavior, McNay suggests that there are many pre-reflexive aspects of masculine and feminine behavior which call into question the idea of reflexive identity.

Crucial to all these theories about gender, and the ways in which we acquire our gender identity, is our understanding of **language**. All language is saturated with meaning: the very terms man or woman carry all kinds of embedded knowledge that we seldom voice but nevertheless use in our social existence. It is for this reason that the use of language, particularly language about gender, has become such an important issue in both the academy and practical politics. In the mid-1960s, the term people was quite widely used to refer only to men; today the term is used to make explicit the absence of bias towards male or female in particular situations. Traditional terms such as husband or wife have been replaced by the term partner, a term which ironically carries with it associations of the formal relations of the marketplace. But in contexts other than the everyday world, language is also crucial for theories of gender, because it is through language that we achieve the means to express our understanding of the symbolic meaning of our bodies. The writer who has contributed most influentially to this debate is the French psychoanalyst **Jacques Lacan** in his *Écrits* (1966 [trans. 1977]), who has argued that a child has to recognize sexual difference before becoming a speaking subject; it is only through recognizing both absence and presence of the phallus that a child can make the necessary progress towards both language and an understanding of the symbolic world. Feminist writers (most particularly the French writer **Luce Irigaray**) have challenged this idea by arguing that what children primarily experience is the "discursive" sexuality of their mothers. For Irigaray it is not male sexuality which constitutes the primary means of entry into language but that of the female. With Irigaray's thesis in "When our Lips Speak Together" (1980, *Signs*) comes the view that femininity resides in female biology: it is a view which has been accused of biological **essentialism** and it is, of course, very different from the ideas of Butler.

Whatever the different views of various writers about the relationship between language and the formation of gender identity, all writers agree on the centrality of the body to theories about gender. Here the spectrum of writers ranges from those who see the body, and its physical characteristics, as definitive in the making of individual identity, to those who would question the idea that the body has a sex at all. This very radical view might seem to challenge all taken-for-granted assumptions about the social world, but the idea is supported by evidence from diverse **communities** which suggests that our western ideas about gender, and gender difference, are not necessarily as straightforward as we might like to suppose. Thus anthropologists (for example Henrietta Moore) have pointed out that male and female are not necessarily the fixed and certain categories that we might suppose but differ between societies and cultures. If the physical definition of the body can be questioned, then it is inevitable that gender identity then becomes a matter of uncertainty and negotiation. This thesis alters our relationship to the body: it is no longer the fixed starting point but actually the unknown, fluid starting point of attempts to define gender. Seen in the light of this, it is possible to surmise that gender identity is as rigid as it sometimes is because what Freud recognized as the "polymorphous perversity" of the psyche is as true of the body as it is of the mind. In his work on the history of the body, Bryan S. Turner in *The Body and Society* (1984) has emphasized the importance of working with an understanding of the "lived body," an approach which opens up the possibility of seeing the body itself as a production of the social world rather than as a fixed constituent of it.

All theories of gender work with the paradox that they begin with the recognition of the impact of gender difference in the social world and then attempt to show that this difference, having been produced, can also be dissolved. The politics of gender have come to be recognized as central to the organization of social life, not because these politics have been articulated for the first time in the latter part of the twentieth century but because gender, and gender identity, has always played a crucial role in the history of the social world. The Bible begins with the drama of the recognition of sexual difference (implicitly suggesting that the concept of sexual difference was created through knowledge rather than corporeal reality) and Homeric epic is organized around the mistaking of the identity of the mother. Both these examples might serve to remind us that the question of gender, and gender identity, is as old as civilization itself.   MARY EVANS

gender studies

This area of interdisciplinary research is concerned with understanding the biological differentiation of male and female, the gender roles that express that differentiation in **society** and **culture**, the development and expression of different types of human **sexuality**, the political representation of **gender** in **feminism**, and the modern expression of sexuality such as lesbian, gay, bisexual, and transsexual **identities**. **Women's studies** and gender studies are interdisciplinary fields of contemporary scholarship that are devoted to the study of women and gender in different historical and social contexts. These areas of study stress the gendered nature of social life.

In sociology, **social constructionism** has argued that gender is not a naturally occurring phenomenon but has to be socially produced and sustained. Sociologists are concerned with understanding how people do, rather than have, gender – that is, by what processes of **socialization** do people learn the practices, **attitudes**, and behavior through which distinctive gender identities are expressed. For example, **masculinity** is itself not a uniform expression of male identity. In *Gender and Power*, R. W. Connell (1987) has argued that masculinity and femininity are normalized gender identities that are hegemonic in modern society. Gender studies are concerned to understand **power** and **inequality** in terms of gender differences.

There are a huge array of gender studies and women's studies programs, especially in higher education in the United States. There are innumerable journals, research centers, and institutions devoted to this field of study, and gender studies in many respects provided a model for the development of **lesbian studies** and **Gay Studies**. Some leading feminist journals include *Signs, Feminist Review, Feminist Studies, differences: a journal of feminist Cultural studies*, and *Hypatia*.

Gender studies is in large measure the academic consequence of feminism and related **social movements** that campaigned for gender **equality**. The success of feminism and its internal political and cultural divisions are also manifest in different forms of gender research. Gender studies was introduced into universities because it was argued that higher education was dominated by men and that the academic disciplines ignored women, gender, and sexuality. There has been a substantial debate about whether gender studies is a special field of research or whether gender as an issue should be part of the mainstream of every discipline. Gender studies have been important in promoting research on the **family**, **marriage and divorce**, **nature/nurture** (see **environment**), **patriarchy**, private and **public spheres**, and **women and work**. Through feminist **social theory**, it has been critical of **biologism** and **essentialism**. Feminist theory has often been associated with **postmodernism** by challenging many of the taken-for-granted assumptions of social science. The study of gender has had a significant impact on the development of the sociology of **health** and illness (for example **Ann Oakley**'s *Women, Medicine & Health*, 1993), the sociology of the **emotions** (such as **Arlie R. Hochschild**'s *The Managed Heart*, 1983), and the sociology of the **body**, in which Emily Martin's *The Woman in the Body* (1987) was important. The study of gender has been significant in sociology, but it has often found a more secure home in literary studies and **Cultural studies**, where the traditional canon has been transformed by the impact of feminist theory.

BRYAN S. TURNER

generation(s)

This term is used in different and sometimes inconsistent ways by social scientists. There are at least five ways in which the term is employed: (1) to designate levels in extended kinship structure; (2) to designate the general stage or segment in the **life-course** that a **group** occupies (for example the current generation of college students); (3) to refer to those who experienced a common historical period (for example the Depression generation, the Sixties Generation, or Generation X); (4) to refer to a subset of a historical generation who share a common political or cultural **identity**; and (5) to denote a circumscribed age **group** in the population. The fifth use is closest to what developmental scientists call a "cohort." The concept of cohort refers to an aggregate of individuals (generally defined on the basis of birth year) whose lives move together through a historical time. Given these varied meanings, it is important to trace the way the various concepts are measured and used.

The confusion of generation and cohort has led some scholars to insist that generation should only be used to designate a kin relationship and genealogical linkage (for examples, parents and children or grandparents and grandchildren). As D. L. Kertzer, in *Generation as a Sociological Problem* (1983), points out, there is often substantial overlapping of age among (kin) generations, and it would be impossible to characterize the generations properly in terms of their common characteristics vis-à-vis other generations. A generation might consist of several cohorts, each of which has encountered different historical experiences that have affected its life-course. Therefore, to examine change over time in generational relations it is necessary to compare cohorts not generations.

With the revolutionary changes in longevity in the advanced industrial world, there is far greater co-survival of generations and this has led family researchers to examine the consequences in terms of intergenerational family **solidarity** and conflict. Much of the contemporary research suggests that obligations are giving way to more negotiation among the generations. Yet, while intergenerational support has been shown in both the United Kingdom and the United States to be more a matter of negotiation than of prescription, there is little evidence to suggest that intergenerational family relations are of less importance than in the past.

The distinction between generation and cohort has been further blurred by the political debates in many western nations about generational equity, a concern about whether the distribution of resources and **power** in **society** among different age groups (cohorts) favors one generation to the detriment of another. This debate was spurred by the United States demographer Samuel Preston's article, "Children and the Elderly: Divergent Paths for America's Dependents" (*Demography*, 1984), in which he claims that elderly people receive more than their fair share of the federal budget, particularly in light of their economic status, and they ultimately receive these benefits at the expense of groups that are more needy and deserving, especially children. Notions of the Third Age, a time of personal fulfillment after retirement, have helped fuel labels like "the SKI generation" (Spending the Kids' Inheritance). The crucial point is about the just distribution of **wealth** between age groups which, according to historical demographer Peter Laslett's *A Fresh Map of Life* (1996), is one of the most urgent issues of contemporary society.

It is the problem of **social change** that has informed much of sociology's concern with generations. **Karl Mannheim**, in his essay "The Problem of Generations" (1928), posed the thought experiment of how human social life would be if one generation lived on forever and none followed to replace it. It was the linkage between "generational replacement" and social change that Mannheim explores in his famous essay. According to Mannheim the biological process that defines generations creates the potential for the development of a shared consciousness that unites and motivates people. It provides them with a similar location, much like **social class**, but does not guarantee that they will form a "generation as actuality." For a generation to trigger social change, they must forge an additional bond that allows a shared consciousness that underpins what he calls a generational unit. Of course, not all respond to historical circumstances in the same way, and the same historical period may provoke different generational units who take quite contrary stances. However, once adopted, consciousness is resistant to revision. Thus societal change takes place partly as a result of cohort replacement, the process by which the older generation dies out and is replaced by the new.

Some forty years later, Norman Ryder, in his article "The Cohort as a Concept in the Study of Social Change" (1965, *American Sociological Review*), revisited Mannheim's analysis. Ryder substituted the concept of birth cohort for Mannheim's generation and largely jettisoned the notion of shared consciousness and the distinction between "generation" and "generation as actuality" that was central to Mannheim's view of the structural linkage between agency and social change. Ryder argues that a comparison of different cohorts is a powerful analytical strategy for studying social change. Cohorts describe age-homogeneous groupings that are clearly bounded. A whole industry of social research (predominantly North American) has grown up looking at cohort change in **attitudes** and behaviors. However, the definition of cohorts according to birth year is convenient but problematic. When we examine the question of why a particular span of years is important in the life experiences of individuals, we are back into the thorny issues of how biography and history intersect. This was the issue that **C. Wright Mills**, in his book *The Sociological Imagination* (1959), identified as the crucial concern of the social science.

Social research on generations, aging, and life-course interconnect in ways that defy any simple overview of sociological work on generations. Glen Elder, in his classic study of *Children of the Great Depression* (1974), makes use both of generations (in the kinship sense) and of birth cohorts to track the influence of the economic crisis of the 1930s on the life-course of two cohorts of children born just eight years apart. He shows the importance of familial processes for mediating the impact of socioeconomic change. As John Clausen stated in his preface to Elder's book, "we know that 'life chances' depend on historical circumstances and one's location in the social structure but we are only beginning to formulate the nature of the linkages between particular kinds of experiences located in time and place, adaptive responses to these experiences and long-term outcomes."

Generational **reproduction** is a complex process, regardless of whether we are looking at kinship relations or societal change. The various meanings of the term generation do at least serve to remind us that biological, biographical, social, and historical reproduction crucially interrelate. This was one of the central insights of Mannheim's essay which has stood the test of time.   JACKIE SCOTT

genetic engineering
– see **genetics**.

genetics

A branch of biology, genetics is concerned with the study of **heredity** and the variability of organisms. The twentieth century has been described by Evelyn Fox Keller as *The Century of the Gene* (2000). From the discovery at the turn of the twentieth century that Gregor Mendel's laws of inheritance could also be applied to those of human heredity, to the recent successful completion of the human genome project identifying all the genes in the human **body**, developments in genetics have accelerated so that they now dominate the science arena. If the field of nuclear physics dominated post-World-War-II science, it is the fields of genetics and genomics that have come to supplant it. These fields are often referred to as "big science," a term used to describe both the scale and complexity of large-scale post-World-War-II scientific endeavors. Commentators have suggested that genetics is not only influential in shaping ideas about human **identity**, but also a powerful economic and political force aligning considerations of **health** and **wealth** and generating new forms of biocapital. As we move into the twenty-first century, genetic science and its associated **technologies** seem likely to have an even greater impact on society and upon understandings of what it is to be human.

The idea of eugenics, a process for selectively breeding humans in order to preserve and promote "desirable" characteristics, was first formulated by scientist and cousin of **Charles Darwin**, Francis Galton (1822–1911). In 1904 at a meeting of the Sociological Society, Galton is reported to have said that, "Eugenics is the science which deals with all influences that improve the inborn qualities of a race; also with those that develop

them to the utmost advantage." Eugenics was defined by Galton as the study of agencies under **social control** that may improve or impair the qualities of future **generations** either physically or mentally. He intended eugenics to extend to any technique that might serve to increase the representation of those with "good genes," in this way accelerating evolution. A major motivation of many eugenicists was an idea of human **progress**. The idea of progress was based not solely on the advancement of scientific knowledge but also on genetic improvement. This was supported by Darwin's **evolutionary theory**, wherein the survival of the fittest was equated with the survival of the best. The best were thought to be the best people to cope with modern life. Galton tended to equate people's genetic fitness with their social position. Social Darwinist **ideology** provided a good climate for eugenic thought, and many qualities such as **intelligence**, temperament, and behavior were believed to be inherited. Galton proposed that the human race might be improved by eliminating society's so-called undesirables and multiplying its so-called desirables. Such ideas became increasingly popular in the political sphere with both democratic and totalitarian regimes.

The eugenic movement was supported by the upper-middle classes, with scientists and geneticists in particular playing an important role in this movement. Research into human heredity was carried out in scientific laboratories to develop eugenically useful knowledge. A human genetics program emerged, focusing on the analysis of various conditions, particularly those seen to be creating a social burden for society. The so-called feeble-minded were a particular focus. Psychologist and eugenicist Henry Goddard was of the opinion that "feeble-mindedness" was a hereditary condition of the brain that made those who had inherited such a condition more prone to becoming criminals, paupers, and prostitutes. Societal problems such as **poverty**, vagrancy, prostitution, and alcoholism were understood by eugenicists as primarily the outcome of a person's genetic inheritance rather than emanating from social, political, and economic factors. The mental and behavioral characteristics of different **"races"** were also a focus of the eugenic movement, and, in genetic science in northern Europe and the United States, eugenics was frequently used to support ideas of the existence of a superior white, middle-class Protestant **elite**, such as the so-called Aryan race. Beginning in 1907, compulsory sterilization laws were passed in many states in the

United States, with Denmark and Germany passing such measures in the 1930s. While these countries adopted compulsory sterilization programs designed to prevent the continued breeding of those deemed to be undesirable, the eugenic movement in Nazi Germany led not only to the sterilization of hundreds of thousands of individuals but ultimately to the death camps where millions of Jews and "undesirables" were murdered.

The story of eugenics is not only characterized by such negative aspects; the eugenic program also included many initiatives that were classified as "positive." Galton originally classified eugenics as consisting of two types: positive and negative. While negative campaigns were concerned with getting rid of the "undesirables," positive eugenics involved the promotion of "desirable" human stock. In Britain, positive eugenic campaigns sought to encourage the middle classes to breed through a system of tax concessions and grants, and in the United States the American Eugenics Society sponsored Better Babies competitions and Fitter Families contests as part of their positive eugenic campaign. Beginning in the 1950s, there was a rise in nondirective genetic counseling in an attempt to dissociate the field from the negative eugenics of the Nazi regime. Such measures were based on the understanding that couples wanted healthy children, and such interventions were seen as important in providing impartial advice to enable couples to make choices concerning **reproduction**.

Scientific endeavors to discover the chromosomal location of genes and their relation to each other initially began slowly at the start of the twentieth century. Scientists understood that a gene was a single unit located on a chromosome, passed from one **generation** to the next, and that this material was coded in cells determining how an organism looked and behaved. In 1913, the first genetic map appeared, identifying the relative location of six genes on one chromosome. In the following decades, this process remained painstakingly slow and difficult. In 1953, two Cambridge University scientists, James Watson (1928–) and Francis Crick (1916–2004), made what is considered to be a landmark scientific breakthrough by discovering the physical structure of DNA (the molecular structure that holds genetic **information**). Nevertheless, scientists still faced a daunting task in identifying all the genes of the human body, particularly as it was incorrectly assumed that there were likely to be in excess of 100,000. However, by the 1980s, genetic maps were good enough to allow scientists to go "hunting" for genes among **families** of people with inherited diseases such as Huntington's disease and cystic fibrosis. In the 1980s, with the invention of a new **technology** called PCR (polymerase chain reaction) that enabled DNA to be replicated and amplified, and the availability of new high-speed computer-sequencing technology, scientists began to consider a global endeavor to map and sequence the entire human genome – that is, to identify the now more accurately assessed 20,000–25,000 genes of the human body and determine the sequences of the 3 billion chemical base pairs that make up human DNA.

The human genome project marks the entry of genetics into the realm of big science and officially began in 1990 with the aim of completing the genetic sequencing of certain forms of bacteria, yeast, plants, animals, and ultimately human beings. It was anticipated that a complete human sequence would be produced by 2005. The scale of the project was such that it was as much a political endeavor as a scientific one. In the United States, the project was headed by James Watson, who played a key role as both scientist and political lobbyist. Although the majority of the research was undertaken in the United States, the project became an international collaboration, involving twenty research groups from six countries. The intention was to divide the mapping of the twenty-four human chromosomes among some dozen or so laboratories around the world. One-third of the human genome was sequenced in the United Kingdom at the Sanger Institute. The scale and cost of the project was huge. It is estimated that work carried out in sequencing the single gene responsible for the disease cystic fibrosis cost between US$50 million and US$150 million.

The human genome project has political dimensions, as could be expected for any project requiring so much funding, with huge potential rewards for the biotechnology industry in terms of the possible application of genetics to medicine and agriculture. The enormous expense of this project was justified primarily on the basis of the likely medical benefits. There was also an implicit understanding that such an enterprise would have economic benefits by helping to fuel a growing **biotechnology** sector. Indeed, as the project progressed, many countries involved, including the United Kingdom, were quite explicit in their plans to use genomics to help generate national wealth. The International Human Genome Consortium (the group which coordinated and managed the human genome project) made extravagant speculations about the practical importance of their work for human health, claiming that the human genome project would lead to profound long-term consequences for medicine, by enabling an understanding of the underlying molecular mechanisms of disease and the design of drugs and other therapeutics targeted at those mechanisms. As the project developed, so too did the "hype," with many speaking of genetics as the key to unlocking the secrets of life and providing a genetic blueprint of what it is to be human.

Many scientists involved were also keen to ensure that scientific competition would not undermine or delay the project. In particular, there was concern that the granting of patents allowing exclusive property rights over **data** would undermine international collaboration. It was therefore agreed that this worldwide, multi-billion-dollar project would be funded solely from public funds and medical charities such as the United Kingdom's Wellcome Trust. Furthermore, information on the sequencing of all human genes was to be made freely available via the internet. The ethos of the policy of publicly funding the human genome project is that it is a democratic resource intended to maximize the benefits for society as a whole. Nevertheless, commercial companies were involved in a race to map and sequence the human genome, and the American company Celera Genomics developed a rapid gene-sequencing technique and subsequently took out commercial patents in order to profit from this work. In response, work being undertaken on the human genome project accelerated and a race between these two groups to be the first to announce the completion of an initial draft of the human genome developed. In June, 2000, President Bill Clinton of the United States and Prime Minister Tony Blair of the United Kingdom made a televised announcement that the work of the human genome project was almost complete. The announcement was made five years before the original estimate of completion, and it was a further two years before the project was officially declared complete. The announcement made headline news around the world and was surrounded by much media-fueled hype, with politicians and scientists variously describing it as the most wondrous map ever made and more important than the invention of the wheel.

The human genome project and recent developments in genetics are surrounded by triumphalist accounts of scientific progress. While there has been little in the way of **sociological theory** to explain the phenomenon of hype that pervades this field, some have noted that such hype plays an important role in generating the necessary funding and investments for projects such as the human genome and other biotech endeavors. Alongside the creation of high expectations that genetics and associated technologies will bring, it is recognized that developments in genetics also raise new ethical problems. While this new form of scientific knowledge has promised to bring about cures for many diseases, and the elimination of inherited disabilities, genetics is also understood to raise new ethical issues and fears about the social consequences of such interventions.

Concerns were voiced from the outset about the ethical, legal, and social implications of the human genome endeavor. In the United States, James Watson successfully argued for the case that 5 percent of the total science budget should be set aside to study and address these issues. There has also been a growing expansion in the funding of similar projects in other countries. These initiatives are understood as playing an important role in the governance of genetic developments. Critical questions have been raised about whether such new technologies for reading our genetic constitution would challenge human **identity** and freedom, create unjust **discrimination**, and invade our **privacy**. Although many sociologists are now working in the field of bioethics alongside philosophers and lawyers, this is an uneasy alliance. There is a growing sociological critique of bioethics, which maintains that bioethics involves a narrowing of debate, is focused too much on individuals at the expense of the social, and too often readily legitimizes genetic developments. Sociologists have in general been more critical of recent developments in genetics. Some have suggested that developments in genetics are promoting a return to eugenic practices and generating genetic determinism. Others are less critical and, while acknowledging that genetics is extremely powerful in shaping ideas, see the emergence of new kinds of identities, forms of personhood, and social relations developing. Various surveys carried out to ascertain public opinion on developments in genetics indicate that, while there is widespread support for developments related to improvements in health, there is also widespread concern about scientists "tampering with nature."

Advocates of projects to map the human genome claim that the information produced will illuminate the causes of human disease, improve treatment, and, in general, increase our health and well-being. Certainly there are now tests available for detecting over 1,000 genetic diseases and conditions. Although not all of these are readily accessible in the clinic, the availability of such tests is growing at a rapid rate. Tests are used variously: to diagnose those suspected of having a genetic disease, to predict the likelihood of the existence of genetic disease in asymptomatic individuals with a family history of genetic disorders, and to identify carriers of a genetic disease (that is, those at risk of passing the disease on to their children but who do not themselves have susceptibility to the disease). Tests are also carried out during pregnancy and after birth. Prenatal testing is performed during a pregnancy to assess the health status of a fetus. Such tests are offered when there is an increased risk of having a child with a genetic condition due to maternal **age**, family history, or fetal ultrasound examination. Preimplantation testing is performed on early embryos resulting from in vitro fertilization (IVF) in order to decrease the chance of a particular genetic condition occurring in the fetus. It is generally offered to couples with a high chance of having a child with a serious disorder. Newborn screening identifies individuals who have an increased chance of having a specific genetic disorder so that treatment can be started as soon as possible. Nevertheless, while the human genome project has helped to identify a number of genetic conditions, there are only a few treatments available. Most genetic conditions cannot be treated and the reduction in the numbers of individuals being born with such conditions is a result of pregnancy terminations or through the selection of healthy embryos identified by genetic testing during IVF. There have also been a number of educational programs aimed at raising awareness among certain ethnic groups (see **ethnicity and ethnic groups**) that have been identified as having increased susceptibility to certain genetic conditions. Those of eastern European (Ashkenazi) Jewish descent, for example, are often targeted, as chances of being a carrier of Tay Sachs disease are significantly higher in these populations.

A number of commentators have expressed concern about the commercialization of genetic tests and testing services. The biotech company Myriad Genetics, for example, has taken patents out on the genetic codes relating to the two genes most commonly associated with hereditary forms of breast cancer and has been successful in creating exclusive rights over these genetic tests. Many other genetic tests are now readily available over the internet, with tests such as those used for establishing paternity being increasingly used in disputes between parents as well as by agencies involved in determining child support.

Many critics of contemporary genetic practices, such as Troy Duster, suggest that the introduction of clinical testing and genetic screening programs that have steadily increased since the late 1980s have created a *Back Door to Eugenics* (1990). Duster clearly warns against the dangers of prenatal detection of birth defects, gene therapies, and genetic solutions to problems associated with various racial minority groups. He also documents an increasing propensity to see **crime**, mental illness, and intelligence as expressions of genetic dispositions. Feminists and disability scholars, too, have expressed concern about the social implications of genetics, especially its reliance upon abortion to prevent the occurrence of genetic disease. In *Genetic Politics* (2002), Ann Kerr and Tom Shakespeare, while acknowledging that the recent implementations of practices and policies related to genetic technologies are very different from those in the past, also warn that there is a fine line between contemporary policies and practices on abortion and diseases and the past practice of compulsory sterilization for deviancy. They argue that genetics reinforces medical-genetic definitions of disability, makes judgments about the social worth of disabled persons, and ultimately involves decisions about what kinds of persons ought to be born.

A number of scholars have criticized the costs of mapping the human genome and the possible discriminatory and eugenic applications of the information it will provide. They have raised concerns such as the implicit assumptions in the biomedical discourse in which the "benefits" of genetics are proposed, and the ways in which genetic tests shape definitions of illness and health, normality and abnormality. The terms geneticization and genetic determinism were first coined in the early 1990s to refer to the ways that social and other environmental conditions that shape the manifestation and meaning of bodily characteristics and behavior have been ignored in preference to biological and genetic understandings. Abby Lippman is credited with first using the term geneticization to build upon the concept of **medicalization**, whereby people come to perceive the body in conformity with biomedical categories. From this perspective, genetics is highly problematic, as it is based on false biological reductionist and deterministic assumptions which generate a sense of fatalism. In a similar vein, Dorothy Nelkin and Susan Lindee in *The DNA Mystique* (1995) argue that the gene has become a very powerful cultural icon and that a process of genetic essentialism is occurring whereby what it is to be human is increasingly understood in genetic terms. Such geneticization, these critics argue, stems from highly exaggerated claims made by scientists and the ways in which powerful metaphors such as "genetic blueprint" and the "book of life" have been used to describe the human genome. The media in particular are seen to play a vital role in conveying and proliferating the iconic status of the gene.

Nevertheless, concerns about geneticization and a return to eugenics are not shared by all scholars in this area. Nikolas Rose and Carlos Novas, for example, maintain that such approaches oversimplify the shifts in the form of personhood that arise as a result of the growing awareness of genetic **risk**. They claim that the new genetics does not so much result in individuals seeing themselves and their lives along predetermined genetic lines, but rather that knowledge of genetic risk transforms their identities and relations with medical experts in novel and unexpected ways. The growth in various forms of patient activism – such as those coalescing around web-based forums and patient **organizations** that not only raise funds to find cures for genetic diseases, but also help direct scientific agendas – are evidence, they argue, of a more active self-actualizing form of personhood.

There has been a great deal of research within the field of medical sociology examining the experience and understandings of those who are understood to be genetically at risk of disease. The new genetics is based primarily on those self-identifying, and being identified, as at risk. Much of this work is based on a phenomenology approach, focusing on descriptive analyses of the procedures of self-, situational, and social constitution of those who have experienced genetic testing or understand themselves as living with an increased risk of disease. While much of this work, too, highlights the ways in which individuals' knowledge of genetic risk may generate a sense of responsibility towards others, in particular family members who may also be at risk, such research also demonstrates the difficulties and dilemmas faced by those at risk.

Risks in the form of the consequences of genetic engineering or genetic modification of human and other living organisms have also been a subject of debate for scholars.

There is concern that genetic engineering of humans, where faulty genes are either repaired or replaced, might alter the germline cells (those cells that have genetic material that may be passed on via reproduction to a child) and irreversibly alter the genetic makeup of future generations. In *The Future of Human Nature* (2003), **Jürgen Habermas** argues that positive eugenics such as genetic engineering, along with other forms of genetic enhancements, should be forbidden. The reason for forbidding such interventions is that they undermine what it is to be human by ignoring the autonomy of future generations and their standing as moral agents. Drawing upon **Max Weber**'s notions of **rationality**, John Evans, in *Playing God!* (2002), examines bioethics and policy debates about genetic engineering. Evans demonstrates that many such debates, although initially broad-ranging, quickly tend to become narrowly defined, focusing more on how best to achieve the scientific aims rather than on the desirability or otherwise of the aims themselves.

Developments in the new genetics raise profound questions about **democracy** and citizen **rights**. Fears about the undesirable social consequences of developments in genetics have prompted governmental and international regulations and statements.

In 1997, for example, the United Nations Educational, Scientific and Cultural Organization (UNESCO) drew up a *Universal Declaration on the Human Genome and Human Rights*. The declaration affirms the human dignity of each individual, regardless of his or her genetic endowment, and sets out ethical principles for the conduct of research, treatment, or diagnosis related to characteristics of a person's genome. It calls upon states to outlaw **discrimination** based on genetic characteristics if such discrimination would have the effect of "infringing human rights, fundamental freedoms and human dignity."

Many indigenous peoples and environmental nongovernmental organizations oppose the granting of patents on biological materials such as genes, plants, animals, and humans. Some commentators suggest that we are witnessing new forms of "biopiracy" and the colonization of life itself. The Human Genome Diversity Project, which proposes to collect blood and tissue samples from hundreds of different indigenous groups worldwide for genetic study, has been severely criticized by indigenous **communities** and human rights advocates. They have raised questions regarding both ownership of the genetic samples and who stands to profit from the commercialization of products derived from the samples. Concerns have also been raised in relation to the collection, storage, and ownership of DNA for the growing number of national genetic databases.

The creation of genetic databases has been surrounded by controversy and debate, attracting worldwide media attention and significant financial investment by both public and private bodies. At national and international levels, policymakers have sought to define and engage with what they see as the considerable social, ethical, and legal issues at stake. These include informed consent, commercialization, ownership, privacy, confidentiality, and public confidence in the governance of research. Many of these are longstanding areas of **public policy** in relation to the new genetics and more broadly.

An Enlightenment model of progress underpins much of this scientific endeavor with an ever-increasing control of nature through **culture**. At the same time, a number of commentators have noted that culture is becoming increasingly biologized. Paul Rabinow, for example, has coined the term "biosociality" to refer to the new forms of subjecthood and social and political practices that are emerging, which he sees as providing a possible basis for overcoming the nature/culture split.

OONAGH CORRIGAN

genocide

While mass killing has been a perennial aspect of human **societies**, the term genocide is a relatively new concept. It was coined by the Polish jurist Raphael Lemkin in his *Axis Rule in Occupied Europe* (1944) as the legal term to describe the atrocities committed by the Nazis in World War II. Lemkin's effort aimed to provide a legal category to make such acts justiciable under international law (see **law and society**). In Lemkin's view, genocide is a coordinated plan that aims to destroy national groups, in whole or in part. This plan includes not only physical destruction, in the form of mass murder, but also the destruction of the group's **culture** and collective **identity**.

Lemkin's definition has served as the conceptual foundation for practically all subsequent efforts to define genocide, including those by sociologists. Among sociologists, there is considerable conceptual confusion about how to define genocide. Some sociologists adhere rather closely to Lemkin's definition and/or legal definitions, while others seek more expansive sociological definitions, which outline the general structural elements of genocide. Legalistic definitions, however, make it difficult to engage in systematic socio-logical research and theorizing about genocide. There is some general consensus among sociologists that genocide is the killing of substantial numbers of people by an institutionalized, superordinate form of **power**, generally a **state** in conjunction with military power. The victims are generally subordinate, both in a material sense (lacking the means of self-defense) and in a symbolic or ideological sense (they are socially constructed as "threatening," "evil," or "dangerous"). For many legal scholars, genocide is characterized by what is called *dolus specialis*, or special intent, but this is a difficult category to conceptualize within existing **sociological theory**. Homicide is the killing of one person, but genocide is the killing of a number of people. There is, however, no consensus, either among legal scholars or sociologists, as to what the numerical threshold for genocide is.

Much of the social science literature on genocide relies on a naturalistic and positivistic frame of reference that aims to predict and prevent genocide. Barbara Harff and Ted Gurr in *Early Warning of Communal Conflicts and Genocide* (1996) have developed an "early warning" model that provides a series of indicators that aims to predict the occurrence of genocide. Such predictions, however, are not at present tied closely to the institutional means of prevention. In recent years, genocide has occurred in Iraq, Bosnia and Herzegovina, Rwanda, and Sudan. Owing to the modern **mass media**, these genocides were widely observed, but were not prevented. This fact indicates that the phenomenon of "bystanding" is also an important aspect of any definition, empirical research, or theory of genocide in the modern world.

For some sociologists, the relationship between **modernity** and genocide is highly significant. In his *Modernity and the Holocaust* (1989), **Zygmunt Bauman** argues that the scale of mass killing in the Holocaust was enabled by the very forms of bureaucratic **rationality** and instrumental reason that characterize modernity. Bauman's sociological view focuses less on the intent and agency of actors or **institutions** and more on the power of **social roles** and institutionalized practices that enable ordinary people to become perpetrators of extreme **violence**. Michael Barnett in *Eyewitness to a Genocide* (2002) notes that the inability of institutions of global governance to prevent genocide is related to bureaucratic decisionmaking procedures, which stress organizational **norms** and imperatives to the detriment of more global ethical norms and genocide prevention.

Since World War II, when the term genocide was coined, there have been numerous genocides, which indicates that this remains a perennial aspect of human collective behavior in the modern world. A recent example of genocide is in Darfur, Sudan, where as many as 300,000 people have been killed in a campaign of mass murder and cultural destruction. This event was recognized by the world community as genocide, but no decisive action was taken to stop it.

TOM CUSHMAN

gerontology

The study of processes of population and individual aging, this draws upon a wide range of perspectives, including disciplines such as biomedicine, the **social sciences**, and the humanities. Gerontology is typically concerned with understanding aging, first, as a biological and social process affecting individuals across the **life-course**; second, as a process influencing **social change** through the movement of birth cohorts; thirdly, as a significant issue for the development of health and **social policy**.

Interest in the nature of human aging is long-standing, reflected in studies of longevity and related themes from Francis Bacon (1561–1626) onwards. Gerontology as a discipline first emerged at the end of the nineteenth century, notably through investigations by Jean-Martin Charcot (1825–93) into the relationship between old **age** and illness, and the development of theories of aging by Elié Metchnikoff (1845–1916), based upon his work in medicine and biology. The study of aging from social as well as biological perspectives took longer to develop, but expanded rapidly from the 1940s – driven by awareness of the economic impact of aging populations. Professional associations concerned with research into aging developed around this time, including the Gerontological Society of America (established in 1945) and the International Association of Gerontology (1948). Key figures in the development of social and psychological studies of aging, from the 1950s onwards, included James Birren, Bernice Neugarten, Clark Tibbitts, and **Matilda White Riley** in the United States, and Peter Townsend in the United Kingdom.

Sociological and social policy perspectives in gerontology were extended during the 1980s with a combination of critical perspectives on aging and fresh investigations into the family and community life of older people. The former (notably through the work of Carroll Estes and Alan Walker) challenged prevailing views about old age as a "problem for society," highlighting structural pressures and constraints affecting older people. The latter confirmed the diversity of social ties in later life, and the continuing centrality of **family** and friends through all stages of the life-course.

Longitudinal research in gerontology has confirmed the complex mix of factors influencing the experience of growing old. On the one hand, interactions between social, psychological, and biological characteristics influence key aspects of aging. On the other hand, these are embedded within the particular historical and cultural experiences of successive birth cohorts. Membership of a cohort may, for example, greatly influence health and financial status as people mature into later life. This point is reflected in approaches such as cumulative advantage/disadvantage theory, which examines the extent to which early advantage or disadvantage may be accentuated over time leading to increased **inequality** at later stages of the life-course. Through models such as these, gerontology has challenged assumptions of homogeneity among old people, with research evidence suggesting that people become less alike with age, given long-term interactions between genetic endowment, social inequalities, and cultural and historical events.

Major influences on gerontological research in the twenty-first century are likely to include the challenge of **globalization** and the impact of population aging on poorer regions of the world. Hitherto, studies of growing old have been dominated by a focus on older people in western society. Global society comprises, however, a range of demographic processes with variations in the experience and likelihood of growing old. Studying such differences and inequalities across the world will undoubtedly produce major challenges and questions for gerontological research over the next phase of its development.   CHRIS PHILLIPSON

ghetto

This term comes from the early modern Italian practice of setting aside urban **neighborhoods** for Jewish people. Over time, the term retained its association with the enforced **segregation** of Jews in Europe, but in the United States in the twentieth century, ghetto was generalized to other social **groups** against which a collective **prejudice** was directed – notably urban blacks confined economically and socially to an isolated residential area. By the early 2000s, the term had entered common language to be applied to any social group cut off from common social life, sometimes by its own preferences (for example, "the academic ghetto" or "the gypsy ghetto"). With respect to urban enclaves of ethnic groups (see **ethnicity and ethnic groups**) other than Jews or blacks, the term ghetto is commonly replaced by expressions like Chinatown or Little Italy. Whether imposed on the segregated by the wider society or assumed by those who cut themselves off, the term generally retains its original pejorative connotation, as in "ghetto-blasting" in reference to the loud music outsiders associate with the cultural tastes of black ghetto **youth**. In academic sociology, "ghetto" may occur as a quasi-technical term borrowed from common language, but it is more accurately used to denote the social practice whereby social groups tend to associate with others of like kind, usually (but not always) residentially, occasionally by their own choice, but usually by force.   CHARLES LEMERT

Giddens, Anthony (1938–)

Born in 1938 in north London, the son of a clerk, Giddens has had two careers, the first as one of the most influential social theorists of our time, the second as a public **intellectual** both in Great Britain and on the global stage. Giddens was trained as a social theorist at the London School of Economics, to which he returned as Director from 1997 to 2003. From 1970 to 1997, Giddens taught at the University of Cambridge where he became a professor and life fellow of King's College. He is the author or editor of over thirty books. He was made a life peer and took his seat in the British House of Lords in 2004.

As a social thinker, Giddens has an exceptional ability to reconcile and synthesize leading arguments drawn from disparate and often rival schools of thought. In doing so he produces novel analytical frameworks and concepts that preserve the strengths of a vast array of sources. Proceeding in this way, Giddens has done as much as any single thinker to set the agenda for an entire **generation** of sociologists. He first rose to prominence in 1971 when he published *Capitalism and Social Theory*. At a time when Anglophone **social theory** was still ill informed about European social thought, Giddens provided surehanded commentaries on the depth and breadth of works by **Max Weber**, **Émile Durkheim**, and especially **Karl Marx**, whom Giddens did much to legitimate for sociologists who previously had avoided his works.

In the next phase of his sociological career, Giddens created a new analytic framework he dubbed structuration theory. Structuration theory is a sociological **ontology**, that is, a set of concepts that propose generic assumptions about the nature of social life that sociologists draw upon when they first think about social life in any given historical, cultural, or local domain. When developing structuration theory, Giddens absorbed the lessons of **Harold Garfinkel**, **Erving Goffman**, and the later philosophy of **Ludwig Wittgenstein,** all of whom concurred on the fundamental importance of enacted practices in social life. It is in part thanks to Giddens's structuration theory that social practices are now regarded as basic units of analysis in sociology. When Giddens first began developing structuration theory at Cambridge in the mid-1970s, **social action** was almost always defined in terms of the subjective meaning the actor gave to his/her own acts. Like Garfinkel, Goffman, and the later Wittgenstein, Giddens recognized that it is what actors do and how they perform that constitutes social conduct.

But Giddens was quite critical of sociologists of practice (also known as sociologists of **everyday life**) for their unwillingness to take on board the reflexive association between enacted forms of conduct and the larger structural properties and morphological patterns of relations in **society**. In his central concept of the duality of structure, Giddens proposes that structural properties of larger and enduring social **groups** are carried by actors as forms of competencies that enable them to act in specific ways in appropriate situations. Actors in such situations may reproduce the general form of the practices they have learned in the past, or they may alter that form in some way. While no single act may sustain or change the structural properties of a **culture** or a group in itself, the manifold reproduction or alteration of practices by numerous actors over extended periods of time will either reproduce the characteristic structured features of a culture or group, or more or less substantially revise the structure of that group. In much the same way, enacted practices may either reproduce or alter the **networks** of contacts and relations, and the more integrated systems, that provide the morphological patterns for society.

In structuration theory, Giddens also offers a new theory of **power** in society. Like Weber, Giddens distinguishes forms of domination from the forms of social power in everyday life. Concentrating on the latter, Giddens breaks sharply with **Michel Foucault** and others who see pervasive domination in social life. In his concept of the dialectic of control, Giddens proposes that in principle all actors, save perhaps for those who are physically disabled, have at least two options, namely to comply or resist the orders of others. Given that the dominant typically require compliance from the dominated, Giddens proposes that dominated groups always have some ability to carve out spheres of autonomy for themselves, however modest or expansive they may be. Recent works by **Michael Mann** and **Charles Tilly** expand upon this point, though only Mann directly acknowledges a debt to Giddens in this regard.

Modernity is the theme in the third phase of Giddens's sociological career, a phase marked by three publications: *The Consequences of Modernity* (1990), *Modernity and Self-Identity* (1991), and "Living in a Post-Traditional Society," in Ulrich Beck, Giddens, and Scott Lash, *Reflexive Modernization* (1994). As the Soviet Union imploded and the information age was about to dawn, Giddens pointed out that dramatic cultural, political, economic, and technological change has been characteristic of modernity since its inception. This did not make the new wave of changes any less disruptive and disorienting. Indeed, Giddens mainly concentrates his attention on the existential problems and the difficulties in maintaining personal relationships that have beset modern western societies since the end of World War II. Two disruptive forces of particular note are, on the one hand, the eclipse of time and (to only a relatively lesser degree) space as barriers to the expansion of social systems and, on the other hand, the erosion of local **authority** and culture by abstract economic and informational systems. But Giddens also notes the countervailing trend of the reappropriation of abstract knowledge by actors in their everyday lives.

As a public intellectual, Giddens is best known as the originator of The Third Way, a set of leading ideas for **social policy** associated with the Labour government of Prime Minister Tony Blair in Britain and several European governments as well. Giddens has published several books for general audiences including *The Third Way* (1998) and *Runaway World* (2000).   IRA COHEN

gift

The giving of gifts has been analyzed as an aspect of social exchange. Gifts generally create or reinforce social **solidarity** by creating obligation, but they can also be used aggressively to demonstrate superior social **power**. In his *The Gift*, **Marcel Mauss** (1923 [trans. 1983]) treated gifts as a form of social exchange which reinforces social solidarity, creating a duty to reciprocate the original gift, but he also examined the "potlatch ritual" of Native

Americans in which a chief might display his power through a ritual destruction of his possessions. This example demonstrates the contradictory nature of gift giving, both creative and destructive.

In the social philosophy of Jacques Derrida (1930–2004), the study of gifts is related more broadly to hospitality and **friendship**. Derrida has drawn on Emile Benveniste's *Le Vocabulaire des institutions Indo-Europeenes* (1969) in his *Of Hospitality* (2000). In the study of reciprocity, Derrida showed that in a variety of European languages there are important etymological connections between "stranger," "enemy," and "guest." Latin *hostis* indicates the notion of a stranger who has an irresistible claim on our hospitality, specifically a claim against the master of the household. While people who dwell outside may be enemies, the guest who has entered our dwelling to sit by the fireside has significant **rights** and can claim our protection. This analysis of the origins of "guest" demonstrates how notions of reciprocity and exchange between the master of a household and the guest emerge from expectations about hospitality. Any consideration of the stranger/guest relationship must take into account the wider realm of gift exchange, and the duties that attach to giving and receiving.

Derrida was influenced by Mauss's discussion of "primitive exchange" in *The Gift*, in which the word *pharmakon* means both poison and cure. In Mauss's analysis of the potlatch ritual of the Native American **communities** of the northwest coast, it is evident that the gift-exchange is typically a challenge that creates a destructive social relationship. In connection with social relations, the gift is both corrosive (poison) and therapeutic (cure). In reflecting on "Plato's Pharmacy" through Mauss's analysis of the *pharmakon,* Derrida used this etymological analysis of the ambiguity of the gift to show in effect that all ethical behavior involves hospitality, because ethics are about the claims which the stranger might have on our **society**.   BRYAN S. TURNER

gift relationship
– see **gift**.

Gilroy, Paul (1956–)

Influenced by the **Birmingham Centre for Contemporary Cultural Studies**, since 1999 Gilroy has been Professor of Sociology and African-American Studies at Yale University. His PhD thesis, "Racism, Class and The Contemporary Politics of 'Race' and 'Nation'" (1986), focused on the British situation and culminated in his first book, *There Ain't No Black in the Union Jack* (1987). His work has been a consistent attempt to combat "raciology" by emphasizing the diasporic character of racial categories of **identity**, **solidarity**, and resistance. *The Black Atlantic* (1993), *Against Race* (2000), and *Between Camps* (2004) reject essentialist approaches to **ethnicity** in favor of a post-identity form of **double-consciousness** that seeks to acknowledge the hybrid form of the various versions of white supremacy and black **power**. The *Black Atlantic* reveals the authoritarian connection between sovereign territory and national consciousness and the contradictions thereof. It argues that for 150 years black **intellectuals** in the West have been diasporic and struggled with the dilemmas involved in being simultaneously black and western. Gilroy's **sociology** makes an explicit link between the quest for territorial sovereignty, **racism**, and **fascism**. At the level of material **culture**, Gilroy has examined black vernacular and **popular cultures** through black music, film, and literature to demonstrate the articulation of diasporic, hybrid forms. His recent work has been concerned with examining the meaning of **multiculturalism** and elaborating non-racial **democracy**. This has climaxed in the concept of "planetary humanism" which he develops from Aimé Césaire and **Franz Fanon**. This rejects liberal humanism on the grounds that it is complicit with racism and calls for an inclusive, global, anti-racist, anti-militaristic, and environmentalist humanism.

By arguing that racial **politics** must transgress the color line and incorporate a critical stance on essentialist thinking per se, Gilroy shows that he is *au courant* with postcolonial thought and the post-identity thinking found in the work of his old Birmingham School mentor, **Stuart Hall**. But critics have questioned whether his politics of double-consciousness and planetary humanism is practically viable.   CHRIS ROJEK

Glazer, Nathan (1924–)

Formerly Professor of Education and Social Structure and currently Professor Emeritus, in the Graduate School of Education, Harvard University, and the co-editor of *The Public Interest*, Glazer has been an influential figure in American public life in terms of his writing on race relations and **multiculturalism**. He has been closely associated with the so-called New York **intellectuals** who included such figures as **Daniel Bell**. He was, as a student, a follower of L. Trotsky, the Russian revolutionary. After the Depression, Glazer, like many Jewish intellectuals, came to regard capitalist

America as a successful **democracy** in which each successive wave of migrants could eventually be incorporated into America, despite **discrimination**. His first publication was on the topic of his dissertation, *The Social Basis of American Communism* (1961), and he collaborated in **David Riesman**'s *The Lonely Crowd* (1950). He came to the attention of the academic **community** through his publications on **race and ethnicity**. He wrote the influential *American Judaism* (1957) and, with D. P. Moynihan, he published *Beyond the Melting Pot* (1963) and *Ethnicity. Theory and Practice* (1975). His essays on these issues were published as *Ethnic Dilemmas 1964–1982* (1983).

Glazer has emerged as a controversial figure in American **politics** because he has questioned affirmative action programs, for example in support of black Americans. These arguments were presented in *Affirmative Discrimination* (1975) – a collection of essays that date back to the early 1970s. Critics of Glazer, for example S. Steinberg (2001) in *Turning Back. The Retreat from Racial Justice in American Thought*, have argued that, not only has he abandoned the socialist principles of his youth, but also it is hypocritical of a person from a migrant Jewish background to criticize black activists for demanding support for their aspirations to succeed in American **society**. For example, Glazer was a student at City College New York in 1940 when tuition was free – a form therefore of **affirmative action**. Critics claim that his policy prescriptions are justified by apparently scholarly arguments from, for example, *Beyond the Melting Pot*, where Glazer argued that, because black Americans had suffered so profoundly in the past from **slavery**, they have not experienced the upward **social mobility** enjoyed by other ethnic **communities** who have prospered in the American Dream. Glazer argues that repairing this historical problem of black Americans is beyond the scope of current **social policy**.

Glazer argued that, despite the civil rights movement, the gap between white and black Americans has persisted, and this **inequality** is associated with declining inner-city schools and the unravelling of the black **family**. He has recently been critical of liberal policies, especially in schools towards a multicultural curriculum, in *We Are All Multiculturalists Now* (1997) and *Sovereignty under Challenge* (J. D. Montgomery and N. Glazer (eds.), 2002), in which he is concerned that multicultural **education** subverts the truth and undermines national unity by the "Balkanization" of the American republic. Glazer and his generation believed that Americanization was unproblematic because ethnic minorities would eventually be assimilated and benefit from growing economic prosperity. However, that optimism has been questioned by the fact that black **progress** appears to have come to an end in the 1970s. For his critics, Glazer apparently offers black **youth** a bleak choice: either negative **social conflict** and disharmony, or passive acceptance of inclusion into American society (on white terms). Despite criticisms, the quality and importance of Glazer's scholarship remains unquestioned.   BRYAN S. TURNER

globalism
– see **globalization**.

globalization
Described as a new world order, some scholars argue that globalization is an unprecedented 21st-century reorganization of **time**, **space**, people, and things. It is variously portrayed, sometimes as "globalism" by advocates and promoters, or as a postmodern form of unrestrained capitalist expansion and **imperialism** by members of anti-globalization movements. In both instances, the object of support or resistance is a global system of interconnected communication and transportation **networks**, economic **markets**, and persons, covering almost the entire planet. An essential feature of this system is that it is deterritorialized, that is, the connections and collectivities exist primarily in electronic networks of communication. Some authors, such as Arun Appadurai in his "Disjuncture and Difference in the Global Cultural Economy," in *Public Culture* (1990), refer to this as a form of pan-locality, with multiple nodes of transaction or "scapes" – ethnoscapes, technoscapes, finanscapes, mediascapes, ideoscapes, linguistically echoing the notion of landscape for segmented networks in this now deterritorialized, fluid, transnational, global social **organization**. Through the electronic connections and diverse scapes, elements of human **culture** move around the globe separately from geographic, institutional, or relational contexts.

A scientific–technological account of globalization describes a world engirded by a finely wrought network of cables, satellites, air, and sea lanes, as well as old familiar land routes, that transport **information**, things, and people from one place to any other on the globe in anything from a minute to a day. This is a world in which boundaries that once had been created by time and space have been eroded by scientific and technological developments, especially in communication and transportation.

These innovations have roots in ancient times when exploration and trade by land and sea was apparent in the Mediterranean basin and Asian seas, and in medieval and Renaissance times when scientific and technological innovations began to spread around the globe. Scientific and technological development escalated noticeably, however, during the sixteenth and seventeenth centuries, and, with exponential rates of both invention and **social change** in the twentieth century, the spatial and temporal distances that had historically moored distinct populations, **languages**, cultures, markets, and political systems have been made porous through regularized and continual communication. In this techno-scientific account, emphasis is placed on the cumulative effects of the **Enlightenment**, and how humans slowly accumulate the knowledge and ability to produce ever increasingly rational forms of social organization and technological innovation, in the end overcoming ignorance, superstition, **myth**, **religion**, and **scarcity** to create relative abundance, human freedom, and worldwide mobility. The mixing of peoples, languages, and cultures has brought about what is now a transparent **hybridity** in human **groups** and cultures. While few human cultures, in history or contemporary times, have been unaffected by exchange with others (enemies or friends), the degree of hybridity and technologically driven hybridization is at a scale and pace heretofore unknown.

A political-economic account of globalization places less emphasis on the technological sources of globalization than on the political and normative claims of capitalist investment. Rather than being a portrayal of the success of science and **technology**, a political-economic account describes the historic triumph of the market **economy**. It is an account of how the market – as a means of coordinating production and distribution – is now worldwide, after more than a century of being confined within national and regional boundaries. This view of globalization depicts markets as both the engine and product of human energy and imagination, now in the twenty-first century overcoming what is described as backward and inefficient systems of centralized planning and socialized ownership that governed a good part of the globe during the twentieth century.

Some accounts of globalization emphasize the international coordination of scientific research to control disease, prolong lifetimes, and improve conditions of **everyday life**. Others focus on the transnational flow of people, goods, and capital that creates a global division of **labor** with an equally global diffusion of material and cultural goods. For example, goods produced with Korean or Chilean labor, from materials mined in Zaire or grown in India, are sold in the shops in Paris, Los Angeles, or Tokyo. People born and raised in Mexico, Guatemala, Turkey, Algeria, Ethiopia, or Zimbabwe travel north to find work to sustain families left behind. At the same time, music from American urban **ghettos** is played in the shops in Japan and Australia or the streets of Budapest and Russia, portable telephones manufactured in Finland adorn the hips of laborers from Santiago to Cape Town, and television stations around the globe fill their schedules with the product of Hollywood studios while munching on American-style fast **food** of Big Macs and French fries.

As the same time as local sites become linked in a global circulation of people, signs, materials, and goods, globalization is understood to be reshaping the parts of the world now joined communicatively and economically. While some people and phenomena are ripped from spatial and territorial moorings, others – for example, social groups based on ethnic, linguistic, or religious practices – become re-territorialized, making claims to specific pieces of geography with newly recognized boundaries as the ground of their participation in the global world order. While some localities experience a marked increase in standards of living (measured in terms of reduced infant mortality, longevity, **education**, and calories consumed), others experience an equally marked decline in material, psychological, and sociological conditions of everyday life. In the techno-science account, the global **community** is linked internally by its actively shared cultures and externally through its collective scientific exploration beyond this globe.

Rather than a portrayal of the success of science and technology, the political-economy account emphasizes the virtues of flexible production, worldwide sourcing, and low-cost transportation and communication. Just as the boundaries between time, space, people, and things are erased in the techno-science account, the economic account emphasizes the erasure of traditional distinctions among market tools – between banking, brokerage, insurance, business, politics, and consumer credit – and the promotion of strict boundaries between economics and politics. Global capital is financialized, that is, like social transactions dis-embedded from geography and social

relations, capital accumulation is also de-territorialized, mobile, residing nowhere more than in cyberspace. Ever liquid, new financial instruments are created as well as markets in these instruments, new markets in commodities, as well as markets in currencies and debts. The capital that fuels the global circulation of goods, services, and people is therefore faceless and rootless, free of national or geographic **identity**, ever mobile, moving from one locale to another, as efficiency and profit demands.

The global markets create both dispersion and integration. Global dispersion is typified by the creation of new producers and sites of production within nations and transnationally. Large and small companies increase their subcontracting, and do so with several geographically distant subcontractors for the same product. Industrial homework spreads into the hinterlands of remote parts of the world at the same time as highly skilled cognitive (mind-work) laborers and professionals move their work from office to home, sometimes also at great distances from the centers of control and **management**. This diffusion of worldwide outsourcing – fueled by low transportation costs and computerized communication linkages – creates flexible production and higher profits for corporate managers and owners, while relegating labor and suppliers to hyper-competition and insecure **income**.

The territorial dispersion is accompanied by a parallel concentration of centralized control to manage and finance the dispersed production. The remotest sites of individual production are tied by centralized management through closely linked chains of financial and design control finding their apex primarily in the global cities such as Tokyo, New York, and London. The global cities produce the specialized services which, according to Saskia Sassen in *The Global City* (1991), are "needed by complex organizations for running spatially dispersed networks of factories, offices, and service outlets," as well as the "financial innovations and the making of markets . . . central to the internationalization and expansion of the financial industry."

The dual processes of dispersion and integration are joined in processes of what some term "glocalization," a neologism joining globalization and localization to describe the customization of globally produced products or services for local cultures and markets. It is also used to refer to the use of global networks, for example in cell phones, to provide local services. It refers in addition to identity marketing that fetishizes local places for the purpose of product branding, associating, for example, coffee with a particular Colombian farmer, or a unique island with the home of a generic product. According to Roland Robertson, who is credited with popularizing the term, glocalization describes the tempering effects of local conditions on global pressures. At a 1997 conference on "Globalization and Indigenous Culture," Robertson said that glocalization "means the simultaneity – the co-presence – of both universalizing and particularizing tendencies." The term, first used by Japanese economists in the 1980s, is also used prescriptively in business circles to emphasize that the globalization of a product is more likely to succeed when the product or service is adapted and tailored specifically to each locality or culture in which it is marketed. Examples of glocalization display the self-conscious cultural hybridization that is at work in global marketing. For example, the American fast-food chain McDonald's replaced its mascot, the clown Ronald McDonald, in French advertising with Asterix the Gaul, a popular French cartoon character.

Accompanying the techno-scientific and economic accounts of globalization, there are political and moral claims about the necessity of a rule of law (see **law and society**) and, at the same time, the inefficiencies of legal regulation. In the political–legal account of globalization, national boundaries are described as inefficient and should cease being barriers to trade: all national economies should be open to trade. In this moral universe, all exchanges, transactions, and engagements should be signaled solely through market prices, which are conceived as the only legitimate form of **social control** for rewarding good action and punishing bad. Public regulation of private enterprise, as an alternative to price regulation, is the enemy of the global economy and its moral universe. As a corollary to the dominant role of prices as the major form of communicating participation in the market economy, domestic prices are supposed to conform to international prices and monetary policies are expected to be directed to the maintenance of price and balance-of-payment stability. These are the basic universal principles of market economics promoted by the International Monetary Fund, the World Bank, and neoliberal economists promoting market globalization.

Although markets depend on law to provide a stable normative environment, ensuring security of **property** and contracts, the global "marketeers" insist that the law do no more. Beyond the assurance of mutual **trust** and normative order, the market or neoliberal account of globalization demands that the rest of economic affairs remain entirely matters of market (price) decisions rather than the consequences of political organization or legal processes. The market version of globalization urges use of law to police a fixed boundary between public and private, between economics and politics. Although national legal orders in western Europe and the United States have, for more than 100 years, created various adjustments to counteract market instabilities and imperfect competition, a key feature of globalization at the end of the twentieth and beginning of the twenty-first centuries is the fury of its critique of legal intervention and its insistence on a natural and necessary divide between public and private, economics and politics. Historical experience and legal precedents notwithstanding, the global marketeers insist that the private law regime of property and contract, at both the national and international levels, is an apolitical realm, merely supportive of private initiative and decision, immune from public or political contestations and without significant or problematic redistributive consequences.

Some observers argue that the global system – embodied primarily in the communication networks – allows direct cultural and economic relationships that bypass and/or subvert – depending on the point of view – traditional power hierarchies like national governments, or markets. There are some who see in globalization the possibilities of a new democratic transformation. Some stress that the circulation of capital and culture is – as the phrase suggests – a circulation, not solely a movement from the center to the peripheries. By dissolving political, temporal, and spatial boundaries, the technological revolutions underwriting this transnational exchange create capacity for movement in all directions and with less investment than was heretofore possible. From this perspective, as illustrated in Boaventura de Sousa Santos's *Toward a New Common Sense: Law, Science and Politics in the Paradigmatic Transition* (1995), globalization enables more diverse participation and more sources of **influence** – forms of enfranchisement – throughout the world-system. Those at the geographic peripheries of the world-system welcome the chance to be regular and possibly influential participants in the virtual global community. In the global networks of communication and exchange, human creativity can be unleashed from traditional cultural and material constraints to find new forms of expression in what seems like an unbounded space of possible interactions and connections. Here, observers point to the importance of human rights discourse, in contrast to the economic rights discourse of marketeers, in shaping actual, not merely a virtual, community, and the empirically documentable changes that discourse has wrought in heretofore authoritarian regimes. Similarly, some note the growing significance of environmental concerns in mobilizing **social movements** across traditional national, political, racial, and gender boundaries. For optimistic observers, globalizing markets pose an opportunity and challenge.

In contrast, others view globalization as a historic process leading to a more one-way relationship between the global realm, inhabited by multinational corporations, global finance, the entertainment industry, international broadcasting, the worldwide web, amoral secular humanism, and a subjugated "local" realm where the identity-affirming senses of place, **neighborhood**, town, locale, **ethnicity**, **religion**, and **morality** barely survive against the global onslaught of globally circulated, professional produced-for-profit identities. Some claim that the techno-scientific account of globalization is a saga of disenchantment, as **Max Weber** predicted. Noting the immediacy with which persons, goods, information, and technologies move across vast distances, and the expanding breadth and accelerating pace of **consumption**, critics of globalization, in anti-globalization movements and elsewhere, emphasize how the loss of sacred illusions and embedded identities has left a corrosive absence at the center of human life where "all that is solid melts into air" (**Karl Marx** and **Friedrich Engels**, *The Communist Manifesto* (1848 [trans. 1968]). Critics note the bombardment by stimuli, the neurological overloads, and the homogenizing consequences of the escalating circulation of signs and **symbols** removed from local experiences and interpretive frameworks. Globalization seems to be characterized by isomorphisms, convergences, and hybridizations that create a sense of pervasive sameness across heretofore-diverse cultures. Some anti-globalization movements emphasize this emptying out of meaning and morality in the global markets, actively seeking a return to a religiously guided morality, **politics**, and economy – sometimes violently, such as in Islamic Jihadist groups (such as the Taliban in Afghanistan) or some anti-abortion movements in the United States, sometimes peacefully, such as among Christian fundamentalists.

Other anti-globalization movements emphasize and attempt to resist the growing **inequality** and erosion of economic security that had been promoted by the twentieth-century welfare politics.

Some observers go so far as to describe globalization as a form of postmodern **colonialism**, where the worldwide distribution and consumption of cultural products removed from the contexts of their production and interpretation are organized through legal devices and markets to constitute a form of domination, as argued by Susan Silbey in "Let Them Eat Cake: Globalization, Postmodern Colonialism, and the Possibilities of Justice" (1996, *Law and Society Review*). In postmodern colonialism, control of land or political organization or nation-states is less important than **power** over consciousness and consumption, much more efficient forms of domination. This is, for anti-globalization critics, the consequence of advanced **capitalism** and technological innovation seeking a world free from restraints on the opportunity to invent and to invest. In this most critical account, globalization describes a world in which size and scale in terms of numbers of persons (who can produce), and in numbers of outlets (to disseminate and place products), and capital (to purchase both **labor** and land) determine the capacity to saturate local cultures. Advocates of free-market capitalism worldwide acknowledge the inequalities produced, urging "measures that enlarge the scope for wage differentials without making it socially unacceptable" (Y. Kosai, R. Lawrence, and N. Thygesen, "Don't Give Up on Global Trade," in the *International Herald Tribune*, 1996). The processes of global economic **differentiation** have led to increased income for some previously poor workers at the peripheries of the system, but also for significant transfers of income from workers to upper-level managers and investors. Alongside the economic differentiation is a division of intellectual labor: the new systems that organize **work** and production are designed by relatively few highly educated, technically trained specialists, with labor and repetitive, minimal skill well distributed across the globe.

SUSAN SILBEY

glocalization
– see **globalization**.

Goffman, Erving (1922–1982)
One of the most original, influential, and exciting sociologists, Erving Goffman found systematic order and moral meaning in the momentary gestures of individuals in the presence of one another

that seem at first glance to be nothing more than unreflective conformity to local custom and cultural etiquette. Goffman characterized this realm of phenomena "the interaction order," and in his essay by that name, published in *American Sociological Review* (1983), saw it as comprising all that is socially structured whenever actors are in sufficiently close proximity to be aware of one another's presence. (He termed this the condition of copresence.) Focused conversations are the most obvious phenomena in the interaction order. However, the interaction order also includes the less involving, small gestures through which actors acknowledge or avoid one another in **everyday life**. At the boundaries of the interaction order, Goffman includes the ways people respect one another's **privacy** in public settings and the ways people maneuver so as to maintain order on crowded city streets.

Readers almost unanimously experience a special sense of discovery in reading Goffman's work. He was outstandingly blessed with the ability to find order and significance in everything from small shifts in body posture to a conversational pause that continues only slightly beyond cultural expectations. But Goffman did not couple his deep insights with sociological breadth. He assumed a controversial theoretical position by maintaining that there is only a loose coupling between the interaction order and larger institutional orders such as the worlds of **work**, commerce, and government.

Goffman was born in 1922 in the Canadian province of Alberta to parents of Jewish-Ukrainian descent who immigrated to Canada prior to World War I. He was educated in sociology and anthropology at the University of Toronto and began his graduate studies in anthropology at the University of Chicago, where he received his doctorate in 1953. His doctoral research, conducted during eighteen months of fieldwork in the Shetland Islands, yielded the data analyzed in one of his most prominent books, *The Presentation of Self in Everyday Life* (1959). Goffman took his first major academic position at the University of California, Berkeley, in 1958, and moved to the University of Pennsylvania in 1968. At the time of his death from cancer in 1982, he was President of the American Sociological Association.

Goffman, together (though not in direct association) with **George Herbert Mead**, **Alfred Schutz**, and **Harold Garfinkel**, transformed the study of **social action** by shifting from a Weberian (and ultimately Kantian) emphasis on subjectivity, **motivation**, and the ascription of meaning, to an emphasis on the enacted performance of social practices. He summarized this shift in a famous apothegm, "Not men and their moments. Rather moments and their men" (*Interaction Ritual*, 1967: 4). By this, he meant that social action in local situations is structured by cultural **rituals** rather than by the psychological motives of individuals.

The majority of Goffman's publications from 1956 to 1971 have a special richness in this regard. Transforming **Émile Durkheim**'s insights in completely unanticipated directions, Goffman demonstrated that apparently inconsequential aspects of social etiquette have deep-seated moral significance. One of his great achievements was to transmute Durkheim's philosophically inspired insights into the cult of the dignity of the individual into studies of facework (that is, the ways in which individuals establish their **identities** during social **interaction**). Though Goffman never strayed into the analysis of the culture of **individualism** at large, he seemed to have a deep intuitive understanding of the fragility of social face within the culture of **modernity**, where interaction rituals and social identities shift from one context to the next. He was keenly aware of the possibilities of error, playfulness, and even attacks upon others during the course of facework. He was extremely sensitive to the structured avenues available in interaction for the protection and repair of one's own face and the defense and repair of others. But these vulnerabilities impressed Goffman less than the fact that interaction rituals generally produce order in everyday life. For example, Goffman understood conversation to create an *unio mystica*, that is, a shared involvement that transcends all other concerns.

But Goffman's interest in order, which is one of his great sociological strengths, is the source of his greatest weakness as well. Other than embarrassment, an **emotion** that he could not ignore, Goffman studied the interaction order by bracketing the actor's existential and emotional experiences. Hence, despite the stunning brilliance of his insights into morally meaningful interactions, his works sometimes lack sufficient human depth. For example, in *Stigma* (1964), Goffman analyzed the nature of profoundly damaged identity in social interaction with no more than perfunctory acknowledgments of the dramatic inner experiences of stigmatic individuals.

In 1974, Goffman published *Frame Analysis*, a sprawling book in which he tried to draw together a systematic approach to the structured enactment of meaning in social life. However, the work is more valuable for its remarkable insights into specific forms of interaction than for its theoretical structure at large. Goffman's genius, and the word is used purposefully here, resided in his ability to find order in the seemingly improvised nature of social action. His methods make reading his work a special delight, thanks in particular to his skill in drawing metaphors from contexts such as religious rituals, dramatic performance, and games, seen as idealized instances of the deeper and more general properties of social practice he wanted us to see. But if his imaginative recourse to these and a profusion of other metaphors to find the order in interaction sets him apart, Goffman stands out as well for his ability to sustain a systematic analysis while allowing for the contingencies available as an interaction scene unfolds. No other sociologist of action has managed to find the balance between order and contingency in local situations nearly as well. When classical **social theory** is redefined to include the twentieth century, Goffman will be one of the first nominees.

IRA COHEN

Goldmann, Lucien (1913–1970)

Born in Romania, Goldmann spent much of his adult life in Switzerland and France. He is best known for his contribution to the study of literature and philosophy and in particular to the discussion of the ways in which literary and philosophical works are related to their social context. Goldmann was much influenced by the Hungarian Marxist **Georg Lukács** and the Swiss psychologist Jean Piaget; the work of both men encouraged Goldmann to attempt to find a way of explaining cultural form without reverting to either **materialism** or **idealism**. The fruition of Goldmann's work was his study of Pascal and Racine, *The Hidden God* (first published in 1956), in which he argued that complex cultural phenomena are formed through what he described as "homologous structures," essentially similar patterns of thought between relatively unformed **ideologies** and more complex and finished intellectual works. For Goldmann, the study of **culture** was not about the identification of **"influence"** or "context," since this enterprise isolated social patterns; Goldmann argued for a method which maintained a "conceptual oscillation" between the parts and the whole. Goldmann wrote widely on seventeenth-century France, the **Enlightenment**, the method of the **social sciences**, and cultural change in the twentieth century. In the latter context he is well known for his assertion

that in modern western societies the great political battles are for the control of consciousness rather than the control of the means of production.

MARY EVANS

Goldthorpe, John (1935–)

A British sociologist, Goldthorpe is best known for his empirical and theoretical contributions to the study of **social mobility** and **social class**, and his trenchant critical essays on a wide range of topics in contemporary sociology. At the center of much of Goldthorpe's work on topics in **social stratification** has been a critical empirical assessment of modernization and industrialization theories. Goldthorpe's first major work, the three-volume *The Affluent Worker* (1968–9), examined the extent to which the best-paid segment of the working class was undergoing a process of **embourgeoisement**, concluding that this core claim of industrialization theory was for the most part unsustainable. From a base at Nuffield College at Oxford University, beginning in the early 1970s, he produced important work on occupational sociology (*The Social Grading of Occupations*, 1974) and the patterning of social mobility in Britain (*Social Mobility and Class Structure in Modern Britain*, revised 2nd edn., 1987 [1980]). Goldthorpe led a pioneering effort to examine systematically the patterns of social mobility cross-nationally in the so-called CASMIN project. The major work of this project, *The Constant Flux* (1992), was co-authored with Swedish sociologist Robert Erikson. It challenged the view that all societies are on a unilinear path of increasing social mobility. The "EG" class schema presented there and in earlier writings has become virtually standard in most contemporary cross-national work on classes in capitalist societies and has even been adopted by the British government. Goldthorpe has also penned a series of sharply and widely debated critical essays on the practice of qualitative and comparative-historical sociology, class analysis, **feminism**, and **Marxism**. Many of these are collected in *On Sociology* (2000). These critiques have in common an insistence upon the importance of rigorous empirical evidence and data analysis in developing and evaluating **sociological theories**, an approach Goldthorpe has consistently applied in his own research across his long career.

JEFF MANZA

Goode, William Josiah (1917–2003)

Emeritus Professor at Stanford University, former President of the American Sociological Association, President of the Eastern Sociological

Society, and an assistant director of the Bureau of Applied Social Research, Goode made major contributions to the cross-cultural study of **marriage and divorce**, and to the theory of social control systems of **prestige**, force, and love. Goode taught at various universities in the United States: Wayne State, Columbia, Stanford, Harvard, and George Mason. His Columbia dissertation was published as *Religion Among the Primitives* (1951), which remains a brilliant introduction to the sociology of **religion**. His *World Revolution and Family Patterns* (1963) set the research agenda on the **family** in twentieth-century sociology by examining the rise of distinctive family patterns in fifty societies during the process of **industrialization**. His other major publications in this field were *After Divorce* (1956), *The Family* (1982), and *World Changes in Divorce Patterns* (1993). Goode developed the theory of **social role** in his *Theory of Role Strain* (1960) and of **social status** in his *The Celebration of Heroes* (1978). He contributed, with his co-author, Paul K. Hatt, to the teaching of **methodology** in *Methods in Social Research* (1952). Underlying much of his work was a theory of social exchange in which he was particularly interested in the role of third parties.

BRYAN S. TURNER

Gouldner, Alvin (1920–1981)

Gouldner made a significant contribution in several areas of sociology, most notably to the understanding of the sociological enterprise itself. In his most important work, *The Coming Crisis of Western Sociology* (1970), he advances the case for a reflexive sociology which, he felt, would address the shortcomings of existing "conservative" and "Marxist" traditions.

Gouldner's most important early work, *Patterns of Industrial Bureaucracy* (1954), deals with conventional themes in industrial sociology and **organization theory**. The influential *Wildcat Strike* (1965), meanwhile, focused on a **case study** of employer–employee relations from which Gouldner constructed a theory of group tensions.

By the 1960s, he had turned his attention increasingly to theoretical commentary on traditions of **social theory** and to its reconstruction. Taking a long time-span, he turned, in *Enter Plato* (1967), to aspects of the legacy of ancient Greece that he saw as having value in the contemporary world. Closer to home in *The Coming Crisis*, he argued against the adequacy of both structural **functionalism** and **Marxism** as models for the sociological project. The former, as exemplified by **Talcott Parsons**, was regarded as conservative, accommodating sociology to new realities of power and **inequality**. Since it is hard for social theorists to reconcile new forms of power built around corporations and the **professions** with **norms** of goodness, Gouldner felt that the conservative option found ways of representing power as positive, changing norms to accord with reality. He rejected this, having more sympathy with radical alternatives that provided a critique of power, and gave a positive normative loading to thoughts and feelings unpermitted by mainstream opinion. Gouldner's commitment to theoretical renewal also led him to found the influential journal *Theory and Society* in 1974.

Marxism was a possible alternative source of radical inspiration, though this had a further difficulty, namely that it was more successful in criticizing other traditions than criticizing itself. In this respect, Gouldner thought of himself as an "Outlaw Marxist." Instead of asking social theorists to choose between "conservative" sociology and "radical" Marxism, Gouldner projected reflexive sociology as an alternative standpoint. This idea was designed as a way of reconstructing the vocation of **intellectual** in a general way, and of sociology in particular. While intellectuals should promote a **culture** of critical discourse, the reflexive sociologist should rise above the role of technical specialist. Reflexive sociology was to be defined not in terms of scientific objectivity towards its subject matter, but in terms of a critical stance to the social and political context in which the sociologist operated. Soul-searching was better than soul-selling.

This position is in one sense a product of its times, sociology seemingly oscillating between canonical (Parsons) and iconoclastic (Gouldner) moments. Marxism, as Gouldner was later to argue in *The Two Marxisms* (1980), contained these tensions within itself, manifested in the contrast between Marxism as science and Marxism as critique. While reflexivity is now very much a mainstream idea – seen in the concept of reflexive modernity – Gouldner's emphasis on social emancipation via critical intellectuals and the culture of critical discourse, advanced in *The Future of Intellectuals and the Rise of the New Class* (1980), has been undermined by the class-like inequalities associated with knowledge holders.

Gouldner's project of a sociology based on critical analysis from a moral standpoint is again a fairly widely held presupposition. Yet he failed to provide much epistemological depth on how a critical position can be reconciled with a realist approach to social analysis. His legacy is therefore a somewhat fragmented one, perhaps as befits a would-be outlaw.

ROBERT HOLTON

governmentality

This encompasses a set of practices, **institutions**, **technologies**, and sciences that enable the exercise of political **power** over a population of individuals. The contemporary study of governmentality derives from the work of **Michel Foucault** whose oeuvre sought to uncover the microsocial processes, techniques, and knowledges associated with governmentality. In his essay "On Governmentality," which appears in *The Foucault Effect* (1991), edited by Graham Burchell, Colin Gordon, and Peter Miller, Foucault dates the origins of the concept to the sixteenth century when self-conscious investigations of the "art of government" were initiated.

Governmentality came to involve by the eighteenth century an economy of **politics** over a population. This relationship between government and governed evolved out of a pastoral model of the **family**, in which a head of a household claimed responsibility for the well-being of its members. The welfare of the population is the end of governmentality. To seek the common good is to ensure that laws (see **law and society**) are obeyed and order maintained. Governmentality is therefore distinguished from other reasons of **state**, in particular the religious and the Machiavellian. While governmentality is associated with a pastoral relationship of shepherd and flock, it explicitly rejects the possibility that a Christian kingdom dedicated to the glory of God could realize governmental sovereignty. Any religious doctrine in which moral or divine ends supersede the rationally understood good of the people will by necessity contradict governmental reasons of state. This lends a distinctly economic character to the notion of the good. The logic of governmentality also eschews Machiavellian premises insofar as it insists that government exists for the sake of the population, and not the power of its leader(s). Economic, familial, and political governance are continuous enterprises that share a triangular relationship in which none is ever entirely subject to either or both of the other two. Therefore, a politics in which a leader occupies a singular position and wields a unique form of power through channels over which he maintains a monopoly cannot support governmentality.

Implicit in a governmental approach to politics is the conclusion that sovereignty is defined primarily by dominion over a population rather than a geographic territory. A population of individuals simultaneously provides a government with both its greatest source of power and gravest potential threat. Therefore the means through which a government can control its population are crucial to asserting governmentality. This requires the regulation of individuals through the threat of direct physical coercion implied by an omnipresent police force as well as indirect and even internalized means of enforcing social **norms**.

The apparatuses, technologies, and sciences capable of controlling a population and realizing the goals of governmentality developed alongside modern politics. Insofar as governmentality prioritizes an economic reason of state, it inevitably relies upon scientific understandings of the population being governed. The good, having been construed in material rather than metaphysical or otherwise transcendent terms, can only be arrived at upon close inspection of those whose good is sought. Thus the science of **demography**, and statistical knowledge more generally, are crucial technologies of governmentality. Because both political and social security are essential to the success of government, a symbiotic relationship develops between the sciences from which statistical knowledge of the population can be gleaned and the military technologies whose purpose it is to ensure the safety of the population. Detailed scientific assessments of the contours and characteristics of a population facilitate the degree of surveillance necessary to identify, inhibit, and punish **deviance**.

A range of forces collude to cause citizens to recognize their **identity** as political beings belonging to specific **communities** to which they owe certain obligations and from which they need and will receive protection. In the modern liberal context, **civil society** becomes the terrain upon which negotiations between government and the governed occur. This implicates an almost endless array of social and economic **institutions** in the process of asserting governmentality. It also suggests that a significant challenge of governmentality will be the reconciliation of social and economic **justice**. The notion of justice exists to distinguish those who recognize and abide by social norms from those who do not, and who consequently must be isolated from the rest of society and/or reeducated. Law provides an articulation of the responsibilities of individuals to society, and vice versa. However, within **liberalism**, various interpretations of economic logic yield vastly disparate notions of these responsibilities, in no small part because social and economic justice are not simply distinct but often contradict one another. Thus social and civil **rights** often come at the cost of one another and hence obstruct both the expression and realization of a conception of justice.

Governmentality is a broader political concept than either the Weberian notion of legitimate **authority** or the Marxian concept of the **state** within any given mode of production (see **Karl Marx**). It is broader than legitimate authority because it embraces processes both within and beyond the administrative apparatus of the state. Foucault explicitly addressed himself to Marxist critics whose work he believed falsely assumed the state to be the inevitable locus of political power in all modes of production. The core concept of governmentality contradicts the Marxian thesis, instead offering a vision of politics in which power constitutes and expresses itself through multiple sources, of which the state is merely one. The confluence of the pastoral model of politics, specific diplomatic and military techniques, and the development of a police force is responsible for the governmentalization of the state. The state in this view, while perhaps uniquely successful, is simply one instrument and manifestation of governmentality.   ELIZABETH F. COHEN

Gramsci, Antonio (1891–1937)

Gramsci was one of the most influential Marxist theorists of the twentieth century. After graduating from Turin University in 1915 he worked as a journalist and regularly spoke at workers' study-circles on novels, the Paris Commune, the French and Italian revolutions, and **Marxism**. In 1919 he was one of the founders of the revolutionary weekly paper *L'Ordine Nuovo*, in 1924 was elected to the Chamber of Deputies for the Italian Communist Party, and became General Secretary of the Party. But after the fascist takeover Gramsci was imprisoned in 1926, and during the following ten years in confinement wrote copious notes on theory and strategy, that were published in translation as *Selections from the Prison Notebooks* (1971). Gramsci was concerned to eradicate economic determinism from Marxism and to develop its explanatory power with respect to cultural and legal **institutions**. He argued that class struggle must always involve work against the dominant **hegemony** of bourgeois ideas and **ideologies**, so that creating alternative cultural forms was essential to the struggle for **socialism**. He stressed the role performed by human agency in historical change since economic crises by themselves would not subvert **capitalism**. As opposed to a war of maneuver (a frontal attack on state **power**, such as the Bolshevik Revolution), a war of position may be more appropriate for liberal-democratic societies, which would involve a long struggle across institutions of **civil society**. Gramsci's

thinking was influential in the postwar Italian Communist Party and in western Marxism – especially in developing theories of **Cultural studies**, for example by **Stuart Hall**.   LARRY RAY

grand theory

– see **C. Wright Mills**.

Granovetter, Mark (dates unknown)

A leading American contributor to the study of economic **sociology** and social **networks**, Granovetter has been responsible for major innovations in thinking about the strength of weak ties in economic life, and about the **embeddedness** of economic relationships in wider social arrangements, both in non-market and in market-based economic systems. His work moves economic sociology beyond the pioneering formulations of **Karl Polanyi** and beyond the generalized emphasis on normative rules in the work of **Talcott Parsons** and **Neil Smelser**, while remaining distinct from the predominant focus on power relations within political economy.

Granovetter's initial empirical work published in *Getting a Job* (1995) focused on how professional, technical, and managerial workers found new jobs. His evidence demonstrated the importance of personal contacts. Granovetter pursued the characteristics of these contacts, and developed in the process a theoretical account of the significance of "weaker" ties with individuals not well known to each other, as compared with "stronger" and closer ties between those who interact frequently. In a major paper "The Strength of Weak Ties" (1973, *American Journal of Sociology*), he argued that such weak ties were especially salient in situations where **communities** contained several ways, rather than one distinct way, in which individuals might interrelate. This made a significant opening for a new kind of micro–macro network analysis, in contrast with the primarily micro focus of existing network theory.

Granovetter's seminal contribution to economic sociology was made in another paper, "Economic Action and Social Structure: Problems of Embeddedness" (1985, *American Journal of Sociology*). This engaged with Polanyi's celebrated discussion of the relations between economy and **society**. For Polanyi, most economic arrangements across history operated through the embedding of economic transactions and price mechanisms with broader social, political, and cultural arrangements. The exception was found in modern capitalist **economies**, where, for the first time, according to Polanyi, the economy became profoundly differentiated from society, around notions of economic freedom or laissez-faire. This, however, threatened social cohesion and the protection of social cohesion, and the pendulum swung back in the epoch of **welfare states** towards a reembedding of markets in political **institutions**.

Many economists have criticized this view by arguing that **markets** through history have been far more autonomous than Polanyi proposed. **Rational choice theory**, even more radically, proposed that a logic of rational choice underlies **social action** across history, rendering the past almost entirely similar to the present. Granovetter, by contrast, took a rather different view. For him, all economic arrangements, markets included, are embedded in wider social arrangements, and in this respect the idea of laissez-faire is a misnomer. This conclusion followed from his earlier work on job search and social networks. In later work in the 1990s he developed this line of thinking regarding all economic institutions as socially constructed, arising as "congealed networks," assisting in flows of **information** and the creation of **trust**. The social dimension here is, however, a very broad one, in which a complex mix of expressive and instrumental aspects of life are included.

Granovetter's ideas have developed one line of thinking about economy and society in very striking directions. What remains unanswered is quite what the social means within a network context, and why it is that markets, networks, and formal **organizations** have emerged as distinct forms of social life.   ROBERT HOLTON

Graunt, John (1620–1674)

A draper and haberdasher, and merchant and citizen of London, Graunt was born in that city on April 24, 1620, to Henry and Mary Graunt. He died in London in poverty, of jaundice, on April 18, 1674. Although lacking higher education and not trained in the sciences and mathematics, he was an active participant in the intellectual life of London and was a charter member of the Royal Society of Philosophers. He published in 1662 the first known **quantitative data analysis** of a human population, *Natural and Political Observations Made Upon the Bills of Mortality*. This small and very influential book has led some to recognize Graunt as a founder of both **demography** and **statistics**.

The "Bills of Mortality" were weekly accountings and reports of the London parish clerks of all the deaths and christenings. The reports were started in response to the plagues of the late sixteenth and early seventeenth centuries and

were published in a nearly unbroken series for decades. Merchants used **data** from the "Bills" as a rough gauge of the likelihood of their clientele to flee to the countryside during epidemics.

Graunt studied this mass of data searching for regularities. He is credited with being the first to recognize that more males are born than females, and that females have greater life expectation than males. He also was one of the first to recognize the phenomenon of rural to urban **migration**. He also developed a crude mortality table that eventually led to the modern life table.

In addition to the above four substantive contributions, Graunt also set a precedent for one of demography's oldest traditions, namely, the thorough evaluation of data to learn the extent, types, and probable causes of errors. P. Kraeger, in "New Light on Graunt" (1988, *Population Studies*), writes that he "carefully evaluated the bills for their numerical consistency and reliability of compilation, and presented his evidence at length so that his readers might judge it independently." Although Graunt died in obscurity, his lasting monument is his *Natural and Political Observations*, a book which to this day is a joy to read.

DUDLEY L. POSTON

grounded theory

Developed by Barney Glaser (1930–) and **Anselm L. Strauss** this theory, put forward in *The Discovery of Grounded Theory* (1967), argues that sociological research should be based on the close observation of social life – **participant observation**, in-depth **interviews**, and **focus groups** – to allow the experience of social life as understood by the actors to emerge out of the **data**. This contrasted with **Talcott Parsons**'s "grand theory" – in which the sociologist derived hypotheses about social life at his or her desk, and then gathered data to test them according to the **hypothetico-deductive method** – and with **Robert K. Merton**'s middle range theory, which sought to examine ways in which specific **social structures** (for example religious beliefs) constrained individuals in their actions. For Glaser and Strauss, **sociology** could not proceed by deduction, nor did an independent social reality or set of social forces exist apart from the individual and his or her interactions. Thus, grounded theory aims to generate theory rather than to verify it. Hence grounded theory was an important early reaction to **positivism** in American sociology and gave impetus to the resurgence of **qualitative research** in sociology in the mid-1970s.

In what we might call the "strong version," grounded theory argued that sociologists should shed all preconceptions about social life before entering the field and allow the data to shape their developing theory. Moving between the data and the **explanation** of what was going on – the constant comparative method – was the only way to produce valid sociological knowledge, which would provide an adequate account of people's understanding of their social situation. Glaser and Strauss developed a system for the close reading of interview and field notes. Open coding is the initial sorting of the material to identify what is going on in a given situation; axial coding is drawing the different codes together and relating them to each other; and, in the final stage, in selective coding, one key category, the core, is identified and ties all the others into it. In addition, they argued that sampling strategies should be driven by the theoretical concerns that emerged out of the research (this contrasts with the random sampling of the hypothetico-deductive method). Once no new data were being found – when the researchers had reached saturation in data collection – then the writing-up of the study could start. Ultimately the research should have a practical outcome and a positive impact on the subjects' understanding of their situation and experiences. The problem with the strong version of this theory is that, without pre-existing hypotheses, research data cannot be gathered or classified. A second problem is that, in the search to provide an emic account (that is, one from the subject's perspective) of social reality, sociologists would only reproduce and record the respondent's views and understanding of reality.

In subsequent developments, major differences emerged between Glaser (*Basics of Grounded Theory Analysis*, 1992) and Strauss (Strauss and Corbin, *Basics of Qualitative Research*, 1990). While Glaser remained committed to a qualitative account of social life, emphasizing a flexible use of qualitative research methods, Strauss moved to codify explicitly the steps researchers must take to ensure that they were doing grounded theory. In Strauss's approach, the emphasis came to be based more on traditional concepts of positivistic social research, emphasizing generalizability, replicability, and theory verification. Glaser objected that Strauss was "forcing" the development of theory rather than allowing it to "emerge" from the data.

KEVIN WHITE

group dynamics

The group dynamics approach to small groups research was perhaps the most influential attempt to analyze the processual quality of group life. The approach was first articulated by German émigré Kurt Lewin (1890–1947) in the 1930s and 1940s, and became institutionalized by Lewin, his students, and colleagues, notably at centers of small group research, such as Michigan, Harvard, and Massachusetts Institute of Technology, in the 1950s.

The group dynamics approach attempts to examine the processes through which group activity occurs. The claim is memorialized in Lewin's famous equation, $B = f(PE)$: behavior is a function of **personality** and **environment**. Lewin treated the relations of people within group settings using the dynamics model of physics, and developed a set of concepts – force fields, vectors, valence – that detail this metaphor.

Lewin's metaphor proved difficult to operationalize precisely and many subsequent experimental researchers used the label while jettisoning the connections to physical forces. The group dynamics tradition was also enriched by Freudian theory, as in the interaction process analysis work of **Robert Freed Bales**, whose approach owed much to both **Sigmund Freud** and the Parsonian tradition of the general theory of action. In all cases, the group dynamics tradition attempts to incorporate theoretical models of larger units, bringing them into the action arena of the **small group**. The leading text treating the approach is the edited collection of Dorwin Cartwright and Alvin Zander, *Group Dynamics: Research and Theory*, first published in 1953 at the height of the movement.

Today, remnants of the group dynamics tradition are evident in expectation states theory, as it was developed at Stanford by Morris Zelditch, Joseph Berger, and Bernard Cohen, who trained in **social psychology** at Harvard during the heyday of the group dynamics approach. Expectation states bring in social categories from outside group life – **gender**, **social status**, or **race** – examining how they are exemplified in behavioral arenas.

GARY ALAN FINE AND KENT SANDSTROM

group(s)

The term group(s) is widely used within sociology, and the **social sciences**. However, the referent of the term may vary, according to whether or not people interact as groups, or share a feeling of group membership, or unity. Social scientists have long recognized the distinction between "a group defined by outsiders" which has no social reality for its members and groups that have social and psychological reality as such, for their members. Henri Tajfel (1982, *Annual Review of*

Psychology: 1–39) notes that there are two distinct theoretical senses of the term:

(1) objective collections of similar individuals as defined by outside observers, that is, objectively defined groupings that may be statistically significant to the researcher, but not subjectively significant for their members (that is, some sociological category, such as single-income **families** in rural areas).

(2) groups defined as such by their members through patterns of **interaction** and shared representations, that is, a dynamic social process in which the capacity of people to represent themselves as members of social categories is part of the process by which sociological categories may become meaningful social groups.

Charles Horton Cooley's distinction between "primary groups" and "secondary groups' or nucleated groups is also a key distinction in sociology. Primary groups are defined by close, face-to-face interaction, unlike secondary or "nucleated groups," which tend to be larger and less congruent. Members of such groups (for example, **political parties**, and **trade unions**) are seldom in direct contact, in contrast to members of primary groups (for example, friendship **networks**, families) who are in regular contact.

A further distinction may be made between closed groups and open groups. This distinction refers to the relative permeability of the boundaries of social groups. Open groups have relatively permeable boundaries, and few barriers to interactions with outsiders, while closed groups have impermeable boundaries, and have little interaction with outsiders. Thus, ostensibly similar social groups (for example clubs or religious **sects** (see **church–sect typology**) may be distinguished by being either open or closed. Further, group membership may be either ascribed and relatively fixed (for example, by **race and ethnicity**, or **gender**), with little possibility of movement out of the group (save in cases of surgical reassignment, gender identity "disorder," or divorce), or relatively flexible, with the possibility of movement between groups (such as occupational groups or nationalities).

Peer groups are collections of individuals who define themselves, and are recognized by others, as a distinct social group. Peer groups may also define themselves through shared social characteristics such as **age**, gender, **sexuality**, **occupation**, or **ethnicity and ethnic groups**. Such groups have shared **norms**, **culture**, and **rituals** and socialize new members according to these. Existing members may be excluded from the peer group with reference to a breach of these group norms and sanctions.

The dynamics of peer groups, and other face-to-face groups, is the subject of both **social psychology** and **sociology**. Within sociology, notable contributions to the study of group dynamics have been made by **Talcott Parsons** (see, for example, *Family, Socialisation and Interaction Process,* 1955, and *Working Papers in the Theory of Action, 1953*); within social psychology, **Robert Bales** made significant foundational observations (see, for example, *Interaction Process Analysis: A Method for the Study of Small Groups,* 1950; and *SYMLOG: A System for Multiple Level Observation of Groups*, 1979).

Pressure groups are a particular kind of social group characterized by a common purpose – to put pressure on governments and decisionmaking bodies, and to influence **public opinion**, such that their aims are supported. These aims may be either for significant reforms to a current system, or for the maintenance of the current or previous status quo. Pressure groups may be distinguished from other groups united in a common interest, such as political parties, in that they aim to influence public opinion, and government decisions, rather than to govern and make such decisions per se. However, the relationship between pressure groups and political parties is often symbiotic, and certain pressure groups have close relations with particular political parties – for example, the relationship between the trade unions and the Labour parties of Australia and Britain; and the relationship between fundamentalist Christian groups and the Republican party of the United States. Further, pressure groups may develop into political parties – for example, the Family First party in Australia – and enter into **politics** and decision-making proper.

There are two general types of pressure groups – broadly, "protective" and "promotional" groups. This distinction is intended to highlight the divergent aims of some pressure groups. Protective pressure groups are united in their aim to protect existing and affiliated members of that group – for example, trade unions and professional associations. By contrast, "promotional" groups seek to promote a cause, rather than to defend a defined group. Promotional groups include the RSPCA, and other societies bound by a goal to promote a cause – for example, environmental groups; pro- or anti-censorship groups; pro- or anti-choice groups. However, this distinction is not always clear-cut. Thus, professional associations have joined with other groups in condemning **prejudice**,

war, and **violence**, for example; and the public interest lobby for an increase in the national minimum wage – a public cause – is a key task of the trade unions in defending their members, and others.

SUSAN HANSEN AND MARK RAPLEY

Gurvitch, Georges (1894–1965)

Born in Novorossisk, Russia, Gurvitch closely observed the Russian Revolution, met **V. I. Lenin**, and knew Leon Trotsky (1879–1940). In 1917 he published a work on Jean-Jacques Rousseau (1712–78) and agrarian **rights** and became a lecturer at the University of Leningrad. He was made a professor at the University of Tomsk in 1919, but in 1920 he left Russia. Between 1921 and 1924 he worked in the Russian Department at the University of Prague, and was particularly influenced by the work of Johann Fichte (1762–1814). Indeed, in 1930 he published in France *Les Tendencies actuelles de la philosophie allemande: E. Husserl, M. Scheler, E. Lask, M. Heidegger*. In 1925 he moved to France, and became a lecturer at the University of Strasbourg in 1935. He spent the years of World War II in the United States, and his *Déclaration des droits sociaux* (1944) was a socialist analysis of self-management.

Returning to Strasbourg, Gurvitch edited *Twentieth-Century Sociology* (1945) with Wilbert E. Moore; although based in France, he was a visiting professor in Brazil, Argentina, Japan, Canada, North Africa, and the Near East, as well as Europe. He was a passionate opponent of French government policy during the Algerian war, and founded the Centre d'Études Sociologiques. He also created the journal *Cahiers Internationaux de Sociologie*, and started the Bibliothèque de Sociologie Contemporaine (Library of Contemporary Sociology). He was concerned with the preservation of the French language. He published *La Vocation actuelle de la sociologie* in 1950, and in 1962 his most complete work, *Dialectique et sociologie* appeared. He spent much of his time battling over the question of dialectics. His *Les Cadres sociaux de la conaissance* (1966) was published posthumously.

JOHN HOFFMAN

H

Habermas, Jürgen (1929–)

Often regarded as the most influential German social theorist of the second half of the twentieth century, Habermas belongs to the **Frankfurt School**, a group of neo-Marxist **intellectuals** who pursue a **critical theory** of **society**. Habermas belongs to the so-called second generation of the Frankfurt School; the first generation consists, for instance, of **Theodor Wiesengrund Adorno** and **Max Horkheimer**. He initially worked under Adorno's supervision, but soon developed his own version of critical theory.

Habermas's project differs from Adorno in a number of respects. First, whereas Adorno's critique was directed at the Enlightenment project, Habermas emphasized its positive features. He recognized the problematic nature of the current sociopolitical constellation, but he insisted that these problems were not intrinsic to **modernity**. He argued for recognition of the liberating features of the shift towards modernity, and the central nature of these features to any critical theory. Second, whereas Adorno's notion of **rationality** was still embedded in the "philosophy of consciousness," Habermas sought to ground reason in the intersubjective context of daily linguistic usage. For this, he drew partly on the speech act theory of J. L. Austin (1911–60) and partly on the theory of psychological development of Lawrence Kohlberg (1927–87), who published *Stages of Moral Development* (1971).

The Structural Transformation of the Public Sphere (1962 [trans. 1988]) was Habermas's first book, and it already expressed his belief in the importance of unconstrained, open debate amongst equals. He called this the ideal of a "discursive will-formation." Habermas argued that the emergence of bourgeois society made possible the potential for realizing this ideal. With the advent of bourgeois society, a **public sphere** emerged: people openly discussed political issues, which appeared in newspapers and magazines. Modern society has not fulfilled this potential, partly because of the way in which the content and role of the media have changed. Several commentators criticized Habermas for overestimating the existence of the public sphere in the nineteenth century. They pointed out that several sections of society were excluded: notably working-class people and women. Some feminist authors add that the emergence of a private sphere for women was constitutive of the public sphere for men.

In *Knowledge and Human Interests* (1968 [trans. 1971]) and other methodological writings, Habermas draws on the pragmatism of Charles Peirce (1839–1914) to criticize **positivism**. Positivist **epistemology** tends to reduce knowledge to one type: empirical-analytical knowledge, directed towards technical control and prediction. Habermas insists that other types of knowledge are also valid; they simply aim at different cognitive interests. Interests are "basic orientations" based in "fundamental conditions" of **reproduction** and self-constitution of the human species. Besides empirical-analytical knowledge, there is also **hermeneutics** and critical theory. Whereas the empirical-analytical approach aims at nomological knowledge, hermeneutics insists on the qualitative differences between the natural and the social sciences. Hermeneutic authors insist that the main objective of the social sciences is to provide understanding – to make sense of different practices or cultural artifacts. Critical theory consists of a combination of empirical-analytical and hermeneutic knowledge, but it is ultimately directed neither towards control, nor towards understanding. Its main goal is emancipation and critique. It seeks to question what was previously taken for granted and it intends to reveal and uplift psychological dependencies and sociological obstacles. Once these are removed, emancipation becomes a realistic political target.

In the early 1970s, Habermas turned his interest towards the question of how governments are able to find **legitimacy** within **capitalism**. In *Legitimation Crisis* (1973 [trans. 1975]), Habermas set out to explain the problems capitalism faces. Capitalism tends to justify itself as a highly efficient socioeconomic system; it avoids referring to higher political, spiritual, or religious **values**. In reality, however, capitalism faces recurrent economic problems. These economic crises are inherent to the capitalist mode of production. Because capitalism justifies itself mainly in terms of instrumental rationality, these economic crises easily lead to a "legitimation crisis." Governments find it difficult to sustain themselves in the light of an **economy** of boom and bust, especially given that their legitimacy relies on their ability to solve technical, economic problems.

Towards the mid-1970s, Habermas developed a growing interest in the accomplishments of the **linguistic turn** in philosophy. This led to his theory of universal pragmatics, which forms the core of his *Theory of Communicative Action* (1981 [trans. 1984]). Central to his universal pragmatics is the idea that, whenever people talk, they make a number of validity claims. Validity claims are presuppositions such as intelligibility, truth, moral rightness, and sincerity. For instance, when I explain to a student how to get to a lecture hall, it is implicit in my account that the instruction is intelligible and that it is correct – that is, it is the right way to reach the lecture hall. Also implicit in it is the assumption that I am morally justified to provide it, and that I am being sincere – I am not explaining the way in order to deflect attention from something else. Habermas talked about undistorted communication in which people can openly criticize each other (and openly defend themselves) with regard to the validity claims. Habermas coins the term ideal speech situation for when there are no obstacles whatsoever in the way of such an unconstrained debate. Although the ideal speech situation never exists in reality, it is a yardstick for a critical theory of society. It allows the critical theorist to judge and compare real settings and to criticize distorted communication.

Habermas used this communication-based approach to tackle various issues. In *The Philosophical Discourse of Modernity* (1985 [trans. 1987]) and *The New Conservatism* (1985 [1989]), he defends Enlightenment principles against **postmodernism** and **conservatism**. In *Moral Consciousness and Communicative Action* (1983 [trans. 1990]) and *Justification and Application* (1991 [trans. 1993]), he applied the theory of universal pragmatics to the ethical domain. Discourse ethics treats normative claims like truth claims: they are considered as having a cognitive meaning. Discourse ethics assumes that the grounding of **norms** requires a dialogue. As such, moral judgments are not simply conclusions reached by isolated individuals (as in the formal approaches), nor do they simply reflect social

codes (as in the communitarian perspectives). In *Between Facts and Norms* (1992 [trans. 1996]), Habermas took the position that legal and political issues should not be left in the hands of the experts. These issues should be subjects of an open discussion, which includes as many people as possible. In his proposal for a "discursive democracy," norms are valid if they are accepted by the individuals who are potentially affected by these norms, and if this acceptance followed procedures of communicative rationality.

PATRICK BAERT

habitus and field

Pierre **Bourdieu**'s sociology of structured **inequality** pivots on these two concepts. (See Bourdieu's "Structure, Habitus, Practices," in his *The Logic of Practice*, 1980 [trans. 1990].) Habitus, the more widely known term, refers to a system of lasting dispositions which integrate past and present perceptions, appreciations, and actions, and also facilitate the achievement of an open-ended array of diversified tasks. It constitutes a component of a field of objective relations, where the term objective signifies independent of the individual's consciousness and will. The objectivity of fields is provided by the distribution of different species of **power**, which Bourdieu characterizes as economic, cultural, and **social capital**. To each field corresponds a tacit struggle over these resources. Fields determine relational positions which impose present and future situations on their more or less powerful occupants. A given population may occupy positions in multiple fields. Multiple fields may impose more or less consolidated relations of domination and subordination.

For fields to operate there must be agents with the appropriate habitus, which operates tacitly (see David Swartz, *Culture and Power*, 1997). Like **Émile Durkheim**, Bourdieu sees the dispositions which constitute habitus as acquired in primary **socialization**. The originality of the idea of habitus stems from its positioning in fields of struggle. This allows Bourdieu to investigate the tacit ways in which the dominant perpetuate their own domination or, in Bourdieu's terms, commit symbolic violence on themselves.   IRA COHEN

Halbwachs, Maurice (1877–1945)

A French sociologist who was much influenced by **Émile Durkheim**, but who modified and extended the claims of the Durkheimian **paradigm**, Halbwachs was an accomplished social statistician, and, in his book *Les Causes de suicide* (1930), he introduced major new findings that Durkheim missed. For example, suicide rates differ between rural and urban **communities**, such that those in more placid and religious rural settings have lower suicide rates than those in densely populated urban agglomerations. Halbwachs was also one of the first French sociologists to write systematically about the nature of **social class**. In his study of the working class he showed that **Friedrich Engels**'s Law, according to which low-wage groups spend a larger proportion of their **income** on **food** than other classes, applies far more widely. He argued that perception of **human needs** is determined by class position. His representation of the working class, however, is too inflexible to be of much use to contemporary class analysts.

Halbwachs's most influential and innovative work concerns collective memory where he goes far beyond Durkheim's concept of collective representations. Halbwachs's thesis is that human memory can only function within a collective context. He shows how collective memory is always selective, and how various **groups** of people have different collective memories which in turn give rise to different modes of behavior. Halbwachs was the first sociologist to stress the important insight that memories of the past are essentially reconstructions in the light of the present. His work has important implications for contemporary studies of the role of collective memory (and collective forgetting) in continuity and **social change**.   JACKIE SCOTT

Hall, Stuart (1932–)

Born in Kingston, Jamaica, Hall migrated to the United Kingdom in 1951 to study as a Rhodes Scholar at the University of Oxford, and is widely regarded as Britain's leading public **intellectual**. He is sometimes erroneously called "the father of **cultural studies**." Actually, he belongs to the second "New Left" generation that took the cultural turn, following the mold-breaking work of **Richard Hoggart**, C. L. R. James (1901–89), **Raymond Williams**, and Edward Thompson. Hall's contribution has been built upon a consistently inventive and exhaustive reading of western **Marxism**, **post-structuralism**, post-colonialism, psychoanalytic theory, and **feminism**. He has combined this with political activism and various media contributions. Hall's ideal for intellectual activity, borrowed from **Antonio Gramsci**, is the organic intellectual, who combines the latest cutting-edge ideas with effective political action.

In 1964 he was invited by Hoggart to join the newly founded **Birmingham Centre for Contemporary Cultural Studies**, where he became Director

in 1974. In Birmingham, Hall's work attempted to fuse central elements from the thought of Gramsci with the Marxism of **Louis Althusser** to elucidate the interpellation of subjects under advanced **capitalism** and the unfolding crisis of the "representative–interventionist" British nation-state (Hall et al., *Policing the Crisis*, 1978, and Hall *et al.*, *On Ideology*, 1978). This involved an ambitious reformulation of the operation of **ideology**, **hegemony**, and normative regulation. Not the least achievement in this respect was his encoding/decoding model of mass communications that purported to reveal how "preferred readings" of news items are orchestrated in the process of political and cultural reproduction. Hall's work on the crisis was based in a trenchant analysis of the roots of welfare interventionism that he traced back to the 1880s, and which he presented as a constant "war of maneuver" designed to co-opt the working class (Hall *et al.*, *Crises in the British State*, 1985).

Writing before the rise to power of the New Right, Hall accurately predicted the drift towards the "law and order" society and a form of democratic state control organized around authoritarian populism (*The Hard Road to Renewal*, 1988; Hall and Martin Jacques, *New Times?* 1990). In 1979 he was appointed Professor of Sociology at the Open University, where he remained until 1997. Hall's later writings focused on questions of **multiculturalism**, new **ethnicities**, identity slippage, and black **aesthetics**, raising a series of urgent questions about **identity** and belonging in the age of **globalization**, but casting doubt on the political realism of his project.   CHRIS ROJEK

Haraway, Donna J. (1944–)

A cultural theorist and scientist concerned with the relations among humans, **technologies**, and animals, Haraway, during her early career studying primate behavior, engaged in a number of feminist debates, and published critical accounts (*Primate Visions*, 1989) of the activities of her male colleagues in the biosciences, ascribing to them the behaviors they ascribed to primate bands, such as competition, aggression, and the pursuit of dominance. Her "A Manifesto for Cyborgs", first published in *Socialist Review* in 1985, has become one of the three most cited articles in the humanities. In it she constructs a socialist-feminist case against essentialist **feminisms**, those that describe femininity as an unchanging quality, often with mystical connections. Instead, through the use of the metaphor of the "cyborg," she argues for a feminist, hybrid cybernetic organism. This imaginary creature (which nonetheless has some practical existence, for example, in wearers of pacemakers and contact lenses) is a construct built from existing components. By analogy, new **genders** may be constructed from the components with which we are surrounded. Rather than embrace a mystical essence, Haraway recommends building new **identities**: "I would rather be a cyborg than a goddess." Though her essays collected in *Simians, Cyborgs and Women* (1991) were especially influential in the first generation of critics responding to the emergence of the worldwide web in 1993 as they began to describe virtual worlds and identities composed of material and electronically constituted components, Haraway herself pursued her interests in the life sciences to produce significant critiques of genetic engineering techniques from socialist feminist perspectives (*Modest Witness @ Second Millennium*, 1997). In her most recent work, she has begun a critique of human–animal relations, initially through an analysis of "companionate" (pet) animals and the institutional discourses that surround them (*The Companion Species Manifesto*, 2003).

SEAN CUBBITT

health

The sociology of health was originally known as medical **sociology**, emerging as a specialized area in the 1950s. "Sociology of health and illness" is now the preferred term, suggesting a wider canvas than the purely "medical," though medical sociology is still often used for convenience. Despite its youth – little more than half a century – it rapidly became one of the most important of the subdisciplines of sociology, in terms of numbers of practitioners, volume of research, and specialized journals.

In part, this is because of the recognition by medicinal authorities of the importance of a sociological perspective on health and illness in helping general practitioners to understand better their **interaction** with patients. The subject is now almost universally taught in medical schools and in the **education** of nurses and other health professionals.

Originally a distinction was made between sociology *in* medicine and sociology *of* medicine. The first described the use of sociology in solving medically defined problems, such as the social distribution of disease (covered by social **epidemiology**), the self-definition of illness which brought people to seek medical help, and illness behavior. The sociology *of* medicine is seen as less oriented to the professional interests of medicine, and treats

the concepts of health and illness as problematic and constructed. Medicine itself is studied as an **institution** and practice, and there is concern with the issue of power relations between doctors and patients. The larger term, the sociology of health and illness, defines the concept positively, and includes not only the **profession** of medicine, but also the whole range of caring **occupations** and activities, and not only the identification, treatment, and experience of illness, but also health-related **lifestyles** and health as general well-being.

What is called, in its stereotypical form, the biomedical model has been the basic **paradigm** of medicine since development of germ theory in the nineteenth century. At the beginning of this modern period, medicine was based almost entirely on the methods and principles of biological science. Four postulates were seen as its basis:

(1) the doctrine of specific etiology, that is the idea that all disease is caused by agents which are at least theoretically identifiable – germs, parasites, trauma, bacteria. Ideally, the search is for single causes;

(2) the assumption of generic disease, that is the idea that each disease has its distinguishing features that are universal within the human species;

(3) the model of ill-health as deviation from the normal, with health defined as equilibrium and disease as a disturbance of the body's functions;

(4) the principle of scientific neutrality, that is, the belief that medicine adopts the values of **objectivity** and neutrality on the part of the observer, and sees the human organism as the product of biological or psychological processes over which the individual has little control.

The actual practice of medicine, as knowledge advanced and medical institutions became more differentiated and complex, threw up many problems relating to these postulates. In his book *Man Adapting* (1966), René Dubos (1901–82) asked, for instance, why infection does not always produce disease. It was realized that for many diseases there are multiple and interacting causes, rather than single ones. The principle of single causes is more easily applicable to acute conditions and infections than to the chronic diseases that became more important in the twentieth century. The assumption of generic diseases stumbled against the realization that diseases are differently defined in different **cultures**, and medical definitions are not simply a matter of advancing knowledge but also of professional choice. Diseases tend to be those things which, at any given time, medicine is able to treat or wishes to treat. Deviation from the normal, though still a foundation of much medical investigation and categorization, is complicated by the fact that it is often unclear where normal variation ends and abnormality begins. What is defined as the normal range (of body mass index, of lung function, of birth weight, of liver function, of blood pressure, and so on) has to be a choice, even if it is one which is scientifically informed. Finally, scientific neutrality was questioned, since the **institution** of medicine is always embedded in the larger society and subject to social, political, and cultural pressures.

Residues of these postulates can be found in modern medical practice. However, the advance of science has directed attention to necessary and sufficient rather than single causes, and biomedicine now stresses multiple and interactive causes, including the state of the **body**'s own defenses. The rise of psychology was influential in altering a purely mechanistic model of illness. The medical model current in medical practice should not be presented as separate or in opposition to the social model of health.

The clearest dissatisfaction with the dominant model offered by biomedicine arose around the mid twentieth century. A mechanistic view of human health, together with the rapid rise in knowledge, had resulted in an ever-increasing use of medical **technologies**. Dubos described the *Mirage of Health* (1959), whereby we are led to believe that science can produce a utopia of disease-free life: scientists look only for a "magic bullet." The American philosopher Ivan Illich (1926–2002), in his *Medical Nemesis* (1976), argued that medical practice had transformed the human condition of pain, illness, and **death and dying** into merely a technical problem. As a result, medicine had prevented people from dealing with these threatening circumstances with autonomy and dignity. Medicine had paradoxically created a new kind of "unhealth" (1974, *Lancet*).

Anton Antonovsky, in *Health, Stress and Coping* (1979), was influential in pointing out that this means more attention to disease than to health – "We do not ask about the smokers who do not get lung cancer, the drinkers who stay out of accidents, the Type As who do not have coronaries" – and advocated thinking "salutogenically," that is, focusing on what facilitates health, rather than what causes or prevents disease.

The focus on stressors as causes of ill-health has led to much study of the mechanisms and possible buffers, such as coping resources and social support **networks**. This literature has shown clearly that social integration is positively linked with mental and physical health and with lower mortality. The most powerful form of support is intimate relationships, and emotional support can provide protection against adverse life events. Most recently this has been associated at the societal or group level with theories of **social capital.**

The concept of social or holistic health is more than simply the recognition that social factors such as **poverty** or behaviors have to be included in any model of the causes of ill-health. It locates biological processes within their social context, and considers the person as a whole rather than a series of bodily systems. It is organic rather than mechanistic and reductionist. Human beings are living networks formed by cognitive processes and purposive intentions, depending on the meanings ascribed to bodily phenomena, not simply machines.

The development of the social model has been accompanied, among the public, by a growing enthusiasm for alternative and complementary therapies, which tend to be more holistic. These have also been incorporated to some extent into mainstream medicine. In the social model, health is a positive state of wholeness and well-being, associated with, but not entirely explained by, the absence of disease or mental or physical impairment. The concepts of health and ill-health are not simply opposites.

In 1948 the World Health Organization defined health as "a state of complete physical, mental and social wellbeing, and not merely the absence of disease or infirmity," and this is generally held to epitomize the social definition of health. This definition has been criticized as difficult to measure and impossible to achieve, and as promoting the **medicalization** of all aspects of daily life. However, it draws attention to the holistic and socially conscious definition of health which is most favored in contemporary western societies and medical systems.

Whether health is considered negatively, in terms of disease, or positively, in terms of holistic health, it is necessary to distinguish between objective and subjective health. In English-speaking countries it is usual to give different meanings to the words disease, illness, and sickness. Disease is the medically defined pathology. Illness is the subjective experience of ill-health. Sickness is the **social role** of those defined as diseased or ill.

There are problems about this usage, since not every language has equivalent words, but it has value in emphasizing that these concepts are not the same.

People may be ill, that is, feel themselves to have something wrong with them, without (known) disease. In the doctor's office, the person with an illness may be transformed into a patient with a diagnosis, that is, a disease. It is possible to be subjectively ill or to be medically diagnosed as having a disease without adopting the role of the sick person – that is, without assuming or seeking permission to give up normal roles. People may have a disease, or be injured or functionally incapacitated, without being ill or claiming to be sick. It is very common, in **surveys** of self-defined health, to find people with severe **disability** claiming that their health is "excellent." Moreover, it has been noted that modern medicine produces many liminal states which are neither ill nor well – potentially ill, but at present well, in remission but not cured, at known risk of disease which has not yet developed. A commonly cited epigram is "disease (and trauma) is what doctors treat, illness, is what patients experience." Though attractive, this is somewhat facile: doctors do treat illness, even in the absence of anything that can be diagnosed as disease, and patients do subjectively perceive and self-define disease.

The distinction between disease, illness and sickness is paralleled by the usage, in the field of disability studies, of the terms impairment, disability, and handicap, as promulgated by the World Health Organization in their "International Classifications" of disabling conditions.

In the early days of medical sociology, the American sociologist David Mechanic, in his *Medical Sociology* (1968), defined illness behavior as the way in which "symptoms are differentially perceived, evaluated and acted upon (or not acted upon) by different kinds of people and in different social situations." The concept included, as well as what **Irving Zola** called the pathway from person to patient, the whole process of seeking help, including the "lay referral system." Classic work, particularly in the United States, mapped out the way in which **groups** in society might differ in their responses. The concept became extended to include their perceptions of the illness and its treatment, and their heath-promoting or health-harming lifestyles. Many models, largely variants of the "health belief model" described by Irwin Rosenstock (*Health Education Monographs*, 1974), were used, especially in health psychology, to formalize the processes by which perceived illness is translated into sickness, and offer explanations of actions taken, or not taken, to promote health.

Certain disease labels carry with them public stereotypes. More generally, in early medical sociology the work of **Talcott Parsons**, defining illness as a form of **deviance** which disrupted the social system by interfering with normal role performance, gave rise (particularly in the United States) to a body of theory analyzing illness as deviance. **Labeling theory** was applied to the secondary deviation resulting from the identification as being ill, especially for particular disease labels such as epilepsy. **Thomas J. Scheff,** for instance, in *Being Mentally Ill* (1966), claimed that labeling was the single most important cause of the manifestations of mental illness. The work of **Erving Goffman** on *Stigma* (1964) was also very influential. These concepts are still important in disability and impairment and are relevant in specific conditions such as HIV/AIDS.

The psychological models of health beliefs and behavior have, in more recent decades, been criticized as abstracted from social settings, and the term illness behavior has become somewhat outmoded. Studies of the perception and experience of illness, based on **phenomenology** and the methods of **qualitative research**, are seen as moving away from the medical model, and turning to the patient's perspective.

The influence of **social constructionism** has become strong in the sociology of health, especially in many countries of Europe. It is argued that medical knowledge is produced by and reflects the society in which it is found. What counts as disease or abnormality is not given in the same sense as a biological fact is given, but depends on cultural **norms** and shared rules of interpretation. It is, as the Polish medical philosopher Ludwik Fleck (1896–1961) suggested, a product of the "thought style" of a particular **community** of scientists and practitioners. In the version of constructionism most favored in the sociology of health, it is not suggested that diseases and pathogens are not "real," but that health is, like other human experiences, at the same time a socially constructed category. Much of the understanding of how people act in illness began to come from studies of groups suffering from particular chronic conditions, including especially diabetes, asthma, hypertension, heart disease, and epilepsy. Self-regulation and control, and adjustment to illness within a family and social context, are prominent themes, as is illness as biographical disruption, that is, the place of ill-health in the **lifecourse**. Interest has increased in the analysis of illness narratives, in which, as Arthur Frank notably described in *The Wounded Storyteller* (1995), individuals make sense of their experience and create new **identities**.

The search for meaning, or the answer to what the French social anthropologists Claudine Herzlich and Janine Pierret in *Illness and Self in Society* (1987) called the "Why me? Why now?" question, became a focus of research. Associated themes are moral discourses of health, lay explanations of disease, and particularly the question of self-responsibility. An earlier, and more specifically psychological, model of **attitudes** to health as either "internal" (health as the outcome of individual behavior) or "external" (health as the consequence of outside **influences** or simply chance) has, largely, been abandoned. Contemporary discussion still very much emphasizes the question of **agency and structure**, however: the debate about the extent to which people can, or feel themselves able to, exercise individuality and free will or are subject to various kinds of constraint. **Max Weber** had provided a theoretical background for these discussions, distinguishing the two concepts of life conduct and **life chances**. The interplay of these is a dominant theme because of its practical and political importance in the fields of health promotion and health **inequalities**.

Relevant to this issue is the popular theme of the commodification of health. This emphasizes the range of dietary, leisure, slimming, and body maintenance and decoration products which modern commerce and **culture** provide, and the emphasis on the young and fit body as a fashionable ideal.

Theorizing health as **consumption** owes much to **Pierre Bourdieu,** who extended analysis to the explanation of class and group differences in health behavior. Individual practices are connected to culture and structure, and ultimately to power, through the concept of **habitus.**

The consultation, as a basic unit of the interaction between health professional and patient, is a topic of particular interest in the sociology of health. A distinction has been made between "doctor-centered" consultations, traditionally paternalistic and controlled by the doctor, and "patient-centered" ones, with greater patient involvement and a more mutual relationship. These, and other suggested models, such as the consumerist relationship which may be applicable in particular circumstances, can be appropriate to different stages and types of illness. Different patient characteristics are also shown to be associated with their willingness to assume a participative role.

Within the earlier and more medical model, there had been many studies of compliance, or

whether the patient accepts the doctor's instructions or takes medication as prescribed. This approach, it was suggested, ignored the lay meanings of medications, and their place in the individual life, and the term adherence began to be preferred, implying a more active, collaborative activity. Non-compliance was demonstrated to be, often, a rational response to experience. Concordance is an alternative term especially popular in primary care, suggesting a course of action agreed upon in negotiation between patient and doctor. Doctors' communication skills are an important topic in teaching and in research, as are decision-making principles and practice, and the characteristics of **health care systems** which may affect interaction and the outcome of consultations. The role of patients in decisionmaking about treatment is an active theme in contemporary western health systems, since the **right** of patients to be involved in making informed choices is an increasingly promulgated **value**.

At a more theoretical level, the relationship of health to social systems has always been one of sociology's major interests. Most of the significant differences in health between countries and groups within countries are not biologically inevitable, but bound up with the particular society, its place and time, its politics, administration, and health services. At the same time, the relationship is reciprocal: the health of a population has economic consequences. Health is part of a society's capital. Two of the most influential founding theorists on the relationship of health and society were Émile **Durkheim** and Parsons, offering "functional" models of society. Durkheim emphasized the importance of societal structures, and norms and processes which were outside the individual but integrated them into the structure. In *Suicide* (1897 [trans. 1951]) he used the example of rates of suicide, developing a three-fold typology of egoistic, where the individual was detached from society; anomic, due to a state of normlessness; and altruistic, a purposive choice. The prevalence of this very individual act of suicide was shown to be determined by ties to society. The concept of **anomie**, in particular, proved of lasting importance in theories about health and society.

The American sociologist Parsons, influenced by Durkheim and by Weber, as well as by early psychoanalytic theory, was concerned to explain value consensus, social order, and stability. In the major work *The Social System* (1951), using the medical **profession** as a model, he analyzed the needs of the system, expressed in the duties and reciprocal entitlements of both doctor and patient. For the doctor, the pattern variables of universalism, performance, or achievement, rather than ascription, specificity, and affective neutrality, were appropriate. The rights, obligations, and privileges of the **sick role** described the norms of being a patient. This ideal-type contract was what would, theoretically, identify medicine as functional in maintaining equilibrium in society and maintaining social order.

However, structural **functionalism** lost influence as a theoretical position in the 1960s and 1970s. The emphasis on consensus seemed to favor the status quo and the domination of the powerful, and the approach was found inadequate in the explanation of change. Social conflict theory, with its roots in **Karl Marx**, suggested that society was not held together by shared norms and values, but by those imposed by economically powerful groups. Weber added that social differences are based not only on economic factors, but also on status and other forms of influence. Conflict theory turned attention, especially, to the sources of ill-health in the economic environment.

In the later decades of the twentieth century, the power and pre-eminence of medicine as an institution, combined with some disillusion about the actual effects of increasingly high-tech medical science, led to an emphasis on a degree of conflict between the interests of patient and of doctor, and on medicine as an instrument of **social control** in society. The medicalization of society became a popular topic of medical sociology.

A separate strand of theory relates to the relationship of economic development to health. This turns attention from the possibly oppressive effects of the system of medicine to its undoubted positive successes, together with economic development, in prolonging life. Obviously, in the long term, the health of populations increases with economic development: even in the already developed nations, life expectancy at birth usually still increases from one **generation** to the next. At present, two or three years are added with each decade that passes. The causes include not only improving material standards of living, but also changing disease patterns (especially the relative disappearance of infectious disease), advances of **public health** and hygiene, and the non-material advances in, for instance, **education** associated with economic **progress**. How much is due to the advances of medical science or improvements in health care is disputed. Once a certain state of development has been reached, the proportion of Gross National Product spent on medical care, or the way in which care is organized, does not seem to have any clear association with differences in the longevity of populations.

Expectation of life has been markedly influenced by the steep fall in infant mortality in the developed world, rather than by much extension of life in old age: this fall has now reached a stage where little more is possible. The possibility of treating ever more diseases does, however, alter the health profile of populations. The shift from acute (infectious, commonly fatal) disease to chronic (long-term, to be controlled rather than cured) means that longer life may mean an increase in the actual experience of ill-health. This has an effect on the burden placed on health services.

A corollary of the political and economic view of the relationship of health to **social structure** is that **capitalism** necessarily creates inequalities between sections of populations. The minimization or correction of these inequalities is a major concern of western health systems, and inequality in health has been one of the most active areas of research and discussion in medical sociology for some three or four decades.

Obviously, simple equality in health is impossible to achieve in any society: differences associated with genetic inheritance, the geographic environment, or pure chance (and of course **age**) are part of the human condition. The patterning of inequality shows that the issue is not related only to the extent of economic deprivation, with deficiencies in such things as **food**, living environments, or medical care. In effect, the term "inequality in health has come to mean a special sort of difference – that difference between individuals or groups which is: socially determined, rather than due to biological factors; felt to be unjust and inequitable, and not the individual's own responsibility; held not to be inevitable, that is, it could, with current technologies and knowledge, be alleviated.

Thus the concept of equality in western societies is highly constructed and dependent on the progress of science and on ethical positions. It is more than equity of health-service provision, though "equality of provision for equal need" is a common way in which policy tries to find a services-relevant description.

The measures of equality most often used are rates of death or life expectancy. Since life expectancy at, say, age 65 and at birth may be differently patterned, years of healthy life, or potential years of life lost (PYLL) before the age of 70, are measures which can be used. Inequalities may also be measured in absolute terms (simple differences between two groups) or in relative terms (for instance, the ratio of death rates in the lowest social group to those in the highest). The latter may appear to exaggerate inequality if rates are low.

Approaches to the problem of inequality in health vary widely throughout the world. In low-income countries, the causes may clearly be material and the urgent questions may be political and economic ones, including the provision of health care. A strong emphasis on equality of access is also found among some of the wealthiest nations, such as the United States, with largely privatized health services. Countries with large ethnic or indigenous groups may also be particularly concerned with the health care of different races.

In the United Kingdom there has been a tradition of public concern about unequal health ever since the mid nineteenth century, when pioneers such as Edwin Chadwick (1800–90) described the living conditions of the poor and noted their low expectation of life. Concern about inequality remained in the early years of the twentieth century, and was offered as one major justification for the setting up of the National Health Service in 1948, following the Beveridge Report of 1942. The rediscovery of inequality was marked by the Report of the United Kingdom Department of Health (known as the Black Report) in 1980, and in the following decades many other countries, especially those of western Europe, took up the issue, and the theme was one of those around which the World Health Organization has based its strategies.

The field has been primarily occupied with understanding why differences linked with socioeconomic status arise, persist, and even grow greater. In Europe, it has been usual to rely on occupation-based measures of **social class** to demonstrate this. In the United Kingdom this classification has been used, sometimes collapsed into the two classes of manual and non-manual, for almost a century, to measure differences by class in mortality rates. Increasingly, however, the classification scheme is seen to have problematic features in modern society, and others are being developed for the purpose of health **statistics**.

The experience of illness health also varies by social class, though not as strongly or as regularly as mortality. Other dimensions of inequality in health include **ethnicity** and region. Certain regions within countries show consistent health disadvantages over others, associated with, but in addition to, their economic or social class composition. Everywhere, minority or migrant ethnic groups tend to show higher rates of many sorts of ill-health than the native population.

Two aspects of the statistics on inequality have attracted particular attention in recent decades. One is that, measured by social class and by death rates, inequality appears to be growing in many developed nations. The second issue relates to what is known as the "continuous gradient" or "fine grain" of inequality. The "threshold model," suggesting that inequality only occurs at a level of deprivation below which health is likely to be affected, does not seem to be correct: there is no sharp discontinuity between the minority who lack the basic needs of life and the majority whose living conditions meet at least minimum standards. Rather, a straight line relationship between socioeconomic status and health is found everywhere.

The main issue of debate in inequality studies is about **causality**, and especially causes of the apparent increase in inequality in developed countries. The 1980 Black Report in the United Kingdom discussed three types of explanation of real inequalities, if the social class differences were not, as is generally agreed, simply artifacts of statistics and the changing composition of social classes over time. These explanations were: natural and social selection and mobility (the healthy move up the social scale and the unhealthy suffer occupational disadvantage); the lifestyles and health-related habits typical of particular groups (in particular smoking, or general lack of health awareness or preventive behavior); the direct materialist effect of living and working conditions.

It is now generally agreed that the types of explanation are interconnected, and each makes a contribution. Simple models stressing only the importance of behavioral patterns, for instance, have to allow for the fact that lifestyles depend on social relationships and the cultures of areas and of groups. Cohort studies, following populations from the day of their birth, have demonstrated in Britain and in other countries how the causes of unequal health begin at birth or even before, and can accumulate through the life-course. A poor start in life, associated with poorer family circumstances and vulnerability to illness, can be reinforced throughout childhood by inadequacies in education and thus lower adult socioeconomic success, less healthy behavior, and poorer health.

This overview has shown that the sociology of health and illness is multifaceted, ranging from the statistical to the qualitative and philosophical, and from concern with social structures and historical processes to individual experience and **social psychology**.

Subspecialities flourish, some with their own institutions and journals. Some of the most important topics have been noted, but others include: the sociology of nursing and the professions allied to medicine; social pharmacy; the sociology of mental health; media and **cultural studies** of medicine and health; community care; death and dying; the sociology of reproductive behavior and the social **epidemiology** of **fertility**; health promotion; and health service organization and evaluation.

Discourses of **risk** are pervasive in health, as in other areas of life. Risk assessment is a key element of public health, and the perception and management of voluntary risks to health, and the relative importance of lifestyle factors and environmentally and socially imposed risks, are central questions of health promotion. Expert and lay concepts of health risk are a topic of particular sociological interest, and **Ulrich Beck**'s *Risk Society* (1986) [trans. 1992] has been influential in discussions of attitudes and responses to global ecological, genetic, nuclear, and economic risks to health.

Currently, sociological research and discussion focuses especially on the consequences of the explosive rate of change and development in medical science and technology. Techniques such as microsurgery and nanotechnology (technology at the level of molecules), and new technologies of imaging, change attitudes to the body. It has been argued that the image is becoming privileged over the actual body: simulations have come to constitute reality. Other technologies which are changing the practice of medicine relate to the information revolution. Telemetry (the transfer of measurements at a distance) and telemedicine (distant, or even automated, contact between patient and professional), alter the doctor–patient relationship.

The application of **genetics** is a very important topic. There is, for instance, much discussion of predictive genetic testing for disease as an ethical issue, how it is perceived by the public, and what changes it may bring to medical practice, family life, and social relationships. Developments in reproductive technology call into question when a new life commences. Technologies such as in-vitro fertilization, cloning, surrogate **motherhood** or the use of fetuses for genetic therapy raise questions about the **family** and person-hood. At the end of life, modern techniques of keeping alive, especially in the context of transplant surgery, blur the boundaries between life and death. The replacement of body parts, including xenotransplantation (where animals are bred to carry genes from another species) and stem cell technology (which is capable of supplying transferable tissue), also blur the distinction between the body and not-body and call human identities into question. The integration of machine parts into the body is sometimes called cybermedicine.

MILDRED BLAXTER

health care systems

Health care can be divided into primary care, taking place in the **community** as a point of first contact, and secondary care, usually taking place in hospitals and delivered by specialists. The term tertiary care is sometimes used to indicate rehabilitation, or restorative rather than curative care. Community care is used to indicate care provided outside **institutions**, not only by doctors but also by social carers. Preventive care systems (such as immunization) are also distinguished from curative care. A distinction is also made between personal clinical health care, provided for the cure or care of the individual, and **public health**, directed at populations.

The ways in which health care is organized, in different societies, range from the extreme of a pure market system in which health is treated as any other commercial commodity, to universal free services provided entirely by governmental funding. In most nations of the world, however, the distinction is becoming increasingly blurred. Patterns of health provision are converging, because aging populations, changing disease patterns, advances in **biotechnology**, growing public expectations, and increasing costs, all introduce common pressures. Market systems have to make provision for those who cannot pay, as in the Medicare for old people or Medicaid for the poor in the United States. In wholly or predominantly state-organized systems, there is a tendency to shift some costs onto the consumer, and introduce types of rationing. In order to gain some of the advantages of a market system, "free at the point of need" services may introduce elements of managed competition, separating the funding of services from their supply while retaining universal access, as in the internal **market** of the British National Health Service.

In most systems, insurance of various forms acts as the buffer between provider and consumer. Health insurance is commonly obtained through employers' schemes, and in some countries these are compulsory. Insurers can limit consumer choice by cost-contained health services, as in the Health Maintenance Organizations of the United States.

In recent decades, all industrialized nations have tried to reform health care. Growth in expenditure, commonly exceeding growth in Gross Domestic Product, has created a heightened interest in efficiency and effectiveness. There is also general interest in increasing patient choice and public participation in the organization of services. A further factor in change is some dissatisfaction about the priority given, in the past, to hospital services at the expense of community care and public health.

However, a wide range of international studies (notably from the regular publications of the World Health Organization and the Organization for Economic Cooperation and Development) suggest that the way in which services are organized, and indeed the level of provision, have little effect on the health status of populations, once a country has reached an advanced stage of development. This is not because medical services are ineffective, but is thought to be due to the overwhelming weight of other, principally economic and social, factors. Nevertheless, the equity and efficiency of services, patterns of patient usage, and medicine as an **institution,** are important topics within the sociology of **health**.

MILDRED BLAXTER

health inequalities
– see **health**.

Hegel, Georg Wilhelm Friedrich (1770–1831)
Born in Stuttgart, the son of a government clerk, Hegel studied theology at the university in Tübingen, working as a private tutor in Berne and Frankfurt, before becoming a university lecturer at Jena, a post he held until 1807.

It was here that he published *The Phenomenology of Mind* (1807 [trans. 1931]) – a work generally regarded as his masterpiece, in which he argued that the power of reason itself is unlimited. While reality is the entire development of everything, it consists ultimately of a world soul or mind. In *The Science of Logic* (1812 [trans. 1929]), which he published in 1812, he elaborated upon the dialectical categories through which this absolute reality passes.

He edited a newspaper during the Napoleonic occupation and was headmaster at a school in Nuremburg until 1816. Hegel was appointed Professor at the University of Heidelberg for two years in 1816, and then acquired the Chair of Philosophy in Berlin that he held until his death in 1831.

He published the *Encyclopedia of the Philosophical Sciences* in three volumes (1817, 1827, and 1830 [trans. 1927–30]), and his lectures on history, philosophy, and **religion** were published posthumously. But arguably his most important work was *The Philosophy of Right*, which appeared in 1821 (trans. 1942). Here he built upon his earlier philosophical work to argue that the modern **state** is an ethical entity. The state incorporates the altruism of the **family** and the self-interestedness of **civil society**, and its universal outlook is guaranteed by a hereditary monarch, by an assembly representing social interests, and by a civil service that constitutes a "universal class." Hegel's philosophy of history had a profound influence on the **sociology** of **Karl Marx**.   JOHN HOFFMAN

hegemony
The process by which a ruling **group** secures the consent of the ruled, this term is identified with the Italian **Antonio Gramsci**. Writing in prison under Benito Mussolini (1883–1945), Gramsci employed an idiosyncratic vocabulary to avoid censorship. However, this term proved a viable alternative to the more commonly used term **ideology**, because it describes a process rather than a result of rule. Faced with the question, "Why has the Italian working class accepted fascist rule?" Gramsci outlined a process of negotiation between rulers and ruled. To secure **power**, rulers may use coercion, but to maintain it they require the active participation of the ruled in the processes of economic and, in many instances, civil life.

With the exception of periods of revolutionary activity, **societies** are characterized by dynamic equilibria in which, normally, one hegemonic group holds sway over several subaltern groups. Subaltern groups may be formed from the residues of a previously hegemonic **social class** or classes, from newly emergent social groups such as the proletariat that emerged during the industrial revolution, or from class fractions striking alliances either against some abuse of power or to gain a particular goal. Hegemony passes through cycles of emergence, establishment, renewal, and decline, and the hegemonic process will necessarily involve alliances and therefore compromises with groups outside the hegemonic class itself. Typical alliances struck by Mussolini's fascist party included those with the Catholic Church, with residues of semifeudal landowners, with the military, with the civil-service **bureau-cracy** based in Rome, and with some elements of the skilled working class, all in the interests of the industrial bourgeoisie of northern Italy. Compromises included recognition of religious **values**, protection of inherited property **rights**, extensive military expeditions and budgets, and enhanced employment prospects.

Gramsci's term was initially specific to the political life of society. The word was taken up, after Gramsci's notebooks were translated as *Selections from the Prison Notebooks* in 1971, in British **cultural studies**. In the **Birmingham Centre for Contemporary Cultural Studies** especially, cultural life could be examined as a dynamic equilibrium in which **mass media** offered entertainment in exchange for loyalty to the nation and a sense of belonging. At the same time, television and popular music provided subaltern groups with the means to assemble alternative and competing **subcultures**. In certain instances, these subcultures served the purposes of hegemony by encouraging disaffected school students to opt for low-paid employment. In others, cultural resistance formed social bonds that allowed emergent subaltern groups, such as black Britons, to articulate their social and political interests. The concept of rule as dynamic equilibrium also served as a powerful analytical tool in analyses of education policy, sports studies, and **gender studies**. A more political variant appeared in the Indian journal *Subaltern Studies*, notably in analyses of the way in which Hindi nationalist histories of the struggle for independence from Britain subordinated non-Hindi and working-class achievements, in the interests of securing the postindependence hegemony of the ruling bloc. Similar concerns engage the Latin American Subaltern Studies Group. The theoretical turn of cultural studies in the 1990s displayed some return to ideological determinism, in Gayatri Spivak's query in her article "Can the Subaltern Speak?" from Cary Nelson and Lawrence Grossberg (eds.), *Marxism and the Interpretation of Culture* (1988), rather than a dynamic process of ideological exchange. Some of the most trenchant contemporary scholarship describes hegemony as that which is taken for granted, uncontested, and unnoticed in social life, leaving ideology to describe the active contests over meaning and interpretation.

SEAN CUBBITT

heredity

This incorporates the idea that characteristics such as **intelligence**, strength, or criminality have a biological basis and can be transmitted between **generations**. Some versions, following the pre-Darwinian biologist Jean-Baptiste Lamarck (1744–1829), suggest that acquired characteristics can be inherited. The idea was highly influential in early forms of sociology, such as the **social Darwinism** promoted by **William Sumner** and **Herbert Spencer**, the latter emphasizing transmission of acquired characteristics. Heredity remains significant today in the **social sciences**, though it is widely considered an **ideology** justifying the social order as natural. There is still no evidence of genes directly affecting intelligence or behavioral characteristics.

In 1865 a Moravian monk, Gregor Mendel (1822–84), established the key principles of **genetics**. He discovered that when plants are crossed the outcome is not simply a blending of characteristics. Discrete characteristics are passed on down the generations, resulting in, for example, a purple plant transmitting inherited white characteristics from future to later generations. Some twenty years later, though not having encountered Mendel's work, **Charles Darwin**'s cousin Francis Galton (1822–1911) coined the term eugenics, derived from the Greek "good in birth." This new science appeared to show that intellectual success runs in **families**; the Galton, Darwin, and Wedgwood families, for example, producing a relatively large number of offspring that were "brilliant." Such insights led to proposals for the active management of human **reproduction**. This would favor the reproduction of the fittest and discourage the reproduction of the less fit.

The new science received widespread support (including encouragement from a broad range of political opinion) during the late nineteenth and early twentieth centuries. Some branches of contemporary social science incorporate, at least tacitly, a notion of heredity as the basis of **social structure**. R. Herrnstein and C. Murray's *The Bell Curve* (1994) was, for example, highly influential and generated considerable debate among those exploring links between genes and intelligence (see, for example, R. Sternberg and E. Grigorenko, *Intelligence, Heredity and Environment*, 1997).

As a political practice, eugenics reached its most horrific conclusion with the Nazi mass extermination of the Jews. The killing of thousands of Croats and Muslims by a Serbian **elite** in the early twenty-first century shows that eugenics persists as an idea. But, despite its deeply sinister history, it would be wrong for sociologists to completely reject biological understandings of heredity. There is, for example, some evidence of genes generating predispositions to certain afflictions, such as Huntington's disease and cystic fibrosis. And some biologists – for example, E. Steele, R. Lindley, and R. Blanden in *Lamarck's Signature* (1998) – claim that certain forms of immunity (even acquired immunity) can be genetically transmitted. Meanwhile, more mainstream epidemiological work – for example, D. Barker in *The Best Start in Life* (2004) – is showing that bad health can indeed be inherited, but as a result of undernutrition in utero, rather than the passing on of specific genes. Genes, according to this literature, are important in terms of governing overall developmental processes. Illnesses are mainly a product of **environment**, especially as encountered in the earliest stages of life, combined with genetically driven processes of development.   PETER DICKENS

hermeneutics

The art of interpretation, hermeneutics was originally meant to adjudicate disputes concerning the authenticity of religious texts. Later, its role was extended to a method or set of tools that help to understand writing in general. Later, again, hermeneutics dealt with the understanding of any type of human action – not just writing.

In the nineteenth century, hermeneutics became a prominent philosophical tradition in Germany with central figures like Friedrich Schleiermacher and Wilhelm Dilthey. Influenced by Immanuel Kant (1724–1804), Herder, and **Georg Wilhelm Friedrich Hegel**, hermeneutic authors emphasized the differences between the study of historical, social phenomena and the natural sciences. The former deal with the understanding (*Verstehen*) of unique events, whereas the latter aim at explaining (*erklären*) and generalizing. The reliving (*Nacherleben*) of people's aims and assumptions is crucial in the understanding of historical phenomena. The nineteenth-century hermeneutic authors became involved in the well-known *Methodenstreit* over the method of the historical sciences. Influenced by positivist views, the opposite camp advocated a unity of method between the social and the natural sciences. **Max Weber** was influenced by hermeneutics but took a balanced view in the debate. For Weber, social scientists need to rely on *Verstehen* (or "interpretative understanding") but this re-enactment of individuals' purposes and assumptions does not exclude the possibility of causal analysis. He was also skeptical of the view that the emphasis on understanding makes history or **social science** a hopelessly subjective endeavor. Although historians and social scientists always adopt a selective

viewpoint, this does not make their research less objective.

Hans-Georg Gadamer's *Truth and Method* (1960 [trans. 1975]) heralded a major shift in philosophical hermeneutics. Influenced by Martin Heidegger, he criticized Enlightenment philosophers for failing to acknowledge the pivotal role of **tradition**. In contrast with nineteenth-century hermeneutics and its emphasis on methods, Gadamer was more preoccupied with ontology. He suggested that we conceive of understanding in a dialogical fashion: we cannot help but rely on our presuppositions to make sense of what we encounter, but the very same presuppositions are also affected by this interaction. In *Philosophy and the Mirror of Nature* (1980), Richard Rorty refers extensively to Gadamer's dialogical model to back up his notion of an edifying philosophy beyond **epistemology**.

For a long time, social scientists ignored the importance of hermeneutics, especially in the heyday of structural functionalism. Since the 1970s sociologists have shown a growing interest in interpretative philosophies, including hermeneutics. **Anthony Giddens**'s *New Rules of Sociological Method* (1976) and **Zygmunt Bauman**'s *Hermeneutics and Social Science* (1978) were crucial in drawing the attention of social scientists to hermeneutics. In *Constitution of Society* (1984), Giddens suggests that the way forward is the structuration theory, an attempt to integrate interpretative philosophies with **structuralism**. Structuration theory conceives of social order as continually produced by "knowledgeable" individuals in everyday settings. In *Knowledge and Human Interests* (1968 [trans. 1971]), **Jürgen Habermas** demonstrated the importance of hermeneutics to **critical theory**: his notion of critical theory draws on a combination of empirical-analytical knowledge (directed towards prediction and control) and hermeneutics (directed towards understanding) and is ultimately aimed at self-emancipation.   PATRICK BAERT

hidden curriculum

In 1971 B. R. Snyder published *The Hidden Curriculum*, containing a chapter by the American sociologist of higher **education**, Martin Trow, on "distraction and the expropriation of learning." Snyder's book was the outcome of research in which, as a student of psychiatry, he investigated in the early 1960s "the paths that students followed during four years at the Massachusetts Institute of Technology." His findings were also informed by his subsequent experience as a senior administrative officer in a university. This was a period in the history of American higher education in which the system seemed to be dominated by regulation and **bureaucracy**, associated with a technocratic model of education and with **credentialism**. In a context of precise regulatory control, Snyder argued that students adopt coping mechanisms which involve acting on the basis of their calculations of what is actually required to succeed and secure accreditation rather than what is officially required. These mechanisms involve restricting study only to those elements of curricula which are assessed and also ensuring that extra-curricular behavior is socially or politically acceptable to the institution. Trow's argument suggested that similar circumstances push staff towards equally "instrumental" rather than "expressive" behavior. Snyder argued that acknowledging the operation of a hidden curriculum recognizes social and cultural factors in learning ignored by rational planners. Arguably, subsequent higher education reforms have sought to make the hidden curriculum more visible and have thus subjected the informal in teaching and learning to more insidious regulation.   DEREK ROBBINS

historical materialism

Materialism and **idealism** offer two contrasting ways of understanding the social world. The former emphasizes the causal primacy of material forces such as climate, **technology**, economic resources, and the institutional arrangements within which they are organized and applied. The latter emphasizes the primacy of ideas and the meanings given by human actors to their actions. Historical materialism, associated with **Karl Marx** and **Friedrich Engels**, is a particular form of materialism designed to account for long-term processes of **social change** across time.

It was first articulated during the 1840s, in *The German Ideology*. German idealism, as reflected in the work of **Georg Wilhelm Friedrich Hegel** and his successors, had seen historical development as the progressive realization of the ideas of reason and freedom in human activities. This position was criticized for ignoring the differing material contexts within which individuals lived, the changing patterns of **power** and exploitation built into human **institutions**, and **social conflicts** between exploiting and exploited **social classes** evident through time. Meanwhile, existing forms of materialism were generally ahistorical and often contemplative in function.

For Marx, the agenda for **social theory** was both to understand and to change the world. This required an activist materialism, in which human actors helped make the world and emancipate humankind from exploitation, though not through the simple imposition of progressive or utopian ideas on the conditions of social existence. The task was rather to bring ideas into harmony with material possibilities. This shifted the burden of human emancipation from philosophers to exploited social classes whose interest lay in overcoming the forms of material exploitation in which they lived.

Within historical materialism the mode of production is the key concept through which the material conditions of existence are articulated. This includes two main elements: the productive forces, such as technology, and the social relations of production, referring to the prevailing form of property **rights** in human **labor** and other economic resources. Such rights included **slavery**, feudal land tenure, and the capitalist wage-labor relationship. Under the capitalist mode of production, the exploited working class would be the bearer of social change through class conflict leading to a socialist and communist future, where labor and **property** were owned in common.

Historical materialism has received significant criticism, and has been subject to revision and reformulation from those more sympathetic to the underlying project. Critics such as **Max Weber** argued that the approach offers far too crude an approach to the interaction of material and ideal elements in social change, as well as downplaying the motivating role of ideas, as proposed in Weber's Protestant ethic thesis on some origins of the spirit of modern **capitalism**. Historical materialism also overemphasizes class **institutions** and class struggle over other social cleavages, and downplays the autonomy of political institutions and structures of legitimate domination. Capitalism, meanwhile, has proven far more robust, a reflection in part of periodic surges of productive new technology, and in part of working-class incorporation into **consumer society**. Attempts to reformulate historical materialism to take these trends into account remain haunted by the failure of material existence to restructure social consciousness in ways that generate revolutionary struggle rather than social passivity.

ROBERT HOLTON

historicism

Deriving from the German *historismus*, this concept has two broad meanings. First, it refers to the belief that **social structures**, events, and texts should be understood within the context of their historical formation and the social conditions within which they arose. Every age and each historical situation, it is argued, can only be understood in its own terms. The applicability of the concept is usually restricted to the **social sciences** and humanities. In contrast to an emphasis on ahistorical universalist assumptions or nomothetic forms of explanation, which are used in the natural sciences, the focus is, as Friedrich Meinecke (1862–1954) argues, on the essential individuality, contingency, and uniqueness of social phenomena. This has two implications: (1) since events are unique and there is no independent means for comparing phenomena, this implies a form of **relativism**; (2) that in order to understand social phenomena a form of empathetic, hermeneutical understanding, or what W. Dilthey and **Max Weber** call *Verstehen*, is required. For **Karl Mannheim** in "Conservative Thought" in his *Essays on Sociology and Social Psychology* (1952) the origins of the term historicism, and a stress on historical **explanation**, have their roots in the conservative and Romantic reaction to the **Enlightenment**, especially in Germany in which a dynamic historical philosophy of life confronted a static philosophy of reason.

Second, the term has been employed by **Karl Popper** to designate explanations of the social world which advocate fixed long-term laws of historical development and argue for their predictability. For Popper, the chief exponents of such a misconceived view were Plato, **Georg Wilhelm Friedrich Hegel**, **Auguste Comte**, **Karl Marx**, Oswald Spengler (1880–1936), and Arnold Toynbee (1889–1975). He argued that such views of historical inevitability were imbued with totalitarian overtones and were, in addition, unscientific.

STEVEN LOYAL

Hochschild, Arlie Russell (1940–)

Hochschild received her undergraduate degree from Swarthmore College and, in 1969, her PhD in sociology from the University of California, Berkeley. She joined the Berkeley faculty in 1971, and is currently Professor of Sociology. She has made significant contributions to the sociology of the **family** and **gender**, and to **social psychology**.

In *The Managed Heart* (1983), she develops the notion of emotional **labor**. According to Hochschild, in the increasingly service-oriented **economy** of the postindustrial world, more and more occupations require that **emotion** be a part of the service offered. Emotional labor demands that the worker produce an emotional state in another person, as workers in jobs from waiting tables to flight attendants are increasingly called upon to create good feelings in their customers. Moreover,

the employer increasingly exercises a great degree of control over his/her employee's emotions.

Hochschild has also explored the intersection of **work** and women (see **women and work**), gender, and family as an increasing number of American women enter the workforce outside the home. In *The Second Shift* (1989), she shows that women are still responsible for housework and child-care, the "second shift," even if they work outside of the home. In *The Time Bind* (1997), she demonstrates that, often, family-friendly policies enacted by corporations fail because people are becoming more comfortable with their work life, finding home life increasingly hectic. In particular women have little "quality time" to spend with their families. Hochschild's most recent research documents the difficult plight of immigrant care workers in the United States. KENNETH H. TUCKER

Hoggart, Richard (1918–)

A lecturer in English at the University of Leicester (1959–62) before gaining the Chair in English at Birmingham University (1962–73), he founded the influential **Birmingham Centre for Contemporary Cultural Studies** in 1964. He left in 1971 to become Assistant Director-General of UNESCO and Warden of Goldsmiths College, University of London (1976–84).

Hoggart's origins betray and compromise much about his position on the register of cultural theory. His hometown was Leeds, and the working-class districts of Chapeltown and Hunslet supplied the **data** and inspiration for his most famous book, *The Uses of Literacy* (1957). In its day, this volume was a much-lauded work. Progressive sections in both the media and the redbrick universities regarded it as holding a set of refreshing insights into working-class life, not least the injunction to take working-class **culture** *seriously*. Today, it is chiefly regarded as a somewhat nostalgic, impressionistic, introspective study, that retains its place in the canon for its historically important, unapologetic insistence that working-class culture *matters*.

This is unjust. In founding the Centre for Contemporary Cultural Studies at the University of Birmingham with a self-ordained tripartite brief to study the historical-philosophical, literary-critical, and sociological aspects of culture, and gaining private funding from Sir Allen Lane of Penguin Books to finance the project, there is reason to claim that Hoggart made a seminal contribution to the development of **Cultural studies**, especially in the two volumes of *Speaking To Each Other* (1970 and 1972). Further, he turned the rejection of the elitist view of Mathew Arnold and F. R. Leavis – that culture is the best that can be thought and done – into a *cause célèbre*. Against this, his revisionist approach sought to recognize that important new cultural forms were emerging around media culture and to honor the value of non-elite cultures.

His work emphasized the policy dimension of Cultural studies, for example in *The Future of Broadcasting* (with Janet Morgan, 1982), *British Council and the Arts* (with others, 1986), and *The Idea of Europe* (1987). With deep roots in adult **education**, Hoggart made a virtue of unostentatious, practical criticism and forms of cultural theory based in realistic involvement with society and culture. This emphasis is now associated with anti-theoretical overtones in his work.

CHRIS ROJEK

Homans, George Caspar (1910–1989)

Between 1939 and 1941, Homans taught sociology at Harvard, then served for four years as a naval officer, and finally returned to Harvard where he made significant contributions to **exchange theory** in *The Human Group* (1950), *Social Behavior: its Elementary Forms* (1961), *Sentiments and Activities* (1962), and *The Nature of Social Science* (1967). He became a full Professor of Sociology at Harvard between 1955 and 1980. He was elected to the National Academies in 1972. He was 54th President of the American Sociological Association and his presidential address was published as "Bringing Men Back In" (1964) in the *American Sociological Review*, in which he argued that social phenomena are to be explained in terms of the characteristics of individuals rather than **social structures**. Homans developed a range of propositions that draw on **social psychology** to examine the ways in which individuals are connected to social **groups**. These propositions (relating to success, stimuli, **values**, satiation, and aggression) explain how social exchange functions at the level of the individual. Homans was critical of what he regarded as the abstract **sociological theory** of his day, and especially the work of **Talcott Parsons**, because it could not be adequately tested by empirical research. Homans insisted on the importance of developing testable hypotheses that explain basic social processes in **small groups**.

BRYAN S. TURNER

Horkheimer, Max (1895–1973)

For many years Horkheimer served as Director of the Institute for Social Research and, with **Theodor Wiesengrund Adorno**, **Herbert Marcuse**, and others, helped develop the critical theory of **society**. In "Traditional and Critical Theory" (1937 [trans. 1972]) in *Critical Theory*, Horkheimer argued that "traditional theory" (which included modern philosophy and science since Descartes) tended to be overly abstract, objectivistic, and cut off from social practice. **Critical theory**, in contrast, was grounded in **social theory** and (Marxian) **political economy**, carried out a systematic critique of existing society, and allied itself with efforts to produce alternatives to **capitalism** and bourgeois society (then in its fascist stage in much of Europe). The goal of critical theory is to transform these social conditions and provide a theory of "the historical movement of the period which is now approaching its end."

A collaborative work with Adorno, *Dialectic of Enlightenment* (1947 [trans. 1972]), sketched out a vision of history from the Greeks to the present that discussed how reason and **Enlightenment** became their opposite, transforming what promised to be instruments of truth and liberation into tools of domination. Under the pressure of societal systems of domination, reason became instrumental, reducing human beings to things and objects and nature to numbers. While such modes of abstraction enabled science and **technology** to develop apace, they also produced societal **reification** and domination, culminating in the concentration camps that generated an instrumentalization of death.

Horkheimer's *Eclipse of Reason* (1947) presents a popularized version of *Dialectic of Enlightenment* for an English-speaking audience, and *Critique of Instrumental Reason* brings together Horkheimer's key essays since the end of World War II. Some of Horkheimer's most important writings are collected in *Critical Theory* (1972) and *Between Philosophy and Social Science* (1993).   DOUGLAS KELLNER

housework
– see **women and work**.

housing classes
– see **social class**.

Hughes, Everett C. (1897–1983)

A Methodist minister's son from small-town Ohio, Everett C. Hughes rose to lead the "Second **Chicago School**." Like his mentor **Robert Park,** his primary impact on sociology was by challenging and inspiring graduate students. Inspired by **Georg Simmel**, he specialized in dazzlingly insightful miscellany.

The method Hughes preferred was "the intensive penetrating look with an imagination as lively and as sociological as it can be made." He directed his own sociological imagination to the areas of **work** and **professions**, **race relations** (see **race and ethnicity**), and such topics as **social movements**, **migration**, and social **institutions**. His sociological eye often reframed subjects in subversive ways – for example, showing how psychiatrists and prostitutes share the problem of distancing themselves emotionally from situations that are highly emotional to clients, or by spotlighting the dark side of respectable **occupations**.

Hughes delighted in locating social facts in larger contexts of meaning. His stream-of-consciousness lectures sparkled with insights drawn from **family**, fieldwork, and **friendships**. **Participant observation** was the keystone of his research ingenuity. He developed and passed on to devoted generations of students, including **Erving Goffman**, a range of techniques on how to do and to interpret fieldwork. **Symbolic interactionism** stemmed from the ideas of Hughes and his colleague **Herbert Blumer**.

His academic works include *French Canada in Transition* (1983), *Where Peoples Meet: Racial and Ethnic Frontiers* (with Helen MacGill Hughes, 1981), *Men and Their Work* (1958), *Education for the Professions of Medicine, Law, Theology, and Social Welfare* (1973), and *The Sociological Eye: Collected Papers* (1984). In 1994, **Lewis A. Coser** edited a selection of his writings, *On Work, Race, and the Sociological Imagination*.   DONALD LEVINE

human capital
– see **social capital**.

Human Genome Project
– see **genetics**.

human needs
These have two related but different definitions. One is grounded in psychology and the other in **sociology** and social welfare. The difference in the two perspectives is the unit of analysis. The psychological approach to human needs focuses on the individual and the sociological and social welfare perspective attends to the needs of the **family**, **group**, and **society**.

The task of psychology is to understand behavior by linking it to the organism's primary needs and the environmental conditions relevant to them. Other approaches have added to this line of inquiry by concentrating on psychological

rather than physiological needs. In the 1950s psychologists developed a model in terms of eight levels. The first four are: physiological needs, safety needs, belongingness and love, and esteem needs. Once these needs are met, individuals seek self-growth by addressing the next four levels of needs: need to know and understand, aesthetic needs, self-actualization, and transcendence. Self-actualized people are characterized by: (1) being problem-focused; (2) incorporating an ongoing appreciation of life; (3) being concerned about personal growth; and (4) having the ability to enjoy peak experiences. The most recent psychological work on human needs is self-determination theory which defines needs as innate psychological nutriments that are essential for ongoing psychological growth, integrity, and well-being. The psychological concept of human needs has served as a means of organizing and integrating a wide range of research related to social contexts, motivational orientations, goals, healthy development, high-quality performance, maintained behavior change, and mental health.

The sociological and social welfare perspective defines human needs in terms of what the family, group, or society needs to enjoy a humane and high quality of life and to have fundamental human **rights**. These discussions are often couched in terms of: avoiding **violence** and **social conflict** (stability, security, and peace being desirable); disparities between racial/ethnic groups, sexes, or age cohorts; social **justice**; equal opportunity; free trade; immigration; **citizenship**; taxes and social welfare (redistribution of resources) policies. The Coalition on Human Needs in the United States, for example, is an alliance of national **organizations** working together to promote **public policies** that address the needs of low-income and other vulnerable populations, such as children, women, the elderly, and disabled people. Human Rights Watch and Amnesty International are two international human rights organizations that monitor human rights abuses around the world. They publish their findings and use publicity to focus the world's attention on human rights abuses. Most of these organizations base their work on the *Universal Declaration of Human Rights* which was adopted by the United Nations General Assembly on December 10, 1948, and which declares:

> Whereas disregard and contempt for human rights have resulted in barbarous acts which have outraged the conscience of mankind, and the advent of a world in which human beings shall enjoy freedom of speech and belief and freedom from fear and want

has been proclaimed as the highest aspiration of the common people. Whereas it is essential, if man is not to be compelled to have recourse, as a last resort, to rebellion against tyranny and oppression, that human rights should be protected by the rule of law.

GARY L. ALBRECHT AND MARK SHERRY

human relations
– see **management**.

human rights
– see **rights**.

human sciences
This term has its origins in the work of Wilhelm Dilthey (1833–1911), who, in his 1883 *Introduction to the Human Sciences*, argued for a conception of the human sciences that contrasted with existing perspectives and practices in many parts of the humanities and nascent **social sciences**. He argued for an interpretivist and hermeneutic approach to socio-historical studies, seeing them as united under the heading *Geisteswissenschaften*, in contrast to *Naturwissenschaften* or the natural sciences. Central to this was his emphasis on the meaningfulness of human lived experience and its primacy in the genesis of human action. Thus the psychology of the individual and individual consciousness are seen as part of broader historical inquiry and many traditional boundaries that now exist between disciplines are avoided. A central part of Dilthey's work was an attempt to provide a secure philosophical foundation for the *Geisteswissenschaften* that would afford them the same integrity and status as *Naturwissenschaften*.

In conducting social-historical research, *Verstehen* was afforded a central role, and a wide variety of materials and sources were brought within the purview of this kind of inquiry. *Verstehen* is a German word which may be roughly translated as "the understanding of meaning," and as a method it has been described as seeking the empathic understanding of the outlook and feelings of others. As an approach and a philosophy, this work has its clearest descendants in social anthropology and interpretative sociologies.

In contrast to Dilthey's original definition, the term human sciences is used very broadly and loosely, and most commonly in the name of university faculties, departments, and research groups. Typically these uses do reflect his desire to bring together the different parts of the humanities and social sciences. A number of them also include various parts of the biological

sciences too, but rarely do they follow the philosophical and methodological precepts which Dilthey sought to establish.   DAVID GOOD

hybridity
The synthesis of different **cultures** or social **identities**, resulting in a new third form, this term originates in horticultural studies to refer to the crossbreeding of two different species which produces a new species. In the nineteenth century, the term was sometimes used to refer to the mixing of races, synonymous with miscegenation. Typically it had a negative connotation. In the early twentieth century, the negative connotations were shed by anthropologists who used it as a descriptive category. Some anthropologists claimed that the mixing of races produced a new "social type" which they called the "hybrid."

In linguistics, hybridity is used to refer to the combination of **languages**. Examples include "pidgin" and "creole" languages. The most recent uses of the term in social analysis have been partially influenced by the work of Mikhail Bakhtin (1895–1975). He argued that linguistic difference also corresponded to differences between forms of social consciousness and **social classes**, such that, in his view, a hybrid refers not only to the combination of linguistic elements but to the social elements as well. Hybrids mark innovation, creativity, and change in social spaces. Bakhtin's idea has been expanded to encompass not only linguistic combinations but also combinations of social identities, ideas, and cultures, typically produced through cultural encounters during **colonialism** or through **globalization**. Culture theorists like **Stuart Hall** have tried to shed the negative connotations of the term and replace them with positive meanings. In this use of the term, hybrids reveal the inadequacy of **essentialism**. The underlying idea is that all cultures and identities are hybrids. There is no such thing as a completely unified culture or identity; they are always formed by a process of negotiation or interrelationships between differences or opposed terms, categories, or ideas. Hybridity therefore emerged as an important analytic concept in culture theory because it highlights that identities and meanings are formed relationally. Some strands of **postmodernism** and **postcolonial theory** have also used the term to show the importance of cultural difference without falling into the trap of essentialism.

JULIAN GO

hybridization
– see **globalization**.

hypothesis

– see **hypothetico-deductive method**.

hypothetico-deductive method

This method is in fact a theory of how science is supposed to work. The scientist makes hypotheses about reality and then tests them by looking for evidence to confirm these hunches. That is, a scientific hypothesis must be testable and based on observable empirical **data**. We deduce from a hypothesis what we should be able to discover as an explicit observable feature of reality. If observed, then the hypothesis is supported; if not, then the hypothesis must be given up. The immediate contrast is with the inductive method that suggests that science proceeds by collecting empirical instances of an event and then producing a hypothesis about what was going on (induction).

However, the hypothetico-deductive method does not resolve problems of what constitutes a scientific **explanation**. In the first place, what is to count as an observation is not clear, and scientists, when confronted with disconfirming evidence, can dismiss it on other grounds, such as, for example, that the measuring instruments are wrong. Following the work of **Thomas Kuhn** on **paradigms**, it is now clear that scientists actively work to protect their theories from disconfirming evidence, rather than actively working to falsify them. The strongest rejection of the hypothetico-deductive method was put forward by the philosopher of science **Karl Popper**. In his account, for a theory to be scientific, any hypotheses it produces must specify explicit observable outcomes that are capable of **falsification**, rather than searching for data that are able to verify the original set of hypotheses.   KEVIN WHITE

I

ideal type

Max Weber defined the nature and use of the ideal type, though many of the elements of his discussion originated with his colleague Heinrich Rickert (1863–1936). Ideal types are pure concepts that make no claim directly to describe or explain empirical events. They are constructed by social scientific investigators as conceptually pure benchmarks for contrasts and comparisons with facts collected from historically specific cases. Thus, one may use several different ideal types to specify the historical significance and cultural meaning of any given constellation of events. For example, in studying socially disadvantaged groups in a modern nation-state, one might use ideal types of both **social class** and **social status**.

According to Weber, sociology as a discipline devotes itself to the construction of ideal types. Though sociological ideal types can make no empirical claims, they gain the advantage in conceptual precision on the level of meaning. Weber's compendium of ideal types in *Economy and Society* (1922 [trans. 1978]) demonstrates this advantage. Each ideal type includes actions defined by typical subjectively assigned meanings, all of which are logically integrated into a complex concept. Beyond conceptual precision, distilling ideal types from historical sources requires great erudition. Ideal types may be developed on many levels of abstraction. Weber's well-known ideal type of **social action** is historically unlimited. His ideal-typical model of the routinization of **charisma** is applicable only in a particular range of situations, and his ideal type of the Protestant ethic applies only to a small group of early modern religious confessions and sects.　　　　IRA COHEN

idealism

A view of the world that sees reality as ultimately composed of ideas rather than a realm existing outside human consciousness, idealism reaches this conclusion on the grounds that, without ideas, humans could not function. Because human activity is conscious activity, the world itself is ultimately composed of ideas.

All religious **attitudes**, conventionally understood, are idealist in character, but they can be described as forms of objective idealism. Objective idealism does not doubt the existence of a reality outside the individual mind, but sees the real world as the creation of gods or God, so that worshipping God or appeasing the gods is essential for human control over nature. In its "deist" form, objective idealism argues that, while the world is ultimately created by God, science studies its regularities and character without assuming any further divine intervention.

Objective idealism needs to be distinguished from subjective idealism. Subjective idealists argue that the real world is created by individual ideas. Since all **data** must be processed by the human mind, it is impossible to prove that there is a world beyond these data. It is difficult to see how subjective idealism can rebut the criticism that it leads to a paralyzing skepticism and an inability to distinguish the subjective from the objective.

Idealism in general is unable to provide an analysis of how consciousness itself is a product of history.　　　　JOHN HOFFMAN

identity

The idea of human beings having an identity or identities has come to replace previous notions of character. Whereas identity is assumed to be socially constructed and invented, character signified individual attributes that were fixed and permanent. Identity then has an intersubjective dimension. In the **social sciences**, the view of **George Herbert Mead** that identity is dependent upon the recognition of others introduced more complex forms of understanding. Mead argued that human identities develop out of a three-way conversation between the I, Me, and generalized Other. It is by "taking the attitude of the other" that we learn reflexively to monitor our identities and present them to others. Identity is formed out of the constant ebb and flow of conversation between ourselves and others. When there is a conflict between the demands of the **community** and the **self**, individuals are thrown back on themselves in a reflective attitude, thereby examining whether their **values** and beliefs are in need of revision. On this reading all identity is reflexively produced.

If all identity is produced in the context of community, many have sought to look at the ways society seeks to regulate and manage its production. Many have sought to criticize Mead's views for neglecting the role of **power** and **culture** in helping shape identity. The modern **state** has been involved in the regulation and monitoring of identities through a number of **institutions**, from prisons to the courts and from the education system to border controls. Further, these features of identity are related to the rise of identity **politics** over the course of the twentieth century. In opposition to the way many of the dominant features of modern societies have sought to police and control identities, many have used claims to identity as a means of organizing themselves politically. The most prominent amongst these movements has been **feminism**, which has historically sought to deconstruct overtly masculine assumptions about human identities, while promoting new forms of inclusion and respect for women. On the other hand, other **social movements** have more explicitly sought to claim an absolutist identity as a means of engaging in politics. The politics of identity includes a number of social movements and **networks**, some of which provoke critical questions, while others defensively reaffirm communal connections.

The impact of more complex models of identity in the wake of Mead (not forgetting the impact of **psychoanalysis**) and identity politics has led to a growing appreciation of the complexity of identity. Indeed many now prefer the term "identities," signifying the idea that no one source can explain the complexity of the modern self. Modern selves are the product of a range of shifting and diverse social and cultural categories and identifications that are rarely stable. For many the capacity to have an identity means the ability to be able to tell a story about the self and related communities. An identity is like a narrative that has to be constantly retold and reformulated in the light of new circumstances. If social and cultural change in respect of **globalization** and **technology** has aided the reflexive capacity of identities, it has also increased the capacity of many to claim more fundamentalist versions of identity. The rise of the internet and new forms of communication have offered new opportunities for new forms of identity conflict and contestation that are no longer contained by the nation-state.   NICK STEVENSON

identity politics
– see **identity**.

ideology
Generally used to point to the ability of ideas to affect social circumstances, the function of ideology has thus been described as the capacity to advance the political and economic interests of **groups** or **social classes** (**Karl Mannheim**, *Ideology and Utopia*, 1936; **Karl Marx** and **Friedrich Engels**, *The German Ideology*, 1846), or, alternatively, the capacity to produce cohesion (N. Poulantzas, *State, Power, Socialism*, 1978) and resolve social strain (**Talcott Parsons**, *The Social System*, 1951). In Marx and Engels's early formulations, ideology belonged to the cultural superstructure of social formations while material forces of production were described as the foundation or base. Contradictions in the mediation between base and superstructure were understood to be signs of strain and class conflict that in turn produce **social change**. This general notion treated ideology as materially effective representation, although it often carried with it a connotation of false representation and concealment of **power**. Ideology was associated with systems of beliefs that naturalized **inequality** through false consciousness. So powerful was the association between ideology and political mobilization that, by the end of World War II, writers such as **Daniel Bell** (in *The End of Ideology*, 1960) described the ensuing period of conformity and political quiescence in some advanced capitalist societies as the eclipse of ideologies, post-political **politics**, broad social consensus, and the emergence of the administrative **state** organized for efficiency rather than contests between opposing claims concerning power and **justice**.

Few contemporary scholars claim that ideology is a grand set of ideas that in its seamless coherence imposes belief. It is not a system of ideas that strictly determines what people think, their consciousness, false or otherwise. The most promising formulations propose that ideology is not a body of abstracted ideas at all (static, coherent, or otherwise). Rather, ideology is a complex process "by which meaning is produced, challenged, reproduced, transformed" (M. Barrett, *Women's Oppression Today: Problems in Marxist Feminist Analysis*, 1980; M. M. Bahktin, *The Dialogic Imagination*, 1987; M. Billig, *Ideology and Opinions*, 1991). Ideology as a process of meaning making is not, however, to be equated with **culture** or structure in general, or with **social constructionism** as a transactional process in general. An ideology always embodies particular arrangements of power and affects **life chances** in a manner that is different from some other ideology or arrangement of power.

Within this constructivist or constitutive framework, consciousness and ideology are understood to be part of a reciprocal process in which the meanings given by individuals – in transactions with others – to their world become patterned, stabilized, and objectified. These meanings, once institutionalized, become part of the material and discursive systems that limit and constrain future meaning making.

Meanings can be said to be ideological only insofar as they serve power; thus ideology is not defined by its specific content but by its contextual construction and function (P. Ewick and S. S. Silbey, *The Common Place of Law*, 1998). This view recognizes that ideology continues as in the nineteenth century to be associated with power, inequality, and domination, but is not simply a tool to hide or create a distraction from the real. Rather, the social meanings we define as ideological are constitutive of domination; they are ideological precisely because they appear to be non-ideological (P. Ewick, *Consciousness and Ideology*, 2004). Ideologies vary, however, in the degree to which they are apparent, contested, or conventionalized. Thus, ideology can be understood in relationship to **hegemony** as the ends of a continuum. At one end of the continuum, the visible and active struggles referred to as ideology. At the other end, the term hegemony refers to situations where these struggles are no longer active, where power is dispersed through **social structures**, and meanings are so embedded that representational and institutional struggles are no longer visible (J. Comaroff and J. Comaroff, *Of Revelation and Revolution*, 1991). Although moments of resistance may be documented, in general subjects do not notice, question, or make claims against hegemony.

In *Ideology and Modern Culture* (1990), J. B. Thompson offers a useful typology of how ideology generates meaning and truth claims by creating ways of knowing and not knowing by suppressing alternative meanings. Focusing on ideology as process and technique, Thompson suggests that ideology produces **legitimacy**, authorizing, sustaining, and reproducing social relations and organizations. By drawing boundaries around objects and processes, ideologies both unify and fragment coalitions and groups, creating and suppressing opportunities for action. Most importantly, ideological processes also reify and deceive. Ideology reifies social relations by masking their social and historical character, treating as concrete what is an ongoing process in the making. By naturalizing and thus making inevitable what is a human process of social construction, ideology not only reifies social relations but also deceives and is mobilized to sustain or achieve domination.

SUSAN SILBEY

imagined communities

A theory of **nationalism**, the phrase entered the lexicon of modern sociology through B. Anderson's *Imagined Communities. Reflections on the Origin and Spread of Nationalism* (1983). Anderson argued, on the basis of a historical study of the struggle for Javanese independence from Japan in *Java in a Time of Revolution* (1972), that nations are created or imagined rather than naturally occurring entities waiting to be discovered. Although nationalists typically like to think of their nation as existing from the dawn of time, nations are the products of modern revolutions. He defined a nation as an "imagined political **community**" that is both limited and sovereign.

It is imagined because, even in the case of small nations, the fellow-members cannot know or meet each other, but they consider themselves or imagine themselves to be members of the nation. This community is limited in having boundaries, and it is sovereign, because the **state** attempts to assert its legitimate **power** over a territory. Finally, it is a community, because irrespective of social class divisions, members of a nation imagine themselves to be what Anderson calls a "horizontal community." For example, Indonesians, who occupy a complex and sprawling archipelago of islands with diverse **cultures** and **religions**, have acquired a national consciousness as a result of their struggle against Japanese and Dutch occupation. The Indonesian nation is an imagined community in this sense.

Anderson also argued that the spread of print culture and the growth of literacy in modern times have facilitated or made possible a situation whereby people can imagine themselves as part of an integrated, horizontal, political community. The growth of the novel (in the eighteenth century) and the spread of the mass newspapers (in the nineteenth century) were both important in the spread of the political imagination of the nation. The Protestant Reformation was especially important in the growth of a literate population who consumed print (for example in copies of sermons), and which contributed to the triumph of vernacular **languages** over the Latin of the Catholic Church.

With Anderson's thesis the idea that nationalism produces rather than discovers nations became the common assumption of sociological and political discussion.   BRYAN S. TURNER

imperialism

In an article on the "Sociology of Imperialism" (1919), **Joseph Schumpeter** defines imperialism as "the objectless disposition on the part of a state to unlimited forcible expansion." In this sense, "imperialism" describes the common tendency of a political unit to grow until it encompasses the earth. In so far as the purpose of any political unit is expansion, all polities are either potentially or actively imperialist. But polities do not all try to expand in the same manner or to the same extent. Only empires aspire to expand themselves indefinitely: both city-states and nation-states are based on a territorial sovereignty, while empires aim directly at a universal sovereignty, a *dominium* over the whole of humanity.

At its best, imperialism is a noble disposition to create a political structure that is both universal and concrete, a desire to unify humanity. At its best, imperialism is also a just disposition: not a disposition to conquer out of an unhealthy *libido dominandi*, but for the sake of peace, for the sake of an equivalent of the *pax romana* which political unity makes possible. However, imperialism has often been seen as problematic. In the book of Genesis, God condemns the project of building a tower "with its top in heaven," Babel, by halting this symbol of human over-reaching with "the confusion of tongues," thereby dividing humanity into many nations, making human attempts to build imperial projects to unify humanity more difficult. Genesis associates imperialism with hubris and pride, with a vain and evil desire to be like God.

Our present unease with imperialism has at least two specific roots. The first is the non-democratic character of empires. In an empire, a ruling individual or a ruling **oligarchy** imposes its will on the rest of the empire. Empires are built around the opposition of a core and a periphery, the periphery being subordinated to the core. In contrast, city-states and nation-states are not built around the distinction core/periphery but around an opposition between internal and external, with more firmly defined boundaries: these political forms are compatible with the idea of a unified people of equal citizens. Whereas empires exclude **democracy** as a political regime, city-states and nation-states are compatible with democracy; they are not necessarily hierarchical. A second

root of our contemporary discomfort with imperialism is **cultural relativism**. In order to justify their imposed order, empires tend to claim that they stand for a higher degree of **civilization**, that this gives them a right to rule "barbarians." In a world like ours, which considers itself to be disenchanted with any claim about the superiority of any aristocracy or civilization, empires appear to be lacking in **legitimacy**.

According to Schumpeter, imperialism is an irrational inclination towards **war** and conquest, and one which he associates with the survival of residual political structures: imperialism belongs to a pre-capitalist era and is an atavism destined to disappear. In order to defend their social position, a ruling class (see **social class**) foments a jingoistic mood in which ideas such as national honor and prestige play an essential part. But, according to Schumpeter, a purely capitalist world can offer no ground for imperialist impulses. Schumpeter belongs to a tradition illustrated by **Auguste Comte** and **Thorstein Veblen** according to which commerce will replace war – a tradition analyzed in **Raymond Aron**, *War and Industrial Society* (1958). One dominant contemporary version of this theory, a theory of **globalization**, has two roots: a belief that commerce will replace war, and an argument turning the ideals of the **Enlightenment**, ideals which underpinned European imperialism, against imperialism itself.

However, imperialism should not simply be confused or conflated with an old-fashioned spirit of conquest, an anti-capitalist and an anti-democratic inclination. Not all empires have been tyrannies, not all empires belong to a pre-capitalist and pre-democratic age. Another school of **explanation** of imperialism stems from **Vladimir Ilich Lenin's** analysis of imperialism as the "highest stage of capitalism." The claims of this school are the converse of Schumpeter's: the accumulation of **wealth** will not be enough to get rid of war, as war is a necessary consequence of economic **inequality**. This argument and its posterity are described in Wolfgang J. Mommsen, *Theories of Imperialism* (1977 [trans. 1980]). The preservation of capitalism requires expansionist opportunities. Imperialism is due to the acute competition of surplus capital which did not find profitable employment on the home market.

Lenin's theory echoes Machiavelli's political philosophy perhaps even more than **Marxism**. According to Machiavelli, imperialism is favored by all those who try to avoid the conflict between the haves and the have-nots, the oligarchs and the people. Imperialism reorients the activity of the city or state in a way which enables it to avoid imploding through civil war. On this account, the sociology of international relations cannot be separated from the sociology of social classes and political sociology. As Machiavelli puts it in his *Discourses On the First Ten Books of Titus Livius* (1531 [trans. 1996]) (an analysis of Rome's imperial past), the passions of those who want to acquire and of those who do not want to lose combine to form a communal passion to acquire the world. The quarrel between the poor and the rich frees an energy that helps in building up the power necessary to conquer. Imperialism sublimates class conflicts into wars of overseas conquest and external expansion.

One can reconcile in part Lenin's and Schumpeter's teachings by noticing that there are various types of empires and imperialisms. Empires are more or less military and more or less formal. Although Britain built the immense empire that became the empire par excellence in modern times, the nation's **power** was ordinarily exercised in an indirect way that made it easy to rule with a comparatively small army and civil service – Niall Ferguson's *Empire* (2003) offers an introduction to its history. In its weakest form, imperialism can be a form of loose economic **hegemony**. Today, deepening the spirit of commercial societies, the United States of America seem to have superseded the indirect character of the British Empire in exercising their empire without the real burden of an empire.

Imperialism is not necessarily incompatible with **capitalism** and democracy: it can be a product of both. Western nations ruled the world because their individual members set sail for science, victory, and gain. The extension of political and economic liberty at home went hand in hand with the extension of the power abroad. The great discovery of Machiavelli, both a republican and an imperialist, is that freedom is not an enemy of power, but what produces it. The acquisitive passion is equally at work in democracy, capitalism, and imperialism: it leads the have-nots to impose their own regime (democracy), a regime that will allow them to acquire more goods (capitalism) and more territory (imperialism).

ÉMILE PERREAU-SAUSSINE

income

In commonsense terms, income refers to the wages that an individual earns through gainful employment (see **work and employment**) over time. In more technical language, it refers to the flow of **money**, goods, or services to an economic unit, which may be an individual or more typically a household. Personal disposable income refers to the income available to a household after taxation and national insurance contributions. The national income refers to the aggregate incomes of the residents of a **society** in a given period of time. Incomes in this national calculation include all payments for the factors of production, that is wages, salaries, profits, rent, and income from abroad.

In economic distribution theory, the incomes of land, **labor**, and capital are determined by the demand and supply for them. This way of looking at income was an aspect of the classical **political economy** of David Ricardo (1772–1823) who sought to determine the economic laws that regulate the distribution of the produce of industry between different **social classes**, namely landowners, capitalists, and workers. In developing these ideas, Ricardo created a theory of income distribution, that is an analysis of the share of the economic output that went to landlords, capitalists, and workers. Whereas landlords depended on rent from land, capitalists seek profit on industrial investments, and workers exist on wages. Ricardo anticipated **Karl Marx** in recognizing the fundamental conflict of interest between these three classes. Ricardo recognized that the value of any commodity will be determined by the amount of labor invested in it, and therefore capitalists have an interest in controlling wages to increase their profits. Capitalists will attempt to replace labor with machinery, because capital-intensive goods will be cheaper than labor-intensive goods. Ricardo's theory of the dynamics of **capitalism** was similar to the demographic theory of **Thomas Malthus** (1766–1834). Ricardo argued that when wages rise above the subsistence level, workers respond by increasing the size of their **families**. As population grows, the supply of labor will increase, there will be downward pressure on wages, and as family size increases the standard of living declines. However, population growth increases the demand for land and increases rent. This Ricardian distribution model described the inherent contradictions of capitalism, thereby anticipating the Marxist theory of capitalist crisis.

Sociologists have been primarily interested in the distribution of income as a measure of social inequality. **Richard Titmuss** in *Income Distribution and Social Change* (1962) showed that in Britain the problems of income distribution and taxation were poorly understood, and that social workers had been too concerned with the basic problem of **poverty** to the neglect of relative income inequality. Titmuss's research was intended to examine whether there had been any equalization of incomes in the postwar period. This question has given rise to much debate, but there is some consensus that, with **neo-liberalism**, income inequality has increased.

Sociologists typically measure income inequality in terms of the gini coefficient. This coefficient is based on the Lorenz curve which shows the extent of inequality in terms of a frequency distribution by reference to personal income. A Lorenz curve is a graphical representation of inequality in which the cumulative percentages of a population of taxpayers are plotted against the cumulative percentage of incomes. A straight line rising at an angle of 45 degrees from the base of the graph will show perfect equality. For example, if 10 percent of the population earned 10 percent of the national income, and 20 percent earned 20 percent, and so on, there would be perfect income equality. When a curve is traced below the 45 degree line, the degree of curvature measures the degree of inequality. The gini coefficient is measured as

$$G = \frac{\text{Area between Lorenz curve and 45-degree line}}{\text{Area above the 45-degree line}}$$

Where the frequency distribution is equal, then $G = 0$.

As the **welfare state** expanded in the postwar period, Britain was characterized by a considerable degree of income **equality** in the 1950s and 1960s. However, the gini coefficient showed that in the mid-1980s income inequality began to increase, and from the late 1980s it increased rapidly. Taxation has an important role to play in income distribution, and with the reduction in direct personal taxation the income of the rich has increased significantly. The number of millionaires in Great Britain has increased dramatically since the 1980s. Sociologists are interested in income distribution because it provides a proxy measure of social class, and the conflict between wages and profits is an indication of the extent of **class struggle**. Furthermore, income inequality is closely associated with poor **health**. In *Unhealthy Societies* (1996) Richard Wilkinson showed how improvements in mortality rates in Great Britain had slowed down after 1985 as income inequality increased.

The economic theory of income distribution assumes perfect competition between factors of production and, in a free **market**, labor, land, and capital will be fully and efficiently employed. Sociologists have, however, been interested in conditions that limit perfect competition such as the growth of **trade unions**, wage bargaining, the institutionalization of **social conflict**, and monopolies over profit. Economic theories of perfect competition between factors of production with constant returns to scale and zero profits have had difficulties explaining such phenomena as waste. Such theories are also limited by their inability to calculate the value of the black market (or **informal economy**) and **crime** to economic activity, because such activities are not or rarely subject to taxation, and hence are not easily measured.

BRYAN S. TURNER

income equality
– see **income**.

independent variables
– see **dependent/independent variables**.

indexicality
– see **ethnomethodology**.

individualism
There are two general perspectives on individualism. First, it is a political doctrine associated with **liberalism** that emphasizes the autonomy, importance, and freedom of the individual in relation to the **state**. Second, it is a particular type of **culture** associated with private property **rights**, personal **consumption** and individual autonomy. It is typically assumed to be an important aspect of western culture as a whole, having its historical roots both in Greco-Roman antiquity and in the Christian **religion**. However, individualism had its modern origins in the theology of seventeenth-century religious sects, and it is often held to be the dominant ideology of **capitalism**. In political theory, **John Stuart Mill** claimed that the individual is sovereign, and in economic theories of **entrepreneurship**, Robinson Crusoe in Daniel Defoe's novel is seen to be the quintessential hero of individualistic capitalism. Individualism is also thought to be a defining characteristic of western culture, in contrast with the emphasis on the **family** and the collectivity in eastern cultures. In *Essays on Individualism* (1986), **Louis Dumont** contrasted the hierarchical caste **society** of India, with its emphasis on the social over the individual, with modern western society where society is subordinated to the individual.

Individualisme was employed in France as condemnation of the rational individualism of the **Enlightenment** and the French Revolution. For the eighteenth-century English philosopher Edmund Burke (1729–97), individualism and the promotion of individual interests would undermine the commonwealth and create an uncivil, unstable, and repressive society. Nineteenth-century French **sociology** can also be seen as a powerful criticism of individualism, and in the notion of the social sociologists emphasized the importance of social **solidarity** against the negative impact of egoistic forms of individualism. **Émile Durkheim** developed a sustained intellectual attack on utilitarian individualism as represented by **Herbert Spencer**. While the analysis of individualism has played a significant role in the development of **sociological theory**, the ideological and intellectual relationship between individualism and sociology is often ambiguous. As a result, understanding the relationship between "the individual" and "the social" remains a perennial issue in sociological theory.

The development of individualism corresponds closely with the emergence of western capitalism from the early seventeenth century. **Max Weber**, in *The Protestant Ethic and the Spirit of Capitalism* (1905 [trans. 2002]), showed how Calvinism challenged traditional **authority** by claiming that the salvation of the individual could not be guaranteed by the **institutions** of the church, such as the Sacraments. Each individual would stand alone before God on the Day of Judgment, and would be held responsible for his or her sins. Protestantism created a radical version of religious individualism that profoundly shaped western attitudes towards political and social institutions. The emphasis on the isolated individual and the anxieties surrounding uncertain knowledge of salvation was part of a "tragic vision" that in France characterized the Jansenist sect, the philosophy of Pascal, and the tragedies of Racine. In early modern history, the Protestant Reformation was a critical turning point, because it made salvation potentially available to everybody, regardless of his or her social standing. This theological differentiation of the individual from society is an important component of the historical development of **religion**.

In theoretical terms, individualism is subject to considerable confusion. It is important to establish a clear distinction between four separate issues. We can distinguish an emphasis on the individual as an autonomous agent with a distinct **identity** as part of the western tradition. Then there is individualism as a social and political **ideology** with various national traditions. Third, in European thought, individuality was a romantic view of the uniqueness of the person and is the product of a long process of **education** and cultivation. Fourth, in modern societies, there is individuation as a process whereby people are standardized by the bureaucratic processes of the modern state. Finally there is in addition an epistemological theory called **methodological individualism** that argues that all sociological **explanations** are reducible to the characteristics of individuals.

The development of sociological theory has involved various attempts to resolve this dilemma of collective and individual concepts of social institutions. Weber, for example, has been criticized for an artificial and historically static construction of the individual and society. In *The Society of Individuals* (1991), **Norbert Elias** criticized Weber for his inability to reconcile the analytical tensions between the individual and society. This failure to deal successfully with this artificial division is a general weakness of sociological theory. Elias offered a solution in which we analyze the two concepts of individual and society as historical constructs that arise from social processes. The balance between society (We) and the individual (I) is not fixed, and hence what he called "processual sociology" or "figurational sociology" was designed to explore the We–I balance in different social configurations, such as **feudalism** or bourgeois society.

In American sociology, there has been a persistent theme claiming that nineteenth-century individualism was undermined by the growth of **mass society.** The debate starts with **Alexis de Tocqueville** who, in *Democracy in America* (1848 [trans. 1968]), believed that the lack of centralized, bureaucratic government in America had encouraged individual initiative and that **voluntary associations** had flourished to solve local, community problems. **Civil society** required these associations to flourish, and as a result individualism had not been crushed by centralized administration. However, the emphasis on **equality**, while a revolutionary doctrine, also threatened the individual with mass opinion. Tocqueville's fears for individual opinion in a mass **democracy** influenced liberals such as Mill towards universal suffrage in Britain.

Critical theorists in the twentieth century continued to study the impact of mass society on individuals. **C. Wright Mills**, in *The Power Elite* (1956), claimed that individuals were increasingly manipulated by **public opinion** in a society where **elites** controlled the channels of **information. David Riesman**, in *The Lonely Crowd* (1950), analyzed the American personality as the other-directed character, because it depends on constant approval and affirmation from others. Other-directed personalities are conformist, and hence American culture was stagnating. In *The Organization Man* (1956), W. H. Whyte described the company executives, who are mobile, disconnected from their local **communities** and families, and dedicated to personal achievement within the **organization**. These organizational commitments encouraged social conformity. In *Habits of the Heart* (1985), **Robert N. Bellah** and his colleagues undertook an influential study of contemporary **attitudes** towards **politics** that was intended to replicate Tocqueville's study. They discovered that Americans were alienated from politics and political institutions, but their commitment to society was expressed through a multitude of local and informal associations.

In the 1950s sociologists created a theory of social standardization and conformity that apparently undermined the raw individualism of early capitalism. Contemporary sociological studies have drawn on the theory of **postindustrial society** to argue that modern patterns of employment, for example in the service sector, are fragmented, and employment does not require loyalty to the company. In the 1990s, **work and employment** have become casualized, part-time, and discontinuous. The alienated individual of mass society has been replaced by a work force that has no sense of identity with the company, and many people no longer have an experience of a life-time career. **Richard Sennett**, in *Respect* (2003), argues that casualized workers have low self-esteem. The implication of these studies is that the rugged individualism of the American frontier is decaying.

BRYAN S. TURNER

individualization theory

Individualization concerns the conversion of **identity** into a task to be achieved. Life is increasingly lived as an individual project. The decline of class loyalties and bonds (along with growing income **inequalities**) means that individuals are increasingly thrown back on their own biographies, with human relations increasingly becoming susceptible to individual choice. This does not mean that the self is being increasingly determined by market **individualism** or by social isolation. In *Risk Society* (1992), **Ulrich Beck** argues individualization means the disembedding of the ways of **industrial society** and the reinvention of new communal ties and biographies. As more areas of social life are less defined by **tradition**, the more our biographies require choice and planning. Individuals are "condemned" to become authors of their own lives.

The partial disintegration of the nuclear **family** and rigid class hierarchies means we are all released from the structures of industrial society into the uncertainties of a world risk society.

There are two main criticisms of these views. (1) The individualized **self** is dependent upon access to material and symbolic resources that are unevenly distributed in modern industrial societies. The argument here is that the individualized self is a middle-class rather than a universal social condition. (2) This view seriously underestimates the extent to which ordinary lives and sensibilities have been colonized by the imperatives of economic reason. NICK STEVENSON

induction
– see **explanation**.

industrial democracy

This phrase refers to worker participation in **management** as both a historical and institutional development within **industrial relations**. The theory of industrial democracy summarizes a range of participatory practices induced by workers, **trade unions**, state legislature, or management. Common organizational forms are worker self-management, cooperatives, codetermination, work councils, and shop-floor programs (for example autonomous work groups). Participation can be indirect (for example representation through trade unions or work councils) or direct (for example individual worker involvement in teamwork schemes). Politically, the term symbolizes ideological commitment to social **rights** and economic or industrial **citizenship** as dimensions of so-called organizational **democracy.** Towards the end of the twentieth century, the European Union developed a range of industrial democracy initiatives, thus creating legislative support for European employee rights.

Collective bargaining by trade unions (to determine wages and conditions) is still the dominant form of industrial democracy, but there has been a decline in the strength, scope, and scale of union action, as well as in the role of the **state** in industrial relations. Changes in production **technologies** and production organization as well as changes to firm and market structures, in the context of the ongoing **globalization** of the **economy,** have also affected nationally instituted structures and produced different sets of actor choices and opportunities. Diverse organizational forms and actor constellations now exist, in which individual-employee participation represents both more direct participation and leverage for managers to bypass labor representatives and collective agreements. Although the power balance is generally understood as shifting in favor of management, industrial democracy remains a salient public issue.

Crucial to understanding contemporary industrial democracy is the recognition that worker participation is no longer confined to labor interests. Worker involvement has been developed as a programmatic component of management theory and practice, and implemented through so-called human resource management (HRM). This form of management helps institute worker participation through widespread practices of worker consultation, without intending to advance democracy. Compared with actual collaborative decision-making and participation in ownership and profit-sharing, this weaker form, generally welcomed by employees and their representatives, has also been analyzed as undermining the more far-reaching, encompassing, or radical, goals of trade unions and collective action by labor movements more broadly.

Distinct national models of industrial democracy exist. There are clear differences between the Anglo-Saxon and German varieties of **capitalism**. For example, in the United States and the United Kingdom, economic competition from Japan led to experiments with high levels of worker participation (for example so-called quality circles and total quality management) and, from the 1980s, financial participation (for instance, profit-sharing and stock-ownership extended to employees). Germany's system of industrial relations, on the other hand, involves a dual system of interest representation, with collective bargaining between unions and employer representatives at the industry level that is kept separate from co-determination (*Mitbestimmung*) at the level of the **firm**. Legal regulation supports industry-level bargaining, determining the practices of negotiation and arbitration without direct state intervention. Work councils on the firm level are increasingly taking over the role of the unions on the industry-level of negotiation, but the essential feature of capital–labor co-determination remains.

ANN VOGEL

industrial relations

These are concerned with the relationship between employers and employees, with its regulation, and with the social, legal, and economic **influences** that shape it. The subject first received systematic study in the late nineteenth and early twentieth centuries, notably with the work of Beatrice Webb (1858–1943) and Sidney Webb (1859–1947) in the United Kingdom, and of John Commons (1862–1945) in the United States. Their interest was a response to the contemporary rise of trade union **power** and to the industrial unrest that increasingly disrupted the developed world. An underlying concern of the subject was, and remains, collective employee behavior and its regulation. The employment relationship was seen to be inherently conflictual because of the open-ended nature of the employment contract, and the imbalance of power between employer and employee. This distinguishes the subject from personnel **management** and human resource management, for which the frame of reference is the management of individualistic relationships with employees.

For most of the twentieth century, and for most industrialized market **economies**, the driving force behind the regulation of terms and conditions of employment was formal bargaining between employers and the **trade unions** representing their employees. This regulatory process, called collective bargaining, gave rise to a patchwork of industrial agreements within countries. Trade unions were seen to play an often controversial role in exacerbating **inflation**, in encouraging or impeding industrial efficiency, and in upholding decent labor standards. Governments, to varying extents, and with varying degrees of political support from trade unions, legislated a procedural framework for collective bargaining. This provided constraints to strike activity, means (such as conciliation and arbitration) for conflict resolution, and rights to trade union organization. Towards the end of the twentieth century, collective bargaining became eroded by intensified national and international competitive pressure for goods and services. As a result, in most market economies, trade union membership and strike action diminished, and concern with industrial relations declined.

In the decades after World War II there was substantial sociological interest in industrial relations. Academic theorists sought to ground their policy prescriptions in sociological analysis – for example, John Dunlop drew on the work of **Talcott Parsons** for his *Industrial Relations Systems* (1958) and Allan Flanders's influential analyses of the breakdown of the British system used conceptions of legitimation and **anomie** taken from **Max Weber** and **Émile Durkheim**. Ethnographic studies such as **Alvin Gouldner**'s *Patterns of Industrial Bureaucracy* (1955), Melville Dalton's *Men who Manage* (1959), and Michel Crozier's *The Bureaucratic*

Phenomenon (1964) inspired a generation of industrial sociologists to explore informal processes and power relationships in industrial relations. Studies such as Alan Fox's *Beyond Contract: Work, Power, and Trust Relations* (1974) and Eric Batstone and his colleagues' *Shop Stewards in Action* (1977) did much to shed light on the rational bases of what was popularly conceived to be the irrational exercise of union power. In the British context, such studies played an important part in drawing attention to the managerial weakness that lay behind disorderly workplace industrial relations, and thereby facilitated its elimination. The economic pressures of subsequent decades have tended to eclipse the pursuit of sociological **explanations** of industrial relations behavior.

WILLIAM A. BROWN

industrial society

Modern **society** is industrial society. When a society undergoes industrialization, it tends to take on the following features. It has an **economy** in which power-driven machinery replaces human and animal power, and steam, gas, or electricity replaces wind and water as sources of power. Handicraft production in the home or small workshop gives way to mechanized production in the factory. The majority of the adult population work in manufacturing or services, rather than agriculture. Work is based on a complex division of **labor**, involving generally a considerable degree of mechanization and **automation** and a strict separation of manual and mental labor. Its **organization** is based on Fordism (see **Post-Fordism**) and **Taylorism.** The industrial way of life also tends to involve a strict separation between home and work, and between work and **leisure**. For **Karl Marx**, such features of industrialism give rise to a high degree of **alienation**.

The industrial population is urban, that is to say that a majority live in towns of over 20,000 inhabitants, and many in towns of over 1 million people. Even rural dwellers are dependent on the **city**, either for work or for most of the required services and amenities.

Industrial life also tends to be secular, with **religion** playing a diminished role in the life of societies. As emphasized in the work of **Max Weber**, industrial society is increasingly rationalized and bureaucratized. For many nineteenth-century sociologists, such as **Ferdinand Tönnies**, such features of industrial society lead to fragmentation and a loss of **community**.

The first society to industrialize was that of Britain in the early nineteenth century, as a result of its "Industrial Revolution." Industrialism gradually spread to the rest of western Europe and, by the late nineteenth century, to America, Japan, and eastern European countries such as Russia. By the mid twentieth century, industrialism had become worldwide, and commentators were beginning to speak of a second industrial revolution and the movement to a **postindustrial society** in the developed world.

Industrial society has been, in the main, capitalist society. That, for Marx, was its most important feature, leading to the development of **social classes** based on ownership or non-ownership of the means of production, and involving more or less permanent class conflict. Eventually, Marx thought, such conflict would lead to **socialism** and a more stable form of industrial society. That has not happened yet in any advanced industrial society, though a number of less developed countries, such as Russia and China, have tried, with considerable success, to industrialize under the banner of socialism or **Communism**. Liberal thinkers past and present, such as **Herbert Spencer**, **Émile Durkheim**, and **Talcott Parsons**, have taken a more optimistic view of industrial society and its future, arguing that the early conflicts and discontents would give way to a more orderly integration as social **groups** adjusted to each other and a normative system governed by fairness and **justice** gradually established itself in the workplace and in the society at large. As industrial society has globalized, largely under capitalist auspices, the socialist dream has largely faded and some form of liberal **democracy** has increasingly become the norm.

KRISHAN KUMAR

industrialization

– see **industrial society**.

inequality

The unequal distribution of opportunities, rewards, and **power** among and between individuals, households, and **groups** is a defining feature of all known **societies**. The study of such differences, or inequalities, is a core concern of much sociological research. The subfield of **social stratification** has as its main task the description and analysis of inequalities, or the makeup of the stratification system of any given society. Many other subfields of sociology also examine particular kinds of inequalities (for example, political sociology examines inequalities in the distribution of power, cultural sociologists study the unequal distribution of cultural capital, and so forth). Inequalities can be seen most clearly in two distinct allocations – who gets what? (inequality of outcomes) and who does what? (inequalities of opportunities) – and across four distinct social levels (individuals, groups, **organizations** and **institutions**). The interaction between allocation processes and the social levels at which they occur defines the contours within which sociological research on inequality proceeds. Sociologists have also paid considerable attention to the consequences of inequality, and the ways in which inequalities are reproduced and transmitted from **generation** to generation. Finally, it is important to keep in mind that research on inequality may concern either the distribution at one point in time or dynamic or intergenerational processes.

The most basic question about inequality concerns the uneven distribution of rewards. Inequalities of **income** and **wealth** are central, but these are fundamentally different concepts. Income refers to the receipt of money or goods over a particular accounting period (such as hourly, weekly, monthly, yearly, or over the **life-course**). For most individuals and households, it is their earned income that primarily defines their well-being and capacity to acquire goods and service. The choice of time period for studying income is important. Take lifetime income flows: the young generally receive little or no income; income typically peaks in middle age, declining later in life. But such generalizations cannot take into account short-term shocks (**unemployment**, health problems, macroeconomic conditions, the birth of a child, good or bad luck) that may radically alter income level at any particular point in time. The use of averages over longer periods (such as yearly) tends to obscure certain kinds of inequalities. For this reason, analysts have typically considered income insecurity an important supplement to analyses of income inequality.

There are multiple possible sources of income: earned income from a job, income received from investments or ownership of income-generating **properties** or business, income transfers from the government, income received from **family** or friends, and illegal or "underground" earnings (such as from **crime** or informal services provided outside a formal labor contract). The source of income is a critical distinction. Individuals who rely solely on paid employment or government transfers have neither the security nor typically the amount of income relative to those who receive income from multiple sources. One may lose a job or a government entitlement and be without income altogether for some extended period of time. For these reasons, analysts of inequality must pay attention to the source of income as well as the amount.

In studying income flows, sociologists have highlighted the importance of **occupations** and/ or aggregations of occupations known as **social classes**. Occupations vary widely in the level of income they provide to their incumbents; professional and managerial occupations provide far greater incomes and employment security than do routine "white-collar" jobs or skilled and unskilled manual jobs. Occupations are powerful predictors of income, intergenerational **social mobility**, **attitudes**, voting behavior, and friendship/ marriage patterns.

Within a single "occupation" (however defined), there is wide variation in the types of labor performed and in the compensation provided. The primary alternative analytical method is to examine classes, broad groupings of occupations and/or individuals with similar **life chances**. Research on class-based inequalities has been a hallmark of the sociological tradition since **Karl Marx**. Class analysis provides a different way of examining the impact of inequalities across a wide range of social domains. A variety of different types of class schema have been developed as analytical tools. Among the most prominent of these in contemporary sociology are the models of **John Goldthorpe**, notably in *The Class Structure in Modern Britain* (1980), and Erik Olin Wright, *Classes* (1985). The Goldthorpe class scheme is built around an analysis of employment relations (such as the degree of **trust** associated with particular kinds of occupations), while the Wright scheme focuses on the differential distribution of assets possessed by different classes (principally skill and organizational, and property, assets).

A different perspective on class inequalities emerges when analysts focus on wealth. Wealth refers to the total stock of capital resources possessed by an individual or family. The most important types of wealth possessed by most households are their homes, while a much smaller subset of the population owns net financial assets (NFAs) in addition to property. Home ownership is the most widespread type of wealth ownership in the developed capitalist world, and, since homes tend to appreciate over time, home ownership has been one way that modest households accumulate wealth. (The difficulties in securing legal title to property and the barriers to wealth accumulation this posed has been identified as one critical source of slow economic growth in less-developed countries.) Significant net financial assets (the total value of savings, investments, and other convertible assets, less outstanding debts), in contrast, are far less widely held. Upper-class families possess vast NFAs, while many families possess little or no NFAs. Wealth is a critical source of intergenerational inequality, something which affluent parents can pass on to their children to provide them with important starting advantages. Wealth differences between individuals and groups are often far larger than income differences, and the sources of wealth inequality has been an increasingly important topic of investigation in recent years. Of particular note is the role of wealth assets in cushioning families against unanticipated crises such as sudden job loss or health catastrophe.

Less commonly thought of in relation to inequality of outcomes is status inequality. Inequality on the basis of status refers not to the amount of income, but rather the **prestige** of a particular social location. In primitive societies, for example, the social position of "medicine man" or tribal elder meant high social prestige even if there was relatively little extra reward associated with possession of that title. In modern societies, status attaches to particular occupations (occupational status), fame (celebrity status), successful performance within a social location (heroic status), and power. While any of these statuses *may* be associated with substantial rewards, it is not necessarily the case. For example, the President of the United States commands a very modest salary in comparison with heads of most large corporations, but has infinitely more status. Occupational prestige is an important area of investigation in relation to status inequality. In the influential research of Donald Treiman and his colleagues, most notably in *Occupational Prestige in Comparative Perspective*, scales for ranking occupations according to the social prestige accorded to them by a cross-section of survey respondents was developed. A robust finding is that, over time and across societies, occupational prestige rankings are remarkably consistent.

Much research on income and wealth inequalities has focused on examining trends over time. One conclusion that is now universally agreed upon is that intracountry inequalities are growing, albeit at different rates in different countries. There are a number of different theories about why inequalities in the postindustrial capitalist world are growing. Among the leading **explanations** are rising returns to **education** (with the gap between college-educated and non-college-educated citizens growing), changes associated

with economic **globalization** in the late twentieth and early twenty-first centuries (including rising levels of trade and more rapid movement of capital across borders), declining union strength, and the decline of medium-wage manufacturing jobs. Although inequality has risen, rates of **poverty** have not significantly increased in most countries, as social provision through the public sector continues to play an important role in shoring up the well-being of low-income households.

A focus on income or wealth inequality is but one side of the sociological examination of inequalities. All known societies are characterized by a division of **labor** in which individuals and groups are vested with different responsibilities and powers in the reproduction of their lives and societies as a whole. This division of labor defines a second-core allocation of inequality, the question of who does what. Two types of human labor are fundamental in defining who does what: **work** (including paid employment) and household labor (housework; see **women and work**). In the Marxist tradition, this distinction is known as production versus reproduction, and feminist sociologists have brought the study of the latter into the heart of the sociological study of inequality.

At the top of any division of labor are social positions imbued with power. In such positions, incumbents are in a position to make decisions that others have to follow whether they want to or not. The most important types of power reside in organizational position (such as in government, the military, or corporate hierarchies), or in command over investment decisions (afforded by the ownership of great wealth). But decision-making power can also exist in much smaller units, such as heterosexual families (where men typically exert far greater influence over household decisions than women).

Autonomy is a second critical concept in defining who does what, especially in the world of work. Occupational hierarchies produce wide variation in the level of autonomy provided to individuals. In high-trust occupations, incumbents work without much supervision and are free to define the pace of their work effort. By contrast, in low-trust occupations, continual monitoring of effort and lack of autonomy are defining features of the daily grind. These issues are core questions in the sociology of work and employment.

Another critical source of autonomy comes from the ownership of assets, which can be invested to create opportunities for self-employment (or, in cases of extreme wealth, provide for a life of **leisure** free from involuntary toil). However, only at the top of the occupational structure is self-employment a vehicle for control over one's working life. High levels of self-employment in many developing countries, and also in some developed countries like the United States, are frequently associated with long hours, low wages, and high levels of income insecurity. In the developed countries, self-employment is often dominated by immigrants seeking a toehold in the economic order.

The division of housework has been a second vital area of inquiry concerning who does what. Feminist sociologists have established that the narrow focus on the world of work, so characteristic of sociologists in the first half of the twentieth century, ignored a second important dimension of who does what in the family. Wide disparities in the division of labor on the "second shift" between men and women, in terms of childcare, elder **care**, cooking, routine housework, and other household chores, constitute a powerful source of gender-based inequality. Recent debates over whether the distribution of household tasks between men and women have become more egalitarian suggest some evidence of convergence, but in most families women still do far more routine and caring work than men.

The link between inequalities in families and inequalities in the workplace has been a widely debated topic. While human capital theorists have postulated that women choose to prioritize family over work and women's smaller incomes and occupational choices reflect those preferences, feminist sociologists have developed alternative theories which emphasize that women's subordinate roles in heterosexual families are disadvantaging women in the workplace. These arguments go beyond sexist attitudes to attribute part of gender inequalities to the disruptive aspects of child-rearing (and care-giving for parents) for women seeking to maintain career tracks.

Research on inequality frequently starts from the analysis of the difference between individuals. In the classical "status-attainment" model of **social mobility**, associated with the work of **Peter Blau** and **Otis Dudley Duncan** (*The American Occupational Structure*, 1967), individual inequalities in opportunity and reward reflect family background, individual attainment (such as education), and sociodemographic attributes (such as **race** / ethnic group memberships), or even such idiosyncratic factors as physical attractiveness. All of these characteristics and attainments inhere in

concrete individuals. Some of these characteristics are rooted in ascribed characteristics fixed at birth. Other characteristics are achieved (such as an individual's level of educational attainment).

But later work has argued that this model does not fully theorize the impact of social groups, organizational settings, and **welfare states** in structuring and altering individual-level attributes. Group membership is in many societies a critical source of advantage or disadvantage. Being a member of a high-status group in a society typically eases access to opportunities. Analyses of the distribution of income frequently draw upon the idea of **social closure**, or the means by which groups protect access to certain scarce resources, to account for why groups are able to gain and maintain advantages over time. **Max Weber** argued in chapter 1 of his *Economy and Society* (1922 [trans. 1968]) that the monopolization of opportunities and/or rewards by particular groups is a vital source of inequality. Examining the history of group-based inequality, Weberians have shown that one of the ways in which groups achieve power is by maintaining formal and informal systems of social closure. Formal systems include legal barriers to entry such as occupational restrictions, while informal systems involve less explicit but nonetheless powerful forms of **discrimination**.

The organizational structure and types of social provision are both a locus of inequality and a potential source of their amelioration. Major institutions such as schools, the health-care system, and the legal system all tend to reinforce the advantages of powerful individuals and groups. For example, public health care or education systems rarely can provide the same quality care or learning as can be acquired by those with the means to acquire private health services or to send their child to private schools. However, public institutions on balance significantly reduce inequality through the welfare state. Welfare states include principally state institutions that provide income transfers on the basis of either a social-insurance model or means-tested benefits based on income or other personal or family attributes. A consistent body of evidence demonstrates that welfare states reduce poverty and inequality, smooth out income fluctuations, and reduce old-age poverty and equalize health-care outcomes, with higher-spending countries (such as the Scandinavian social **democracies**) getting more of these outcomes than lower-spending countries (like the Anglo-American liberal welfare states). In many postindustrial capitalist countries, market-based inequalities are growing sharply but these continue to be reduced by welfare state interventions.

Finally, it is important to underscore the global character of inequalities. Individuals and households are embedded not just in local and national **economies**, but also in a world-system that significantly influences the patterns of inequality. The global economy is based on an unequal set of trading relationships between countries that makes some countries far richer than others. However, the most careful recent research (adjusted for **demography**) suggests that inter-country inequalities are declining, as previously poor but very large countries like China move closer to the global mean. The patterns of global capital investment are also changing in ways that encourage firms to seek profitable sources of investment outside the core developed countries. Globalization may also set limits on the capacities of welfare states to reduce intracountry inequalities, although thus far the impact on welfare effort in the developed capitalist countries has not been manifested in the way anticipated by some globalization theories.   JEFF MANZA

infant mortality rates
– see **mortality**.

inflation
This refers to an overall increase in the price of goods and services so that the purchasing power of **money** declines. It is an episodic feature of **capitalism**, but became a focus of sociological debate in the 1970s when inflation in many advanced capitalist **economies** exceeded 10 percent per annum. This tended to redistribute purchasing **power** between social **groups** in ways that lacked obvious **legitimacy**, fueling competition between them (though anti-inflationary state policies could have similar repercussions).

Economists offer varied analyses of inflation. These highlight the role of increases in raw materials prices; the capacity of workers or **trade unions** to gain wage increases above productivity growth; the market power of employers to pass on costs through increased prices; or the role of the **state** in increasing the money supply to fund state expenditure. Neo-classical economists, however, often view the collectively organized, institutional features of these processes (especially state policies and union leverage) as illegitimate distortions of market mechanisms. By contrast, economic sociologists (and some political economists) argue that analyses of normative orientations, in-

stitutional frameworks, and forms of collective **organization** must be integrated with analyses of market mechanisms to provide adequate accounts of inflationary processes.

Thus, M. Gilbert, in *Inflation and Social Conflict* (1986), compared different advanced capitalist **societies** in terms of normative expectations, institutional arrangements, productive capacities, and power relations, tracing their implications for the generation, escalation, or mitigation of inflation. Such analyses lead into wider debates about the character, scope, and limits of alternative variants of capitalism, reviewed by D. Coates in *Models of Capitalism* (2000), where inflation and anti-inflationary state policies are analyzed within a more encompassing international and comparative **political economy**.   TONY ELGER

influence
A form of **power**, influence arises in the context of relationships, between individuals, within an individual, and between individuals and the wider world of nature.

Influence (when placed in a purely human context) can be defined as a pressure that gets someone to do something that they otherwise would not have done. But the problem with a broad definition like this is that it does not distinguish between the threat of force and social pressures to which people tacitly comply without necessarily being under duress. It is extremely difficult to distinguish sharply between different forms of power since all pressures, short of force, require agency on the part of the recipient. Technically, when asked for "your money or your life" by the proverbial highway robber, a choice is given and the victim must choose. Force is qualitatively different from power, since when force is implemented the recipient becomes a "thing" and no agency is involved.

Influence can be more precisely defined as pressures that get someone to do something they would not otherwise do, when this "someone" acts in a conventionally voluntary manner. When we say that a doctor influences a patient, we mean – on this argument – that they employ persuasion rather than the threat of force, so that the person thus influenced believes that they are acting with autonomy. It is complicated by the fact that, whereas a doctor does not threaten force of a kind that he or she would use, it would be wrong to say that no force of any kind is involved. After all, illness can threaten a person's life, and a doctor might warn that, unless a dangerous operation is undertaken, then force of a "natural" kind would ensue. Hence, what makes influence persuasive is that sanctions would certainly follow, even if they are not sanctions that a doctor has deliberately and intentionally orchestrated.

Hence, influence need not be intentional. A newspaper editor might not intend to influence readers in the way they vote, but this might be the result, nevertheless. Indeed, we are becoming increasingly aware that malign influences on the **environment**, for example, arise although the people causing them did not intend them to be such.

Indeed, it could be argued that, given the fact that we live in a society, it is impossible for an individual to undertake any action that does not influence another. Is it then possible to distinguish between positive and negative influences? The only coherent way of addressing this problem is through an ethic of development – that which influences a person positively is a pressure that enables them to develop, as opposed to a negative pressure that distorts and arrests development. An ethic of development needs to be tied somehow to a concept of autonomy and self-government, so that, rather than imagine that individuals can exist without influence, it should be acknowledged that we are influenced and influencing all the time. The question that arises is basically: do these influences help or hinder us in governing our own lives?   JOHN HOFFMAN

informal economy

This refers to aspects of economic activity that lie outside visible, official, and legally recognized forms of production, distribution, and **consumption**. While the existence of this kind of activity has been known to social investigators since the nineteenth century, the term informal economy first entered the social scientific vocabulary in the late 1960s.

Sometimes known as the black, shadow, or cash economy, this sector of economic activity generally operates outside forms of legal regulation affecting company registration, taxation, and workforce protection. It may involve illegal activity and forced **labor**, though this is not a necessary feature since forms of cashless exchange and community self-help have also been included under the umbrella term. The term informal economy has therefore been applied to a very diverse range of activities in terms of employment status, sectoral location, and geographical incidence. It embraces forms of self-employment as well as wage labor and applies to survival activities such as rag-picking and scavenging, as well as domestic

service work, small-scale manufacturing, and illegal people-smuggling and criminal extortion.

The scale of the informal economy is hard to determine precisely because it remains unregulated and, to a degree, invisible. Variations in definition also complicate analysis of its spatial distribution. International Labour Organization data from the late 1990s suggest that the highest levels of informal employment occur in West and East Africa, South East Asia, and Latin America, at levels of from 30 to 70 percent of total employment. However, informal activity has also been identified with many unregulated or deregulated economic sectors in western Europe and North America, notably in larger cities. Much of this is associated with sweatshops and low-grade service work, employing both native-born and (often illegal) immigrant labor.

Geographically, then, the informal economy applies to the developed as well as developing worlds, though in both cases it is associated with significant **inequalities** of **income** and lack of access to social regulation and protection. Its ubiquity has prompted some analysts to see it less as a marginal feature of the capitalist periphery, and more as a key feature of **capitalism** – both historically and contemporaneously. What has come to be seen as informalization emerges wherever producers seek to evade or bypass a regulatory framework to reduce costs and optimize profits. Just as much production in early modern Europe was informally "ruralized" to escape urban guild regulation, so a good deal of contemporary production and service work has been informally "urbanized" in small to medium-sized inner-city locales largely hidden from the gaze of national regulators of large-scale public enterprises. Access to the informal sector is therefore often through **networks** rather than publicly available information.

Contemporary informalization is also disproportionately concentrated among women (see **women and work**) and ethnic minorities. It is thereby indicative of inequalities that **markets** have helped to create rather than alleviate. Overall, the persistence of the informal economy renders problematic theories of capitalism that focus solely on large rationalized production units and the public world of organized interests.

        ROBERT HOLTON

information

Information may be considered on three different levels: (1) uncertainty reduction, (2) patterned abstraction, and (3) knowledge. The term connotes the recognizing, creating, encoding, transmitting, decoding, and interpreting of social patterns – in a word, communication – and often involves **technology** in some way. Information also may be considered at a meta-level: how and for whom the information is created, to what uses it may be put, and with what consequences.

By creating, modifying, and framing information, people can use it to alter the opinions and actions of others, and thus future states. Archeological and ancient textual evidence demonstrates that an enduring concern of rulers and sages alike has been the crafting of messages to achieve desired effects. Aristotle and other ancient Greeks systematically analyzed the social context of information construction and delivery as well as its anticipated effect, including how various **groups** might be served or disadvantaged by its forms of public presentation. Many ancient **elites**, perhaps as much as modern ones, realized that information exists not as an essence but within a context.

In contrast to rhetorical analyses, **Paul Lazarsfeld**'s empirical studies of information transmission among groups in *The People's Choice* (1944) must be considered foundational. He held that there was a two-step flow in interpersonal **influence** related to political opinions, with local opinion leaders playing a pivotal role. Lazarsfeld and long-time collaborator **Robert K. Merton** emphasized, in *Social Theory and Social Structure* (1949), the importance of Weberian concepts of social location, **social class**, **religion**, opportunity structures) over mass mobilization processes in political decisionmaking. The dynamic tensions between personal and public information, on the one hand, and social and political structures on the other, have been profitably investigated by Harold Lasswell in *World Politics and Personal Insecurity* (1935), Hugh Duncan in *Communication and Social Order* (1962), and Walter Lippmann (Barry D. Riccio, *Walter Lippmann – Odyssey of a Liberal*, 1994). These scholars have shown how **power** and **leadership** influence what comes to be considered knowledge from among various possibilities, and the importance of framing information.

From a quite different (and highly technical) tack, Bell Labs mathematician Claude Shannon characterized information as being measured in bits and probabilities. He defined information theory as the problem of "reproducing at one point either exactly or approximately a message selected at another point." Information therefore reduces uncertainty, and the more uncertainty that is removed, the more information any signal or piece of **data** contains. Shannon helped spawn several domains of inquiry, including theories of encryption and data transmission, and also showed how a variety of technical factors (such as bandwidth, reliability, channel numbers, and signal-to-noise ratios) limited certain system functionalities.

An essential part of Shannon's analysis was the concept of entropy in communication systems. He demonstrated that, as the amount of uncertainty that exists in a communication channel increases, the amount of information that can be transmitted also rises (and that the inverse also applies). His work has proven invaluable in information theory for helping determine optimal technical designs for communication technology systems under various practical scenarios. His ideas influenced control theory, which emphasizes coding, sender, receiver, noise, and feedback. Yet Shannon is far more cited than understood in the **social sciences**, and his definition of information is too technical to be of substantial interest to the sociologist. Yet his parsimonious notions, so elegantly proven in mathematical terms, have some intriguing implications for the social sciences, a point returned to at this entry's conclusion.

Turning to the social structural and process levels, information is also linked to the notion of change – in theory and practice. Information alters lived reality. Information works to reduce uncertainty and thereby increases control over **environments**, both natural and social. On a macro-level, **Manuel Castells** in *The Informational City: Information Technology, Economic Restructuring, and the Urban–Regional Process* (1989) links information-processing to **culture**, seeing it as symbolic manipulation. Information technologies are the systems, devices, and techniques that produce and augment relationships among culture, productive forces, and scientific and other knowledge, and they operate within a cultural or mental setting.

Fritz Machlup in *The Production and Distribution of Knowledge in the United States* (1962) emphasizes the distinction between transmission (information) and understanding (knowledge), yet this traditional distinction has come under siege by some in the Cultural Studies movement who see knowledge as power – power invoked not by Plato's benign philosopher-king but by exploitative interests. These interests are often exercised along the lines of militarism, **capitalism**, **gender**, and social class, and are exploited along the lines of decomposition (Horowitz, *The Decomposition of Sociology*, 1994) and statism. Mark Poster holds that "information has become a privileged term in our culture . . . and society is divided between the information rich and the information poor" (*The Mode of Information: Poststructuralism and Social Context*, 1990). In a related vein, **Jean-François Lyotard** asserts, in *The Postmodern Condition: A Report on Knowledge* (1979 [trans. 1984]), that information is not simply scientific knowledge but also encompasses narrative knowledge.

Although Peter Nilsson in "The Distortion of Information," in J. Berleur, A. Clement, R. Sizer, and D. Whitehouse (eds.), *The Information Society: Evolving Landscapes* (1990), links information to change on the level of either real-life practice or thought patterns, it is because information is affecting processes within the human mind. For Castells in *The Informational City* (1989), information is intrinsically linked to culture because information-processing is actually the symbolic manipulation of existing knowledge.

Communication theorists deal with information as a substance that, like other forms of discourse and nonverbal communication, conveys a meaning. For the 1969 Japanese Information Study Group, information "was not merely what is in print, but also any **symbol**, signal, or image having meaning to the parties at both the sending and receiving ends" (Y. Ito, "The 'Johoka Shakai' Approach to the Study of Communication in Japan," in G. C. Wilhoit and H. de Bock [eds.], *Mass Communication Review Yearbook*, 1981). In addition, information has a directional utility. Nilsson in "The Distortion of Information" defines the goal of electronic and communication systems as providing quality information, or useful information "in a given problem area for a given subject and all effects on any subject and/or object." As with the socio-cultural definitions, information is again held to be a social factor that expresses a particular worldview and has discernible effects on social actors.

If knowledge is to serve as an intermediary in contemporary society, then the information that it interprets must be transferable. James Boyle argues in *Shamans, Software, and Spleens: Law and the Construction of the Information Society* (1996) that the easy conversion from one form into another is a central marker of an information society. Ironically, though, Boyle says that, as information expands to include "anything," it is commoditized to restrict its dissemination and manipulation. While digitalization in theory allows for infinite copies that are identical to the original, copyright laws and technical enhancements can restrict and possibly prevent such copying, and what one has a right, ability, and permission to do continue to be tested.

The two opposing views concerning the ability to copy and reuse information are drawn from a similar inspiration: that society should be regulated to advance the interests of **society** as a whole and that intellectual property laws should return the greatest good possible to society. Thus the length of time that a copyright restriction may be in force is checked, and some fair use is allowed even of copyrighted material. As an inducement for investing effort to create valuable intellectual property, however, those who create the works are rewarded for their efforts and control the copying and use of their creations.

From a social-relativistic view, **justice** demands that those who are least able to pay for materials ought to be able to use those materials. Advocates often argue that the poor would not have bought the intellectual property anyway or that another digital copy can be made cost-free. These arguments are often used by students or by people in less-developed countries to justify making copies of software. Advocates of copyright-free approaches also hold that worthwhile intellectual property should be created for its own sake and that society benefits by not having barriers to information.

This argument for copyright-free reproduction is countered by those who feel that those who create works should decide who gets to use them. Without some incentive, effort (and investments), which allow information to be brought forth to the public, would not be made. In the area of computer operating-system software, one company (Xerox) created approaches that another company (Microsoft) later reengineered and used, leading to the birth of one of the world's largest commercial empires. But at the same time, open systems that are based on freeware (Linux) have been used on a no-cost basis and a proprietary basis (Red Hat). This area will undoubtedly continue to be contested.

No single definition of information society has been universally accepted, but there is convergence on several elements. The term itself seems to have originated in Japan. A society generally is characterized as an information society when information becomes its most significant product. According to a 1997 report by the IBM Community Development Foundation, *The Net Result: Social Inclusion in the Information Society*, an information society has high levels of information usage by people in their ordinary lives and in most **organizations** and workplaces; uses common or compatible technology for a range of personal, social, educational, and business activities; and has a widespread ability to transmit, receive, and exchange digital data rapidly between places irrespective of distance.

For most of human history, societies have been concerned with subsistence or, if they were fortunate, with material pursuits. Technological limitations made moving information from one place to another difficult. Many societies were nonetheless deeply concerned with patterned abstraction in the form of religious practices and beliefs, as the great pyramids of Teotihuacán and Egypt attest. Institutions of major religions, such as the Catholic Church, were centrally concerned with pattern interpretation and the communication and reinforcement of these interpretations, and they devoted enormous human and material resources to that end. However, manuscript copying, messengers, heralds, and fire towers were cumbersome systems for distributing information and gaining feedback on that distribution.

Technological innovations have yielded tremendous advances in the way that information is produced, processed, and consumed, with important economic, political, and social ramifications. Notably, they have enabled information to be moved more easily (that is, communicated), which has allowed the creation of **markets** to supply the information and the means for its transmission. By strategically controlling the creation, transmission, and application of information, enormous commercial empires could develop in the fields of telegraphy, telephony, newspapers, television, and radio. Secondary markets quickly developed to use information to adjust for **risk**; today these take the form of the stock markets and the insurance industry. Tertiary markets also opened to gather and apply information in the institutions of scientific research, higher **education**, financial accounting, and consultancies. These yielded quaternary markets – including the byproducts of transactions (such as frequent-flyer programs) and location information (such as mobile telephone monitoring systems) – that can be useful for applications including marketing and law enforcement.

The most important questions concerning social equity in the information society involve the **digital divide** – the division between those with and without access to digital data. Increasingly, the utility of information and thus the quality of its meaning are coming to be measured in its price. At the same time, there is continuing policy pressure to adjust marketplace dynamics in light of concerns over differential access to information and to what extent information equity across demographic groupings should be a target of governmental (by nation-state or international bodies) action.

Lyotard, like Poster, sees a progression in the function of knowledge and predicts the increasing commodification of knowledge, losing its "use-value" to become an end in itself. He goes so far as to claim that learning will circulate as **money**. In a parallel vein, Lawrence Lessig in *The Nature of Ideas: The Fate of the Commons in a Connected World* (2001) and other theorists write that technology does not directly lead to the production of original knowledge but creates more paths and links between information – such as linked webpages or Wikipedia functions online – which becomes the source of new knowledge.

Indeed, it is possible that the personal, mediated communication typical of the internet, especially when it is further enhanced with mobile applications, will be a qualitative change of a magnitude that equals the change from the industrial era to the information society. In this regard, Irwin Lebow's criticism in *Information Highways and Byways: From the Telegraph to the Twenty-First Century* (1995) that the phrase "information superhighway" confuses "information" with "communication" is worth noting: networked information access actually includes communication and entertainment, and from the user's viewpoint these applications are often the central attractions.

The following section highlights some major theoretical perspectives on the social role of information. Of course the various perspectives may be classified in a number of different ways. One general way is to look at information within the context of its ambient society. Alistair S. Duff in *Information Society Studies* (2000), for instance, examines the information sector, the information explosion, and the information technology diffusion, which contribute to his methodology for finding valid grounds for the phenomenon of the information society. Another general way is to focus on information in a societal setting, that is, in the "Information Society." Thus Frank Webster in his article "What Information Society?" in *Information Society* (1994) isolates five analytical approaches to defining the information society (their theorists are in parentheses): technological innovation (Williams, *Measuring the Information Society: The Texas Studies*, 1988; Michael J. Piore and Charles F. Sabel, *The Second Industrial Divide: Possibilities for Prosperity*, 1984), economic means (Machlup, *The Production and Distribution of Knowledge in the United States*, 1962; Porat, "Communication Policy in an Information Society," in

G. O. Robinson (ed.), *Communications for Tomorrow: Policy Perspectives for the 1980s*, 1978), occupational breakdown (**Daniel Bell**, *The Coming of Post-Industrial Society: A Venture in Social Forecasting*, 1973), and spatial (Goddard, "Networks of Transactions," in K. Robins (ed.), *Understanding Information: Business, Technology and Geography*, 1992) and cultural definition (Baudrillard, *In the Shadow of the Silent Majorities*, 1983; Poster, *The Mode of Information*). In a blended approach, eight classification categories are used below to sketch understandings of how information shapes and is shaped by social forces.

The economic approach, as its name denotes, defines information and the society in which it exists through a lens that emphasizes production, market, and consumption aspects. Researchers pursuing this approach highlight the rapid expansion of the number of people who work in the information sector of the **economy**. F. Machlup introduced this approach with his study of national data, where he defines knowledge as a state of knowing that "is produced by activities such as talking plus listening, writing plus reading, but also by activities such as discovering, inventing, intuiting." Knowledge producers transmit or communicate information, receive and process information, invest knowledge, and create instruments for the production of knowledge (such as typewriters, photocopiers, and computers). As a result, according to Machlup, the information industry is composed chiefly of workers in the educational sphere, other white-collar-industry workers who participate in managerial tasks, and some blue-collar workers (such as pressmen, lithographers, and typesetters). Machlup's 1962 seminal contributions have yet to be superseded.

Expanding on Machlup's argument for socioeconomic transformation through information, theorists have formulated the idea of the "postindustrial society." Its two most widely recognized proponents – **Alain Touraine**, *The Post-industrial Society: Tomorrow's Social History – Classes, Conflicts and Culture in the Programmed Society* (1969 [trans. 1971]), and Bell, *The Coming of Post-industrial Society: A Venture in Social Forecasting* (1973) – are influenced by Marxist interpretations of class movement and hold that, in the postindustrial society, the production and processing of information are core activities that are engaged in at all levels of production, distribution, **consumption**, and **management**. Touraine's "programmed society" is structured by its production methods and economic organization. He claims that the present social conflict is between economic and

political decision making, that this new society is "technocratic" (as defined by the nature of its ruling class), and that the working class is no longer a unified political agent. Similarly, for Bell, the labor shift away from goods-producing industries and towards white-collar service and information-producing industries moves society towards sexual **equality** and communal consciousness. Bell identifies a "knowledge class" that is composed of a dual axis of technology and knowledge as fundamental resources. While Bell takes a more economic approach and Touraine writes through a sociopolitical lens, both theorists see the sociologist as having a privileged place as a "seer" of sorts who can understand and direct the postindustrial society. Marc Porat and Michael Rubin in *The Information Economy: Development and Measurement* (1977) also see the transition of the labor force from manual to informational work as the foundation of the informational society, as does Robert B. Reich in *The Work of Nations: Preparing Ourselves for 21st-Century Capitalism* (1991), who writes about jobs that involve symbol manipulation and the international trade issues that arise from this global class.

For Bell, scientific knowledge and **values** will be involved in the political process in the postindustrial society, and intellectual work will be bureaucratized. While he calls this new society "postindustrial" rather than "knowledge-based" or "informational," clearly one source of power in it is possession or ownership of knowledge. Jacques Ellul in *The Technological Society* (1954 [trans. 1964]) also posits the coming society as a technological society – not entirely based on technology but rather using carefully planned "techniques" to achieve its goals.

Following closely after these theorists, Porat identifies two information sectors – the major information goods and services producers (industries that produce, process, or distribute information) and the secondary public and private **bureaucracies** (organizations that engage in research, development, record keeping, and governmental planning). Like Machlup and Bell, Porat uses economic **statistics** to support his claims.

While most theorists agree in principle that trends in social and economic organization can be identified and assessed, they have different opinions about the social effects of these trends. For liberals such as **Ralph Dahrendorf** in *The New Liberty: Survival and Justice in a Changing World* (1975), economic growth and **social change** are necessary prerequisites to social improvement and require a free flow of information. For

Marxists, such as Herb Schiller in *Information and the Crisis Economy* (1984) and *Information Inequality: The Deepening Social Crisis in America* (1991), however, information is associated with advanced capitalism in crisis. His three themes are that market criteria and pressures are important in information developments; that class **inequalities** play a large role in the distribution of, access to, and generation of information; and that society, which is undergoing many changes in information and communication systems, is marked by corporate capitalism. For libertarian and conservative advocates such as Peter Huber in *Law and Disorder in Cyberspace* (1997), the information society has unbounded potential for raising standards of living, increasing comfort, and sparking creativity, if only the hamstringing efforts of governmental entities would get out of the way and stop seeking to impose their collectivist values on others. Those theorists who see the information society as radically different from past societies are inclined to be optimistic about its possibilities, whereas those who see the information society as a progression from past societies tend to predict a downward spiral.

The political-regulation-school approach to examining the information society is similar to the economic approach but is linked to political processes. Regulation-school theorists, such as Michel Aglietta in *A Theory of Capitalist Regulation: The US Experience* (1979) and Alain Lipietz in *Mirages and Miracles: The Crises of Global Fordism* (1987), examine the mode of accumulation in a given society and the relationship of accumulation to its mode of regulation. After a period characterized by the mass production of goods by blue-collar industrial workers, the mass conception of goods, nation-state oligopolies, and the prominent role of planning increasing **globalization** brought about a state that was denoted by Lipietz in "Fordism and Post-Fordism," in W. Outhwaite and Tom Bottomore, *The Blackwell Dictionary of Twentieth-Century Social Thought* (1993), as post-Fordist. This post-Fordist period has witnessed the disintegration of vertical organization, a strategy of outsourcing, an international division of **labor**, and an assault on organized labor as a whole, and is marked by flexibility in production, consumption, and employment. When mass production declines, the individual emerges as much more individualistic and consumption-centered, and information takes on an individualistic representation as people find their own information and even become information producers on their own.

There are, of course, other approaches to regulation. One of them is the regulation-analytic school, which focuses on influences on policymakers and the values that come into play. In this vein, Gerald Brock in *Telecommunication Policy for the Information Age: From Monopoly to Competition* (1998) examines what he calls a theory of decentralized public decision making. According to Brock, this model generates rational outcomes consistent with public preferences.

By contrast, neo-Marxist Dan Schiller in *Digital Capitalism: Networking the Global Market System* (1999), as well as theorists across the political spectrum, fears the convergence of control over all information media in a few large multinational corporations. The nature of public life, the autonomy of consumers, and the quality of education would be the big losers. Schiller holds that cyberspace will be the handmaiden of this unprecedented centralization of power, which will advance consumerism on a transnational scale, particularly among privileged groups in various countries.

Other theorists see information as intrinsic to political processes and even the nation-state as a whole. **Jürgen Habermas** in *The Structural Transformation of the Public Sphere: An Inquiry into a Category of Bourgeois Society* (1962 [trans. 1992]) builds a theory that information is the center of the **public sphere**, which is the hub of information *qua* social knowledge in a democratic society. The public sphere is the source discourse, it functions to construct knowledge, especially political knowledge, out of the information input of its members.

Information – while perhaps always a fundamental element of political processes, public spheres, and the nation-state – is playing a larger role in defining the political realm. Webster points out the increasing frequency of information warfare that uses intelligence and informational technologies on the battlefield. This is not simply a metaphor. Rather, information, as has always been the case, is critical to military success.

The information-explosion approach to defining the information society looks at the amount of scholarly literature on this topic (Price, *Little Science, Big Science*, 1965) and the ways that information and knowledge play roles in **everyday life**. Sometimes this approach joins qualitative understandings to quantitative baselines. This was the case with Derek deSolla Price, an early exponent of this approach, who adopted the term "scientometrics" to describe his efforts. As such, he was part of the first generation of information scientists, and is most remembered for having documented the exponential rise of scientific publications and knowledge across the globe and across several centuries.

On an even grander scale, Manuel Castells uses a world-systems perspective to explore the recent historical transition from development by capitalism to development by information. He posits a strong link between knowledge and economic growth, showing that the heretofore intermediate stage of technological development is unnecessary. Instead, he holds that knowledge can perform the technological function of producing informatization – knowledge alone may be the basis of production in the informational society. How is this new development to take place? According to Castells, information is both the raw material and the outcome of technological change. Information-processing activities in the industrial mode of development were fostered by two major factors – the central organizational capacities of the large corporation and the shift in the sources of productivity from capital and labor to factors such as science and technology. Information-consumption activities were fostered by two additional factors – the need for information-gathering and -distributing flows to connect between buyer and seller in the mass-market environment and the state's role in assuming collective management of goods and services. The **state**, in turn, establishes information systems that set the codes and rules that govern citizens' lives.

Reich echoes Bell by observing what he calls the rise in "symbolic-analytic services" as a job category. These services trade not in concrete things but in the manipulation of symbols and visual representations. Workers are problem solvers: "they simplify reality into abstract images that can be rearranged, juggled, experimented with, communicated to other specialists, and then, eventually, transformed back into reality." Whereas "professionals" of the earlier regime attained mastery of a particular knowledge domain, symbolic-analysts work by using, not learning, knowledge. They draw on established bodies of knowledge to rearrange and analyze information that already exists. In this way, the symbolic-analyst is changing the nature of information from static and isolated to dynamic and integrated. Additionally, the rise of the symbolic-analyst leads to a breakdown in traditional hierarchies of information provision. Workers rise in the job market not because of hard work or technical expertise but because of inventiveness and creativity: "the only true competitive advantage lies in skill in solving, identifying, and brokering new problems." For these theorists, the widespread availability of information, and not technology itself, has far-reaching social implications. Perhaps one of the most striking is the way that ideas can flow easily across borders, even while people cannot, which will impact the international economic order and spill over into the quality of lives for millions in both the developed and developing nations.

One common framework for interpreting the information society is technological innovation, especially in telecommunications. "Information technology (IT) diffusion" can be measured by the scope of the IT revolution and the proliferation of computer technology (Duff, *Information Society Studies*). Frederick Williams remarks that the information society "is a society where the economy reflects growth owing to technological advances." Piore and Sabel use the term "flexible specialization" to refer to independent, small businesses that analyze and respond to markets far more efficiently than large corporations can.

Simon Nora and Alain Minc in *The Computerization of Society: A Report to the President of France* (1980) were the first to propose the term "informatization" to represent the union of computers, telecommunication systems, and social organizations that leads to a greater informational society. Their report presented knowledge as the "engine of growth" and warned of the dangers of noninformational paths of development. Herbert S. Dordick and Georgette Wang in *The Information Society: A Retrospective View* (1993) enlarge this interpretation to define "informatization" along three dimensions – infrastructural, economic, and social. Informatization therefore is measured by the number of telephone lines, newspapers, computers, and television sets in a society, as well as the number of workers who are engaged in information technology and the size of the information sector's contribution to a nation's gross domestic product.

As with the economic definition of the information society, the technological-drivers approach treats the information society as an objective, quantifiably measurable entity that has both positive and negative implications.

Cultural theorist Mark Poster provides a semiotic account of studying the information society: "an adequate account of electronic communications requires a theory that is able to decode the linguistic dimension of the new forms of social interaction." His term "mode of information" (which parodies **Karl Marx**'s notion of the mode of production) suggests that history can be characterized by stages marked by differing structures of symbolic exchange and that society currently provides a fetishistic dimension to "information." He criticizes the approach of Bell for making the "postindustrial" idea a model for modern society and for treating information merely as an economic entity. Bell's perspective thereby ignores the ways in which electronic technology disseminates information through communication. Instead, Poster seeks to interrogate cultural forms of information technology in their modern and postmodern contexts and to examine the role of communication systems in postindustrial society.

Within this stream of thought, **Jean Baudrillard** views information as being produced equally by all people and as having no singular meaning or interpretation. Information can thus be seen as meaningless. However, he sees that people impose their meanings on the information, and the structure, which is created, is largely arbitrary. As yet another meta-framing, Ron Day shows in *The Modern Invention of Information* (2001) that there have been many information ages, and that the concept itself tends to divorce power from its historical context, thus banishing a troubled history of winners and losers in information's construction and application.

When cheap, digital information is combined with networked computers, new social forms and interaction patterns can emerge. Some predict negative consequences for social **interaction** from these changes. Sherry Turkle in *Life on the Screen: Identity in the Age of the Internet* (1995) sees a wilderness of mirrors in which identity is produced through online interactions, and is basically synthetic. As a result, senses of **community** and integration are lost as people flee unpleasant "real-world" social situations for a "life on the screen," that is, for online pretending.

James E. Katz and Ronald E. Rice in *Social Consequences of Internet Use: Access, Involvement, and Interaction* (2002) offer a brighter picture in their study of the social consequences of internet use. Their conclusions are based on surveys of both internet users and those who do not use the internet. These surveys include the earliest comparative public-opinion surveys about the internet as well as cross-national comparisons between the United States and the United Kingdom. They conclude that the internet does not reduce **social capital** but rather contributes to it and also enables novel

forms of social interaction and self-expression. One such novel form of information and self-expression they discuss is the web log (or blog) phenomenon. Blogs are a novel blending of diary and self-expression that erase the lines of public and private spheres. While blogs have been decried as a "wasteland of self-important nobodies" (Anon., *Wall Street Journal Online*, 2004), Katz and Rice hold that they provide a valuable opportunity for people to express themselves and create new relationships. While Katz and Rice agree that misuse can occur with any information system, including the internet, they conclude that the internet fosters opportunities for satisfying individual interests while providing collective benefits to society.

Incisive social critic and sociologist **C. Wright Mills** anticipated many of the arguments presented above. He held that "knowledge is no longer widely felt as an ideal; it is seen as an instrument. In a society of power and wealth, knowledge is valued as an instrument of power and wealth." He went on to identify numerous ways in which this proposition was supported, most famously in *The Power Elite* (1956).

The ancient view that knowledge is power was also picked up by **Michel Foucault** in *Discipline and Punish: The Birth of the Prison* (1975 [trans. 1977]), who advanced provocative ideas about information in a social context and about why information (and resulting knowledge) is such a coveted commodity. According to him, knowledge is synonymous with power. He presents the Panopticon, a prison in which guards can see into every cell but prisoners see neither guards nor other prisoners. The guards therefore have the advantage of knowledge of the prisoners' activities. As the prisoners internalize the idea that they are constantly under surveillance, they begin to self-regulate, and thus the guards have attained power over their inmates. However, if a prisoner learns that he is not being watched, he may try to escape; the prisoner attains power over the guard as a result of this knowledge. For Foucault, the relationship between power and knowledge is inseparable, so that knowledge always grows out of power relations and vice versa. In the context of the information society, a reading of Foucault may sensitize us to the inherent power relations that underlie flows of information and the effects that information and social knowledge can have on social order and form.

While Foucault takes a highly theoretical approach to power and society, Bell draws a more concrete relation between knowledge-holders and the ruling class. For Bell, the codification of knowledge, especially in the technical and scientific **professions**, plays an increasingly important role in maintaining society. As a result, a highly trained and intellectualized elite will lead further social **progress**.

On the other hand, Boyle maintains that the information society may actually lead to horizontal social progress and that the idea of information has become so fluid and pervasive that it completely dissolves disciplinary boundaries. For example, gene-mapping as a topic has escaped from biological discourse to pervade discussions of social scientists, engineers, and artists. At the same time, information has become a value-added dimension of commercial products that needs to be protected. As technological materials (such as DVD disks) become cheaper to use and own, their informational or intellectual content makes up a greater part of the end product's value.

This shift is echoed by Lyotard, who believes that knowledge is increasingly becoming an informational commodity. Because knowledge as a commodity is vital to maintaining productive power, nation-states may "fight for the control of information, just as they battled in the past for control over territory, and afterwards for control of access to and exploitation of raw materials and cheap labor." The state no longer has a monopoly on the distribution of knowledge and information: as the need for transparent and clear information begins to underpin society, economic interests butt heads with the state, and the state grows powerless to control information and knowledge dissemination and must reexamine its traditional role in guiding technological progress.

For the optimists of the information society, notably Yoneji Masuda in *The Information Society as Post-Industrial Society* (1981), information access encourages people to participate in **democracy** and to improve the environment by working from home and spending more time in creative, intellectual work. For him and other optimists, informatization can redress and prevent **social problems** like the unequal distribution of wealth and slow economic development. Melvin Kranzberg in "The Information Age: Evolution or Revolution?," in B. R. Guild (ed.), *Information Technologies and Social Transformation* (1985), likewise believes that the increased production of knowledge in the information society will allow people to understand their options and the consequences of their actions better, thus preventing catastrophic wars. Even earlier, the theorist Kenneth E. Boulding

in *The Meaning of the Twentieth Century: The Great Transition* (1964) proposed the term "postcivilization" to describe the freedom that he expected the information society to bring out of the Marxist socioeconomic class revolutions of the past. According to Boulding, as the information society builds up the sphere of the self-conscious social against the individual, general mental evolution will guide further social progression.

Wireless mobile communication promises to be the next information revolution as it changes people's work and study habits and their activities in public space (Katz, "A Nation of Ghosts? Choreography of Mobile Communication in Public Spaces," in K. Nyiri [ed.], *Mobile Democracy: Essays on Society, Self and Politics*, 2003). When mobile communication is combined with the internet, new problems arise, but so do novel social and economic opportunities that are comparable to those precipitated by the computer and that can enrich the lives of vast numbers of people, from all backgrounds and all regions of the world.

For many centuries, various experts thought that increased information would lead to better lives, and that enhanced communication would lead to harmonious social interaction, perhaps even an end to strife and **war**. In terms of material lives, improved technology based on better information has eased many material burdens, so that an ordinary worker in industrial society typically has a life of comfort (air conditioning, antibiotics, TV) that was beyond the reach of the richest mogul. In terms of the second contention, it may be that the opposite is true. While faster flow of information can lead to enhanced material lives, it also speeds misinformation. It is possible that a corollary obtains, namely that new information technologies, such as the mobile phone, can give rise to anxiety: one must be in touch and ready to react. Or that making more information available, such as is the case with internet websites and blogs, can keep alive, and even stimulate, the growth of dissident political movements and attacks on even the largest media empires.

Moreover, information flows can lead to demands for transparency and accountability at every level from institutional to micro-social. So instead of being a fountainhead of freedom, increased information can lead to demands for increased constraints and monitoring. From a sociological perspective, there are many ironies in information flow.

It is worth noting too that much attention has been paid to sociological analyses of information that emphasize potential monopolistic and exploitative practices among the owners of media content. Yet the Marxist-inspired view that the centralized control of the means of production, in this case of information, determines material conditions is being turned on its head due to technological advances. This line of argument was pioneered by Ithiel de Sola Pool, who declared in *Technologies of Freedom* (1983) that technologies of freedom aim at **pluralism** of expression rather than a dissemination of prefabricated ideas. Pool's prescient ideas have become realized, perhaps more profoundly than even he might have imagined. The novel and ever-increasing array of alternative communication systems continues to surprise and amaze social scientists. These range from internet steganography and web-cams to mobile phone videos, alterative reality games and geopositional monitoring. These proliferating and ingenious applications have severely eroded dominant **paradigms** of elites and the power of traditional monopolistic "one-to-many" technologies (such as newspaper publishing, broadcast TV, and studio films).

Because of personal communication technology, information has lost its relevance as part of a Marxist superstructure of production that sits atop society. It has instead become a form of struggle within society. Despite efforts to the contrary at the level of policymaking, information is becoming ever more fungible as a commodity even while its meaning and interpretation becomes more contested. More voices are raised in every quarter, and there is an open contest over knowledge claims. Even while more data is collected at the level of the individual social actor, dictators around the world are confronted by information they would wish to banish.

The ultimate irony, though, may be that, while the narrow definition of information discussed above – that information is uncertainty reduction – is germane at local levels, the larger-ranging impact may be the opposite: knowledge leads to growth in uncertainty and psychological tension. Shannon's axioms, as it turns out, are extremely apposite to **social science** and **public policy**: increased information also leads to increased uncertainty. It does this in the soft terms of human lives lived, every bit as much as in the hard terms of communication network efficiencies achieved.   JAMES E. KATZ

information society
– see **information**.

information superhighway
– see **information**.

information technology
– see **information**.

inner-directed character
– see **David Riesman**.

instinct
– see **genetics**.

institutional theory
– see **institution(s)**.

institutionalization of conflict
– see **social conflict**.

institutionalized racism
– see **race and ethnicity**.

institution(s)
Émile Durkheim defined **sociology** as the scientific study of institutions. In everyday language we refer to institutions in terms of a heterogeneous array of concrete social forms such as the **family**, the church, or the monarchy. Departments of sociology traditionally had mainstream courses that were called "**social theory** and social institutions" indicating that sociology was the study of the principal institutions that make up what we call **society**. There is, however, a second and more subtle meaning in which institutions are conceived as regular patterns of behavior that are regulated by **norms** and sanctions into which individuals are socialized. Institutions are thus an ensemble of **social roles**.

In mainstream sociology, it was conventional to recognize five clusters of major institutions in society. These are: (1) economic institutions for the production, distribution, and **consumption** of goods and services; (2) political institutions that regulate and control access to **power**; (3) institutions of **social stratification** that regulate access to prestige and **social status**; (4) **kinship**, **marriage**, and family that control **reproduction**; and finally (5) cultural institutions that are concerned with religious, symbolic, and cultural practices.

The analysis of these clusters was a central feature of **social systems theory**, and it can be said that the functionalist sociology of **Talcott Parsons** was a major contribution to this branch of sociology. In *The Social System* (1951: 39), Parsons defined an institution as "a complex of institutionalized role integrates (or status-relationships) which is of strategic structural significance for the social system in question." Parsons argued that institutions are fundamental to the overall integration of social systems.

The contemporary analysis of institutions has, however, been decisively influenced by the sociological writings of **Peter L. Berger**, whose general sociology was in turn influenced by the philosophical anthropology of the German sociologist **Arnold Gehlen**. Berger did much to introduce the work of Gehlen to English-speaking social science, for example in his introduction to Gehlen's *Man in the Age of Technology* (1957 [trans. 1980]). In general terms, Gehlen argued, following Friedrich Nietzsche (1844–1900), that human beings are "not yet finished animals." By this expression, Gehlen meant that human beings are biologically ill equipped to cope with the world into which they are born and they have no finite instinctual basis that is specific to a given natural environment, and depend upon a long period of **socialization** in order to acquire the knowledge and skills to exist in the world. Gehlen claimed that, in order to cope with life, human beings have "world-openness," that is human beings have to create and maintain a cultural world to replace or to supplement their instinctual world. It is this incompleteness that provides the anthropological explanation for the origins of social institutions. Berger and **Thomas Luckmann**, in *The Construction of Social Reality* (1967), developed this position to argue that, since human beings are, as it were, biologically underdeveloped, they have to construct a social canopy or **religion** around themselves in order to complete or supplement their biology.

Institutions are the social bridges between human beings and their natural **environment** and it is in terms of these institutions that human life becomes coherent and meaningful. Institutions, in filling the gap created by instinctual deprivation, provide humans with relief from the tensions generated by their undirected instinctual drives. Over time, these institutions come to be taken for granted and become part of the implicit background of **social action**. The social foreground is occupied by reflective, practical, and conscious practices. With **modernization**, however, there is a process of de-institutionalization with the result that the taken-for-granted background becomes less reliable, more open to negotiation, culturally fluid, and increasingly an object of critical debate

and reflection. Accordingly the social foreground expands, and the everyday world becomes risky and precarious. The objective, sacred institutions of **tradition** recede, and modern life becomes subjective, contingent, and problematic. According to Gehlen, we live in a world of secondary or quasi-institutions. There are profound psychological changes that are associated with these social developments. In premodern societies, human beings had character that is a firm, coherent, and definite psychological structure that corresponded with reliable social roles and institutions. In modern societies, people have personalities that are fluid and flexible, like the precarious institutions in which they live. The existential pressures on human beings are significant and to some extent modern people are confronted with the uncertainties of what Berger, B. Berger, and H. Kellner called *The Homeless Mind* (1973).

This theory of institutions and their decline presupposes a theory of **secularization** in which the traditional sanctions behind institutions decline with the advent of modern, risk-ridden **cultures**. However, the contemporary revival of religion suggests that this melancholic picture of uncertainty requires some correction. Berger's early sociology was also influenced by the work of Helmut Schelsky who, in an influential article, asked the question "Can Continuous Questioning be Institutionalized?" in Norman Birnbaum and Gertrud Lenzer (eds.), *Sociology of Religion* (1957 [trans. 1969]). His conclusion was that a process of continuous reflectivity was not humanly possible, if enduring and reliable social relationships were to survive. While a number of sociologists, such as **Ulrich Beck** and **Anthony Giddens**, have argued that "de-traditionalization" and "reflexive modernization" are the predominant trends of late **modernity**, there are valid counterarguments, both sociological and psychological, to suggest that people in their **everyday lives** need stable **social structures**. Where there is de-traditionalization, there will also be countervailing movements of re-institutionalization.

Whereas traditional sociology was the study of institutions, the speed of **social change** in contemporary society and the apparent flexibility of social arrangements have meant that sociologists have sought to avoid treating institutions as if they were things, and have looked more towards social processes – that is towards processes of institutionalization, de-institutionalization, and re-institutionalization – than towards stable clusters of roles. Institutions should not be reified, but rather treated as maps by which to read social processes.   BRYAN S. TURNER

instrumental rationality
– see **rationality**.

intellectuals
Three notions are intertwined in the idea of the intellectual: intellectuals, the intelligentsia, and intellectual **labor**.

The term intellectual came into common usage with the Dreyfus affair in France (1894–1906), during which the novelist Émile Zola wrote a politically charged open letter in a popular periodical. In the public controversy which followed this crossing of the boundary between **culture** and **politics**, Zola was accused of being a mere "intellectual," a publicity-seeking dilettante, a popularizer who degraded cultural values in seeking a wider audience. In response, the term intellectual became a *nom de guerre* for those who wished to do public battle with the establishment, be they cultural or political.

The intelligentsia is historically older, having its roots in sections of the Russian and Polish **elite** in the middle of the nineteenth century who identified themselves with European **modernity**. The intelligentsia achieved even greater social cohesion in taking on the missionary task of bringing enlightenment to what it considered the darker regions of eastern Europe and central Asia.

As a sociological concept, the idea that the working population could be divided and defined by a division between intellectual and manual labor emerged later as part of an attempt to operationalize the concept. The idea of intellectual labor as the defining characteristic of the intellectual has, however, been projected backward in time by those seeking to identify a material and objective basis for empirical investigation. It has served as a means of distinguishing various strata of the middle class, for example. The "intellect" is here treated as a source of **income** and **social status** and "intelligence" as a personal attribute, a form of rent-bearing property: human capital. From this perspective, one may speak of "intellectual **professions**," as well as attempting to divide intellectual from manual labor.

Common to these three notions is the attempt to define the intellectual as a distinctive social category and to make some judgments about its functions and its behavior. In the 1920s, Julien Benda (1867–1956) railed against the "treason of the intellectuals," because in his eyes this social group was not fulfilling its proper role as social reformers and critics, while **Antonio Gramsci** distinguished "organic" and "traditional intellectuals" on the basis of their role in **social change** as much as their allotted class position. Decades later, the American sociologist **Alvin Gouldner** spoke of the intellectuals as a "new class," to which Georgy Konrad and Ivan Szelenyi, in their *Intellectuals on the Road to Class Power* (1979), developed the idea that intellectuals, expecially in central and eastern Europe, were moving towards class power. The opposite point of view was proposed by **John Goldthorpe** in "On the Service Class" (1982) in **Anthony Giddens** and G. Mackenzie (eds.), *Social Class and the Division of Labour*, where he defined intellectuals as a service class with conservative rather than radical political orientations.

Another point of view is offered by Ron Eyerman in *Between Culture and Politics* (1994), who defines intellectuals as an assumed **social role**, rather than an assigned social category or personality type. The intellectual from this point of view mediates and reinvents ideals and **traditions** in new historical contexts. Facilitating factors in this process are often **social movements**, which provide opportunities for those without formal "intellectual" qualifications to assume the functions traditionally associated with intellectuals, mediating culture and politics.   RON EYERMAN

intelligence
The publication of Francis Galton's *Hereditary Genius* (1869) pre-dates by several decades the period which is normally taken to be the moment marking the beginning of modern sociology. Writing in the aftermath of **Charles Darwin**'s *Origin of Species* and *The Ascent of Man*, Galton maintained the real objective existence both of racial differences and of social class differences in mental ability. **Émile Durkheim**'s insistence, in *Suicide* (1896), that this phenomenon was to be explained primarily by collective rather than individual factors can be seen as a deliberate reaction against the prior tendency to suppose that human behavior is biologically or genetically determined. The question of the "heritability of intelligence" was critical in resolving whether or not a sociology of **education** might be necessary or possible and whether it was justifiable to expend public finance in order to expand educational provision. The acceptance in general that human behavior is at least partly modified by social **interaction**, that human character is at least partly the product of "nurture" rather than wholly determined by "nature", is a *sine qua non*

for sociological research, and the debate about intelligence has provided a **case study** for this larger issue at significant moments in western social history since 1869.

In 1953, Brian Simon wrote a small book entitled *Intelligence Testing and the Comprehensive School*. In the Preface to the text, a teacher asked: "Have we achieved 'secondary education for all,' the reform that was the keystone of the Education Act, 1944? If not, why not? What are the fundamental misconceptions and practices that stand in our way?" What was at stake was the widening of opportunity within the British educational system that was projected immediately at the end of World War II. The teacher believed that Simon had exposed the obstacle to **progress** towards egalitarianism: "He shows how the practice of intelligence testing is used to justify the curtailment of opportunity from the junior school onwards; he shows also how theories based on intelligence testing uphold a form of school organization, and forms of teaching, which make secondary education for all impossible." The book was reproduced in entirety in Simon's *Intelligence, Psychology and Education. A Marxist Critique* (1971) and he asked in a new introduction why a publisher should want to reprint the earlier text, since the reorganization of secondary education on comprehensive lines was "now well under way." He indicated, however, that victory was far from secured in the United States. He suggested that "attempts to reanimate the ideology of 'intelligence' testing in the United States, as a barrier to the declared policy of desegregating schools, indicate that there are powerful social and political forces in favor of reinstating the doctrine that intelligence is innate and impervious to educational influences, to the detriment of social and educational advance." He was especially referring to the article by Arthur Jensen which appeared in the *Harvard Educational Review* in 1969 with the title: "How Much Can We Boost IQ and Scholastic Achievement?" This article relied on **data** on identical and fraternal twins reared apart which had been accumulated by Cyril Burt from the 1920s and presented in his *Factors of the Mind* (1940). Simon's text of 1971 criticized Burt's work but, in the second edition of 1978, he was able to quote L. J. Kamin's *The Science and Politics of I.Q.* (1977) to suggest that Burt's research had "fudged" the evidence.

Nevertheless, the debate continued and still continues. Robert B. Joynson's *The Burt Affair* (1989) questioned Kamin's criticisms, and a new statement of the heritability thesis appeared in 1994, occasioning much comment and political dispute. In *The Bell Curve* (1994), Charles Murray and Richard Herrnstein asserted, on the basis of **statistics** derived from the National Longitudinal Survey of Youth in the United States, that intelligence is largely inherited and that genes play a part in the fact that African Americans score lower than whites on intelligence tests. The debate about intelligence has always had important implications for developments in social and educational policy (see **social policy**). **Michael Young**'s satire of 1958 entitled *The Rise of the Meritocracy, 1870–2033* was sub-titled "An Essay on Education and Inequality." The book coined the word meritocracy which then became part of the language of subsequent thinking about education and **society**, linking with the assumption of **credentialism** that occupational and social advancement are the consequence of individual merit. Young proposed the formula that IQ + Effort = Merit and expressed skepticism that social engineering might be achieved without reference to class assumptions or **prejudices**. The implications of the debate now seem more serious as rapid developments occur as a result of research in **genetics**, cognitive neuroscience, and molecular biology. After some discussion in the late 1920s of Charles Spearman's postulate that there must be a general factor of intelligence, labeled "g," that is the underlying cause of an individual's performance in varied tests, Francis Fukuyama commented in his *Our Posthuman Future. Consequences of the Biotechnology Revolution* (2003) that scientific advances will soon generate a more refined understanding of this phenomenon, and that there is a possibility that the consequences of such good knowledge will be beneficial. He suggests that brain imaging techniques can chart blood flow and neuron firings and that it may then become possible to correlate these with different kinds of mental activities so as to determine with some finality whether "g is one thing or many things." Bad science has been used for bad ends in the past but, as Fukuyama optimistically concludes his discussion of the sciences of the brain and the heritability of intelligence, this should not rule out the possibility that good science may serve us well in the future.

DEREK ROBBINS

intelligence task
– see **intelligence**.

intentionality
This is a subject with philosophical origins and identifiable roots, according to some authorities, as far back as Parmenides in the fifth century BCE,

and certainly of importance in classical and medieval writings before the contemporary interest, which is usually dated to the work of the phenomenologist Franz Brentano (1838–1917). Mental states are said to be intentional insofar as they have a content. Beliefs, **attitudes**, desires, purposes, and the like, that are about something – for example, *I believe that extraterrestrials are among us, I am in favor of government by extraterrestrials, and I plan to vote for extraterrestrials in the next election* – are thus distinguished from other kinds of mental state – for example, affective states such as *I am depressed* – which do not require a specified content for them to be coherent or intelligible. This particular technical use is to be distinguished from a related use in ordinary **language** and legal judgments, where the focus of interest is the intended effect of an action. The former became a subject of philosophical and sociological inquiry through John L. Austin's (1911–60) work on "speech acts," and the latter have been the subject of work by many jurists including Austin himself.

Brentano's focus on what he termed intentional inexistence – which is to say mental content that is not tied to any known existing state of affairs as in the case of the extraterrestrials above – raises interesting conceptual challenges. For him, the argument from the observation that mental states do not depend on existing cases or experiences and the claim that mental states are qualitatively different to physical states led to a conclusion in favor of dualism, but left open the problem of how a mental state thus defined can become a physical cause.

Others, while not subscribing to an overtly dualist position in seeking to avoid this problem have argued that intentionality inheres in computational states of the brain which are themselves physical. However, this account is vulnerable to the problem that there is no necessary correspondence between physical state and belief state, nor between the belief states of two physically matched entities as Hilary Putnam (1926–) argued with his Twin Earth thought experiment.

One response to the problems raised by intentionality has been the proposal that it is an epiphenomenon and plays no role in the determination of individual action. Another, which derives from both certain behavioral and hermeneutical positions, has been to argue that intentional talk effectively attributes intentional states to individuals, by themselves or by other individuals, and is part of the public calculus on which we base the prediction of our own and each other's behavior. Fundamental to what some refer to as the intentional stance (Donald Davidson [1917–2003] and Daniel Dennett [1942–]) is the mutual recognition that individual actors have of each other's interpretations of their actions as intentional. In this view, the analyst's focus on intentionality is drawn away from unobservable internal psychological states to public events and the external environment. DAVID GOOD

interaction

In general, the term interaction is associated with micro-sociological studies of social processes involving face-to-face encounters, and of contexts in which people act in relation to one another. But the term also has a broader sociostructural import, involving a macro-sociological orientation, in that many sociologists view social systems as built upon systems of interaction. Such systems arise out of the production of both face-to-face interaction and interaction with others who are physically absent; they thus stretch away in time and space in terms of their wider implications for analysis of the social field.

The micro-sociological analysis of interaction derives its central impetus from **Max Weber**'s concept of ***Verstehen*** (understanding), by which Weber sought to underscore the basic role of subjective interpretation in human doing and human action. To understand what a social agent is doing in any particular social context, according to Weber, demands some minimal consideration of how that agent subjectively grasps the meaning of their own behavior. Applying this insight to the normative character of **social action**, **Talcott Parsons** wrote of the "double contingency" that shapes interaction. For Parsons, the reactions of the other(s) always frame the acts of the social actor, because the nature of contingent responses is such that it serves as a potential sanction in the broader context of power relations.

The micro-sociological study of interaction has taken different forms. One of the most influential has issued from **ethnomethodology** and analysis of "turn-taking" in conversational interaction. When we engage in conversational talk, for example, much of what we do is based on our recognition that only one person usually speaks at a time (termed the seriality of participants) in order to constitute interaction as meaningful.

Another tradition which focuses upon the conventions whereby the communication of meaning in interaction is achieved is that of **critical theory**, specifically the work of **Jürgen Habermas**. The reproduction of social life unfolds, according to Habermas, not only through technological modes of action but also through "symbolic interaction." In this sociological communicative framework, interaction is contextualized in terms of the symbolic structuring of communication, with reflection upon human action arising in and through reflexive linguistic interaction.

Other sociologists have been critical of the micro-sociological neglect of the role of temporality and social reproduction in grasping how interaction, the social field, and history are closely intertwined. Other sociologists suggest that the micro- versus macro-sociological distinction fails to grasp the radical extension of human interaction in space and in time as a consequence of the overall development of **modernity**. In this respect, **Anthony Giddens** has argued that, rather than contrast small-group interaction with larger forms of communal interaction, sociologists should focus on the more profound difference in interaction between face-to-face encounters and interpersonal communication with others at a distance. The development of writing, according to Giddens, radically extends the scope of "distanciated interaction" whereby agents can access the past through interaction with texts. Writing and its technologies also fundamentally alter the nature of the social interactions that can be carried out: the temporal gap between agents engaged in dialogical interaction is obviously much less in the case of someone sending a fax to someone on the other side of the world than would be the case in an exchange of letters.

A persistent theme in contemporary sociology is that **globalization** is reconstituting interaction in complex and uneven ways, principally as a result of radical transmutations in structures of signification. This extension of interaction in time and space concerns not only the new information technologies that people deploy in their day-to-day lives, but also the mediated representations we have of others distant in time and in space. Here the focus is on individuals or groups of people we do not interact with on a daily basis, but with whom, through mediated interaction, we come to forge some sense of cognitive and emotional connection – however minimal. ANTHONY ELLIOTT

intergenerational mobility
– see **social mobility**.

intergenerational processes
– see **generation(s)**.

internal colonialism
– see **colonialism**.

internet society

The term internet society has two general meanings. The first is a physical society that has a large proportion of its populace online and active in consuming, communicating, or producing **information** via the internet. The second refers to the activities of people online, and the extent to which such activities may be perceived as reproducing, imitating, or extending in a virtual sense the activities that are carried on in a physically real society. This second sense is a new layer on an older discussion of the "information society."

In terms of the first sense – a society whose members spend a great deal of time using the internet – two visions are usually offered: optimistic and pessimistic. The optimistic or even utopian vision is that internet **technology** will enable societies to overcome the **digital divide** and increase social, political, and economic participation. Use of traditional, often stigmatizing, categories will disappear because users become unable to use such categories and instead will deal with each other on an unbiased basis. The other vision is pessimistic, or even dystopian. It foresees a loss of **privacy** and other civil **rights**, "cyber-ghettoes," exacerbation of **inequality**, and dominance of modes of communication by malevolent corporations or governments.

Clearly, there are some important changes taking place as more activities are transplanted from real-world social settings to online ones. For instance, dating and match-making have a long tradition. These arrangements were carried out via each new communication technology, including the mail, newspapers, telephones, and computers. With the internet, millions of people are now involved in seeking new personal relationships. The combination of the power of the computer with **networks** means that one can search the world over for a relationship candidate. The seeker is offered unprecedented choices. There are important ramifications for the establishment, maintenance, and termination of real-life relationships. It has been speculated that, as online options increase, people will be less willing to invest in the emotional tasks of real-life relationships, which will suffer as a result. So an internet society, it seems, follows the rubric that applies to other areas of life: when new opportunities arise, they often entail costs to existing structures.

As to the second meaning of internet society, theorists have examined social relationships that have grown out of a technology based on physically stationary computers and wire-based communication links among them. Inquiry has focused on the nature and number of online **communities**. Boundary creation and reinforcing mechanisms, the motives for participation in virtual societies, and the relationship between these societies and physical ones are central analytical constructs in this endeavor.

At the same time, R. S. Ling, in *The Mobile Connection* (2004), makes clear that the trajectory of use is towards mobile internet, which in turn will require a conceptual modification on the part of scholars. The questions of the use of public space and social relationships stemming from this change have been little studied. One line of reasoning concerning this is that a "walled garden" will develop, in which people become more tightly linked to their primary relationships and exclude those outside these relationships, and also reduce their psychological if not physical presence in public places. Such technological changes will also transform the use of public space as more people physically occupy restaurants and other public venues while being mentally absorbed in the world of the distant other.

JAMES E. KATZ

interpellation

A term developed and made popular by the French Marxist philosopher **Louis Althusser**, this describes the process by which **ideology** addresses the individual. The word shares the root of the word "appellation" (name) and interpellation is a hailing, according to Althusser. If a policeman shouts "Hey, you there!" at least one individual will turn around to "answer" that call. At the moment of realization that the addressee is oneself, one becomes a subject of the ideology of law (see **law and society**). This almost instantaneous process operates not simply at the level of individual **interaction**, but also is the point at which the police officer, representing an arm of the **state**, weaves the subject into a web of law. For Althusser this is generally how ideology operates: we are always caught up in processes in which we voluntarily acknowledge the validity of the ideological practices. Interpellation draws on the structuralist theory that the notion of an autonomous human subject is an illusion, since human beings are enmeshed in discursive and **social structures** that shape their identity.

Film theorists in the 1970s used the concept of interpellation to suggest that mainstream cinema acts as an "apparatus" to position the viewers to "misrecognize" themselves through identification with the fictional characters on the screen. They thus appear to possess coherent, autonomous personalities solving conflicts, moving from disunity to unity. Ideology is understood here not in the sense of false beliefs but as constructing the nature of experience itself, thus creating an imaginary relation to the real.

LARRY RAY

interpretation

– see *Verstehen*.

interpretive repertoires

– see **discourse analysis**.

interval scale

– see **measurement**.

interview(s)

These are widely used forms of **data** collection, not only within sociology but across the **social sciences**. Although intuitively an attractive and inherently "truthful" source of data about matters of sociological interest, data derived by researchers from talking to people (or via the analysis of research participants talking to each other) may also be subsumed under the category of **low-inference descriptors** – that is, as the sort of data that should always be treated with circumspection. Some critiques from within **feminism** have dismissed the use of interviews in principle as necessarily reproducing relationships of patriarchal dominance, given the power differential in the roles of interviewer and interviewee, respectively.

Interviews are used for a variety of purposes, and may be employed in a variety of forms. Interviews are a routinely used technique in the pilot-study phase of larger-scale research endeavors where they may be employed to trial alternative questionnaire item wordings or to assist in item generation for larger-scale research. Increasingly, interviews are employed in their own right as a stand-alone research tool: for example to permit the identification of the interpretative repertoires of particular **groups** regarding social issues by the use of **discourse analysis**; to survey public perceptions of specific political matters; or to develop novel theoretical understandings of issues via the use of **grounded theory**.

Interview methods vary in terms of the rigidity of the requirement for the interviewer to adhere exactly to a pre-scripted schedule. In terms of this requirement – inspired by a concern for quasi-statistical reliability – interviews may, broadly, be characterized as structured, semi-structured, and "conversational"/open-ended. Absolute fidelity to pre-scripted questions is demanded by structured interviews, a degree of flexibility – for example paraphrasis and clarification of items – is allowable in semi-structured approaches, and under open-ended interviewing the simple provision of a number of probe questions permits respondents to elaborate on issues of research interest. Interviews may be employed as individually administered research devices or, less commonly, via the use of carefully selected small groups of participants, as a tool for the generation of data from a number of respondents simultaneously. The **focus group** may be distinguished from a group interview, in that the moderator of a focus group is usually concerned to *facilitate* a group *discussion* via a series of open-ended questions and probes, rather than to *elicit* a group's *answers* to a sequence of predetermined interview questions.

Data collected by interviews also varies, that is, respondents' answers to pre-scripted questions may be field coded and simply recorded as a number (see Extract 1 for an example of problematic field coding); alternatively, the interview may be tape-recorded and transcribed either verbatim (as, for example, are Hansard and court transcripts) or using the more finely grained conventions of **conversational analysis** which record linguistic details such as prosody, inflection, and emphasis. Whatever the purpose, administration format, and eventual representation of the interview, for the most part the contemporary use of the social scientific interview as research tool depends upon, or rather implicitly accepts, a number of usually unexamined key assumptions. Thus it is assumed, for example, that: all interview questions veridically represent the intent of the designer of the interview schedule and are delivered by interviewers precisely as such; that all interview questions have the same semantic meaning to all respondents; that all interviewer utterances are questions and all interviewee utterances are more or less well-formed responses; and, most crucially, that interview talk is an essentially unproblematic means of transmitting the contents of one mind to another. This frequently unstated belief has been termed the conduit metaphor, or, less kindly, the telementational fallacy.

Although the empirical study of a variety of specific settings in which interviews are used as sense-making practices (for example in doctor–patient encounters, psychotherapy sessions, or news interviews) has a long history in **ethnomethodology**, more recently – particularly since the work of **Ludwig Wittgenstein** (see *Philosophical Investigations*, 1958) and the **linguistic turn** in the

---

Extract 1 (from M. Rapley and C. Antaki, "A Conversation Analysis of the 'Acquiescence' of People with Learning Disabilities," 1996, *Journal of Community & Applied Social Psychology*; transcription simplified):

INTERVIEWER: D'you feel out of place out an' about in social situations?
ANNE: No.
INTERVIEWER: Anne? Never?
ANNE: No.
INTERVIEWER: Sometimes?
ANNE: No.
INTERVIEWER: Or usually?
ANNE: Sometimes I do.
INTERVIEWER: Yeah? OK, we'll put a 2 down for that one then.

---

social sciences – not only have interviews become an increasingly prevalent research method but also, through the use of conversational analysis, a body of work has begun to examine critically the ways that social science interviews themselves are used as academic sense-making practices. For example, Hanneke Houtkoop-Steenstra's work (*Interaction and the Standardised Interview: The Living Questionnaire*, 2000) focused on the administration of market-research **questionnaires**, and Rapley and Antaki's work (1996) has examined the delivery of psychological tests as interactional practices, rather than as neutral probes into the **attitudes**, beliefs, or intentions of respondents. This work has started to cast doubt on long-cherished social-scientific notions that interviews offer an unproblematic "window to the soul."

Extract 2 (from Rapley and Antaki, 1996; transcription simplified):

INTERVIEWER: Erm and I'd like you to answer some questions to tell me how you feel about the –
ARTHUR: They're not 'ard ones are they?
INTERVIEWER: Not very hard
ARTHUR: No
INTERVIEWER: No and if you don't understand them Arthur you can just tell me
ARTHUR: Yeus
INTERVIEWER: And I'll I'll say them differently. . .
INTERVIEWER: So there's no hurry do you have any questions to ask me?
ARTHUR: Yeers
INTERVIEWER: What would you like to ask me?
ARTHUR: I like being I like being er in 'ere
INTERVIEWER: You like: being
ARTHUR: Living in 'ere like I like living in 'ere

Rather, from this perspective, with interviews understood as being no different to any other piece of talk-in-interaction, it becomes clear that the local interactional business of "doing interviewing" and "doing being interviewed" may itself become highly salient in its own right; see Extract 2 for an example of how the very business of the interview and its consequences becomes a difficult topic.

Interviews remain a staple method in the social scientific armamentarium. However, the canonical assumptions about the precise replicability of interview protocols across respondents – upon which the reliability and validity of aggregate data gathered via interviews rely – warrant critical review. Close attention to the social organization of **interaction** revealed by interview transcripts suggests that these assumptions are simply not borne out by the data.

MARK RAPLEY AND SUSAN HANSEN

intimacy

This is a relatively new word in the sociological lexicon and, although sociologists have long researched the "private sphere," or **families**, or **marriage**, they have not seen intimacy as a proper focus for **sociological theory**. This changed, initially with the rise of feminist research which began to identify close personal, heterosexual, relationships as possible sites of oppression for women. In some senses feminist work prized open the black box of close personal relationships and began to challenge the assumption that intimacy was simply personal and/or the realm of **psychoanalysis** or psychology. The mainstream sociological revolution in understanding intimacy came, however, with **Anthony Giddens**, in *The Transformation of Intimacy* (1992), who called to attention the ways in which the qualities of personal relationships were changing in late modern times. He introduced concepts of "confluent love" and the "pure relationship." The former refers to the quality of a relationship in which it is the mutual sharing of thoughts and feelings that matters most. Confluent love is said to be based on **equality**, while the more traditional idea of romantic love is based on gender **inequality**. The pure relationship signifies one which will only last as long as it is mutually fulfilling. Under such a regime it is seen as acceptable to end a relationship which no longer meets one's needs and interests. In constructing these models of contemporary relationships, Giddens owes much to earlier feminist work which criticized the power imbalances between men and women. Indeed, he argues that it is

women who are demanding these "new" kinds of relationships and who are leaving marriages if they are not satisfied with the quality of intimacy, that is established. Moreover, Giddens argues that it is same-sex relationships which are in the vanguard of the new form of intimacy, because they are not based on traditional understandings of gender difference.

Giddens's intimacy is, however, mainly a sexual intimacy; his focus is on the couple, whether heterosexual or homosexual. Other sociological discussions of intimacy have broadened the concept to include **friendship**, intergenerational relationships, and parent–child relationships. Thus Lynn Jamieson in *Intimacy* (1998) speaks of "disclosing intimacy" which is of a different sort to bodily or sexual intimacy and can encompass rather different sorts of close relationships. Work on friendship is perhaps the most interesting development because the predominant sociological emphasis on family life and relationships has tended to obscure the significance of intimate friendships. Friends have been treated as being of less significance than family members, and friendships as less enduring than marriages. Social factors such as high rates of divorce, the growth of single-person households, and the rise of childlessness have combined to ignite a re-appraisal of friendship as an important sociological category. Studies of friendship and friendship **networks** (often based on the workplace) have replaced studies of **communities** (based on where people live), and contemporary friendships are now understood to be relationships which endure notwithstanding the fact that individuals may have relationships based on sexual intimacy as well.   CAROL SMART

invisible religion
– see **religion**.

Irigaray, Luce (1932–)

Born in Belgium, Irigaray has made her home since the 1960s in France, where she trained in **psychoanalysis** with **Jacques Lacan**. Her first, and most famous work, *Speculum of the Other Woman* (1974 [trans. 1985]), argued that women have been excluded from both philosophy and psychoanalytic theory. This exclusion is explained by Irigaray in terms of the identification of women with nature and the association of women with **motherhood** (an identification which applies whether or not women are mothers). In contrast to this, men are identified with **culture** and subjectivity, a subjectivity which women support. In this analysis, Irigaray employs that distinction between men/culture and women/nature which has become a familiar premise of feminist theory, and she emphasizes – as **Simone de Beauvoir** had done in *The Second Sex* (1949 [trans. 1972]) – that the only form of subjectivity in western culture is male.

Irigaray's theoretical antecedents lie in a number of disciplines, of which psychoanalysis and philosophy are perhaps the most dominant. But Irigaray's own work crosses conventional disciplinary boundaries, in that her concerns are less with specific institutional changes in the **social status** and position of women (she is not concerned, for example, with social rearrangements of the **social role** of mothers) than with a rethinking of the ways in which women and men encounter the **body** and their physical existence. For Irigaray, the most important shift in the reconfiguration of **gender** is the recognition by men that nature / the body do not have to be controlled and that the "imaginary body" (a concept inherited from Lacan) is not to be identified with that of men. Thus welcoming the possibilities that **Sigmund Freud** opened up for the study of **sexuality**, Irigaray also wishes to counter Freud's theories about women and their sense of loss.

MARY EVANS

iron law of oligarchy

– see **Robert Michels**.

J

James, William (1842–1910)

An American psychologist and philosopher, James was the founder of **pragmatism**. Born in New York City, unconventionally educated in America and Europe and a qualified MD, James never practiced medicine. He started his career at Harvard, first as Instructor in Physiology and Anatomy, and, at different times, Professor of Psychology and Professor of Philosophy. Of the books published in his lifetime, the most enduring and of interest to sociology include *The Principles of Psychology* (1890), *The Varieties of Religious Experience* (1902), and *Pragmatism* (1907). All are still in print.

James's **influence** in sociology is through a number of routes. *The Principles of Psychology* includes a chapter, "The Consciousness of Self," that is thoroughly sociological and strongly influenced both **Charles Horton Cooley** and **George Herbert Mead**. James proposes the notion of a social **self**, later elaborated by Cooley as the looking-glass self, and also the distinction between the I and the Me, later developed by Mead. Through his influence on Mead, James contributed to the emergence of **symbolic interactionism**. But this is not the only route through which James enters sociology. James was also a source and inspiration for **Thorstein Veblen**, especially in the conception of human evolution directed by consciousness and also the characteristic Jamesian understanding of human instinct, both of which featured in Veblen's evolutionary approach in economic sociology. Additionally, James's discussion of **religion** (1902) was much more important to both **Max Weber**'s *The Protestant Ethic and the Spirit of Capitalism* (1905 [trans. 2002]) and **Émile Durkheim**'s *The Elementary Forms of the Religious Life* (1912 [trans. 1954]) than a mere index check could reveal.

JACK BARBALET

Jameson, Fredric (1934–)

Professor of Comparative Literature at Duke University, cultural critic, and the key exponent of Marxist **postmodern theory** and interpretation of contemporary cultural trends, Jameson is best known for his *Postmodernism or the Cultural Logic of Late Capitalism* (1991), and his broad, innovative, and radical cultural criticism, especially *The Cultural Turn* (1998). **Postmodernism**, according to Jameson, represents a new mode of representation, life experience, and aesthetic sensitivity, all of which reflect the latest stage of capitalist development. The key features of this stage, which evolved out of market **capitalism** of the nineteenth century and monopoly capitalism of the early twentieth century, are the global division of **labor**, intensified **consumption**, especially consumption of images, a proliferation of the **mass-media**, and an increasing saturation of society with information **technology**. Above all, late capitalism integrates aesthetic production into general commodity production, thus intensifying mass consumption of ever more novel goods. Jameson identifies the features of postmodern cultural configuration, a new "mode of production" in late capitalism, as including the blurring of distinction between popular/commercial and highbrow/classic culture; the weakening of the historical dimension with the emphasis on current experience (here and now), and the organization of **space** (most conspicuous in contemporary architecture); the spread of electronically reproduced images ("the simulacra" in **Jean-François Lyotard**'s terms); a wide use of pastiche; and a decline in affectivity that reduces the need for emotional engagement in cultural consumption. In his quest for the "cognitive mapping" of contemporary **culture** in relation to late capitalist **economy** and society. Jameson links **postmodernity** with the popular ethos, **lifestyle**, and mentality of "the yuppies," the young segments of a professional–managerial class, and with a new wave of American economic, cultural, and military domination.

JAN PAKULSKI

justice

The question "What is justice?" is at the center of political philosophy but not at the center of **sociology**. Famously raised by Plato in *The Republic*, it is a question which sociologists deal with in an anti-Platonic fashion. Plato analyzes justice with respect to the soul. His work is organized around an analogy between the city and the soul, suggesting that a proper understanding of justice requires a philosopher to transcend the narrow boundaries of society, portrayed as a cave, an obscure place where little can be understood: for Plato, the truly just can be grasped only in the light of the eternal, beyond the social here and now. Sociologists aim to start not from beyond the cave but, most emphatically, from within the cave itself: when they do study the question of justice in itself, they aim to do so by giving morally detached accounts of the notions of justice held in particular societies. In the preface of his *Injustice. The Social Bases of Obedience and Revolt* (1978), Barrington Moore notes that, for a while, he thought of calling his book "a study of moral outrage"; but he adds that, after all, "moral outrage suggests too strongly the agonies of **intellectuals** trying to interpret, judge, and change the world." Sociologists offer descriptions and analysis of existing **ideologies** rather than a normative "theory of justice," an analysis given in terms of **values**, of ideology, of history, of context. Such accounts of justice often depend on or express **historicism** and/or **relativism**.

This is why, in spite of acknowledging **Montesquieu**'s role as a founder of sociology, **Émile Durkheim** criticizes him for remaining too much of a political philosopher. Montesquieu treats despotic or tyrannical regimes as anomalous, but Durkheim argues in *Montesquieu and Rousseau, Forerunners of Sociology* (1892 [trans. 1960]) that, from a scientific point of view, every regime must be treated as having its own perfect form. The injustice inherent in a despotic regime does not or should not matter from the politically neutral point of view of a sociologist. Considered as a unified enterprise, sociology offers an alternative to political philosophy, an analysis of the human condition which does not start from the political question of justice.

The main reason why sociology tends not to address the question of justice directly goes back to its origins. Sociology was born as a result of the eighteenth-century separation between **state** and **civil society**. Originally, sociology took as its proper object civil society, aiming to treat this

independently from the activities of the state; in this sense, sociology began with a critique of the primacy of the political. It aimed to show that societies obey laws or belong to types that can be described and understood without reference to laws (see **law and society**) enforced by the state. However, this very critique of the primacy of the political has political consequences, and bears on the understanding of the question of justice.

In this respect, Durkheim's focus on Montesquieu's legacy is significant. Montesquieu distinguishes law and mores (see **norm[s]**), developing an account of the autonomy of mores, of the complexity of social phenomena, of a "spirit" of laws that is required to avoid despotism and injustice. To the extent to which Montesquieu can be counted among the founders of sociology, he founds it because he thinks that it will be politically useful. Sociology is the science which, in the hands of rulers and lawyers, should foster political moderation through an understanding of the comparative narrowness of the political category and of the resilience and relative autonomy of social phenomena. A ruler cannot make *any* law, and become a tyrant: he needs to take into account the "spirit" of the laws – that is, the sociology of law. Besides, a proper understanding of the autonomy of mores paves the way for a proper account of the balance of powers, that is the balance between the state and the representatives of civil society in dealing with the state. From this liberal point of view, an insistence on the limits of the political sphere helps to protect civil **rights** and minimize injustice. At the other end of the political spectrum, **Karl Marx**'s theory offers a good example of sociology put in the service not of political moderation but of revolution. Marx's sociology is built around a critique of the category of the political in the name of the primacy of the **economy**. The state and its laws are denounced as instruments of the bourgeoisie, developed for the oppression of the proletariat. Although Marx plays on the demand for justice, on a revolt against the fate of the poor in the context of the industrial revolution, he remains faithful to the sociological critique of the category of justice, which he tries to avoid as overly ideological.

ÉMILE PERREAU-SAUSSINE

K

Keynes, John Maynard (1883–1946)

One of the leading economists of the twentieth century, Keynes held academic positions at the University of Cambridge and also worked from time to time within the British civil service. His significance lies both in his contribution to economic theory and in his influence on **public policy**.

Keynes's major work is *The General Theory of Employment, Interest, and Money* (1935). Writing in the context of global economic depression and mass **unemployment**, Keynes rejected the prevailing assumption that economic recovery could be left to market forces. In the orthodox view, **markets** were seen as creating and recreating equilibria through changes in the demand for and supply of goods and services. Keynes argued that, under certain conditions, the market search for equilibrium was incapable of resolving depression and alleviating unemployment. If aggregated demand was low, then depression would remain endemic. In such circumstances, one should look to government action in the form of public spending, rather than market forces, to create economic revival.

This theoretical insight had a significant impact on public policy from the 1930s until the 1980s. Government demand management became a pillar of Western economic policy, and the basis for **welfare states** and national economic planning. Under the impact of Keynesian economics, social programs to promote welfare had an economic as well as a social rationale. In addition to this emphasis on the Keynesian welfare state and Social Keynesianism, Keynes strongly influenced the architecture of global economic recovery after World War II. **Institutions** such as the International Monetary Fund and the World Bank originated in the Bretton Woods conference of 1944 which Keynes attended. They were designed, in large measure, to provide an interventionist framework at the international level, to parallel national economic policy initiatives.

Keynesian approaches fell out of favor from the 1970s. This occurred in part through the simultaneous onset of **inflation** and stagnation (stagflation), not anticipated in Keynes's theoretical framework, and in part because demand management neglected supply-side reforms of labor markets and public-sector efficiency. Deregulation and the rolling back of state activity were more widely advocated as means of optimizing national competitiveness and reaping the benefits of **globalization**. The Washington consensus on neoliberal economic policy rather than Keynesianism has dominated the Bretton Woods institutions since the mid-1980s, though this has been challenged very recently by Joseph Stiglitz and George Soros, who argue for a return, if not to Keynesianism, then at least to a more interventionist approach to market failure and instability.   BOB HOLTON

Keynesian welfare state
– see **John Maynard Keynes**.

Khaldun, Ibn (1332–1406)

A Muslim social philosopher who is often described as "the father of sociology," Khaldun was born in Tunisia into an upper-class Andalusian family, the Banu Khaldun. He traced his ancestry back through an Arabic-Yemeni tribe from Hadhramaut. He lived at various times in Spain, Tunisia, and Egypt, where he died, in Cairo, shortly after becoming an Islamic judge or *qadi*.

His work concerned the social and political determinants of the rise and fall of **civilizations**. His **sociological theory** was presented in *The Muqaddimah: An Introduction to History* (1958). This "prolegomena" to world history was composed around 1375 when he had withdrawn from **politics**. This prolegomena concerns the circulation of **elites** between town and desert in North Africa. The town elites over time grow lazy, rich, and corrupt, while tribal elites remain disciplined and enjoy greater **social integration** or **solidarity**. This greater social unity allows them periodically to replace town elites, but in turn they become corrupt, and are replaced by fresh elites. This Khaldunian theory of social and political change was used to great effect by **Ernest Gellner** in

Muslim Society (1981) to explain different forms of Islam (puritanical and egalitarian versus mystical and hierarchical) in relation to political change, for example in Morocco. The development of modern communications **technology**, especially the telegraph, telephone, and radio, eventually gave urban elites a military advantage over the countryside, and the ancient political oscillation was transformed. Radical reform movements in Islam such as the fundamentalist Wahhabi movement, which was inspired by Muhammad b. Abd-al-Wahhab (died 1791), are often said to exhibit the **social changes** that were originally described by Ibn Khaldun's sociology. Muslim **intellectuals** often complain that most histories of sociology neglect Ibn Khaldun, because they are written within the framework of **Orientalism**.

BRYAN S. TURNER

kinship

Socially universal, this is probably the most basic of institutional modalities of human organization. Anthropology has consistently treated kinship as its special theoretical preserve, and its preoccupations with kinship have consistently focused on three overlapping thematic issues. One of these is typological. From Lewis Henry Morgan's *Systems of Consanguinity and Affinity in the Human Family* (1871) onward, the field of kinship studies has preserved the distinction between classificatory (or "merging") kinship terminologies, which assign a general rubric to relatives of differing genealogical distance from any given ego, and descriptive terminologies, which in their most expansive versions provide each relative with a rubric of his or her own. Morgan's efforts have given way to the distinction among six terminological schemas, from the expansively classificatory Hawaiian to the meticulously descriptive Sudanese.

Another thematic focus has rested on the question of the generative principle of kinship. Its star curiosity is the taboo against incest. **Claude Lévi-Strauss** underscores the taboo's proscription of **marriage** within the elemental family group in arguing that kinship systems are before all else not systems of descent but of intergroup alliance.

A final focus falls on the substantive ground of kinship. David Schneider's *Critique* (1984) of the naturalism of even the most ardently conventionalist theories of kinship has not discouraged every psychoanalyst or sociobiologist since, but it has inspired a new effort to establish the grounds of kinship in strictly socio-cultural phenomena. Leading contenders include the symbolization of **fertility**, the articulation of domesticity, and the dynamics of self-formation.

JAMES D. FAUBION

Komarovsky, Mirra (1905–1986)

Born in Baku in the Caucasus, Komarovsky emigrated to the United States in 1922 and attended Barnard College in New York where she was taught by Franz Boas, Ruth Benedict, and William Ogburn. She became a research assistant on the Westchester Leisure Project (1931–3) that resulted in George L. Lundberg, Mary M. McInerny, and Komarovsky's *Leisure, A Suburban Study* (1934). From 1934 to 1936 she was a research associate at the International Institute for Social Research, directed by **Paul Lazarsfeld**, and on the basis of that work she published her PhD thesis in 1940 on *The Unemployed Man and his Family*, with an introduction by Lazarsfeld. Komarovsky became an associate professor (1948–53) and later full professor (1954–70). She was influential in the development of the sociology of **gender**, through articles such as "Cultural Contradictions and Sex Roles," in the *American Journal of Sociology* (1946), and "Functional Analysis of Sex Roles," in the *American Sociological Review* (1950). Her books, such as *Dilemmas of Masculinity* (1976) and *Blue-Collar Marriage* (1964), were highly influential. Her works on **social class** criticized American sociologists for neglecting the working class and for applying generalizations from the middle class to blue-collar families. The principal theoretical focus of her empirical work – inconsistencies in **social roles** – was influenced by **Robert Merton**'s role theory and William Ogburn's concept of social lag. She had three scientific objectives, namely to understand the functional significance of sex roles, to locate their cultural contradictions, and to assess the possibilities of **social change**. Her monograph on unemployed men has also been recognized for its methodological contribution to the use of personal documents. She made important contributions to feminist theory in *Women in the Modern World* (1953) and *Women in College* (1985). She was the second female President of the American Sociological Association (1972–3); her presidential address that year was, suitably, on "Some Problems in Role Analysis."

BRYAN S. TURNER

Kristeva, Julia (1941–)

Born in Bulgaria, Kristeva has spent her life in France since 1965. She is best known for the distinction that she makes between what she calls the "semiotic" and the "symbolic," and for her assertion of the centrality of the mother (see motherhood/mothers) in human biography and the social world. Kristeva defines the "semiotic" in terms of the drives and rhythms of the human body, and in particular the maternal body. The "symbolic," on the other hand, is the frame of reference that we use to make sense of our experience. The "symbolic" and the "semiotic" combine to produce signification, and it is Kristeva's contention that the structure of signification comes from what she describes as maternal regulation.

In emphasizing the place of the mother in both the individual and the social world, Kristeva follows Melanie Klein (1882–1960). She takes the centrality of the mother forward in her texts *Powers of Horror* (1980) and *Black Sun* (1987) to argue that, within patriarchal cultures, the mother, and maternity, are subject to what she describes as "abjection," a form of subjectivity in which women become depressed and develop a depressed **sexuality**. In order to change the degradation of the feminine, Kristeva does not propose ideas of universal **equality**, nor the development of a specific female **language** and **culture**. Kristeva validates what she sees as multiple possible sexualities and a recognition within cultures that there is a need to heal what she describes as wounded **narcissism**. One of the characteristics of Kristeva's work is the links she makes between **psychoanalysis** and the social world: for example, *Strangers to Ourselves* (1992) considers some of the reasons for **racism** and the fear of other cultures.   MARY EVANS

Kuhn, Thomas Samuel (1922–1996)

An American historian and philosopher of science, Thomas Kuhn was an undergraduate and graduate student in physics at Harvard, where he came under the influence of the university's powerful president, James B. Conant, who was himself a physical chemist as well as a member of a small group of politically important scientists. Conant had a strong concern for undergraduate science education. His new strategy was based on the popular Harvard method of the **case study** that focused on historical cases of far-reaching conceptual changes in scientific disciplines. Kuhn began teaching this course and was asked to develop his own historical research. After a few years at Harvard, he took up a teaching position at Berkeley where he turned this study into his first book, *The Copernican Revolution* (1957), and worked on *The Structure of Scientific Revolutions* (1962), a summary

and overview of far-reaching conceptual changes in science.

The book proved difficult to publish but was eventually accepted in the logical positivist *International Encyclopedia of Unified Science* (1955). It was also published as a separate volume and became one of the best-selling scholarly books of all time and was the most frequently cited book in the late twentieth century. Kuhn's key term **paradigm** passed into common usage. Kuhn did not develop the implications of his argument for the **social sciences** and was shocked by some of the sociological interpretations of the text. He spent much of the rest of his life responding to issues concerning incommensurability and meaning-change in science.   STEPHEN P. TURNER

Kymlicka, Will (dates not known)

Professor of Philosophy at Queens University, Ontario, Canada, and recurrent Visiting Professor in the Nationalism Studies program at the Central European University in Budapest, Kymlicka has contributed extensively to the analysis of **citizenship**, ethnic minorities, and cultural **rights** in liberal **democracies**. His most influential publication in this field was *Multicultural Citizenship* (1995). His principal argument is that modern democracies have sought to accommodate national and ethnic differences under the broad umbrella of **multiculturalism** through the creation of "group-differentiated rights." He identified three forms of these rights. First, self-government rights recognize some degree of self-determination, for example through federalism. Secondly, polyethnic rights recognize the entitlement of minorities to practice their own customs, **religion**, and **language**, such as the in-principle right of Muslim girls to wear the headscarf in secular schools. Finally, there are special representation rights, which would give representation to minorities, for example by allocating a certain number of seats to them in representative chambers (of parliament). Kymlicka's arguments are controversial because he claims that these group rights are perfectly compatible with the individualistic rights of **liberalism**. His other publications include *Politics in the Vernacular: Nationalism, Multiculturalism and Citizenship* (2001), and *Contemporary Political Philosophy* (2002). He has co-edited Kymlicka and Wayne Norman (eds.), *Citizenship in Diverse Societies* (2000) and Kymlicka and Magda Opalski (eds.), *Can Liberal Pluralism be Exported?* (2001).

BRYAN S. TURNER

L

labeling theory

Labeling represents not a single **sociological theory**, but a number of different ideas relating to the notion that no behavior is deviant or criminal unless so labeled. Labeling thus refers to the process by which behaviors come to be categorized as deviant or criminal. Each society makes rules whose breach will constitute **deviance** or criminality.

Labeling is a derivative of the widely used sociological idea of **symbolic interactionism**. Interactionist theory analyzes the way in which individual actors develop conceptions of themselves on the basis of their **interactions** with others. This gives meaning to the behavior of individuals and places their actions and behavior in the context of their understanding of the world. **Culture**, sex, **age**, and other elements of **identity** all shape self-conception, of course, but the interactionists give particular emphasis to the meanings which the individual places on various occurrences and interactions. Labeling theory is drawn from this, but focuses on the impact of being labeled in a particular way on behavior.

Early 1930s work on juvenile **gangs** led sociological writers to recognize that the official label of "deviant" had potentially negative effects on the young people concerned. In the 1950s, **Edwin Lemert** in *Social Pathology* (1951) refined the thinking by distinguishing between primary and secondary deviation. While primary deviance might be a temporary aberration, secondary deviance was created as a reaction to the reaction of others to the initial deviance. But labeling theory is most strongly associated with **Howard S. Becker** in his *Outsiders: Studies in the Sociology of Deviance* (1963). His perspective on labeling revolved around the social reactions of a **group** rather than individual reactions. In a series of studies he described the processes of *becoming* a prostitute or a marijuana smoker and so on. In each case, it was the stigma attached to the label that was critical in shaping future behavior. Thus the labeling processes created "outsiders" and a self-fulfilling prophecy ensued. The processes of criminal justice are thus perceived to be instrumental in making matters worse.

By focusing on definitional issues, labeling theory has injected important critical thinking into criminological theorizing. It has revealed how the concepts of **crime** and deviance are not universally agreed but socially constructed. But labeling theory itself has attracted criticism for being ahistorical, astructural, and atheoretical. First, it is argued that labeling fails to explain why some behaviors are labeled as deviant in the first place; second, it is suggested that labeling theory gives too little attention to the concept and exercise of **power**; and third, it is thought that labeling theory is hard to test empirically. More pointedly, it is thought that the key question of whose interests are being protected in the labeling of some people's behavior and actions as "deviant" has been neglected. Other criticisms relate to the neglect of the victim in the analysis.

Despite criticisms, labeling theory has had far-reaching effects in sociological thinking that go well beyond the sociology of deviance; for instance, labeling theory has been applied to **witchcraft** and mental **health**.
                                            LORAINE GELSTHORPE

labor

This concept has several standard referents in sociology, covering specific forms of paid employment (such as manual labor); generic features of such employment, often conceived as one pole of a relationship between labor and capital; the differentiation and relationships between the whole range of different sorts of paid work (representing the division of labor); and the collective organization of workers in a **labor movement** or party. All these concepts were formulated in the specific context of the development of **capitalism** and its associated forms of waged employment, and analyses using these concepts are particularly associated with theoretical traditions (both Marxist and non-Marxist) that have addressed the character and dynamics of social class relations in industrial capitalism.

However, analyses of labor have moved beyond these core debates about capitalist industrialism in several ways. First, "free" wage labor has been compared with forms of unfree labor (such as **slavery** and bonded labor), both outside and within capitalism, as in R. Miles's *Capitalism and Unfree Labour* (1987). Second, analyses of the social division of labor and specific forms of labor have been extended beyond the formal sphere of paid work to include work in the household (that is, domestic labor), and voluntary and **informal economies**, as in C. Tilly and C. Tilly's *Work Under Capitalism* (1998). Finally, there has been attention to expanding forms of paid work in **postindustrial societies**, such as knowledge work, insecure employment, and emotional labor, and the extent to which they can be analyzed within a labor **paradigm**.

First, then, labor usually refers both to paid work and to those who do that work, as one side of the relationship between labor and capital or employees and employers. This relationship is central to arguments about the fundamental features of waged employment (see **work and employment**) and hence the organization of work and **industrial relations** in capitalist **societies**. Such features are addressed in different conceptualizations of the **labor market**, the labor contract, and the **labor process** in such societies, and link directly with debates about changing social class structures and forms of class mobilization. The growth of labor markets, in which workers become available for hire to work for specified periods for a wage, sets capitalism apart from earlier societies. However, the implications of this development for relations between employers and workers are contentious: some economic accounts treat such markets as the guarantors of equivalent choices and reciprocity between employers and workers, while most sociological accounts emphasize that **inequalities** of **power** are intrinsic to the labor market and to social relations between employees and employers within the capitalist labor process.

At the nexus of the relationship between the labor market and the labor process is the labor contract, which in formal legal terms summarizes the exchange between employer and employee, specifying such matters as job title, hours, and payment. Different and changing legal frameworks have defined the form, scope, and detail of such contracts in very varied ways. But a fundamental argument of many sociological analyses of labor is that any such summary is necessarily incomplete, with important implications for the character of employment relations. Sometimes this argument rests on the claim that all market exchanges depend upon more than the stipulated terms and conditions of exchange, because they rely on wider institutional and normative frameworks which are often taken for granted and would be impossible to specify completely. This theme relates to **Émile Durkheim**'s notion of the "noncontractual elements in contract" in which informal assumptions and agreements are seen to be a necessary precondition of formal contracts and agreements.

More crucially, however, it rests on the claim that the labor contract is quite distinctive in ways that set it apart from the purchase and sale of other commodities, for two related reasons. First, workers do not sell their labor and depart, but have to perform their work through their working hours; thus what they sell is their own capacity to labor, what **Karl Marx** termed the purchase and sale of their labor power. Second, the demands that employers make of their workers are not fixed, but flow from the changing circumstances of their business, as they exercise "management prerogatives" to reconfigure the duties workers perform while at work.

This conception of the open-endedness of the labor contract is central to Marxist accounts of the relationship between labor and capital, setting the scene for an analysis of the changes and conflicts that arise as capitalists seek to impose the requirements of capital accumulation upon workers, and workers experience and oppose the damage this inflicts upon them. However, it has a more general relevance across a spectrum of social science analyses of employment and industrial relations. It excludes those economists who argue that the equivalence of the labor market transaction persistently guarantees reciprocity between employers and workers, and those sociologists who abstract from the labor contract and employment relations in their study of other aspects of work and **occupations**. But it defines common ground between many other Marxist and non-Marxist materialist and institutionalist approaches, all of which attend to the power relations and social processes implicated in filling out the labor contract, as P. K. Edwards shows in *Conflict at Work* (1986). Where these positions differ markedly is in their specification of the character and extent of the uncertainties and conflicts that arise around the performance of paid work, and in their analyses of the ways in which, and the extent to which, such uncertainties and conflicts are successfully managed or negotiated. Indeed, some of these approaches (such as industrial relations pluralism) devote relatively little attention to analyzing underlying sources of uncertainty and conflict, but concentrate on the processes through which empirically identified contention in the workplace is managed.

One way in which these disagreements can be illuminated is by considering the ways in which work processes within capitalist **firms** are structured and restructured over time, through analyses of **management**'s organization of the labor process and labor discipline within the workplace. One example is Marx's analysis of the effective subordination of workers and work processes to the requirements of surplus extraction and capital accumulation. However, during the twentieth century, other sociological traditions – such as those which focus on the institutionalization of formal **rationality** in **bureaucracies** or those that see organizational arrangements as heavily influenced by the **technology** required for particular work processes – have provided alternative bases for analyzing the imperatives governing the organization of the labor process in capitalist (and sometimes noncapitalist) societies. In turn this has prompted extensive debate on the changing character of management strategies and worker responses in the organization of the labor process.

These debates have important implications for analyses of the division of labor. From Adam Smith (1723–90) onward, commentaries have distinguished between the social division of labor in the **economy** as a whole and the *technical* (or, to avoid implicit technical determinism, the organizational) division of labor in the enterprise and workplace. The former is portrayed as directly subject to the vagaries of market relations, with the growth and decline of demand for different types of product and associated occupations. The latter is seen as only indirectly subject to market relations but directly subject to management prerogatives and strategies.

Labor process debates have focused primarily upon analyses of the organizational division of labor. In particular, they have debated the extent to which management strategies have forged relatively homogeneous or heterogeneous workforces in terms of skills, autonomies, and job security. There has also been substantial disagreement about how any heterogeneity is to be conceptualized, in terms of stable hierarchies, or patterns of polarization, or as a shifting kaleidoscope of forms of labor. For example, it has been argued that an important feature of the capitalist transformation of the labor process has been an increasing separation of manual and mental labor, in which

mental labor conceptualizes and plans work tasks while manual labor performs those tasks. However, it has also been recognized that the extent of such separation, how far it might constitute a basis for hierarchy or polarization in the organizational division of labor, and its implications for wider processes of class formation and conflict, have been varied rather than uniform, while explanations of these outcomes remain controversial.

Indeed, some accounts of emergent forms of employment have suggested that networked, rather than hierarchical, relations within organizations and the growth of high-discretion knowledge work have so changed work and employment relations that all analyses using the conceptual apparatus outlined above have lost their relevance. However, the extent and character of these transformations have been strongly contested by commentators who have sought to demonstrate the continuing salience of these analytical approaches for contemporary forms of work and employment, as in the work of H. Beynon and his colleagues on *Managing Employment Change* (2002). Such controversies relate not only to **explanations** of key features of the division of labor but also to diagnoses of the possibilities and conditions for ameliorating, transforming, or abolishing those features.

Sometimes accounts of the organizational division of labor within enterprises have been set in a wider context, of the changing relations between enterprises and sectors, to address the social processes that constitute the wider social division of labor, as in A. Sayer and R. Walker's *The New Social Economy* (1992). This involves analyses of: (1) the ways in which management strategies in recruiting and organizing labor in different enterprises contribute to the structuring of wider labor markets, at a variety of spatial scales from localities to national economies and beyond; (2) the implications of major sectoral shifts, from agriculture to manufacturing to service employment, and also between small-firm, large-firm, and state employment; (3) the changing relationships between enterprises and workplaces, mediated not only through competitive market relations but also through alliances, **networks**, and production chains. All these aspects of the analysis of the social division of labor can be seen, for example, in debates over the new international division of labor, the proposition that leading enterprises in advanced capitalist societies have sought to relocate labor-intensive production processes to developing societies characterized by low labor costs and poorly organized workers, while retaining knowledge-intensive activities at home. The ensuing debate, outlined in R. Munck's

Globalisation and Labour (2002), explored different ways in which such changes were organized, sometimes coordinated within **transnational corporations** but also mediated through production chains involving hierarchies of enterprises. It also emphasized that corporate policies were often contradictory, and that the outcome was usually more complex than a stable polarization of production activities and forms of employment between advanced and developing capitalisms.

Such analyses of the dynamics of the social division of labor have primarily been developed in interdisciplinary research, though with significant contributions from economic sociology. More specifically, sociological commentary has focused on the consequences of the organizational and social division of labor for patterns of social consciousness, **solidarity**, and conflict. Here intellectual influences range from neo-Marxist and neo-Weberian explorations of the scope and limits of the formation of wider class solidarities from the varied experiences of wage labor, to symbolic interactionist and social constructionist analyses of the negotiation of occupational **identities**, boundaries, solidarities, and rivalries. However, there has been little recent reference to the more ambitious but problematical Durkheimian program which explored the occupational bases and limitations of modern forms of social solidarity.

Meanwhile, one major sociological critique of conventional analyses of the social division of labor grew out of feminist analyses of the sexual division of labor. These analyses problematized biological accounts of the gendered division between male workers in paid employment in the **public sphere** and women engaged in unwaged household and caring work. At the same time, they emphasized the significance of the latter forms of work in terms of time, tasks, and consequences for societal reproduction. This was conceptualized in terms of domestic labor to emphasize the parallels and linkages between work in paid employment and unpaid work in the household, but also involved discussion of the distinctiveness of the power relations and patterns of work characteristic of gender relations in households and **families**, often conceptualized in terms of **patriarchy**. In turn, and in the context of a major change in women's involvement in paid employment, this has prompted analyses of the ways in which gender, and in related ways **ethnicity**, have been constitutive features in the restructuring and hierarchization of *both* paid labor and unpaid work. To address these features, M. Glucksmann has developed the concept of the total social organization of labor, in "Why 'Work?'"

(1995) in *Gender, Work and Organisation*, to analyze the varied and changing patterns of articulation and dislocation between different forms of paid, unpaid, voluntary, and forced labor over time and across different social scales.   TONY ELGER

labor, social division of
– see **labor**.

labor aristocracy
– see **social class**.

labor-market segmentation
– see **labor market**.

labor markets
These involve the purchase and sale of a peculiar commodity, as what is bought and sold is actually the capacity of a worker to perform paid work, and the exercise of that capacity is not separated from workers but depends on their conduct at work. The supply of such capacities is influenced by wider institutional arrangements (for example welfare policies, family structures, or professional associations). Similarly, demand is influenced by employment relations within workplaces (for example strategies for securing worker compliance, training arrangements, and negotiations with workers).

From this vantage point, labor markets represent an appropriate focus for sociological research. Often, however, they are seen as the specialist preserve of economists, while sociologists focus on social relations within the workplace and treat labor markets as exogenous variables. This leaves unchallenged the dominant economic treatment of the labor market as a competitive arena in which employers and workers freely exercise choices according to their talents and preferences. This neoclassical model views the labor market as a mechanism which, unimpeded, will generate both reciprocity between buyers and sellers of labor and an efficient allocation of labor to different activities. Thus social **institutions** that influence the supply of or demand for labor are treated as exogenous givens or as distortions that should be removed to allow the market to perform its proper role. In response, some sociological approaches to labor market analysis seek to marry sociological analyses of **values** and institutions to existing economic models, but others challenge such economic models more directly.

Historical sociologists have analyzed the historical conditions in which extensive labor markets were formed, while also insisting that labor market mechanisms necessarily remain embedded in and conditioned by wider forms of social regulation. However, more specific challenges to neoclassical economic models of labor markets were developed from the late 1960s, initially by institutionalist and neo-Marxist economists critical of the mainstream but then taken up by other social scientists. J. Peck, in *Work-Place: The Social Regulation of Labor Markets* (1996), identifies several phases in the development of this alternative analysis. The first phase, concerned especially with the experience of advantaged workers, developed a dual labor market model. The primary labor market involved internal job ladders, usually within large **organizations**, with access to many jobs governed by internal administrative rules and bargains. The secondary labor market remained outside the **firm**, offering access to insecure jobs with little scope for progression. This model emphasized the role of **management** in structuring the demand for labor: technical imperatives encouraged managers to retain those workers trained within the firm, who might be tempted to move elsewhere, while those who were deemed unsuitable for training were consigned to the insecure periphery.

The next development also addressed the institutional logic of the demand for labor, but within a wider historical framework. This suggested that multiple labor market segments arose from the efforts of capitalist managers to divide and rule the workforce, as recruitment was structured in terms of occupational, gender, and ethnic divisions. Such accounts sought to integrate segmented labor market models into a historical analysis of changing "social structures of accumulation." This represented a more radical repudiation of orthodox economics, but left considerable scope for arguments about the coherence and consequences of such segmentation.

These early analyses were primarily attempts by American scholars to explain and critique entrenched ethnic and gender **inequalities**. The next phase was primarily European and particularly influenced by feminist accounts of gender inequalities in employment. This drew upon the earlier work on the social organization of the demand for labor by management, but noted that organized workers could also influence this process. More distinctively, it was emphasized that such accounts must be complemented by analyses of the social organization of the supply of labor. Labor supply was influenced by existing institutionalized patterns of labor demand, but also by developments in state policies (involving training, welfare, or **industrial relations**) and relatively autonomous features of the social organization of gender relations and households. These arguments prompted particular attention to the ways in which labor market segmentation took distinctive forms within specific local and national contexts, linking to wider debates on varieties of capitalism and changing structures of opportunity and inequality across societies, as in J. Rubery and D. Grimshaw's *The Organization of Employment* (2003).

Early segmented labor market models were primarily designed to understand enduring divisions and inequalities in the labor market. However, recent analyses have also addressed changing forms of labor market segmentation, especially as employers and state policymakers embraced policies of deregulation and flexibilization of labor markets, but also as "equal opportunity" policies opened possibilities to widen access to internal job ladders. In the late 1980s, the "flexible firm" model provided one influential account of the dynamics of such labor market change. It recommended the strategic construction of a dual labor market: employers would gain labor flexibility by constructing multifunctional teams (rather than job ladders) for "core workers" and extending various forms of disposability (such as part-time, temporary, or agency work) among "peripheral workers."

However, this prescriptive model faced powerful theoretical and empirical critiques, especially from A. Pollert in "The 'Flexible Firm': Fixation or Fact?" (1988) in *Work, Employment and Society*. First, there were important continuities in the institutional structuring of labor market inequalities, while management policies often remained reactive rather than strategic. Second, contemporary developments were poorly captured by the contrast between secure "core" and insecure "peripheral" workforces. Some core workers were becoming increasingly insecure, while the periphery included employees with very different labor market prospects (from well-paid, self-employed "consultants" to day laborers in the shadow economy). Current segmented labor market analyses of the growth of different forms of "nonstandard" employment have built on these criticisms. In these accounts, the boundaries and internal composition of existing labor market segments may be reconstructed by new state and management policies, but such policies remain characterized by unresolved tensions, while the outcomes are also influenced by wider institutional arrangements and social settlements, as shown in A. Felstead and N. Jewson (eds.), *Global Trends in Flexible Labour* (1999).

TONY ELGER

labor movement

This refers to a major type of **social movement,** traditionally addressing socioeconomic **inequality** by means of its members' engagement in **collective action** to improve the living and working conditions of its constituency. Historically, the phenomenon emerged with western industrialization (see **industrial society**), but its structure, functions, and **ideologies** have changed with the arrival of **postindustrial society**. Aside from the United States, most advanced industrial countries have well-institutionalized national union federations, and labor or socialist parties. Industrialization, however, is not a sufficient condition for the emergence of labor movements, as the national histories of developing and export-intensive **economies** in the twentieth century show.

Before the rise of the labor movement, workers' actions and industrial conflict mostly took the form of disputes about pay and working-conditions, with contenders asking fellow workers from other craft shops to join, while awaiting the outcome of negotiations between strike leaders and trade masters. Nowadays, the labor movement manifests itself in its bargaining agents' negotiations, through formal **organizations**, with employer, and often state, representatives. The labor movement has long been studied as a central force of welfare state expansion; post-World War II economic growth is interpreted as conditional upon deals between business, government, and labor. Social policy programs decrease the economic vulnerability of the workforce and stimulate a sense of social responsibility and **solidarity** among workers. Generous **welfare states** raise wage floors and increase labor costs, which, in the era of economic **globalization**, together with complex labor regulation, has been taken by capitalists as a prime argument to relocate production to low-wage and low-regulation economies. Welfare state policies have also brought about new organized constituencies, often autonomous from the labor movement and thus having the perverse effect of weakening the labor movement.

Trade unions represent the traditional core of the labor movement, with collective bargaining as their most routinized function, and strikes (see **industrial relations**) and demonstrations as their preeminent political tactics. First emerging in England in the early nineteenth century, their efforts to create alliances across trades soon became part of a greater political landscape. The national and international labor movement came to involve participation from **political parties** as well as **voluntary associations** concerned with workers' **rights**, and these became integral, and often respectable, elements in the industrial relations systems of the nation-states where they emerged.

De-unionization is often used as a shorthand for the erosion or disappearance of the labor movement as a consequence of the shrinking of the working class (both in terms of new recruitment and retention) and of changes in identity, class consciousness, and **ideology**. Recent studies of specific industries, for example by Beverly Silver in *Forces of Labor* (2003), show that patterns of labor unrest shift together with geographic changes in production locations around the globe, and thus collective labor interest reemerges in relocated as well as wholly new industries. Labor movements in some parts of the world have become part of anti-globalization movements, and their international strength much depends on how they navigate the North–South divide, particularly as to their role in industrial protectionism, and the extent to which labor interest can form coalitions with other interest-group-based movements.   ANN VOGEL

labor process

This process occurs when labor power is expended to produce goods and services. Many scholars investigate the labor process mainly in terms of its technical dimensions but explicit concern with its organization in different sites and at different scales is largely associated with studies inspired by **Marxism.** There is also significant feminist work on the gendered dimensions of the labor process and more general work on its broader social and cultural dimensions.

The labor process involves both a technical division of labor (see **labor**) and a social division of labor. A complete account should consider the articulation of both aspects in specific contexts. The technical division of labor concerns the relation among direct laborers (those who are directly engaged in appropriating and transforming nature), the instruments of production (such as tools and machines), and the matter (raw materials or intermediate products) on which they work – all considered from the viewpoint of specific embodied skills and specific products. It can be studied at particular sites (for example individual plants, offices, shops, or universities) or for particular commodity chains (the entire labor process for a given product from the initial appropriation of nature through to its final **consumption**). The production of services (for example live performances, sexual services, pedagogy, emotional labor) also has a technical division of labor, even if there is no enduring material product. The social division of labor concerns control over the allocation of labor power within the labor process, over the organization of the labor process, over decisions about what to produce, and over the allocation of any surplus production beyond what is required to renew labor power, instruments of production, and inputs. This raises issues of social domination, class exploitation, and aspects of the labor process that are not directly or primarily grounded in technical aspects of production.

Analyses of the labor process in the modern world are often restricted to commodity production in a profit-oriented, market-mediated process of economic organization. But there are also important studies of substantive provisioning outside the cash nexus, such as self-provisioning, unpaid domestic labor, or activities in the informal **economy**; and of the labor process in the state sector or precapitalist societies. Some argue that only free market competition ensures an efficient technical division of labor and rational allocation of scarce resources to competing ends. Others dispute this. There are also major debates on the normative dimensions of production.

Karl Marx analyzed the articulation of the technical and social divisions of labor and argued that this impelled the continual reorganization of the labor process. He shows how capital, driven to incessant innovation as the condition for its own existence in competitive **markets**, transforms **technology** and the technical division of labor. Marx's key innovation here is the distinction between labor and labor power. Labor occurs when the laborer expends energy in production; *labor power* is the laborer's capacity to labor. Marx argues that capitalists purchase labor power and must then mobilize this potential to ensure that value is added in production. In doing so they are subject to the pressures of capitalist competition. Marx distinguished analytically between two forms of such mobilization: (1) extending working hours and/or increasing the physical intensity of labor – this increases output based on "absolute surplus value"; and (2) enhancing labor power's productivity by reorganizing the labor process so that less time is needed for a given commodity – resulting in relative surplus value. Capitalists compete to reduce the socially necessary labor time involved in commodity production and thereby gain extra profits relative to their rivals – but, as new ways of organizing the labor process

become generalized, these extra profits are competed away. This creates permanent pressure to reorganize the labor process, putting capitalists and workers alike on an apparently unstoppable treadmill. Whereas the younger Marx studied the capitalist labor process in terms of **alienation** and dehumanization, the later Marx did so in terms of exploitation and capitalist laws of motion. One feature of the labor process relevant to both approaches is the separation between manual and mental labor that occurs in capitalism, especially during the phase of machinofacture. Marx's analyses also provide a basis for studying class struggle, trade union organization, capitalist competition, and attempts to control the innovation process.

In addition to work on the generic features of the capitalist labor process, there are many studies on its different stages. These include the transition from manufacture based on the use of tools in simple or complex forms of cooperation (for example pin manufacture), through machinofacture (where the worker becomes an appendage to the machine), to new forms of knowledge-based (or postindustrial) production. There is also continuing interest in various labor-process **paradigms** (for example craft production, mass production, continuous flow production, diversified quality production, **flexible specialization**).

Marx rarely discusses what occurs once workers enter the workplace, apart from allusions to their subordination to the machine, "barrack-like discipline," and "factory codes." But industrial sociologists have made many studies of the labor process in fields such as mining, fishing, agriculture, automobile production, offices, schools, and so forth; they have also examined unskilled, semiskilled, skilled, supervisory, nonmanual, professional, and managerial labor. Recent work has also drawn on **Michel Foucault**'s analyses of disciplinary power: organizing individuals in **space**, organizing movement in **time**, and the training of aptitudes, for example in Richard Marsden, *The Nature of Capital: Marx After Foucault* (1999). There are a few studies on the labor process and the (de) formation of the **body**.

Marx also compared the labor process in class societies with the potentialities of work under **Communism**. Work would be freely undertaken rather than dictated by demands of nature (essential needs) or the logic of the market (profitability); skills would be acquired as a chosen prowess rather than tied to an assigned function in a rationalized division of labor oriented to a stipulated output;

and work **groups** would form voluntarily, based on intrinsic pleasure and **solidarity** rather than an external goal. Thus Marx argues in Volume I of *Capital* (1867) that, while Communism cannot abolish the need for humans' interaction with nature, it can bring that process under the **community**'s conscious control and deprive it of its independent, coercive force.   BOB JESSOP

labor process approach
– see **labor process**.

labor theory of value
– see **Karl Marx**.

Lacan, Jacques (1901–1981)
An influential interpreter of **Sigmund Freud**, Lacan had a major impact upon modern European thought and **social theory**. A highly unconventional psychoanalyst, he delivered a famed seminar at the École Normale Supérieure (formerly attended by philosophers such as **Michel Foucault**, **Roland Barthes**, and Jacques Derrida), as well as founding his own psychoanalytic organization, the École Freudienne de Paris. In addition to his work as a practicing psychoanalyst, Lacan wrote many papers on a range of theoretical issues.

He made two major contributions to the analysis of human subjectivity: first, in "The Mirror Stage as Formative of the Function of the I", which was published in *Écrits. A Selection* (1949 [trans. 1977]), he proposed the thesis of the self-deception of the ego by considering the infant identifying with a mirror image of a complete unified **body**. Following closely Freud's proposition that the ego is fundamentally narcissistic in character, Lacan focused on the notion of a "mirror stage" which, he argued, provided the subject with relief from the experience of fragmentation, by granting an illusory sense of bodily unity through its reflecting surface. Second, in "The Agency of the Letter in the Unconscious, or Reason Since Freud" (1957), published in *Écrits*, he argued, drawing upon structural linguistics, that the construction of the unconscious, and hence by implication **culture** and society, is dominated by the primacy of **language**. The signifier represents the subject for Lacan; the primacy of the signifier in the constitution of the subject indicates the rooting of the unconscious in language. In Lacan's infamous slogan, "The unconscious is structured like a language."

Along with *Écrits*, his principal works included *The Four Fundamental Concepts of Psychoanalysis* (1973 [trans. 1994]).   ANTHONY ELLIOTT

language
There are at present about, 6,000 languages in the world, 4,000 of which have been recorded or documented. Present estimates suggest that 96 percent of these languages are spoken by a mere 4 percent of the world's population, and that half of them will become extinct within the next century. Underlying causes for these accelerating extinctions include ecological collapse, military conflict, and political, social, and economic hegemonic **influence**, whether deliberately wielded or not.

Despite the obvious significance of language as a basis of social **identity** and **culture**, the topic has not received much attention from sociologists. **Karl Marx** in the *Economic and Philosophical Manuscripts* (1844 [trans. 1964]) observed that language was a form of what he termed "practical consciousness." Fifty years later, **Émile Durkheim** declared it to be an exemplary instance of what he called "social facts" and took an interest in its role in systems of social classification. Subsequently, **George Herbert Mead** identified language as the crucial means by which persons can "take the role of the other" and thereby become objects to themselves, an insight which was foundational for **symbolic interactionism**. Finally, the notion of **habitus** popularized by **Pierre Bourdieu** serves as a valuable conceptualization of the ingrained skills and practices associated with language use and identity and their resistance to change. These contributions notwithstanding, the theoretical invocation of language within **sociology** has tended to be holistic and underspecified, and, perhaps because the sociologists of the early twentieth century stressed the significance of acculturation and **assimilation**, while the anthropologists of the same period celebrated linguistic, cultural, and ethnic diversity, interest in language has comparatively shallow roots within the discipline.

The sociological study of language has thus remained somewhat sequestered from mainstream sociology. In keeping with the perspective sponsored by Durkheim, it focuses on the ways in which language serves as a bridge between individual identities and the social **group(s)** to which persons belong. Its primary interests have centered, at the macro-level, on the relationship between language and identity in the context of **race and ethnicity** and the nation-state, and, at the middle-range level, on the ways in which **social** class, community, and gender function as causes and consequences of sociolinguistic variation.

At the most macro-level are studies of language shift and maintenance. A number of conditions have been identified as creating the potential for language shift. An essential precondition is bilingualism. A monolingual society will remain monolingual (though its language may evolve over time), until the arrival of an additional language that can influence the economic or power balance among language users. Migration, industrialization, urbanization, government sponsorship of particular languages in schools and elsewhere, and the relative prestige of different languages are all factors that impact language maintenance and shift. Perhaps the most important factor promoting language maintenance is linguistic nationalism, defined by Joshua Fishman, for example, in the Handbook of Language and Ethnic Identity (1999) as the values, attitudes, and behavior of societies acting on behalf of their explicitly stated ethnocultural self interest. Linguistic nationalism involves political organization, language policies that promote chosen vernacular languages, and language codification (the creation, where necessary, of a written form of the language).

At the meso-level, sociolinguistics studies the relationship between language use and a wide variety of sociological variables. Emerging out of the study of dialect variation, contemporary sociolinguistics was born with William Labov's The Social Stratification of English in New York City (1967) which used random sampling of informants, tape-recorded data, and quantitative measurements of linguistic data to build a complex but orderly picture of language use. Subsequent research has shown the significance of geography, ethnicity, social networks, class, gender, and age in language variation. The reliability of linguistic markers of group membership means that, for other individuals, sociolinguistic variation can be a sensitive measure of the person's place in social space, and for sociologists it can be a subtle unobtrusive measure of a variety of social indicators.

In the end, sociolinguistics as a field is underwritten by the fact that people speak the way they do because the people they identify with also speak that way. Practices of thinking, acting, and speaking using a particular language constitute a linguistic habitus for each person, and cannot easily be changed. Nonetheless, they are subject to maintenance or change through interpersonal processes. Social psychological research by Howard Giles and others suggests that persons adapt their use of fundamental components of dialect – vocabulary, grammatical choices, and pronunciation – so as to converge or diverge from their interlocutors. Convergence in any or all of these may occur when a speaker is conversing with a person of higher social status, or from the same geographical area, or simply a person who is likable. Conversely, a speaker may accentuate dialectal divergences when speaking with a social inferior, or with a stranger, or with someone towards whom they entertain feelings of hostility. Accumulations of convergences and divergences can result in a change in habitus at the individual level, and language change at the societal: the recent shift in the direction of so-called estuary English as a dominant dialect of the English spoken in the United Kingdom is a case in point.

Languages are not only methods of communication, but systems of classification and conceptualization. While the notion that language influences thought is an old one, it is most associated today with the anthropological linguists Edward Sapir (1884–1939) and Benjamin Lee Whorf (1897–1941). Their thesis, which was based on anthropological studies of the conceptualization of space, time, and matter among Hopi Indians, asserted that language determines our perceptions of the world. Different languages produce different conceptual maps of reality. The original formulations of the Sapir–Whorf hypothesis were dogged by circularity and by a lack of evidence for the cognitive side of the claim. Subsequent work during the 1960s on subjects' ability to discriminate colors and shapes gave modest but questionable support to their ideas. However, work by Stephen Levinson and others in the 1990s that examined the representation of space in language and cognition appears to give solid support to claims that, in the 1980s, were viewed as far-fetched and tendentious.

The most important sociological contribution to the study of language may yet turn out to come from new trends in conversational analysis and discourse analysis. These analytic streams insist on the idea that speaking is a form of social action and that it is subject to the normative constraints that shape and drive action. Since it is within interaction that language choices are made and modified, family-resemblance-based classificatory decisions are indexically attuned, linguistic and conceptual habitus are adjusted, and social solidarity is sustained or undermined, social action and interaction are surely the engine room of language maintenance and change. Moreover, this conceptualization of language as action may contribute to releasing studies of language from their traditional written language bias and open the way for a rapprochement between linguistics and the **social sciences** which is long overdue.　　JOHN HERITAGE

language games

Developed by **Ludwig Wittgenstein** in his *Philosophical Investigations* (1953) to focus attention on language use and its social context, the concept was a useful means with which to repudiate the exclusive focus on the representational functions of **language** which dominated his early philosophy. In place of this focus, the language game concept invited attention to the immense variety of uses to which language is put: for example giving and obeying orders; describing the appearance of an object; reporting an event; telling a story or a joke; asking questions; greeting someone; praying, and so on. In his discussion of these uses of language, Wittgenstein stressed both that language games are interwoven with ordinary aspects of **everyday life**, and that understanding the meaning of utterances involves knowing the nature of the activity in which the utterances play a role. He also observed that language games are malleable: new language games are invented and others become obsolete. Part of this malleability arises because the meanings of words, **symbols**, sentences, and utterances are lodged, through use, in networks of similarity and dissimilarity which lack an essence.

Although the notion of language game is not much employed today, it has been a fecund influence on contemporary linguistic semantics and pragmatics, and has important implications for computational models of language. Within sociology, the concept had a potent influence on **Harold Garfinkel**'s **ethnomethodology** and continues to influence a wide range of sociological and cultural analyses of language use.　　JOHN HERITAGE

language rights

– see **rights**.

Laslett, Peter (1915–2001)

A historian and sociologist, who also worked in political philosophy and on the history of social and political thought, Laslett was elected in 1948 to a fellowship at Cambridge and began his pathbreaking research on the social and political upheavals of seventeenth-century England. He went on to edit and provide a new critical commentary on the work of Robert Filmer (1588–1653) and John Locke (1632–1704).

As a result of his engagement with Locke's writings on the nature of **power** within the **family**, he moved towards demographic historiography and during the 1960s cofounded the Cambridge Group for the History of Population and Social Structure with E. A. Wrigley. His work questioned assumptions concerning the nature of the family and household in early modern western Europe. In *The World We Have Lost* (1965), basing his evidence on local historical documents, he argued against the widely held view that three-generation stem families predominated in preindustrial England, and that the small nuclear family was a product of industrialization. For Laslett, preindustrial families were also predominantly nuclear, and were in addition highly mobile; resident unmarried servants were the only non-nuclear element within them.

In the 1980s he became interested in the aging process, which he discussed in *A Fresh Map of Life* (1989). As well as his work on social and political demographic history and political philosophy, he was interested in opening up academic life to a wider audience, and with **Michael Young** he cofounded the Open University.　　STEVEN LOYAL

Latino/a studies

Despite their long presence in the United States, and being the nation's second largest minority group in the 1960s, relatively little was known about Latinos at that time. In many ways, Latinos were strangers in the United States. However, **social movements** of the civil rights era (1954–68) called attention to the plight of Latinos in the United States, particularly that of Chicanos and Puerto Ricans, the largest Latino subgroups, both of which were incorporated into the United States through conquest. During the 1960s and early 1970s, these social movements would be instrumental in the development of academic programs and advocacy **organizations** within the Chicano and Puerto Rican **communities**. The roots of Latino/a studies can be traced to this period.

This entry provides an overview of the development of Latino/a studies with particular attention to the institutional arrangements, curriculum, research, professional associations, and publication outlets related to the study of Latinos. To understand the development of Latino/a studies, we turn to a historical discussion of its beginnings.

During the period surrounding the civil rights era, Chicanos and Puerto Ricans protested against **discrimination** and **racism**, and demanded **equality** and dignity. Because Latinos lacked easy entrance to higher education, affirmative action programs helped them gain a modest degree of access to colleges and universities. On their respective campuses, Latino students found few Latinos as students and, especially, as faculty. Further, they often found academic climates devoid of attention to the social and intellectual needs of Latinos. In a number of campuses in the southwest and northeast, Latino students pressed for the recruitment of Latino students and faculty and for the creation of Chicano studies and Puertoriqueño/Boricua studies, respectively. The formation of these programs represents the roots of Latino/a studies.

Latino sociologists played an important role in the establishment of institutions that focus on issues central to the Latino/a population within and outside academia. We highlight here two key sociologists who trained Latino/a students and developed organizations that advocated for the Latino/a population. Julian Samora, who received his PhD in 1953 from Washington University, is recognized as the first Chicano to earn a doctoral degree in sociology and anthropology, as noted in *The Julian Samora Virtual Collection* maintained by the Julian Samora Research Institute (2005). Samora, who died in 1996, mentored approximately fifty-five Chicano graduate students at the University of Notre Dame before he retired in 1985. He also had a major impact in the development of important Latino organizations outside academia. For example, he was one of the three cofounders of the National Council of La Raza (NCLR) and was instrumental in the formation of the Mexican American Legal Defense and Educational Fund (MALDEF).

While Samora is a pioneer in the Chicano community, his colleague, Frank Bonilla, played an equally important role in the training of Puerto Ricans and in building advocacy groups to promote the Puerto Rican cause. A detailed account of Bonilla can be found in an article entitled "From the 'Bulge' to the Halls of Academia: Frank Bonilla's Hunger for Education Opened His Eyes to the World," published in *Narratives* (2004). Bonilla received his PhD in sociology from Harvard University in 1959. He was instrumental in the formation of the Puerto Rican Hispanic Leadership Forum which would eventually become Aspira, an organization focusing on the educational needs of Puerto Rican **youth**. After stints as a researcher in Latin America and a professor in the United States, Bonilla took a faculty position in 1973 at the City University of New York (CUNY) where he became the Director of CUNY's Center for Puerto Rican studies. The scholarship

and activism of Samora and Bonilla embody the mission of the Latino/a studies programs that emerged in the late 1960s and 1970s and serve as a legacy for many Latino scholars today.

The early Chicano studies and Puertoriqueño/Boricua studies programs originating in the late 1960s and early 1970s had broad missions that were student- and community-oriented. For example, these programs emphasized the institutionalization of courses and a curriculum for students interested in Latino/a studies. Additionally, the programs helped in the recruitment and retention of Latino students through both their outreach efforts and the provision of social, academic, and cultural services, which emphasized **social change** and the betterment of local Latino communities. Finally, a distinct feature of Latino/a studies programs continues to be their interdisciplinary focus. Faculty members participating in such programs tend to be drawn from a broad array of social and behavioral sciences, and arts and humanities disciplines.

As the Latino population experienced greater diversity associated with immigration from the Caribbean, Central America, and South America, some programs have maintained their focus on the Chicano and Puerto Rican populations. However, many others have broadened their focus to encompass the greater Latino variation with the establishment of pan-ethnic Latino/a studies programs. The latter emphasize the linkages between Latinos in the United States and Latin Americans more generally, and they recognize the transnational and diaspora experience of Latinos and Latin Americans.

There are also variations in the academic focus of Latino/a studies programs (note that, for the sake of simplicity, we use the term "Latino/a studies" to encompass the diverse types of specific programs just outlined). One set of programs has continued to serve the primary mission of teaching and is located institutionally as independent academic departments or as programs within academic departments or colleges. In other cases, Latino centers and institutes have the primary mission of generating research on the Latino population. Finally, teaching and research related to Latinos takes place beyond the confines of Latino/a studies programs and Latino research centers and institutes, as courses are taught within sociology and related departments, and research on Latinos is conducted by researchers without affiliations to Latino research centers and institutes.

Themes such as "border" or "border-crossing" often emerge within course content of Latino/a studies. These themes are important reminders of the global and transnational, as well as the transformative, nature of Latino communities in the United States, Latin America, and the Caribbean. Further, these metaphors permit an analysis of the historical and contemporary relationship of Latino communities to the economic, political, and **social structures** of **inequality** in the United States. These structures are rooted in the social construction of **race and ethnicity**, **gender**, and **sexuality** and these constructs often serve as catalysts for social change.

The ability to understand race/ethnicity as a social construct is evoked in the introduction of the syllabi. Many Latino/a studies instructors recognize that while the term Latino/a connotes themes of similarity and shared interest across groups falling within this socially constructed label, these courses highlight differences that exist within and across demographic, historical, social, economic, and political domains. The diversity within, and multiple experiences of, the Latino community allow for a departure from strict disciplinary boundaries into interdisciplinary and multidisciplinary lenses, allowing the discussion of topics, such as **culture** or assimilation, to take place beyond the confines of a single discipline. This permits students to view "the Latino/a experience" as one that is diverse, complex, and dynamic, versus one that is narrow, monolithic, and static.

The American Sociological Association (ASA) has teaching and instructional materials geared to assisting faculty members who teach Latino courses. In its fifth edition, *Chicano/a and Latino/a Studies in Sociology: Syllabi and Instructional Materials*, by José Calderon and Gilda Ochoa (2003), is an important source for engaging faculty and students in the understanding of Latino/a studies. A sampling of topics covered in the syllabi comprising the sourcebook include "Introduction and Overview of Latino Population," "Mexicans: Immigration, Conquest, and Work," "Caribbean: Immigration, Colonialism, and Work," "Gender, Sexuality and Women's Studies," "Queer Identities in Contemporary Cultures," and "Institutions and Political Activism." As suggested by these topics, Latino/a studies courses expose students to **sociological theories** and analytical frameworks to understand the production, reproduction, and perpetuation of social inequalities that shape the **life chances** of Latinos.

Consistent with the social change theme of Latino studies, courses related to Latinos frequently require students to get involved in their local communities. For example, students in such courses tend to be involved in service learning, internships, and volunteer work. Such teaching approaches emphasize the intersection between theory and practice and attempt to enhance the academic experience by providing students with experiential training.

The major absence of Latino scholars prior to the 1970s is responsible for the dearth of research about Latinos before this time. Rogelio Saenz and Edward Murguia, in their article "The Latino Experience: Introduction, Context, and Overview" in *Sociological Focus* (2004), observe a steady increase in the amount of sociological research produced about Latinos from the early 1970s to the present. In their general assessment of research on Latinos, Saenz and Murguia highlight four areas that have generated a significant amount of research: gender, immigration, **education**, and **labor markets**.

One major source for the production of research on Latinos is the Inter-University Program for Latino Research (2005), or IUPLR, a consortium of eighteen Latino research centers based in major universities across the United States. Through our examination of research projects that are being conducted through these partnerships, based on information from the various websites, we find evidence of up to fifty research projects. This list is by no means an all-inclusive summary of research projects that are connected with the various research centers. Rather it is a brief overview from various sites, which allows us to assess the most common research areas focusing on Latinos.

We broadly classify the fifty research projects into the following categories: community development; cultural and literary studies; demographic trends; economic issues; education; ethnic relations; evaluation research; health and delivery services; history and political economy; identity politics; and immigration. Of these categories, education receives the most attention, constituting 20 percent of the total research projects, with health and delivery issues accounting for 18 percent, and art and **cultural studies** also receiving substantial attention. Many of these research projects evaluate current policy initiatives or programs but also encourage other scholars to generate more research. Much of the attention in the area of education is geared towards creating a new generation of educated Latinos. For example, one project assists students with college applications and another assists educators who work with Latino parents and their children. The most common research topics demonstrate the interdisciplinary and action-oriented nature of Latino studies.

The development of Latino/a studies has also assisted in the establishment of professional associations that have helped further develop this branch of inquiry. The oldest of these organizations is the National Association for Chicana and Chicano Studies (NACCS), originally established in 1972. Two decades later, the Puerto Rican Studies Association (PRSA) was established to focus on academic concerns related to Puerto Ricans. Moreover, Latino caucuses / special interest groups have been formed within larger disciplinary associations. For example, the Section on Latino Sociology within the ASA was formed in the early 1990s. More recently, in the mid-1990s, the Latino Studies Section of the Latin American Studies Association (LASA) was formed, illustrating the transnational and diaspora links between Latinos and Latin America.

While there have been various academic journals that originated in the late 1960s and early 1970s to disseminate research results on Latinos, currently there are a few journals that specialize in the reporting of evidence from sociological research investigations relating to Latino communities. These include *Aztlan*, *Hispanic Journal of Behavioral Sciences*, and *Journal of Latino and Latin American Studies*. Among the mainstream social science outlets, *Social Science Quarterly* is the undisputed leader in publishing research on Latinos. Of particular significance are the three special issues that the journal produced in 1973, 1984, and 2000. More recently, *Southern Rural Sociology* produced a special issue on "Latinos in the South" (2003) and *Sociological Focus* published a special issue on "The Latino Experience" (2004). This article traced the emergence of Latino/a studies during the late 1960s and 1970s.

Pioneering Latino scholars and students forged the development of institutional arrangements, curricula, research, professional associations, and publication outlets. Their efforts, combined with the growth of the Latino population, have contributed to the evolution and continued expansion of Latino/a studies and its contribution to sociology and wider social science disciplines.

ROGELIO SAENZ, MERCEDES RUBIO, AND
JANIE FILOTEO

Latour, Bruno (1947–)

Educated in philosophy and anthropology, Latour, Professor at the École des Mines in Paris, has been one of the most active contributors to the field of **science and technology studies**, which emerged in the 1970s as an alternative to more traditional approaches to the theory and philosophy of science. Latour has combined a playful, polemical tone with conceptual and methodological innovations, as he has sought to disclose the hidden realities of science in his *Laboratory Life* (1979), with Steve Woolgar.

Latour made seminal contributions to the social and cultural study both of science in *The Pasteurization of France* (1984 [trans. 1988]), most especially through his book *Science in Action* (1987) and of technology (among other places in his book *Aramis*, 1992). He is also well known for his critique of modernism in his *We have Never been Modern* (1993). Latour has characterized the contemporary world in terms of the "proliferation of hybrids" and has argued that nonhumans – both living and nonliving things – should be considered "actors" and be attributed agency by social scientists. His work is associated with **actor network theory**.

His writings have often been attacked by the defenders of traditional approaches to science, and he was one of the central protagonists in what came to be called the "science wars" of the 1990s, when the kind of science studies that Latour promoted were criticized by writers such as Paul Gross and Norman Levitt (in *Higher Superstition*, 1994).

ANDREW JAMISON

law and society

This phrase refers to an association of scholars, a journal of academic research, and a collection of empirical approaches to understanding how law works. As a multi-disciplinary **paradigm** within twentieth-century scholarship, law and society focuses on what legal **institutions** do rather than what they ought to do. In place of the normative and policy orientations of most jurisprudence, the law and society approach claims that law can be understood best empirically, as a social institution embedded within and connected to all other social institutions. Using what are believed to be the more reliable research practices of empirical social scientific inquiry, law and society scholarship moved beyond purely subjective interpretations and the doctrinal argumentation of traditional legal scholarship by systematically collecting **data** and developing empirically grounded theory; at the same time law-and-society scholarship offers critical judgment about legal practices because it is independent of the **authority** and interests of the legal **profession**.

In 1964, a group of sociologists, political scientists, psychologists, anthropologists, historians, and law professors formed the Law and Society Association; in 1967, they began publishing a research journal, the *Law and Society Review*; and following two national meetings in the 1970s, since 1979 they have been holding annual conferences for scholarly exchange and debate. In the early years, the association and the journal, as well as four research centers located on the campuses of the University of California at Berkeley, the University of Denver, Northwestern University, and the University of Wisconsin, were supported by generous grants from the Russell Sage Foundation, whose interest in **social policy** and change found a happy target in this nascent intellectual movement. Recognizing law as the central governing mechanism and language of the modern **state**, the foundation sought to explore ways in which the legal profession might, or might not, provide **leadership** for progressive **social change**. Drawing upon diverse historical sources, and the pioneering work of contemporaries such as **Philip Selznick** at Berkeley, Harry Kalven, Hans Zeisel, and Rita Simon at Chicago, and Willard Hurst at Wisconsin, the birth of the law-and-society group as a formal membership association signaled an organized, long-term commitment to interdisciplinary empirical work that would transcend the boundaries of distinct disciplinary fields and traditional legal scholarship. The Russell Sage Foundation, the Law and Society Association, and the *Law and Society Review* created a field in which "social science disciplines could be brought to bear on . . . law and legal institutions in a systematic manner." The Foundation was, as expressed by Christopher Tomlins in *Framing the Field of Law's Disciplinary Encounter* (2000), "both responding to and contributing to [a] moment of striking change" as epitomized by the civil rights, anti-war, and emergent women's and gay rights movements.

Because law is a system of both **symbols** and action, structured reason and regulated force, this social scientific study of law draws from diverse traditions that attend to both normative aspirations and social organization. Attention to the relationship between law and society, the role of reason, ideas of **justice**, and the regulation of force can be found in ancient and medieval works of philosophy from Plato (427–347 BC), through Thomas Hobbes (1588–1679) and John Locke (1632–1704), to **Baron Charles de Montesquieu**'s canonical work, *The Spirit of the Laws* (1748). These classical works display European philosophy's preoccupation with knowledge as a synthesis of universal, timeless truths. The cultural, social, and variable dimensions of law became more prominent in the nineteenth century, when jurisprudential thinkers, such as Friedrich Karl von Savigny

(1814–75), in Germany in 1831, described law as the slow, organic distillation of the spirit of a particular people, and when historians, such as Henry Maine (1822–88), in Britain in 1861, described the development of social relations over the millennia as a movement from status to contract.

At the beginning of the twentieth century, legal scholars in major North American and European institutions were devoting increasing attention to the sociological aspects of law. The Austrian scholar Eugen Ehrlich (1862–1922) in 1913 described what he called "the living law," the complex system of **norms** and rules by which the members of **organizations**, **communities**, and **societies** actually live. Formal law emanating from the state is dependent in large part, he argued, on its informal concordance with the living law. Judge and jurist Oliver Wendell Holmes, Jr. (1841–1935) perfectly expressed the movement towards a social understanding of law when he described the law as a grand anthropological document, writing in *The Common Law* (1881) that the life of the law is not logic but experience, a word he used for **culture**. Roscoe Pound (1870–1964), Dean of the Harvard Law School, pushed the sociological perspective yet further when, in 1910, he named the informal practices of legal institutions the "law-in-action," contrasting them with the "law-in-the-books," legal doctrines formally enacted and ideally in force. American legal realists, a collection of law professors and philosophers writing in the 1920s and 1930s, made the exploration of this gap between the formal law and the law-in-action the central focus of their research. Alongside their efforts to expose the illogic of ostensibly logical arguments, the legal realists began the work, taken up by the law and society movement three decades later, to describe the law-in-action.

By the end of World War II, the **social sciences** had developed empirical tools for data collection and analysis (for example **surveys** of legal use and need, statistical analysis of court records, interviews with jurors and judges) that moved the study of the law-in-action forward with energy and effectiveness. The social sciences had become a respectable third wing of higher education, finally standing abreast the historically more prestigious humanities and the more recently institutionalized sciences. From some perspectives, the social sciences, in adopting methods from the physical sciences, especially experimental techniques and quantitative methods of data analysis (see **quantitative data analysis**), had begun to pull ahead of the humanities as sources of reliable social knowledge.

Turning their gaze to legal processes and institutions, social scientists could also draw upon their own disciplinary traditions to authorize their research. The most important social theorists writing in the nineteenth and early twentieth centuries had already recognized law as a central means of rationalized coordination and regulation in modern societies no longer governed as tightly by custom and **religion**. Post-World War II social scientists were encouraged to look closely at how law accomplished this role as the general societal manager. In this work, they drew upon **Émile Durkheim**'s models of the different functions of law in societies with lesser or greater divisions of **labor** and sought evidence of varying degrees of repressive law or restitutive law in more or less industrialized societies. Following **Max Weber**, others described patterns of litigation and legal doctrine associated with different types of economic and cultural development.

In its more than thirty-five years of history, this interdisciplinary movement has produced a body of reliable knowledge about how the law works. Law-and-society research has discovered the role of law everywhere, not only in courtrooms, prisons, and law offices but also in hospitals, bedrooms, schoolrooms, in theatres, films, and novels, and certainly on the streets and in police stations and paddy wagons. At times, socio-legal scholarship, another term for law-and-society research, has also mapped the places where law ought to be but is not. In historical studies of litigation, policing, the legal profession and delivery of legal services, court cultures and judicial biographies, the effectiveness of legal regulation of workplace and business transactions; in reports on access to law and the structure of both professional and popular legal consciousness; and in histories of how particular legal doctrines and offices developed, law-and-society research demonstrates how organization, social **networks**, and local cultures shape law. This research has also demonstrated how law is recursively implicated in the construction of social worlds – of organizations, social networks, and local cultures – and thus contributes to both the distribution of social resources and the understandings of the world so constituted.

These accounts describe how in doing legal work, legal actors and officials respond to particular situations and demands for service rather than to general prescriptions or recipes provided by legal doctrine. Although law claims to operate through logic and formal **rationality**, it is no different from most other work and, thus, rather than following invariant general principles, proceeds on a case-by-case basis. This is evident in the production of law through litigation and in the creation of precedent through decisions in individual cases; it is true of law enforcement as well. Most participants, professional and lay, operate through reactive, situationally specific rationality. And even in instances of organized campaigns by civil rights organizations, **trade union**, or the women's movement for pay equity, legal strategies rely on the ability to aggregate the outcomes of individual cases. While they may not produce specifically material outcomes, they often achieve cultural, conceptual transformations as described in M. McCann's *Rights at Work* (1994).

Because legal action is not rule-bound but situationally responsive, it involves extralegal decisions and action; thus, all legal actors operate with discretion. Documenting the constraints and capacities of legal discretion has occupied these several generations of law-and-society scholars, whose research provides evidence about how discretion is invoked, confined, and yet ever-elastic. In exercising this inevitable discretion, legal actors respond to situations and cases on the basis of typifications developed not from criteria of law or policy alone but from the normal and recurrent features of social **interactions**. These folk categories are used to typify variations in social experiences in an office, agency, or professional workload and to channel appropriate or useful responses. These typifications function as conceptual efficiency devices.

By relying on ordinary logics, local cultural categories, and norms, legal action both reflects and reproduces other features and institutions of social life. On the one hand, as a tool for handling situations and solving problems, law is available at a cost, a cost distributed differentially according to **social class**, **social status**, and organizational position and capacity. On the other hand, law is not merely a resource or tool but a set of conceptual categories and schema that produce parts of the **language** and concepts people use for both constructing and interpreting social interactions and relationships. These ideological or interpretive aspects of law are also differentially distributed. The most well-cited piece of law and society research summarizes much of these findings by creating a model of the variable capacity of legal actors based on their status as one-time or repeat players in the legal system, concluding that despite ambitions for **equality** under law, "the 'haves' come out ahead," according to Marc Galanter in his "Why the 'Haves' Come Out Ahead" (*Law and*

Society Review, 1974). This observation does not undermine legality but has become part of the common understanding that helps to sustain the **power** and durability of law, just as the common knowledge of the limitations of legality serves to protect the law from more sustained critique.

In addition to developing a growing body of empirical knowledge about how law works, law and society has also been successful in institutionalizing its field of scholarship. Although the sociology of law in Europe remains a predominantly theoretical and normative enterprise, it is, nonetheless, a required subject for the education and training of European lawyers. In the United States, the original centers of law-and-society research in the law schools of Berkeley, Wisconsin, Denver, and Northwestern remain strong, with additional concentrations of law and society at the University of California at Los Angeles, at Irvine, and at Santa Barbara, the State University of New York at Buffalo, the University of Michigan, and New York University.

The influence of law-and-society research on legal agencies is probably much more significant. Most courts, agencies, and legal organizations collect **data** about their activities. Most recognize the role of non-legal factors in shaping their work and use social variables, among other indicators, to analyze and explain legal work. Law and society scholars regularly serve as expert witnesses in litigations on capital punishment, witness reliability, and gender and racial **discrimination**, among other topics. Newspapers also report the results of socio-legal research. Thus, alongside a picture of the law as a system of words and documents, law and society has succeeded in painting a picture of law as a social system, an understanding that has been documented in popular and professional consciousness.   SUSAN SILBEY

Lazarsfeld, Paul (1901–1976)

Born in Vienna, Paul Lazarsfeld received his PhD at the university there in 1925. He emigrated to the United States in 1933, became Director of the Bureau of Applied Research at Columbia University in 1940, and became a member of the Columbia faculty from 1949 to 1969. Lazarsfeld is best known for his contributions to **methodology**, political sociology, and mass communications research.

Lazarsfeld was a pioneer in the development of quantitative sociology, first through survey research and later through such sophisticated mathematical techniques as latent structure analysis. He helped change sociological research from the qualitative study of **communities** to the systematic, quantitative explanation of individual characteristics and outcomes. **Surveys** and other research techniques demonstrated that measurable variables could be causally linked with one another and explain the social influences on individual attitudes.

He utilized surveys in studies of voting behavior and audience research. In *The People's Choice* (1944), with Bernard Berelson and Hazel Gaudet, and *Personal Influence* (1955), with Elihu Katz, he developed the idea of the two step flow of communication. Though Lazarsfeld recognized that **mass media** were increasingly powerful in the modern world, he found that many people's choices, especially regarding **voting**, were influenced by the viewpoints of powerful individuals in their communities.

Through his directorship of the Bureau of Applied Research, Lazarsfeld helped to inaugurate university based large-scale sociological studies. His association with **Robert Merton** at Columbia contributed to a theoretically sophisticated, quantitative sociology that moved into the mainstream of the discipline.   KENNETH H. TUCKER

Le Bon, Gustave (1841–1931)

A physician and polymath whose writings ranged from studies of Arab and Indian **civilization** to treatises on photography and theoretical physics, Le Bon is best known today as the author of *The Crowd* (1895 [trans. 1896]) and as the founder of a school of **social psychology** that became linked to twentieth-century practices of propaganda and public relations. Born in Rogent-Le-Routrou, Le Bon studied medicine at the University of Paris and traveled in Europe, North Africa, and India before becoming Director of the French military ambulance division. Influenced by **Charles Darwin**, **Auguste Comte**, and **Herbert Spencer**, as well as by Johannson Herder and nineteenth-century race theory, Le Bon became interested in the part played by collective psychology in the character and development of different civilizations. For Le Bon, what united and distinguished a nation or "race" was not biological (since "today there are no pure races") but a shared depository of beliefs and sentiments, which he conceived as a pre-rational collective unconscious. Changes in ideas – "the only true revolutions" – involved ferment at that level. Hence, as he explained in *The Crowd*, the historical importance of crowds and crowd psychology. Le Bon had already laid the grounds for this analysis in *L'Homme et les sociétés* (1881) and *Les Lois psychologiques de l'évolution des peuples* (1884); he further developed it in *Les*

Opinions and les croyances (1910), *Psychologie politique* (1910), and *La Révolution Francaise et la psychologie des révolutions* (1912). Both with regard to peoples and crowds, a category that extended from street riots to legislative assemblies to the rising cultural weight of urban masses, Le Bon parallels **Émile Durkheim** in his stress on the emergent and irreducible properties of **groups**. He differed, however, in his insistence on the non-rational and unconscious elements of collective consciousness, and also in his recognition, which anticipated mass society theorists, that industrial **modernity** was an "era of crowds."

ANDREW WERNICK

Le Play, Pierre Guilliaume Frédéric (1806–1882)

The son of a customs officer from Normandy, Le Play was the founder of an influential school of empirical sociology. He had a multifaceted career and rose to become one of the most prominent figures in the France of Louis Napoléon (1808–73). Besides his voluminous sociological writings (many of which were field reports in connection with administrative assignments), he was a Professor of Metallurgy at the École des Mines from 1844 to 1856, a member of the 1848 provisional government, and in the Second Empire was appointed a Senator and Grand Commissioner of Expositions. Influenced by **Claude Henri de Rouvroy, Comte de Saint-Simon**, **Auguste Comte**, Charles Fourier (1772–1837) and Louis Gabriel de Bonald (1754–1840), and horrified by the violence of the 1830 revolution, Le Play campaigned for a social-science-based reform program that would promote social peace in a new class-divided and individualistic **industrial society**. The focus of much of his research was on the economic and social conditions of the working class **family**, particularly as affected by technological, economic, and geographic determinants. His method combined **fieldwork**, survey research, classification systems, and multi-sided studies of representative cases. To further his scientific work, in 1856 he established the Société d'Économie et de Science Sociale, and in 1871, to promote his schemes for inter-class **solidarity**, the journal *La Réforme*. Among his chief works were *Les Ouvriers européens* (1855), *La Réforme sociale en France* (1864), *L'Organisation de la famille* (1871), and *La Méthode de la Science Sociale* (1875).

ANDREW WERNICK

leadership

The notion of "leadership" arises as a necessary part of a relationship. The only bodies of thought that can deny the necessity of leadership are those that deny that individuals need to develop through relationships with one another.

The notion of leadership is taken for granted by preliberal thought since hierarchy is seen as natural and people are differentiated according to the roles they play. Rulers lead the ruled; men lead women; lords lead their serfs; citizens lead slaves; and so forth. The exercise of leadership is linked to factors that cannot be changed. Leadership is permanent and static – it is preordained. Leaders and followers cannot change places. Indeed, the very designation of the leadership role implies that it is irreversible. It sounds absurd to speak of slaves leading citizens since the very notion of a "slave" implies someone who follows. Once a leader, always a leader.

It is therefore historically valuable that these notions are challenged by **liberalism**. In the place of hierarchical relationships, there is abstract **equality**. Thus the liberal theory of representation argues that, when one person acts as the representative of another, he or she is acting on their behalf. The representative is authorized by those they represent, and therefore the relationship is not one of difference, but of sameness. The individual is re-presented at a "higher" level. No hierarchy is involved.

Hence liberalism places individuals outside relationships. Abstract **individualism** makes the notion of "leadership" theoretically impossible, and it is this abstract individualism that leads anarchists to argue that individuals can spontaneously govern themselves without organization or hierarchy. In fact, since people can identify themselves as individuals only through their relationships with others, real individuals are always in hierarchical attachments to others.

Postliberal or relational argument accepts leadership as inevitable, since what makes a relationship possible is that *on a particular issue* one person leads and the other follows. For this reason, relationships are necessarily hierarchical – two people can relate to one another only because they are both the same and different – and this difference must generate deference of some kind. But although postliberalism stresses the relational character of human activity, it differs from preliberal thought in that the notion of leadership as natural is tied to a concept of nature that is developmental and not static. It is natural for a parent to "lead" a three-year-old across a busy street; it would not be natural for a parent to lead a thirteen-year-old.

Moreover, leaders and followers continually change places. The doctor who "leads" a motor

331

mechanic on medical matters follows such a person when he or she wants a vehicle repaired. Leadership, conceived of in a postliberal manner, is always provisional and specific: a leader who is developmental in one area becomes oppressive when he or she seeks to guide in every issue. Leaders in a **democracy** dedicate themselves to enhancing and not diminishing the capacity of people to govern their own lives.   JOHN HOFFMAN

legal-rational authority
– see **authority**.

legitimacy
The **authority** of an **institution**, person, or practice to command obedience can derive from a sense of its rightfulness or legitimacy. People often go along with the commands of others, rules of law or **organization**, or taken-for-granted **norms** because of a sense of obligation or moral necessity rather than any immediate or general threat of coercion or promise of reward. Legitimacy, according to **Max Weber,** can derive from age-old norms (or **tradition**), from consciously enacted rules (such as law), or from a sense of devotion to an exceptional sanctity, heroism, or magical characteristic of an individual person (**charisma**). At their core, all forms of legitimacy provide an **explanation** for the social world as it is, or as it is hoped to be. This explanation or reason provides the meanings that ground **social action**, for the fortunate and unfortunate alike. According to Weber, human beings are prepared to tolerate extraordinary deprivation, suffering, and torment. What is unacceptable, however, to the unfortunate, is the meaninglessness of suffering, and to the fortunate the meaninglessness of life itself. "Legitimating explanations seek to justify the distribution of fortunes by showing that it conforms to a coherent normative conception of some sort, a conception which not only makes the differences in human fates intelligible but justifies them in an ethical sense as well" (Anthony Kronman, *Max Weber*, 1983). Thus, legitimations, whether from history, reason, or mysticism, offer accounts of social arrangements and events that make life meaningful and therefore tolerable.

Legitimacy attaches not merely to individual actions and relationships but to institutionalized systems of **power** and domination. If power consists of the probability that one actor within a social relationship will be in a position to achieve intended and foreseen effects (**Dennis Hume Wrong**, *Power*, 1969), authority rests on the belief in the rightfulness or legitimacy of that action. Although authority is only one form of power, it is the most stable and enduring according to Weber, because it requires fewer physical or economic resources to sustain. Obedience and deference to authority are secured by its legitimacy, deeply sedimented in social relations and beliefs, through the "internalization of symbolically represented structures of expectation" (**Jürgen Habermas**, *The Legitimation Crisis*, 1973 [trans. 1976]). In this sense, legitimacy is a question-begging avoidance technique that works only to the extent that it is unquestioned and unnoticed, that is, it constitutes a **hegemony.** Once questioned, the ability of legitimacy to secure obedience is threatened because the belief in a person, organization, or institution as legitimate derives from its being unquestionably right. Once the subject of ideological contest, however, a social order can experience a legitimation crisis, the revelation of a disjuncture between the claims of legitimacy and the validity or actual empirical facts of that order. Embedded in legitimacy claims, therefore, is a truth claim, which, once challenged, undermines the deference legitimacy otherwise secures.

In his analysis of types of social orders and legitimations, Weber described a historical development from traditional to increasingly rational systems, punctuated by charismatic eruptions. The systemic **rationalization** of advanced capitalism and loss of tradition and magic would lead, he suggested, to pervasive disenchantment. **Rationality** would undermine its own legitimating capacity by its unceasing inquiry, continually eroding the grounds of social construction and thus eroding the possibilities of legitimating narratives capable of commanding unquestioned deference and obedience.   SUSAN SILBEY

legitimation crisis
– see **legitimacy**.

leisure
The term derives from the Latin word *licere,* meaning "to be allowed." The concept was undertheorized in classical sociology, yet, arguably, it constituted a meta-theme in much progressive and revisionist thought of the time. For example, the **Enlightenment** looked forward to the leisure society in which individuals would have the freedom at their disposal to explore and cultivate their diverse interests. **Karl Marx** regarded leisure under **capitalism** to be constrained by class exploitation, commodification, and **alienation**. His theory of communist society envisaged the expansion of leisure and the development of **social**

capital. Max Weber's sociology implied that leisure was subject to the rationalization process and the bureaucratization of society. **Ferdinand Tönnies**'s distinction between *Gemeinschaft* and *Gesellschaft* carried with it a critique of work-centered existence and, in as much as this is true, connoted leisure with social well-being. However, most classical sociologists followed **Émile Durkheim** in regarding leisure as belonging to "the less serious side of life."

The exception was **Thorstein Veblen**, whose *Theory of the Leisure Class* (1899) is of axial importance in the emergence of the sociology of leisure. Veblen defined leisure as "the non-productive consumption of time." He argued that leisure in **industrial society** is bound up with the allocation of social distinction, which, in turn, reflects social hierarchy. Industrial society is dominated by a leisure class of propertied citizens, who devote themselves to non-pecuniary **labor**. By engaging in the equestrian arts, cultivating etiquette, learning dead languages such as Latin or Greek, and other non-pecuniary work, the leisure class articulate their exemption from the need to engage in wage-labor. Distinction in leisure forms and practice is further expressed through "conspicuous **consumption**," that is, lavish expenditure on **fashion**, entertaining, and other forms of social display. Veblen predicted that the development of industrial society would intensify conspicuous consumption and erode the work ethic.

Sociological interest in leisure expanded in the postwar period. It was first organized around industrial sociology in the 1950s which held that the a priori of leisure was held to be wage-labor. A variety of studies examined the work–leisure relationship and developed compartmentalized/segregated and spillover/extension models of leisure. They also produced a meliorist strain in the study of leisure that essentialized leisure as holding the characteristics of freedom, choice, and self-determination, and related leisure practice narrowly with life fulfillment and social integration.

By the 1960s, the coming of the leisure society was a central element in postindustrial society theory. It was assumed that science and **technology** were on the verge of solving the problems of want and the requirement to spend a large percentage of adult life in paid employment. Leisure Society was presented as a pluralist **democracy** in which the requirement to work would be minimized and a corresponding efflorescence of the arts, **sport**, and social capital would ensue. This approach is now regarded as unrealistic and inadequate in its treatment of **power** and **justice**.

Questions relating to the relationships between leisure and **identity** and between leisure and **citizenship** were peculiarly neglected until the 1970s. Interactionist approaches developed a perspective that stressed the situated character of leisure action and explored choice in relation to a variety of social, economic, and cultural constraints. However, the main units of analysis were the individual and the **group**, and this led to criticisms that the approach could not deal satisfactorily with structural influences of **social class**, **gender**, and **race and ethnicity**.

The Marxist tradition revitalized the Frankfurt School perspective that proposed that leisure is a fundamental means of social control. The distribution of free time was directly related to class, and the proposition that leisure is free time for the expression of individual choice was challenged by emphasizing the preeminence of commodification and corporate domination in consumer culture. Leisure forms and practice were analyzed in relation to their ideological functions. The contribution of the **Birmingham Centre for Contemporary Cultural Studies** led to leisure being directly related to **hegemony**. Leisure forms and practice were studied as contested social processes.

At the same time, **feminism** castigated "malestream" dominance in the allocation of leisure time and the organization of leisure studies. Feminists related leisure to **patriarchy** and the tendency of commodity culture to fetishize the female **body**.

All of these positions challenged meliorist overtones in the sociology of leisure by emphasizing structural **inequalities** in access to leisure **time** and **space** and by positioning **myth** and **ideology** in relation to leisure experience.

Recent work in the field has concentrated on questions of embodiment, classification, and **globalization**. Juliet Schor's "overwork thesis" raised the profile of the relationship of leisure to embodiment through a critique of the culture of overwork and its consequences for physical and mental **health** and mortality, such as in her *The Overworked American* (1991). Overwork was analyzed as a consequence of the general addiction to the acquisitive **values** of consumer **culture**. The creation of a revised work–leisure balance is portrayed as the solution to overwork and the ills of the **consumer society**.

Robert Stebbins's distinction, in *Amateurs, Professionals and Serious Leisure* (1992), between "serious" and "casual" leisure revitalized the interest in classifying leisure forms and practice. Serious leisure refers to a trajectory of activity based in the concept of a **career** and the progressive improvement of skills. Casual leisure refers to desultory, opportunistic practice which is associated with low attention spans and multi-tasking.

Globalization was recognized as a foundational issue in the development of leisure studies in the São Paulo Declaration issued by the World Leisure and Recreation Association in 1998. Citing Article 24 of the United Nations *Universal Declaration of Human Rights* which articulated the right to leisure for every member of the world's community, the *Declaration* pointed to the need to study the global dimensions of inequality and injustice in leisure forms and practice. One urgent research issue here is the dynamics of sourcing leisure commodities for retail by western leisure multinationals from low-wage developing **economies**.

CHRIS ROJEK

leisure class
– see **leisure**.

leisure society
– see **leisure**.

Lemert, Edwin M. (1912–)
An American sociologist, Lemert has been influential in the development of a social-psychological level of analysis in relation to the onset of delinquency and **crime**. His particular contribution has been to refine **labeling theory**. According to Lemert, in order to describe the process of labeling, it is important to distinguish between primary deviation and secondary deviation.

Primary deviation refers to the initial deviant action or behavior. Lemert acknowledged the very wide range of reasons for this: social, cultural, and psychological reasons. More particularly, he acknowledged that many people do engage in deviant or delinquent behaviors (underage drinking, smoking cannabis or petty shoplifting) and that for the most part engagement in activities does not lead to a psychological reorientation in terms of self-identity (that is, individuals do not immediately see themselves as a drunk, a pothead, or a thief). There is no fundamental change in **identity**.

Secondary deviation relates to the official or social reaction to the primary deviant behavior which involves the labeling of the individual (as a "young offender" or as a "criminal," for instance). Lemert's thesis was that individuals so labeled would begin to engage in deviant behavior

based upon the new **social status** of "young offender" or "criminal" conferred on them by the criminal justice system. Through formal name-calling, stereotyping, and labeling, a deviant identity is confirmed. Lemert's subsequent assertion that **social control** causes **deviance** not only provided impetus for the development of a radical and critical **criminology** that has flourished since the 1960s, but fueled the abolitionist movement. The "naming and shaming" tactics so favored by politicians in the United Kingdom may thus have unintended adverse consequences.

LORAINE GELSTHORPE

Lenin, Vladimir Ilich (1870–1924)
Famous for his leadership of the Russian Revolution, and for his theory of the party and **imperialism**, Lenin was born in Simbirsk, Russia. He was expelled from the University of Kazan in 1887 for political involvement, and, after being sentenced to three years of internal exile, he wrote *The Development of Capitalism in Russia* (1899).

In 1900 he became involved with *Iskra*, the official paper of the Social Democratic Labor Party, and two years later Lenin presented the case for a party of professional revolutionaries in *What Is To Be Done?* (1902). He returned to Russia during the abortive 1905 revolution. In 1917 (in Switzerland), he published *Imperialism: The Highest Stage of Capitalism*.

When the tsar abdicated in March, 1917, Lenin argued the case for a socialist revolution in his *April Theses*. This was successfully engineered in October. Lenin became head of the Soviet Council of Peoples' Commissars, and land was distributed to **peasants**, banks were nationalized, and workers' control of factory production introduced. An assembly, elected to draw up a new constitution, had a socialist but not Bolshevik majority. It was closed down and other **political parties** were banned, and, although the Bolsheviks won the civil war, they were faced with an uprising at Kronstadt. Lenin then introduced the New Economic Policy that allowed some market trading and denationalization.

His health declined after an attempt was made on his life. Three days after dictating a "will and testament," in which he called for the removal of Joseph Stalin (1879–1953) from the post of General Secretary of the Communist Party, he died in 1924.

JOHN HOFFMAN

Leninism
– see **Vladimir Ilich Lenin**.

Lenski, Gerhard (1924–)

An American sociologist, Lenski contributed significantly to the study of **inequality**, **social change**, and **religion**. In *The Religious Factor* (1981) he made an important contribution to the development of the sociology of religion in the United States. He is best known for his attempt at synthesizing the functional and conflict explanations of social hierarchy through broad historical comparisons, and for his contribution to the theory of status crystallization (see **social status**). In *Power and Privilege* (1966) and *Human Societies* (1982) Lenski outlined an ecological–evolutionary **social theory**. All desirable resources, including food, **money**, **prestige**, and **power**, are scarce, and therefore obtained through competitive struggles by the best-endowed individuals and **groups**. This competitive struggle is reduced owing to routinization of unequal distribution systems. Such systems, legitimized by custom and **tradition**, reflect the operation of two parallel "laws." The "law of needs" reflects largely the functional needs of society, such as survival and maintenance of the productive efficiencies of all social groups, including the lower strata. The "law of power" applies mainly to the distribution of "surpluses," that is resources exceeding basic functional needs. The surpluses are distributed proportionately to differential power, and therefore are concentrated in **elites** and privileged classes. The implication of this argument is that the less technologically advanced societies have more egalitarian–functional distribution systems, and that social hierarchies become steeper with the advancement of **technology** and surplus production. This regularity, argues Lenski, does not apply to modern **industrial societies** owing to enhanced productivity, increasing legal regulation, and democratic **ideology**. The rule of law changes the power balances in modern **societies** to the advantage of the lower strata by increasing their bargaining power and widening their access to welfare. Therefore **social stratification** in advanced societies is multidimensional and complex, and power hierarchies are open.   JAN PAKULSKI

lesbian feminism

In the early 1970s, in the period of **feminism** usually described as "second-wave **feminism**," a number of feminists argued that the only way to end the oppression of women was for women to identify themselves as lesbians. Any other form of sexual **identity** was, for many writers, merely a way of prolonging sexual **inequality** and abandoning the possibilities of female autonomy and emancipation. Prominent among the writers who suggested this was Jill Johnston, who published two collections of essays (*Marmalade Me*, 1971, and *Lesbian Nation*, 1973). In both collections (drawn from essays which Johnston had written for New York's *The Village Voice*) liberal feminism, or any feminism which accepted heterosexuality, was seen as merely an extension of **patriarchy** by other means. Johnston's vivid prose was very influential at the time and her work contributed considerably to the ideas of her contemporaries **Kate Millett**, Andrea Dworkin, and Adrienne Rich. All these writers were to follow Johnston in her analysis of heterosexuality as "compulsory" (as it was to be described by Adrienne Rich) or inherently based on male **violence** towards women (as Dworkin was to argue).

The influence of these writers has been considerable, but two other forms of lesbian feminism have been equally important. The first is the integration of the idea of the strength of relationships between women (sexually active or not) into academic literature: Terry Castle in *The Apparitional Lesbian* (1993) and **Eve Kosofsky Sedgwick** in *Epistemology of the Closet* (1991) are two examples of writers who have pointed out the hidden **tradition** of relationships between women in literature. The second is the considerable strength of the tradition of lesbian feminism which has been influential in campaigns about violence against women and legislation about **marriage**. In both cases lesbian feminists have pointed out – as have some French feminists – the importance of women, rather than men, defining female **sexuality**.

MARY EVANS

Lesbian Studies

Like **gay studies**, this is a product of the identity **politics** of the 1960s and is closely associated with **lesbian feminism**, which argued that women could still be marginalized and silenced even within the women's movement. Radical lesbian activists argued that the interests of women were not best served without the rejection of female heterosexuality, and hence lesbian studies is not identical with **women's studies**.

In the United States the National Organization of Women adopted a resolution in 1971 that supported lesbians. In 1991 the Center for Lesbian and Gay Studies was founded in the Graduate Center of the City University of New York. A non-profit **organization**, the Lesbian Studies Institute was formed in 1995. The first National Lesbian Conference in the United Kingdom took place in Canterbury in 1974 and a Coordinating Committee was established in

1975. In the 1970s therefore lesbian **communities** sprang up and were influenced by "second-wave feminism" viewing lesbianism as an expression of alternative **values** such as co-operation, a caring ethic, and egalitarianism. Lesbianism rejected the competitive and aggressive **culture** associated with **masculinity** and **patriarchy**. Lesbians came to reject the heterosexuality of traditional female **social roles** embracing androgynous styles such as T-shirts and blue jeans, and rejecting bras, lipstick, and jewelry.

In *Sex and Sensibility* (1997) Arlene Stein has examined how lesbian **identities** were constructed in the 1970s, but by the 1990s a narrow lesbian identity had become much more diverse, fragmented, and complex. Many black women felt excluded by the primarily middle-class, white lesbianism of the 1970s. There was also a tendency to reject lesbianism as a political category in order to explore sexual desire within a lesbian framework. Lillian Faderman in *Odd Girls and Twilight Lovers* (1991) describes the diverse **subcultures** of the lesbian movement, such as "lipstick lesbians," "punk lesbians" and "s&m lesbians." The lesbian community is also fragmented around generational differences. Older lesbian women, like older gay men, face special difficulties since they have spent much of their lives hiding their **sexuality** prior to the lesbian **social movements** of the 1970s.

Several academic journals now publish research on lesbian life and culture. The *Journal of Lesbian Studies* examines the cultural, historical, and interpersonal impact of the lesbian experience on **society**. Another journal is *GLQ – a journal of lesbian and gay studies* (launched in 1994). *Hypatia* and *Lesbian Ethics* deal with philosophical and ethical issues. *Handbook of Lesbian & Gay Studies* (2002), edited by Diane Richardson and Steven Seidman, provides a rich guide to this diverse field of social science research. Research related to lesbianism is organized and promoted by the National Consortium of Directors of Lesbian Gay Bisexual and Transsexual Resources in Higher Education in the United States.

Lesbian Studies faces the same dilemma as gay studies. There is a need to criticize mainstream social science literature for its neglect of gay and lesbian cultures, but there is also the problem of the academic co-option of lesbian politics and identity. Despite the proliferation of books about lesbian and gay studies, relatively little is known empirically about how gay and lesbian people organize their daily lives, including their sexual practices. While the sociology of sex is underdeveloped, historical, philosophical, and literary studies of sexuality experienced a vigorous growth in the late twentieth century.   BRYAN S. TURNER

Lévi-Strauss, Claude (1908–)

The leading French anthropologist of the second half of the twentieth century, Lévi-Strauss has had a discernible impact on thinkers as diverse as **Simone de Beauvoir**, Fernand Braudel (1902–85), **Mary Douglas**, and Jacques Derrida (1930–2004). In the first of some dozen major works, *The Elementary Structures of Kinship* (1949 [trans. 1969]), he demonstrates that unilineal kinship systems prescribing the **marriage** of cousins are logically equivalent to systems of reciprocal exchange. Against the consensus at the time, he argues that the incest prohibition is not merely the first of all cultural rules but also a prescription in negative form to marry outside the **family**; hence, kinship systems generally should be understood first as systems of alliance and only derivatively as systems of descent.

He is most widely known as part-founder, and the leading exponent, of **structuralism**. For Lévi-Strauss, function rarely if ever exhaustively determines structure. Structure properly speaking is the property of logical models of a finite number of elements, each of which stands in a fully determinate relationship to every other. Those of proper interest to the anthropologist are generative of meaning. None is more instructive than the linguistic model of the phonemic system, a matrix of binarily opposed phonic qualities specific to each **language** that in their several permutations yield the minimal functional building blocks of words and sentences. In *The Savage Mind* (1962 [trans. 1966]), Lévi-Strauss accordingly offers a portrait of the primitive *bricoleur* or "tinkerer" whose habits of mind tend spontaneously towards the ordering of the finite **data** of sensory experience into a closed, atemporal totality of analogical pairings of the elements of two fundamental, binarily opposed series, one natural and the other cultural. In the four magisterial volumes of *The Mythologiques* (1964 [trans. 1969], 1966 [trans. 1971], 1968 [trans. 1978], 1971 [trans. 1981]), he presumes that the same habits of mind and the same binary opposition between nature and **culture** underlie the genesis of **myth**. He replaces the model of the source-text and its diffusion with that of the version and its permutations; he rejects psychoanalytic, cosmogonic, and all substantialist interpretations of mythological symbolism and defends instead the thesis that mythology is a recoding of ordinary language, the meaning of whose elements is determined exclusively by the relations they bear to other elements of the same recoding. Because myths resolve and so mask at the symbolic level metaphysical and **social problems** that cannot be resolved in fact, they function "ideologically" in the Marxist sense of that term. Lévi-Strauss indeed pronounces his anthropology a contribution both to the science of superstructures and to theoretical psychology. Critics such as **Pierre Bourdieu** thus object to his relative neglect of human **interaction**. Others object to his formalistic and speculative excesses. Still other criticisms such as poststructuralism reject in principle his attempt to accord theoretical primacy to structure over history and the event.   JAMES D. FAUBION

liberalism

Liberalism is essentially a modern outlook, although aspects of liberalism can be found among the Sophists of ancient Greece with their argument that the **state** is not natural, but conventional.

Thomas Hobbes (1588–1679) was one of the earliest liberals in Britain, and what makes Hobbes a liberal is the abstract individual premises underpinning his argument for a strong sovereign state. Classical liberalism, until the late eighteenth century, subscribed to a state-of-nature thesis, in which humans were seen as naturally equal, living outside both state and **society**, and consenting to form the latter through a **social contract**. It is the universality of this freedom and **equality** that makes liberalism so subversive historically. All individuals are in theory free and equal, so that liberalism refuses to accept that repressive hierarchies are natural. Hobbes is quintessentially liberal in his argument that people, by nature, seek to govern themselves: they have inalienable **rights**. Although Hobbes supported the conservative side during the English Civil War, it was the liberal premises of his argument that accounted for the reservations felt towards him by the royalists.

Much more conventionally liberal is the work of John Locke (1632–1704). Locke makes the case for a constitutionally governed state. Whereas both he and Hobbes saw the state as authorized through consent and contract, Locke limits the prerogatives of the state to a defense of private **property** and allows radically dissatisfied citizens the right to overthrow an oppressive state.

While the classical liberals argued that the state is conventional and artificial, they all take the view that the state is necessary, because, for one reason or another, a state of nature cannot be sustained. Even Jean-Jacques Rousseau (1712–78), who argues that the individual is reconstituted by the social contract, states that individuals have a freedom that is natural and inalienable. For this reason, he too is a liberal, even though his critics fear that a "legitimate" state, governed by the general will, might exercise extensive powers in making people "free."

Towards the end of the eighteenth century, liberals came to reject the notion of the state of nature. They accepted that individuals have always lived in a society, and the idea that the state is the creation of a social contract was seen as implausible. Nevertheless, liberals continued to operate with a notion of the individual that abstracts him or her (it is usually a him) from social relationships. Rousseau is unashamedly patriarchal in his assumption that the citizen must be a man (and much else besides), and this led Mary Wollstonecraft (1759–97) to complain bitterly that Rousseau's support for autonomy and freedom did not apply to women. While the utilitarians may have rejected the notion of "natural rights," they too accepted that individuals should be conceived as separate, atomistic beings whose freedom can be expressed in a purely abstract way. Society remains external to the individual, even when liberals speak of the social nature of humanity.

It is the abstraction of individuals from social relationships that make them what they are, that accounts for the necessary tension between the universal theory preached by liberals and the reality of their actual practice. Liberals historically supported **slavery** (a property right, after all), elitism, **patriarchy**, **colonialism**, and the political **power** of the middle classes, and it is only in the twentieth century that liberals have supported the case for democratic rule. The key to understanding this apparent paradox is the liberal view that the **market** is natural and the desire to appropriate private property is linked to human nature. By property is meant not simply possessions, but possessions that can generate sufficient **income** to sustain people independently.

It is because individuals naturally appropriate property privately that men are favored over women; the **family** is seen as a mechanism for transferring property from father to son; **rationality** is identified with appropriation; the propertyless are excluded from the franchise; "lesser" people are colonized by the "civilized"; and, given the conflicts that the private ownership of property generates, liberals support the case for the state. It is revealing that **John Stuart Mill** could argue in his famous *On Liberty* (1859) that not only is force necessary when individuals harm society, but certain individuals (like Native Americans, for example) are not "ready" for self-government and must be ruled by others. Just how freedom and the state are to be reconciled remains an insoluble problem for liberals, since freedom is (rightly) deemed the absence of force, and yet the state, though artificial in most liberal accounts, is seen as necessary.

Critics of liberalism argue that its notion of freedom allows for license and even self-destruction, but we should not take abstract premises of liberal concepts at face value. They are tied to the notion of private property, and therefore the exercise of liberal **values** is linked to this institution. It is not surprising that liberalism has unwittingly generated a whole range of **ideologies** that seek to bring liberal theory into accord with social practice. Anarchists argue that the state is a barrier to freedom; socialists, that freedom and **equality** must be social as well as political and legal. Feminists protest that individuality, if it is to be universal, must apply to women as well as men, while environmentalists and animal rights supporters contend that egalitarian attitudes need to extend well beyond humanity.

Modern liberals have extended the notion of freedom into social spheres so that in Britain, for example, the architect of the **welfare state** was a liberal. Nor do modern liberals see the market as an autonomous, self-regulating entity, but make the case – **John Maynard Keynes** was another great British liberal – for intervention by the state, and the role of collective institutions such as **trade unions** and cooperatives, to secure social **justice**. Social liberals can be quite close to socialists, but arguably social liberals seek to make a capitalist society fair and humane, rather than transform it. The notion of the individual seeking to realize their freedom through the acquisition of private property remains at the heart of the theory.

JOHN HOFFMAN

life chances

This notion refers to the access that an individual has to valued social and economic goods such as **education**, health care, or high **income**. For **Karl Marx**, life chances were determined by social class position, with members of the working classes having structurally determined poorer life chances than those in the ruling class. **Max Weber** agreed with Marx that the individual's relationship to the means of production were an important determinant of life chances. However, he argued that there were other sources of **power** that could also determine them. In particular he

referred to the formation of status **groups**. High-social-status groups are accorded honor and esteem and have a **lifestyle**, based on **consumption** rather than production, which gives them a privileged position in society, independently of their economic position. While economically dominant classes will successfully consolidate themselves as high-status groups, Weber argued that this was not always the case. For example, some economically successful groups, such as the nouveaux riches, still find themselves excluded from the higher reaches of society. Alternatively, impoverished aristocrats in European societies are accorded high **social status** and esteem, allowing them to benefit from their access to the economically successful. Weber's fundamental point in developing the concept of life chances and status groups was to balance Marx's economic **determinism** with an account of social life that emphasized that it was the meaning individuals gave to their life experiences that shaped their formation into **communities**.

KEVIN WHITE

life-course

Although the life-cycle follows a linear biological trajectory from birth to death, sociologists and gerontologists emphasize the role of historical, social, and cultural context in aging and in shaping trajectories of individual development. Indebted to the insight of the German sociologist, **Karl Mannheim**, who argued in *Ideology and Utopia* (1936) that different social and historical settings produce different perspectives, life-course researchers investigate how the timing of sociobiographical events, such as graduation or **marriage**, at a particular **age** interfaces with specific historical or generational events and the social context in which they are experienced (for example, G. Elder, "The Life Course as Developmental Theory," 1998, *Child Development*). They examine how variation in, among other contextual characteristics, family structure and background, **gender**, **race**, **religion**, **occupation**, and **social class** differentially impact how aging and life-course transitions (for example, adolescence, getting a first job, parenthood, **retirement**, or chronic illness) are negotiated. Life-course researchers pay attention to how the contextual specificity of, for example, being a college-age student rather than a preteen or the middle-aged parent of a college-age student in the 1990s will lead to different constellations of experiences that in turn may differentiate the subsequent demographic and other life-course events of these different individuals (and their age peers). The biggest challenge confronting studies of the life-course is disentangling the discrete effects of, and interactions between, age, cohort, and historical period on life-course patterns. Longitudinal studies that follow the same individuals from multiple cohorts and across time allow researchers to identify what trajectories may be specific to a particular cohort growing up in particular sociohistorical context and what may be generalizable primarily to age or to a particular life-course transition or event.

MICHELE DILLON

life-cycle
– see **life-course**.

life expectancy
– see **age**.

lifestyle
This refers to relatively distinctive patterns of action and **culture** that differentiate people. In this respect, the study of lifestyles is less concerned with individual idiosyncrasy than with expressive modes of behavior that forge collective patterns of living. Many sociologists have utilized lifestyle rather than other terms like **subculture** as it does not necessarily imply a deviant relationship to the dominant culture. Instead the study of lifestyle is employed to emphasize distinctions at the level of practice within wider frameworks of culture and **power**.

In particular, many sociologists following **Pierre Bourdieu** in *Distinction* (1979 [trans. 1984]) sought to emphasize how, in modern class-based **societies**, lifestyles serve to distinguish some **groups** from others as well as providing the conditions for in-group **solidarity**. Hence some lifestyles are able to gain a wider social **legitimacy** at the expense of other ways of life. In this sense, lifestyle is closely connected to the unequal distribution of symbolic resources and power in society. Further, having a lifestyle depends upon certain cultural markers and the ability to establish boundaries on the basis of taste. However, the cultural codes that serve to legitimize some lifestyle groupings are not fixed and are the subject of intense contestation and cultural change. More recently, following the work of **Anthony Giddens** in *Modernity and Self-Identity* (1991), there has been a trend to view lifestyle as a reflexive product and to argue that it has certain political connotations that are not limited solely to the competition over **social status**. Lifestyles in this understanding are still concerned with wider questions of social legitimacy, but become increasingly focused on "how we should live" in a global world.   NICK STEVENSON

lifeworld
This refers to the taken-for-granted world of our experience. It is our "common sense," our everyday **attitude** about ourselves, others, and the objective world. It is shaped by shared meanings, **symbols**, and **language**.

The philosopher Edmund Husserl (1859–1938) developed the idea of the lifeworld in *The Crisis of the European Sciences and Transcendental Phenomenology* (1936 [trans. 1970]). He founded the philosophy of **phenomenology**, which investigates the rules of consciousness which structure experience, the ways in which we organize our reality so that it appears to us as integrated and authentic. For Husserl, the lifeworld supplies the underlying cultural harmony and the rules that govern our beliefs about what is real and normal. The lifeworld also provides the background for science, which extends taken-for-granted beliefs in a systematic manner.

Yet Husserl did not explore the social and cultural dimensions of the common lifeworld experience in depth, as he was interested in formal philosophical issues. **Alfred Schutz** developed a sociology of the lifeworld and a social phenomenology. For Schutz, the lifeworld is a shared, common world of **culture**. Our lifeworld beliefs are based on typifications, the assumptions and taken-for-granted knowledge through which people interpret and classify one another in **everyday life**. Individuals draw on their life experience, their biographies, to understand one another.

Social scientific research confronts a lifeworld rich in meanings and interpretations. For Schutz, the categories of science derive from the lifeworld. The **ideal types**, the most general ideas about the social world which social scientists utilize, are based on everyday typifications. All knowledge begins from commonsense and cannot be separated from the social context in which it emerges. Schutz argues that a satisfactory **social science** must begin with an understanding of the subjective world of its subjects; it must study their lifeworld. The idea of the lifeworld has influenced many sociological perspectives. **Harold Garfinkel**, the founder of **ethnomethodology**, explores the activities and performances by which people construct a taken-for-granted lifeworld. Other authors have taken the lifeworld concept in different directions. **Peter Berger** and **Thomas Luckmann**, in *The Social Construction of Reality* (1967), argue that we inhabit multiple lifeworlds. Moreover, people with social **power** can impose their definition of reality on others.

The contemporary German sociologist and philosopher **Jürgen Habermas** has also utilized the concept of the lifeworld. Habermas distinguishes between the "system" and the lifeworld. The system is the economic and bureaucratic spheres of social life, ruled by the criteria of efficiency and calculability. The lifeworld is the arena of **family** and **voluntary associations** outside these bureaucratic **institutions**. It is a realm of background, intuitive beliefs from which people draw the knowledge that they use to reach mutual understanding. The lifeworld is oriented towards unconstrained communication and the development of shared **values**. Habermas argues that the system has begun to "colonize" the lifeworld, as corporations increasingly shape everyday life, and consumerism and **mass media** influence social interactions. He fears that more and more aspects of the lifeworld are controlled by the system criteria of **money** and efficiency.

KENNETH H. TUCKER

liminality

– see **religion**.

linguistic turn

This is a description of the revolutionary movement in twentieth-century western philosophy, popularized by the American philosopher Richard Rorty who edited a book with the same title, and embodying the view that philosophical analysis is vitiated by unexamined uses of ordinary **language**. Reformers (such as Moritz Schlick, Rudolf Carnap, and the early **Ludwig Wittgenstein**) aimed to construct the basis for an ideal language whose undefined descriptive terms would refer to objects that are directly known, while ordinary language philosophers (John Austin, the later Wittgenstein, and others) maintained that language requires detailed analysis so that the ordinary connotations of linguistic expressions do not become unexamined contaminants of philosophical investigation.

The failure of the reformers' program, most forcefully articulated in Wittgenstein's *Philosophical Investigations* (1953), opened the way to widespread recognition of the extent to which language and symbolic systems are intricated in every form of social analysis. In the Anglophone **social sciences**, this movement issued in the Austin/Searle theory of speech acts which formed the basis of **Jürgen Habermas**'s theory of communicative competence, and in **ethnomethodology**, **conversational analysis**, and a focus on the significance of discourse and narrative in social organization. In European **social theory**, it

powered an assault on **phenomenology** that emerged in the **structuralism** of **Claude Lévi-Strauss** and the **poststructuralism** of **Michel Foucault**, Jacques Derrida, and others. The methodological questions raised by the linguistic turn remain largely unresolved, though the structuring of subjectivity and social relations by linguistic and symbol systems that are themselves open and revisable is a common theme in most forms of social science influenced by it.

JOHN HERITAGE

Lipset, Seymour Martin (1922–)

A leading American sociologist, a past professor at Harvard and Stanford, and former President of both the American Sociological Association and the American Political Science Association, Lipset is the author and co-author of over two dozen books, including *Agrarian Socialism* (1950), *Union Democracy* (1956), *Social Mobility in Industrial Society* (1959), *Political Man* (1960), *The First New Nation* (1963), *Revolution and Counter-Revolution* (1969), *The Politics of Unreason* (1971), *Consensus and Conflict* (1985), *Continental Divide* (1990), *Jews in the New American Scene* (1995), *American Exceptionalism* (1996), *It Didn't Happen Here* (2001), and *The Paradox of American Unionism* (2004). These writings cover a broad range of topics. Perhaps best known are Lipset's contributions to political sociology, such as the theories of **democracy** (especially **industrial democracy**) and **authoritarianism**, **social stratification** and mobility, revolution, nation formation, and the trade union movement. According to the original scheme formulated by Lipset and Stein Rokkan in their *Party Systems and Voter Alignments* (1967), the major social and political cleavages in modern societies – left versus right, urban–industrial versus rural–agricultural, religious versus secular, and national versus local – were formed during a series of revolutions – industrial, national, and political – between the eighteenth and nineteenth centuries. These cleavages gave rise to stable party-ideological divisions common to all modern western societies. Together with other students of **social mobility**, Lipset also formulated a thesis that the absolute rates of social fluidity increase with industrial **modernization**, and he helped to demolish some **myths** concerning the unique social openness of the American society. *The Encyclopedia of Democracy* edited by Lipset (1998) remains the key source in political sociology.

JAN PAKULSKI

Lockwood, David (1929–)

A British sociologist best known for his contributions to sociology of **social class**, occupational stratification, and **social conflict**, in his study *The*

Blackcoated Worker (1958) Lockwood argued that the clerical occupational strata in Britain were losing **social status** but maintaining social distinctiveness vis-à-vis skilled manual workers. This was followed by a classic study in England, *The Affluent Worker* (1969), in which Lockwood participated as a senior researcher. It confirmed an internal differentiation within the British working class, and identified a new segment of privatized, home- and family-centered manual workers, who displayed an instrumental orientation towards work and weak communal ties.

In his early work on social conflict and change, Lockwood made an important distinction between social and system integration. The former concerned the relationship between social collectivities (classes, strata, and ethno-racial **groups**); the latter referred to the relationship between the elements of the social system, that is **institutions** and their clusters, such as the law, the **family**, and the **economy**.

Lockwood's latest theoretical work, especially *Solidarity and Schism* (1992), focuses on the deficiencies of the Marxist theory of change, and the Durkheimian and Parsonian integrative **functionalism**, especially the functionalist account of social conflict. While **Marxism** needs a more explicit theory of action, the functionalist account, argues Lockwood, needs a supplement on the sources of the "systematic distribution and redistribution of material resources" (1992: 97). Popular images and classifications that underlie class and status–occupational divisions have to be causally linked with the actual patterns of resource distribution in society. **Norms** and perceptions perpetuate social order but do not explain it.

JAN PAKULSKI

log linear analyses

These are a form of multivariate analysis particularly suited to categorical variables. Unlike true measures, such as life expectancy or **income**, many sociological variables are naturally categorical, such as **gender**, ethnic group, or economic status (employed, unemployed, full-time carer, student, or retired). For bivariate analyses, the relationship between two categorical variables can be examined by looking at a cross-tabulation of the two variables and calculating the appropriate row or column percentages. However, for more complex problems (for example, to examine the different patterns of economic status in men and women in different immigrant groups) more advanced analyses are necessary to explore the relationships and interactions between variables. Log

linear analyses are a class of **statistics** that can analyze such multi-dimensional tables.

One particular type of log linear analysis, logistic **regression**, is used more than any other in sociology. This can be seen as a direct equivalent of multiple regression, but with a dichotomous dependent variable, instead of a continuous dependent variable.

Log linear analyses are a relatively new innovation in sociological statistics. Whereas other statistical techniques were developed at the start of the twentieth century, log linear analyses have only entered common usage since the 1980s. Although functionally similar to regression techniques, log linear analyses are based on more advanced mathematics than correlations or linear regressions.

BRENDAN J. BURCHELL

logical positivism

– see **positivism**.

lone-parent family

The terminology used to depict parents (typically mothers) who have borne or who raise **children** outside **marriage** has changed considerably since 1900. This shifting terminology reflects changing social **attitudes** and is a kind of cultural barometer of the acceptance of alternative family forms in Western societies. One longstanding term was "the unmarried mother," and her child might have been referred to as a "bastard" or, more recently, as illegitimate. This terminology did not depict the mother and child as constituting a **family** at all, because a socially acceptable family required both a husband and a marriage certificate. From "unmarried mother" the terminology changed to "single-parent" family. This reflected the recognition that fathers too could raise children alone, as well as acknowledging that parents and children living in a household together were, in fact, a family. The subsequent shift to the terminology of "lone-parent family" was an acknowledgment that the most common route into this form of parenthood was divorce rather than nonmarital conception. This means that the status of lone-parent family in the United Kingdom and the United States today is reached through marital breakdown, rather than through contraceptive failure; it also means that lone parents are now much less likely to be teenage (or young) mothers than in the 1950s or 1960s (Kiernan *et al.*, *Lone Motherhood in Twentieth-Century Britain*, 1999). To complicate this picture further, it is now recognized that many unmarried mothers are not really lone parents at all. They may be unmarried,

341

but they are often living with a partner in a cohabiting relationship.

This shifting terminology may reflect a changing moral climate and a greater degree of acceptance that families come in a variety of shapes and sizes, but lone-parent families remain a particular concern for **social policy** and governments. Lone-parent families are much more likely to live in **poverty** than two-parent families, which means, in turn, that their children are more likely to face material hardship than children born and raised in two-parent households (K. Glendinning and J. Millar, *Women and Poverty in Britain*, 1992). So although moral condemnation may have waned, lone parents are often still depicted as "problem families." Of course this definition relates to whether the poverty that lone-parent families face is seen as being a consequence of their "choice" to leave marriage or never to marry (that is fecklessness) in which case they are problem families, or whether it is seen as being a consequence of the difficulty for mothers of going out to work while raising children alone, combined with inadequate rates of state benefits, in which case they are families with problems. Right-wing commentators have raised fears that an underclass is developing, with mothers raising sons without discipline or work ethic and daughters without sexual morals (Karen Struening, *New Family Values*, 2002). Others, who are more left-leaning, point instead to Nordic societies where lone parenthood is much less likely to be associated with poverty and disadvantage because of the state provision of child-care, family-friendly work policies, and higher rates of welfare benefits for those who cannot work. The status and material well-being of lone-parent families (particularly those headed by mothers) is therefore highly dependent on state policies and the extent to which governments wish to discourage lone parenthood in preference for married parenthood (J. Millar and K. Rowlingson, *Lone Parents, Employment and Social Policy: Cross-national Comparisons*, 2001).   CAROL SMART

longitudinal study
– see **panel study**.

looking-glass self
– see **Charles Horton Cooley**.

low-inference descriptors
These descriptors are one of a range of strategies used to promote the validity of **qualitative research**. Other strategies include **triangulation**, **deviant case analysis**, and reflexivity. Specifically, low-inference

descriptors entail the use of summary descriptions based closely on participants' accounts, and the use of field notes. A commonly used low-inference descriptor is verbatim quotation.

There are, however, a number of potential problems with the use of low-inference descriptors as a strategy for ensuring a study's validity. Researchers are divided as to the relative merits of descriptive summary and isolated verbatim quotation versus the use of detailed transcripts and conversational- or discourse-analytic commentary. In *Discourse Analysis Means Doing Analysis* (2003), Charles Antaki *et al.* identify six possible analytic shortcomings for qualitative researchers working with discursive **data**. These are: (1) under-analysis through summary; (2) under-analysis through taking sides; (3) under-analysis through over-quotation or through isolated quotation; (4) the circular identification of discourses and mental constructs; (5) false **survey**; and (6) analysis that consists of simply spotting features.

As **Harvey Sacks** noted, we make inferences by a deceptively simple activity: that of giving a description. Herein lies a potential concern for qualitative researchers. By giving a description of a description, one can, at best, lose vital information, through eliding the detail and conversational nuances of the original. Low-inference descriptors, such as summary paraphrasing may, on close inspection, themselves be replete with (high-inference) descriptive psychological language – imputed motives, beliefs, emotions, and so on. This may be problematic in that the interactional details of participants' own accounts of psychological matters may be obscured.

Further, the use of transcribed verbatim quotes, though laudable, and a necessary precursor to analysis, does not, in and of itself, constitute analysis as such. Indeed, the extraction of participants' utterances from their original conversational context may actually prohibit some variants of discourse analysis (including **conversational analysis**).

     MARK RAPLEY AND SUSAN HANSEN

Luckmann, Thomas (1927–)
Born in Germany, Luckmann is a sociology professor at the University of Konstanz. Influenced by **Alfred Schutz**, he played a significant role in making **phenomenology** more accessible to sociologists through *The Social Construction of Reality* (co-authored with **Peter L. Berger**, 1966) and *Phenomenology and Sociology* (1978). Luckmann sought to bridge the increased **differentiation** of disciplines, itself the product of **modernity** and of the **secularization** of **social theory** from the

control of religious interpretations. He was especially interested in reintegrating sociology's philosophical foundations with the **positivism** of **social science**. Luckmann's various writings emphasize the centrality of human experience in **everyday life** and the lived, reflexive intersubjectivity of everyday communication (thus influencing **Jürgen Habermas**'s theory of communicative action). Extending his modernity/secularization thesis to **religion**, Luckmann argued that religion would become deinstitutionalized and lose its functional monopolization of social life as a result of the increased differentiation of society. In *The Invisible Religion: The Transformation of Symbols in Industrial Society* (1963 [trans. 1967]), he described how the religious dimensions of human experience would be forced out of the **public sphere** and into the privatized inner-directed **self**, thus making for a new individualized religious consciousness. In later work in R. Fenn, *Sociology of Religion* (2001), Luckmann highlighted how the "moralizing sermon," that is instruction in what constitutes a good life – assumed to be a staple in shaping worldviews in traditional Christian societies, though it may have declined within the churches – is intrinsic to human life, and thus variants on it have become part of the communicative stock of public discourse in modern society.   MICHELE DILLON

Luhmann, Niklas, (1927–1998)

Making a substantial contribution to the development of **social theory**, Luhmann studied at Harvard with **Talcott Parsons**, who influenced his work. His other influences include general system theory, **Émile Durkheim**'s evolutionary perspective, **Arnold Gehlen**'s philosophical anthropology, and **phenomenology**. He was Professor of Sociology at the University of Bielefeld. Luhmann developed a system theoretical approach to **society**, which in many respects was at loggerheads with the **critical theory** of **Jürgen Habermas**. This led to heated intellectual exchanges between Luhmann and Habermas. Luhmann's later work was heavily influenced by Humberto Maturana and Francisco Varela's notions of autopoiesis, and he began treating society as a self-organizing system. Especially influential among his works are *Social Systems* (1985 [trans. 1995]) and *Essays on Self-Reference* (1990).

In Luhmann's theory, systems can range from the physiological to the social. Systems always operate within an **environment** and have to reduce its complexity. Complexity depends on the number of actual or possible events; the reduction of complexity refers to the process by which relevant events are selected. In the case of social systems, the reduction of complexity is achieved through communication of meaning (*Sinn*). Central to this process is "double contingency": the process by which, in **interactions**, individuals have to take into account the orientation of other individuals towards them. For Luhmann, it follows that a social system is an autopoietic or self-referential system: that is, a system that interprets the environment, potentially undermining its autonomy, so that it reinforces its autonomy. There are three components to any self-referential system: the code, the structure or program, and the process. Codes are binary oppositions through which **information** is processed (for example, true versus false). Structure refers to the central **values**, normative regulations, and expectations, and process refers to the ongoing interaction. In self-reproducing systems, the code remains identical. The structure and process can change.

Modernity implies more contingency and complexity, so more sophisticated techniques are needed to reduce complexity: for instance, social **differentiation** and self-reflexive procedures. Differentiation can be either "segmental" (the different parts fulfil the same functions) or "non-segmental" (the different parts fulfil different functions). The non-segmental type can be either "hierarchical" or "functional" (with no hierarchy between the different parts). For reducing complexity, functional differentiation is superior to hierarchical differentiation, which in turn is better than segmental differentiation. Historically, the segmental type comes first and functional differentiation comes last. Examples of self-reflexive procedures are: teaching how to teach, or studying how research is done. They allow for continuous adjustment of the social system to an increasingly unpredictable environment.

Luhmann is critical of sociologists who describe differentiation and the shift to modernity in negative terms. Many of them use a premodern logic to describe modernity. Differentiation does not necessary lead to disorder and conflict; it is central to the creation of order and cohesion in modern society. Likewise, it is problematic to talk about contemporary society in terms of **alienation** or mass **culture**. Impersonal relations provide us with unprecedented levels of freedom.   PATRICK BAERT

Lukács, Gyorgy (Georg) (1885–1971)

A Marxist philosopher and literary critic, Lukács was born in Budapest, and between 1919 and 1929 he was one of the leaders of the Hungarian Communist movement. He made important contributions to **social theory**, the study of class consciousness, and the sociological study of literature. Before World War I he was the intellectual leader of the "Sunday Circle" that included **Karl Mannheim**, **Karl Polyani**, Arnold Hauser, and others. In 1918 he joined the Communist Party, and during the Hungarian Commune he was, in 1919, Minister for Education and Culture. In this early stage of his career, he was interested in the historical development of various forms of literature such as the novel, and published *Soul and Form* (1910 [trans. 1974]), *History of the Development of Modern Drama* (1911), *Aesthetic Culture* (1913 [trans. 1963]), and *The Theory of the Novel* (1920 [trans. 1971]).

After the collapse of this revolutionary movement, Lukács spent his exile in Austria, Germany, and Russia, becoming a friend of **Georg Simmel**, **Max Weber**, and Ernst Bloch. In the period 1919–29, Lukács wrote several interpretations of Marxist philosophy that had a major influence on European **sociology**. His work had particular significance for the theory of class consciousness, the sociology of knowledge, and the **Frankfurt School**. In his *History and Class Consciousness* (1923 [trans. 1971]), he emphasized the importance of the work of the young **Karl Marx** on **alienation**, and noted the role of the **reification** of beliefs in **capitalism**. His study of Marx promoted the importance of dialectical thinking and rejected the deterministic and mechanical theories of **society** promoted by orthodox **Marxism**, which predicted the inevitable collapse of capitalism through revolutionary struggles. As a result, Lukács had an ambiguous and unstable relationship with the Communist Party. He was criticized by party **intellectuals** in the 1940s for his views on **culture** and, in 1956, he was briefly Minister of Culture in Imre Nagy's government in Hungary, but he was deported to Romania when the government was suppressed. When Lukács withdrew from political life, he turned increasingly to the study of **aesthetics** and ontology, publishing *The Specific Nature of the Aesthetic* (1962) and *Towards an Ontology of Social Being* (1971).

He made a major contribution to the sociology of literature in *The Historical Novel* (1955 [trans. 1962]), *Essays on Thomas Mann* (1964), and *Goethe and his Age* (1968), in which he treated the novel as a reflection of the life of the bourgeois class.

BRYAN S. TURNER

Lynd, Robert Staughton (1892–1970), and Helen Merrell Lynd (1896–1982)

Born in Indiana, Robert Lynd received his PhD at Columbia University in 1931. He served on the Columbia faculty from 1931 to 1961. His wife, Helen

Merrell Lynd, was born in Illinois, receiving her MA from Columbia in 1922 and her PhD in 1944. She was on the faculty of Sarah Lawrence College from 1928 to 1964. They collaborated on *Middletown* (1929), and *Middletown in Transition* (1937), two important studies of changing American **values** in the face of **industrialization**.

These studies of Muncie, Indiana (under the pseudonym of Middletown), demonstrated the vast changes sweeping the United States through the experiences of a typical Protestant, predominantly white middle-American town. They catalogued the rise of a new **culture** based on consumerism and competitive **individualism** which eclipsed more traditional values of thrift, prudence, and public spiritedness. The increasing importance of **wealth** as a measure of **social status** was illustrated in the disappearance of a shared sense of **community**, and its replacement by a class-based hierarchical **social structure**, in which differences between a business class and the working class became more pronounced.

Middletown and *Middletown in Transition* were the first studies of the corporate, **consumer society** based on new forms of industrial capital that was arising in the United States in the 1920s. The Lynds demonstrated that the Great Depression of the 1930s only helped to consolidate this new society. Robert Lynd criticized this new culture's influence on the **social sciences** in *Knowledge for What?* (1939).

KENNETH H. TUCKER

Lyotard, Jean-François (1924–1998)

A French philosopher and social thinker, one of the leading exponents of **postmodernism** in philosophy and **social theory**, Lyotard is best known to sociologists for his *Postmodern Condition* (1979 [trans. 1984]), a critical reflection on the state of knowledge in **postindustrial society**. It contains a radical criticism of the epistemological foundations of scientific knowledge, and a sociological account of commodified knowledge under the impact of new **technology** and **information**. Knowledge, according to Lyotard, consists of narratives, that is a mixture of **norms**, stories, popular wisdoms, fables, and **myths**. The "postmodern condition" is characterized by increasing public realization that scientific knowledge is no exception: like all social knowledge, it is a type of discourse, a "metanarrative," or a grand story of a totalizing type. Claims of those who see scientific knowledge as uniquely objective, true, and universal are greeted with incredulity or skepticism. This incredulity extends to all metanarratives, including **Marxism** (a story of human emancipation) and modern social theory (a story of progress, **secularization**, and **rationalization**). Their **legitimacy**, and their claims to privileged epistemological status, are questioned; and their true nature as **language games** opens the way for critical revaluation of their substance and social function. Postmodern skepticism permeates **popular cultures** in contemporary postindustrial or (computerized) societies, in which information and communication technologies undermine the capacity of state **elites** to control public discourses and legitimize metanarratives. Knowledge turns into a commodity that circulates among increasingly diverse audiences. This increases the diversity of language games and the accompanying **pluralism**, fragmentation, and eclecticism of knowledge.   JAN PAKULSKI

M

MacIntyre, Alasdair (1929–)

From his early twenties onwards, MacIntyre's work has been dominated by criticism of moral **individualism** and moral **relativism**. The critique of moral individualism led him to sociology, which he taught at the University of Essex in the 1960s. Keen to strengthen a contextual understanding of practical reason in the wake of **Ludwig Wittgenstein**'s *Philosophical Investigations* (1953), he has also been concerned to avoid the relativism to which such contextualism led in the work of Peter Winch. Their debate is to be found in Bryan R. Wilson (ed.), *Rationality* (1970). In *After Virtue* (1981) and in *Whose Justice? Which Rationality?* (1988), MacIntyre developed his own position, reconciling contextualism and moral realism on a neo-Aristotelian basis, using an idiosyncratic theory of **tradition**. MacIntyre denounces the moral emptiness of advanced liberal **societies**, arguing that their individualism undermines the social practices and **communities** required for the development of a proper sense of virtue. Turning away from sociology per se, MacIntyre argues that rigorous sociology must engage with moral and political philosophy.

His other works include (with Paul Ricoeur) *The Religious Significance of Atheism* (1966), *A Short History of Ethics* (1967), *Secularization and Moral Change* (1967), *Marxism and Christianity* (1968), *Marcuse* (1970), and *Dependent Rational Animals* (1999).

ÉMILE PERREAU-SAUSSINE

macrosociology

The sociological study of large processes and **social structures**, it can be illustrated by such prototypical examples as studies of revolutions (see **theory of revolutions**), the **state**, the **economy**, the social system, and the world-system. Macrosociology is often contrasted with microsociology, which is the sociological study of small-scale phenomena – the prototypical example is the study of face-to-face **interaction**.

In practice the difference between macrosociology and microsociology not only lies in the size of the unit of analysis, but also in their theoretical and epistemological commitments. Macrosociology comprises diverse approaches, including structural **functionalism**, **Marxism**, and **world-systems analysis**. Nevertheless, it is with comparative-historical sociology that the label macrosociology has come to be principally associated. Characteristic contemporary exponents are **Barrington Moore**, **Reinhard Bendix**, **Charles Tilly**, and **Theda Skocpol**.

With regard to **epistemology** and **methodology**, macrosociologists often rely, more or less explicitly, on two of **John Stuart Mill**'s canons of induction: the method of agreement and the method of difference. Substantively, they have been more interested in political and economic issues than in cultural ones. In fact, Skocpol's *States and Social Revolutions* (1979) delineated the contours of the field for nearly two decades. However, a new generation of scholars is increasingly moving away from this **paradigm** in terms of both their substantive and their epistemological preferences.

In contrast, microsociology focuses on interpersonal situations and the contexts in which they occur. Within microsociology, there are two main theoretical orientations: **rational choice theory** and social **exchange theory** on the one hand, and **symbolic interactionism** and **ethnomethodology** on the other. The former tradition – influenced by microeconomics and the economic approach to human behavior – places the emphasis upon individual preferences and choices, constraints, transactions, and costs and benefits. The latter tradition – whose intellectual resources include **Max Weber**'s *Verstehen* and Edmund Husserl's **phenomenology** which was channeled through the work of **Alfred Schütz** – is concerned with individuals' subjectivity and the construction of meaning.

The opposition between macro and micro used to be conceived as a dispute over which one is "more fundamental" or "ontologically prior," and was often similar to the contrast between collective and individual and to the debate over **agency and structure**. Nevertheless, this essentialist construal of the micro–macro "problem" is now largely rejected. The point is not to reduce one to the other, but to search for theoretical and methodological linkages. Macrosociology stands on microfoundations and microsociology stands on macrofoundations. In any case, the distinction maintains its value as a linguistic convention by means of which types of inquiries and levels of analysis are classified.

One set of criticisms against macrosociology is methodological. Given the magnitude of the objects studied under its auspices and the inclination to study processes over long periods of time, macrosociologists' samples are generally small. Thus, Stanley Lieberson in "Small N's and Big Conclusion," in C. Ragin and H. Becker (eds.), *What is a case?* has argued that in small-N studies Mill's methods do not yield valid causal inferences. According to him, this strategy requires implausible assumptions, such as that there be no interaction effects, mono-causality, and that **sociological theories** be deterministic rather than probabilistic. A second set of criticisms calls macrosociology to task for having conceptualized history as a mere repository of **data**, thereby failing to historicize social reality and its own conceptual tools in a manner that is convincing.

GABRIEL ABEND AND JEFF MANZA

magic
– see **religion**.

Malinowski, Bronislaw (1884–1942)
A scion of the Polish aristocracy, Malinowski studied engineering before pursuing a degree in anthropology at the University of Cambridge. He was not the first anthropologist to undertake **fieldwork**, but in his classic *Argonauts of the western Pacific* (1916) was the first to provide it with an articulate **methodology** and rationale. He urged impartiality, attention to the "imponderabilia of everyday life," and rigor in investigating "the native's point of view." His research among the peoples of the Kiriwana Islands was itself the benchmark of ethnographic excellence for many decades and his reputation survived the sometimes unflattering revelations of the posthumously published *A Diary in the Strict Sense of the Term* (1967) largely intact.

From the social organization and collective psychology of the *kula*, the periodic sailing expeditions that bound the Kiriwanans into a dynamic inter-island ring of trade and alliance, Malinowski extracted the persuasive model of a reasonable, industrious, and practical economic actor who remained "primitive" only in having less passion for profit than for **prestige**. The model informs Malinowski's instrumentalistic treatment of magic (see **religion**) and **myth** and, in "Group and Individual in Functional Analysis" (1939), a broader argument that each of the basic institutional components of **culture** is so much technological service for the satisfaction of a correlative psycho-biological **human need**. The argument risks circularity and oversimplification, but is also the manifesto of a pure **functionalism** resolutely opposed to the Durkheimian **reification** of **society** as a thing having needs of its own.

Malinowski contributed significantly to the study of religion in *Magic, Science and Religion and Other Essays* (1948) and to the study of **sexuality** in *Sex and Repression in Savage Society* (1972) and *The Sexual Life of Savages* (1929).   JAMES D. FAUBION

Malthus, Thomas Robert (1766–1834)
Educated at Jesus College, Cambridge, where he won prizes for Latin and English declamation, at the age of twenty-two Malthus became a curate near his family home in Surrey and later in Lincolnshire. In 1805 he was appointed a professor of history and political economy at East India College, Haileybury, a position he occupied until his death in 1834.

During his early tenure as a rural clergyman, he published anonymously in 1798 the first edition of his famous book, *An Essay on the Principle of Population as it Affects the Future Improvement of Society, with Remarks on the Speculations of Mr. Goodwin, M. Condorcet, and Other Writers*. W. Petersen in his *Malthus* (1979) writes that this publication "immediately established its anonymous author as a controversial figure." Five years later, in 1803, this time under his name, Malthus published the second edition of the essay, with a different subtitle, as *An Essay on the Principle of Population; or a View of Its Past and Present Effects on Human Happiness; With an Inquiry into our Prospects Respecting the Future Removal or Mitigation of the Evils which It Occasions*. Petersen notes that this was indeed a new book. The first edition was mainly a "deductive book" of around 55,000 words, whereas the second edition expanded the theory and provided a great deal of illustrative **data**, resulting in around 200,000 words. Subsequent editions, the final being the seventh edition which was published posthumously in 1872, included relatively minor changes. The best edition is the second, with revisions, contained in two volumes and edited by Patricia James as *An Essay on the Principle of Population (with the Variora of 1806, 1807, 1817, 1826)* (1989).

The principle of population stated that, if left unchecked, populations would tend to grow geometrically, while **food** and subsistence would grow arithmetically. But Malthus argued that population growth was held in check by two kinds of controls, preventive checks and positive checks. Malthus referred to the major preventive check as "moral restraint," or the postponement of marriage. As a clergyman he was not able to recognize birth control as a check. Indeed he was "opposed to birth control on the grounds that such 'unnatural' experiments ran contrary to God's design in placing humankind under the right degree of pressure to ensure its development" (D. Winch, *Encyclopedia of Population*, 2003). The positive checks included **wars**, famine, pestilence, and other forms of misery. The positive checks kept the death rate high, the preventive checks kept the birth rate low.

Malthus's essay needs to be placed and considered in historical context. It opposed two very influential schools of thought, mercantilism and **utopianism**, and cast doubt on the hope of human perfectibility. Winch writes in the *Encyclopedia of Population* that "Malthus showed that any attempt to create an ideal society in which altruism and common property rights prevailed would be undermined by its inability to cope with the resulting population pressure."

The writings of Malthus are said to have influenced the work of **Charles Darwin**, **Herbert Spencer**, David Ricardo (1771–1823), **John Maynard Keynes**, and many others. For instance, Darwin wrote in his *Autobiography* (1887) that:

> Fifteenth months after I had begun my systematic enquiry, I happened to read for amusement Malthus on population, and being well prepared to appreciate the struggle for existence which everywhere goes on from long-continued observation of the habits of animals and plants, it at once struck me that under these circumstances favorable variations would tend to be preserved and unfavorable ones be destroyed. The result of this would be a new species. Here, then, I had at last got a theory by which to work.

Scholars hold mixed views with respect to the **influence** of Malthus on **demography**. W. Petersen argues that in the writings of Malthus, modern population theory was born. D. Bogue on the other hand, in *Principles of Demography* (1969), states that although the writings of Malthus "have attracted worldwide attention and have dominated the thinking of many students of population, his contribution to the development of demography as a science was rather modest."   DUDLEY L. POSTON

Malthusian theory
– see **Thomas Robert Malthus**.

management
Engineers have long been fascinated by **work and employment**. Engineering has a natural affinity with work in a profit-based **economy**, because it is oriented to getting more output from less input as its definition of efficiency. It was an engineer, Frederick Winslow Taylor (1865–1915), whose *Principles of Scientific Management* (1911) first defined management systematically.

Taylor proposed "four great principles of management": (1) developing a science of work by observing and measuring **norms** of output, using a stopwatch and detailed observation of human movements to improve effectiveness; (2) scientifically selecting and training the employee; (3) combining the sciences of work and selecting and training of employees; and (4) management and workers specializing and collaborating closely. Taylor regarded science as equivalent to making systematic **measurement** and observation, after which work would be redesigned on the basis of the **data** generated and inferences made about existing procedures and how they might be improved. A famous example, which is discussed critically by H. Braverman in *Labor and Monopoly Capitalism* (1974), was the example of the Dutch worker Schmidt, and the art of shoveling pig iron. Taylor established that even a rather stupid worker, with a carefully designed tool, could increase productivity significantly, as long as what scientific management said should be done was done. Armed with a checklist and a stopwatch, Taylor observed and timed work, and then redesigned it, so that tasks could be done more efficiently. Taylor proposed designing the best way of performing any set of tasks on the shop floor, based on detailed observation, selection, and training. **Time** was of the essence.

Taylor's ideas had the advantage of being quite easy to grasp and so were as easily adopted as they were opposed. However, it is worth noting that employers tended to adopt his ideas piecemeal: they were keen on the efficiencies from time measurement but not as keen on the rewards in the form of bonuses that Taylor proposed under his recommendations for the use of piece-rates.

Taylor and the movement for systematic management were opposed by a number of forces. First, there were internal contractors – people who provided and supervised labor to work within factories owned by remote robber barons, financiers, entrepreneurs, and industrialists – who stood to lose their livelihoods if scientific managers triumphed and replaced them with systematic managers. Second, there were the owners of capital, particularly those with small workshops, who were already fearful of being devoured or driven out of business by big businessmen, such as the "robber barons" (Andrew Carnegie and Theodore Vanderbilt), gobbling up their assets into new centers of financial control; they were also fearful of the dilution of the **power** of ownership. Third, the workers, increasingly organizing in **trade unions**, railed against the loss of craft skills that the project of standardization and systematization of work entailed. Standardization became a wedge that opened the door for a wider adoption of systematic scientific management through linking individual remuneration to individual effort in scientifically framed tasks. Managers would be a new breed of practical scientists managing corporations and **organizations** empirically, on the basis of facts and techniques, rather than experience, privilege, or an arbitrary position. Functions and responsibilities would be aligned in a scientifically proven manner by engineers trained in the management of things and the governance of people working with and on them.

Taylorism did not die with Taylor – it became sedimented deep inside organizations, wherein, eventually, many people would be replaced by robots, in which scientific management would find far better raw material: there were no sources of uncertainty in designing and calibrating pure machines, as compared to the person/machine interface. Of course, one does not have to go to a factory to find Taylorism: check out the system for manufacturing fast food in any burger restaurant such as McDonald's (see **McDonaldization**).

Another engineer, Henri Fayol (1841–1925), is often regarded as the most significant European founder of modern management, because he provided a basis for systematic **authority** in the fledgling **occupation**. In 1916, he published *Administration industrielle et générale*, in which he argued that better management not only is concerned with improving output and disciplining subordinates but also must address the training of the people at the top. Although other early management theorists (such as Elton Mayo [1880–1949] and Mary Parker Follett [1868–1933]) and many subsequent ones (such as James March and Karl Weick) were to take a less systematic and mechanical view, these early foundations for management thinking have proven remarkably resilient – especially as the thrust towards the

rationalization of the world has been carried forward by the managerial project.   STEWART CLEGG

managerial revolution

James Burnham wrote *The Managerial Revolution* in 1941. Aware that **economies** based on **capitalism** had inherent structural flaws, he – as a former adherent of Trotskyism – was nonetheless disenchanted by the Soviet **state**. The post-World War I years had seen the decline of many of the huge corporations that had dominated United States economic life, particularly as effective anti-trust legislation took shape from 1932. A concern with the concentration of **power** and the dispersion of share ownership was to become allied with the view that a "managerial revolution" had occurred in United States corporate life. Real power was no longer to be found concentrated in the hands of the robber barons. Power had shifted to the stewards of capital – the managers – and the major concentrations of capital held by the dominant stockholders.

With limited liability, the shareholders of a corporation elect a board of directors who then choose the top management officers to run the business. Burnham suggested that, with this split between ownership and control, a new **society**, neither capitalist nor communist, would develop: a managerial society. Burnham's central argument was that ownership means control. Without control there is no ownership. If ownership and control are separated, the separated ownership becomes purely a legal fiction and real control will reside in the day-to-day stewards of capital, the managers. Senior executives, however, generally hold major consolidated blocks of shares, so potential conflicts between the interests of the principals, the shareholders, and the interests of the agents, the hired managers, may not be as extreme as one might expect. Shareholders – often professional and institutional investors – frequently have little interest in influencing the way business is run; they use the share price as a proxy of quality management. Managers typically dominate boards of directors as well as being significant shareholders.

More recently, Alfred Chandler in *The Visible Hand: The Managerial Revolution in American Business* (1977) has revised the managerial revolution thesis. He argues that modern organizations arose because administrative coordination was better than the **market** at enhancing productivity and lowering costs. Administrative coordination created a managerial hierarchy, one that became increasingly technical and professional, with a preference for long-term stability and growth over short-term gains (although the markets would sometimes favor these). The move to a rational managerial system encourages growing professionalization, which increasingly saw personal and family-owned enterprises replaced by professionally managed firms.

There has been a managerial revolution – but it has not seen family **firms** disappear: indeed, some of the world's largest companies remain family firms. However, those that do not employ professional managers are unlikely to be sustainable. A new and significant stratum of professional managers has been created as the custodians of capital and the driving forces behind an increasing **rationalization** and **globalization**.

STEWART CLEGG

Mann, Michael (1942–)

Professor of Sociology at the University of California, Los Angeles, Mann has been particularly influential in historical sociology and **macrosociology**. His analytical framework is a theory of **power** that is in part derived from **Max Weber**. Mann argues that there are four types of power: military, political, economic, and ideological. He has examined the historical development of these four types of power in *The Sources of Social Power, Volume I: A History of Power from the Beginning to A.D. 1760* (1986) and *The Sources of Social Power, Volume II: The Rise of Classes and Nation-states 1760–1914* (1993). Volume III will examine **globalization**. He has applied this framework to the contemporary United States and its foreign policy in *Incoherent Empire* (2003), arguing that American power cannot be coherently exercised in these four dimensions. His earlier research in political sociology was on **politics** and **ideology** in the western working class in *Consciousness and Action Among the western Working Class* (1973), and he has argued that **citizenship** is an institution to regulate and incorporate the working class in **capitalism** in his article in *Sociology* on "Ruling-class Strategies and Citizenship" (1987). In his *Fascists* (2004) Mann developed a controversial interpretation of **fascism**, arguing that, particularly in Germany, it was not supported by a specific **social class**, was not attractive necessarily to downwardly mobile or marginal men, and was not initially or overwhelmingly characterized by anti-Semitism.   BRYAN S. TURNER

Mannheim, Karl (1893–1947)

Born in Hungary, Mannheim fled to Germany in 1919 after the failure of the revolutionary government in Budapest. With the emergence of **fascism**, he moved to Britain in 1933, eventually becoming a professor at the London School of Economics. He made a major contribution to the development of the sociology of knowledge in *Ideology and Utopia* (1936), *Essays on the Sociology of Culture* (1956), and *Conservatism: A Contribution to the Sociology of Knowledge* (1986). He argued that rising **social classes** embrace utopian systems of knowledge, whereas declining social classes will embrace romantic or reactionary **ideologies**. Against cultural **relativism**, he defended the idea that the "free-floating intelligentsia" can be relatively independent of social determination. Against the Marxist emphasis on social class, Mannheim developed the concept of **generation** as representing the **life chances** and experiences of age cohorts passing through **time**. Members of a generation are held together by experiencing events from the same vantage point. This phenomenon of a common experience he referred to as the "stratification of experience" and he conceived of this experience as the dynamic aspect of generational consciousness.

Mannheim also wrote extensively on **education**, social reform, and **social policy** in *Man and Society in an Age of Reconstruction* (1940), *Diagnosis of Our Time* (1943), and *Freedom, Power and Democratic Planning* (1951). In this work, he argued that sociology can make an important contribution to social planning.   BRYAN S. TURNER

Marcuse, Herbert (1898–1979)

A philosopher by training who studied with Martin Heidegger (1889–1976), Marcuse joined the Institute for Social Research in Frankfurt in 1934 and worked with **Max Horkheimer**, **Theodor Wiesengrund Adorno**, **Erich Fromm**, and others in developing a **critical theory** of contemporary **society**. During the 1960s, Marcuse ascended to the unlikely role of guru of the New Left. His book on **Georg Wilhelm Friedrich Hegel** and **Karl Marx**, *Reason and Revolution* (1941), introduced a younger generation to critical and dialectical **social theory**, and he provided an excellent philosophical interpretation of **Sigmund Freud** in his 1955 *Eros and Civilization*.

In 1964, Marcuse published a wide-ranging critique of both advanced capitalist and communist societies in *One-Dimensional Man*. This book theorized the decline of revolutionary potential in capitalist societies and the development of new forms of **social control**. Marcuse argued that "advanced **industrial society**" created false needs that integrated individuals into the existing system of production and **consumption**. **Mass media** and **culture**, advertising, industrial **management**, and contemporary modes of thought all reproduced the existing system and attempted to eliminate negativity, critique, and opposition. The result was a "one-dimensional" universe of thought and behavior in which the very aptitude and ability for critical thinking and oppositional behavior were withering away.

During the 1960s and 1970s, Marcuse had worldwide influence on the student and anti-war movement. Later works include his 1969 *Essay on Liberation, Counterrevolution and Revolt* (1972) and *The Aesthetic Dimension* (1979), while the collections *Technology, War and Fascism* (1998), *Toward a Critical Theory of Society* (2001), and *The New Left and the 1960s* (2005) collect some of his most important work.

DOUGLAS KELLNER

manual and mental labor
– see **labor**.

market(s)
In classical economic theory, the market not only establishes the price of commodities, but the economic exchanges it coordinates are also seen as a means of **social integration**. Specialization and the division of **labor** require the exchange of goods and services which replaces the self-sufficiency of traditional **societies** with the mutual advantage of economic interdependence. For economic **liberalism**, market exchange produces the **wealth** of nations and simultaneously reconciles self-interest and **individualism** with social integration. In Bernard de Mandeville's (1670–1733) aphorism in *The Fable of the Bees* (1714), "private vices" bring "public benefits," later more famously described by Adam Smith (1723–90) as the mechanism of the "invisible hand."

Sociology developed to a large extent as the result of a critical dialogue with this liberal economic theory, as in **Talcott Parsons**'s *Structure of Social Action* (1937). From **Auguste Comte**'s early nineteenth-century critique of the "invisible hand" to today's concern with the social and political consequences of **globalization**, sociologists have pursued two related lines of attack. First, the market was not a viable basis for social order; indeed, impersonal calculative exchange relations inhibit the formation of social bonds based on **trust** and cooperation, as **F. Tönnies** argued in his analysis of the transition from **community** (*Gemeinschaft*) to association (*Gesellschaft*). Second, Adam Smith's explanation of the existence of markets as the natural outcome of a universal and primitive predisposition to "truck, barter, and exchange" was rejected as being inconsistent with the wide historical and cultural variability in the existence of markets. **Karl Polanyi** observed that the allocation of goods according to **norms** of either reciprocity and/or redistribution has been more prevalent throughout human history than allocation by the mechanism of market price. Thus, the existence of markets as social **institutions** required a historical and sociological **explanation** – that is, how they came into being and how they worked.

Until recently, however, sociology gave more attention to the socially and politically corrosive impact of market exchange. A classic exposition is contained in **Karl Marx**'s analysis of **alienation** and the "cash nexus." Market exchange mediated by **money** involves the estrangement of individuals from their products and from the social relations into which they enter in the process of production. Most importantly, labor becomes a commodity to be bought and sold and, consequently, people become alienated from their essential humanity, or "species being." Modern society is based on the fragile "cash nexus" rather than the more robust norms of traditional society. The same general theme is pursued from somewhat different perspectives in **Émile Durkheim**'s analysis of **anomie**; Polanyi's discussion of land, labor, and money capital as "fictitious commodities"; and, more recently, for example, in **Amitai Etzioni**'s communitarian critique of the "free market."

In *The Architecture of Markets* (2001), Neil Fligstein systematizes the literature on the macro-sociological structure and historical development of modern markets. Markets are social institutions comprising four kinds of rules: (1) property rights; (2) governance structures; (3) rules of exchange; and (4) conceptions of control. (Note also that the existence of stable money, in the form of a stable "money of account," is necessary to enable the calculations that make large-scale impersonal exchange a possibility.) First, property rights define who has claims, or not, over the profits or surplus of economic enterprise – that is, shareholders, patent holders, creditors, and workers. Property rights are continuously contested in a political process that produces different legal forms of enterprise structure – for example, family **firm**, corporation, partnership, cooperative. Second, governance structures consist of the rules that define the cooperative and competitive relations within the market. These are either laws, such as monopoly legislation, or informal norms that define unfair practices such as "cutthroat competition." Third, rules of exchange specify the transacting parties and the conditions under which the transactions are carried out – for example, contract law, accounting standards, product standards, and health and safety legislation. Without such rules, exchange will remain fragmented. For example, the harmonization of exchange rules is seen clearly in the creation of the European Union's single market. The continued absence of harmonized accountancy standards across the world inhibits globalization. Fourth, and finally, conceptions of control are the largely informal normative and cognitive definitions of the situation held by the participants in a particular market. These shared understandings concern, for example, competitive and cooperative tactics, the internal structure of firms, and their status ranking. They create a "social field" that enables firms to reproduce themselves routinely, and a stable market order.

Max Weber was one of the first to see that the development of extensive markets in **capitalism** required an explanation. Quite different in scale and scope from the limited exchanges in traditional communities, large impersonal markets became one of the axial bases of society as the result of changes in the social and political structures of early modern western Europe. In his economic lectures (*Wirtschaftgeschichte*) which were published as *General Economic History* (1923 [trans. 1927]), he showed that rules for establishing markets as **institutions** for regularizing the exchange of particular goods, as opposed to relatively disorganized "truck and barter," were established through political struggle and state power. Capitalist property **rights** were the result of struggles which produced a balance of **power** between multiple political **elites**, economic interests, and classes. With such a dispersion of power, the various interests agreed to rules that established routine competition that prevented any one group from monopolizing power and economic advantage. For a similar analysis, see Douglass North, *Institutions, Institutional Change and Economic Performance* (1990). The competition that, for Weber, ensured social and economic dynamism also applied to economic competition between nations. So long as these did not give way to a world empire, capitalism would endure.

Weber also noted that traditional society's economic transactions contained an "ethical dualism." On the one hand, within the communal in-group, transactions were governed by an ethic of charity, comprising norms of fairness defined by **tradition**, ritual exchange, customary **consumption**, and prohibition on usury. On the other hand, outsiders were treated according to the opposite ethic, and routinely cheated and charged exorbitant interest and prices. Both dimensions of the ethic were inimical to large mass markets and a commercialization of economic life in which strangers are treated with an impersonal ethic of fairness. The breakdown of the dualism was the unintended result of modern bureaucratic state administration and the concomitant institution of formally equal **citizenship**. Citizenship eroded the **social closure** of traditional status **groups**, with their substantive sumptuary restrictions, and enabled the mass consumption that made mass production viable and, in turn, made mechanization profitable (note that this analysis reverses the conventional account in economic history in which the sequence of changes is driven by technological developments). Weber's account may be compared with Polanyi's analysis of the **state**'s role in creating markets in land, capital, and labor.

On a micro-level, recent economic sociology has criticized economic theory's "perfect competition," or "general equilibrium," models of how markets actually operate. In formal economic models, originally developed in the late nineteenth century by economists such as Alfred Marshall (1842–1924, England) and Leon Walras (1834–1910, Switzerland), the forces of supply and demand interact to produce an equilibrium price for a good at which all demand is satisfied and all supply is exhausted. That is to say, the market "clears." In order to model this outcome, a number of assumptions are made concerning the structure of the market. It comprises: (1) a myriad of rational, utility-maximizing individuals making independent decisions on the basis of "exogenously" given preferences and tastes; (2) individuals possessing perfect information about the quality and quantity of a uniform good; (3) there is market **equality** – that is, all participants are "price-takers," not monopolistic "price-makers"; and (4) there are frequent and regular exchanges.

Paradoxically, however, there is no competition in the perfect competition model. Perfect information and foresight would render any competitive bargaining process redundant. In fact, the model describes an end state of equilibrium, but cannot satisfactorily explain how this comes about as a result of the utility-maximizing decisions of independent, isolated individuals. To solve this problem, the early proponents of the supply and demand model had to add further components in order to make it function. Walras introduced the "auctioneer" to initiate and coordinate the competitive bidding. (Note that real auctions have estimated and reserve prices to "frame" the market interaction.) Marshall realized that myriad uncoordinated actions of producers and buyers with less-than-perfect **information** and **rationality** would result in price volatility. He introduced the middleman, or wholesaler, into his example of the corn market to hold buffer stocks in order to balance supply with demand and thereby maintain a stable price and an orderly market. In other words, Walras and Marshall were giving the market a **social structure** that would enable it to operate, as opposed to the instability that they recognized in the model of the interaction of the subjective preferences of myriad atomized individuals.

Alternatively, "Austrian" economic theory advocates markets as the most efficient means of economic decisionmaking and coordination on the grounds of the contrary assumption of *imperfect* information. According to Ludwig von Mises (1881–1973), for example, it was precisely because we could never have adequate information to plan an economy centrally that decentralized markets were necessary. Competitive market struggle was the best means of establishing the relative **scarcity** of goods and of ensuring dynamic change. Weber's incorporation of these ideas into his ideal type of capitalism as a "struggle for economic existence" and the "economic battle of man against man" led him to reject **socialism** as a viable form of **economy**.

Modern-economics recognizes the existence of "market failure" and "imperfect markets," but sees them as exceptions or corrigible deviations. Market failure is said to occur when the existence of a competitive market cannot establish a price for a good that will clear the market – that is, brings supply and demand into equilibrium. Three types are identified: (1) "public goods" exist when property rights cannot be established securely enough to exclude "free-riding," which deters the production of the good in question – for example, lighthouses shed light on all passers-by; (2) "externalities" refer to the unintended social costs that are "external" to the private production or exchange of a good and that are not included in its price – for example, pollution and road congestion (in general, economics considers externalities to be exceptions, whereas the deleterious unintended effects of markets are the focus of sociological critiques); (3) "perverse

outcomes" such as "moral hazard" in which the production of a good with a single price has contradictory unintended consequences that destabilize the market – for example, single-premium fire insurance that encourages negligence; or "adverse selection" in which a single price stimulates a demand that perturbs the market – for example, the single-premium health insurance that attracts demand from the unhealthy; and a single interest rate for bank loans can never be high enough to balance the costs of defaults without at the same time discouraging low-risk borrowers. Both circumstances give rise to social processes of risk assessment and, in the case of bank loans, credit-rating.

Modern economics explains the existence of real-world imperfect markets in terms of "asymmetric information." This problem was clearly illustrated by George Akerlof in his "The Market for Lemons" (1970, *Quarterly Journal of Economics*), in which the average buyer's inability to distinguish good from bad cars ("lemons" in American parlance) depresses the average price and deters the owners of good used cars from putting them on the market. In contrast, **John Maynard Keynes**'s analysis of the failure of the labor market to "clear" is inherently more sociological in its recognition of capitalism's asymmetrical power relations. He argued that workers cannot create more employment by accepting lower wages because employers may choose to take advantage of the lower costs to reduce prices and, thereby, gain a competitive advantage. This would result in the same levels of *ex ante* production and employment. Or, with lower wage costs, monopoly producers might simply take higher profits.

All the above problems derive from the inadequate understanding of the market as a socially and politically constructed institution, and from the fact that different kinds of market – labor markets, consumer markets, and production markets – have different **social structures**. In an "Interview" with Richard Swedberg in *Economics and Sociology* (1990), Harrison White has gone so far as to say that the "perfect-competition," or "general-equilibrium," model is not a theory of the market as such, but rather a theory of "pure exchange." This might describe the operation of a bazaar or medieval fair where individual buyers and sellers haggle over prices, but this theory of pure exchange does not apply, for example, to capitalist producers' markets. A producers' market cannot be understood as the result of discrete independent calculations of cost, revenue, and profit maximization by individual isolated producers that converge to fit objective economic constraints. Rather, White argues in *Identity and Control* (1992) and with Robert Eccles in "Producers' Markets" (*The New Palgrave*, 1987) that producers' markets can operate only after two "control projects" have been successfully completed. First, the firm's internal power struggle must be resolved. Second, the potentially destabilizing effect of price competition has to be dealt with; stable markets are socially constructed by the participants' comparisons of their similarities and differences and their search for a segment of the market. Either existing prices are taken as benchmark terms of trade which individuals try to better; or they may attempt to differentiate their product by quality in a particular niche which is relatively immune from competition. This can create a stable social structure, which is destabilized when participants actually behave like those modeled in the economic theory, by either calculating marginal costs and revenues and thereby creating "price wars" and "cutthroat competition," or by imitating a successful strategy and creating overcrowding, which has the same consequence. Not all markets are successfully stabilized – for example, those for haircuts and restaurant meals where intense price competition leads to a large turnover of market participants. A further implication of this approach is that oligopoly, rather than the myriad producers of the perfect competition model, is normal in production markets in order that they can make the structure-producing comparisons. In *The Architecture of Markets*, Fligstein has interpreted White's work on production markets in terms of **Pierre Bourdieu**'s "theory of fields." As actors can never have the information or market power that will enable them to determine what will maximize profits, activity is directed towards the creation of a "field" in which the participants attempt to produce the social order that will maximize their chances of survival.

This kind of approach is developed in Mitchel Abolafia's ethnographic study, in *Making Markets* (1996), of the social construction of different levels of competitive behavior in Wall Street money markets. For example, as an outsider, the bond trader, Michael Milkin, was able to make large profits by selecting those stocks – the "fallen angels" – that established elite investment banks had neglected. They responded with imitation that created destabilization and the designation of the underpriced bonds as "junk" bonds. With the market having been destabilized, Milkin was accused of the malpractice that eventually resulted in his imprisonment on accounting offences. A restabilization of the market followed his removal.

It has been noted by the French "sociology-of-convention" school and **actor network theory** – for example, Michel Callon, *The Laws of the Market* (1998) – that the economic theory of perfect competition is now used to construct the "fields" that constitute a market capable of reaching an equilibrium price. M.-F. Garcia's study of the construction of the strawberry market in the Solonge region of France in the early 1980s shows how economic textbooks had a "performative" role in bringing about the very same conditions that they described. The product was standardized; demand and supply organized into a competitive structure; and the transactions mechanism established to frame a situation in which the participants were able to calculate prices more efficiently.

Modern economic sociology has gone some way towards explaining what are seen conventionally in economic theory as the problems of imperfect information and uncertainty which prevent the achievement of market equilibrium. Information and certainty are not merely found in discoverable objectively given external conditions – for example, costs of production, marginal productivity, consumers' demand, and so on. Rather, the information that produces an intelligible and shared social world and the certainty, or relative predictability, of the market consist in the socially constructed fields and rules that structure competition.   GEOFFREY INGHAM

marriage and divorce

Although finding a (sexual) partner and forming a couple may appear to be a "natural" or even biologically driven activity, marriage is a social **institution** defined by laws, **culture**, **religion**, and of course historical and social context. This means that what marriage is (and what it might mean to the people who marry) changes over time and can reflect very different social contexts. At present, in most western societies, marriage is regarded in law as an essentially heterosexual contract, entered into with the express purpose of raising children and with the equally important function of joining **families** together. It is a contract between individuals, but it also involves the **state** and extended families. So although marriage is popularly seen as the way in which couples can proclaim their love and commitment to each other exclusively, the state has a very strong interest in marriage and has operated, with varying degrees of vigor at different times, to support and buttress marriage as a social institution. Moreover, extended families maintain a close interest in who their children marry, with arranged and vetted marriages being the norm in some **cultures** and **social classes**. Marriage is therefore both deeply personal and private, yet also the business of families, relatives, legislators, politicians, judges, policymakers, and social commentators.

Sociological interest in marriage has waxed and waned over the last half-century. Typically, discussions of marriage have been combined with sociological work on "the family," and the two social institutions tended to be treated together, with marriage being conventionally treated as little more than the threshold to family life. Sociological interest in marriage was understated, and was reflected more in the study of **social problems** such as unmarried **motherhood** or divorce, which were, at least in the 1950s and 1960s, seen as deviant forms of behavior. Because marriage was so taken for granted as something that everyone did (which was fairly true in England in the 1960s at least) it was not seen as worthy of specific analysis or debate. For example Ronald Fletcher's influential work *The Family and Marriage in Britain*, originally published in 1962, had little to say about marriage, but rather more to say about divorce. On marriage itself, Fletcher was rather complacent in his depiction:

> In the modern marriage, both partners choose each other freely as persons. Both are of equal status and expect to have an equal share in taking decisions and in pursuing their sometimes mutual, sometimes separate and diverse, tastes and interests. They live together permanently and intimately in their own home and in relative independence of wider groups of kindred.

Yet there was an earlier tradition of more critical work on marriage; although it was not strictly sociological, it ultimately provided the basis of later challenges to the taken-for-granted character of marriage and the presumed **equality** between spouses. These critical perspectives came from the work of nineteenth-century radicals, feminists, and suffragists like Cicely Hamilton, **John Stuart Mill**, Harriet Taylor, Caroline Norton, and **Friedrich Engels**. Cicely Hamilton wrote *Marriage as a Trade* in 1909, in which she outlined the gender **inequalities** in **society** which led women to have no alternative but to "snare" a husband in order to achieve economic security and **social status** in society. Women, she argued, were part of a trade which actually demeaned them and gave too much power to men. Caroline Norton, in the mid nineteenth century, pointed out that in marriage

men had absolute legal control over children and could deprive mothers of contact with them, while Mill, Taylor, and Engels all pointed to the economic inequality between husbands and wives, giving rise to tyrannical powers and absolute control over women in the private sphere. Victorian and Edwardian marriage was depicted variously as a form of virtual **slavery**, as a form of **feudalism**, and inevitably as a site of inequality and oppression.

Such depictions of marriage did not sit well with mainstream sociology of the 1950s and 1960s. **Talcott Parsons**, taking a structural functional approach, did not see inequality between the **genders**, rather he saw complementary **social roles** in the form of the breadwinner husband and the housewife. By this time the sociological gaze was more firmly fixed on "the Family," with marriage being left to the anthropologists who could study the marriage practices of less-developed societies and different religions, while the "modern" marriage depicted by Fletcher was treated as a pinnacle of achievement. It took the polemical work of Jessie Bernard in 1976 to disaggregate the unity of husband and wife, to challenge the presumption of equality once again, and to rediscover that, behind the unified front created in the functionalist approach, there could be a man's marriage and a woman's marriage, and that these were two very different, uneven lived experiences, albeit going on under one roof.

The work of Jessie Bernard was part of a new wave of feminist writing which occurred simultaneously in the United States and the United Kingdom, and which brought a very different perspective on marriage. As with the earlier suffragist writings, the second-wave feminists focused on the legal disparities that were entailed in marriage. Thus it was pointed out that only husbands could sign mortgage documents and so were the sole legal owners of the couple's home; they revisited the problem of **violence** against wives and stressed the fact that the law did not take domestic assault seriously; they pointed out that rape in marriage was perfectly legal; they also pointed to the double burden assumed by women who increasingly worked outside the home, yet were required to carry on with all the usual housework and child-care obligations. While Engels had depicted marriage as a form of capitalist exploitation with the husband as the capitalist and the wife as worker, feminist sociologists depicted marriage as a form of patriarchal exploitation in which the husband benefited not only financially from the appropriation of his wife's labor, but also materially, physically, and psychologically from her oppression. Intense debates between different strands of **feminism** ensued, with some feminists arguing that men were the primary beneficiaries of women's oppression in marriage, while others argued that **capitalism** benefited because women's unremunerated domestic labor supported and renewed the labor power of men in the **labor market**, to the benefit of capitalism.

The legal contract of marriage was seen as the device that served primarily to lock women into subservience and to remove many of their basic civil **rights**. It was, for example, lawful for the teaching profession to sack women on marriage in England and Wales, and, long after this became unlawful, the custom of leaving work on marriage continued in many parts of the United Kingdom. In the United States, Betty Friedan referred to "the problem with no name" in her book *The Feminine Mystique* (1963). By this she meant the problem of the bored housewife whose horizons in the United States of the 1950s and 1960s had shrunk to encompass little more than finding washing detergents of an adequate power, or buying Tupperware containers to keep **food** fresh. She depicted women existing on Valium and other tranquilizers in order to get through the meaninglessness of their days, awaiting the return of their husbands and serving his dinner on time.

The critical analyses that feminist sociologists developed of marriage were closely linked to political activism in the 1970s and 1980s: for example the Y B A WIFE? campaign in the United Kingdom in the 1970s. The boundaries between scholarly enterprise and political campaigning were blurred in a way similar to the relationship between **Marxism** and class struggle and the trade-union movement, or studies of **racism** and anti-racist and/or Black Power movements. These links were controversial. In the academy it meant that feminist analyses were not seen as serious or scholarly, and for a time a kind of parallel universe developed where mainstream **sociology** continued to be largely indifferent to what might happen in the "private sphere" of family life. It appeared almost as if marriage and the family became an issue for women academics, while the men concentrated on the **public sphere** and more global issues, this division of labor ironically mirroring the very problem in the "real" world that feminist academics were trying to critique.

The feminist focus on marriage as an oppressive institution, combined with the associated criticisms of romantic (heterosexual) love as **ideology** and/or a form of false consciousness led ultimately to a kind of intellectual cul-de-sac. This was because it became "unnecessary" to look into the interiority of married relationships because they were always already known to be oppressive. Much evidence was collected on the problems of marriage, but few were concerned to understand its enduring popularity or what this form of **intimacy** might signify for couples in a positive way. This meant that some early sociological insights were lost, only to be rediscovered again in the 1990s when mainstream sociology became interested once again in issues of intimacy and the private sphere. An example of what I mean is to be found in Ronald Fletcher's work. He wrote in 1966 of the way in which marriage had been transformed over time from a contractual alliance between families, designed primarily to produce legitimate heirs, into a love relationship based on choice and dependent for its continued existence upon mutual compatibility. He went on, "It is clear, therefore, that the modern relationship between husband and wife must be an extremely intense affair and, as such, is potentially unstable."

This theme is central to his work and it bears a striking similarity to the arguments put forward by **Anthony Giddens** in *The Transformation of Intimacy* (1992) and by **Ulrich Beck** and E. Beck-Gernsheim in *The Normal Chaos of Love* (1995 [trans. 1995]). A striking difference is the fact that Fletcher speaks only of husbands and wives while, by the end of the twentieth century, contemporary sociologists spoke of couples or partners – in order to include unmarried couples in their remit. Rates of cohabitation were much lower when Fletcher wrote at the start of the 1960s, and unmarried cohabitation was then still seen as shameful or something to be secretive about. But the theme of intensity and intimacy being the core of contemporary relationships, and the commensurate instability that ensues from this, is one that has returned to dominate sociological thinking. The rise of the companionate marriage/relationship is identified as an inevitable outcome of greater equality between the genders, as well as reflecting changing mentalities, but it is also seen as having major social consequences, because the compassionate relationship is paradoxically identified as increasing the chances of divorce or separation with all their attendant hardships.

What Fletcher, Giddens, and Beck and Beck-Gernsheim also have in common is their understanding of the relationship between a particular form of marriage and **modernity**. Fletcher speaks of "modern" marriage, which is not quite the same terminology as was deployed in the 1990s; yet the idea that the late modern era produced new styles of marriage based on choice and love is common to all these authors. Unfortunately this analysis tends to condemn other forms of marriage to a less modern form or to a more traditional mentality. Arranged and vetted marriage, and various forms of "sponsored courtship," are inevitably seen as less desirable, based on a lack of choice and freedom, and as devoid of (romantic) love. The social evaluation of these marital arrangements is now complicated by the prevalence of internet dating. These other forms of marriage are depicted through a very ethnocentric lens, and the meaning and significance of these forms for minority ethnic or religious **groups** are given little consideration. The significance of arranged marriages for transnational families who may be highly disadvantaged in a dominantly ethnically white **community** does not seem to have generated much sociological interest, for example.

One other silence in much of the sociological work on marriage has been the core fact that marriage is a legal contract that can only be entered into by a man and a woman. This issue became central to the feminist critique in the 1980s because the privileged status of marriage was understood to demote lesbian and gay relationships to insignificance. But the solution to this was envisaged as a rejection of marriage per se. Moreover, for a considerable time after the 1970s it appeared as if marriage was falling out of favor, with the average age of marriage in the United Kingdom rising to almost thirty years at the start of the twenty-first century, and rates of cohabitation rising annually. However, it is no longer clear that these statistics indicate a rejection of marriage. Rather marriage might be postponed, or it might happen when **children** are born, or it might happen much later in a cohabitation when issues of inheritance and **property** begin to loom as salient. Marriage may be something that people do at a specific point in their **life-course**, but it no longer has to occur as a kind of **rite of passage** into adulthood, as it was in the 1950s or 1960s.

The fact that people can actively choose to reject marriage, or elect to marry when it suits them rather than in their early twenties, indicates that the meaning of marriage is changing. It is no longer "compulsory" and many of the legal and personal disabilities that attended marriage for women have diminished. In this context, gay and lesbian groups have begun to challenge the "heteronormative" assumptions that are still the basis of marriage. Because marriage brings with it certain privileges (such as recognition by the state in terms of social benefits, tax and exemptions, and residence) it is seen as a denial of human **rights** for a sector of the community to be denied the right to marry. Marriage has therefore become the site of political activism again in both the United States and the United Kingdom, and also throughout Europe, Australia, and New Zealand. Some countries, such as the Netherlands, now recognize gay and lesbian marriage, while others such as the United Kingdom have created a parallel legal institution called "civil partnership" which carries all the rights and obligations of marriage, but which is not given the title of "marriage." In the United Kingdom and the United States religious groups reject strongly the idea that gay men and lesbians should be entitled to have their relationships recognized and celebrated in the way reserved for heterosexual couples, seeing it as contravening basic religious teaching. Moreover, some gay and lesbian groups also reject the idea of marriage and state recognition of relationships, because they see this as a way of being co-opted into conventional family life when they would prefer to subvert the normative order. Others argue that to offer gay men and lesbians "civil partnership" when heterosexual couples retain the option of "marriage" merely confirms homosexual relationships as second-rate, and they demand absolute equality as a matter of basic civil rights. Marriage is therefore back on the political agenda in much the way it was in the 1970s and at various points since the mid nineteenth century.

Sociology (along with political commentators and the media) has had a fascination with divorce rates and **statistics** since the 1950s. Divorce rates have become the modern equivalent of É. Durkheim's suicide rates, in as much as they are treated as the measure of the stability of family life and ultimately a measure of social cohesion. This approach to divorce rates originates with functionalist thinking in which "the family" is treated as the foundation of other social institutions. This gave rise to the understanding that instability in the family led to both personal instability (through poor **socialization** of children) and social instability (through the knock-on effects of underachieving, anti-social young people, and personal and economic disruption). Divorce has therefore occupied a particularly significant place in the study of contemporary **social problems** not only because it has been seen as a problem in itself, but because it has been seen as giving rise to a host of other difficulties.

The tradition of treating divorce as a social problem (rather than a solution to a problem) stems from sociology's general lack of a critical perspective on the family in the past. Because gender relations in the private sphere were not a matter of (much) sociological interest until second-wave feminist scholarship forced them onto the agenda, divorce could only be envisaged as a threat to social cohesion. Even Fletcher, who did write more positively about divorce in the 1960s, saw it as a route to remarriage and hence a means of re-establishing proper family life, rather than a potential liberation from the institution of marriage itself.

Control over the exit from marriage has been closely regulated in western societies, and the Catholic and Protestant Churches strove hard to retain this control, even in increasingly secular societies. In the Republic of Ireland, for example, legal divorce became available only in 1996, and in England and Wales it was only in the 1960s that the Church of England gave up its opposition to the introduction of divorce on the grounds of mutual consent. Prior to this, divorce was only available on the basis of proof of matrimonial offense, and one spouse had to be identified as a guilty party. Divorce courts were full of details of spousal cruelties, adulterous relationships (sometimes faked), and minute details of incompatibilities. Divorce was a kind of public spectacle and humiliation, with details published in the print media, and with "innocent" and "guilty" parties named and shamed.

Some early sociological work was critical of this spectacle, and also of the class basis of divorce, since the wealthy could afford to divorce, while the poor could not. There also grew up a pre-second wave feminist critique of the **poverty** and hardship caused to women who were denied divorce, yet were unsupported by their husbands who had deserted them. In the 1960s the apparently new problem of lone mothers (see **lone-parent family**) was gradually recognized and, although the poverty of women raising children alone was actually not new at all, it gained a new name and a new urgency because of the increasing numbers of formerly married women in this situation after World War II. While mothers alone with children had formerly been divided into the deserving poor (namely widows) and the undeserving poor (namely unmarried mothers), the advent of deserted mothers and then divorced mothers created a new category of women who were obliged to look to the public purse for support.

In both the United States and the United Kingdom divorce rates climbed steeply in the 1970s and 1980s and, although rates of increase have declined, divorce has become a common feature of family life and it increasingly involves children under sixteen years of age. This of course means that more young people reaching marriageable age come from families where either their own parents have divorced, or there has been a divorce within the extended kinship network. The availability of divorce is therefore part of the context of marriage in the twenty-first century.

It is this context that has given rise to a new level of concern over divorce as a social problem, namely the problem of the lack of commitment in modern relationships. Divorce is seen to have generated a new psychology in which younger **generations** "fail" to recognize that they have to work at relationships to make them last, and that much self sacrifice is required. What pro-family commentators depict as a lack of commitment and moral fiber, some sociologists have labeled the **individualization theory**. Thus authors such as Giddens, Beck, and Beck-Gernsheim have identified a changing mentality in which communication and mutual support become key elements of relationships and where the lack of such components is seen as adequate motivation for leaving one partner to find another. The debate over divorce and commitment reflects wider debates in sociology about the impact and significance of the decline in personal life of external **authorities** to govern behavior and whether this has led to a form of moral anarchy, or to a new normative order which has different modes of demonstrating responsibility and commitments. The rise in rates of divorce and cohabitation are, for example, for some indicators of the demise of the moral family, while for others they merely indicate that in a more open society, with greater equality between the genders, people can mold new forms of commitment and mutual support. It seems unlikely that there will be a ready resolution to this debate because the social landscape of marriage and divorce is constantly changing and different implications and consequences of changes to personal relationships emerge as social, cultural, and economic conditions change. Two new developments are discussed below, the first being the changing perception of childhood and the second being the changing position of fathers.

Until the 1990s children were depicted in divorce literature as the "innocent victims" of parental divorce. This victim status did not require children to speak, although the children might be assessed in terms of their academic achievements, their social skills, and their conformity to a series of life-course expectations. It was of course expected that the sons of divorced parents would become delinquent and the daughters would become unmarried, teenage mothers. In the rush to calibrate the harms of divorce there was little room for more qualitative or ethnographic research that would seek to understand divorce from the standpoint(s) of children. However, such approaches have begun to emerge and children are increasingly seen as actively engaging with the problems of family transformations and in seeking to find solutions and coping mechanisms, often giving support to their parents, and often critical of their parents' behavior. The perspectives of children reveal their powerlessness (particularly because children are rarely consulted about their futures when parents separate) but also their growing demands for greater attentiveness from parents in the evolution of post-divorce family life.

This concept of post-divorce family life, sometimes referred to as the divorce-extended family, is a recent development. Almost all sociological work on divorce took it for granted that divorce meant family breakdown, indeed the terminology was used interchangeably. It was assumed that children's family horizons were diminished through the loss of a father (usually) and paternal kindred. But the new attentiveness to children and the possibility of divorce by mutual consent has meant that children can, in some circumstances, retain their family links (including grandparents on both sides). Sociological research now embraces concepts such as "parenting across households" or "shared parenting" in order to capture the ways in which parents continue to be parents notwithstanding divorce and the establishment of different households. The idea that divorce leads automatically to lone motherhood and fatherless children, and that the best solution is for mothers to remarry and create the re-constituted nuclear family with the introduction of a step-father, is no longer seen as accurate. Indeed the new morality of divorce seems increasingly to embrace the idea that parenthood is for life, and that this should be valued regardless of the quality of the relationships between former spouses.

These shifts in the moral ordering of divorce are related to another important shift in the landscape of marriage and divorce: the position of fathers. While mothers were seen as the economic victims of marriage and divorce throughout the 1970s and 1980s, during the 1990s fathers started to be redefined as the victims of the system. Having been depicted as "deadbeat dads" who fail to pay child support and to maintain contact with their children, fathers are now redefined as being the ones who lose most from divorce because of the tendency for mothers to have the residence of children after separation. The Fathers' Rights Movement has become one of the fastest-growing and most politically influential single-issue campaigns at the turn of the twenty-first century. This movement requires that, on divorce or separation, fathers should be allocated 50 percent of their children's time to ensure equality between parents, and also that children maintain their relationships with their fathers. This movement is a complex one. At one extreme it may be seen as a reassertion of paternal authority in which fathers insist on their genetically based rights to a child, quite independent of the quality of any relationship that they may have with the mother of the child. At the other extreme it may be seen as a positive reflection of the new fatherhood in which men seek to share both the burdens and the joys of raising children. In the former model, fatherhood is imposed regardless of the views of mothers and/or children, in the latter, fatherhood arises from relationships of equality and mutual support with both mothers and children. While the impact of this movement is still unknown, it has already reshaped the debates that currently surround the issue of divorce.   CAROL SMART

Thomas H. Marshall (1893–1982)

Fellow of Trinity College Cambridge and subsequently Professor of Sociology at the London School of Economics, Marshall is famous for his analysis of **citizenship** in *Citizenship and Social Class and Other Essays* (1950), in which he showed how in Britain social **rights** had evolved through three stages, namely civil, political, and social rights. These rights had been recognized in such **institutions** as the jury system, parliament, and the **welfare state**. He argued that citizenship modified the class system by some redistribution of entitlements to resources, primarily through the welfare state. In his *Social Policy in the Twentieth Century* (1965), he analyzed the growth of social rights through policy development between 1890 and 1945. In *The Right to Welfare and Other Essays* (1981), he argued that modern **societies** are 'hyphenated' because there is a permanent contradiction between liberal **democracy** and the capitalist system. His theory of citizenship was essentially a description of the postwar reconstruction of Britain in terms of the tension between **social class** and citizenship. He has subsequently been criticized for neglecting such issues as **gender** and **race and ethnicity.** Marshall was not a prolific sociologist, but his framework has been the foundation of the sociology of citizenship in both the United States and the United Kingdom.

BRYAN S. TURNER

Martin, David (1929–)

An Emeritus Professor of Sociology at the London School of Economics, and Honorary Professor in the Department of Religious Studies at Lancaster University, Martin was in 1948 a conscientious objector and did his national service in the "noncombatant corps". This experience influenced his early contribution to the sociological analysis of *Pacifism* (1965) and to the understanding of the Christian challenge to **violence**, but his major research has been in the sociology of **religion**, in which he has been a leading critic of the contention that **industrial societies** are characterized by an inevitable process of **secularization**. In *A Sociology of English Religion* (1967), *The Religious and the Secular* (1969), and *A General Theory of Secularization* (1978), he showed that the evidence on belief and practice does not support a theory of uniform secularization in modern societies. He challenged the implicit historical and sociological assumptions behind this analysis of secular society.

In *Tongues of Fire* (1990) and *Pentecostalism: The World Their Parish* (2002), he explored the global development of charismatic Christianity, drawing a productive comparison between the growth of evangelical Methodism in the early nineteenth century and the expansion of Pentecostalism in Latin America in the twentieth century. Martin argues that there is an important consonance between Pentecostalism and the spread of global liberal **capitalism** and "the expressive revolution" (see **Talcott Parsons**). Pentecostalism, which is devolved, voluntary, local, and fissiparous, works within a religious **market** that offers spiritual uplift, social success, and emotional gratification. While Methodism supplied the work ethic of early capitalism, Pentecostalism is relevant to the work skills and personal attributes of the postindustrial service **economy**, especially in terms of self-monitoring and a refusal to accept failure. He has throughout his career been concerned with the relationship between sociology and theology, as illustrated in his *Reflections on Sociology and Theology* (1997).

BRYAN S. TURNER

Marx, Karl (1818–1883)

The most influential of the socialist thinkers, Marx changed dramatically the way we view **society** and the world. Although he dedicated his life to writing a critique of **political economy**, he also pioneered a theory of society and history, and a view of the world that were truly revolutionary. It is impossible to think of a criticism of capitalist society that does not refer centrally to his work.

He was born in Trier, Germany. Although often referred to as a Jew – he came from a long line of rabbis – Marx was technically a Protestant. He grew up in a professional middle-class home, and his father, a lawyer, supported the **Enlightenment**. His uncle, the Baron von Westphalen (whose daughter Marx married), was enthusiastic about the **socialism** of the French writer, **G. H. Saint-Simon**.

After schooling in Trier (1830–5) – a schoolboy essay showed him committed to the development of humanity – Marx entered the University of Bonn to study law. At university he spent much of his time socializing and running up large debts. His father insisted that he move to the more sedate University of Berlin. Here he came under the influence of one of his lecturers, Bruno Bauer (1809–82), who introduced Marx to the writings of **Georg Wilhelm Friedrich Hegel,** who had been the Professor of Philosophy at Berlin until his death in 1831.

In 1838 Marx decided to become a university lecturer. After completing his doctoral thesis on ancient Greek philosophy at the University of Jena, Marx hoped that Bauer would help find him a teaching post. However, in 1842 Bauer was dismissed as a result of his outspoken atheism and was unable to help.

Marx's notion of philosophy was practical and down-to-earth, and he distanced himself from the empty radicalism of many of the Young Hegelians. From Berlin he moved to Cologne where the city's liberal opposition movement was fairly strong. In 1842, Marx was appointed editor of the newspaper *Die Rheinische Zeitung*, and interestingly he denied at this stage any sympathy with **Communism**. The newspaper was committed to **liberalism**, and Marx certainly demonstrated a deep concern with social questions, as in his defense of **peasants**' right to collect wood, or his concern about the **poverty** of the Mosel wine growers. In 1843, the paper was banned by the Prussian authorities.

Warned that he might be arrested, Marx moved to Paris and in the spring and summer of 1843 he wrote a detailed critique of Hegel's *Philosophy of Right* (1821 [trans. 1942]) in which he not only identified himself as a democrat, but saw a tension between **democracy** and the **state**. He now talked about the need to dissolve **civil society** – society based upon private **property**, the **market**, and the state.

He was greatly influenced by the **materialism** of Ludwig Feuerbach (1804–72) in his *Essence of Christianity* (1841 [trans. 1957]), although he felt that Feuerbach had placed too much stress upon nature and not enough on **politics**. In a letter to Arnold Ruge (1802–80) in 1843, Marx emphasized the need to work with social and political realities as they were actually constituted. He became the editor of *Franco-German Yearbook*, and it was here he published *On the Jewish Question* (1844 [trans. 1932]), in which he argued that emancipation must not merely be political: it must be social. This text is crucial because it establishes Marx's concern with transcending the state (which is linked with **religion**), the market, and commerce, and contains his celebrated attack on liberal notions of **citizenship** as abstract and limited. His second piece in the *Yearbook* proclaims the need for the principles of radical philosophy to be realized by the proletariat: for the first time Marx identified the agent that will move humanity beyond civil society and the state. The proletariat is the **social class** with radical chains, and his piece – an introduction to the critique of Hegel's *Philosophy of Right* – contains the famous characterization of religion as the "opium of the people."

Mixing with members of the working class for the first time, he now described himself as a communist. He championed the revolt of the Silesian weavers in Germany, because it emphasized the importance of a social, and not merely political, solution to their problems. In 1844 Marx wrote *Economic and Philosophic Manuscripts* (first published in English in 1932), which consisted of a critical assessment of the work of economists like James Mill (1773–1836) and Jean-Baptiste Say (1776–1832), and a critique of Hegel's dialectic. The work is famous for its characterization of exploitation as a process of **alienation**, and the argument that religion, the **family**, state, law, **morality**, and science are (in their conventional forms) expressions of this alienation. Humans are enslaved by their own creation, and communism is seen as the riddle of history solved. While in Paris, he became a close friend of **Friedrich Engels**, whose essay on political economy greatly impressed him, and they decided to work together, writing a fierce critique of Bruno Bauer (and his brothers) in a work entitled *The Holy Family* (1845 [trans. 1932]).

In 1845 Marx was deported from France and went to Brussels, where he (with Engels) wrote *The German Ideology* (1845 [trans. 1965]), a work not published in his lifetime. Before writing this work, Marx drafted his *Theses on Feuerbach* (1845 [trans. 1970]) where he argued that Feuerbach saw abstract theoretical solutions to practical problems. The famous eleventh thesis refers to the fact that, whereas the philosophers have interpreted the world, the point is to change it. *The German Ideology* elaborates the criticisms of Feuerbach, and deals at great length with the latest manifestations of Young Hegelian **idealism**, including Stirner's anarchist theory of egoism. Marx explicitly identifies his position as one of "new materialism," and the work contains general arguments for a conception of history, society, politics, and **culture** rooted in the relations of production. While writing this volume, Marx and Engels established a Communist Corresponding Committee (the embryo of subsequent Communist Internationals). One of the socialists he was anxious to recruit was Pierre Joseph Proudhon (1809–65), but by 1847 he had written a fierce critique of Proudhon's ideas (which he denounced as abstract and doctrinaire) in *The Poverty of Philosophy*.

In November 1847 Marx attended a meeting of the Communist League's Central Committee in London (it had originally been the League of the Just), and this was the organization that commissioned *The Communist Manifesto* (1848 [trans. 1968]). Although Engels had written some earlier drafts, the *Manifesto* in its published form was written primarily by Marx and is the most famous of Marx's works. With extraordinary brevity and poetic intensity, the work contains a hymn of praise to **capitalism** as a dynamic productive system, and establishes the argument that communism must arise on the basis of capitalism as a system that becomes increasingly crisis-ridden as it progresses. The *Manifesto* refers to the way in which more and more sections of society are "proletarianized," although in Marx's more specific writings (like the political analyses on France) the uneven nature of this process receives more stress. The work also contains highly suggestive comments on the need for communists to organize as a "party" (although the meaning of this is far from clear), and it contains a denunciation of other forms of **socialism** and a radical ten-point program, as well as a famous argument that the liberal ("bourgeois") revolution in Germany must be supported, as a prelude to "the immediately following" proletarian revolution.

News of the revolution in Paris reached Brussels in February 1848. Marx briefly decamped to Paris but moved to Cologne where he founded the *Neue Rheinische Zeitung* which published reports of revolutionary activity all over Europe. The program of the paper was a united democratic Germany (democracy interpreted in a left-liberal fashion) and a war with tsarist Russia. But the revolutions were all defeated and the *Neue Rheinische Zeitung* closed down. In 1849 Marx settled in Britain. He was initially convinced that the defeats were only a temporary setback, and Marx rejoined the Communist League. In his March circular to the League, Marx espouses the strategy of "permanent revolution" – a strategy of continuing an antifeudal revolution until capital itself is overthrown. This rather "optimistic" perspective was continued in the June circular, although Marx was to warn in 1850 that up to fifty years might have to pass before a revolution could succeed. After a split within the League, Marx moved "his" wing of the Communist League to Cologne and had it wound up in 1852.

Often depending on the money that Engels could raise, the Marx family lived in poverty. The *Neue Rheinische Zeitung Revue*, produced in 1850, contained among other things Marx's analysis of French political developments. These essays were subsequently edited by Engels and published in Germany as *The Class Struggles in France* (1895 [trans. 1964]) and *The Eighteenth Brumaire of Louis Napoleon* (1852 [trans. 1934]), often considered his most brilliant political pamphlet. In these works Marx showed the importance of producing a concrete analysis of the nuances of political struggle and the way in which a ruling bloc of different class fractions has to be stitched together to make up state **power** in a particular instance. After completing his book on the Communist Cologne Trial, Marx turned to his economic studies and during the 1850s he published the first two chapters of what was to be *Capital*. Despite decades of mid-Victorian prosperity passed in Britain, Marx made an attempt to get to grips with class structure there in a review he wrote of the pamphlet of 1850 (*Pourquoi la révolution d'Angleterre a-t-elle réussi?*) by François Guizot (1787–1874).

Between 1852 and 1862 Marx published – although in many instances the actual articles were written by Engels – for the *New York Daily Tribune* as their London correspondent. He tackled the questions of India, the Crimean War, and upheavals in China. Marx wrote an "Introduction to the Critique of Political Economy" in 1861. In this introduction or outline, which was not published

until 1941 as the *Grundrisse*, he dealt with the questions of **money** and capital, with important asides about, for example, **alienation** and the division of **labor** in a capitalist society. In 1859, he published *A Contribution to the Critique of Political Economy*, which contains the famous "guiding thread" that outlines what came to be called his "materialist conception of history." He identifies the "Asiatic, ancient, feudal and capitalist modes of production" so that a mode of production embraces both the forces and relations of production of a given system. Critics argue that this analysis "fits" capitalism far more easily than it does precapitalist modes of production.

Much of the argument here was rewritten in *Capital*, but before his magnum opus could be tackled, Marx spent eighteen months attacking Karl Vogt (1817–95) who had been a leader in the Frankfurt parliament. In November, 1866, Marx personally took the manuscript of Volume I of *Capital* over to his publisher in Germany. The first section deals with the nature of commodities and money; the second, the transformation of money into capital; the third, with the nature of surplus value. Marx argues that what makes it possible for commodities to exchange is that they are the product of labor, but this theory of value is seen by many commentators (including Marxists) to be rather archaic and implausible. This was followed by Marx's far more readable history of capitalism and the effect of machinery on the worker, and culminated in his assessment of capital accumulation.

The other two volumes of *Capital* have none of the polish of the first. Volume III deals with the relationship of values and prices.

By the 1860s, working-class activity was reviving. In September 1864, the First International was formed with Marx as its president. The first years of the International were taken up with arguments against the followers of Proudhon, who were opposed to strikes and political involvement. One of the affiliates to the First International was the newly constituted German Social Democratic Workers Party. Marx supported the causes of Polish and Irish independence. After the defeat of France by Prussia, the Paris Commune was proclaimed. Marx saw this as a heroic if doomed attempt to storm heaven, presenting the commune (which was brutally crushed after seventy-two days in office) in *The Civil War in France* as a "working-class government," a state ceasing to be a state. However, after 1870 Marx became increasingly preoccupied with a struggle against the Russian anarchist,

Mikhail Bakunin (1814–76), and the International was transferred to New York where it died a natural death.

Capital was translated into Russian in 1872, and Marx learnt Russian in order to read original sources. He became familiar with Russian socialists and declared in the 1882 Preface to the Russian translation of the *Communist Manifesto* that a revolution in Russia could avoid capitalism and spark a revolution in the West. In 1875 he wrote a critique of the German socialist party program, accusing the latter of liberal formulas and abstractions. But his health continued to deteriorate, and he died in 1883.   JOHN HOFFMAN

Marxism

Karl Marx famously declared that he was not a Marxist, and it is arguable that there is an inherent tension between his ideas and the movements that arose in his name.

Marx never saw a Marxist movement seize power during his lifetime. The relationship between Marx's theory and the Russian Revolution of 1917 is highly contentious. There is evidence to suggest that Marx thought that socialist revolutions could emancipate humanity only if they took place in developed capitalist countries, and western Marxists have held to this view, although without practical results.

Soviet Marxism used Marx's ideas to establish a highly authoritarian form of **socialism** that replicated itself after World War II in the Communist Party states of eastern Europe. Chinese Marxism emphasized the importance of national independence, the centrality of will-power, and economic self-sufficiency, and Cuban Marxism arose out of the unwillingness of the United States to tolerate radical **nationalism**. It is certainly true that Marxism has been much more successful where it has been able to integrate itself with anti-colonial and anti-imperialist struggles in the so-called Third World, but only in South Africa has Marxism expressed itself through an independent Communist Party; and even here it is closely integrated into a movement of national liberation.

Marxism as a political movement has usually been anti-liberal, except in western Europe where the ideas of the Italian Marxist **Antonio Gramsci** led to a Marxism that emphasized the importance of winning popular consent and infusing Marxism with liberal **values**.   JOHN HOFFMAN

Marxist sociology

Marxism is a theory of **society** as well as a theory of economics. In its classical form, Marxist sociology argues that people enter into social relationships independent of their will. This does not mean that they lack agency, but rather that what people wish to do can never be the same as what they actually do. This is why a Marxist sociology is materialist in that it assumes that even though people act consciously, their consciousness is not a reliable guide to the course of action they pursue.

In order to survive, people must produce goods and services, and this fact has particular significance for Marxist sociology. Production is possible only if people have **technology** – what are referred to as the forces of production – and they cooperate with one another in particular ways – what are called relations of production. The forces and relations of production collectively constitute the basis of society: they have primary significance in accounting for events.

Marxist sociology assumes that there is always a tension between the forces and relations of production. Hence relationships must continually change, since the technology people employ is itself always changing. This tension occurs in all societies, so that it would be wrong to assume that social development can ever cease.

On the other hand, this tension becomes an "antagonism" when society is divided into **social classes**. Classes arise where those who produce are not the same people as those who benefit from production. Classical Marxism assumes that there is a relationship of exploitation between classes. This makes it impossible for changes in the forces of production to be reflected relatively smoothly in changes in the relations of production, since a particular class has a vested interest in a given set of productive relations. In class-divided societies, the collision between the forces and relations of production creates the necessity for revolution.

Marx and his supporters are well aware that production cannot occur on its own. Its organization requires a **culture**, a legal and political framework, a set of **values**, and a family structure; these are seen as constituting a "superstructure" not because they are irrelevant, but because they cannot be understood on their own terms. Hence Marxist sociology is not a theory of "economic reductionism" since this would imply that, whereas the base molds the superstructure, the superstructure does not impact on the base.

In class-divided societies, the "superstructure" works to entrench a particular set of productive relations, giving the latter religious, political, and ethical **legitimacy**. This is why class is political and cultural as well as economic, even though the roots of class lie in the way society produces. While certain elements of the superstructure (such as **religion** and the **state**) are particular to class-divided societies, others (such as **culture**, political and social organization, family structure) exist in all societies. They are in tension with the base but this tension can be resolved without the need for revolution (see **theory of revolution**), since no one has an entrenched interest in a particular set of productive relations.

JOHN HOFFMAN

masculinity/masculinities

At a general level masculinity is understood as the ways of being and becoming a man. As with many of the key terms in sociology, masculinity and femininity were developed against the background of biological definitions that suggest that these concepts are based in nature. Recently, sociobiological and evolutionary psychology theorists have gained increasing popular appeal with their focus on the power of nature over **culture** in determining gender differences between men and women. Since the mid-1980s, particularly, as a result of feminist, gay, and lesbian writing, and AIDS activism, the changing nature of men's lives and their experiences have been much debated within a range of literatures, drawing upon sex roles, gender **identity**, **psychoanalysis**, and **gender** and power relations.

Sex-role theory, which developed alongside theories of **socialization**, has been highly influential in the **social sciences**. Through socialization, sex-role theorists argue, males and females are conditioned into appropriate **social roles** and behavior. **Norms** and expectations that are polarized between the genders are central to the definition of masculinity. Sex-role theory assumes that these ahistorical gender essences are quantifiable and measurable. Consequently, attitude tests can be used to measure levels of socialization by the amounts of masculinity that males possess. Within this perspective, masculinity is subject to objective measurement through an index of gender norms. For example, strength, **power**, and sexual competence are expected of boys in western societies. Hence a wide range of individual men and male **groups**, such as effeminate boys and gays, are seen as not having enough masculinity, which is explained in terms of deficient levels of testosterone, inadequate role models, or overpowering mothers. In contrast, black boys and working-class boys are seen as having too much masculinity. Second-wave **feminism** challenged the conceptual and political implications of

the commonsense view that biology is destiny. In response, a distinction was made between biologically based sex (females and males) and culturally based gender (femininity and masculinity). Such work opened up masculinity to critical scrutiny, understanding masculinity as situated within a structure of gendered hierarchies, in which particular social practices are used to reproduce social divisions and **inequality**.

Earlier theories of **patriarchy** (male dominance) used a unitary notion (one style) of masculinity. Later feminist theorists emphasized that gender relations are multidimensional and differentially experienced, and are responded to within specific historical contexts and social locations. In other words, differentiated forms of male power can be explained only by an analysis that takes into consideration the specific conditions that give rise to these situations. Sociological perspectives have been used to explore the social organization of masculinity and the active cultural production of masculinities within institutional sites. One of the most influential theorists, R. W. Connell, building on feminist analysis, suggests that men occupying a hegemonic masculinity are asserting a position of superiority. They do this by winning the consent of other males and females, in order to secure their (hegemonic) **legitimacy**. Men are able to position other men by way of their subordinated, complicit, or marginalized relationships. This suggests a move away from talking about a single masculinity to that of a plurality of masculinities. In *Masculinities* (1995), Connell acknowledges the social and cultural variations in being and becoming male. Multiple masculinities is a term used to convey the diversity of ways of enacting masculinity, individually and/or collectively. For example, emerging male gay identities/subjectivities provide concrete evidence that masculinity is not something one is born with or an inherent possession, but rather an active process of achievement, performance, and enactment. Furthermore, the development of a wide range of gay male styles makes clear that the meaning of the living out of fractured masculinities involves a diverse range of men's investments, anxieties, fantasy identifications, and contradictory **emotions**.

More recently, poststructuralists and psychoanalysts have produced texts that address the perceived limitations of sociology around issues of the self, subjectivity, the **body**, and gender and sexual identity formations. For example, J. Butler's contemporary theorizing on gender as performative, in *Gender Trouble* (1990), in which she rejects stable categories, has opened up ways of understanding notions of femininity and masculinity. This emphasis on gender as performative has problematized the cultural formation of sex and the interconnections between sex and gender. For example, it provides a framework within which to focus on uncoupling masculinity from male bodies, that is, uncoupling *what men do* from *what men are*. Masculinity and femininity in this way can be understood as something that cannot simply be equated with biological sex. The implication of this is that, at particular historical moments, female bodies are able to take on and live out particular masculinities. In particular, this highlights the inadequacy of contemporary theories of gender in accommodating female masculinities. Anthropologists are also critical of the conceptual development of masculinity in the context of western academia, which they argue tends to construct a set of insular concepts and reified types that inadequately describe gender relations in other cultures. This cross-cultural analysis illustrates the limitations of generalizing about what it means to be a man from a western model of masculinity. Work on masculinities has tended to concentrate on the localized production of men's meanings and experiences. However, recent anthropological studies suggest the need to understand masculinities within a broader social and cultural framework that includes such issues as international **politics**, intranational economic relations, and globalized desires.

Presently, across western societies, the main representation of men and masculinity is that of crisis. For example, masculinity is intimately linked to wider social and cultural transformations within the British nation-state, and the assumed crisis of masculinity can be read as an effect of the wider crisis of late **modernity**. It is suggested that socio-cultural change is marked by the disintegration of older social collectivities – such as **social class** – and increased fluidity of social relationships, with an accompanying interest in identity and subjectivity. This is part of a more general trend whereby the ascendant social category in established binaries (for example, men, heterosexuals, and whites) are becoming the new objects of critical appraisal.

MAIRTIN MAC-AN-GHAILL AND CHRIS HAYWOOD

mass media and communications

During the **Enlightenment** and the period of eighteenth-century revolutions, the press was perceived as a progressive source of **information**, debate, and political transformation. The nineteenth century, however, saw the rise of a commercial press and sensationalistic pandering to the masses that evoked critique of emergent mass media and communication. With the rise of mass entertainment, broadcasting, and a proliferation of new media in the twentieth century, there were a series of critiques of mass culture and communication, from the right and left. Mass media and communications were linked to the rise of what critics saw as **individualism** and **mass society,** which were in turn interpreted as threats to **democracy**, freedom, and other positive **values**.

Critiques of mass culture and the press began emerging during the late eighteenth century. Leo Lowenthal in *Literature, Popular Culture, and Society* (1961: 20) cites the comment of J. W. Goethe (1749–1832) that the press constitutes a squandering of time wherein the reader "wastes the days and lives from hand to mouth, without creating anything." Anticipating Søren Kierkegaard (1815–55), he criticized the ways that modern entertainment and the press promoted passivity and conformity, noting in a ditty how the press is eager to provide its readers with almost anything except dissenting ideas:

Come let us print it all
And be busy everywhere;
But no one should stir
Who does not think like we.

Others had more optimistic appraisals of the impact of mass media, and particularly the press. **Georg Wilhelm Friedrich Hegel**, famously, compared reading the daily newspaper with morning prayer. **Karl Marx** in *Collected Works* (1975, vol. I: 165), had an especially high opinion of the press in the promotion of **democracy** and civil liberties, writing in 1842 that:

The free press is the ubiquitous vigilant eye of a people's soul, the embodiment of a people's faith in itself, the eloquent link that connects the individual with the state and the world, the embodied culture that transforms material struggles into intellectual struggles and idealizes their crude material form. It is a people's frank confession to itself, and the redeeming power of confession is well known. It is the spiritual mirror in which a people can see itself, and self-examination is the first condition of wisdom. It is the spirit of the state, which can be delivered into every cottage, cheaper than coal gas. It is all-sided, ubiquitous, omniscient. It is the ideal world which always wells up out of the real world and flows back into it with every greater spiritual riches and renews its soul.

By the 1840s, the press was thus a contested terrain with fervent defenders and critics. Some saw it as an instrument of progress and enlightenment, while others saw it as an instrument of distraction and banality. Different political groupings were developing their own distinct presses and attempting to shape **public opinion** in various ways. While Goethe and others made some critical remarks concerning the press of the day, one of the first systematic and sustained attacks on the press is evident in Danish philosopher/theologian Kierkegaard's polemic *The Present Age* (1846 [trans. 1982]), with the satirical Danish review *The Corsair*, which published articles making fun of him in late 1845, inciting him into a literary duel with the journal. Kierkegaard's efforts constitute one of the first critiques of print media as an instrument for the creation of mass audience and political manipulation, producing an early assault against the media and foreshadowing later critical theories of mass media and society.

Anticipating later Marxist and conservative critiques of the media, Kierkegaard argues that when "passion and commercial interest determine the issue," when "the rattle of money in the cashbox" is at stake, the propensity for corruption increases (1982: 172). Kierkegaard reveals insight here into the economic roots of the features of the press that he finds scandalous, arguing that "immoral slander" is "of no benefit whatsoever" and "does great harm because it seduces the unstable, the irresponsible, the sensate, those who are lost in earthly passions, seduces them by means of ambiguity, lack of character and the concealment of brash contempt under the pursuit of the comic" (1982: 179–80).

Interestingly, Kierkegaard's privileged metaphor for the press is that it is a vicious attack dog. He does not theorize the press as a guardian of the public's interests, as it was initially conceived to be in democratic theory, but rather as a predator that goes after individuals in a contemptible way. The press, he argued, is fundamentally irresponsible because its writers were anonymous and did not assume responsibility for what they wrote. In addition to undertaking an ethical critique of the press, Kierkegaard was one of the first to see that the press is a mass medium which addresses its audience as members of a crowd and that itself helps to create a mass society. The press plays a fundamental role, Kierkegaard suggests, in producing a public, a crowd devoid of individuality and independent judgment, their thought determined by the **authority** of printed words and editorial fiat. The average man in the street, Kierkegaard suggests, "believes that what appears in the newspapers is public

opinion, the voice of the people and of truth" (1982: 186).

Kierkegaard thus points to the ways that the press simulates **authority** and **objectivity** and can thus make a lie appear as truth, or an opinion as fact. Inverting the liberal theory of public opinion (which is supposed to protect the interests of the public against corrupt authority), Kierkegaard claims that the press creates a phantom public devoid of character and individuality. Consequently, Kierkegaard, like later **postmodern theory**, ascribes to communications media a tremendous role in producing a mass society without distinction, individuality, or conviction. Devoid of individuality, the masses themselves are an abstraction and the main effect of modern society is a leveling of the population into a mass.

Friedrich Nietzsche (1844–1900) believed that modern society had become so chaotic, fragmented, and devoid of "creative force" that it had lost the resources to create a vital **culture**, and that ultimately it greatly advanced the decline of the human species that had already begun early in western history. In Nietzsche's view, two complementary trends were evident that were producing contradictory processes of "massification" and fragmentation – the extreme consequences of which would be a central theme of some postmodern theory. On one hand, for Nietzsche, modern society was fragmenting into warring **groups**, factions, and individuals, without any overriding purpose or shared goals. On the other hand, it was leveling individuals into a herd, bereft of individuality, spontaneity, passion, and creativity. Both trends were harmful to the development of the sort of free, creative, and strong individuality championed by Nietzsche, and thus he was sharply critical of each.

In their groundbreaking work *Dialectic of Enlightenment* (1948 [trans. 1972]), **Max Horkheimer** and **Theodor Wiesengrund Adorno** coined the term culture industry to signify the process of the industrialization (see **industrial society**) of mass-produced culture and the commercial imperatives that constructed it. The critical theorists analyzed all mass-mediated cultural artifacts within the context of industrial production, in which the commodities of the culture industries exhibited the same features as other products of mass production: commodification, standardization, and massification. The culture industries had the specific function, however, of providing ideological legitimation of the existing capitalist society and of integrating individuals into its way of life.

For the **Frankfurt School**, mass culture and communications therefore stand in the center of leisure activity, are important agents of **socialization**, mediators of political reality, and should thus be seen as major **institutions** of contemporary societies with a variety of economic, political, cultural, and social effects. Furthermore, the critical theorists investigated the cultural industries politically as a form of the integration of the working class into capitalist societies. The Frankfurt School theorists were among the first neo-Marxian groups to examine the effects of mass culture and the rise of the **consumer society** on the working classes that were to be the instrument of revolution in the classical Marxian scenario. They also analyzed the ways that the culture industries and consumer society were stabilizing contemporary **capitalism** and accordingly sought new strategies for political change, agencies of political transformation, and models for political emancipation that could serve as norms of social critique and goals for political struggle.

The positions of Adorno, Horkheimer, Lowenthal, and other members of the inner circle of the Institute for Social Research were contested by **Walter Benjamin**, an idiosyncratic theorist loosely affiliated with the Institute. Benjamin, writing in Paris during the 1930s, discerned progressive aspects in new **technologies** of cultural production such as photography, film, and radio. In "The Work of Art in the Age of Mechanical Reproduction" (1934 [trans. 1968]), Benjamin noted how new mass media were supplanting older forms of culture. In this context, the mass reproduction of photography, film, recordings, and publications replaced the emphasis on the originality and "aura" of the work of art in an earlier era. Freed from the mystification of high culture, Benjamin believed that mass culture could cultivate more critical individuals able to judge and analyze their culture, just as sports fans could dissect and evaluate athletic activities. In addition, Benjamin asserted that processing the rush of images of cinema helped to create subjectivities better able to parry the flux and turbulence of experience in industrialized, urbanized societies.

Collaborating with the prolific German artist Bertolt Brecht (1898–1956), Benjamin worked on films, created radio plays, and attempted to utilize the media as organs of social progress. In the lecture in 1934 on "The Author as Producer" (1966 [trans. 1978]), Benjamin argued that radical cultural creators should "refunction" the apparatus of cultural production, turning theatre and film, for instance, into a forum of political enlightenment and discussion rather than a medium of "culinary" audience pleasure. Both Brecht and Benjamin wrote radio plays and were interested in film as an instrument of progressive **social change**. In an essay on radio theory, Brecht anticipated the internet in his call for reconstructing the apparatus of broadcasting from one-way transmission to a more interactive form of two-way, or multiple, communication – a form first realized in CB radio and then electronically mediated computer communication.

Moreover, Benjamin wished to promote a radical cultural and media politics concerned with the creation of alternative oppositional cultures. Yet he recognized that media such as film could have conservative effects. While he thought it was progressive that mass-produced works were losing their "aura," their magical force, and were opening cultural artifacts to more critical and political discussion, Benjamin recognized that film could create a new kind of ideological magic through the cult of celebrity and techniques like the close-up that fetishized certain film stars or images via the technology of the cinema. Benjamin was thus one of the first radical cultural critics to look carefully at the form and technology of media culture in appraising its complex nature and effects.

Horkheimer and Adorno answered Benjamin's optimism concerning the mass media in *Dialectic of Enlightenment*. They argued that the system of cultural production dominated by film, radio broadcasting, newspapers, and magazines was controlled by advertising and commercial imperatives, and served to create subservience to the system of consumer capitalism. While later critics pronounced their approach too manipulative, reductive, and elitist, it provides an important corrective to more populist approaches to media culture that downplay the way the media industries exert power over audiences and help produce thought and behavior that conforms to the existing society.

Jürgen Habermas, a student of Adorno and Horkheimer, provided useful historical perspectives on the transition from traditional culture and the democratic **public sphere** to a mass-produced media and consumer society. In *The Structural Transformation of the Public Sphere* (1962 [trans. 1989]), Habermas historicized Adorno and Horkheimer's analysis of the culture industry. Providing historical background to the triumph of the culture industry, Habermas discussed how bourgeois society in the late eighteenth and nineteenth centuries was distinguished by the rise of a public sphere that stood between **civil society** and the **state** and which mediated between public and private interests. For the first time in history, individuals and groups could shape public opinion, giving direct expression to their needs and interests while influencing political practice. The bourgeois public sphere made it possible to form a realm of public opinion that opposed state power and the powerful interests that were coming to shape bourgeois society.

Habermas analyzed a transition from the liberal public sphere that originated in the Enlightenment and the American and French Revolutions to a media-dominated public sphere in the current stage of what he calls "welfare state capitalism and mass democracy." This historical transformation is grounded in Horkheimer and Adorno's theory of the culture industry, in which giant corporations have taken over the public sphere and transformed it from a site of rational debate into one of manipulative **consumption** and passivity. In this transformation, "public opinion" shifts from rational consensus emerging from debate, discussion, and reflection, to the manufactured opinion of polls or media experts. For Habermas, the interconnection between the sphere of public debate and individual participation has thus been fractured and transmuted into that of a realm of political manipulation and spectacle, in which citizen-consumers ingest and passively absorb entertainment and **information**. "Citizens" thus become spectators of media presentations and discourse which arbitrate public discussion and reduce its audiences to objects of news, information, and public affairs.

As communication studies began emerging in the 1930s and 1940s, and as theorists noted the power of propaganda in World War II, a wide range of texts began appearing on the social effects of the media, promoting debate over the media and **social problems**, and the media as a social problem. Some of the first empirical studies of the effects of film, for instance, criticized the cinema for promoting immorality, juvenile delinquency, and **violence**. The Motion Picture Research Council funded the Payne Foundation to undertake detailed empirical studies of the impact of films on **everyday life** and social behavior. Ten volumes were eventually published and a book, *Our Movie-Made Children* (1933), sensationalized the Payne findings, triggering debates about the media and how they inflamed social problems like **crime**, youth problems, sexual promiscuity, and what was perceived as undesirable social behavior.

The first models of mass communication built on studies of propaganda, film influence, advertising, and other media studies, assumed a direct and powerful **influence** of media on the audience. This model became known as the "bullet," or "hypodermic," theory, asserting that the media directly shape thought and behavior and thus induce social problems like crime and violence, rebellious social behavior, mindless consumption, or mass political behavior. Based on research by Harold Lasswell, in *Propaganda Technique in the Modern World* (1927), there were a number of studies in the 1930s and 1940s of the propaganda role of the media in World Wars I and II, reflecting concern about the roles of film, advertising, and other media in intensifying a number of social problems ranging from crime to growing numbers of teenage pregnancies.

This model of powerful and direct media effects was questioned in *The People's Choice* (1944) by **Paul Lazarsfeld** and his colleagues Bernard Berelson and Hazel Gaulet who, in a study of the influence of the media on voters, determined that it was "opinion leaders" who were the primary influence in voting behavior, while the media exerted a "secondary" influence. Lazersfeld and Elihu Katz expanded this model in *Personal Influence: The Part Played by People in the Flow of Mass Communication* (1955). Their "two-step flow" model claimed that opinion leaders are the primary influence in determining consumer and political choice, as well as **attitudes** and **values**. This model holds that the media do not have direct influence on behavior, but are mediated by primary groups and personal influence, thus in effect denying that the media themselves are a social problem because they merely report on issues and reinforce behavior already dominant in a society.

Yet both conservatives and left-liberal media critics argued that the media had harmful social effects and promoted social problems. Growing juvenile delinquency in the 1950s was blamed on comic books, such as Fredric Wertham's *Seduction of the Innocent* (1954), and rock and roll was broadly attacked for having a wide range of subversive effects. In the 1960s, many different studies of the media and violence appeared throughout the world in response to growing violence in society and more permissive public media that increased representations of implicit sex and violence in film, television, and other media.

In addition to seeing the media as a social problem because of growing media and societal violence, from the 1960s to the present, left-liberal and conservative media critics coalesced in arguing that mainstream media promote excessive consumerism and commodification. This view is argued in sociological terms in the work of **Daniel**

Bell, who asserted in *The Cultural Contradictions of Capitalism* (1978) that a sensate–hedonistic culture exhibited in popular media and promoted by capitalist corporations was undermining core traditional values and producing an increasingly amoral society. Bell called for a return to **tradition** and **religion** to counter this social trend and saw media culture as undermining **morality**, the work ethic, and traditional values.

In *Amusing Ourselves to Death* (1985), Neil Postman argued that popular media culture has become a major force of **socialization** and was subverting traditional literacy skills, thus undermining **education**. Postman criticized the negative social effects of the media and called for educators and citizens to intensify their criticisms of it. Extolling the virtues of book culture and literacy, Postman called for educational reform to counter the nefarious effects of media and consumer culture.

Mass culture and communication was of great interest in the United Kingdom and Europe, as well as the United States. While the Frankfurt School arguably articulates cultural conditions in the stage of state monopoly capitalism or Fordism that produced a regime of mass production and consumption, British **cultural studies** emerged in the 1960s when, first, there was widespread global resistance to consumer capitalism and an upsurge of revolutionary movements, and then emergence of a new stage of capital, described as **post-Fordism**, **postmodernity**, or other terminology that attempted to describe a more variegated and contested social and cultural formation. Moreover, the forms of society and culture described by the earliest phase of British cultural studies in the 1950s and early 1960s articulated conditions in an era in which there were still significant tensions in Britain and much of Europe between an older working-class-based culture and the newer mass-produced culture whose models and exemplars came from American culture industries.

The initial project of cultural studies developed by **Richard Hoggart**, **Raymond Williams**, and E. P. Thompson attempted to preserve working-class culture against onslaughts of mass culture and communication from the culture industries. Thompson's inquiries into the history of British working-class institutions and struggles, the defenses of working-class culture by Hoggart and Williams, and their attacks on mass culture were part of a socialist and working-class-oriented project that assumed that the industrial working class was a force for progressive **social change** and that it could be mobilized and organized to struggle against the **inequalities** of the existing

capitalist societies and for a more egalitarian socialist one. Williams and Hoggart were deeply involved in projects of working-class education and oriented towards socialist working-class **politics**, seeing their form of cultural studies as a progressive instrument for change.

The early critiques in the first wave of British cultural studies of Americanism and media culture in Hoggart, Williams, and others, during the late 1950s and early 1960s, thus paralleled to some extent the earlier critique of the Frankfurt School, yet valorized a working class that the Frankfurt School saw as defeated in Germany and much of Europe during the era of **fascism**, and which they never saw as a strong resource for emancipatory social change. The 1960s work of the **Birmingham Centre for Contemporary Cultural Studies** was continuous with the radicalism of the first wave of British cultural studies (the Hoggart–Thompson–Williams "culture and society" tradition) as well as, in important ways, with the Frankfurt School. Yet the Birmingham project also eventually paved the way for a postmodern populist turn in cultural studies.

During this period, the Centre developed a variety of critical approaches for the analysis, interpretation, and criticism of cultural artifacts. Through a set of internal debates, and responding to social struggles and movements of the 1960s and the 1970s, the Birmingham group came to focus on the interplay of representations and **ideologies** of **social class**, **gender**, **race and ethnicity**, and nationality in mass culture and communication. The Birmingham scholars were among the first to study the effects of newspapers, radio, television, film, and other popular cultural forms on audiences. They also focused on how various audiences interpreted and used media culture in different ways and contexts, analyzing the factors that made audiences respond in contrasting ways to media texts.

Like the Frankfurt School, British cultural studies observed the integration of the working class and the decline of its revolutionary consciousness, and studied the conditions of this catastrophe for the Marxian project of revolution. Like the Frankfurt School, British cultural studies concluded that mass culture was playing an important role in integrating the working class into existing capitalist societies and that emergent consumer and media culture was forming a new mode of capitalist **hegemony**. But John Fiske in *Understanding Popular Culture* (1989) and other writings attacked the concepts of mass society and mass culture which were said to be overly homogenized and monolithic, neutralizing cultural contradictions and dissolving oppositional groups and practices into a neutral concept of "the masses" which many in the British cultural studies tradition found overly contemptuous and elitist.

Both traditions, though, see culture as a form of resistance to capitalist society, and both the earlier forerunners of British cultural studies, especially Williams, and the theorists of the Frankfurt School see high culture as forces of resistance to capitalist **modernity**. Later, British cultural studies would valorize resistant moments in media culture, and audience interpretations and use of media artifacts, while the Frankfurt School tended, with some exceptions, to see mass culture as a homogeneous and potent form of ideological domination – a difference that would seriously divide the two traditions.

Negative depictions of the media and consumerism, youth hedonism, excessive **materialism**, and growing violence were contested by British cultural studies which claimed that the media were being scapegoated for a wide range of social problems. In *Policing the Crisis* (Hall *et al.*, 1978), **Stuart Hall** and colleagues at the Birmingham Centre analyzed what they took to be a media-induced **moral panic** about mugging and youth violence. The Birmingham group argued for an active audience that was able to dissect critically and make use of media material, arguing against the media manipulation perspective. Rooted in a classic article by Hallen titled "Encoding/Decoding" (1980), British cultural studies began studying how different groups read television news, magazines, engaged in consumption, and made use of a broad range of media. In *Everyday Television: Nationwide*, Charlotte Brunsdon and David Morley (1978) studied how different audiences consumed TV news, and Fiske wrote a series of books celebrating the active audience and consumer in a wide range of domains throughout the world.

Yet critics working within British cultural studies, individuals in a wide range of **social movements**, and academics from a variety of fields and positions began criticizing the media from the 1960s to the present for promoting **sexism**, **racism**, homophobia, and other oppressive social phenomena. There was intense focus on the politics of representation, discriminating between negative and positive representations of major social groups and harmful and beneficial media effects, debates that coalesced under the rubric of the politics of representation.

The groundbreaking work of critical media theorists like the Frankfurt School, British cultural studies, and French structuralism and **poststructuralism** revealed that media culture is a social construct, intrinsically linked to the vicissitudes of the social and historically specific milieu in which it is conceived and that gender, race, class, **sexuality**, and other dimensions of social life are socially constructed in media representations. Media and cultural studies engaged in critical interrogations of the politics of representation, which drew upon feminist approaches and multicultural theories to analyze fully the functions of gender, class, race, ethnicity, nationality, sexual preference, and so on in the media. The social dimensions of media constructions are perceived by cultural studies as being vitally constitutive of audiences who appropriate and use texts.

While earlier British cultural studies engaged the progressive and oppositional potential of working-class and then youth culture, under the pressure of the social movements of the 1960s and 1970s many adopted a feminist dimension, paid greater attention to race, ethnicity, and nationality, and concentrated on sexuality. During this period, assorted discourses of race, gender, sex, nationality, and so on circulated in response to social struggles and movements and were taken up in cultural studies to engage critically the politics of representation. An increasingly complex, culturally hybrid, and diasporic global culture and networked society calls for sophisticated understandings of the interplay of representations, politics, and the forms of media, and theorizing global culture has been a major focus of the contemporary era.

Many critics emphasized the importance of connecting representations of gender, race, class, sexuality, and other subject positions to disclose how the media present socially derogatory representations of subordinate groups. bell hooks, in *Black Looks: Race and Representation* (1992) and other writings, has been among the first and most prolific African-American feminist scholars to call attention to the interlockings of race, class, gender, and additional markers of identity in the constitution of subjectivity. Early in her career she challenged feminists to recognize and confront the ways in which race and class inscribe women's (and men's) experiences. In "Eating the Other" (1992), hooks explores cultural constructions of the other as an object of desire, tying such positioning to consumerism and commodification as well as to issues of racial domination and subordination. Cautioning against the seductiveness of celebrating "otherness," hooks uses various media cultural artifacts – clothing catalogs, films, rap music – to debate issues of cultural appropriation versus cultural appreciation, and to uncover the personal and political crosscurrents at work in mass media representation.

Since the 1960s, a broad range of theories and methods to analyze the production of media texts, their polysemic meanings, and their complex uses and effects have been developed. Critical theories were developed within **feminism**, **critical race theory**, gay and lesbian theory, and other groupings associated with new political movements, making critical theory part of political struggle inside and outside the university. Feminists, for instance, demonstrated how gender **bias** infected disciplines from philosophy to literary studies and was embedded in texts ranging from classics of the canon to the mundane artifacts of popular culture. In similar ways, critical race theorists demonstrated how racial bias permeated cultural artifacts, while gay and lesbian theorists demonstrated sexual bias.

These critical theories also stressed giving voice to groups and individuals marginalized in the dominant forms of western and then global culture. Critical theory began going global in the post-1960s disseminations of critical discourses. **Postcolonial theory** in various parts of the world developed particular critical theories as a response to colonial oppression and to the hopes of national liberation. **Franz Fanon** in Algeria, Wole Soyinka in Nigeria, Gabriel Marquez in Latin America, Arrundi Roy in India, and others all gave voice to specific experiences and articulated critical theories that expanded their global and multicultural reach.

Focus on the politics of representation thus calls attention to the fact that culture is produced within relationships of domination and subordination and tends to reproduce or resist existing structures of power. Such a perspective also provides tools for cultural studies whereby the critic can denounce aspects of media forms and artifacts that reproduce class, gender, racial, and diverse modes of domination, and positively valorize aspects that subvert existing types of domination, or depict resistance and movements against them.

Issues of the politics of representation and violence and the media intersect in the impassioned debates over pornography. For a school of **feminism** and cultural conservatives, pornography and violence against women are among the most problematic aspects of media culture. Anti-porn feminists argue that pornography objectifies women, that the industry dangerously exploits them, and that pornography promotes violence against

women and debased sexuality. Pro-sex feminists and defenders of pornography, by contrast, argue that pornography exhibits a tabooed array of **sexuality**, provokes fantasy and awakens desire, and can be used by consumers in gratifying ways.

Hence, while there is widespread agreement that the media has multiple effects and that its representations are an important part of the social world, there is heated debate over whether the media have positive or negative social effects. Many critics argue that one-sided pro or con positions tend to be simplistic and reductive and that contextual analysis needs to be made on specific media effects of certain technologies or artifacts on specific audiences. This position also asserts that, in general, media have contradictory effects and that in many cases it is impossible to discern accurately or distinguish positive or negative features that are often interconnected. Contemporary debates thus reflect the bifurcated positions on the media and mass communications first debated in the early nineteenth century.

DOUGLAS KELLNER

mass society

A type of society based on social conformity, political complacence, the decline of **community**, mass production and mass communication, this concept was most influential in the 1940s and 1950s when it was related to theories of social order and manipulation. Following in the footsteps of Matthew Arnold, T. S. Eliot, in *Notes Towards the Definition of Culture* (1948), refined the distinction between **elite** and mass **culture**. Eliot argued that it is the duty of the elite to protect the values of high culture from the onslaught of mass culture, which he associated with pandering to the lowest common denominator.

C. Wright Mills argued in *The Power Elite* (1956) and *The Sociological Imagination* (1959) that the **pluralism** upon which **democracy** depended was being replaced by the standardization of opinion, **values**, and behavior. Individual freedom was being replaced by programmatic behavior orchestrated by the centralized **state** and the business corporation. In the popular sociology of Vance Packard in *The Hidden Persuaders* (1957), ordinary men and women were subject to the "hidden persuaders" who controlled advertising and operated the levers of public opinion formation. The argument paralleled key themes in the **Frankfurt School** critique of society, especially the proposition that mass culture had become one-dimensional in **Herbert Marcuse**'s *One-Dimensional Man* (1964). But it was given a fillip in these years by the Cold War and the increasing knowledge about the centralized regulation and orthodox value systems that operated in the Soviet command state.

David Riesman, in *The Lonely Crowd* (1950), argued that a new general personality type was emerging in mass society. The first settler communities and the **generations** that succeeded them up to the 1940s were characterized by "inner-directed" personality types based in self-reliance, personally defined convictions, and a strong sense of place. Under mass society they were being replaced by "other-directed" types who assimilated opinions and values from the mass media, were susceptible to advertising, marketing, and other forms of public opinion manipulation, and who expressed a weak sense of belonging and community.

Mass society theory came increasingly under fire after the 1960s. It was held to sponsor a dominant ideology thesis that exaggerated the manipulative power of ruling formations and failed to grasp social and cultural diversity. Critical thought shifted to questions of **social class**, **gender**, and **race**, all of which destabilized the proposition of a homogeneous mass of citizens, producers, and consumers. The rise of interest in **multiculturalism** projected issues of **hybridity**, **diaspora**, **postmodernism**, and postcolonial **identity** to the forefront of **sociological theory**. The effect was to expose the over-simplification and inflexibility of mass society theory.

Covertly, mass society theory underwent a massive revival in the 1990s in the guise of George Ritzer's thesis in *McDonaldization of Society* (1993). Taking over and modernizing **Max Weber**'s rationalization thesis, Ritzer argued that social life was succumbing to penetrating standards of efficiency, calculability, predictability, and control. The argument invoked again the notions of standardized social practice and mass conformity. Following the train of classical mass society theory, Ritzer concludes that the prospects for resistance are dim. The fate of advanced **industrial society** is to subject citizens to various processes of standardization of **emotions** and practice in the conduct of everyday life.   CHRIS ROJEK

materialism

This concept can be understood in two rather different ways. In everyday language, it is used as a moral judgment of a person or philosophy, ascribing to them an excessive devotion to possessions or sensory pleasures. In a more technical vocabulary, it means any secular philosophy or system which accepts only **explanations** grounded in material reality. The most widespread materialist system is that of western science, which seeks an account of the physical world without recourse to spiritual or supernatural forces. Anglo-Saxon **social sciences** and French *sciences humaines* derive their inspiration from scientific materialism. Typically such approaches emphasize observable behaviors, notably **language**, rather than intangible elements such as psychological **motivations**. Equally significant is the scientific **socialism** of **Karl Marx**. Marx sought a scientific basis for understanding human history and social formations, and found it in the economic activities of societies. Marx's dialectical variant of materialism identified the contradictions arising within economic orders as the motor of history. Moreover, in his earlier writings, Marx claimed that the cultural products and symbolic and political systems of a society were products of its economic organization. Later materialists, often inspired by **phenomenology**'s interest in embodiment, inquired into the material force of communication, **power**, **sexuality**, and other factors. One core challenge for materialism is to avoid the mechanical determinism common in Indian and classical materialism and some versions of Newtonian scientific reasoning. Marx's dialectical materialism, the phenomenological emphasis on lived experience, and developments in contemporary science, especially in **cybernetics**, have lessened the more extreme determinist aspects of early materialism. A second challenge, to describe structure and change without recourse to abstract ideas, which are difficult to use without ascribing agency to them, still proves elusive. SEAN CUBITT

maternal deprivation thesis

This thesis originally arose in Britain from the work of John Bowlby, a child psychologist and psychoanalyst, in the 1940s and 1950s, most notably from *Child Care and the Growth of Love* (1953). The idea of maternal deprivation has been much used and abused since he developed his thesis, and so it is important to contextualize his work. As a clinician Bowlby worked with disturbed **children** and he began to relate the delinquent behavior he witnessed to the quality of parenting, particularly mothering, that children received. These ideas developed in a more focused way when he observed the treatment of children in hospitals and residential institutions and, also, of those who were separated from their mothers by wartime evacuation. Hospital practices at that time entailed a complete separation of mother and child, and, while in the institution, the infant was neither cuddled, comforted, nor played with. Bowlby observed that this resulted in an inability of the child to attach to other human beings. The idea of maternal deprivation was therefore an important component of Attachment Theory. He argued that if the child did not learn to respond to other key individuals, most particularly the mother or mother substitute, s/he could not learn to trust or interact in a normal way. To achieve attachment, Bowlby argued that mothers must form affective bonds with their children and that these bonds should not be disrupted by long absences, or by the introduction of multiple carers. His work was part of a trajectory of work which sought to protect children and to improve their **life chances**.

However, the maternal deprivation thesis became popularized through the growth of social work and health visiting in the 1950s and 1960s, and Bowlby's originally humane ideas became sedimented into virtual rules for how mothers should raise their children. Mothers were criticized for going out to work, especially if their children were under five, and the idea that mothers were solely responsible for the delinquency or disturbed behavior of their children also became an *idée fixe*. Feminist work in the 1970s became very critical of the maternal deprivation thesis because it was seen as responsible for closing nurseries in the postwar era and condemning mothers to long, lonely hours of virtual imprisonment with their infants. The thesis was used to deny employment to women with children, and alternative **care** was also frowned upon. Fathers too became insignificant in this process, with all the attention being on the quality of the mother–child bond and the father being seen solely as the economic support to allow the mother to be a full-time carer. However, Denise Riley, in *The War in the Nursery* (1983), has argued that much of the criticism against Bowlby was misplaced because, from a sociological perspective, it is essential to distinguish between the original ideas taken in context (such as the importance of bonding) and the ways in which these ideas were popularized and utilized by others who might have had different purposes. In other words, she suggests that the thesis was treated instrumentally to keep mothers at home, whereas the original aim was to recognize the importance of the mother–child bond and to improve the treatment of children. CAROL SMART

matriarchy

An anthropological term which describes a **society** in which descent and lineage are traced through the mother rather than the father; an example of matriarchal descent patterns is that of Judaism, in which it is the mother who confers the status of Jew on her **children**. It is, however, not the case that matriarchy can be read as the opposite to **patriarchy**, since many matriarchal systems do not confer on women the same **authority**, nor access to **property**, as patriarchal systems do on men. It is also the case that matriarchy can exist in certain contexts within patriarchal societies; the most obvious and well-known example would be the matriarchal household, in which women dominate the social and personal arrangements of the domestic space, but in which power outside the household belongs exclusively to men. As is the case with the term patriarchy, matriarchy is often used in a more general sense to denote a pattern of female control and authority.

MARY EVANS

Mauss, Marcel (1872–1951)

Mauss was born in Epinal, also the birthplace of **Émile Durkheim**, who was his uncle and became his teacher and mentor. Mauss led, so to speak, the anthropological wing of the Durkheim school, at any rate after the death in World War I of other anthropologists (or ethnographers, as they generally called themselves) associated with it. His numerous and significant contributions derived their **data** chiefly from the study of pre-literate **society** but on Durkheim's death he took over the editorship of the *Année Sociologique*, and in 1931 he was called to a chair in **sociology** at the Collège de France. With his uncle he wrote a seminal essay on *Primitive Classification* (1903 [trans. 1963]); with H. Hubert, a "Sketch of a General Theory of Magic"; with H. Beuchat, a very successful "Essay on Seasonal Variations within Eskimo Societies." The latter two essays were published as *Sociologie et anthropologie* (1906). Some of Mauss's other writings addressed classical anthropological themes, such as sacrifice, **myth**, and **ritual**. Others, however, owed their impact to the novelty of their themes, such as laughter and tears, the "techniques of the **body**," and, most especially, the **gift**. Mauss addressed the latter phenomenon, in *The Gift* (1924 [trans. 1954]), as a major instance of what he called "a total social phenomenon," that is one comprising at the same time juridical, economic, religious, and aesthetical aspects, none of which should be studied in isolation from the others. His sophisticated handling of all these topics constituted a major inspiration for the development of **structuralism**, especially in anthropology as practiced and theorized chiefly by **Claude Lévi-Strauss** after Mauss's own death.

GIANFRANCO POGGI

McDonaldization

This term was successfully deployed by George Ritzer in his book *The McDonaldization of Society*, first published in 1993, and promoted in several other volumes by the same author. He defines McDonaldization as "the process by which the principles of the fast-food restaurant are coming to dominate more and more sectors of American society as well as of the rest of the world." He continues by maintaining that this process affects "not only the restaurant business, but also **education**, work, health care, travel, **leisure**, dieting, **politics**, the **family**, and virtually every other aspect of society." The practices of the McDonalds restaurant chain are thus used metaphorically to describe and illustrate more general societal tendencies. According to Ritzer, McDonalds operates in accordance with four basic principles: efficiency, calculation, predictability, and control. These principles, being applied to workers and work organization and to customers, account for the company's success. Their single-minded pursuit in a business organization have had some detrimental consequences for personnel, work, and their products. Work is boring, and their goods are uniform just as they were in factories engaged in the industrial production of standardized commodities. Applied to other domains of existence, like education or personal **care**, the principles often have irrational effects, damaging to the social relationships between providers and recipients. The concept is primarily a rhetorical device for redescribing processes which in earlier sociological literature would be described as **rationalization**.

ALAN WARDE

McLuhan, Marshall (1911–1980)

In the 1960s and 1970s, McLuhan was read as one of the most influential media theorists of our time and is once again becoming widely discussed and debated in the computer era. His 1964 work *Understanding Media* dramatized the importance of television and electronic broadcasting and entertainment media on contemporary **society**. The eventual decline of influence of McLuhan's work perhaps resulted in part from his exaggeration of the role of television and electronic **culture** in effecting a break from the print era and producing a new electronic age. Yet, in retrospect, McLuhan anticipated the rise and importance of computer culture and the dramatic emergence and effects of personal computers and the

internet that provide even more substance to McLuhan's claim that contemporary society is undergoing a fundamental rupture with the past.

Indeed, McLuhan can be read in the light of classical **social theory** as a major theorist of **modernity**, with an original and penetrating analysis of the origins, nature, and trajectory of the modern world. Furthermore, he can be read in retrospect as a major anticipator of theories of a postmodern break, of a rupture with modernity, of leaving behind the previous print–industrial–urban-mechanical era and entering a new postmodern society with novel forms of culture and society. McLuhan's work proposes that a major new medium of communication changes the ratio of the senses, the patterns of **everyday life**, modes of social **interaction** and communication, and many other aspects of social and individual life that are often not perceived. "Understanding media," thus, for McLuhan, requires understanding the form of the media and its structural effects on the psyche, culture, and social life.

McLuhan's analyses of book and print **technology**, newspapers, roads, modern industry and mechanization, **war**, radio and television, computers, and other modern technologies and phenomena all illuminate the constitution of the modern world and provide new insights into modernity and the emergence of a postmodern era. His description of specific technologies and how they produced the modern era and anticipation of how new emergent electronic technologies are fashioning a new postmodern era are often highly illuminating. McLuhan, like **Jean Baudrillard**, **Fredric Jameson**, and other theorists of the postmodern, presents an ideal-type analysis in which modernity is marked by linearity, **differentiation**, explosion, centralization, homogenization, hierarchy, fragmentation, and **individualism**. **Postmodernity**, by contrast, is marked by implosion or dedifferentiation, decentralization, tribalism, synaesthesia, and a new media and computer culture that would be called cyberspace which would be theorized by Baudrillard and other postmodern theorists.

As with **Karl Marx** and certain versions of **postmodern theory**, there have been criticisms of McLuhan's notion of stages of history and his ideal-type delineation of premodern, modern, and postmodern societies. His depiction of premodern societies as "primitive" and "savage" is highly objectionable from the standpoint of contemporary **critical theory**. Unlike more dialectical theorists, McLuhan does not mediate between the **economy** and technology in the construction of contemporary media industries, although he provides unique insights into media form and the powerful effects of specific media. McLuhan thus remains important for **social theory** and **cultural studies** as we enter a new millennium.

DOUGLAS KELLNER

Mead, George Herbert (1863–1931)

Best known in sociology as the progenitor of the symbolic interactionist school, which builds upon his ideas on the social nature of the act and its relation to the human **self** and **society**, he was actually one of the most original thinkers in twentieth-century American philosophy. In addition, he dedicated much thought and effort to movements for progressive social reform.

As David Miller observes in *George Herbert Mead: Self, Language and the World* (1973), Mead's pivotal philosophical concept of sociality, which he explicitly articulated only late in his life, refers to processes of interaction among and between phenomena of all kinds throughout the natural universe. Mead developed this idea by referring to such disparate intellectual developments as, among others, Einstein's special theory of relativity or **Charles Darwin**'s evolutionary principles. That Mead's thought is only partially understood by most sociologists is due, at least in part, to his well-known writer's block. Most of his influential works, including *Mind, Self, and Society* (1934), were not composed for publication, but rather were compiled from course notes taken by dedicated students. This group included **Herbert Blumer**, who transmitted edited statements of Mead's ideas into sociological circles. But there may be other problems as well. It is unclear if Mead modeled his philosophical notion of sociality on his social psychology of human **interaction**, or vice versa. In addition, Mead never worked out an epistemological position adequate to understanding interactions between phenomena with different properties. Indeed, the absence of an epistemological position in Mead's thought is reflected in the absence of a unifying method in **symbolic interactionism** today. Not only are there two methodologically distinct schools of symbolic interactionism, the Chicago and Iowa Schools, but the **Chicago School** often relies on methods much richer in elegant ethnographic description than in generalized sociological analysis.

Mead's thought has experienced a renaissance in recent years led by Hans Joas, Gary Cook, and Dmitri Shalin. **Jürgen Habermas**, more ambitiously, has reframed and reconstructed sociological elements of Mead's thought and incorporated them into his theory of communicative action. Habermas emphasizes Mead's focus on the coordination of interaction via significant **symbols**. Mead, in turn, was inspired, with regard to the significance of communication, by C. S. Peirce (1839–1914), one of the founders of the philosophy of **pragmatism**.

Mead was born in 1863, the son of a Congregational minister father and a mother who became President of Mount Holyoke College after her husband's death. Mead graduated from Oberlin College in 1883 and enrolled at Harvard University in 1887. Though he studied with **William James**, he had a higher regard for Josiah Royce (1855–1916). The strongest influences on Mead's thought were **Charles Horton Cooley** and John Dewey (1859–1952), both of whom Mead met at the University of Michigan, where he took a position in 1891. Three years later he joined Dewey, who accepted a chair in philosophy, as a member of the Department of Philosophy at the University of Chicago, where he spent the rest of his career.

IRA COHEN

Mead, Margaret (1901–1978)

A student of Franz Boas (1858–1942) and *protégée* of Ruth Benedict (1887–1948), Mead was an anthropologist of unrivaled international celebrity during her long and multifaceted career. She opposed **cultures** to races (see **race and ethnicity**) and pointed to the diversity of practices of enculturation as the key to any adequate account of the behavioral diversity of different human populations. Yet she shared with Benedict a **relativism** tempered by a humanist psychology which licensed the rebuke and even the pathologization of the culture that failed to accommodate the whole array of putatively natural psychosexual **human needs** and temperamental inclinations of its members. The part-relativist, part-humanist thrust of her critical pedagogy is already at work in *Coming of Age in Samoa* (1928). It is a motif in more than forty books and hundreds of essays that she would subsequently publish. Mead's terrains of investigation were many and far-flung; her critical attention consistently returned to the intolerance and the Puritanism of her native United States.

Quiet but sustained discomfort with the quality of much of Mead's ethnographic research erupted into controversy after her death with Derek Freeman's *Margaret Mead and Samoa: The Making of a Myth* (1984). Her enduring stature owes more to her long curatorial career at the American Museum of Natural History, her early and persistent advocacy of the use of multiple media of ethnographic documentation and multiple genres of ethnographic writing, her leadership as a public scientist and **intellectual**, and her great success in rendering anthropology accessible to a mass audience.   JAMES D. FAUBION

mean
– see **distribution**.

measurement

In the **social sciences**, measurement consists in the application of numbers to persons, social objects, or events. An identical number may have a radically different meaning, depending on the predetermined rules for its application in a particular measurement context. There are three qualitatively different ways that numbers can be applied to effect such measurement: nominal **scales** are used to *name* things, people, or events; ordinal scales are used to *rank* things, people, or events; and cardinal (interval and ratio) scales are used to represent quantity. First, nominal scales may be used to name, or label, things, people, or events. Scores assigned according to a nominal scale could just as easily be letters, or words. The numbers employed in a nominal scale operate to distinguish between observations – but have no *cardinal*, or real, value. Examples of the use of a nominal scale include the assignment of a "1" for females and a "2" for males, in a dataset. A student number or social security number is also an example of a nominal scale. The assignment of numbers according to a nominal scale does not permit the sophisticated statistical interpretation of collections of such scores. For instance, it does not make sense to infer that males are twice as valuable as females, according to the scores accorded to each (for it would be equally sensible to accord a "2" to females and a "1" to males). Similarly it would be nonsensical to compute the average social security number. For this reason, variables that are measured according to a nominal scale are termed qualitative variables.

Second, numbers assigned according to ordinal scales provide the researcher with more information than do numbers assigned according to nominal scales. In addition to performing the basic function of categorization, such numbers also provide a sense of the relative position of a number in relation to other numbers. In this sense, ordinal scales are quantitative, in that they give a rough indication of the quantity of the entity in question, relative to other entities. A common instance of an ordinal scale is the activity of ranking persons, events, or objects.

Thus, it may be stated that X is more popular than Y, and that Y is more popular than Z; however, an ordinal scale can tell us nothing about the intervals between X, Y, and Z. That is, the consistency of the intervals between adjacent ranks cannot be assumed, according to an ordinal scale.

There are two kinds of cardinal scales: interval scales and ratio scales. Interval scales provide a third level of measurement. Interval scales, like nominal and ordinal scales, may be used to categorize things, events, or people. In addition, like ordinal scales, scores reflect the property of quantity. That is, different numbers reflect more or less of a particular variable. However, interval scales differ from ordinal scales in that they have the property that numerical distances on the scale represent *equal* distances on the dimension argued to underlie each scale. Temperature (whether measured by Fahrenheit or Celsius) is an example of an interval scale. The distance between 5 and 10 degrees is identical to the distance between 20 and 25 degrees. Similarly, a log-interval scale of measurement is one in which numbers are assigned so that the ratios between values reflect ratios in the attribute being measured. In log-interval ratio scales, the logarithms of the scale scores form an interval scale, as the ratio $a/b = \log a - \log b$. Common examples of log-ratios are density (mass divided by volume) and fuel efficiency in kilometers per liter. The application of interval scales within the social and behavioral sciences is more contentious than within the natural and physical sciences. Many statistical tests rely upon the assumption that the **data** represent an underlying dimension of equal intervals. As early as 1946, Clyde Coombs in his "A Theory of Psychological Scaling," urged social scientists to stick with lower levels of measurement, rather than "quantifying by fiat." The process of transforming data into higher levels of measurement is known as "scaling" or "quantification." Critics have argued that quantification or scaling can, if applied without consideration, impose nonsensical numerical values on non-numerical dimensions. In turn, the ubiquity of this practice raises questions about the transferability of scaling, as a concept, from the physical sciences to social phenomena, with the risk of otherwise information-rich qualitative data being subjected to the imposition of a single, linear, underlying dimension.

Ratio scales are argued to provide the most sophisticated level of measurement. In addition to possessing all of the properties of an interval scale, a ratio scale also possesses an absolute zero point. Time and length are instances of ratio scales. Temperature is not, as "0" does not equal the complete absence of heat.

A discontinuous or discrete variable, or dimension, of interest is one that usually increases by increments of one whole number. Pregnancy and number of children are discrete variables. That is, while it may be true that the average number of children per Australian couple is 2.21, and that the average number of live births per single mother per year is 0.18, these expressions do not reflect any particular real-world pregnancy or child. One cannot be a little bit pregnant; just as one cannot raise 0.21 of a child. In the interpretation of averages based on discontinuous variables, one should identify the closest sensible denominator. For instance, in the above example, we should expect to find 221 children per 100 Australian couples.

A continuous variable, or dimension, in contrast, can in theory have an infinite number of increments between each whole number. Height and weight are common examples of continuous variables. When measuring continuous variables, it is always possible to achieve a more precise measurement – and any measurement taken is always an approximation. In consequence, the measurement of continuous variables typically involves the specification of a particular unit of measurement, which specifies the desired level of precision. This specification will result in all measurements taken that fall within a particular interval being recorded as an instance of that interval. The upper and lower real limits of a number are typically one half of the specified unit of measurement. Thus, if one were recording height in centimeters, the real limits for the figure 164 would be 163.5 cm (lower limit) and 164.5 cm (upper limit). If the unit of measurement were tenths of a centimeter, then the real limits for the figure 164 would be 163.95 cm (lower limit) and 164.05 cm (upper limit).

Measurement gives rise to consideration of the issues of reliability and validity. Reliability refers to the ability to repeat the results of a measurement accurately (common forms include inter-rater reliability; test–retest reliability; and measures of internal consistency, including split-half and coefficient alpha). Validity refers to the degree of fit between the measurement taken and the underlying analytic construct (construct validity); or to the resemblance between the measurements taken and their "real-life" equivalent (ecological validity). The measurement scale employed may have consequences for both these issues. Particular

caution may be necessary when combining extremely qualitative, or "subjective" social issues, such as **racism**, or homophobia, with higher-order measurement approaches.

Measurement raises a number of issues for sociologists. It engenders at least two basic challenges: the question of finding an appropriate fit between indicators and analytic concepts, and the search for sufficiently accurate data. Sociological forms of measurement are more diverse than those found within other social sciences, including psychology, where the variables of interest are often articulated at an individual, rather than a societal, level. In consequence, sociological researchers encounter issues of measurement in the context of the collection and organization of both primary and secondary sources of data. Census-based data, including Severe Acute Respiratory Syndrome (SARs), offer sociologists a rich resource for the measurement of a range of social variables, such as socioeconomic status and **poverty**, quality of life, and well-being, and other social indicators.

The measurement of socioeconomic status is a central activity for sociologists and policymakers alike. However, the precise methods by which socioeconomic status are measured is, at the outset, a reflection of a particular theoretical approach to understanding socioeconomic status and **social class**. Divergent methods of measuring socioeconomic status tend to be, in turn, based on divergent theoretical approaches. For instance, Marxist and Weberian approaches tend to produce, respectively, categorical and categorial/continuous variables. That is, the very qualities of the underlying dimension may alter, according to the theoretical approach taken. Measures developed using a Weberian framework, which emphasizes a three-fold definition of socioeconomic status (ownership of wealth-producing enterprises and materials; skills, credentials, or qualifications; and social **prestige**) tend to conceptualize this dimension as either a categorical (discrete) *or* a continuous variable. In contrast, measures constructed using a Marxist or neo-Marxist approach produce, without exception, *categorical*, or discrete, variables. This is a product of the centrality of the criterion of ownership or non-ownership of the means of production. Marxist and neo-Marxist measures accordingly take the form of at least three distinct class groups: large employers; the self-employed; and workers.

Thus socioeconomic status may, in practice, be calculated from either a single measure or from several closely related variables. Single measures tend to be based upon the classification of occupational status. Multiple measures may be drawn from a range of sources, including educational attainment, father's (and increasingly) mother's **occupation**, **income**, possessions, and home ownership. Multiple measures are often treated as more reliable measures of socioeconomic status than single measures, as these correlate more strongly with such closely related variables as school achievement.

However, even single measures based on occupation may be refined. Some systems of measurement (for example the 501 categories of the United States Census Occupational Classification) are capable of classifying occupations into hundreds of categories. These categories, when hierarchically ranked according to criteria such as the prestige, income, entry-level qualifications, and typical workplace injury rates associated with each occupation, may be transformed into instances of a continuous variable, which in turn enables a greater range of statistical operations to be conducted on such data.

Within sociology, measurement has long been a topic of critical reflection. In *Method and Measurement in Sociology* (1964), **Aaron Cicourel** developed a critique of the unacknowledged reliance of the sociologist as a coder – responsible for assigning numerical values to social phenomena – on "common sense knowledge":

> if we must rely on human judges, then we should know as much as possible . . . about how the "human computer" goes about encoding and decoding messages . . . Instead it is often assumed that such meanings are self-evident, that native-speakers of a language are more or less interchangeable, that the manifest content is sufficient for study, or that judges are interchangeable. The structure of common-sense knowledge remains a barely recognizable problem for sociological investigation.

Further, the order created by the use of formal instruments is, according to critics, often created by the very administration of such scales and the comparability between units of measurement that they produce. Thus, scales measuring a certain social variable may correlate with other measures of related variables (thus demonstrating construct, or convergent validity) but may bear little resemblance to the lived orderliness of respondents' lives (thus lacking *ecological validity*).

More recently, Michael Lynch, in his "Method," in G. Button (ed.), *Ethnomethodology and the Human Sciences* (1991), studied ordinary and scientific measurement as ethnomethodological phenomena. Lynch has examined the practical accomplishment

of categorization and classification. He argued that an ethnomethodological approach to the practice of measurement, following **Harold Garfinkel** and **Harvey Sacks**'s formulation of "ethnomethodological indifference," would operate to place matters of **methodology** back into the everyday settings they emerge from, as "ethnomethodological indifference turns away from the *foundationalist* approach to methodology and that gives rise to principled discussions of validity, reliability, rules of evidence, and decision criteria." However, as he notes, many sociologists may find the upshot of these debates unsettling.

MARK RAPLEY AND SUSAN HANSEN

measurement levels
– see **measurement**.

media
– see **mass media and communications**.

median
– see **distribution**.

mediascape
– see **mass media and communications**.

medical dominance
Defined as the enormous social, financial, and political **power** medicine has over the organization and practice of health care, medical dominance is a concept that has been used to explain why doctors asymmetrically have more power than patients in their **interactions**, but also why doctors have more power than allied health-care professionals such as nurses, social workers, and therapists who use alternative or complementary medicine.

Medicine gains much of its power through its exclusive knowledge about the operation of certain mechanisms of the **body**. The emphasis placed on specialist medical knowledge, as opposed to the subjective opinions of an untrained lay person, is central to medical dominance. The notion that medical diagnoses are scientific, objectively verifiable, and replicable, and the way health care is hierarchically organized, reinforce medical dominance.

The professional nature of a **career** in medicine profoundly affects the interactions between doctors and patients and may reinforce medical dominance. For instance, the professional can control the amount of time spent with a patient, can interrupt the patient's conversation, or can control the flow of **information** to a patient in a way which exacerbates **inequalities** in their relationship. The power to label a patient is also a fundamental source of medical power. As well, doctors have significant power over patients because of their position as gate-keepers of entitlement to certain welfare benefits and ability to influence medical costs and insurance payments.

Some authors, such as Paul Starr in *The Social Transformation of American Medicine* (1982), suggest that changes in the organization of the health-care industry, including the corporatization of medicine and the rise of managerialism, may result in a decline in medical dominance, because doctors' clinical decisions are influenced by corporate goals of profitability and efficiency.

MARK SHERRY AND GARY L. ALBRECHT

medical model
– see **medicalization**.

medicalization
Defined as the way in which the scientific knowledge of medical science is applied to behaviors or conditions which are not necessarily biological, this concept was developed (originally in the United States) in the early 1970s, associated with the view of medicine as an instrument of **social control**.

Critics of the medical model, particularly in the last decades of the twentieth century, suggested that this model was increasingly being applied in situations where it was not appropriate. Historically, it is common for the medical model of the **culture** and period to find application in wide areas of life beyond the **body** and its diseases. Nevertheless it is true that the twentieth century saw the increasing attachment of medical labels to behaviors then regarded as morally or socially undesirable (alcoholism, delinquency, and homosexuality) as well as to many normal stages of life (such as pregnancy and old age).

Ivan Illich (1926–2002) in his *Medical Nemesis* (1976) promulgated the idea that society was becoming increasingly medicalized. Doctors were becoming the new priesthood, and modern medicine was creating overdependence on technical fixes. **Irving Zola** in his article "Medicine as an Institution of Social Control" in The *Sociological Review* (1972) analyzed the increasing pervasiveness of medicine in terms of: (1) expansion into more and more areas of life; (2) absolute

control over techniques; (3) access to intimate areas of life; and (4) medical involvement in ethical issues.

For instance, the medicalization of behavior extends the concept of **addiction** to include a variety of activities such as shopping, gambling, and promiscuous sexual activity. Alcoholism offers a particularly clear example of the effects of this, with some divergence of **attitude** between experts about behavioral models of the condition and the addiction model, which sees it in physiological or psychological terms.

The medicalization thesis has been particularly important to feminist sociologists, who have seen expansionist tendencies in medicine applied to women's bodies and women's lives, defining natural processes such as pregnancy and childbirth, menstruation and menopause, as illness conditions. Recognition of the major part which medical **technology** has had in reducing maternal and infant mortality has gone hand in hand with longstanding dissatisfaction with maternity services. Feminist criticisms, such as the British sociologist Ann Oakley in her book *The Captured Womb* (1984), have accused a medicalized system of ignoring women's own preferences and experiences. In other contexts, women are similarly seen as the object of patriarchal medical control, for instance over drugs (especially the prescription of tranquillizers) and surgery, and in general the treatment of women within the medical system is accused of serving to enforce passivity and dependence.

The labeling of problems as "disease" may have the positive consequence that the individual is absolved of moral responsibility, and offers the prospect of treatment or help. Sociologists point out, however, that the labels do carry moral evaluation with them, defining behaviors which may be normal in particular circumstances as things which should be cured.

The French social philosopher **Michel Foucault** saw medicalization not as the simple exercise of personal power by a **profession** intent on extending its boundaries, but as a historical process deriving from the power of clinical knowledge and the redefinition of medicine to include psychological, economic, and social "health." Although the development of holistic medicine is generally welcomed, all aspects of life become medicalized, in need of continual monitoring, self-examination, and **education**. The British sociologist David Armstrong, in *Political Anatomy of the Body* (1983), described this as a shift from the biological anatomy of disease to the political anatomy of disease in which medicine focuses on social life.

In late modern society, it is now generally agreed that a degree of demedicalization is taking place, whereby lay knowledge and experience are being given a more important place, and lay people's knowledge about the body allowed more legitimation.   MILDRED BLAXTER

men's health
– see **health**.

mental health
– see **health**.

meritocracy
– see **credentialism**.

Merleau-Ponty, Maurice (1908–1961)
A French philosopher who held professorships at the University of Lyon and the Sorbonne, Merleau-Ponty was the editor of the journal *Les Temps modernes* which had been founded by Jean-Paul Sartre (1905–80). He broke with Sartre and the Communist Party after the Korean War, becoming increasingly detached from **politics**.

He developed the **phenomenology** of the everyday world, and was concerned to understand human consciousness, perception, and **intentionality**. His work was original in applying the phenomenology of Edmund Husserl (1859–1938) to intentional consciousness but from the perspective of corporeal existence. He wanted to describe the lived world without using the conventional dualism between subject and object. Hence, Merleau-Ponty was critical of the dualism between mind and **body**. He developed the idea of the "body-subject" that is always situated in a social reality. He sought to develop an **epistemology** that would avoid the dualism between **realism** and **social constructionism**. He also rejected behavioral and mechanistic approaches to the human body, and worked towards the development of a phenomenology of the body as a lived experience of the everyday world. He attempted to show that **identity** and consciousness of **self** cannot be divorced from our embodiment. For sociologists, his most influential work was *Phenomenology of Perception* (1945 [trans. 1962]), which has been important for contemporary approaches to the sociology of the body, and therefore his approach is often contrasted with **Michel Foucault**'s treatment of the body in his concept of **governmentality**.

BRYAN S. TURNER

Merton, Robert K. (1910–2003)
Born in Philadelphia, Meyer Schkolnick changed his name to Robert Merlin in adolescence when he was already a gifted magician in need of a stage name. Robert King Merton came later, but his youthful talents for plying the line between the apparent and the real were a promise of things to come. After education in the public schools and libraries of South Philadelphia, Merton attended Temple University where he discovered **sociology** (BA, 1931). His graduate studies were at Harvard (PhD, 1936), where he distinguished himself both in sociology and the history of science. As a graduate student he published eight articles in the leading journals in academic sociology and science studies, which were the groundwork for his first major book, *Science, Technology and Society in Seventeenth-Century England* (1938), and his most important scholarly article, "Social Structure and Anomie" (1938).

Merton's place in the history of twentieth-century science and culture is assured by four among his many accomplishments: (1) the founding of the sociology of science; (2) his **leadership** (with **Paul Lazarsfeld**) of one of academic sociology's most important centers of training and research at Columbia University; (3) the introduction of theoretical ideas, always empirically grounded, that simultaneously turned American sociology into a mature social science and renewed its appreciation of the European traditions; and (4) by writing the English language with such clarity and elegance that concepts of his invention (such as "self-fulfilling prophecy," "**focus group**" and "role model") entered the vernacular. Merton's genius is most simply described as a devotion to empirical social science conveyed without sacrifice of his formidable learning in literature, history, and philosophy.

If there was a single handbook for **sociological theory** and research in sociology in the middle of the twentieth century, it was Merton's *Social Theory and Social Structure* (1949), in which he developed concepts like manifest and latent functions, **anomie** as a structural effect, theories of the middle range, the self-fulfilling prophecy, and reference group theory, among others, including the key ideas upon which the sociology of science was established. Though he is thought of as aligned with **Talcott Parsons** as a structural functionalist, Merton's thinking was first and foremost structuralist: for example, in "Social Structure and Anomie," he revised **Émile Durkheim**'s theory of anomie to demonstrate how structures can invent new, if deviant, forms of social behavior when **society** fails to provide the normal institutional means. He was, thus, the master of discerning the hidden behind the apparent.

Merton published some thirty books between 1938 and the year of his death in 2003, the last of which, *The Travels and Adventures of Serendipity* (2003), stands with *On the Shoulders of Giants: A Shandean Postscript* (1965) as a work that will long be read by literary and cultural critics as well as by sociologists. Among his many distinctions were twenty-nine honorary degrees, a MacArthur Prize Fellowship (1983–8), a presidency of the American Sociological Association (1957), and the National Medal of Science (1994). Merton was a man of consummate generosity who helped countless people with their work and lives.

CHARLES LEMERT

Methodenstreit

This was a controversy over the method and **epistemology** of economics in the late 1880s to 1890s between supporters of the Austrian School led by Carl Menger (1840–1921) and the German Historical School of Gustav von Schmoller (1838–1917). The Historical School argued that economists could develop social laws from the collection and study of **statistics** and historical materials, and distrusted theories not derived from historical experience.

The Austrian School believed that economics was the work of philosophical logic and could only ever develop by deriving abstract, universally valid rules of conduct from first principles. Human motives and other causes for concrete interaction were far too complex to be amenable to statistical analysis. At a general level the *Methodenstreit* was a question of whether there could be a science, apart from history, which could explain the dynamics of human action. The dispute began in 1884 with Schmoller's critical review of Menger's *Principle of Economics* (1871) and Menger's reply, *The Errors of Historicism in the German Political Economy* (1884). It subsequently involved thinkers such as Lujo Brentano (1844–1931), **Max Weber**, and **Werner Sombart** for the Historical School, and Eugen von Böhm-Bawerk (1881–1914), Friedrich Wieser (1851–1926), and Ludwig von Mises (1881–1973) for the Austrian School. Politically there were overtones of a conflict between the classical **liberalism** of the Austrian School and the advocacy of welfare state provisions by the Historical School. In sociology the issues were central to Weber's approach, which attempted to steer a pragmatic course between the pursuit of generalizations and historically grounded and specific analysis.

LARRY RAY

methodological individualism

This concept was introduced by the philosopher of science **Karl Popper** in his influential work *The Poverty of Historicism* (1957), one of the two most influential books in the twentieth-century history of the philosophy of the **social sciences**. The main thesis of this book, developed in the 1930s, was an attack on the notions of the forces of history and ideas of historical inevitability in **fascism** and **Communism**, but also in the thinking of academic scholars such as **Karl Mannheim** and, before him, **Ernst Troeltsch**, who employed similar "holist" or supra-individual concepts and argued that they referred to concrete realities of a special kind.

The use of these concepts was typically associated with the philosophical claim that understanding these concrete phenomena required a special kind of knowledge or **methodology** beyond that of science. Popper's point was that such things as **society** were theoretical constructions, of a kind familiar from science, which were abstract concepts used to interpret our experience, but that the experience which they construct can be adequately captured in the terms that apply to individuals, such as **attitudes**, expectations, decisions, and relations. This did not imply, however, methodological psychologism, the claim that **sociology** could be reduced to the laws of psychology.

Max Weber is the most prominent and consistent methodological individualist in the history of sociology. In recent years the term has been associated with rational choice theorists who have argued that many social processes formerly explained in terms of society could be better understood as the product of individual choices or decisions which produce collective results through the processes of an "invisible hand."

STEPHEN P. TURNER

methodology

This term refers to the specialist study of procedures of empirical investigation. Traditionally, in sociology as in other sciences, it is the reliability of the research method which is thought to assure the validity of the research **data** and the generalizability of the research findings: it is methodology that differentiates sociology from mere anecdotage. A distinction is regularly made between quantitative and qualitative methods. Quantitative methods are primarily those of **censuses** and surveys, both structured **interviews** and postal **questionnaires**, but other examples are content analysis in studies of documents and mark-recapture methods of population estimation. Qualitative methods are primarily those of in-depth interviews, **ethnography**, **focus groups**, and **discourse analysis**, but other examples are life histories, group interviews, and rapid assessment techniques.

The growth in popularity of qualitative methods in the 1960s and 1970s – and the concomitant dissatisfaction with quantitative methods – was part of a revolt against **positivism**, a concern that sociology was studying what could be measured, rather than developing measures for social reality. However, the distinction between quantitative and qualitative methods has been overdrawn. Thus, qualitative methods of data collection have often been subjected to realist/positivist methods of analysis (see, for example, Rory Williams's use of "logical analysis" in *A Protestant Legacy*, 1990, his ethnography of the health beliefs of elderly Aberdonians). And best practice in large-scale quantitative surveys has long embraced the need for complementary qualitative work. This is seen most obviously in **pilot studies**, such as focus groups used to develop and refine measures and to test the comprehensibility of research instruments, but the best examples of such complementarity are found in the multi-disciplinary, community-based, randomized controlled trials of health services research, where qualitative methods are typically deployed to generate the "process evaluation" component of the study, that is, to explain why the service being evaluated appears to be more effective in some service-delivery settings – or with some subgroups of clients – than others.

The criticisms of a preoccupation with research method have continued to multiply. Critics have suggested that such preoccupations lead to a disabling scientism and political quietism, manifested in a failure to engage with oppressions such as **racism**. Or they have suggested that the claim to scientific status based on methodological expertise is a political claim to the privileges and rewards associated with professional autonomy; or that the same claim of expertise serves to distance the sociologist from his/her research subjects who lose the right to influence the research findings and collaborate in the scientific representation of their social world; or that the claim that one can accurately analyze the social phenomena of late **modernity** by carefully following rules of scientific practice, is simply a *claim*: a postmodern analysis would seek to examine how

representations of method serve to advance claims to scientific status.

Yet sociological research flourishes despite these buffets from activists and action research, from **Science and Technology Studies**, from **discourse analysis**, and from **postmodernism**. It flourishes under two dispensations, that of counter-reformatory **realism**, and that of a reformed methodology which incorporates reflexive awareness of its own limitations. The counter-reformatory position draws on the philosophy of **Karl Popper** to argue that, by following rigorous methodological procedures, sociologists can be led to reject a pre-existing theoretical assumption or hypothesis as negated by the research evidence and therefore false: research methods assure us of the scientific basis of the investigation because they provide for the possibility of the **falsification** of a hypothesis. The reformist position recognizes that the unthinking application of rules of methodology cannot of itself guarantee scientific reliability, that no rule can specify all the occasions of its use, and that the everyday application of scientific methods is a matter for pragmatic interpretation by researchers in the situation of action. Instead, the reformist position commits the researcher to the skillful use of certain practices to ensure outcomes such as relatively complete descriptions of the setting/activity, "saturation" of the analytical categories derived, and the demonstrable credibility of the provisional findings for collectivity members and/or other fellow sociologists. In effect, the reliability of the findings depends on the practical accomplishment of a reflexive researcher, keenly aware of the pitfalls and the limitations inherent in the research process: research methods (including the analysis and write-up) are craft skills practiced with varying degrees of success. The reformist position has been defended from a philosophy-of-science perspective, most notably by Roy Bhaskar's "critical realism" in *Reclaiming Reality* (1989) and by Martin Hammersley's "subtle realism" in *What's Wrong with Ethnography?* (1992). Of course, much sociological research takes place owing nothing to Popper on the one hand or Bhaskar and Hammersley on the other, but strictly speaking such research employs the methods, not of sociology but of **cultural studies**, the methods of textual **deconstruction**.

The study of research methods has progressively broadened from a preoccupation with procedures of research design, data collection, and analysis. Good ethical practice has become a matter for external regulation and professional self-regulation as well as academic writing. Methodological writing now also embraces topics such as the negotiation of research access, fieldwork relationships, leaving the field, researcher safety, and public participation in the research process. Much recent writing has been concerned with the authorial voice and the processes of sociological representation, so that reflexive awareness of research practice now extends to the writing of research itself.

MICK BLOOR AND FIONA WOOD

metropolitan fringe

This concept describes a region between 16 and 64 km outside major urban centers where traditional rural industries are giving way to residential, commercial, and industrial development. This new development is mainly located along highways and in the countryside rather than in established settlements. It is often unclear where suburbs end and the fringe begins. One criterion is to register changes in the size of parcels of land through the use of a GIS map in order to identify transformations of relatively small plots to larger parcels of four or more hectares. Many people who live in the fringe have suburban **lifestyles**, commuting long distances to jobs in the suburbs, edge cities, and the central **city**. The fringe is attractive because it offers open space, potentially cleaner air and water than a city or suburb, less congestion and noise, and less **crime**. In the information economy these features give the fringe significant economic development potential. **Firms** are more mobile than previously, and workers prefer to live in a pleasant environment with access to cultural amenities. The fringe combines environmental advantages with proximity to suburban and urban activities. Since the 1980s developed societies have seen population movement from the suburbs (the predominant growth area of the mid twentieth century) to the fringe, sometimes called "exurbia." There is a debate about whether this new growth is substantively different from what preceded it and some dispute claims that counter-urbanization in developed societies represents a dramatic break from previous growth patterns. Rather, the development on the metropolitan fringe may be simply the latest incarnation of continued suburbanization.   LARRY RAY

Michels, Robert (1856–1936)

A cosmopolitan political theorist, Michels made an enduring contribution to sociology in his

"iron law" of **oligarchy** as developed in his book *Political Parties* (1911 [trans. 1966]). His argument, which is neither a law nor as unyielding as the word iron implies, nonetheless offers acute insights into the general relation between **bureaucracy** and **democracy**. Using an empirical **case study** of the German Social Democratic Party (and associated **organizations**) to illustrate his general point, Michels observes that bureaucracies, which are organized solely for their effectiveness, can be effective only by relying on a small group of officials with specialized knowledge and skills. These upper-level bureaucrats ultimately become indispensable to administrative operations, especially when bureaucracies are under competitive or political pressures to achieve goals. Even organizations founded on democratic ideals ultimately cede day-to-day **authority** to these bureaucratic oligarchies. Though the idea is now ubiquitously known as the "iron law of oligarchy," it was anticipated in many other works, beginning with the arguments regarding democracy made by Jean-Jacques Rousseau (1712–78) in *On the Social Contract* (1792 [trans. 1913]), and including Moisei Ostrogorski (1854–1919) in his brilliant comparative study *Democracy and the Organization of Political Parties* (1902 [trans. 1964]), and **Max Weber**'s analysis of bureaucracy. *Union Democracy* (1956) by **Seymour Martin Lipset**, M. Trow, and **James S. Coleman** demonstrated the (uncommon) structural conditions for the persistence of democracy in a bureaucratized **trade union**. **Alvin Gouldner** went so far as to coin a counter concept of the "iron law of democracy," which maintains that oligarchy always generates opposition from the dominated (see "Metaphysical Pathos and the Theory of Bureaucracy," *American Political Science Review*, 1955).

Because of its stress on the unassailability of **elites**, Michels's thought is often associated with a broad theoretical tendency, the so-called theory of elites.   IRA COHEN

microsociology

– see **macrosociology**.

micro–macro theory

For several decades, sociological theorists have been concerned with how to link conceptualizations of face-to-face interpersonal processes to theories about more meso- and macro-level processes. This concern is often seen as a micro–macro theory "gap" because no theory in sociology fully integrates various levels of social organization. If we visualize the social world as unfolding at three basic levels — the micro-level of face-to-face **interaction** in encounters, the meso-level of structures revealing a division of **labor** (**groups**, **communities**, **organization**) and social categories (**social class**, **ethnicity**, **gender**, **age**, and the like), and the macro-level of institutional systems, **societies**, and inter-societal relations — theories tend to focus on one of the three levels. Despite sociology's concern about the lack of theoretical integration across levels of social reality, the problem is not unique to sociology; all sciences, including the most advanced theoretical science of all, physics, have been unable to develop a unified theory that explains the operative dynamics at all levels in their respective universes.

Within sociology, there are several basic strategies for trying to close the micro–macro conceptual gap. At opposite extremes are micro- and macro-chauvinists who posit the primacy of one level of social organization. Micro chauvinists view meso- and macro-reality as ultimately constructed from microsocial processes, such as symbolic interaction or interaction rituals, aggregated over **time** and across **space**, whereas macro-chauvinists argue that all micro-processes are constrained by macro-socio-cultural systems. Between these extremes are a variety of alternative strategies.

One approach involves building "a conceptual staircase" from conceptions of elementary actions and micro-level units to conceptualizations of ever-more-macro processes and structures, and vice versa. A related approach employs simulation techniques to posit an elementary dynamic at both the micro- and macro-levels that, through iterations, generates, respectively micro- and macro-outcomes. Still another approach comes from formal sociology and revolves around conceptualizing common processes that are isomorphic across levels of reality, ignoring the nature of the unit and, instead, focusing on the form of social relations among all micro-, meso-, and macro-units. Still another mediating approach tries to use the logic of deductive theory to cut across levels of reality by positing axioms about the behavior of individuals from which all propositions about meso- and macro-structures and processes can be deduced. Yet another approach is to invoke the *ceteris paribus* clause to bracket out, for purposes of analysis, other levels of reality in order to focus on the dynamics of one level, with the presumption that what is bracketed out can be incorporated later into a more robust theory. Another approach is to emphasize the **embeddedness** of social phenomena whereby micro-units are embedded in meso-level units that, in turn, are embedded in macro-level units, with the emphasis on how the more inclusive unit constrains the operation of the forces driving the formation and operation of embedded units and processes.

All of these approaches have produced interesting theory, but none has fully integrated at a theoretical level the dynamics operating at the micro-, meso-, and macro-levels of social organization. Perhaps the most important strategy is to recognize that social reality unfolds at all three levels and, while there are isomorphic processes across all three levels, there are also dynamics unique to each level. The goal should be, first of all, to theorize the dynamics of each level and, then, to see how the values of the variables in propositions and models explaining one level are influenced by the values of variables in propositions and models of the other two levels. In this way, bridging propositions are created that can, on the one hand, recognize what is unique to each level of social organization while, on the other, making the theoretical connections among levels. In this way, the micro–macro "gap" can be closed or, at least, reduced.

JONATHAN TURNER

middle class
– see **social class**.

middle-range theory
– see **sociological theory**.

migration
A change in permanent residence, often of a year or more in duration, migration involves a geographical move that crosses a political boundary. It is common to distinguish two basic forms by whether the move involves the crossing of an international boundary from one country to another, that is international migration, or whether the geographical move involves the crossing of a political boundary, usually a county, within a country, that is internal migration.

Several migration concepts require attention: in-migration (or out-migration) refers to the number of internal migrants moving to an area of destination (or from an area of origin); the analogous concepts for international migration are immigration and emigration. Return migration is the number of internal migrants who return to the area of origin; at the international level the analogous concept is remigration. Net migration refers to the migration balance of an area, consisting of the number of in-migrants (or immigrants) minus the number of out-migrants (or emigrants); the net balance may be positive (representing a net population gain to the area) or negative (representing a net loss) or, conceivably, zero. Gross migration is the sum total of migration for an area and comprises the in-migration into the area and the out-migration from the area. Rates of migration are developed by dividing the above by the number of persons in the area at the beginning of the migration time interval. Migration efficiency is an area's net migration divided by its gross migration. A migration stream is a body of migrants departing from a common area of origin and arriving at a common area of destination during a specified time interval. A migration counter stream is the migration stream, smaller in size, going in the opposite direction during the same interval. This entry now focuses on internal migration, and next on international migration.

With respect to internal movement, if the permanent change of residence does not involve crossing a county boundary, it is referred to as spatial mobility but not as internal migration. Thus all migrations are instances of spatial mobility, but not all instances of spatial mobility are migrations. In the United States during the one-year period between March 1, 2001, and March 1, 2002, 14.8 percent of the population aged one year or older changed residences, that is, they were spatially mobile. Of this nearly 15 percent, fewer than half – 6.3 percent of the totol population – were migrants, that is, their changes in residence involved the crossing of a state boundary. The reason for making such a distinction is that a migration is meant to involve a change in one's community of residence.

Migration from one area to another has the effect of decreasing the size of the population in the area of origin and increasing it in the area of destination. A migrant is at the same time both an out-migrant from the area of origin and an in-migrant to the area of destination. With regard to the growth dynamics of human communities, internal migration is the single most important of the demographic processes (**fertility**, **mortality**, and migration). Differences in birth rates and death rates in communities of the same country are typically small compared to differences between the communities in migration. Migration is thus the major method for redistributing the population within a country.

Among the many theoretical models developed to explain internal migration are: (1) the effects of distance; (2) **income** and migration; (3) the

physical costs of migration; (4) information and migration; (5) personal characteristics and the decision to migrate; (6) individual expectations and migration; and (7) **community** and kinship ties.

The distance model states that long distance discourages migration because the costs involved in migration are substantial and closely related to distance. The income and migration model argues that income (and job) opportunities provide a better explanation of in-migration than out-migration; destination characteristics also help determine the location to which the migrant will move. The physical costs model suggests that physical costs influence resource allocation and migration by influencing the private costs of migration. According to Michael J. Greenwood, in "Research on Internal Migration in the United States: A Survey" (1975, *Journal of Economic Literature*), the information model emphasizes that "the availability of information concerning alternative localities plays a prominent role in the potential migrant's decision regarding a destination." The personal characteristics model argues that personal demographic characteristics (such as **age**, **gender**, **education**, number of dependents, **networks**, and **race and ethnicity**) exert important influences on the individual's decision to migrate. The individual expectations model assumes that the dynamics of migration decision making are based on individual expectations about the advantages and disadvantages of the home community versus possible alternative destination communities. P. N. Ritchey, in "Explanations of Migration" (1976, *Annual Review of Sociology*), notes that the community and kinship ties model points out that "the presence of relatives and friends is a valued aspect of life [that] . . . encourages migration by increasing the individual's potential for adjustment through the availability of aid in location at an alternative area of residence."

International migration is the permanent movement of people from one country to another for a year or longer time. According to Rainer Münz, in "Immigration Trends in Major Destination Countries" in the *Encyclopedia of Population* (2003), twentieth-century immigrants to most of the major destination countries may be broadly grouped into four categories: refugees and asylum seekers; migrants from former colonies; economic migrants; and ethnically privileged migrants.

Refugees and asylum seekers emigrate involuntarily because of persecution, **violence**, or extreme deprivation and usually move to a neighboring state. Postcolonial migration began in the 1950s as a result of **decolonization**. Indigenous people moved from former colonial countries to the European countries that had colonized them. Economic migrants are voluntary migrants motivated by economic aspirations and are likely to move from less to more developed countries. Some countries, such as Israel, give priority to migrants with the same ethnic and religious origins as those of the majority population.

Douglas Massey and his colleagues, in Massey *et al.*, "Theories of International Migration: A Review and Appraisal" (1993, *Population and Development Review*) and "An Evaluation of International Migration Theory: The North American Case" (1994), focus on several of the most important theories of international migration, most of which focus on the determinants of voluntary migration. The neoclassical economic model posits that migration results from individual cost–benefit decisions to maximize expected incomes by moving. Workers are attracted from low-wage countries with adequate labor, to a high-wage country with limited labor.

The new economics-of-migration theory challenges some of the hypotheses and assumptions of neoclassical economics. It argues that migration decisions are made not only by isolated individuals but also by larger units, such as **families** and households.

The dual-labor-market theory argues that migration results from the labor demands of **industrial societies**. International migration is caused not only by the push factors of the origin countries, but also by the pull factors of the destination countries. **Capitalism** tends to separate **labor markets** into two sectors, the primary sector that produces jobs with tenure, high pay, and good benefits and working conditions; and the secondary sector, with the opposite. Employers turn to immigrants to fill the jobs in the secondary sector.

World-systems analysis argues that international migration is the natural result of the **globalization** of the **economy**. A large number of people are released from traditional industries, such as farming, creating a pool of people ready to move, both internally and internationally. The market economy attracts human capital to a relatively small number of global cities, among them New York, Los Angeles, and Chicago.

Migration network theory focuses on **networks**: that is, the interpersonal ties that connect migrants, former migrants, potential migrants, and nonmigrants in the origin and destination countries. Networks increase the likelihood of international movement by decreasing migrant risks and costs and increasing the gains. Networks make it easier for new migrants to find jobs in destination countries.

The above theories and others endeavor to account for the causal process of international migration at different levels of analysis, namely, the individual, the household, the country, and the world. They are not necessarily incompatible.

DUDLEY L. POSTON

military
– see **war**.

Mill, John Stuart (1806–1873)

Born in London, Mill was educated by his father, with the assistance of the celebrated legal and utilitarian theorist, Jeremy Bentham (1748–1832). By the age of seventeen, he began publishing in his father and Bentham's *Westminster Review*. When he was twenty, he suffered a nervous breakdown and, questioning his father and Bentham's ideas, he turned to Romantic influences in general and the work of Samuel Coleridge (1772–1834) in particular.

In 1843, he published *System of Logic* in which he argued that scientific method applied to social as well as purely natural phenomena. In 1848 he published *Principles of Political Economy* and he also championed worker-owned cooperatives. His work *Utilitarianism,* published in 1861, argued that the pursuit of happiness was to be assessed not merely by quantity but by quality.

Most influential of all, however, was *On Liberty* (1859) – a book influenced by **Alexis de Tocqueville**'s *Democracy in America* (1835 and 1840 [trans. 1968]), in which he warned that freedom can be undermined as much by a "coercive" **public opinion** as by arbitrary laws. In *Considerations of Representative Government* (1861), Mill spoke of the "infirmities" to which universal suffrage is subject, while *The Subjection of Women* (1869) argued that women's "nature" cannot be known until women live in a world of freedom.

He was elected as a Radical candidate to parliament in 1865, introducing an amendment to the 1867 Reform Act (which he lost) arguing for women's suffrage. He criticized Governor Eyre's brutality in Jamaica and was defeated in the 1868 general election.

JOHN HOFFMAN

millenarianism
– see **religion**.

Millett, Kate (1934–)

Born in Minnesota, Millett was educated at the University of Minnesota, Oxford University, and Columbia University; it was at Columbia that Millett wrote her doctoral thesis, which was to be published as *Sexual Politics* in 1970. The book was an immediate bestseller and is one of the best-known of the works that became known collectively as second-wave **feminism**. The thesis of the book is that western **culture** (and in particular its literature) is essentially misogynist; using the fiction of D. H. Lawrence, Henry Miller, Jean Genet, and Norman Mailer as illustrative, Millett argues that heterosexuality is used by men to degrade women. This process of degradation is facilitated by **ideologies** of romantic love and the patriarchal structure of the nuclear **family**.

Millett's success with *Sexual Politics* has been followed by a number of other works: *The Prostitution Papers* (1973), *Flying* (1974), and *Sita* (1977). The last two works were largely autobiographical and trace the impact on Millett both of her considerable fame and of her shift in sexual **identity**, from that of the wife of the Japanese sculptor Fumio Yoshimura to the lover of the woman who is the subject of *Sita*. The pressures and demands of fame resulted in the mental breakdown which became the subject of Millett's *The Loony Bin Trip* (1990), a searing account of time spent in institutions for the mentally ill. Millett continues to write and speak on feminist issues and her work provides a radical corrective to some of the more liberal politics of feminism in the United States. Millett has not been afraid to confront issues of **gender**, **poverty**, and powerlessness, while her own work contains much on the confrontational sexual politics which she has so forcefully contested.

MARY EVANS

Mills, C. Wright (1916–1962)

One of the most influential sociologists of the twentieth century, Mills is perhaps best known for his trilogy on the changing character of political **power** in the United States. In the three books, *The New Men of Power* (1948) about the labor movement, *White Collar* (1951) about **intellectuals** and the middle classes, and *The Power Elite* (1956) about the convergence of interests among the military, big business, and the government, Mills developed one of the most sustained critiques of what he and others came to call **mass society**. In attempting to explain the new sort of **society** that had emerged in the period after World War II, Mills also provided important sources of inspiration for the student movement of the 1960s.

Mills was a self-proclaimed outsider, an "academic outlaw" in the postwar United States, and throughout his life he was critical of what he saw as the subservience of his fellow sociologists to those in power.

Mills grew up in Texas, and wrote a doctoral thesis in sociology on **pragmatism** at the University of Wisconsin. He was Professor of Sociology at Columbia University in New York, and, in addition to his academic work, he wrote articles for such publications as the *Nation, Dissent,* and *Partisan Review*. Mills was known for having a colorful personality, and took an active part in the political debates of his times, writing popular books about the Cold War and the arms race (*The Causes of World War Three*, 1958), and the Cuban Revolution (*Listen Yankee*, 1960) which he strongly supported, much to the disapproval of his academic colleagues.

Throughout his short life – he died in 1962 at the age of forty-six – Mills sought to combine indigenous American **social theory**, deriving from **populism** and pragmatism, with the theories of **Karl Marx** and **Max Weber**. In addition to his own writings, he edited anthologies on **Marxism** (*The Marxists*, 1962) and Max Weber (*From Max Weber: Essays in Sociology*, coedited with H. H. Gerth, 1946).

He presented his own approach to sociology in a short volume, entitled *The Sociological Imagination* (1959), which was based on lectures that he had given in Europe. In that book, he outlined his approach to sociological research, distinguishing himself from what he termed grand theory, on the one hand, and "abstracted **empiricism**," on the other. He associated the one style with the work of **Talcott Parsons**, and the other with the interest in quantitative methods that was becoming the dominant form of sociological research in his day. For Mills, sociology was best seen as a kind of "intellectual craftsmanship," and the sociological imagination that he tried to foster was meant to help people become conscious of their place in history, as well as the social nature of the problems that they faced. He wrote that such an approach was not "ascendant" at the time, but, in the intervening years, Mills has continued to serve as a model for politically engaged and socially committed **sociology**.

ANDREW JAMISON

minority rights
– see **rights**.

Mitchell, Juliet (1940–)

Born in New Zealand, Mitchell has been a widely influential writer who is responsible for having reclaimed **Sigmund Freud** for **feminism** and for enabling feminism to use the insights of **psycho-analysis** to illuminate the understanding of the social and, more particularly, the symbolic world. A long-time student of **Marxism**, Mitchell in 1971 published *Woman's Estate*, which used the work of **Friedrich Engels** to argue that women, across **cultures** and **social classes,** were – as Engels had suggested – the proletariat of the world. But it was *Psychoanalysis and Feminism* (1974) which made a lasting contribution to the study of **gender**; Mitchell's subtle and nuanced reading showed the possibilities of Freud's ideas about the instability of gender and the dynamics of the formation of gender **identity**. Contrary to previous readings of Freud (for example, those of **Kate Millett**), which had assumed that Freud took a rigid view of gender divisions, Mitchell showed that Freud understood the acquisition of gender identity as a fluid and always uncertain process. Mitchell's work enabled later feminists to use psychoanalysis as a way of exploring literature and the **arts**: Mitchell's understanding of the term woman, like Freud's, was of a possible, rather than a fixed, state.

Since the publication of *Psychoanalysis and Feminism*, Mitchell has continued to work on the politics of feminism (*Women: The Longest Revolution*, 1984) and on the social pressures that shape ideas about gender (*Mad Men and Medusas*, 2000). In all her work, Mitchell has maintained a recognition of the divisions of class, as much as of gender, in the social world, and a commitment to a politics of radical and more egalitarian social transformation.   MARY EVANS

mobilization
– see **collective behavior**.

mode of production
– see **Karl Marx**.

modeling
In its general sense, a model is an attempt to depict or describe in a dynamic manner a social reality, process, or institution. At this general level, a model is synonymous with a theory. A good model should be essential – in that it covers the important characteristics and/or processes of that which it is attempting to model – and simple – the model should be less complex and easier to comprehend than the reality itself.

What is essential will depend upon the purpose of the model; for instance, an econometric model that attempts to depict the workings of a nation's

economy will highlight features and processes quite different from a model of the diffusion of popular culture fads through the same society. The use of ideal types – the conceptualizations of social phenomena in their abstract or pure (hence ideal) form which then form a base against which to compare the actual phenomena – can be considered as a form of essentialist modeling.

Models imply heuristic prediction and it is for this reason that their attempts to depict must be dynamic rather than static explanations. The ultimate test of a model is not how well it describes the present or the past, but rather how well it is capable of providing reliable predictions of its future as parameters change.

Regarding types, models may either be opaque or transparent. An opaque model makes no attempt to duplicate the actual processes that occur during the interim phases between input and result. In effect, the true interim processes are seen as a black box and the estimation procedures of the model do not necessarily in any way resemble what may be occurring in actuality within the box. All that is required for a successful opaque model is that it produces reliable predictions (outputs) for any given change in parameters (inputs) that accurately mimic what occurs in reality. In contrast, transparent models do attempt to depict internal interim phases. In this latter case, the workings of the model itself may be of more interest than the eventual outcomes that it predicts.

Statistical or multivariate causal modeling is a more specific instance of modeling in which the principles of modeling are applied to quantitative data. All multivariate statistical models seek to summarize **information** from a group of individual cases (typically the "cases" are individuals responding to a large sample survey) into an equation or a set of predictive equations. Usually the simplification is taken further by attempting to eliminate redundant measures of characteristics ("variables") and redundant associations between variables. Some statistical modeling techniques ("measurement models") go even further by positing the hypothetical existence of ideal-type variables that are essential representations of concepts rather than actual measured variables. The success of the application of a statistical modeling technique can be measured by the amount of variance it explains in its solution.

Statistical models are "opaque" models since they are using abstract mathematical formulas to depict qualitatively different social processes. However, there are aspects of "transparency," in that analysts can: observe the dynamic shifting of coefficient estimates as variables are introduced; evaluate conceptual constructs by the combinations of variables included in a model; discover unanticipated complex patterns of multiple causality through identifying statistical interactions between two or more variables; and construct more elaborate models by stringing a number of equations together.

An early use of multivariate techniques in sociology that explicitly claimed to be a model was the use of path analysis by **Otis Dudley Duncan** and **Peter M. Blau** to introduce the "status-attainment" model of **social mobility** in the United States (*The American Occupational Structure*, 1967). Working with **data** from a large-sample **survey** of United States men, Blau and Duncan put together the display of results of a series of regression equations into a single figure, a "path diagram." Their basic diagram is an attempt to depict the process of intergenerational (inheritance) and intragenerational (career) social mobility in the United States. In it, an index of current occupational position (indexed by a scale of status) is seen as being driven by point of entry into the labor market (indexed by "first job"), educational attainment (indexed by "years of schooling"), and social origin (indexed by "father's job" and "father's educational attainment").

The original status-attainment model has prompted four decades of subsequent work and controversy about its validity around issues such as its exclusion of women, the basic conceptualization of its core **values**, and its implicit stance on **social stratification**. The salient point here, however, is that it displays the characteristics of a multivariate causal model: a vastly complicated process of social mobility is distilled down into a set of essential relationships. Furthermore, the construction of the model displays dynamic characteristics since it is possible to trace indirect causal effects along the "paths" of coefficients in the model (for example, **education** may have a direct effect on current occupational position but also could have an indirect effect since education can affect level of "first job," which in turn affects current **occupation**). In addition, a change in a parameter, such as increasing the level of education attained, would result in a change in an "output" estimate: for example, the predicted level of "first job" would be higher.

The number of multivariate statistical techniques is legion, including: (1) analysis of variance techniques; (2) techniques of regression analysis (general linear analysis of parametric data; logistic regression techniques where the dependent variable is a quality, a nominal category; multilevel modeling where the independent variables exist on at least two levels of aggregation, such as individual data plus group, area, and/or organizational data) that have in common the prediction of the values of a dependent variable based upon the values of one or more independent predictor variables; (3) techniques of data reduction, such as factor analysis in which the values of a number of observed variables are assumed to reflect the presence of a smaller number of unobserved "essential" variables; (4) "measurement models" that are a combination of prediction of regression with data reduction; and (5) loglinear analysis techniques for the multivariate modeling of relationships between non-parametric data. Like modeling in general, all of these multivariate techniques have simplification and essentialism in common.

BERNADETTE HAYES AND ROBERT MILLER

model(s)

– see **modeling**.

modernity

Modernity is a civilizational epoch in the same sense as Greco-Roman antiquity. Though modernity originated in western Europe and North America over two centuries ago, today it extends to cosmopolitan centers around the globe and its consequences affect all but the most isolated **communities** in every country on earth. Modernity, like all epochs, includes distinctive forms of economic and political organization, characteristic cultural **institutions**, and persistent tensions between antithetical civilizational trends. It is also an epoch that generates a distinctive set of ambivalent reactions. A number of these tensions and ambivalent reactions will be discussed in itemized fashion in later sections of this entry.

Social theory as we know it today developed when **intellectuals** began trying to make sense of modernity as it matured during the nineteenth century. However, early modern theorists disagreed on how modernity should be defined, and many of these disagreements have continued in subsequent generations, albeit with numerous additions and revisions. The parameters of modernity can be grasped by noting the dynamic forces that various early modern theorists maintained were the prime movers of the history of modernity. For Adam Smith (1723–90) and **Karl Marx**, **capitalism** in the form of **markets** (Smith) or profit-oriented production (Marx) was the mainspring of modern social life. **Henri Saint-Simon** and **Auguste Comte** maintained that scientific knowledge and **technology** ultimately would direct modernity in a rational, orderly manner. **Alexis de Tocqueville** stressed the transition from aristocratic political **organizations** and the cultural **values** of aristocratic **elites** to representative democratic institutions and a **culture** based upon egalitarian values. **Émile Durkheim** stressed the modern culture of **individualism** and the division of **labor**. Until quite recently (see especially Michael Mann's *The Sources of Social Power: Volume I*, 1986, and *Volume II*, 1996), social theorists had dealt with the intensively developed and extensively organized nation-state as a central feature of modernity only obliquely (see especially the works of **Max Weber**). However, most contemporary theorists consider the nation-state, including its military forces, social services **bureaucracies**, judicial system, educational systems, and sources of revenue, as yet another dynamic force of modernity.

Each of these dynamic forces contributes to modernity's most obvious defining trait: namely its endless bouts of disruptive change. In fact, it can be said without hyperbole that modernity is the most unstable epoch that humanity has ever known. The radical mutability of modernity is most easily understood against the backdrop of premodern cultures and **civilizations**, most of which did not welcome dramatic change. Prior to modernity, most rulers discouraged all but the most pragmatic changes in the societies they controlled. Abrupt change, with its unforeseeable results, might threaten their dominion. (The conduct of **wars** and the construction of empires were notable exceptions in this regard.) Rulers sought the stabilizing support of orthodox **religions** and they also encouraged stable customs and **traditions** that made commoners as suspicious of change as were the rulers themselves. Only incremental changes were quietly absorbed into **everyday life**.

Modernity makes the sharpest possible break with the propensity for stasis in premodern social epochs. Each of the dynamic forces of modernity, capitalism, scientific technology, the nation-state, and the culture of individualism not only pushed through the cake of custom during the historical transition to modernity, but also proceeded to foster change after change so that the social circumstances of each generation differed from those of its predecessors.

Intellectuals have been profoundly impressed by the sharp contrast between the tradition-bound cultures of the past and the ever-changing social conditions of modernity. For example, Marshall Berman entitled his influential commentary on modern cultural ways of life *All That Is Solid Melts into Air* (1982), echoing the powerful closing trope of a passage from Marx and **Friedrich Engels**, *The Communist Manifesto* (1848), that evokes the agitation and disruption caused by capitalism and, by extension, modernity at large. Agitation and disruption were on the minds of other early modern thinkers as well. In *Democracy in America* (1835 [trans. 1966], p. 298), de Tocqueville correctly foresaw that the rise of democratic political institutions would generate chronic instability in which governmental regimes and even basic principles of government would recurrently come and go without relief. In his well-known essay, "The Metropolis and Mental Life" (1903 [trans. 1971]), **Georg Simmel** went so far as to propose that human beings were incapable of taking in all of the rapidly changing experiences they encountered in a typical urban environment. To fend off excessive stimulation, individuals were forced to distance themselves psychologically from many of the people they encountered and the events they observed.

Until the last decades of the twentieth century, social theorists were divided on a key question about the history of modernity: does modernity have a historical teleology with a foreseeable destination, a *terminus ad quem*? The question itself is thoroughly modern. No other epoch in any civilization has ever been as unsettled by what the future might hold. If social thinkers knew where modernity was headed and if they knew the mechanisms that were propelling it in this direction, then they could recommend rational steps to hasten the day when the best possible organization of society would finally emerge. Smith, **Georg Wilhelm Friedrich Hegel**, Comte, Marx, **Herbert Spencer**, Durkheim, and **Talcott Parsons** all did their best to discern systematic trajectories in the history of modernity. However, even in the nineteenth century, de Tocqueville and Weber maintained that the history of modernity rarely runs true to a teleological course for very long. By the late twentieth century, most social theorists had come around to the open-ended historical view that modernity has no ultimate destination. The disintegration of the Soviet Union marked a theoretical watershed in this regard, since very few social scientists foresaw these world-historical events. But, in retrospect, no theorist of modernity foresaw the onset or the profound consequences of two world wars, multiple instances of **genocide**, the rapid collapse of colonial rule in the Third World, and the transformative power of information processing and global communications technologies.

No single force is responsible for the relentlessness of modern **social change**. Capitalism is subject to cycles of expansion and contraction in all of its markets from investments and finance to job markets and markets for consumer goods. Equally important, capitalism endlessly seeks to increase profitable operations and reduce costs, a trait that leads to swift transitions between geographical locales of operation, constant searches for cheaper sources of labor, and a host of other propensities to change as well.

Modern scientific technology is a vast engine of unpredictable change. Members of modern societies in the nineteenth century had to adjust to the steam engine, the industrial factory, the railroad, the telegraph, and electrical power. In the first half of the twentieth century, people had to adjust to the mechanized assembly line, automobiles, movies, radio, and telephones. And today we are adjusting to computerized information processing, global communication via satellites and the worldwide web, and new forms of **biotechnology** that have the potential in the not-too-distant future to change the definition of human life itself.

Modern **states** are engines of change as well. From global and regional wars fought with mechanical weapons of previously unimagined power, to more benign changes such as state-run schools and social health and welfare institutions, the modern state recurrently transforms the social circumstances in which its citizens live. Even modern culture, with its multivalent emphases on the **rights**, prerogatives, and opportunities that encourage individuals to pursue changes for the better in their own lives, creates expectations that the future will not be the same as the past.

Not only is it impossible to foresee where the open-ended history of modernity will lead, it is also impossible to say when modernity began. If we again focus independently on each of modernity's dynamic forces, the exception to the rule is the modern state, which many historians believe emerged in its distinctively modern (albeit not very democratic) form in Otto von Bismarck's (1815–98) Germany after 1870. Beyond this there is little consensus on when any of the principal forces of modernity began. Consider modern capitalism. Some elements of capitalism, such as long-distance trade and short-term profit-seeking investments, were already on the scene before 1500. According to Weber in *The Protestant Ethic and the Spirit of Capitalism* (1905 [trans. 2002]), the cultural ethos of the profit-oriented entrepreneur first evolved during the seventeenth and

eighteenth centuries. However, capitalism as the primary system for the provision of material goods in **everyday life** did not fully supplant local agrarian production until sometime after 1750, and then only in the most advanced cosmopolitan centers of Europe and North America.

Next, consider technology. According to Lewis Mumford (1895–1985) in *Technics and Civilization* (1934), the development of the modern machine predates the industrial revolution of the late nineteenth century by at least 700 years. But modern machinery entered the factories of western Europe only during the nineteenth century, and only during the period from 1880 to 1920 did modern technology reach into the households and everyday lives of modern populations at large.

The origin of the culture of modern individualism is difficult to date as well. According to Jacob Burckhardt (1818–97) in *The Civilization of the Renaissance in Italy* (1860 [trans. 1954]), the humanistic appreciation of the power and the beauty of the individual began in the time of Michelangelo (1475–1556). But the belief in the **equality** and liberal rights of human beings as citizens moved from the pages of political philosophy to the constitutions of governments only following the American Revolution of 1776, and even today these values are still partially ideals rather than realities. The idea that every individual should be entitled to realize her or his own potentials and choose her or his own **lifestyle** is more recent still. Even in the 1950s cultural critics such as **David Riesman** worried about the degree to which modern, middle-class individuals conformed too closely to homogenizing cultural **norms**. It is only in the current generation that theorists such as **Anthony Giddens** and **Ulrich Beck** highlighted new trends towards alternative lifestyles and self-identity that carry the culture of individualism into how citizens of modernity pursue their personal lives.

One final point on the history of modernity. While it is true that modernity is driven by multiple engines of social change, what makes the history so difficult to predict is that all of these forces interact with one another in complex ways. For example, it is easy to see that capitalists were already investing in potentially profitable developments in industrial technology as far back as the late eighteenth century. But technology has produced surprises to which capitalists have had to adjust as well. This is no more evident than in the transformative effects of modern information and communications technology which have dramatically accelerated everything from the intensity of economic competition, to the rapid intensification of global markets and **networks** of production, to new means of data gathering and analysis that enable sophisticated **firms** to market their wares in different forms to targeted consumer groups in every corner of the world. Equally complicated interactions are found between capitalist industries and nation-states. On the one hand, nation-states depend upon a prosperous capitalist **economy** for their economic well-being. Therefore they must adapt and adjust to changing commercial and industrial conditions. However, when states are engaged in warfare, capitalist firms are compelled to support the war effort even if this reduces their profitability. Nation-states also adjust their operations to new technologies as well. However, states also sponsor a great deal of technological innovation. This is especially true with regard to the military. Indeed, things as various as computers and global satellites were promoted and perfected to suit military needs.

Modernity as an epoch may have no determinate starting point nor a historical destiny, nor even a predictable historical trajectory, but if the epoch at large lacks a teleological pattern, modernity has generated a number of less enveloping developmental trends. Some of these trends emerge in many institutional contexts; others are confined to a specific institutional order. But the most important trends almost inevitably encounter paradoxical opposition. Paradoxical opposition refers here to trends and countertrends that are each evident in the fabric of modernity, yet radically inconsistent with one another.

Democratic ideals such as equality, liberty, and impartiality in the **public sphere**, and the right to **privacy** in personal life, are modern values. Though never fully realized, they are proclaimed in the constitutions of most modern states and judicial levers that **social movements** use for social change. If modernity has a creed, it is grounded in what Durkheim terms the cult of the dignity of the individual, where human dignity is the lowest common denominator for all of the values. But the paradox is that, though these values apply universally as ideals, state policies determine to whom they apply. All modern states leave some populations unprotected. Some exclusions do minimal harm. But many render certain groups (for example, racial and ethnic minorities, immigrants, gays and lesbians) vulnerable to damaging **discrimination** and harsh stigmatization. Even worse, states sometimes pursue barbaric policies to punish and slaughter peoples they leave unprotected. Modern states have been responsible for the worst genocides in history. **Michael Mann**, in a controversial argument in his *Dark Side of Democracy* (2005), argues that strong modern states, mainly in the northern hemisphere, may now be less inclined to genocide than weak states south of the equator. Even if this speculation proves true, modern states are still capable of ruthless war, systematic torture, and callous oppression of minority groups. Paradoxically, the only institution that can pursue democratic ideals can sometimes cynically forsake or ignore them with cruel, inhumane results.

Weber coined the phrase "disenchantment of the world," by which he meant the replacement of belief in other-worldly forces such as the will of God that once were held to govern the world by impersonal scientific laws and formal **rationality** that leave no room, at least in public life, for unfathomable forces of any kind. Disenchantment need not imply an end to religious faith in private life, but it does signify the end of religious faith as a basis for modern forms of jurisprudence, legitimate government, economic enterprise, and knowledge of the natural world. The accent placed on spirituality in public life in many premodern societies disappears.

As demonstrated by recurrent waves of religious **fundamentalism** in western societies, even a trend as broad and seemingly ineluctable as disenchantment cannot sweep through modernity without encountering paradoxical opposition. Such waves are nothing new. Papalist political and cultural movements have been a recurrent feature in reaction to the rise of modernity in Spain and France, and waves of Protestant fundamentalism have opposed the disenchantment of public life in the United States periodically since its origin. Fascist **ideologies** (including Hitler's Nazi ideology) stem from passionate sacralization of secular **symbols** (for example, the motherland, ethnic purity) in opposition to the disenchantments of modernity as well. Less inflammatory **civil religions** and **nationalism** may serve as vehicles for reactions to disenchantment as well.

Material **inequalities** are not unique to modernity; however, as Karl Marx observed, material inequality takes a unique form in capitalism. The bourgeoisie and the managerial classes are not just rich, as were aristocracies in the past: these classes systematically prosper, their **wealth** expands. Classes in poverty lack structural possibilities to prosper. Though some individuals may increase their wealth, the entire class cannot escape in this way. Like all elements of capitalism, today poverty must be understood globally. Large populations of the desperately poor reside in every Third World conurbation. Meanwhile, local and global capitalist enterprises generate prosperity for the upper classes.

In *The Great Transformation* (1944), **Karl Polanyi** identifies a historical cycle in the relations between capitalism and the state that can be generalized as one of the great paradoxes of modernity. Capitalism as an economic system prefers unregulated **markets** for wage-labor, which generally allow capitalists to pay the lowest possible wages and thereby increase their profitability. However, when wages sink too far (and/or the cost of living rises), workers mount political movements (often in alliance with other **groups**) to enlist the state in protecting them from impoverishment. States often respond with extensive welfare services for the economically disadvantaged. This constitutes the first phase of Polanyi's double movement. The second phase develops on two fronts: on the one hand, workers ultimately become excessively reliant on state aid and withdraw from the labor markets. On the other hand, states reach certain practical limits to the amount of funds they can spend on social services to the poor. In a very simplified sense, over time the double movement operates like a pendulum pushing towards free labor markets until a reaction sets in and the pendulum moves back towards the protective policies of the state, and then a counterreaction sets in and the pendulum begins to swing back the other way. Though Keynesian policies of state regulation seemed to moderate the double movement for a period after World War II, reactions set in against the **welfare state** in the mid-1980s, and the "double movement" once more asserted itself.

Consider a paradox of modern development that was already evident 100 years ago. On the one hand, the increasing division of labor in capitalist production and in bureaucratized organizations of all kinds was dividing labor into a vast array of highly specialized tasks and establishing deep divisions between public and private life. But counterposed to these trends towards **differentiation**, there were also trends towards centralization, the most obvious being the centripetal forces that drew (and still draw) people from the countryside into densely populated **cities** and conurbations.

The same paradox is evident on a global scale. On the one hand, capitalism, both historically and in recent times, has established regional sectors of global inequality based upon what **Immanuel Wallerstein** terms the principle of unequal exchange. There are shifting global divisions based upon

military and diplomatic alliances as well. Moreover, as peoples come into closer contact with one another around the globe, certain cultural differences (for example between China and the West) loom larger than they did in premodern times. Yet there is no denying that modern modes of communication and transportation, from the telephone and the steamship to data transmission by global satellites and transportation by jet aircraft and high-speed pipelines and ships, increase both the velocity and intensity of global interaction that enable durable economic and political **networks** to concentrate the control of many resources on a global scale.

In the early days of the modern era, technology was often welcomed as an unalloyed good. No one regards technology as thoroughly evil today. Very few critics would completely eliminate industrial production or modern medicine. But technology now seems a two-edged sword. Pollution, the most obvious byproduct of technology, threatens our **health**. Global warming is changing our climate with as yet unforeseeable consequences. And it is already evident that biotechnology will change the very meaning of life during the twenty-first century. But there is more. Technology facilitates unprecedented forms of total war in which the object is to destroy civilian populations. Moreover, though genocide is possible without technology, the Nazis demonstrated the horror of genocide by industrial means. Technology is simply a means to make tools, and, as with all tools, the virtues and vices of technology depend upon how it is used.

From Marx's notion of the **alienation** of the proletariat to **Jürgen Habermas**'s writings on the excessive colonization of cultural life-worlds by impersonal and lifeless social systems, social theorists have been sharp, sometimes hostile, critics of the inequalities, injustices, and oppressive conditions and consequences of modernity. Modernity is certainly open to criticism on many counts, from capitalism's exploitation of labor to the practice of total war, where the object is not to defeat a rival military force but to destroy the homeland of the enemy by lethal technological means. Yet even the most comprehensive and justified criticism of modernity contains a certain degree of ambivalence. Modernity, as previously said, is easily the most comfortable set of material circumstances human beings have ever established for themselves. Where is the Luddite who would forfeit central heating in the winter or air conditioning when the temperature is high? Modernity has also spawned a portfolio of political and cultural values such as the equality and rights of individuals, and the notion of social justice to which even the most acerbic critics of modernity subscribe, even as they use these values to highlight modernity's shortcomings and its hypocrisies.

As Durkheim observed, the moral ideals of modernity treat the rights and prerogatives of individuals as sacred. Each of us should possess these rights to an equal extent. But these ideals are contradicted by some very deep-seated modern realities. Capitalism intrinsically generates vast inequalities between the rich and the poor, whether it is in the British slums Dickens described in nineteenth-century England or the slums found in every Third World conurbation today. Merely noting the vast difference between average age of death among modernity's rich and poor alerts us to how dramatic these inequalities are. But, as **Pierre Bourdieu** observes, modernity also includes many forms of cultural inequality that are insidious insofar as people unselfconsciously reproduce their **habitus**, even though in doing so they may put themselves at a cultural disadvantage vis-à-vis dominant groups. Some prominent inequalities between women and men, racial and ethnic minority groups, and minority groups based upon sexual differences can be understood in this way. But critics of these inequalities have had a measure of success. From socialist movements a century ago to women's movements today, periodic rebellions against inequality are as modern as the forms of inequality to which they object.

Social estrangement has been a recurrent theme in **social theory**. Marx's notion of alienation refers both to the loss of control over labor by workers and to the estrangement of workers from their material relations with fellow workers and members of their community. In *Suicide* (1897 [trans. 1951]), Durkheim conceived estrangement in two forms: anomie, which is the sense of profound confusion brought about by the social disruptions to which modernity is prone, and egoism, an excessively selfish, utilitarian form of individualism which is the unappealing underside of the moral individualism of which Durkheim approved. **Georg Lukács** saw modernity in Kafkaesque terms as subject to **reification**, that is, the sense that we live a social world with hard realities that seem too vast and powerful to change. Habermas's notion of the colonization of the life-world speaks to estrangement in the sense that the instrumental policies of capitalism and the modern state invade areas of public culture and private life, suppressing meaningful ties of social integration in favor of calculations of organizational

advantages and efficiencies. (A good example is the bureaucratization of universities and schools.)

Though each of these notions of estrangement makes a specific point, all of them underscore one of modernity's enduring problems, the inability of modern **civilization** to generate groups to replace the local communities that provided cultural meaning, moral **solidarity**, and spiritual assurance in premodern forms of social life. There is no single great impediment to the maintenance of communal ways of life in modernity. Capitalism, the bureaucratized **social policies** of the state, the impersonality of scientific technology, and modern individualistic culture – each adds its own share of obstacles in this regard. However, estrangement is not an all-or-nothing matter. Community groups, stable intimate relationships and personal **friendships**, and close extended **families** remain a part of the modern social scene. But, then, there is no denying that feelings of powerlessness, meaninglessness, loneliness, and insecurity are common experiences in modern social life. And to the extent that these feelings are found, the critics of estrangement in modernity are right.

Ironically, all of these complaints hinge on modern values. Other epochs had different complaints.

IRA COHEN

modernization

As the United States emerged as the world's hegemonic **power** after World War II, the structural–functionalist modernization **paradigm** became the dominant perspective in United States **sociology** and world **social science**. Elaborated by Harvard's **Talcott Parsons**, the lead figure in American sociology, the modernization paradigm saw **societies** as a relatively stable set of interrelated parts changing along similar lines, from traditional agricultural to modern **industrial societies**, part of a global pattern. The models for this transition from developing to developed societies were the industrialized **states** of western Europe and their settler offshoots in Australia, Canada, New Zealand, and the United States, along with countries such as Japan. Poor underdeveloped traditional societies were believed to be in the earlier phases of this transition, having yet to go through the modernization process. Here, the weight of traditional cultural beliefs and practices supposedly inhibited the industrialization, **differentiation**, and specialization of occupational roles necessary for success. Parsons aimed to provide a holistic analysis of this process, discussing the host of structural requirements necessary for the orderly functioning of the social system, so as to promote their diffusion worldwide.

Nils Gilman's important book, *Mandarins of the Future: Modernization Theory in Cold War America* (2003), analyzes how United States social scientists and policymakers converged on this model in the context of American superpower competition against the Soviet Union, including in the struggle for the hearts and minds of those in the Third World. Third World states were seen as being held back by traditional beliefs and cultural practices, thought to be barriers inhibiting the steps required for successful growth.

Perhaps the classic work of modernization or **development theory** and its vision of elite-guided **democracy** was economist Walt W. Rostow's *The Stages of Economic Growth: A Non-Communist Manifesto* (1961). Rostow argued that all countries could pass through these stages to achieve high mass **consumption** as had the United States. Rostow, a former Rhodes Scholar, became an important member of a host of United States presidential administrations, playing a significant role in planning the Vietnam War as part of the group of men David Halberstram called *The Best and the Brightest* (1993), eventually becoming President Johnson's National Security Council adviser. As critics pointed out, many social scientists working within the modernization framework, from Rostow to Parsons to Samuel Huntington, saw their task not just to analyze reality but to try and shape it to the benefit of the capitalist nation-states of which they were a part. In the context of the Vietnam War, such dual roles raised many questions about the objectivity of social scientists, and became an important part of the critique of modernization theory.

While the modernization perspective dominated United States and world social science up until the 1960s, the tumult of this period, from civil rights through the anti-war movement, to the related worldwide revolts of 1968, ushered in a sharp critique of this view and the forwarding of radically different perspectives. Forming an influential critique here were the various brands of international **political economy**, including **world-systems analysis** formulated by **Immanuel Wallerstein** and followers, which borrowed from Third World radicalism and a host of critical perspectives in world social science. Wallerstein and others traced the rise of the modernization paradigm to the shift from biological to cultural **racism**, not surprisingly given the horrors of the Holocaust, the political context of the civil rights movement, and the progress of **decolonization**.

Rather than simply arguing for the racial inferiority of the colonized as during the heyday of **colonialism**, now Third World backwardness was seen instead as the result of cultural differences and **traditions**, views critiqued most recently in Jared Diamond's landmark *Guns, Germs and Steel* (1999). This culture of poverty argument also saw cultural traditions as the cause of minority **poverty** in the advanced core states. While modernization was thus seen as an ideological formulation designed to uphold **power** and **inequality**, Wallerstein nonetheless recognized that there were many liberal scholars honestly concerned with the plight of world poverty and seeking to add knowledge that could aid in its overcoming. That being said, it was argued, the modernization view seriously distorted the actual history of the capitalist world-system, within which development and **underdevelopment** were part of a single historical process, whereby the minority in powerful core states benefited from the exploitation of the great majority in the periphery, the semi-periphery and the internal peripheries of the core.

There were many critical blows to the paradigm which represented the dominant consensus in sociology and the social sciences. In particular, profound criticisms of the underside of modernization came from the **Frankfurt School** of **critical theory** – **Walter Benjamin**, **Theodor Wiesengrund Adorno**, **Max Horkheimer**, and **Jürgen Habermas** – and from **Zygmunt Bauman**'s *Modernity and the Holocaust* (1989). There were also periods of revival, expressed in the 1980s and 1990s, as in Francis Fukuyama's *The End of History and the Last Man* (1992). Today, modernization theory appears to be making something of a comeback, this time not so much by analyzing national backwardness, but in the clash-of-civilizations discourse.

Increasingly, in the aftermath of the September 11, 2001, terrorist attacks, United States scholars such as Bernard Lewis have sought to explain the failure to modernize of Islamic civilizations in ways that provided ideological support to the Anglo-American argument that it is necessary to bring **democracy** to the Islamic world, if necessary through force, as with the United States' and United Kingdom's retrospective justification of the 2003 invasion of Iraq and subsequent military occupation. Yet in spite of the nominal transfer of sovereignty and elections, the revelations of United States torture in Iraq and elsewhere have undermined American claims of promoting freedom and modernization. Sociologists such as Paul Lubeck criticized this new modernization approach, relating the decline of Islamic civilization and its contemporary resurgence as a form of ethno-national political mobilization to culture and issues of global wealth and power. The rise and demise of modernization theory formed a critical part of the changing structures of knowledge in what observers have called "the American Century," and thus in the twenty-first century the modernization project will likely be subject to an increasingly fierce debate.   THOMAS REIFER

money

As a medium of exchange, money has been a pivotal social **technology** in the development of human **societies**. With numbers and writing, money was a basis for the world's first large-scale complex societies in the ancient Near East during the third millennium BC. (Note that these societies did not possess coinage, but used an abstract money notation – money of account – for making budgetary calculations and expressing prices and debts in monetary value.) Today, **globalization** is driven by the electronic transfer of money across national boundaries and by the rapid changes in the value of money wrought in the foreign exchange markets.

According to the familiar economic textbook list, money performs the following crucially important functions: medium of exchange, means of unilateral payment (settlement), store of value, and money of account (measure of value). (Note that these functions describe, but do not explain, the origins and existence of money.) A medium of exchange makes possible the operation of the division of labor and the subsequent exchange of products in **markets** of large-scale impersonal multilateral exchange. Second, money is a store of value – that is, of abstract purchasing power. It enables decisions to be postponed, revised, reactivated, or canceled. In his *An Inquiry into the Meaning of Money*, John Buchan (1997) defined it as "frozen desire." Third, as **Max Weber** and **John Maynard Keynes** emphasized, money's most important attribute, upon which the others are based, is as a measure of value. The abstract notation of money of account (pounds and pence, dollars and cents) enables the calculation of prices, costs, benefits, debts and credits, profits and losses – that is to say, the **rationalization** of economic life. However, money has a dual nature. This useful social technology expands society's capability, or infrastructural **power**; but it can be appropriated by particular interests and used as their despotic power. The power of money is not simply found in the form of amassed **wealth**; but also in the power to control the actual production

of money in mints and banks. Today, for example, the interplay between central banks' interest-rate decisions and the money markets' reactions to them in their pricing of currencies and every kind of financial asset is one of the most important institutional axes of modern **capitalism**.

Two problems have beset the sociological analysis of money, which has remained relatively underdeveloped. First, there is considerable disagreement about the nature of money between and within the different **social sciences**. Second, sociology has taken money's existence for granted and, rather, has focused on its social and cultural consequences, especially as an expression of the "disembedded" economic relations of "**modernity**," as in **Anthony Giddens**, *The Consequences of Modernity* (1990). With some exceptions – for example, Geoffrey Ingham, *The Nature of Money* (2004) – modern **sociology** mistakenly assumed that economics offered an adequate explanation of money's existence. Two developments account for this situation: the division of intellectual **labor** in the social sciences after the *Methodenstreit* during the late nineteenth and early twentieth centuries, in which money was deemed to be within economics' province; and the general influence of **Karl Marx**'s **political economy**.

During the *Methodenstreit*, **Joseph Schumpeter** observed that there were two theories of money – the commodity theory and the claim (or credit) theory – and that they were incompatible. Orthodox economic theories of money are based on the commodity theory in which money is seen as a thing that functions as a medium of exchange in order to overcome the inconveniences of barter that arise in the absence of a double coincidence of wants. According to this theory, barter transforms myriad bilateral exchange ratios between goods into a single market price for a uniform good. Money originates as one of the commodities in barter transactions that eventually function as media of exchange – for example, cigarettes in prison. As a commodity, the medium of exchange can have an exchange ratio with other commodities. As a medium of exchange, money is a neutral veil that has no efficacy other than to overcome the inconveniences of barter.

In Karl Menger's classical formulation in "On the Origins of Money" (*Economic Journal*, 1892), money is the spontaneous result of market exchange and the unintended consequence of individual economic **rationality**. In order to maximize their barter options, traders hold stocks of the most tradable commodities which, consequently, become media of exchange – beans, iron tools, cigarettes. Precious metal has additional advantageous properties – durability, divisibility, portability. By being weighed, struck into uniform pieces, and counted, precious metal becomes money. The progressive dematerialization of money and eventual disappearance of precious metal coinage broke this explanatory link between individual rationality and system benefits. Why should the individual, Menger asked, be ready to exchange his goods for useless base metal disks or notes? Modern neoclassical economics tries to resolve the problem by showing that using (noncommodity) money reduces transaction costs for the individual.

There are three major problems with this analysis. First, this **methodology** cannot distinguish money from any other commodity – that is to say, it does not specify the moneyness of money. In this regard, economics misunderstands the significance of the abstract, or nominal, money of account – that is, pounds and pence, or dollars and cents. Medium of exchange is the key function of money and it is assumed that the others (money of account, means of payment, store of value) follow from it. The **market** spontaneously produces a transactions-cost-efficient medium of exchange that becomes the standard of value and subsequently the nominal "money of account" – as in the above example of precious metal coins. However, there are both a-priori and empirical grounds for reversing the sequence. In *A Treatise on Money* (1930), **John Maynard Keynes** argued that money of account, or the abstract measure of value, was the "primary concept of a theory of money." Money of account provides the description of money, and specific forms – coins, notes, cigarettes – "answer the description." Similarly, according to John Searle in *The Construction of Social Reality* (1995), we know that various material objects – coins, notes, plastic, electronic impulses, and so forth – are forms of money because of the monetary functions that we have "collectively assigned" to them. In this view, money of account is logically anterior and historically prior to the market, but cannot be produced by it. It is improbable that a measure of value (money of account) could emerge from myriad bilateral barter exchange ratios based upon discrete subjective preferences. One hundred goods could yield 4,950 exchange rates. What transforms discrete barter exchange ratios of, say, 3 chickens = 1 duck, or 6 ducks = 1 chicken, and so on, into a single unit of account? A "duck standard" cannot emerge spontaneously, as the equilibrium price of ducks established by supply and demand,

because, in the absence of a money of account, ducks would continue to have multiple and variable exchange values. Moneys of account are authoritatively fixed abstract measures of value. In order for a duck to be a measure of monetary value, it is necessary that a sovereign power declares that one duck is equal to two chickens and promises to exchange ducks and chickens at this rate. (The gold standard was not based directly on the market price of gold, but on the central bank's promise to buy gold at a fixed monetary price per ounce.) But how did agreed measures of value originate? Can an intersubjective scale of value (money of account) emerge from myriad subjective preferences? The question is at the heart of a problem that distinguishes economics from sociology. Is social order the result of the individual calculations of advantaged interdependence or of supra-individual social **norms**? (See **Talcott Parsons**, *The Structure of Social Action*, 1937. For an account of the social origins of money of account, see Ingham, 2004.)

Second, the explanation of money's existence in terms of transaction-costs reduction exposes the problem with **methodological individualism**. It is only advantageous for an individual to use intrinsically worthless money tokens if all other agents do likewise. The advantages of money for the individual *presuppose* the existence of money as a social **institution**.

Third, the model of the barter **economy** with its neutral veil of money is inappropriate for the understanding of capitalism. Financing of production with bank loans of credit-money does not take place in the model of the barter exchange economy, where money exists only as a medium for gaining utility through the exchange of commodities. Capitalist banks are not merely intermediaries between savers and borrowers; they create new money by extending loans that are not directly matched by incoming deposits. As the bank's debtors spend their credit, it is transformed into money, which may then be deposited as money in other banks. Thus, the banking system as a whole creates a money multiplier (Ingham, 2004).

Neoclassical economics' explanation of money's existence was tacitly accepted in Parsons's early work, which confirmed the division of intellectual labor between economics and sociology. Later, in *Economy and Society* (1956) with **Neil Smelser**, he saw money as a generalized medium of communication that facilitates the integration of the functionally differentiated parts of the social system – in an analogous way to prices in the economy. They followed neoclassical economics' axiom that value is only realizable in the actual process of exchange and that money is no more than a **symbol** of "real" value. This does not acknowledge the obvious fact that money is socially constructed as abstract value; it is, according to **Georg Simmel**, "the value of things without the things themselves" (*The Philosophy of Money*, 1907 [trans. 2004]: 121).

The production of money as a social institution was also neglected by Marx, who was more concerned with money as an expression of **alienation** in capitalism. He starts with the classical economic labor theory of value in which precious metal can be a measure of value because the labor of mining and minting can be expressed in "the quantity of any other commodity in which the same amount of labour-time is congealed" (*Capital*, vol. I, 1976: 186). However, in a critical departure from classical economic theory, Marx argued that money is a double "veil." As orthodox economics maintains, it veils the real relations between commodities; but for Marx this also masks the underlying unequal social relations of production that appear as monetary relations. For example, the level of money wages appears to be the result of an equal economic exchange between capital and labor, but is in fact an expression of exploitative power relations. Tearing away these monetary veils will demystify the alienation and capitalism will become "visible and dazzling to our eyes" (187). This points to money's role in the ideological naturalization of capitalist social relations – as, for example, in modern economic theory's concepts of the "natural" rates of interest and **unemployment**. But Marx follows classical economics in not granting a relative autonomy to the value of money; it is fundamentally a commodity whose value cannot be separated from the material base of either its costs of production or the embodiment of labor **time**.

The other side in the *Methodenstreit* – the German Historical School – advanced the credit, or claim, theory of money. Here money's role as a final "means of payment" for the unilateral settlement of a debt is emphasized. A "means of payment" denominated in money of account stores abstract value in the form of purchasing power, which enables it to be removed temporarily from the circulation of commodities. This gives freedom and flexibility to the modern world. As Simmel noted in *The Philosophy of Money* (1907 [trans. 2004]), when a feudal lord demanded a specific quantity of honey or poultry from his serfs he directly determined the nature of their labor. But as soon as a money levy is imposed, the peasant is free to pursue any

activity that will raise the sum. But there is another side to this capacity to store abstract value. Saving money removes it from the process of production and, according to Keynes's "paradox of thrift," may cause unemployment.

From this perspective, money is a token credit that is assigned a nominal value by a money of account – pounds, shillings, dollars, cents, euros. Money does not take its value from its substantive commodity content, but from the existence of goods that can be bought and, more importantly, debts that can be discharged. This alternative theory stems from attempts to understand early capitalist credit instruments – private bank notes or bills of exchange – and from works such as Georg Knapp's *The State Theory of Money* (1924 [trans. 1973]). **States** issue money to pay for their purchases, which the population must accept in order to meet their tax payments. Moneyness is assigned by the issuers' (banks and states) denomination of credit in abstract value (money of account) and in their promise to accept it back in payment of a debt – the repayment of a loan or a tax demand. The promise may be backed by precious metal, or some other commodity; but this is not essential – as modern dematerialized money demonstrates. Money is constituted by the social relation of credit–debt. As Ingham (2004) argues, for something to be money it has to be issued as a liability of the issuers – that is to say, the issuer promises to accept it in payment of a debt owed.

Weber's analysis of money was influenced by both sides of the *Methodenstreit* dispute: by von Mises's economic theory and also, more importantly, by Knapp's historical "state theory." In *Economy and Society* (1978), Weber notes that, as the largest maker and receiver of payments, the state's role in the creation of money is inevitably paramount. Moreover, for Weber, money is not a "neutral" medium of exchange, but a "weapon" in the "struggle for economic existence." The production of money and the regulation of its "scarcity" and the value of money are socially and politically determined by the clash of interests. "The public treasury does not make its payments simply by deciding to apply the rules of the monetary system which somehow seems to it ideal, but its acts are determined by its own financial interests and those of important economic groups" (172).

Money consists in abstract value (media of exchange and means of payment) which is also its own measure (money of account). According to Simmel, "Money is one of those normative ideas that obey the norms that they themselves represent" (*The Philosophy of Money*, 1907 [trans. 2004]: 122). Money is essentially a promise, denominated in the money of account, made by the issuer that the issued tokens will be accepted back in payment of a debt. This makes it acceptable for the discharge of any debt within the sovereign monetary space, circumscribed by the state's imposition of the money of account, in which prices are posted and debts contracted. This quality of moneyness has been made more obvious with the disappearance of all precious metal monies and monetary standards. States pay for goods and services with their issue of tokens which become sought after because they are the only means of discharging tax liabilities. Private issues of bank notes are also accompanied by the promise that they will be accepted in payment of any debt owed to the bank. But, until banks joined the giro network headed by a state-sponsored public, or central, bank, their issued money was unstable. Money is an expression of sovereignty (Michel Aglietta and André Orléan, *La Monnaie souveraine*, 1998). Weak monetary systems are as much the result of a weakness of the state as they are of any economic weakness – for example, post-Soviet Russia and Argentina.

After moneyness has been established this way, it can become a commodity whose value is determined by its exchangeability for goods (purchasing power) and other moneys in foreign exchange markets (exchange rate). In other words, once money has been produced, then economic analysis is applicable; but it cannot explain money's existence. Furthermore, the economic analysis of the exchange value of money in relation to goods, and other currencies, needs to be supplemented by sociological analysis because the *scarcity* of money is socially and politically determined. At the macro-level, the supply of money is structured by the rules and norms governing fiscal practice (for example, sound money principles), which are the outcome of a struggle between economic interests in which economic theory plays a performative role. In capitalism, the major struggle between creditors and debtors is centered on forging a real rate of interest (nominal rate minus inflation rate) that is politically acceptable and economically feasible. On the one hand, too high a real rate of interest will deter entrepreneurial debtors and inhibit economic dynamism. On the other hand, too low a rate or, more seriously, a negative rate of interest (inflation rate in excess of nominal interest rate) inhibits the advance of money-capital loans. On the micro-level, credit-rating produces a stratification of credit risk that regulates the demand for money by means of differential interest rates and the refusal of loans. This has an autonomous impact on the reproduction of **inequality** through "Matthew Effects": the rich receive low-interest credit and the financially excluded fall prey to "loan sharks." Other important areas that require sociological analysis are the social and political construction of inflation expectations by central bankers and the financial press. A sociology of **inflation** flourished in the 1970s in Fred Hirsch and **John Goldthorpe**, *The Political Economy of Inflation* (1978), but waned with the decline of its subject matter. This was closely related to Keynesian theories of "cost-push" inflation which reverses the implied causal sequence in the quantity theory of money. Rather than the quantity of money determining the price level, it is the market power of economic interests, in the Weberian "struggle for economic existence," to bid up their prices and (especially) wages that triggers inflation. This increased demand for money is met in the capitalist system by the power of banks to create money by extending loans. This monetization of private debt is a distinctive characteristic of the capitalist system, as Ingham has argued. This depiction of the monetary process in capitalism is now acknowledged insofar as monetary policy does not attempt directly to control quantities of money, but rather attempts to dampen the demand for money by the manipulation of interest rates.   GEOFFREY INGHAM

monogamy
– see **family**.

Montesquieu, Baron Charles de (1689–1755)

A political theorist, social critic, and an early precursor to sociological analysis, Montesquieu was born into a wealthy French aristocratic family and studied natural history, law, and physiology, before becoming a lawyer. As a result of a generous inheritance, he traveled widely in Europe, spending considerable time in England. In 1721, he published the *Persian Letters*, ostensibly a satirical portrait of French and especially Parisian manners as seen from the perspective of two Persian travelers, but on a deeper understanding a caustic social critique of the church, Louis XIV, and the aristocracy. In 1734 he published his *Reflections on the Causes of the Grandeur and Declension of the Romans*, which charts the historical rise and decline of the Roman Empire using **ideal types** as a methodological device. His major work, however, remains the *Spirit of the Laws* (1750 [trans. 1914]), which, written over twenty years, comprises thirty-one books. Among the achievements of this great work was to delineate the laws of society (see **law and society**) as well as to classify governments according to their underlying principles: the republic based on virtue; the monarchy based on honor; and despotism based on fear. As a leading Enlightenment liberal, he championed republicanism and, as a means to prevent despotism, advocated the separation of powers – that judicial, executive, and legislative powers should remain independent – modeling his arguments on what he had witnessed in England.

As well as examining universal laws, he also sought to explain the differences between societies, seen holistically, in terms of the **influence** of various ecological and social factors such as climate, **religion**, **education**, and the maxims of government. He also made significant contributions to the study of law and **demography**.

STEVEN LOYAL

Moore, Barrington, Jr. (1913–)

One of the few American-born sociologists to pursue questions of classical dimensions, Moore was a contributor to themes as disparate as Soviet studies, the history of **privacy**, and social scientific method. Moore's preeminent work is his historical sociological study, *Social Origins of Dictatorship and Democracy* (1966). The legacy of this book extends into the twenty-first century on two fronts. First, Moore's works (in company with those by **Reinhard Bendix, Jr.**) renewed the Weberian tradition of comparative historical **sociology**, which had been almost brought to a halt as the Nazis came to dominate Europe before and during World War II. Second, in an era when Marxist theory set the standards in left-wing sociology and normative political theory, Moore concentrated on the semiautonomous rise of the **state**, in addition to **capitalism**, as a key to understanding the development of **modernity**. Subsequent comparative historical sociological studies of political **power**, the state, and social revolution, notably including works by **Michael Mann** and **Theda Skocpol**, owe enormous debts to Moore's extraordinary work.

In *Social Origins*, Moore explains the differing paths towards the modern nation-state taken as the result of the political movements of lords and **peasants** – independently and in relation to one another – in premodern agrarian states. Spanning six major cases (England, France, the United States, Japan, China, and India), with secondary observations on Russia and Germany, Moore asked one simply stated question of the utmost

significance: under what conditions do lords or peasants, or both, push historical developments towards parliamentary **democracies** or authoritarian regimes or communist systems? In the course of his work, he identifies three historical paths. The first two are "top-down" paths – the bourgeois revolutions leading to (in his terms) capitalist democracy and the abortive bourgeois revolutions leading to **fascism**. He also finds one "bottom-up" path: the peasant revolutions leading to communist regimes. In all cases he finds that the ways in which lords and peasants reacted to the challenge of commercial agriculture played a leading role.

But this summary is much too schematic to do justice to Moore's sensitivity to the variations between historical cases. Like **Max Weber**'s comparative studies on economic ethics of the world **religions**, Moore refuses to sacrifice the messiness of history for the sake of analytical clarity. His work poses challenges to readers, but it has a stronger ring of truth as a result.

Another of Moore's works, *Injustice: The Social Bases of Obedience and Revolt* (1978), takes a different methodological approach. Here Moore concentrates on one case, the German working class from 1848 to 1920, to ask: why do people quietly accept being victims of society in many instances, yet passionately rise to take action in certain situations? In a reflective epilogue, Moore suggests as one lesson of his book that obligations between rulers and the dominated should be reciprocal. Here again, the lesson of the book gains its credibility from the detail. Other books include *Morality and Persecution in History* (2000), *Privacy: Studies in Social and Cultural History* (1984), and *Political Power and Social Theory* (1958).

IRA COHEN

moral panics

A disproportionate public reaction in response to actions deviating from established social and cultural **norms**; such actions range from acts of provocation of cultural and historical sensibilities to criminal offenses. Moral panics often arise in relation to subcultural **groups** and youth **culture**, **addiction** and religious deviations such as satanic **rituals**. Further targets of moral panics have been other marginalized or disadvantaged social groups such as welfare recipients or refugees. A distinct set of moral panics surrounds acts of sexual transgression and **violence**.

Moral panics are based on a perceived threat to mainstream **society**. Often this threat is constructed in relation to third parties, usually **children** and adolescents, who are seen as potential victims of illicit practices (sexual abuse, or drug pushing) or deemed liable to deviant practices themselves (for example, the panic surrounding violence and homosexuality in American comics sparked by Frederic Wertheim's *Seduction of the Innocent*, 1954).

While moral panics as a response have an original cause for concern and are thus to be distinguished from forms of mass hysteria or delusion, they, as Stanley Cohen observes in *Folk Devils and Moral Panics* (1972), diverge from other forms of public reaction to a perceived moral or social malaise, such as the formation of **social movements** in relation to ecological risk, gender **discrimination** or **poverty**, in that they are based on an exaggerated threat: exaggerated either because the actions that trigger moral panic are represented inaccurately or because the threat itself is portrayed as more serious than it is in comparison to other problems.

The different processes and actors that are involved in the exaggeration of perceived threats are detailed in Cohen's study of Mods and Rockers in 1960s Britain which first coined the phrase moral panic. Crucial to the portrayal of **subcultures** as "folk devils" are, according to Cohen, both legislative and executive sections of the **state** and the **mass media**, both impacting on public perception. The mass media in particular have been implicated in the formation of moral panics in subsequent studies: Stuart Hall's *Treatment of Football Hooliganism in the Press* (1979), Chas Critcher's *Moral Panics and the Media* (2003), and Sarah Thornton's *Club Cultures* (1995) all highlight the indispensable role of mass media, and the (British tabloid) press in particular, in creating moral panics. Thornton's study furthermore highlights the complex interplay between subcultures and mass media in which subcultural credibility is derived from hostile media coverage, whereas mainstream media approval spells the death of subcultures.

CORNEL SANDVOSS

moral statistics
– see **social pathology**.

morality
This is a term that refers to injunctions of what to do, and how to behave, in particular circumstances.

All societies require notions of morality, since individuals cannot conduct their lives without **norms** to guide them. It is tempting but erroneous to divorce moral norms from the time and place in which they arose: hence the institutions of **slavery** or cannibalism, while repellent to modern mores,

cannot be regarded as inherently immoral, since they seemed normal and natural in particular societies. Behavior *becomes* immoral when **groups** in society begin to question particular lines of conduct and espouse practical alternatives.

This is not, however, a purely relativist view of morality since underlying particular historical examples are wider notions of autonomy and self-government which are crucial to morality. The point is that these absolute **values** emerge and it would be wrong to think of them as having "stopping points" as if they are to be fully realized in one society or another. Indeed, the notion of morality has been bedeviled by **religion** and the idea that an absolute value has to be timeless in order to be absolute. God is seen as embodying this absolute and is conceptualized as the repository of a timeless absolute truth. There are absolute values (autonomy and self-government have been mentioned), but these absolute values can only express themselves in relative form, that is, in a particular time and place. The influence of theology on morality has been to instill a dualistic divide between the absolute and the relative so that the individual is to "choose" one or the other.

Contemporary public debates often polarize around relativists who argue simply that "beauty lies in the eye of the beholder" and "there is nothing good or bad but thinking makes it so," and fundamentalists who react against this **relativism** by seeking to abstract values from their historical context. The modernist belief in timeless absolutes is not adequately dealt with by simply turning it inside out, so that morality is merely denied. The modernist view of morality must be transcended, moved beyond, so that morality is seen as the combination of the absolute and the relative, the utopian and the realistic.

The problem with expressing morality as a timeless absolute is that it inevitably becomes imbued with a perfectionism that cannot be matched by historical practice. A gulf between theory and practice acts not as a stimulant to activity, but as a paralyzing frustration – a distinction becomes a dualism, an unbridgeable gulf that inevitably generates cynicism and despair. Of course, every individual acts in a way that breaches morality, and the more serious the breach, the more explicit the articulation of the moral norm. But where morality is expressed in a historically conscious fashion, this gap is an incentive to develop and improve, not a source of impotence and passivity.

Morality becomes problematic when focused upon the **state**. It could be argued that it is difficult to see how the state can act morally when its distinctive attribute is the use of **force** to tackle conflicts of interest. The "morality" of the state is of a distinctively propagandist quality, designed to bully and coerce people into compliance.

As long as society was seen as "naturally" divided into citizens and slaves, Christians and atheists, men and women, and so on, then the use of force against the others is not problematic. However, once all are deemed to be individuals – all equally entitled to natural **rights** – then the force of the state becomes problematic from a moral point of view. Liberals are right to see force as antithetical to morality since it is impossible to act autonomously and govern your own life if you are subject to the coercive will of another. The use of force destroys relationships since, to form a relationship with another, one needs to be an agent and one cannot be an agent if one is damaged, to a great or lesser extent, by the acts of another. To use force against another is to see them as a thing, an inanimate object, and not a fellow human being.

The use of force by the state can be "justified" as the lesser of two evils since there are all kind of contexts in which the failure to employ counterforce against a bully or thug makes a bad situation worse, but it is hard to see how the use of force itself can ever be moral. The problem with **liberalism** is that it seeks to justify the unjustifiable since its postulates of freedom and **equality** are themselves projected as timeless absolutes. Antisocial behavior cannot be given a historical **explanation**. It is "naturalized," that is, illicitly presented as natural in the sense of being unchangeable, so that the need for a state, an **institution** claiming a monopoly of legitimate force, is presented as eternal and inevitable.

Morality is sometimes seen as norms that are imposed from on high. This accounts for the view by youth in liberal societies that morality is inherently hypocritical and corrupt. The word moral is used pejoratively – a bad thing. There is something to be said for this argument since state functionaries cannot practice what they preach, and religious figures present a theoretical piety which their practical behavior belies. But it is important not to see morality through the eyes of those who deform it through hypocrisy and equivocation. It is better to say that those who say one thing and do another are negating morality since neither they nor their victims can be said to be governing their own lives or acting autonomously. When morality is imposed from above, threats accompany it. Those who abide by norms out of fear of the consequences cannot be said to be acting morally. Morality cannot be treated as a

purely subjective attribute: "I am moral because I think I am." Although it is true that a person must intend to be moral in order to be so, it would be naive to suppose that the consequences of an act can be ignored: the use of physical chastisement in our contemporary world by authority figures may be intended to instill morality, but its effects are crippling and deforming.

The same can be said about the lack of knowledge of the alternatives. Of course **relativism** makes an input here, since knowledge that is withheld must exist and be available. One can hardly say, in a world in which research into lung cancer and passive smoking has not taken place, that smoking is inherently immoral; it *becomes* immoral when knowledge is available but not utilized. This point is crucial in linking morality to an objective interest. An act is contrary to objective interests if an individual would act in a different way if he or she knew what others know. There have to be what some call "counterfactuals," that is, meaningful alternatives which can be chosen.

Authoritarian deformations of morality divorce the objective and subjective in a dualistic way. The norm is imposed from on high – the authority figure knows best – or, as a reaction to this explicit authoritarianism, the norm is not advocated at all on the grounds that each must do as they please even if this destroys the individual concerned or the well-being of others. This holds whether moral norms are being developed in children or adults. Context is crucial, and the way that a moral norm is expressed for a three-year-old obviously differs dramatically from the way in which it would be expressed for a young person of thirteen. Morality is both objective and subjective, since an individual must believe in the rightness of an action and that action needs to contribute to their autonomy and capacity to govern their own lives. The "moral" injunctions associated with authoritarian rule – whether of a personal or institutional kind – undermine rather than further morality.

The attempt to present the study of society as a science devoid of moral or normative implications is misguided. Science itself, whether natural or social, has moral implications. It is true that the natural sciences study a realm outside human activity, and it would obviously be perverse for a zoologist to describe a queen bee as autocratic or dictatorial. But this does not mean that the study of nature is value-free. Humans are part of and interact with the wider world of nature, and therefore the study of nature cannot but affect their lives. The discovery that the earth went around the sun was seen understandably as a threat to a medieval outlook, and extraordinary lengths were taken to repress those taking this view. To this day, **social Darwinism** has proved controversial to those who cling in fundamentalist fashion to what they see as the letter of their holy text. Modern ecology rightly poses the human–nature relationship as crucial to our well-being, even though there is sometimes the temptation to invert traditional attitudes so that our equality with nature is treated as though we were the *same* as the rest of nature. This leads to the inversion of traditional humanism rather than to the development of a new and more concrete humanist position.

The point is that the notion that factual statements must be morally neutral treats the facts in an atomistic way. Factual statements pose relationships. Skeptics dismiss these necessary relationships as purely metaphysical (that is, subjectively imposed) while philosophical idealists present these relationships as evidence of a higher spiritual power. In fact, relationships derive from movement in the material world and it is impossible for an entity to move if it has no relationship with its **environment**. All factual statements imply relationships: sometimes these relationships are commonplace in our **culture** and therefore they are not controversial, but a lack of controversy does not mean that there is an absence of values. It merely means that the values are shared. The statement that the World Trade Center in New York was destroyed on September 11, 2001, is agreed by terrorist and state functionary alike, and the relationships which this statement postulates between an act and a point in time are not particularly important (although those who argue that the act was somehow created by the media may inject controversy into a statement even like this).

Values derive from the relationships which factual statements imply. There is therefore no qualitative difference between the statements of natural and social scientists in this area, although (as the example of the zoologist illustrates), the language appropriate to actions of humans differs significantly from that appropriate to the behavior of other natural beings and entities. At the height of the behavioral revolution (a movement that rejected the difference between humans and the rest of nature), it was common to argue in voting studies that apathy among ordinary members of the public was functional for a **democracy** because it enabled politicians to take decisions with unimpeded expertise. Whatever one thinks of this statement, it is not, as was claimed at the time, a value-free discovery, since the notion of **functionalism** smuggled in a moral judgment. If apathy was functional, it was in practice a good thing. The relationship that the functional implies contains the values – whatever the intention of the author.

Morality is thus inherent in society because relationships are inherent in society. This morality is both relative and absolute. It links to our autonomy and capacity to govern our lives – a value that we can only move towards but never absolutely realize. Morality is subverted if values are expressed in timeless fashion. Morality cannot be developmental unless it is integrated into human practice so that it helps us to improve and does not stand over the individual us an alienated set of unattainable ideals. Morality is inherently all statements; it is a positivist argument that scientific statements must be value-free. This position ignores the relational character of factual statements, and the way in which values derive from the relationships implied. This position holds for the natural as well as the social sciences for, although there are undoubtedly differences between the two, neither are morally neutral.

JOHN HOFFMAN

mores
– see **norm(s)**.

mortality
The relative frequency of death in a population, mortality is both a biological and a social phenomenon. Demographers distinguish between two aspects of mortality, namely, the life span, that is, the oldest age to which humans survive; and longevity, that is, the capability to survive from one year to the next. Longevity has both biological and social components, whereas life span tends to be mainly biological.

An easily understood and interpreted method for quantifying mortality is the crude death rate (CDR), that is, the number of deaths in a population in a given year, per 1,000 members of the population. It may be expressed as follows:

$$CDR = \frac{\text{Death in the year}}{\text{population at mid-year}} \times 1,000$$

Using **data** for China for 2004, the equation becomes:

$$CDR = \frac{7,800,000}{1,300,000,000} \times 1,000 = 6$$

This means that in China in 2004, there were six deaths for every 1,000 persons in the population. Crude death rates among the countries of the world in 2004 ranged from lows of 2 in Kuwait and the United Arab Emirates to 26 in Botswana and 29 in Sierra Leone. The range of crude death rates is narrower than that for crude birth rates. Crude death rates, however, must be interpreted with caution. When crude death rate comparisons are made between countries, differences are sometimes due to differences in age composition. Countries with high proportions of young people will usually have lower crude death rates than countries with small proportions of young people.

When the countries of the world are categorized into more developed and less developed and their crude death rates examined, countries with low death rates are found in both groups. This does not mean that the more and less developed countries have the same mortality experiences. For although crude death rates are low in many countries of the world, members of the populations of the more developed countries have greater longevity, that is they live longer, than those in the less developed countries. Age-specific death rates and age-standardized death rates should be used to compare the mortality experiences of countries with known differences in age composition.

The quantification of mortality is central to **demography**. A key measure of the mortality experiences of a population is the life table, and this dates to **John Graunt** and his analyses of the *Bills of Mortality*. The life table starts with a population (a radix) of 100,000 at age 0; from each age to the next, the population is decremented according to age-specific mortality probabilities, until all members have died; the mortality schedule is fixed and does not change over the life of the population. The basic life table consists of seven columns including the probability of dying between age x and age x + n ($_nq_x$), the number of survivors at exact age x (l_x), the number of deaths between age x and age x + n ($_nd_x$), years lived between age x and age x + n ($_nL_x$), and life expectancy after exact age x (e_{x0}).

Alfred J. T. Lotka (1880–1949), whom many refer to as the person most responsible for the development of modern demography, used life tables in his development of the theory of stable population. The concept of a stable population was actually first set forth by L. Euler in "General Research on Mortality and Multiplication," *Mémoires de l'Académie Royale des Sciences et Belles Lettres* (1760 [trans. 1970]), but its current development stems from the work of Lotka, who first introduced the concept in a brief note in 1907. Later, F. R. Sharpe and A. Lotka in "A Problem in Age Distribution" (1911), proved mathematically that

if a population that is closed to **migration** experiences constant schedules of age-specific fertility and mortality rates, it will develop a constant age distribution and will grow at a constant rate, irrespective of its initial age distribution. The mathematical bases and foundation of stable population theory are laid out and discussed in many places, one of the better expositions being A. J. Coale's masterpiece, *The Growth and Structure of Human Populations* (1972). A. J. Coale and P. Demeny, in *Regional Model Life Tables and Stable Populations* (1983), developed model life tables to generalize about mortality under various different conditions.

A primary aspect of quality of life, directly derived from the life table, is life expectation. In 2004, life expectation at birth in the world was 65 for males and 69 for females. In more developed countries it was 72 and 80, and in less developed countries, 63 and 67. The highest life expectation at birth was in Japan, 78 for males and 85 for females; the lowest was in Sierra Leone (34 for males, 36 for females), Zambia (35 for both males and females), and Botswana (35 for males and 36 for females) (*Population Reference Bureau*, 2004). Maximum potential life span refers to the theoretically highest known age. The longest known life span is 122 years and 5 months authenticated as the age at death of Frenchwoman Jeanne Louise Calment who died in August, 1997.

Another aspect of quality of life is the infant mortality rate (IMR), or the number of deaths in a year of infants under 1 year per 1,000 live births. It is expressed as:

$$IMR = \frac{\text{deaths in the year to persons under age 1}}{\text{live births in the year}} \times 1,000$$

The infant mortality rate is a combination of the neonatal mortality rate (NMR) – deaths to babies of 28 days of age or less per 1,000 live births – and the post-neonatal mortality rate (PMR) – deaths to babies of 29 days to 1 year of age per 1,000 live births.

A major explanation of mortality change has its origins in demographic transition theory (DTT). DTT proposes four stages of mortality and fertility decline that occur in the process of societal **modernization**. The first is the pre-industrialization era with high birth and death rates along with stable population growth. With the onset of industrialization and modernization, the society transitions to lower death rates, especially lower infant and maternal mortality, but maintains high birth rates, with the result of rapid population growth. The next stage is characterized by decreasing population growth due to lower birth and death rates, which lead then to the final stage of low and stable population growth.

Epidemiological Transition Theory (ETT) focuses on the society-wide decline of infectious disease and the rise of chronic degenerative causes of death. According to epidemiological transition theory as postulated by A. R. Omran in "The Epidemiologic Transition: A Theory of the Epidemiology of Population Change" (1971), there are three stages. The first is the age of pestilence and famine in which the primary causes of mortality were influenza, pneumonia, smallpox, tuberculosis, and other related diseases, with a high infant and childhood mortality and a life expectancy averaging between 20 and 40 years. The second is the age of receding pandemics in which there was a decline in mortality due to improved sanitation, increases in standards of living and **public health**, resulting in a steady increase in life expectancy to between the ages of 30 and 50 years. According to R. G. Rogers and R. Hackenberg in "Extending Epidemiologic Transition Theory: A New Stage" (1987), the stage of receding pandemics was around 1875–1930. The third stage is known as the era of degenerative and man-made diseases (heart disease, cancer, and stroke), in which mortality declines are due to medical advances in the prevention and treatment of infectious diseases. The life expectancy at birth rises rapidly so that fertility becomes the primary factor in population growth as life expectancy exceeds 70 years. About three-quarters of deaths in this stage are the result of degenerative diseases in the advanced years. Rogers and Hackenberg have noted a fourth "hybristic stage" where mortality is heavily influenced by individual behavior or lifestyle choices, and deaths are due to social pathologies such as accidents, alcoholism, **suicide**, and homicide, as well as lifestyle issues such as smoking and diet.

The impact of mortality has been shown to vary significantly according to social demographic characteristics. People in higher social classes live longer than those in the lower classes. In the United States, Asians and whites live several years longer than blacks and Hispanics, with blacks having the shortest life expectancy. Married people live longer than the single, separated, or divorced.   DUDLEY L. POSTON

Mosca, Gaetano (1858–1941)

An Italian jurist and political theorist, Mosca was active in **politics** and administration. With **Vilfredo Pareto** he contributed to the theory of **elites**.

Mosca was the author of two works of abiding significance, *Elementi di Scienza Politica* (1896) which was translated as *The Ruling Class* (1939) and *Lezioni di Storia delle Istituzioni e delle Dottrine Politiche* (1933 [trans. 1972]). In his critique of parliamentary **democracy**, he argued that all political regimes exhibit, or seek to hide, one fundamental fact: the superiority/inferiority relationship between the political class or ruling class, who possesses political **power**, and the remainder of the population. But the possession of power itself is gained through a "struggle for prominence" between competing groups, and a significant aspect of that struggle is constituted by the political formula employed by each **group** to assert itself over the others, and to justify its own tenure of power. Democracy is one such formula, capable of generating **legitimacy**, although, like all other formulas, it is at bottom irrational. However, there are significant qualitative differences between political regimes, and Mosca maintained his own preference for a liberal one even when its Italian version was destroyed by **fascism**.

GIANFRANCO POGGI

motherhood/mothers

By its very nature, the term motherhood is a relational category. Thus women who are defined as mothers are primarily understood in terms of their relationships with their **children**. This means that studies of motherhood can tend to focus solely on the dyad of mother/child relationships. However, from a sociological perspective, analyses of motherhood have attempted to locate themselves in the context of the social organization of much broader themes such as (hetero)sexuality, conception, birth, child rearing, child care, and paid work. Because becoming a mother tends to be understood to be a natural or biological process, it has been the task of **sociology** to reveal the ways in which motherhood changes in relation to other social transformations and, within this, to explore how different elements of motherhood (such as the **ideologies** of motherhood or the experiences of motherhood in different class or ethnic contexts) shift and adjust over time.

Early functionalist sociology treated motherhood as a self-evident role for women in the context of the married, nuclear **family**, and the sole component of this role was seen to be the proper **socialization** of children. This narrow perception was challenged by feminist research in the 1970s and 1980s when motherhood started to be analyzed as a form of women's oppression. This oppression was seen to encompass two forms, in line with the influential neo-Marxist framework of the time. These forms were the material conditions of motherhood and the ideology of motherhood. The former paid attention to the fact that motherhood isolated women from the labor market and made them dependent upon the male breadwinner for their economic survival. The latter identified the ways in which women were seduced into becoming mothers through a belief system which imposed the idea that women could not be fulfilled without children and which insisted that it was natural for all women to be mothers (and hence unnatural not to be). Radical feminists coined the term "compulsory motherhood," used by Adrienne Rich in *Of Woman Born* (1977), thereby suggesting that in a heterosexist and patriarchal **culture** women had little choice but to become mothers – not least because they could not refuse to have sex with men, but also because they did not have control over contraception and **reproduction**. Alongside these structuralist approaches to motherhood there developed an interest in women's experiences of being mothers, as illustrated by **Ann Oakley** in *Becoming a Mother* (1979), and these accounts gradually shifted the concentration away from just the oppressive elements of motherhood, towards some of the everyday benefits and problems associated with becoming a mother, such as negotiating with the **professions** who take charge of motherhood, and combining motherhood with paid employment. Mothers themselves were increasingly seen as agents in the process of mothering, rather than just the victims, and emphasis was given to the idea that mothers' voices should be heard, in particular by the medical and health care professions. More recently, research on motherhood has taken into account the significance of new reproductive **technologies** which are seen as disruptive of the taken-for-granted genetic link between mothers and the children to whom they give birth. The rise of surrogacy, embryo and egg donation, and post-menopausal childbirth is changing further the idea that motherhood is simply a natural phase of women's life course.   CAROL SMART

motivation

Central to both lay and technical uses of this term is the conception that motivation is why people do what they do. None of the abilities or potential of an individual will result in action without him or her being motivated to act.

The range of meanings included in everyday talk encompass the full range of meanings to be found in the academic literature, and thereby foreshadow the conceptual difficulties and wrangles present in analyses of motivation. Standard dictionaries refer to conscious and unconscious stimuli, which are characterized either in terms of internal psychological desires or beliefs, or in terms of physical or social environmental conditions leading to behavior which may be novel or habitual, and learned or innate. While these different elements can be used promiscuously and speculatively in daily conversation, substantial and different theoretical consequences follow from each of them. Careful technical use needs to bear in mind five important distinctions.

First, does a person do something because of an internal need or desire which must be satisfied, or are they stimulated to action by an external event? Second, are they pursuing specific goals, or are they motivated by general drives? Third, is their motivation based on a cognitive calculation or judgment, or on an emotional reaction? Fourth, is it something of which the individual is conscious and aware, or something of which he or she has little awareness? Finally, is it a function of innate and inherent properties of the individual, or is it developed over time?

Many otherwise quite incompatible theories, for example, **psychoanalysis** and **sociobiology**, have argued that there are fundamental underlying drives which are part of a person's biological endowment. Individuals seek the satisfaction of these drives through the pursuit of pleasurable stimuli and the avoidance of noxious ones with highly significant consequences for the character of persons, their social relations, and the social order that follows. Necessarily, an account of a generalized drive towards, for example, sexual engagement, presumes a cognitive apparatus that can organize one's behavior in the light of a specific demand or opportunity, but often these theories are less forthcoming on this matter. In contrast, many more cognitive accounts – for example, expectancy value theory – prioritize the cognitive component in the individual's pervasive motivation to maximize benefits and minimize costs without paying much attention to how value is determined.

Many authors have proposed that motivation may be an important area of individual difference. Abraham Maslow (1908–70) proposed that **societies** as a whole will vary as a function of a hierarchy of **human needs**. In this, individuals will first be motivated by physiological needs such as **food** and water. When that need is satisfied, the motivation will be for safety, followed by social engagement, then personal esteem, and finally self-actualization. As a society or social group enables the easy satisfaction of these needs, so the individuals will be motivated by the higher levels in the hierarchy.   DAVID GOOD

multicultural citizenship

– see **citizenship**.

multiculturalism

There are two tensions within multiculturalism that sociology inherits. First, multiculturalism has come to define a set of state policies to manage (neutralize, nullify, subdue, or conquer) difference (multiculturalism as policy). Second, it also has come to define those strategies that mount resistances to state management policies of difference (multiculturalism as **politics**). Thus, multiculturalism has come to express both a will to difference and a will to sameness (equity, **equality**, fairness) simultaneously.

These tensions are not unique to multiculturalism. In the second half of the twentieth century, many struggles for social **justice** have mobilized **identity** and difference and placed new demands on **citizenship**. There are two reasons for this. First, which may be called the politics of identity, many **social movements** (civil rights and women's and indigenous peoples' rights being principal examples) called into question the shortcomings of the ideal of universal citizenship in practice, signaling that, while being formally citizens, their identities still excluded them from rights of citizenship. Second, which may be called the politics of difference, many social **groups** articulated rights that accrued to them on the basis of their difference. Struggles for minority rights in **language**, schooling, and public appearance were often waged on this basis. The politics of recognition (combining the politics of identity and difference) has, therefore, increasingly mobilized itself as simultaneous and conflicting claims to sameness and difference, inclusion and exclusion, and **rights** and obligations.

Multiculturalism, both as policy and politics, inherited these tensions from other forms of politics of recognition but displayed unique characteristics (see, for example, Danielle Juteau, "Beyond Multiculturalist Citizenship: The Challenge of Pluralism in Canada," 1997). These tensions can be traced to the origins of the concept itself (for example, Mark Lopez, *The Origins of Multiculturalism in Australian Politics 1945–1975*, 2000). On the one hand, multiculturalism meant rights for cultural minorities but, on the other, their **assimilation** into the dominant culture. Both these tensions can be observed in its official incarnation when, on October 8, 1971, Canadian Prime Minister Pierre Trudeau spoke in the House of Commons to proclaim Canada's policy of multiculturalism. He said, "There is no official [Canadian] culture, nor does any ethnic group take precedence over any other. No citizen or group of citizens is other than Canadian, and all should be treated fairly." With astonishing clarity, what Trudeau was proclaiming was both the absence and presence of a dominant (in this case, "Canadian") culture.

This proclamation announced the acceptance of the material conditions of the politics of recognition, which was brewing in North American but also European and Australian cities. The shifting patterns of global **migration** and immigration resulted, within a few decades in the second half of the twentieth century, in cities such as Toronto, New York, Los Angeles, Chicago, Amsterdam, London, Sydney, and Melbourne becoming home to large numbers of foreign-born residents with ostensibly radically different cultural backgrounds from those of their host **cities** and nations, as illustrated by Leonie Sandercock, *Towards Cosmopolis: Planning for Multicultural Cities* (1998). Yet, this pattern was not so different from the massive sea-change experienced in almost all those cities at the turn of the twentieth century when their populations had "welcomed" vast numbers of foreign-born residents. It is often forgotten that, proportionally speaking, there were more foreign-born residents in New York and Chicago at the turn of the twentieth century than at that of the twenty-first. Yet at the turn of the twentieth century the decisive requirement was assimilation.

This is probably the source of the paradox of multiculturalism. While, at the turn of the twentieth century, sociology, especially what came to be known as the **Chicago School** and its **urban ecology**, emerged out of a milieu that had asked assimilation of its minorities, by the late twentieth century society could no longer do so, at least not explicitly (for example, Bhikhu C. Parekh, *Rethinking Multiculturalism: Cultural Diversity and Political Theory*, 2000). If, at the turn of the twentieth century, the service that sociology was pressed into was the achievement of the assimilation of these minority cultures into the dominant host culture, by the end of the century confidence in that possibility, for various complex reasons, was shaken, and thus was born the policy and politics of multiculturalism. As policy, multiculturalism still clung to "integration," "cohesion," and "inclusion" as euphemisms to stand for assimilation but, as politics, multiculturalism also increasingly articulated demands for differentiated citizenship as rights and obligations, as shown by Seyla Benhabib, *The Claims of Culture: Equality and Diversity in the Global Era* (2002) and Will Kymlicka, *Multicultural Citizenship: A Liberal Theory of Minority Rights* (1995). The sociology of multiculturalism embodies these tensions by pressing itself, on the one hand, in the service of integration, cohesion, and inclusion, and, articulating, on the other, new ways of being different yet equal in postnational **states** and their cities.

Multiculturalism, either as policy or politics, may well have exhausted its possibilities. It was never as accepted and embraced in the United States and Europe as it was in Canada, and it has had a variegated history in Australia. The growing securitization of the state and politicization and racialization of borders, and the growing conflicts between Muslim minorities and dominant **cultures**, have already shifted the discourse in the United States and Europe from multiculturalism to euphemisms of "integration" and "cohesion." Whatever the concepts deployed, the tensions of the politics of recognition will continue to influence the research and political agendas.

ENGIN ISIN

multilevel models
– see **modeling**.

multilevel regression model
– see **modeling**.

multiple level regression
– see **regression**.

multivariate analysis
This is the generic term for analyses that involve many variables, such as multiple **regression, cluster analysis**, or **log linear analyses**. Typically, they are used to determine the relative importance of a number of **independent variables** on one **dependent variable**. An example of this is given in the description of **regression**. The most important reason for using multivariate analyses in sociological research is that many sociological phenomena have multiple overlapping causes, and it is difficult to unravel the relative importance of each of them by simply examining the correlations between pairs of variables (bivariate analysis). (The other type of analysis, alongside multivariate and bivariate is univariate analysis – looking at just one variable at a time, such as when examining the averages of individual variables.)

It is often noted that **children** whose parents get divorced during their childhoods experience disadvantage later in their lives (for instance, in their educational outcomes or the status of their jobs as adults). But this simple correlation tells us little about the relative importance of a number of factors that could have brought this about. Is being brought up by one parent inherently inferior to being raised by two parents? Or could it be that other factors are to blame? For instance, many single-parent families live in **poverty**, are forced to live in poorer **neighbourhoods** where the schooling might be of lower quality, or experience **prejudice** in society. Or perhaps it was living in households with higher levels of conflict *before* the separation or divorce that caused the disruptions to the children's development?

Such a complex web of interrelated variables would be nigh impossible to unravel with simple bivariate analyses. But, given an appropriate dataset (for instance, a birth cohort study) and multivariate analyses, the relative importance of each of these factors, and many more, can be understood in detail, as in, for example, B. J. Elliott and M. P. M. Richards, "Children and Divorce: Educational Performance, and Behavior, Before and After Parental Separation" (1991, *International Journal of Law and the Family*).

Another great advantage of multivariate interactions is that they permit the investigation of the complex way in which independent variables combine to influence other variables. For instance, there is evidence that individuals with larger social **networks** cope better with stressful life events, such as **unemployment**. So unemployment or social networks might only have mild effects by themselves, but, for those individuals with limited social networks, unemployment might have a greater effect on their well-being. In this case there is an interaction between unemployment and social support affecting well-being – a relationship that cannot be adequately described by the bivariate relationships between social networks and wellbeing or unemployment and wellbeing.

Multivariate analyses can also be performed where there are several dependent variables that might be considered simultaneously. For instance, in medical sociology, if one is interested in health outcomes, rather than analyzing a whole raft of health measures separately (such as blood pressure, body mass index, cholesterol levels, cortisol levels, and self-rated depression), they could all be analyzed simultaneously using multivariate analysis of variance.

Before the advent of computers, multivariate analyses were considered an advanced technique, only attempted by the statistically most competent social scientists. More recently, computer packages such as the Statistical Package for Social Scientists (SPSS) have made them more accessible to all social scientists, and multivariate analyses are taught in most sociology undergraduate degrees.   BRENDAN J. BURCHELL

Mumford, Lewis (1895–1990)

Recognized as an architectural critic, Mumford's most enduring legacy may well have been as a social and political critic, raising fundamental questions about **modernity** and its drive towards technological **progress**. An independent scholar, he followed his *The Story of Utopias* (1921) with imaginative and original books including *Sticks and Stones: A Study of American Architecture and Civilization* (1924), the widely acclaimed *The Culture of Cities* (1938), and the trenchant *The City in History: Its Origins, Its Transformations, and Its Prospects* (1961). His *Technics and Civilization* (1934) provided the first glimpse of his developing critical views on **technology**. His later *The Myth of the Machine: Technics and Human Development* (1967) and *The Myth of the Machine: The Pentagon of Power* (1971) fully developed these early critical thoughts on technology, **power**, and democratic imagination.

Mumford was independent in at least two senses. According to D. L. Miller, *Lewis Mumford, a Life* (1992), he did not have an institutional employment all his life and, perhaps consequently, developed an original and prodigious mind along with a powerful literary style. This combination gave him an independent voice that was as resolute as it was agile, highlighting, in equal measure, the darkest and brightest aspects of being social throughout human history. In his *The Culture of Cities* (1938), he had already developed an idea of the **city** both as being the **institution** for fulfilling the brightest possibilities of being social and as enacting its darkest nightmares. He did not flinch from calling the city a war machine right from its inception and yet believed that it could, and indeed it did in certain periods of human history, become the crucible of the outmost possibilities of being social. Similarly, his views on the increasing reliance on technological **progress** did not deter him from investing in human capacities for collective responsibility, whether that meant planning urban regions or stopping nuclear proliferation.   ENGIN ISIN

Myrdal, Gunnar (1898–1987)

A Swedish economist and sociologist, Myrdal was educated and subsequently taught at the University of Stockholm and held a Chair in **Political Economy** and International Economics. He was also active in Swedish **politics** and was elected to the Senate as a member of the Social Democratic Party in 1934, and again as Minister for Commerce in 1945–7. In 1974 he was jointly awarded the Nobel Prize for Economics together with F. A. Hayek.

He, together with a research team of thirty-eight members, was commissioned by the Carnegie Corporation to study the social, economic, and lifestyle conditions of black Americans in the United States. The result was a carefully and extensively documented 1,500-page report which was published as *The American Dilemma* (1944). The report pointed to the gap between the American democratic ideal of the **equality** of man, and the reality of racial **segregation** and denial of civil and political **rights** that American blacks experienced. It discussed the caste-like relations between blacks and whites and the processes of cumulative causation that maintained and reinforced **racism**. The work was crucial in the Supreme Court's decision to rule against the "separate but equal" law in the 1954 *Brown* versus *Board of Education of Topeka* case, which outlawed racial segregation in public schools.

His other major publications include *The Political Element in the Development of Economic Theory* (1930) and a three-volume study of South Asia, *Asian Drama: An Inquiry into the Poverty of Nations* (1968).   STEVEN LOYAL

myth

From the Greek *muthos* (plot or story), this term now circulates in religious studies and in anthropology largely free of the association with error, delusion, or childish flights of imagination that it had for many scholars of the nineteenth century and still has in popular usage today. **Bronislaw Malinowski** is transitional; myths are for him primarily functional instruments deployed in ritual contexts to lay claim to specific properties or titles, but their specific messages are barely interpretable at best. From **Sigmund Freud** to Bruno Bettelheim (1903–90), myths are collective displacements onto the symbolic plane of common but illicit desires whose literal representation would be unbearable. For Carl Gustav Jung (1875–1961) and his still considerable following, the motifs found so widely in mythologies throughout the world arise from a collective – indeed, pan-human – unconscious of a less exclusively libidinous nature and serve less defensive than therapeutic purposes. Both of these psychoanalytic approaches must be distinguished in turn from the existentialist approaches of religionists such as Mircea Eliade (1907–86) and Joseph Campbell (1904–87), who claim to find in mythologies everywhere a common store of enduring human concerns and virtues. Methodologically, psychoanalytic and existentialist interpretations of myth are largely substantialist; most presume that the same **symbol** conveys the same meaning in every one of its occurrences. In this respect, they are typically at odds with **Claude Lévi-Strauss**'s **structuralism**, which rests in a positionalist theory of meaning and whose decryptions uncover in myths themselves socially specific messages having a specifically ideological function and force.

JAMES D. FAUBION

N

narcissism

Associated with the doctrines of **Sigmund Freud** and **psychoanalysis**, the term has come to enter sociology as an account of certain pathological trends of modern social life. Often interpreted as a consequence of **consumer society** and the West's obsession with surface appearances, the rise of narcissism is said to have played a significant role in the shrinkage of public political life, thus promoting a defensive, painfully empty search for self-gratification.

The sociological analysis of narcissism has been plagued by lack of conceptual precision. It is important to distinguish between three related issues: first, psychodynamically, narcissistic disorders have their origin in what Freud termed "primary narcissism" – with the child remaining stuck in a destructive omnipotence, which thus prevents the development of healthy boundaries between **self** and others. Second, in terms of **generations**, narcissism is reproduced in capitalist society through parents relating to their **children** primarily as "investments." Third, culturally, narcissistic pathology is said to arise not only from **capitalism** but as a result of **globalization**, mass communications (see **mass media and communications**), and the decline of **tradition**. Contemporary patterns of narcissistic identity-formation are thus conceptualized in sociology as at once thin and precarious, as the self is outstripped by the dislocations and terrors of **modernity**.

The sociological critique of narcissism is best known through the writings of **Richard Sennett**, Christopher Lasch, and Joel Kovel.

ANTHONY ELLIOTT

narrative analysis

Narrative as a topic of sociological investigation has a long and diverse history. Interest in narrative has always been predicated on the assumption that to grasp adequately the nature of some aspect of the social world one must analyze one's research subjects' own understandings of their circumstances. However, many different approaches to accomplishing this project have emerged over the years. The earliest exemplars for narrative analysis in sociology used a combination of data sources including oral histories, biographies, **interviews**, diaries, letters, and archival records to construct life histories of research subjects. These life histories were sometimes held up as important sociological chronicles in their own right, but they were usually valued for the contributions that could be made to more general sociological topics by their use. Hence, individual life histories have been compared to more general narratives either to enrich what is known about the experiences of ordinary people in particular historical periods or to evaluate critically more general theoretical claims about those periods. Narrative analysis has thus been used as a prominent resource in fulfilling the mandate for sociology to understand the relations between history and biography which **C. Wright Mills** famously set in his book *The Sociological Imagination* (1959). More recently, theoretical and political trends within the discipline have further invigorated narrative analysis while simultaneously shaping the direction of its development.

During the 1960s, several theoretical movements converged to suggest **language** is the medium through which personal experience is made meaningful. This **"linguistic turn"** in sociological research highlighted the "storied" character of personal experience and inspired research on the structural characteristics of both oral and written narratives. While still flourishing, the structural approach to narrative analysis has been criticized for reifying narrative structures and under-emphasizing how narratives are accomplished in the ongoing course of social **interaction**. It is much more common now for analysts to consider narratives not for their intrinsic structural characteristics but for the ways in which these characteristics are themselves socially contingent. Most analysts now appreciate that both oral and written narratives are best understood as collaboratively constructed by storytellers and the myriad **audiences** for whom stories are told. Therefore, most contemporary narrative analysis seeks to discover how the work of storytelling is itself responsive to the wider round of social activities within which storytelling is embedded.

Narrative analysis has also been profoundly influenced by political developments both within the discipline of sociology itself and in neighboring disciplines. Social scientists once prided themselves on their professional ability to use the information they elicited from their research subjects to generate superior understandings of those people and their social worlds. Without necessarily forsaking their claim to **objectivity**, many researchers are now a good deal more attentive to the fact that they do not possess a monopoly on the capacity to describe social events objectively. Feminist scholars, in particular, have promoted the view that narrative analysis is not merely a project of generating scientific accounts of the narratives of others but of giving "voice" to those historically denied the authority to speak for themselves.   DARIN WEINBERG

nation

– see **nationalism**.

nationalism

This is an **ideology** that holds that the nation is the natural basis of social life and that the best and most natural political units are states based on nations, that is, nation-states. Correspondingly, it gives rise to movements in which groups which define themselves as nations demand that they have their own independent national **state**.

Thus understood, nationalism is unproblematic. The difficulties have to do mainly with the concept of the nation, and the different understandings of nationhood. Who belongs to the nation? In one tradition, the nation is seen largely in political, civic, and territorial terms. This has been the dominant understanding of nationhood in such countries as Britain, France, Spain, the Netherlands, the United States, and Canada. To belong to the nation, in this view, has nothing to do with **religion**, **race and ethnicity**, or any other cultural marker, and everything to do with political membership of a particular, territorially defined, state. In principle, all one needs to be a national of, say, Britain or France, is to be born on the territory of the state or to become naturalized as a citizen. National belonging and **citizenship**, in this tradition, are more or less synonymous. Hence the famous commentary by Ernest Renan in his lecture "What is a Nation?" at the Sorbonne in 1882 (published in G. Eley and R. Suny, *Becoming National*, 1996) emphasized the willed, voluntary nature of civic membership (*What is a Nation?*, 1889).

The other tradition of nationhood puts the stress on blood and belonging, on deep or primordial ties of race, ethnicity, religion, history, and other cultural factors. Membership is a hereditary, involuntary, matter, especially as this concept tends to stress an assumed common descent. Nations, in this view, are born, not made. This is the cultural or ethnic understanding of the nation. It had its birth in eighteenth-century Germany, from where it spread to eastern Europe and other parts of the world. The power of the ethnic concept of the nation is that, though it normally aims at statehood, it can exist without statehood. It therefore has wide appeal to those peoples who feel themselves to be nations but who do not have their own states or who exist as – often subordinate – **groups** in states dominated by other nations. There can in this concept be nations without states, commonly given examples being the Catalans of Spain, the Scots of Britain, and the Québécois of Canada. Not all such nations necessarily want states, and whether or not they actually get their own states is largely a matter of power **politics** – the 20-million Kurdish nation, for instance, has been waiting and fighting for a very long time for statehood, but international politics have stood in the way and are likely to do so for the foreseeable future.

Nationalism as a doctrine arose in the late eighteenth century in Europe, and received powerful definition in the course of the French Revolution. This was also the time when the two principal concepts of nationhood were identified, though the French themselves tended to promote the civic concept – leading, by reaction, Germans and others to stress the ethnic concept. But whether the nation was politically or ethnically defined, in the first half of the nineteenth century nationalism was widely identified with the progressive currents of **democracy** and **liberalism**. Its earliest and one of its greatest prophets, Giuseppe Mazzini (1805–72), saw individual nations as subdivisions of a larger family of mankind, and envisaged a future world order in which nations would live peacefully and harmoniously together. In the later nineteenth century, nationalism, affected partly by the **Social Darwinism** of the time, took on a sharper edge. It now tended to be hijacked by right-wing thinkers and statesmen, and to become aggressive and intolerant (a form of nationalism known as integrative nationalism). Nationalism in this period was often allied with **imperialism**, and sought through the acquisition of colonies the aggrandizement of national **power** at the expense of other nations. This form of nationalism reached a climax in the 1930s in Europe, when it was often transformed into **fascism** and other totalitarian ideologies and movements. With the defeat of fascism, nationalism also suffered a rebuff, the more so as liberal hostility to nationalism was also echoed by the left-wing movements of **socialism** and **Communism**. Socialism historically had always been opposed to nationalism as a bourgeois, class-based, ideology with which the international proletariat should have no truck (which did not stop most socialist parties from supporting their nations during the two world wars).

But while nationalism was under a cloud in the post-Second World War western world, it was the central inspiration behind the liberation movements of the developing, non-western, Third World as they sought to throw off colonial rule. Even where the movement took a communist form, as in China, Vietnam, and Cuba, its driving force was clearly nationalist. In some cases, especially in Africa and the Middle East, the nationalism was made problematic by the fact that many of the nations were of recent invention, usually the creation of western powers under **colonialism**. They might contain several ethnic groups of widely differing character, though usually one managed to achieve dominance during the independence struggle. This threw up a welter of conflicts after independence as different ethnic groups claiming national status tried to free themselves from "alien" rule. Examples were the Biafrans in Nigeria, the Tamils in Sri Lanka, and the East Timorese in Indonesia.

But it was not only in the developing world that nationalist conflicts continued to flourish. In the West too, after a relatively short period of quiescence, nationalism revived vigorously, with strong movements in such places as Britain, Belgium, Spain, and Canada. Further East, the collapse of communist regimes after 1989, and the break-up of the Soviet Union in 1991, were accompanied by a powerful surge of nationalism throughout the region – leading, for instance, to the separation of Czechs and Slovaks and, in a bitter and bloody conflict, to the disintegration of Yugoslavia and the rise of five new nations in its place. Nationalism, it is clear, far from being the passing phenomenon that most nineteenth-century thinkers assumed, remains one of the most powerful forces in the world, overriding most other distinctions of **social class**, **gender**, and region, and apparently thriving even amidst the current currents of **globalization**.   KRISHAN KUMAR

nature
– see **environment**.

nature/nurture debate
– see **genetics**.

neighborhood

In sociology, neighborhood is a largely undertheorized and commonsense term referring to urban locales based on residential proximity. The context for neighborhood studies in urban sociology was provided by early twentieth-century sociologists (for example **Georg Simmel**, **Ferdinard Tönnies**, and **Louis Wirth**), who emphasized the impersonality and anonymity of the modern **city**. Against this view, neighborhood studies (for example **Michael Young** and Peter Willmott's *Family and Kinship in East London,* 1957) found that neighborhoods can be the site of close kinship and personal ties that are not a residue from the past but, on the contrary, have been facilitated by modern cities. Urban living enables people to form associations based on **kinship**, or religious, ethnic, political, or other interests which become the basis of local **networks** and **subcultures**. Cities may thus facilitate a level of diversity not found in rural areas. In recent work the idea of neighborhood decline or regeneration has been linked to the concept of **social capital** drawing on the work of Robert Putnam and **James S. Coleman**. This has focused on the neighborhood's potential as a site of integrative social networks and **solidarity**. The level of social capital in a neighborhood is often related to factors such as stability, integration, **trust**, solidarity, and tolerance, which in turn are used to explain such things as differential economic growth or levels of **crime** between regions. Two problems should be noted. The specific influences of the local environment may now be mitigated by global factors. The argument is often circular in that the evidence *for* and conditions *of* social capital in neighborhoods may be the same.
                                                        LARRY RAY

Nelson, Benjamin (1911–1977)

A sociologist and historian who trained as a medieval historian at Columbia, Benjamin taught **social sciences** at Chicago, Minnesota, and the State University of New York, before becoming a professor of history and sociology at the New School for Social Research.

His classic work remains *The Idea of Usury: From Tribal Brotherhood to Universal Otherhood* (1949), which engages with and extends **Max Weber**'s historical and comparative work on **religion** and **rationalization**. Nelson examined the expansion of the moral **community** and the problems of conscience and moral regulation. Drawing on numerous medieval books, he elucidates the manner in which the original dualistic injunctions against usury, found in Deuteronomy 23:19–20, were inverted and extended by the rise of Christian universalism. An ethic of tribal brotherhood and communalistic association, which excluded the quest of gain and treated outsiders as enemies and morally out of bounds, was first extended to universal brotherhood from the twelfth century onward, and again by John Calvin (1509–64) in the sixteenth century, to an ethic of universal otherhood in which "all become brothers by becoming equally others." The breakdown of the inherited structures of consciousness – where a triangulated regulation of "conscience, casuistry, and the cure of souls" existed – resulted in competition and calculation replacing cooperation.

His later work emphasized the intracivilizational study of **social action** and cultural change, and highlighted the necessary interconnection between sociology and **psychoanalysis**. Both of these preoccupations are evident in his comparative historical sociology of science which compares the development of science in the West with that in China, and extends his discussion of the two great revolutions in the sixteenth and seventeenth centuries, the Reformation and the scientific revolution.   STEVEN LOYAL

neoliberalism

Referring to a broad range of economic policies adopted since the 1970s by western capitalist nations, this doctrine advocates measures to promote economic development, and is used to guide the transition from planned to market economies in former communist countries. In the United States, neoliberalism is often referred to as "neoconservatism," thereby creating some confusion in social-science debates. This "new" economic **liberalism** is based on the late eighteenth- and early nineteenth-century classical **political economy** of Adam Smith (1723–90) and David Ricardo (1772–1823), and on Austrian economic theory – especially, that of Friedrich von Hayek (1889–1992). It came to prominence in the wake of the demise of the Keynesian macroeconomics that had informed economic policymaking after World War II. In a critique of the two older approaches, Keynesian theory argued that the labor market was not self-adjusting and that it could not secure full employment unless the government

manipulated its expenditure and fiscal policy to maintain the necessary aggregate demand in the **economy**.

Following classical political economy, neoliberalism maintains that the most efficient allocation of resources is achieved by the competitive **market**. To function effectively, the market requires that property **rights** are clearly defined by law and that prices are not distorted by the **power** of monopolies – such as governments and powerful **trade unions**. Thus neoliberal policies advocate the reduction of direct government participation in the economy; the privatization of the supply of goods and services; and the reduction of trade union power and job security in order to create labor markets that are "flexible" enough to exert a downward pressure on wage levels if economic conditions dictate. Rather than spending to maintain demand and employment and thereby fueling inflation through an increase in the money supply, governments should try to maintain balanced budgets and a stable supply and, consequently, stable value of **money**. Direct control of the money supply by means of "monetarism" failed, but the anti-inflation goal is now pursued by interest-rate policy administered by central banks that are independent of government. These policies of privatization, competitive markets, and stable money are advocated by the International Monetary Fund and World Bank as the framework within which individuals, and not governments, in underdeveloped economies can create **wealth**. Von Hayek's contribution to neoliberalism was in arguing that economic planning would inevitably fail because **states** could never have sufficient knowledge. Only competing individuals could establish the real scarcity value and prices of goods.

At the international level, neoliberalism takes a pro-globalization stance in following Ricardo's advocacy of free trade based on "comparative advantage." Global economic welfare will be maximized in the long run if there is an international division of **labor** in which nations produce and then trade the goods for which they are best suited.

The neoliberal policy-set is often referred to as the "Washington Consensus" and is frequently criticized for ignoring, in the same way as classical political economy, the fact that economies are characterized by a power structure in which freely competitive markets tend to increase the power and wealth of the powerful at the expense of the weaker participants.   GEOFFREY INGHAM

network theory

– see **networks**.

networks

The study of social networks first emerged within postwar sociology and anthropology as a way of studying multi-centered micro-level connections between individuals. Since then the network idea has expanded in scope and significance as a means of characterizing macro-level qualities of **social structures**, and as a means of linking micro- and macro-levels. The controversial idea of network society advocated by **Manuel Castells** in *The Rise of the Network Society* (1996) and *The Internet Galaxy* (2001) represents a leading contemporary example of social network theory, linking large structures to individual settings.

The recently expanded scope of network theory is connected, at least in part, with new information **technology** and the creation of virtual communication networks such as the internet, e-commerce, and broader processes of **globalization**. While debates continue on the precise connection between electronic and interpersonal networks, a proliferating typology of social networks has emerged, focusing on one or more areas such as business and commerce, policy and governance, advocacy, knowledge, science and the **professions**, **migration** and **diaspora**, **religion**, empire, and **terrorism**. Despite all of this, skeptics ask what exactly is distinctive about networks. Are we dealing with a metaphor that simply alludes to informal patterns of social connectivity, or does the concept carry more analytical purchase?

In its original form as micro-level sociology, network analysis was applied to phenomena such as the support systems at work in rural–urban migration, or interactions within the classroom. A major landmark was **Mark Granovetter**'s "The Strength of Weak Ties" (1973, *American Journal of Sociology*) on how people gained **information** about job opportunities in professional and technical **labor markets**. He found this typically occurred less through intimate associates than through more distant acquaintances. This generated the micro-level insight that "weak ties" could have "strong" social consequences.

A neglected application of network theory to larger social structures was undertaken by Ira Lapidus in "Hierarchies and Social Networks; A Comparison of Chinese and Islamic Societies" (1975) in F. J. Wakeman (ed.), *Conflict and Control in late Imperial China*, which developed a theory of social organization in Islamic societies by comparison with China. While he saw Chinese society as dominated by a hierarchy of levels binding together lineage, gentry, **bureaucracy**, emperor, and world order, in Islamic society, in contrast, there was a vast mosaic of small **groups** with little unity. These are better described as networks.

This distinction between hierarchies and networks anticipated a major development in social scientific approaches to organization, systematized by, amongst others, W. W. Powell in "Neither Market nor Hierarchy: Network Forms of Organisation" (1990) in *Research in Organisational Behaviour* (12:295–333). This argument distinguished three organizational forms: **markets**, hierarchies, and networks. While markets are high on flexibility and spatial reach they are by themselves low on **trust**, and prone to opportunistic self-interest and exit. Hierarchies are stronger on co-ordination and formal control but often inflexible and poor at incubating innovation. Between the two stand networks which typically combine the flexibility of markets with some of the co-ordinating capacity of hierarchies, albeit based on interpersonal trust. This is the nearest network analysis has come to a general theory.

Castells's recent work offers an alternative perspective on network society. This proposes a new form of global **capitalism** that draws on network flexibility, enabled by information technology and digitalization. Flows of capital, **information**, organizational interaction, images, sounds, and **symbols** occur through the hubs and nodes of virtual networks. For Castells, the centrality of virtual networks extends to **politics**, which is increasingly conducted through electronic media, and to **culture**, where the new technology encourages networked **individualism**. Network society, however, is dominated by mobile cosmopolitan **elites**, and creates new forms of **social exclusion** of the immobile poor.

This powerful body of work may, however, be stronger on speculative plausibility than empirical accuracy. Critics point out that most economic communication is not transacted electronically. Even those transactions that are electronically enacted are not usually interactive. Nor is activity on-line strongly networked since much of it takes the form of mundane interpersonal emails. Even more damaging, there is no necessary connection between information technology and globalization.

A contrasting, more historically informed approach to networks is provided by **Randall Collins** in *The Sociology of Philosophies* (1998). Philosophical ideas are neither engendered by heroic individuals nor do they arise spontaneously from the operation of structures or cultures. Rather they develop within a finite number of interpersonal networks. Particular networks link the relatively small core of key individuals that constitute schools, while debate and conflict between schools is mediated through networks. Network analysis helps explain why only a relatively small number of philosophical schools form in any given epoch, since ideas require articulation and reproduction through teachers to pupils and through wider connections between peers, in order to be sustained in a robust and distinctive form.

In the work of Castells and Collins, social network theory offers two contrasting approaches to micro–macro linkages. The empirical research programs entailed by these approaches remain underdeveloped however.   ROBERT HOLTON

new class theory
– see **social class**.

New Deal
– see **welfare reforms**.

new institutionalism
The relationship between **institutions** and **society**, long a central concern for sociology, was revitalized in the 1990s with the growth of interdisciplinary theories of institutions known as the "new institutionalism." The new institutionalism is diverse, with different versions found in economics, international relations, political science, and sociology (and differences within disciplines between rational choice variants, comparative-historical institutionalism, and organizational institutionalism).

At the core of the new institutionalism in sociology are several key insights. At the level of organizational field, new institutionalists have argued that **organizations** operate in distinctive environments which exert pressures for conformity, a process known as institutional isomorphism (see the influential collection of Walter Powell and Paul DiMaggio, *The New Institutionalism in Organizational Analysis*, 1991). Over time, institutional environments become coherent, predictable, and ordered as organizations inexorably respond to isomorphic pressures. A second set of insights examine institutional **influences** on individual behavior within organizational settings. Institutional rules and **norms** have long been understood to shape individual behavior, irrespective of the beliefs or orientations of an individual before s/he enters the organization.

To this traditional focus of institutional analysis, however, the new institutionalists have added a focus on cognitive factors. In particular institutional settings, taken-for-granted understandings of acceptable behavior rule out alternative choices. In this way, institutions exert cognitive control over actors' range of possible actions. Most notable here have been the contributions of Richard Scott and his colleagues; see his *Institutions and Organizations* (2001). In historical institutionalism, the role of institutions in shaping political actors' strategies and influencing political outcomes is emphasized. Political institutions create certain kinds of "path dependence" that favor some outcomes and discourage others. These institutional constraints influence the strength of contending **groups, public opinion**, and the content of specific political or policy proposals that actors may propose, as illustrated in Sven Steinmo and K. Thelen *et al.* (eds.), *Structuring Politics: Historical Institutionalism in Comparative Analysis* (1992). In all of these ways, the new institutionalism has argued that institutions have independent, autonomous impacts on organizations, individuals, and social and political conflicts. They are powerful carriers of embedded social norms and rules, and modes of acceptable behavior.   JEFF MANZA

new religious movements
The term new religious movements (NRMs) usually refers to the diverse range of religious groups that emerged mostly in western countries in the 1960s and later. Although the presence of new religious movements or sects (see **church–sect typology**) has a much longer history, especially in the United States, the phrase is customarily applied to movements that are seen as outside the culturally established religious **traditions**. As part of the broader critique and declining **authority** of social **institutions** associated with the political protest and identity movements of the 1960s, many college-age **youth** in particular were drawn towards participation in the alternative or countercultural **norms** articulated by NRMs and the alternative **values** and **lifestyles** they promoted and/or required of members (see C. Glock and **Robert N. Bellah** [eds.], *The New Religious Consciousness*, 1976). Within Christianity, these movements included Jesus-oriented groups such as "The Children of God" (now called "The Family") and the Charismatic Renewal Movement (which revolved around Catholic prayer groups seeking a more biblically grounded and emotional Catholicism), as well as crossing religious traditions (such as "Jews for Jesus"). The increasing appeal of eastern

religious traditions was exemplified by the visibility and popularity of the Hare Krishna movement, the Nation of Islam, and the Unificationist movement of followers of the Korean spiritual leader, Sun Myung Moon, popularly known as the Moonies.

Although new religious movements represent a small proportion of religious adherents in any given society, their cultural exoticism relative to the routines of institutionalized churches and to accepted norms allows them to achieve a mass-mediated presence in the **public sphere** that bears little relation to their numerical strength. Part of this attention derives from the recruiting strategies (such as indoctrination and allegations of brainwashing) and the somewhat volatile charismatic **leadership** associated with many of the movements, and more generally from the disruption these movements, to a greater or lesser extent, pose, or are seen as posing, to the moral order (see E. Barker, *The Making of a Moonie: Choice or Brainwashing?*, 1984). The communal living and the values of communal **property** and inter-family parenting that characterize some NRMs challenge established definitions of private property, **marriage**, and the functions of the **family**.

The disruptive power of new religious movements is illustrated most visibly by the **violence** associated with some movements, notwithstanding the many complexities that may surround the specific circumstances of any particular movement's recourse to violence. Most notably, the mass **suicide** of followers of Jim Jones at Jonestown in Guyana in 1978; the fire that killed the Branch Davidian leader, David Koresh, and some of his followers during the stand-off with federal law-enforcement agents in Waco, Texas, in 1993; the subway gas attacks in Tokyo in 1995 by the Japanese movement, Aum Shinrikyo; and the Heaven's Gate suicides in southern California in 1997 – all these insure that the typification of violence with new religious movements becomes imprinted in the public imagination (see J. Hall, P. Schuyler, and S. Trinh, *Apocalypse Observed: Religious Movements and Violence in North America, Europe and Japan*, 2000). Such negative associations, in turn, attenuate efforts to shift attention to the sociohistorical reasons why particular religious movements emerge at the time and place and in the form that they do, and to why they succeed, however temporarily, in attracting followers.

MICHELE DILLON

new reproductive technologies
– see **reproduction**.

new social movements
– see **social movements**.

new working class
– see **social class**.

Nisbet, Robert (1913–1996)
American sociologist and historian of ideas who emphasized the importance of conservative ideas for sociology, Nisbet attended the University of California, Berkeley, where, under the supervision of the cultural historian Frederick J. Teggart, he pursued his doctorate on the thinkers of the "Reactionary **Enlightenment**." The arguments and ideas of a number of these thinkers, including E. Burke, **A. de Tocqueville**, J. de Maistre, L. Bonald, and F. R. Chateaubriand, formed the basis for the rest of his work, which attacked rationalism, **individualism**, and **socialism**, whose exemplary embodiment he considered to be Jean-Jacques Rousseau (1712–78).

In his first major work, *The Quest of Community* (1953), he examined the disappearance of intermediate associations, such as the **family**, the church, and the local **community** – which existed as a crucial buffer between the individual and **society** – as a result of the growing concentration of **power** in a centralized, and potentially totalitarian, political **state**. The ensuing personal **alienation** and cultural disintegration that followed led to a broadly based quest by individuals for moral guidance and community. These arguments were reworked in his classic study of *The Sociological Tradition* (1966), in which he examined five "unit ideas," all deriving from **conservatism**, and which formed the nucleus of the sociological tradition: community, **authority**, **social status**, the sacred, and alienation.

As well as examining the adverse consequences of politicization for the university and the **social sciences** in *The Degradation of Academic Dogma* (1971) and *The Idea of Progress* (1980), he edited two influential books, *Contemporary Sociological Problems* (1961) with **Robert K. Merton**, and *A History of Sociological Thought* (1978) with Tom Bottomore.

STEVEN LOYAL

nominal measurement
– see **measurement**.

non-parametric statistics
– see **statistics**.

non-profit organizations
– see **voluntary associations**.

non-response
– see **sampling**.

normalization
Defined as those social processes which pressure individuals to conform to culturally desirable or appropriate **norms** of behavior, the practice of normalization produces certain ideals or standards against which the members of a society are judged. Through this process, individuals are socialized into believing that certain forms of behavior or self-presentation are acceptable and valuable, while other behavior that transgresses social expectations is not as acceptable or legitimate. Normalization is a key concept in the study of **social control**. It helps sociologists understand how societies develop rules governing conduct, how they deal with **deviance**, how individuals resist or challenge such norms, and how social **values** and expectations within a society change over time.

One way of defining norms is through simple **statistics**. However, the standards which are produced and reinforced through the process of normalization are often regarded as more than statistical averages. They are often socially valued and presumed to be good, or even ideal. Certain rewards (such as esteem, **money**, or access to resources) are often provided to those who conform to, reinforce, or exceed, social norms. However, those who do not conform to social norms may be punished, socially excluded, or stigmatized. They may be defined as "deviants" or "non-conformists" and they may also be pathologized, and treated as if they had a disease or disability.

Within the area of disability service provision, the idea of normalization has a more specific meaning. It is commonly identified with the work of Wolf Wolfensberger whose theory of "social role valorization" revolves around ways to find normative **social roles** for disabled people. This approach to disability makes a strong effort to ensure that both service delivery and the social relationships which disabled people have reinforce their image as "normal," socially valued citizens.

Much of the sociological interest in the process of normalization can be traced to the influence of **Michel Foucault**, whose work suggested that normalization is reproduced through various institutional frameworks (including **education**, medicine, the military, and the judicial system). Foucault argued that these social **institutions** are involved in various disciplinary practices which overlap and support one another, with the overall effect of producing bodies that conform to certain ideas, which he called "docile bodies." Normalization is not only created through pressure from social institutions though, Foucault's later work suggested that a major element of normalization stems from the way people think about their own **bodies** and their own behavior. An example of the self-regulation of individuals in this manner can be found in Susan Bordo's discussion of the behavior of anorexics in *Unbearable Weight* (1993). She suggests that anorexics are not only victims of gendered social pressures to have slender bodies, but are also engaged in self-regulation that requires considerable will, and self-determination. The behavior of anorexics can be understood, Bordo argues, by focusing on the normalizing pressures which lead women to have a preoccupation with fat, diet, and slenderness. In this way, social norms about the physical body are seen to reflect wider cultural codes around **gender** and other social vulnerabilities.

The study of normalization begs the question, "Who defines the norms?" Sociologists are therefore very interested in unpacking the power dynamics that underpin normalization. They study the ways individuals are encouraged, compelled, and coerced to regulate their behavior so that it seems "normal," but also how people resist such pressures (both collectively and individually). In this way, a study of normalization shows how pressure to conform to social norms operates within social **interactions**, as well as through a person's own desires to control their behavior or image.   MARK SHERRY AND GARY L. ALBRECHT

norms
These are expectations shared by members of a **group** or collectivity that more or less effectively determine individual behavior. Norms typically attach to **social roles** rather than human individuals, who in performance of their roles conform to a greater or lesser extent to norms. The concept of norm is located in various categories associated with the development of **sociology**.

William Graham Sumner, for instance, in *Folkways* (1906), holds that collective life, necessary for individual survival, requires the preservation of efficacious experience, stored in and communicated as custom. Custom is the collective form of individual habit. Folkways are produced, according to Sumner, in the frequent repetition of petty acts. Folkways are accepted because of the conviction that they are conducive to societal welfare and can therefore be defined as systems of persisting expedient customary behavior. Sumner says that, within a group, folkways are uniform, universal, imperative, and invariable; over time they become increasingly arbitrary. Socially formed and selected inferences derived from folkways, Sumner calls mores. Mores consist largely but not exclusively of taboos (see **sacred and profane dichotomy**), things that should not be done. A characteristic of mores, as coercive ethical principles, is the likelihood that they will contain an explicit **rationalization** or reason for adherence to them, for example don't eat pork because pigs are unclean. Sumner's approach was related to **Social Darwinism**. Believing that **social change** is achieved through the evolution of folkways and the development of folkways into mores is no longer in vogue.

Talcott Parsons argues that, through social **interaction**, persons are able to communicate because signs and **symbols** acquire common meaning. By virtue of a shared meaning system there arises a mutuality of expectations and sanctions that constitutes what Parsons calls a normative order in *The Social System* (1951). Thus norms operate through internalization of a standard of group expectations and are maintained by the reactions of others, both positive and negative. These reactions are sanctions that reward conformity to role expectations and punish departure

from expectation such as **deviance**. For Parsons, the institutionalization of both expectation and sanction constitutive of norms is achieved in varying degrees. **Anomie** occurs in the absence of institutionalization. Norms therefore are not to be located at the level of individual social actor but necessarily function in the institutionalized activity of a plurality of social actors.

While the notion of norm can adequately describe the habitual institutional patterns of a **society**, explanations of societal processes in terms of norms risks accounting for regularities of social action in terms of expectations. In fact, interaction in groups or societies may result from a number of possible factors, of which norms are only one. One alternative approach to **explanation** of social process points not to the system of norms, but to power relations and the balance of **power** that is the outcome of **social conflict** between groups. Exponents of this approach include **Ralph Dahrendorf** in *Class and Class Conflict in Industrial Society* (1959) and **John Rex** in *Key Problems of Sociological Theory* (1961). **David Lockwood**'s *Solidarity and Schism* (1992) developed a sophisticated critique of the normative approach that avoids the problems of conflict theory.   JACK BARBALET

nuclear family
– see **family**.

O

John O'Neill (1933–)

A distinguished research professor emeritus at York University, Canada, and a Fellow of the Royal Society of Canada, O'Neill developed a critical interpretation of **sociology** in his *Sociology as a Skin Trade* (1972) and *Making Sense Together* (1974). His work is characterized by an attempt to bridge the gap between the humanities and the **social sciences**, which is illustrated in his *Essaying Montaigne. A Study of the Renaissance Institution of Writing and Reading* (1982). He contributed to the development of the sociology of the **body** in his *Five Bodies. The Human Shape of Modern Society* (1985) and *The Communicative Body* (1989). He was critical of **postmodernism** in his *The Poverty of Postmodernism*. More recently, he has made two important contributions to the sociology of **citizenship** in which he has been concerned to examine the status of **children** in modern **society** in his *The Missing Child in Liberal Theory* (1994) and *Civic Capitalism. The State of Childhood* (2004). He is a founding editor of the *Journal of Classical Sociology*.

BRYAN S. TURNER

Oakley, Ann (1944–)

A British sociologist who has worked on diverse issues related to the specific condition and experience of women, Oakley's earliest work was a study of the **politics** and gender relations of housework (*The Sociology of Housework*, 1972, and *Housewife*, 1974). Informing both those texts was a concern with the isolation of women in the home and what was – at the time – a refusal of the social world to recognize the unpaid domestic work of women (see **women and work**). Oakley's later work has been concerned with medical aspects of women's lives, particularly childbirth and the transition to **motherhood**. In a number of studies (*Becoming a Mother*, 1979, and *The Captured Womb*, 1984), Oakley criticized the male control and **medicalization** of childbirth and the loss of an autonomous female voice in questions related to women and **reproduction**. Oakley's work has been widely influential in the management of childbirth in the United Kingdom.

In recent years, Oakley has written fiction (for example *The Men's Room*, 1991) and studies of the way in which **gender** informs global politics and the universal organization of social life (*Gender on Planet Earth*, 2003). Throughout her work Oakley has argued that it is **socialization** that creates and maintains the social prioritization of the male and the masculine; her many crosscultural references demonstrate her awareness of cultural difference in the construction of gender roles and behavior. Oakley has worked with **Juliet Mitchell** on collections of essays discussing the meaning of **feminism** and has maintained a consistent loyalty to a politics which affirms the voices and concerns of women.

MARY EVANS

objectivity

A quality of mind such that the investigator is enabled to discern the true properties of the phenomenon being studied by remaining free from **bias** or **prejudice**, objectivity is often considered to be a goal of scientific investigation.

Researchers have deployed a number of strategies to aid impartial investigation. These include attention to validity, reliability, and **sampling**. Finally, because published research reports are available for public scrutiny, and in many cases have been peer reviewed, the authors' claims can be critically assessed for personal prejudices.

The distinction between scientific facts and social (or political) **values** was important for both **Émile Durkheim** and **Max Weber**. Weber argued that scientists can only report on facts and, while they may involve themselves in political polemics, they may maintain objectivity through compliance with scientific protocols and proceeding in accordance with standard rules of evidence and proof. In **Alvin Gouldner**'s 1962 analysis of Weber in *Social Problems*, "Anti-minotaur: The Myth of a Value-free Sociology," interpretation of facts may be infused with personal values, but the research techniques that produce those facts are value-neutral.

The quest for objectivity has been met with resistance on a number of points. One of the arguments against objectivity concerns the debate between **realism** and **relativism**. Relativists argue that scientific truth may be different seen from different perspectives, thus there can be multiple and non-contradictory reports of the same phenomenon.

There is also opposition to the positivistic notion that sociologists should seek to imitate the natural sciences. While sociology may employ systematic methods of inquiry and evidence-based theories, human activity and **interactions** may require different approaches to investigation from objects of nature. The reality of sociological research means that access and rapport with one's informants is often a consequence of a personal approach from one human being to another rather than from scientist to subject. If sociologists are determined to maintain their objective stance they are at risk of damaging their fieldwork relationships. Emotional distance will in turn affect what the subject allows the researcher to observe or hear about their lives. Feminist research has led the main challenge to the positivist orthodoxy that sociology should strive to be objective, arguing that it is only by a transition to **friendship** and a collaborative approach to research that a more insightful account of women's experiences will be generated.

It has also been argued that sociological work cannot be objective in that it is influenced by sociologists' own experiences and values. Sociology is by its very nature ideologically driven, thus the notion of value-free social inquiry is unsustainable. Thus, **Howard S. Becker**, in his paper in *Social Problems*, "Whose Side are we on?" (1967), maintained that sociologists are constantly presenting someone's point of view and have traditionally been unable to remain neutral in the face of moral and political controversies. The issue therefore focuses less on whether objectivity has been maintained but rather whose interests are served by the sociologists' subjectivity. Sociologists may therefore be caught in an ethical tension between a desire to present themselves as objective to their audiences and their commitment to principles of social justice.

MICK BLOOR AND FIONA WOOD

occupational segregation

– see **occupations**.

occupations

In complex societies with a high division of **labor** specialized work roles develop. On the one hand, **Émile Durkheim** argued in the *Division of Labour in Society* (1893 [trans. 1960]) that this increased interdependence of each of us on others leads to **social integration**. On the other hand, **Karl Marx** claimed that such specialization leads to **alienation** and the fragmentation of the **self**. What is clear, however, following the work of **Max Weber**, is that occupational roles provide the basis for a social hierarchy, with some being positively valued status groups and others negatively valued. The Registrar General in the United Kingdom explicitly recognizes this hierarchy, providing a list of **social classes** based on occupation. These are: I. professionals; II. managerial; IIIN. skilled non-manual occupations; IIIM; skilled manual occupations; IV. partly skilled occupations; V. unskilled occupations; and VI. the armed forces. Occupational **inequalities** thus provide sociologists with a proxy measure of class differences. For example, sociologists use this classification to examine the impact of occupation on **life-chances**, and sociologists of **health** and illness have demonstrated that people in socio-economic classes V and VI have lower life expectancy and higher morbidity than people from the non-manual classes (I, II, and IIIN).

Feminist sociologists have also demonstrated that occupations are structured by **gender**, with women pooling in the "pink-collar occupations" of nursing, teaching, and service and secretarial work, a phenomenon known as "occupational segregation." Even where women participate in male occupations, they find it difficult to rise to the top, either because of the existence of a "glass ceiling," as informal sanctions are applied, or the "mommy effect" as they break their careers to rear a **family**. Women also tend to be concentrated in the "caring occupations." This impact of gender on the structure of occupations is reflected in the fact that, even when women medical practitioners go on to specialize, they do so, for example, in psychiatry and pediatrics, reflecting wider social assumptions about their caring and nurturing roles.

Occupational groups protect themselves to enhance their **social status** and **income**, a process known as **social closure**, through **credentialism**. That is, they set entry criteria, usually marked by tertiary-sector qualifications, that are not necessary to the performance of the occupational role. This closure has the effect of keeping out lower social-status **groups**, and especially ethnic minorities, who do not have access to the resources (such as time and **money**) to pursue these qualifications. The occupational structure of **society** thus both reflects and maintains patterns of social **inequality** based on class, **gender**, and **race and** ethnicity. Participation in an occupation is less likely to be structured as a **career**, as is the case for the **professions**, to be more discontinuous, and in **postindustrial society**, to be insecure and, increasingly, part-time.　　　　　KEVIN WHITE

Ogburn, William F. (1886–1959)

A lifetime proponent of empirical **positivism**, Ogburn pioneered the study of **social change** and the systematic use of **social indicators**. Born in Butler, Georgia, and raised in a middle-class home, Ogburn studied under Franklin Henry Giddings (1855–1931) at Columbia University and received his PhD in sociology for a statistical analysis of child labor laws in 1912. He spent most of his career at the University of Chicago (from 1927 until retiring in 1951) where, during a time of ascendant qualitative studies, his quantitative approach attracted a number of distinguished scholars, including Samuel Stouffer and **Otis Dudley Duncan**.

While he was skeptical about the value of **social theory**, Ogburn's work *Social Change* (1922) had a huge impact on the theory of social **evolution**. He argued that social change is brought about not by **social action** but by "inventions" – novel combinations of existing cultural material. **Social problems**, in turn, emerge from disjunctures, or "cultural lags," between one aspect of **culture** that changes due to invention, and another aspect of culture that must adjust accordingly.

In his 1929 presidential address to the American Sociological Society, Ogburn predicted that **sociology** would become increasingly a science of "verification and proof." The methodological domains he cultivated include ambitious projects of interdisciplinary cooperation, techniques to measure social change, and large-scale government **surveys** to inform policymakers (largely through work as Director of the President's Research Committee on Social Trends [1930–3]). Through his study of secular social trends, Ogburn came to argue that such trends usually persist even in the face of disruptive events – so much so that deviations from these trends are more noticeable than the overall course of change.

　　　　　　　　　　　　　DONALD N. LEVINE

oligarchy

According to the classic Aristotelian typology, oligarchy is a system of rule by a few, exercised in their own interest. It is contrasted with monarchy, aristocracy, tyranny, **democracy**, and polity. Classic elite theorists **Vilfredo Pareto**, **Gaetano Mosca**, and **Robert Michels**, who popularized the term,

saw oligarchies as synonymous with consolidated elites. Michels in *Political Parties* (1958) coined a famous "iron law of oligarchy": all complex **bureaucracies** give rise to **elites**. For some social analysts, oligarchy acquires a more specific meaning.

In *The Class Structure of the Advanced Societies* (1973), **Anthony Giddens** analyzed effective **power** in relation to elite formation (consolidated versus diffuse power), and "issue-strength" (broad versus issue-specific). He defined oligarchic rule as involving consolidated "strategic" elites with power over a restricted/specialized set of issues. Such oligarchic elite power was contrasted with autocracy (consolidated elites and broad power), **hegemony** (diffused and broad), and democracy (diffused and restricted). Traditional oligarchies consisted typically of top aristocratic **families** (magnates) controlling ·monarchs. Modern oligarchies take many forms. Power elites involve the leaders of big business, the top government officials, and the top echelons of the military. Strategic elites include a number of well-integrated but sector-specific elite **groups**. Ruling class (see **social class**) is an oligarchy consisting of owners and controllers of corporate capital. The inner circle consists of executives of the largest corporations. Some students of communist elites refer to "party–state" power oligarchies (the *nomenklatura*). The term oligarchy is seldom used in contemporary sociology of politics; it has been largely superseded by the term elite(s).　　　JAN PAKULSKI

online communities

Both the idea and practice of **communities** have always been an essential component of sociological theorizing. Such communities were originally location-based constructs. But as studies of them deepened, another category has developed, namely the idea of conceptual communities. Thus, one could for instance speak of the scientific community. The enormous growth in online activities has led scholars to question whether communities could exist online, and what differences might arise between traditional physically based communities and their online counterparts.

C. Arensberg and S. Kimball in *Culture and Community* (1965) identify three elements to the concept of community: environment, social form, and patterned behavior. I. Sanders in *The Community* (1966) asserted there were four: a place to live, a spatial unit, a way of life, and a social system. Using the former, it can be argued that online groupings that have these elements can qualify as a community. Reliance on the physical and spatial dimensions of the term, by, for example, Sanders, would force one to dismiss the possibility of online communities at all. Yet despite their lack of physical reality, it seems plausible that, since communities are mental constructs in the first place, they could be virtual as well as physical in their nature. Interestingly, the absence of the necessity of overcoming geographical distance, combined with computer processing power, makes many new types of communities possible.

J. Meyrowitz in *No Sense of Place* (1985) has argued that communities, both online and off, can be viewed in a context that is both upward to **institutions** and downward to **social roles**. He analyzes social roles and **identities** in terms of information systems that comprise patterns of access to social **information**, determined by the mix of physical settings, media, and mental constructs. Regarding mental constructs, he extends **George Herbert Mead**'s notion of the generalized other to the mediated generalized other. He describes how people gain a sense of who they are in part by imagining how others, both live and mediated, view them. Additionally, he anticipated much discussion of virtual life by advancing the notion of the generalized elsewhere, wherein one imagines how distant others imagine one's own location and general environment. With considerable variation, this schema allows one to have a grasp of the general theoretical outlines possible in attempting to pin down, then contrast, online communities to their physical counterparts.

JAMES E. KATZ

ontology

In sociology, an ontology responds to generic (that is transhistorical and transcultural) questions about the properties of social life. Though quite fundamental to all disciplinary concerns, ontological issues in sociology are more modest than ontological issues in the broadest philosophical sense. In philosophy, ontology refers to metaphysical issues concerned with the nature of existence and the structure of reality at large, a concern that has intellectual precedents reaching as far back as Aristotle (384–322 BC). Whereas most philosophical schemes are hierarchical, with some form of human "being" or "existence" at the top, sociological ontologies may be more loosely structured and do not concern themselves with "being" at all. Thus, the twentieth-century ontologies by Martin Heidegger and the early Jean-Paul Sartre have no correlated sociological ontologies. Examples of sociological ontologies include structuration theory, which identifies structured social

practices as the basic constituents of all aspects of social reality. **Karl Marx**'s preface to *Critique of Political Economy* (1849 [trans. 1859]) includes a crude materialist ontology. The well-known first chapter of **Émile Durkheim**'s *Rules of Sociological Method* (1895 [trans. 1958]) makes an elementary case for a collectivist ontology. Some commentators interpret Max Weber's basic concepts of **social action** in ontological terms, though others disagree.

Though social theorists have always relied upon ontologies, the term only recently entered the lexicon in the wake of the declining influence of **positivism** in the 1970s. Positivists tried to deny that what they termed metaphysical issues had any legitimate place in scientific thought. The term ontology gave these issues a place to stand in post-Kuhnian **sociological theory**.   IRA COHEN

Operationalization
– see **Falsification**.

organic anology
– see **organicism**.

organicism

Sociology has often linked human **society** to organisms. **Herbert Spencer**, for example, drew attention to the fact that low animals or the embryos of high animals have few distinguishable parts, their elements becoming more numerous and differentiated during evolution or lifetime development. Similarly, he suggested, societies become increasingly complex and subdivided as they grow. **Émile Durkheim**'s well-known distinction between "mechanical" and "organic" forms of sociology also relies on an organic analogy, one in which society becomes more complex as it develops. In the middle of the twentieth century, **Talcott Parsons** argued for a general evolutionary law, change again taking the form of increasing **differentiation** between elements of the social "subsystem" – the home and the factory, for example. Forms of organicism are alive and well, especially among German sociologists strongly influenced by Parsons. **Niklas Luhmann**, for example, envisaged society as a set of distinct subsystems with their own rules and codes, making society very complex and difficult to manage.

Analogies between societies and organisms were important in establishing sociology as a new discipline. But they are highly misleading when carried too far. Organicism can easily become teleological, **social change** apparently having a direction, purpose, and maturity, processes analogous to human growth and which all societies must inevitably experience. Another questionable implication is that of an unproblematic "progress" being steadily made, "simple" societies being replaced by more complex social forms. More generally, organicism can be criticized for implying that human societies, with all their power relations and divisions of **labor**, are somehow a product of nature. Despite such criticisms, however, organicism has had an important heuristic value, suggesting new hypotheses about social change and social organization.

PETER DICKENS

organization man

William H. Whyte's *The Organization Man* (1956) was a famous commentary on American business **culture**, but it belongs to another era: one in which **careers** could be foreseen in a large organizational **bureaucracy**, in an era before **feminism**, with its demands for a new type of man as well as the equal participation of women, a new approach to parenting, and a new set of commitments. It was also an era before downsizing, **rationalization**, and outsourcing threatened individual careers and lives. The organization man of the title was expected to be a loyal and conformist member of the **organization**. Indeed, in mid-1950s America, he was expected to be a loyal and conformist American.

Whyte was doubly well placed to produce an outstanding **ethnography** of the organization man. First, the times were right: he wrote during the height of the Eisenhower administration (1953–61), when corporations appeared to provide all the necessities of modern life – careers, consumer goods in abundance, and suburban **lifestyles**. Second, as an editor of *Fortune*, Whyte could observe corporate America up close, and what he saw belied what he and many others believed. America was shifting from a land of individual initiative to one of corporate control.

Whyte observed that the young men who entered organizations saw their whole working lives as being committed at that point: their interests were inexorably tied to those of the organizations that employed them. The assumption was that they would be rewarded in their career for the time they invested in the organization. *The Organization Man* showed the white-collar employee as increasingly shaped by employer demands: focused on advancement through the firm, he became narrow, conformist, and unwilling to innovate. This figure's fear of original thought and his lifestyle (situated in rationalized

suburbs and marked by **consumption** rather than **community**) stood in direct opposition to the **ideology** of American competitive **individualism**.

As recently as the 1980s, Whyte revisited the organization man and claimed little had changed. Today he would have to draw different conclusions. The **social contract** has been broken. Managers and professionals work harder than ever – but more often than not for their individual as much as organization interests. While organizations seek to align individual and organization interests with inducements and salaries, they do not promise lifelong careers. Project-based careers are increasingly becoming the order of the day. Downsizing does not produce loyalty but survivor syndromes, where loyalty is contingent, bought with high salaries, bonuses, and stock options, until a better offer comes along or until the manager is dismissed. Pay is performance-related, and managers cannot afford to slacken the intensity of their work if they are to maximize their **income**. The expectation is, increasingly, of a career in projects and parts, rather than a commitment to one organization, with the expectation of the pursuit of central life-interests occurring outside work rather than through the job. Organizations have increasingly become de-bureaucratized and more marketized, with correlative shrinkage of organization-man opportunities. While cultural consent may still be valued, it is increasingly bought and specifically contingent on the risk/reward package negotiated.

STEWART CLEGG

organization theory

The work of **Max Weber** was initially influential in shaping the sociological analysis of **organizations**. It offered a unifying frame – the theory of **bureaucracy** – within which to research organization processes and, unlike early management theory, did not offer prescriptive and mutually contradictory principles. Typically, researchers first started to interpret organizations using Weber's ideas, which they then revised as they attended to features of reality that were not captured in his model, producing an influential body of postwar work (see, for example, that reviewed in S. Clegg, M. Kornberger, and T. Pitsis, *Managing and Organizations*, 2005). Until the mid-1950s, the **case study** was the dominant method of research and Weber a central resource. These were based on substantive aspects of specific cases, and thus their generalizability was low and hard to cumulate into a consistent body of interrelated theoretical knowledge.

In the 1950s, after the emergence of the journal *Administrative Science Quarterly*, the systems perspective came increasingly to dominate organization analysis. The perspective solved some problems inherent to the typological approaches. Systems perspectives such as that of **Talcott Parsons** promised a general approach to any and every organization, conceived as a system of inputs, transformation processes, and outputs. General systems theory was scientifically influential and organizations became a specialist domain of its analysis.

Emerging out of systems theory in the 1960s was the approach known as contingency theory. Organizations were still seen as systems but they had to deal with specific contingencies that shaped their structure, such as their size, **technology**, environment, and the national **culture** in which they were embedded. While the earlier generation of researchers used case studies, contingency research was characterized by survey methods and larger samples, seeking to operationalize factors identified in the earlier literature, such as Weber's fifteen dimensions of bureaucracy.

From the 1970s onwards, a number of new currents emerged. First, the influence of the labor process approach, derived from H. Braverman's *Labor and Monopoly Capitalism* (1974), spawned a renewed fascination with case studies, such as the work of M. Burawoy on *Manufacturing Consent* (1979), many of which were reported in a series of edited volumes that represented the work of the labor process conference, held annually from 1983. Second, from the early 1980s onwards, there was a renewed interest in Weberian theory, as a result of two related trends. One was the reemergence of institutional theory, after the publication of P. DiMaggio and W. W. Powell's seminal paper on the "iron cage" in the *American Journal of Sociology* (1984); the other was the popular success of G. Ritzer's Weberian-inspired analysis of organizational **rationalization** in *The McDonaldization of Society* (1993).

Further, from a sociological perspective, one would have to count the influence of population ecology, an approach influenced by general ecological theory, which concentrates on populations of organizations and changes at the population level, typically dealing with big changes over large datasets, across significant periods of time, often using datasets that were not generated by the researchers themselves but which were available or constructed from available sets. The approach was based more on the statistical testing of relations between constructs than upon intimate research knowledge. It was a sociological approach

premised on biological models but one whose peak of **influence** seems to have passed. More recently, in the 1990s and beyond, the influence of Foucauldian-inspired genealogical analysis has begun to make an impact on the field, perhaps best represented in A. McKinley and K. Starkey's *Foucault, Management and Organization Theory* (1997). Closely related, but hotly contested, are more postmodern approaches, debates about which may be found in E. Locke's *Postmodernism in Organizational Thought* (2003).

All of the above may safely be thought of as a part of sociological approaches to organizations. However, with the massive growth in business and management programs across the world in the recent past, today the vast majority of organization theory is taught not in sociology but in business and management faculties. Typically, the definition of what constitutes organization theory in such places may be less sociological than the currents identified here. For instance, a number of economic approaches to organization theory have developed, the most significant of which is known as transaction-cost analysis, as seen for example in O. E. Williamson's *The Economic Institutions of Capitalism* (1985). Increasingly, organization and management theory is being taught by people with little or no trained capacity as sociologists – a situation quite dissimilar to the generation of work done in the aftermath of World War II. Nonetheless, organization theory remains one of the more populous and significant homes of applied sociology.   STEWART CLEGG

organizational culture

T. Peters and R. Waterman's *In Search of Excellence* (1982) placed organizational culture center stage. The message was simple: great companies have excellent **cultures**. Culture was typically defined in terms that stressed a pattern of learned and shared basic assumptions, framing how organization members perceive, think, and feel. It was presumed that if you forged a strong culture – one that incorporates all organization members in shared beliefs and commitments – then everything else – good morale, performance, and results – should follow. Having such a widely shared and integrative culture in organizations became seen as a panacea for **management** and an algorithm for corporate success.

Organization theorists were relative latecomers to the consideration of culture in the pantheon of **social science** but may be said to have discovered it quite early in the development of their field.

F. W. Taylor sought to create a single utilitarian culture to minimize employee resistance and maximize productivity – and, of course, earnings. However, it is clear that Taylor in his *Principles of Scientific Management* (1911) did not have an explicit analytical focus on culture. The earliest confirmed sighting seems to be when F. Roethlisberger and W. Dickson realized, in *Management and the Worker* (1939), that the most significant variables governing the output at the Hawthorne Plant appeared not to be physical but social. As N. Mouzelis pointed out in *Organization and Bureaucracy*, they defined the "culture of the group" (1967: 99).

Since at least E. Mayo's *The Social Problems of an Industrial Civilization* (1975), managers have had available the use of various types of expert knowledge (psycho-technological and managerial) for the management of culture. Increasingly, managers have sought to regulate workers through attending to their thoughts and **emotions** as well as securing compliance for shaping workers' **attitudes** and sentiments.

Recent approaches argue that organizational culture will always be fragmentary (and contingent on **identities** deriving from occupational, regional, **social class**, ethnic, **gender**, and other forms of social marker, under highly variable local conditions). However, all approaches understand cultures (whether fragmented or homogeneous) as extremely important patterns that shape organizational realities. Understanding organizations means understanding their culture.

STEWART CLEGG

organization(s)

Although the medieval monastery became the template for rational bureaucratic organization, the transfer of the organization form to secular society occurred primarily through the modern **state** developing extensive **bureaucracies**, in areas such as **education**. These forms were later replicated in commerce and industry.

In industry, the central issue became the maximization of private profit. Owners of capital had to be able to exercise regular and routine dominion and sway over the working lives of those on whom its reproduction depended. Industrial property owners could not rely on feudal fealty to deliver able and willing bodies, as did the lords of old; however, it was a matter of record that they often found religious deference and piety to be invaluable assets. **Authority** that could claim it had God on its side stood a better chance of success, as **Max Weber** realized in *The Protestant Ethic and the Spirit of Capitalism* (1905 [trans. 2002]).

In the early days of industrialism, a combination of heavy doses of **paternalism**, rough discipline, and an efficient **labor market** buttressed less secular sources of moral authority with sheer necessity. More traditional relations could often overlie the wage relations that mostly bound production. In lieu of internalized religious **ritual** or deference to feudal hierarchy, management control seemed best assured through the routine disciplining of those employed.

In small craft workshops, discipline was relatively easy to enact, organized around mastery of a specific knowledge, such as how to make barrels, fabricate metal, or weave wool. In such a structure, the master was presumed to know the craft, which apprentices were presumed not to know and had every motive for learning, so that they too could become skilled workers. The master exercised **power** by getting the apprentice to do things in the favored way. Authority was based on power unified with knowledge: masters owned the workshop as well as expert knowledge of how to work in it. Effective oversight was by direct control of people in the workshop. The early days of modern management and organizations were bootstrapped. Primitive methods of surveillance and drill were adapted, panopticons proposed, and elements from preindustrial craft relations incorporated. Bootstrapped solutions worked appropriately for as long as the scale of enterprise remained small.

There were two distinct shortcomings associated with expanding scale. To grow large meant expending capital. The capital in circulation in the early industrial **economy** was relatively small compared to that invested in landed estates. It was raised mostly through merchants combining credit with rented buildings and machinery, together with cheap sources of **labor**. Keeping costs low meant that, if the enterprise were to fail, the liability and exposure of the emergent entrepreneurs would be limited.

It was the institutional innovation of limited liability legislation, pioneered first in Britain in 1856, but widely copied internationally, that enabled enterprises to grow by separating the private fortunes of entrepreneurs from their investments in business; if the latter failed, personal fortunes were sequestered and the debtors' prison was avoided.

Limited liability legislation did not resolve the problem of how to manage the vastly expanded enterprise. How was the master to achieve effective governance over a vastly increased scale of operations? Two resolutions to the puzzle of how to ensure mastery were proposed: one adopted a market solution while the other copied what had already occurred in the large-scale public service of the day and threw in its lot with bureaucracy.

In **firms** that were taken over by use of the new financial instruments, owners of previously independent businesses were re-employed as internal contractors to oversee the processes of labor. One consequence of internal contracting – where the contractor used materials, plant, and equipment supplied by the owners but managed the labor contracted to deliver a certain quantity of product – was that quite different methods of internal control could flourish in different plants in the same industry. Standards were highly variable. However, under pressure for more standardization from both financial controllers and emergent unions, internal contracting gave way to a bureaucratization of relations of production in large concerns, such that, by the early twentieth century, Weber noted that bureaucracy had become the fate of our times. Weber argued that no special proof was required to demonstrate that military discipline was the ideal model for the modern capitalist factory in the early twentieth century. Since that time, standardization – as the blueprint for designing modern organizations – has increasingly stressed being disciplined and being visible. Order, discipline, and authority were to become the organizational watchwords of the new world under construction, and have remained at the core of much organization ever since.

STEWART CLEGG

Orientalism

The modern debate about western views of the Orient was significantly influenced by **Edward Said**'s *Orientalism* (1978). However, the anthropological controversy about "other **cultures**" can be traced back to the European encounter with its colonies, and hence, over an even longer period, between Christianity and its antagonists. Said's controversial **paradigm** had the effect of establishing the notion of "Orientalism" as a specific and pervasive **ideology** about Asian societies. His critique has laid the contemporary foundation for an extensive inquiry into the problematic relationships between **power**, sexual desire, religious **identity** and cultural dominance.

Orientalism is a largely implicit paradigm within which Oriental civilizations have been understood by the West. It makes a clear distinction between the Orient and the Occident, emphasising the **rationality**, reflectivity, and dynamism of the latter. In its sociological versions, Orientalism has been associated with theories of **modernization**, in which the Orient is regarded as stationary and unchanging. One illustration is the comparative **sociology** of **Max Weber** who regarded **rationalization** and asceticism in Christian sects as unique characteristics of western modernity. The general argument of Orientalism has been that the Orient has not experienced the revolutions that shook the West, and hence has not experienced an independent form of modernization. Orientalists argue that, for example, Islam is inherently incompatible with **democracy**. Orientalism has been criticized, for example by **Andre Guider Frank**, on the grounds that the paradigm seriously underestimates the dynamic nature of economic and **social change** in India and China.

In recent sociological debates about "otherness," Said's criticisms of the Orientalist tradition are typically associated with the critical **social theory** of **Michel Foucault**. Representations of the Orient are seen to be manifestations of an enduring ideological paradigm that constructs the Orient as an object of scientific knowledge. Said's analysis of Orientalism was also influenced by Erich Auerbach's *Mimesis* (1946 [trans. 1953]). Written in Istanbul between 1942 and 1945, and published in German, it was a study of the literary practices by which reality was represented through definite stylistic conventions. Said's *Orientalism* can be said to do for French literary representations of the Orient what *Mimesis* attempted more generically to do for western literature as a whole. Said also relied heavily on Raymond Schwab's *The Oriental Renaissance* (1950 [trans. 1984]) that first provided the concept of Orientalism in a study of western **attitudes** towards India. In short, Said's account of Orientalism belongs to a recognizable heritage of western self-reflection in the context of the engagement with other cultures.

Said's account of Orientalism has been criticized because it failed, for example, to differentiate clearly between French, British, and Spanish views of the Orient. His work was largely focused on the Middle East, and had little to say about Asia. Despite the criticisms of Said, the debate about Orientalism has produced a rich, critical literature on the consequences of **colonialism**, and the attempt to explain modernization comparatively still remains a major task of the **social sciences**.

BRYAN S. TURNER

Ossowski, Stanislaw (1897–1963)

A Polish sociologist writing on **social structure**, **methodology**, social psychology, **aesthetics**, and art, Ossowski led the post-Stalinist revival of Polish sociology, served as a President of the Polish Sociological Association (1956–63), and cofounded the International Sociological Association. While his analyses cover a wide range of topics, Ossowski is best known for his synthesis of humanistic (interpretive) sociology with rigorous empirical analysis, and for his influential study of *Class Structure in the Social Consciousness* (1957 [trans. 1963]). He analyzed the three major interpretations of the class structure: the functional, stressing complementarity; the gradation ("social ladder") highlighting hierarchy; and the polar one (owners versus workers) emphasizing social antagonism. He identified the social functions of these three interpretations: while functional and gradation schemes were typically embraced by the supporters of the social order in the upper strata, the polar schemes served as idioms of radical social contestation. The concept of "classlessness" was used by Ossowski in his analyses of gradation schemes popularized in the United States and the "non-antagonistic" class visions promoted in the then Soviet Union. In this context, he pointed to the inadequacy of Marxist class schemes for the analysis of social hierarchy and division in modern **industrial society**. Anticipating the criticism of class orthodoxy by the students of industrial society, he suggested that **modernization** brings increasing complexity of social divisions. The social distribution of privilege and disadvantage reflects not only the control of the means of production, but also – and increasingly – the control of the means of compulsion (**authority**), and the means of **consumption**.   JAN PAKULSKI

other-directed character

– see **David Riesman**.

oversocialized conception of man

– see **Dennis Hume Wrong**.

P

panel study

These studies offer researchers the opportunity to follow the same group of research participants over time; they differ from cross-sectional studies (although they may represent sub-components of some cross-sectional studies) in that they allow researchers to track changes in the views, **attitudes**, and reported behaviors of a defined panel on a longitudinal rather than "snapshot" basis. Panel studies promise to analyze the effect of "real-world" events on particular social groupings. For classic examples of such studies, see the British Household Survey or the University of Michigan – Institute for Social Research's Panel Study of Income Dynamics (PSID), which has followed a representative sample of 8,000 United States households, or 65,000 individuals, since 1968.

Panels may be any social unit with a sufficient degree of theoretical homogeneity to make the study empirically compelling: thus panels may consist in households, university graduates of a given year (otherwise known as age-cohorts), or other groupings with a common and date-sensitive life experience such as the birth of a first child. Panels, once constituted, are regularly mined for **data**, most often using **interviews** or other standardized **surveys**, to explore the relationships between lived experience, social factors, and period effects.

Difficulties with panel studies are attrition (if people are followed over months and years some leave the area forgetting to provide a forwarding address, emigrate, or die) a difficulty that may be ameliorated by the adoption of a dynamic sample panel whereby matching "replacement" panel members are substituted for those who drop out. Alternatively, the dynamic **methodology** may be used to control for "experience **bias**" – that is to say, respondents becoming practiced at providing material that the researchers wish to hear.

MARK RAPLEY AND SUSAN HANSEN

panopticism

– see **Michel Foucault**.

paradigm

The concept of paradigm, used by **Thomas Samuel Kuhn** in his classic book, *The Structure of Scientific Revolutions* (1962), was taken from its use to describe model "correct" sentences in Latin. Kuhn argued that in science, scientific discourse was rooted in exemplary achievements, such as experiments, which served as models of the correct way to approach scientific problems. Kuhn further argued that major conceptual changes in science, which he called scientific revolutions, typically consisted of changes in what constituted a paradigmatic achievement, what constituted a scientific problem, what counted as evidence, and the meanings of the terms themselves, which derives from their place in practice and in the conceptual scheme. He used psychological terms such as *Gestalt* and sociological terms such as worldview to characterize paradigms, emphasizing their pervasive world-constituting role, and emphasized the role of scientific **communities** in sustaining them.

The most distinctive of the ideas making up the concept of paradigm was also the most problematic to Kuhn, namely incommensurability, meaning non-comparability.

Kuhn's notion of scientific revolution raised the question of what sense could be given to the notion of **progress** in science or to the notion of science as increasingly approaching higher degrees of truth.

STEPHEN P. TURNER

Pareto, Vilfredo (1848–1923)

An Italian economist and sociologist, active also in Switzerland, his contributions to **sociology** fall into two components. The first consists in aspects of his outstanding work as an economic theorist which have a direct bearing on questions of **social policy** – for instance, a notion of "optimality" which still bears Pareto's name, or a statement of the narrow limits within which policies for redistributing **wealth** must operate. The second aspect largely coincides with his expressly sociological work, the massive *Trattato di Sociologia* (1916) which was translated as *The Mind and Society* (1935).

Pareto considered sociology a science complementary to economics. The latter deals with rational conduct oriented to the maximization of individual utility, while sociology deals with all other forms of conduct, where non-rational motivations and reasonings prevail. The *Trattato* transcended this negative understanding of the near totality of social experience by classifying the accounts of actions generally given by actors or observers. It distinguishes between the few fundamental, most recurrent accounts (the "residues") and their multiple, less significant variants (the "derivations").

The resulting classification is clumsy and unworkable; but the process of producing it yielded further significant results, particularly a theory of **elites**. These small **groups**, all distinguished from the masses by some outstanding quality and attainment, differ according to the respective weight in their makeup of two contrasting types of "residue" – those leading to "combinations" (the foxes) and those favoring "the persistence of aggregates" (the lions). This difference leads to competition between elites and their inevitable "circulation."   GIANFRANCO POGGI

Park, Robert Ezra (1864–1944)

Perhaps best known as the key figure of the **Chicago School** of sociology, Park led the University of Chicago sociology department from 1914 to 1934. Born in Harveyville, Pennsylvania, he studied under luminaries John Dewey (1859–1952) and, at Berlin, **Georg Simmel**, whom he introduced to American audiences. He also worked for twelve years as a journalist, experience that shaped his methodological penchant for scrupulously accurate reporting.

Park held a clear view of sociology as genuinely scientific, a view manifest in the classic text he co-authored with **Ernest W. Burgess**, *Introduction to the Science of Sociology* (1921). By directing his many students towards accurate reporting of events observed first-hand, he notably extended the use of ethnographic methods in early American sociology.

Park's major theoretical contributions include the notion of "self-conception" and how it relates to the organization of **social roles**; the idea of the "marginal man" – one who moves in plural social worlds, where he is nowhere at home; and clarification of the concept of the public and how it differs from the crowd.

Several areas of modern sociology owe a huge debt to Park. He pioneered the field of race relations, owing in good part to his earlier work with

Booker T. Washington (1856–1915) and his eye-opening accounts of Belgian atrocities in the Congo. His definition of the modern American urban setting as a natural laboratory formed a point of departure for the sprawling field of urban studies. Relatedly, his work on human ecology foregrounded the understanding that humans both compete for resources and are interdependent. Even so, he balanced a purely economistic view of urban **communities** by insisting that they are constituted by a moral as well as a spatial order.   DONALD N. LEVINE

Parsons, Talcott (1902–1979)

A leading social theorist of the twentieth century, Parsons's work is much criticized. However, his contribution to sociological thought is immense and has seen something of a revival since the mid-1990s. Parsons, while justly noted as a general theorist of **society**, also made influential contributions to particular areas of sociology, including medical sociology, the study of the self and the human condition, economic sociology, **family** and **socialization**, and the sociology of **religion**. These contributions attain a level of concreteness that contrasts with the high levels of analytical abstraction found in the general theory.

Born in the United States, Parsons studied in North America, Britain, and Germany, before taking up a position at Harvard. Deeply influenced by European sociology and social thought, Parsons may also be seen as a distinctly American contributor to the evolution of **social theory**, providing a new set of priorities and emphases within a tradition previously dominated by Europeans.

Parsons's overriding ambition was to provide a systematic general theory of the social. This meant the establishment of boundaries between the social and what lay beyond, as well as accounts of the most salient features of social life, embracing **culture, personality**, and **social structure**. Reflecting an early interest in biology, Parsons maintained an interest in the boundaries between social life and the biological organism, and between social life and the metaphysical world of ultimate **values**.

His first and possibly most important book, *The Structure of Social Action* (1937), argued that a general theory of social life could be constructed, taking into account the strengths of previous traditions, while remedying their weaknesses. The task was one of reconciling positivist thinking that saw action determined by external structures with idealist thinking that emphasized individual and interpersonal constructions of meaningful action. While the former emphasized analysis of the means by which objectives were pursued, the latter stressed the significance of the values or ends that were pursued. A general theory, for Parsons, should pursue patterned means–ends relationships, and sociology was par excellence the discipline equipped for the task. In contrast with current attempts of economics to colonize sociology via **rational choice theory**, Parsons saw economics with its utilitarian emphasis on choice of means, as a subfield within a broader social theory, able to analyze ends and their connection with means. For sociology, ends were endogenous not exogenous to social analysis.

The building of a general social theory that was neither exclusively materialist nor idealist was Parsons's major intellectual task, and in this he followed the multidimensionality of **Max Weber**, whose work he helped make widely known in the United States. Further key elements in the development of this theory include the pattern variables, and concepts of social **differentiation** linked with the so-called four-function **paradigm**. Parsons's pattern variables offer a striking set of conceptual dichotomies, between universalism and particularism, achievement and ascription, diffuseness and specificity, neutrality and affectivity, and lastly self-orientation and collectivity-orientation. The first term in each pair signified for Parsons a constitutive element in the nature of **modernity**. This involves a higher level of freedom of individual action from what went before, but set within a normative framework founded on generalized values, such as universalism and achievement. Modernity is therefore very far from a free-floating **individualism**, though Parsons's ostensibly universalistic account was strongly inflected with North American versions of the secularized individual vocation.

This pattern of modern variables was linked with the performance of a set of social functions, which Parsons believed were necessary for any social system to survive and develop. There were four of these, namely *adaptation* [A] (the securing of material resources available for distribution), which might be called the economic function; *goal-attainment* [G], akin to the political allocation of resources; *integration* [I], involving the development of a stable set of **norms**, as, for example, embodied in law; and *latent pattern-maintenance* [L], involving ordered patterns of value-commitment. For Parsons, all social systems, whether national, supranational, or subnational, can be analyzed in terms of functional differentiation into four subsystems corresponding to the AGIL

paradigm. The further task is then to explain interaction and integration between them through mechanisms of exchange such as **power** and **influence**.

This highly abstract and much-criticized theoretical edifice, widely referred to by others as structural **functionalism**, was developed via both theoretical commentary and analysis of empirical phenomena, as exemplified in *The Social System* (1951). Empirical themes included the development of the modern **professions** as exemplars of modern pattern-variables, and the emergence of the sick role as a normative regulator of sickness and health. The sick role draws on a distinction between feeling sick and being sick, the latter carrying social expectations including temporary withdrawal from normal **social roles**, a responsibility to work for recovery on the incumbent, and a duty to seek out appropriate professional advice, embodied in the neutral universalistic modern professional. This argument made a striking contribution to the development of an autonomous medical sociology distinct from the perspectives of the biomedical model.

Parsons's pattern variables and four-function paradigm also fed into his evolutionary approach to **social change**. Contrary to those who argue that Parsons had no adequate theory of change, his two books *Societies: Evolutionary and Comparative Perspectives* (1966) and *The System of Modern Societies* (1971) argued that certain human **institutions** such as **markets**, **democracy**, and the rule of law possessed an evolutionary advantage over alternative types of economy, polity, and **social integration**, in meeting social functions. This provided much of the intellectual grounding for modernization theory in the 1950s and 1960s.

Many critics of Parsons have attacked structural functionalism for a variety of reasons. Some of these are very wide of the mark, while some are damaging. The most misconceived criticisms impute to Parsons a structural **determinism** in which human agency is lost, while Parsons aimed at what he called an action-systems perspective in which norms and values are central. Other problematic criticisms include the idea that Parsons saw integrative values as the prime mover of social life, to the exclusion of material issues and conflicts of interest. While he opposed Hobbesian and Marxist accounts of society as a war between constellations of coercive power, he was mindful both of the centrality of economic functions to system survival, and of the existence of forms of **social stratification**, such as **racism**, that inhibited equality of opportunity.

More telling criticisms may be made of his assumption that the integration of social systems typically occurs through normative integration (that is, if it occurs at all). More specifically, he was criticized for making the following assumptions: that socialization processes are typically successful in binding individuals to the social order, that the nuclear family offered ideal solutions for women's domestic roles within it, and that **modernization** on the western model would unambiguously enhance the welfare of Third World populations. The advent of political and student unrest throughout the western world in the second half of the 1960s was but one of a number of instances of more fundamental value conflict that challenged Parsons's optimistic liberal world-views, requiring revisions and additions to his sociological position. One instance here is the idea of the expressive revolution, whereby new value orientations were seen as emerging around forms of countercultural expression, beyond the work ethic and family-centeredness.

Even so, Parsons's system remained incapable of providing accounts of coercive and discursive **power** functional to the self-interest of economic and social **groups** rather than to overall normative order. Similarly the emergence of a rich social history of social and political contestation has rendered Parsons's accounts of human agency unduly abstract and formulaic. What does remain intact is the breadth of his synthetic program for a unified social theory, a resource drawn on even by other thinkers of a more radical disposition such as **Jürgen Habermas**.   ROBERT HOLTON

participant observation

A technique used by adherents of interpretative methods in sociology in which the researcher participates in the practical activities of **institutions**, social **groups**, or **communities** in order to ground observations in naturally occurring practices. The method may vary according to the setting and the disposition of the observer. The observer may become a full participant in the practical action (for example Susan Krieger in *Mirror Dance: Identity in a Woman's Community*, 1983); or he/she may be unable to pass as a full participant (for example Elliott Liebow, in *Tally's Corner*, 1967).

The strength of the method is that participation allows the observer to examine social events at close hand, which can lead to additional sources of information such as informants, members of the group observed who are willing to disclose their understandings of the local practices. The weakness of the method is that the validity of the observations is limited to the setting studied, making it difficult to generalize in precise language. This problem can be ameliorated somewhat by **triangulation,** the technique of crosschecking observations in the local setting against **data** acquired by more formal methods including **surveys** and **demography**, such as in **William Julius Wilson**, *When Work Disappears* (1996).

Participant observation is widely used by academic sociologists, though at the beginning of the twenty-first century it became common to call it **ethnography**, which had long been in use by anthropologists. The method can also lead to a romantic attitude whereby the observers overstate the **realism** of their accounts of groups; see Patricia Clough, *The End(s) of Ethnography* (1991).

CHARLES LEMERT

paternalism

This term has two important meanings: the first is the set of informal expectations and codes of manners held by men about how to behave towards women, and the second is the assumption that the more powerful and the better-off in any society have obligations towards the less powerful and the poor. What unites these two assumptions is the idea that it is the responsibility of the more powerful to demonstrate concern for the less powerful, but without disturbing existing power relations or taking steps to ensure that those in weaker social positions are enabled to improve their situation. Paternalism is frequently associated with nineteenth- and twentieth-century attitudes towards the poor: paternalistic strategies advocated acts of individual charity to alleviate **poverty** while rejecting more radical attempts to provide social assistance that did not depend on acts of individual goodwill. In the latter part of the twentieth century, western **feminism** has identified paternalism as a masculine pattern of conduct that maintains male **power** and is essentially random and individualistic. At the same time, other critiques of paternalism have identified it as a set of expectations that are always organized around the presumption of the **authority** of the powerful (whatever the source of power) over the less powerful.   MARY EVANS

path analysis

This describes a class of **statistics** that aim to understand how a set of variables relate causally to each other. The analysis typically starts by sketching out a diagram consisting of variables joined by arrows to represent the researcher's conception of a particular system. The statistical analysis is then computed to evaluate the relative importance of each of those causal links, by assigning them a coefficient representing the strength of the relationship.

The computations of those paths can be done by simple multiple regression, but increasingly now it is done through a more advanced technique called "structural equation **modeling**" (SEM), that permits a more complex analysis of the **data** and the error that is inherent in the measurement of many sociological variables. By isolating the effects of this error, truer estimates of the size of the relationships between variables can be obtained.

In more conventional statistics, the focus is on using the data to develop a model. Path analysis reverses that order. One starts by carefully theorizing a model (or several models) that describes the links between variables in one's theoretical view of the world. Only after that theorizing has been done is the data then used to test how well it fits the model, or which of several models best fits the data.

Until the 1990s structural equation models were the preserve of the most mathematical social scientists. But more recently, the advent of user-friendly statistical software packages that perform structural equation modeling have made them commonplace in many areas of research.

BRENDAN J. BURCHELL

patriarchy

The concept of patriarchy is one which is widely used across a number of disciplines in both the **social sciences** and the humanities, even if the way in which the term is used differs between particular contexts (for example, **Karl Marx** and **Friedrich Engels** write about the "patriarchal" **family**, whereas literary critics might employ the term to indicate a bias towards the masculine). Whatever the discipline, however, the term always indicates the rule of men, not just over women but also over the general structure of social relations. The term is therefore about the **power** of men, a power which extends to the individual jurisdiction of men (or a man) over a family and its members, as well as the more general power of "the male" over the organization of a social **group** or a society.

The discussion of the term patriarchy, and its general use within social and political theory, can be traced to the seventeenth century. In 1680 Sir Robert Filmer's *Patriarchia. A Defence of the Natural Power of Kings against the Unnatural Liberty of the People* asserted the right of one man to rule the

many; an assertion challenged by John Locke (1632–1704) in *Two Treatises of Government*. The liberal tradition, of which Locke was a crucial founder, consistently challenged the assumption of the "natural," patriarchal, **rights** of the monarch. However, it was not until the nineteenth century that the discussion of the term was widened to include the context of gender relations. Engels, writing in 1884 in *The Origin of the Family, Private Property and the State* (1972) wrote of the defeat of "mother right" but also claimed that in monogamy and individual sexualized love (coupled with the entry of women into social production) lay the basis for the emancipation of women. For Engels, there were crucial relationships between the power of men in the private realm (the family) and in the **public sphere**, a connection which has been consistently important in mary of the social sciences. The emphasis on the loss of the power of the mother and the appearance of the father as the crucial authority figure in human social relations is drawn from the work of the German writer, Jacob Bachofen, who, in 1861, wrote of the historic struggle between the old order of matriarchy (the social **authority** of mothers) and the newer, emergent, authority of fathers in *Myth, Religion and Mother Right* (1861 [trans. 1967]). The struggle, Bachofen suggested, was articulated in Greek tragedies, for example Aeschylus' *Eumenides* in which Orestes murders his mother, Clytemnestra, in revenge for her murder of his father, Agamemnon. The Greeks were to be a later source of inspiration for **Sigmund Freud**, who drew on the story of Oedipus for his conjecture about the nature of psychic competition between father and son, a competition fueled by their mutual wish for primary access to, and control of, the mother. The power of the mother, as interpreted by Freud and others, was a power to attract men, and excite their wish to control, rather than an autonomous power which allowed authority over others.

The development of the social sciences in the nineteenth and twentieth century saw an emphasis on the study of different societies, in both historical and geographical terms. The term patriarchy became a crucial organizing concept for social anthropologists, whose discipline placed a particular emphasis on the study of **kinship** and kinship relations. By the second half of the twentieth century, anthropologists had generally concluded that the majority of human societies were explicitly patriarchal, in that authority, lineage, and descent were situated in men, the social function of women (as **Claude Lévi-Strauss** was to point out) being as objects of the exchange process which cemented and continued social relations and structures of power. Nevertheless, there were some societies (for example in regions of West Africa) where kinship was inherited through the mother. These societies, undeniably matriarchal in their patterns of inheritance, nevertheless invested other forms of social power in the mother's brother, ensuring that even in apparently matriarchal societies it would be wrong to conclude that social relations were represented and ordered as the reverse of patriarchy.

In the second half of the twentieth century the authority of patriarchy, and the patriarchal, has come to be contested in a number of ways. Patriarchy was identified by second-wave **feminism** as the conceptual apparatus, both symbolic and material, through which the social inferiority of women was maintained. In this re-thinking of the ways in which male power is both socially and psychically reproduced, **psychoanalysis**, post Freud, has questioned his emphasis on the part of the father in the life of the infant and the child. Although debates still continue about the meaning of the father, there is a general consensus that his authority cannot be understood without a more dialectical account of relations between women and men, mothers and fathers. This discussion provides the context for work on **language** and the recognition that it is saturated with assumptions about the relative power of women and men. These exchanges (involving figures such as **Jacques Lacan** and Monique Wittig) have informed the study of literature, just as the recognition of the almost universal authority of men has informed studies of the law (see **law and society**), work, the **body** and **politics**. For example, it was through the recognition of patriarchy as a crucial research term that feminist historians were able to demonstrate the ways in which patriarchy was a form of authority which crossed class and ethnic boundaries: as Barbara Taylor was to write in *Eve and the New Jerusalem* (1982), her study of gender and labor relations in Britain at the beginning of the nineteenth century, "the men are as bad as their masters." For many feminist historians and social scientists this comment reflected their own findings on the ways in which human society worked and represented itself: in a wide range of contexts and meanings it was the male, and the interests of men, which were given priority over those of women. At the same time it was also observed that the recognition, from the eighteenth century onwards, of the detailed biological differences of men and women made possible the

emergence of social understanding which did not understand women as, in biblical terms, "Adam's Rib." Many parts of the West have now attempted to produce "gender neutral" (and non-patriarchal) forms of social practice and regulation, although in other societies the patriarchal authority of men, endorsed by **religion**, remains dominant.

MARY EVANS

patrimonialism

This term is used to describe relationships that distribute **power** and **authority** within **organizations**. Usually referring to **Max Weber**'s use in *Economy and Society* (1922 [trans. 1968]), patrimonialism is a system of rule that is based upon personal–familial, rather than rational–legal relationships. Central to the notion of patrimonialism is that the leader of the organization distributes power and authority according to his or her wishes. At the same time, patrimonialism also refers to systems in which authority may be claimed, based upon birth right, heritage, or **tradition**. Patrimonialism derives from the Latin *patrimonium* that refers to a "paternal estate" and the model of the traditional patriarchal **family**, where a man, in a system of patrilineage, is the ruler of the household. As relationships with the patrimonial organizations are based upon personal patronage (or lack thereof), the exercise of power is highly informal, subjective, and open to change. In contrast, state **bureaucracies** in western democratic societies operate through the formal separation of public and private spheres. Such organizations insist on the primacy of rational or technical competency as legitimate sources of authority and **social status**. More recent work has blurred the neat distinction between the two forms of organization by suggesting a notion of neopatrimonialism. In these accounts, organizations (often implicitly or clandestinely) combine both rational–legal sources of authority and those of patrimonialism. An example of this might be where the head of a privately financed company nominates or promotes close friends or family members.

MAIRTIN MAC-AN-GHAILL AND CHRIS HAYWOOD

pattern variables

– see **Talcott Parsons**.

peace studies

Peace studies is an interdisciplinary academic enterprise that is the institutional outgrowth of various political and ideological programs of the global left in the 1960s. As an intellectual field, peace studies focuses on the development of nonviolent strategies for redressing interpersonal, institutional, national, and global conflicts. As such, peace studies represents a significant challenge to dominant perspectives in **social science** and philosophy, such as **realism**, elite-centered analyses of conflict, and just war theory. In contrast to such perspectives, peace studies stresses ideas such as pacifism, mercy, reconciliation, constructive engagement, and forgiveness, and has been primarily concerned with nuclear disarmament, the avoidance of international conflict (especially **war**), and redistributive efforts in the name of social **justice**. The field is characterized by a strong activist agenda: knowledge about various types of conflicts is seen as a means towards conflict resolution at all levels of social life. Peace studies is a utopian intellectual movement, characterized by a historicist and teleological view of **progress** defined as the absence of war, a preference for nonviolent means of conflict resolution, and the desire for more equitable distribution of economic resources. Much of the discourse of peace studies focuses on the critique of western political and cultural formations, to the detriment of understanding other systems of social, political, and cultural domination, such as communist **totalitarianism** (see **Communism**) and religious **fundamentalism**. While a widespread movement with many notable practitioners, the overtly ideological agenda of peace studies has made it difficult for the field to gain **legitimacy** as an intellectual endeavor in the contemporary academic environment.   TOM CUSHMAN

peasant society
– see **peasants**.

peasants
For centuries, peasants were the internal other of European society but also its "folk," lingering repositories of primitive innocence but also of superstition and dull **conservatism** in the midst of a progressive and enlightened **civilization**. In classical **social theory**, they are of central concern first to the Marxists, who from Marx onward had little confidence in their revolutionary potential. **Max Weber** addresses them most systematically in *The Agrarian Sociology of Ancient Civilizations* (1909 [trans. 1976]). They become the specific subjects of ethnographic research only in the 1920s and not in significant numbers until the later 1940s. Their politico-economic condition is the key to their typological distinctiveness. Thus, in *Peasants* (1966), Eric Wolf characterizes them as "rural cultivators whose surpluses are transferred to a dominant group of rulers that uses the surpluses both to underwrite its own standard of living and to distribute the remainder to groups in society that do not farm but must be fed for their specific goods and services in turn" (1966: 3–4). As A. V. Chayanov in *The Theory of the Peasant Economy* (1986) was the first to underscore, the peasant **economy** is further a family economy. Its labor units are households. Its goal is not profit but securing the survival of the household through the course of its yearly cycle. In *The Moral Economy of the Peasant* (1976), James Scott characterizes its attendant ethic accordingly as a "subsistence ethic." Wolf appropriately notes that subsistence itself demands more than the provision of a nutritional minimum over and above what must be expended as tribute or the rental of land. It further requires the production of a surplus sufficient to cover the expenditures of sociality and the ceremonial life, including those associated with such central **rites of passage** as **marriage** and **death and dying**.

Peasants are indeed noted for their religious devotion around the world, but also for a devotion that is often at odds with the churches to which they might belong. Their systems of belief tend to be syncretic, relatively informal, and practically oriented – popular heterodoxies at the fringes of the cultivated orthodoxy of a clerical or elite **tradition**. Such a tendency led Robert Redfield in *Peasant Society and Culture* (1956: 70) and elsewhere to press a broader distinction between the "little tradition" of the typical peasantry and the "great tradition" of "the philosopher, theologian, and literary man." The distinction is an appropriate register of stratification not merely of a political but also of a cultural order. Spatially, such stratification is often manifest as the distinction between the countryside and the **city**, but peasantries can and do exist in societies, such as that of early feudal Europe, having no urban centralization at all. Temporally, it is almost always manifest as what in *Vasilika* (1962) Ernestine Friedl describes as "cultural lag" (see **W. E. Ogburn**). In their beliefs and practices alike, peasantries reveal the **influence** of the great traditions that encompass them and frequently seek to emulate their stylistic and even intellectual standards. Distortions in the processes of cultural diffusion, however, leave them stylistically and intellectually behind or out-of-date, even in the age of effectively simultaneous media of transmission such as television.

That peasants are inclined to emulate the advanced cultural **fashions** with which they happen to come into contact suggests, after **Norbert**

Elias's and **Pierre Bourdieu**'s work, that they harbor certain **values** more similar to those of aspiring middle classes than those stereotypically ascribed to them. There are in any event no clear empirical grounds for declaring the destiny of peasants in developing or developed capitalist economies to point any less to embourgeoisement – at least the petite **embourgeoisement** – than to proletarianization. The egalitarian but sometimes proto-fascist **populism** of which peasants everywhere are putative carriers is similarly ambiguous. In part, these ambiguities reflect the often notable socioeconomic diversity of peasant populations, whose better-off and sometimes even rich members may find themselves in overt **social conflict** with their poorer relations. In another part, however, they inhere in what even charitable analysts judge to be a political sensibility that remains as personalistic and short-sighted as its economic counterpart. Peasants can and do rebel; as Wolf (1966: 107) and others have pointed out, and in further contrast to their stereotypical conservatism, they often heroize the rebel figure. What galvanizes them when they rebel, however, is rarely the unbroken domination and exploitation to which they are subject, but instead the unexpected imposition of some particularly onerous collective burden. What inspires them is rarely an articulate program of socioeconomic change, but instead a millenarian vision of imminent and total redemption. Norman Cohn in *The Pursuit of the Millennium* (1957) and Eric Hobsbawm in *Primitive Rebels* (1959) document the long European history of peasant millenarianism (see **religion**), and examples are readily available from elsewhere. Peasants so inspired have almost never furthered their practical interests. Most often, they have been brutally repressed.

Yet the destiny of the peasants of the future is probably neither redemption nor complete failure. It may rather be much the same as the destiny of the majority of the peasants of the past – to drift towards other socioeconomic positions, of greater or of lesser means and **prestige**, that only add to the ambiguities of the position from which they began. As Michael Kearney has argued in *Reconceptualizing the Peasantry* (1996), typologization can do more to obscure than to elucidate the frequency and the ubiquity with which peasants keep one foot in the household but another squarely planted in the **market**. It can also obscure the frequency and ubiquity with which petits bourgeois and proletarians do the same – and with the advent of consumption-driven and flexible **capitalism**, the higher reaches of the

middle classes seem in ever greater numbers to be joining them. The future may not thus bring the disappearance of the peasant; it may instead bring the peasantification of ever broader fractions of the market **society** as a whole.

JAMES D. FAUBION

pedagogical practices

The sociology of **education** took a specifically practical turn in the 1960s and 1970s in relating to the problems of the science of pedagogy – the science of the communication of knowledge content. Whereas the political sociologist Harold Dwight Lasswell (1902–78) had developed a theory of mass communication, arguing for distinct kinds of control, content, audience, and effect analyses, the work of **Marshall McLuhan** destroyed this neat categorization, claiming that the "medium is the message." The study of the transmission of knowledge raised questions about the a-priori status of curriculum content as well as about the status of **language** as a medium of transmission. These issues related to those highlighted by **poststructuralism**. The work of **Pierre Bourdieu** at this time focused more on the epistemological dimension of pedagogy, while the work of **Basil Bernstein** was part of the contemporary **linguistic turn** of analysis. These forms of sociological pedagogy defied the attempts made to absorb it into the science of **sociolinguistics** or, by **Jürgen Habermas**, to generate a theory of autonomous communicative action. The most systematic attempt to produce a sociological pedagogy was made by Bourdieu and J.-C. Passeron in *Reproduction in Education, Society and Culture* (1970 [trans.1977]). They defined pedagogic action (PA), pedagogic authority (PAu), pedagogic work (PW), school authority (SAu), educational system (ES), and the work of schooling (WSg), in order to present a framework within which the functioning of pedagogical practices can be understood, both within the confines of institutionalized education and in relation to more general processes of cultural communication within society.

DEREK ROBBINS

peer group

– see **group(s)**.

penology

This term is used to refer to theories of punishment, forms of punishment, and penal conditions. It refers to the systematic application of clinical, social scientific, or managerial expertise to the study and evaluation of penal measures, especially prisons.

The birth of the modern prison or penitentiary occurred in the eighteenth century. Prior to industrialization, life was cheap, and capital and corporal punishment predominated. The modern prison represented progress from a brutal and barbaric system of punishment to benevolent discipline. The social role of the prison has been of considerable interest to Marxist historians such as George Rusche and Otto Kirchheimer in *Punishment and Social Structure* (1939), to historian David Rothman in *The Discovery of the Asylum: Social Order and Disorder in the New Republic* (1971), and to philosopher/historian **Michel Foucault** in *Discipline and Punish: The Birth of the Prison* (1975 [trans. 1977]) among others. Certainly, it is thought that the prison might have an ideological function as well as representing **progress** from previous barbaric punishments.

The inception of modern penological thinking with questions such as "what is punishment for?" can be partially attributed to Christian reformers such as John Howard (1726–90) – who believed that punishment should be about the religious reformation of the offender and reflect humanitarian magnanimity – and utilitarian rationalist Jeremy Bentham (1748–1832), who thought that punishment should be directed more instrumentally at the refinement of techniques of behavioral control – hence his idea of the Panopticon: a circular architectural structure in which complete surveillance of the offender was possible. Thus, while Howard traveled the world denouncing poor prison conditions that would arguably militate against the reclamation of the offender's soul, Bentham was concerned with the formation of discipline via prison architecture as if surveillance would lead to order within and without prisons. Bentham's thinking went beyond this, however, and he promulgated consequentialist theories of punishment.

Consequentialist theories of punishment are essentially those that justify punishment by making claims about the desirability of its future consequences. These theories are sometimes known as reductivist, because they claim that the incidence of crime will be less than it would be if no penalty were imposed. Bentham's "felicific calculus" is thus that punishment of the individual is justified if it can be shown that the good derived thereby outweighs the pain. Such consequentialist theories include those of general deterrence, individual deterrence and incapacitation, and rehabilitation. Nonconsequential theories of punishment revolve around retribution and desert theory. The idea of retribution derives historically from the Roman concept of *lex talionis*, illustrated by the biblical phrase "Wherever hurt is done, you shall give life for life, eye for eye, tooth for tooth, hand for hand, foot for foot, burn for burn, bruise for bruise, wound for wound" (Exodus 21: 23–5). Classical desert theory was predicated upon the assumption that offenders are rational, autonomous individuals who, having made the decision to offend, "deserved" punishment for their wrongdoing. Modern desert theorists focus on notions of proportionality in sentencing according to the seriousness of the crime, and on desert theory as a communicative device for censuring wrongful behavior in such a way that it permits the offender to rejoin the moral consensus.

For much of the twentieth century, penological projects focused on the monitoring of sentencing and the manipulation of penal regimes both within and outside custodial settings. Optimism that penal interventions could work were at their highest in the 1960s (the so-called rehabilitative ideal), but this was short-lived because systematic analysis of the effects of such interventions led to the sobering conclusion that "nothing works." Since the mid-1990s there has been a resurgent international interest in "what works?" Research findings from meta-analytical studies have prompted the development of a panoply of institutional and community-based programs based on cognitive-behavioral ideas. The findings from these studies, however, are not encouraging and early 21st-century penological thinking indicates moves away from such programs towards **education and training** for offenders.

LORAINE GELSTHORPE

personality

The study of personality builds on the everyday recognition that people around us are different in their social behavior, and seem to be disposed to react in particular ways. It seeks to characterize in a rigorous way the basis of that difference by identifying characteristic patterns of behavior that are distinctive and consistent across time. Some accounts of personality try to use these characterizations as a basis for predicting future behavior by establishing lawlike generalizations about factors that underpin variation in all people. These accounts, sometimes referred to as nomothetic statements, adhere to a scientific model of inquiry which sees the testing of predictions, ideally in an experimental setting, as the best way to establish a secure understanding. They are part of a tradition in psychology that focuses on individual differences, for example **intelligence**. Other accounts, sometimes referred to as idiographic accounts, focus on the individual in depth and pursue an understanding of that individual using a variety of interpretive or phenomenological approaches.

Many nomothetic theories have antecedents in classical descriptions, and many can ultimately be linked to Hippocrates (470–410 BC) who defined the four humors: yellow bile, black bile, phlegm, and blood. This system had two dimensions (hot and cold, and dry and wet) on which all people could be placed, with different individuals being characteristically hotter or colder, and wetter or drier. These terms still exist in everyday speech as choleric, melancholic, phlegmatic, and sanguine, but in personality theories the humors are now referred to as "traits." Five traits (extraversion, neuroticism, agreeableness, conscientiousness, and openness) are widely accepted as defining the essential descriptive framework that best captures individual variation. Idiographic theories have often drawn on the same tradition, but in the modern era are much more closely associated with clinical work and individual psychotherapy. The clinic is where many of them were first developed, and the best known is **Sigmund Freud**'s work on **psychoanalysis**.

The personality literature is very diverse in terms of its theoretical and methodological assumptions, and most of the critical debates from across the **social sciences** are to be found here. One important critical line that intervenes in these debates concerns how much of the individual's behavior is to be understood in terms of personality. At one time, grand claims were made for the range and types of behavior that personality theories could explain, but now personality theorists are more circumspect, and recognize the significance of other social characteristics such as **age, gender**, and **race and ethnicity**, or other personal determinants of behavior, such as **attitude**.

Apart from the application of idiographic accounts in psychotherapy, personality theories from the nomothetic tradition are of interest and value to those selecting people for different roles in **organizations** and teams, or advising individuals on career choices. Personality tests such as the Myers–Briggs test, which identifies four dimensions akin to the five traits mentioned above, is typical in this regard, and in over sixty years of use and development it has a reasonable degree of reliability and validity in many eyes.

DAVID GOOD

petite bourgeoisie
– see **social class**.

phenomenology
A philosophical school, which gained prominence in the course of the twentieth century, etymologically speaking, phenomenology refers to the study of phenomena or of how the phenomena appear to the individual. It investigates the structure of various forms of experiences and assumes that this analysis provides a better foundation for philosophy than, for instance, **epistemology** or metaphysics. Amongst phenomenological philosophers, Edmund Husserl (1859–1938), Martin Heidegger (1889–1976), and **Maurice Merleau-Ponty** are particularly well known. Some hermeneutic philosophers like **Hans-Georg Gadamer** and Paul Ricoeur (1913–2005) partly draw on the phenomenological tradition. Existentialist philosophers like Jean-Paul Sartre (1905–80) and Karl Jaspers (1883–1969) also rely on insights from phenomenology. Phenomenology had a significant impact on **sociology**, especially through the work of **Alfred Schutz**. Phenomenological sociology is a particular version of interpretative sociology. It shows affinities with other types of interpretative sociology such as **ethnomethodology** (which was strongly influenced by phenomenology), **symbolic interactionism**, and **hermeneutics**. Phenomenology also influenced the writings of **Peter L. Berger, Harold Garfinkel, Georges Gurvitch, Thomas Luckmann**, and Maurice Natanson. Phenomenological sociology pays attention to the ways in which people make sense of social reality and act accordingly. It tends to oppose neo-positivist appeals for a unity of method between the social and the natural: contrary to the natural, the social is already "pre-interpreted," and this begs for an interpretative **methodology**. In American sociology, phenomenological sociology emerged in the 1960s in opposition to the dominant orthodoxy of structural **functionalism**.

The aim of Husserl's phenomenology was to capture the universal structures of people's subjective orientation towards their external **environment**. Schutz was a student of Husserl and very much influenced by him. Where Husserl's preoccupation was purely philosophical, Schutz on the other hand explored the sociological relevance of phenomenology. **Max Weber** and **George Herbert Mead** also impacted on Schutz's thought. In *The Phenomenology of the Social World* (1967) and in his *Collected Papers* (1962–6), Schutz was particularly interested in the way in which individuals use interpretative schemes to make sense of their everyday surroundings. This "stock of knowledge" enables them to attribute meaning to what others say or do. People are not normally aware of the stock of knowledge they employ; it is part of tacit knowledge. In this context, Schutz talked about everyday **rationality** as opposed to scientific rationality. Whereas scientific rationality is characterized by theoretical knowledge and systematic doubt, everyday rationality draws on practical knowledge and suspension of disbelief. Schutz's phenomenology paves the way for a sociological inquiry into how people attribute meanings to their surroundings. Influenced by Schutz and Sartre, Berger and Luckmann's *The Social Construction of Reality; A Treatise in the Sociology of Knowledge* (1967) focused on how everyday conceptions of reality are constructed and maintained.

Harold Garfinkel and **Aaron Cicourel**'s ethnomethodology drew on Schutz's writings, but unlike Schutz – who remained a pure theorist – their research was empirical. In *Studies in Ethnomethodology* (1967) Garfinkel investigated the interpretative procedures that people employ to make sense of their social environment. In a number of experiments, Garfinkel and his team also studied what happened when these encounters do not square with people's expectations. In those situations, they discovered that people did not question their presuppositions. Rather, individuals drew on their presuppositions to make sense of their surroundings, and they did so in ways that maintained or reinforced those very presuppositions. Garfinkel called this the "documentary method of interpretation."

For a long time phenomenology remained on the margins of sociology, because its premises were in opposition to the reigning orthodoxy. Phenomenology contradicted **Émile Durkheim**'s guidelines in his *Rules of Sociological Method* (1895 [trans. 1958]), notably his dictum that social facts need to be treated as "things." In the 1970s sociologists became interested in phenomenology, partly through the writings of **Anthony Giddens** and **Pierre Bourdieu**. Ironically, this interest went hand in hand with a growing recognition that this philosophical tradition was one-sided. Phenomenology focused too much on how individuals make sense of the world, and it ignored the constraining and external nature of **social structures**. Sociologists became preoccupied with bridging the gap between phenomenological approaches and **structuralism**, taking insights from both. In *The Constitution of Society; Outline of the Theory of Structuration* (1984), Giddens proposed a structuration theory, which investigated how people draw on tacit, practical knowledge in their **everyday**

life, and, in so doing, contribute to the reproduction of society. Likewise, Pierre Bourdieu's *Outline of a Theory of Practice* (1972 [trans. 1977]) attempts to transcend the opposition between "subjectivism" (phenomenological approaches) and "objectivism" (structuralist approaches). Bourdieu's notions of **habitus** and hexis rely on phenomenology. The habitus is a set of "dispositions" that allow for the perception and account of the world in a particular way. The hexis points at the bodily aspects of the habitus. In Bourdieu's writings, however, the habitus is linked to broader structural concerns and to the reproduction of **inequality**.

More recently, sociologists have been drawn to Merleau-Ponty's phenomenology at the expense of Schutz's, especially Merleau-Ponty's *The Phenomenology of Perception* (1945 [trans. 1962]). In this work, Merleau-Ponty paid attention to the role of the **body** in perception. His notion of the "phenomenal body" (in opposition to the "objective" body) undermined the objectivism at the core of the natural sciences. Although in some respects close to Sartre, the closing chapters of *The Phenomenology of Perception* include strong criticisms of Jean-Paul Sartre's ideas. The increasing interest in the body explains why sociologists have recently been drawn to Merleau-Ponty's work. Bryan Turner's *Sociology of the Body* (1984) was one of the first books to point out the relevance of Merleau-Ponty for sociological purposes.   PATRICK BAERT

Phillips curve

In A. W. Phillips's famous article "The Relationship between Unemployment and the Rate of Money Wages in the UK 1861–1957," in *Economica*, he argued that when the unemployment rate was low, the **labor market** was tight and employers had to offer higher wages to attract scarce **labor**. At higher rates of **unemployment**, there was less pressure to increase wages. When the **economy** was expanding, **firms** would raise wages faster than "normal" for a given level of unemployment; when the economy was contracting, they would raise wages more slowly.

Policymakers used the Phillips curve to determine economic policy. For example, if unemployment increased, the government might stimulate the economy to lower it. Monetarist economists challenged the theory by arguing that only real wages mattered: the inflation-adjusted purchasing **power** of money wages. Thus, the more quickly worker expectations of price **inflation** adapt to changes in the actual rate of inflation, the less successful governments will be in reducing unemployment through monetary and fiscal policy.

There are more fundamental objections: the meanings of both unemployment and inflation are not constant over time. The former is measured by the definition of what being employed constitutes: in Australia today, for instance, if employees are employed for more than one hour a week, they are classified as "employed," and thus the unemployment rate can be represented as 5.3 percent. If the measures used to define unemployment twenty years ago were still used, it would be closer to 15 percent. Similarly, inflation is constructed from an index that measures the price of a bundle of commodities. As these items are changed, or their weights change, then what is being measured ceases to be constant. The measures are socially constructed.   STEWART CLEGG

philosophy of the social sciences

Philosophy of the social sciences is a meta-theoretical reflection on the workings of the **social sciences**. Some philosophers of social science prescribe guidelines for social researchers, for instance about how to make research scientific or how to make it a proper critique. Some philosophers focus on other issues, for instance, the relationship between **values** and facts or the validity of particular theoretical frameworks.

Initially, sociology had strong links with a positivist philosophy of social science. **Positivism** assumed a unity of method between the social and natural sciences. If the social sciences employ the method of the natural sciences, then they will uncover scientific laws or law-like generalizations. In addition, some positivist authors argued that we should keep a clear separation between facts and values (one cannot be inferred from the other) and between theory and observation (observations ought to be theory-independent). Since the mid twentieth century, various schools within the philosophy of the social sciences have developed in reaction to positivism.

Karl Popper introduced falsificationism or critical rationalism. According to this view, scientific theories are falsifiable rather than verifiable. That is, they can, in principle, be refuted. Various psychological and sociological theories purport to be scientific but are not, because they are immunized against refutation. For example, Alfred Adler (1870–1937), **Sigmund Freud**, and **Karl Marx** present non-falsifiable theories.

Influenced by **hermeneutics** (see, for instance, Charles Taylor) or **Ludwig Wittgenstein** (see, for instance, Peter Winch), some anti-naturalist authors stress the differences between the study of the social and that of the natural. According to

this view, there are no significant laws or law-like generalizations in the social realm.

Critical **realism** rejects the positivist "regularity" notion of causality, according to which the regular observation that "X is followed by Y" is both sufficient and necessary for saying that X causes Y. Critical realists argue that both natural and social sciences try to uncover the underlying structures or **powers** that affect the observable level. These structures or powers are not necessarily immediately accessible to observation.

Critical theory disagrees with the view that social research is a purely descriptive or explanatory endeavor. Critical theorists like **Theodor Wiesengrund Adorno**, **Max Horkheimer**, or **Jürgen Habermas** contend that social research should also aim at a critical assessment, possibly leading to self-emancipation. This calls attention to the question of what criteria or procedures can be used in order to arrive at a judgment. Habermas believes that the notion of an open, unconstrained debate provides the key to answering this question.

Pragmatism argues against foundationalism (any attempt to find atemporal foundations of reliable knowledge) and against the spectator theory of knowledge (any view that sees knowledge as representing the inner nature of the external world). Instead, pragmatists prefer to see knowledge as active and tied to cognitive interests. Habermas's critical theory relies heavily on Charles Peirce's pragmatism. For Habermas, different types of knowledge accomplish different goals. Empirical-analytical knowledge aims at prediction and control, hermeneutics is directed towards understanding, and critical theory combines both to achieve self-emancipation.

PATRICK BAERT

pilot study

Just as naval pilots guide larger vessels safely into port, so too are pilot studies intended to secure the passage of research projects from a tentative and questioning approach to the issue in question, to a secure berth as a substantive contribution to knowledge in sociology. As such, pilot studies are often designed to act as either small-scale replicas of a much larger research project and/or to act as a "test bed" upon which potentially problematic methodological or procedural issues can be tried out and resolved. The size of any pilot study will be variable, and determined by the nature of the research **methodology** being used. Some pilot studies may thus be much larger than full-scale studies using tried and tested instruments.

For example, if a study in a new area of enquiry wished to examine the relationship between, say, religious affiliation and car-buying intentions, **questionnaires** may be designed to effect the **measurement** of both variables via a representative **sampling** of the wider population to which inferences are to be drawn. A pilot study, using a small (possibly even a convenience) sample, may then be used to trial the newly minted questionnaires to ensure that items are not infelicitously phrased, ambiguous, or incomprehensible to research respondents. Should problems be identified at this stage of the research process (via debriefing of interviewers, for example), steps may be taken to rewrite or otherwise disambiguate the measures in question prior to the execution of the full-scale study. It is not unknown for *second* pilot studies to be required to confirm the successful rectification of methodological, study, and measure design difficulties.

MARK RAPLEY AND SUSAN HANSEN

plural society

This concept refers to a **society** that respects differences. In one sense, all societies are plural since it is impossible for individuals to relate to one another unless they have differences that each respects. But a plural society is one in which these differences are explicitly and consciously accepted, and they are seen as a strength rather than a weakness.

But differences generate conflict and these conflicts have to be resolved. A plural society is not therefore a society without conflict, but a society in which conflicts can be managed, rather than suppressed, in which compromise and conciliation prevail over the use of force and **violence**. Should conflicts be violent, then the case is likely to be made for a strong **state** able to employ counterforce, so that instead of a plural society we have an authoritarian one in which differences are seen as disloyal and problematic.

In an increasingly globalized world, societies are becoming more and more obviously plural as people from different **cultures** and language groups come together in large, heterogeneous **communities**. However, it would be naive to imagine that differences can be respected unless there is toleration and accommodation. People need to have common **values** if differences are to strengthen a society, and not cause it to break down and divide.

Living within a society has to be both a unifying and diversifying experience. Without conscious plurality, society becomes suffocating, but without mechanisms for accommodation, a society ceases to exist.

JOHN HOFFMAN

pluralism

Arguments about the virtues or otherwise of pluralism span from the works of ancient philosophers to recent times. It stands as a protest against "monism" or one-ness, and emphasizes that difference and multiplicity must be taken seriously.

In its more recent social science form, pluralism is identified with the argument that, in a liberal **democracy**, interests are diverse so that, although some groups may (say) be wealthier than others, it is wrong to regard one factor as ultimately predominant since other groups may enjoy popularity or represent large numbers of people. This doctrine became discredited in the late 1960s and during the 1970s. The notion that in liberal societies different **groups** "balanced" themselves out was considered to be propagandistic and inaccurate. A pluralist view of **politics** and society excluded the idea that, in the liberal form, a particular interest might prevail in the form of an **elite** or ruling class.

More recently, critiques of the liberal pluralism of the 1960s have themselves been criticized on the grounds that an emphasis upon underlying structures that unify society generates dogmatism, exclusivity, and **authoritarianism**. Feminists, for example, argued that society consisted of two sexes, not just one, and that liberal (and left-wing) notions of the individual and humanity viewed the world through the lenses of men. Some feminists (the "radicals") turned **liberalism** inside out and argued for the primacy of women and their outlook, and argued that women need to keep aloof from men. But why should plurality "stop" with the acknowledgment that individuals can be either male or female?

The postmodernist argument enshrines pluralism as its key **value**. People can identify themselves only through their difference from others, so that it becomes invidious to privilege one difference over others. Postmodern **feminism** argues that not only are women different from men, but they are different from one another. An infinite range of other factors need to be taken into account – a person's **social class**, **religion**, **language**, **culture**, and region. Traditional concepts like the **state** and conventional religion, and thought systems like **Marxism** and liberalism, are challenged since they appear to ascribe primacy to one particular factor over all others. The search for the Truth or the belief in Reason are dogmatic and authoritarian postures that must be challenged and rejected.

The problem with pluralism is that it can operate its own system of "privileging." The danger with a dogmatic pluralism is that differences themselves are seen as more important than similarities. All forms of unity become dissolved into differences, and these differences lack anything to hold them together. If women differ among themselves, does this mean that feminism itself is impossible since the whole notion of "women" has been dethroned? If individuals are plural and each individual may have numerous **identities**, does this mean that individuals no longer exist, so that the concept of the subject becomes redundant?

Pluralism can only be sustained as an outlook and approach if it operates alongside, and not to the exclusion of, a monist stress upon sameness.

JOHN HOFFMAN

pluralization

This involves an ethos of deep diversity, as in, for example William E. Connolly, *The Ethos of Pluralization* (1995). While **pluralism** can be seen as either accommodation and tolerance of differences or distribution of **power** among competing interest **groups**, pluralization is an ethos to deepen and multiply differences that involves a refusal to flatten them under any kind of pretense or goal: unity, common ground, or union. The concept of pluralization emerged out of a discontent with various forms of **politics** of recognition that either essentialized **identities** (**multiculturalism**, integration, **assimilation**) or imagined their boundless proliferation (tolerance, accommodation). By contrast, pluralization aspires to recognize the depth and multiplicity of differences while recognizing the necessity for crossing them, for example, Paul A. B. Clarke, *Deep Citizenship* (1996). As such, it remains as a research and activist ethos rather than a celebrated policy or avowed politics.

ENGIN ISIN

Polanyi, Karl (1886–1964)

Born in Vienna and brought up in Budapest, as a student Polanyi knew **Georg Lukács** and **Karl Mannheim** and became acquainted with the works of **Karl Marx**, **Max Weber**, and **Georg Simmel**. While he did not, strictly speaking, profess sociology, these **influences** and those of **Émile Durkheim** are to be found in his major work, *The Great Transformation: The Political and Economic Origins of Our Time* (1944), which was started during his stay in England in the 1930s and finished after emigration to the United States.

He sought to explain the breakdown of nineteenth-century liberal **capitalism** which led to the turmoil of the 1920s and 1930s. In a critique of orthodox economic theory, he argued first that its analysis did not apply to all forms of **economy**, and, second, that the **market** was not self-regulating. Before market capitalism, economic exchange had been embedded in **social structures** regulated by **norms** of either "reciprocity" and/or "redistribution." The determination of economic exchange exclusively by market price destabilized social and political order; and the fundamental economic "factors" – land, **labor**, and money-capital – were, in fact, "fictitious commodities." The free market in land created environmental degradation; in labor, human misery; and in **money**, **inflation** and financial crises. This led to a "double movement" in capitalism between, on the one hand, **states'** creation of these socially and politically "disembedded" markets and, on the other, the efforts to regulate their worst effects. Thus, by the end of the 1930s, there was a swing towards regulation in all sectors of the economy and the beginnings of the modern **welfare state**. Polanyi's critique of the self-regulating market has experienced a revival following the economic liberalization and **globalization** of the late twentieth century.

Other important works by Polanyi are, with Conrad Arensberg and Harry Pearson, *Trade and Market in the Early Empires* (1957), and the posthumous *The Livelihood of Man* (1977).

GEOFFREY INGHAM

political economy

Classical political economy emerged as a distinct field of scholarship and policy-oriented analysis during the eighteenth century, in rough parallel with the development of a distinct sphere of profit-oriented, market-mediated economic activities that was nonetheless seen as dependent on a wider nexus of legal, political, social, and moral conditions. In contrast with the later discipline of neoclassical economics, which studies such activities in isolation, classical political economy was a predisciplinary field of inquiry insofar as it tried to put the emerging capitalist **economy** in its wider social context. Adam Smith (1723–90) is exemplary here, writing not only *An Inquiry into the Nature and Causes of the Wealth of Nations* (1776) but also *A Theory of Moral Sentiments* (1759) and studies of jurisprudence, **politics**, logic, and **language**. Other key figures in this tradition are David Malthus (1766–1834), and David Ricardo (1772–1823) whose work *On the Principles of Political Economy and Taxation* (1817) made him its leading figure.

Classical political economy is linked to the rise of a commercial and industrial bourgeoisie that sought to challenge the economic, political, and ideological domination of **feudalism** and the absolutist **state**. It is part of the more general European **Enlightenment**. A parallel tradition in Germany, which was an economic laggard, was more oriented to the political dimension of the emerging system of political economy – reflected in the *Polizeiwissenschaften* ("police" or policy sciences) that were concerned with good economic, political, and moral government on behalf of the population of a given state.

Following the rolling back of feudalism and the consolidation of **capitalism**, the rise of organized working-class resistance, and the recurrence of capitalist crises, classical political economy was slowly displaced by vulgar political economy. This downplayed the class relations between capital and **labor** and the origins of **value** in the **labor process**, began to focus on the efficient allocation of scarce factors of production to competing uses, and sought the causes of economic crisis in factors external to the nature and dynamic of capitalism itself.

Although their work is often mentioned as a key part of the tradition of political economy, **Karl Marx** and **Friedrich Engels** developed an explicit critique of classical and vulgar political economy both as scholarship and as the basis of economic policy and practice. They elaborated an alternative account of the capitalist mode of production based on radically different philosophical assumptions and a political commitment to the proletariat rather than the bourgeoisie. Thus a significant part of their studies was concerned to critique the economic categories and analyses of orthodox political economy. Two major examples are Marx's *Economic and Philosophical Manuscripts* (1844 [trans. 1964]) and the three-volume *Theories of Surplus Value* (1861–3 [trans. 1963]). They also built on this critique to provide an alternative account of the capitalist mode of production, its social foundations, its dynamic, and its crisis tendencies. Marx's *Contribution to the Critique of Political Economy* (1859), the *Grundrisse* (1857 [trans. 1973]), and the incomplete analysis in the three volumes of *Capital* (1867, 1885, 1894 [trans. 1970]) are his best-known work here. Their guiding theme is that capital is not a thing (a simple, transhistorical factor of production) but a social relation that is a historically specific class relation between persons, mediated through the instrumentality of things.

Marx argued that the best starting point for such a critique was to ask why **wealth** in societies where the capitalist mode of production is dominant presents itself as an immense accumulation of commodities. He regarded the commodity as the "cell form" of capitalism and, on this basis, unfolded the key contradictions of capital as a social relation. He defined the historical specificity of capitalism in terms of the generalization of the commodity form to labor power, arguing that the nature and dynamic of capitalism were rooted in the inhuman treatment of labor power as if it were a commodity. Capitalism is the first mode of production based on the existence of formally free wage-labor and a **labor market** in which workers sell their labor power in a formally free and equal commercial transaction to the owners of the means of production, who in turn need this labor to set the labor process into motion. The resulting goods and services belong initially to the capitalists for whom the proletariat works, who are therefore free to sell these commodities in the marketplace. Beneath the surface appearance of free and equal market exchange, however, lay a despotic world of production in which capital sought to maximize the production of surplus labor as the basis for economic exploitation and the accumulation of capital.

Marxism became a crucial reference point for the subsequent development of radical, heterodox, and more orthodox forms of evolutionary and institutional political economy. This trend is sometimes signified in the idea that authors such as **Max Weber**, **Werner Sombart**, **Joseph Schumpeter**, and **Karl Polanyi** engaged in a debate with the "ghost of Marx." Evolutionary political economy holds that time matters: there can be no valid transhistorical analysis of economic activities because the nature of economic **institutions** and conduct, the sites and stakes of economic conflict, and the scope for economic change depend on their prior developmental trajectory. And institutional political economy argues that institutions matter: there can be no pure, isolated economic calculation and conduct because these are always shaped by specific economic institutions and market relations and their embedding in a complex extra-economic environment. It is on this basis that political economy has not only studied the development of different forms of economic **organization** but has also identified a number of more or less distinct varieties of capitalism.

Vulgar political economy was the basis for neoclassical economics. This tries to develop a universal, transhistorical analysis of economic activities based on a general model of rational economic calculation about the most efficient allocation of scarce resources (factors of production) to competing ends. Neoclassical economics is associated with "economics imperialism," that is, the extension of economic analysis to social spheres that are not dominated by profit-oriented, market-mediated economic activities but are nonetheless marked, it is claimed, by individual utility maximization within defined rules of the game. The extension of this model is the basis for rational choice institutionalism, theories of constitutional design and **public policy**, and a new form of political economy.   BOB JESSOP

political parties

A political party is an association of like-minded individuals that seeks to gain **power** in a **community** (usually a **state**) in order to promote its chosen social order. As a social **organization**, a political party has two main functions: interest articulation and interest formation. Interest articulation is simply the process of bringing together within a single organization all the members of a community who share relatively similar political views on an issue or set of issues, and to voice this position in such a way that existing political **institutions** heed it. Interest formation is the process by which a party is able to shape and influence the political views of the members of the community at large. This dual function that political parties perform creates internal tensions that are solved in different ways according to the political and organizational outlook of the parties. At the interest articulation end of this spectrum, populist parties behave in a demagogic way and shape their political discourse and program of governance primarily according to what is popular in the community at any one time. At the interest formation end, by contrast, authoritarian party systems claim that the party's primary function is to teach the population how to behave in a politically enlightened way. In between are competitive party systems, such as the ones present in most contemporary electoral **democracies**, where this tension is resolved through compromise.

In modern electoral systems, the **legitimacy** of the government rests principally on political parties. However, party **politics** acquired a bad reputation as it came to represent the (sometimes violent, sometimes petty) struggle between different factions vying for power. During the period of formation of modern democracies, key thinkers and politicians such as James Madison (1751–1836)

and **Alexis de Tocqueville** saw this factionalism as one of the main drawbacks of the new era of democratic politics. From outside the political establishment, **Karl Marx** took an equally dim view of the (bourgeois) political parties that dominated the scene in his days. In *The Eighteenth Brumaire of Louis Napoleon* (1852 [trans. 1934]), he equated them with propaganda tools that the ruling class used against the proletariat to give the latter the illusion of participation, while entrenching their own interests. Marx's followers on the Leninist side would take this characterization of party politics as the starting point for their construction of the one-party political model that came to symbolize socialist and communist states in the twentieth century. In pluralist political systems, however, political parties have become the most common form of social mobilization for participation in politics. As **Max Weber** pointed out in "Politics as Vocation" (1919 [trans. 1994]), with the bureaucratization of the state and the growth of mass politics, political associations had to manage more effectively the drawbacks of electoral competition, and the professionalization of their party machinery was an effective means of ensuring the survival of the organization over time. Today, therefore, the vast majority of politicians are professional politicians, paid by states (if elected) or parties to fulfill their role.

In modern multiparty systems, the most common distinction between parties is that between left and right. Historically, this terminology referred to the physical location of the parliamentary groups in the French Assembly after the revolution of 1789. Those on the right side of the assembly represented principally the interests of the nobility, while those on the left side of the assembly represented the bourgeoisie and the Third Estate. The right tended therefore to be more conservative and the left more reformist. This left–right distinction was compounded throughout the nineteenth century by the industrial revolution. In effect, the right came to represent principally the interests of the upper classes (the former aristocracy) as well as those of an increasingly wealthier section of the middle classes (the petite bourgeoisie), while the left represented the former Third Estate, which became the working class. Throughout most of the twentieth century, this left–right opposition dominated pluralist political systems, be they based on a two-party model or a multiparty one. In the late twentieth century, however, with the apparent weakening of class distinctions, this left–right configuration began to lose its sharpness. At the same time, helped by the drop in electoral participation in most advanced industrial democracies, single-issue parties as well as new political movements (for example green parties) began to reshape the parameters of party politics.

The level of predictability that multipartyism gave, to electoral democracies particularly, proved wrong many of the earlier assumptions about the negative influence of party politics on political stability. Although the debate about the pros and cons of party politics is still alive in many developing countries, the arguments put forward by Robert Dahl (1915–) in *A Preface to Democratic Theory* (1956) and in *Polyarchy* (1971), concerning the stabilizing influence of political parties, remain powerful explanations of this phenomenon today. According to Dahl, what political parties provide is a multitude of powerful minorities that ensure that pressure is applied to the faction in government to take into account the interests of many different social **groups** in **society**. In order to rule effectively, parties in government find it practical to reach out to some of the opposition factions and to create as wide a consensus on their policies as possible. Besides directly entering ruling coalitions, what political parties (and the bargaining process in which they repeatedly enter) create is a cohesive political **culture** that underpins the formal institutions of the polity and strengthens a consensual model of political rule. This phenomenon is most obvious in mature party systems with a strong tradition of **pluralism**. In developing countries, as granting the franchise to vote to the population at large is often a recent development, the competition between mass parties and cadre parties (which do not rely on mass support but simply represent a political front for groups of powerful interests), remains a source of instability.   FREDERIC VOLPI

politics

This term refers to the process of organizing social **power** in a **community**. Politics takes place at various levels of social **interaction**, from the microlevel – the politics of **friendship**, family politics, and so on – to the macro-level (international politics and global politics). Most commonly, within its broad field of application, politics is concerned with the activities of human beings, as Aristotle's (384–322 BC) description of human beings as political animals (*zoon politikon*) indicates. However, in the late twentieth century, biologists and specialists in animal behavior – particularly primatologists – have argued that non-human animals living in complex **societies** could also be described

as having political activities. Aristotle's *The Politics* (*c.* 350 BC) introduced the terms politic into our vocabulary from the word *politikos* meaning "of, or pertaining to, the *polis*" (city-state). For Aristotle, the object of politics was the good of the community and social order embodied in the *polis*. As a practical activity, it was therefore prescriptive in nature. And the role of the politicians, whom Aristotle likened to craftsmen, was to ensure the good functioning of the polity in order to allow the community to reach its normative goals. The task of those involved in politics was, and remains, to establish and implement laws and rules of government that promote the good of the community (though not necessarily or systematically that of each single individual within it).

Because politics is concerned with harnessing the social forces of a polity into an effective **organization**, those models of **collective action** that can achieve this feat on a large scale have traditionally been highly valued. The highest organizational units for politics have varied significantly over time, from small city-states to large empires. In the contemporary context, however, the most complex form of institutionalized political order is the nation-state. Today, we may be witnessing the emergence of an international community (for example the United Nations) and of powerful supranational regional organizations (for example the European Union) but the ability of these **institutions** to dictate the rules of the political game remains tied to the behavior of the states that compose them. Because of the enormous power that the state can muster, its political institutions have always received a high degree of attention. In this respect, politics is tightly connected to the science (or art) of government. It is this art that all the great political thinkers have tried to describe in new and ingenious ways over time.

Probably the foremost question that political thinkers have traditionally been asking regarding the politics of government is whether a rule ought to be moral in order to be effective. Classical Greek philosophers like Plato in *The Republic* (*c.* 360 BC) or Aristotle in *The Politics* generally argued that it was so – and so did most Roman humanists and Christian medieval thinkers in their footsteps. It is not until the Renaissance that the notion that a political rule needs not to be just to be successful began to take the ascendancy. At this juncture, the works of Niccolò Machiavelli (1459–1517), such as *The Prince* (1513 [trans. 1988]) and *The Discourses* (1531 [trans. 1996]), were of particular importance. From this conceptual transformation comes the notion of *raison d'état* – the idea that, for the greater good of the political community, the state (and its representatives) could and should behave outside the moral framework that applies to ordinary individuals. As theorized in works such as *Six Books of the Commonwealth* (1576 [trans. 1955]) by Jean Bodin (1530–96) and, most notably, *Leviathan* (1651) by Thomas Hobbes (1588–1679), this rationale for politics was increasingly put to the service of the absolutist powers that ruled Europe and its growing number of colonies in the early modern period. The inadequacy of absolutist politics and of **authoritarianism** were highlighted by thinkers like John Locke (1632–1704) in *Two Treatises of Government* (1690) and **Baron Charles de Montesquieu** in *The Spirit of the Laws* (1748 [trans. 1989]). However, it is only in the late eighteenth century with the French Revolution and the diffusion of writings such as the *Social Contract* (1762 [trans. 1997]) by Jean-Jacques Rousseau (1712–78) that politics increasingly became a matter and an activity for the people as much as for the aristocracy.

In the nineteenth century, with the extension of the voting rights to an increasingly larger proportion of the **population** (the poor, women, slaves, and so forth) politics truly became a mass phenomenon. This transformation of the nature of the political community had important implications for earlier notions of "government," conceived as the greater good of the state and the monarch. Now, the state was redefined to include the nation and a new brand of *raison d'état* was introduced, which was influenced by the philosophy of classic **utilitarianism** – often known as "the greatest happiness for the greatest number." The notion of utilitarian politics developed from works such as the *Introduction to the Principles of Morals and Legislation* (1789) by Jeremy Bentham (1748–1832) and **John Stuart Mill's** *On Liberty* (1859), but also in a different vein from those of **Karl Marx**. Under various guises, utilitarianism and the notion of the good of the people have remained important justifications of the politics of government throughout the twentieth century and up to the present day. It is only towards the end of the twentieth century, most notably under the impulse of John Rawls's *A Theory of Justice* (1971), that the utilitarian logic that underpinned politics slowly began to be partially superseded by a more ontological and procedural approach to the political good, grounded on notions of fairness and **justice** for each member of the community. This conceptual evolution, in its turn, reinforced the articulation of identity politics by minority

groups who were forcefully incorporated in the nation, and who increasingly began to challenge the political organization of the contemporary nation-state from within.

Historically and geographically, the issues that have been deemed political always varied enormously. In western Europe, for over a millennium, **religion** was a political issue par excellence. However, with the rise of secularism in the nineteenth and twentieth centuries, particularly in western **democracies**, religious preferences increasingly became an essentially private matter, which political actors endeavored to maintain outside the boundaries of the political debate. (But the revival of religious politics at the beginning of the twenty-first century illustrates clearly that any such historical trends are always susceptible to being reversed.) If some issues can become de-politicized over time, other previously nonpolitical matters can also enter the political debate. Some issues have long been recognized as having political implications without being self-reflectively acknowledged as a political matter. **Gender** is one of them. In most political systems, political opportunities are influenced by gender status (typically to the detriment of female participants), but it is only with the rise of women's movements in the nineteenth century and of **feminism** in the twentieth century that gender issues have become legitimate political concerns. Finally, other issues acquired a political status simply because of the realization that the requirements for the survival of a growing human population in limited spatial settings demanded that such concerns be formulated in political terms. The **environment** is one such aspect; and the rise of environmental movements and green politics increasingly contributes to redefining the boundaries of the political in the twenty-first century.

The boundaries of politics are always and necessarily highly contested because of the range of issues that can potentially be considered as political – from the **economy** to the environment, and from **morality** to sex. Drawing from the genealogy of the term, it is generally acknowledged that politics is an activity that concerns the *polis*, in other words the **public sphere**. But even such a general statement about public affairs is not easy to sustain systematically The identification of public goods and the distinction between the public and the private, in particular, have been continuously questioned by social groups arguing for a better (more effective, fairer, and so on) organization of **wealth** and power in the community. These debates and challenges underscore the fact that an element of force is always necessarily involved in politics. From this perspective, politics can be conceived in the terms of Harold Lasswell's book *Politics: Who Gets What, When, How* (1936) (or encapsulated by **Vladimir Ilich Lenin's** saying, *Kto? Kogo?* [Who? Whom?] – who does what to whom?). Yet, in so far as politics, as a social activity, is distinct from the exercising of brute force, it also consists in the art of resolving public disagreements and conflicts by engaging collectively in dialog and bargaining. The boundary between politics as a means of resolving **social conflict**, and politics as a cause of conflict, is a porous one. As the military strategist Carl von Clausewitz pointed out in *On War* (1832), in international affairs it is often the case that **war** is the continuation of politics by other means – even though this difference of means cannot be underestimated from a social perspective. Even in domestic settings, politics, and particularly party politics for the followers of Marx, involves an element of oppression of the masses by the ruling classes in the ongoing struggle between the proletariat and the bourgeoisie for the control of the means of production and the institutions of the state. Yet, in contemporary political systems, as the discourse on **democracy** has come to dominate the global debate on politics, this activity tends to be seen as more discursive and consensual than might otherwise be thought.

In the contemporary context, one can distinguish at least four main levels of political interaction for analytical purposes: global/transnational, international, domestic, and local/intimate. Despite appearances, these categories cannot be neatly located along a well-defined spectrum as the two ends often meet – religion, for example affects politics on a global scale, as well as intervening in this process at a very intimate level, and so do economic issues that have both macro- and micro-political implications. Traditionally, state politics has been at the heart of people's understanding of what politics stood for. State politics has two main aspects: an internal dimension (domestic politics), and an external one – international politics or international relations. In domestic politics, the ordering of society by the state is probably the most common yet intense form of political activities in which individuals are repeatedly involved, as well as being subjected to. In this context, politics is simply the way in which individuals act collectively (usually by joining political associations) in order to mold the political community in to the shape that they see fit. Whether this process is in fact bottom-up or top-down depends on the type of political system that is in place at any one time – for example democratic on autocratic contexts. In the field of international politics, individuals outside the ruling circles hardly have any direct involvement in the decisionmaking process, except in the form of the proverbial **public opinion**. International politics, especially at its war-like end, can, however, have a massive and direct impact on all the members of the political community. Local and even intimate politics, by contrast, represent the sphere of political activities in which social interactions are the most common for most individuals, most of the time. The **networks** composed by the **family**, friends, kin, neighbors, and other formal or informal proximity associations constitute a ready-made receptacle for politics, albeit one with usually limited resources for action. Finally, the process of **globalization** of politics – be it through the activities of transnational non-state actors (for example Al-Qaeda) or supranational institutions (such as the International Monetary Fund) – increasingly has such an impact on every aspect of life that it is becoming the one single set of factors that redefines the concept of politics in the interdependent global system that is emerging in the twenty-first century.

FREDERIC VOLPI

polyethnic rights
– see **rights**.

Popper, Karl (1902–1994)
Born in Vienna, Karl Popper attended the University there, and worked as a cabinet maker and primary school teacher. He received his PhD in 1928. From 1937 to 1945 he taught at Canterbury University College, New Zealand, and from 1945 to 1969 at the London School of Economics.

Popper is best known as a philosopher of science and defender of open societies. In books such as *The Logic of Scientific Discovery* (1959), Popper contends that the study of nature and society share similar logics. Yet social scientists and philosophers often misinterpret the logic of natural science while attempting to imitate it, creating pseudo-scientific theories that cannot be refuted. Popper counters such claims with his theory of critical rationalism. In Popper's view, scientific theories must be falsifiable. Any theory can find evidence to support it. Only those theories that can stand the rigors of empirical testing and attempted refutation can claim to be scientific.

Popper devoted *The Open Society and Its Enemies* (1945) and *The Poverty of Historicism* (1944) to the analysis of theorists such as Plato and **Karl Marx**, who assert their discoveries of universal truths. Popper criticizes such theories as unscientific and anti-democratic. They do not promote open discussion, tolerance of opposing views, or a pragmatic and piecemeal approach to **social change**, the ingredients of a good society. For Popper, the growth of knowledge is tied to a **community** of scientists who freely and rationally criticize one another's viewpoints. **Institutions** guaranteeing such debate and dialog are crucial for the advancement of science and an open, democratic society.

KENNETH H. TUCKER, JR.

popular culture

The early waves of studying popular culture emerged out of Great Britain during the 1950s and 1960s. Figures such as the literary and cultural critics **Raymond Williams** and **Richard Hoggart** and the historian E. P. Thompson (1924–93) sought to discover within the study of popular culture the political contestation of **values** and ways of life. If high culture was enjoyed by the few, then most popular culture, it seemed, reproduced the dominant orientations of a capitalist-dominated marketplace. However, historically the working class and the Romantic movement had sought to produce alternative forms of popular art and **culture** that had sought to criticize the status quo. These arguments led many in sociology, **cultural studies**, and history to investigate how the people had been actively involved in making their own culture (or cultures) from below. Such views were at this time contrasted with the ideas of the early **Frankfurt School**, that tended to reduce the study of popular culture to that of mass culture. Whereas mass culture captured the way in which the production of culture was centrally organized in terms of the needs of a culture industry (rise of mass **audiences** for television, press, and consumer goods), a genuinely popular culture was made by and for ordinary people.

From the 1970s onward, the work of Italian Marxist **Antonio Gramsci** and his conception of **hegemony** were to influence these debates deeply. The idea here was that popular culture was constituted by a set of **institutions**, practices, and forms that aimed to win the consent of the people. This was more than a simple act of dominant **groups** establishing their domination, but always required the active incorporation of subordinate groups and cultures. This approach became strongly connected with a number of writers who associated with the **Birmingham Centre for Contemporary Cultural studies** (including **Stuart**

Hall, Angela McRobbie, and Paul Willis). The study of youth cultures, popular magazines, **sport**, and the media then were undertaken to reveal processes of containment and resistance in respect of the dominant culture. In particular this tradition has placed intellectual emphasis upon the various and contested meanings of popular culture and its role in disrupting or securing relations of domination. There are three main criticisms of these arguments: the emphasis on meaning leads to a relative neglect of changing institutional features which organize the production and distribution of popular culture; the critical role which the avant-garde or more elite forms of high culture have played in creating critical consciousness historically tends to disappear from the analysis; and little of the actual theorizing about cultural resistance pays much attention to the need to formulate more adequate social and political environments that would seek a more just settlement between competing cultures.

Since the early 1990s many have become aware of the need to promote more global understandings of the operation of popular culture. The new mode of popular cultural studies has sought to understand its formation both within and in opposition to cultural **nationalism**. This has further broken with the idea of homogeneous national cultures in order to investigate the ways in which, in an increasingly global culture, different groups have been able to maintain interconnections with one another. In particular the development of transnational forms of mobility in respect of **tourism** and the media, as well as the development of counter-publics on the basis of **race** and **gender**, have pushed the analysis of popular culture beyond the nation-state.

Paul Gilroy, in *There Ain't No Black in the Union Jack* (1987), argued that black popular music has been the key cultural location for the articulation of a sense of diasporic connection between Africa, America, and Britain. This has operated in a number of ways, including the borrowing of musical styles and **influences**, protesting about injustice, the recording of struggles, and in certain rap songs the display of misogyny. Through the fostering of a distinctively black aesthetic, Gilroy argues that music has provided a uniquely connective culture in a globalized civil society. Such features have not only proved to be important in the study of the complexity of popular forms but have also warned against many postmodern arguments which simply assumed that distinctions between high and popular culture had evaporated.

However, many remain critical of these and similar studies for neglecting to analyze the continued power of the nation-state and popular discourses of nationhood that continue to exert a considerable amount of influence over the organization and meaning of popular culture.

Further, many are now less concerned with the meanings of particular popular texts and more with how a diversity of audience members actively constitutes the popular. John Fiske, in *Reading the Popular* (1989), has gone farthest in this respect, arguing that the art of **everyday life** is commonly involved in the transformation of consumer products. All popular culture is the site of struggle where meanings are never controlled by the producers, but are actively and pleasurably produced by the consumers. These irreverent forms of *jouissance* erupt from below and are opposed to the disciplinary techniques utilized by the power bloc. Here there is a double pleasure involved in the audience's reading of popular texts. The first is the enjoyment involved in the symbolic production of meanings that oppose those of the power bloc, and the second concerns the actual activity of being productive. In this scenario, the **market**, by contrast with the declining high culture of the powerful, brings certain cultural products within the critical horizons of the people. Many have been extremely critical of these developments, arguing that, unlike those who first sought to study popular culture in the 1950s and 1960s, such views end up endorsing an uncritical culture of **consumption**. If popular culture depends upon what we do with culture rather than what it does to us this would seemingly cancel any criticisms we might want to make of the **power** of cultural producers. Most popular culture continues to be shaped by the practices of a dominant capitalist culture, whatever role it might play within the domains of everyday life. NICK STEVENSON

population studies

– see **demography**.

populism

This began as a movement of small farmers in the South and Midwest in the late nineteenth-century United States who desired control of the federal government, which they believed was dominated by northern industrialists and bankers. Populism has resurfaced as an ambiguous political concept, designating political positions from a call for a more equitable distribution of **wealth** to criticisms of liberal beliefs regarding abortion, gun control, **affirmative action**, and the like.

Late nineteenth-century agrarian populism attempted to preserve a way of life against an encroaching **industrial society**. During this era, technological growth was unprecedented, as railroads, the telegraph, and eventually the telephone increased the scope and pace of business activity. Immigrants from southern and eastern Europe streamed into the United States, transforming the countenance of the working class. Large corporations and an aggressive federal government centralized economic and administrative **power**, and local **communities** lost control over their destinies.

As wealth flowed into railroad and manufacturing industries, the **incomes** of many small farmers declined. They were driven into debt by falling agricultural prices, increased transportation costs, and a shortage of credit. The populist movement grew as many farmers banded together in order to pool resources and break the monopoly on lending held by banks. Populists developed a political and economic program, advocating a more egalitarian economic system. They attempted to democratically reform federal and state governments, supporting a progressive income tax, the direct election of United States senators, and more reliance on popular initiatives and referendums to change government policy. Many of these demands were stripped of their radical impulse and incorporated into the platform of the Democratic Party, as populism faded in the early years of the twentieth century.

The populists called for the power of the people versus the **elites**. It provided a distinctive language of American radicalism, different from **Marxism** more popular in Europe. Yet the definition of who constituted the "people" was ambiguous. Many populists harbored nativist **prejudices**. **Racism** against African Americans sometimes intertwined with a fear that a vast conspiracy of moneylenders, often either Catholic or Jewish, controlled the **economy** and the government.

This ambiguity continues to haunt the meaning of populism. Many politicians embrace populism, calling for a more egalitarian economy, and criticizing the power of large corporations. But a conservative cultural populism has arisen in the United States in the wake of the controversial era of the 1960s. Often tied to a fundamentalist view of **religion**, contemporary cultural populism feeds on animosity towards government taxation and affirmative action programs, and policies aimed at helping the (largely nonwhite) poor. Yet it favors government action to suppress forms of behavior considered immoral, from restricting abortions to controlling the distribution of pornography.

Scholars such as **Seymour M. Lipset** in *Political Man* (1960) contend that populism arose as the United States political center broke down, and people embraced authoritarian beliefs that gave voice to their economic and cultural frustrations. Progressives such as Thomas Frank in *What's the Matter with Kansas* (2004) state that American conservatives have convinced many working-class people that their enemy is an ambiguous cultural elite, rather than the wealthy.

KENNETH H. TUCKER, JR.

positional goods
– see **consumption**.

positivism

The term positivism was coined in the 1830s by **Auguste Comte** as the name for his philosophy of science. *Philosophie positive*, as the theory and history of the positive sciences, whose full range was deemed to have been completed by Comte's own **sociology**, would provide the mental framework for **industrial society**. In contrast with theology and metaphysics, positive (or scientific) knowledge was based on *impressions externelles*, and was oriented to the discovery of laws, understood as regularities in phenomena, rather than ultimate causes. Positivism thus had a relative rather than absolute view of truth. "Positive," at the same time, meant affirmative and constructive, as opposed to critical and negative. The "metaphysics" that Comtean positivism sought to expunge was not only an obfuscatory residue of religious belief. In the context of the *grande crise* that marked the birth of industrialism, it expressed the rising up of individual reason, which, in itself, was abstract, anarchic, and "incapable of building." By the same token, positivism adopted a social, rather than individual, viewpoint, a shift that was not only epistemological but linked to the *altruisme* that gave knowledge its ends and fixed the mind on objects outside itself.

While positivism has continued to be associated with Comte, his totalizing philosophy and program have long been abandoned, and the term has come to have a more generic meaning. In this wider sense, positivism encompasses a diverse spectrum of positions which champion a scientific viewpoint, and insist that knowledge claims, including in the social domain, should confine themselves to what can be derived from observable phenomena. Such positions range from the classical positivism of Comte and his followers, to

the more astringent logical positivism of the Vienna Circle, as well as, more generally, to operationalist, quantitative, and statistics-based tendencies in sociology and other **human sciences**.

Whether sociology itself, as Comte claimed, can be a positive science, and in what sense, has been hotly debated throughout its history. Besides issues about causality and agency, and about the constructed nature of "facts," there are difficulties conceiving and treating the social as an objectively knowable domain. Social reality has an interior, subjective, dimension, and sociology itself is a social phenomenon, so that, for sociology, the subject of knowledge is part of its object. For classical sociology, which grappled with these issues, a science of society was not impossible, but it had special features, and could not be modeled on other sciences without reductionism. **Karl Marx** thought that the capitalist economic base could be analyzed with the precision of natural sciences, but not the superstructure where "social antagonisms become conscious and are fought out." In Germany, sociology came to be classified among the *Geisteswissenschaften*, implying an interpretative and non-quantitative approach which **Max Weber** sought to imbue with a "value-neutral" spirit through an emphasis on formal structures, chains of cause and effect, and comparative civilizational analysis. In France, **Émile Durkheim** criticized Comte's sociology as itself metaphysics, and adopted a neo-Kantian conception of knowledge, but still affirmed that social facts could be studied "according to the methods of the natural sciences" so as to establish "laws of concomitance and succession." However, the Post-Durkheim **Annales school** shifted from laws to structures and abandoned developmentalism, while philosophical issues about positivism in the **social sciences** were raised anew by **phenomenology** and **critical theory**. These resurfaced in the 1960s with a new round of the late nineteenth-century "positivism debate" (*Positivismusstreit*) between **Jürgen Habermas** and **Karl Popper**, as well as in the controversies surrounding **Louis Althusser**'s intervention "for Marx," which resurrected Comtean themes in a Marxist form.

ANDREW WERNICK

post-Fordism

This is an ambiguous term that describes a relatively durable form of economic organization that happens to follow Fordism and/or resolves the crisis tendencies of Fordism. A basic problem is that this concept lacks any positive content – its chronological prefix indicates only that it comes *after* Fordism. This is why some theorists propose substantive alternatives such as Toyotism, Fujitsu-ism, Sonyism, and Gatesism or, again, informational **capitalism**, the knowledge-based **economy**, and the network economy. However, to understand the rationale behind such terms, we must first consider Fordism and its crisis tendencies.

Fordism is widely used to describe the system of mass production pioneered in the early twentieth century by the Ford Motor Company and/or the typical postwar mode of growth in North America and western Europe. In the latter respect, Fordism has been analyzed, often without adequate distinction, in terms of four dimensions. First, the Fordist industrial **paradigm** involves mass production of standardized goods on a moving assembly line using dedicated machinery and semi-skilled **labor**. Second, as a national accumulation regime, it involves a virtuous cycle of mass production and mass **consumption**. Third, in line with **regulation theory**, it has been analyzed as a mode of regulation with five dimensions: (a) an institutionalized compromise between organized labor and big business such that workers accept capital's right to manage in return for wages indexed to productivity and **inflation**; (b) monopolistic competition between large **firms** based on cost-plus pricing and advertising; (c) centralized financial capital, deficit finance, and credit-based mass consumption; (d) state intervention to secure full employment and enable all citizens to share in mass consumption; and (e) the embedding of national economies in a liberal international economic order. Fourth, as a form of social life, it involves a mass **society** with mass consumption, **mass media**, mass transport, mass **politics**, and so on.

Despite (or perhaps because of) its wide use, the notion of "Fordism" is contested. Key disputes concern: (1) the extent and significance of mass production for postwar advanced capitalist economies; (2) whether economies as varied as the United States, Germany, Denmark, Italy, or Britain can all be usefully described as Fordist; (3) the extent to which the social and political contexts in which mass production and mass consumption developed were similar, and, in turn, how far the growth of mass production and mass consumption was shaped by these contexts; and (4) whether social phenomena such as **McDonaldization** derive from the Fordism industrial paradigm or from broader social processes.

The Fordist accumulation regime and mode of regulation allegedly became dominant in advanced capitalism during postwar reconstruction and then facilitated the long postwar boom. During the 1970s, however, crisis tendencies

started to show in each of its four dimensions. This is seen in the gradual exhaustion of the growth potential of mass production and an intensified working-class resistance to its alienating working conditions; an emerging market saturation for mass consumer durables; a declining profit rate combined with stagflation; a growing fiscal crisis and a declining state capacity for economic management due to internationalization; a popular rejection of standardized, bureaucratic treatment in the **welfare state**; and a weakened international order due to declining American economic dominance and political **hegemony**.

These conditions promoted various economic and political actors to search for solutions to the crisis of Fordism, either by restoring its typical growth dynamics to produce a neo-Fordist regime and/or by developing a new accumulation regime and mode of regulation. Social scientists have adopted three main approaches to giving a positive content to such a new, hence post-Fordist, regime: (1) focus on the transformative role of new **technologies** and practices in regard to material and immaterial production – especially new information and communication technologies and their facilitation of a new, more flexible, networked global economy; (2) focus on the leading economic sectors that enable a transition from mass industrial production to postindustrial production; and (3) focus on how major crisis tendencies of Fordism are overcome through the consolidation of a new and stable series of economic and extra-economic regulatory fixes corresponding discursively and materially to new and profitable growth potentials. Even thirty years after the crisis of Fordism became apparent, debate continues over whether a stable post-Fordist order has yet been consolidated and, indeed, whether the stability of Fordism was an exceptional period in an otherwise typically disorderly and crisis-prone pattern of capitalist development.

Those who are committed to the assumptions of a stable post-Fordist order regard its key features as: (1) a flexible production process based on flexible machines or systems and an appropriately flexible workforce; (2) a stable mode of growth based on flexible production, growing productivity based on economies of scope, rising **incomes** for polyvalent skilled workers and the service class, increased demand for differentiated goods and services favored by the growing discretionary element in these incomes, increased profits based on technological rents and the full utilization of flexible capacity, reinvestment in more flexible production equipment and techniques and/or

451

new sets of products, and a further boost to economies of scope; (3) a post-Fordist wage relation based on polarization between multiskilled workers and the unskilled and a decline in national or industrial collective bargaining; (4) the rise of flexible, lean, and networked firms oriented to their distinctive core competences and strategic alliances; (5) the dominance of hypermobile, rootless private bank credit and forms of cybercash that circulate internationally, and the subordination of government finance to international money and currency **markets**; (6) a shift from the primacy of the postwar Keynesian national welfare state to a political regime concerned with international competitiveness and innovation, with promoting a flexible workforce and full employability rather than jobs for life, with coordinating economic and **social policies** on local, regional, national, and supranational scales, and with developing new forms of economic and social governance to compensate for state as well as market failure; and (7) the shift from international regimes that secured the conditions for the survival of national economies and sovereign **states** to supranational or even global regimes that address economic and political problems that transcend national boundaries.

These supposedly generic features of post-Fordism are very unevenly developed and, where they exist, they assume quite different forms – neoliberal in some contexts, statist or social democratic in others. There is also continuing debate over the extent, significance, and durability of these features in the face of the continuing contradictions in global capitalism. Nonetheless, attempts to identify the positive content of post-Fordism have contributed to the emerging shape of an after-Fordist economic and political order.

BOB JESSOP

postcolonial theory

This is a field of inquiry and collection of concepts aimed at illuminating, as well as criticizing, the cultural, intellectual, literary, and epistemological dominance of the modern West over countries previously colonized by western imperial powers. Postcolonial theory is not a theory in the tradition of **positivism** or **realism** but rather a range of premises, analytic approaches, and conceptual tools for understanding the legacies of **colonialism** and **imperialism** in formerly colonized societies, with a primary focus upon cultural legacies. Postcolonial theory also carries an explicit political agenda. It examines the cultural bases and legacies of imperialism in order to identify

and support resistances to them. Its main contributions include: advancing colonialism and imperialism as categories of social analysis on a par with categories like **social class**, **gender** and **race and ethnicity**; identifying the cultural processes involved in colonialism and imperialism; and questioning the position that European knowledge and **culture** has normative supremacy.

The origins of postcolonial theory are disputed, but three sources from the humanities are typically identified. One lies in Commonwealth literary studies, a field of study that began in the 1960s in former British colonies among literary critics seeking to contribute their voices to an academy seen as "Anglocentric." Another source is **Edward Said**'s *Orientalism* (1978), which argued that imperialism had been facilitated by forms of knowledge and categorical binaries. A final source is the field of Subaltern Studies, advanced by historians of British colonialism in India seeking to uncover the voices and agency of peasant **groups** in the making of colonial history. Further proponents of postcolonial theory include literary critics: Homi Bhabha and Gayatri Spivak are among the most notable. Writers in the field of postcolonial theory have also sought to expand the base of its founders by turning to African **intellectuals** like **Franz Fanon**, Ainé Césaire (1913–), and Albert Memmi (1920–).

Given these diverse origins and developments, postcolonial theory does not offer a unified theory or a single **methodology**. There are, however, at least two key theoretical claims upon which its key concepts and lines of inquiry are based. The first is that imperialism did not only involve the use of coercion or economic domination but also discourse and associated forms of knowledge and representation. Said's *Orientalism* is seen as the foremost innovator of this thesis. Said argued that British imperialism in the Middle East was enabled by a "style of thought," field of academic study, or "discursive formation" called "Orientalism." Orientalism constructed a fundamental "ontological and epistemological distinction . . . between 'the Orient' and 'the Occident'" or "the West" and "the East," akin to the social-psychological distinction between **self** and other. It likewise portrayed westerners as "rational, peaceful, liberal, [and] logical" while portraying Orientals as uncivilized, irrational, inferior, and lacking and therefore in need of control by the West (1978: 2). According to Said, Orientalism was critical for imperialism and colonialism because it enabled the West "to manage . . . the Orient politically, sociologically, militarily, ideologically, scientifically, and imaginatively" (1978: 3). Said therefore identified a cultural or epistemological dimension to imperial domination that worked in conjunction with other dimensions of **power**. One of his targets was **Marxism**, which was seen as either overlooking the importance of Orientalism in facilitating imperialism or reducing it to mere **ideology**. Said instead drew upon **Michel Foucault**'s theory of power and knowledge to argue that Orientalism did not reflect the economic bases of imperialism but was productive of imperialism itself. Orientalism allowed for a "flexible positional superiority, which puts the westerner in a whole series of possible relationships with the Orient without ever losing him the relative upper hand" (1978: 6–7).

The other key claim of postcolonial theory is that **decolonization** did not bring the dissolution of political, social, and economic **inequalities** between former imperial powers and previously colonized societies. Postcolonial theory insists that those inequalities have continued through the postindependence period. World-systems and **dependency theories** make a similar argument, but the contribution of postcolonial theory is to suggest that persistent inequalities are related to the epistemological and cultural legacies of colonialism. The dominating discourses and knowledges that facilitated imperialism persist into the post-independence period, contributing to a form of cultural **hegemony** and rendering postcolonial peoples without the cultural tools or critical consciousness to challenge western dominance. The persistence of colonialism's effects is important for postcolonial theory because it underlies one of its key suggestions: that the former colonial status of societies could be seen as a category of social analysis alongside race, class, and gender. It also led postcolonial theorists to employ the term "postcolonial" rather than "post-colonial." The latter hyphenated term posits the end of colonialism, but the unhyphenated term is meant to signify the continuation of colonialism's effects despite formal decolonization.

The main lines of research and thinking in postcolonial theory have been guided by these two main insights. The idea that colonialism and imperialism were facilitated by knowledge and discourse set the basis for colonial **discourse analysis**, which seeks to examine colonial forms of representation and their relationship to power. Literary critics, for example, examine novels and other forms of popular representation for the ways in which they portray colonized peoples. Historians working from a postcolonial perspective extend

Said's analysis by arguing that the idea of "history" itself, like Orientalism, has served to portray postcolonial societies and peoples as inferior and lacking. Western historical knowledge is rooted in a Hegelian logic that encourages further binary distinctions between the Occident and the Orient while privileging the former as the agent of history. Other postcolonial theorists have stressed the incoherence of colonial discourse and representations. These theorists accuse Said of portraying Oriental discourse as uniform and monolithic and argue that colonial discourse was fractured and incomplete. H. Bhabha drew from **poststructuralism** and **deconstruction** to argue that colonial stereotypes were contradictory and "ambivalent" or "undecided": they offered images of the colonized that were presumably fixed and natural but the images themselves were shifting and at times contradictory. The colonial subject is portrayed as "savage (cannibal) and yet the most obedient and signified of servants (the bearer of food); he is the embodiment of rampant sexuality and yet innocent as a child; he is mystical, primitive, simple-minded and yet the most worldly and accomplished liar" (*Location of Culture*, 1994: 82).

The premise that the cultural effects of colonialism persist through the postindependence period also guides postcolonial studies. Some postcolonial theorists turned to the work of Fanon and Memmi as a new source of inspiration. Fanon and Memmi argued that colonialism had psychological effects that were detrimental to colonized peoples and which continued even after decolonization, and so postcolonial theorists extend this theme in various ways. A. Nandy's *The Intimate Enemy* (1983) argued that the superiority of the West portrayed in Orientalism became deeply rooted in the psyche of the colonized. While Fanon argued racial hierarchies were internalized, Nandy argued that geographical and civilization hierarchies were also internalized. Nandy also took up Memmi's idea that the psychological effects of colonialism extended to colonizer and colonized alike.

Postcolonial theory's key insights have also guided its explicit political project. If imperialism was supported by discourse, forms of representation, and knowledge, and if its cultural legacies persist through the postcolonial period, postcolonial theory aims to construct an alternative basis of knowledge that might challenge or resist those effects. In *Orientalism*, Said raised one of the key questions to which postcolonial theory has tried to respond: "How can we know and respect the other?" To meet the challenge, literary critics who work with postcolonial theory look for ways in which literary representation might subvert Eurocentrism. Historians advancing postcolonial theory aim to write historical narratives that highlight the experiences, agency, and voice of colonized subjects so as to question in turn the authority of European experiences and perceptions. Here postcolonial theory can be seen as having an affinity with **postmodernism** in that it questions rather than presumes linear narratives of historical **progress** and development. Yet its distinct contribution is to stress that those narratives have helped to subjugate colonized peoples in particular.

The key dilemma for postcolonial theory, as G. Spivak pointed out, is to produce alternative knowledges without reproducing the forms they aim to resist. How can one write a history of colonialism and postcolonialism while "history" itself is a form of knowledge that facilitates imperialism? To meet this challenge, some have turned to deconstruction. Postcolonial theory cannot cast off western knowledges and so the best it can do is show that those knowledges are incomplete and fractured. Bhabha expanded his analysis of colonial discourse to introduce the idea of **hybridity** as a potentially resistant form. As colonial discourse was fractured and ambivalent, colonized subjects were able to appropriate it and use it in ways that challenged its authority. The task of postcolonial theory is to examine these instances. Others, employing the genealogical method of analysis proposed by Foucault, suggest that proper postcolonial histories should offer narratives that "provincialize" Europe, that is, treat European dominance as a contingent or accidental rather than a necessary or linear outcome, thereby challenging the West's representation of itself. Marxist critics, however, suggest these methods run into difficulties because they lead to a self-referential textualism that ignores the material bases of domination. These debates with **Marxism** constitute one of the main turning points for postcolonial theory in establishing its research agenda and orientation.   JULIAN GO

postcommunist societies

This concept refers to the countries of eastern Europe and the republics of the former Soviet Union which, during the anticommunist revolutions of 1989–91, gained full sovereignty and autonomy, and introduced comprehensive regime change towards western models of political **democracy**, market **economy**, and open, pluralistic **culture**. They include two groups of countries.

First, those which fell under the political, economic, and ideological domination of the USSR after World War II as the result of the Yalta and Potsdam agreements among the Allied powers: Poland, Hungary, Czechoslovakia, the German Democratic Republic (central–eastern Europe), Albania, Bulgaria, Romania, and Yugoslavia (Balkan states). Their number has grown in the 1990s owing to the separation of the Czech Republic and Slovakia, as well as the breakdown of Yugoslavia in the wake of Balkan wars into Slovenia, Croatia, Macedonia, and Bosnia-Herzegovina, only Serbia and Montenegro retaining the label of the Yugoslav Republic. The second group consists of the fifteen successor states to Soviet republics: the Russian Federation, plus Ukraine, Belarus, and other members of the Commonwealth of Independent States (CIS), with Lithuania, Latvia, and Estonia (the Baltic states) remaining outside the CIS.

After World War II all these countries became part of the Soviet Empire, and were ruled or dominated by the largest and most powerful country of the region. The republics of the Soviet Union constituted an internal empire, over which Russia exercised direct rule, whereas the countries of eastern Europe constituted an external empire, whose countries had limited sovereignty and imposed regimes patterned on that of the Soviet Union (they were satellite countries). The chief commonalities of these regimes were the one-party **state** and monocentric **authority** in the area of **politics**, and central planning and state ownership in the area of the **economy**. These features were combined with a controlled official **culture** (marked by extensive censorship), and the suppression and limitation of **civil society**. Apart from these principal similarities, there was great diversity in their concrete implementation. In the Soviet Union itself there were temporal differences in the repressiveness of the regime, ranging from the dictatorial Stalinist period on one hand, to a relatively liberalized system under Mikhail Gorbachev (1931–). Among "satellite" countries Yugoslavia under Tito (Joseph Broz) (1892–1980) was the first to obtain political sovereignty, and approximate a market economy, but it retained strong ideological control. From the middle 1950s Poland under Wladyslaw Gomulka (1905–82) and Hungary under Janos Kadar (1912–89) became exceptional in allowing the rudiments of an economic market and **entrepreneurship**, as well as some liberalization of politics, for example the unique phenomenon of the Polish Catholic Church possessing considerable autonomy, or the emergence of organized democratic opposition in Poland and Czechoslovakia as early as the 1970s. Romania under Nicolae Ceaucescu (1918–89) was able to conduct relatively independent foreign policy, otherwise sticking to communist orthodoxy. At the other extreme, tight political and ideological control and direct Soviet influence were characteristic of the GDR (East Germany – the frontier country against the West), Albania, Bulgaria, and – after 1968 – Czechoslovakia.

The breakdown of the communist empire started from eastern Europe, with the revolutions of 1989 typically originating from below and mobilizing pro-democratic and opposition movements (Poland's Solidarity movement being the biggest and most powerful). The concrete processes of extrication from the communist regime differed markedly: for example in Poland and Hungary it was by means of round-table talks and the peaceful, gradual exit from power by communist **elites**; in Czechoslovakia, by means of a bloodless "velvet revolution" in the streets; in Romania, by means of the bloody uprising against the communist dictatorship; in the GDR by direct incorporation into the political and economic system of West Germany, through the process of unification. The disbanding of the Soviet Union itself followed soon after, in 1991, as the result of a process initiated from above, by Gorbachev's reforms of *glasnost* and *perestroika*, and carried further in the direction of democracy and **capitalism** under the leadership of President Boris Yeltsin (1931–).

Calling the societies which emerged in these processes "postcommunist" draws attention to their continuing dependence on the communist past and their incomplete reshaping into the western model. The legacies of **Communism** are to be felt in four areas. In the political domain, there are deficiencies in the operation of the democratic system, which are most pronounced in the countries devoid of earlier democratic **traditions** (for example in Russia, some post-Soviet republics, Bulgaria, and Albania), and relatively smaller in the countries which had experienced periods of democratic rule in their earlier history (for instance Poland, Hungary, and the Czech Republic). But everywhere one observes: incompetent, ill-prepared, often corrupt, and nepotistic political elites, chaotic and amorphous party systems, lack of an independent apolitical civil service, weak rule of law, continued **influence** of former communists able to convert their earlier political capital into personal enrichment ("new nomenklatura" or "oligarchs"). In the economic domain the consolidation of the **market** has been favored by the existence of earlier capitalist traditions (as present, for example, in the Czech Republic), as well as where the initial economic reform was of the radical, "shock therapy" variety, while gradual or evolutionary steps have proven less effective. But everywhere it was slowed down by the continuing presence of inefficient large state sectors, resistance to privatization, an overgrown agricultural sector, as well as unresolved issues of restitution of private **property** nationalized under the communist regime. In the cultural area, the readiness to embrace the western way of life depends on the strength of earlier pro-western orientations (higher, for example, in the countries existing formerly in the orbit of the Habsburg Empire, with a dominant Catholicism, than in those which were in the orbit of the Ottoman Empire and the Orthodox Church). But everywhere there are mental and value deficiencies covered by the concept of civilizational incompetence: in particular, attitudes not adapted to the new conditions of democracy and capitalism, such as collectivism, egalitarianism, avoidance of responsibility, aversion to **risk**, claims to social security and welfare directed towards the state, system-blame for personal failures, and indifference to the public good. In the area of civil society, its suppression under Communism, and the flight of citizens to the private sphere of the **family**, friends, and "connections," results in the persistent opposition between "us" and "them" and a reluctance to engage in public participation and in voluntary associational activism.

Nevertheless the process of development and consolidation of democracy, capitalism, and free culture proceeds consistently, and has already led to the rebuilding of key institutional structures, to new cultural and mental orientations and to changes in the **everyday life** of postcommunist societies. A significant role has been played in this process of shedding of the legacies of the communist past by the incorporation of leading countries of the region into supranational economic and political **organizations** of the western world: the Organization for Economic Cooperation and Development (OECD), the World Bank, and most significantly NATO (with Poland, Hungary, and the Czech Republic joining first, in 1999, and Bulgaria, Estonia, Latvia, Lithuania, Romania, Slovakia, and Slovenia invited in 2004), and the European Union (with the accession of Poland, Hungary, the Czech Republic, Slovakia, Slovenia, Estonia, Lithuania, and Latvia in 2004).

In sociology the complex **social changes** occurring in postcommunist societies have become the subject of various theoretical accounts. They describe the process under the headings of transition, transformation, **modernization**, and traumatic sequence. The idea of transition assumes that we witness the simple replacement of one regime by another, and that by imitating western **institutions** the postcommunist societies will quickly reshape themselves in the likeness of leading societies of the West (namely the United States and western Europe, and westernized countries such as Japan, and so forth). The idea of transformation sees the process as a more complex, path-dependent, and open-ended construction of a new form of **society**, partly patterned on the West, but also revealing specific historical experiences within the region. The idea of modernization focuses on the continuation and extension of the incomplete, "fake modernization" under Communism – limited to industrialization, **urbanization**, and educational emancipation – into the political and cultural domain, as well as on the reemergence of civil society. The idea of traumatic sequence emphasizes the negative, unintended side-effects of the process: a certain disorientation and **anomie** in the domain of **values**, adverse effects of reforms (for example **unemployment**, raised levels of **crime**, and impoverishment of considerable segments of the population), and the resulting post-traumatic moods of the people (distrust, apathy, and nostalgia for the past). The key process is conceived as a long-term effort to cope with such traumas, by mobilizing entrepreneurial energies, educational aspirations, and citizens' activism. And the fulfillment of the ultimate promise of success is entrusted to the turnover of **generations**, where young people are already immune from communist legacies.

PIOTR SZTOMPKA

postfeminism

This has two meanings. First, it is used as a comment on what some writers see as the disappearance of **feminism** in the West, and, second, it can be used as a description of societies that have changed various social practices as a result of what is known as the "second wave" of feminism in the 1970s. In the first case, the term postfeminism can be interpreted as a fervent hope by some critics of feminism that this **social movement**, which they find to be profoundly disturbing, has lost its impact and support and that feminism no longer exists as a viable movement. Right-wing critics of feminism have been quick to assume, report, and state the "death" of feminism while hailing a return to the halcyon days of

more traditional relationships of **gender**. The evidence of the demise of feminism is usually anecdotal information about women choosing to become full-time mothers; other arguments (for example, that the current arrangements of the **labor market** are rarely supportive of parents) are seldom part of the same discussion. Tabloid newspapers throughout the West have played a considerable part in the popularization of the idea that feminism is dead and that it was only ever a minority social movement, associated with lesbian **sexuality**.

The second use of the term postfeminism recognizes the impact of feminism on the social world (for example, the calculation of unpaid work in the household as part of the Gross National Product, the greater equalization of the law in relation to women and men), but tacitly assumes that the work of feminism has been done. A "postfeminist" society is thus one that has put into place equal rights legislation, recognized disparities in social **power** between women and men, and questioned practices that were related to the social inferiority of women. For many feminists, the term postfeminism has been created out of the backlash against feminism from the political right and the rise, most significantly in the United States, of a religious right which has increasingly challenged the liberalization of laws relating to **reproduction** that were achieved by feminists in the 1970s. Postfeminism can thus be read as a construct of those social groups that were always opposed to feminism.

MARY EVANS

posthistoire

A theorem associated with **postmodernism** and notions of the end of history, *posthistoire* refers to the analysis of the social beyond the horizon of the Enlightenment self-understanding of **modernity**. The term was first made popular by Lutz Niethammer in his *Posthistoire Has History Come to an End?* (1989 [trans. 1992]). Often interpreted as spelling the collapse of modernity, its analysis has played a central role in sociological debates about the exhaustion of ideas stemming from the European **Enlightenment**.

Posthistoire has taken two key sociological forms. **Arnold Gehlen** argued that, in an age of intensive **modernization**, there is an uncoupling of **rationality** on the one side and the cultural self-understanding of modernity on the other. For Gehlen, *posthistoire* means the guiding assumptions of the Enlightenment are dead; only their consequences live on, and unpredictably so. From this perspective, processes of **modernization** have become unhinged from any internal connection with the conceptual horizons of western rationalism in which the project of modernity was founded.

The idea of *posthistoire* also arises in sociology as a result of the postmodern turn, but in this reading it is both **society** and **culture** that are deconstructed. In postmodern sociology, the end of cultural modernity spells a similar eclipse of advanced modernization. In *posthistoire*, society is directionless, producing itself only in the fleeting transparency of pluralistic discourses.

ANTHONY ELLIOTT

posthumanism

Associated with **postmodernism** and **poststructuralism**, posthumanism is a form of postmodern philosophy predicated on the notion that the human species is self-limiting. Posthumanists seek to promote a radical political agenda, pushing beyond the ideas and images from the European **Enlightenment** on the "natural" constraints of the body and towards alternative utopias promoting artificial **intelligence**, nanotechnology, cyber **technologies**, and biomachines. In this sociology beyond humanism, in which society is said to have entered a post-Darwinian era, the political aim is to eradicate distinctions between humans and machines.

The historical emergence of posthumanism is closely connected with the philosophy of Friedrich Nietzsche (1844–1900) and his unearthing of an imminent process of continual self-overcoming, such that an erasure of the "subject of man" was the theoretical premise from which the Overman (*Ubermensch*) might be conceptualized. Yet whereas Nietzsche's analysis of evolution – human and nonhuman – was concerned with the spontaneous growth of productive desire, posthumanists focus on the mutations of machine intensities, biomachine becomings, bodily transpositions. Specifically in terms of sociological analysis, there is an emphasis on radicalizing human forms through the use of technological and other means. Developments in artificial life, particularly neural networks and biomorphs, promise a nonlinear conceptualization of evolutionary life; so, too, computer models and digital technologies offer a revaluation of the fundamental sociological concepts through which self-organization and sociality are constituted.

These arguments advanced by posthumanists suggest that sociology needs to embrace interdisciplinarity in order to engage critically the dynamism of configurations of nature, sociality, and technology. In *Simians, Cyborgs and Women: The Reinvention of Nature* (1991), **Donna J. Haraway** noted that human and nonhuman "actants" are mixed in "material–semiotic entities"; these are biotech knowledge objects, such as the database, the chip, the neural net, the ecosystem. Haraway suggests that, from this perspective, complex socialities can be analyzed otherwise, from the micro-physical to the macro-physical.

A persistent theme in posthumanism is that social memories and socialities are multiple. Gilles Deleuze and Felix Guattari argue in *A Thousand Plateaus* (1980 [trans. 1987]) in favor of molecular memories, of open, complex systems, where mutant "lines of flight" initiate forms of becoming that call into play novel forms of communication between heterogeneous phenomena. Refiguring established **epistemologies** and **ontologies** in terms of the posthuman, some argue – like Hans Moravec in *Robot. Mere Machine to Transcendent Mind* (1998) – that **biotechnologies** can expand human horizons indefinitely, refiguring our understanding of speed, vision, strength, and intelligence. However, there are other posthumanists who caution against the more extreme flights of utopian vision concerning the transhuman condition. Keith Ansell Pearson argues in *Viroid Life* (1997) against the biotechnological vitalism of cybergurus. While the posthuman condition involves sociology in thinking beyond the "beyond," as Pearson argues, the intellectual task concerns, above all, mapping creative intelligences and productive becomings.   ANTHONY ELLIOTT

postindustrial society

This argument is that, following a period of almost two centuries of industrialization, some societies of the advanced industrial world have undergone further changes which require that we now speak of "postindustrial societies." The most important exponent of this view is the American sociologist **Daniel Bell**, though it has also been echoed by several European sociologists such as **Alain Touraine**. According to these thinkers, postindustrial societies are characterized by the following features: economically, a move from a goods-producing to a service **economy**; occupationally, the decline of the manual working class and the rise of a professional, managerial, and technical class; culturally, the growing importance of universities and other research **institutions**, to some extent replacing the business enterprise as the source of innovation and growth; in **politics** and decision-making, the creation of a new "intellectual **technology**" involving computer-simulations, **game theory**, scientific forecasting, and other types of theoretical systems that increasingly displace the deliberations of "amateur" politicians. Overarching all this, what Bells calls the "axial principle" of the new society, is "the centrality of theoretical knowledge" as the source of innovation and policy formation for society as a whole. In later writings, moved by the rapid developments in computers and communications technology, and the links between them, Bell has increasingly come to see postindustrial societies as information societies. Others, such as Peter Drucker (1909–2005), for similar reasons have spoken of "the knowledge society," for example in his *Post-capitalist Society* (1993), while Zbigniew Brzezinski (1929–) writes of "the technetronic society" in his *Between Two Ages* (1970). In all these accounts, central features are the emergence of a new type of worker, the "knowledge worker," the significance to the economy and society as a whole of the new information technology, and the increasing proportion of Gross National Product that is devoted to research and development.

The United States, western Europe, and Japan are the countries that by common consent have advanced farthest in the direction of postindustrialism. But east European theorists, putting a Marxist slant on it, have also hailed the advent of the "scientific–technological revolution" in their region, incorporating many of the central changes identified by Bell and others. It is seen as heralding a new mode of production in industrial societies, whether socialist or capitalist. Certainly there is no doubt that the majority of workers – somewhere between two-thirds and three-quarters in most cases – in all industrial societies are now service workers; nor that between 30 and 50 percent of the tertiary education age cohort now goes on to some form of higher **education**. At this most basic level no-one can deny that there have been fundamental changes in industrial society, leading, for instance, to a significant decline in the **power** of **trade unions** and forcing traditional socialist parties to modify their programs away from an exclusive focus on the proletariat. Many of these changes have been discussed under the heading of **embourgeoisement**.

The question is whether these changes add up, as Bell and others claim, to a new principle of society. Here there can be serious doubts. The driving forces of the postindustrial society appear to be much as they were in industrial society: capital accumulation, technical innovation, and **rationalization**. Neither **Karl Marx** nor **Max Weber**

would have been much surprised at the new developments, which were indeed implicit in their theories of industrial society.   KRISHAN KUMAR

postmodern theory

As the very prefix post- indicates, postmodern theory reflects uncertainty as to the direction of change and critical skepticism about the grand narratives of **modernization**, including ideological constructs of **socialism**, **liberalism**, **conservatism**, and welfarism. The term refers both to a postmodern theorizing, that is a specific form of analysis and **explanation** of contemporary society, and to the theoretical accounts of postmodern understood as either a new socio-cultural configuration (**postmodernity**) or a new trend in **social change** (postmodernization). The former usage (postmodern theorizing) has been associated with such thinkers as **Michel Foucault** and **Jean-François Lyotard** who analyze the discursive and narrative foundations of knowledge (**language games**). This predisposes them towards cultural criticism and philosophical reflections that engender postmodern sensitivity to language–power relations. The latter usage (theory of postmodernity or postmodernization) is associated with writings of such thinkers as **Fredric Jameson**, **Zygmunt Bauman**, and David Harvey, who analyze **postmodernism** as a new configuration, and **Jean Baudrillard,** Stephen Crook, Jan Pakulski, and Malcolm Waters in *Postmodernization* (1992), who study postmodernization as an ongoing process and directional trend.

Postmodernism typically refers to changes in cultural representations, mentalities, feelings, and lived experience. While the idea of postmodernism has been gaining currency since the 1970s in relation to the visual arts and architecture, its origins reach back to the second decade of the twentieth century, when radical artistic avant-garde movements, such as Dada, attempted to link art back to life through the use of images drawn from **popular culture** and found objects, such as the hatstands of Marcel Duchamp (1887–1968). It has been argued that this makes Dada an early forerunner of postmodernism. However, the Dada avant-gardism is usually seen as a failure in the sense of its confinement to the isolated modernist establishment. By the 1950s, modernist art started to lose its isolation and radical edge, becoming sanitized, popularized, commercialized, and internationalized – a step in a postmodern direction. The Pop Art of the 1960s has also been seen as a forerunner of postmodernism. Pop used images from popular culture, hyperrealism, collages, jokes, and parodies (for example *Soft Toilet*). Recent decades have seen a bewildering variety of postmodern styles: a resurgence of figurative work, **realism** and hyperrealism, **historicism**, and a deliberate superficiality that rejects the psychological depth of modernism.

Postmodern architecture, like postmodern art, rejects the elitist and avant-garde orientation of modernism. It is programmatically popular, immediately attractive to the eye, diverse, and eclectic. The term has been applied to decorative designs, neo-classicism, neo-vernacular, parody, and pastiche. These styles are united in their double coding of modernist techniques and materials, and contain stylistic references to something else. In one view, postmodernist architecture and art are welcomed as popular, accessible, and playful. In another view, they are deplored because they become the decorative façade of contemporary niche-marketed consumerism.

While there seems to be a consensus on what constitutes postmodernism in art, there is no agreement about contemporary notions of social postmodernity. Some (like Mike Featherstone) contrast the postmodern epoch with the modern era; postmodernity implies a break with and shift away from the organizing principles of modern society. Others such as Jameson in *Postmodernism or the Cultural Logic of Late Capitalism* (1991) see it as a continuation of modern trends; postmodernism constitutes just the cultural reflection of modern **capitalism**, an expression of American domination, and a lifestyle of the "yuppies." **Jean Baudrillard**, in turn, sees social postmodernity as a correlate of expanding **mass media and communications** and mass consumption, and as a new era brought by the proliferation of mediated communication, symbolic **consumption**, and the compression of **time** and **space**. This results in a proliferation of self-referential signs, intensified consumption of signs (for example brands), and the emergence of social order based on symbolic consumption.

There are differences in the view of how widespread the postmodern features are and how advanced the postmodern trends are. Bauman and Jameson see the advanced societies as already postmodern. By contrast, Crook and his colleagues analyze postmodernization as an ongoing – and by no means even or complete – social process. Postmodern trends include social fragmentation, **differentiation**, and the increasingly ephemeral nature of social formations; flexible specialization; progressing cultural **pluralism**, depthlessness, commercialization, and **populism**; widening

eclecticism and syncretism of styles; and generational libertarian shifts in **values** and sensitivities. Critical culturalists, such as Ronald Inglehart, focus on changes in values and the rise of diverse identity **politics**. Others, like Lyotard and Baudrillard, highlight the decline of ideological meta-narratives and the return to the local and vernacular, and the ascendancy of autonomous but empty symbols or simulacra. For Baudrillard, the world is saturated by sounds and images from mass media, eroding the distinction between representation and (social) reality and producing the "end of the social."

Postmodernization typically means the processes that accelerate and reverse modern trends. One can see the accounts of postmodernization as ranging from less radical, pointing to some continuities, to more radical, suggesting discontinuities. Jameson and Harvey, for example, analyze postmodernization as involving continuities: a gradual commodification of **culture**, collapse of styles and high/low cultural tastes, populism of standards, fragmentation of **social classes**, and political realignments as reflected in the proliferation of ephemeral movements. Crook, Pakulski, and Waters (1992) see postmodern trends in the "reversal through acceleration" of the key processes of modernization: commodification to hypercommodification, social differentiation to hyper-differentiation, and **rationalization** to hyper-rationalization. They identify postmodern trends in the domains of culture and **identity**, the role of the **state**, **politics**, work and production, and weakening class relations. Hypercommodification extends market relations to formerly non-commodified regions (for example intellectual **property**, and televangelism). Hyperdifferentiation breaks up **institutions** into fragments that combine in an unpredictable manner (for instance syncretic **lifestyles**, multimedia, transdisciplinary science). Hyperrationalization splits off inaccessible "expert cultures," produces "irrational" social responses and pluralizes **rationalities** (for example **fundamentalism** and new age cults). On this view, postmodernization involves also the blurring of the boundaries between social, cultural, and political domains. For Crook and his colleagues this means that flows of **social action** (as in new **social movements**) are no longer contained in social institutions.

JAN PAKULSKI

postmodernism

Associated with **postindustrial society** and **poststructuralism**, postmodernism arises as a consequence of advanced **modernization**, in particular the fragmentation of the West's institutionalization of unilinear history and systems of meaning. A conception of history as having a single direction, the endeavor to develop a rational program of collective emancipation, the grounding of all human experience and representation in reason: these are some of the key criteria of **modernity**. Yet in our own time, paradoxically, it is precisely such modernist aims for self-mastery and control that fall victim to the very social processes they seek to colonize. Recent decades have powerfully shown that the ethos of modernity has come to haunt us. Global **risks**, threats, and pandemics, from AIDS to **terrorism**, have served to highlight the gross limitations of modernist perspectives, generating in turn the emergence of new social and political agendas.

Postmodernism confounds **identity**, theory, and **politics** in a scandalous way, with its leveling of hierarchies, its dislocating subversion of ideological closure, its interpretative polyvalence and its self-reflexive **pluralism**. In this sense, postmodernism refers to certain currents of cultural and critical discourse which seek to deconstruct the ideological affinities of totalizing thought, the operations of **power**, the legitimating functions of knowledge and truth, and the discursive practices of self-constitution.

A growing appreciation of the limits of rationality, various postmodernists have argued, has led to the abandonment of the epistemological illusions of emancipatory declarations made in the name of freedom, truth, **equality**, liberty, and so on. As the pioneering postmodern analyst **Jean-François Lyotard** put this in *The Postmodern Condition* (1979 [trans. 1984]), postmodernism is defined as an "incredulity toward metanarratives." The grand narratives that unified and structured western science and philosophy, grounding truth and meaning in the presumption of a universal subject and a predetermined goal of emancipation, no longer appear convincing or even plausible. Instead, in the anti-totalizing, postmodern perspective, knowledge is constructed, not discovered; it is contextual, not foundational.

Social transformations are understood to be of central importance in this erosion of the grand narratives of the modern era. **Globalization** and especially the proliferation of new information **technologies** introduce a qualitative transformation in the experience of **space** and **time**, the result of which is a dramatic acceleration in the turmoil and flux of personal and cultural life. The overall effect, as **Jean Baudrillard** argues, is an implosion of all boundaries, an erasure of the distinctions of high and low **culture**, of appearance and reality, of past and present. Postmodernity is thus inherently decentered and dispersed: everything is of the same **value**, which means that nothing much counts in terms of meaning, distinction, hierarchy.

There are two major criticisms of postmodernism, one sympathetic, one critical. The sympathetic argument is that sociology should remain critical of the postmodern turn by attempting to develop a sociology of postmodernism, rather than succumbing to a postmodern sociology. This case has been vigorously argued by **Zygmunt Bauman**. The second response within sociology has been to reject the view that postmodernism spells the end of modernity.   ANTHONY ELLIOTT

postmodernity

The idea of postmodernity has until recently been the focus of a contested debate amongst **intellectuals**. Those seeking to defend the concept (it has many detractors) use it as a way to imply a change in modern social conditions and a new way of relating to **modernity**. The changes in modern social conditions usually include the development of new **technologies**, the decline in the power of **tradition**, the erosion of a strong version of secularism, **globalization**, the role of **culture** and communications, and the emergence of ecological issues and of other world regions challenging Euro-American modernities. New ways of relating to modern times have led to an enhanced questioning of ideas of **progress** and a reflection upon the limits of reason.

These arguments and others have begun to emerge in a political and intellectual context that has begun to debate the limits of specifically western modernity. A growing realization that there are other non-western civilizations and the idea that Euro-American forms of development have a number of negative side-effects, making them unsuitable for universal application, have aided thinking on these questions. In addition, the cultural turn in sociology has led to an increasing recognition of both the complexity and cultural plurality of modern societies. **Zygmunt Bauman** has arguably gone the farthest in pressing the claim that the condition of postmodernity is more than just changing social conditions. Postmodernity articulates a particular crisis for intellectuals who have suffered a period of relative displacement.

First, intellectuals are unable to offer authoritative solutions to questions of truth, the normative claims of **justice**, and taste. Their position of influence in modern society then can be said to be in decline. In this respect, Bauman suggests that they become interpreters of knowledge rather than legislators of new social systems. Second, the recognition of the inevitably pluralistic features of modern life disrupts universal claims and introduces questions of **relativism** into the production of knowledge. Finally, modern social conditions have also changed, introducing the development of a society based upon **consumption** rather than production. This means that the system now requires the pleasurable consumption of commodities rather than the deferral of gratification and thrift. Political domination is no longer achieved through the legitimation of social **values** as much as through a combination of seduction and repression. The requirement that we recall our unconditional responsibility towards the other without trying to reinvent the existential security of rules and expert systems takes us to the heart of postmodernity. In this respect, processes of globalization and individualization offer new opportunities for responsible political engagement beyond the now permeable walls of the nation-state.

Many intellectuals have sharply disagreed with these and similar ideas. They have suggested that ideas of postmodernity signify not so much a new social order, but a form of intellectual defeatism. The failure of intellectuals to offer up new blueprints for alternative social orders exhibits a lack of social responsibility. The global triumph of **capitalism**, new imperialist **wars**, the continuation of nationalist **violence**, and a planet that is being pushed beyond its ecological limits are reason enough to reject the label of postmodernism. Rejecting any notion of new times, many point to both the continuation of a largely capitalist-driven modernity and the need to develop solutions to **social problems**.   NICK STEVENSON

poststructuralism

This is concerned with the relations between human beings, the world, and the process of making and reproducing meanings (see Catherine Belsey, *Poststructuralism. A Very Short Introduction*, 2002). There are at least two historical narratives which relate to this definition, offering different routes leading to the intellectual position which became dominant in France in the last quarter of the twentieth century and, by extension, globally significant through the translations into English of the work, in particular, of **Louis Althusser**, **Roland Barthes**, **Jean Baudrillard**, **Pierre Bourdieu**, Jacques Derrida (1930–2004), **Michel Foucault**, **Julia**

Kristeva, and **Jean-François Lyotard**. One route tends to locate poststructuralism in the context of **language** and literature, whereas the other associates it with philosophy and the **social sciences**.

The first account takes the work of **Ferdinand de Saussure** in linguistics as the main starting-point. In analyzing "signs," Saussure distinguished between the "signifier," which is the sound or appearance of words being deployed, and the "signified," which is their meaning. Linguistic signs are arbitrary. Particular combinations of signifiers and signifieds are arbitrary entities. There is no natural correspondence between signifiers and what they signify (the signified). To analyze language, one has to analyze the relations between signs rather than the relation between those signs and any prior reality which they might be thought, fixedly, to represent. Language is not a nomenclature but a relational system of signs. But Saussure also distinguished between "langue" and "parole," between the systemic structure of language and contingent speech-acts. It was his contention that the primary purpose of linguistic science was to understand the structure of the non-contingent system of non-referential signs. In this account of the origins of poststructuralism, the work of Barthes was critical in following Saussure's notion of signification while rejecting his attempt to generate a universal analysis of signs. At the beginning of his *S/Z* (1970 [trans. 1975]), Barthes has commented that there are said to be Buddhists whose ascetic discipline enables them to perceive a whole landscape within a single bean. He asserted that the first analysts of narratives worked on this premise, attempting what is ultimately undesirable because the text as a result loses its distinctiveness and difference.

Barthes's science of signs, semiology, was poststructuralist in emphasizing "difference" rather than structural uniformity, but for a poststructuralist social scientist like Bourdieu, Barthes persisted in operating with the fundamentally structuralist assumption that an a-priori, systemic "langue" regulates speech practice. Bourdieu wanted to de-regulate "langue" as well as liberate signs from referential constraint. The second account of the development of poststructuralism incorporates the **influence** of Edmund Husserl's **phenomenology** and the **ontology** of Martin Heidegger (1889–1976). These influences from philosophy pushed the social sciences towards a recognition of the primacy of agency, towards the recognition of difference at the level of signifying actions rather than at the level of objectivized signs. There is a close relationship between the development of poststructuralism and **postmodernism**. One could say provocatively that postmodernism exposed the extent to which poststructuralism remained parasitic on structuralist assumptions.   DEREK ROBBINS

poverty

This concept describes an empirical reality, both globally and in individual societies, but the meaning of which is contested. What constitutes poverty depends on how it is defined and measured. The main debates around definition concern the role of material resources, in particular **income**, and whether poverty should be understood in absolute or relative terms. The nature of the debates differs according to context, in particular that of the global South or North.

Disagreements about the role of income revolve around a number of issues. One concerns the relative importance of income versus living standards, which may also reflect factors such as access to services and quality of the local **environment**. Another raises wider questions about the significance of nonmaterial aspects of poverty that are often raised by people in poverty in both the North and the South. These include disrespectful treatment, loss of dignity, lack of voice, and of **power**. With regard to nonmaterial aspects, it is possible to resolve any disagreement by making a distinction between the (narrower) definition and (broader) conceptualization of poverty. The latter is better able to embrace the relational aspects of poverty while the former focuses on poverty as a material condition.

The other key definitional debate has revolved around whether poverty should be understood in absolute or relative terms. Definitions deployed in the late nineteenth and early twentieth centuries by Charles Booth (1840–1916) and Seebohm Rowntree (1871–1954), the pioneers of modern poverty research, were supposedly absolute in the sense that poverty was said to be understood as lack of sufficient money to meet basic physical needs to subsist and survive. The alternative, relative definition was pioneered by Peter Townsend. In his major study *Poverty in the United Kingdom* (1979), he defined poverty in terms of exclusion from the living conditions, and inability to participate in the activities, taken for granted by the wider society because of lack of material resources. Central to his approach was the concept of **relative deprivation**, but understood as an objective condition rather than a subjective feeling as in **W. G. Runciman**'s formulation.

In judging whether relative poverty exists, comparison is made with others living in the same society at the same point in history. This means that historical and global North/South comparisons are misplaced. Such a comparison also highlights any **inequality** of resources between **groups** in a society, although relative poverty and inequality are not synonymous. The latter does not necessarily imply the inability of some members to participate fully in society because of lack of material resources. A relative definition also involves a particular reading of **human needs** not merely as physical but as socially and culturally constituted. One implication of an understanding of even the most basic physiological needs as socially conditioned is that the conventional notion of absolute poverty falls apart. Indeed, contemporary scholarship questions the conventional wisdom that Rowntree promulgated a definition of poverty, in terms of subsistence, that was absolute.

There have also been attempts to develop a framework that treats absolute and relative as complementary rather than competing formulations, which can be applied to both North and South. The first was by Amartya Sen (1933–). He identified an absolutist core to poverty, the most obvious manifestation of which is starvation and malnutrition. He suggested that what one is able to do or be (capabilities) is a question of universal absolutes, whereas the goods (or commodities) needed to translate this ability into actual being or doing (functionings) takes us into the sphere of relativities because commodities vary according to cultural and historical context. A heated debate with Townsend ensued in the early 1980s, which was confused because of a failure to clarify different interpretations of absolute and relative. More recently, Townsend and colleagues have promulgated a two-part definition of poverty – absolute and overall – which emerged from the 1995 United Nations (UN) Copenhagen summit. This, it is argued, can be applied to both industrialized and poorer countries.

The capabilities approach has been developed by Sen and Martha Nussbaum (1947–) in numerous books and papers, most recently, *Development as Freedom*, 1999. Their approach has been particularly influential in development circles, providing the framework for the annual UN Development Program *Human Development Report*. The essence of Sen's thesis is that what matters is not income or living standards as such but the kind of life that a person is able to lead (functionings) and the choices and opportunities open to people in leading their lives (capabilities). **Money**, Sen argues, is just a means to an end and the goods and services (commodities) it buys are simply particular ways of achieving functionings. Thus, poverty should be defined in terms of failure to achieve minimally acceptable capabilities.

In order to identify and count those defined as poor, measures are needed. These too generate controversy, involving choice of indicators and the standard, often called the poverty line, against which indicators are assessed. Questions include whether poverty should be measured in terms of income, living standards / **consumption**, or expenditure; increasingly the view is that a combination of approaches is needed to improve the accuracy of measures. Official measures tend to use income levels to establish a poverty line. Examples are 60 percent of median national income, as used within the European Union, and the World Bank's (much-criticized) $1, $2, or $4 a day. In addition to headcount measures, poverty-gap measures have been devised to gauge the extent to which people fall below the poverty line, although these are used less frequently. A focus on the numbers below the poverty line or on the poverty gap can point to different policy priorities.

This is one of the criticisms made by those who query the very construction of poverty lines. At the heart of such criticisms is the question as to whether there exists a clear threshold which neatly divides the poor from the nonpoor or whether the relationship between the two is better understood as a continuum, with gradations among both groups. The idea of a simple dichotomy between poor and nonpoor has also been questioned in the light of the growing use of longitudinal datasets to measure the dynamics of poverty. These show considerable movement in and out of poverty (although not usually very far), which is obscured by traditional snapshot measures. The length of time in poverty also affects the degree of deprivation of necessities experienced.

An alternative approach to drawing a poverty line is based on estimates of the income levels at which people are unable to afford items specified as essentials by either experts or the population at large. Typically, budget standards are calculated, based on the cost of a basket of goods and services. In the United Kingdom, a number of poverty studies have used a list of necessities agreed by a survey of the general population. Yet another device is to ask a sample of the population directly a question aimed at gauging what they think the poverty line should be for their household.

Although poverty estimates generally refer to individuals, they are typically based on measures of combined household/family resources. This is problematic where resources are not shared fairly within households, as research indicates can be the case. The result can be hidden poverty experienced primarily by women. It is one example of the ways in which poverty is gendered, although this was largely ignored prior to the intervention of feminist scholars. Even on conventional measures, women are more likely than men to be in poverty. They also tend to take the main responsibility for managing poverty and often go without to protect other family members, especially children, from its full impact. The stress involved can damage both physical and mental health.

Poverty is also racialized in terms of its incidence, racialized stereotyping, and the effects of **discrimination** and **racism**. This dimension is most marked in the United States where **race and ethnicity** and urban **segregation** figure prominently in the sociological poverty literature. Segregation is one aspect of the geography of poverty, which is a manifestation of wider spatial inequalities.

Explanations of poverty can broadly be understood as behavioral or structural. Behavior-based explanations attribute poverty to the **values**, **attitudes**, and behavior of the poor. An example is Charles Murray's writings on the underclass (including *The Emerging British Underclass*, 1990). In the United States, the earlier notion of a culture of poverty drew attention to the ways in which a **subculture**, marked by fatalism, an inability to defer gratification, and pathological behavior, was passed down through the **generations**. Although Oscar Lewis, who coined the term in the 1960s, emphasized that the culture of poverty represented an adaptation to rather than cause of poverty, it was used to argue with the latter meaning by others who blamed the poor for their poverty, as both supporters and critics of Lewis have observed. A related notion in the United Kingdom, in the 1970s, was that of the cycle of deprivation.

In *The Other America* (1967), a pivotal intervention in the United States, Michael Harrington linked the culture of poverty to a structural analysis. Structural explanations of poverty focus on economic, social, and political structures and processes – from the global to the local/familial. Examples are **unemployment**, low pay, and women's position in the **family**. Another perspective is institutional, which points to the failure of government policies. For example, the term poverty trap was coined in Britain to highlight the way in which means-tested benefits can trap the working poor: the interaction of the withdrawal of means-tested supplements with taxation and insurance contributions meant that a pay rise could leave a low-paid worker worse off. Although the system has since been reformed to avoid this extreme situation, large numbers of lower-paid workers can still lose a significant proportion of a pay increase because of the poverty trap. An example of an explanation that combines the behavioral and institutional is that which locates the cause of poverty in a dependency culture said to be created by welfare benefits.

Recently, some poverty analysts who subscribe to a structural explanation have married this approach with a sociological account of agency in order to understand better the ways in which people cope with poverty. One formulation, taken from the development literature, is of people deploying a range of resources (personal, social, cultural, and material) to compose their livelihoods. Structure and agency also combine in some sociological accounts of the concept of **social exclusion**, which emphasize the agency of the more powerful in excluding the less powerful.

Labels such as "socially excluded," "poor," and "underclass" are examples of how the more powerful name those without **power**. They are not labels with which those experiencing poverty necessarily want to identify. **Organizations** of people in poverty are, however, developing alternative discourses that have also been promulgated by some more powerful bodies such as the United Nations. This is a discourse of human **rights**, **citizenship**, voice, and power. Two key principles underpin the conceptualization of poverty in terms of human rights and citizenship: recognition of the dignity of all humans and the interdependence of civil, political, social, and cultural rights. In addition, this perspective emphasizes participation in society and the polity and the right to be heard in decisionmaking. In both North and South, people in poverty identify lack of voice and associated powerlessness as critical to understanding their situation. Calls for their voices to be heard in policymaking and campaigning are becoming more emphatic. In the South and, to a lesser extent, the North, the case is being made for participatory research that involves people in poverty as experts in their own lives. The argument is that sociological accounts will provide a better understanding of poverty if they reflect the analyses of those with experience of poverty. RUTH LISTER

poverty line
– see **poverty**.

poverty trap
– see **poverty**.

power

In a discipline such as **sociology**, notorious for the difficulty it experiences in establishing widely and durably agreed definitions of its concepts, that of power (at any rate social power, which is our only concern here) stands out as one whose definition is particularly contentious and unstable. This in spite (or perhaps on account) of the fact that, however understood, this concept signals a particularly significant social phenomenon, arguably entitled to a central position in the discipline's vocabulary and discourse.

The most significant of the controversies taking place among sociologists and political scientists in the twentieth century around the concept-of-power concern, expressly or otherwise, concerns the definition of power (*Macht*) offered at the beginning of the century by **Max Weber**. In *Economy and Society* (1922 [trans. 1968]), that definition characterizes power as "the chance of a man or a group of men to realize their own will in a communal action even against the resistance of others who are participating in the action."

In fact, some expressed or implied elements of this definition were not widely considered as controversial. In particular, it was generally agreed that one should think of (social) power not as a substance but as a relationship – a point implied in Weber's reference to both parties' "participation" in "communal action." In other terms, power is not something to be held, so to speak, in one's hand or pocket, but as something obtaining between two parties, such that A may hold it vis-à-vis B, but not vis-à-vis C.

Weber's expression "chance" entails two further plausible, closely related characteristics of power. First, power refers to a probability, not so to speak to a "dead cert," to the complete assurance of a given party's success. Second, power is always potential because it refers not so much to the doing of something (to the actual "production of effects," proposed by others as an alternative definition of power) but to the capacity of doing something, of producing effects if and when one chooses.

In other words, power does not need to be exercised (by overcoming opposition or otherwise) in order to exist. Paradoxically, the exercise of power may consume it and/or expose it, when actually brought to bear, to the risk of being found wanting, of failing to do its number as it were. Rather, power is at its most powerful when those subject to it practice their subjection to it without its being actually exercised, when it operates through the power subjects' memory of past exercises of it or their imagination of future ones, when it needs to be at most symbolically represented rather than actually put into action. (One may connect to this intuition a number of enlightening discourses by political scientists, historians, and sociologists, on the symbolism of power – and of related phenomena.)

Other aspects of Weber's definition became controversial in a wide ranging post-World War II discussion of the power concept, involving both political scientists – for instance Robert Dahl, *Modern Political Analysis* (1963) – and sociologists such as Steven Lukes in *Power: A Radical View* (1974) and Dennis Wrong in *Power: Its Forms, Bases, and Uses* (1979). In particular, Weber's reference to the "will" of the party in power became an issue. It was questioned whether that reference implied intentionality. Does the existence of a power relationship depend on the powerful party's awareness of its own preference for a given, existent, or future state of things and its conscious commitment to obtaining it? Does it depend on its ability to superimpose its own over the other party's will? Is the overcoming or the potential overcoming of actual or virtual resistance an essential component of the relationship? What of situations where the asymmetry between the parties is so great that the inferior party is not even aware of having interests contrary to those of the superior party, but routinely cooperates in the attainment of the latter, or at any rate does not seek to hinder that attainment? Is not the superior party's ability to keep certain present or future states of things from becoming an issue between itself and the other party – its ability to control the agenda, it was said – a particularly privileged condition?

Some contributors to the debate, while assuming that Weber's conceptual construct was essentially acceptable – whatever the qualifications and modifications to it suggested by the answers to some questions we have mentioned – labored to establish its boundaries by comparing and contrasting it with cognate concepts, such as **authority** (or domination), **influence**, force, or manipulation.

In the second half of the twentieth century the concept of power, with reference to the Weberian definition or otherwise, was also the object of methodological arguments concerning the possibility of grounding it empirically. The discussion involved both sociologists and political scientists, especially those associated with the behaviorist approach, itself much inspired by sociology. It

often concerned, besides the power concept itself and its elaboration in the notion of "power structure," the analysis of **elites**. Attempts to put such concepts to use in empirical research, through varying methodological approaches, were conducted both at the local level – for instance by Floyd Hunter, *Community Power Structure: A Study of Decision Makers* (1953), and Robert Dahl, *Who Governs? Democracy and Power in an American City* (1961) – and at the national level – for example by **C. Wright Mills**, *The Power Elite* (1956). This led to interesting developments, for instance the study of "interlocking directorates," carried out with reference to numerous corporations or other economic units, such as banks and **firms**, or the study of decisionmaking within political bodies.

Some scholars went further in the attempt to operationalize the power concept and indeed to measure various parameters of a power relationship. Some aspects of these are in principle amenable to quantitative assessment. For instance, over how many subjects can the holder of power exercise that power? Over how many aspects of their existence? How significant are those aspects?

Also, assuming that power entails the ability to inflict negative sanctions on those subject to it, one can put those sanctions in some kind of ordinal sequence. The power over life and death which Roman law attributed to the *paterfamilias* can plausibly be assumed to stand at the high end of that sequence, although there are variations in the manner in which a subject can be put to death. This side of killing lies, for example, banishment from the polity, often accompanied by the confiscation of the patrimony of the banished. The sequence goes down to a rich variety of less and less blatantly damaging sanctions, such as the dismissal from employment of a worker, the blackballing of someone seeking admission to a club, or the exposure to gossip of a member of a social circle. But it is a demanding task to subsume this ordinal arrangement of sanctions into a more sophisticated metric, comprising other aspects of the power relations, and allowing their comparison – the comparison, say, between the threat of a lockout and the threat of a strike. In fact, some scholars adopting high standards of methodological rigor were led by the difficulty of measuring power to the conclusion that one might as well dispense with the concept itself!

Fortunately, few scholars took that suggestion seriously. The rest continued, more or less explicitly and consistently, to abide by the notion that power was an indispensable concept, pointing to a most significant social experience or indeed a critical dimension, overt or covert, of all **social structures**. From the late 1950s through the mid 1970s, in the protracted sociological argument over a theoretical perspective focused on order versus one focused on conflict, the power concept was often invoked by students associated with the latter perspective. However, it could be employed also to challenge that alternative, arguing that order need not be grounded on normative consensus among all involved in systematic **interaction**, but rather on the pressure which one part of society, the powerful part, imposed upon the other, powerless part. Even those situations where significant structures were in fact underwritten by some kind of normative consensus valid across society could be interpreted as outcomes of particularly protracted, routinized, long-unchallenged power **inequalities**.

Another advantage of the emphasis on these was that it gave some conceptual purchase even on **social change**, on situations where existent arrangements were called into question and order broke down. In its Weberian framework, the concept of power implied the possibility of resistance. It thus allowed that sometimes the power-less but resistant part of society could gain the upper hand and succeed in restructuring society to suit its own interests. Or, a group not favored by the existent power structure could challenge it by developing alternative power sources. Finally, even within a stable power structure, its very existence gave rise to contentions over the occupancy of the favored positions within it, and thus to further occasions for change.

Arguments of this kind, as we have seen, often appealed to Weber's intellectual authority. The debate became more intense, and more significant, when the central imagery of the Weberian construction was called into question. To simplify matters, an intrinsically tough-minded view of power was challenged by a tender-minded one.

The Weberian imagery, we have suggested, emphasized the asymmetry between individuals or between **groups** acting in the presence of one another, and the advantages enjoyed by those located at the upper end of the asymmetry. It implied that, at any rate in a stable and consistent power relationship, whatever its sources and scope, all the power there was lay at that end – in other words, the relationship was a zero-sum one.

Yet Weber himself had connected that relation with the involvement of both parties in "communal action." Whether Weber meant this or not, this consideration suggested to some authors that one could view the power relation, in spite of its intrinsic asymmetry, as a functional feature of that communal action, a fixture, as it were, of a shared social space, rather than something appropriated by one party and by the same token denied the other party and used to keep it at bay. A given party's power over the other could be viewed also as something both parties benefited from, as a component of their power to attain some shared end, as a collective facility.

This bold reconceptualization of power was put forward in the late 1950s by **Talcott Parsons**, in a belated but impressive rebuttal of a criticism often made of his theories, to the effect that these ignored the phenomenon of power and the related reasons for conflict and change. It was taken further by **Niklas Luhmann**, who expressly reproached Parsons's critics, and his own, for their bloody-minded insistence on the asymmetry of power, on the distribution of power within a group. The time had come to consider the extent to which the institutionalization of power relations empowered the group as a whole, made it more capable of pursuing collective goals.

Power should be considered as a medium through which selections made in one part of society could be transmitted to others, and thus as analogous to **money**. In the same way that money allows and fosters the **rationalization** of economic activities in a society where it has been invented or adopted, the development within it of power relations could strongly assist a society's pursuit of non-economic goals.

The gain a group or society derives from being the locus of a power relationship deserves serious consideration, irrespective of the way in which or the extent to which such a relationship favors in the first instance one part of society over the others. It allows the society as a whole to respond more promptly and energetically to new opportunities and dangers in its environment, to promote and manage new modes of cooperation. It can be likened to a cybernetic device, monitoring the environment, collecting, storing, elaborating **information**, forming decisions which can be the more promptly, coherently and predictably implemented, to everybody's advantage, the more they are backed by sanctions available in principle exclusively to one part of society – the superior part. Put otherwise, power does not empower only those who hold it.

The fact that power can be, and, according to this argument, typically is, generated and accumulated on behalf of the whole society, although managed by one part of it, is suggested by one significant aspect of political power, namely its tendency to seek **legitimacy**, that is to generate in those subject to power a disposition to obey, grounded on a sense of moral obligation. Yet, Parsons's own strong emphasis on legitimacy (and the attendant processes of legitimation, and its variety), while in keeping with his own strongly normative (and Durkheim-inspired) conception of the social process at large, is only to a limited extent supported by Weber's own discourse on power. Here, the ideal-typical discussion of the subjective processes presiding over the subjects' obedience points also to other motivations to obey – a subject's totally unreflected, automatic habit of submission, or a subject's calculation of the advantages and disadvantages of obedience versus non-obedience and of the probability of the attendant application or non-application of sanctions. Obedience grounded on a sense of moral obligation comes in only as a third answer – though one on which Weber himself lays emphasis, by offering a particularly creative treatment of it.

Weber in fact treats legitimacy itself as a significant but contingent qualification of a power relation previously established on strictly factual grounds, and which can if necessary reassert itself and maintain itself, at any rate in the short to medium term, even in the presence of a legitimation crisis. Furthermore, in the context of big-time politics – the context, that is, of international relations, where the competitive interactions between sovereign polities take place – there is not much place for legitimacy, which is instead a property, if of anything, of domestic political relations. In the international realm, instead, sheer, military might is necessarily the ultimate stake and medium of political action. Because legitimacy is irrelevant to such might, only its effectiveness counts.

Furthermore, Weber was keenly aware that political power itself, that to which the notion of legitimacy could apply, as we have seen in the domestic context, was only one form of social power. Weber argued that **social classes**, status groups, and **political parties** are all phenomena of the distribution of power within a **community**. In Weber's view, power exists between a community's component groups if, and to the extent that, one of these secures exclusive or highly privileged access to and control over a critical social resource. This allows the group to lay enforceable boundaries on the activities of the other groups. The powerful group can induce the others to desist from opposing or hindering the pursuit of its own interests, or indeed direct them to commit

some of their own activities, willy-nilly, to that very pursuit.

The power phenomenon, then, can be differentiated conceptually by considering the social resources a group must appropriate in order to gain this degree of control over others. In Marxian language, those resources are of three kinds: means of production (on which is based economic power, the main theme of the relations between classes); means of **violence** (these ground political power, and the possession and employment of them is contended over by parties – in a very broad meaning of this expression); and means of interpretation.

This last concept needs some further elaboration, for it points to the elusive domain of the imaginary. **Michael Mann**, in *The Sources of Social Power* (1986), without using the expression "means of interpretation," convincingly argues its significance on the basis of three "anthropological" considerations. Human beings need cognitive frameworks by means of which to experience and to handle reality; need normative frameworks to sustain and routinize their cooperative activities and to moderate and settle their contentions; and need ritual and aesthetic practices by means of which to express particularly meaningful **emotions** and symbolize and sustain their **identities**. "Ideological" power emerges to the extent that a distinctive group establishes privileged control over the social activities and the cultural artifacts relating to the satisfaction of these needs, and to that degree can direct those social activities and the access to those cultural artifacts.

Mann, however, dissents from this tripartite classification of the power phenomenon by giving separate conceptual status also to military power. Other students dissent from it by explicitly or implicitly subscribing to the identification of power itself with political power.

A sustained argument to the effect that social power can manifest itself in different ways was developed, towards the end of the twentieth century, by the German sociologist Heinrich Popitz (1925–2002). The title of his book, *Phänomene der Macht: Autorität, Herrschaft, Gewalt, Technik* (1986) conveys this meaning, for *Phaenomene* is a plural noun. In particular, Popitz argues, power can be acquired and managed also to the extent that, through "technical action," some people can shape and modify to their own advantage the objective circumstances under which other people live, the constraints under which they operate.

Technical action has three essential moments, all in the first place relating individuals with things:

"making use of," "modifying," and "producing" objects.

But such subject-to-object relations always affect also those between subject and subject. This does not simply mean that technical action has social conditions and consequences. Rather, such action plays a role in establishing the social conditions of human beings. Behind the "making use" of objects necessarily lies the question of property claims, behind the "modifying" of objects a particular form of the exercise of power – and not just power over the objects themselves – and their "producing" entails the **differentiation** of activities and thus a form of division of **labor**.

Another of Popitz's significant contributions, however, is chiefly concerned with political power, which he, with Weber, grounds in violence, and particularly with its institutionalization. He conceptualizes three main aspects of this process: the depersonalization of power, the formalization of its exercise, and its integration (the latter meaning the increasing extent to which power gears itself into other social activities, is supported by them, and contributes to them).

Popitz also outlines an ideal-typical sequence of phases in the institutionalization of political power. The recourse to violence (or the threat of it) as a way of inducing others' compliant behavior may go beyond its sporadic phase insofar as means of violence are made ready for repeated uses, and brought to bear on recurrent situations, from which those threatened with violence cannot easily escape. Power can then move on to a norm-making phase, where it does not just induce the subjects to momentary compliance but seeks to program and routinize their compliant activities and dispositions. Further, it can be positionalized, that is, connected with the occupancy of distinctive **social roles** (the earliest of which have been those of the patriarch, the judge, and the war leader). In the next phase, those and other such positions come to be surrounded and supported by a staff, an apparatus – a set of individuals who steadily and reliably collaborate with each position's holder. The final phase sees the emergence of a **state**. Here the ensemble of the holders of power positions and of the related administrative agencies effectively claims the monopoly of three essential functions: norm-making, jurisdiction, and enforcement.

The recognition that social power has different sources and takes different forms, including at least political and economic power, brings to bear a specifically sociological perspective on a phenomenon – power itself – which for centuries has been attributed primarily or indeed exclusively to the political sphere. Indeed, according to Luhmann, until the advent of **modernity** western philosophers and other students of social and cultural affairs "thematized" **society** itself chiefly in its aspect as a polity, as a "realm," as the bounded territory whose inhabitants are perceived in the first place as suitable objects for rule.

Only in the course of **modernization** has the sphere of the **economy** strongly asserted its autonomy from that of politics, and economic power has separated itself institutionally from political power. But according to Franz Neumann, this historically unique development has by the same token posed the problem of how those two power forms would relate to one another, whether and how they would assist or contrast with one another, establish alliances with one another or seek to maximize their own autonomy over one another, their own superiority over one another.

This problem cannot be settled by conceptual fiat, for it has different aspects, and finds different solutions, in varying empirical circumstances. For instance, the Marxian characterization of the state as "the executive committee of the bourgeoisie" was not wide of the mark when it was proposed, but it needs at the very least strong qualifications and modifications, if one wants to apply it in later circumstances. Here it became more enlightening to think of politics and the **market** as the institutional loci of intrinsically different, and potentially competing, power processes. The title of **Thomas H. Marshall**'s *Citizenship and Social Class* (1950) points in this direction.

The duality in question finds an echo in other contemporary theoretical debates in the **social sciences**. The superiority of the economy is implicitly asserted in the extension of the rational choice approach to spheres of social existence, including the polity, where previously other approaches prevailed. In particular, the economist Oliver Williamson construed the emergence of hierarchy itself (the key political phenomenon) as the outcome of particular circumstances where the individuals' purely market behavior, which he viewed as the **paradigm** of all social conduct, generated inefficiencies. These are remedied by complementing the mechanism of coordination constituted by mere exchanges by a different one – "do as I say."

Whatever the insights yielded by these economic perspectives, one must note their persistent tendency to identify power with political power, and thus to treat the power phenomenon itself as something in principle extraneous to the economic realm. Power so conceived can be at best complementary to that realm, servicing its need for political support and regulation. At worst, it tends to prey upon it, and thus to damage its unique capacity to produce efficiency (once more an intrinsically economic criterion, unproblematically put forward as the one criterion by which to judge all social arrangements).

As long as such perspectives prevail, they do little to prepare the sociological imagination to deal with the continuing story of the relationship between economic and political power. The main content of that story is, in the early twenty-first century, the **globalization** process. This can be roughly conceived as a (partly) novel way in which economic processes seek to proceed with a maximum of support, and a minimum of interference, on the part of political power centers. The novelty lies in the ever-growing availability to economic forces of largely deterritorialized spaces and resources. This deeply challenges the still prevalent power centers – states which exercise jurisdiction over distinctive territories, and extract resources from economic units stably located within those spaces.

An appreciation of the extent to which these ongoing phenomena find in social power both their target and their medium requires among other things the continuing awareness of the significance and complexity of the power concept itself. Once more it is not a conceptual question whether the relationship between political power and economic power, in particular, is primarily one of collusion or collision. But one can assume that the answer to that question – or indeed the answers, since these will continue to vary from time to time and from place to place – will throw light on historical phenomena of great human significance.   GIANFRANCO POGGI

pragmatism

This philosophical school, founded in the United States in the nineteenth century, originates in the belief that philosophical standards, and especially the standards of truth, should be grounded in the efficacy of the practices that would result from their use. Pragmatism is averse to all metaphysical, moral, and social ideals that claim priority over the solutions to practical problems.

While several current sociological projects draw inspiration from C. S. Peirce (1839–1914), the father of modern pragmatism and the scholar who made communication central to pragmatic thought, **Charles Horton Cooley** and John Dewey (1859–1952) built more well-established bridges to

topics of sociological interest from pragmatic philosophical positions. **George Herbert Mead** expanded and extended these bridges. Thereafter, some of Mead's leading insights were institutionalized in sociology via **Herbert Blumer**'s interpretations of him. The **Chicago School** of **symbolic interactionism** followed Blumer's lead.

However, the influence of pragmatism in sociology extends beyond the symbolic interactionist school. After arriving in the United States, **Alfred Schutz** worked several pragmatic insights into his social **phenomenology**, paying special attention to the works of Dewey and the pragmatically inspired psychology of **William James**. **Erving Goffman** was inspired by James as well when writing *Frame Analysis* (1973). **Arlie Russell Hochschild** draws central elements of her groundbreaking conception of emotion work from Mead, which is quite helpful because most pragmatists other than James are inclined to emphasize cognition over **emotion**. On a more abstract level, Mead's pragmatic analysis of **social action** is reworked and plays a central role in **Jürgen Habermas**'s extraordinary model of communicative action.

Though Mead is far more widely cited by sociologists than any other pragmatist, John Dewey's analysis in *Human Nature and Conduct* (1922) provides the most clear-cut illustration of the application of pragmatic principles to **sociological theory**. Dewey builds a theory of social action upon an insight into social praxis that more recently has figured prominently in **Anthony Giddens**'s structuration theory and the ideas of **habitus and field** devised by **Pierre Bourdieu**. The insight is that most actions in **everyday life** are performed with only tacit consciousness in habitual ways. This widely shared view does not derive from pragmatism per se. But Dewey takes the pragmatic turn when he observes that, when habitual routines are blocked, sharply focused thought concentrates on eliminating the blockage, whether by removing it or by creative innovation. Dewey proposes that basic human psychic impulses become associated with habits. Their frustration motivates the actor to conscious thought. However, these efforts may be derailed through various kinds of dissipation. Drug abuse, promiscuous **sexuality**, daydreaming, and psychological distress all follow from the dissipation of impulses to overcome frustrating problems. The proper aim of scientific practice is to expedite an end to these frustrations. Dewey, like most pragmatists, underrates the role of domination in both social routines and focused thought. His **social psychology** also lacks a deep appreciation of the structured nature of social conduct. Moreover, unlike Peirce and Mead, Dewey neglects communication. Nonetheless, his emphasis on cycles of routine and frustration in action epitomizes the pragmatic view of social conduct.   IRA COHEN

prejudice

In sociology the concept of prejudice refers broadly to systematic and durable subjective assessments of **groups**, or members of those groups, in unfavorable terms. The concept has been at the center of sociological research on **race and ethnicity** for many years but has also played an important role in sociological research pertaining to **age**, **social class**, **disability and impairment**, **gender**, and **sexuality**. Research on prejudice overlaps to a considerable extent with research on the closely related phenomena of **discrimination** and **stigma**. However, the study of prejudice tends to focus more on the causes and characteristics of people's prejudicial **attitudes**, discrimination research focuses more on their prejudicial or injurious behavior, and research on stigma tends to focus on the experiences and behavior of those who are victimized by prejudice, discrimination, and stigmatization. While some social scientists believe prejudice entails evaluations based on erroneous preconceptions regarding an out-group, others suggest it can be based on objective conflicts of interest between in-group and out-group members. Scholars belonging to the first school of thought tend to take a more optimistic view of the prospects for overcoming prejudice insofar as they see the problem as essentially one of changing people's attitudes through a sustained campaign of enlightened **education**. Proponents of the second school of thought see the problem as more deeply entrenched in people's social structural circumstances and relationships, and hence are rather less optimistic about the prospects of remedies that do not attend to the social structural, as well as the social psychological, causes of people's prejudices.

Another important and pervasive distinction in the literature on prejudice concerns the extent to which prejudicial attitudes are conscious or unconscious. The earliest research on prejudice tended to focus on overt forms of bigotry or the explicit espousal of prejudicial attitudes towards various out-groups or individual out-group members. However, it is now much more common for social scientists to consider how systematic biases against particular out-groups or systematically discriminatory behaviors towards them are maintained despite research subjects' conscious commitments to an image of themselves as non-prejudiced against that group. This issue is particularly salient in debates as to whether prejudice is maintained primarily by social psychological or by social structural processes. Those who lean towards social structural **explanations** of prejudice tend to be more amenable to the view that individuals may often be unwitting, or unconscious, agents of prejudice and discrimination despite consciously espousing egalitarian **values**.

At least as far back as **Émile Durkheim**'s classic work on the value of deviance ascriptions for the maintenance of in-group **solidarity** in his analysis of **crime** in *The Rules of Sociological Method* (1895 [trans. 1958]), sociologists have recognized a certain social functionality in explicitly designating, and discriminating against, groups other than one's own.

While sometimes drawing on this longer legacy from classical sociology, research on prejudice has more recent origins. It was only in the wake of World War II, following revelations about the Holocaust and other horrors of Nazi Germany, that social scientists began to investigate how it was possible for such powerfully chauvinistic sentiments to arise. While **ethnocentrism**, xenophobia, and chauvinism were certainly recognized features of the social landscape before this time, they were not made the topic of systematic sociological analysis until World War II. One early approach to explaining prejudice against minority groups in society drew upon the frustration–aggression hypothesis formulated by John Dollard and his colleagues in *Frustration and Aggression* (1939), wherein it was argued that an agent frustrated at the hands of a more powerful actor will sublimate the sentiments of aggression created by these frustrations by focusing them on less powerful scapegoats. Thus, met with the frustrations surrounding World War I, the Versailles Treaty, and subsequent reparations, Germany was held to have taken this out on the Jews because they could not express their aggression directly towards the Allies. Another major theoretical approach to emerge on the topic of prejudice was that put forward by **Theodor Wiesengrund Adorno** and his colleagues regarding what they called the **authoritarian personality**. Drawing upon the principles of Freudian **psychoanalysis**, Adorno focused on early childhood learning processes to explain the propensities of some people to adopt rigid, inflexible, and prejudicial attitudes towards certain minority groups and their members. According to this theory, the early childhood experience of growing up in a highly regimented, strictly disciplined household could often produce a personality structure in children that is highly submissive to the dictates of established authority figures and intolerant of people(s) who do not conform to those dictates. This personality structure predisposes individuals to chauvinistic persecution of people who do not subscribe to the ethnic and/or cultural values to which they were compelled to adhere as children. Once established in the deep psyche of the individual, this personality structure becomes relatively impervious to rational critique and hence relatively resistant to change. These earliest approaches tended to locate the cause of prejudice in psychopathological learning processes and thereby to delimit the focus of analyses to only those people thought to have undergone them. While certain segments of the human population were held to be guilty of prejudice, the vast majority were not seen to be implicated in the reproduction of prejudice and discrimination.

Research following on from the pioneering work of Harvard social psychologist Gordon Allport (1897–1967) has suggested that prejudice is not only the result of psychopathology but also results from much more routine and pervasive learning processes. This research opened the door to much more encompassing theories concerning both the causes and the prevalence of prejudice. According to Allport, the human mind cannot dispense with what he called categorical thinking, and what is now more commonly known as stereotypical thinking, because it is the function of the mind to simplify and systematize the diverse sensory and cognitive inputs to which it is exposed. Were it not to do so, we would be hopelessly ill-equipped to act in the world. However, this natural mental function can serve to create significant **social problems** when our stereotypes are based on flawed information and are applied indiscriminately to whole minority groups and their members. While acknowledging the role played by psychodynamic pathologies in creating prejudice, Allport insisted in *The Nature of Prejudice* (1954) we must supplement psychodynamic explanations with explanations that speak to the whole spectrum of processes, both normal and abnormal, that figure in the development of our personalities. These include social, cultural, and economic processes as well as psychodynamic ones. Allport properly insisted that any adequate understanding of prejudice must allow that it can be caused by many different kinds of things occurring in a person's life. However, as a social psychologist he was quite understandably predisposed to focus on the personality of the individual actor as the critical apparatus upon which these various processes must act if they are to become manifest as prejudice. For Allport and his followers, prejudice was most fundamentally an "antipathy based on a faulty and inflexible generalisation." And just as he focused on the social psychological processes that give rise to prejudicial attitudes, his proposals for alleviating prejudice focused on efforts to correct the erroneous mental predispositions of individual actors rather than the social structural circumstances that compel those mental predispositions. From this social psychological perspective, the basic nature of prejudice is seen to reside in the mistaken judgments of particular individuals rather than in the inter-group conflicts and tensions endemic to a social system. As one might imagine, sociologists have sometimes been dissatisfied with what they have taken to be the over-emphasis on individuals in this approach and the concomitant under-emphasis on macro-structural causes of persistent prejudice and discrimination.

Several theoretical approaches have been taken in research aimed at exploring such macro-structural causes. One suggests that prejudicial attitudes express what are in fact realistic group conflicts. Far from expressing mistaken understandings of the threat posed by out-groups and/or their individual members, members of in-groups are prejudiced against members of those out-groups with whom they actually, or might potentially, struggle over objectively scarce resources. Another related theoretical approach follows in the tradition of **Herbert Blumer**'s group position model. According to Blumer, in a variety of publications relating to "Collective Behavior" in A. M. Lee, *New Outline of the Principles of Sociology* (1946), and "Social Movements" in A. M. Lee, *Principles of Sociology* (1955), members of an in-group must share an outlook comprised of four key features for prejudice to arise: (1) a feeling of superiority, (2) a belief that an out-group is intrinsically different and alien, (3) a sense of proprietary claim to certain privileges and resources, and (4) a sense of threat from members of subordinate groups upon the dominant group's prerogatives. In contrast to the realistic group conflict model, Blumer's group position model focuses on the perceptions of in-group members that their prerogatives are under threat rather than the objective reality of the threat itself. This highlights not only that prejudice may arise from perceptions that may or may not be accurate, but also the notion that there is an affective, as well as a purely instrumental, dimension to the felt conflict between members of an in-group and an out-group. More than merely observing an objective conflict of interest, in-group members feel a normative sense that this conflict ought to be resolved in favor of their own group and that not only their own personal prerogatives but the prerogatives of their group as a whole ought not to be threatened. This highlights how prejudice must be understood as not just the negative attitudes of an individual towards an out-group, but negative attitudes necessarily mediated by a sense of group membership and commitments to the well-being of that group as a whole in comparison with other groups. Other important approaches to the study of prejudice include the ideological control and paternalism model, the social dominance model, and social identity models. While not necessarily conflicting with the realistic group conflict and group position models, these models tend not to focus as much attention on overt conflict and threat. The ideological control and paternalism model argues that prejudice arises when efforts are made by members of a dominant group to legitimize their expropriative relationship with a subordinate group ideologically. In this effort they will seek to minimize overt hostilities by proffering deflated images of the aptitudes of subordinated group members and a paternalistic sense of obligation to look after them. This approach suggests that prejudice may not always be expressed in hostile terms but may also be expressed in terms connoting warmth and concern for the welfare of subordinated group members. The social dominance model highlights a sense of entitlement felt by in-group members to dominance in their relations with out-group members, but does not call so much attention to their felt sense of competition with and threat from members of an out-group. Finally, social identity models point to the fact that prejudices against out-groups and their individual members may often arise as a consequence of in-group loyalties as such and the wide range of instrumental and affective satisfactions that come from our self-categorization as members of an in-group.   DARIN WEINBERG

pressure group
– see **group(s)**

prestige
Referring to **influence**, reputation, or popular esteem, this concept is often mistakenly treated as a synonym for **social status**. Status refers to the social position a person occupies in a social hierarchy. Prestige refers to the esteem assigned to social position. Prestige comes in two general forms. Ascribed prestige refers to the generation of esteem based upon rank. For example, a people assign prestige to a monarch by virtue of bloodline; or to a physician on the basis of the honorific **value** of the **occupation**. Achieved prestige refers to the assignment of esteem on the basis of the accomplishments of the individual. For example, John Lennon (1940–80) of the Beatles was esteemed as a result of his success as a popular entertainer and campaigner for peace, and Nelson Mandela (1918–), the founder of the African National Congress in south Africa, is honored for his stance on human **rights** and anti-racism. The trend in modern **democracies** is for ascribed prestige to be replaced by achieved prestige. However, because democracies create opportunities for achievement that generate unequal rewards in economic **wealth** and distinction, they support new types of ascribed prestige. For example, in the United States, Caroline Kennedy does not occupy a formal rank in society. Nonetheless, she commands a type of ascribed prestige by virtue of the accomplishments of her parents, John and Jackie Kennedy. Democracies weaken traditional status hierarchies, but they create the conditions for new hierarchies based on achievement, which in turn confer prestige through inheritance.

Because esteem has value it is subject to contrivance and imposture. In traditional society this often took the form of illegal claims to bloodline. In contemporary society they more commonly take the form of the tabloid media constructing celebrities for public **consumption** and pecuniary gain. The magnification of celebrity **culture** is often held to result in the leveling down of prestige and is linked with **secularization**, **rationalization**, and bureaucratization.

Prestige may wax and wane according to the performance of the individual who occupies a status position. For example, a monarch may behave in ways that offend his people, or a doctor may misplace the **trust** placed in his occupation by behaving in a way that is harmful to others. In cases like this, we speak of dissonance between prestige and **social status**. The inverse of prestige is notoriety, which is a condition in which the dissonance between status and performance has been scandalized.

In mainstream American sociology the concept is more narrowly associated with research on occupation and occupational ranking. Quantitative sociology has devised a series of **scales** which purport to measure prestige.   CHRIS ROJEK

primary group

– see **group(s)**.

primitive society

In prototype, primitive society was an explicit object of philosophical speculation and natural-historical curiosity from the moment that the first European explorers returned from Africa and the Americas. By the middle of the nineteenth century and until the 1920s, it was the analytical preserve of anthropology and analytical attention accorded it was anthropological by definition. As Adam Kuper points out in *The Invention of the Primitive* (1988), it was, for nineteenth-century theorists, of a piece with **ancient society**; if distinguished from the latter at all, it was distinguished as the most ancient of the forms of **society** that, as a matter of historically particular fact or general evolutionary law, had preceded the modern present. Examples of it survived, but they were in the present without being of it, "living fossils" that had somehow refused or failed to change.

If the first hallmark of primitive society was thus its primordiality, the second was its simplicity or elementariness. It manifested little if any institutional **differentiation**. Its primary matrix of the distribution of roles and statuses was that of **kinship** and its typical system of kinship a classificatory system that pressed relationships of differing degrees of mutual propinquity into a common pigeonhole. Technologically, it constrained its members to hunt and gather. Cognitively and intellectually, it exhibited an analogous lack of rigor and discernment. Most theorists could agree that primitive man was endowed with the same basic powers of perception and judgment as his modern counterpart, but those powers had yet to develop beyond those of a child. He might be practical enough to survive, but not yet sufficiently astute to recognize even the principle of physiological paternity. He could engage in the wildest flights of mythological fancy, but had no sense of history and no means either of fashioning or of grasping moral and conceptual abstractions.

The concept of primitive society underwent three notable changes in the course of the twentieth century. At the vanguard of the first are **Bronislaw Malinowski** and American cultural anthropologists such as Ruth Benedict (1887–1948). With them, primitive society is divested of its primordiality and retains a simplicity no longer differing in kind but only in degree from the societies that abut or otherwise invite comparison with it. The second change owes something to the

ethnography of India but even more to **Claude Lévi-Strauss**. In its aftermath, primitive society is neither bereft of **intellectuals** nor ignorant of history. It instead joins its qualitatively more complex but still traditional societies in resisting the existential and social significance of the difference between the past and present and future. The third of the changes comes with the rejection of the subliminal evolutionism and the subliminal progressivism that inform the distinction between primitive and modern. Its key texts remain Renato Rosaldo's *Ilongot Headhunting* (1980), Richard Price's *First-Time* (1983), and Johannes Fabian's *Time and the Other* (1983).

JAMES D. FAUBION

Privacy

The importance of privacy is often associated with the "quarrel between the ancients and moderns." This expression came from the title of a famous lecture on "The Liberty of the Ancients Compared with that of the Moderns" in 1819 by the French political philosopher Benjamin Constant (1767–1830), which is reprinted in his *Political Writings* (1988). This lecture compared the respect for public **institutions** and public space in the ancient world with the emphasis on conscience and individual subjectivity in modern society. Constant argued that the liberty of the ancients, which arose from their active engagement in **politics**, required the sacrifice of their personal interests to those of the polis. By contrast, the moderns pursue their personal pleasures, regarding politics as merely a means to protect their private lives. The concept of privacy is thus interconnected with a range of other key concepts in political and **social theory**, such as individual **rights**, the **state** and the **social contract**.

In contemporary thought, privacy is closely associated with **individualism**, because private space outside the public realm is assumed to be important for cultivating and protecting the individual from social scrutiny and political surveillance. In the liberal theory of John Locke (1632–1704), the protection of the rights of individuals is held to be essential to guard against the threat of arbitrary rule by authoritarian governments. Civil rights refer to the legal entitlements of free and rational agents, who combine, by means of a social contract, to form a **state**, whose sole purpose is to guarantee their enjoyment of these privileges. The minimalist theory of the state, for example the night watchman state, is a product of **liberalism**, because the only justification for the state is the protection of the liberties of individuals to do as they please, namely to enjoy their privacy.

In classical Greece, private affairs were often negatively defined in opposition to the **public sphere** and public duty. The private arena was associated with deprivation (*privatus*), while the public sphere was one of freedom and reason, where citizens congregated for political debate and economic exchange. The autonomous individual could only exist and develop in the public domain. In political philosophy, this contrast has been an important aspect of the modern theory of **totalitarianism**. In *The Origins of Totalitarianism* (1958), **Hannah Arendt** argued that in modern society people are forced out of a shared public world into a lonely, isolated, and interior space. In their isolation, pressures towards social uniformity undermine their individual autonomy, and they are psychologically exposed to totalitarian forces.

According to Arendt, this clear distinction between private and public has been confused in modern times by the emergence of "the social." In modern society, people are bound together, but these common threads are paradoxically the private desires of **consumption** and a common mass **culture**. In a **mass society**, the social becomes the basis for mass conformity and the moral calling of the political sinks into petty **politics**. The noble art of politics as a life of virtue becomes merely a trade in **power** and **influence**.

Arendt's vision of modern society was debated by **David Riesman** in *The Lonely Crowd. A Study of the Changing American Character* (1950), in which he contrasted the tradition-directed **personalities** who are conformists and merely reproduce traditional culture with the inner-directed personality who emerged with the Renaissance and the Reformation. By contrast, the other-directed personality of modern America (and other societies dominated by the **mass media**) craves approval from others. The social relations of the other-directed character are mediated by the flow of mass communication, and their demand for social approval is an aspect of liberal, middle-class **socialization**. Riesman's criticisms of American society in the 1950s bore a close resemblance to **Herbert Marcuse**'s analysis of the 'happy consciousness' in his *One-Dimensional Man* (1964), but they were also related to the study of individualism in colonial America by **Alexis de Tocqueville**. In his *The Idea of the Self* (2005), Jerrold Seigel has shown how, especially in the social philosophy of J.-J. Rousseau (1712–78), there is a well established view that the conscience of the individual requires protection from **public opinion**, and this protection is an important aspect of privacy.

In contemporary sociology, writers like **Amitai Etzioni** in *The Limits of Privacy* (1999) have raised critical questions about the benefits of the protection of privacy for public life, but one can also argue that privacy has been further transformed by modern **technologies** (such as closed-circuit television) which allow the individual to be under constant surveillance. In addition, changes to the law relating, for example, to notions of sexual harassment in the workplace mean that the private /public distinction has broken down, because the law can intervene into people's "private" sexual activities.   BRYAN S. TURNER

private and public spheres
– see **public sphere**.

process sociology
– see **Norbert Elias**.

professionalization
– see **profession(s)**.

profession(s)
A group of **occupations** (for example, doctors, lawyers, and clergy) who provide highly specialized services, based typically on an esoteric body of knowledge, which only they can assess. They thus experience autonomy over their own work, and direct others in the conduct of their occupations. They have monopolistic control in their area of expertise (only doctors can practice medicine), and they exercise dominance over subordinate occupations. Their claims to monopoly and dominance are backed by state legislation. In return for this autonomy, they govern themselves by abiding to a code of ethics by which they are required to put their client's interests ahead of their own, are in a fiduciary relationship with their client (that is, one of **trust**), and put their client's needs ahead of any self-interested profit-making.

For **Émile Durkheim** professional associations played a central role in fostering trust and stability in a society otherwise driven by utilitarian self-interest, an argument captured in the title of his work *Professional Ethics and Civic Morals* (1957), a posthumous translation of the *Leçons de sociologie* (1950). This line of analysis was further developed by **Talcott Parsons** in the *Social System* (1951, especially chapter 10). Taking the medical profession as an example, Parsons argued that it was characterized by a number of distinctive practices which distinguished medical practitioners from other **occupations** in a market **economy**. They are universalistic in their orientation; they provide services independently of the particular characteristics of their patients, such as **gender**; they are affectively neutral in that they do not stand in moral judgment of their patient's condition; they are oriented to the good of the collective; and they are functionally specific, dealing only with the issue at hand and using the best scientific knowledge. In contrast, contemporary sociologists of the professions emphasize their self-interested practice of **social closure**, thereby maintaining occupational autonomy to enhance their **incomes** and keeping competitors out. While Parsons pointed to the long period of training for professionals as central to their **socialization** into the profession's ethical standpoint, contemporary sociologists regard such training as a protracted gate-keeping exercise. Eliot Freidson in *Profession of Medicine: A Study of the Sociology of Applied Knowledge* (1970) and *Professional Dominance: The Social Structure of Medical Care* (1970) argued that the medical profession dominates in the health sector, not as a consequence of its scientific, humanitarian ethos, but because it is politically well organized. Medicine maintains its aura of high standing, despite the often degrading nature of its work, effectively passing such dirty work onto subordinate occupations such as nursing. Sustained analysis of the actual ways in which doctors practice, carried out by sociologists in **grounded theory**, demonstrated that doctors were not universalistic in their orientation to treatment, with significant variations in their dealings with women and ethnic minorities. In fact, the profit motive was a significant factor in their clinical decisionmaking. Overall then, the positive evaluation of the professions that is the legacy of Durkheim and Parsons has not fared well following empirical analysis of the ways in which the professions actually operate in society.

Other **social changes**, particularly the rise of **neoliberalism** in the political sphere, are having a substantial impact on the structure and work of professionals. Economic policymakers in the state sector are now disposed to view professional associations as anti-competitive cartels, and to regard professional self-regulation and exclusion of competitors (who may perform the same services more cheaply) as merely self-interested. Other social changes, such as the rise of an educated public, make consumers of professional services more cautious and skeptical of professional knowledge claims. The organization of consumer **groups** provides a platform to question such expert systems. Furthermore, the inability or lack of will on the part of professional organizations to discipline

errant members has led to far greater legal control over practitioners as the public takes to the courts as the first line of action. Technological changes have led to the routinization of much professional work and the claim to practice on the basis of an esoteric body of knowledge has been considerably weakened, especially in medicine, engineering, and architecture as computer programs replace professional judgment. Linked with a decline in self-employment and the rise of corporate employers, it has been argued, following **Karl Marx**, that the professions are being proletarianized. This proletarianization can take two forms: ideological proletarianization refers to the loss of autonomy over the setting of policies, goals, and objectives of and by the profession; and technical proletarianization refers to the loss of control over work practices by the professional. While there is considerable debate over this claim, it is clear that there has been significant de-professionalization as doctors, lawyers, and architects, for example, perform work under the control of bureaucratic superiors. Furthermore, under these conditions of employment their responsibility is not to their client but to the shareholders who expect a profitable return on their investment. In turn the professions themselves have started to fragment, a process in which the **elite** within the profession continues to enjoy considerable autonomy, and a dependent stratum are supervised by superiors. This erosion of autonomy occurred especially in law and general practice, where, increasingly, female employees perform routine tasks that are monitored by superiors in the professional hierarchy. These changes in professional medicine were clearly documented in Paul Starr's *The Social Transformation of American Medicine. The Rise of a Sovereign Profession and the Making of a Vast Industry* (1982). While the professions may still enjoy reasonable **social status**, high incomes, and have more freedom than those in other occupations, they have also experienced significant inroads into their autonomy and all indications are that this will increasingly be the case.

KEVIN WHITE

progress

The view that the human world has advanced, is advancing, and will continue to advance in the future. It is opposed to all ideas of a past Golden Age, or the sense of decadence and decline. It expresses a basic optimism and confidence in the ability of humans to resolve their problems, and to increase in prosperity, **morality**, and understanding with the passage of time.

Historically speaking, the idea of progress is relatively new. It first arose in western Europe in the second half of the seventeenth century. In a battle of the books between the Ancients and the Moderns, the Moderns achieved a decisive victory in arguing that modern people could advance as far and indeed farther than the ancient Greeks and Romans, who for much of the past thousand years had continued to be accepted as the unsurpassable leaders in learning and **civilization**. What made the arguments of the moderns convincing then, in a way that they had not been earlier, was undoubtedly the dazzling achievements of the seventeenth-century Scientific Revolution. The work of scientists such as Kepler (1571–1630), Copernicus (1473–1543), Galileo (1564–1642), and especially Newton (1643–1727), with their unlocking of the basic mechanisms of the universe, indicated that modern societies had the capacity to be as enlightened and creative as any past society. The philosophers Bacon (1561–1626) and Descartes (1591–1650), with their call for a new method in the understanding of nature and **society**, also expressed a sense of the originality and novelty of the times, together with a confidence that the modern age had within it the seeds of unlimited progress.

The idea of progress became a central feature of most of the leading social philosophies of the eighteenth and nineteenth centuries. It was accepted by most Enlightenment thinkers, even as they criticized the conditions of their own societies and times. Their faith in reason gave them the confidence that they could discover and remedy the outstanding abuses in their societies. Nineteenth-century thinkers, such as **Herbert Spencer**, **Auguste Comte**, and **Karl Marx**, similarly looked forward to a future of freedom, **equality**, and prosperity for all, even as they lambasted the forces holding back progress in their own times. The idea of progress appeared to find satisfyingly scientific confirmation in the **evolutionary theory**, in which a misunderstood **Social Darwinism** was applied to the idea of the ascent of man from savagery to civilization.

There was, from the time of the French Revolution onwards, always a contrary current of thought that radically questioned the idea of progress, which in the case of some thinkers of a religious persuasion, such as Joseph de Maistre (1754–1821), was thought actually impious and blasphemous. European Romanticism, with its criticism of industrialism and **materialism**, and its idealization of the Middle Ages, added its own passionate and persuasive critique. Towards the end of the nineteenth century, a *fin-de-siècle* pessimism became a distinct and increasingly powerful strand of thought among European thinkers, such as Friedrich Nietzsche, **Max Weber**, and **Sigmund Freud**. World War I and its aftermath, with the unprecedented slaughter of men followed by two decades of economic depression and the rise of totalitarian dictatorships, buried the idea of progress for most artists and **intellectuals**. But the defeat of **fascism** in World War II, and the strong economic recovery of the postwar era, brought about a significant revival of the idea of progress, though it has never regained the central position that it held in previous centuries, being subject now particularly to the criticisms of ecologists.   KRISHAN KUMAR

proletarianization
– see **profession(s)**.

proletariat
– see **Marxist Sociology**.

property
Property implies ownership, to which may be attached **rights**. In **liberalism**, property rights have a distinctive and foundational role. Distinctive because since John Locke (1632–1704) property rights have been attached, not just to possession of land and movable objects, but also to a human being's own person and the person's capacities, especially the capacity to **labor**. The notion of a person's proprietorship of their own capacities has become foundational in liberal theory for other rights of the person, including civil and political rights. In **Marxism**, on the other hand, property is not primarily a right but a relationship, especially a production relationship. Thus property is concerned with (but not reducible to) **power**.

Karl Marx holds that ownership or possession of property is the principle of **organization** within relations of production and distribution. Those who possess property have direct access to the means of **consumption**; those who do not must offer their labor services to owners, who pay them wages in order to bring their property into productive use. In this exchange the reciprocity between property owners and property-less workers is asymmetrical, with the material benefits being greater for owners and the opportunity costs being greater for non-owners. This Marx characterizes as exploitation. Marx adds that the form of property yields to historical variation, corresponding to historical stages of societal development, namely primitive **Communism**, Asiatic society, **feudalism**, and **capitalism**.

Sociological discussions of property typically derive from either liberal or Marxist accounts. **Max Weber** offers an account of property in his *Economy and Society* (1922 [trans. 1968]) in terms of appropriation and closed social relationships or closure. The appropriation of economic opportunities, from which others are excluded, is the basis of an advantage, according to Weber, which may take the form of a right. If this right is enduring and can be transferred between individuals, then the appropriated advantage is property. Weber goes on to discuss how appropriation and property have taken different forms under different historical conditions and in different economic settings. **Émile Durkheim** argues in *The Division of Labor in Society* (1893 [trans. 1960]) that inheritance of property is responsible for a forced labor, through which a natural distribution of talents is distorted and **anomie** results. Apart from this, Durkheim does not develop a theory of property, even though his largely descriptive account of property rights in *Professional Ethics and Civic Morals* (1950 [trans. 1957]) is historically insightful.

Frank Parkin in *Marxism and Class Theory: A Bourgeois Critique* (1979), following Marx, distinguishes between personal property and property as capital. Property as capital, he argues, following Weber, is exclusionary closure. Out of these relations arises class exploitation. The problem with Parkin's account is its exclusive focus on distributional relations and competition for resources; it considers only the production of **life chances** and fails to address the question of the production of means that are necessary to bring those **life chances** into existence. Marx does this by treating property as an economic relation, and Weber and Durkheim by treating property as possessing a legal dimension. Parkin treats property as an essentially political facility.   JACK BARBALET

Protestant Ethic Thesis

– see **Max Weber**.

psychoanalysis

This refers to the type of psychotherapy that was founded by **Sigmund Freud**. In psychoanalysis the therapist, or analyst, seeks to aid patients to recognize their unconscious **motivation**. According to psychoanalysts, all people have unconscious desires and thus everyone would benefit from undergoing psychoanalysis. The term psychoanalysis is also sometimes used to describe the ideas of Freud and his followers about the unconscious structure

of the mind. It is in this second sense, as a theory of mind rather than as a psychotherapeutic practice, that psychoanalysis has had a major effect on sociological thinking.

Initially Freud began his career as a psychiatrist using hypnosis to treat patients who displayed neurotic symptoms. He found that the symptoms often disappeared when patients could be induced to recall forgotten memories under hypnosis. Freud, with his colleague Josef Breuer (1842–1925), hypothesized that the symptoms were related to painful memories or shameful desires that the patients had pushed, or repressed, from conscious awareness. Although the experiences and desires may have been repressed from awareness, they continued to exert an unconscious influence. If the patients could be encouraged to recognize their unconscious thoughts, then, according to Freud, it would be possible to treat their neurotic symptoms. Thus, there could be a talking cure.

Freud and Breuer published their results in *Studies on Hysteria* (1893–5 [trans. 1953–74]). In this book, Freud outlined the concept of repression, which he later was to call the key concept of psychoanalysis. Increasingly, Freud became convinced that the most important repressed desires were sexual ones originating in **childhood**. Following his own "self-analysis," Freud concluded that all adults had unconscious sexual and aggressive desires that had their roots in infantile desires. Young boys, he suggested, desired their mothers and harbored aggressive hatred towards their fathers. These desires needed to be repressed. Freud was to call this pattern of childish desire "the Oedipus complex."

In 1896, Freud first used the term psychoanalysis to describe the practice by which the unconscious could be brought into conscious awareness. The analyst had to be trained to de-code dreams, neurotic symptoms, and the stories told by the person undergoing analysis. Freud set into place professional structures for the training and recognition of analysts. It was a condition that all psychoanalysts had themselves to be analyzed by an experienced analyst. In the first half of the twentieth century, psychoanalysis became an international movement with recognized associations across the world.

At the root of psychoanalytic practice lay a theory of the human mind. According to Freudian theory, the mind was split between the conscious self (ego) and the instinctual unconscious element (id). The ego itself was split – it, too, had unconscious parts. As the child begins to repress its own childhood sexual feelings, so the ego becomes further divided: the rational part of the ego becomes split from a punitive sense of **morality** and duty (the superego). Freud outlined these ideas in a series of books such as *The Interpretation of Dreams* (1900 [trans. 1991]), *Three Essays on the Theory of Sexuality* (1905 [trans. 1982]), and *Introductory Lectures on Psychoanalysis* (1917 [trans. 1973]).

Psychoanalytic theory, as developed by Freud, contained a vision of the relations between the individual and society. In later works such as *Group Psychology* (1921 [trans. 1992]) and *Civilization and its Discontents* (1930 [trans. 1992]); Freud argued that social life demands the repression of the basic human instincts of **sexuality** and aggression. This is why children come to repress their childish instincts. In repressing their instincts, they come to identity with the opposite-sex parent. However, the boy at the conclusion of the Oedipal period adopts the punitive voice of the father as his own superego: this is the origin of moral conscience. In this way, repression ensures that children tame their instincts and accept the social codes of society. The result is that social life, especially modern society, demands that humans become alienated from their instinctual nature.

Many psychoanalysts have sought to reinterpret basic Freudian ideas. This has led to a succession of schisms within the psychoanalytic movement. Although Freud was developing a highly original psychology of the mind, his influence has been greater amongst social scientists than amongst academic psychologists, who have tended to view his theories as being insufficiently grounded in experimental evidence.

The theorists of the **Frankfurt School** were particularly influenced by psychoanalytic ideas. **Max Horkheimer** and **Theodor Wiesengrund Adorno** argued that orthodox Marxist theory could not explain the rise of **fascism** because fascist propaganda appealed to irrational unconscious motives rather than to rational economic interests. In their work, and in that of **Erich Fromm**, who, unlike most members of the Frankfurt School, was a practicing psychoanalyst, lay the roots of the theory of the **authoritarian personality**. Fromm also criticized Freud for overemphasizing sexual motives, and ignoring motives such as the need for a secure **identity** to counteract the **alienation** of modern **capitalism**.

Feminism has a great impact upon recent understanding of psychoanalysis. Feminist social theorists have emphasized how Freud's theories are marked by patriarchal assumptions and how the practice of psychoanalysis has permitted powerful male analysts to impose patriarchal interpretations upon female patients. Feminists have argued that Freud failed to provide a convincing account of women's psychic structure, claiming that women's experience does not match the Oedipus complex. However, there is a division between those feminists who entirely reject psychoanalysis as irredeemably sexist and those, like **Juliet Mitchell**, who believe that basic Freudian ideas can be reformulated in non-sexist ways. Feminist psychoanalysts, such as Mitchell, argue that the young girl's psychic structure and her relationship with her mother may not be Oedipal, but tensions and repressions are nevertheless involved.

Of late, one of the most famous theorists has been **Jacques Lacan**, the controversial French psychoanalyst who saw the "mirror stage," rather than the Oedipus complex, as the decisive event in childhood. Lacan's ideas have been particularly influential in **cultural studies**, especially in film theory. Although Lacan claimed to be "returning to Freud," his obscure, evasive writings contrast with the precision and clarity of Freud's prose.

MICHAEL BILLIG

public administration

The development of independent public **bureaucracies** was vital to the rise of the modern **state**. Nonpartisan public servants carrying out directives according to a set of rational rules and procedures are ideals of the modern bureaucracy. For **Max Weber**, the rise of such bureaucracies is a defining feature of **modernization** itself. Public administration is the science and professional practice of civil service. In theory, the goals of public administration are straightforward: efficiency and effectiveness on the one hand, and fairness and incorruptibility on the other. But achieving these goals, in the face of social and political pressures on civil servants, has proved extremely difficult in practice.

While important vestiges of public administration can be found in ancient and feudal societies, most notably in the Chinese dynasties, the rise of bureaucracies grounded in civil service rules took hold in early modern Europe. This is where the current concept of public administration began to develop. Professional civil services have been associated with the rise of **capitalism** and **industrial societies**, as well as the transition from monarchical and authoritarian proto-democratic systems of governance. In particular, the rise of market-based exchanges created the need for state administrative apparatuses capable of enforcing contracts and imposing rules on newly emerging **markets**. By the late nineteenth century, governments throughout Europe and elsewhere had adopted civil service reforms that increased the independence of public bureaucracy and required that appointments be made based on demonstrated competence rather than patronage.

The establishment of public administration as a professional field is a twentieth-century development. Public administration today has its own knowledge base, schools of public administration and **public policy** to train practitioners, and professional associations – all hallmarks of professional status. Civil servants are trained in universities, and appropriate expert credentials are prerequisites for **careers** in public bureaucracies. Methods of program evaluation, cost–benefit analysis, and the integration of legal and economic analyses are now part of the core training of public administrators. While such requirements vary widely across developed and less-developed countries, civil service professionalization has become a de facto standard. The largest variation tends to be at the top of public bureaucracies. Some countries, such as France, have long-serving professional civil servants in charge of government bureaucracies, while other countries, such as the United States, have senior administrators appointed by elected leaders. Even in the latter cases, however, lower-level bureaucrats often still retain considerable control over administrative decisions of vast bureaucracies – which can pose difficulties for bureaucrats at the top. Incentives for bureaucrats at all levels of the hierarchy to maximize the resources under their control have given rise to theories of the "budget-maximizing bureaucrat."

The theoretical underpinnings of public administration rest on the possibility of a separation of policy implementation from the **politics** of policymaking. A science of public administration requires the capacity for administrators to implement policies based on calculable rules and nonpartisan evaluation. This is a controversial assumption, however. The goal of insulating bureaucracies from political **influence** has in practice proved exceptionally difficult. Indeed, it is perhaps impossible in democratic societies. Integrating political analysis into the routines of public administration is thus an essential task, albeit a controversial one in the world of public administration. Budgetary pressures and calls for spending cuts are another source of interference. A virtually universal feature of the operating environment of public bureaucracies in all countries,

such pressures impose further constraints on public administrators.

One of the critical questions relating to public administration today is the status of bureaucracies in the less-developed world. Many observers view persistent corruption and patronage in the public sector as the main impediments to development in those countries where they occur. International lending agencies have sometimes considered the degree of professionalization in the civil service as a factor in the worthiness of prospective recipient nations. Whether public bureaucracies can attain and sustain independence in the face of **poverty** and political turmoil is likely to remain a key question in the future.

JEFF MANZA

public health

This term includes the separate notions of a perspective, infra-structure, and philosophy of government. In 1988, the Institute of Medicine in the United States defined public health as "the science and art of preventing disease, prolonging life and promoting health and efficiency through organized community effort." This definition reflects the public health thinking behind the World Health Organization's Alma Ata *Declaration of Health for All* (1978) and the Ottawa Charter (1986) which were endorsed by the United Kingdom Association of Public Health and the American Public Health Association as well as by many governments.

The public health perspective emphasizes: **health** rather than medicine; the public good rather than that of the individual; and, prevention rather than intervention after the problem has occurred. Public health efforts are focused on **communities** at the local, regional, and national levels, emphasizing partnerships among government agencies, **states**, municipalities, industry, and non-government **organizations**. In most countries, public health efforts are conceived and organized under the direction of government ministries of health and delivered by local and regional health authorities. The role of the **state** is a key variable, because public health problems and interventions are closely linked to the larger **political economy** of the nation, socioeconomic disparities, **poverty**, immigration, **health care systems**, and how the state builds and maintains health infrastructures.

Public health consists of three domains: health protection, health improvement, and health services. Health protection involves monitoring and oversight of clean air, water, **food**, infectious diseases, emergency responses to disasters, **war** and **terrorism**, radiation, chemicals and poisons, and environmental health hazards. Health improvement focuses on improving health, reducing **inequalities**, employment, housing, **family** and community, **education**, and **lifestyles**. Health services refer to service planning, clinical effectiveness, clinical governance, efficiency, research, audit, and evaluation. The exercise of responsibility in these domains requires a substantial infrastructure, including a trained workforce, knowledge and **information**, organizations, research institutes like the United States Center for Disease Control, facilities to monitor and deliver vaccinations, and testing of air, water, food, and the **environment**.

The critical functions of the public health system are to assess potential problems, develop policies to address these **risks**, and institute monitoring and intervention strategies to assure the health safety of the public. For example, the United Kingdom response to "mad cow" disease, the European attention to genetically engineered crops, and the United States efforts to acknowledge and react to the obesity epidemic are instances of public health at work in western countries where there are well-established public health infrastructures. In non-western countries, China has struggled with but coordinated a public health plan to deal with SARS (Severe Acute Respiratory Syndrome) and Asian and African countries are struggling with the HIV (Human Immunodeficiency Virus) and the AIDS (Acquired Immunodeficiency Syndrome) epidemic, but often without the resources of richer countries. Public health efforts are also evident on a worldwide level. Because of global warming, inexorable growth in the world population, and increased use of fossil fuels, the world has looming public health problems associated with basic resources like water, clean air, and the food supply. Familiar diseases like tuberculosis have re-emerged in drug-resistant forms and potential scourges like ebola virus and new forms of influenza have emerged to challenge global public health efforts. The World Health Organization usually takes the lead in such initiatives, supported by the World Health Assembly composed of the Ministers of Health of the United Nations member states. The outcomes of these prevention and intervention efforts are measured in terms of numbers of identified cases, morbidity, **disability**, mortality, and cost to the community or nation. Cost–benefit analyses show how much benefit public-health interventions produce on health and quality of life outcomes per unit cost. Historically, research on the health of nations indicates that public health measures are the most cost-beneficial forms of health interventions. These results are calculated in terms of deaths, morbidity, and disability avoided due to the application of public-health measures. For example, reducing the amount of obesity in a population through education, changes in nutrition, and exercise will save billions of dollars of lost **income** and medical care costs due to associated conditions like diabetes, heart disease, cancer, and vision problems. At a basic level, large improvements in the health of a population are realized by just having a clean water supply, sewage disposal system, vaccinations and prophylactic drugs for infectious diseases, and effective health education programs about maternal and child health and **reproduction**.

The response to public health problems is contingent on the resources, infrastructures, and political economic climates of individual nations and communities. Resources are usually measured in terms of amount of money spent per capita on health, the facilities, workforce, equipment, and supplies available for the task. Infrastructures refer to basic transportation and communication systems, the ability to deliver public health interventions when needed, and stable political economic systems. Political economic systems reflect the **values**, political organization, and market dynamics of a country. For instance, the United Kingdom is a **democracy** with a public health system that is closely articulated with the National Health Service. As a result there can be integrated intervention efforts between the two systems to address problems like smoking, alcohol use, road rage, and obesity. In contrast, the United States is a capitalist **democracy** where public health is organized and delivered through government agencies but this system is not well articulated with a patchwork of for-profit and not-for-profit medical care delivery organizations and **institutions**. In addition, there is a heated debate in the United States around religious values that are expressed in discussions about sex, alcohol, drugs, and the "right to life." As a consequence, even though the United States has considerable resources, sex education, use of condoms, clean needle exchange programs for drug injectors, and adolescent pregnancy cannot be addressed in the United States as they can in the United Kingdom, continental Europe, or Japan. Public health efforts are, then, dependent on local values and circumstances.

There is a strong interplay in theory, methods, research, and applications between sociology and public health. Sociology analyzes the social world in terms of the **interaction** between individuals, **groups**, communities, and the larger social, political, economic, and physical environment. Thus, in **methodology**, there is considerable interest in considering activity within context through multilevel **modeling**, mixed models, and network analysis. Public health uses the sociological perspective in analyzing and pragmatically addressing problems, dealing with the health of groups and populations. Public health can contribute to sociology through its development of environmental models, focus on translating theory and research into practice, use of participative action research, and in research methods such as evaluation research and **statistics** such as Cox regression and mixed models. There is much to be gained by maintaining a close working relationship between these two fields.

GARY L. ALBRECHT AND MARK SHERRY

public opinion

This concept describes either a single set or the sum of shared beliefs, assessments, and **attitudes** within a given society. In **modernity**, public opinion has reflected common or prevalent convictions among the population of nation-states. However, we find illustrations of the existence and significance of public opinion from the ancient world in the Athenian *polis*, the rhetorical manipulation of public opinion by Marcus Cicero (106–43BC) and the early Renaissance where the notion of "public opinion" plays an important role in foundational work on the **state** and social organization.

Not least because of the adaptation of the concept of public opinion across different disciplines and by theorists of distinct and contradictory philosophical foundations, an absence of a common definition of public opinion is widely acknowledged. The differences concern the question of how public opinion is constituted and what purpose public opinion serves. In its liberal interpretation, public opinion functions as a regulatory control of state actions through the need of executive powers to base their actions on public support, as is evident in parliamentary **democracies**, where public opinion is assumed to form the basis of voters' electoral decisions. In this interpretation, public opinion is in fact the sum of private opinions which might not actually be articulated in the public realm and which are measured through quantitative **surveys** conducted by polling institutes. This assumption of a free formation of public opinion in contemporary indirect

democracies is rejected in **Jürgen Habermas**'s criticism in *The Structural Transformation of the Public Sphere* (1962 [trans. 1989]), in which he sketches out the decline of public discourse as the basis on which rational opinion can be formed. Habermas draws in this context on **C. Wright Mills**'s distinction between "public" and "mass" to illustrate how the formation of public opinion shifts from an unrestricted communicative environment to a state of mass communication in which opinions are expressed by a small **elite**, excluding the public from the opinion-making process.

Such concerns are shared at the other end of the political spectrum, where they form the basis of a very different conclusion. Grounding her work in social-psychological assumptions about the individual's need to conform with the views of a larger social **group**, Elisabeth Noelle-Neumann has coined the notion of the *Spiral of Silence* (1980 [trans. 1984]). According to Noelle-Neumann the opinion leadership of largely liberal mass media creates a climate in which individuals are reluctant to voice diverging opinions (about, for instance, **ethnicity**, **migration**, or the **welfare state**) breaking a seemingly dominant social consensus. Opinion polls thus account not for respondents' actual opinions but for those they believe to be socially acceptable. These polls are subsequently misconstrued as evidence of a dominant public opinion as favored by opinion leaders, which in turn further deepens the spiral of silence.

The extent to which public opinion can be formed freely and how it can be measured continues to form the key sociological concerns in public opinion research. CORNEL SANDVOSS

public policy

The sociology of public policy has been strongly conditioned by the different ways in which policy-making has been organized and conducted. In North America, the **public sphere** has been comparatively smaller, and the **state** less interventionist, than in many European countries, and this has had an influence on how sociologists and other social scientists have come to approach the subject.

In North America, a separate discipline of policy analysis emerged after World War II in an attempt to improve the effectiveness of government and **public administration**. Based on rationalist and pragmatic assumptions, the study of public policy was often linked fairly closely to the practice of policymaking, and in particular to efforts to extend the scale and scope of the public sphere in relation to the private sector. With precursors in both the progressive era at the turn of the century and the New Deal era of the 1930s, students of public policy have tended to share a common commitment to social reform and to the importance of scientific expertise in the making of public policy.

There are institutions of policy analysis both inside and outside the universities, and practitioners tend to conceive of their field as an applied, rather than a basic, or academic, science. In Europe, the legacy from the nineteenth century's more theoretically minded sociologists contributed to giving the study of public policy a somewhat more "critical" identity, with its practitioners often attempting to keep a certain distance from the actual policymakers. The applications of policy research were more to be found in the separate policy sectors, which, because of the more ambitious role of the state in many European countries, were usually more substantially developed than in North America.

In Europe the study of public policy has been subdivided into its various component parts – formulation, implementation, evaluation, assessment, contention – as well as into its various societal sectors – for example, health policy, education policy, environmental policy, innovation policy, economic policy.

As a result, instrumental approaches, such as **rational choice theory** and cost–benefit analysis, that have been widely used in the United States, have been comparatively less influential in Europe. Instead, the study of public policy outside North America has generally made use of theories and concepts that are not specifically oriented to policymaking.

The differences began to dissipate in the 1970s, and in recent decades, particularly with the expansion of the European Union, the domain of public policy has tended to grow more uniform. At the same time, there has been a challenge to public policy in general in the name of privatization and deregulation. This is most evident in politically charged fields such as the **environment** and **health**, where the various policy discourses have become a popular subject for social scientists. In recent years, there has been an interest, throughout the world, in what are sometimes called "post-positivist" approaches to the study of public policy, which make use of one or another form of **discourse analysis**, as discussed in Frank Fischer's *Reframing Public Policy* (2003).

ANDREW JAMISON

public sphere

Referring to the **institutions** and spaces within which **public opinion** is formulated outside the government, this term acquired a specific historical significance in **Jürgen Habermas**'s *The Structural Transformation of the Public Sphere* (1962 [trans. 1989]), in which he argued the concept was specific to late seventeenth-century Britain and eighteenth-century France. A public sphere presupposes **urbanization,** the evolution of **civil society** and **civic culture**, and the spread of literacy. These developments were important for the creation of debating societies, literary clubs, salons, and coffee houses where **intellectuals** would assemble for discussion and debate. In England, the philosopher Edmund Burke (1729–97), on the eve of the French Revolution, argued that in free societies there was more public wisdom in shops and the workplace than among princes and their cabinets. This public wisdom came to have the modern meaning of public opinion in 1781, according to the *Oxford English Dictionary*. In Germany, similar associations developed such as the "table societies" (*Tischgesellschaften*) and "literary societies" (*Sprachgesellschaften*). In political terms, these societies created spaces for the rising middle class to give expression to their social and economic interests.

This association between the bourgeoisie as a **social class** and the public sphere is clear in German whose *bürgerliche Öffentlichkeit* is translated as "bourgeois public sphere." In fact Habermas distinguished between the liberal model of middle-class associations of the educated social strata and the plebeian public sphere of the working class. This public sphere of the uneducated lower class was characterized by, for example, the Chartist Movement, the working-class Protestant chapels, craft guilds, and eventually **trade unions**. This plebeian alternative was associated in France with the French Revolution and the revolutionary Maximilien de Robespierre (1758–94). In social history, a brilliant account of these plebeian associations has been given by E. P. Thompson in *The Making of the English Working Class* (1963) according to which, for example, the Methodist chapels provided educational and associational opportunities for working-class **communities**.

The bourgeois public sphere has declined with changes to **education**, the monopolistic ownership of the media, the impact of television on reading habits, and the decline of **voluntary associations**. Habermas argues that in the "social-welfare state" there is an increasing **rationalization** of the **lifeworld** and, as a result, public life is managed by the **state** through its civil servants, scientists, and experts, rather than through the informal **network** of associations in civil society. Habermas recognized that this situation could change under the impact of new **social movements** which articulate new needs around environmentalism, sexual **identity**, animal **rights**, and **globalization**. Habermas's provocative and broad analysis of modern society has given rise to a general debate on new social movements, **citizenship**, **democracy,** and the changing nature of social participation and political engagement in civil society, for example in Jean L. Cohen and Andrew Arato, *Civil Society and Political Theory* (1994).

BRYAN S. TURNER

Q

qualitative data analysis
– see **qualitative research**.

qualitative research
These methods are comprised of a diverse array of epistemological orientations (such as **positivism**, **realism**, and **social constructionism**), data gathering techniques (for instance **participant observation**, **interviews**, audio and video tape recording, and textual analysis), and analytic procedures (for example, **grounded theory**, analytic induction, or negative case analysis). While they share a general regard for the subjective dimensions of social life, qualitative research methods are also marked by significant divergences and sometimes even disputes among their various practitioners. These divergences and disputes are best understood as a reflection of the maturation and flourishing of qualitative **social science** rather than any failure to develop beyond pre-scientific or pre-paradigmatic disagreements.

Whereas sociological research that employs numerical approaches to the collection and analysis of **data** tends to emphasize objective **social structures** and their objective relationships with one another, qualitative research methods tend to emphasize the subjective meanings social actors find in their lives and the interactional processes through which they engage one another and the wider world. Qualitative research is overwhelmingly predicated on the presumption that meaning and human practice merit scientific interest as important phenomena in their own right and not merely as reflections of more general and anonymous social structural relationships. Though this presumption hails from a variety of distinct historical sources, its most commonly cited source in the annals of social science history is the *Methodenstreit*, or "dispute over method," which took place in late nineteenth-century Germany.

The *Methodenstreit* came to embroil some of Germany's finest social thinkers in debate concerning the specific nature of social life and its amenability to the methods of analysis found in physical sciences. Thinkers like Wilhelm Dilthey

(1833–1911), **Hans-Georg Gadamer**, **Georg Simmel**, and **Max Weber** became figureheads for an intellectual movement that sought to distinguish the social sciences decisively from the physical sciences, on the grounds that their methods and/or subject matters were irreducibly unique. Scholars argued that whereas physical scientists study lower life forms and inanimate objects, social scientists study people. Unlike the behavior of inanimate objects or lower life forms, the behavior of human beings is not caused by uniform laws but by sentient, creative subjects imbued with an understanding of the worlds within which they live and act. Hence, any effort to grasp the nature of social life must begin with an appreciation of one's research subjects' own understandings of their circumstances.

These ideas were appropriated by the pioneers of qualitative research methods in the social sciences. But unlike some of the more romantically inclined among the German theorists, the pioneers of qualitative research methods generally insisted that we combine an appreciation of human creativity with an equally serious regard for scientific rigor. Though committed to understanding the subjective dimensions of social life, early proponents of qualitative research methods, like Franz Boas and **Bronislaw Malinowski** in anthropology and **W. I. Thomas** and **Robert Ezra Park** in sociology, were equally committed to the idea that they must do so scientifically. Theirs was decidedly not a campaign to critique science and exalt the humanities. Instead their aim was to distinguish the nature of the social sciences from orthodox understandings of the physical sciences. It must be said, however, that, despite programmatic pronouncements of scientific rigor, the earliest excursions into systematic qualitative field research were rather woolly by contemporary standards. They were usually predicated on a diffusely holistic sense of social **groups** as relatively situated, relatively distinctive, and relatively homogeneous both in terms of the objective conditions under which members of the group were compelled to live and in the customary mental **attitudes** and practical responses to those conditions they developed. Empirical research was designed to illuminate these dimensions of a particular group's existence and facilitate efforts to link them to one another theoretically. At first such efforts were fairly unselfconscious, opportunistic, and eclectic. Data were drawn from a variety of sources and analysis was often miscellaneous and more implicit than explicit. Eventually, though, a variety of historical events converged to constrain this original eclecticism.

The two most salient of these historical events were the rise of scientism in American sociology, and the progressive expansion of the academy and its division into an ever larger number of distinct disciplines and sub-disciplines. As the discipline of sociology grew larger, more diverse, and more thoroughly ensconced in the academy, disputes arose among sociologists as to the kinds of investigations that were to qualify as genuinely scientific studies of social life. These disputes often focused on the comparative strengths and weaknesses of qualitative and quantitative research methods. During the 1930s and 1940s, the largely qualitative case study tradition associated with the University of Chicago came under serious attack from a coterie of sociologists fiercely committed to fashioning sociology in the image of the natural sciences. A confluence of several complex changes within the Department of Sociology at the University of Chicago, in the discipline of sociology more generally, in academia, and in American society as a whole, eventually tipped the balance of power between practitioners of qualitative and quantitative approaches towards the latter. Whether they opposed them, endorsed them, or strove for some other manner of conciliation, qualitative sociologists have experienced powerful institutional pressures to attend to the methodological arguments of their quantitative colleagues. This has had profound effects on the development of qualitative research methods in sociology.

The survey researchers who rose to power in the 1940s and 1950s tried to measure the value of qualitative research in terms of their own positivistic philosophy of science. By suppressing or ignoring issues of meaning and human agency, positivist sociologists ascribed a second-class status to qualitative research. Though the doctrines that sustained the positivist ascendancy have long since been discredited among philosophers of science themselves, news of their demise has traveled slowly through the social sciences. Regrettably, some still disparage qualitative research for its putative non-conformity to an antiquated and hopelessly flawed conception of scientific work. But there can be little doubt that the situation is rapidly improving. Virtually every major social theorist since the mid-1970s has come down in opposition to the positivism that alienated qualitative research from the mainstream of the social sciences. And at an institutional level, qualitative researchers have successfully carved out niches for themselves throughout the academic world. Beyond sociology and anthropology, one can now find growing qualitative contingents in such fields as business administration, communications, **education**, folklore, linguistics, nursing, political science, and **public health**. And, indeed, there is growing interest in qualitative research beyond the confines of the academy.

In order to illustrate the variety of qualitative approaches now flourishing in the social sciences, the rest of this entry will briefly describe four distinct genres of contemporary qualitative research: (1) qualitative interviewing; (2) ethnographic observation; (3) **conversational analysis**; and (4) the study of material artifacts.

Qualitative **interviews** are distinct from **questionnaires** insofar as they rely to a greater extent on open-ended questions. Whereas survey questionnaires generally provide a fixed range of answer options, qualitative interviews invite respondents to answer questions in whatever fashion they like. Of course, this difference is one of degree rather than kind. Many qualitative interviewers variously delimit the nature of the answers they elicit and survey questionnaires can also include open-ended questions (though such questions do complicate numerical analysis).

Some of the advantages of the qualitative interview are: (1) it reduces the risk of putting words in respondents' mouths; (2) it allows investigation of unanticipated themes that emerge in the course of the interview; (3) it allows the study of people or themes about which very little is already known; (4) it allows us to maximize the extent to which respondents' "own voice" may be preserved in our data; (5) it allows analysis of not only what respondents tell us but how they do so; and (6) it allows us discretion to pursue particular themes with respondents in depth.

Ethnography entails placing oneself in direct personal contact with a social group as they go about their routine affairs. In contrast to interview techniques, wherein we ask people to tell us about their lives, ethnography entails observing people's lives and circumstances first-hand. While combining interviews and observations remains pervasive (and is very often extremely useful), qualitative researchers have more recently begun to distinguish ethnographic research from studies that rely on qualitative interviewing. One reason for this is simply that interviewing and observation require different sorts of skills. Good interviewers are not necessarily good observers and vice versa. Secondly, when we interview people we must always contemplate *what* they are including and what they are leaving out of their responses to our questions, *how* it is being included and how it is being left out, and, of course, *why*. When we observe directly, however, our encounter with local meanings and practices is not mediated by respondents' personal judgments regarding what should and should not be discussed. Moreover, much of what we might find interesting and distinctive about our research subjects' lives simply may not occur to them as interesting or worthy of mention at all. Furthermore, as the old saying goes, actions often speak louder than words – what people do may indicate how they orient to certain things better than what they explicitly tell us. Often what people consider meaningful and important they nonetheless find difficult to put into words. Indeed, sometimes people find certain things hard to discuss precisely because they consider those things so profoundly meaningful. Firsthand observation can often help us to grasp such matters in ways that other research methods cannot.

Conversational analysis is concerned with the study of **language** as a social practice. Though there are exceptions, conversation analysts usually insist that analysis be confined to audio- or video-tape-recorded instances of natural language use. Hence, most conversation analysts decline to use interviews, **surveys**, experiments that require the manipulation of people's behavior, observational methods that resort to field notes or precoded schedules, the use of native intuitions to generate exemplary interactional scenarios, or any other data source that includes artificial recreations of naturally occurring talk. Such data sources are held to distort inevitably the specific details of naturally situated interactional conduct and to install in their place mere idealizations about how interaction actually works.

Conversation analysts are also wary of relying on received categories of sociological analysis to make sense of conversational data. This wariness is predicated on the empirical observation that in studying conversation, descriptively adequate claims about the participants and the context of their interaction are not always relevant to interactants themselves nor procedurally implicated in

their talk itself. Moreover, too much emphasis on the role of social structures in **interaction** risks masking and thereby pre-empting the discovery of important conversational structures.

Compared to other sorts of data, artifacts (that is documents and material objects) endure. Hence, for those who wish to study historically distant peoples and events, documents and material objects are often the only data available. Moreover, such data may possess a special relevance to those who wish to study people who have historically been muted or denied voice. But, just as with other types of data, the analysis of documents and material artifacts must be accomplished with respect to the particular forms of life in which they were produced and/or used. And it is here that methodological puzzles begin to emerge. Just like other elements of **culture**, documents and material artifacts may be analyzed with respect to both their symbolic and their mundane utility. One major challenge of analysis is thus to infer the extent to which the former or the latter should be emphasized in any particular instance. Another distinctive complication arises from the fact that artifacts produced in one context may be put to use in ways that were not originally anticipated. Many objects we have inherited from our forebears are meaningful/useful to us in ways quite different from the ways they were meaningful/useful to them. Though the use of artifacts as data undeniably presents unique analytic challenges, these challenges can generally be handled with techniques familiar to those acquainted with other varieties of comparative social research. DARIN WEINBERG

quantitative data analysis

Quantitative data are data that have been measured numerically. A number of other entries in this dictionary describe particular statistical techniques for quantitative data analysis (for example **regression**, **factor analysis**, **correlation**, **cluster analysis**, **log linear analyses**, **path analysis**).

In the natural sciences, advances were often associated with being able to quantify, or measure, aspects of the physical world, for instance temperature, electrical voltage, or the speed of light. Some sociologists (often associated with **positivism** in the philosophy of science) have assumed that **social sciences** will also progress most effectively through developing measures of sociological phenomena. For instance, the social capital **paradigm** has been distinctive in attempting to develop measures of such social investments that would permit one to chart changes in these forms of capital over time, or to compare countries in terms of their levels of social involvement. Similarly, a great deal of effort has gone into developing precise numerical measures of **social class** and **social stratification**.

An opposing view is that reducing complex sociological phenomena to numbers over-simplifies our accounts of those phenomena and limits or distorts our understanding. For instance, in making the claim that social capital has fallen in the United States since the mid twentieth century, researchers have measured the change in the average number of clubs and societies that American citizens are members of. Or, in making claims about the differences in the level of social capital in different countries, researchers have typically relied on **questionnaires** that ask how much individuals trust each other or important public **institutions**. Critics of such approaches argue that the nature and role of clubs and societies has changed over time, and that people in different countries assign a different meaning to the word **trust**, so these measures are flawed.

The alternative to quantitative research is termed **qualitative research**, in which typically the investigators are more concerned with understanding the nature and meaning of people, or the complexity of social institutions – for example **Clifford Geertz**, or proponents of **hermeneutics**). Examples of their research styles would be their attempts to understand the meanings individuals assign to phenomena by in-depth interviews, or the nature of institutions by conducting **ethnographies**.

The methods of analyzing quantitative and qualitative **data** are very different, employing **statistics** for the former, or qualitative research for the latter.

Throughout its history, sociology has spent much time preoccupied by disputes between advocates of quantitative and qualitative research **methodologies**. More recently, many researchers have taken a pragmatic approach and considered, for any given research problem, which approach (or what combination of the two) will lead to the most satisfactory understanding of the research question. In other cases, both are used simultaneously, for example in **triangulation**.   BRENDAN J. BURCHELL

queer theory

The term queer has an interesting history. In the United Kingdom, colloquial and ironic expressions such as "there's now't as queer as folk" indicate that the term has been defined in terms of strangeness. It is also used as a pejorative label for people who participate in nonheterosexual relationships, such

as gays, lesbians, and bisexuals. More recently, with its impetus mainly from lesbian and **Gay Studies** in the United States, queer theory engages with sex, **gender**, and **sexuality** in two key ways.

First, at a scholarly level, queer theory seeks to destabilize socially given **identities**, categories, and subjectivities, around the commonsense distinctions between homosexuality and heterosexuality, men and women, and sex and gender. It does this by establishing the social and historical specificity of sexual categories, linking them to processes of state and institutional control. Queer theorists also seek to collapse the boundaries that separate sexual normality and abnormality, suggesting that separate discrete oppositions are mutually constitutive rather than exclusive. Furthermore, they contest the adequacy of matching existing sexual categories to the complexity of people's lived-out experiences. Queer theorists develop the possibilities of sexual being and doing outside the conventional identities and subjectivities (including gay, lesbian, and bisexual identities).

Second, at a political level, queer activists argue that the established gay **community**, in campaigning for community identity recognition and validation by straight society, has adopted an assimilationist position. The perceived limitations of this political strategy are resonant of those voiced by black radicals in the 1970s concerning the state setting the agenda on which racialized ethnic minority **groups** were to be included within white society, on terms of liberal acceptance rather than human **rights**. A major concern for queer activists, operating from an anti-essentialist identity position, is that mainstream inclusion involves state regulation and surveillance of a sexual minority identity that implicitly produces the homosexual–heterosexual boundary of a fixed subcultural type. Furthermore, for queer activists, the gay movement, in targeting its political energies towards straight society, has not addressed a wide range of internal sexual exclusions, including bisexuals, transsexuals, and transgendered groups, alongside **social closures** – around **age**, **ethnicity**, and **disability** – arising from the narrow conception of gay identity itself. In contrast, queer **politics**, adopting a utopian stance, is open to all dissident eroticized minorities, while simultaneously claiming that the effect of transcending the homo/hetero divide is to challenge the sexual regulation and repression of the sexual majority – heterosexual desire.

There are a range of criticisms of both queer theory and politics, including that it is a development of a social-constructionist tradition rather than a radical break with established **social theory**; and that, in privileging significatory systems, discourse, and discursive **power**, it colludes with **postmodernism** in underplaying the importance of socioeconomic structural differences. It is also seen as the downplaying of gender, in the critical discussion of heterosexual relations being viewed as the norm. Queer theory remains highly abstract, disconnected from the way people are living their lives within the institutional constraints of economics, the **state**, and cultural **traditions**. However, as a postmodern politics, it celebrates the transgressive potential, both discursive and social, of the implosion of existing gender and sexuality categories, enabling us to reimagine inhabiting a range of **masculinities** and femininities and the full diversity of sexual desire.

MAIRTIN MAC-AN-GHAILL AND CHRIS HAYWOOD

questionnaire

The *Webster's Dictionary* definition for questionnaire is "A prepared set of written questions for purposes of statistical compilation or comparison of the information gathered; a series of questions." It is sometimes assumed that questionnaires refer to the documents that people fill out for themselves (self-completion questionnaires), but that is too narrow a definition. The administration of questionnaires can be self-completion or by face-to-face or telephone **interview**. Questionnaires can be administered manually but, in the last decade or so, many survey organizations have begun to use computer-assisted personal interviewing (CAPI). This **technology** makes it more feasible to tailor questions so they are suited to different respondents (for example different questions about employment would be asked depending on the respondent's current employment status and past employment histories). Computer-assisted interviewing also allows for complex computing checks to be built in that indicate when answers are inconsistent or incomplete.

In the modern world, governments rely heavily on **information** that is gathered through questionnaires. Most countries have an Office of National Statistics or its equivalent, which is responsible for compiling the various social and economic indicators needed to inform **social policy**. The most comprehensive **survey**, from the viewpoint of sample and population coverage, is the Census. Significant resources are put into questionnaire design for the Census, and, before any new question is added, there is widespread debate and testing. This is necessary because social measures are rarely straightforward. Take **ethnicity**, for example – this might

involve place of birth, place of parental origin, language, or self-identity.

Questionnaires are widely used because they appear deceptively easy to construct and relatively cheap to administer. This view, however, needs qualification. Even apparently straightforward "factual" measures like ethnicity or employment are often quite complex to capture, given the range of issues and meanings. The challenges become even more daunting when the researcher wants to gather subjective information concerning beliefs and **attitudes**, where responses can be influenced by question wording and question format as well as the context in which the question is posed. The quality of questionnaire surveys relates directly to the resources available (both money and time) and large and complex surveys involving representative samples can be extremely costly to administer. Cutting costs (for example using mail, rather than face-to-face modes of administration) can increase sample **bias** and reduce data quality.

Despite not being cheap to administer or easy to design, questionnaires will remain a key methodological technique for **social sciences** because they can provide invaluable information about personal characteristics, experiences, behavior, activities, attitudes, and beliefs. The question-and-answer process is a remarkably efficient way of obtaining information. However, two qualifiers are essential. First, respondents have to be available and agree to cooperate with the survey. If the response rate is poor, this jeopardizes the representativeness of the sample. Second, informants have to be able to provide the required information.

To ensure high-quality surveys, researchers must strive to reduce response error or bias that can result from poor questionnaire design, unwanted interviewer effects, or respondent problems. Much of questionnaire design involves a trial-and-error process. For example, overly long questionnaires can result in respondent fatigue, which diminishes the quality of information. However, the appropriate length of a questionnaire varies enormously with subject matter and respondent characteristics. It is often in pilot work that problems of design are identified and hopefully rectified.

There are numerous methodological books that describe "best practice" in questionnaire design. Question writing is usually depicted as more of an art than a science. However, scientific experimental methods have been used to explore systematically how different question constructions affect responses. Respondents differ greatly in their susceptibility to being influenced by different question wordings and question contexts. **Education**, for example, matters. More educated respondents are less likely to display what is known as the "acquiescence bias" (a tendency to agree with questions, whether or not agreement is the appropriate response). Good examples of the uses of experimental **methodology** can be found in Howard Schuman and Stanley Presser's *Questions and Answers in Attitude Surveys* (1981).

There is little point in asking respondents for information that they cannot provide. However, it is not always easy to identify the limits of respondents' knowledge. Respondents often provide answers even when posed questions that make no sense. Experiments have demonstrated that respondents will give opinions about fictitious issues, and guess rather than admitting that they "don't know." There are other sources of response bias. Retrospective questions, for example, are prone to biases of memory. People's accounts of the past tend to be shaped by present-day experience. In addition, memories are selective and people forget stressful events. Memory is also subject to forward telescoping (thinking that something happened more recently than it did). Cognitive biases also affect the answer process. If people are presented with a list of options to choose from, they will often select the first (primacy) or last (recency) and middle options are overlooked. Survey researchers have invested much effort in finding ways of posing questions that take account of and help assuage such cognitive biases.

Interviewer effects can also influence the question-and-answer process. The very characteristics of the interviewer, including **gender**, **age**, and ethnicity, can affect the way respondents answer questions. Research to date on interviewer effects suggest that they are relatively modest. However, for some purposes, particularly when asking for sensitive information, the interviewer matters enormously. Interviewers are a crucial intermediary between questionnaire and respondent. Good interviewers can probe answers to questions to ensure that the response captures clearly what the respondent thinks. However, poor interviewers may pose questions in ways that alter their meaning, or record responses inaccurately.

Questionnaires are sometimes portrayed as being a superficial way of collecting social information. However, this is often a matter of poor practice rather than a flaw in the question-and-answer method. Questionnaires have supported some of the most innovative and imaginative social science research on a diverse range of subjects including **social class** and **social mobility**, **poverty**, **migration**, racial attitudes, family change, social and cultural capital, cross-national **values**, and information **technology**. Questionnaires are an invaluable tool for social science, when used appropriately.   JACKIE SCOTT

R

race and ethnicity

These terms are political constructs that have been used to classify humans into ethnic groups (see **ethnicity** and **ethnic groups**) based on socially significant and identifiable characteristics. These groupings, in turn, have worked to structure societies and regulate social relations. Race generally refers to genetically transmitted characteristics popularly associated with different human groups (such as skin color, facial features, hair texture, body type, and so forth), while ethnicity is generally used to distinguish between groups with a salient array of culturally acquired characteristics (such as **language**, **religion**, or nationality). However, the use of the two terms has been less than uniform. Some scholars have conceived of race as a dimension of ethnicity and/or use the terms interchangeably. Others have conceptualized race as a phenomenon or quality theoretically and substantively distinct from ethnicity.

The history of race and ethnicity as analytical constructs, indeed, reveals a lack of consensus in the literature and in popular discourse. Ethnicity, for instance, is a relatively new term that emerged in the 1920s and 1930s. Because the term connotes a set of cultural characteristics often associated with immigrants from specific nations, it traditionally has been linked to perspectives predicting the eventual melting away of ethnic differences as immigrants settle into their new national homes, or to perspectives predicting and/or advocating the mediation of these differences by universalistic political principles. The notion of race, by contrast, is much older. While there is much disagreement about the historical origins of race as a political phenomenon, distinctions have been made between human groups for centuries, based on their continents of origin and on phenotypical traits popularly associated with these environmental contexts (for example Europe, Asia, Africa, North America, and South America). Adding to the confusion, perhaps, the term race has also been used for millennia to describe specific cultural groups that today are more commonly referred to as ethnic groups (for example biblical references to "races").

Regardless of how the relationship between race and ethnicity is conceived, it should be underscored that both phenomena are socially constructed. That is, both race and ethnicity acquire their meanings and register their impacts through social **interaction** – through contact and competition between racially and/or ethnically defined groups embedded in specific social contexts. Indeed, pure races do not exist as there is often as much phenotypical difference within so-called races as there is between them. Racial categories, in the end, are a creation of the socially situated observer, not of nature. Similarly, because interaction between different peoples throughout history has resulted in substantial cultural exchange, mixing, and **hybridity**, the boundaries of so-called ethnic groups are typically quite porous. Ethnic boundaries are drawn rather arbitrarily, usually in accordance with geographic considerations, historical accident, or political convenience.

Sociologists are interested in race and ethnicity not because either exists in an objective, bounded sense, but because people think and act as if they do. This thought and action results in race and ethnic relations, interaction between people who have been assigned to different racial and/or ethnic categories, usually at birth. Interaction between the groupings is subject to the established societal **norms** and expectations about the nature of the various groups, which results in a patterning of such interaction and the allocation of resources, **power**, and privilege in society.

What may be identified today as race and/or ethnic relations have existed throughout much of human history and in societies around the globe. However, the tenor of these relations between groups has varied considerably, ranging from comity to complete antagonism and marked by six distinct patterns: **assimilation**, **pluralism**, legal protection of subordinate groups, population transfer, continued subordination, and extermination.

Assimilation refers to intermarriage between different groups to the point where socially significant phenotypical and cultural differences are blended together, incorporated by the mainstream, and become meaningless. The early twentieth-century ideal of the "melting pot" in the United States, for example, represented a vision of ethnic assimilation in which English, Irish, German, Italian, and other European immigrants would be blended into a hybrid nation of undifferentiated "Americans." In large measure, these groups were eventually assimilated into the nation's dominant "white" population, while other more racially defined groups (such as "Asian Americans" and "African Americans") were excluded from this level of incorporation on the basis of physical distinctions.

Pluralism, by contrast, refers to the coexistence of separate and distinct racial and/or ethnic groups based on **equality** and cultural tolerance. A contemporary example of this pattern is found in Canada, where the relatively large British and French ethnic groups that founded the nation share **power** and governance with several other racially and ethnically defined groups. While inevitable group tensions arise in Canada as they do in most societies, an official state policy of **multiculturalism** – which includes the support of several languages and ethnic-group-based media outlets – works against the kind of cultural assimilation evident in the United States.

The legal protection of subordinate groups is a pattern reflected in laws ostensibly enacted to insulate subordinate groups against the lingering effects of past racial and/or ethnic antagonisms, as well as against contemporary conflict with dominant groups. The United States and its civil rights laws (for example the Voting Rights Act, affirmative action legislation, and so forth) represent a case in point: these laws were advocated as necessary correctives for a social order that regularly disadvantages certain racial and ethnic groups relative to the dominant group.

Population transfer has occurred throughout history when dominant groups successfully removed and relocated subordinate groups they perceived as barriers to their plans to exploit fully the resources of a given territory. The United States establishment of reservations for the original natives of the North American continent is an example of population transfer designed to move peoples considered different and inferior to less desirable territories and out of the way of "**progress**."

Continued subjugation is a pattern in which a dominant group freely exercises its power to oppress and exploit subordinate groups with which it coexists in a given society. An exemplar of this pattern is the apartheid regime that structured South African society throughout much of the second half of the twentieth century. By establishing and policing a firm line in the law, **politics**, and social relations between the Dutch ethnic group that had colonized the nation, the British, and aboriginal inhabitants of the region, the oppression and exploitation by the settlers was unabashedly executed with the support of state policy.

Finally, biological extermination has been advocated by dominant groups when it was no longer profitable to exploit particular subordinate people and when the dominant group did not successfully assimilate subordinated communities or choose peacefully to coexist with them. A classic example of this pattern is the **genocide** of 6 million Jews in Nazi Germany's concentration camps during World War II.

When race and ethnic relations in a given society are characterized primarily by ongoing conflict between groups – and they usually are – several specific practices and institutional arrangements are likely to mark these group interactions. **Prejudice** factors into group interactions when prejudged negative attitudes about one of the groups are transferred to individual members of the group solely on the basis of their group membership. **Discrimination** occurs when a prejudice is acted upon, particularly when a social actor refuses to grant opportunities to a member of a negatively valued group that he or she would make available to similarly qualified members of his or her own group. When a substantial power imbalance exists in the relations between differently defined groups, a majority group and minority group(s) (which are not necessarily in minority numerically) emerge and the impact of race and/or ethnicity on **life chances** becomes more systemic. "Institutional discrimination" is an indirect form of discrimination that is rooted in the routine use of unjustifiable prerequisites and standards that results – often without immediate intent – in the exclusion of a disproportionate number of minority-group members from participation in valued **institutions** or from access to coveted resources. Finally, **racism** refers to the overall relations of domination and subordination between groups that flow from the hierarchical structuring of a given society based on racial distinctions. In racist societies, prejudice,

491

discrimination, and institutional discrimination are common elements that differentially shape the **life chances** of individuals from dominant and subordinate groups on a day-to-day basis.

To be sure, the **culture** of a given racist society is likely to be permeated by an **ideology** of racism, which works to reproduce racial and ethnic **inequalities** in a manner that resembles self-fulfilling prophecy. Even in a racist society that officially denies the salience of race, a system of majority dominance and minority subordination is often reinforced at the level of ideology through a circular chain of five logically connected societal assumptions and normative expectations. First, racist societies by nature define (officially or unofficially) subordinate racial groups as somehow inferior to the dominant group. Second, because subordinate groups are generally perceived as inferior, members of these groups are considered to be less suited for advanced **education**, high-status jobs, or key positions in society. Third, relatively low expectations about minority qualifications work to discourage members of the dominant group from considering minority-group members for coveted opportunities, particularly when other candidates are available and when competition for the opportunities is fierce. Fourth, because of these racially influenced practices, minority-group members do tend to be more poorly educated, hold lower-status jobs, and fill fewer of the key positions in society. Finally, **statistics** regarding the overrepresentation of minorities at the lower levels of academic achievement and in lower-status jobs, combined with the underrepresentation of minorities in key positions in society, seem to prove for many that minorities are indeed inferior. The chain of assumptions and expectations thus comes full circle.

The classic writings of **Karl Marx, Max Weber**, and **Émile Durkheim** have shaped sociological thought and practice for more than a century. All three theorists were in essential agreement over the significance of race and/or ethnicity in the structuring of society: each treated the phenomena as remnants from early forms of human organization that would disappear as society modernized. Marx, for example, treated race or ethnic consciousness as false consciousness, ideology exploited by the ruling class in order to maintain **hegemony** over the masses. For Weber, the rise of legal–rational **authority** as the dominant form of societal organization would eventually lead to the rule of impersonal law, which would necessarily result in the decline of racial and/or

ethnic significance. Finally, Durkheim argued that race and/or ethnic **solidarity** could be conceptualized as a manifestation of a deeper need for societal order, a phenomenon that would fade in significance as **modernization** transformed mechanical and particularistic solidarities into universalistic ones.

However, a fourth figure centrally implicated in the development of sociology, **W. E. B. Du Bois**, adopted an altogether different stance on the societal importance of race and ethnicity. Having earlier pioneered the empirically based community study with his analysis of black Americans in Philadelphia, Pennsylvania, Du Bois underscored the centrality of race in the structuring of society by proclaiming in 1903 that the problem of the twentieth century is "the problem of the color line." Indeed, more than a century later, race and ethnic phenomena continue to structure societies around the globe, and the writings of Marx, Weber, and Durkheim that had predicted the demise of race and ethnic relations have instead combined with Du Bois's work to inspire a barrage of studies that seek to explain the emergence and persistence of these conditions. At the root of important "conflict" theories of race and ethnicity, for example, can be found key Marxian conceptualizations of **social class** and mode of production. At the core of influential "order" theories about these phenomena are important Weberian and Durkheimian concepts, such as elective affinity, legitimation, organic solidarity, and collective representation. Meanwhile, Du Bois's early community studies prefigured a vibrant tradition of empirically based inquiries that has sought over the years to map the social, cultural, and political effects of race and ethnic relations.

For the purposes of comparison and contrast, the resulting sociological scholarship on race and ethnicity can be crudely organized into three major approaches: (1) those that conceptualize race and/or ethnicity in primordial terms; (2) those that conceive of race and/or ethnicity as artifacts of economic relations; and (3) those that theorize race and/or ethnicity in cultural terms. In the spirit of Weber, these approaches should be viewed as **ideal types**, as many of the scholars so classified also employ elements of the other categories in their conceptualizations, albeit in relatively minor ways.

Theories that treat race and/or ethnicity as primordial phenomena conceive of the categories as essential qualities intrinsic to the nature of specific human groups. These qualities can take several forms: biological traits, psychological complexes, or a combination of the two. Primordial theories often share the notion that race and ethnicity will persist as significant variables in the structuring of society because the conditions that first gave rise to group distinctions are rooted in nature or otherwise quite stable. Against the conventional sociological wisdom that race and ethnicity are socially constructed phenomena, these theories understand the phenomena as qualities that were always there or that naturally evolved out of preexisting physical conditions. Studies of cranial capacity or body type as socially meaningful distinctions between human groups, for example, represent early incarnations of this approach. These (failed) attempts to locate scientifically fixed boundaries between naturally occurring racial groups eventually spawned studies that rooted racial difference in hardwired social responses to biological differences, if not in the differences themselves.

For example, in "The Significance of Skin Color in Human Relations" in J. Franklin's *Color and Race* (1968), Kenneth Gergen roots **ethnocentrism** in the primordial love of self. This instinctual love, he argues, leads to the attraction to and favoring of others who resemble the self. He proposes that the popular association of blackness with negativity is the result of associative learning and color symbolism – particularly for groups who experience darker skin as distinct from their own. The universal phenomenon of day and night, he argues, provides the proverbial model for the symbolic meanings of white and black that permeate many languages around the globe. That is, a child soon learns to associate day with nurturing and care and to associate night with neglect and hunger. These associations, it follows, are internalized and carry over into later life in the form of a color symbolism that influences how phenotypically similar and distinct groups are perceived and evaluated.

In a more complex variation of the primordial approach, Pierre Van den Berghe's *The Ethnic Phenomenon* (1987) synthesizes elements of earlier, Darwin-inspired biological approaches and later sociological and psychological approaches. The primordial goal of fitness, Van den Berghe argues, leads to three different strategies for genetic adaptation: kin selection, reciprocity, and coercion. Ethnicity is defined as an extension of kinship, and racism is the product of the widespread practice of nepotism between kinsmen. The study analyzes human behavior at three interrelated levels: the genetic, the ecological, and the cultural. In the

end, it presents ethnicity as a phenomenon that is both primordial and situational.

While the previous approach to race and ethnicity roots the phenomena in relatively stable, primordial conditions, another more influential approach holds that economic relations constitute the primal force in society, and that race and ethnicity are mere artifacts of these more basic human relations. For these studies, the form of economic relations – preindustrial versus industrial or postindustrial modes of production – is critical because it determines the pattern of racial and/or ethnic relations. Theories characteristic of this approach often postulate that, as economic relations become more advanced, racial and ethnic solidarities will decrease in significance and eventually give way to class solidarities.

In *Caste, Class and Race* (1970), for example, Oliver C. Cox conceptualized race as a modern phenomenon, historically rooted in the genesis of world **capitalism**. His model essentially argued the following: the labor requirements of capitalism sparked a drive to proletarianize the masses; **slavery** was seen as the ideal mechanism for labor manipulation, and appeals to ethnocentrism were used to legitimate the arrangement; when the efficiency of this system began to falter, capitalists used the same ethnocentrism to divide and conquer the "free" workforce, creating, in the process, racial antagonisms. In short, racial conflict, for Cox, amounted to masked class conflict – conflict that promotes the interests of the capitalist class. Walter Rodney's *How Europe Underdeveloped Africa* (1982) echoed this Marx-inspired interpretation of race. Here, of course, the focus was on establishing the links between white racism, the worldwide expansion of capitalism and colonization, and the concomitant decline in the standard of living throughout Africa relative to the conditions in colonizing nations.

In "A Theory of Ethnic Antagonism: The Split Labor Market" (1972, *American Sociological Review*), Edna Bonacich focuses on ethnicity rather than race because the former is viewed as the more general category. Like Cox's theory, this theory identifies economic relations as the basis for interethnic relations. But unlike Cox and other orthodox Marxist approaches to race and ethnicity, Bonacich's split-labor market model does not single out the capitalist class as the promoter of ethnic divisions and antagonisms. Instead, the workers themselves foment ethnic divisions and antagonisms as they pursue their own narrow economic interests. Bonacich contends that a split-labor market is created when higher-paid

labor is able to protect its privileged status in the **market** by monopolizing access to key resources. A common manifestation of this development consists of the banding together of higher-paid labor – usually along ethnic lines – into guilds and other associations, blocking the access of out-groups to education and job skills, thereby lessening the threat that these groups could compete for the same privileged jobs in the **labor market**. All things being equal, the argument goes, higher-paid labor would become relatively scarce, allowing it to demand of employers higher wages than possible if other groups had equal qualifications and skills. It is this exclusion of subordinate groups from labor guilds and associations – combined with the threat of subordinate group members as cheaper, replacement labor (or even as strikebreakers) – that fuels ethnic antagonism.

In many respects, **William Julius Wilson**'s *The Declining Significance of Race: Black and Changing American Institutions* (1978) advances a model of race relations that synthesizes key tenets of contemporary Marxian studies like those discussed above with ideas inspiring culture-based studies like those discussed below. Wilson uses American census **data** and other evidence to argue that the historical period determines the system of production, which leads to specific patterns of inter-group relations (for example, race relations). These relations, in turn, lead to legitimating norms and stereotypes that reinforce the racial order through cultural means. Wilson divides the history of the United States into three distinct epochs of production: preindustrial, industrial, and postindustrial. The preindustrial epoch, he argues, was one in which black–white relations were essentially relations between master and slave. Wilson refers to this as an era of symbiosis and **paternalism**, when the planter class exploited slave labor while protecting their captive labor force against the threat of displaced Southern workers. The emergence of the industrial epoch, however, sealed the doom of this "peculiar institution," leading to a transformation in race relations. In this emergent period, former slaves were perceived by white workers as potential competitors for the industry jobs that were growing in importance. This perceived threat, Wilson suggests – and the absence of planter-class protection for the former slaves – led to increases in anti-black racial **ideology**, Jim Crow legislation, and, ultimately, a split-labor market where blacks occupied the bottom realm. In this period, though, race was still more important than **social class** in the structuring of society. But in the postindustrial era, Wilson argues, the role of the polity increased relative to that of the market in the structuring of society, leading to increased racial **equality** and an environment where class is more important than race in the shaping of **life chances**.

While approaches that treat race and ethnicity as cultural phenomena often give great importance to economic relations between groups, these approaches are distinctive in the centrality they attribute to the relative autonomy of ideas, of ways of life, and of experiences, in the shaping of social relations. This grouping of approaches might itself be broken into two subgroups: works that treat race and/or ethnicity as static concepts and those that treat them as dynamic concepts. Static approaches are more characteristic of earlier works in the field, works that tend to define categories from the perspective of the analyst and impose the meaning of these categories backwards in time to the relations under study. In contrast, dynamic approaches are usually more recent in origin and attempt to derive meaning from the context of the relations under study, ultimately conceiving of race and ethnicity as fluid phenomena whose connotations change over time within a given context. In an ironic way, perhaps, dynamic-culture studies often employ Durkheimian concepts to argue – contrary to Durkheim himself – that race and ethnicity are likely to persist as meaningful social phenomena.

Robert Ezra Park, **Gunnar Myrdal**, and **E. Franklin Frazier** are important, early representatives of the static-culture approach. In *Race and Culture* (1950), Park's race-relations cycle proposed that as racial and ethnic groups come into contact with the dominant American **culture**, three stages of **interaction** would necessarily ensue: competition, accommodation, and assimilation. Frazier's *The Negro in the United States* (1957) also conceptualized race relations as an evolutionary process. The process of integrating Negroes into American society, he argued, is represented by a sequential gradient, with assimilation coming first in sectors of secondary (secular) rather than primary (sacred) contact. Similarly, Myrdal's massive study of American race relations, *An American Dilemma: The Negro Problem and American Democracy* (1944), underscored the importance of cultural factors that might be managed over time – in this case, the **attitudes** that white Americans held about blacks. Despite his acknowledgment that white Americans held virtually all economic, social, and political power in society, he argued that the "Negro problem" in the United States could be resolved simply by bringing the attitudes of whites in line with an "American Creed" of **democracy** and basic equality. This cultural achievement, he concluded, would go a long way towards breaking the chain of cumulative causation in American race relations – the vicious cycle by which disadvantage begets more disadvantage for blacks, further dividing the races in the United States. In the end, each of these works is of the static-culture variety because they treat the content of racial categories as a given, something either to be assimilated in a one-way, transhistorical process or to be tolerated by the broader, mainstream culture. None of the works endeavors to theorize changes in the meaning of race and/or ethnicity as relations between groups progress.

By contrast, in *Racial Formation in the United States from the 1960s to the 1990s* (1994), Michael Omi and Howard Winant posit a racial-formation model that exemplifies the fluid-culture approach. This work conceptualizes race as a social and historical concept whose meaning changes relative to specific social relations embedded within specific historical and geographic contexts. Economic and political forces matter, the argument goes, but primarily in terms of how each shapes the social meaning of existing racial categories. Indeed, racial categories are understood to be in a perpetual process of formation (that is, creation, destruction, and realignment), composed at any given point in time of common-sense etiquette, ideologies, and representations. The theory conceives of racial projects (for example, colonization, slavery, or anti-racism) as the building blocks of racial formation; these links between the cultural realm of ideas and the material simultaneously provide common-sense **explanations** for prevailing racial dynamics and support efforts to (re)distribute resources along racial lines. The racial state, which is composed of countless institutions infused with race-based assumptions and policies, regularly intervenes to stabilize contemporary racial dynamics. At base, racial formation theory is heavily influenced by **Antonio Gramsci**'s notion of **hegemony**. Accordingly, the theory conceives of the racial order at any given moment as an unstable equilibrium fashioned by interaction between the racial state, interest groups, and organic consciousness. It conceives of race as distinct from ethnicity in that the former is read off human bodies (which are less malleable than cultural characteristics) for the purposes of grounding social **identities**, maintaining social boundaries, and protecting social privilege. The theory thus presents race as a relatively permanent, central axis of social relations that cuts across class lines. Indeed, it understands racial dynamics as determinants of class relationships, not – as the economic approaches argue – the other way around.

Echoing Omi and Winant's focus on the role meanings play in the trajectory of racial dynamics, a recent body of scholarship on race and ethnicity has emerged, which is rooted in the **cultural studies** tradition. A key figure associated with this movement is **Stuart Hall**, whose empirical studies and theoretical writings have underscored the increasingly important role played by media in racial formation processes. Hall conceives of race as a "floating signifier," as a discursive category that links the otherwise random physical characteristics that we read from human bodies with important social assumptions, expectations, and outcomes. Indeed, Hall argues that the political function of race as a signifier is to establish a system of equivalences that allows social actors to read culture (that is character, capabilities, and so forth) from nature (that is, the **body**), thereby naturalizing and fixing differences that are actually socially constructed and fluid. The formation of "black" and "white" races as a binary opposition represents the quintessential expression of this process, as the perceived location of each racial group at an opposing end of the meaning spectrum, by default, anchors the meaning of the other. That is, what is "black" is "not white," and what is "white" is "not black." Floating (or fluid) signifiers associated with "black" and "white" bodies, Hall argues, resonate with an important system of equivalences that continues to shape racial politics in many societies:

white = European = civilized = rational = superior = free = good

versus

black = African = savage = emotional = inferior = slave = bad

These basic equations have worked to reinforce systematically at the level of ideology, the relative positioning of persons considered "black" and "white" throughout a number of societies around the globe, including the United States and the United Kingdom. Hall's studies of news, motion pictures, and other media – as well as several other important media studies inspired by his work – interrogate how these equivalences reinforce racial commonsense and stereotypes. Collectively, these studies trace the cultural processes by which popular ideas contribute to a reproduction of racial **inequality**.

Contrary to **sociological theories** that reduce race and ethnicity to other social phenomena, or that predict they will either decline in significance or eventually disappear as meaningful social categories, race and ethnicity continue to shape societal and global relations in profound ways. This is because race and ethnicity have taken root in cultures around the world and exert their force, on a regular basis, as irresistible social representations. To be sure, these naturalized mental frameworks have ordered and continue to order the way social actors see the world before them. In the case of race, people notice otherwise arbitrary differences on the surface of the human body and imbue these differences with social meanings. These meanings, in turn, reinforce the significance of the otherwise nonessential social construction, giving it a rather objective weight. In many societies, race is a fundamental component of social actors' ongoing efforts to establish who they are, who they are not, and who they hope to be. Social actors in these societies regularly affirm and police the boundaries of race, in their own little ways, as a means of bringing necessary order to their social experiences. In other societies, ethnicity might be more salient in these meaning-making processes.

But meaning-making processes related to race and ethnicity ultimately involve much more than just attitudes about in-groups and out-groups. Race and ethnicity are also about group resources, about group security, and about group power. As commonsense ideology, race and ethnicity have been exploited by **elites** as a potent means either for masking their own privilege or for naturalizing their group's dominant position in society (and, by extension, their own personal privilege). At the same time, however, subordinate groups have relied upon race and/or ethnicity in order to mobilize participants into oppositional, identity-based movements for **social change**. These observations reveal the fundamental social utility of race and ethnicity, while echoing their many contradictions. Whether it is the ethnic cleansing of non-Serbians in Bosnia, movements to institute affirmative action protection for blacks in Brazil, or anti-immigrant sentiments in the United States, contemporary events around the globe underscore both the complexity of race and ethnicity and the sense of urgency surrounding race and ethnic relations. As long as there is conflict in the world, it appears, race and ethnicity will serve as important axes of group antagonism.

DARNELL HUNT

race relations
– see **race and ethnicity**.

racial discrimination
– see **race and ethnicity**.

racial orders
– see **race and ethnicity**.

racism

As distinct from **prejudice**, a psychological **attitude**, **racism** is an enduring, salient aspect of social and global structures. It is based on demonstrably false theories of racial differences appropriated by a **culture** in order to deny or unjustly distribute social privileges, economic opportunities, and political **rights** to the racially stigmatized **groups**. Racism, thus, structures social differences, **power**, and culture, as when, according to George Fredrickson, "one ethnic group or historical collectivity dominates, excludes, or seeks to eliminate another on the basis of differences that it believes are hereditary and unalterable" (*Racism*, 2002).

Historically, the concept came into use late in the modern era, principally in reference to the Nazi program for the elimination of Jewish people and to the **segregation** of blacks in South Africa and the United States. Racism stops short of **genocide** when the dominant classes depend on the labor power of the segregated. In recent international discussions, for example at the World Conference Against Racism, Racial Discrimination, Xenophobia, and Related Intolerances in 2001 in Durban, South Africa, it has become increasingly clear that "racism" often includes extra-racial factors. In sociology, where the distinction between race and ethnicity is uncertain, it is best to limit "racism" to structures in which race is explicitly used to effect social domination. The foundations of racial domination were laid in the sixteenth-century slave trade and Euro-American colonization. Racism, thereby, applies most accurately to structures historically dominated by the European diaspora. The expression "reverse racism" is thus ironic. There is no scientific evidence that race is a meaningful way to identify social or biological differences.   CHARLES LEMERT

radical feminism
– see **feminism**.

random sampling
– see **sampling**.

rational choice theory

In sociology, theories based on rational choice assumptions borrow many of their core ideas from the Scottish moralists (classical economics) as the ideas have been recast in neo-classical economics, **game theory**, and efforts by economists to sort out the "logic" of **collective action**. In its most extreme form within neo-classical economics, actors are seen as participating in a free, open, and competitive **market** in which individual actors seek to maximize their utilities in transactions with other actors. In this extreme form, it is assumed that actors have access to all relevant **information**, that they can consider all available alternative courses of action, that they can calculate the potential utilities relevant to the costs associated with each alternative action forgone, and that they will seek to maximize their utilities (rewards less costs in getting these rewards and alternatives forgone). From classical economics comes the assumption that if actors behave in this "rational" manner, the "invisible hand of order" proposed by Adam Smith (1723–90) will create the most just and fair society, although it should be noted that Smith, more than other neo-classical economists, had a view of the importance of moral sentiments regulating the rational actions of individuals. Some forms of sociological **exchange theory** relax these extreme assumptions, assuming only that individuals use what information they have available to generate a profit (utilities less costs) in exchange relations with others, although those within the rational choice tradition proper (rather than the more general exchange-theoretic tradition in sociology) tend to retain most of the extreme assumptions of neo-classical economics.

Game theory has added to this conception of individuals in markets mathematical models of the payoffs to be gained or lost by various behavioral strategies by one actor or set of actors in relation to the potential behavioral strategies of other actors. By modeling various "games" through computer simulations, various behavioral and social structure outcomes of different behavioral strategies can be documented. Another approach within economics that has had considerable influence on **sociological theories** invoking rational choice assumptions is Mancur Olson's *The Logic of Collective Action* (1965) in which the production of "public" and "private" goods from the coordinated actions of individuals, coupled with the problem of free-riding (or not contributing to the production of a joint good), determines the nature of actors' organization into group structures.

Within **sociology** proper, these ideas have been incorporated into theories that try to explain the emergence of **social structures** and associated systems of cultural **symbols** as outcomes of efforts by individuals to maximize utilities in exchange relations with others. These approaches conceptualize the individual as purposive and goal-oriented, as revealing a clear hierarchy of preferences, as making calculations about likely payoffs relative to their hierarchy of preferences for each potential line of conduct, as assessing the costs for each line of conduct, and as trying to maximize utilities (rewards less costs in getting them and in alternative utilities forgone). What makes these rational choice assumptions sociological is the view that emergent social phenomena – social structures, collective decisions, collective behavior, and systems of cultural ideas – are ultimately the result of rational choices made by utility-maximizing actors. Once socio-cultural phenomena emerge, however, they operate as parameters that constrain subsequent rational choices because they affect the distribution of resources among actors, the distribution of opportunities for payoffs among actors, and the distribution and nature of normative obligations constraining actions.

In trying to explain the emergence of **norms** and social structure, rational choice theories borrow the notion of "negative externalities" from neo-classical economics. When individuals are engaged in collective action to produce some joint good, the problem of free-riding inevitably emerges because it is rational for actors not to contribute to the production of a good while still enjoying the utilities that come with its production. Of course, if all actors free-ride, the joint good does not get produced; and as a result, the more actors free-ride, the greater are the negative externalities for all actors engaged in collective action. Under these conditions, it is rational for actors to create normative agreements that limit free-riding and, thereby, guarantee maximum payoffs to all individuals. This is the basic argument for why and how social structure and normative agreements are created by rational actors working in their self-interest – a sociological version of Adam Smith's invisible hand of order.

Various theories within this tradition add important propositions. Individuals become more interested in creating normative agreements to the degree that negative externalities are experienced collectively, the rate of free-riding is high, and the level of dependence of actors on the utilities that come from the production of a joint good is high. The power of the norms created under these conditions will be greater to the extent that each actor's dependence on the production of a joint good is high, actors consume the joint goods that they produce (making the good a "private" as opposed to "public good" that can be consumed by all), rates of communication among actors are high, network density among actors is high, and a high proportion of actors receive utilities from jointly produced goods. The ratio of prescriptive to proscriptive content of norms regulating the production of a joint good increases when the costs of monitoring conformity to norms are low and when the ratio of positive to negative sanctioning is high. And these conditions together promote high levels of social **solidarity** among collectively organized actors producing a joint good.

The goal of all rational choice theory is to demonstrate that macro-level outcomes can be explained by micro-level conceptions of rational actors. There is a persistent critique of sociological theories that simply assume social structure and norms without explaining how they are generated and without documenting the forces by which they are sustained. The critique of normative and structural sociology emphasizes that structural and normative theories do not posit a mechanism or set of dynamic processes by which meso- and macro-level structures and associated cultural symbols are generated. In contrast, rational choice theorists argue that they are able to specify the mechanisms – rational decisions among actors producing joint goods but experiencing negative externalities and free-riding – that generate and sustain social structures and norms. Yet, critics of rational choice theory argue that this specificity is more elusive than real because, in the end, what rational choice theorists posit is that people create social structures and **culture** because it is rational, without specifying in detail the exact sequence of processes by which negative externalities, free-riding, and norm creation operate or by obscuring the actual processes in the equations guiding computer simulations.   JONATHAN TURNER

rationality

In philosophy, reason refers to the human capacity to acquire knowledge and/or make intelligent decisions. Reason contrasts with habit, **emotion**, blind faith, and **tradition**. Aristotle distinguishes theoretical and practical reasoning, where practical reasoning culminates in action rather than in a proposition or a new belief.

Though **Max Weber** refers to theoretical rationality, sociological uses of rationality broadly favor Aristotle's sense of practical reasoning.

Utilitarianism supplied the first sociological accounts of rational action during the **Enlightenment**, and **rational choice theory** continues the utilitarian tradition today. In its most elementary form, utilitarian, or instrumental, rationality refers to actions undertaken by individual actors in pursuit of their interests by the most effective available means.

Weber introduced a more nuanced view of rational action by distinguishing a second, value-rational form of action. Here, actors act upon a belief in the ultimate **value** (for example, religious, ethical, aesthetic) of the behavior in question. Weber clarifies the rationality of these forms of action by introducing two contrasting forms of action, traditional action (for example, habit or custom) and affectual behavior based purely upon emotion.

Weber conceived the preceding concepts as abstract and limited **ideal types**. They are abstract because they apply universally, and they are limited because they refer to the actor's subjective understanding of individual acts. However, as a historical sociologist, Weber was most concerned with studying patterns of action on levels ranging from actions of members of religious sects to actions in institutional orders such as **capitalism** or feudal principalities. Weber ultimately (often only obliquely) referred to four ideal types of patterns of rationality. Two points about these patterns must be borne in mind. First, in reality each pattern comprises individual actions. Second, in any given historical case, two or more patterns of rationality may merge and diverge in kaleidoscopic configurations.

The four ideal types of patterns of rational action include: (1) formal rationality – comprising actions oriented to instrumental goals by efficient means. Formal rational patterns are extremely disciplined, involving calculations according to generally applicable **norms** or rules. Ideal-typical **bureaucracies** and capitalist enterprises incorporate formal rational patterns of action; (2) substantive rationality – patterns comprising actions oriented to constellations of values. Ideal-typical religious **communities** adhere to substantive rational patterns of action; (3) practical rationality – comprising actions by which individuals solve problems relevant to self-interest or survival without regard to formal discipline; and (4) theoretical rationality – confined mainly to dedicated thinkers, these patterns of action are dedicated to producing systems of thought as means to master reality. Theologians and philosophers adhere to theoretical-rational patterns of action. Though they are rarely dominant, Weber believed that in specific historical settings theoretical-rational patterns of action can influence the course of development for entire **cultures** and **civilizations**.

Weber's notions of patterns of rational action, and his inclusion of value-rational action in patterns of substantive rationality was one inspiration (among others) for **Talcott Parsons**'s *The Structure of Social Action* (1937).　　IRA COHEN

rationalization

In **social theory** today, rationalization refers to the historical development of institutional orders such as the law, the **market**, capitalist enterprise, and the bureaucratic **state**, all of which are organized by impersonal and amoral principles that facilitate the instrumental pursuit of means and ends. **Max Weber** is the classical source for the idea of rationalization. His well-known metaphor of the iron cage suggests the existential experience of being encased in formal rules that allow no moral or humane relationships. Franz Kafka's (1883–1924) image of a defendant trapped in a judicial system beyond his control captures the experience of living in a rationalized world from a more literary point of view. The most recent sociological conceptualization of rationalization appears in **Jürgen Habermas**'s notion of the colonization of the **lifeworld** by impersonal social systems. Other ideas associated with rationalization include **Georg Lukács**'s notion of **reification**, and interpretations of the Holocaust by Richard Rubenstein and **Zygmunt Bauman**.

Weber's account of rationalization processes remains unsurpassed in its historical sensitivity. Not only did he distinguish different rationalization processes in the history of every modern institutional order and cultural sphere, but he also recognized moral (substantive) limits to rationalization in every order except **capitalism**, where formal **rationality** goes unchecked. For example, though the bulk of any body of modern law is formal and hence rationalized, the precepts of any legal system are grounded in moral axioms (see **law and society**). In **bureaucracy**, the overarching policy decisions are always subject to moral evaluation. They cannot be made on the basis of strictly rule-guided formal procedures.　IRA COHEN

realism

This is a philosophy of science that seeks to establish that scientific theories refer to real objects that are independent of representations of them, even where the postulated entities and processes are unobservable. Scientific realism emerged as a critique of **positivism**. Realists argue that positivism is concerned only with regularities, or the empirical association of events. However, merely knowing that events are associated tells us little. We want to know how the events are associated; that is, we wish to identify causal mechanisms that operate as real forces, even if those mechanisms cannot be observed. Where the theory that invokes such mechanisms is empirically well confirmed, we have good reason to believe that the mechanisms are real.

An important distinction is made between closed and open systems. Closed systems are mostly the product of the activity of scientists who perform experiments in order to isolate a particular structure and its effects. Open systems are systems of the real world where many structures operate and may cancel the effects of other structures. The non-occurrence in open systems of the necessary effects of a real structure could not in itself falsify that structure. Mechanisms and their causal laws are only claims about tendencies; the real effects of structures need not become actual and there is an ontological gap between causal laws and their empirical manifestations.

These arguments are used to criticize the positivist concern with prediction, with important implications for **social science**. Prediction is only possible in closed systems – for example, the structures that are responsible for the weather may be known, but we may not be able to predict it because of the inherent complexity of the open system that is the weather. Realists argue that the social sciences deal with similarly complex open systems and, therefore, prediction is an inappropriate and misleading objective. The social sciences can, however, achieve *retrodictive* explanation, where knowledge of effective structures is used to make sense of events in the past and the present.

Realism became influential in the social sciences following Thomas Kuhn's *Structure of Scientific Revolutions* (1962). Kuhn challenged the view that science proceeded in a linear and accumulative manner, arguing that there are fundamental changes in world-views and that different scientific **paradigms** are incommensurable. He was seen as presenting a social constructivist and relativist view of science, albeit one which challenged the positivistic prescriptions that many thought had severely constrained social science.

The implications of realism for social inquiry have been developed by Roy Bhaskar (1944–) and **Margaret Archer**. They use the term critical realism, arguing that naturalistic social inquiry can follow an ontology implicit in **Karl Marx**. **Social structures** are less enduring than natural structures. Whereas natural structures are independent of human action, social structures are reproduced and changed through human action. This does not mean that they are the intended outcome of human actions; social structures should be understood as the unintended outcome, and unacknowledged condition, of human action. However, actors' own understandings of the world must be part of the **explanation** of structures, their reproduction, and change. For critical realists, a realist philosophy of science must be supplemented by an interpretive understanding of the social world. Realist social science, then, is not fully naturalist and subsequent developments in critical realism by Archer have concentrated on setting out a formal approach to social inquiry that captures this dualism of **agency and structure**.   JOHN HOLMWOOD

realist criminology
– see **criminology**.

reception theory
– see **audience**.

reciprocity
– see **exchange theory**.

reductionism
A term usually used to denounce descriptions of **society** that over-simplify it by treating a limited number of its constituent components as if they make up the whole; society, it is said, is thereby illegitimately treated as nothing but (reduced to) the parts that are singled out. This would be true of a crude interpretation of **Marxism** that treated the social whole as if it could all be explained in terms of, reduced to, the economic realm. Reductionist accounts are thus often contrasted with pluralist accounts in which respect is given to many explanatory factors.

The charge of reductionism is also used, in a logically connected way, to criticize those writers who make no distinction between the many parts that go to make up a social phenomenon and the intrinsic properties of the phenomenon itself. Thus, if it was claimed that there is nothing more to be said about water once one breaks it down into its constituent elements, of two parts hydrogen and one part oxygen, then this would be a reductionist statement. It would deny all the emergent properties and powers of water that emerge out of the combination of the elements of hydrogen and oxygen. The same is true of **methodological individualism**, often associated with **Max Weber**'s explicitly methodological writing, which denies the emergent properties of society. As the approach breaks everything down into the actions of individuals, it cannot account for those differential capabilities that depend upon their situation with respect to emergent social properties, which may include a range of conditions from institutional infrastructures through monetary or transportation **networks** to inherited cultural **traditions**. Gregor McLellan (1996, *New Left Review*) has argued for a form of "weak" or "loose" reductionism in which prior social parts, such as the class system and class interests, are seen as causally connected to, say, a political party's agenda for social transformation, but not as completely explaining it or somehow effacing its own emergent significance.   ROB STONES

reference group
This term refers to a "collectivity" that an individual uses either to evaluate their own position – a comparative reference group – or to set norms and standards of behavior – a normative reference group.

In either instance, the group only needs to be an imagined collectivity of the individual and does not necessarily have to be an actual collection of interacting individuals.

The classic study of a comparative reference group comes from Samuel Stouffer *et al.*, *The American Soldier* (1949). Soldiers in units that had a high promotion rate saw their chances of advancement as poor, while soldiers in units with low promotion rates, such as the military police, saw their chances as good. The comparative reference group of soldiers was the explanation for this apparent paradox. Soldiers in units with high rates of promotion evaluated themselves against other members of the same unit who had been promoted more often or sooner than they had been. High promotion appeared typical, so anything other than that was relatively worse. In contrast, in units where promotion prospects were low, not being promoted was typical, so soldiers did not feel worse off than their compatriots. So, the feeling of deprivation is relative. This idea of **relative deprivation** can be applied generally. For instance, while **poverty** can be defined objectively by criteria such as having an **income** below a certain level or lacking access to basic amenities or necessities of life, poverty can also be defined subjectively by how individuals perceive themselves in relation to what they see as a typical or adequate standard of living.

In its normative sense, a reference group was defined by Tamotsu Shibutani, "Reference Groups as Perspectives," in the *American Journal of Sociology* (1955), as "any collectivity, real or imagined, envied or despised, whose perspective is assumed by the actor." Used in this manner, the reference group is employed as a source of patterns of behavior or ways of acting that are to be emulated or shunned. The concept of a normative reference group came from **symbolic interactionism** and relates to **George Herbert Mead**'s "generalized other." It differs, however, in that, while the "generalized other" refers to the standards and customs of the whole society, a normative reference group refers to a smaller, more specific collectivity within the society. The normative reference group's mores may differ from those of the general society or even be in diametric opposition to it. Hence, normative reference groups can be used as a means of explaining how social deviance, such as criminality, can be rule-bound.

In both these senses, reference groups can be either positive or negative; collectivities that an individual can either hope to join or emulate or seek to avoid or rise above.   ROBERT MILLER

reference group theory
– see **reference group**.

reflective modernization
– see **Ulrich Beck**.

regression
A statistical technique to investigate the relationship between two or more variables, in its simplest sense, regression can be used to predict the score of one variable from another variable, if those two variables are correlated. For instance, regression can be used to predict the adult height of a baby when it will become an adult. This could be done from just one variable, such as the mother's height. But more accurate predictions would be possible if other variables were also taken into account, such as the father's height and the baby's sex. Regression (or, more exactly multiple regression) can easily do this: predict one outcome or **dependent variable** from

a number of causal or independent variables simultaneously.

As social scientists, we are rarely interested in making predictions. More often, we are interested in the nature of the relationship between several variables. For instance, we might want to know why, in the United Kingdom, men are still paid more per hour, on average, than women? Is it because men are better educated, more skilled, physically stronger, choose higher-paid **occupations**, have more experience in the **labor market** because they are less likely to take time out of employment to care for children, and so on? Or is it partly due to raw **discrimination** against women? A multiple regression would be able to answer such a question by seeing how much of the difference in hourly pay (the dependent variable) between men and women was explained in terms of each of the independent variables (skill, **education**, or occupation), and how much remained unexplained, which could be attributed to discrimination.

There are many different statistical forms of regression. The most common form, simply referred to as multiple regression (or sometimes OLS or ordinary least squares regression), is best suited to situations where all of the variables are continuous, interval, and Gaussian, involving two independent random variables. Other forms of regression, such as logistic regression, are also available for when the variables are categorical (such as male/female). Some more advanced forms of regression can cope with situations where the errors in variables are themselves correlated, so simple regression could give misleading results.

Like correlation, multiple regression is not suitable for determining the causal direction of a relationship in cross-sectional **data**. In those cases other research methods may be required, such as cohort or **panel studies**.   BRENDAN J. BURCHELL

regulation school
– see **regulation theory**.

regulation theory
This theory (also known as the regulation approach and the regulation school) is a major **paradigm** in institutional and evolutionary economics, and is especially concerned with the contradictory and conflictual dynamics of contemporary **capitalism**. Its several schools examine the role of extra-economic as well as economic **values**, **institutions**, and practices in securing, if only temporarily and always in specific economic spaces, the inherently

improbable and always crisis-prone process of capital accumulation. This process involves alternating periods of relatively stable accumulation and of crisis-induced restructuring, rescaling, and reregulation. In examining the extra-economic aspects of the regularization of economic activities, regulation theorists draw on, and provide links to, other **social sciences**. This has enabled them to make important contributions to the study of advanced capitalist economies and, more recently, to dependent capitalist **economies** and the dynamics of global **capitalism**.

Regulation theory originated with French heterodox economists in the mid-1970s, whose work is collectively identified as the Parisian School. Representative early work in English includes Michel Aglietta's pioneering study, *A Theory of Capitalist Regulation* (1976), Robert Boyer's critical introduction, *The Regulation School* (1990), and Alain Lipietz's essays on *Mirages and Miracles: The Crises of Global Fordism* (1987s [trans. 1987]). There are two less well-known French regulation schools dating from the 1960s and 1970s. One is linked to the French Communist Party and focuses on the ways in which profits in privileged sectors are protected by reducing returns in other sectors; and the Grenoble School focuses on the internal regulation of distinctive plurinational productive systems organized under the dominance of one national capital and on the anarchic relations between such systems. The Amsterdam School explored how national and transnational economic relations are regulated according to hegemonic "concepts of control" associated with either **money** or productive capital. The West German School focused on the **state**'s role in securing capitalist reproduction and on the repercussions of different growth regimes for the wider society. Finally, an American radical school focused on the "**social structures** of accumulation" that secured growth in different periods of American economic history and applied this analysis to other economies (these schools are surveyed by Bob Jessop and Ngai-Ling Sum in *Beyond the Regulation Approach*, 2006).

The variety of such schools means that, rather than involving a single, homogeneous approach, regulation theory is better seen as a broad, progressive economic research program with major implications for critical social science more generally. As such it denies that there is anything automatic about periods of economic stability (capitalism is not self-stabilizing) or about capitalist restructuring in response to crises (capitalism is not self-healing). Social agency is crucial in both

respects – behavioral regularities are essential for relative stability until the inherent contradictions and crisis tendencies become too intense, and new patterns of conduct are required during the institutional restructuring that may eventually reregularize economic expansion.

Thus, regulation theory explores the interconnections between the institutional forms and dynamic regularities of capitalist economies. Unlike orthodox economics, it rejects any general, transhistorical account of economics or rational economic conduct. Instead it focuses on the historical specificities of capitalism and regards its continued growth as inherently improbable due to its crisis tendencies and associated class struggle. While first-generation regulationists tended to cite the fundamental contradictions and conflicts generated by capitalism's distinctive dynamics, later studies pursue more middle-range analyses of the self-limiting or self-undermining nature of particular accumulation regimes and modes of regulation defined in more institutional terms. Overall, while far from neglectful of the essentially anarchic role of exchange relations (or market forces) in mediating capitalist reproduction, regulationists also stress the complementary functions of other mechanisms (including **institutions**, collective **identities**, shared visions, common values, **norms**, conventions, **networks**, procedures, and modes of calculation) in structuring, facilitating, and guiding accumulation. In addressing these issues, regulationists have developed a wide array of concepts to study the institutions and practices of capitalism, explain the various crisis tendencies of modern capitalism and/or likely sources of crisis-resolution, distinguish among different stages (periods, phases, and so forth) of capitalist development, compare and contrast different accumulation regimes and modes of regulation within a given stage of world capitalism, and examine the social embedding and social regularization of economic institutions and conduct.

The dominant Parisian School developed four key concepts for analyzing capitalism and its regulation. First, an industrial paradigm is a model governing the technical and social division of **labor** (for example, mass production). Second, an accumulation regime is a complementary pattern of production and **consumption** that is reproducible over a long period. The Fordist regime based on mass production and mass consumption is the most famous example. Third, a mode of regulation is an emergent ensemble of norms, institutions, organizational forms, social networks, and patterns of conduct that can stabilize an accumulation regime. This is a more meso-level concept and is generally analyzed in terms of five dimensions: the wage relation (**labor markets** and wage-effort bargaining, individual and social wages, and **lifestyles**); the enterprise form (its internal **organization**, the source of profits, forms of competition, ties among enterprises, links to banking capital); the nature of money (its dominant form and its emission, the banking and credit system, the allocation of money capital to production); the **state** (the institutionalized compromise between capital and labor, forms of state intervention); and international regimes (the trade, investment, monetary settlements, and political arrangements that link national economies, nation-states, and the world system). Fourth, a model of development comprises a complementary industrial paradigm, accumulation regime, and mode of regulation that together secure for a time the conditions for a long wave of capitalist expansion. All four concepts are typically defined to take account of the conflictual and antagonistic nature of capitalism.

Regulation theory remains a progressive research program (see, for example, the comprehensive survey in Robert Boyer and Yves Saillard's 2002 collection, *Régulation Theory: The State of the Art*). But it has also been criticized by fundamentalist leftwing critics for appearing to treat capitalism as inevitable (crises are always eventually overcome) and hence for supporting reformism; and by more mainstream social scientists for its one-sided concern with the economic logic of capital accumulation. There has also been critical historical and econometric work challenging the original analyses of Fordism and its crisis on empirical grounds. Regulation theorists have responded by developing new analyses, extending the approach to other national cases, examining more sites and scales of economic organization, developing alternative scenarios for post-Fordism, and returning to some of the basic categories of economic analysis (Jessop and Sum, 2006).

BOB JESSOP

reification

In its broadest sense, reification is the logical fallacy of regarding an abstract concept (such as **society**) as if it were a concrete thing, and consequently treating fluid and mutable entities as though they were natural and immutable. Sociological usage of the term is associated with the Hungarian Marxist, **Georg Lukács**. In *History and*

Class Consciousness (1923 [trans. 1971]) he argued that in capitalist society the fetishistic commodity form becomes universal. People appear to be confronted by a world of autonomous things (commodities and social relations) rather than by historically contingent and socially produced forms of life. Reification for Lukács involves a methodological error that generates a fragmented view of the world and loses sight of the dialectical totality of capitalist society. Marxist **intellectuals** (who take "the standpoint of the proletariat") avoid this error, but reified consciousness will disappear only at the point of revolutionary transformation when social relations will appear fluid and transparent. Again within the Marxist tradition, **Theodor Wiesengrund Adorno** used the concept to refer to the social determination of thinking (in, for example, *Negative Dialectics*, 1966 [trans. 1973]) in which concepts either impute properties to the object that are absent (such as freedom) or distort existing properties so that they appear objective. In particular, the commodity creates an illusory identity between concept and object. However, in *The Social Construction of Reality* (1966), **Peter L. Berger** and **Thomas Luckmann** suggest that only insofar as humans forget that social reality is constructed does it attain permanence; this implies that reification might be to some extent necessary.

LARRY RAY

relative deprivation

This concept focuses on comparisons between the levels of deprivation suffered by different **groups**. Deprivation can be absolute, when it is determined against an independent standard of measurement, or relative, when it is based on a comparison with the resources of other groups. The term relative deprivation was initially coined by Samuel Stouffer *et al.*, the authors of *The American Soldier* (1949), a large-scale social-psychological study carried out during World War II by a specialist research branch within the United States War Department. Soldiers posted overseas, for example, experienced a sense of deprivation relative to soldiers still at home, but felt less deprivation relative to the combat soldier. Similarly, black soldiers stationed in the American South felt privileged in terms of **wealth** and status compared with black civilians.

In *Social Theory and Social Structure* (1957), **Robert K. Merton** linked *The American Soldier*'s treatment of relative deprivation to the theory of **reference groups**, noting the way in which groups orient themselves to an array of membership and non-membership groups in shaping their behavior and evaluations, but particularly emphasizing the latter. Drawing on empirical inquiry he also emphasized the counterintuitive implications of such relative comparisons for subjective states of mind, such that a family experiencing a great loss in a mass disaster would feel less deprived than others elsewhere suffering similar losses, if, in the immediate circumstances, they were surrounded by people whose losses were much more severe than their own.

W. G. Runciman's *Relative Deprivation and Social Justice* (1966) linked relative deprivation to social **inequality** along the three dimensions of **social class**, **social status**, and **power**, and insisted that the subjective "sense" of felt deprivation was essential to the concept. Linking his analysis to the conception of distributive **justice** in John Rawls's *A Theory of Justice* (1971), Runciman argued that there was a difference between comparative **inequalities** experienced subjectively as unjust, and thus felt as unnecessary deprivations, and those that could be seen as benefiting the social whole.

In his path-breaking analysis of household resources and standards of living, *Poverty in the United Kingdom* (1979), Peter Townsend systematically applied the concept of relative deprivation to the issue of **poverty** but moderated the social-psychological emphasis on felt deprivation. He distinguished poverty narrowly defined in terms of current low **incomes** from material and social inadequacies that may or may not be directly linked to these low incomes. The latter, poverty as relative deprivation, was seen in terms of a person's lack of resources to obtain the kind of diet, to enjoy the living conditions and amenities, and to participate in the social activities considered customary in the societies to which they belong. These necessities could be anything from damp-free housing or properly fitting shoes to the resources to invite relatives around for a meal, to send children on a school trip, or to have a garden for them to play in. While all of these have a subjective dimension, Townsend was adamant that the importance of this could not be assessed independently of the actual, objective, deprivation of a group relative to others.

ROB STONES

relativism

The strongest and crudest form of the relativist attitude to knowledge is that any claim to knowledge is as good as any other. This kind of relativist does not believe that some knowledge claims are more adequate than others. He/she does not recognize the qualitative difference between an unsubstantiated opinion, for example, and a belief that has been subjected to current critical and self-corrective methods and rational standards of inquiry. It is important to understand that it is possible to be a voluntarist in **Max Weber**'s sense of the word without being this kind of relativist. Voluntarism for Weber indicated an acknowledgment that the critical and rational standards applied to knowledge claims are the result of hard-fought and ongoing battles, and choices (hence the voluntarism), between differing positions within the social scientific **community**. This entailed a concession that such standards were culturally and historically situated. This differs, however, from strong relativism as there remains a clear distinction between theoretically framed, conceptually consistent, logically coherent, claims that are empirically substantiated, on the one hand, and vague unsubstantiated views, opinions, rhetoric, and **prejudice**, on the other.

In conceding the weak form of relativism that accepts that knowledge is culturally and historically situated, Weber, in effect, subscribes to what Rom Harré and Michael Krausz in *Varieties of Relativism* (1996) refer to as ontological relativism. This indicates the relativity of beliefs about existence to a particular conceptual system. This can be seen when, in *Madness and Civilization* (1961 [trans. 1967]) **Michel Foucault** tells us that a scientific description of a brain, commonplace around 1780, bore little resemblance to the description offered twenty-five years later by the new physiology of the very "same" organ on the marble slab. It is also the case for the electric fluids that existed for Benjamin Franklin (1706–90) but not for us, or for the witches that existed for the Azande but not for us. The conceptual systems that are used to judge the objectivity of knowledge are irremediably situated both culturally and historically. Harré and Krausz list three other forms of relativism besides the ontological. These are, first, semantic relativism, associated with **Ludwig Wittgenstein**, and, in a different way, with **poststructuralism**, in which words take their meaning from the form of life or **language game** in which they are embedded. So, for example, a word could not be translated into another language without loss of meaning. Second, there is moral relativism, in which conceptions of right and wrong alter according to the times and places in which one lives. And, finally, there is aesthetic relativism where "the music of classical Chinese opera might well be judged cacophonous relative to the standards of Bel Canto." **Pierre Bourdieu** in *Distinction* (1979 [trans. 1984]) showed how the aesthetic tastes of different groups within the national cultural formation of 1970s France were further stratified along the lines of classes and class fractions.

In the recent debates around **postmodernism**, those writers who took what Pauline Rosenau in *Postmodernism and the Social Sciences* (1992) refers to as an "affirmative" postmodernist position accord with Weber's combination of voluntarism and ontological relativism. They consolidate the emphasis on cultural and historical variability, however, by emphasizing that viewpoints change and differ not only according to academic **paradigm** or along with the received scientific wisdom of the age but also with respect to race, **gender**, **ethnicity**, **sexuality**, **culture**, and so on. Those whom Rosenau labels "skeptical" postmodernists took the stronger and more radical relativist position as they rejected any difference at all between fiction and truth, and so implicitly rejected the claims made by Weber, and by contemporary realists, that there are epistemic gains to be had through respecting the regulative frameworks provided by ongoing academic debate, critique, and counter-debate.   ROB STONES

reliability
– see **Sampling**.

religion
Sacred things are believed to be so extraordinarily important, powerful, and different from mundane or profane affairs that they need to be protected by special rules and restrictions or taboos (see **sacred and profane dichotomy**). Religion elaborates on experiences of the sacred, building them into systems of belief, **emotion**, action, and social relations oriented towards higher realities that supposedly transcend the level of empirical experience and thereby confer ultimate meaning on life. The sense of ultimacy may be associated with belief in such states as eternal life, salvation, rebirth, reincarnation, the transmigration of souls, immortality, and everlasting torment or nothingness. These beliefs entail religious practices as diverse as worship, prayer, meditation, purification, preaching, study, sacrifice, pilgrimage, charity, healing, and exorcism. A sense of obligation usually attaches to these beliefs and practices, and they confer a sense of collective **identity** on believers – unlike magic, which tends to involve the manipulation

of hidden forces for the benefit of individual clients or practitioners.

This is a generic definition of religion that is adequate for many purposes but it gives no clue to the seemingly endless disputes about the term's meaning. For, although religion is often claimed to be universal in human societies, agreement about its defining characteristics is far from universal. Some definitions insist that religion must involve belief in supernatural beings or divinities; others are content to define religion in terms of the type of functions that it allegedly fulfils for individuals or societies. Another possibility is to focus on how the meaning of religion is constructed and challenged in different times and social contexts. Indeed, the very notion that the disparate phenomena associated with world religions such as Buddhism, Hinduism, Islam, Judaism, and Christianity all belonged to the single category of religion gained currency only in the eighteenth century. The question of how well the primal beliefs and practices of indigenous peoples in the more remote parts of the world conform to the generic model of religion remains open.

In short, the meaning of religion cannot be taken for granted and must be understood in relation to the contexts in which it is used. The boundary between religion and non-religion, para-religion, and quasi-religion therefore affords a particularly interesting insight into shifts of meaning. Furthermore, religions are not monolithic entities but are complex amalgams of components that are official, in the sense of being warranted by formal authoritative **institutions**, and, on the other hand, a host of unofficial beliefs and activities that lack formal authorization. The latter include folk religion with its deep roots in premodern **cultures**; customary or common religion with its selection of highly attenuated extracts from official religion; invisible religion with its belief that the human condition is inherently religious; and implicit religion with its informal expression of the sacredness sensed in **everyday life**. Each world religion displays huge variations in the extent to which its forms of expression are formal, official, and visible. Moreover, individuals can express their religious commitments in dimensions as varied as knowledge, **ideology**, ethics, experience, and **ritual**. Their personal orientation to religion can be extrinsic and instrumental or intrinsic and an end in itself; and their types of religious experience can be confirmatory, responsive, ecstatic, or revelational. Finally, their attitude towards the truth of their religion's sacred scriptures can be literalist or relativist.

In spite of these problems of definition and variation, all the major contributors towards the foundational works of modern sociology saw reason to attribute significance to the category of religion, or to particular religions, in their widely differing depictions of the social formations emerging in western Europe and North America in the late nineteenth and early twentieth centuries. **Karl Marx** and **Friedrich Engels** conceded that religion had inspired some rebellions against injustice but claimed that, as an obstacle to the elimination of the exploitative social relations of **capitalism**, religion was bound to wither away in the face of **socialism**. By contrast, **Max Weber** argued that religion could serve both conservative and progressive interests, although he expected that its societal significance would be gradually sapped by **rationalization**, bureaucratization, and **modernization**, despite the occasional eruption of charismatic religious leaders. **Émile Durkheim** was more sanguine about the fate of religion, believing that it would continue to fulfill the function of sacralizing and symbolizing **industrial societies**, albeit in individualistic rather than collective terms. And **Georg Simmel**, in *Essays on Religion* (1898–1918 [trans. 1997]), regarded religion as one of the abiding forms of social relations encapsulating interpersonal **trust** and faith.

The influence of these classical contributions to a sociological understanding of religion remains strong on subsequent work in the sociology of religion. For example, there is strong continuity between early thinking about the dynamics of **modernity** and the vitality of conservative evangelical and fundamentalist forms of religion in the early twenty-first century. Similarly, Weber's thesis about the affinity between *The Protestant Ethic and the Spirit of Capitalism* (1905 [trans. 2002]) underlies sociological analysis of the political, economic, civil and personal consequences that flow from the global diffusion of charismatic and Pentecostal forms of Christianity. In addition, the predominantly individualistic character of religious commitment at the dawn of the new millennium elicits many of the theoretical concerns raised 100 years previously about the social **solidarity** of the industrial society that was emerging in the West. For example, Durkheim's highly influential books on *The Division of Labor in Society* (1893 [trans. 1960]) and *The Elementary Forms of Religious Life* (1912 [trans. 2001]) offer a framework for interpreting phenomena as varied as **new religious movements** and New Age practices in terms of their capacity to reconcile **individualism** with collective **identity**. The long-term legacy of **historical materialism** in the interpretation of religion in conditions of capitalism is less clear, however, especially in view of the apparent revivals of religion after 1989 in Russia and the formerly communist states of eastern Europe. Nevertheless, the concern with the social conditions that might overcome **alienation** and exploitation, as argued in Marx's *Economic and Philosophic Manuscripts* (1844 [trans. 1959]) and the "Introduction to a Critique of Hegel's *Philosophy of Right*" (1843 [trans. 1978]), finds an echo not only in Liberation Theology and other theologies of struggle but also in analyses of the religious component of present-day **social movements** against **globalization** and against the abuse of human **rights**.

Nevertheless, religion has continued to stimulate sociological imaginations for reasons that are far from exclusively concerned with theorizing about capitalist, industrial, or modern forms of society. The results will be discussed in various sections, although the interactions between them should not be overlooked. First, religions are human and social phenomena regardless of whether the ultimate reality to which they are supposedly oriented has a basis in truth. Consequently, if "the gods have feet of clay," the social forms assumed by religions are interesting in themselves. Second, social factors such as demographic change, **gender**, and **social class** help to shape the social forms that religions take. It does not follow that religion can necessarily be reduced to a matter of the social factors that shape its expression. It is simply a fact that religions are practiced in social contexts. Third, religions are not simply a product of their contexts: they also have active implications for the **cultures** and societies in which they operate. In fact, an interchange of mutual influence is evident between the social factors that shape religions and the implications that religions have for their social contexts. The leading debates about the interplay between the social shaping of religions and the religious shaping of the social world in the early twenty-first century are the topic of the fourth heading. Religion lies at the heart of some heated debates and theoretical disputes about social life in the future.

The social forms of religion include **organization** and ideology. Religious organizations are structures of social relations, power, and other resources that control the practice of religion. They not only give practical expression to religious ideas but they also aim to defend and promote them. Forms of religious organization and ideology are strongly interrelated, as Max Weber and **Ernst Troeltsch** showed in their respective studies of the development of Christianity. They explained the distinctions between the church-type and the sect-type of Christian organizations in terms of contrasting theological ideas about social ethics and access to salvation. Whereas the church-type offers objective means to salvation to all its members, the sect-type regards salvation as something to which only religiously qualified volunteers can aspire. These differences are associated with many other aspects of religious organization, although it is debatable to what extent the social forms of religions other than Christianity make sense in church–sect terms (see **church–sect typology**). Further elaboration of this fundamental dichotomy, and of Troeltsch's third **ideal type** of mysticism, has introduced refinements such as established churches, **denominations**, established sects, and sub-categories of sect. Deployment of the concept of the **cult** was a response to the perception that some of the new religious movements that became controversial in the late twentieth century differed from the church-type and the sect-type to the extent that they cultivated individualistic and, in some cases, magical notions of salvation. Some of the most controversial movements also showed that it was possible, but difficult, to resist or delay the institutionalization of their leaders' **charisma**. Distinctions between audience cults, client cults, and cult movements have refined the concept of cult even further, along with the notion of the cultic milieu. Nevertheless, many scholars still find the term inappropriate because journalists and the opponents of controversial religious movements tend to use cult in a derogatory fashion.

Organizational forms of religion extend well beyond church, denomination, sect, and cult. They include temples, monastic orders, shrines, brotherhoods, mosques, Sikh gurdwaras, parishes, congregations, chaplaincies, and missions. In keeping with the increasing pace of communication, however, social **networks** are proving to be the key to the successful mobilization of people and resources in religious organizations as well as in religious movements. Relatively loose, segmented networks are crucial for the spread of New Age spirituality, new religious movements, and transnational Pentecostal churches such as the Universal Church of the Kingdom of God which originated in Brazil and is active in many

other regions of the world. Effective use of the internet, satellite broadcasting, and video **technology** has also enabled relatively small religious organizations to flourish worldwide. These developments have important implications for the distribution of authority in religious organizations. The growing importance of managers and communications specialists presents challenges to traditional hierarchies and to the authority of religious professionals such as priests, pastors, rabbis, gurus, and imams, or religious specialists such as healers, preachers, exorcists, diviners, and prophets. Nevertheless, the distinction that Weber drew between "mass" and "virtuoso" styles of religion remains valid. This means that most participants in religious activities practice their religion in ways that do not require rigorous training or extensive separation from the rest of the world. In contrast, religious virtuosi aspire to higher forms of religious knowledge, experience, and devotion that tend to isolate them in, for example, monastic orders, brotherhoods, or esoteric cabals. It is not yet clear whether the worldwide spread of electronic means of communication has made it easier or more difficult to maintain virtuoso styles of religion.

The immense variety of ways in which religions can be defined and put into operation in social forms is not arbitrary but is subject to the influence of social forces or factors. Leaving aside the claims about the super-empirical realities to which religions are supposedly oriented, there is extensive evidence that social factors help to shape religious belief, experience, practice, and organization. This does not mean that religions are merely the dupes of their circumstances; it simply asserts that individual and collective expressions of religion develop in a complex interrelationship with societies and cultures.

The probability that religion will be salient in the lives of individuals will vary with many social factors and with particular configurations of them. For example, women tend to consider themselves to be more religious than men; adults under the age of eighteen and over the age of sixty are the most likely age groups to be involved in religious activities; people with relatively low levels of **wealth**, **income**, educational attainment, and **social status** display lower levels of engagement in religion than do their better-off counterparts; levels of reported religious belief tend to decline with each passing **generation** despite the fact that adolescents tend to be more religious than young adults; with the principal exception of the United States, national levels of religious practice tend to be negatively correlated with national levels of prosperity; and postcommunist countries of eastern Europe display wide differences in their levels of religious belonging and practice that reflect their religious history before 1945. Taking into account the inherent difficulties of defining, operationalizing, and measuring religion in the questionnaire **surveys** on which many of these findings are based – and the subtle qualifications that scholars have made to them – the **data** provide ample support for the view that religion is socially patterned.

The religion of migrant groups shows particularly interesting patterns. The processes of international **migration** from the relatively poor countries of the global South to the relatively prosperous countries of the North, which began to accelerate sharply in the 1960s in western Europe and North America gave rise to cross-generational change in the religious practices of migrants, settlers, and their descendants. Many of the first-generation migrants from South Asia to Europe were men who came from rural areas and retained their traditional beliefs, but second- and third-generation Muslim, Hindu, and Sikh settlers in Europe – especially young women – are developing new understandings of their **identity** and their faith. Moreover, many migrants from South to North America had previously had contact with Protestantism and were not therefore averse to breaking their family ties to Catholicism. "Ethnic congregations" are flourishing among Christian settlers who retain strong attachments to their ethnic and national origins as well as to their religion. The descendants of migrants lead religious lives that reflect their social contexts in the West as well as the cultural **traditions** of their ancestors.

The social contexts in which religions operate are legal, political, economic, and cultural. Religions have long been subject to regulation by various agencies of the modern **state**, but the growing religious diversity of many countries has created fresh challenges. Gender relations, marriage customs, methods of slaughtering animals for food, separate spaces for burial, and the display of ostentatious symbols of religious identity in public institutions have become some of the most contentious issues in the legal regulation of religions. Similar issues arise in relation to prisoners' access to opportunities to practice their religion during incarceration. International legal instruments such as the European Code of Human Rights protect individuals' freedom of religion, but high-profile legal cases concerning such religious minorities as Jehovah's Witnesses, Scientologists,

Muslims, and Falun Gong still occur in, respectively, Greece, Germany, France, and China.

Relations between the realms of religion and **politics** are virtually inevitable given that strong convictions about ultimate **values** and power are common to both of them. Strong correlations therefore exist between certain kinds of religious belief and support for political ideas about, for example, pacifism, just **wars**, abortion, birth control, the death penalty, and environmentalism. For the second half of the twentieth century, Christian **Democracy** in various European countries represented a clear combination of non-traditional Catholicism and centrist politics. Elsewhere internecine conflicts have racked countries where the major divisions or fault lines in society coincided with religious differences. Israel/Palestine, the former Yugoslavia, Sri Lanka, Cyprus, Sudan, and Northern Ireland are only a few such places. International tensions between Greece and Turkey, India and Pakistan, or Iran and the United States are also aggravated, if not actually caused, by religious differences.

The economic context of religion is often overlooked, but religious organizations clearly need to compete for resources within the terms of their own highly variable teachings about the relative merits of wealth and **poverty**. Some of Japan's New Religions, for example, regard their displays of wealth as indicators of their spiritual power, whereas Protestantism has spawned numerous denominations that prize plain living. Nevertheless, Weber's essay on *The Protestant Ethic and the Spirit of Capitalism* (1905 [trans. 2002]) is only the best-known of various commentaries on the irony that some early modern Protestant movements, in inspiring their followers to look for signs that their destiny was to go to heaven, incidentally inculcated such habits of sobriety, abstemiousness, and diligence in them that they became successful capitalists – and scientists – in spite of themselves. Similarly, Islam's prohibition on lending money at interest used to be considered an obstacle to capitalistic enterprise among Muslims, but alternative ways of financing businesses are proving successful. Meanwhile, the individualistic "prosperity gospel" is popular among conservative Evangelicals and some Pentecostals in Africa, South Korea, parts of Latin America, and the United States.

Although all religions operate in cultural contexts, the responses of particular religious organizations to the influences emanating from **elite** and mass cultures range along a spectrum from enthusiastic embrace to outraged rejection. For example, the **individualism** and subjectivism that pervade culture in most western societies are reproduced and enhanced in various new religious movements and New Age spiritualities. At the other end of the spectrum, pietistic and mystical movements in Islam, Christianity, and Hinduism reject individualism, **consumer society**, and **materialism**, preferring to live in strong tension with popular values. Religious attempts to defy the influence of dominant culture are often hampered by the power of the **mass media** to shape **public opinion**. Popular television programs, newspapers, magazines, and films tend to reinforce conservative stereotypes of normal and deviant religions. This is partly why well-resourced religious organizations invest heavily in their own media productions and websites.

Social and cultural factors help to explain how religions operate in human societies. But they are only one side of the coin: religions also contribute towards shaping their social and cultural contexts. The implications that religions have for society and culture require separate discussion.

History provides many dramatic instances of the capacity of religions, often in alliance with political forces, to shape society and culture in certain circumstances. For example, millenarianism, or beliefs about the imminence of the end of ordinary **time** and the arrival of 1,000 years of peace and prosperity, was at the base of many rebellions and revolutions in medieval Europe. The Iranian Revolution of 1979 and the contribution of Christian groups towards the collapse of communist regimes in eastern Europe after 1989 showed that religion retains the power to influence the transformation of societies. Admittedly, it is rare in late modernity for religions to be decisive in such major transformations, but there is plentiful evidence of the everyday involvement of religious organizations, personnel, and ideas in attempts to steer social life in certain directions.

To begin with the political sphere, the Japanese state Shinto tradition and Roman Catholicism both served as symbolic resources for and vehicles of fascist ideology in the 1930s and 1940s; Hinduism in India, Buddhism in Sri Lanka, Sikhism in the Punjab, Protestantism in apartheid South Africa, and Catholicism in Poland have all nourished varieties of **nationalism**; religious ideologies of various kinds underlie the global distribution of religious **violence** and **terrorism** in places as diverse as Indonesia, Afghanistan, Chechnya, and the United States (Mark Juergensmeyer, *Terror in the Mind of God*, 2000); Catholic Liberation

Theology has inspired numerous movements against oppression in Latin America and the Philippines; non-denominational Christianity underlies the **civil religion** of many countries; and **social movements** for peace and **justice**, human rights, animal protection, reproductive rights, the rights of unborn children, environmentalism, and **feminism** all draw, to varying degrees, on religious inspiration and support. The involvement of religious organizations in cross-national efforts to relieve suffering at times of acute drought, famine, disease, and civil war – as well as in varieties of charitable and welfare work – is on a massive scale. The religious factor is not the sole ingredient in any of these examples of the political implications of religion, but they all demonstrate the uses to which religion can be put in the national or international exercise of political power.

The implications of religious ideas have historically been strong for the control of **sexuality**, gender roles, family formation and divorce, the **socialization** of children, **social stratification**, and the transmission of **property**. Divisions of theological and moral opinion about sexuality and **gender** are particularly threatening to the unity of some major Christian Churches, but ironically successive United Nations conferences on women have revealed some unexpected alliances between, for example, Catholic and Muslim interests. Other lines of division are apparent in world religions over the use of nuclear power, genetically modified organisms, and embryonic stem cells in medical research.

The consequences of religious ideas have also affected the classification, regulation, and nurture of human **bodies**. Questions of diet, clothing, hair covering, disease, healing, birth, death, funerals, punishment, and the consumption of stimulants have all emerged from religious traditions. Not surprisingly, many Christian Churches invested heavily in the provision of health care in their home countries as well as in mission fields. In addition, some strands of Buddhism nurtured martial arts; and urban churches were influential in organizing the game of soccer in nineteenth-century Britain, while the Young Men's Christian Association did the same for basketball in the United States. There is also some statistical support for the claim that people with active involvement in religion are more likely to live longer, stay healthier, and feel happier than other people, although the direction of causation may be questionable. Finally, studies of Christian revivals, conversion processes, and ritual states of liminality, during which participants are temporarily stripped of their normal **identities** and expected to show obedience and humility, have documented the variable impact of religious ideas and activities on **emotions**.

Education has taken many different forms in all the world's religions, ranging from elementary instruction in Christian Sunday Schools and catechism classes to Muslim *madrasas* or seminaries and monastic training in Buddhism. Religious **institutions** of higher learning have produced some sublime examples of scholarship, literature, music, architecture, and art. But states now provide most forms of public education, either separately from religions – as in France and the United States – or in partnership with them – as in the United Kingdom. Opposition to the involvement of religious **organizations** in either public or private education is strong in some quarters, especially at times of growing religious diversity. Nevertheless, religious interests try to influence school curricula and, in some countries, they provide schools based on religious values as an alternative to the state's educational system. For example, the Soka Gakkai Buddhist movement in Japan and the Roman Catholic Church in many parts of the world run their own kindergartens, schools, colleges, and universities.

The differentiation of social institutions that accompanied **modernization** had two main effects. One was to reduce the significance of religion for political and economic spheres for the integration of whole societies; the other was to confine matters of religion largely to the sphere of **voluntary associations**, **families**, **neighborhoods**, and private life. It is in this private sphere of relative independence from the state and profit-seeking activity that religion continues to have implications for the self-identity of individuals and the collective identity of ethnic **groups**. In advanced industrial or **postindustrial societies**, in particular, individuals are expected to choose a religious identity – or none – and to use it in accordance with their own wishes. It is assumed to be a subjective choice, and religious groups accused of "brainwashing" or manipulating their recruits face stiff criticism. On the other hand, some defensive reactions against the impersonal, rapidly changeable, centrally managed, and mobile character of societies in the early twenty-first century have taken the form of collective identification with ethnic and ethno-religious identities. This is particularly the case with ethno-religious migrants to prosperous countries in the North, for whom integration into their new societies may entail or force a heightened appreciation of their religious and ethnic distinctiveness. **Public policies** in the United Kingdom favor societal integration on the basis of ethno-religious **community**, whereas more centralized **states** such as France discourage the deployment of collective religious identity in public institutions. Tensions are evident concerning the place of ethno-religious identities and interests as the European Union becomes increasingly diverse in terms of **ethnicity** and religion.

Sociological theories about religion present bewilderingly different landscapes that reflect differing assumptions, perceptions, and impressions of religion's social significance. Theoretical debates about religion from sociological perspectives center on **secularization** or the restructuring of religion, the **rationality** of religious actors, the implications of **globalization** for religion, and the growing significance attached to spirituality.

The most general theory of secularization holds that the significance of religion for the guidance, integration, and symbolization of societies declines as a consequence of processes of differentiation, **rationalization**, and modernization. There are Marxist, Freudian, and functionalist variations on the general theme, but none of them anticipates the total disappearance of religion or denies the possibility that religion could occasionally be revived. Refinements of the theory have been numerous. **David Martin**, for example, argued in *A General Theory of Secularization* (1978) that secularization varied with the religious and political frameworks operative in each country; and Karel Dobbelaere insisted in *Secularization: A Multi-Dimensional Concept* (1981) that analytical distinctions should be made between laicization, religious change, and declining levels of religious involvement. Objections to the general theory of secularization charge it with being motivated by anti-religious ideology, based on inadequate evidence, applicable only to Christianity, and limited to the history of Europe. Replacements for, or alternatives to, the general theory of secularization have grown in number and assertiveness since the 1980s. The most radical ideas are that, globally, the significance of religion has increased, especially in the form of Pentecostal Christianity, and that, in any case, human beings are "hard wired" for religion. Another proposal is that, although levels of participation in formal religious activities have declined in many countries, levels of religious belief remain high. An alternative view is that religion is not in decline: it is merely being restructured in new forms. A final argument against secularization is that **postmodernity** heralds a re-enchantment of the world in which religion is expected to flourish.

A second set of theoretical debates about religion also have implications for thinking about secularization. These debates center on the claim made by Rodney Stark and Roger Finke in *Acts of Faith: Explaining the Human Side of Religion* (2000) that human beings employ their "subjective rationality" to "weigh the anticipated rewards against the anticipated costs" when making choices about religion. The assumption is that, as the greatest rewards are scarce or not attainable in life, it is rational to seek general compensators for them by entering into exchanges with deities. Since this theory considers the practice of religion to be a rational choice (see **rational choice theory**) for individuals, it follows that levels of involvement in religion are not expected to decline. Moreover, when the same theory is applied to religious organizations it predicts a process of continuous decline and renewal as those that offer relatively poor rewards for the costs incurred by members are replaced by new organizations with low start-up costs that can offer relatively high rewards. The expectation is that, in the "religious **economy**," high-demand organizations with few "free riders" will triumph over less demanding ones. Competition for market share is expected to perpetuate the cycle, thereby ruling out secularization in the sense of the withering away of religious organizations. But criticisms of this rational choice approach are numerous. They include the claims that it rests on questionable and highly individualistic psychological assumptions; it mistakenly takes for granted that religious costs and rewards can be unproblematically measured and compared; it fails to acknowledge that the religious economy is far from being a free market in many societies; and it has very little to say about the factors that determine the changing significance of religion in the **public sphere**. The debates about the merits of rational choice theory in relation to religion are contentious and polarized with no sign of resolution.

Globalization means that transnational forces are helping to make the world appear to be a smaller place and to raise consciousness of what Roland Robertson terms "globality" in his *Globalization* (1992). In these circumstances, religions can be expected to make significant contributions towards the identification and sanctification of global processes and structures without necessarily coalescing into a single global religion. In fact, Robertson and others have emphasized that globalization involves not only the emergence of would-be universalist themes but also the filtering of universal themes through "local" cultures, resulting in hybrid globalization. Certainly, religious movements such as the Unificationists, the Baha'is, and Soka Gakkai International – to say nothing of the Catholic Church's long tradition of ecumenical outreach – aspire to embody ideals of global peace and unity through symbols rooted in their own national origins. Moreover, James Beckford argues in *Social Theory and Religion* (2003) that would-be global **norms** governing the freedom of religion are emerging from international codes of human rights. But critics of globalization theory point to the fact that control over each movement remains firmly in one country, although their operations are undoubtedly transnational. Other critics point out that the global surge of Pentecostal and charismatic Christian groups is actually promoted mainly by interests in the United States, especially in the case of denominations using satellite communications technology. Nevertheless, there is little doubt that the availability of global communications networks has enabled some religious organizations to strive for effective global outreach and to achieve unprecedented levels of international activity. This may be another reason for skepticism about theories of radical secularization. On the other hand, it remains to be seen how far religious ideas about the global circumstance and globally active religious organizations can influence the development of other cultural, political, and economic processes at the global level.

The final theoretical debate echoes the opening discussion about the definition and the diversity of religion. A new development is occurring against a background of declining levels of participation in formal religious activities in many western countries, the growing popularity of charismatic forms of Christianity, the vitality of so-called ethnic congregations, the rising salience of Islam outside its heartlands, and the continuing strength of commitment to conservative evangelicalism and **fundamentalism**. In this context, fundamentalism refers to a loose bundle of characteristics including the rejection of **relativism** and secularism and the insistence on rigorous application of "true" knowledge and sacred law to all areas of public and private life. It concerns the rapidly swelling interest in spirituality – primarily in advanced industrial societies. According to Robert Fuller's *Spiritual but Not Religious* (2001), "Spirituality exists wherever we struggle with the issue of how our lives fit into the greater cosmic scheme of things." New Age practices of, for example, channeling, Reiki healing, dynamic meditation, or aura therapy cultivate spirituality as an individualistic form of self-development that draws upon forces in the human body, mind, and spirit, as well as in the natural **environment**. The spiritual dimension is said to add depth and significance to human life without necessarily invoking ideas of the sacred or of ultimate meaning. This is why some commentators, distinguishing clearly between religion and spirituality, regard the growth of interest in spirituality as an indicator of secularization. Others prefer to consider spirituality as evidence of the long-term process of the privatization of religion: not the decline of religion. Their argument is that the focus on spirituality permits "real" or authentic religion to escape from its captivity in forms of official, organized religion. Again, this disagreement highlights the difficulty of assessing the long-term development of religion as a social and cultural phenomenon in the absence of an unambiguous definition. It also underlines the need to keep firmly in mind the diversity of religion and the complexity of its place in societies and cultures.

JAMES BECKFORD

replication
– see **sampling**.

reproduction
This term has two major uses in sociology: social and physical reproduction. That there is a close relationship between the two has been emphasized by both **feminism** and those sociologists who have identified and investigated the continuity across time not just of social **inequality** but also of the human beings who make up **social classes**. In Britain the sociologist A. H. Halsey (1923–) has described what he defines as the cultural capital which is an intrinsic part of individual circumstance. In France, **Pierre Bourdieu** has developed a very similar thesis in terms of the **politics** of cultural reproduction. What both these sociologists note is that social inequality is not just a matter of the inheritance of economic capital; it is also a question of the way in which **children** acquire from their parents specific social understandings and skills which have a value in the social world.

The sociological understanding of the term reproduction was further enhanced in the 1970s and 1980s by debates, arising within feminism but subsequently not confined to that context, about the part that women play, specifically in

the form of domestic and caring **labor**, in the reproduction of the labor force. The politicization of the private world (epitomized by the feminist slogan "the personal is political") enlarged the sociological understanding of the meaning of the social world. Previous understandings, which had tended to focus on the performance of social acts in the public world (and, prior to the wider inclusion of women in the paid work force, those acts were largely the acts of men), were replaced by a view of the social world that included relations within, as well as outside, the household. Within the household, detailed ethnographic studies pointed out the part that women played in "reproducing" the work force, in both the physical and the social senses.

The transformation of many western **economies**, in the last thirty years of the twentieth century, towards service-sector, rather than manufacturing, industries has emphasized the importance of certain social skills traditionally assumed to be held by women. In that sense, the reproduction of feminine patterns of **socialization** has been given an added importance, with an accompanying decline in the importance (and viability) of what were assumed to be masculine patterns of behavior. The so-called crisis of **masculinity** (for which, as Linda McDowell, in *Redundant Masculinity*? (2003), and David Morgan, in *Discovering Men* (1992), have pointed out, there is relatively little evidence) is, however, an instance of the way in which the cultural reproduction of the social world does not follow a consistent pattern and can be closely related to changes in economic and material social conditions. At the same time, sociologists such as **Anthony Giddens** have suggested that the changes in intimate and household relations brought about by shifts in the pattern of the **labor market** can have a wider effect on political ideas and, in *The Transformation of Intimacy* (1992), he relates what he describes as the greater **democracy** of the household to greatly increased political aspirations for democracy.

Although the term reproduction has focused largely on the reproduction of individuals and their place in the social world, there is also a sense in which sociologists have long recognized the ways in which social **institutions** are subject to changing patterns of reproduction. For example, the sociologist Robert Putnam, in *Bowling Alone* (2000), has suggested that the sense of **community** in the United States is not being reproduced as individuals order their lives in more exclusively social ways. Equally, sociologists of **culture** have defined the processes through which cultural assumptions and habits are both reproduced and interrupted. E. J. Hobsbawm (1917–) has, in his *The Invention of Tradition* (1983), observed that **tradition** cannot be regarded as an enduring, unchanging aspect of social life; sociologists, as much as historians, have to recognize that the social world is as constantly invented as it is reproduced.   MARY EVANS

retirement

Since the mid-1970s, retirement has been a major focus for research and debate in social **gerontology**. Its significance has been acknowledged in a variety of ways: as a mechanism for assisting the individual's withdrawal from social life; as an **institution** helping to redistribute work from older to younger people; as part of the movement to a "leisured society"; and, from a critical perspective, as a contributory element in the creation of dependency in old **age**.

Different criteria may be used to define retirement, with the most common including reduced labor-force participation, receipt of a pension, withdrawal from main **career**, self-definition as retired (or a combination of any of these). In the United Kingdom, people tend to redefine their **social status** as they move past state pension age (SPA). A representative **survey** of adults by Alun Humphrey *et al.*, *Factors Affecting the Labour Market Participation of Older Workers* (2003), found 90 percent of men aged 65–9 describing themselves as retired, compared with 26 percent of men aged 60–4; among women, 73 percent of those aged 60–4 described themselves as retired, compared with 13 percent of women aged 55–9. This change in perception appears not just to be related to retirement from paid work; rather it reflects acceptance of retirement as a natural and inevitable part of the life-course.

Although there is no state retirement age in the United Kingdom, on reaching state pension age workers lose the majority of their statutory employment **rights**. Most employers can, and usually do, set a compulsory retirement age as a condition of service. The European Equal Treatment Directive (to be implemented in 2006) will, however, outlaw age **discrimination** in the workplace. Responses to this on the part of the British government are currently under consideration, these including prohibiting compulsory retirement altogether, or allowing employers to set retirement ages above 70. In the United States legislation to prohibit discrimination against older workers was first passed in 1967.

Modern retirement policy is a product of the last quarter of the nineteenth century as large private companies and branches of the civil service adopted pension policies. Subsequently, at key periods in the twentieth century (usually in periods of economic slump or through the impetus of **war**), pension coverage, as Leslie Hannah in *Inventing Retirement* (1986) shows, has been extended to cover virtually all sections of the population. Behind this development can be traced a range of economic and political influences. The growth of the factory system accelerated the introduction of retirement, with the development of assembly-line methods reducing the status of older workers. From another perspective, retirement also provided industrial **capitalism** with a means of challenging security of tenure or jobs for life. It was a reaction against the persistence of personal modes of behavior (*Gemeinschaft* versus *Gesellschaft* in the classic terms of **Ferdinand Tönnies** in *Community and Association*, 1887 [trans. 1957]), providing a mechanism for discharging loyal workers. As a further advantage it also assisted the stabilization of corporate hierarchies, creating a permanent flow of employees and guaranteeing promotion through the ranks.

The **value** and social meanings attached to retirement tend to vary over time. In the 1950s, with panics about an aging population, shortage of labor, and the priority of postwar reconstruction, pressure was placed on people to delay leaving work. Older workers were eulogized for their steadiness and reliability, in contrast to the 1930s when politicians were praising older people's ability to withstand idleness and their willingness to be pensioned off. By the 1980s, retirement was once again in vogue as a means of redistributing jobs to the young and was the target of a powerful leisure and consumer industry. From the 1990s onwards the emphasis has been on extending work life, in the context of fears about the apparent costs associated with population aging.

Retirement has now emerged as a significant phase in the life-course. In the United Kingdom around half of men will leave the labor force at 63 years and then spend another 17 years in retirement; the equivalent figures for women are 60 years and 22 years. The reasons given for retirement vary substantially according to factors such as age, **social class**, and **gender**. Men are more likely than women to expect to retire early, and this appears to be especially the case among those in professional and managerial **occupations**. The desire to spend more time "with the family," according to Alun Humphrey *et al.* (2003), is common among early retirees, with couples taking joint decisions about the appropriate point to retire. Poor **health** and **disability** are common reasons for retiring ahead of SPA, although the individuals affected are unlikely to define this in terms of "early retirement."

Manual workers are more likely than their skilled and professional counterparts to enter retirement in a poor state of health. According to Stephen McNair *et al.* in *Changing Work in Later Life* (2004) they are also likely to have lower **incomes** and to have experienced insecurity (redundancy, job losses) in the period leading to retirement. Pressure to provide informal **care** – for a partner or an elderly relative – will be a factor for some, with women often finding new care responsibilities as they enter their fifties and sixties. Men and women show contrasting retirement patterns in most western societies. Men's retirement typically comes at the end of a work role that has dominated a major part of their life. Women, in contrast, tend towards discontinuity over the life-course, experiencing a number of moves in and out of paid employment, this resulting in lower incomes and less extensive pension coverage in comparison with men.

Longitudinal **data** from the United States has found no evidence that retirement necessarily leads to social isolation or low morale. Most retirees find new forms of social engagement or continue with lifelong interests and activities. Studies such as the Boston Normative aging Study also show that retirement does not significantly affect quantitative or qualitative measures of support (cited in Kenneth Ferraro, *Aging and Role Transitions*, 2001).

Different theoretical models have been used to explain **attitudes** and behavior in the transition to retirement. In the 1950s and 1960s functionalist perspectives such as the theory of the **social role** stressed the extent to which loss of a primary role such as work deprived the individual – men in particular – of status and **identity**. Retirement was viewed as a "roleless role" which placed the retiree in an ambiguous social position (**Ernest W. Burgess**, *Aging in western Societies*, 1960). Another functionalist approach, the disengagement theory of Elaine Cumming and William Henry in *Growing Old: The Process of Disengagement* (1960) took a different view, arguing that retirement could be interpreted as permission to disengage from demanding social roles.

By the 1970s, other theoretical models were beginning to challenge the assumptions of role and disengagement theory. Robert Atchley's identity continuity, in his *Retirement and Leisure Participation: Continuity or Crisis* (1971), suggested an underlying stability in **lifestyles** through the retirement transition. For example, individuals might still view themselves as teachers or coalminers even though they were no longer actively performing such roles. At the same time, people will draw upon their existing interests, or develop new ones, to form a bridge between work and retirement.

In the 1980s and 1990s, new insights about retirement emerged from **political economy** and life-course perspectives. The former focused on the way in which retirement was shaped by the **social structure** and by the social and economic factors that affect the individual's place in society. This approach emphasized the impact of **social class**, **gender**, and **race and ethnicity** in influencing the experience of retirement. Events such as retirement were presented, in papers brought together in *Critical Gerontology* (1999) edited by Meredith Minkler and Carroll Estes, as socially constructed, that is varying according to lifelong social status and state policies and **ideologies**. Life-course perspectives view retirement as a process rather than a "one-off" event, with links to other institutions such as **education**, work, and family life. With this approach, past experiences – notably those relating to employment history – are viewed as crucial in influencing factors such as the timing of retirement, morale in retirement, and the degree of control experienced in the transition to a new phase in life, as shown in Karl Pillemer *et al.*, *Social Integration in the Second Half of Life* (2000).

Despite pressures to encourage people to continue working for as long as possible, retirement is now firmly embedded within the life-course. Some slowing in the rate of withdrawal from work will certainly occur in the years ahead. On the other hand, changes over the last decades have generated expectations and aspirations that may prove hard to change. What appears likely is that the range of transitions and experiences associated with retirement will almost certainly grow: from baby boomers ready for an extended period of **leisure**, low-income groups facing an extended period of work to supplement their pension, and women (and some men) balancing a mix of work and caring roles. Phyllis Moen in *Midcourse: Reconfiguring Careers and Community Service for a New Life Stage* (2003), reviewing data from the United States, identifies an emerging life stage between the years of career building and old age, a period stretching roughly from age 50 through to age 75.

She sees this new phase as creating a mixture of uncertainties and opportunities: the former reflected in pressures and insecurities in the workplace (with downsizing and forced early retirement); the latter developed through a broadening in the range of productive activities (with combinations of work, caring, and leisure activities). Both developments indicate major changes in the relationship between work and retirement, a relationship which is likely to be a focus of attention in sociological research.   CHRIS PHILLIPSON

revolution, theory of

It was not until the eighteenth century, largely as the result of the American and French Revolutions, that the word revolution acquired its modern meaning. Before that, its use in **politics** and **society** had reflected the classical concept, as used for instance by Plato (428–348 BC) and Polybius (203–120 BC), of revolution as a cyclical movement – a movement, just as in nature or among the heavenly bodies, that was one of several turns of a wheel – revolutions – that eventually returned one to the original starting point. So, for instance, the English Revolutions of 1640 and 1688 were widely conceived as attempts to return English politics to its original, pristine state, after the unwise innovations of English monarchs. By the same token, and with the same significance, the Restoration of 1660 was also described by its proponents as a revolution – a return to an original state after the disturbances of the Civil War.

With the eighteenth century revolutions, above all that of the French in 1789, the word revolution came to mean what we now mean by it today: the attempt to create something completely new, a new beginning, a new order of things. Moreover, it was clear to the French revolutionaries, and to all who inherited their **tradition**, that revolution was a progressive thing, the construction of a society based on liberty, **equality**, and **justice**. As Marie Jean Marquis de Condorcet (1743–94) put it, "the word revolutionary can only be applied to revolutions which have liberty as their object" (*On the Meaning of the Word "Revolutionary"*, 1793). Any other goal, as Condorcet again stated, would be a "counter-revolution, a revolution in reverse." Nineteenth- and twentieth-century revolutionaries have mostly accepted this, even if, as with **Karl Marx** and his followers, they argued that the purely political liberty of the French Revolution needed to be completed by social and economic liberty. One consequence of this has been the difficulty of talking about "right-wing revolutions," such as those of Benito Mussolini (1883–1945) and

Adolf Hitler (1889–1945), which self-consciously opposed the democratic legacy of the French Revolution. The predominantly secular, left-wing, meaning of revolution has also made it problematic to deal with the new religious revolutions of our time, such as the Iranian revolution of 1979, inspired by religious **fundamentalism** and a desire to return to an older and purer order of things.

The French Revolution also gave rise to theories about the course of revolution, what happens when a revolution breaks out. Here what seemed apparent to many observers was a certain "logic" of revolution, a certain inevitability to the course of revolution. Using the terms derived from the French Revolution, it was said that revolution begins with the rule of the moderates, moves on to a more radical phase – the Girondins – culminating in the rule of the Jacobins and a Reign of Terror, in which the revolution is defended by extreme means against threats from within and outside the society. The reign of terror leads to a reaction – "Thermidor" – followed by a return of the moderates. But the forces unleashed by the revolution are too turbulent to be led by moderates, hence the tendency for this period to lead to a military coup – an "Eighteenth Brumaire" – and the establishment of a military dictatorship – a Napoleonic phase. For some theorists this too was but a prelude, as in the English and French Revolutions, to defeat of the revolution and a restoration of the old regime, though never completely in its original form. But this has not been the experience of several twentieth-century revolutions, such as the Russian and the Chinese, though the collapse of the Soviet Union in 1991 might be seen as a long-delayed restoration.

What causes revolutions? Marx, the most influential theorist, argued that a revolution comes about as a society undergoes a change in the mode of production, leading to the rise of a new class which seizes power, in a political revolution, from the old ruling class. In this view, both the English and the French Revolutions can be seen as bourgeois revolutions, the victory of the new bourgeois class over the landed aristocracy. This account can be made to fit several major revolutions, but only by a rather problematic dissociation of the actual act of revolution from the much slower and long-drawn-out change in the mode of production. It is also difficult to apply Marxist theories to the Russian Revolution of 1917, as well as to many other twentieth-century revolutions, where the principal agents appear to have been not so much **social classes** as a revolutionary party led by radical **intellectuals**, and where the change in the mode of production appears to have followed rather than preceded the revolutionary seizure of power.

More persuasive as an account of the causes of revolution has been **Alexis de Tocqueville**'s theory, as outlined in the *Ancien Régime and the Revolution* (1856 [trans. 1955]). Revolutions break out, says Tocqueville, not when things go "from bad to worse," when people come to suffer from great oppression or utter **poverty**, but rather when they experience a real improvement in their condition which, however, is then abruptly cut short or, which comes to the same thing, they think it will be interrupted or stopped. Revolution, in other words, is not caused by absolute but by **relative deprivation**: "The evils which are endured with patience so long as they were inevitable seem intolerable as soon as hope can be entertained of escaping from them" (1856 [trans. 1955]). It is hopes cruelly disappointed that provide the fuel for revolution. If we combine this with Plato's insight in the *Republic*, that "in any form of government revolution always starts from the outbreak of internal dissension in the ruling class" – that, in other words, it is divisions in the ruling class that precipitate the revolution – we are in command of a theory of revolution that fits most of the main instances with remarkable accuracy.

Some have claimed that, at least in the liberal **democracies** of the West, the age of revolutions is over. The events of May 1968 in Paris, a kind of play-acting of revolution, is seen as the best the West can do. Over in eastern Europe, where there was more serious oppression, the events of 1989 that brought down Communism are generally seen as true examples of revolution. Less confidently, the rise and rule of Islamic fundamentalists in Iran and Afghanistan are seen as heralding a new wave of religious revolutionary sentiment in the non-western world. Revolution has always had a tendency to surprise; it should be no surprise if its announced demise in the West also turns out to be premature.   KRISHAN KUMAR

Rex, John (1925–)

Born in South Africa, Rex held a number of key professorial positions in the United Kingdom: Professor of Social Theory and Institutions at the University of Durham (1964–70), Chair of Sociology at the University of Warwick, Research Professor in Ethnic Relations at the University of Aston, Birmingham, and subsequently Professor of Ethnic Relations in the University of Warwick. He made important contributions to classical

sociology and to the study of **race and ethnicity**. As an influential interpreter of **Max Weber**, he was critical of **functionalism**, because it could not develop an adequate theory of **social action** and it neglected the study of **power**, both of which, for Rex, were necessary for an effective understanding of **racism**. His publications on **sociological theory** included *Key Problems in Sociological Theory* (1961), *Discovering Sociology* (1973), *Approaches to Sociology* (1974), and *Sociology and the Demystification of the Modern World* (1974). In his work on **social class** and race relations, Rex came to be closely associated with "conflict sociology" publishing *Social Conflict: A Conceptual and Theoretical Analysis* (1981). His work on the study of racial conflict was equally influential and wide-ranging. With R. Moore, he developed the concept of housing classes in his study of mortgage **inequality**, housing allocation, and ethnic divisions in Birmingham in *Race, Community and Conflict: A Study of Sparkbrook* (1967). A spate of publications on sociological theory and race followed: *Race, Colonialism and the City* (1973), *Race Relations in Sociological Theory* (1982), *Race and Ethnicity* (1986), and (with S. Tomlinson) *Colonial Immigrants in a British City* (1979).

BRYAN S. TURNER

Rieff, Philip (1922–)

A seminal American analyst of the sociology of **values** and **morality**, Rieff was Benjamin Franklin Professor of Sociology at the University of Pennsylvania until his retirement in 1993. He has also held a number of distinguished posts in the United States (including at Princeton and Yale) as well as a Visiting Fellowship at All Souls College, Oxford. His social vision is strongly informed by Freudian theory, which he has used to develop a powerful critique of "therapeutic culture" and the strains of **consumer society**.

Rieff has made two principal contributions to sociology and **social theory**. In *Freud: The Mind of the Moralist* (1959), he compellingly argued that **psychoanalysis** is primarily a doctrine of tragedy and forbearance – with political implications for the ways in which society seeks to deal with loss and destruction, but nonetheless a vision of the human spirit opposed to blueprints of revolutionary political transformation. His other key contribution came in 1965, with *The Triumph of the Therapeutic*, in which Rieff analyzed the rise of therapeutic **culture**. Inextricably linked to a social crisis of **authority**, Rieff argued that the whole terrain of therapy systems was a search for consolation and one reducible to the risks of illusion. In his most recent work, *My Life Among the*

Deathworks (2006), he explores the fleetingness of culture, arguing for the necessity of God as the final authority.　　　　　　ANTHONY ELLIOTT

Riesman, David (1909–2002)

Riesman was Henry Ford II Professor of the Social Sciences at Harvard University (1958–80) and author (in collaboration with Nathan Glazer and Reuel Denney) of the influential *The Lonely Crowd. A Study of the Changing American Character* (1950). Riesman argued that tradition-directed **personalities** are conformists who reproduce the **culture** of their ancestors. The inner-directed personality emerged with the Renaissance and the Reformation, and is most suited to **individualism**. The other-directed personality of modern America (and other societies dominated by the **mass media**) craves approval from others. The social relations of the other-directed character are mediated by the flow of mass communication. The other-directed personality creates a shallow form of emotional **intimacy** and their demand for approval is an aspect of liberal, middle-class **socialization**. Riesman's criticisms of American society in the 1950s bore a close resemblance to **Herbert Marcuse**'s analysis of the "happy consciousness" in his *One-Dimensional Man* (1964), but they were also related to the study of individualism in colonial America by **Alexis de Tocqueville**. Riesman was awarded the Prix Tocqueville of the Sociétié Tocqueville in Paris. *The Lonely Crowd* was part of a more general appraisal of the changing nature of **power** and **social class** in the United States in the 1950s by Riesman, **C. Wright Mills**, and **Talcott Parsons**. Through his study of popular beliefs and **attitudes** in America, he is often credited with founding the sociology of **popular culture**.

BRYAN S. TURNER

rights, human

It could be said that nearly the entire discipline of sociology is fundamentally concerned with issues of human rights, even though sociologists represent a minority in the more formalized interdisciplinary field of the study of human rights. The central fields of sociology (social **inequality**; the differential allocation of resources; **discrimination** along the lines of **race and ethnicity**, **social class**, and **gender**; **social movements**; and the more generalized problems of **modernity**) deal fundamentally with issues of human rights, but the core of both classical and contemporary sociological discourse is practically devoid of discussions of human rights, as that concept has been used historically and in other **social sciences** and the

humanities. In other words, with a few exceptions, sociology as a discipline has not as yet articulated an autonomous subfield called the sociology of human rights.

Contemporary global **civil society** is currently characterized by an expansion of discourse on human rights to which sociology as a discipline is, in general, quite marginal. These facts themselves pose interesting questions for the sociology of knowledge, which will be addressed here. This entry outlines some of the central issues and questions which might serve as the basis for a more fully developed and autonomous sociology of human rights.

The classical grounding of sociology lies primarily on the work of **Karl Marx**, **Max Weber**, **Émile Durkheim**, and **Georg Simmel**. Discussions of rights in the works of the classical theorists were not central and for the most part were critical of the ideas of Natural Law which informed most discourse on human rights at the time (see **law and society**). As a political liberal, **Émile Durkheim** was concerned about the "rights of man," as discussed, for example, in W. S. F. Pickering and W. Watts Miller (eds.), *Individualism and Human Rights in the Durkheimian Tradition* (1993), and about the relationship between **individualism** and human rights, but for the most part his attempt to form a positivist science independent of philosophy distanced him from the idea of rights – a development which is considered by Bryan Turner, "Outline of a Theory of Human Rights" (1993, *Sociology*). Sociologically, he might have seen rights as important representations of "the collective conscience," as important models for the formation of social **solidarity**, or simply as "social facts" which served as the new normative bases for social order and individual **identity** in **modernity**. Durkheim was well aware of the French Revolutionary **tradition**, which constructed the rights of man as secular forms of the sacred which were functional equivalents of the sacred in modernity: the rights of man thus could be considered as models for individual identity in place of traditional **religion**. Some time before Durkheim, other French theorists such as **Claude Henri de Rouvroy, Comte de Saint Simon** and **Auguste Comte** clearly articulated new secular representations of human rights as part of their respective "new religions of humanity."

As Fritz Ringer has shown in his *Max Weber: An Intellectual Biography* (2004), as a political liberal Weber believed in fundamental human rights, and yet his sociology does not include a specific sociology of human rights; rather, his focus was on the sociology of *Recht*, or law, rather than *Menschenrechte*, or human rights, per se. Weber's value-free sociology would have insisted on not deriving any value positions from sociology, and therefore it is entirely understandable that his sociology was distant from issues which were articulated more clearly in the tradition of normative theorizing about rights. Nonetheless, a Weberian sociology of human rights might see the latter as subjectively meaningful forms of substantive-ethical rationality, which guide **social action**. Correspondingly, Weber's analysis of the historical process of **rationalization** might be extended to understanding the tensions between human rights as meaningful cultural forms which sought to re-enchant the world in the face of such disenchanting modern processes of formal **rationality** as **bureaucracy**, state **power**, and the law. Some of these issues are explored in Thomas Cushman, "The Conflict of the Rationalities: International Law, Human Rights, and the War in Iraq" (2005, *Deakin Law Review*). In any case, the core of a Weberian perspective on human rights would proceed at some distance from the often overly romantic **utopianism** of the contemporary human rights movement, and perhaps provide a more pessimistic view about the possibilities of human rights in an increasingly rationalized world in which a variety of substantive rationalities competed for attention.

It was Marx for whom the discussion of rights was most central, although it was central in the sense that he criticized and rejected the idea of human rights as an ideological legitimation of bourgeois capitalist society. Marx believed that the ruling ideas of an age were the ideas of the ruling class. In this sense, he viewed classical liberal ideas of individual rights – especially the Lockean idea of the right to **property** – as **ideologies** which legitimated the privileged position of the bourgeois classes and maintained class society. In his controversial essay on the problem of **citizenship** in the French Revolution, in "On the Jewish Question" in the *Deutsch-Französische Jahrbücher* of 1844, reprinted in *Early Writings* (1992), Marx criticized the assimilationist aspiration of Jews and other minority **groups** to become French citizens. He claimed that such a process would merely serve to incorporate such groups into the existing system and thus to perpetuate new forms of false consciousness and the **alienation** of man's "species-being." For Marx, "human rights revolutions" were merely cosmetic revolutions which brought to **power** a new ruling class with new ideas which legitimated its power and class position.

This incidentally was also Marx's understanding of the American Revolution. Rights claims were not seen as liberating from power, as most classical liberal theorists would have it, but reproductive of power and existing social relations. This is an important distinction, since most liberal theorists of rights from the time of the American and French Revolutions until now have viewed individual rights as the central driving force for political and personal emancipation.

Marx, on the other hand, viewed aspirations to bourgeois rights as impediments to such authentic emancipation. This Marxian line of thought has continued on very strongly in the modern world in the emergence of the idea of social and economic rights, which are aimed at guaranteeing basic rights such as **food**, shelter, water, health care, and the like. In much contemporary debate on human rights, social and economic rights have taken precedence over classical liberal ideas of individual rights and liberties, which, proponents of such views would argue, can only be claimed and exercised by those with high social status and power. Indeed, the fault lines between liberal conceptions of rights and Marxian critiques of rights remain very much alive in the early twenty-first century in the heated debates about **neoliberalism** and **globalization**, with so-called neoliberals championing classical liberal ideas of freedom, property, and **capitalism**, over and against more Marxian-inspired theorists who see globalization as yet another form of predatory and exploitative social process. These issues are explored in Richard Falk's *Human Rights Horizons* (2000).

One of the most significant contributions of **sociological theory** to the study of human rights, and one which has not hitherto been made, would be the analytical focus on the relationship between the individual and **society**. All of the major classical theorists were interested in this issue, and this focus remains central to much contemporary sociological theory. If there is one central point of articulation between sociology and human rights, as it is studied outside of the field, it lies in the recognition that human rights represent individual and collective aspirations for human freedom. The idea of freedom has been articulated in various times and places as emancipation, liberty, autonomy, authenticity, or agency. As a result, wherever we see expressions of human rights, we see discourses of freedom, but also a discourse of power, coercion, restraint, or tyranny, that is, something which freedom is declared from or for. Historically, cultural representations of human rights emerge dialectically in relation to oppressive **social structures** and they are central to processes of human emancipation and freedom.

While his work was not directly relevant to human rights, Simmel's formal sociology, which examined the dialectical interplay between *Geist* (spirit) and form, is especially important as a theoretical underpinning for this dialectical conception of human rights. As Simmel noted in *The Philosophy of Money* (1900 [trans. 1978]), "negative freedom" is the absence of structural impediments to human agency. "Positive freedom" represents the active construction of social-structural arrangements to provide for basic **human needs** and to alleviate the condition of human vulnerability so that agents may claim their full agency as human beings. This Simmelian conception of freedom captures well the distinction between negative rights and positive rights which is central in the history of human rights. Negative rights – as expressed, for instance, in the American Bill of Rights – are primarily concerned with specifying the limitations of the power of the **state** over individuals and might be conceived in sociological terms as proscriptive **norms** which set the preconditions for the enablement of human agency, liberty, and freedom. Positive rights, in contrast, are prescriptive norms which specify the duties or obligations of powerful entities, such as states and economic systems, to provide resources and opportunities for individuals to protect them from both natural and social forces which make them vulnerable. In the modern **welfare state**, positive rights have taken a more central place in various global human rights projects.

Human rights movements are cultural projects which struggle to negate or temper powerful social forms, such as tyranny, despotism, or unrestrained market forces. At the same time, and especially with the rise of the modern welfare state, human rights projects aim to affirm human existence by providing people with first-order needs, such as food, shelter, housing, living wages, medical care, and the like. There is considerable debate in modern human rights movements about whether negative rights or positive rights ought to be primary. Proponents of negative rights are more traditional in rooting their idea of freedom in the alleviation of structural impediments to individual agency. Proponents of positive rights, however, counter this with a more sociological view which holds that not all individuals are equally placed within society and thus are not equally as free as others to claim individual rights, liberties, and freedoms. The object of most rights movements based on positive conceptions of rights is to redress social injustices and structured **inequalities**, which will then create a situation of equal opportunity for individuals to claim the more abstract types of individual rights and freedoms which comprise the core of liberal conceptions of rights.

In this theoretical sense, various conceptions of human rights, at various times and places, are, to use Weber's terms, forms of re-enchantment which express themselves in dialectic relation to disenchanting forms of social order. This is not an entirely new process: while **modernity** has witnessed an increase in the cultural expression of ideas of freedom in the form of human rights discourse, the struggle between **agency and structure** has been a perennial aspect of human societies. Yet the idea of human rights is one of the most powerful cultural constructions of modernity.

As documented by Lynn Hunt in *The French Revolution and Human Rights* (Hunt [ed.], 1996), for many theorists of human rights the experience of the French Revolution is a crucial starting point for thinking about how human rights claims have been made in relation to power. The French Declaration of the Rights of Man and the Citizen (1789) specifically tied the question of rights to the status of **citizenship**. The Declaration was notable for specifying what rights should be accorded "the man and citizen," but one of the most crucial debates was about who would be able to acquire the status of citizen and as a consequence make valid claims to enjoy the rights and freedoms specified in the Declaration. In this sense, rights were privileges which were tied to the status of citizenship. Indeed, Turner, in his *Sociology* article of 1993 has noted that, to a large extent, the sociology of human rights has been part of the sociology of citizenship. The French Revolution provided the impetus for a wide array of groups – slaves and former slaves of African origin, women, Jews, actors, and executioners – who had been excluded from enjoying "the rights of man" by virtue of their ascribed or acquired statuses to mobilize to claim the status of citizenship which would thereby confer upon them the privilege and protection of human rights. The sociological importance of the French Revolution is that it established general grounds for both the exercise of rights and exclusion from their enjoyment: first, rights were a certain kind of privilege to be enjoyed by individuals; second, the recognition, which is now seen very clearly in the theory of group rights, that not every individual is in a position to enjoy such rights by virtue of being a member of a subordinated group; and third, that human rights were not so much about the process of creating social representations called rights, but about the process of making claims to human rights by disenfranchised groups, once such cultural representations of rights had been made.

In thinking about various human rights projects in modernity, the French Revolution provides an important historical model of the process by which people, who define themselves as excluded from citizenship, nevertheless make claims to that juridical status, from which they then might legitimately claim, and subsequently be given, the protections and liberties which such a status formally confers. The process of the mobilization of groups in the modern world follows this same model to a large extent, with the notable exception that the substantive nature of the groups has changed. In recent years, lobby groups such as gay and lesbian **communities**, **children**, criminals, and members of indigenous groups – just to name a few – have made human rights claims in the form of **social movements**. These groups, which could not have made any legitimate claims in the historical context of the French Revolution, have proceeded along similar lines by making claims to the status of being "fully human," and by virtue of that to enjoy the privilege of certain rights.

The reticence of sociology as a discipline to engage more fully in the study of human rights may have something to do with sociology's insistence that it is a value-free science. Discussions of human rights are for the most part normative, and therefore would not be considered to be central to scientific sociology. The influence of **positivism** in sociology probably has much to do with the distancing of the field from the field of human rights, since positivist conceptions of human beings cannot understand the dialectical interplay between agency and structure which, as argued above, is central to a theoretical understanding of expressions such as rights in terms of agency over and against structure. But even more fundamentally, there is hostility between the dominant philosophical tradition in human rights and those philosophical traditions that form the foundation of sociology.

While certainly not as important as it once was, the natural-law tradition has been central to thinking about human rights. Historically, theorists of rights relied on the idea of the existence of a "natural law," which holds that human rights exist across time and space, are universally valid

for all people, and can be understood and enacted by all human individuals through the application of reason. This metaphysical understanding of rights was crucial in the **Enlightenment** to such thinkers as Immanuel Kant (1724–1804) and John Locke (1632–1704), and was in addition the basis for the American and French Revolutions. Even Marx relied to some degree on the logic of Natural Law theory with his dream of building a communist utopia based on the purely scientific understanding of **historical materialism**. Yet, the Natural Law tradition is directly at odds with the basic sociological axiom that all **culture** is socially constructed and this is one reason why both classical and contemporary sociology have resisted the foundational claims of the natural law tradition.

From the perspective of **social constructionism**, human rights can only be seen as cultural representations, which are projected, objectified, and internalized by social actors to varying degrees at various times and places in world history. The understanding of such processes could provide a firm footing for the sociology of human rights, but would also place it a distance from the fundamentally normative underpinnings of most human rights theorizing outside of the discipline. Most approaches in the formalized study of human rights would not see human rights as simply interesting "social facts," which exist merely to be explained scientifically, but as normative ideas and concepts which are regarded as valuable in some way for ordering human societies. The study of human rights is not a value-free enterprise, but a value-full one, and for the most part those who study human rights generally tend to be strong advocates of rights as a normative framework for social order. Because of its radically constructivist theoretical logic, **sociology**, like anthropology, would naturally find itself at odds with other conceptions from other disciplines, especially philosophy, which have no problem with and are predominantly concerned with the creation of normative theory.

The existence of a value-free sociology is a matter of much debate in sociology and has been called into question by many leading theorists, and specifically by **Jürgen Habermas** in *Knowledge and Human Interests* (1971). Most sociologists are political liberals whose choice of topics is conditioned by their ideological commitments and **values**, and whose research aims at producing knowledge which is helpful in the amelioration of various **social problems**, especially those related to subordinated classes and groups.

Notwithstanding the ideological predisposition towards social amelioration, the theoretical assumptions of both **structuralism** and macro-sociological approaches, the concept of individual agency, much less that of individual rights, would not logically be the focus of sociological research and practice. In this sense, the conceptual distance between sociology and other fields on the issue of human rights is more intelligible.

It is useful to see the distance between sociology and mainstream work on human rights as a product of the tensions between philosophical debates over universalism and **relativism**. Universalism is the belief that there are human rights, values, norms, and ethics that exist across time and space. Relativism is the idea that rights, values, norms, and ethics are the product of particular cultures and contingent historical forces. Sociology is firmly grounded in relativism, as is anthropology. It was in anthropology, however, that a sharp tension between universalism and relativism emerged in the mid twentieth century, and many of the intellectual lessons learned from this tension remain relevant to understanding sociology's position in relation to human rights.

Following World War II, the *Universal Declaration of Human Rights (UNDHR)* was finally ratified by the newly formed United Nations on December 10, 1948. The UNDHR specified a range of both individual and social and economic rights that were held to be universal for all individuals, regardless of their location in time and space. The Declaration was met with hostility in the academic field of anthropology when the Executive Board of the American Anthropological Association issued a statement in 1947 denouncing the UNDHR as a form of western cultural **imperialism** and decrying it for failing to affirm a central "right to culture" and the importance of cultural differences in determining specific values, norms, and rights. The reaction by anthropologists to the universalism of the UNDHR was strongly defensive and did more to sharpen than resolve the tensions between universalism and relativism. In fact, this debate only served to create a more polarized theoretical dichotomy between universalism and relativism than is now considered the case in contemporary anthropology. While it seemed counterproductive at the time, these early debates on rights established the presence of anthropology rather than sociology in the history of ideas on human rights and set the stage for a well-developed contemporary anthropology which far outpaces sociology in terms of its theoretical and empirical level of development in the field of human rights research.

Recent work in anthropology on human rights serves as a valuable reference point for a sociology of human rights. For example Jane Cowan, Marie-Bénédicte Dembour and Richard Wilson (eds.), *Culture and Rights: Anthropological Perspectives* (2001), and Sally Merry, *Human Rights and Gender Violence: Translating International Law into Local Justice* (2006) have developed new conceptions of culture and human rights which focus on how universal conceptions of human rights interact with local cultures to produce cultural outcomes which are neither universal nor particular. In this sense, they have recast the fruitless and dichotomous debate between universalism and relativism by observing through ethnographic detail how globalized conceptions of human rights intersect with local cultures, and how this process is affected by the various processes of globalization. The solution to the relativist–universalist debate is not to be found in any abstract considerations, but in the re-conception of the idea of culture as a process, where the focus is on the empirical details of how human rights and local cultures interact dialectically in specific locations to produce new hybrid and contingent cultural outcomes.

These new anthropological approaches have produced some of the most important contributions to understanding human rights outcomes as a negotiated process. Nonetheless, they do not solve the problems for human rights posed by relativism more generally. If such cultural practices as female genital mutilation, torture, and **genocide**, which are generally assumed to be gross violations of human rights in the normative discourse of human rights, are simply seen as normal behaviors which cannot be judged by any universal standards, then it is virtually impossible for social scientists or activists to advocate any form of social intervention against these practices without contradicting themselves or adhering to some form of universal **morality**, albeit a very minimalist morality. For the most part, most contemporary theorists of human rights have developed the idea of a minimal morality, a set of rights which the majority of people, regardless of their location in space and time, might consider to be not subject to derogation. Such a set of peremptory norms might serve as a basic common position for a global project of human rights advancement. This "minimalist argument" has been advanced by both Michael Walzer in *Thick and Thin: Moral Argument at Home and Abroad* (1994) and by Michael Ignatieff in *Human Rights As Politics and Idolatry*

(2001). Yet even such minimal moralities have not secured themselves as the basis of a common global morality: serious violations of human rights, including torture, **slavery**, gross violations of women's rights, and genocide continue unabated in the modern world. It is worth pointing out, as well, that, quite outside of any theoretical or empirical arguments for or against it, relativism falls apart on logical grounds as well, since the relativist position is itself put forth in the form of a general statement of value, thereby refuting its own foundational proposition that there can be no such general statements of value. Relativism is a self-defeating argument.

When the *UNDHR* came into force, the dominant paradigm in American sociology was **functionalism**. Functionalist sociology is ostensibly guided by a form of methodological relativism that would look at any given society in terms of how its values, ethics, norms, and laws are functional or dysfunctional for the maintenance of social order or the production of social disorder. From a strictly functionalist perspective, for instance, it might be possible to argue that certain human rights are denied to people in societies out of functional necessity and that the provision of rights constructed from outside of the society would throw the society into disequilibrium. In this sense, functionalism can be seen, in some ways, as a modern analog to classical conservative critiques of rights, such as that presented in 1790 by Edmund Burke in *Reflections on the Revolution in France* (1955). In his strident attack on the Enlightenment arguments underpinning the French Revolution, Burke argued that abstract and universal rights such as those produced by the French radicals, when transposed to other societies, were a direct threat to the traditions and values which held such societies together. While Burkean conservatives had attacked the Revolution's formulation of rights, in general sociologists offered virtually no reaction to the UNDHR. If there was any reaction at all, it was one of acceptance and celebration of the new universal ideas which were touted as the basis for a new world order, for instance by R. M. MacIver in *Great Expressions of Human Rights* (1950).

In the 1960s, the idea of group rights began to emerge as a strong criticism of classical conceptions of human rights and this idea was attractive to sociologists whose main area of focus was the structural subordination of groups, classes, and minority cultures, and who felt that the assumptions of structural-functionalist perspectives ignored, or even justified, such social subordination in their theories.

Advocates of group rights argued that traditional conceptions of rights, especially those derived from the Natural Law tradition, were almost completely concerned with the rights of individuals. In such documents as the UNDHR, the rights specified refer to abstract, idealized individuals who exist outside specific locations, and historical and group processes. As such, proponents of individual rights ignore the central sociological fact that individuals exist as members of cultures and groups, which fundamentally structure and condition individuals' abilities to claim their human rights. For instance, in the everyday world, people do not interact with each other based solely on considerations of the individuality of the other person. The **interaction** is conditioned by perceptions of the groups, classes, or other categories to which people belong. As an example of this, one of the most celebrated documents in the history of individual rights, the Constitution of the United States which was created in the Virginia convention of 1787, provided a set of sacred ideals for individual rights without even considering women's rights, and redefined the humanity of African Americans with the result that they were not seen as being fully human. In the so-called three-fifths rule, African slaves in the United States were counted as only three-fifths human for purposes of political apportionment of representation in the new republic.

The idea of group rights would seem, on its face, to be immensely attractive to sociologists and there is little question that the discipline has much to offer theorists of group rights from its substantial literature on differential treatment of social groups and classes. A large part of the stock of knowledge of sociology is relevant to these debates and one major task of sociology is to articulate its knowledge about social class, group dynamics, **social status**, and differential treatment of subordinated groups more clearly with the discourse on human rights occurring in other fields. American sociology is extremely provincial in its focus on American society, and within American society the discourse on human rights, as opposed to the notion of civil rights, is not a major cultural narrative used to describe problems in that society. In general, human rights have been a global description and **explanation** of events outside of the United States, and this global narrative has failed to make significant inroads into American sociology. One of the more interesting questions in the field of human rights is why human rights violations are considered something which happens outside the boundaries of the United States, whereas human rights violations within the United States are not articulated within the more general discourse of human rights.

The most comprehensive recent programmatic statement for an autonomous field of the sociology of human rights has been put forward by Gideon Sjoberg, Elizabeth Gill, and Norma William in their "A Sociology of Human Rights" (2001, *Social Problems*). This work is the most useful starting point for acquiring an extensive understanding of how contemporary sociological thinking can be made more relevant to human rights, which, at present, is at the center of cultural discourse on global **civil society**. However, one of the boldest new attempts to construct a new theoretical program for a sociology of human rights has been put forward by Bryan S. Turner, in a variety of works but most recently in his *Vulnerability and Human Rights* (2006). Turner attempts to provide a foundationalist, as opposed to a constructivist, sociology of rights and argues that all human beings are vulnerable and exist in a precarious relationship to the social and natural world. This vulnerability is a cultural universal which challenges both cultural relativism, which holds that there are no such universals, and the idea that there are no universal grand narratives which are applicable to the amelioration of human rights violations. Turner argues that our common vulnerability makes us dependent and interdependent on others and that a sociological theory of human rights must focus on this vulnerability and the various ways in which different human societies develop **institutions** which both alleviate and exploit vulnerability. Turner argues that mutual recognition and sympathy based on a common awareness of human vulnerability is a fundamental precondition for a viable liberal democratic order. He develops the idea of sympathy alongside the notion of **cosmopolitanism**, and both concepts are in turn related to recent work on "recognition ethics," which were originally outlined in **Georg Wilhelm Friedrich Hegel**'s *Philosophy of Right* (1821 [trans. 1952]). These claim that no ethical relationship can exist between two individuals without their prior mutual recognition of each other as free, moral agents. Slavery is the extreme example of the absence of recognition.

In this sense, Turner's emergent work is in the best tradition of sociological theorizing which seeks to establish a foundationalist basis for the study of human rights and which aims at practical normative outcomes. He outlines a new theoretical perspective which serves as the basis of an ethically engaged and politically viable strategy for understanding and alleviating human frailty and vulnerability in modern social life. Turner's work represents one of the most useful and important starting points for a new phase of sociological theory on human rights. In its interdisciplinary scope and aspirations to bring the most important traditions of sociology to the study of human rights, Turner's work provides a grounding for the development of an autonomous sociology of human rights, one which affirms that a universal aspect of the human condition is vulnerability and which establishes the fact that sociological theory, informed by the advances in other disciplines, has an important role to play in understanding the origins and consequences of institutionalized responses to human vulnerability.   TOM CUSHMAN

Riley, Matilda White (1911–2004)

First Executive Officer of the American Sociological Association (1949–60), Chief Consulting Economist for the US War Production Board (1942–4), and University Professor of Rutgers University (1950–73), Riley was a pioneering figure in the development of the sociology of aging. She worked at the Russell Sage Foundation (1974–7), was founding Associate Director (1979–91) of, and subsequently Senior Social Scientist (1991–7) for, Behavioral and Social Research at the National Institute on Aging in the United States. She finished her career as a professor at Bowdoin College Maine (1973–81).

Riley developed the age stratification theory in which society is stratified into various age cohorts, and each age cohort has life-course and historical dimensions. Different age cohorts age differently. To express these processes, she developed the "aging and society **paradigm**" which articulates cohort flow and **social change**, and explicated **age** as a feature of **social structure**. Social structure and **ideology** combine to exercise constraints on the human capacity for living and aging successfully and productively. One aspect of the **power** of social structure and ideology over individual lives was age **segregation**. Her aging and society paradigm demonstrated that cohort membership does not simply influence people as children, but affects them through the life-course in terms of the **groups** to which they belong, the people with whom they interact, and the cultural conditions to which they are exposed. Her contribution to the sociological study of aging was published in the three-volume edited collection *Aging and Society* (1968–72).   BRYAN S. TURNER

risk

The concept of risk has been elaborated in a variety of social science disciplines, generating distinct but overlapping literatures in anthropology, economics, and sociology. **Joseph Alois Schumpeter**, in *The Theory of Economic Development* (1934), famously characterized **entrepreneurship** in terms of a propensity for risk-taking behavior. In his *Risk, Uncertainty and Profit* (1921), Frank Knight formulated the benchmark distinction between risk, in which a random process generates an outcome which, though unpredictable, is determined by parameters that are known in advance, and uncertainty, where such probabilities are not known. Following on from this, in economics the variance of possible outcomes is often used as a measure of risk.

Since the mid-1980s the idea of risk has also been taken up in sociology, becoming an increasingly central concept in the characterization and investigation of **modernity**. In a general sense, risk is an intrinsic part of the human condition, arising necessarily from the capacity of sentient minds to envisage, anticipate, and understand the meaning of **death and dying** and injury, to evaluate rationally different courses of action, and to empathize with the **lifeworld** of other thinking, feeling selves. In relation to this, superstition, **ritual**, and magic in traditional societies can be understood, at least in part, in terms of the strategies and belief systems through which individuals and social **groups** attempt to deal with, contain, and prevent anticipated danger. In the same way many modern practices and behaviors, though nominally grounded in a more rational-scientific understanding of causation, are also to be understood in terms of the sense of empowerment and agency that they engender in an otherwise chaotic and uncertain world of random and unpredictable events.

However, this psycho-anthropological continuity notwithstanding, sociologists and historians have also charted a series of significant transformations in the nature and social perceptions of risk over the last three centuries. In premodern, medieval societies the idea of risk was coterminous with fate or fortune and understood in terms of acts of God: risk as the unpredictable consequence of a radically indeterminate cosmos. In the wake of the **Enlightenment** a new **paradigm** emerged with the concept of risk being extended to cover the social world and being seen to derive from human action. In this new understanding, risk came to denote a calculable, mathematical probability and was in this sense transformed into something knowable, predictable, and to some extent manageable – contrasting with a situation of uncertainty in which probabilities remained inestimable. In this developing, insurance-based paradigm, risk was a neutral concept and could be good or bad. In the eighteenth and nineteenth centuries calculable risk in this sense was linked closely with the new science of **statistics** and can be understood as an aspect of the Enlightenment vision of an objective world, knowable, and manageable through the extension of scientific **explanation**.

More recently, during the period characterized variously in terms of **postmodernism, post-Fordism**, and **postindustrial society**, the colloquial meaning of risk has narrowed, the term becoming synonymous with a vaguely specified sense of danger or threat; an undesirable outcome per se, divorced from any statistical notion of probability. In *Risk* (1999), Deborah Lupton relates this narrowing of meaning to the information-technology-driven expansion of routinized data-gathering, the availability of large datasets, and the resulting proliferation of risk calculations in all areas of socioeconomic and cultural life. The pervasive language of risk probability in popular discourse makes it difficult for individuals to accommodate the older, neutral concept of risk in the development of personal life strategies. This cultural saturation is reinforced at a deeper level by increasing awareness of the global and potentially devastating nature of what **Ulrich Beck,** thinking about nuclear **technology** and global ecological problems, calls "civilizational risks." Such risk-related anxiety corresponds with the more general uncertainty about the benefits of industrial–scientific **progress** diagnosed by postmodernist commentators. In a similar vein, sociologists have linked the declining **trust** in social **institutions** and traditional **authorities** to the undermining of the insurance paradigm based on the modernist conception of risk. **Niklas Luhmann** characterizes late-modern risk awareness as a fascination for improbable circumstances with grave outcomes.

Recent approaches to risk can usefully be divided into three categories. Technoscientific (realist) approaches continued the modernist preoccupation with risk measurement and management. The cultural-symbolic approach associated particularly with Mary Douglas and Aaron Wildavsky, *Risk and Culture* (1982), emphasized the cultural processes through which certain risks are given greater weight than others. Focusing on the role of experts in constructing and mediating discourses on risk as a peculiar feature of modern societies, Foucauldian/governmentality approaches, arguments such as F. Ewald's "Insurance and Risk" in *The Foucault Effect* (1991), take **social constructionism** the farthest, thereby undermining any claims as to the objective nature of risk.

Sharing a great deal with the work of **A. Giddens** and occupying a "realist" position that lies somewhere between these poles, Beck's *Risk Society* (1986 [trans. 1992]) was published in the same year as the nuclear accident occurred at Chernobyl. This macro-perspective focuses on three processes – individualization, reflexivity, and **globalization** – which in combination engender a process of transition towards "risk society." In conditions of post-scarcity, the production of **wealth** (economic goods) continues alongside a parallel production of risks ("bads"), some of which threaten global **civilization**. Late-modern risks are characterized by a "boomerang" effect: their impacts cannot be limited spatially, socially, or temporally to particular **communities** but ripple across **social class**, national, and even generational boundaries. Beck's work has been highly influential, not least because of his success in linking widely separated processes such as individualization, the feminization of **labor markets**, and the growth of information **technology** to what he calls reflexive **modernization**. The progressive loosening of the traditional ascriptive patterning of **social class** and **gender** contributes to the expanding field of sub-politics, characterized variously by the activism of new **social movements**, single-issue campaigns, an increased role for courts and the legal system, and a corresponding decline in the salience of the traditional class–party system. And it is the negotiated management of the problems and risks of late-modern society in these more fluid spaces of **civil society** that create the feedback loops underpinning the new reflexivity. For Beck the new risks are systematic (unavoidable and intrinsic to the process of modernization), impersonal, global, and imperceptible. Emanating from the scientific industrial system, they undermine the public authority of science while increasing public dependence on scientific expertise not only for their detection and management, but also for supporting particular perspectives or campaigns in the proliferating sub-politics. In this sense the risk society thesis echoes familiar postmodern themes of public disaffection with the meta-narrative of **progress**, while positing an ongoing modernization process in which, increasingly, reflexivity offers the prospect of an ongoing management, if not resolution, of the techno-

ecological and **social problems** of post-industrial society.   STEPHEN QUILLEY

risk society
– see **risk**.

rites of passage

These comprise a wide array of schematic sequences of action that symbolically mark and effect a change of **social status** or **identity**. Their distribution is universal. The most familiar and ubiquitous include rites of initiation, of **marriage**, and of graduation, investitures, baptisms, and funerals. In their majority, rites of passage mark enhancements of status, but as part of a process of criminalization or of the sorts of social disqualification on which **Erving Goffman** focused in *Asylums* (1961) they can serve to mark precisely the opposite.

In his classic *Rites of Passage* (1909 [trans. 1960]), philologist and folklorist Arnold van Gennep (1873–1957) discerned in the typical rite of passage three formal stages. The first stage results in the "disaggregation" – often the literal removal – of the ritual patient from the collectivity of which he or she is ordinarily a member. The second stage imposes a condition of liminality, of social ambiguity or indeterminacy in which the ritual patient leaves behind his or her former status and acquires a new one. The final stage culminates in the "reaggregation" of the ritual patient with the collective of which, thus transformed, he or she can or must henceforth be part. Van Gennep's analysis has proven remarkably durable, if not beyond critical development. Most notably, in *The Ritual Process* (1969), Victor Turner sought to render rites of passage as derivative elaborations of a more basic binary opposition between "structure" and the liminal interstitiality of "anti-structure."   JAMES D. FAUBION

ritual

Often scripted, always iterable action whose effectiveness rests essentially on its being properly formed and performed, ritual belongs to the most incidental as well as to the most significant episodes of human life. The concept of ritual most broadly rendered includes the casting of spells as well as the Eucharistic transubstantiation of bread into the body of Christ, the furtive washing of the hands as well as the public conferral of an academic diploma. In "Obsessive Practices and Ritual Actions" (1907), reprinted in the *Standard Edition*, volume IX, **Sigmund Freud** preserves such breadth in inaugurating a psychoanalytic theorization of ritual as a defensive reaction against anxiety. His perspective has its converse in the structural **functionalism** stemming from the work of **Émile Durkheim**. For the rigorous Durkheimian, anxiety is not the cause of ritual but the regular symptom of anticipating the great occasions that it marks. Private ritual, whether obsessive or merely arcane, is incommensurate with collective ritual. The former is mere magic, nonsocial, and perhaps even anti-social. The latter has its *raison d'être* in the maintenance of both social conformity and social **solidarity**. With both Freud and Durkheim, such early anthropologists as James Frazer (1854–1941) and **Bronislaw Malinowski** saw in magical ritual an arrogant or ignorant attempt to deploy **symbols** in order to alter the material world. More appreciative of the effectiveness of symbols as such, Arnold van Gennep saw, in the transformation of status wrought in the typical **rite of passage**, the service of ritual symbols in achieving symbolically constituted social ends. A half-century later, **Erving Goffman** returned to rites of passage as mechanisms of the transformation of **social status** but also emphasized the substantial similarities between theatrical and ritual performance in casting the individual actor as the dramaturge of the social self and ritual devices his or her primary means of "impression management." Analysts of shamans and other ritual therapists typically count either van Gennep or Goffman among their intellectual ancestors.

Semioticians familiarly posit that **myth** expresses and asserts what collective ritual manifests and enacts. As the performative figuration of cosmogonic or cosmological reality, ritual action is sacral action and, as Durkheim insisted, its cardinal arena is the arena of the religious life. Following both Durkheim and van Gennep and inspired by **Claude Lévi-Strauss**'s **structuralism**, Victor Turner argued in *The Ritual Process* (1969) that the suspension of mundane **norms** of conduct and the erasure of distinctions of rank and status that are characteristic of the specifically transformative or liminal phase of rites of passage point to a more fundamental binary contrast between the rule-burdened *societas* that human beings must endure and the liberated and egalitarian *communitas* that, periodically at least, they seek. Turner the dualist has his skeptics. He is also guilty of downplaying the systematic frequency with which the transformations of ritual are wrought with and through oppression and **violence**. Yet his elaboration of liminality even so has the enduring virtue of articulating and

accounting for the ritual and sacral aura that so often and perhaps necessarily attends occasions of profound social upheaval, creative and destructive alike.   JAMES D. FAUBION

routinization of charisma
– see **charisma**.

ruling class
– see **social class**.

Runciman, Walter Garrison (1934–)
A senior research fellow of Trinity College Cambridge since 1971 and the Third Viscount Runciman of Doxford, generally known as Garry Runciman. He was President of the British Academy from 2001 to 2005. He made important contributions to the study of social **justice** in *Relative Deprivation and Social Justice* (1966), but he has made equally significant contributions to theoretical **sociology**, for example in *Social Science and Political Theory* (1963). He has made influential contributions to the study of **Max Weber** in *A Critique of Max Weber's Philosophy of Social Science* (1972) and edited *Weber. Selections in Translation* (1978). His magnum opus is the three-volume *A Treatise on Social Theory* (1983–97). In his recent work, he has defended "the selectionist **paradigm**," arguing that social evolution involves the selection of **institutions** that are best adapted to **social change**. For example, Runciman contends in "Was Max Weber a Selectionist in Spite of Himself?" in the *Journal of Classical Sociology* (2001), that we can interpret Weber's Protestant Ethic thesis as saying that there was a historical process of selection in which inner-worldly asceticism came to fit the economic needs of the capitalist **economy**.
                                              BRYAN S. TURNER

rural–urban continuum
A notion which proposes a linear depiction of the contrasting natures of social relationships characteristic of rural and urban settlements, this was a popular conceptual tool for classifying different types of **community** and the transition between them. It arose from early twentieth-century sociology trying to understand the **social changes** consequent upon rapid urbanization. Life in the countryside occurred in small, geographically isolated settlements which were socially homogeneous, with high levels of mutual communication and social **solidarity**, and which changed very slowly. Urban communities were attributed the opposite characteristics: L. Louis

Wirth (1897–1952) of the **Chicago School**, in his highly influential essay "Urbanism as a Way of Life" (*American Journal of Sociology*, 1938), thought **cities** distinctive because they were large, dense, and heterogeneous and that this produced the transient, disorderly, anonymous, and cold associational relationships of urban living. Such understandings had affinities with **F. Tönnies**'s a-spatial distinction between *Gemeinschaft* and *Gesellschaft*. In principle, if all settlements could be placed on such a continuum we would have a strong account of how spatial arrangement affected social life. However, subsequent research largely undermined that idea. Spatial arrange-ments themselves are not determinant of social relations; even if some parts of cities are rather anarchic, most, for instance the suburbs, do not conform to the model. One can also find traditional and interpersonally intimate relationships in cities, as exemplified by the working class **community** of Bethnal Green described by **Michael Young**, and conflicts and isolation in the countryside. Moreover, both city and village contain culturally distinct groups, suggesting that there are no dominant cultural forms typical of settlement type and that settlement type does not determine the character of interpersonal social ties.

ALAN WARDE

S

Sacks, Harvey (1935–1975)

An American sociologist, early collaborator with **Harold Garfinkel**, seminal ethnomethodologist and conversation analyst, Sacks received his AB from Columbia University in 1955, LLB degree from Yale University in 1959, and PhD from the University of California, Berkeley, in 1966. He lectured in sociology at the University of California at Los Angeles, and at University of California, Irvine. While Sacks published some landmark essays during his lifetime, including "An Initial Investigation of the Usability of Conversational Data for Doing Sociology" (1972) in Sudnow (ed.), *Studies in Interaction*, "On the Analyzability of Stories by Children" (1972) in R. Turner (ed.), *Ethnomethodology*, "On Formal Structures of Practical Action" (1970, with Harold Garfinkel) in J. Mckinney and E. Tiryakian (eds.), *Theoretical Sociology*, and "A Simplest Systematics for the Organization of Turn-taking in Conversation" (1974, with Emanuel Schegloff and Gail Jefferson) in *Language*, the bulk of his work remained unpublished until after his death. Sacks is best known for systematizing the formal study of **language** use by means of audiotape recordings of naturally occurring conversations, though his work is by no means confined to this approach. Most prominent among his many contributions to sociology is the identification of turn-taking systems in conversation. He also introduced the study of what he called membership categorization devices (MCDs) in conversation. The study of MCDs provides a highly nuanced analytic appreciation of how interactants utilize characterizations of their own social **identities** and those of others in the course of social **interaction**. This research technique allows analysts to identify empirically how social actors incorporate social status ascriptions into the conduct of social interaction at a level of empirical detail still unmatched by any other analytic approach.

DARIN WEINBERG

sacred and profane dichotomy

Symbolic (as opposed to technical) classification towards understanding the hierarchical relations between things in society was a central interest of **Émile Durkheim**, initially outlined in his co-authored essay with **Marcel Mauss** (*Primitive Classification*, 1903 [trans. 1963]). In *The Elementary Forms of Religious Life* (1912 [trans. 2001]), Durkheim elaborated on two universal categories of things: the sacred (that is, things set apart and forbidden), and profane things from which the sacred must be isolated and protected. As defined by Durkheim, anything can be consecrated as sacred, and not just beliefs, ideas, and **symbols** that might commonly be thought of as **religion**. The sacred and profane are not predetermined but are contingent on the specific communal and historical context in which ideas and things are so categorized by the society's members; sacred things are continually being created out of ordinary things. The taboos or boundaries separating the sacred from the profane are especially evident in the myriad **rituals** by which individual and social deference to the sacred are maintained. Churches are sacred places wherein rites demand clearly defined disciplined behavior in regard to sacred ideas and things; but the sacred can also be found in a wide range of ceremonial and ritualized behavior apparent across **everyday life** (for example sports events). The plurality of sacred things points to the many ways humans affirm the meaning of, and impose order on, social relations. Although the sacred functions to unify people by objectively representing their shared ideas regarding specific things, what gets defined as sacred (or profane) in everyday life is frequently contested and a source of **social conflict**. In contemporary times, the sacred–profane dichotomy frequently underlies the demarcation of domains of knowledge and activity: religion versus science, **emotion** versus **rationality**, and **progress** versus the conservation of **tradition** (as in definitions of **marriage**), as well as taste distinctions (as in **foods**) in everyday life.

MICHELE DILLON

Said, Edward W. (1935–2003)

Born in West Jerusalem in 1935; his family left Palestine in 1948. Said was the Parr University

Professor of English and Comparative Literature at Columbia University from 1963. Said made important contributions to literary and **social theory**. Broadly speaking, his work can be divided into four components. First, he made major contributions to literary studies, especially to the study of literature and **colonialism**, such as *Joseph Conrad and the Fiction of Autobiography* (1966), *Beginnings* (1975), *The World, The Text and the Critic* (1983), and *Culture and Imperialism* (1993). Second, he formulated a view of the committed and oppositional role of the **intellectual** in *Representations of the Intellectual* (1994). Third, he explored the question of **Orientalism** in *Orientalism* (1978), *Covering Islam* (1981), and *Culture and Imperialism* (1993). Finally, he was critical of the state of Israel and worked towards creating a democratic, reformist Palestinian political movement in *The Question of Palestine* (1979), *The Politics of Dispossession* (1994), and *The End of the Peace Process* (2000). Said, who supported a two-state solution in the Middle East conflict, was critical of the Camp David peace process and the Oslo Accords of 1994 which resulted eventually in a political compromise between the state of Israel and the Palestinian Authorities

Said became a significant figure in **postcolonial theory**, and while he made no direct contribution to sociology, his interpretation of Orientalism had an important influence on the interpretation of Islam, the understanding of other **cultures**, and on the critique of **prejudice**. His most significant and enduring contribution was *Orientalism* – a sustained critical analysis of western attitudes towards the Orient.   BRYAN S. TURNER

Saint-Simon, Claude Henri de Rouvroy, Comte de (1760–1825)

Claude-Henri de Rouvroy, comte de Saint-Simon (1760–1825), was a visionary social thinker who produced an original synthesis of Francis Bacon, the Encyclopédistes, and Scottish **political economy** (among others), and is now best known as an influential precursor of **socialism** (via Ludwig Feuerbach and **Karl Marx**), **sociology** (via **Auguste Comte** and **Émile Durkeim**), and technocracy. An aristocrat who renounced his title during the French Revolution, Saint-Simon led a turbulent life as an adventurer, soldier in the American War of Independence, speculator, and patron of artists and **intellectuals**. Through his writings, especially the journals *l'Industrie* and *l'Organisateur*, he campaigned energetically for a reconstructive reform of post-revolutionary French society. This

would complete the transformation negatively begun by the Revolution by providing the framework for a newly emerging form of society based on science and *l'industrie* (organized work), rather than on theistic **religion** and military rule. Saint-Simon first sketched his program in *Lettres d'un habitant de Genève à ses contemporains* (1803), which argued for a reconstructed polity in which parasitic remnants of the old regime would be ousted and the leaders of science and industry would rule. This reform, though, needed to be complemented by an intellectual one. Hence his call in *Mémoire sur la science de l'homme* (1813) for a science of **society** that would both provide a road-map for reform and complete the scientific revolution, making it possible to forge a fully scientific world-view as the basis for a "terrestrial" **morality** to hold the new order together. His last work, *Nouveau christianisme* (1825), gave these ideas religious form, proposing that the old Catholicism should be replaced by an anthropocentric **communitarianism** dedicated to the principle that "we should love one another as brothers."

ANDREW WERNICK

sampling

In survey research, sampling usually involves "people sampling." It is a method for collecting **information** from a number of individuals (the sample) and drawing inferences about a larger number of individuals (the population or universe) from an analysis of this information. The key concepts therefore are the population (the total target group to which the results of any analysis are to apply) and the sample (the actual **group** of people in the study and from whom the **data** are collected). For example, we may be interested in finding out what the relationship is between **religion** and **attitudes** towards political **violence** in Northern Ireland. Because it would not be possible or practical to investigate this relationship in the total population, we take a sample of the population and study this relationship in the sample.

A sample perfectly represents a population when the relevant characteristics of the individuals sampled are present in the sample in exactly the same way as they are in the population. In other words, the sample does not need to be representative in all respects but it must be so in terms of those characteristics that are of substantive interest to the study. For example, if you were interested in studying gender differences in attitudes towards abortion, a sample will perfectly represent the population with respect to gender if the proportion of males and females in the sample is exactly the same as in the population. If the same can be said for all relevant characteristics of the sampled individuals, then the sample perfectly represents the population. Such an ideal situation is never achieved in practice. Samples, as subsets of the population, are always imperfect in that some relevant characteristics are present in the sample in a way that does not match how they are present in the population. Such imperfections in the sample are referred to as error in sampling because they are produced by the sampling procedure. Error in sampling, or nonrepresentativeness, threatens the validity of generalizations in that, if there is enough sampling error present, it will be impossible to reach any valid conclusion about the population. In practice, there are two types of error in sampling: sample error and sample **bias**.

Sample error is a special case of random error produced by chance owing to the sampling procedure. The presence of such error means that at least one relevant characteristic will be imperfectly represented in the sample, but the direction and size of the imperfection are unpredictable, as it has been created by chance. For example, if **gender** is evenly divided in the population, one might draw a random sample that consists of 65 percent females. Such an outcome is unlikely but it could happen given the traditional tendency for more women than men to be at home during the day when many opinion poll **surveys** were previously undertaken. If it does happen then clearly the sample is in error with respect to gender and needs to be corrected.

The second type of error is sample bias, which is a special case of constant error produced by the sampling procedure. As in the case of sample error, the presence of sampling bias means that at least one characteristic of the population will be imperfectly represented in the sample. Again assuming that gender is equally divided in the population, an example of sampling bias would be a researcher who is supposed to sample randomly an equal proportion of males and females but every now and then he or she abandons the selection technique and simply chooses a female. Whenever this error in sampling occurs, it always favors females. Therefore it is a sample bias. Sample bias means that the sample does not adequately represent the target population. Therefore, any generalizations from the sample to the population may be invalid. Once a sampling bias is present, it is very difficult to correct unless radical steps are taken to improve the quality of sample selection. If this is not done, the sample is flawed and must be abandoned. This is not the case in relation to sample error, which can be reduced by simply increasing the size of your sample. As sample size approaches population size, sampling error must approach zero. After all, when sample size equals population size, you no longer have a sample but a population, which represents itself perfectly.

An important source of sampling bias is a sample bias. This is the list of the members of the total population of interest from which the sample for study is drawn. In practice, however, the sample frame usually does not in fact cover all of the intended population. For example, there are systematic differences between people who do or do not enter themselves on the electoral register or own a telephone – in these cases, young adults, those in privately rented accommodations, and the unemployed tend to be underrepresented – so that lists of such persons are not completely representative of the adult population. Another common source of sampling bias also associated with the selection process is nonresponse error. Nonresponse is a good indicator of response bias in that, as a general rule, the higher the proportion of nonrespondents in a study, the greater the degree of bias among those who participate. Although nonresponse error can occur for a number of reasons, the largest component of nonresponse is usually made up of people who refuse to participate in a survey, in terms of either agreeing to be interviewed or completing a **questionnaire**. Rules of thumb for acceptable levels of survey response vary, but 60 percent is usually regarded as the bare minimum. Whatever the magnitude of nonresponse, all surveys should identify the nature and extent of any bias and seek to address it. This can be done by a variety of means, the most common being further follow-ups in terms of personal callbacks or additional telephone calls to the sample address in an attempt to "retrieve" the nonrespondents.

The sample size is the number of cases or individuals in the sample studied. It is usually represented with the symbol n. Usually, the larger the sample size in a study, the more likely it is that the results will accurately reflect the universe, or population, from which the sample was obtained (all else being equal). Nevertheless, there are trade-offs when sample sizes are increased. In particular, larger samples usually add time and expense to data collection, coding, and data entry. In attempting to balance the increased accuracy of a survey against the additional time and expense that accompanies larger sample sizes, you need to keep in mind the law of diminishing returns. This basic law of probability means that the larger your sample size already is, the less likely that there will be a notable increase in accuracy by adding more individuals. By the way, contrary to common sense, the size of the universe basically has no bearing on the size of the sample needed to achieve accuracy at a given level. Normally, samples are, in fact, tiny fractions of the populations from which they are drawn. For example, 3,000 adults is the usual sample size employed by nationally representative opinion poll surveys, such as the General Social Survey (GSS) in the United States.

There are two general types of samples, probability samples and nonprobability samples. A probability, or scientific, sample is a sample that has been selected using random selection methods so that each individual (element) in the target population is chosen at random and has a known, nonzero chance of selection. The sampling fraction (SF) is the chance of selection of each element of the population. It is calculated from the sample size (n) divided by the population size N, that is, $SF = n/N$. It is generally assumed that a representative sample is more likely to be the outcome when this method of selection from the population is undertaken. The aim of probability sampling is to keep sampling error to a minimum. Once the sample fraction and the sample size are known, probability theory provides the basis for a whole range of statistical inferences to be made about the characteristics of the population, from the observed characteristics of the sample drawn from it. For example, the standard deviation of the distribution of sample means, which is referred to as the standard error of the means for any one characteristic (such as age), can be calculated to assess the reliability of the sample data. Large standard errors reduce our confidence that the sample is fully representative of its target population. In calculating the standard error, the size of the sample is crucial, in that the larger your sample, the smaller your standard error.

The most common type of a probability sample is the simple random sample. As in all probability samples, selection is based on the equal probability of the selection method (EPSM) in that each member of the population has an equal chance of being selected. For a long time, the two most common techniques for obtaining a pure random sample involved literally throwing the names of every member of the population into a hat and

drawing out names one at a time, or using what is called a "table of random numbers," which is found in the back of most statistics texts. Today, it is commonly done by a computer, which is programmed to generate random lists of names from sampling frames. Whatever the method of selection, it is first necessary to obtain a sampling frame, which uniquely identifies every member of that population. This is not as straightforward as it first appears, in that not only is it often difficult to obtain a complete and accurate listing of your intended population, but it can also be surprisingly difficult to define exactly who is the target population. For example, in examining the relationship between religion and attitudes towards political violence in Northern Ireland, how do we define our target population? Is it the total population of Northern Ireland or just the adult population in private households, usually defined as individuals aged eighteen years or over?

Because taking a simple random sample can be a long and tedious process, particularly when a large population is to be sampled, researchers often use a modification called systematic or interval sampling. Systematic sampling takes sampling units directly from the sampling frame at designated intervals (such as every tenth name in a telephone directory) or at designated positions (such as the third name from the top of each page). Although systematic sampling cannot be considered random sampling in the strictest sense – once the interval has been designated, most members of the universe no longer have any chance of being chosen – nevertheless, no one seriously questions that systematic sampling methods are as representative as pure random sampling methods.

Another common variation on the simple random sample is the stratified sample. This is a special type of random sampling that is often undertaken to make sure that groups (such as female professors) with low representation in a target population (for instance, British universities) are adequately (or highly) represented in the sample. Users of this sampling method take a sample frame (for example, a list of all professors in British universities) and divide the constituents up according to one or more characteristics (such as the proportion who are male and female), and then randomly sample individuals from the resulting sample lists. Of course, a necessary precondition is that the researcher must know how the stratified variable (gender) is distributed in the target population (British universities). If the sampled proportions fit the population proportions exactly, this sort of sampling is known as proportionate stratified sampling. Alternatively, if extra cases (additional individuals) are selected, this is known as disproportionate stratified sampling, where the sample proportions on the characteristics of interest exceed the population proportions. Disproportionate stratified sampling usually occurs if the number that would appear in the sample is too small to allow any reliable conclusions to be drawn. In general, however, stratified random samples are used to ensure that the sample matches the population in all crucial respects.

Another common variation, which is particularly suitable for studying populations spread over a large geographical area, is cluster sampling. The word "cluster" refers in this context to what might be called naturally occurring groups of subjects, such as church congregations or students in a university. In its most elementary form – a simple cluster sample – a researcher picks a few clusters, and then collects data from respondents in each of the clusters. Say, for example, a researcher was interested in studying the views of particular religious groups about whether women should be ordained as priests. Here the researcher selects a number of church congregations geographically dispersed throughout Britain and, at each location, interviews a random sample of its members about their opinion in relation to this issue. Thus, although the church members are randomly picked, the congregations to be sampled are not. Nevertheless, this sampling procedure will normally approximate a representative sample.

In many situations, there is no obvious sampling frame that can be used or compiled. This means that it is not possible to draw random samples. In these circumstances, nonprobability sampling methods are used. One of the most commonly used forms of nonprobability sampling methods is a convenience or haphazard sample. This involves building a sample almost by accident from those who are conveniently at hand, such as interviewing friends and neighbors, or just stopping passers-by on a street corner. Because of its convenience nature, this method leaves the researcher open to all sorts of bias in the selection of respondents and, thus, should be avoided if at all possible. An improvement on this method is the adoption of a purposive sample. Here, the researcher deliberately seeks out those who meet the needs of the study. This kind of sampling is often associated with so-called snowballing techniques, in which those in an initial sample are asked to name others who might be willing to be approached. This type of sampling is often used in studies of deviant or closed groups, such as heroin users, where the initial respondents themselves provide the names of additional study members.

Because purposive or snowball samples are not very useful in most large-scale surveys, a method that tries to approximate random selection procedures is most often used. This is what is known as a quota sample. This method is superficially similar to stratified random sampling, but does not involve any statistically random procedures. In quota sampling, the population is divided into categories that are known to be important, such as gender and **age**, and for which it is possible to get some basic information, either from a census or a similar source. This method is very widely used in large-scale marketing surveys, as it is an economical and efficient way of achieving a sample that matches the broad and known features of a population. The individuals chosen, however, are not randomly selected and, thus, it is not strictly legitimate to apply probability statistical techniques to the results.

BERNADETTE HAYES

sampling error
– see **sampling**.

sanction
– see **norm(s)**.

Saussure, Ferdinand de (1857–1913)

A professor of general linguistics at the University of Geneva, Saussure is widely regarded as the founding figure of French **structuralism**. But, significantly, Saussure did not use the term "structure"; he preferred "system" for conceptualizing the relation between **language** and **society**. The key elements of his doctrines, set out in his posthumously published *Course in General Linguistics* (1916 [trans. 1974]) which was reconstructed from students' notes, include: the distinction between "langue" (language) and "parole" (speech); the arbitrary character of the sign; and the function of difference in the constitution of meaning through the conjunction of signifier and signified.

For Saussure, language rather than speech is the object of the science of structural linguistics. The preexisting language system is assimilated, he argued, by the speaker and reproduced through the heterogeneous production of speech.

The production of meaning does not arise from a pregiven connection between the sign and the real world of objects. Rather, Saussure argued that signs are made up of a signifier (a sound or image) and a signified (the concept or meaning evoked). The meaning of a word arises through its differences from other words: a pencil, for example, is not a pen. Language creates meaning only through an internal play of differences.

Structuralism, and particularly poststructuralism, came to put more emphasis on the productive role of the signifier and less on the signified. The impact of Saussure's thought is especially evident in the work of **Claude Lévi-Strauss**, **Roland Barthes**, and **Jacques Lacan**.   ANTHONY ELLIOTT

scales

The investigation of **attitudes** is a prominent area in social research. One of the most common techniques for conducting such an investigation is through the use of scales. A scale consists of answers to a number of statements. The most widely used scale in social research is the Likert scale, named after Rensis Likert (1903–81) who developed the method in the 1930s to provide an ordinal-level measure of a person's attitude. In constructing a Likert scale, respondents are presented with a number of statements ("items"), some positively and some negatively phrased, and asked to rate each statement in terms of their agreement or disagreement. The reason for including both positively phrased and negatively phrased statements is to avoid the problem of the response set. The response set, otherwise known as the acquiescent-response **bias**, is the tendency for some people to answer a large number of items in the same way (usually agreeing) out of laziness or a psychological predisposition. Typically, responses are scored using five-point bipolar categories, such as strongly agree, agree, neither agree nor disagree, disagree, and strongly disagree. An "alpha coefficient" can be calculated to assess the reliability of the item battery.

The following two statements, designed to measure attitudes towards providing sex **education** for young people, will illustrate this process.

1 Sex education helps young people prepare for married life.
2 Sex education encourages experimentation and promiscuity among young people.

For each item, respondents were asked whether they: strongly agree, agree, neither agree nor disagree, disagree, strongly disagree, or don't know. Note, in this example, the additional category of "don't know" was included in the response set. Although researchers have debated whether or not to offer a "don't know," or no-opinion category, as a general rule it is better to offer this nonattitude (no opinion) choice, as it allows researchers to distinguish between those who hold a genuinely neutral opinion (neither agree nor disagree) from those without any opinion.

Likert scales are called summated-rating or additive scales because a person's score on the scale is computed by summing the number of responses the person gives. In other words, each item is assumed to have equal weight and the final score is determined by simply adding up the various subscores to all the separate items. Thus, while simplicity and ease of use of the Likert scale is its greatest strength, some important limitations include the assumption of equal intensity in opinion (all items are weighted equally) as well as its lack of reproducibility (different combinations of several scale items can result in the same overall score).

The Bogardus scale, otherwise known as a social-distance scale, is now one of the most widely used techniques in measuring attitudes towards ethnic **groups**. Developed in the 1920s by Emory Bogardus (1882–1973) to measure the willingness of members of different ethnic groups to associate with each other, it can also be used to see how close or distant individuals feel towards some other group (for example, religious minorities or immigrants). The scale has a simple logic. People respond to a series of ordered statements: those that are the most threatening are at one end, and those that are least threatening are at the other end. The scale is considered unidimensional in that each item is assumed to measure the same underlying concept and there is no set number of statements required; the usual number ranges from five to nine. An example of a Bogardus scale to assess how willing individuals are to associate with immigrants would ask respondents how comfortable they feel with the following statements:

1 Immigrants entering your country;
2 Immigrants living in your **community**;
3 Immigrants living in your **neighborhood**;
4 Immigrants as personal friends; and
5 Immigrants marrying a member of your **family**.

Social-distance scales are considered cumulative scales in that, unlike Likert scales, there is a relationship between the pattern of item response and the total score. In other words, the logic of the scale assumes that individuals who refuse contact or are uncomfortable with the more socially distant items (immigrants entering your country) will also refuse the socially closer items (an immigrant marrying a member of your family).

Another form of cumulative scaling is the Guttman scale. Developed by Louis Guttman (1916–87) in the 1940s, these scales are considered strictly unidimensional and list items in order of favorableness. A frequently cited example of a Guttman scale measuring attitudes towards abortion is the following:

1 Abortion is acceptable under any circumstances;
2 Abortion is an acceptable mechanism for family planning;
3 Abortion is acceptable in cases of rape;
4 Abortion is acceptable if the fetus is found to be seriously malformed; or
5 Abortion is acceptable if the mother's life is in danger.

A respondent who agrees with the first statement is assumed to agree with subsequent statements. In fact, if you know a respondent's final score, it should be possible to reproduce his or her responses to all the scale items. This feature is called reproducibility and, when constructing Guttman scales, a coefficient of reproducibility is calculated to determine the extent to which the scale conforms to this requirement.

The semantic differential was developed by Charles E. Osgood (1916–) in the 1950s to provide an indirect measure of how an individual feels about a concept, object, or person. The technique measures subjective feelings towards a person or thing by using adjectives. Because most adjectives have polar opposites – good/bad – it uses polar opposite adjectives to create a rating measure or scale. To use a semantic differential, respondents are presented with a list of paired opposite adjectives, usually with a continuum of seven to eleven points between them. Each respondent marks the spot on the continuum between the adjectives that expresses their feelings. The adjectives can be very diverse and should be well mixed. In other words, positive items should not be located mostly on either the right or the left side. The semantic differential has been used for many purposes. An example of a semantic differential scale measuring attitudes towards political parties would include the following:

Weak __ __ __ __ __ __ __ Strong
Right-wing __ __ __ __ __ __ __ Left-wing
Loser __ __ __ __ __ __ __ Winner.

BERNADETTE HAYES AND ROBERT MILLER

scarcity

In economics and classical **political economy**, this concept is central to **rational choice theory**.

Scarcity is the key assumption behind the notion that in the **market** the competition between individuals over scarce resources forces them to specialize and to economize. The principal criterion of **rationality** involves the rational allocation of resources in a context of scarcity of means to satisfy **human needs** in order to maximize outcomes. Marginal utility theory is the rational allocation of an extra unit of effort for the satisfaction of a want or need via scarce means, and market equilibrium is achieved when individuals' wants are satisfied. What causes scarcity? In classical economics, it was assumed that scarcity is a consequence of the fact that nature cannot provide enough resources to satisfy human wants. In the classical demographic argument of **Thomas Robert Malthus**, nature is a constant, and unregulated population growth results in pestilence and famine. Human beings must exercise sexual restraint in order to match population growth against fixed resources. Scarcity compels people to limit their (sexual) desires. The alternative view, which was implicit in much of the work of the **Frankfurt School**, is that scarcity is socially produced and that **capitalism** artificially inflates human propensity to consume. The crises of the capitalist mode of production are often interpreted therefore as consequences in the unstable relationship between production and **consumption**. The British economist **John Maynard Keynes** argued that economic slumps could be resolved by state investment in utilities, such as building roads to stimulate the **economy** during depressions. Both **Karl Marx** and Keynes rejected Say's Law in which a given level of supply necessarily created a specific level of demand. The problem of the capitalist economy was the tendency to underconsume. In mature capitalist economies, **unemployment** is caused by a deficiency in effective demand because over-saving occurs as a result of the relative abundance of capital. The correct anticyclical government policies included the creation of "cheap money" through interest rate manipulation and the use of budget deficits through deficit financing.

In a **consumer society**, desires are created by advertising and capitalist goods are important, not because they satisfy our primary needs for **food** and shelter, but because they satisfy our desire for **social status**. Contemporary **culture** does not appear to require the Protestant Ethic of **Max Weber**'s sociology of the ascetic spirit of economic growth, namely abstaining from consumption in order to save. The idea that in modern society people struggle for control of symbolic goods has been developed by sociologists such as **Pierre Bourdieu** in the theory of cultural capital. Some social theorists such as **Jean Baudrillard** have argued that modern society is based on waste and excess rather than scarcity, and hence the economy of an advanced capitalist society operates on a different logic of production and consumption.

Whereas classical economics, including Marxian economics, was based on the assumption of limited natural resources (such as agricultural land), contemporary sociological analysis has begun to raise important questions about waste and non-renewable resources that challenge conventional notions about development and economic growth. N. Georgescu-Roezen in *The Entropy Law and the Economic Process* (1971), employing the second law of thermodynamics (the so-called entropy law) and developing the notion of "entropic depletion," argued that the exhaustion of the earth's resources cannot be ultimately overcome because waste is unavoidable. To some extent, we can regard pessimistic assessments of an environmental crisis, depletion, and exhaustion as a neo-Malthusian vision of global scarcity.　　　　　　　　　　BRYAN S. TURNER

scatter diagram
– see **regression**.

Scheff, Thomas J. (dates unknown)
An emeritus professor at the University of California, Santa Barbara. Scheff obtained his PhD in 1960 from Berkeley. He has made substantial contributions to the sociology of mental illness and to **social psychology**, and is a pioneering researcher and the theorist in the sociology of **emotions**. His contributions to sociological **methodology** are also significant. His first book, *Being Mentally Ill: A Sociological Theory* (1966), introduced an interactionist frame to the study of mental illness, by accounting for clinical symptoms in terms of **social role** and proposing "societal reaction" as a determinant of entry into that role. From the late 1980s, Scheff's contribution to the then new sociology of emotions was highly significant. A landmark paper, "Shame and Conformity" (1988) in the *American Sociological Review*, argued that **shame** is the predominant social emotion, operating below the threshold of awareness in determining behavior. Practically all of Scheff's work since is an exploration of the nature and consequences of shame in **social systems**, both theoretically and historically. In *Microsociology: Discourse, Emotion and Social Structure* (1990) the determining importance

of pride and shame for a range of social processes is demonstrated. The application of Scheff's approach is later extended to the macroscopic level, covering the historical orgins of World Wars I and II in *Bloody Revenge: Emotions, Nationalism, and War* (1994) and of destructive conflicts more generally in *Emotions and Violence* (with Suzanne Retzinger, 1991). Among his other works are *Catharsis in Healing, Ritual and Drama* (1979) and *Emotions, the Social Bond, and Human Reality* (1997).

JACK BARBALET

Schumpeter, Joseph Alois (1883–1950)
Born in the Austro-Hungarian Empire and educated as an economist at the University of Vienna, Schumpeter served as Finance Minister of Austria in 1919–20. In 1932 Schumpeter left for the United States, where he worked at Harvard University till his death.

Joseph Schumpeter's ideas about **entrepreneurship** and his theory of **democracy** constitute his two most important contributions to **social science**. Schumpeter is also the author of two well-known works on business cycles and the history of economic analysis.

Schumpeter's most important work in economics is *The Theory of Economic Development* (1911 [trans. 1934]), which contains his famous theory of entrepreneurship. Entrepreneurship, Schumpeter suggests, can be defined as the putting together of a new combination of already existing elements. Innovations include the creation of a new **market**, a new product, and the like. What drives the entrepreneur is not so much money as the desire to be creative, to outdo one's competitors, and to create one's own empire.

Capitalism, Socialism and Democracy (1942) contains a famous analysis of "creative destruction" and the United States **economy**. It is most famous, however, for its critique of the existing theory of democracy and for Schumpeter's related attempt to create an alternative theory. According to the old theory, democracy is about realizing the will of the people. The new theory, in contrast, views democracy as a competition among leaders for the vote of the masses.

At the time of his death Schumpeter was working on a massive history of economics that was published posthumously as *History of Economic Analysis* (1954). This work is remarkable in many respects, including the fact that it is rare that a major figure in social science writes the history of his own discipline; Schumpeter's work also contains a full vision of what he terms "social economics," consisting of economic theory, economic history, economic sociology, and economic **statistics**.   RICHARD SWEDBERG

Schutz, Alfred (1899–1959)

Born in Austria, Schutz emigrated to the United States in 1939. He was instrumental in the development of phenomenological sociology, and his academic work was devoted to improving the sociological understanding of the **lifeworld**. He used the resources of the **phenomenology** of the German philosopher Edmund Husserl (1895–1938) to provide a better understanding of the philosophical underpinnings of the **social sciences**. He was critical of **Max Weber**'s theory of **social action** and interpretation, and he sought to understand how a theory of action could become scientific. His central argument was that sociology must understand how social actors use typification to organize their commonsense knowledge of the lifeworld and to grasp the basic differences between everyday and scientific knowledge. This phenomenological research involves the study of the relevance of different forms of knowledge to social action.

His principal publications were posthumously collected in four volumes as *Collected Papers* (1971). These were *The Problem of Social Reality* (1962, vol. I), *Studies in Social Theory* (1964, vol. II), *Studies in the Phenomenology of Philosophy* (1966, vol. III), and *Collected Papers* (1996, vol. IV). His other publications include *The Structures of the Life World* (1973 and 1989, 2 vols.) and *Reflections on the Problem of Relevance* (1970).

Schutz served at the New School for Social Research in New York from 1944 to 1951 as Visiting Professor, and from 1952 as Professor until his death in 1959. Despite his involvement in the New School, Schutz was marginal to professional sociology in the United States, partly because his commitment to European phenomenology was increasingly incompatible with the growth of **empiricism**.

He has had a profound influence on the theory of action, for example in his debate with **Talcott Parsons** in *The Theory of Social Action: The Correspondence of Alfred Schutz and Talcott Parsons* (1978) and *Philosophers in Exile: The Correspondence of Alfred Schutz and Aron Gurwitsch 1939–1959* (1989). He was also influential in the development of the sociology of knowledge in the work of **Peter L. Berger** and **Thomas Luckmann**.   BRYAN S. TURNER

Science and Technology Studies

This title names a heterogeneous body of research, scholars, journals, professional associations, and academic programs that focus on the history, social organization, and **culture** of science and **technology**. Begun in the 1960s in response to the recognizable growth in science in the contemporary world and to the educational and economic policy implications of this explosion of scientific research and development, Science and Technology Studies (STS) also responded to issues of public responsibility that seemed to be engendered by technological innovation.

Significant accounts of the work of scientists, the accumulation of scientific knowledge, and the impact of technological innovation had been produced in each of the **social sciences** from their distinctive disciplinary perspectives by the 1960s, generating a "focused confluence" begging for integration, according to David Edge in "Reinventing the Wheel" (*Handbook of Science and Technology Studies*, 1995: 3–24). Across the diverse research traditions, there seemed to be, however, a shared or received view of science as the work of great minds, usually male, discovering nature's hidden patterns and mechanisms. This is often viewed as a bounded activity in which science impacts society, technology – as applied science – develops linearly from (basic) science, and the entire process is regarded as a value-free, amoral enterprise that is legitimated by the claims both that its truths exist independent of, and prior to, any social **authority** and that it provides the grounds of human **progress**. This "internalist" account describes an essentially autonomous and asocial process consistent with positivistic philosophies of science as a self-regulated search for timeless, universal, irrefutable facts. Facts are themselves understood, in this received or traditional conception of science, to exist independent of the procedures for making or discovering them. Sal Restivo in *Science, Technology and Society* (2005) has argued that "Scientific facts were considered to exist in a realm outside of the blood, sweat and tears of our everyday sensual and material world, outside of history, outside of society and culture."

By the 1960s, however, few realms of human action were immune from acknowledgment of their historicity, including science. Within each of the traditional social science disciplines (history, philosophy, sociology, economics, anthropology, and political science), germs of a more complex understanding of science and technology were developing. Despite diverse theoretical, pragmatic, and disciplinary sources, science and technology studies seemed to force an orienting consensus that science is a social **institution**. Although it had long been clear that science and technology impact society, an impact that was already documented in historical scholarship and economic development, science and technology studies began by exploring the ways in which social forces constitute not only the context of science (for example the organization and dissemination of science) but also the content and substance of scientific knowledge itself.

Importantly, science and technology studies developed not only a more complex but also a more critical stance towards science and technology, emerging simultaneously with periods of intense public skepticism towards the roles of science and technology as an aspect of the growth of anti-military sentiments against American involvement in the Vietnam War in the United States in the 1960s and 1970s, and the growing anti-nuclear and environmental movements in the United Kingdom and Europe in the 1980s. The constructivist position that social forces constitute not only the context but also the content of science developed first in Europe and spread from there. Alongside this more socially engaged scholarship (for example in Donald MacKenzie's "Tacit Knowledge, Weapons Design and the Uninvention of Nuclear Weapons," *American Journal of Sociology*, 1995: 44–99), research moved away from the more traditional periodization and research foci (for example the scientific revolution, Darwinian revolution, or Quantum Revolution) that occupied historians of European science. As STS develops, scholars become interested in science outside of Europe and also more interested in activities not heretofore categorized as science by contemporary scientists, such as the alchemical interests of both Newton and Boyle, and the relationship of these to the works that are taken to have made the scientific revolution, or the ways in which mathematical equations are understood in some African cultures (Betty Jo Teeter Dobbs, *The Foundations of Newton's Alchemy*, 1975; Lawrence Principe, *The Aspiring Adept: Robert Boyle and His Alchemical Quest*, 1998; Helen Verran, *Science and an African Logic*, 2001). No longer do scholars regard it as appropriate to isolate the elements of scientists' work that have over time proven useful and scientifically productive, discarding what modern science has rejected as aberrational or simply wrong. STS attempt to produce fuller, more comprehensive and complex accounts of science, its methods, and its subject matter.

By the 1980s, it was well understood, and in some scholarly networks taken for granted, that science is in this regard the same as all other human activities, a socially constructed phenomenon: the product of collectively organized human **labor** and decisionmaking.

> Facts do not fall out of the sky, they are not "given" to us directly, we do not come to them by means of revelation . . . [W]ork is embodied in the fact, just as the collective toil of the multitude of workers in Rodin's workshop is embodied in *The Thinker*. This is what it means to say that a fact is socially constructed. (Restivo, 2005: xiii).

This does not mean that any statement can secure the status of scientific fact; social construction is not a recipe for cognitive solipsism or moral relativism. Nor does it mean that scientific facts are completely arbitrary accidents. It means only that scientific facts are contingent: the ways in which a fact is produced – the choice of topic, location of research, the constraints of resources, the accumulation of empirical evidence, the transparency of methods – are part of the constitution or construction of the fact. Scientific facts are produced under constraints that vary historically and culturally; thus scientific inquiry is both enabled and constrained by what is already known, by technological capacity and the material resources that are available, and human capacity for work, imagination, collaboration, and communication. Those constraints shape the content of the science as well as the process of producing that content.

Considerations of organization, resources, and human capacity seemed obvious with respect to technological innovation, but in the traditional disciplines were usually relegated to the boundaries of science or the social conditions of its making. STS rejected the notion of a natural or fixed boundary between science and its context. What became known as "boundary work" – the discourses and practices of institutional **legitimacy** and exclusion – became a central focus of STS research tracking the human transactions – symbolic and material – that shaped scientific facts and membership in scientific **communities** (for example in Thomas Gieryn, *The Cultural Boundaries of Science*, 1999). Similarly, any hard and fast distinction between basic science and applied technology became difficult to sustain, once the work of scientists and engineers is closely observed. The advance of modern physics, for example, is described as a productive collaboration between theory, instrumentation, and experiment in Peter Galison, *Image and Logic* (1997). Finally, any hard and fixed division between the disciplinary approaches to the production or reception of science began to merge in important studies. Steven Shapin and Simon Schaffer's influential book, *Leviathan and the Air-Pump* (1985), encouraged scholars to move among the historical, anthropological, and sociological approaches to the study of science and technology.

Yet this social constructivist orientation probably claims more than some in the field would admit, and has been the source of shared interests as well as extended controversy among science and technology scholars and between the field and the practitioners they study: scientists, engineers, and policymakers. As in any other field of cultural production, as described by **Pierre Bourdieu**, STS is constituted more by its oppositions and debates than by any shared theoretical **paradigm**, set of research questions, or canon of readings. However, STS may be more fractious than many other scholarly fields or interdisciplinary engagements. Because STS scholarship takes the creation of knowledge as its subject of study, it has been hyper-reflexive about its own knowledge production practices, leading to extended yet insightful debate. Sometimes referred to as the science wars, these scholarly disputes suffused much of academia in the 1990s where they went by a more generic label as culture wars. One line of cleavage developed about the strength and depth of the constructivist position and the sufficiency of internalist histories of science. Another derives from the conjunction of science and technology within the same intellectual rubric, and yet other lines of cleavage develop from epistemological debates and professional competitions among the constituent disciplines. This self-reflexive critique in a heterogeneous joining of topics and disciplines has produced an abundance of shorthand expressions and acronyms to describe the distinctive camps and orientations. For example, some observers distinguish the scholarship of STS from the subject being studied, the latter a subject that can be studied via STS or through any traditional discipline such as history, sociology, or philosophy without adopting any particular epistemological position with regard to the social construction of science. Those who focus on the sociology of scientific knowledge (SSK) distinguish themselves from those who examine the social construction of technology (SCOT) or the social history of technology (SHOT). The STS coalition probably bespeaks more about the marginality of science and technology to the central concerns of the constituent disciplines than to any necessary or comfortable marriage between the study of science and of technology or across the disciplinary perspectives. Because

the history, social organization, and logic of science has been a topic of minor interest for each of the disciplines – in comparison, for example, to concerns about state development, inequality, freedom – scholarly communities addressing science and/or technology in each discipline were relatively small and perhaps particularly guarded.

Nonetheless, the divergent perspectives and heated debates have energized the field, producing an abundant literature in books and academic journals (for example *Social Studies of Science* for science studies generally, *Isis* for the history of science, *Science, Technology and Human Values* covering contemporary science, policy, and culture, *History and Technology*, *Science in Context*, *Minerva*, *Osiris*, *Technology and Culture*, *Studies in History and Philosophy of Science*, and a wide range of specialized and regional publications such as *Metascience*, *Science Studies*, *Knowledge and Technology in Society*, *Public Understandings of Science*, *History of Science*, *Philosophy of Science*, *British Journal of the Philosophy of Science*, *British Journal of the History of Science*, *Science for the People*, and *Science Technology and Société*); a substantial network of professional associations (for example the Society for the Social Studies of Science, Society for the History of Technology, ICOHETEC [International Committee for the History of Technology], HSS [History of Science Society], IASTS [International Association for Science, Technology and Society]); and dozens of departments offering undergraduate and advanced degrees in STS.

STS research covers an enormous array of topics, most of which can be subsumed within two very general rubrics: (1) the institutionalization, reception, and appropriation of science and technology; and (2) the production of science and technology. With respect to the first aspect, interest in science and technology policy animated some of the first STS studies in the 1960s and led to a flourishing industry on scientific and technological controversies (for example Dorothy Nelkin, *Controversy, Politics of Technical Decisions*, 1979; Nelkin, *Atom Besieged*, 1982; and H. Tristan Engelhardt and Arthur L. Caplan, *Scientific Controversies*, 1987). Such work exposes the divergent theoretical assumptions, rival experimental designs, and contrary evidentiary interpretations, at the same time displaying the communally developed procedures for reaching closure on debate to restore continuity and consensus (Harry H. M. Collins and Trevor Pinch, *The Golem: What Everyone Should Know About Science*, 1993, 1998; *The Golem at Large: What Everyone Should Know About Technology*, 1998). Other lines of research in this general rubric focus on science institutions and funding; science **education** and public understandings of science; and, technological innovation, planning, and assessment. Closely related are studies of the role of science and science advising in government (for example Chandra Mukerji, *A Fragile Power*, 1989; Sheila Jasanoff, *The Fifth Branch*, 1990) and the role of scientific evidence in law (such as Roger Smith and Brian Wynne, *Expert Evidence: Interpreting Science in the Law*, 1989; Sheila Jasanoff, *Science at the Bar*, 1995; and Simon Cole, *Suspect Identities*, 2001). Using science to make policy, law, and property constitutes a thick strand of STS scholarship (see **law and society**). Since the 1980s, when American law changed markedly, allowing the results of publicly funded research to be patented and licensed, the institutional and distributional issues associated with technology licensing and transfer have been the subject of extensive research. These topics were present in the pre-STS work, primarily in political science and policy studies. STS contributed a critical dimension, revealing and unpacking the embedded, often unreflective claims of scientific expertise in law and elsewhere; at the same time, research explores the ways in which such expert **authority** is constructed and legitimated in and through government policies and programs (for instance in Brian Wynne, *Risk Management and Hazardous Wastes*, 1987; or Stephen Hilgartner, *Science on Stage*, 2000). STS scholars also study public and private systems of risk analysis in such diverse fields as weapons, environmental management, and financial **markets** (for example, Donald MacKenzie, *Inventing Accuracy*, 1990; Mackenzie, *Mechanizing Proof: Computing, Risk, and Trust*, 2001; Hugh Gusterson, *People of the Bomb*, 2004). Some, not all, of this research adopts a distinctly progressive, democratic stance, worrying about the consequences of concentrated expertise and public exclusion from critical decisions and the public responsibilities of science. This is an outgrowth of movements such as Science for the People that emerged as organized opposition to the American war in Vietnam; the movement and publications continue to this day in studies concerning such issues as genetically modified foods, explosion in the use and marketing of pharmaceuticals, as well as global warming and worldwide environmental degradation, unplanned growth, resource depletion, and **inequality**. Other works look at the human–machine interface from the point of view of instrument design as well as the role of technology, for example computers, in human relations and development (Sherry Turkle, *The Second Self*, 1984), while yet other research focuses on human

relations with animals or nature in general (for example Donna Haraway, *Primate Visions*, 1990; Bruno Latour, *Politics of Nature*, 2004). In essence, this thread of STS scholarship marries in-depth technical knowledge of particular scientific fields or pieces of technology with examinations of the public and private uses for business, management, government, and interpersonal relations.

The second general rubric of STS research looks more centrally at the production of science and technology than at their appropriation, distribution, regulation, and use. Beginning in the 1970s, anthropologists and sociologists undertook closely observed, ethnographic studies of laboratory practices, processes of scientific discovery, and technological invention. Subjecting scientists, and later engineers in work groups, to the same scrutiny and in-depth analysis of social organization, culture, and **epistemology** that anthropologists had long applied to small-scale, often pre-industrial **societies** and human **groups**, STS researchers produced rich descriptions of the unarticulated and often tacit understandings that made science and scientists. In this way, they demonstrated that science is not a distinct realm of **social action**, but is like other social settings, rife with conflict, compromise, pragmatic adjustments, and **power**, as well as taken-for-granted habits that make social settings transparent and familiar to socially competent members but alien and uninterpretable to non-member outsiders (**Bruno Latour** and Steve Woolgar, *Laboratory Life*, 1979; Sharon Traweek, *Beamtimes and Lifetimes*, 1988; Karin Knorr-Cetina, *The Manufacture of Knowledge*, 1981; Michael Lynch, *Art and Artifact in Laboratory Science*, 1985; Lynch, *Scientific Practice and Ordinary Action*, 1993; Harry Collins, *Changing Order*, 1992; Collins, *Gravity's Shadow: The Search for Gravitational Waves*, 2004; Joseph Dumit, *Picturing Personhood*, 2004). These studies built on and critiqued earlier research in the history and sociology of science that had identified functional, normative requisites for scientific communities (**Robert K. Merton**, *The Sociology of Science*, 1979) and the paradigmatic development of scientific theories (**Thomas Samuel Kuhn**, *The Structure of Scientific Revolutions*, 1962). While both Merton and Kuhn had described the structures of normal science, for example dialectical developments among theory, experimentation, and career advancement, STS scholars adopted insights from European **critical theory** to pay particularly close attention to the cumulative consequences of micro-transactions, discursive strategies, and forms of representation, as they produced a particular scientific fact or practice (for example David Kaiser, *Drawing Theories Apart*, 2005). These same perspectives and research methods were also adopted to study technological innovation, engineers, and designers (Hugh Gusterson, *Nuclear Rites*, 1996; Gary Lee Downey, *The Machine in Me: An Anthropologist Sits Among Computer Engineers*, 1998; Stefan Helmreich, *Silicon Second Nature: Culturing Artificial Life in a Digital World*, 1998; Katherine Henderson, *On Line and On Paper*, 1999; Trevor Pinch (with Frank Trocco), *Analog Days: The Invention and Impact of the Moog Synthesizer*, 2002; David Mindell, *Between Human and Machine: Feedback, Control and Computing before Cybernetics*, 2002). These closely observed studies of scientific and engineering practice have led to extensive research on processes of cognition and categorization (G. C. Bowker and S. L. Starr, *Sorting Things Out: Classification and Its Consequences*, 2000). Important work, such as Shapin and Schaffer (1985) showed that the mechanical experiments of Robert Boyle did not satisfy Thomas Hobbes's criteria for philosophical truth, and hence their work is a bridge between the philosophy of science and the sociology of knowledge.

These categories are organizing tools for identifying the variation within science and technology studies more than means for identifying the **information** and analysis within any particular text. Many studies can fit within both families of scholarship, looking at the production of science as well as its distribution, appropriation, and implications for particular groups or classes (for example, Londa Schiebinger, *The Mind Has No Sex? Women in the Origins of Modern Science*, 1989; *Has Feminism Changed Science?* 1999). Steven Epstein, for example, described the ways in which gay rights activists became expert analysts of the existing medical knowledge concerning AIDS when the epidemic first took hold and eventually became co-producers of new knowledge, especially treatment protocols in drug trials (Epstein, *Impure Science: AIDS, Activism, and the Politics of Knowledge*, 1998). The research of Emily Martin and Anne Fausto-Sterling responded to critiques of both the science and pseudo-science of **gender** and reproductive medicine while exploring both the production and appropriation of scientific knowledge (Martin, *Woman in the Body*, 1992; Anne Fausto-Sterling, *Myths of Gender*, 1992; Fausto-Sterling, *Sexing the Body*, 2000). The scholarly work on reproductive medicine and technology, like the work on AIDS (Acquired Immunodeficiency Syndrome), followed upon grass-roots activism that exposed the limitations, and often ideological or biased assumptions, of the then conventional

science in these areas. Similarly, Troy Duster has shown how biological research can be inadvertently used to feed racist policies, and how tacit assumptions can feed a research agenda (Duster, *Backdoor to Eugenics*, 1990, 2003).   SUSAN SILBEY

scientific management

This is the theory of **management** advanced by Frederick Winslow Taylor (1856–1915) in his book *The Principles of Scientific Management* (1911). This approach to the **rationalization** of the production process, as well as its modern-day successors, is often called **Taylorism.** Taylor proposed systematic management as a method for achieving national prosperity based on productivity growth. The economic-organizational context of the development of scientific management is the rise of the large **firm**, large-scale mechanized production, and the shift from control by ownership to control by the professionalizing class of managers in the late nineteenth- and twentieth-century industrial division of **labor**. Within this context the notion of scientific management represented by Taylor was not so much a complete innovation as it was a bringing-together and popularizing of a number of existing trends and new practices, including new methods of accounting, the employment of less-skilled workers (particularly in the United States), and moves to rationalize and formalize management methods. Unlike sociological **paradigms** that assume (group or individual-level) conflict, scientific management takes the true interests of employers and employees as identical. From this point of view, industrial conflict and its solution appear as a matter of proper **organization** through the application of scientific methods to work organization. Taylor's approach promised higher profits, long-term beneficial organizational development, and higher wages (based on the then fairly novel idea of systematic incentive pay) as the outcomes of efficient cooperation.

In scientific management, **automation** is not limited to machinery but extended to workers' behavior through extensive standardization. Taylor's system rests on close observation and control of the **labor process**. Applying time-and-motion studies to industrial organization (initially in one plant in 1881, where he developed his main approach), Taylor studied and proposed the breakdown of tasks into the smallest possible units of movement that could then be made quickly and repetitively. To obtain optimum output levels, the "one best method" identified in this way was to be applied by the person best suited to the task: Taylor's protagonist, a worker named Schmidt, showed a high work-rate and obedient following of procedure and for Taylor represented the best traits that a worker should possess. The **deskilling** and loss of autonomy implied by this procedure had the greatest effect on a specific class of workers, that of skilled craftsmen.

Taylor's book also implicitly presents a theory of **leadership**; it asserts the role of the new professionalizing group of managers, so the theory is also a legitimization project for the managerial class. Severe criticisms over the a-social view of humans, specifically non-managerial employees, in work organizations have been raised throughout the twentieth century from a range of social science disciplines, including from management scholars who have deemed Taylorism morally indefensible. Nevertheless, contemporary management theorists broadly regard Taylor's work as a classic of management theory, and consultancy. Taylor himself lectured and consulted widely with managers and academics and was responsible for the early spread and uptake of a range of methods of scientific management. ANN VOGEL

sect
– see **church–sect typology**.

secularization
This term is conceptualized differently by different scholars but for the most part refers to the constellation of historical and modern social processes that allegedly bring about the declining significance of **religion** in social **institutions**, public **culture**, and individual lives. The secularization thesis has its roots in the classical theorizing of both **Max Weber** and Émile Durkheim. Most notably, Weber argued that the increased **rationalization** of society – bureaucratization, scientific and technical **progress**, and the expanding pervasiveness of instrumental reason in all domains of **everyday life** – would substantively attenuate the scope of religion, both through the increased specialization of institutional spheres (of **family**, economy, law, **politics**) and as a result of disenchantment in the face of competing rationalized value spheres. Durkheim, although a strong proponent of the centrality of the sacred to society, nonetheless predicted that the integrative functions performed by church religion in traditional societies would increasingly be displaced in modern societies by the emergence of differentiated professional and scientific membership **communities** (see **sacred and profane dichotomy**). The secularization thesis, especially its Weberian understanding, was highly influential in the **paradigm** of **social**

change articulated by modernization theorists in the 1960s. These theorists argued that among the inevitable and linear societal processes associated with **modernization** – including **urbanization**, industrialization, the expansion of **education** and mass communication (see **mass media and communications**), and the increased autonomy of law and politics from traditional **authority** – religion would no longer have the authority that it allegedly commanded in traditional societies; it would become socially invisible (**Thomas Luckmann**) and lose plausibility (**Peter L. Berger**).

The modernization–secularization thesis was widely accepted by western sociologists and, though there were some exceptions (for example A. Greeley, *Unsecular Man*, 1972), many assumed a priori that religion had lost its significance in modern societies; whatever empirical evidence suggested otherwise was largely a vestige of a cultural lag that would soon disappear. Various societal factors, such as the increased public visibility of religious **social movements** in the United States, Iran, and Poland and intradisciplinary theoretical challenges to modernization theory, converged in the late 1970s and resulted in more complex and nuanced approaches to the study of secularization. Sociologists have been particularly vigorous in debating its meaning and measurement and investigating evidence for and against various indicators of secularization. The application of **rational choice theory** to religion has resulted in an intense debate about the ways in which competitive religious environments (religious economies) produce religious vitality and church growth. This paradigm rejects the assumptions of secularization theory as being more appropriate for the historically monopolized religious markets found in Europe but at odds with the American context of religious **pluralism** (R. S. Warner, "Work in Progress Toward a New Paradigm for the Sociological Study of Religion in the United States," 1993, *American Journal of Sociology*). Philip S. Gorski argues that credible empirical claims for either secularization or religious vitality need to be grounded in longer historical and broader geographical perspectives in assessing changes in religion over time ("Historicizing the Secularization Debate," in M. Dillon [ed.], *Handbook of the Sociology of Religion*, 2003).

Secularization today, then, should be understood in terms of a balance between extensive empirical evidence in favor of the continuing sociological significance of religion in the public domain and in individual lives, and the coexistence of these trends with equally valid empirical evidence indicating selectivity in the acceptance of religion's theological, moral, and political authority. Both sets of trends must necessarily be interpreted with a cautious and differentiated understanding of the nature and place of religion in earlier sociohistorical contexts, and with greater attentiveness to how the contextual meanings of religion and religious commitment change over time. Given the importance of religion, especially in political life, some sociologists, such as Berger, have argued against the secularization thesis that contemporary societies are going through a process of "resacralization."   MICHELE DILLON

Sedgwick, Eve Kosofsky (1950–)

A theorist who has made a major contribution to the understanding of the theoretical, conceptual, and emotional scaffolding of modern sexual sensibilities, Sedgwick was educated at undergraduate level at Cornell University and received her PhD from Yale University. Working from within the discipline of literary studies, Sedgwick's early work *Between Men: English Literature and Male Homosocial Desire* (1985) establishes the complexity of men's relationships in the Victorian era and focuses on the structured limits of homosocial relationships and homosexual desires. For example, Sedgwick highlights how male-to-male desire became channeled into a competing love triangle for the love of women. Sedgwick argues that increasing social circumscription of the expression of desire led to a reshaping of **gender** and sexual relations, something that is explored in greater depth in *Epistemology of the Closet* (1990). In this book, Sedgwick delivers an analysis of how the male homosexual–heterosexual binary has operated to authorize the possibilities of sexual **identities**. Central to this binary is a tension between a "minoritizing view" in which gay **identity** is part of an identifiable minority and a "universalizing view" in which same-sex desire is inherent in all men. Thus the "closet" is emblematic of gay identity operating to "haunt" and police an already fractured contemporary male heterosexuality. Deconstruction of the binaries that fail to hold sexual and gendered categories is explored further in her collection of essays, *Tendencies* (1994). More recently, her autobiographical work *A Dialogue on Love* (1999) is a more personal exploration of the tensions and incoherency of gender/sexual categories in her own **everyday life** and her hidden desires and fantasies.

MAIRTIN MAC-AN-GHAILL AND CHRIS HAYWOOD

segregation

This is a naturally occurring practice whereby **groups** or **social classes** in a dominant position enforce the social isolation of groups or classes stigmatized as inferior. The isolation is imposed to limit or deny access to basic social needs, including housing, jobs, **voting**, public accommodations, or the right to travel outside the segregated region or **ghetto**. The stigmata are arbitrarily made with reference to social differences such as **race**, **gender**, sexual orientation, class, **ethnicity**, or **politics**, or position in the world-system. Segregation is ubiquitous, occurring in virtually any social arrangement where there are identifiable marks of differences that can be used by those in **power** to enforce their social, economic, or political advantages or to limit their contact with the disadvantaged; such marks include physical or mental **disability**, **age**, and body weight. The practice is commonly *de facto* (for example social avoidance of persons with discrediting physical deformities), but more often is *de jure* (for instance, codes excluding children from **neighborhoods** reserved for the elderly).

The structural cause of segregation is the **scarcity** of social goods – for instance, **income**, social status, political power. The social goods may be material needs necessary to survival (for example water, **food**, shelter, health care) or immaterial desires (for example, status, respect, recognition, or club memberships). There is no known enduring **social structure** without scarcities of one or many kinds. Segregation is, therefore, a social means for organizing social **inequality** which, in academic sociology, is commonly referred to as the stratification system. In the modern era, segregation was thought to be a practice internal to discrete nation-states, but as **globalization** became more salient sociologists have come to understand segregation as a global practice (e.g., the economic and social segregation of impoverished, debtor nations in the global periphery by creditors in the core of the world-system).

The most notorious instances of segregation in the modern world were based on official policies of racial **discrimination**, for example in Zimbabwe (until 1980), South Africa (until 1991), and the American South (until after 1964). Racial segregation has its structural roots in the colonial system of the *de facto* or *de jure* slave **economies** extracting **wealth** and labor power from the colonized regions. Historically, *de jure* segregation has been ended by political, legislative, or judicial action (for example the independence of Rhodesia from British control [1980], the overthrow of the Group Areas Act in South Africa [1991], and the United States Civil Rights Act [1964]). With rare exceptions, de facto segregation seldom ends when discriminatory codes or laws are overturned; and in some instances legal or quasi-legal segregation is reestablished under a different name: for example, in the United States after the 1877 collapse of federal efforts to lend social and economic assistance to freed people, the Southern states restored a system of racial segregation known informally as Jim Crow. In effect the legalized slave-holding system was replaced with a quasi-legal system of social degradation that led to economic and political segregation. Racial segregation was recodified in the "separate but equal" ruling of the United States Supreme Court in *Plessey* v. *Ferguson* (1896), which remained in force until 1954. The Supreme Court's 1954 *Brown* v. *The Board of Education of Topeka* decision was, in effect, a reversal of *Plessey* v. *Ferguson* declaring segregated public **education** to be unconstitutional **discrimination**.

Desegregation seldom occurs without direct and frequently violent political action on the part of the segregated. In the United States, the civil rights movement began late in 1954, after *Brown* v. *The Board of Education* committed the federal government to desegregation. The civil rights movement mobilized **public opinion**, which led to the Civil Rights Act of 1964 (ending *inter alia* the segregation of public accommodations) and the Voting Rights Act of 1965 (striking down state laws preventing blacks from voting). Yet, the formal legal **rights** gained in 1964–5 did not extend to other segregated areas, notably economic rights. When the legal basis for segregation ends, de facto segregation usually continues until the social and political structures catch up with the law. Very often the interim is a period of renewed **violence** and social turmoil: for example, the end of the nonviolent phase of the American civil rights movement and the emergence of the more aggressive Black Power movement after 1966, the continuation of economic violence against blacks in South Africa under black majority rule after 1991, or the establishment of a totalitarian regime under Robert Mugabe in Zimbabwe after 1980.

In academic sociology, social movement theory and research was invigorated in the 1970s by the study of the struggle to end racial segregation. The civil rights movement inspired other social groups to engage in legal or political actions to end segregation as it affected them. As a result, the Black

Power, feminist, and gay rights movements, among others, are commonly referred to as new **social movements** and distinguished from the more traditional political movements by an emphasis on identity politics. New social movements are, thus, those in which political action is organized with respect to the recognition of the rights and differences of the segregated groups (for example "Black is beautiful"), with a corresponding decline in emphasis on universal principles of common humanity (for example integration of the races). The new social movements led, thereby, to discord in the ranks of liberal academics and political activists – between those favoring a politics of distribution after the traditional socialist or reform politics of the early decades of the twentieth century and those favoring a politics of recognition after the identity politics in the post-1960s era. Differences notwithstanding, both types of social movement are concerned with desegregating access to social goods, including rights; both are, therefore, movements intent upon advancing the inclusion of the segregated in the distribution of social goods which, in turn, can only occur when they are recognized as legitimate members of the social whole.

Under the political and legal conditions resulting from globalization, segregation is not as amenable to change because there is no court of international law with legitimate enforcement **authority**. Consequently, global segregation is primarily economic, as opposed to political. Yet, its social consequences are just as severe in the effects on women, **children**, homosexuals, and others who are more exposed to the segregating effects of **poverty** and its *sequelae*: hunger, disease, and civil strife. One recursive effect of global segregation is the rebirth of social segregation in **states** that require immigrant workers, who bring with them social differences unfamiliar or repellent to the host society.   CHARLES LEMERT

selection
– see **evolutionary theory**.

self
Insofar as **sociology** is defined as a science of **social action**, it will implicitly and more often explicitly develop an analysis of the agent and agency. The idea of the agent in sociology is related to more general philosophical debates about the self. Many undergraduate lecture courses in universities will have a foundation course that is called "The Self and Society," and the juxtaposition of self and **society** typically creates an

intellectual arena where there is an interdisciplinary interaction between psychology and sociology. Perhaps the most elegant presentations of the self and society notion have occurred in **symbolic interactionism**, but the debate about the characteristics of the self is obviously highly developed in philosophy, for example in accounts of the problem of free will and moral responsibility. Finally, it is often argued that the idea of an autonomous self is a specifically western development, and that Asian **traditions** have a more prominent notion of the collective and social **identity** of the individual. These contrasts between eastern and western notions of the self were explored by anthropologists such as **Louis Dumont**. Western **individualism** was probably best summarized in the famously provocative observation of the British Prime Minister Margaret Thatcher that there is no such thing as society, there are only individuals and their **families**.

In *The Idea of the Self*, Jerrold Seigel (2005) has argued that any theory of the self will have three components. To be a self, we need self consciousness, that is we must be able to reflect upon our identities, our actions, and our relationships with others. This consciousness requires **language** and memory. Selfhood must have a capacity for continuous self-assessment and monitoring. Second, the self is not a free-floating consciousness, because the self is also defined by embodiment. Recognition of the self depends not simply on memory and consciousness but also on the peculiar physical characteristics of the individual. This aspect of the discourse of the self is obviously the **body**, and recent sociology has insisted that the self involves an embodied subjectivity towards the world. In the theories of **Pierre Bourdieu**, the individual is expressed through a particular **habitus** that contains their dispositions and tastes. The final dimension of this model is the notion of the self as a historical product of society and that the self is always situated within social relationships. The western self has often been represented in the isolated figure of Robinson Crusoe, but sociology has interpreted the self as inextricably social. Although different theories tend to emphasize particular aspects of the self – reflection, embodiment, or social relationships – most theories of the self have necessarily to address, directly or indirectly, all three aspects.

While Seigel's theory is concerned mainly with the analytical dimensions of the self, these three dimensions can be seen from a historical perspective. Thus, the reflective self was dominant in the eighteenth and nineteenth centuries as a consequence of the **Enlightenment**, after the challenge from Immanuel Kant (1724–1804) to throw off traditional, especially religious, constraints on the individual self. The Romantic reaction placed greater emphasis on individuality, subjectivity, and embodiment, against the rational world of Kantian Enlightenment. The rise of the idea of the social in **industrial society** and the emergence of **sociology** as a science were criticized by **Hannah Arendt** as signs of modern **totalitarianism**. **Modernization** paved the way for sociology and the view that the individual is merely a product of social forces. This view of the passive self which dominated the middle of the twentieth century was articulated in **sociological theories** of **mass society**, the **managerial revolution**, and the other-directed self. The individual became reflexive rather than merely reflective. The corporeal self is the dominant **paradigm** of contemporary society, because the scientific revolutions in information science, microbiology, and **genetics** have created a language of genetic determinism in which the self no longer exercises agency. The "criminal gene" and the "divorce gene" now obscure any recognition of individual reflexivity and responsibility. The individual self is now thought to be driven by whatever genes they have fortuitously inherited.

Sociology has characteristically defined the self as simply the product of **socialization** and social relationships (such as **Charles Horton Cooley**'s "looking-glass self"). **Émile Durkheim** is the classical representative of this **tradition**, because he argued that the moral life of the individual was completely dependent on society, and that without such social regulation the life of the individual would be one of **anomie**. For Durkheim, the individual was the product of the collective, and morals had a decisive force because they are social facts – they have the moral **authority** of the collective. In Durkheim's sociological theory, this position is worked out in *Suicide* (1951) where too little integration results in egoistical behavior and too much regulation produces fatalistic suicide. The moral individual has to balance excessive egoistical and excessive altruistic behavior. This tradition was later reinforced in **Erving Goffman**'s *The Presentation of the Self in Everyday Life* (1959) in which the self merely learns a social script that has to be delivered within a dramaturgical setting. But this interpretation of the sociological tradition is superficial. Like the western tradition as a whole, sociology has struggled conceptually with the contradictions between **social action**, **social structure**, and the reflective self. The analytical solutions to this theoretical quandary of **agency and structure** have in recent sociology been extensively explored by **Anthony Giddens** in his structuration theory.

The idea of the self can be distinguished from, but is related to, the notions of "the individual" and "individualism." N. Abercrombie, S. Hill, and B. S. Turner, in *Sovereign Individuals of Capitalism* (1986), made a conceptual distinction between notions of the individual or self, the rise of individualism, and the processes of individuation. The rise of the idea of the individual self is associated with the development of **capitalism**. The relationship between Protestantism, individualism, and capitalism was explored by **Max Weber**. Modern sociology has, in approaching the self, emphasized issues relating to **intimacy, sexuality**, and subjectivity. Giddens, *The Transformation of Intimacy* (1992) and Ulrich Beck and Elizabeth Gernsheim-Beck, *The Normal Chaos of Love* (1995) are pertinent illustrations. The self in modern society is charged with emotional eroticism. Beck and Gernsheim-Beck (1995) argue that love is now our "secular **religion**," and claim that as religion loses its hold, people seek solace in private sanctuaries, but this sociological interpretation fails to recognize that modern erotic, sentimental love is itself part of the legacy of the Protestant conversionist sects. This emotional component of religious experience entered Protestantism in eighteenth-century England specifically from the evangelical preaching of John Wesley (1703–91) and the emotional hymns of Charles Wesley (1707–88). This emotional trend in Christian spirituality depends on German pietism. Friedrich Schleiermacher (1768–1834) defended religion against the rationalist criticisms of the Enlightenment, and argued that religious feelings of dependence on God are the foundation of religious faith. This religious tradition was the foundation of the modern notion that private and intimate experiences are fundamental to the authentic self, and that social relations such as **marriage** are primarily about establishing satisfactory social **interactions** of companionship.

What **Talcott Parsons** in "Religion in Postindustrial America: The Problem of Secularization" (*Social Research*, 1974) called "the expressive revolution" was closely related to subjective individualism in popular **culture** and the importance of choice in **lifestyles** and **values**. The new quest cultures have been critically evaluated as forms of expressive individualism. This American religious revolution involved a shift from the cognitive-instrumental values of early capitalism to an affective–expressive culture. Individuals are free to reinvent themselves and refashion themselves constantly and self-consciously. The expressive revolution signified in the student rebellions of the 1960s a new cultural movement that was a significant departure from the asceticism that Weber had described in *The Protestant Ethic and the Spirit of Capitalism* (1905 [trans. 2002]). The expressive revolution celebrated hedonism, self-expression, and hostility to conventional **norms** and social **institutions**. The language of personal freedom in the 1960s had largely evaporated by the end of the century, and had been replaced by a return to determinism in the language of genetic causation.

BRYAN S. TURNER

self-government rights
– see **rights**.

Selznick, Philip (1919–)
Selznick's work brings together questions about **organizations**, law (see **law and society**), and moral philosophy to explore the fate of ideals, their realization in the world, and the moral competence of **institutions**. *TVA and the Grass Roots* (1949), a classic of institutional theory and analysis, extended and critiqued extant theories of **bureaucracy** by identifying modes of co-optation to dominant **authority**, but also resistance that could counteract the centralizing authoritative tendencies of bureaucratic organizations. His central foci – on rules, procedures, purpose, **value**, authority, responsiveness, and the significance of institutionalization – in early studies, including *The Organizational Weapon* (1952) on the strategies and tactics of the Communist Party, and *Leadership in Organization* (1957), were specifically elaborated in *Law, Society and Industrial Justice* (1980). Selznick describes legality, a term he uses for the rule of law, as an imperfectly institutionalized ideal for limiting arbitrariness. Legality is a practical **norm** of variable instantiation. Selznick argued that when an aspect of the law does not meet a set of ideal standards, it can be said to be wanting in legality. However, it does not as a result cease to be part of the law. *Law and Society in Transition* (1976, with Philippe Nonet) attempts to reintegrate legal, political, and **social theory** through an analysis of the development of distinct legal/political orders by recasting "jurisprudential issues in a social science perspective." In *The Moral Commonwealth* (1992) and *Communitarianism and Citizenship* (1998), Selznick explores the possibilities for social connection in **community** as the basis of well-being. After brief appointments at the University

of Minnesota and the University of California, Los Angeles, Selznick has since 1952 been a professor at the University of California, Berkeley, where he was the founding Chair of the Center for Jurisprudence and Social Policy and the Center for Law and Society. Selznick's cumulative work has been a search for responsive law and governance, humane institutions, and a sensible balance between freedom and communal life. SUSAN SILBEY

semiotics

A science of signs that seeks to understand how signification occurs in **language**, this term was invented by the English philosopher John Locke (1632–1704). Modern theories of signs are concerned with how human communication is possible. Language is regarded as a system of signs or a discourse, and this general notion of language allows sociologists to regard all cultural communication as a language. For example, a boxing match can be defined as a language in which the blows falling on the boxers are also forms of communication, in which the boxing match can be read as a language of competition or **violence**. Specific semiotics refers to such local languages, whereas a general semiotics is the theory of what these various languages have in common. In European philosophy, semiotics is often referred to as "semiology" which was developed by the linguistic philosopher **Ferdinand de Saussure** in *Course in General Linguistics* (1916 [trans. 1974]) and in many respects laid the foundation for modern **structuralism**. He distinguished between "langue" (the grammatical rules of language) and "parole" (the actual production of speech), and between the signifier (the sound or expression) and the signified (the concept). He also argued that signs are arbitrary, their functions are determined by the structure of the sign system, and language involves a system of differences. The meaning of a particular unit of communication only makes sense in terms of its relationship to all the other units, and in particular to its opposites. **Émile Durkheim**'s distinction between the sacred and the profane in *The Elementary Forms of Religious Life* (1912 [trans. 2001]) can be regarded as a semiotic analysis of religious mythologies. Saussure's semiology ignores the social context of language, and hence social semiotics emerged to understand how discourses operate in their social context. Saussures's theory of semiotics came eventually to have a significant impact on the development of **cultural studies** and media studies. In cultural studies, anthropological **methodology** was applied to the understanding of urban **cultures**, which were interpreted through structuralist

methods that exposed the "cultural plots" that inform the "narratives" of modern cultural phenomena (such as football matches, films, and festivals). These methods were also called "narratology" because they sought understanding through unweaving the stories of modern societies. For example, **Roland Barthes** employed semiology to analyze contemporary cultural practices such as **fashion**. Modern society can be interpreted as a system of such languages or *Mythologies* (Barthes, 1957 [trans. 1972]) and hence semiotics has contributed to the contemporary reformulation of the notion of "**ideology**." BRYAN S. TURNER

Sennett, Richard (1943–)

Born in Chicago, Sennett began his career as a musician. Having taught in New York, he is currently Professor of Sociology at the London School of Economics. His research has been concerned with the changing nature of **work** in **capitalism** and its impact on the working class, especially on their **emotions**, aspirations, and expectations. Four publications have studied the negative impact of work and its organization on workers: *The Hidden Injuries of Class* (Sennett and Jonathan Cobb, 1972); *Authority* (1980); *The Corrosion of Character. The Personal Consequences of Work in the New Capitalism* (1998); and *Respect. The Formation of Character in an Age of Inequality* (2003). Sennett has also been interested in the changing quality of urban life and the organization of the **city** in *Families Against the City* (1970), *The Uses of Disorder* (1973), and *Flesh and Stone* (1994) in which he explored the sensory deprivation of individuals in the modern urban environment. His sociology as a whole can be described as an inquiry into the emotional bonds of modern society, and their erosion by the transformation of industrial capitalism. His most influential book was *The Fall of Public Man* (1974) in which he argued that the loss of formal codes of behavior in public and the growth of superficial forms of **intimacy** between strangers have produced a loss of civility. BRYAN S. TURNER

service class
– see **social class**.

sex
– see **sexualities**.

sexism

This term is used to describe those social processes and **social structures** that demonstrate a **prejudice** towards the interests of one sex rather than another. The term is most generally used to describe the ways in which women have been depicted in derogatory and demeaning ways by a particular **culture**, the mass media (see **mass media and communications**), or particular social **institutions**. The term acquired a general resonance in the West in the 1970s when feminists campaigned against the use of highly sexualized images of women in advertising and the media; similarly general campaigns at the same time targeted those visual images of women which were either deliberately pornographic or part of the more subtle male "gaze." At the same time as numerous targets throughout the media were found to be "sexist," the public awareness of the term – and the issues related to it – enhanced a more general social understanding of the ways in which **language**, all forms of communication, and cultural assumptions can contain ideas which prioritize the interests of men rather than women. The campaigns of the 1970s about the unthinking acceptance of the male as the definitive human form have now given way to a more complex understanding of the way in which individual behavior is shaped by conventional expectations of **gender**. The majority of western societies have now accepted the existence of sexism as an unacceptable part of social behavior and have attempted to put in place "gender-blind" practices and language for public institutional contexts. These practices have, in certain contexts, been reinforced by legislation that effectively criminalizes any explicit **bias** towards one sex, or sexual **identity**, rather than another.   MARY EVANS

sexual abuse

The concept of sexual abuse covers a wide range of behaviors from rape to indecent molestation; it also covers physical acts which may be life-threatening, as well as forms of verbal harassment which may be psychologically and emotionally damaging rather than physically harmful. The current social concern with sexual abuse dates back to the 1970s in the United Kingdom and the United States, although it should not be forgotten that throughout the twentieth century there were recurrent concerns about such things as stranger abuse, the sexual predator, and what used to be referred to as "interference" with **children**. The scientific study of what is now called sexual abuse began in the 1880s with the work of Krafft Ebing, who in *Psychopathia Sexualis* (1886) created a taxonomy of sexual deviations. His taxonomy listed behaviors which would now be defined as abusive alongside practices which would now be seen as harmless or simply unusual. In this way he set the tone for later research which treated harmful

behavior such as father/daughter incest as a sexual perversion rather than as an abuse of **power** and **trust**. Treating sexual abuse as if it was a sexual deviation had the effect of eliminating the "victim" from social concern; indeed the victim was often just seen as a partner in immoral behavior. This means that a person who, in the twenty-first century, might be understood to be a victim of a **crime**, was in the nineteenth century more likely to be seen as immoral and culpable. Social and cultural definitions of sexual behavior are therefore central to the sociological analysis of sexual abuse, because it is not only the behavior per se that is of concern or interest, but also the ways in which certain forms of behavior come to be defined or redefined as harmful or problematic.

In contemporary sociological research sexual abuse is defined predominantly in terms of the concept of harm (both physical and emotional). It is understood as an inappropriate exercise of power, and feminist contributions have argued that this power is also gendered. Thus, it is argued that men typically abuse women, not simply because they are physically stronger but because **masculinity** is culturally constructed as sexually aggressive and predatory. Moreover, it is argued that men are more usually in positions of economic or situational power over women in places of employment, the **public sphere**, and even the domestic arena. Some feminists such as Susan Brownmiller, in *Against our Will* (1977), have argued that all men are potential rapists because of their physiology and their biologically driven sex drive. This argument is no longer widely held, however, because of its overly deterministic orientation which robs men of the capacity to make conscious decisions about their behavior.

Sociological studies of subjects like rape and sexual assault have tended to avoid the question of why men rape in order to focus more on issues of how such offences are dealt with (especially in the legal system) and on how victims are treated. Sociological enquiry therefore tends to ask why so few official complaints of rape are made, or why there are so few successful convictions of men charged with sexual offenses (compared with men charged with property offenses for example). The answers to these questions have revealed the extent to which juries are still reluctant to convict men of sexual offenses because criminal trials hinge on whether the victim's account can be believed beyond all reasonable doubt in a context where it is usually her word against his (Sue Lees, "Judicial Rape," 1993 *Women's Studies International Forum*). It is also in this area that it becomes apparent that many women (and also male victims) are reluctant to admit to having been sexually abused because it still carries shameful connotations and because there is still a tendency to blame the victim. Sexual assaults and rape are therefore crimes which are unlikely to be reported and which, if reported, are unlikely to lead to convictions.

Following the growing interest in research on the sexual abuse of adults came the "rediscovery" of a yet more controversial issue, namely the sexual abuse of children. Florence Rush, in *The Best-kept Secret: Sexual Abuse of Children* (1980), is often credited with drawing attention to this form of abuse in the context of second-wave feminism. Following the popularization of Freudian psychoanalytic theories, there had grown up a dogma in the 1950s and 1960s which insisted that children's claims to have been sexually abused (and adults' recollections of abuse in childhood) were statements of fantasy and wish-fulfillment rather than statements of truth. The victims of this abuse were therefore pathologized and even punished, while the perpetrators remained virtually invincible. Sociological research has drawn attention to the extent to which children are the focus of adult sexual attention and has shown that there is a continuing international sexual trade in children (Judith Ennew, *The Sexual Exploitation of Children*, 1986). As evidence has grown that child sexual abuse is a widespread problem (from the priesthood in the Catholic Church to residential social workers in children's homes, as well as in the **family**) so the victims of this abuse are redefining their experiences into a collective sense of harm. Increasingly, adults who were abused as children are taking legal measures to gain compensation and to achieve a symbolic reversal of the power imbalance they suffered as children.

More recently, attention has turned to the way in which the internet has increased the availability of visual images of child abuse, and the rise in prosecutions for downloading child pornography has demonstrated the extent to which this is a global phenomenon. The expansion of sex **tourism**, particularly from the West to poorer countries where children are more vulnerable to sexual exploitation, also indicates that this sexploitation is a huge industry and that child sexual abuse, rather than being a rare perversion as once thought, is now part of the global economy.

CAROL SMART

sexual citizenship
– see **citizenship**.

sexual discrimination
– see **prejudice**.

sexual division of labor
– see **labor**.

sexualities
The study of different types of sexual **identity** has emerged in contemporary sociology, because **social constructionism** has argued that the binary division between male and female is too restrictive to capture the great array of human sexual expression. The sociology of "sexualities" in the plural recognizes the biological differentiation of male and female, but goes on to emphasize the variety of gender roles that express the complexity of human sexual orientation in society and **culture**. Sociological categorization of sexual preference takes note of lesbian, gay, bisexual, and transsexual identities. This complexity in human sexual expressivity is indicated by the variety of interdisciplinary areas that undertake research on **gender**, namely **gay studies**, **gender studies**, **lesbian studies**, and **women's studies**. These different areas of study have in common the notion that the binary division between male and female is an oppressive, hegemonic system of classification that is based on **essentialism** and **biologism**. It is not just that this rigid binary system is oppressive to women through **patriarchy**, but that it is also oppressive to men. For example **masculinity** is itself not a uniform expression of male identity. In *Gender and Power* (1987) R. W. Connell has critically examined the hegemonic nature of masculinity and femininity as normalized gender roles that function as an **ideology**.

The emergence of the idea of sexuality as a concept distinct from sex and gender was influenced by **Simone de Beauvoir** who claimed that women are made not born. Understanding the complexity of sexuality in human development was further developed by **Sigmund Freud** in his contribution to **psychoanalysis**. Further contributions were made to modern **social theory** and the analysis of sexuality by **Jacques Lacan** and **Michel Foucault**. Sexuality is now seen to be a dimension of our knowledge about the social world, and hence sexuality is inextricably linked to the emergence of the **self** through the acquisition of **language**. These themes of knowledge, language, and **power** have been embraced by **queer theory** and **postmodernism** in gay studies, in which sexualities are free-floating and forever-changing discourses that frame a variety of positions in social identities. The role of language in constructing gendered identities has been emphasized by Judith Butler in *Gender Trouble* (1990) and *Bodies that Matter* (1993). Butler argues that when, shortly after birth, we exclaim "It's a girl" we set in place a social process of naming which allocates and confirms a sexual identity and sexuality that has the effect of "girling" (or making into a girl) the subject. Sexualities are thus ultimately determined by a process first described by **Louis Althusser** as "interpellation."

In sociology, there are classic illustrations of research on homosexuality, such as Laud Humphrey's *Tearoom Trade* (1975). **Anthony Giddens** has written creatively about the nature of intimate interpersonal relationships in *The Transformation of Intimacy* (1992). Eva Illouz has studied the impact of consumerism on love in her *Consuming the Romantic Utopia* (1997), and Ken Plummer has explored narratives in *Telling Sexual Stories* (1995). There is also now a journal devoted to the field, namely *Sexualities* (1998). Sociologists have studied some of the **subcultures** that provide a social vehicle for the exploration of sexual desire outside the conventional distinction between male and female sexualities. For example, Lillian Faderman in *Odd Girls and Twilight Lovers* (1991) examined the transformation of the lesbian movement to include a variety of lesbian **groups** such as "lipstick lesbians," "punk lesbians," and "s&m lesbians."

Despite these developments in **sociological theory**, mainstream empirical sociology has somewhat neglected the study of human sexuality. However, a range of sociological, psychological, and anthropological literature has been edited by Christine Williams and Arlene Stein in *Sexuality and Gender* (2002).   BRYAN S. TURNER

shame

Variously defined both as an emotional state and as a form or mechanism of **social control**, shame may be defined by a self-awareness of the deviant, inappropriate, or morally problematic nature of one's conduct. The sociological study of **emotions**, including shame, emerged as a subfield of sociology in the 1970s. **Thomas Scheff** has argued that "shame is the primary social emotion." and examines the life of shame (and associated rage) in social **interaction** in his *Microsociology: Discourse, Emotion and Social Structure* (1990). Scholars often draw a distinction between the social emotion of shame and the "private" or "inner" emotion of guilt.

Social scientists have noted that shame is a highly effective means of social control, and may guide the self-regulated behavior of members of society. Ruth Benedict in *The Chrysanthemum and the Sword: Patterns of Japanese Culture* (1989) argues that, around the world, different **cultures** regulate the social conduct of their members through drawing primarily on either shame- or guilt-based approaches. Thus, for example, European and North American cultures are considered "guilt-based" cultures, that rely on the internalization of the aversive experience of engaging in morally problematic conduct. By contrast, some Asian cultures, such as the Japanese and Chinese, are based instead on the aversive experience of "shame" – or the social consequences, rather than the inner individual experience – of morally problematic conduct.   SUSAN HANSEN AND MARK RAPLEY

shame cultures

– see **shame**.

Shils, Edward A. (1910–1995)

An influential figure in research on the role of **intellectuals** in the formation of **public policy** and the exercise of **power** in *The Intellectuals and the Power* (1972), *The Calling of Sociology* (1980), and *The Academic Ethic* (1983), Shils was associated with the University of Chicago for over fifty years, but he also held a fellowship at Peterhouse College Cambridge. He defended the traditional research university throughout his career. In 1962, he founded and edited the journal *Minerva*. During the course of his career, he received many awards and honors, including the Balzan Prize in 1983 for his contribution to a "truly universal, general sociology." Shils was renowned for his wide-ranging sociological analysis and was a prolific writer, editor, and researcher. His main substantive interest was the formation of "personal, primordial, sacred and civil ties," that is, social **solidarity**; these themes appeared in *Center and Periphery. Essays in Macrosociology* (1975) and *Tradition* (1981). He also collaborated with **Talcott Parsons** in *Toward a General Theory of Action* (1951). Through his translations and editions, he made many contributions to the development of **methodology** and theory, for example in his publication of collections of **Max Weber**'s sociology, such as *The Methodology of the Social Sciences* (1949, with Henry Finch) and *Max Weber on Law in Economy and Society* (1954, with Max Rheinstein).

Shils wrote on higher **education** in *The Calling of Higher Education. The Academic Ethic and Other Essays on Higher Education* (1997) and *Max Weber on Universities. The Power of the State and the Dignity of the Academic Calling in Imperial America* (1973). He opposed the student activism of the 1960s, rejected the argument that universities should become directly involved in **politics**, and promoted the ideal of the university as an independent, autonomous research **institution**. From the 1970s onwards, Shils continued to defend the "calling of higher education" in a climate where government policies, media coverage, and **public opinion** continued to undermine his defense of the university.

BRYAN S. TURNER

siblings

The focus of the sociology of the **family** has been predominantly on relationships between parents, and between parents and their children. Relationships that matter therefore tend to be seen as those between adults and/or those between the **generations**. Horizontal relationships between children in families have not evoked much interest. This is quite possibly because children per se have not been seen as sociologically significant until recently, and it may also be related to the fact that the quality and nature of siblings' relationships with each other is not identified as having socially significant consequences. **Juliet Mitchell** in *Siblings: Sex and Violence* (2003) has, from a psychoanalytic perspective, argued the opposite case and suggests that how we relate to our siblings is extremely formative, since it is with our brothers and sisters that we often have our most intense, early emotional relationships. Although her work is essentially a critique of **Sigmund Freud** and his insistence on the primacy of the parent/child dyad (*Three Essays on the Theory of Sexuality*, 1905 [trans. 1910]), the recognition that siblings may be important also disrupts the traditional sociological view that it is parents who socialize their **children** and who control children's emotional environment. It introduces the idea that **socialization** may be just as much influenced by brothers and sisters as by parents, which disrupts the classic presumption that parents are the more powerful members of a family grouping. Where sociological work has turned its attention to siblings (including step- and half-siblings) has tended to be in the context of divorce or some other kind of family "breakdown." This suggests that siblings are understood to be important to one another only at times of stress or in the absence of parents. Sibling relationships have therefore become sociologically visible only in the context of a perceived problem.

CAROL SMART

sick role

This concept was first developed by L. J. Henderson in "Physician and Patient as a Social System"

(1935) in the *New England Journal of Medicine* and further elaborated by **Talcott Parsons** in his *The Social System* (1951). It has four components. The first aspect is that the role legitimates social withdrawal from social obligations, such as those relating to work and family duties. The second feature is that a sick person is exempted from responsibility for their medical condition. The third component is that the person has a social obligation to improve and get better; the legitimation of sickness as a basis for social withdrawal from roles is conditional on the patient's full acceptance of an obligation to get better by co-operating with the professional recommendations of a competent doctor. The fourth element is therefore an expectation that the person will seek out competent health care from a trained physician. As a consequence, the sick role describes patient compliance and the role-set of the doctor–patient relationship which is structured in terms of the pattern variables which Parsons had outlined in his analysis of the **professions**.

The concept of the sick role was elaborated by Parsons against a background in which the American medical profession was beginning to take some notice of the idea of psychosomatic illness and to realize that the emotional connection between the doctor and the patient was an important aspect of both the diagnostic and therapeutic processes. Parsons had become aware of the relevance of **psychoanalysis** for the study of sickness, especially **Sigmund Freud**'s notion of transference. There was a significant issue of motivation in the process of becoming sick and getting better. Given the concept of the action frame of reference with its voluntaristic premises in Parsonian sociology, there was an important sense in which the individual decides to adopt the sick role. Voluntarism was important because sickness could not be considered merely as an objective condition of the organism without some discussion of the motivation of the individual in relation to the social system. To be sick required certain **norms** such as exemptions from social obligation and a motivation to accept a therapeutic regime. Parsons classified sickness as a form of deviant behavior which required legitimation and **social control**. While the sick role legitimizes social deviance, it also requires an acceptance of a medical regime. The sick role was therefore an important vehicle for social control, since the aim of the medical regime was to return the sick person to conventional **social roles**.

In terms of Parsons's pattern variables, the doctor–patient relationship is characterized by its affective neutrality, universalism, functional specificity, and orientation to collective norms. The point of this description is to show how the doctor and patient are committed to terminating their relationship rather than forming a social connection as a result of psychological trans- ference. The sick role is intended to be a tempor- ary role and it is important that the patient does not become emotionally dependent on the doctor or the doctor become involved in a particularistic relation with the patient.

The theory is open to criticism in that it cannot provide a satisfactory account of the differences between acute and chronic illness. While acute illness was an implicit assumption of the sick- role concept, we need to examine how people attempt to live normal lives while coping with chronic illness and how these experiences affect their **family** and friends. Many medical conditions are ambiguous in this respect – are pregnancy or alcoholism sick roles?

Parsons's approach has also been criticized be- cause it is in effect a description of the patient role rather than the sick role. Not all who are sick become patients, and not all patients are sick. The so-called "abnormal sick role" might include Munchausen's syndrome in which a person in- flicts self-harm in order to become a patient. The concept does not pay sufficient attention to con- flicts between patient and doctor; in other words, it does not explain lack of compliance. Empirical research has shown that people typically consult friends or relatives about their condition long before they consult a professional doctor – this pattern is described as the lay referral system. Doctors do not invariably behave in a neutral or universalistic manner towards their clients; they are influenced by the **gender, social class**, and **ethnicity** of the patient.

Despite these criticisms, Parsons's concept of the sick role has played an important part in the development of medical sociology, and has re- mained influential in understanding doctor– patient **interaction**.   BRYAN S. TURNER

significance test
– see **statistics**.

Significant others
– see **George Herbert Mead**.

Simmel, Georg (1858–1918)
In recent years, the philosopher and social theorist Georg Simmel has increasingly been recognized as a key figure in the development of sociology in the late nineteenth and early twentieth centuries. He is the author of over 20 monographs and over 300 essays and other pieces; his work extends over philosophy, sociology, psychology, cultural analysis, **aesthetics**, literature, and art, though his contribution to sociology and **social theory** is associated with other areas of interest.

However, his early monographs already revealed a social scientific interest. In his first book, *Uber Soziale Differenzierung* (1890), Simmel considered the nature of social **differentiation** and sought to identify sociology as the study of forms of social **interaction** or reciprocal effect, as well as provid- ing early examples of the application of this framework to specific social phenomena. In the first edition of his *Problems in the Philosophy of His- tory* (1892–3 [trans. 1977]), he sought to argue against the notion of universal historical laws. In his *Introduction to Moral Science* (1892–3 [trans. 1977]), Simmel critiqued the then-common at- tempt to establish a-priori ethical principles and philosophies and argued instead for an empirical investigation of moral **values** and ethical phenomena.

Like his contemporary, **Émile Durkheim**, Sim- mel also sought to establish sociology as an inde- pendent discipline in the 1890s, though on different foundations. In essays from 1890, 1894, 1895, and 1908, Simmel developed his own foundation for sociology on the basis of a series of propositions: in the world, everything interacts with everything else. This is true of the social world, too, where the fundamental inter- relatedness of the most diverse phenomena per- tains. The concern with relations between phenomena is a concern with the reciprocal effect or interaction (*Wechselwirkung*) of phenom- ena with one another. From 1890 onward, soci- ology is defined as the study of "forms of social interaction." By the mid-1890s, Simmel defines sociology's task more precisely as the study of "forms of social interaction [*Vergesellschaftung*]," that is, the process by which we engage in, and are members of, society. This sociology is con- cerned with the forms rather than the contents of social interaction and sociation because other **social sciences** already deal with these contents. Hence, sociology is defined not in terms of its sub- ject matter – society – but in terms of its method. If sociology is the study of forms of social inter- action, then sociology can and should examine any form of sociation. The fact that none is too insignificant means that Simmel explores not merely major features of interaction, be they conflict, group enlargements, and so on, but also mealtime interaction, the rendezvous, flirtation, and so on. All forms of interaction and sociation may be studied historically and comparatively in order to discover their general features.

Simmel's conception of sociology has important implications for the way in which we study **society**. First, Simmel rejects the notion of society as a totality as the immediate object of sociology. In opposition to **Herbert Spencer** and Durkheim, for whom society is an absolute entity, Simmel views society as the sum total of interactions, and only when we have investigated all the forms of social interaction can we know what society is in this total sense. It follows, therefore, that society is a constellation of forms of sociation, whether temporary or more enduring. Specifically, there is a crucial minimum number of interacting persons, which involves "I" and "you," but also the wider network of other social actors. Simmel explores ideal forms of social interaction in sociability and in exchange relations. Second, Simmel sees society as grounded in the experience and knowledge of its participants, thus anticipating a **phenomenology** of society and a sociology of knowledge. Society presupposes our consciousness of sociation. These dimensions emerge out of Simmel asking the question of how society is possible. Third, the aesthetic dimensions of society and social interaction form one of the distinctive features of Simmel's sociology, as evidenced in his essay "Sociological Aesthetics" (1896 [trans. 1968]), in his major *Philosophy of Money* (1900 [trans. 1978]), and in many other essays.

Not surprisingly, therefore, Simmel was and is viewed as a major contributor to a sociology of **culture**. In part, this contribution is to be found in his explorations of the two interrelated sites of **modernity** – the developed money **economy** and the modern metropolis. Both are conceived as **networks** and labyrinths of social interaction accompanied by increasing social differentiation (though in the value form of the money economy, dedifferentiation too), increased functionalization of social relations, and a widening gap between subjective (individual and creative) culture and the objective culture of things. In several respects, the focus in both sites is upon the spheres of circulation, exchange, and **consumption**. The increasing autonomy of the sphere of circulation is matched by a growing autonomy of the cultural sphere. In the metropolis, the individual is confronted by an objective culture of material objectifications, shocks of abstract confrontation. The individual responds to the tumult of the metropolis through social distance, dissociation, and a blasé **attitude**. The individual freedom gained in the metropolis is paid for by increasingly abstract functional relations with others. The very complexity of interactions and sense impressions requires precise differentiation, functionality, intellectuality, exactitude, and calculability.

These same features are present too in interactions within the money economy, where individuals must respond to the **reification** of exchange relations and the dynamic flux of commodity and money circulation.

Simmel's explorations of modern culture rest upon three concepts of culture that relate both to his interest in the "fragments of reality," in the "dedicated individual threads" in social interaction, and to his more general dialectic of subjective and objective culture. His concepts are the crystallization (*Verdichtung*) of interactions into cultural forms, both transitory and enduring; the creation or cultivation (*Kultivierung*) of cultural forms through the transcendence of subjectivity and the creation of objective forms; and the dialectic of subjective and objective culture (whose disjunction Simmel identifies variously in several essays as the conflict crisis and the tragedy of modern culture). In his essay on female culture (1902), Simmel declares that this objective culture is gendered and thoroughly male. Elsewhere, he radicalizes **Karl Marx's** theory of commodity fetishism to include cultural production as also existing in an "autonomous realm" with its own "immanent developmental logic."

Simmel's contribution to sociology and the analysis of modern culture appeared both in individual monographs and in essay form. In particular, his major work *Soziologie* (1908), which contains contributions to his investigation of forms of sociations that extend over the previous decade, explores significant social processes such as subordination and domination, conflict, the size of social **groups** and their self-preservation, the intersection of social circles, and the first major contribution to the sociology of **space** and spatial relations. His analysis of processes of social interaction are replete with instances from **everyday life**. Hence, Simmel is a sociologist who explores not merely significant social processes such as social distance and social differentiation but also face-to-face interactions in the everyday world. Instances of the latter are found in his essays on the sociology of the senses, interaction at mealtimes, flirtation, the aesthetic significance of the face, and many others. In his *Philosophy of Money* (1900 [trans. 1978]) and in short essays, Simmel makes early contributions to a sociology of the **emotions**, examining – variously – greed, avarice, gratitude, **shame**, love, the blasé attitude, and pessimism. He also made original contributions to the study of the structure of experience in his essay on the adventure. Furthermore, because our social interactions often rest upon our and others' typifications of the **self**, social typifications of the poor or the stranger are investigated.

As an early sociologist of modernity, some of these themes, such as the blasé attitude or social distance, are often located within his study of metropolitan modernity or the modern mature money economy. In the latter, Simmel examines not merely the role of **money** and exchange in the transformation of social relations but also modern consumption and display forms, such as exhibitions. Relevant to both sites of his theory of modernity are his essays on **fashion**, style, and adornment.

The breadth of Simmel's sociological and cultural interests and the fragmentary nature of much of our experience of modernity are also revealed in these investigations not only in the character of everyday interactions but also in the form of their presentation too. Simmel was recognized by his contemporaries as a master of the essay form, a form reflected upon subsequently by his student **Georg Lukács** and also by **Theodor Wiesengrund Adorno**. His essays are not closed off from further reflection, nor do they have the apparently definitive content of the academic article. Rather, they remain open to interaction with other essays (his student Siegfried Kracauer [1889–1966] suggested that from any point of Simmel's work one could arrive at any other). They all commence with antinomies or contradictions that are then developed in a kind of incomplete dialectic. They often conclude with unresolved oppositions that, perhaps, invite the reader to provide the resolution through the intervention of the third position of the reader him/herself.

The fate of some of these essays has been varied. In some cases, hypotheses have been derived from them and been empirically investigated, as in the essays on number and the distinction between dyadic and triadic interactions, or on the nature of secret societies. In others, notably on the stranger and the metropolis and mental life, they have become much-cited texts utilized in a variety of contexts, often far from their original ones. At the same time, other essays are increasingly recognized as contributing to the development of what Simmel terms a sociological aesthetics,

whose sociological significance has become increasingly apparent. It is important, nevertheless, for us to recognize that Simmel was, ultimately and foremost, a philosopher. The aesthetic dimensions of social life are explored in essays on the landscape and the ruin, the handle, and the picture frame, as well as on places such as Florence, Rome, and Venice or specific writers and artists such as Rodin (whose work he judged to be the epitome of modernity) or Rembrandt, to whom Simmel devoted a whole monograph (1916 [trans. 2005]).

This recognition, albeit only partial, of the breadth of interests and the contemporary relevance of his sociology ensured that Simmel was regarded as a theorist of modernity. His conception of modernity is not that of a unilinear process but of interaction between unresolved contradictions. The experience of modernity is fragmentary, in motion, and problematical. This is true of Simmel's two sites of modernity: the metropolis and the money economy. The focus is therefore upon something much more elusive than the mode of production or the rational economic enterprise. Yet out of that dynamic flux, Simmel seeks to explore the forms of interaction constitutive of that flux, in order to capture general properties of social interaction.

There are a number of features of the analysis of modernity that make Simmel's work relevant to more recent theories of modernity and **postmodernity**. The shift from a focus upon production to one located in the sphere of circulation, exchange, and consumption allows him to concentrate upon the dynamics of circulation of commodities and individuals. The interest in modes of **leisure** and consumption anticipate more contemporary sociological developments. Second, the theme of the widening gap between subjective and objective culture that runs through his explorations of the metropolis and the money economy highlights the cultural sphere whose objectivity becomes increasingly autonomous and subject to its own laws. Finally, the focus upon the aesthetic sphere, which marked him out from his sociological contemporaries, has given his work an affinity with strands of contemporary cultural analysis. At the same time, many of these themes are framed in the context of contributions to the sociological analysis of forms of social interaction and a general theory of modern society.   DAVID FRISBY

single-parent family

– see **lone-parent family**.

Situationists

Situationist thinking began in Paris in the early 1950s when **Guy Debord** and others devoted themselves to "dérives" – drifting through the **city**, seeking to isolate its psychogeography and to fashion a new version of **everyday life**. The endeavor related both to the Dada and the Surrealist movements but, in his *The Society of Spectacle* (1967 [trans. 1973]), Debord insisted that Dada "wanted to suppress art without realizing it" while Surrealism "wanted to realize art without suppressing it." The Situationists strove for the "supersession of art," wanting to generate artistic creativity which would not be routinized. Creativity involved new forms of action which would continuously defy the kind of appropriation which characterizes modern life where "all of life presents itself as an immense accumulation of spectacles." The Situationist International was founded in 1957 and disbanded in 1972. Debord defined its central purpose as the construction of situations, that is, "the concrete construction of temporary settings of life and their transformation into a higher, passionate nature." The movement produced a journal – *Internationale Situationniste* – and supported interventions such as, notably, the events of May 1968 in Paris. There were affinities with the sociology of Henri Lefebvre (1901–91) and, hence, with the **Annales School**, as well as with the Socialisme ou Barbarie (1949–65) movement, associated with Cornelius Castoriadis (1922–97) and **Jean-François Lyotard** (one of whose earliest texts is a "dérive"). The influence of the Situationists is also clear in **Pierre Bourdieu**'s attitude towards "consecrated art" and in **Jean Baudrillard**'s development of the notion of "simulacra."   DEREK ROBBINS

skewness

– see **distribution**.

Skocpol, Theda (1947–)

Victor S. Thomas Professor of Government and Sociology, and Director of the Center for American Political Studies, at Harvard University, Skocpol was President of the American Political Science Association (2002–3).

In *Vision and Method in Historical Sociology* (1984), she has advocated the use of secondary **data** and sources to undertake macro-historical and comparative work – an approach that she pioneered in her major work *States and Social Revolutions in France, Russia and China* (1979), which received the C. Wright Mills Award of the Society for the Study of Social Problems in 1979 and the American Sociological Association Award for a Distinguished Contribution to Scholarship in 1980. Skocpol has produced a distinctive theory of revolutions through an examination of social revolutions in three *ancien régimes* (see **revolution, theory of**). Revolutions occur because **states** are vulnerable to endogenous socioeconomic processes, particularly the management of internal class conflict. Her theory rejects any role for human agency in revolutions. For example, revolutions are not produced by the revolutionary will of revolutionaries themselves; revolution is the unintended consequence of the decomposition of the state and its agrarian **bureaucracy**. Instead she examines the causal constraints imposed by objective historical circumstances. The three principal forms of constraint are class relations, the repressive character of the state, and the external military and other constraints on the state. Perhaps the key aspect of her argument is to reject any attempt to absorb the state into society. The repressive actions of the state have independent causal consequences for revolutions.

She has conducted historical research on the origins of American **social policy** in *Social Policy in the United States: Future Possibilities in Historical Perspective* (1995), *Protecting Soldiers and Mothers. The Political Origins of Social Policy in the United States* (1992), and *The Missing Middle. Working Families and the Future of American Social Policy* (2000).

In *Diminished Democracy. From Membership to Management in American Civic Life* (2003), Skocpol criticized those liberal theories that claim the vigor of civic life depends on the absence of the state. In contrast, her study of **voluntary associations** demonstrates that vigorous democratic **politics** nourishes a participatory **civil society**. She has contributed to the study of contemporary American political life in *Boomerang. Clinton's Health Reform and the Turn against Government* (1997) and (with Morris P. Florina) *Civic Engagement in American Democracy* (1999).   BRYAN S. TURNER

slavery

A condition of subordination and domination involving forced **labor** and servitude, which has been present from the dawn of **civilization**; it is a condition made possible through distinguishing insiders and outsiders, creating social **groups** who are possible to enslave, to dominate, and to make use of. Slavery thus involves a process of social **differentiation** as well as subordination, turning outsiders into subordinates to labor for "over-ordinates." In the process, legitimating **ideologies** are drawn upon and created to justify this distinction. While associated with physical labor, slavery also has a symbolic dimension, as rulers surrounded themselves with slaves to mark themselves as powerful.

While many definitions treat slavery in reference to property relations and contrast it with freedom, Orlando Patterson in *Slavery and Social Death* (1982) defines slavery as a form of "social death," a social condition characterized by the "permanent, violent domination of natally alienated and generally dishonored persons." The slave is an other, existing outside the communal **politics** of **trust** and reciprocity. This is an opportunistically imposed externality, created firstly through **social conflict**, especially **war**. Combat and conflict create others as outsiders who may then be defined as marginal.

Being other or "not one of us" opens the possibility not only of enslavement and domination but also of dehumanization, being treated as an animal, and exploited in similar fashion to livestock or in other cases as a pet. An ideal slave, rather like a domestic pet, is one who has internalized a docile, obedient, and willing **attitude** towards his/her master. In the Bible, Paul remarks "Tell slaves to be submissive to their masters and to give satisfaction in every respect; they are not to talk back, not to pilfer, but to show complete and perfect fidelity."

Religion has played a central role in legitimating slavery and, later, in its abolition. The Old Testament drew a distinction between the limited servitude of Jews and the lifelong, hereditary servitude of gentiles. Islam was most explicit in its conviction that freedom, not slavery, is the natural status of mankind, yet Islamic law also sanctioned the enslavement of infidels, and Arabs and Muslim converts were the first to make use of sub-Saharan African blacks. Resistance and revolt were common occurrences, and a massive slave revolt occurred between 869 and 883 in what is now Iraq.

From its origins, the enslavement of whites was as common as that of blacks. It was medieval Arabs who first came to associate the most degrading forms of labor with black slaves. The Arabic for slave, *abd*, came with time to mean only a black slave and modern racial stereotyping of blacks has its origin in medieval Islam, while the Latin designation *sclavus* is the root of the English word "slave." *Sclavus* was used to denote the **ethnicity** of those inhabitants captured along the Dalmatian coast and sold by Italian merchants to Muslims in the Middle East. These were white Christians, who later were called "slavs" in English.

Northern European nations, France, Holland, and England, were the first free-labor nations in world history and were also the major beneficiaries of the Atlantic slave system. The abolitionist Thomas Clarkson's *The History of the Rise, Progress, and Accomplishment of the Abolition of the African Slave Trade by the British Parliament* (1808) provides an account of the history of the Atlantic slave trade and traces its origins to 1503, "when a few slaves were sent from the Portuguese settlements in Africa into Spanish colonies in America," while English participation began in 1562 "in the reign of Elizabeth." Sugar, rice, cotton, and tobacco were the prime crops which drove the Atlantic slave trade. It has been argued that sugar, the first consumer nutrient for a mass market, provided the extra nourishment which drove the early stages of the industrial revolution in Great Britain.

Slavery was never unproblematic in the United States and its spread was always a matter of moral concern, even where the early founders, including Presidents George Washington (1732–99) and Thomas Jefferson (1743–1826), were slave-holders. Few, however, allowed these moral concerns to interfere with their practical concern for profit. One exception was the great patriot Patrick Henry (1736–99), who immediately after the War of Independence declared that he could no longer justify his own involvement in the ownership of slaves.

Although grounded in religion and the First Great Awakening (a series of religious revivals starting as early as 1679, along the eastern seaboard of America), movements to abolish the slave trade and slavery itself coincided with the **Enlightenment** and the emergence of **nationalism** and democratization, that is, with **modernity** itself. Abolitionists and the accompanying doctrine of abolitionism drew inspiration from Enlightenment philosophers such as John Locke (1632–1704) and from the scientific theories of Isaac Newton (1642–1727), as well as Christianity, evangelical Protestantism, and the dissenting sects, such as Methodists and Quakers. John Wesley (1703–91), the founder of Methodism, published his *Thoughts on Slavery* in 1774, which contained ideas linking religion and the Enlightenment: "Liberty is the right of every human creature as soon as he breathes the vital air and no human law can deprive him of that right which he derived from a law of nature." Many of those involved in abolitionist movements were ministers. "Among the evils, corrected or subdued, either by the general influence of Christianity on the minds of men, or by particular associations of Christians, the African Slave-trade may very properly be considered as occupying the foremost place": such are the opening words of Thomas Clarkson's testimony before the British Parliament. American abolitionism was formalized with William Lloyd Garrison's founding of the *Liberator* in 1831. Women, excluded from formal political participation, also played a very forceful role in these movements, both in Britain and its former colonies, such as the United States.

Slavery was outlawed in the British Empire in 1833 after a struggle of more than fifty years. During the American Civil War (1861–5), fought over the individual states' rights to slavery, President Abraham Lincoln's Emancipation Proclamation of 1863 formally freed all slaves within the United States.

Though slavery is currently banned in all parts of the world, it still continues, and current debate concerns the extension of the concept to include such practices as sex trafficking.   RON EYERMAN

Small, Albion W. (1854–1926)

The son of a Baptist minister, Small has a unique position in the development of North American sociology as its first professor of sociology and the founder of the first Department of Sociology in North America at the University of Chicago in 1892. In 1895, he founded the *American Journal of Sociology*, the first sociology journal in the United States. He was President of the American Sociological Society (the forerunner of the American Sociological Association) in 1912 and 1913. His main influence was on the institutional development of North American sociology.

Small saw **social science** as having an essential role in **democracy** and social reform, a combination of concerns that was to flower sociologically after 1915 in the **Chicago School**, although his own interests tended to general **sociology** rather than specific empirical studies. His primary interest was in the relation of sociology and economics and he was particularly influenced by German writers such as **Werner Sombart**. He also translated many essays by **Georg Simmel**. His key writings are: *General Sociology* (1905), *Adam Smith and Modern Sociology* (1907), *The Cameralists* (1909), *The Meaning of Social Science* (1910), *Between Eras: From Capitalism to Democracy* (1913), and *Origins of Sociology* (1924).   JOHN HOLMWOOD

small groups

The study of small groups has been a part of social psychology since the pioneering studies of Norman Triplett (1861–1910) in the late nineteenth century. Triplett argued that the presence of others affected individual performance. This led to the recognition of the importance of social **influence** in interpersonal relations. The small groups approach – sometimes called the group dynamics approach – flourished in the 1950s and 1960s – under the leadership of such figures as Kurt Lewin (1890–1947), **Robert Freed Bales**, and Dorwin Cartwright, particularly at universities such as Michigan, Harvard, and Massachusetts Institute of Technology.

In general, the groups approach analyzed social **interaction** as a part of a system, and focused more directly on behavior, in contrast to cognition or **emotion**. Important studies attempted to determine the roles, structures, and contexts of group life that led some groups to be more effective than others in task completion or in producing satisfaction of members. Much research was observational, conducted in experimental laboratories, but some important studies, notably the Robbers Cave experiments at the University of Oklahoma in 1954 by of Muzafer Sherif and his colleagues, had an ethnographic component, and others, such as the self-analytic groups organized by Bales, had a strong psychoanalytic component.

With the rise of cognitive and human information-processing models in the 1970s, research on small groups fell out of favor. However, studies of small groups are still to be found in the sociology of **culture** in studies of idioculture / small group culture, in organizational sociology in studies of work-group effectiveness, and in science studies in studies of individual laboratories.

GARY ALAN FINE AND KENT SANDSTROM

Smelser, Neil (1930–)

A leading American sociologist based for many years at the University of California, Berkeley, with wide-ranging accomplishments, Smelser's interests range from **social change** and modernization theory, through the sociology of economic life and collective behavior, to understandings of **personality** and **psychoanalysis**. As a close associate of **Talcott Parsons**, with whom he wrote *Economy and Society* (1956), Smelser went on to become a leading member of the postwar generation of American social scientists who developed modernization theory. His work has, however, continued to develop, and he has played a major role in the consolidation of economic sociology as a distinct field of study within sociology, writing the first textbook and reader in the area.

One of the major difficulties with modernization theory was the sharp dichotomy proposed between traditional and modern **societies**. Faced with criticism that this grossly exaggerated discontinuities in social change, Smelser, in *Social Change in the Industrial Revolution* (1959), proposed that the idea of social **differentiation** allowed a more nuanced way of analyzing gradual and complex patterns of change. The idea of social differentiation and related challenges of integration or fragmentation remain a major theoretical theme in **postmodernism** and neofunctionalism, without any current sense of an emerging consensus.

A further important theme running throughout Smelser's life and work is that of the articulation of psychoanalysis with sociological inquiry. In *The Social Edges of Psychoanalysis* (1998), he notes that a range of theorists from **critical theory**, through **feminism**, to **postmodernism** have looked to psychoanalysis. This has been in part to link issues of personality more closely with social analysis. In this manner Smelser continues the Parsonian interest in an integrated **social theory**, capable of bridging the macro–micro divide. ROBERT HOLTON

snowball sample
– see **sampling**.

social action
All forms of human behavior other than physiological reflexes are profoundly influenced by the cultural settings and the social circumstances in which they occur. Sociologists conceive the social qualities of action from several different points of view. The oldest sociological accounts of social action hinge on subjective meaning. Utilitarians, and subsequently in **rational choice theory**, emphasize action subjectively motivated by actors to maximize their interests or advantages and/or to minimize their losses or discomfort. **Max Weber**, who was influenced by neo-Kantian philosophy, defined as social action only behavior that involves the attachment of existential meaning by an actor when she orients to other actors past, present, or future.

Émile Durkheim made a point of emphasizing how cultural conditions shape the form and content of social action. For Durkheim, our everyday actions, such as speaking a certain **language** or exchanging currency in certain ways, are structured by collectively shared ways of life. The collectivist aspect of Durkheim's take on action influenced the thought of **Talcott Parsons** and is implicitly reconstructed by certain French post-structuralist thinkers, including **Pierre Bourdieu** and **Michel Foucault**.

During the twentieth century, sociological accounts of social action took a new, praxiological

turn. Unlike philosophy, where praxis takes on normative and political connotations, in sociology praxis refers simply to enacted social conduct. Hence, instead of questions about the subjective meaning or motivation of action, praxis-oriented sociologists ask how social action is produced or performed. The pragmatist philosophers John Dewey (1859–1952) and **George Herbert Mead** exerted a strong praxiological influence on sociology through the symbolic interactionist school. Dewey emphasized the significance of routinely enacted behavior and behavior involving thought that occurs when routines are disrupted. Mead, more ambitiously, saw social action in terms of interactive patterns of sociality. For Mead, actors produce **interaction** by emitting and reacting to symbolic gestures. Symbolic gestures and the learned responses they evoke are channeled through the human mind where some greater or lesser degree of personal autonomy is introduced.

The shift towards praxis-oriented accounts of social action acquired both inspiration and momentum in the works of **Erving Goffman** and **Harold Garfinkel**. Goffman was influenced by Durkheim. For Goffman, the social actions that matter occur as **rituals** during interaction. These rituals exhibit moral meaning and create small-scale local systems of moral order. Goffman's praxiological attention to the subtle, tacit performance of small but ritually significant gestures is a highlight of his accounts.

Garfinkel took the praxiological turn about as far as it could go. For him, action is always locally situated, reflexively taking its meaning from the unfolding context produced in a given setting and thereby sustaining or redirecting the nature of that setting. His research demonstrates the great significance of the moment-by-moment production of all kinds of social action, from sorting bureaucratic files to making new discoveries in the natural sciences. **Anthony Giddens**'s structuration theory combines the Durkheimian with the praxis-oriented accounts of social action. A logical step that has yet to be taken is to combine the subjective and the praxis-oriented accounts.

IRA COHEN

social administration
– see **social policy**.

social capital
This form of capital arises from relationships between individuals, **families**, **groups**, or **communities** that provide access to valuable benefits and/or resources. It is one of several forms of

capital – including human, symbolic, and cultural capital – developed by sociologists as homologies to economic capital. Although less tangible than economic capital, these other capitals share many characteristics with economic capital: they have **value** to their holders, they can be accumulated, and – most importantly – they can be "invested" in ways that produce other social rewards or advantages. Capital in all its forms is important to study because it provides insight into otherwise hidden forms of the **reproduction** of social **inequality**. For example, social capital has been shown to be associated with a wide variety of outcomes, such as socioeconomic attainment, educational attainment, political participation, juvenile delinquency, and the success of ethnic entrepreneurial enclaves.

Though its roots have been traced to a diffuse set of classical theorists – from **Karl Marx** and **Alexis de Tocqueville** to John Dewey (1859–1952) and Alfred Marshall (1842–1924), to name a few – the concept of social capital was introduced into the **social sciences** through the work of **Pierre Bourdieu** and **James S. Coleman**. There are, as discussed below, some key differences in the conceptions of social capital outlined by Bourdieu and Coleman. Bourdieu views social capital as a resource that individuals possess in various quantities and qualities, which can be used strategically to gain access to other, especially economic, resources. Coleman's functional theory of social capital, on the other hand, focuses on groups and the collective nature of social capital. It highlights the benefits accrued by dense **networks** characterized by **trust** and mutual obligation. These different orientations have given rise to divergent research programs and are thus important to distinguish. The concept of social capital has recently come into vogue because of Robert Putnam's deployment of it in his widely discussed work *Bowling Alone* (2000).

In a series of essays and books in the 1970s and 1980s, Bourdieu argued that social capital is one form of capital, closely tied to other forms he called "symbolic" and "cultural" capital. This line of theoretical and empirical research arose out of Bourdieu's general concern with the role that noneconomic forms of capital play in the transmission of social advantages across **generations**. According to Bourdieu, these various forms of capital, although often ignored because they are less tangible than economic capital, are nevertheless significant because they disguise the processes by which power relations and material inequalities are reproduced.

Symbolic capital is the ability to make certain kinds of relationships of **power** and privilege seem disinterested or natural. The transmission of cultural capital is one way in which this is accomplished. Expressed both in embodiment (etiquette, language style, or, more generally, one's **habitus**) and cultural resources (such as knowledge about art, books, classical music, or scientific ideas), cultural capital produces competencies that can contribute to success in such areas as educational achievement, occupational attainment, and **marriage**. These processes are largely invisible to the actors involved.

Social capital is a second way in which unequal advantages may be disguised as merit. Bourdieu defines social capital as a resource consisting of durable social obligations or connections, such as group or network memberships, that can be called upon to access other valuable resources. As such, social capital can be accumulated, the amount of social capital held by an actor (most often an individual for Bourdieu) depending on two factors: the size of the network of connections that can be effectively mobilized, and the volume of capital (economic, cultural, or symbolic) possessed by the other members of the network. A key aspect of Bourdieu's conceptions of social and cultural capital are their instrumentality; they can be converted into other forms of capital. Social capital, like cultural capital, is a force that helps to create, and sustain preexisting, social advantages.

There are several fruitful lines of empirical research that have been inspired by, or draw upon, Bourdieu's model of social (and other) capitals. One strand of this work provides strong evidence tying social capital – in the form of connections or ties to resources outside the family – to the attainment of better jobs, earlier promotions, higher earnings or bonuses, and physical and mental health outcomes. Another important line of research has examined how the lack of social capital exacerbates the problems of the poor. "Social isolation" is a shorthand for the lack of social capital that would allow individuals, families, and/or disadvantaged subgroups to escape **poverty.** Finally, this approach provides a better understanding of the benefits of dispersed **networks** of contacts that holders of high levels of social capital typically possess. In the influential work of **Mark Granovetter**, *Getting a Job* (1974), such "weak ties" provide important benefits in a variety of social settings, especially in employment.

A second prominent conceptualization of social capital was developed by Coleman, most notably in his *Foundations of Social Theory* (1990). While Coleman's and Bourdieu's definitions of social capital are similar at the most general level – they both believe that social capital exists in the relations between actors and that these relationships facilitate the achievement of ends that would be otherwise unattainable – they focus on very different aspects of these relations. Instead of viewing social capital as a resource, Coleman's model views social capital in terms of **social structure**. It is primarily concerned with analyzing the relationships between social capital and the positive outcomes that result from dense family and community networks. The key innovation of the Coleman model is the role of social trust in these relationships. Coleman emphasized the important role that social capital plays in the creation of human capital – investments, such as **education**, training, and other forms of skills and knowledge, that increase the productive potential of individuals. Coleman argues that social capital within the family (for example, strong relations between children and parents that provide children access to the parents' human capital), and within the community (for example, parents' relationship with the **institutions** of the community), are critical types of social capital resources.

Two distinct lines of empirical research have grown out of Coleman's model of social capital. Both examine close-knit groups or communities and their outcomes. The first of these approaches emphasizes the value of intrafamilial social capital for **children**. This type of social capital manifests itself in the development of human capital mentioned above. Specifically, the more of their own human capital that parents invest in their children through the time and attention they give them, the better the development of human capital (that is, educational attainment and personality advancement) in their children. A series of studies in this area has demonstrated, for example, that the outcomes for children of families with higher amounts of this type of social capital (two-parent households, parents who spend a lot of time with their children, and families with fewer children) tend to do better in terms of, among other things, success at school, avoiding teenage pregnancy, and emotional adjustment.

A second strand of research that has grown out of Coleman's conception of social capital emphasizes the value of dense social networks outside the family. These networks produce relationships of trust and reciprocity among their members that, especially in smaller networks, enmesh members in mutual and mutually beneficial obligations and provide a powerful form of informal **social control**. High degrees of this type of social capital, for example, foster contexts of trust in which children are felt to be safe when they are not with their parents, or valuable goods can be exchanged without expensive security measures. Coleman and later analysts used such explanations to account for why children in Catholic schools tend to outperform their state school peers in the United States.

Subsequent research in the Coleman tradition, most notably that of Robert Putnam, has generalized the concept of social capital to large communities, regions, and even nations. Putnam sees social capital as a public good which is not zero-sum (one person's use does not diminish another's). Like other public goods, such as national defense, water supply, and public education, that benefit the entire community, social capital contributes to overall well-being. According to Putnam, participation in community groups and civic associations enhances collective **norms** and trust and this in turn has positive effects on democratic participation and collective well-being. Using large-scale survey **data** on individuals' feelings of trust and participation in groups and other public activities (such as **voluntary associations** and, most famously, bowling leagues), Putnam argues that the reserve of social capital in the United States has become depleted in recent years. This argument has been applied widely to explain such phenomena as declining political participation, neighborhood involvement, and parental participation in schools, as well as falling church attendance. Some later analysts have been critical of this popular treatment of social capital, arguing, for example, that Putnam conflates key concepts such as trust, association membership, and social networks, and that his explanation is often tautological and provides a weak account of how social capital is generated. Putnam's perspective has nonetheless been a lively source of research and debate about the broader impacts of social capital.

JEFF MANZA

social change

All societies recognize social change. Three questions arise: is this change natural and normal?; what is its source?; and what is its tempo?

Premodern societies regard change as external and problematic. The way things have been done in the past is a powerful indicator as to how they should be done in the present, and this sense of continuity is understandable. To venerate others in the contemporary world, one needs to venerate their ancestors, since each of us is a product of the past – our parents and grandparents, and so on, physically and culturally produced us – and therefore disrespect to them is also disrespect for their progeny.

Such a position, despite its valid and valuable features, runs the risk of idealizing the past, and it leads to a paralyzing **relativism** (whatever happened in the past was good) and an authoritarian absolutism (the past reflected a timeless truth that contemporary society foolishly disregards). It is important not to take these attitudes at face value, for veneration of the past is linked to the needs of the present, and traditionalists may distort the past in order to justify present practices. Change is seen as either the tragic disintegration of a golden age or at best a cyclical process. "There is nothing new under the sun" and new social forms replace one another in merry-go-round fashion.

The modern age takes a much less hostile view of change. Change is seen as natural and necessary – something that is positive rather than negative. Each **generation** faces new and different challenges to those of the previous one, so that it seems implausible to imagine that continuity with the past is all-important. With the European **Enlightenment** in the eighteenth century, liberals begin to postulate a doctrine of **progress** – change is celebrated and admired. This doctrine of progress is contradicted by perfectionism, which ascribes animating change to a timeless creator, so that inevitably at some point in the future the perfect society will arrive. Some conservatives reject the notion of progress itself as though the idea is an inherently perfectionist one. It is important to subject the argument about progress to an internal critique: it is not that the notion of progress is problematic, but rather the idea that this progress has a beginning and an end – concepts which undermine the dynamism of change.

The conservative condemns change as a bad thing, the radical sees it as good, but each position betrays a numbing one-sidedness. Change to be meaningful must be expressed through continuity with the past so that newness can be critically appraised. Change must be tied to absolute as well as relative standpoints – do new ideas and practices help us to govern our own lives in a more satisfactory fashion? The concepts of self-government and autonomy express a longstanding aspiration – inherent in all systems of morality – and they enable us to decide whether change is positive and developmental, or negative and self-destructive.

It is also important to tackle the question of the source of change. Why do societies change? It is perfectly true that people develop new ideas and **attitudes** – but why? The idealists treat ideas as autonomous agents with an origin in mystical genius – either of the outstanding individual or of a supernatural creator. Materialists rightly insist that change derives from forces outside the consciousness of people – that is, change occurs whether people like it or not. But the problem with this position is that it is sometimes interpreted as an **idealism** turned inside out. Ideas, from being the source of change, become irrelevant – change is rooted in **technology** or physiology. It is clear that cultural and political **institutions** are themselves important agents of change, but it is also true that what we think is happening is never identical to what is going on. Ideas and institutions express this change, but we should never assume that what the creators of change intend is the same as the actual outcome. This is as true as regards changes in the law (see **law and society**) as it is for changes in technology and the forces of production.

But, flexibly and concretely used, the materialist argument is a powerful one, for it seeks to locate change in circumstances that operate structurally, that is, in collective "forces" that people can never wholly control. Thus, the demand by women for social as well as political **equality** arises not simply because greater equality is a "good idea." More and more women work outside the home and undertake **occupations** of a nontraditional kind. This breaks down patriarchal stereotypes, although it also provokes fundamentalist backlashes. The point is that, although the change is expressed in debate and argument, these new ideas (and new language) cannot simply be understood on their own terms. They seem plausible because they correspond to changing realities in society itself.

What of the tempo of change? Changes are always incremental in the sense that society is always evolving. In modern societies this change is built into structures so that it is seen as natural and normal: new ideas; new institutions; new practices. Is this change revolutionary or gradual in character? This is in a dualism that we need to overcome, for change is both. Each change is in a particular area, and affects the operation of society as a whole. The development of the internet in contemporary society has enormous implications for other institutions and ideas – it affects psychology, **ideology**, the political system, industry, **education**, and the media. It is a revolutionary force, but it builds upon previous developments so that it is both gradual and insurrectionary. It is a mistake to identify revolutions with transformations of the **state** – although these occur as well.

Social change is apparently accidental in premodern societies, but it is seen as normal in modern orders. The notion that this change is governed by higher powers (which are timeless) is contradictory and seeks to impose limits on change. Change occurs at every level in society and those who create change never see the full implications of the process they instigate. Change is neither simply evolutionary nor revolutionary: it is always both.   JOHN HOFFMAN

social class

All complex **societies** are characterized by some kind of structured social **inequality** (or stratification system). The totality of **social stratification** will be made up of a number of different elements that will vary in their importance between different societies – for example, old **age** is accorded more respect in some societies than others. Class makes a significant contribution to structured social inequality in contemporary societies. However, it is a multifaceted concept with a variety of different meanings. There is no correct definition of the concept, nor any single correct way of measuring it. Nevertheless, questions of both definition and **measurement** have been endlessly contested over the years. Broadly, three dimensions of class may be identified. These are the economic, the cultural, and the political. The economic dimension has a focus on patterns and **explanations** of material inequality; the cultural dimension a focus on **lifestyle**, social behavior, and hierarchies of **prestige**; and the political dimension addresses the role of classes, and class action, in political, social, and economic change. Common to all sociological conceptions of class is the argument that social and economic inequalities are not natural or divinely ordained, but rather emerge as a consequence of human behaviors.

Modern ideas of class are inextricably associated with the development of capitalist industrialism (or **industrial society**). The development of **capitalism** was accompanied by the emergence of the "two great classes" identified by **Karl Marx** and **Friedrich Engels** (*The Communist Manifesto*, 1848 [trans. 1968]) as the bourgeoisie (the owners and controllers of capital or the means of production) and the industrial working class or proletariat (those without capital or access to productive resources who were forced to sell their **labor** in order to survive). This does not mean that indus-

trial capitalism was ever a two-class society, as many other groupings, distinguished by a variety of relationships to both production and the **market**, have always existed in capitalist societies. For example, in the *Eighteenth Brumaire* (1852 [trans. 1934]), Marx identifies (in addition to the proletariat) finance, landholding, and industrial capital (different fractions of the capitalist class), as well as the peasantry, the petite bourgeoisie (shopkeepers and small owner of private capital), and the lumpenproletariat. Thus Marx defined class in economic and political terms, and **cultures** and **ideologies** were held to be largely determined by class processes.

A key issue relating to class (deriving largely, but not entirely, from the work of Marx) is that of class **identity** or consciousness. Marx argued that, as different classes had conflicting interests, deriving from their position in relation to production and markets, these interests would find their expression in political action. Indeed, Marx saw class conflict as the major driving force of **social change**. In preindustrial (feudal) societies, the dominant class was the feudal aristocracy, whose **power** and **authority** was challenged by the rise of the industrial bourgeoisie. The conflict between these classes resulted in the emergence of capitalism. In capitalist society, Marx argued, the proletariat (or working class) assumed the role of the revolutionary class. He argued that the bourgeoisie exploited the proletariat via the extraction of the surplus **value** created by their labor. Marx predicted that the conflict brought about by growth of class consciousness and action amongst the proletariat (its becoming a "class for itself"), together with the weaknesses engendered by successive crises of capitalism, would eventually lead to the victory of the proletariat and their allies and transformative social change. These changes would usher in first **communism**, then **socialism**.

The work of **Max Weber** has also been influential (*Class, Status and Party* [trans. 1940]). Like Marx, Weber emphasized the economic dimension of class. However, besides property ownership (Marx's major axis of class differentiation), Weber also emphasized the significance of market situations. These included individual skills and qualifications, the possession of which will result in enhanced **life chances** as compared with those groups possessing neither property nor skills. Weber's account of class, however, was radically different from that of Marx in that it was not linked to any theory of history and, although Weber recognized the likelihood and persistence of class conflict, he did not see such conflicts as necessarily leading to radical social change. Weber also identified the independent significance of **social status** (social honor or prestige), that is, hierarchical systems of cultural **differentiation** that identify particular persons, behaviors, and lifestyles as superior or inferior, more or less worthy. Weber identified class and **social status** as different bases for claims to material resources. Subsequently, many sociologists have insisted on the analytical separation of the two concepts. The class concept, it is argued, describes the relationships giving rise to inequalities; it is a relational concept. Hierarchies of prestige or status, on the other hand, only describe the outcomes of underlying class processes, as described in gradational class schemes. However, as we shall see, although, analytically, class and status are distinct concepts, there are difficulties in separating them empirically.

From the nineteenth century onwards, different class interests, reflecting ownership and market position, were increasingly represented by a range of different bodies including the **political parties** of left and right, as well as **trade unions** and employers' **organizations**. Thus, there were good reasons to argue that the interest groupings representing different classes could be broadly mapped onto the material groupings identified by the classic theorists of class – owners and non-owners of the means of different elements of production, as well as occupational groupings. By the late nineteenth and early twentieth centuries (albeit to varying degrees), the greater majority of the population in industrial capitalist societies had come to rely on paid employment of some kind. Official statisticians (as well as social investigators) sought to classify these populations in some kind of meaningful fashion. Increasingly, the occupational order began to emerge as a useful axis of classification that gave a summary indication of standard of life as well as life chances. In all such schemes, managerial and professional employees are located at the apex, and unskilled workers in the lower-level groupings.

Thus the convention developed of describing the different occupational groupings created by the application of classificatory schemes as social classes (for example, the Registrar-General's six-fold social-class classification in Britain). Such classifications were often criticized as atheoretical. The Registrar-General's classification, which was at its inception a **scale** of social standing, was held to be a commonsense status scale rather than a measure of class relations. However, it proved to be remarkably robust in policy-oriented research and in the mapping and investigation of inequalities of various kinds (for example, in **health**).

Thus, for many investigators, the occupational order became synonymous with the class structure. This assumption did not go unchallenged and alternative bases of classification were proposed. **John Rex** and R. Moore (*Race, Community and Conflict*, 1967), for example, developed the notion of housing classes deriving from variations in house ownership and tenure, giving rise to conflicting (housing) class interests. This approach to class was taken up by a number of urban sociologists (for example, P. Saunders in *Social Theory and the Urban Question*, 1986).

Despite the sociological insistence on the analytical separation of class and status, material differences and cultural and social distinctions are, invariably, intertwined (**P. Bourdieu**, *Distinction*, 1979 [trans. 1984]). This has been recognized in a number of classic **case studies** focusing on particular localities (for example, M. Stacey, *Tradition and Change*, 1960), and in the " affluent worker" series, an influential British study carried out in the 1960s (**John Goldthorpe**, **David Lockwood**, F. Bechhofer, and J. Platt, *The Affluent Worker in the Class Structure*, 1969). The affluent-worker thesis had argued that, with rising prosperity in the years after World War II, the wages of "working-class" employees were now at the same levels of those of the middle classes (that is, those around the middle of the occupational structure), thus a process of embourgeoisement (or "the worker turning middle class) was held to be underway. Goldthorpe and his colleagues identified three dimensions of class, the economic, the normative, and the relational. They demonstrated that, although manual workers might have achieved **incomes** equal to those of some middle-class occupations, this was achieved by working longer hours. Furthermore, patterns of association and aspirations (for promotion) continued to differentiate middle-class and working-class employees; thus their research rejected the embourgeoisement thesis.

From the 1970s, class theory and research were affected by a number of different, and sometimes contradictory, **influences**. In particular, debates in class theory became increasingly characterized by a separation between economic and culturalist approaches. Theoretical discussions also became distanced from empirical research, which from the 1970s was dominated by quantitative class analysis focusing on occupational aggregates (or classes) as revealed in large datasets. This employment aggregate approach was dominated by two major crossnational projects, the CASMIN (Comparative Analysis of Social Mobility in Industrial Societies) project, led by Robert Erikson and Goldthorpe, and the Comparative Project on Class Structure and Class Consciousness, coordinated by Erik Olin Wright.

The revival of interest in **Marxism** in the 1960s and 1970s generated highly abstract theoretical debates, often with a focus on the contested middle class. For writers influenced by Marx's work (N. Poulantzas, *Classes in Contemporary Capitalism*, 1975), a key issue lay in the identification of the actual interests (or location within the class structure) of the middle classes. As propertyless employees, they had features in common with the proletariat, but their **labor** did not directly create a surplus (so how could they be exploited?), and both their levels of material reward, and the **power** and **authority** associated with their employment situation, served to differentiate them from the working class. Did their interests, therefore, lie with the bourgeoisie or with the proletariat? One reason why this question appeared, to some, to be crucial was the manifest failure of a unitary proletarian or working-class consciousness to materialize in any sustained form in western industrial societies. Some writers (often influenced by the upsurge of political activism in France in 1968) identified elements of the middle classes (for example, scientific and technical workers) as a new working class that might assume the revolutionary vanguard. Others argued that both the interests and **politics** of the middle classes lay closer to those of the employers. Rather than being in the middle, this class was described as the service class, rewarded for faithful service to employers by career progression and material benefits.

The identification of class with employment and property relationships emphasizes the economic dimension of the class concept. However, throughout much of the twentieth century, explorations of the economic and the cultural dimensions of class were linked via a continuing interest in class consciousness or **identity**. In the nineteenth century, Engels had identified the presence in Britain of an aristocracy of labor, that is, the better-paid elements of the (skilled) working class who were thereby induced to disidentify with the proletariat. In a similar vein, the failure of a unitary working-class consciousness to emerge as capitalism developed was widely attributed to the fragmentation of class identities dependent on diverse community and employment experiences or cultures (Lockwood, "Sources of

Variation in Working-Class Images of Society," 1966, *Sociological Review*). For example, the relational proximity of some employees (such as agricultural workers) to their employers was held to generate a "deferential" class identity, whereas the employment and community experiences of, say, miners were more likely to generate a "traditional proletarian" consciousness. The protagonists in these debates were not necessarily Marxists, but in respect of consciousness, these kinds of arguments implicitly employ a structure → consciousness → action model of social behavior, in which structure (that is, material circumstance) is assumed to be causally dominant.

This broadly materialist approach to class and the generation of identities was buttressed by H. Braverman's influential *Labor and Monopoly Capital* (1974). Although Braverman was explicit that he was describing a class in itself rather than a class for itself, nevertheless, his account of the inexorable **deskilling** of work in the circumstances of monopoly (large-scale) capitalism apparently seemed to resolve a number of issues for materialist, Marxist-influenced approaches, which were enthusiastically taken up by a number of authors (R. Crompton and G. Jones, *White-Collar Proletariat*, 1984). The processes of deskilling were seen to be leading to the potential homogenization of proletarian employment, thus removing the barriers to working-class unity. Moreover, the deskilling of clerical (conventionally assigned to "middle" occupational categories) employment would increase the ranks of the proletariat itself. Nevertheless, the question of actually existing class consciousness remained problematic. Some writers (notably social historians; see E. P. Thompson, *The Making of the English Working Class*, 1963) had never subscribed to the distinction between classes in and for themselves. For these authors, classes were called into being by the generation of consciousness itself, rather than any deterministic structural factors. Besides the apparent failure of consciousness to materialize, however, during the 1970s wider **social changes** were calling into question the utility of the class concept in sociology.

The origins of many critiques of class as an analytical tool lay in the global economic and political transformations that followed successive economic crises from the 1960s onwards. C. Crouch (*Social Change in Western Europe*, 1999) has described the period after the end of World War II as the "mid [twentieth] century social compromise." This was in a broad sense a class "compromise." Governments of left and right supported social protections and increasing welfare, and left-wing ("working-class") parties and their representatives did not seek to destabilize existing social arrangement in any radical way. An important argument that captures the prevailing mood of these times is expressed in **Thomas H. Marshall**'s (*Citizenship and Social Class and Other Essays*, 1950) identification of the rise of "social **citizenship**," that is, those rights which enable the citizen "to share to the full in the social heritage and to live the life of a civilized being according to the standards prevailing in the society." In an oft-quoted phrase, Marshall described the ideals of citizenship as being at war with the class system.

These arrangements may be described as characteristic of Fordism, a term that has been widely employed to describe the industrial and social order that emerged in many advanced capitalist societies after World War II. Fordism was characterized by mass production, full employment (at least as far as men were concerned), the development of state welfare, and rising standards of **consumption**. However, no sooner had it been identified than western Fordism began to unravel. Rising prices (in particular for oil) and **inflation** in the West were accompanied by rapid industrialization in South East Asia and an influx of cheaper goods to the West. Pressures on government revenues as well as a sharp increase in **unemployment** (associated with deindustrialization) put considerable strains on welfare spending. In the West, the election of Ronald Reagan's administration (1981–9) and Margaret Thatcher's government (1979–90) signaled a turn to economic neoliberalism, while, in the eastern bloc, state socialist regimes began to collapse from the end of the 1980s.

These political developments were accompanied by the shift of academic Marxism in a more culturalist direction. Post-Marxists E. Laclau and C. Mouffe (*Hegemony and Socialist Strategy*, 1985), for example, rejected the notion of objective (that is, structurally determined) class interests and emphasized the variable and discursive construction of such interests. Indeed, this turn to culture was reflected in sociology more generally. In any case, the utility of class for the analysis of postmodern societies (in which, it was argued, consumption had assumed greater significance than production) had already been challenged. Following from the identification of housing classes in the 1970s, a developing strand of argument took the position that consumption had become a more useful axis than class via which to explore group cleavages and patterns of identity in contemporary societies. J. Pakulski and M. Walters

(*The Death of Class*, 1996), for example, argue that culture and its consumption constitute the major axis of stratification in postmodern societies. Individual wants and desires, it is suggested, are in the process of replacing past collective **solidarities**. The current emphasis on **individualism** and its consequences for class theory and analysis is an issue to which I will return later, but first the implications for class analysis of changes in the occupational structure will be examined.

Deindustrialization in the West was associated with a dramatic decline in what had been viewed as unambiguously working-class occupations – in steel-working, manufacturing, mining, and so on. Lower-level jobs in the service sector (for example, in retail, fast food, and caring occupations) have expanded, but so have the number of professional and managerial occupations – by convention, service-class occupations. The numerical decline in the working class was also associated with the erosion of locality and community structures that had been argued to generate the collective proletarian identities of the structure → consciousness → action model. More importantly, the expansion of women's employment raised important questions as to how women, as employees, should be located within the occupational (class) structure.

Both the CASMIN and Comparative Class Structure projects had devised alternative, sociologically informed class schemes for the analyses of their data (large-scale, random-sample **surveys** conducted in a number of different countries). Both of these occupational classifications are argued to reflect patterns of economic class relations, and both sets of authors distinguish their classifications from commonsense status scales such as those of the Registrar-General. Erikson and Goldthorpe's scheme (CASMIN) has been described as "neo-Weberian," although this is perhaps a somewhat misleading description, as Goldthorpe's (*On Sociology*, 2000) *post-hoc* account of the theoretical underpinnings of his class scheme, grounded in employment relations, can be seen as drawing insights from both Weber and Marx. However, Wright's occupational class classification (Comparative Class Structure) was unambiguously Marxist in its inspiration. There are two versions of Wright's class scheme. The first version is structured around ownership, as well as authority and control in employment. The second version of the scheme, deriving from game-theoretic Marxism, is based on relations of exploitation deriving from the possession of different assets, including capital, organization assets, and skill or credential assets. As many critics have noted, this second version of Wright's scheme has many parallels with Weber's account of class.

The major objective of the CASMIN project was the investigation of social mobility. In the United States, **Peter M. Blau** and **Otis Dudley Duncan**'s research (*The American Occupational Structure*, 1967) had apparently demonstrated that educational background and early work experiences were more important than social origin (class) in determining mobility chances. These findings confirmed the positive industrial-society thesis (C. Kerr et al., *Industrialism and Industrial Man*, 1960). This thesis argued that industrial development would be associated with rising living standards, middle-class expansion, and the triumph of achievement over ascription. All of these factors, it was argued, would lead to a less polarized class structure and a decline in class conflict. However, Goldthorpe and his colleagues (R. Erikson and J. Goldthorpe, *The Constant Flux*, 1992) demonstrated that, although rates of absolute social mobility had increased, this was largely due to changes in the occupational structure, as the expansion of professional and managerial occupations (together with the decline in working-class occupations) will mean that an increasing proportion of higher-level jobs will have to be filled from below. However, relative rates of social mobility, that is, the relative chances of achieving a service-class occupation depending on class of origin, had remained remarkably stable. Thus, despite outward appearances, the class structure of industrial societies had not become more open.

Wright's original research objectives differed considerably from those of Goldthorpe and his colleagues. One of the major issues explored was the characteristics of and variations in the class structure itself (Goldthorpe and his colleagues took the occupational structure as largely given, and the statistical techniques employed controlled for structural variations between countries). Inspired by Marx's analysis, Wright examined the question of whether the class structure was, in fact, becoming increasingly proletarian. In fact, Wright found that, in the United States, the working class was actually declining as a proportion of the labor force, apparently confirming aspects of the industrial-society thesis. However, the composition of the working class has changed in that women, and members of ethnic minorities, are now in the majority. Wright also investigated the interaction between sex and class, as well as the question of class consciousness, which showed considerable variation across different societies

(Wright, *Class Counts*, 1997). In general, this explicitly Marxist class project has not served to demonstrate the robustness of Marx's predictions, but Wright nevertheless continues to argue that Marx's analytical framework provides the theoretically most coherent account of capitalism.

It might be suggested that both the CASMIN project and Wright's Comparative Project were from the beginning relatively limited in what they were able to achieve given their chosen methods, for there are problems with the operationalization of class via an occupational measure. Most obviously, occupation gives no indication of wealth holdings; thus the owners of capital are lost to sight. The occupational structure is also stratified by **gender**, **race and ethnicity**, and **age**; that is, the occupational structure is shaped by status as well as class. Indeed, the same occupation may be associated with different life chances depending on whether the employee is male or female, old or young, black or white. There will be an inescapable arbitrariness in the allocation of **groups** to particular categories – for example, the owner of an enterprise with fewer than twenty-six employees would be placed in a different class to the owner of a firm with twenty-six or more in Goldthorpe's scheme. A further problem lies in the class allocation of individuals without an occupation – for example, the long-term unemployed, or women carrying out domestic work in the home. It must be stressed that these kinds of difficulties do not invalidate the employment-aggregate approach to class analysis, but they impose limitations on its scope.

However, one negative outcome of the dominance of quantitative class analysis during the 1970s, 1980s, and into the 1990s was that debates within this strand became increasingly focused on measurement issues. As Mike Savage argues, "The 'point' of class analysis was rarely discussed, rather attention focused on how best to define class in occupational terms" (*Class Analysis and Social Transformation*, 2000). In fact, occupational measures of class (including status scales) intercorrelate quite highly and, for the individual researcher, the best measure may be a pragmatic rather than a theoretical choice. One point that should be emphasized, however, is that, despite the many criticisms that have been directed at occupational class schemes, they remain one of the most effective tools available for the mapping and exploration of social and economic inequalities.

Debates within employment-aggregate class analysis tended to be rather self-contained (and self-referential), although they ran parallel with broader arguments as to the significance of class in contemporary societies (see Rosemary Crompton, *Class and Stratification*, 1998). The general tenor of these wider debates (for example, C. Clark and S. M. Lipset, "Are Social Classes Dying?" 1991, and **Ulrich Beck** and E. Beck-Gernsheim, *Individualization*, 2002) has been to argue that, although the class concept might have had some value as far as the analysis of earlier phases of capitalist development was concerned, it had lost its cutting edge in relation to the understanding of postmodern, late modern, or **postindustrial societies**. These arguments might be summarized as follows: first, class no longer serves as a basis for the organization of politics or social protest more generally; rather, **social movements** with a focus on particular issues (ecology and the **environment**, antiwar, antinuclear, and antiglobalization) had taken their place. Second, it was argued that class no longer made a significant contribution to the construction of collective and individual identities. Rather, gender, **sexuality**, and **ethnicity** (and age) have become more important in defining the individual as well as in providing a focus for collective belonging. Finally, it is argued that class is no longer relevant as societies have become increasingly "individualized." Thus Beck states that: "Individualization is a concept which describes a structural, sociological transformation of social institutions and the relationship of the individual to society . . . Individualization liberates people from traditional roles and constraints . . . individuals are removed from status-based classes . . . Social classes have been detraditionalized."

It might seem paradoxical that social theorists were arguing for the redundancy of the class concept at precisely the same moment as material and social inequalities were expanding very rapidly, in part as a consequence of the adoption of neoliberal economic and **social policies** by national governments and international institutions. The erosion of the "mid [twentieth] century social compromise" was accompanied by increasing pressures on welfare benefits. Indeed, neoliberal commentators (C. Murray, *Losing Ground*, 1984) argued that the collective welfare provisions developed during the period after World War II had contributed to the undermining of individual capacities and thus the emergence of a welfare-dependent "underclass." Welfare reforms, it was argued, had taken away the incentive to work, giving rise to marginal groupings (lone mothers, the long-term unemployed, and people living off fraud and **crime**) who lived in a different world from that of mainstream society. Trapped in poverty and with no incentive to work, the **attitudes** and behavior of these groupings simply serve to reproduce disadvantage across the generations.

Right-wing commentators, therefore, have emphasized the moral and cultural deficiencies of underclass groupings, which are seen as having been brought into being by the excessive generosity of postwar **welfare states**. Critics of the underclass thesis, however, have emphasized the structural developments that have served to increase the numbers of those in poverty, as well as being highly critical of the underclass concept itself. In the United States (where the "underclass" is overwhelmingly black), **W. J. Wilson** (*The Truly Disadvantaged*, 1987) argued that economic restructuring and the decline in manufacturing employment had a particularly significant effect on the inner **city**. Lacking in job opportunities, inner cities in the United States became black **ghettoes**, deprived of a resident ethnic middle class which, taking advantage of the opportunities offered by equal opportunity and affirmative action programs, had moved out to the suburbs. More generally, the underclass concept has been criticized for its overemphasis on the moral deficiencies of the very poor. This reflects the political differences between the protagonists in the underclass debate. It is often argued controversially that an important justification for persisting inequality is that the more successful and better-rewarded are actually intrinsically and individually superior to the less successful, and thus deserving of their good fortune. However, critics of the underclass thesis argue that the identification of a (morally deficient) underclass effectively does no more than blame the victims. In fact, survey evidence has demonstrated that people without employment are no less committed to the idea of work, and no more fatalistic in their attitudes, than those in employment.

In my concluding arguments, it may be suggested that many contemporary criticisms of the utility of class analysis may be seen as deriving, ultimately, from the failure to establish a consistent and enduring link between structure and action, class and consciousness. The rapid increase in inequality since the 1970s, for example, was not accompanied by any sustained class action or resistance. Survey data suggest that the majority of the population does not consciously locate itself in class terms. The position taken here is that, while there may be numerous examples whereby a link between structure and action might be demonstrated (most would want to argue that capitalists have been remarkably effective in furthering their own interests, for example), this linkage is contingent upon circumstance, and the absence of such a link should not be assumed to undermine the validity of class analysis in all of its many aspects.

The insistence on a rigid separation of class and status or culture runs the risk of inadequately acknowledging the role of cultural and status hierarchies in the creation and **reproduction** of class inequalities. Recent work on class has emphasized the intertwining of these two dimensions, rather than their separation. The work of Bourdieu has been developed to demonstrate how cultural processes are embedded within specific socioeconomic practices. Socioeconomic locations are themselves accompanied by fields within which classed agents operate, guided by habitus (see **habitus and field**), that is, mental structures and dispositions that are socially inculcated and go largely unremarked. These practices (for example, the middle-class consciousness of the benefits of education and practical awareness of the competitive system) serve to ensure the reproduction of class advantage (F. Devine, *Class Practices*, 2004). Savage has reworked the thesis of individualization to argue that the increasing dominance in contemporary societies of middle-class, individualized culture lies behind the absence of collective expressions of class; that is, class practices have themselves become individualized. However, in emphasizing the interdependence of class and social **differentiation** more generally, there is a danger that class is simply conflated with the diffuse practices of social hierarchy.

A reemphasis on cultural class practices is in part a reaction to the growing **influence** of the cultural turn within the **social sciences**. However, the turn to culture, with its emphasis on individualized identities and the politics of recognition, resonates positively with neoliberal defenses of the market and the importance of individual **rights**. Furthermore, a stress on the primacy of recognition may effectively sideline issues of redistribution, which have always been central to class analysis. Moreover, there are important ontological issues that have implications for recent culturalist discussions of class. In particular, if it is argued that culture and the economy cannot be separated (or if class is conflated with hierarchy), then how can the different elements that contribute to structures of social inequality be identified?

N. Fraser ("Rethinking Recognition," 2000, *New Left Review*; see also J. Scott, *Stratification and Power*, 1996) has recently suggested a resolution to these problems that returns to the Weberian distinction between class and status. Her argument rests on the analytic separation of culture and economy. She suggests that class and status reflect two, analytically distinct, dimensions of social **justice**. Class relates to the distribution of disposable resources, status the allocation of recognition. The cultural definition of different categories of social actors (status groups) can result in social subordination and thus a lack of full partnership in social **interaction**. Fraser argued that claims for both economic redistribution and cultural recognition can be appraised against the same evaluative standard of participatory parity, that is, the social arrangements that permit all adult members of society to interact with one another as peers (it may be noted that this argument implicitly resurrects Marshall's idea of citizenship).

In conclusion, recent debates in class theory and analysis suggest a continuing need to recognize both that stratification systems are multi-stranded and that social class is a vital component of these systems. The way ahead for class analysis is to recognize the increasing complexity of inequalities in modern societies, without either beating a retreat in the face of this complexity, or attempting to resolve the issue by dissolving the boundaries between the contributory elements.

ROSEMARY CROMPTON

social closure

The terminology of closure and the closely related language of exclusion and monopolization appears first in **Max Weber**'s *Economy and Society* (1922 [trans. 1968]). A relationship that is closed against outsiders is one in which the "participation of certain persons is excluded, limited, or subjected to conditions." Weber noted that many relationships, including the exclusive erotic monopoly of **marriage**, membership of sects, personal relations of loyalty, the caste system, exclusive clubs, guilds, monastic orders, and various kinds of hereditary **groups** which asserted rights also used the means of closure. In the context of the **economy**, the idea of closure as monopolization is related to the concept in economics of rent-seeking, and Weber noted that there was a tendency for the economically successful to preserve their position by closure. The concept of closure, however, had little impact until it was revived in the 1970s and 1980s, when it was applied and elaborated in two different ways.

The first of these uses arose in a specific historical situation, in which the traditional Marxian criterion of class membership no longer corresponded to the distribution of **wealth** and **life chances**, and where social position was transmitted and preserved between **generations** by means other than the inheritance of **wealth**. Among the intellectual sources of the idea of social closure as a solution to this and related problems about the nature of **power** was a book by **Randall Collins** entitled *The Credential Society: An Historical Sociology of Education and Stratification* (1979), which suggested that modern society was a "credential society," in which such credentials as academic and professional certification, which were more accessible to the children of the successful, had become primary determinants of **income** and social power. Another early source was Frank Parkin's *Marxism and Class Theory* (1979), in which he argued, against the Marxian concept of exploitation, that exclusion from the work force rather than the exploitation of the employed was the major determinant of life chances. Raymond Murphy in *Social Closure: The Theory of Monopolization and Exclusion* (1988) later developed these ideas by arguing that the power to exclude or monopolize better explained the phenomenon of economic power than Marxian notions and avoided their difficulties, notably with the labor theory of **value**. Murphy also argued that many **social conflicts** could be understood in terms of the creation and defense of monopolies, which were then contested by those who were excluded, who attempted to gain access to their benefits, or, in Murphy's terms, to "usurp them."

The second major use is associated with **James S. Coleman**, in *Public and Private High Schools: The Impact of Communities* (1987), who applied the notion of closure to informal processes of social contact, to explain an important and anomalous empirical finding in the study of American schools. He had discovered that students in Catholic schools did significantly better than state-school students on standardized tests, and that controlling for differences in the students and the schools did not explain the discrepancy. He argued that the relatively closed social relations between parents in Catholic schools enabled the development of **norms** for student behavior, and that this was a valuable form of **social capital** that raised and enforced expectations, leading to improved **life chances**. He later applied this insight to norm-generation in general.

STEPHEN P. TURNER

social conflict

The contrast between conflict and consensus as interpretations of **society** was at one stage fashionable as a criterion for classifying **sociological theories**. For example it was argued that an emphasis on social conflict was the defining characteristic of **Marxism**, whereas an emphasis on social consensus was the defining characteristic of structural **functionalism**. More specifically, this classification contrasted the legacy of **Karl Marx** and class analysis with the influence of **Talcott Parsons** who allegedly ignored or neglected conflict in favor of the study of how shared **values** underpin social order. This simple classification is now regarded as inadequate because any theory of conflict will imply a theory of consensus, and therefore sociologists will inevitably have to address both aspects of social life. As **David Lockwood** argued in *Solidarity and Schism* (1992), whereas consensus theory overstated the normative integration of society, conflict theory depended too heavily on a utilitarian model of **social action** and could not explain how **norms** were important in the **explanation** of social conflict.

Marx's theory of social class conflict continues to be a foundation of any general analysis of conflict in **capitalism.** Whereas classical economists had recognized that a major source of conflict in society was the struggle over resources, and hence **scarcity** is the principal driving force behind conflict over access to goods in a competitive **market**, Marx concentrated on the emergence of **social classes** in capitalist societies, where there is a structural contradiction between the interests of workers, who want higher wages, and those of capitalists, who want higher profits. Conflict in modern societies, according to this theory, is primarily economic conflict. Marx's analysis of capitalism was modified by **Ralph Dahrendorf** in his *Class and Class Conflict in an Industrial Society* (1959) who argued that in modern industrial relations policy there had been an institutionalization of conflict because industrial disputes were often settled by negotiation between trade union officials and the managers of **firms**. In the early stages of capitalism, disputes between workers and capitalists could always escalate into strikes, social disruption, or revolution. In advanced capitalist societies, such disputes were managed through bargaining processes that avoided the revolutionary potential of industrial conflict, but such industrial settlements, when they resulted in a wages spiral, often resulted in inflation. As a result, postwar British society was characterized by industrial disruption, wage inflation, and low productivity that, in policy terms, resulted in classic "stop-go" economic crises. Inflation can be seen therefore as an alternative to class conflict. In more general terms, it is often claimed that the growth of social **citizenship** – as described, for example, by **Thomas H. Marshall** (1963) in his *Sociology at the Cross Roads* – brings about a reform of capitalism by the inclusion of workers in society, and thereby reduces their propensity for social conflict.

In contrast with **Marxism**, **Max Weber**'s sociology was seen to provide a more flexible and subtle understanding of conflict over **power**. Resources in human societies are diverse; they include economic, cultural, and honorific or status resources. In Weber's conflict sociology, **groups** attempt to monopolize access to resources through various strategies of power that involve some form of **social closure**. One example of social closure involves **credentialism** as an aspect of professional closure: that is, occupational groups will seek to protect their advantages in the marketplace by preventing competition from groups who are deemed to be unqualified. The historical competition between barbers and surgeons, and between homeopaths and allopaths, in the history of medicine is a classical illustration of social closure. The professional conflicts between registered doctors, bone setters, apothecaries, and quacks was brilliantly described by Roy Porter in his *Bodies Politic. Disease. Death and Doctors in Britain 1650–1900* (2001). The idea that conflict can occur over any resource has been developed, in differing forms of social capital theory, by Robert Putnam in *Bowling Alone* (2000) and by **Pierre Bourdieu** in *Distinction* (1979 [trans. 1984]), in which he distinguished between cultural, economic, social, and symbolic capitals. Conflict will occur in every field of the distribution of capital in society where groups struggle to gain competitive advantage. Bourdieu saw intellectual disagreements between academic **traditions** as conflicts over the control of symbolic and cultural capital in the academy in his *Homo Academicus* (1984 [trans. 1988]).

In the study of **race and ethnicity**, Weber's conflict sociology was employed by **John Rex** to develop a conflict theory of the competition between ethnic **communities** over resources. While Rex drew inspiration from Weber in the development of his *Social Conflict. A Conceptual and Theoretical Analysis* (1981), he also followed the British colonial administrator John Furnivall who, in his *Colonial Policy and Practice* (1968: 304), wrote that there is a "medley" of different ethnic communities in the market, but socially they "mix but don't combine." Race relations theorists have subsequently argued that in a **plural society** social conflict will be along racial rather than class lines. This argument raises serious questions therefore about the possibility of **multiculturalism**. Contemporary societies are consequently characterized by various forms of conflict in terms of **ethnicity**, class, and **gender**. These contemporary conflicts are, in plural or multicultural societies, seen to be conflicts over **identity**, especially in societies where **religion** comes to dominate **politics**, giving rise to identity politics. These conflicts, insofar as they appear to involve major conflicts between **civilizations**, have been described by Samuel Huntington in a famous article in *Foreign Affairs* (1993) as the "clash of civilizations". Because conflict is ubiquitous, it is assumed that a special theory of social conflict is redundant.

BRYAN S. TURNER

social constructionism

A set of theories and concepts in **sociology** and other disciplines that seek to explore and explain social phenomena and occurrences on the basis of their historical context and social framing, constructionism thereby traces how seemingly natural occurrences are constructed through a history of human actions and **interactions**. It refutes assumptions of **essentialism** and **realism**, namely that an external, objective world exists outside our categories of perception and interpretation. Social constructionism is thus part of a relativist turn in **social sciences** in which categories and forms of knowledge are contextualized, debunking **myths** of their transcendental quality.

Peter L. Berger and **Thomas Luckmann**'s *Social Construction of Reality* (1965), generally recognized as the major social constructionist work of modern sociology, explores the social construction of reality as the basic category of human perception and interaction. While they do not argue that the material world is in itself constructed, our realities within this world are. Subsequent **case studies** identify instances of social constructionism across the spectrum of social classifications, **identities**, and material objects, including **nationalism**, physical and mental illness, **moral panics**, **social class**, taste, **technology**, **sexuality**, **gender**, and knowledge.

In the sociology of science, studies focusing on the construction of scientific knowledge in disciplines such as mathematics (for example

P. Ernest, *Social Constructivism as a Philosophy of Mathematics*, 1998) and physics (for instance A. Pickering, *Constructing Quarks*, 1984) have been met with hostility by other scientific **communities** in the so-called "science wars." Ian Hacking, in *The Social Construction of What?* (1999), attempts to reconcile contrary positions on whether scientific facts or laws, such as the concept of Quarks, are universally true – in other words based on discoveries of facts that exist independent of human cognition – or socially constructed. He proposes a spectrum of possible positions between these polarities depending on responses to three questions about the particular idea or fact that is assumed to be constructed. First, are alternative **explanations** or concepts possible ("contingency")? Second, do the ordering and structure of knowledge follow from our own and hence constructed systems of perception or reflect an independent structure of the material world ("nominalism")? Third, how do we explain the stability of certain facts and ideas? Natural scientists may claim that such stability derives from the accuracy of knowledge whereas social constructionists point to the context of scientific research (the institutionalization of research, and the economic and political framing of research funding). Hacking's argument is that, in all three positions, we find a mixture of both constructionism and essentialism, and both epistemological perspectives inform scientific knowledge.

Hacking also seeks to define the objects and the purpose of social constructionist studies. Social constructionism in particular focuses on occurrences and classifications that are perceived as "natural," despite being not inevitable but a product of human action and interaction. The aim of social constructionism is therefore to "unmask." In particular, studies on the social construction of gender and sexuality, which have formed the foundational core of **gender studies**, serve this purpose of unmasking. **Simone de Beauvoir** in *The Second Sex* (1949 [trans. 1984]) first documented the historical, cultural, and social context through which gender is formed, and thereby undermined the understanding of gender as biological fact which was prevalent until the mid twentieth century. Numerous feminist scholars have followed de Beauvoir in unmasking the ideological function of a perception of gender, and associated roles such as **motherhood**, as naturally given as a tool of **patriarchy**. Equally, **queer theory** has aimed to expose heterosexual **norms** and legislation as repressive instruments. The implication in this and other social constructionist

work is that the socially constructed objects, classifications, or categories they investigate are undesirable and should be transformed or abolished. Hence, social constructionism has been particularly popular in areas of sociology that address questions of **power**, **inequality**, and **discrimination** and propose **social change**.

Whereas the purpose of social constructionism appears obvious, its objects of study are more difficult to define. Hacking distinguishes in this context between "objects" and "ideas," arguing that objects exist independently of human classification and social construction, whereas ideas, as the way we represent and comprehend these objects, are socially constructed. The concepts of Quarks or child abuse, for example, are constructed, yet Quarks and child abuse are also actual objects that exist beyond this construction. These examples reveal two problems: Quarks can only be encountered and verified through the idea of quarks; we cannot see or experience them otherwise. Child abuse, in contrast, is a relatively new idea, yet we find an extensive historical documentation of child abuse prior to the rise of the idea. However, the rise of the idea of child abuse has in itself impacted on the phenomenon. The consequential distinction between "indifferent kinds" and "interactive kinds" seeks to separate between objects such as Quarks which are oblivious to our classifications and objects involving social actors that are impacted by the construction of ideas.

The balance between essential and constructed aspects of non-social objects also forms the key concern of social constructionist studies in the sociology of media and **technology**. They explore the question of whether to assess the interaction between technology and history through the prism of discovery and innovation of such technologies, or by emphasizing their history of adaptation and use. Various qualitative studies of the social shaping of communication technologies have thus sought to counter the claims of medium theory and **technological determinism** which, following **Marshall McLuhan** in *Understanding Media* (1964), propose that the inherent essence of technologies shape human history and behavior; in McLuhan's example, there is only one, very definite meaning of the atom bomb. Social constructionists in contrast point to the specific socio-historical and cultural circumstances that formed the necessary preconditions and contexts that made the adaptation and proliferation of particular technologies possible. In a social constructionist sense, the history of television, for instance, is hence not a history of mere technological advances (involving radio transmission or the Braun tube) but a product of a wider process of individualization, suburbanization, and the rise of **consumer society**.

CORNELL SANDVOSS

social contract

This concept derives from political theory to explain the acquiescence of free citizens in the political **authority** of the **state**. Under the unwritten contract, the citizen trades unfettered freedom for the freedom that derives from the **rights** and obligations of **citizenship** under the protection of the state. The concept is associated with political philosophy in the seventeenth century, especially with liberal theorists such as Thomas Hobbes (1588–1679) and John Locke (1632–1704), and with the eighteenth-century republican Jean-Jacques Rousseau (1712–78).

In the twentieth century, the liberal social and political philosopher John Rawls (1921–2002) developed the idea of a hypothetical social contract in *A Theory of Social Justice* (1971). Using the device of the "veil of ignorance," he argued that people would agree to an equitable principle of distribution without knowing their own position in society and hence the implications of the principle for themselves. More recently, the metaphor of the contract has been central to work-focused welfare reform in a number of **welfare states**, notably the United States and the United Kingdom. In the former, the Republican Party's "Contract for America" framed the debate about welfare reform in the Clinton era. The outcome was the Personal Responsibility and Work Opportunity Reconciliation Act 1996, which, with bipartisan support in Congress, replaced Aid to Families with Dependent Children with the highly conditional Temporary Aid to Needy Families. In the United Kingdom, the New Labour government promoted its reform agenda in the late 1990s as "a new contract for welfare." Under this contract, social security recipients are expected to fulfill their obligations, especially in relation to paid **work**, in exchange for social benefit rights and also opportunities, such as training, offered by government. Such developments have led to the suggestion that a process of "contractualization" is increasingly governing the relationship between government and individual citizens.

There is a strong feminist critique of the social contract, developed most comprehensively by Carole Pateman in *The Sexual Contract* (1988). Her argument is that women were not party to the social contract, which was also a sexual contract. As such, it established men's political and sexual rights over women. The social contract thus spelt patriarchal subjugation, not freedom, for women. Although the social contract was represented as applying only to the **public sphere,** the feminist critique emphasizes the interrelationship of public and private (domestic) spheres and therefore that the sexual social contract regulates both spheres. The notion of a "gender contract" has also been proposed, initially by Scandinavian theorists, to describe the pattern of implicit rules that govern social relations between women and men and the organization of production and **reproduction** and associated social **institutions**.

RUTH LISTER

social control

This term has been used to describe anything from nursery social-skills training to incarceration in prisons and closed-circuit television surveillance systems. It is one of the key concepts in the lexicon of political and **social sciences** and is present in a range of fields including **education**, the **welfare state**, workplaces, psychiatry, and, more obviously, crime control. The concept is intimately linked to issues of social order – how individuals, **groups**, and **societies** organize their lives together. Today, the term social control is often used to refer to some form of organized reaction to deviant, criminal, worrying, or otherwise troublesome behavior. One key writer, Donald Black, has argued in *The Behaviour of Law* (1976) that social control generally refers to the normative aspect of social life and to prohibitions, accusations, and punishment.

The term came into frequent use in the 1960s when academic and professional critics alike focused on the idea that the **state** was less benign in its intentions than previously understood. Indeed, reactive and reparative criminal justice system interventions came to be seen as repressive. Fueled by protest movements in the United States and in Europe and an emerging (often Marxist-inspired) left-wing **politics** in Britain, coercive aspects of social control were identified in social work, medicine, psychiatry, law, probation work, and schooling, for instance. The state was thought to be intruding into the private lives of individuals, with frequent surveillance and regulation. As Stanley Cohen put it in *Visions of Social Control* (1985), "social control has become Kafka-land". **Michel Foucault**'s subsequent recognition of the processes of diffuse societal **power** in the 1980s added analytical sophistication and broadened the concept to include the discursive construction, **ideology**, and production of meaning, as well as institutional practices. Foucault refers to a continuous disciplinary discourse, for example, in which power emanates as much from forms of knowledge that shape social relations as from the state or a mode of production. Cohen's work on the "punitive archipelago" (1985) has also been influential in deepening our understanding of the nature and meaning of social control. As discipline is dispersed from custody into the **community**, and as new **technologies** and professional interests are developed, we are all drawn into the control enterprise. Gated **cities**, zero-tolerance, exclusion zones, and new laws to regulate "anti-social behavior" in the street all feature here. It is also of significance that a good deal of control has been removed from direct state oversight and become privatized, with private security **firms**, voluntary agencies, and communities all playing a part in the commodification of social control.

Social control theory reflects a sociological approach to the nature of conformity. Early social control theorists suggested that juvenile delinquency occurred when individuals had a weak ego or poor self-concept. Thus delinquents were deemed to lack the requisite personal controls to produce conformity. Later studies explained conformity in terms of "ties" to the conventional social order. F. Ivan Nye in *Family Relationships and Delinquent Behavior* (1958) identified four types of control: direct (based on the promise of rewards and the threat of punishment), indirect (based on affectional ties to conventional persons), internalized (based on the development of individual **personality** and conscience), and control over opportunities (for deviant and conventional activities).

Travis Hirschi's notion of "social bonds" outlined in *The Causes of Delinquency* (1969) is probably the most widely known version of social control theory. There are four components: attachment (to significant conventional others), involvement (in conventional activities), belief (respect for society's laws), and commitment (having a stake in conformity). Subsequent researchers have sought to refine the theory by looking at the nature and quality of attachments. The theory is at its weakest when it comes to thinking about the interactive effects of the different components, but Hirschi's version of social control theory is widely perceived to have been hugely influential.

LORAINE GELSTHORPE

social Darwinism

This extends the theory of natural selection to the human social world. As **Charles Darwin** himself argued, humans are a form of animal. They, like all other animals, must have been subject to the processes of evolution (see **evolutionary theory**). They must have competed among themselves and with other species for survival in the context of limited resources. And those humans with special characteristics (those with, for example, special physical or intellectual resources) must have prevailed and reproduced future **generations**. Such ideas predated the publication of the theory of natural selection by **Charles Darwin** and Alfred Russel Wallace (1823–1913). **Herbert Spencer** is particularly well known in this regard. The weakest members of what he called a "race" have died out in the process of human evolution. Meanwhile, the average fitness of a race has improved as those surviving pass on their characteristics to future generations.

One strong implication of this argument is that humans have evolved as naturally competitive. Furthermore, social **care** for the sick and weak should be strictly limited. Such care, particularly by governments, would only stop the winnowing process and reverse the process of steady social improvement. The fittest would thereby not survive and the stock of people would be weakened and die out. This is the version of social Darwinism which is perhaps best known. It was Spencer's view and one which Darwin himself occasionally reiterated. Furthermore, it found widespread support, particularly amongst those, including **William G. Sumner**, promoting free trade in nineteenth-century America.

But Darwinism has been recruited in different ways by other kinds of **politics** and in other kinds of society. Sidney Webb (1859–1947), the British Fabian socialist, concluded from Darwin's and Wallace's theory that state intervention be implemented. It is not individuals who are competing for survival, Webb believed, but whole societies. And perpetual struggle between societies for domination would, in the long run, only be damaging to individuals. It was therefore up to governments to step in, providing jobs, housing, and social security on a scale allowing society to remain fit and healthy. Such well-being was particularly required by a society then at the center of the biggest empire the world had seen.

The Russian anarchist writer Prince Kropotkin (1842–1921) interpreted Darwin in yet another way. He argued that it is in all animals' very nature to be collaborative. They are not predisposed to compete for survival. His survey of the animal kingdom concluded that collaboration in the interests of survival is the rule rather than the exception. In a similar way, the modern anarchist Murray Bookchin argued that it is only humans which compete for survival. The early domination of males over females during the process of human evolution has led to a culture of domination, one spreading to the domination of children and nonhuman species. These anarchist writers would still not call for state intervention, and they would be equally opposed to the use of Darwin to promote laissez-faire philosophy, free trade, or the "natural" superiority of men over women. The lesson of Darwinism was that people should be left to their own devices. They will make their own peaceful and collaborative societies without either state intervention or the widespread extension of free trade.

These varying interpretations of Darwin suggest that the application of Darwin's ideas to particular social and political projects is largely misconceived. Darwin and Wallace identified underlying causal mechanisms operating over millennia but these are overlaid by social and political relations which deeply affect whether, how, when, and where they operate. A central feature to humans is their immense flexibility; indeed, this is perhaps the main reason why they and not other species have survived for so long. Humans have shown themselves capable of living in many different types of physical and social setting. Furthermore, they have demonstrated themselves capable of being either competitive or collaborative, of successfully living in either free-trade or state-administered societies. Whether they thrive equally well under all these settings, however, is a somewhat different matter, one for further careful empirically based research. Richard G. Wilkinson (*Unhealthy Societies*, 1996) and others have produced growing evidence, for example, that human beings suffer from psychic and physical disorders under conditions of relative **inequality**. Constant exposure to stressful circumstances can severely affect the body's immune system, leaving it open to infections and diseases such as cancer. D. J. P. Barker in *Mothers, Babies and Health in Later Life* (1998) points to widespread epidemiological evidence that **children** from the poorest backgrounds are left with bodily structures and forms of metabolism which leave them open to relatively short lives and diseases such as diabetes. Humans and other animals have probably inherited during their evolution mechanisms which ensure that in straitened circumstances the most basic of organs (such as the brain) are not too damaged while others (such as the pancreas) are left in a poor state. And these problems can be passed on over time as a woman's own intrauterine experience affects her children, and so on down the generations.

Evolutionary and biological processes are therefore still combining with social relations, albeit in complex and varied ways. Developing a new social Darwinism would entail sociologists and natural scientists working together to track how inherited biological and psychic mechanisms combine with social systems to produce some people who are fit while others live short and relatively unhealthy lives. As Peter Dickens (*Society and Nature*, 2004) suggests, this could imply a realist perspective, one which acknowledges real causal mechanisms and processes but explores how these are developed and realized in different social settings.   PETER DICKENS

social distance

Analogous to the idea of physical distance, which is the degree of separation between two physical entities in terms of units of length, social distance is the degree of separation between two social entities in terms of an appropriate social metric. The analogy is easy to appreciate, and ideas of personal closeness and distance are common in everyday language. The organization of **ritual**, ceremony, and **everyday life** in very many societies leads different people of different social categories to be located in a way that maps social space onto physical space, which in turn radically affects the possibility of communication and **interaction** between them. It also has consequences for conceptions of **privacy** and the **public sphere,** and resonances with conceptions of **sociometry**. However, despite the richness of the metaphor given these correspondences, the nature of the social entities and what metrics should be used in defining social distance are not simple matters.

The concept has its roots in the work of **Georg Simmel**, who articulated a complex linkage between physical and metaphorical social **spaces**. His ideas were greatly simplified and operationalized in the Bogardus social-distance scale. This asked respondents whether they would admit someone from another social, ethnic or racial **group** to various groupings of which the respondent was part. The closest was admittance to one's **family** by **marriage**, and ranged through being in one's **neighbourhood**, **profession**, or country. Some variants of the scale even had as the most distant extreme the willingness to allow members of the target group to be alive. In each category of closeness, there is a clear implication of physical distance and in turn of the frequency with which one might interact with that person. The impact of social distance on linguistic form has been explored in studies of conversation, and is used to account for why different modes of expression are used by speakers to achieve what are ostensibly the same interactional purposes in different situations. The variable use of second-person singular and plural forms when addressing a single other person, for example *tu* (a familiar "thou") and *vous* (a formal "you") in French, is typically explained in terms of horizontal and vertical social distance, that is, familiarity and comparative **social status** respectively.

The correspondence between physical and social distance is greatly affected by **technologies** that change our capacity to interact with one another when not copresent. By permitting interaction at a distance, they seemingly undercut the effect of physical distance on social distance. This began with the invention of writing, and has been greatly extended by the development and spread of numerous communication technologies. It is widely observed, however, that these technologies, which permit high-quality visual and auditory connections between people in different parts of the planet, still do not permit one to have the same sense of being together as actual physical copresence permits. Whether this will still prove to be the case as more **children** grow to adulthood in a world in which these technologies are a commonplace remains to be seen.

DAVID GOOD

social economy

This term denotes the social character of economic life and rejects the idea that the **market** and the **economy** generally can operate independently of social life as a whole. In premodern society, it is obvious that the way that **wealth** was appropriated affected one's social position, so that one's relationship to the means of production had obvious ideological and cultural implications.

Liberalism, however, has traditionally argued otherwise. Indeed, classical liberalism postulated the existence of individuals in a "state of nature" in which these individuals acted as isolated atoms, without relationships or social ties. Some took the view that this **individualism** made economic life impossible; others held the view that individuals could trade and even agree to the use of **money**,

before establishing a social order. The latter version, associated in particular with the work of John Locke (1632–1704), assumed that the **state** was the product of a **social contract**, and that trading and the acquisition of wealth could occur "naturally" and independent of society as such.

Even when liberals abandoned the notion of the state of nature (at the end of the eighteenth century), they still continued to believe that the market was autonomous and independent of the state, and in practice, if not always in theory, they saw individuals as "abstracted" from society. Indeed, one could argue that the exchange process creates the illusion that individuals enter into transactions as autonomous individuals: by law, individuals are deemed "equal" even though they may have dramatically different amounts of social **power** at their disposal. The very notion of contract assumes an **equality** that may be purely formal, and belied by real differentials in wealth and power.

In reality, economic life has always been social in character. It is impossible to produce without cooperation, but a stark division of **labor** between those who work and those who command the services of others may create the illusion that the creation of wealth occurs outside society. Production of wealth is not only a social process; it also dramatically influences the wider character of society, so that, strictly speaking, the concept of a "social economy" is pleonastic, that is, the word social is redundant since an economy cannot be other than social in character.

Many liberals in the late nineteenth century became conscious of the social character of wealth creation, and they expressed concern about the social divisions that had accompanied the production process. Indeed, **sociology** as an academic discipline arises on the assumption that human activity in all its forms is inherently social in character, so that it makes no sense to see the economy as somehow separate from society.

New liberals, social democrats, and many conservatives stressed the need to integrate individuals into society, and this meant reforming the market so that a stake in society could be more widely shared. Individualism became less and less abstract and it is increasingly seen that, when people enter into market relations, they do so as real people with differential amounts of wealth and social power.

JOHN HOFFMAN

social exclusion

This is a concept that has become increasingly dominant in European poverty discourses (and to a lesser extent in international development) in recent years. However, the concept has little purchase in the United States. The concept's theoretical roots lie in the sociological thought of **Max Weber** (as a process of **social closure**); of **Émile Durkheim** and **Robert K. Merton** (as undermining **social integration**); and of **Thomas H. Marshall** (as the denial of citizenship **rights**).

The concept's modern usage is, however, more political than sociological in origin. It was deployed in France in the 1970s and early 1980s to denote what had happened to marginalized **groups** who had fallen through the net of the social insurance system, and was then applied more broadly to conditions of precariousness. The term was adopted by the European Commission in the late 1980s and is now firmly embedded in European Union policy. It was appropriated by the United Kingdom's New Labour government when it came to power in 1997, with the establishment of the Social Exclusion Unit. This adopted a problem-oriented approach to social exclusion focused on particular vulnerable groups and **neighborhoods**.

Social exclusion is a concept with multiple meanings. Ruth Levitas (*The Inclusive Society*, 1998) identifies three competing discourses: redistributive egalitarian (RED); moralistic underclass (MUD); and social integrationist (SID). The last is most prominent in European policy, with its emphasis on paid **work** as the route to social inclusion.

Social exclusion is not a synonym for **poverty**, even though it is often treated as such. There is considerable debate as to the exact empirical and conceptual relationship between the two and around their political usage. Empirical research has identified a number of dimensions of social exclusion in the spheres of the **labor market**, social integration/isolation, **politics**, and service provision. These dimensions overlap to varying degrees with material poverty, with social isolation showing only a weak association. Research in the United Kingdom has not yet identified a significant group excluded on all the dimensions of social exclusion. This has led some analysts to conclude that it is better to talk about specific dimensions of exclusion rather than an undifferentiated category of socially excluded people.

Skepticism has been expressed in some quarters as to what the concept of social exclusion adds to our understanding of poverty. There are fears that it can be used politically to downplay the significance of material poverty itself. Some exponents of the concept view it as a significant conceptual shift from poverty, while others contend that it constitutes a valuable lens illuminating aspects of poverty itself. These aspects, identified in the literature, are: an emphasis on relationships and **rights**; a broader framework of analysis, which embraces social divisions such as **gender**, **race and ethnicity**, and **disability**; a multidimensional and multilevel understanding that also incorporates a spatial dimension; a focus on dynamics and process, including an understanding of process as causal mechanism at the societal and institutional level. Those who focus on process in this way ask questions about the **agency** and **power** of both excluders and excluded.

RUTH LISTER

social indicators

Regularly collected social **statistics** can be used to track trends in society, such as crime rates, health outcomes, educational attainment, divorce rates, and family composition. Such social indicators parallel the more widely known economic indicators, such as retail prices or the unemployment rate. Governments have long collected national social statistics through **censuses** and other regularly collected large-scale **surveys**. These **data** provide policymakers with the means to assess how policies will impact on societies in the future, and are central to the functioning of modern governments. Improvement and expansion of social-indicator data-collection efforts are a hallmark of the **modernization** of **states**. Policymakers today have at their disposal vastly improved sources of **information** about social and economic trends compared to a century ago.

Measurement issues are a critical component of social indicators. Good indicators must be capable of measuring the same thing at different points in time. Problems arise in one of two ways. First, **social changes** influence the meaning of categories being measured (for example, the current definition of rape differs greatly from that of several decades ago). Second, changes in data-collection techniques produce false impressions of trends (for example, improvements in police recordkeeping may give the impression of rising **crime** when only improved reporting of crime has occurred).

The visibility and urgency of **social problems** are closely linked to the collection of social indicators. Potential problems without regularly measured indicators may go unheeded by the **mass media** and policymakers. Conversely, well-measured problems more easily attract the attention of key actors, especially when negative trends appear (for example, rising crime rates, falling educational test scores, or rising levels of teenage pregnancy).

Social indicators are frequently misused, misunderstood, or manipulated in a variety of ways. Short-term trends may indicate a larger long-term pattern of change, or they may merely reflect "trendless" fluctuation. Mistaking the latter for a true long-term trend is a common misuse of such indicators. Critical scrutiny of claims about trends based on social indicators by social scientists and policy activists is thus an important part of the larger dialogue over **public policies** designed to address social problems. JEFF MANZA

social integration

One of the central postulates of **functionalism** is that the very idea of a **society** means that there is a tendency towards integration among its parts. Since the different parts of a society are maintained by human action, this was frequently interpreted to mean the integration of the subjective meanings and motives of actors. Functionalists, such as **Talcott Parsons**, argued that actors operated within a common **culture** that both generated the definition of role expectations and provided them with internalized need dispositions that served to define wants. Actors respond not only to positive rewards, but also to internalized feelings of guilt, anxiety, and the need for approval; a functioning social system is also a normative order.

For conflict theorists, such as **Ralph Dahrendorf** and **John Rex**, functionalism was too one-sided. It gave greater emphasis to **values** and **norms**, than to **power** and **social conflict**. For Dahrendorf, it was a "consensus" model. Its emphasis on social processes tending towards integration was part of a longstanding conservative tradition in **social theory** going back to Plato. It was also unrealistic and utopian in proposing a model of society from which change is absent; social conflict was more typical of society than social integration.

These criticisms struck a chord, but the position was unstable for a number of reasons. Parsons had sought to account for both power and consensus in his model. It was difficult to argue that the two models could be kept entirely apart and used separately for different purposes, as Dahrendorf and Rex argued, while expressing a preference for the conflict model. The issues of conflict and cooperation, and **power** and legitimation, are intertwined.

David Lockwood went further. He argued that conflict theorists were too concerned with overt conflict between actors. Drawing on **Karl Marx**'s analysis of **capitalism**, Lockwood suggested that what was missing was a concept of system contradiction. Simply put, functionalism had no place for the idea that the parts of a social system may contain tendencies towards malintegration, or contradiction (the exception, perhaps, is **Robert K. Merton**'s idea of dysfunction). According to Lockwood, those tendencies may eventually come to the surface in the form of oppositional interests and conflicts among actors. These conflicts may or may not be contained by the normative order (for Lockwood, this is an empirical question).

Rather than proposing two separate models, Lockwood argued that it is necessary to consider the question of cooperation, conflict, and **social change** in terms of two distinct, but interrelated, sets of processes. One concerned normative processes of social integration, the other concerned material processes of system integration. The problem with functionalism was that it conflated the two and emphasized the mutual operation of both sets of processes. Lockwood's ideas have been taken further in **Jürgen Habermas**'s development of the concepts of system and **lifeworld**.

JOHN HOLMWOOD

social keynesianism
– see **John Maynard Keynes**.

social mobility

The movement of individuals and **groups** within a stratification order, the comparative study of social mobility, especially in industrial societies, is a major area of empirical sociology. Part of the ideological **legitimacy** of industrial societies has been that they are open and meritocratic and the study of social mobility has been central to the evaluation of this claim.

Social mobility was first examined systematically by **Pitirim Sorokin** in his book *Social Mobility* (1927). His fundamental concern was with the **social structure** within which movements take place, and he conceived it to be a structure of classes. Mobility might be a matter of the rise and decline of whole classes or other large social groups (as, for example, in caste mobility), or of the relative openness of classes to movements across their boundaries. Before Sorokin, **Max Weber** had defined **social class** in *Economy and Society* (1968: 302) as the "totality of those class situations in which individual and generational mobility is easy and typical," while **Vilfredo Pareto** had written on the circulation of **elites** in *The Rise and Fall of the Elites* (1968).

Within advanced industrial societies, the study of social mobility is more usually concerned with a structure of **occupations**, ranked in terms of their relative advantages and disadvantages. Intergenerational mobility compares **children**'s occupational achievements with those of their parents, while intragenerational mobility is concerned with an individual's movement within their own lifetime. The greater the mobility between **generations** or over the **life-course**, the more open the society is regarded to be, and the less durable its system **inequality**.

According to Robert Erikson (1938–) and **John Goldthorpe** in *The Constant Flux* (1992), the liberal theory of industrialism (which they associate with **functionalism**) proposes that industrial societies, when compared with preindustrial ones, are characterized by high rates of social mobility; upward mobility predominates over downward mobility, mobility opportunities are more equal across groups, and rates of mobility and the degree of **equality** of opportunity increase over time. Social positions in preindustrial society are largely ascribed, whereas in industrial society they are increasingly achieved through meritocratic selection.

Feminists have criticized the emphasis on male heads of household and father-to-son mobility, arguing that it misses the performance of gender-ascribed roles in the household and their impact on the wider stratification order.

Social mobility raises serious issues of conceptualization and **measurement. Peter M. Blau** and **Otis Dudley Duncan** analyzed mobility in terms of occupations ranked in a continuous hierarchy of socioeconomic standing. In contrast, Marxist and Weberian class theorists, such as Erik Wright and Goldthorpe, argue that what should be studied is movement between bounded groups defined in class terms. Class theorists downplay the idea of movement within a hierarchy, though there are undoubted implications of a continuous hierarchy of positions in the way in which occupations are assigned to "classes" on the basis of "more or less" **income** or **authority**. In this conceptualization, there is interclass mobility as well as intraclass mobility.

The occupational structure itself has changed with the development of industrial society (for example, there has been a decline in the number of manual jobs and a corresponding rise in the number of white-collar jobs). Some mobility would necessarily follow from changes in the occupational structure, if there were an increase in the number of higher-class locations compared with lower-class occupations. This seems to have taken place, despite attempts by some Marxists to assert a general thesis of the proletarianization of occupations. Increased measurement sophistication, with the development of log-linear **modeling**, has enabled the analysis of rates of relative mobility as a more appropriate measure of openness; that is, the chances of an individual with origins in one class finishing up in a particular destination class rather than another, when compared with individuals from a different class of origin. Equally, the comparison could be with relative positions in a hierarchy.

Class theorists suggest that high rates of social mobility in industrial societies are largely an artifact of changes in the class structure. Mobility opportunities became more equal relatively early on in the process of industrialism, but for much of the twentieth century they have remained stable and rates of relative mobility have remained unchanged. Critics of class-based schemes have argued that they tend to overemphasize rigidities and that, while inequality is very durable and the early thesis of industrial society was overstated, there is a secular weakening of family **influence** that continues through the twentieth century.

The argument that meritocratic selection should be the basis of achievement in industrial societies is also strongly associated with the view that **education** is a vehicle of selection. In 1960, Ralph H. Turner suggested two **ideal types** of sponsored versus contest mobility for considering differences between the British and American educational systems, respectively, though with wider application beyond those two systems. In sponsored mobility, there is early selection by the **elite** of promising candidates from lower echelons, while in contest mobility candidates self-select themselves through effort and compete on an equal footing for available elite positions. The difference reflects the greater role of traditional, status aspects within the British system (for example, in selective schools, the role of Oxford and Cambridge Universities), compared with that of the United States.

In contest mobility, the availability of elite positions places no restriction on the provision of educational qualifications or their pursuit; other sociologists, most notably **Randall Collins**, have identified the tendency towards **credentialism** in the American educational system and have attributed this to competition among ethnic groups. Turner draws attention to the psychological consequences of the two systems in terms of their impact on feelings of worth and "phantasy aspirations." While Turner's types are overstated – he calls them ideal types – they draw attention to cultural elements in the **reproduction** of social inequality and its hidden injuries. These themes were developed by the French sociologist **Pierre Bourdieu** and his idea of the **habitus** of social classes; the unequal social order determines the experiences and ways of thinking of those differently located within it, such that their **attitudes** and behavior serve to reproduce inequalities and thus limit mobility.   JOHN HOLMWOOD

social movement theory
– see **social movements**.

social movements
These are relatively spontaneous forms of collective political action which break everyday routines and challenge established political **norms**; the term originated in the circle around **Claude Henri Rouvroy, Comte de Saint-Simon** in the aftermath of the French Revolution. From the middle of the nineteenth century, it became associated with the working class and the **labor movement**. In their *Communist Manifesto* (1848), **Karl Marx** and **Friedrich Engels** identified the working class and the labor movement as the prime historical agents of **social change** in modern society. It was Lorenz von Stein who, in the mid-1840s, coined the German phrase which later translated into the English "social movement" and **Werner Sombart** who established its study as a legitimate object of research.

Max Weber and **Émile Durkheim** conceptualized social movements in relation to problems of **social integration**, as forms of behavior associated with periods of societal transition. The central concern was with integrating the working class and creating a new social order within the nation-state. Social movements, conceived in terms of **social classes** or masses, were forces demanding to be recognized by and integrated into the institutional framework of the nation. This set a pattern for later interpretations.

The rise of **fascism** as a mass movement provided the next phase in the conceptualization of social movements. Rather than seeking integration, these movements presented a threat to established political **institutions**. Knowledge of them was considered essential not to the promotion of social integration but to prevent societal

disintegration. Influenced by theories of crowd behavior developed by **Gustav Le Bon**, social movements were interpreted as a form of collective behavior and understood on a scale of **rationality**, from the irrational behavior of the crowd to the more rational social movement. Opposed to Le Bon, this approach called for a social rather than psychological explanation of group behavior. While displaying similar characteristics to a crowd, a social movement was considered more rational because of an underlying goal-orientation and the potential for new **norms** to emerge as it developed. **Herbert Blumer**, who was closely associated with **symbolic interactionism**, was a significant figure in this theoretical development. Blumer attributed a degree of creativity and social learning to social movements.

Also significant in the development of the collective behavior perspective, **Talcott Parsons**'s article "Sociological Aspects of Fascist Movements," in *Social Forces* (1942) made use of classical **social theory** to explain the emergence of contentious collective behavior as due to "strains" relating to the **rationalization** of society which accompanied **modernization**. Social movements were conceptualized from a macro-perspective as collective behavior caused by the strain stemming from rapid social change, which both marginalized and then constituted certain **groups**.

The collective behavior perspective focused on the strains of societal transition and the **alienation** and marginalization of groups in relation to them. The social movements of the 1960s called this into question, given the number of middle-class college students involved in them. What came to be called the resource mobilization perspective emerged with an organizational and institutional focus. Far from marginal and irrational crowd behavior, social movements were conceptualized as structured, purposive–rational action. As the name indicates, resource mobilization called attention to the efficient and effective mobilization of resources as the prime indicator of success in social movement. Key actors in this process were called "movement entrepreneurs," whose role was the management of resources within social movement **organizations** (M. N. Zald and J. D. McCarthy, *Social Movements in an Organizational Society,* 1987). As opposed to collective behavior, resource mobilization conceptualized social movements in structured settings and as themselves already structured. Besides forms of organization, central issues concerned **leadership** and the management and effective use of available recourses, including ideas as well as the traditional **money** and people.

Utilitarian cost/benefit calculations and game-theoretical models were introduced and the issue of the "free rider" and the risks of participation were of central concern. Internal developments in this perspective were carried out by **Charles Tilly** in *From Mobilization to Revolution* (1978), who added wide-ranging historical scope by conceptualizing social movements as engaged in protest and producing protest events that could be mapped and codified. Another internal development introduced the term political opportunity structure, and related mobilization to an interplay between movements and their external political environment.

The idea of "new" social movements developed in Europe related to the emergence of environmentalism and the women's and peace movements in the 1970s. The idea was that there might be a fundamentally new type of social movement, as opposed to a new way of studying them. New social processes produced new conflicts and new collective actors. New social movements, it was argued, were triggered by concerns with the quality of life and emerge in the sphere of daily life, rather than in the sphere of production. They are characterized by a concern with personal **identity**, rather than the redistribution of **wealth** or **power**, making their forms of action more symbolic and expressive than instrumental and strategic. In the work of **Manuel Castells**, the idea and significance of urban social movements with a more fluid and transitory structure were also proposed as new.

One can identify a strong and weak version of this thesis. The strong version, associated with **Alain Touraine** and Alberto Melucci, was couched in macro-theories of societal transformation linking new social movements to the emergence of a "**postindustrial society**" or "programmed, information society." Ronald Inglehart's survey-based research (*The Silent Revolution: Changing Values and Political Styles Among Western Publics*, 1977), claiming to reveal a fundamental value shift favoring "postmaterial" values, proved influential in grounding ideas that a new **politics** emerged with new movements. The weaker version argued for a new perspective, rather than a new theory of **society** or a fundamentally new politics. While agreeing that something significant had happened in the form and content of social movements, it was proposed that a change in perspective focusing on the more symbolic and expressive dimensions of collective action – primarily questions of identity – was sufficient.

This cultural turn has continued. While **values**, ideas, and **ideology** had been a central concern of early approaches to social movements, the structural and organizational focus of resource mobilization tended to downplay their role. A new focus on cognition and on frameworks of meaning and interpretation resulted. The concept of framing taken from **Erving Goffman** was introduced to the study of social movements in the mid-1980s. Social movements, it was pointed out, offered new ways of interpreting the world, of defining the social situation and attempting to convince others in the process. The ability to modify and affect meaning and interpretation, to change, align, and coordinate, were thus made central to social movement activity. Protest and changing the world, it was argued, necessarily involved changing the way people looked at the world. Social movements offered new frames to make this possible.

A meaning struggle, the struggle to define the situation, was seen as a central site of a conflict in which social movements engaged. Movements struggled cognitively and rhetorically to align the understandings of activists, attract potential supporters, convince the general public, and, at the same time, counter the frames offered by their opponents. Attention to the means, the media, through which this process occurred was also a central topic of research.

The role of narratives and stories as they relate to the formation of the **rituals**, collective imagination, and consciousness of social movements has recently become an additional research focus. Recent research has called attention to the role of **emotions** in protest and mobilization, as well as the interplay between social movement "**cultures**" and **popular culture**.

The student protests of the 1960s triggered a conceptual crisis which eventually led to a shift in perspective; the emergence of "new" social movements in the 1970s–1980s, the women's movement, environmentalism, and a revived peace movement had a similar effect. The rise of ethnic and religion-based movements and a new right has spurred similar modifications. Many of those engaged in the analysis of social movements had their academic coming of age in the 1960s–1970s and took a broadly sympathetic stance to the movements they studied, conceptualizing them as "progressive" and "universalistic" or, at worst, as "particularistic" and "defensive." Newer, more conservative mobilizations and movements have proved more problematic and difficult to classify. The same can be said for the so-called antiglobalization, or global justice, movement, but for different reasons. The latter is most often looked at with sympathetic eyes and through a traditional – that is, 1960s – lens. Because of this, questions about whether or not antiglobalization protests constitute a "movement" or not are frequent.   RON EYERMAN

social pathology

This perspective stresses the importance of social factors in accounting for social or moral decline. Such a perspective on **crime**, for instance, reflects a sociological understanding that the causes of crime lie in **anomie**, social disorganization, and economic recession rather than in individual biological or psychological factors. The interest is in establishing patterns of criminality rather than individual motivations. The perspective reflects sociological **positivism** – first developed by philosophers such as **Auguste Comte** and **Claude Henri de Rowroy, Comte de Saint-Simon** in the early nineteenth century. Comte's belief that **society** both predates and shapes the individual psychologically provided a foundation for sociological **criminology**.

One element of the social pathology perspective on crime involves the scientific **measurement** of indicators of social disorganization such as rates of **suicide**, drunkenness, the age and sex of offenders, educational levels, and crime in particular urban areas. This approach itself has roots in the work of the nineteenth-century "moral statisticians," Adolphe Quételet (1796–1874) in Belgium and Andre-Michel Guerry (1802–66) in France, and their social-campaigning colleagues in England (Henry Mayhew, 1812–87, for instance), who used early empirical methods to investigate the urban slums where crime and **deviance** flourished. **Émile Durkheim**'s work has also been critical to developments here. Durkheim argued in *The Rules of Sociological Method* (1895 [trans. 1958]) that, in any given social context, the inevitability and predictability of crime rates must mean that they are social facts, and thus a normal feature of collective life. Thus it follows that the volume of crime is likely to increase as societies evolve from mechanical to more complex, organic forms of organization.

One of the most significant forms of sociological positivism was developed by the **Chicago School** in the 1920s and 1930s. The University of Chicago sociologists suggested that crime rates were determined by certain economic, environmental, and spatial conditions. They observed that the highest crime rates occurred in those areas characterized by declining populations and deteriorating **neighborhoods**. Their observations thus led them to conclude that it was the nature of the neighborhoods rather than the nature of the individuals who resided therein that determined levels of criminality.

Social pathology perspectives were further developed in the 1940s and 1950s under the heading of "strain theory." By this time, many of the advanced capitalist societies had entered an economic boom, and there were high standards of living and optimism about the future. But crime persisted in the face of apparently good social and economic conditions. The answer was thus to examine more closely the distribution of opportunities in society and it was this analysis that led to the conclusion that there was a strain between the "ideal" and opportunities that were actually available. Thus the social strictures here or wider social pathology helped explain crime.

Social pathology and social disorganization reappeared in the 1950s in the context of functionalist **sociological theory**. Here, behavior that transgressed social **norms** threatened the supposed unity of a social system.

Social pathology perspectives have come under critical scrutiny, not least because of the assumption that there is a single good society which is being pathologically undermined or disorganized. **C. Wright Mills** in *The Sociological Imagination* (1963) suggested in a classic phrase that there was a "professional ideology of social pathologists" – indicating assumptions about the shared social mores and rules of a middle-class American **lifestyle**.   LORAINE GELSTHORPE

social policy

This is an area of social scientific study as well as a description of the actions of (mainly) government that address social issues, generally in the name of meeting **human needs** and promoting social welfare or well-being. The roots of social policy lie in the nineteenth century but its development as a subject mirrored the development of the **welfare state** in the twentieth century. Until the late 1980s it was more typically called social administration, **Richard Titmuss** held the first Chair in Social Administration, established at the London School of Economics in 1950. The change of name to social policy, which was controversial, reflected both a broadening of the subject beyond a focus on welfare-state policies and the development of more theoretical and cross-national perspectives. Today, social administration usually refers more specifically to the study of the development and implementation on the ground of welfare-state policies.

Although generally treated as a social science discipline in its own right, social policy can also be understood as an interdisciplinary field of study, which draws on, for example, **sociology**, economics, and **politics**. The boundaries between it and the other disciplines are not clear-cut or fixed, and indeed in some countries it does not exist as a separate academic subject. A distinguishing feature of British social policy, in particular, has been a tendency to policy prescription as well as analysis. More generally, social policy and social administration have traditionally been concerned with the **values** and principles that underlie policies as well as with their practical implications.

It is not only the disciplinary boundaries of social policy that are fuzzy. There are also ongoing debates as to where the boundaries around the subject should be drawn. Some social policy textbooks, for instance, confine themselves to welfare-state policies such as social security, **health**, housing, and personal social services. Others define the subject more widely to embrace other **institutions** and **organizations** that affect welfare and well-being, such as the **family**, **voluntary associations**, and the **market** (including the **labor market**), and to take on board issues such as the **environment** and the impact of social divisions such as **race**, **gender**, **disability**, and **sexuality**. A key focus is the distribution of different kinds of resources, notably **money** but also **work** (paid and unpaid), **care**, and **time**.

An underlying issue is whether defining social policy in terms of needs and well-being provides an unduly benign reading of the motives behind and effects of certain welfare-state policies. Some analysts therefore emphasize the regulatory nature of policy and the ways in which social policies serve as tools of **social control** and reinforce social divisions.   RUTH LISTER

social problems

One of the more commonly used phrases in sociological inquiry is that of social problems. However, in common parlance its meaning is somewhat ambiguous. According to Earl Rubington and Martin S. Weinberg in *The Study of Social Problems* (2002: 4), a social problem is "an alleged situation that is incompatible with the values of a significant number of people who agree that action is needed to alter the situation." For example, **racism** and **discrimination** remain social problems in the modern-day United States. The year 2005

marked the fiftieth anniversary of the refusal of Rosa Parks (1931–2005), a black woman, to give up her seat on a segregated bus on that fateful day in Montgomery, Alabama. The event marked the beginning of the civil rights movement in America. Until that time, racial **segregation** and discrimination were commonplace and quietly accepted. However, when African-Americans gained social and political momentum, their efforts brought into focus the practices that would be forever unacceptable.

How social problems are defined is dependent upon the sociological perspective from which they are analyzed. For example, **functionalism** views **society** as a system of interrelated parts whose activities have consequences for survival implications for the whole. If the activity promotes survival, it is considered functional, whereas if the activity lessens survival, it is dysfunctional. Within functionalism, there are three vantage points from which to analyze the concept of social problems: **social pathology**; social disorganization; and cultural-lag perspective. According to the perspective of social pathology, social problems occur as a result of unintentional actions by ill-advised people. Social disorganization theorists view the existence of social problems as being attributed to an imbalance among the interrelated parts of the system. The solution of any social problem would be to find a way back to equilibrium. **Norms** and **values** guide the cultural lag perspective. There exists a coherent view of the world because of a shared sense of **culture** and meaning. Social problems evolve when technological changes proffer new opportunities for behavior at a time when the cultural norms have not yet evolved or adopted an acceptable way of behaving, given the new circumstance. The main criticism of the structural-functionalist school of thought is that the status quo is seemingly the preferred state of being. Consensus is taken for granted as the way to keep the entire system operating in balance.

The second perspective is that of conflict theory, which views social problems as emanating from a power differential between **social classes** or other social **groups**. Societies are not orderly systems designed to promote the balance of the collectivity. Rather, society is a collection of different groups of people who have differing interests, which necessitate a struggle for resources and **power**. From the perspective of **Marxism**, **capitalism** and its consequences constitute the heart of these struggles, hence they are the underlying causes of social problems. The only solution to these social ills is to overthrow the capitalist system and to inaugurate a communist **state**, in which all people would share equally in **wealth** and prosperity. Conflict theorists such as **Ralph Dahrendorf** believe that the struggle for power is evident in society and thus the cause of social problems. However, the struggle is less about economic imbalances and more about differentials of power and **authority**.

Symbolic interactionism conceptualizes social problems in terms of the processes by which the subjective meaning of "problems" is created. Conditions of social life shape people's perceptions and interpretations. Social problems are, therefore, social constructs. They are neither good nor bad, neither desirable nor undesirable until and unless someone assigns the situation some meaning. In the study of social problems, the main condition of concern is the process by which some social conditions become social problems while others do not. For example, child abuse prior to the 1970s no doubt occurred; however, it was not until a group of physicians brought attention to it as an emergency room phenomenon that social policymakers and practitioners began attending to the issue.

Social problems are those social circumstances that appear to affect, or are believed to affect, a significant proportion of the population. The affect, by definition, has adverse consequences for collective life. However, it is possible to bring about positive change in order for these negative effects to be reversed and conditions improved. Social problems are considered to be by-products of given social practices, including economic, political, social, or technological practices. These practices are usually valued by society. The consequences of the practices can be predicted or unanticipated. It is typically the case that social problems do not arise as a consequence of deliberate or malicious activities. According to **Robert K. Merton** in his article, "The Unintended Consequences of Purposive Social Action" (*American Sociological Review*, 1936), specific social problems correlate with particular sets of institutionalized societal values and available means to achieve those values. Social problems are therefore the social price a society pays for promoting those values such as prosperity without providing the appropriate means to realize them.

Social problems can be persistent or re-occurring. Once social conditions are recognized, identified, and acknowledged as being problematic, their solutions are dependent upon calculated, purposeful social interventions. It is important to note, obviously, that not all social conditions are social problems. A social condition that is eventually defined as a social problem is so deemed because someone has defined it as such. There must be an acknowledgment by someone with **influence** that the social conditions have deteriorated to such a point that a significant segment of the population is adversely affected. The influence or authority does not have to rest in the hands of policymakers, but can be based on social, economic, or political capital.

The invention of a social problem is guided by the sensitivities of the collective. There must be an agreement, however implicit, upon a series of definitions and perspectives. As a result, social problems are socially defined and constructed. They are based on conceptual ideals and perceptions of a given set of social circumstances at a particular point in time. According to Armand L. Mauss in *Social Problems as Social Movements* (1975: xv) "social problems originate in public opinion rather than in objective reality." Social problems emerge as a result of collective decisionmaking, albeit the decision is at times implicit. In other words, as social constructs, social problems are defined through a collective process of **interaction** rather than being defined by a set of independent objective measures against which social conditions are gauged.

Defining something as a social problem entails a process by which members of the collective identify a supposedly undesirable condition as a problem. At that stage, collective forces move towards seeking solutions. The key to understanding social problems is that governments do not have particular policy tools or measurement instruments that monitor social conditions as they approach the realm of social problems. The existence of social problems lies within people's perceptions, within their construction of reality, regardless of the sociological perspective used to study the phenomenon. Social problems rely on the reaction of a critical mass that monitors social conditions and that will identify when the condition becomes a social problem.

In 1955 the Society for the Study of Social Problems was founded in the United States with the aim of promoting scholarly critical research on issues that influence social life. Through research, open dialog, and regular publications, for example in the Society's own journal *Social Problems*, attention has been drawn to the more endemic and prolific issues that erode quality of life. For example, the principal social problems plaguing American society include: **addiction**, crime, drug abuse, **poverty**, HIV/AIDS, **racism**, **sexism**, legal immigration, urban decay and gang **violence**.   JACQUELINE SCHNEIDER

social psychology

Existing as a sub-discipline within both **sociology** and psychology since the early twentieth century, the first textbooks on social psychology were published independently in 1908 by a sociologist, Edward Ross (1866–1951) (*Social Psychology: An Outline and Source Book*), and a psychologist, William McDougall (1871–1938) (*Introduction to Social Psychology*). Social psychology continues to straddle the border between sociology and psychology. However, despite a number of theoretical concerns in common, sociological social psychology and psychological social psychology remain largely independent endeavors.

Psychological and sociological social psychology are distinct in scope and focus. Contemporary work in social psychology is dominated by American research in the area of social cognition, which draws heavily on the **experimental method**, and applies instruments such as attitude **scales** to such topics as stereotyping and **prejudice**, **cognitive dissonance,** and **relative deprivation**. In contrast, sociological social psychology has been historically influenced by **phenomenology** and **symbolic interactionism**, and has investigated the impact of social structural variables on human behavior and/or **personality**. Sociological social psychology employs a range of non-experimental methods such as **surveys** and fieldwork methods, including **participant observation**.

Psychological social psychology acquired **legitimacy** as a science through the application of the experimental method during the 1930s, and was influenced by the tenets of **behaviorism**, in which experimental manipulations were used to effect and measure changes in **attitudes** and behavior. Although foundational studies in the field would be considered unethical by modern standards – for instance Stanley Milgram's studies of **authority** in 1961, and Philip Zimbardo's prison experiments of 1971 – a more conservative variant of this laboratory-based research **tradition** continues to exemplify American social psychology.

Sociological social psychology is marked by its rejection of experimental laboratory methods in favor of naturalistic **fieldwork** and survey methods. This tradition encompasses the foundational work of **Erving Goffman, George Caspar Homans**, and **George Herbert Mead**, as well as the **Frankfurt School**'s amalgamation of **Marxism** and **psychoanalysis**, especially as realized by

Theodor Wiesengrund Adorno, Erich Fromm, and **Paul Lazarsfeld**. Sociological social psychology eschews the **individualism** of the experimental tradition to focus on the study of social behavior from an interactional perspective, such as in work in **ethnomethodology** on the intersubjective accomplishment of **identity**, or the investigation of the dynamics of **groups** and **organizations**. While the social psychology of **authoritarianism** was of common concern to both sub-disciplines between the 1930s and the 1960s, the epistemological conflict between the two psychologies came to the fore in the 1970s, in what was known as the "crisis." During this time, the laboratory-based experimental methods of psychological social psychology became the subject of sustained critique.

More recently, discursive social psychology, with roots in ethnomethodology and **conversational analysis**, and the work of **Harold Garfinkel** and **Harvey Sacks**, has introduced sociological concerns into psychological social psychology. In turn, research methods employed by discursive social psychologists – such as **discourse analysis** and the study of interpretative repertoires – have since been adopted within sociology. The social constructionism movement provides a middle ground for the development of communication between sociological and psychological social psychology.   MARK RAPLEY AND SUSAN HANSEN

social rights
– see **rights**.

social role

The concept social role refers to the repertoire of possible behaviors associated with social position in cooperative relations, that is social standing or **social status**. The terms role and status are associated, on the one hand, with **functionalism** in **sociology**, put forward by **Talcott Parsons** and **Robert K. Merton**, and, on the other hand, with **symbolic interactionism**, associated with **George Herbert Mead** and **Erving Goffman**. Whereas the functionalist notion of role emphasizes socially prescribed behavioral and attitudinal expectations that attach to a particular status, symbolic interactionist understandings of role focus on the elaboration of practices available to a role incumbent. Neither approach has much currency in sociology today. Indeed, the term role is more likely to be used in everyday conversation than in sociological writing. There are a number of reasons for this. First, the co-relative concept of status has been diminished since the mid twentieth century. If it survives at all it refers to position in a scheme of **social stratification**, and the associated conditions are unequal distributions of resources not roles. Also, in a social climate of supposed individual autonomy, the concept of role has come to suggest a much higher degree of plasticity than the notion of social status itself could permit. In late capitalist society, roles appear to be freely chosen, and their performance determined solely by the personal interpretations their incumbents invent. Here the social character of status is almost totally lost through the highly ideological connotations that have attached themselves to the role concept.

JACK BARBALET

social sciences

Theoretically, methodologically, and institutionally broad-ranging and diverse in character, the social sciences aim at nothing less than the analysis and understanding of human **society**. In pursuit of this goal, social scientists have studied the structures, practices, and processes of many elements of society including, *inter alia*, its **economy**, **religion**, law (see **law and society**), **politics**, **language**, and beliefs; how these are manifested in the daily lives of people, in both their mentality and their **social actions**; and how individuals are socialized into the ways of acting and believing which enable them to be competent members of that society. This breadth has given rise to the study of a multitude of specific phenomena, ranging from broad large-scale issues such as the class structure of societies and patterns of advantage and disadvantage, to very specific detailed matters such as how conversationalists organize their turns at speaking in a conversation.

Some social science disciplines are motivated by specific fields of interest, for example, in the case of politics and economics, while others are driven by a more synthetic approach, as in the case of anthropology or **sociology**. While some of its disciplines are comparatively new as distinct perspectives, for example, **social psychology**, all of them can trace the origins of their ideas and investigative practices to much earlier periods. Every discipline can find a classical precursor when necessary, and many lay claim to the same figures even though nowadays they are often seen to be quite distinct. While Thomas Hobbes (1588–1679) is most often seen as a figure of importance within the field of politics, it is quite easy to see within his work many psychological and sociological claims that are reflected in contemporary work. More recently, **Karl Marx** is seen as a precursor for more or less every social science discipline, according to some.

The disciplinary specialization we see nowadays is very much a phenomenon of the period from the late nineteenth century onwards. It is often decried as inhibiting the proper study of social phenomena, and interdisciplinarity repeatedly comes into vogue. However, the institutional, professional, and theoretical positions of many social scientists ensure that the disciplines have become a fixed and enduring fact of life. This will continue to be the case as long as the social sciences do not have an agreed position on what constitutes secure knowledge and how it might be acquired, as is to be found within the natural sciences. The comparative success of the latter has led some to success by imitating its practices. Others, in contrast, have sought to prove on a-priori grounds that any such project for the discovery of secure social scientific knowledge is bound to fail. These led to one British government minister requiring the United Kingdom Social Science Research Council to change its name on the grounds that there could be no such thing as a social science. Ironically, the idea of evidence-based policy is very much in favor in the United Kingdom nowadays, but the name has not been changed back again.

Specifying the boundaries of the social sciences can also be problematic. On the one hand, many disciplines have components that clearly sit within and without, for example, psychology, history, and law. Some of these have elsewhere been characterized as more properly called the "human sciences." On the other hand, other disciplines, most notably biology, have sought to arrogate to themselves the explanation of social phenomena such as **violence**, aggression, and competition, and thereby deny a role for the social sciences.

Ultimately, the quintessential social sciences are synthetic disciplines such as sociology and anthropology, but it is quite clear that many of the phenomena they seek to explain are in part dependent on biological and other phenomena that currently lie outside their remit. A successful social science will be one that finds the basis of a felicitous integration of cultural, historical, and biological accounts.

DAVID GOOD

social status

This term is used in three analytical contexts with quite different meanings. In the analysis of **social structure** and **differentiation**, social status refers to (1) a position in social relations (for example student, parent, or priest) that is socially recognized and normatively regulated. This generic usage is often contrasted with a more specific one, associated with sociological studies of **inequalities**, and meaning, (2) a hierarchical position in a vertical social order, an overall social rank, standing, and social worth. In this context, individual statuses are associated with privileges and discriminations. Finally, in contemporary studies of **social stratification**, especially those inspired by **Max Weber**, social status refers to (3) an aspect of hierarchical location in the social order derived from established cultural conventions (traditional beliefs and popular creeds). It is contrasted with class (market position in the economic order) and party (authority or command position in the political/organizational order). In this Weberian context, hierarchical status positions reflect the unequal conventional distribution of honor (esteem) and the accompanying **life chances**, while class positions reflect unequal distribution of market endowments and the accompanying lifechances. The occupants of these positions form status **groups** characterized by common **lifestyles**, tastes, social proximity, and intermarriage. Traditional aristocracies, ethnoracial groups, and lifestyle **communities**, such as "yuppies," are all examples of status groups. In **Edward Shils's** view (*Center and Periphery*, 1975), all societies engender status inequalities, and these inequalities reflect distance from the center which represents the shared value standards. This echoes **Émile Durkheim**'s proposition that status represents a distance from "the sacred" – the symbolic representations of society (see **sacred and profane dichotomy**). This link with the sacred gives strong **legitimacy** to status distinctions. Status group members reinforce these distinctions by claiming monopolies over certain privileges, titles, occupational roles, and styles of dress.

The penetration of traditional status distinctions into the fabric of modern society was the main theme of **Thorstein Veblen**'s *Theory of the Leisure Class* (1899). Social esteem enjoyed by the upper strata, argued Veblen, did not depend on their **wealth** or **power**; it had to be earned through conventional social practices, in particular the avoidance of vulgar forms of labor, especially services, engagement in "vicarious leisure," and conspicuous **consumption**. Earning and cultivating esteem was a task pursued by **families**, rather than individuals. While the *paterfamilias* led and provided, his wife and children cultivated social **networks**.

The processes of **modernization** have weakened status conventions and undermined established status hierarchies. The social distance scores – the most popular sociological measures of status

divisions between ethno-racial categories – have been showing a steady decline since they were first applied in the 1920s. However, new status hierarchies and divisions emerge around **occupations**, **citizenship** (or lack of it), and civic activism, as well as cultural consumption, tastes, and lifestyles. Thus the occupational status rankings and occupational prestige scales, constructed mainly by American sociologists, show a change, rather than a decline. The old arguments about the salience of **race and ethnicity**, and **gender** as the key determinants of social status were supplemented by new arguments about the importance of **education**, civic/citizenship status, consumption, and taste. New theories of status, principally in the work of European sociologists, such as Bryan S. Turner in *Status* (1988), re-opened the issue of the role of the modern **state** in managing status inequalities by granting citizenship rights to all its members. Turner followed in the footsteps of **Thomas H. Marshall** in exploring the expansion of citizenship **rights**, and he pointed to an expansion of more universalistic human rights in the context of globalizing trends. Efforts to identify the new status hierarchies of consumption and taste were fueled by **Pierre Bourdieu,** especially in *Distinction* (1979 [trans. 1984]). Bourdieu purposefully fused (some critics say conflated) status and class, and highlighted the importance of gender, race and ethnicity as core status distinctions. His book on **masculinities** (*Masculine Domination*, 1998 [trans. 2000]) carries indelibly the signature of his distinguished predecessor and countryman, Durkheim. Bourdieu, like Durkheim, saw status inequalities as constituted hierarchically through collective representations and symbolic classifications in relation to the "legitimate culture" – a close equivalent to the sacred in classic Durkheimian analyses. While popular, studies of taste and consumption illustrate the numerous difficulties in constructing synthetic status hierarchies with more than local scope and applicability.

There seems to be an agreement among contemporary sociologists that the key determinants of social status (standing, esteem, and **prestige**) in advanced societies are occupation/class, education/skill, race/ethnicity, gender, citizenship, and cultural consumption. They show quite different dynamics. While the ascribed and traditional sources of status distinction (primarily race and gender) decline in importance, the status-leveling impact of citizenship continues, and the status-stratifying impact of education and cultural consumption have been increasing. There also seems to be an agreement that postmodern trends weaken further traditional status distinctions and blur status hierarchies. The hierarchies of consumption and taste, in particular, seem to fragment and decompose. They show less clarity, stability, and anchoring in "communal norms and values" than the old status divisions. Lifestyles are so diverse and fickle that they defy attempts at a clear status ordering – the point made by all students of postmodernization. The new status hierarchies based on consumption and lifestyle are fragmenting under the impact of value polytheism, rampant consumerism, and increasing commercial pressures. Intense **social mobility**, combined with the increased interpenetration of diverse value systems (and tastes) that accompanies globalization, also contribute to blurring and fragmentation of status hierarchies in advanced societies.   JAN PAKULSKI

social stratification

Social stratification is usually contrasted with social **differentiation**. Differentiation involves the formation of horizontal social divisions; stratification involves vertical (hierarchical) ranking of social strata. Some sociologists also contrast stratification, which implies gradation, with social class divisions, which are seen as polar and antagonistic. Stratification implies persistent gradation of **social classes**, occupational **groups**, and ethno-racial categories. Strata may be nominal, constructed by sociologists, or real, reflecting actual social distances. Real strata are divided by social distances and systematic exclusions. Sociologists also distinguish closed stratification systems, such as the Hindu caste system, from open ones, such as modern occupational/class systems. In the former, **social mobility** is discouraged and restricted by traditional conventions. In the latter, mobility is typical, intense, and socially approved. In the functional theory of stratification, sociologists portray stratification as socially beneficial and consensual. Conflict theorists perceive stratification as contested and accompanied by domination. Marxists see it as an outcome of economic exploitation engendered in class relations, while Weberians treat it as an outcome of multifaceted domination in combination with socioeconomic class, sociocultural status and sociopolitical power/authority hierarchies.

Modern stratification systems are open – social mobility is frequent and expected – and they emphasize achieved characteristics, such as **education**/knowledge, skills, performance, and experience. They are also increasingly complex, with various criteria and dimensions of stratification interacting and cross-cutting each other. The rankings of individuals and groups in various dimensions of social hierarchies seldom coincide, thus resulting in status inconsistency. The most popular representation of modern stratification systems is in the form of national occupational status gradations, often scaled. Such status schemes prove most popular in the United States; European sociologists seem to prefer synthetic occupational class maps. While there is a wide consensus that occupational and employment statuses form the backbone of modern stratification, it is accepted that social strata may also develop around other assets and locations:

- political **influence**, **authority** (as in **Ralph Dahrendorf**);
- ethno-racial status, **prestige** (as in W. Lloyd Warner or **Edward A. Shils**);
- **education**, skills, human capital, expert knowledge (as in Gary Becker and **Daniel Bell**);
- social **networks**, ties, **social capital** (as in **James S. Coleman**);
- "cultural capital," taste, **lifestyle**, **gender** (as in **Pierre Bourdieu**);
- **rights**, entitlements, privileges (as in Bryan S. Turner).

Contemporary students of social stratification typically combine class, occupational status, and authority dimensions into synthetic gradations (stratification schemes and class maps). **Anthony Giddens** (*The Class Structure of the Advanced Societies*, 1973) and **Ralph Dahrendorf** (*The Modern Social Conflict*, 1988), for example, draw stratification maps that include occupational classes, **elites**, and socially marginalized strata (underclasses). Similarly, **John Goldthorpe** (*Social Mobility and Class Structure in Modern Britain*, 1987) synthesizes class and occupational schemes into an eleven-class map. Erik Olin Wright (*Class Counts*, 1997), in turn, juxtaposes class analysis to a study of race and gender stratification. His class/stratification schemes also incorporate the dimensions of managerial control and skill/expertise. Finally, **Bell** (*The Coming of Post Industrial Society*, 1973) and Gøsta Esping-Anderson (*Changing Classes*, 1993) accommodate in their postindustrial class maps the dimension of power/authority (elite or political directorate), economic integration, and citizenship rights (outsiders and underclass). With advancing **globalization**, many sociologists see the whole world as stratified, typically along the economic/developmental and power dimensions. Thus the dependency and world-system theorists distinguish the global power strata between countries of the core, semi-periphery, and periphery.   JAN PAKULSKI

social structure

The product of human agency, social structures express the fact that what people intend should never be confused with what results.

Premodern thought is basically structural in character. People act through **social roles** that determine their action, and great stress is laid upon executing a particular role according to the **norms** governing it. A male feudal lord is expected to act quite differently from, say, a female servant. These structures are seen as timeless, and are usually ascribed to the creative interventions of a higher divinity.

With the onset of **modernity**, all this dramatically changes. People are presented as individuals who can choose which role they play and change from one role to another. Structures seemingly dissolve into agency, so that what matters is the will of individuals to alter the world in which they find themselves. The problem with this position is that not only is agency presented abstractly – that is, as outside society – but the same abstract force that enables some to be actors condemns others to passivity. Hence the classical liberals limited the notion of the individual to men who owned **property**, were Protestants, and had the correct **ethnicity**. Timeless structures had not disappeared – they were merely assigned to others.

The emphasis upon agency and the individual is important, but it needs to be linked dynamically and historically to the notion of structure. People became conscious actors not simply because they had changed their ideas, but because they acquired through the **market** the **wealth** that enabled them to command the services of others. They may have imagined that social structures simply affected others – women, the poor, the residents of the colonies, and so forth. But this is an illusion. The market is itself a social structure and, as such, dictates to beneficiaries and victims alike how they are to conduct themselves. Social structures are the product of agency. Without conscious action, there would be no structures. But what makes a practice structural is that the patterning which results has implications and imposes constraints that correspond only imperfectly to the intentions of those who created them.

The structural argument that people enter into social relations independent of their will cannot mean that these relations are the product of automatons – creatures without intention and purpose. What it means is that the result of activities undertaken is never the same as the intention of those who undertook those activities: it is this gap between intention and consequence that creates the structural character of activity. It is not that these structures are brought about by the will of some higher power: they are creations of human activity, but human activity in which intention and result never coincide.

Being aware of this makes it possible to try and organize our activities with greater consideration of their likely consequences. It is, however, a mistake to imagine that any society, no matter how enlightened and well regulated, can extinguish the gulf between intention and result, since the fallibility of humans and the complexity of social practices make it inevitable that **agency and structure** will remain distinct. JOHN HOFFMAN

social systems

– see **social systems theory**.

social systems theory

The theory of social systems was strongly influenced by systems theory in other fields, especially **cybernetics**, engineering, and biology. General system theory was particularly influential in the 1950s and 1960s. It was proposed by the biologist Ludwig von Bertalanffy (1901–72) as the basis of a unified science, avoiding the older mechanistic view of physical science under which it had proven difficult to include the human sciences.

The basic postulate of any systems theory is that the particular phenomenon under investigation is made up of elements and parts that are organized and interdependent. This organized interdependence is what constitutes a system, and it operates as a relatively bounded entity in **interaction** with an **environment**. System theorists are interested both in the organization of the system and in the organization of its relations with its environment. Emphasis is upon self-regulation and the processing of **information** and learning via feedback mechanisms.

The functionalist sociologist, **Talcott Parsons**, developed a theory of the social system in the 1950s; from the 1960s onwards, he increasingly used the language of cybernetics and biological systems theory. In "Some Problems of General Theory in Sociology," in Edward Tiryakian (ed.), *Theoretical Sociology* (1970: 230), Parsons describes the social system as a structurally differentiated system of **social roles** and expectations that is maintained by four functional imperatives (adaptation, goal-attainment, integration, and latency) as it operates in its environment(s), writing that, "the concept function is central to the understanding of all living systems . . . [and] is simply the corollary of the concept living system, delineating certain features in the first instance of the system–environment relation and in the second, of the internal differentiation of the system itself." The social system operates in an environment of other systems, including the system of the organism, the personality system, and the cultural system. Parsons outlines a "cybernetic hierarchy," ordered with the cultural system, highest in **information**, at the top and the system of the organism at the bottom. In that sense, Parsons declares himself to be a "cultural determinist."

Parsons analyzes social systems in terms of an analytical postulate of perfect integration, arguing that this is to be distinguished from concrete social systems as such, which are to be analyzed in terms of their tendencies towards integration, and not in terms of integration as a fully realized state. This has been restated by Jeffrey Alexander in his "Introduction" to *Neofunctionalism* (1985) as the basis of a neofunctionalist **paradigm** of social systems, where "equilibrium is taken as a reference point for functionalist systems analysis, though not for participants in actual social systems as such."

Nonetheless, critics argued that this analytic emphasis on integration neglects conflict, and overemphasizes equilibrium theoretically, if not concretely. For some systems theorists, the problem is the overgeneralized nature of Parsons's theory. According to Walter Buckley (1921–), systems theory could be applied directly to concrete systems without any assumption of the priority of equilibrium over "chaotic complexity," or of consensus over conflict, and without the artificial constraint of just four functions with which to account for **differentiation**.

Parsons developed his theory of the social system on an action frame of reference; his aim was to integrate the analysis of systems of action with that of the agency of individuals. Critics such as **Anthony Giddens** and **Jürgen Habermas** argue that he came to neglect action and overemphasized systems. Nonetheless, each comes to offer a very similar account of social systems to that of Parsons. Giddens's theory of **structuration** sets out a level of social **interaction** whose internal differentiation is organized by four structural principles, those of allocation, authorization, legitimation, and signification. Habermas, for his part, sets out a level of society and a

division between the system and the **lifeworld,** where each operates in terms of two functions defined similarly to those of Parsons and Giddens.

The Chilean biologists, Humberto Maturana (1928–) and his student Francisco Varela (1946–2001), coined the term autopoiesis in the 1970s to describe the self-regulation of living systems. This concept was developed by the German sociologist and student of Parsons, **Niklas Luhmann**, to develop a constructivist, or self-referential, account of systems. Unlike Habermas, with whom he was engaged in debate, Luhmann argued that the structure/agency and system/lifeworld divisions were false ones. The divisions can be appropriately conflated within a systems theory based on the communicative coupling of actors and systems. Communication, not action, should be the core concept of sociology; modern societies, or social systems, are too complex to be reducible to actors' reasons for acting, which can be multifarious. According to Luhmann, autopoietic social systems construct themselves self-referentially as social relationships made up of differentiated subsystems. These subsystems interact, but have their own relatively autonomous logics, and are not limited by a pregiven set of functions.

Differentiation increases communication and the scale and complexity of society. Like Buckley, Luhmann argues that this form of system theory avoids the priority given to integration in the Parsonian scheme. His theory is not about the reestablishment of equilibrium in the face of contingent disturbances from the environment, but about the renewal of system elements; all elements must pass away in time and **reproduction** is a matter of "dynamic stability." According to Luhmann in his *Social Systems* (1984 [trans. 1995: 48]) disintegration and reproduction are intertwined: "systems with temporalized complexity depend on constant disintegration. Continuous disintegration creates, as it were, a place and a need for succeeding elements; it is a necessary, contributing cause of reproduction."

JOHN HOLMWOOD

social theory

The systematic reflection on the nature of society and social relationships, social theory is intimately tied to the fate of **sociology** as a discipline concerned with the empirical study of social life. Historians of **social science** frequently associate both social theory and sociology with the rise in the late eighteenth century of capitalist **modernity** and its distinctive institutional separation of **state** and **civil society.** Associated with this "transformation of the public sphere" by **Jürgen Habermas** (1962 [trans. 1989]), **society** – as distinct from the more standard concern with the nature of political obligation – became an object of attention for a new stratum of public **intellectuals**, concerned with the underlying conditions of civility and social life.

As **capitalism** matured and developed more complex **institutions**, the expansion of universities provided the conditions for the development of disciplinary social science. In *Structure of Social Action* (1937), **Talcott Parsons** famously associated the 1890–1920 **generation** of European social scientists and social theorists with the founding of sociology as an empirical discipline based on the theoretical presuppositions of an action frame of reference. He believed this had come to fruition in the post-World War II period of affluence and political consensus; the end of **ideology** coincided with a new "age of sociology." **Sociological theory** would replace social theory, which remained tied to ideological concerns that had been transcended. Even those who disagreed with Parsons's particular conception of sociological theory frequently shared his view that a scientific, discipline-based sociology would provide useful knowledge that could be harnessed to address the **social problems** of advanced welfare capitalism.

In this period, social theory as a distinct field was frequently regarded as a historical throwback, under the continuing **influence** of European **Marxism**, or something pursued by lone individuals posing as social critics. The latter – for example, **Robert Staughton Lynd** and **David Riesman** in the United States – frequently decried professional sociology's lack of public purpose. The rapid expansion of higher **education** in the postwar period, however, not only gave rise to disciplinary consolidation, but also created opportunities for posts outside **networks** of professional patronage. This coincided with the breakdown of the postwar social and political consensus and the rise of new **social movements**, associated with women's **rights**, **race and ethnicity**, struggles against **colonialism**, environmental rights, and alternative **sexualities**.

In his *Coming Crisis of Western Sociology* (1970), **Alvin W. Gouldner** criticized the claim to professional expertise on the part of disciplinary sociology and called for "new theoretical communities" to be formed with links to these new social movements. Similar arguments were made by **Alain Touraine** in France. Others, such as **Anthony Giddens** and Habermas, argued for a

reengagement with the classical **tradition** in social theory to reinvigorate the discipline, while the work of **Michel Foucault** was important in identifying the **politics** of knowledge claims and the techniques of **power** to which expert knowledges were allied. The women's movement and the movement for gay rights developed feminist and queer critiques of sociology (see **queer theory**) and developed distinctive forms of social theory. **Edward Said** utilized Foucault to develop **postcolonial theory.**

Increasingly, social theory has reemerged as a distinctive field to displace sociological theory. Where the latter is concerned with the development of distinctive **paradigms** and collective programs of research, the former tends to be focused on a small number of prominent thinkers, is weakly integrated, and is concerned with novel interpretations of social issues, such as **Ulrich Beck**'s idea of risk society, or **Manuel Castell**'s information society. This new generation of social theorists advocates the role of public **intellectual**, rather than that of professional expert.

JOHN HOLMWOOD

socialism

Socialists come in so many shapes and forms that some argue that there is no socialism: there are only socialisms. Despite differences over questions of **religion**, **nationalism**, parliament, **democracy**, and **liberalism**, all socialists have an optimistic view of human nature, stress the importance of cooperation, see freedom in terms of material resources, and support **equality**. Socialism is more than a notion that individuals can only survive in a society since socialists challenge both conservative ideas of hierarchy and the liberal notion that humans can only flourish when they acquire private **property** and produce through a **market**.

Marxists divide socialists into those who are utopian and those who are scientific. Utopian socialism, Marxists argue, is a creed that links socialism to supposedly timeless **values** like equality and **justice**. Nineteenth-century utopians sought to establish egalitarian **communities** rather than transform whole societies, but Marxists also criticize utopian socialists for their failure to connect socialism to a particular group in society, a particular period of history, and a revolutionary political project.

Marxism claims to be a scientific socialism on the grounds that socialism is tied in an empirically demonstrable way to the material interests of workers. Although individuals from other **social**

classes can join the socialist cause, only the working class has the organizational experience to bring about a socialist society. Attaining socialism is not simply a matter of will-power, as utopians suppose, but can be established only when a capitalist society has demonstrated its productive strengths and weaknesses. The stark incompatibility between the material interests of the bourgeoisie and those of the workers means that **capitalism** has to be transformed through revolution – although not necessarily by force – and this process requires workers to form a new **state**. However, as a classless society is established, the state itself would "wither away." Although Marxists see capitalism as an immoral system, socialism is not merely ethically desirable, but historically necessary.

Anarchists expressed concern about the Marxist emphasis on the need for **political parties** and the state, and towards the end of the nineteenth century a German socialist, Eduard Bernstein (1850–1932), argued that the notion of a capitalism increasingly paralyzed by its internal contradictions did not fit the historical facts. A revolutionary overthrow of capitalism was now irrelevant as workers had shown that they could win seats in parliament, and establish valuable reforms. Indeed, the whole notion that socialism is tied to one class in society was archaic, since **democracy** and **citizenship** demonstrated that people across the class divide can cooperate. Moreover it was wrong to think of socialism as some kind of hermetically sealed alternative to capitalism. The formation of **trade unions** and cooperatives had already shown that socialist elements could be introduced into a capitalist society so that a more democratic and socially fairer order was emerging. Socialism was not, as the Marxists argued, the stern antithesis of liberalism, but a **liberalism** put into practice, and extended to those sections of society, in particular the women and workers, whom traditional liberalism had "left out." Finally Bernstein challenged the idea that socialism was "inevitable." It was certainly desirable, but socialist reforms depended upon moral **values** and not some kind of "natural" process that would necessarily create a socialist society.

Bernstein's arguments generated fierce controversy and he was accused of "revisionism." But he was influential not just in his native Germany: his arguments seem to fit British experience. Bernstein, who lived in Britain for a number of years, had been impressed by the Fabian Society, which took its name from the Roman emperor, Fabius, a commander famed for his gradual approach to military campaigns. The Fabians argued that socialism is a highly focused concern with the organization of industry and the distribution of **wealth**. The Society still exists today. Examine its pamphlets, and what do you find? There are specific proposals on organizing the civil service, the health service, tax reforms, social security benefits, European Monetary Union, and the like.

The British Labour Party grew out of the Labour Representative Committee – a body formed by trade unions in 1900 since they felt that they needed a political voice. The party received a constitution in 1918, but the famous Clause IV that spoke of common ownership of the means of production was not intended to be taken seriously.

The Labour Party supported "its" side during World War I, entered into a national government, and opposed **V. I. Lenin**'s Russian Revolution. Not surprisingly, when the Bolsheviks formed the Third International, urging socialist parties to rename themselves "communist" and affiliate to the new body, the Labour Party declined to do so, nor would it work with the newly formed Communist Party of Great Britain. Its 1922 program made it clear that it stood for "common sense and justice," and Labour's **politics** have always been of a liberal and constitutional nature. When Labour won a landslide electoral victory after World War II, it adopted a policy of domestic reform and American-aligned foreign policy. Harold Wilson (1916–1995), who led the party in the 1960s, argued that **Karl Marx** should remain buried at Highgate cemetery, and Tony Blair (1958–) succeeded in doing what an earlier Labour leader tried, but failed, to achieve: the removal of the "symbolic" Clause IV from the party's constitution.

Although a controversial figure among traditional "Labourites" such as Roy Hattersley (1932–), Blair has stressed the ethical values of a democratic socialism – social **justice**, fairness, and **community**. What emerged after 1914 as the social democratic version of socialism – before then all socialists had called themselves social democrats – has been endorsed internationally by European, Asian, and Latin American socialists, and social democrats still attend an international gathering from time to time.

There are of course numerous currents of socialist thought within the broad camps of social **democracy** and **Communism**, and the collapse of so many of the Communist Party **states** in 1989 dented the **prestige** not only of "scientific socialism," but also of socialism generally. Nevertheless, socialism remains a significant theory and practice, and arguably will continue as long as a capitalist society exists.   JOHN HOFFMAN

socialist feminism

This term is used to describe the western **feminism** of the 1970s onward, which maintained a commitment to **social class**, as much as **gender**, divisions in the social world. The history of socialist feminism is, however, much longer than a part of the twentieth century, since, from the early nineteenth century, women had organized collectively as part of working-class movements. In Britain, Sheila Rowbotham (in *Hidden from History*, 1971) had argued that the history of working-class women had been largely ignored; that comment encouraged the work of feminist historians such as Barbara Taylor, Sally Alexander, and Anna Davin. In the work of all these authors there was a determination to show that class is as much a part of social **identity** as gender and that **social change** is not merely accomplished by the renegotiation of gender **norms**.

Other feminist writers (for example, Sonia Kruks) have outlined the transformation of women's situation by socialist regimes (such as Cuba and China) while still others (for example, Barbara Einhorn) have suggested that state **socialism** gave women advantages not known by women in capitalist societies. The fall of the Berlin Wall in 1989 and the disappearance of the command **economies** of state socialist regimes have marginalized the position of socialist feminism as a major theoretical position within feminism, as have significant changes in the structure of western **labor** markets, which have seen the eradication of traditional workplace divisions of **gender**, together with related – and deeply gendered – trade unions. In the United States, debates about social class and gender have emerged in the exchanges between Nancy Fraser and Judith Butler, the former arguing that a crucial element of any discussion of gender has to be a recognition of the existence of capitalist social relations.

MARY EVANS

socialization

Historically both sociology, for example **Charles Horton Cooley** in *Human Nature and the Social Order* (1902), and psychology — for example **Sigmund Freud**'s *The Ego and the Id* (1923 [trans. 1927]), reissued in *The Standard Edition* (1961: 3–66) — have been preoccupied with the question of "human nature," and, more specifically, with the manner in which, and process whereby, neonates come to be recognized as more-or-less competent members of a shared social order. The term socialization has, most usually, been employed to refer to this (developmental) process (sometimes referred to as primary socialization). It has been used to examine the **social roles** of parents, peers, and social **institutions** such as the school as agents of socialization. The term has also focused on locally specific issues such as **work**, **occupation**, **social role** (such as parenthood), or political socialization (often referred to as secondary socialization). Similarly, socialization is now increasingly understood to be not a one-off, once-and-for-all, matter, but rather, via the **differentiation** of the concept, issues such as anticipatory socialization or re-socialization (the anticipatory rehearsal, or instantiation of new, patterns of conduct [re-socialization], when circumstances change as persons move through the **life-course**) have been explored. **Erving Goffman**'s early work (such as *Asylums*, 1961) on "degradation ceremonies" had a major influence on these developments.

The problem of socialization has been understood in two essentially different ways. The first, and dominant, way has been concerned to conceptualize socialization by asking how it is that persons come to learn, or to internalize, the **values**, **attitudes**, and **norms** of the **culture** or society (or local setting such as a workplace in which they live) and how it is that they come to be able to enact culturally congruent social roles and culturally appropriate practices. This approach has tended to see socialization as a something that *happens* to people, rather than understanding socialization as a process which (even young) people *take part in* as active agents. A second approach to socialization, often associated with the work of **George Herbert Mead** in *Mind, Self, and Society* (1934) and the symbolic interactionist **tradition**, has been to see socialization as being a matter of the development of a linguistically mediated reflexive self(-concept). This tradition, and more recent developments drawing from it, such as **ethnomethodology** and discursive psychology, represent an interesting recapitulation of Cooley's notion (1902: 2) that societies and their members are "collective and distributive aspects of the same thing." This tradition rejects the idea that "self" and "society," or "identity" and "culture," are separate or separable things and dismisses the commonsense assumption that they are binary contrasts. Instead each informs and co-produces the other.

Most mainstream sociological and psychological work on socialization has, however, begun from the presumption that the process of producing recognizably human beings out of infants (or new versions out of extant adults) is a deeply puzzling matter, especially given the hugely variable detail of the experience of individual members of any given society. The work of **Harvey Sacks** (namely *Lectures on Conversation*, 1995) has recently become important in questioning this assumption. Conventional work has most usually adopted an approach which has sought to separate out (and often to quantify) the relative importance of individual and environmental factors or variables for human development and patterns of sociality (a binary frequently referred to as the nature versus nurture debate) – hence psychological work since Freud on socio-cognitive development (for example *The Language and Thought of the Child*, 1923 [trans. 1926], by Jean Piaget (1886–1980), moral development (such as Lawrence Kohlberg's *The Meaning and Measurement of Moral Development*, 1981), or identity development (for instance Erik Erikson's *Childhood and Society*, 1950); sociological / social psychological work on structural variables such as **social class** (for example A. H. Halsey, Anthony Heath, and John Ridge Halsey on *Origins and Destinations*, 1980) or institutional forms (such as Phillip Zimbardo's *The Power and Pathology of Imprisonment*, 1971) or on social conduct, the **life-course**, and social outcomes; and, more recently, the highly contentious studies in sociobiology and evolutionary psychology by Edward O. Wilson (*Sociobiology*, 1975) and Steven Pinker (*The Blank Slate*, 2002), which attempt to demonstrate the hardwired nature of human sociality. MARK RAPLEY AND SUSAN HANSEN

society

Human beings are social animals and organize their activities in **groups**. The term "society" is used to describe a level of organization of groups that is relatively self-contained. However, the boundedness of groups is always relative and so sociologists may refer to human society, where the reference is to the interdependencies among all social groups, or to subgroups such as family society, where the reference is to the typical interactions among the individuals making up a grouping of close kin. Equally, the term society may be used to indicate the wider activities of those under the **authority** of a particular **state**, for example, French society or Indian society.

The term society came into usage in the eighteenth century with the rise of European **modernity** and its distinctive **public sphere** of **civil society** and **state**. Here the relative openness of association

and the range of cultivated activities available created a space for social intercourse among the better-off, who would go out into "society," meaning "high society." This period coincided with the emergence of **social theory** and its differentiation from political theory, as writers became interested in the distinctiveness of modernity and its **institutions**. With the development of disciplinary **social science** and the formation of sociology as a distinct discipline, sociation and its differentiated forms were seen as the special object of sociology.

The German sociologist **Ferdinand Tönnies** proposed a highly influential distinction between *Gemeinschaft* and *Gesellschaft* (usually translated as "**community**" and "association") to capture the difference between premodern and traditional types of societies. The former are characterized by ties of reciprocity and mutuality; custom predominates and they are largely rural. The latter are characterized by voluntary association and exchange relationships; rational calculation predominates and such societies are urban and cosmopolitan.

Functionalist and associated structurally oriented sociologies provide an analytical definition of society. It is associated with the level of the social system. Each social system must meet functional imperatives (or structural principles) and societies are classified according to the degree of specialized institutional development around each function. Modern society is characterized by specialized and separated institutions of **economy**, polity, legal system, and societal community (of voluntary association); each is a subsystem and the ensemble of subsystems makes up modern society.

In **Marxism**, where the mode of economic production is held to dominate, other institutions of law, **politics**, and **ideology** are sometimes characterized as the social formation. The term society is rejected as obscuring the real determinations at work. In **liberalism,** which also gives priority to the market economy, albeit seeing this as positive, there is also suspicion of the term society, on whose behalf the **state** might act in order to restrict the **market**.

Feminists and postcolonial theorists have criticized the dominant sociological representations of society. For the former, the sociological concept of modern society neglects gendered relationships within the family household and how these structure other social institutions. For the latter, the idea of society as a relatively self-sufficient entity has meant the neglect of the colonial relationships integral to modernity. JOHN HOLMWOOD

sociodrama

Originally, and sometimes still also, known as "psychodrama," sociodrama refers to a set of group-work practices that originate in the theory of Jacob Levry Moreno (1889–1974), who had a diverse background in Viennese psychiatry, general practice, health work with postwar refugees, and theatre. He also worked in **sociometry** and he subsequently founded the journal *Sociometry. A Journal of Interpersonal Relations.* This diverse background was brought together in a series of books such as *Das Stegreiftheatre (The Theatre of Spontaneity,* (1923 [trans. 1947]), *Who Shall Survive? A New Approach to the Problem of Human Interrelations* (1934), and *Sociometry in a Cooperative Community* (1938). He worked to establish sociometrics as a method of studying group relations and also as an innovative approach to group psychotherapy, the inception of which he officially dated from April 1, 1921.

Finding **Sigmund Freud**'s **psychoanalysis** of limited utility, particularly given its individual focus, psychodrama was intended to draw upon the creativity of **groups** to help solve interpersonal and individual difficulties. It is perhaps of note here that Moreno is commonly credited not only with having set up the world's first self-help group (of prostitutes) in 1912, but also with coining the terms group therapy and group psychotherapy. Psychodrama is based, then, in concepts from spontaneity research, social role theory, and the empirical study of groups, to provide a forum within which, by taking on different roles and acting out difficulties, problems, or conflicts in interpersonal relations, patients or actors can be assisted to develop alternative understandings of their problems and – via group process – to develop new, and more constructive, ways of relating to themselves and other people.

While psychodrama concentrates on individual personal concerns, sociodrama takes as its site issues that belong to the group. Sociodrama, then, represents the transfer of the concepts, techniques, and practices of psychodrama (for instance, role playing, doubling, role reversal, and sculpting) into group, community, and non-clinical organizational settings. Sociodrama has been widely used in a range of organizational settings such as **education**, social work, **management**, the military, the police, and health care.

Sociodrama may, then, be described as a way of simulating "real life" in order to facilitate social learning in a group with shared (organizational) goals. Sociodramatic techniques may be used to develop consensual group understandings of the social issues facing and affecting the group, to foster more effective group problem-solving, planning, and decisionmaking; to innovate, develop, experiment with, and test alternative procedures; and through the rehearsal of novel practices or strategies, to assist in the identification of a range of potential outcomes.

MARK RAPLEY AND SUSAN HANSEN

sociogram

– see **networks**.

sociolinguistics

Usually regarded as originating in the work of William Labov (1927–) (in his seminal study, *The Social Stratification of English in New York City*, 1966, but also in *Principles of Linguistic Change*, 1994, and *Principles of Linguistic Change*, 2001), this approach was also important in his work on the varieties of American English (such as *Atlas of North American English*, 2001). Sociolinguistics has become a highly diverse field of study in contemporary sociology. Broadly speaking, sociolinguistics can be understood as the study of the effects of social and cultural variables on language usage, language change and development, and the way in which **language** is used in local contexts.

Sociolinguistics developing from this work is primarily quantitative, may employ **experimental methods**, and applies sophisticated multivariate statistical analyses to the study of variation in the (social and geographical) distribution of linguistic variables, or language usage. As Labov himself, in his chapter on "Quantitative Reasoning in Linguistics" in Peter Trudgill, *The Social Differentiation of English in Norwich* (1974), puts it, operationalizing or defining "linguistic variable[s] is the first and also the last step . . . [T]he most common first step in quantitative analysis of a linguistic variable is the binary division of the population (of speakers or utterances) into salient groups: men vs. women, middle class vs. lower class, preconsonantal final clusters vs. pre-vocalic clusters, and so on." As such, sociolinguistic studies document variations in a range of both "speech particles" and also higher-order phenomena such as "lects" (for example "dialects" – geographically constrained forms of talk), "sociolects" (class-based linguistic patterns), and "ethnolects" (ethnic/culturally distinct vocabularies, syntax, and grammar, for example New York English, or Southern English). Sociolinguistics also examines the variation in use of other sociolinguistic variables at the phonetic, phonological, morpho-logical, grammatical, lexical, and paralinguistic levels of analysis across the usual range of macro-sociological variables such as **gender**, **race and ethnicity**, level of **education**, religious affili-ation, socio-economic status, and so on.

Thus work illustrative of the immense diversity of current quantitative sociolinguistics might in-clude studies as apparently unrelated as Kristin Anderson and Campbell Leaper's "Meta-Analyses of Gender Effects on Conversational Interruption" (1998, *Sex Roles*) on the use of conversational interruption, which suggests that men are statis-tically significantly more likely than women to interrupt their interlocutors, and L. Koch, A. Gross, and R. Kolts's study of "Attitudes Toward Black English and Code Switching" among African-American college students in the *Journal of Black Psychology* (2001).

Quantitative sociolinguistics has come to be complemented by work sharing the concerns of the ethnological, ethnomethodological, conversa-tion analytic, and ordinary language philosophy **traditions**. This stream of work, often associated with key, but divergent, scholars such as J. L. Austin (*How to Do Things with Words*, 1962), John Gumperz and Dell Hymes (*Directions in Sociolinguis-tics*, 1972), John Searle (*Speech Acts*, 1969), Deborah Schiffrin (*Approaches to Discourse*, 1994), and Em-manuel Schegloff ("Discourse, Pragmatics, Conver-sation, Analysis," 1999, *Discourse Studies*), which is often referred to as interactional sociolinguistics, has sought to explicate "the linguistic and socio-cultural knowledge that needs to be shared if conversational involvement is to be maintained" (Gumperz, *Discourse Strategies*, 1982: 3). The diver-sity of the field since inception may, however, be appreciated by reference to one of the canonical texts edited by Gumperz and Hymes in 1964. Although originally a special issue of the journal *American Anthropologist* (1964) which was called "The Ethnography of Communication," this was later republished as *Directions in Sociolinguistics* as a collection of papers by authors with disciplinary affiliations as diverse as anthropology, psycho-logy, philosophy, linguistics, and sociology.

Subsequent scholarship that is recognizably re-lated to interactional sociolinguistics has broad-ened into a diverse, and far from homogeneous, field of research. Increasingly, attention has been paid to **discourse analysis** as an analytic site, with the incorporation of poststructuralist theor-etical **influences**, for example the work of **Michel Foucault**, in the development of areas such as "critical discourse analysis" (for example in

Norman Fairclough's *Discourse and Social Change*, 1992) and discursive psychology (for instance Derek Edwards and Jonathan Potter's *Discursive Psychology*, 1992). That is, a number of different strands of scholarship, with widely differing methodological and analytic emphases, may sens-ibly be described as sharing in a common concern with a relatively small set of issues. Key themes in this field are: questions of how meaning is con-structed and conveyed in talk-in-interaction — for example in the study of judicial settings in J. Max Atkinson and Paul Drew's *Order in Court* (1979); how and to what extent shared cultural know-ledge is employed in the co-creation of in-tersubjectivity; the influence of contextual cues on the success or otherwise of **interaction**, as well as attention to more "obviously" linguistic features of talk such as grammar, syntax, and the normative sequential structure of conversa-tion (for example in **Harvey Sacks**, Emmanuel Schegloff, and Gail Jefferson's "A Simplest Sys-tematics for the Organisation of Turn-taking for Conversation," 1974, *Language*).

Thus, for example, scholars such as Deborah Cameron ("Theoretical Debates in Feminist Linguis-tics: Questions of Sex and Gender," in Ruth Wodak [ed.] *Gender and Discourse*, 1997: 21–35) have attended to the way in which a feminist (socio)linguistics may explicate the relations be-tween **gender**, interaction, and **power**. At a more micro-level, and drawing directly on the micro-sociological work of Emmanuel Schegloff, scholars such as Celia Kitzinger (for example C. Kitzinger and H. Frith, "Just Say No? The Use of Conver-sation Analysis in Developing a Feminist Pers-pective on Sexual Refusal," 1999, *Discourse and Society*) have examined the ways in which claims made in talk about knowledge can be understood. Here the explicitly and self-consciously political usage of **conversational analysis** to intervene in what is both an academic and a social debate (in this case concerning the extent to which mis-communication about sexual consent between men and women is a matter of gender-specific "lects") becomes apparent (for example Deborah Tannen's *You Just Don't Understand*, 1992).

It is in this subfield, however, that the key difference between quantitative and qualitative sociolinguistic work can be seen. That is, the issue of the effects of "context" has a long and conten-tious history (see Alessandro Duranti and Charles Goodwin [eds.], *Rethinking Context*, 1994; John Heritage, *Garfinkel and Ethnomethodology*, 1984; and D. Lawrence Wieder, *Language and Social Reality*, 1974), and while quantitative and qualitative sociolinguistics are both concerned with context, in the latter area — under the influence of the Schegloffian variant of conversation analysis — attention to contextual sociological variables such as gender, **ethnicity**, or **social class** is dismissed unless made explicitly relevant in the interaction in hand by the members in question. However, even within interactional sociolinguistics, conversation analysts argue that "context" is so over-determined as to provide only analytic glosses, with no empirically secure specification of local relevance, whereas critical discourse analysts (such as Fairclough, 1992) contend that aspects of context which are essential to comprehending social interaction are identifiable, a priori, by socio-politically committed analysts. Between these positions some have attempted to outline a way of reading work inspired by **ethnomethodology** in terms of either rhetorical analysis or poststructuralist thought, and vice versa (for example Mick Billig's *Arguing and Thinking*, 1987; Mark Rapley's *The Social Construction of Intellectual Disability*, 2004, and Margaret Wetherell's "Positioning and Interpretative Repertoires: Conversation Analysis and Poststructuralism in Dialogue," 1998, *Discourse and Society*). There is much controversy that remains unresolved.

MARK RAPLEY AND SUSAN HANSEN

sociological imagination
– see **C. Wright Mills**.

sociological theory
Any form of sustained reasoning or logic that endeavors to make sense of observable realities of social life via the use of concepts, metaphors, models, or other forms of abstract ideas may be legitimately classified as sociological theory. The need for theoretical reasoning is particularly acute in sociology because of the remarkable complexity and diversity of observable realities within any given social group, among comparable **groups**, and between dramatically different historical epochs and culturally distinct **civilizations**. Though several methodologists, most notably **John Stuart Mill** in his *System of Logic* (1843), have proposed inductive means to develop **social theory** via generalizations from empirical research, most methodologists agree with **Auguste Comte**, who declared in his six-volume *Course of Positive Philosophy* (1830–42 [trans. 1855]) that social facts, while always numerous and easily observed, are too vague and incoherent to be useful in the absence of theory. However, in practice sociological theorists need not confine themselves to abstract

reasoning. Theory is often developed by shuttling back and forth between abstractions and empirical evidence. Moreover, a number of extraordinary works, including **Max Weber**'s *The Protestant Ethic and the Spirit of Capitalism* (1905 [trans. 2002]), **Émile Durkheim**'s *Suicide* (1897 [trans. 1951]), and the *Elementary Forms of Religious Life* (1912 [trans. 2001]), and **Erving Goffman**'s *Interaction Ritual* (1967), develop theory by incorporating highly abstract sociological insights in the abstract analysis of empirical examples.

But whatever the relationship between theory and facts, logical reasoning never makes sense of social realities on its own. All original theories begin with an inspiration of some kind, for example novel insights that bring the prosaic background of social events into the foreground of sociological interest, new ways to discover or explain puzzling **social structures** or forms of behavior, or morally compelling visions of **society** and its discontents. These inspirations are only intuitions in themselves. Intuitions are transformed into theory via the disciplined analytical reasoning that follows.

Sociological theories may be classified in any number of ways. Perhaps the most familiar distinction is that between classical and contemporary social theory. This entry begins with an extended discussion of this distinction, followed by more specific treatment of salient themes on each side of the classical–contemporary divide.

Sociological theory written prior to 1930 is referred to as classical sociological theory. Much of it was written well before 1890 when the academic discipline of sociology began to emerge. Theory written from 1930 to the present is referred to as contemporary social theory. Though both forms of theory share a common purpose in making sense of observable realities, they otherwise differ in so many respects that they can be regarded as separate genres, and this is how they are taught in academic **institutions** around the world today.

The historical transition from classical to contemporary theory marks a large cultural shift in how thinkers go about making sense of society. The extraordinarily learned classical theorist Max Weber observed in *Economy and Society* (1922 [trans. 1968]) that **intellectuals** have always been driven by an inner compulsion to understand the world as a meaningful cosmos. For much of human history, this need was inspired by the apparent senselessness of human suffering in light of religious teachings as well as by the desire to discover ways and means of release or relief from the social and material miseries of human life. Over many centuries and across many civilizations, intellectuals created systematic theologies and ethical philosophies to serve these ends. But these theologies and philosophies are too removed from observable social realities to qualify as sociological thought even in the broadest sense.

The classical era in sociological theory began when thinkers stopped trying to make sense of the world exclusively in terms of theological and ethical concepts and began searching for the underlying principles that organize the realities of social life. Isaac Newton's stunning discovery of a small set of laws that explained the motions of the material universe motivated social thinkers to find similar devices in their fields as well. Considered in this way, Adam Smith's *The Wealth of Nations* (1776) may well be the earliest work in classical social theory to be well received by a large audience. Smith's theories assumed a truly Newtonian form with little regard for ethical inspiration. However, other classical theorists began with an ethical vision of the meaning of social life even as they sought to discover how social life actually operates and is organized. From dramatically different ethical positions, Comte and **Karl Marx** drew inspiration from their respective moral visions, systematically integrating into their work philosophies of history that proceeded from dysfunctional societies of the past and present, to the radical reduction of socially created human suffering in a utopian society – a *terminus ad quem* preordained ultimately to emerge. Although classical theorists such as Weber and **Alexis de Tocqueville** saw human history as too complex and too dependent upon local events to constitute a single trajectory (in Marx's metaphor, a single riddle), or to possess a single ethical meaning of any kind, the residual influence of theology and ethical philosophy was still evident in most classical theoretical works.

The important change after 1930 was that the majority of social theorists relinquished the compulsive search for theological or ethical meaning in social life, and fixed their gaze more narrowly on making sense of social life as a realm of multiple, diverse structures and processes that we do not understand. The shift is quite evident in the career of **Talcott Parsons**, who constructed several vast and systematically integrated conceptual schemes, none of which made the kind of ethical prophecies or social critiques that are so evident in Marx, Comte, and other classical theorists such as Durkheim. Parsons believed that his purely abstract theoretical reasoning ultimately would

be supported by a large body of empirical research. Others had their doubts. **Robert K. Merton**, for one, believed that **sociology** had yet to find a major thinker who would transform sociology into a discipline with both an adequate empirical methodology and an analytical framework. In light of the difficulties in connecting sociological reasoning with empirical fact, Merton devised what he termed theories of the middle range in order to understand the organizing principles of distinctive, conceptually defined sectors or moments of social life.

Merton was not the only contemporary sociologist to find that sociology's greatest challenge was to make as much sense as possible of specific segments of the social world in the absence of a comprehensive conceptual scheme. Beginning in the 1920s and 1930s with the pragmatic philosophy of **George Herbert Mead** and the phenomenological sociology of **Alfred Schutz**, social theorists became intrigued by the intricate, half-hidden contingencies of social **interaction**. Indeed, one prominent theorist of interaction, the ethnomethodologist **Harold Garfinkel**, went so far that in his work empirical contingencies often seem to overshadow theoretical reasoning altogether. However, **Erving Goffman**, arguably as close to a "genius" as anyone contemporary social theory has so far produced, set the study of social interaction on a somewhat more abstract course, with exquisitely chosen metaphors that suggest sociological correspondences as well as literary resemblances.

If students of interaction find contingencies in locally produced encounters, contemporary historical sociologists find contingencies on a much grander scale in the developmental patterns of societies and civilizations, especially those patterns and contingencies associated with the rise of **modernity**, first in western civilization and then across all cosmopolitan regions around the globe. Weber established the **legitimacy** of historical sociology in the classical era and his example inspired other European theorists, most notably **Norbert Elias. Barrington Moore, Jr.**'s *Social Origins of Dictatorship and Democracy* (1966) reinvigorated the Weberian tradition in contemporary sociology, shedding new light on the much-neglected development of alternative organizational forms of the modern **state**, a topic that attracted the interest of other contemporary historical social theorists including **Reinhard Bendix, Theda Skocpol**, and **Michael Mann**. Other contemporary historical sociological theorists such as **Charles Tilly** and Perry Anderson draw inspiration from

Marx. **Immanuel Wallerstein** has developed the most ambitious of contemporary Marxist-based historical social theories by charting the rise and projecting the ultimate demise of the capitalist world-economy.

The vestiges of classical theory, and even pre-classical philosophy, are not entirely absent in other areas of contemporary sociological theory either. Some theorists, such as **Karl Mannheim** and **Daniel Bell**, thought in classical ways about contemporary themes, combining vast erudition with great sensitivity to grasp how modernity has developed in recent times. A number of theorists have been inspired by the classics to make sense of socially generated misery and injustice. Until the fall of the Soviet Union and the uprising in Tiananmen Square, Marxist sociologists dedicated themselves to theory in service to social ethics as Marx had done before. Whereas some post-1989 Marxist theorists struggled valiantly to retain Marx's redemptive philosophy of history, others, taking an implicitly Nietzschean turn originated by **Georg Lukács**, **Theodor Wiesengrund Adorno**, and **Max Horkheimer**, assumed the role of sociological Jeremiahs, interpreting twentieth-century western civilization both sociologically and ethically as a spiritual wasteland that would nourish no truly meaningful ways of life. Just when it appeared that the ethical mission of social theory might disappear from contemporary sociological theory altogether, the ethical criticism of modern social **institutions** was renewed in two different forms. On the one hand, drawing on and uniting a vast array of social theories and philosophies, **Jürgen Habermas** sought to transcend Horkheimer and Adorno's pessimism by developing a new systematic theory of western modernity grounded in a conception of communication that claims to identify ethical universals of human life. On the other hand, sociologists of **gender** and **sexualities**, inspired by new developments in feminist **politics** and philosophy, began to theorize forms of **inequality** that sociology at large had previously ignored. Though these sociological perspectives have yet to be systematized, the commitment to egalitarian ethics and the critique of **discrimination** and injustice are quite evident among many thinkers, including **Arlie Russell Hochschild**, Dorothy Smith, and W. R. Connell.

Why did classical social theorists turn away from pure philosophy and begin the move to analytical themes capable of sustained empirical reference? It was more than just science that inspired this turn. Of equal importance was the radical disruption of premodern forms of social organization and the rapid emergence of new forms of institutional orders that marked the first phase of modernity. In their own lifetimes, classical theorists witnessed feudal and aristocratic institutions overpowered by **capitalism** and the nation-state, human-powered **technologies** rendered obsolete by the industrial revolution, and tradition-bound, communal **cultures** severely weakened by the rise of the culture of **individualism**. The political, economic, and social arrangements that were in decline were still too recent to forget. But the modern institutions that were replacing them were so different, so powerful, and so difficult to control that the supreme intellectual task for all social thinkers at the time was simply to comprehend the nature of modernity as a civilizational form.

Perhaps it says something about the enduring features of modernity that the agenda of themes contemporary sociology inherits from classical sociology continues to shape so much sociological thought today. This is not to say that the classical theorists got everything right. They exaggerated some features of modernity, underemphasized others, and could not have anticipated more recent developments at all. For example, no classical theorist anticipated twentieth-century **genocide** or world **wars**; the end of **colonialism**; or the information technology that has facilitated the **globalization** of numerous **networks** of production, distribution, and finance, transnational political **organizations** and alliances of nation-states around the world, and global competition and specialization among academic scientists, as well as industrial designers and engineers.

Both Adam Smith and Marx saw that capitalism would shape and reshape every aspect of society. No contemporary sociological theorist addresses capitalism today without drawing upon the enduring legacies of these two sociological masters from the past. De Tocqueville, in *Democracy in America* (1835 and 1840 [trans. 2003]), which is classical sociology's most underappreciated masterpiece, saw that egalitarian **values** and democratic institutions would transform states on the one hand and civic culture on the other. Though he focused on the United States in the Jacksonian era, his insights are relevant in all parts of the world where democratic institutions organize political life, or where egalitarian values are regarded as cultural ideals. Durkheim understood several things about modernity that remain with us today. He was vitally concerned with the tension between the ubiquitous human need for **solidarity** with others and the more specifically modern need for individual autonomy. A century after he wrote, the tension between integration and autonomy remains as fraught with consequences as ever in every region where the modern seeds of individualism have found fertile ground. Weber introduced yet another point of view on modernity that remains with us today. He focused most of the historically rich concepts he termed **ideal types** on institutional and cultural orders rather than entire societies or civilizations at large. Nonetheless, in one realm after another, from the rule-governed **bureaucracies** of the state and the profit-oriented practices of capitalists to the self-interested motives of modern politicians and the efficiencies of scientific technology, Weber perceived the displacement of ways of life with ethical substance by instrumental motivations and rigid, formally defined routines. The roster of classical theorists whose visions of modernity remain influential today does not end here. **Claude Henri de Rouvroy, Comte de Saint-Simon**, **Herbert Spencer**, and **Georg Simmel** should appear on everyone's classical list. Furthermore, a number of European sociologists might well have sustained the classical way of doing social theory into the middle of the twentieth century were it not for their displacement from their native lands by the ominous ascension of Nazism to state **power** prior to World War II. This last set of classical theorists includes **Joseph Alois Schumpeter** on **democracy**, capitalism, and **socialism**, and **Karl Polanyi** on the contradictions of the market society.

The transition from classical to contemporary sociological theory was accompanied by, and in some ways induced by, an increasing methodological self-consciousness. Prior to 1930, sociology in many academic cultures lacked the legitimacy of rival disciplines such as history, philosophy, theology, and **political economy**. Like newcomers to any cultural organization, sociologists were anxious to demonstrate their respectability. Given the unrivaled **prestige** of science at the time, social theorists sought to establish their discipline by adhering to strict codifications of the scientific method. Indeed, it may well be that no other discipline has ever tried as diligently as sociology to emulate the rules of scientific method in their purest form as reconstructed by logical empiricist philosophers of science. **Charles Darwin** felt no need to write a philosophical treatise on scientific method in biology in order to justify his theory of evolution, nor did Albert Einstein frame his theories of relativity with a methodological legitimation of any kind. But when Parsons wrote *The Structure of Social Action* (1937), he concluded with a fifty-page discussion of the methodological status and implications of his work. Merton was even more methodologically self-aware than Parsons, devoting five long essays, which ultimately appeared together as the opening chapters in *Social Theory and Social Structure* (1968), to erudite and engagingly written accounts of the scientific status and techniques of what he termed (following **Thomas H. Marshall**) theories of the middle range. In doing so, Merton stressed a tight integration between theoretical concepts and models on the one hand, and systematically collected and analyzed empirical evidence on the other. This tight integration between theory and **data** was highly prized in American sociology at the time, and it remains a hallmark of self-consciously scientific American sociology today. Indeed, in the period from 1945 to 1970, American sociologists produced a long shelf of volumes on the **methodology** of scientific theory construction. As guides for their work, most of these authors adopted logical empiricist philosophies of science prepared by **authorities** such as Ernest Nagel and Carl Hempel. Few of these methodological schemes yielded actual sociological theories of enduring **value**. However, the logical empiricist approach at large has successfully shaped a number of notable sociological works. These include **Peter M. Blau**'s *Inequality and Heterogeneity* (1977) and **James Coleman**'s *Foundations of Social Theory* (1990), as well as the works of four **communities** of theorists who work on expectations, theories of the state, theory, network, and **rational choice theory**.

Methodological self-consciousness is by no means confined to those devoted to logical empiricist philosophies of science. Even in the classical era, Wilhelm Dilthey, Heinrich Rickert, and other German scholars advocated a **social science** focused prevalently on the cultural meaning of historical constellations of events, artworks, and moral or spiritual beliefs. These arguments entered sociology via Weber's methodological writings. However, Weber's methodological views did not influence the mainstream of social theory, which remained enthralled by formal scientific methods. Indeed, the Canadian American theorist **Dennis Hume Wrong** put the situation quite well when he spoke of a Weberian underground that resisted the scientific methods which reached their highwater mark in the late 1950s.

Two intellectual currents arose in the early 1960s that stemmed the scientific tide. The first was the growing interest in the highly contingent nature of locally produced social **interaction**. The symbolic interactionist **tradition** founded by Mead's student **Herbert Blumer**, the ethnomethodological community founded by Garfinkel, and those who loosely expanded upon Goffman's works actively resisted rigidly rationalized guidelines for scientific theory. Newly released from methodological dogma, these theorists created new ways and means to analyze the social construction and cultural meaning of interpersonal relations. The best of these theorists devised new techniques for observing social life, thereby renewing the connection between theory and data that is a necessary condition of sociology, whether or not it conforms to any well-specified account of the scientific method.

The second current that stemmed the dogmatic view of scientific methods in social theory emerged quite suddenly with the publication of **Thomas Samuel Kuhn**'s relatively brief and not very well-written book, *The Structure of Scientific Revolutions* (1962). Kuhn, who was trained first as a physicist and then as a historian and philosopher of science, recognized that philosophical reconstructions of scientific method lacked authenticity in terms of how scientific theories are actually produced. His historically evidenced and sociologically informed analysis demonstrated that scientific knowledge includes an element of communal agreement on concepts and exemplars that is not subject to empirical dispute. One implication of Kuhn's work was that the integration of theory and data was never as tightly integrated as logical empiricist philosophers liked to suppose. Indeed, Kuhn went so far as to challenge the notion that science proceeds by progressive accumulation and consolidation of empirically documented propositions. Instead, unanswered questions in one scientific community challenge the most original thinkers to see the world that they study in new ways. Ultimately these new studies induce what Kuhn terms a shift in **paradigms**. By the late 1960s, a new **generation** of sociological theorists already recognized that Kuhn's arguments licensed a new methodological priority for theoretical developments vis-à-vis the analysis of empirical data.

One of the great challenges of sociological theory is to determine the most incisive ways to conceive society, **social structures**, and **social action**. No other mode of thought was ever as widely accepted in this regard as was the functionalist model during the period from 1945 to 1975. **Functionalism** is a generic term for an array of theories, all of which begin with the idea borrowed from biological theory that any given social phenomenon is theoretically significant in terms of its consequences for society or other large social systems such as the capitalist **economy** or the nation-state. Thus, to cite a common example, social **inequality** was said by many functionalists to make a positive contribution to society by attracting the most talented and energetic individuals to positions of great importance for the well-being of a social group as a whole.

Though functionalist models were extensively employed by Comte, Spencer, and Durkheim, functionalism reached its zenith in contemporary sociology when it was elaborated in Parsons's famous AGIL format for theoretical analysis. According to Parsons, every social system has four basic functional requisites: adaptation to the environment or the economic subsystem (A), the determination and pursuit of goals or the political subsystem (G), the integration of its constituent members or parts or the cultural subsystem (I), and the maintenance of latent social patterns via **socialization** and other means, or the subsystem concerned with problems of motivation (L). Parsons ultimately developed concatenated models of systems within systems, each of which required means to satisfy its own functional needs even as it contributed to satisfying certain functional needs of larger systems.

Parsons's functional models ultimately tested the limits of sociological plausibility. But by the time he reached this point, functionalism was already in trouble. Merton's essay on manifest and latent functions in *Social Theory and Social Structure* (1949), though widely regarded as an extremely subtle elaboration of functional thought, was also a cautionary analysis of the numerous pitfalls that made functionalist reasoning a logically suspect form of analysis. But, though weakened by internal criticism, functionalism might have survived were it not for ideologically inspired attacks from left-wing groups who objected to its concern for order and stability rather than injustice, exploitation, and **discrimination**. In recent decades, only **Niklas Luhmann** has revised the functionalist model to take account of these criticisms, arguing that the reduction of complexity is a primary need of all social systems.

With the eclipse of functional reasoning, social theorists had to devise new means to conceptualize large social collectivities. Some turned to structuralist models, importing analyses of collective phenomena that had proven useful in linguistics (for example **Ferdinand de Saussure**) and anthropology (for example **Claude Lévi-Strauss**). But logically rigorous structuralist models were difficult to associate with observable social realities. Those who turned to the analysis of positional and relational patterns had greater success. **Mark Granovetter** and Ronald Burt, two students of Harrison White, have used network analysis to good effect in subtle demonstrations of surprising patterns of network relations with consequences for the organization of collective life. Network analysis has served as a tool for theories of many kinds, including Tilly's in *Durable Inequality* (1999). One theorist, **Manuel Castells**, has gone so far as to make **networks** the primary units of the analysis of **modernity** in his recent trilogy, *The Information Age* (1996–8).

A concentration on the relationship between the properties of collectivities and the enactment of social practices, commonly called the problem of **agency and structure**, has emerged since the mid-1970s as a highly original way to make sense of the realities of social life. Anticipated in certain respects in the pragmatic philosophies of John Dewey (1859–1952) and Mead, this new mode of theorizing has been advanced by **Pierre Bourdieu**, **Margaret Archer**, and **Randall Collins**, and the association between collective structures and social practices has been a central theme in Habermas's analysis of the relationship between systems and **lifeworlds**, and Tilly's theory of the persistence of **inequalities** in the scripts of **everyday life**.

Anthony Giddens's structuration theory is the most prominent account of this new sociological point of view. For Giddens, collectivities are associated with social practices in two ways. First, social practices are connected in networks, systems, and other circuits of **reproduction** that maintain the morphological properties of collective groups. Second, common social practices, many of which are reproduced in a large collectivity millions of times each day, are structured by pragmatic skills that actors have acquired in the past. When these practices are reproduced anew, they reestablish familiar forms of structuration and thus help to perpetuate the structures received from the past. Thus, when people coordinate their activities via standard clock time, they help to reproduce the chronological structuration of modern social life.

Two things are obvious about contemporary sociological theory today. First, whereas theory fifty years ago centered on formal scientific ambitions and functionalist models, social theory today has no obvious center of gravity at all. Some sociologists long for more theoretical coherence. Others glory in the intellectual freedom that is a concomitant of this diversity. Yet one thing has not changed: every sociological theory is still motivated by the need to make sense of social life, the most complex, diverse, and mutable of all empirical domains.   IRA COHEN

sociology

Both an academic field and a practical accomplishment, it may be understood as the competence by which ordinary participants in social settings recognize and obey (or violate) rules and **norms** that are widely shared by others. The performance of sociological competence leads to the practical accomplishment of the salient and enduring **social structures** that organize social life into **institutions**. How practical sociological competence is acquired remains a mystery, though it seems to operate in much the same way as language acquisition in that the ability to respond to social settings in a normal (or deviant) manner arises suddenly at a relatively young age in early childhood. Even preverbal infants know how to please (or irritate) care-givers in practically competent ways. Practical sociological competence is not necessarily discursive in that participants may or may not be able to discuss or explain the reasons they behave as they do. This is sometimes called the naive, natural attitude of **everyday life**.

Academic sociologies can be distinguished from practical ones by the trained ability to describe the discursive properties of regularities in the competent achievements of social **groups**. The child as a practical sociologist cannot say how she gets a care-giver to change a diaper. An academic sociologist, however, uses a disciplinary **language** to account for how regularities in a society's family structure may affect the **interactions** of **children** and their care-givers. From its beginnings in the 1890s, academic sociology has developed along two lines. Explanatory sociologies seek to follow the lead of pure sciences by offering discursive **explanations** in formal, preferably mathematical, languages. Interpretative sociologies, by contrast, believe that, unlike events in the natural world, social things cannot be reduced to their formal properties because social performances seldom conform exactly to competency rules. Thus, while explanatory sociologies take the analytic **risk** of making their discursive statements too precise and overly general, interpretative sociologies risk giving up the advantages of formal analysis in order to investigate the natural irregularities in practical aspects of social behavior. The two methods, never fully comfortable with each other, have enriched the field by reminding sociologists that a science of social facts depends on the practical sociologies of untrained persons in natural settings (called by some "ethnomethods" – for example **Harold Garfinkel**, *Studies in Ethnomethodology*, 1967).

Academic sociology began in earnest in the 1890s when the early industrial era made it difficult to neglect the practical consequences of urban conflict, political instability, and rapid economic change. The earliest academic sociologists did not choose sides between explanatory and interpretative methods; for example, **Émile Durkheim**'s *Suicide* (1897 [trans. 1951]) was a formal explanatory study of the practical consequences of **anomie**, as **Max Weber**'s *Protestant Ethic and the Spirit of Capitalism* (1905 [trans. 2002]) was an interpretative explanation of the practical consequences of formalization in society. Also in the classical period, American sociology pursued empirical work that used formal methods to study the practical accomplishments of marginal social groups; such as **W. E. B. Du Bois**, *The Philadelphia Negro* (1896), and **W. I. Thomas** and Florian Znaniecki, *The Polish Peasant in Europe and America* (1918–20).

Scientific sociology did not begin to mature until the 1940s in the United States. The key texts at the beginning of the scientific era were **Talcott Parsons**'s *Structure of Social Action* (1937), which emphasized the independence of formal analytic concepts, and **Robert K. Merton**'s *Social Theory and Social Structure* (1949), which insisted on embedding of concepts in empirical research findings. Yet, the differences notwithstanding, the two approaches inspired empirically formal research that came to dominate the field.

In the 1960s and 1970s, academic sociology, responding to the political turmoil of the times, began to restore the balance between formal explanatory and practically interpretative sociologies. After World War II, the United States had been the global hegemonic **power** in cultural and economic matters. But, after 1968, the new **social movements** in the global core and semi-periphery and the resistance of newly decolonized peripheral regions challenged the United States' cultural **authority** in sociology as in most areas. In the 1970s, European sociology reasserted its independence from America's narrowly scientific

sociology. In Germany, critical sociology was defined as a third sociological way beyond the limitations of formal and interpretative methods; for example, **Jürgen Habermas**, *Knowledge and Human Interests* (1968 [trans. 1971]). In France, **Pierre Bourdieu** challenged the very idea that objectivist formal methods were opposed to subjectivist interpretative ones, as in *Outline of a Theory of Practice* (1972 [trans. 1977]). Some time later, in Great Britain, **Anthony Giddens** also defied the pure science ideal in sociology in an unmistakably European way, for example, in *New Rules of Sociological Method* (1976). Though these developments differed in important ways, they sought to rethink sociology as the study of the consequences of ordinary social practices.

Meanwhile, in the United States, a native **pragmatism** reasserted itself by emphasizing the study of the natural **attitudes** of people in everyday life; for example **Erving Goffman** in *Presentation of Self in Everyday Life* (1959) and **C. Wright Mills** in *The Sociological Imagination* (1959). Slightly later, the easing of Cold War tensions encouraged an appropriation of structural, including Marxist, ideas that supported a more global perspective. **Immanuel Wallerstein**'s *The Modern World-System* (vol. I, 1974) is the prime example of a critical sociology of global structures that is formal without being empiricist and interpretative without being local. Also in the 1970s, feminist sociology and other sociologies associated with the new social movements defied the prevailing scientific norms in the United States, for example in Dorothy Smith's "Women's Experience as a Radical Critique of Sociology" in *The Conceptual Practices of Power* (1974) and **Nancy Chodorow**'s *Reproduction of Mothering* (1978). In the 1970s historical sociologies such as **world-systems analysis** and feminist sociologies significantly broadened academic sociology's ability to account for global and personal issues of practical social life by encouraging a new wave of research into racial and sexual **identities**, economic change, and **globalization**.

Over the last decades of the twentieth century, sociologies with balanced commitments to explanatory and interpretative methods began to surface, notably in modernizing regions like East Asia, for example in Young Hee Shim, *Sexual Violence and Feminism in Korea* (2004). Early in the twenty-first century, academic sociology had achieved a scientific maturity that did not require the sacrifice of its natural reliance on practical sociologies: for example **Zygmunt Bauman**, *Liquid Modernity* (2001), and **Ulrich Beck**, *World Risk Society* (1999).

CHARLES LEMERT

sociometry

This term was coined by Jacob L. Moreno (1889–1974) and is true to its Latin roots which mean "social" and "measure." For Moreno, the social was the relatedness between the members of any social **group** or **organization**, and the **measurement** was to be based on the perception by the members of that group of their relations to others from their own individual perspectives. The result was to be the mathematical study of the psychological properties of populations.

At the time of its coinage in the early 1930s, Moreno was one of a number of writers who had an interest in the use of spatial metaphors to describe **society**. In his and their view, society was best analyzed through the sets of personal relationships in which they were involved, and which in turn underpinned the larger **social structures** with which other writers were concerned. Various sociometric techniques were developed in the light of this view, which enabled the creation of what are called sociograms. These offer a visual representation of the degree of connectedness between members of a group, and of the extent of **social distance** between them.

At the practical level, sociometric techniques were designed to support a variety of therapeutic and managerial interventions into groups, organizations, and **communities**, reflecting Moreno's own background in psychiatry and psychotherapy, particularly **sociodrama**, of which he was a key exponent and important innovator. It is in these areas that these techniques see continuing use today. Their validity is viewed as being due to their phenomenological grounding, which renders the outcome of their application meaningful to the members of the group from which they are derived.

At the theoretical level, sociometry was adopted within a variety of disciplines in the 1930s, and was, in part, the offspring of the very fruitful mixing of North American and European intellectual **traditions** which resulted from the waves of immigration from European universities at that time. The abiding focus was interpersonal relationships, the flow of **information** between persons, its affective significance, and the consequences that followed. A line of thinking that is pursued currently is the study of social distance.

Moreno and others founded the journal *Sociometry* to take their work forward, but not in any narrow sense. The editorial foreword to the first issue in 1937 is remarkably, and perhaps depressingly, prescient in its recognition that many of the challenges that face the study of human societies can only be approached by an interdisciplinarity that rises above "a glib scrambling of fashionable texts from biology, psychiatry and ethnology." In the 1960s, the journal was briefly transformed into the journal *Social Psychology* before that too was absorbed into another publication.   DAVID GOOD

solidarity

Whereas economic accounts of collective phenomena typically operate in terms of individual-level capacities or inclinations, sociological accounts function in terms of factors not reducible to individual qualities. Whereas economic accounts of **markets**, for instance, refer to self-interested exchanges between individuals, sociological accounts may operate at the level of societal **organization**, such as **capitalism**, or institutional arrangement, such as property **rights** or consumer legislation. Social or group solidarity in sociological **explanation** is the factor that gives reality to collective entities that are more than the mere aggregation of individuals who make up or populate them. **Émile Durkheim**, with whom the notion of solidarity is originally associated, famously insisted that solidarity is "[not] amenable to exact observation and especially not to measurement" in *The Division of Labor in Society* (1893 [trans. 1960]). It can be known only by its effects.

As the basis of group formation and cohesiveness, solidarity is responsible for the sense of belongingness that individuals experience in social life, and for the direction of their conduct towards mutuality or interconnectedness that characterizes social behavior and **interaction**. For the concept of solidarity to be meaningful, it must be distinguished from others that might have the same consequences for group cohesiveness. Solidarity cannot be reduced to coercion, for example. Durkheim holds that solidarity implies collective **norms** through which group members are obliged but not forced to participate in group activities. Neither is the social obligation inherent in solidarity to be confused with expediency, through which an individual will submit to group-defined requirements in exchange for a benefit that compensates for that submission. Rather, the individual's obligation to the **group** is a consequence of their acceptance of the group's entitlement to demand their commitment. Durkheim agrees that the level or intensity of solidarity varies between types of groups.

Solidarity, as a basis of social order, has been sociologically explained in a number of different ways. One indicator of the nature of the prevalent solidarity identified by Durkheim, for instance, is law, in which different types of law, repressive or restitutive, determine different types of solidarity (*The Division of Labor*, ch. 1, section 3). Few sociologists have followed Durkheim, however, in a legal approach to solidarity. Many who focus on **culture** as the foundation of solidarity nevertheless see norms, also emphasized by Durkheim, as its source. **Talcott Parsons**, for instance, in *The Social System* (1951) holds that solidarity (which he also calls loyalty) has two aspects; attachment and **symbols** (involving both meaning and value-orientation). An alternative to the cultural perspective on solidarity is the structuralist perspective, with **Karl Marx** as its chief exponent. Marx accounted for class solidarity, for instance, in terms of consciousness, and the absence of societal solidarity under capitalist conditions in terms of divergent economic interests and social organization between **social classes**. Conflict theory, for example **Georg Simmel**, *Conflict and the Web of Group-Affiliations* (1955) offers another possibility of solidarity, as arising not primarily from culture or structure internal to the group, but from external pressure caused by conflict with another group.　　　　　　　　JACK BARBALET

Sombart, Werner (1863–1941)

An economist and sociologist, Sombart edited one of the main journals of **social science** in Germany, namely the *Archiv für Sozialwissenschaft und Sozialpolitik* with **Max Weber** and Edgar Jaffe. He wrote extensively on the nature of modern **capitalism** in the six-volume history of the European capitalist **economy** *Der Moderne Kapitalismus* (1902). Sombart is best known for his dispute with Weber over "the spirit" of capitalism, in which Sombart in *The Jews and Modern Capitalism* (1911 [trans. 1951]) emphasized the role of Jewish entrepreneurs against Weber's emphasis on Calvinism. Further aspects of his analysis of **entrepreneurship** and the nature of capitalist production appeared in *The Quintessence of Capitalism* (1913 [trans. 1967]) and *Luxury and Capitalism* (1913 [trans. 1967]). Sombart also departed from Weber's **liberalism** in talking a nostalgic and romantic view of the importance of the **family, community**, and the folk in German history in his account of the "communal economy" in *Die deutsche Volkswirtschaft im neunzehnten Jahrhundert* (1905). Sombart defended **socialism** and the economic theories of **Karl Marx** in his account of socialism

and **social movements** in his *Sozialismus und soziale Bewegung in 19. Jahrhundert* (1896), but he came to embrace **fascism** in his later career. He also contributed to the debate about the political history of the United States in *Why is There No Socialism in the United States?* (1906 [trans. 1976]). Sombart also favored, against Weber's political views, a traditional and patriarchal approach to **social policy**. In 1915 Sombart published the influential and controversial pamphlet on *Handler und Helden: Patriotische Besinnungen* in which he compared the trader's spirit of English **utilitarianism** with the heroic ethos of German **culture**. This image was an early version of two stereotypes in which, while the British spirit was represented by an "island of shop-keepers," the **civilization** of Germany was forged by heroic warriors. Because Sombart saw European history as a movement from **feudalism** to capitalism or from Christian community to Jewish association, his work is often criticized as anti-Semitic and as an example of "reactionary modernism."　　　　　　　　BRYAN S. TURNER

Sorokin, Pitirim (1889–1968)

Born in the north of Russia, the son of an itinerant icon-maker – appropriate for an iconoclast – Sorokin was involved in revolutionary activities and arrested while a school pupil and again while at university in St. Petersburg, where he also became acquainted with sociology. He was Chair of the Sociology Department between 1919 and 1922, despite having been under threat of execution from the Bolsheviks in 1917. He went into exile in 1922, arriving in the United States in 1924, holding a number of posts before being invited to Harvard in 1930, where he became founding Chair of the new Department of Sociology (to be replaced in 1946 by **Talcott Parsons**, with whom he had a bitter feud).

Sorokin wrote prolifically, making a major contribution to **sociological theory**. His *Systematic Sociology* (1922) was published clandestinely in Russia, and was followed by a highly influential critical **survey**, *Contemporary Sociological Theories* (1928). His book *Social Mobility* (1927) was the first systematic study of the topic (see **social mobility**). With his colleague Carl Zimmerman, he wrote *Principles of Rural–Urban Sociology* (1929). His four-volume *Social and Cultural Dynamics* (1937–41) was his magnum opus. Famously combative, he was stinging in his attacks upon his sociological colleagues and his reputation suffered from it, though he was elected President of the American Sociological Association in 1965. With support from a drug company, he set up a Research Center in Creative Altruism at Harvard and wrote many more books, mainly concerned with social prophecy, that had little impact in sociology. He returned to his earlier sociological interests with another dismissive attack on his contemporaries in *Fads and Foibles in Modern Sociology* (1956).

JOHN HOLMWOOD

space

The question of space is among the most perplexing questions in sociology. It is true that **sociology** studies objects in space, but should or could space as such be an object of sociological analysis? What would space as such mean? If it means anything at all, does not human geography deal with it? So perhaps sociology abstracts from space and geography studies space. But these assumptions of a fundamental division of **labor** between sociology and geography have been effectively repudiated. Whatever the specific cultural and social history of organization of disciplines, whether social objects can be studied within neatly delineated disciplinary boundaries, where geographers stop at the moment of abstraction from space and sociologists take over to theorize beyond space, is now considered a vacuous question. That said, the best sociological work on space has been accomplished by geographers in the last few decades, for example by Edward W. Soja in *Postmodern Geographies: The Reassertion of Space in Critical Social Theory* (1989). The question is, then, why have sociologists lagged behind geographers in producing sociological analysis of space? Before we proceed to give an answer to that question, we need to elaborate on what we mean by sociological analysis of space.

Consider the sociological analysis of sexual or ethnic **identities**. There have been excellent studies on the ways in which sexual identities are constructed and how these identities enact and perform themselves in and through **social action**. But, as many have been quick to emphasize, sexual or ethnic identities are not constructed, enacted, and performed the same way everywhere (or everywhen). In other words, space matters. But it matters in a more complex way than it appears – for example Andrew Sayer, *Space and Social Theory* (1991). First, it matters obviously because such identities differ in different places. That is fairly easy to grasp and perhaps agree with. But space matters also because specific arrangements that constitute a space are not arrangements in which social action takes place but they constrain, enable, influence, form, articulate, render, and

condition such social action – for example Doreen B. Massey, *Space, Place, and Gender* (1994). Sociological analysis that grasps spatiality would take into account both these ways in which space matters. Thus, studying space as such sociologically would mean studying both these aspects.

Why have sociologists lagged behind geographers in investigating space sociologically? Some have argued that the reason was in the origins of sociological thought and that classical sociologists did not have interest in space – for example Peter Saunders, *Social Theory and the Urban Question* (1981), and John Urry, *The Sociology of Space and Time* (1996). While that argument might be sustained for **Karl Marx**, it is difficult to see it especially in **Max Weber**, *The Agrarian Sociology of Ancient Civilizations* (1909 [trans. 1976]), **Georg Simmel**, "Metropolis and Mental Life" in *The Sociology of Georg Simmel* (1903 [trans. 1977]) and "The Sociology of Space" in *Simmel on Culture* (1903 [trans. 1997]), and **Émile Durkheim**, *Professional Ethics and Civic Morals* (1890 [trans. 1957]). Rather than assuming that classical sociologists did not have interest in space, it is more accurate to argue that subsequent sociologists held a specific conception of space, a static and "container" view of space, and, as a result, associated society as their ostensible object of analysis coterminously with the **state** and, perhaps more appropriately, the nation-state. The study of the **city** in urban sociology illustrates this well. For much of the twentieth century, urban sociology was largely occupied with those things that happened in cities rather than studying the essence of the city, despite notable exceptions such as **Manuel Castells**, *The Urban Question: A Marxist Approach* (1977), David Harvey, *Social Justice and the City* (1973), and Saskia Sassen, *The Global City: New York, London, Tokyo* (1991). That meant understanding and interpreting the city as a container that staged events rather than a space that both enabled and enacted social, political, and cultural relations. As Mark Gottdiener in *The Social Production of Urban Space* (1994) argued, the modern city appears as a container within a container, the state.

But the age of assuming a world that reveals itself in contiguous containers called states, or more problematically, nation-states is all but over. For those who understand sociality of space and spatiality of the social, boundaries, flows, frontiers, camps, borders, and margins have become both social metaphors and spatial objects of sociological and geographical investigations. Questions of **diaspora**, transnational identities, and crosscultural and cosmopolitan spaces are slowly but forcefully becoming central questions of sociological thought.   ENGIN ISIN

spatial inequality
– see **space**.

spatial processes
– see **space**.

spatial turn
– see **space**.

spectacle
– see **Guy Debord**.

Spencer, Herbert (1820–1903)

Widely regarded as the most important proponent of **social Darwinism**, Spencer's evolutionary ideas were first formulated before **Charles Darwin**'s *Origin of Species* (1859). His writings were very considerable and wide-ranging. They covered the rearing of **children** (*Education*, 1861), **political economy** (*Man Versus the State*, 1884), **social theory** (*The Study of Sociology*, 1873; *The Principles of Sociology*, 1893), and psychology (*Principles of Psychology*, 1870), as well as the natural and life sciences (*Principles of Biology*, 1864–7). Central to Spencer's thought is the idea that a common form of evolutionary development underlies all forms of animal and plant life and human society. It is often forgotten that Spencer's work was based on an interpretation of the First Law of Thermodynamics. This states that the total inflow of energy into a system must equal the total outflow from the system. Energy cannot therefore be created or destroyed, it can only be converted from one form to another.

This concept was seen by Spencer as underlying social and organic evolution throughout the entire cosmos (see **evolutionary theory**). Biological systems therefore survive and reproduce by transferring energy between their component parts. Similarly, a social system survives and changes through interacting with its **environment**: changing not only its overall structure but the flow of energy and resources between its **institutions**. Spencer's application of the First Law of Thermodynamics made him one of the first proponents of a systems understanding, one which saw social as well as physical and biological entities as self-balancing and adapting. It is a view taken up and developed by later sociologists such as **Talcott Parsons** and **Neil Smelser** in their *Economy and Society* (1956).

As regards human society, Spencer argued that individuals, like all organisms, are constantly struggling to survive. They also undergo change in order to adapt to the forces and environments which they confront. Those individuals with the most advantageous characteristics survive and propagate in the struggle for survival. But, whereas Darwin argued that natural selection was the main mechanism underlying all organic evolution, Spencer believed this only applied to the earliest stages of evolution and to the most inferior organisms. Like many Darwinian writers in the nineteenth century, Spencer's version of evolution, especially as it applied to humans, strongly depended on a notion of **heredity** and on acquired characteristics being handed down between **generations**. Humans, like other higher animals, acquire structures and **powers** during their lives (the blacksmith's muscles, for example) which can be passed on to their offspring. This raises a central feature of Spencer's sociology. This is his **determinism**: people having to adapt to the society and environment in which they live. There is little sense here of human autonomy within the evolving social system.

Spencer also argued that societies change in a certain direction. They develop from unstructured homogeneity to a structured heterogeneity. Simple, homogeneous **societies** are therefore displaced by heterogeneous compounded societies, a process that is parallel to the change from simple amoeba-like organisms to complex beings such as humans. Spencer also distinguished between militant and **industrial societies**, arguing (unlike one of his main supporters, **William G. Sumner**) that the overall tendency is towards a harmonious industrial society and away from endless **war**. This is because industrial society fosters and perpetuates sentiments such as kindness, forgiveness, and truthfulness. Like Sumner, however, Spencer believed it was a mistake for governments to intervene in the social winnowing process. Such intervention runs counter to the survival of the fittest, leaving the intellectually and physically inferior to survive and propagate. Spencer therefore belongs to the classical liberal tradition, one insisting on limits to state power.

Spencer was the most widely read social scientist of his era, but his work finds a relatively small readership today. "Spencer is dead," Parsons famously wrote and asked "Who reads Spencer now?" (*The Structure of Social Action*, 1937: 3). But Spencer has been important in the development of sociology. His emphasis on the ways in which natural organisms and societies differentiate into elements (each element having a particular function to play in its survival) was important in the development of **Émile Durkheim**'s sociology. Spencer's work also prefigured today's arguments that social and economic achievements are largely a product of heredity.

Developing a sociology sensitive to the links between social and environmental systems is clearly of major importance today. But Spencer's approach is not especially helpful. His grand theorizing, his overemphasis on the First Law of Thermodynamics, and his analogies between biological and social evolution do not offer adequate insights into the detailed and complex links between social, physical, and biological systems. While the disciplinary scope of his work is to be admired, his synthesis of these disciplines is highly problematic. This is one reason why Spencer remains largely unread.

PETER DICKENS

sponsored mobility
– see **social mobility**.

sport
Organized play, a pastime, or a diversion – according to Johan Huizinga (1872–1945) in *Homo ludens* (1938 [trans. 1950]) and Louis Mumford *The Myth of the Machine* (1967), play is an elemental feature of human **groups**. Both writers associate it with creativity, the development of self-discipline, the team spirit, and the origins of **civilization**. However, until the 1960s, the subject featured as a relatively minor part of the curriculum in sociological study. In the late nineteenth century, the rational recreation movement, various youth movements, and imperialists promoted sport as a central mechanism in self-improvement and social **solidarity**. Baron de Courbetin's revival of the Olympics in 1896, as an international festival of amateur sports, provided a global stage for the cultural awareness of sport and for financial sponsorship through advertising, media coverage, and government subsidy.

The cultural profile of sport was vastly enhanced in the twentieth century by the professionalization and commercialization of games. This generated the adhesion of strong patriotic emotions to national teams and the emergence of a variety of personality **cults** around sporting heroes. **Rationalization** and bureaucratization are also evident in the organization of national leagues, international competitions, scientific training and management programs to improve performance, and commercial sponsorship deals

with the sports "celebritaariat." More recently, the development of satellite broadcasting has turned sport into a staple of television **culture** and sports stars into icons of **popular culture**. This has been reinforced by the cult of the **body** and the popularity of diet and fitness regimes.

The increasing financial price of spectatorship and the monetization of major sports have resulted in some critics claiming that sport has become commodified. Similarly, the financial stakes involved in high achievement, together with the cultural **prestige** attached to sporting success, have made the issues of match-fixing and the use of performance-enhancing drugs central topics of debate and research. However, despite these various developments, professional sport retains powerful popular cultural connotations with authenticity, spontaneity, glamor, and social solidarity. It has been theorized as a compensation for the deprivations of the work ethic and a safety valve which permits the discharge of pent-up **emotions** caused by the requirements of the civilizing process.

While scholarly attempts to classify and analyze modern sport reach back to the eighteenth century, the first sociology of sport is generally acknowledged to be *Soziologie des Sports* (1921) by Heinz Risse, a student of **Theodor Wiesengrund Adorno**. Risse's book failed to achieve significant impact, perhaps reflecting the emphasis on economic production, rather than leisure, in European sociology at that time.

It was not until the mid-1960s that the sociology of sport became institutionalized. The key developments here were the foundation of the International Committee of Sport Sociology (ICSS) and the establishment of the journal *International Review of Sport Sociology* (IRSS). The growth of the sub-discipline produced multiparadigmatic rivalry. The main theoretical approaches today are **functionalism**, **Marxism**, **cultural studies**, **feminism**, interactionism, figurational sociology, and **postmodernism**. As interest in the subject has matured, sports studies has emerged as a synthetic interdisciplinary discipline drawing on sociology, political science, psychology, business, **management**, and bio-mechanics.

CHRIS ROJEK

SPSS
– see **statistics**.

standard deviation
– see **statistics**.

state

The term state is treated as synonymous with modern state, for its understanding presented here applies only to polities which have arisen, or have been extensively refashioned, in the course of **modernization** – although of course one can find precedents and similarities elsewhere.

The state represents a distinctive way of structuring a particular form of social **power**, namely political power. Here a **group** exercises some control over the activities of other groups with which it interacts, thanks to its privileged access to facilities for the organized use of **violence**, which allows it to threaten those groups with strong negative sanctions. In routine situations, however, that threat remains in the background, and political power operates chiefly through commands issued by those who hold it, and which find more or less prompt and willing obedience on the part of those to whom they are directed. The probability of this occurring is increased to the extent that political power becomes institutionalized – that is, according to H. Popitz in his phenomenological study of violence such as, *Phänomene der Macht* (1986), it undergoes three processes: depersonalization – formalization – integration.

The raw will that a person's command may otherwise express, is filtered through that person's occupancy of a role, that is a more or less elaborate set of entitlements and obligations. The state takes this strategy much further than other polities, for it consists in a vast ensemble of highly differentiated organs, each endowed with expressly conferred (and regulated) faculties and facilities of rule. They are all integrated, ideally, both by a commitment to a shared (though highly abstract) interest – the public order, the country's security – and by the unique social resource they accumulate and deploy – the monopoly of legitimate violence.

To be legitimate, commands must comply with certain expectations concerning their formation and their execution, which to a greater or lesser extent restrict their discretionality. In the state, this standardizing of activities of rule is chiefly done by law – not, as was the case, for instance, in the Chinese Empire, chiefly by **ritual**. Western law has been used to perform (besides other tasks common to law in all **cultures**) in addition, a peculiar task – instituting and activating political entities, framing their policies, and arranging for the implementation of such policies.

Jurisdiction was seen to characterize the essence itself of rule, and doing **justice** was recognized as a primary task of rulers. Constitutionalism – a critical component of political **modernization** – refers in the first instance to a distinctive legal instrument (written or otherwise). Together with other such instruments, constitutions were widely employed to establish the roles we have referred to above.

The creation of a body of public law setting up offices, specifying their competences, assigning them facilities and faculties of rule, arranging how those manning them would be selected, monitored, and rewarded, constituted the driving edge of a phenomenon of great cultural significance: the positivization of law. Law, that is, could be purposefully made, not just found and sanctioned, by political actors (see **law and society**).

Yet, while laying down the law became the prerogative par excellence of the holders of political power, legal instruments not only instituted and activated the state's organs and agencies, but also constrained and limited their activities. The expressions rule of law and *Rechtsstaat* are not synonymous, but both signify that some of the **norms** the state produces are (or should be) binding on the state itself.

This means, according to Popitz, that political power "gears itself" into the broader social order, imposing burdens on it but also delivering services to it. The state does this chiefly via its complementarity to **civil society** – a complex of social processes and structures not themselves political in nature, and which the state acknowledges as not only autonomous of itself but as needing to be politically safeguarded, even if their workings generate forms of social power (economic, ideological) distinct from the political form.

The formation of western civil society is signaled by two most significant developments. First, the **secularization** of the state: the state, that is, progressively disclaims responsibility for fostering religious interests and ceases to privilege one Church over against the others, and to attach political and juridical significance to the individuals' confessional memberships and loyalties.

Second, after the mercantilist phase, the state progressively ceases to perform economic tasks directly through its own **institutions**. The absolutist monarch claims all *imperium*, that is all expressly political faculties and facilities of rule. But at the same time he recognizes and validates the *dominium* (in the Roman sense of private **property**) of private individuals. Generally, the state attaches high priority, in its own legislative and judicial activities, to securing, in particular, the **rights** of property and of contract. More generally, individuals pursuing their varied interests within the civil society are seen by the state as the bearers of subjective rights.

A further critical step in the process of integration consists in the formation of a **public sphere**. Not only does the state oversee and secure the civil society from above, as it were, and allow the forms of social power operating within it to interact with one another, it also allows them to communicate legitimately with itself from below. Arrangements such as the freedom of opinion and association allow individuals to form and communicate opinions on public affairs. Typically, elections are employed for the selection of the political class, and public competitions for the selection of administrative personnel. In availing themselves of these possibilities, the members of a state's population begin to operate no longer *just* in the capacity of its subjects but *also* in that of citizens.

Of course, all this takes place within divided societies, which raises the problem of which social interests will be favored by the state's activities. For instance, the state's commitment to the protection of private property will unavoidably favor groups in possession of it, conferring on them an advantage as they interact in the **market** with groups deprived of significant property. But the state's policy may also counteract this situation, without subverting it, by conferring also on the latter groups the entitlement to *public* goods and services, thus expanding and enriching the content of **citizenship**. As if to counter the centrifugal pull exercised by contrasting social interests, the state often, particularly from the nineteenth century onwards, projects itself as the political expression of the nation. This is construed as an intrinsically unitary entity, whatever the basis of that unity – ethnic origin, **language**, cultural **traditions**, **religion**, territory, historical experience, or historical destiny. Each nation is seen as entitled to self-rule, and asserts its distinctiveness (often construed as superiority) vis-à-vis other nations. Such entitlements, however, are often contended over between nations, and have to be made good through political means.

This is where the nation-state comes in. Its institutions (from the education system to the army) promote and sustain the nation's awareness of its uniqueness and of the righteousness of its contested claims. Its internal policies keep **social conflicts** from destroying a sense of oneness within the national population. Its external policies identify and pursue the nation's particular interests, often in potential or actual contrast with those of other nations. In the discourse of nationhood, the state's own institutional **identity** as a form of political *Herrschaft* ("domination") of men over men is seen as redeemed and justified by its service to a higher entity.

The emphasis laid so far on the significance of law applies chiefly to a state's domestic arrangements and affairs, not to those relating to its foreign policy. Each state exercises exclusive jurisdiction over a bounded territory, lying next to territories over which jurisdiction is exercised by other states. Thus, the modern political universe is constituted by a plurality of states, and the relations between them are of a different nature from the relations within them. The institutionalization processes we have discussed so far concern the latter relations, and affect much less those between states. Here, political power manifests itself in a much more naked form, related ultimately to the sheer might each of the states can bring to bear, if necessary, in its contentions with the others.

In spite of various arrangements for the formation and implementation of an international order, the modern political universe is not very similar to the state, for it is, one may say, "open at the top." The system generated by the policies of states vis-à-vis one another is capable of reaching an equilibrium, as the imagery of the balance of power suggests. But from time to time that equilibrium must be re-set, as it were, through the threat of or the actual recourse to warfare.

These considerations, it barely needs to be said, amount at best to a highly conventional understanding of the state. These issues are elaborated in Gianfranco Poggi, *The State: Its Nature, Development and Prospects* (1990). The vicissitudes of actual state-making, and their outcomes, have varied considerably even in the European context, not to mention those other parts of the world which have sought, or have been compelled, to put their arrangements for rule through processes similar to those outlined above. Furthermore, it is claimed on some counts that the story of the modern state itself, and particularly of the nation-state, is going through its final phase, under the impact of such phenomena as economic **globalization** and the formation of one political "hyper-power" seeking to promote and control globalization over the world as a whole.

GIANFRANCO POGGI

statistical control
– see **statistics**.

statistical significance
– see **statistics**.

statistics
This term has two distinct meanings, both of which are relevant to sociology. The original meaning of the term refers to facts about society. This is what government statisticians produce, as they measure the ways in which societies change by monitoring births, deaths, **marriages**, employment, the balance of trade, and so on. To this end, social **data** are collected, for instance through the registration of births and deaths, and through the **census**. Having accurate and up-to-date **information** about a society is seen as essential to efficient government, so that policies are targeted to those areas where the need is most acute, and problems are spotted at an early stage. Statistics are also seen as having an important democratic function that permits the success or failure of a government to be evaluated against the facts – for instance, have literacy rates improved and hospital waiting lists reduced?

However, the Office for National Statistics (ONS) is far from being an uncontroversial government department. Social scientists have often been critical of the ways in which statistics have failed to provide a true reflection of society. For instance, unemployment statistics are regularly attacked from both the left and the right. Right-wing critics claim that the government over-estimates the number of people who are unemployed, as many of those claiming benefit on the grounds of **unemployment** could find **work** if they wanted to, or actually work informally or illegally. Left-wing critics have argued that the figures are under-estimates of the true level of unemployment, because many individuals who would work if they could find jobs (such as married women and early retirees) are excluded from the numbers. And feminists have often argued that statistics highlight the more male aspects of life, such as the formal **economy**, while ignoring the importance of domestic work and childrearing for the well-being of a society.

Many social phenomena are perhaps too complex to be adequately measured by figures. But many claim that governments deliberately manipulate figures to highlight their achievements and hide their failures. Sociologists have often been at the forefront of these debates, and have

often used their **influence**, for instance through the Royal Statistical Society (RSS), to hold governments to account.

Over time a second meaning of the term statistics has emerged and many people who have no interest in society at all call themselves statisticians. In this meaning, statistics can be seen as a branch of mathematics that deals with the analysis of data. In the extreme, some pure statisticians are interested only in the development of tools to analyze data and have no interest whatsoever outside of their mathematical properties.

Within sociology, there is a strong historical **tradition** of using empirical data to understand **social change**, going back to **Émile Durkheim**. Now, this type of analysis is seen as an integral part of sociology and the ability to analyze numerical data is seen as an important sociological skill.

There are a number of functions that statistics perform within sociology. Perhaps the simplest and most important is the ability to explore numerical data and apply the sociological imagination. This approach to statistics, known as exploratory data analysis (EDA), emphasizes the way in which a good researcher can look at data, with a combination of openness to new ideas and skepticism about the way in which data can mislead, and gain new insights into the social world. EDA often uses graphs to explore the features of a dataset. How one determines the way in which the **distribution** of variables should be investigated is an example of EDA, with the emphasis on an enquiring mind rather than on mathematical complexity.

A more conventional approach to statistics, termed inferential statistics, is concerned with generalizing results from a sample to a population. Providing that the sample is drawn randomly, or in some other way which assures its representativeness, then conclusions can be drawn about a whole population, instead of just the sample that was interviewed. So, for instance, a general election result can be predicted from **interviews** with just a few hundred or a few thousand voters. But there is statistical error, or sampling error, involved in making such predictions. Often we want to know whether the patterns we observe in a sample can be confidently generalized to a population. If they can, the result is said to be statistically significant. In most cases where researchers analyse datasets (for instance with correlations, **multiple regressions**, or **log linear analyses**) as well as describe the relationships within the data, the results will also indicate whether the results are statistically significant.

This is often done by assigning a "p" value to any statistic, indicating the confidence that the result has not occurred by error alone. For instance, the terminology "$p < 0.05$" signifies that the chance of the result being false and brought about only by sampling error is less than 0.05, or 5 percent, or 1-in-20. This is usually taken as the minimum level of certainty that makes a quantitative finding acceptable as a fact.

Beyond the calculation of statistical significance, more theoretically interesting work involves the **modeling** of data, as a way of understanding the causal structures that account for sociological phenomena, for example in **multivariate analysis** or **path analysis**. Such approaches have attracted criticism, much of it for being positivist and reductionist. But much of this criticism is really aimed at the poor use of statistics, rather than its use per se. Sociologists would simply be unable to understand many sociological phenomena, or to detect many forms of **social change**, without being able to measure and analyze them statistically.

The use of statistics in the **social sciences** has been revolutionized by the advent of user-friendly statistical software able to perform complex analyses on a personal computer. Analyses that would have taken weeks can now be computed in seconds, and many tasks have now been deskilled, so that knowledge of the mathematics underpinning the statistics is no longer necessary.

The most widely used statistical package in sociological research is SPSS (Statistical Package for the Social Sciences), a commercially available software suite. However, many others are also available, ranging from freeware to advanced packages better suited to the needs of advanced statisticians. As well as performing the calculations for descriptive and inferential statistics, these packages can also produce illuminating and insightful graphical representations of data – for instance scatterplots or box-and-whisker diagrams. The appropriate use of graphs can be a powerful tool for the researcher in understanding their data, and also in communicating their findings to wider audiences.

Statistics is seen as a distinct career path for some individuals and some quantitative research projects will employ a specialist statistician. But many social statisticians see themselves as primarily social scientists, who happen to specialize in quantitative data analysis skills.

There are a number of types of statistical tests commonly used in sociology and others are constantly being developed. One of the most important considerations in determining which type of statistical test to use is to examine carefully the nature of the **measurement** of the independent and dependent variables. In some cases they are, arguably, not measurements at all but simply categorizations – for instance into ethnic **groups** or voters for different **political parties**. In other cases, the variables can rank-order cases: for instance, many measures of **social class** derived from **occupations** can *order* the classes from the most advantaged to the least advantaged, but cannot claim to be able to measure the size of the gap between any two classes. Finally, some measures in sociology claim to be similar to measurements of the physical world, in that they can tell us the size of the interval between two cases – for instance, the **income** of individuals, or the fertility rates of countries. Each of these types of measurement, categorical, ordinal (or ranked), and interval, require different types of tests to understand adequately the relationships between variables.   BRENDAN J. BURCHELL

status crystalization
– see **social status**.

stereotypes
– see **prejudice**.

stigma
As **Erving Goffman** noted in *Stigma: Notes on the Management of Spoiled Identity* (1963), the concept of stigma refers to a deeply discrediting attribute or "mark of social disgrace" that is likely to become the focus of others' attention and concern, making it difficult for a person to engage in smooth or pleasant **interactions**. Certain types of attributes are especially likely to evoke stigma.

One set of attributes includes physical or mental impairments. We tend to assume that others will appear to be normal; that is, they will walk normally, talk coherently, see and hear adequately, have a standard level of physical stamina, and have the ability to participate in a normal conversation. If someone does not possess these attributes, they are vulnerable to stigmatization. Those individuals who have particularly noticeable bodily aberrations, such as a physical deformity, debilitating illness, or deteriorated mind, are especially likely to be defined as deviant. Although they have not committed a deviant act, others view them as tainted because their bodily appearance falls outside the bounds of normalcy.

A second set involves signs of a flawed character. As Goffman observed, people are likely to be seen as deviant if they display attributes, such as dishonesty, selfishness, or unnatural desires, regarded as indicators of a blemished character, especially when these attributes are linked to a known history of criminality, mental illness, alcoholism, drug **addiction**, child abuse, **unemployment**, or political extremism. What is considered an emblem of flawed character changes over time and is a function of society standards.

Finally, stigma may result from membership in a discredited or oppressed **group**. People also have a higher probability of being recognized as deviant if they belong to an ethnic, racial, religious, or political group that is defined as undesirable by members of the mainstream society. This is clearly illustrated in the case of Jews, who have been persecuted and killed in various times and places because of their religious heritage and ethnic characteristics. Whether a group is targeted as deviant depends in large part on the amount of political **power** they possess within a society or **community**. If they have relatively little power, they are more apt to have stigmatizing definitions imposed upon them by dominant groups – and these definitions are more likely to stick.

Goffman emphasized that nearly all of us possess traits, or combinations of traits, that fail to live up to the appearance norms of our society. As a result, almost all of us are potentially vulnerable to the threat of stigma. Our situation differs significantly, however, depending upon the visibility of our nonnormative traits. If they are hidden and not easily detected, we can draw upon various protective strategies, such as passing or covering, to control the **information** that others receive about us and avoid having a "spoiled identity" imposed upon us. On the other hand, if our deviant traits are clearly visible to others, we have a more limited range of identity strategies available. In our efforts to address others' stigmatizing attributions and avow desirable features of the self, we are likely to turn to defensive strategies, such as neutralization and destigmatization, or transformative strategies, such as embracement. We are not passive in the face of stigma. Instead, we actively manage our self-presentations in an effort to avoid, deflect, or transcend stigma and the burdens of a spoiled **identity**.

GARY ALAN FINE AND KENT SANDSTROM

stigmatization

– see **stigma**.

Stinchcombe, Arthur Leonard (1940–)

A professor of sociology at Northwestern University, Illinois, since 1983, Stinchcombe is currently Professor Emeritus. He has made substantial contributions to the study of **slavery** in *Sugar Island Slavery in the Age of Enlightenment* (1995), to the analysis of administration and organization in *Creating Efficient Industrial Administration* (1974) and *Information and Organizations* (1990), and to the study of the **economy** in *Economic Sociology* (1983).

Stinchcombe is famous, however, for his contributions to teaching and constructing **social theories** in his *Constructing Social Theories* (1968), which was awarded the Sorokin Prize in 1969. He was a founder of the theory construction movement. Stinchcombe argued that, while the theories of classical **sociology** such as those of **Karl Marx** and **Émile Durkheim** were complex, they can be represented by relatively simple systems models. He promoted commitment to hypothesis testing, the **falsification** of theories, and theoretical models such as system feedback loops. To some extent he followed **Robert K. Merton** in calling for theories of the middle range that could be tested and that illuminated actual social processes.

BRYAN S. TURNER

Strauss, Anselm L. (1916–96)

An emeritus professor at the University of California, San Francisco, much of Strauss's academic work was published jointly with Barney G. Glaser. In *The Discovery of Grounded Theory* (1968), they developed an approach to empirical research which involves a general method of comparative research in which theory is discovered through inductively exploring research findings. Strauss's **grounded theory** was inductive, cumulative, and middle range. He contributed to the study of **professions**, medical **organizations**, and the experience of **death and dying**.

Strauss interpreted the social world as a negotiated order and this perspective characterized his approach from the early essay on "The Hospital and its Negotiated Order" (1963) and *Mirrors and Masks. The Search for Identity* (1959) to his later work on *Negotiations* (1978). In *Social Organization of Medical Work* (1985), Strauss and colleagues studied the negotiation of workplace settings, such as hospitals – specifically how the social interconnections between **technology**, work organization, and occupational clusters are managed. **Symbolic interactionism** has an irreverent tone towards the professions, and in *The Boys in White* (Becker *et al.*, 1961), Strauss and his colleagues demystified the hospital as a place of work and showed that physicians, like other workers, were subject to the vagaries of interaction settings, including endless negotiations.

Strauss remains influential through his analysis of trajectories, in which social relations involve a series of biographical transformations of **identity** through distinctive status passages. These concepts were elaborated in influential empirical studies of death and dying with Glaser, such as *Awareness of Dying* (1965) and *Time for Dying* (1967). Different conditions or diseases have different trajectories, involving different forms of expressive and instrumental work. A lingering dying trajectory was described in the **case study** published as *Anguish* (1970). Their empirical work on these trajectories was partly summarized in a formal theory on *Status Passage* (Glaser and Strauss, 1971).   BRYAN S. TURNER

strikes

– see **industrial relations**.

structuralism

A theoretical **tradition** whose formation and **influence** can be seen as much in the fields of linguistics (**Ferdinand de Saussure**), literature (**Roland Barthes**), psychoanalysis (**Jacques Lacan**), history (Fernand Braudel), anthropology (**Claude Lévi-Strauss**), and philosophy (**Louis Althusser)** as it can in sociology. It is associated with the search for deep and relatively abiding structures that lie beneath the flux and change of surface events and apparent contingencies. In sociology the work of **Émile Durkheim** and **Marcel Mauss** is often associated with structuralism, as is the work of later writers such as **Pierre Bourdieu, Anthony Giddens**, and **Stuart Hall**, who are all clearly marked by the tradition.

Most commentators relate the founding of structuralism as a distinctive tradition to the *Course in General Linguistics* (1916 [trans. 1974]) written by the Swiss linguist Saussure and published posthumously in 1916. Saussure argued that, instead of focusing on language change, linguistics should concentrate on the language system which endured through the surface changes. To this end he distinguished between the diachronic and the synchronic axes of language. The diachronic was the historical, whereas the synchronic pointed to those aspects of a **language** that existed as a system at any one point in time. By suspending time and taking a snapshot of a language system, one could examine the internal relations between the various

grammatical, functional, and meaningful elements of a language. The distinction between "langue" (the stock or system of language as a whole) and "parole" (instances of speech) takes this further. Any one instance of speech ("parole") is generated by the language system that both provides its conditions of possibility and places limits on what can intelligibly be said.

For Saussure, and for later structuralists such as Lévi-Strauss and Barthes, language is a system in which each term relies on its relations with other terms. The distinction between the signifier (the written word, image, or sound) and the signified (the meaning carried by the signifier) as joint components of the sign is central, as is the fact that neither term involves the referent (the real object referred to). The signification system is markedly autonomous from the world of referents. Meaning, as for example within a chess game, relies on differences between arbitrary signifiers (for example, a queen shape and a rook shape) which are in turn converted into differences between signifieds (for example, what they allow the player to do on the basis of underlying generative or paradigmatic rules).

The sense of an underlying system with its own generative rules is central to the investigations of the anthropologist Lévi-Strauss into kinship structures, art, totemism, **ritual**, and **myth**. Just as Saussure divided language up into its component parts on both the systemic and speech-event levels, Lévi-Strauss divided myths up into their surface constituent elements or "mythemes," each with their own deeper function within the myth. His conclusion is that there are a limited number of patterns and types of transformations within myths. In his *Tristes Tropiques* (1955 [trans. 1968]) he suggested that, from an inventory of all cultural customs either observed or imagined, one could distill a limited number of elements and form a periodic table akin to the one used for chemical elements. Diversity could be reduced to a limited number of possible combinations of enduring elements. His analysis of Caduveo body-painting in this account is also typically structuralist in being built upon core sets of differences or binary oppositions – men/women, carving/painting, representationalism/abstraction, angles/curves, symmetry/asymmetry – which underlie the surface variety.

Barthes's treatment of the popular *Mythologies* (1957) of contemporary French life likewise invokes the signifier and signified distinction to reveal how the surface meanings of phenomena as diverse as washing powder, wrestling, wine, and the face of Greta Garbo all share a similar underlying structure. Signification works in each case to suggest the kind of inexorability associated with nature rather than the transient constructions of **culture**. Barthes famously discusses a cover of *Paris Match* from the 1950s in which the relational signifiers are those of a black soldier in French uniform saluting the flag. Placed together like this, the associations conjured up by the elements signify that all Frenchmen, regardless of race, are loyal subjects ready to serve and die for their country. Alongside these mythical connotations, binary oppositions are also created between loyalty and disloyalty, friend and enemy, insider and outsider.   ROB STONES

structuration

This is the process whereby enduring structural properties and relational patterns of social **groups** and **cultures** are either reproduced or altered during the enactment of social practices. Though the term was coined for other purposes by **Georges Gurvitch**, it is now ubiquitously defined with reference to **Anthony Giddens**'s structuration theory. Giddens most extensively develops structuration theory in *The Constitution of Society* (1984). Giddens's theory is explored in Ira Cohen's *Structuration Theory* (1989), and it is criticized by J. Clark et al., *Anthony Giddens* (1990).

The concept of structuration rejects the notion that **social structure** and **social action** are two ontologically distinct aspects of social reality. If it is true that all social realities are generated in social practices and through the consequences of these practices, as leading contemporary theorists of social action and **everyday life** maintain, then it must be true that social structures and patterns are somehow generated in and through social practices as well. But one must also recognize the lesson taught by structuralists that the enduring structural properties of groups and cultures shape the generation of action on any given occasion. Finding means to take these two points into account is known as the problem of **agency and structure**.

Giddens's notion of structuration solves this problem by regarding the competencies to perform actions, as well as the competencies to recognize actions performed by others, as repositories of the structural aspects of social reality. However, it is not until actors draw upon those competencies to perform instances of conduct that structure becomes real. For example, as I write these words, I reproduce the structured elements of academic prose as well as more generic elements of the grammatical and syntactical structure of the English **language**. Of course, the English language would survive very nicely if I never wrote at all. But matters would be otherwise if all Anglophone actors left their competencies unused and began speaking other languages. English would be a dead language when it was seldom reproduced at all. One can make analogous points about the reproduction of bureaucratic procedure, capitalist trade, artistic genre, or legal codes. In order for any of these social realities to endure, they must be reproduced. The same holds true for **networks**, systems, and other patterns of social relations. All relational patterns are structured by the practices through which – in the language of network analysis – nodes are linked together. Structuration adds an original and much-needed twist to the **reproduction** of relational patterns by insisting that the links between nodes be conceived as bridging time and space.

Structuration can refer to **social change** as well as reproduction. Indeed, some degree of variation is found in every instance of structuration. However, when processes of structuration change across large groups of practices over extended periods of time, then all associated structural properties and relational patterns will change as well.

Structuration theory also includes a sophisticated theory of **power** that synthesizes modes of domination and a dialectic of control between the dominant and the dominated.   IRA COHEN

subculture

This concept was first employed by anthropologists. In this traditional conception, subcultures refer to subgroups of local **cultures**; in a more critical perspective, they refer to symbolic representations of social contradictions and offer a symbolic eschewing of the established order. In the area of delinquency, subcultures refers to distinctive sets of **values** and behavior.

Two early American sociological studies by Albert Cohen (*Delinquent Boys*, 1955) and Richard Cloward and Lloyd Ohlin (*Delinquency and Opportunity: A Theory of Delinquent Gangs*, 1961) were influential in directing attention to the idea of a deviant subculture of juveniles as an adaptation to the problems of **alienation** and marginalization thrown up by social, structural, and economic arrangements in society.

Cohen saw the **gang** as a subculture with a value system different from that of mainstream American culture. He viewed it as a working-class attempt to come to terms with a dominant middle-class society. Membership of the gang involved a special vocabulary, shared internal beliefs, and distinctive ways of acting and dressing. Subcultures of delinquency were characterized by **masculinity**, group loyalty, and pleasure-seeking behavior. Thus, here, **Émile Durkheim**'s concept of **anomie** was synthesized with **Sigmund Freud**'s idea of "reaction formation" in an attempt to explain the manifestly expressive and nonrational nature of much delinquency. The prospect of failure was depicted as bringing about a major psychological rejection of what had formerly been sought, so that the once aspiring working-class adolescent pointedly turned his back on the middle-class society that spurned him and adopted a style of behavior that was its systematic inversion. Put simply, Cohen developed the notion of status-frustration to explain how working-class boys find a solution to the lack of status in middle-class American society.

Cloward and Ohlin (1961) described the consequences of boys being pushed into **crime** by the difficulties of acquiring **money** and position in conventional ways. Their version of the theory, however, involves three types of delinquent subculture, relating to the differential opportunity to engage in legitimate and illegitimate means to gain material and status success: criminal subculture (developed in lower-class **neighborhoods** as a response to a lack of conventional role models and the availability of successful criminal models), conflict subculture (which arises where the lack of legitimate and illegitimate opportunities for material success is solved by achieving status through **violence** and crime), and retreatist subculture (which arises where the gang resorts to hustling and drug usage in the absence of either of the preceding options).

Subcultural theory helped shift the analytical focus from individual problematic behavior to collective solutions to societies' social and economic **inequalities**. But there have been strong criticisms because of an overdelineation of values between the dominant culture and subcultures. Empirical studies in the 1960s in the United States and the United Kingdom showed that the sharp separation in values that characterized dominant culture and subculture was overstated. Also, working-class youths are more likely to dissociate themselves from the **labor market** and deflect their energies and aspirations into leisure pursuits rather than a straightforwardly "delinquent solution."

The **Birmingham Centre for Contemporary Cultural Studies** in the United Kingdom published a series of studies of subcultures in the 1970s. Various ethnographic and semiological analyses of the meaning of subcultural style, and political analyses of **deviance** that explain why it is that the structural and class position of various subcultures can lead to **moral panics**, were produced.

LORAINE GELSTHORPE

suicide

A profoundly disturbing phenomenon that raises important ethical and practical issues. How many people take their own lives? Why do they do it? What can sociology teach us about this phenomenon and how can we reduce it?

The World Heath Organization (WHO) has estimated that in the year 2000 approximately 1 million people died from suicide. Between 1970 and 2005, suicide rates have increased by 60 percent worldwide. Although suicide rates have traditionally been highest among elderly males, rates among young people have been increasing to such an extent that they are now the group at highest risk in a third of all countries. Males are four times more likely to die from suicide than are females. However, females are more likely to attempt suicide than are males. Suicide is the third leading cause of death for young people aged fifteen to twenty-four. Mental disorders (particularly depression and substance abuse) are associated with more than 90 percent of all cases of suicide.

Each of these categories provides insight into the failure of contemporary societies to integrate their inhabitants in a meaningful way. It is true that a person stricken by some fatal disease may seek to take their own life, and there may well be a case (under strict constraints) for assisted suicide. But even here the physiological source of the problem does not exist on its own. It is inextricably linked to social pressures and conventions.

When we look at the WHO **statistics**, they tell us a good deal about the divisions within contemporary society. Why should it be elderly males who traditionally commit suicide rather than elderly females? Men in contemporary societies are generally more fearful of pain and discomfort than women. They see their bodies as objects to be instructed, rather than organisms to be respected, so that when the body becomes problematic they seek obliteration. Men are also more likely in contemporary society to see themselves as self-contained individuals, so that when ill-health prevents them from playing "natural" leadership roles life seems to have lost its purpose.

The vulnerability of young men to suicide is particularly revealing. They have been socialized by patriarchal **norms** to play a dominant role and they see this domination threatened by the movement towards female **equality**. If young women can lead and innovate, defend their country, and undertake skilled employment, then dominant males feel redundant. The point is that general problems express themselves in gender-skewed ways. Young women feel a lack of self-esteem when confronted by cultural norms (often highly superficial) which prevent them from conforming. The attempted suicide is a cry for help, a desperate attempt to secure assistance in a world that seems indifferent to those in pain. Young people understandably feel a sense of despair about the future of a world in which grave ecological damage has already been inflicted. There is concern about job prospects in a world in which market projects impose short-term solutions to structural problems. The increased access to consumer goods may simply generate boredom in a world in which plenitude of resources may coexist with poverty of activity. It is clear that there are social causes for the tragic phenomenon of suicide, and each category of victims demonstrates the particular character of the problems faced.

Of course, suicide is not a purely modern phenomenon. In premodern societies suicide may have occurred as the result of certain social norms which dictated, for example, that a Hindu widow must destroy herself on the funeral pyre of her husband, or that military commanders were expected to take their own lives when they "failed" their troops. But it is not difficult to see that the atomism of contemporary liberal societies makes difficulties more life-threatening and adjustments more painful. Social ties are increasingly tenuous and individual self-assertion operates not to strengthen social bonds but to weaken them.

In 1897 **Émile Durkheim** wrote an important work on suicide in which he argued that suicide arises because humans have unlimited desires that their needs cannot fulfill. Suicide can be regulated only if these desires are socially controlled. But, although his argument sounds as though this is an eternal and insoluble problem, in fact Durkheim was highly sensitive to the character of society as a source of **anomie** – that sense of isolation and frustration that leads to suicide. Suicide is ascribed to **social problems**, and

Durkheim regarded the possessive **individualism** of a market society as a factor that aggravated rather than diminished the problem.

Contemporary neoliberalism sometimes expresses itself in a libertarianism in which individuals can treat themselves as they please. Choice is abstracted from constraint and development. The old religious argument – that suicide is impermissible because we are all creations of God and no one is entitled to destroy his **property** – has rightly been discredited. But what do we put in its place? We need to grasp the social nature of the individual in its fullest implications. Individuals develop in the context of a **network** of relations, and it is an illusion for individuals to think that they have developed through resources that owe nothing to anyone but themselves. Individuals "belong" not merely to themselves but to society at large – for society has in a sense created and empowered them, and they are not entitled to assume that they can do as they please with themselves.

The distinction between what pertains to oneself and what pertains to others justifies social intervention, but the distinction between the self-regarding and the other-regarding advanced by **John Stuart Mill** is a developmental ethic. It is intended to assist individuals to acquire greater autonomy and self-government, to exercise those choices that facilitate this process. The distinction implodes if it is taken to justify acts of self-destruction (suicide being the most dramatic example), since individuals need space to develop, not to take their own lives.

Suicide should therefore be seen as a social as well as an individual failure. When individuals take their own lives, it is because society has failed to provide them with the resources and faith that makes continued existence worthwhile.

JOHN HOFFMAN

Sumner, William (1840–1910)

Professor of Political and Social Science at Yale University from 1872, Sumner is best known as the most active and influential proponent of **social Darwinism** in the United States. His best-known work is *Folkways* (1906).

Sumner extended the ideas of **Herbert Spencer** by combining evolutionary thought with classical laissez-faire economics and a belief in the key role of the industrious, frugal, and temperate individual. Social evolution and social **progress** depend on individuals competing for survival, the "fittest" hard-working persons being those who succeed financially while advancing society as a whole. The **family** and inherited **wealth** were, Sumner believed, of central importance. Inheritance offers assurance to the industrious individual that it is worthwhile working hard. And the family is a central means by which the virtues of hard work can be passed on to future **generations**.

Like Spencer, Sumner insisted that good government should be minimal. All forms of **socialism** should therefore be resisted since they merely nourish the least fit and those unprepared to work. Government should be limited to the provision of peace, order, liberty, security, and **equality** before the law. Such is the social context in which industrial development and personal freedom can best flourish and the best setting in which the fittest individuals can provide for their own and their **children**'s welfare. But while Spencer envisaged progress and social struggle between the "fit" and "unfit" eventually being conducted in peaceful forms, Sumner was much less optimistic. **War**, he believed, is unavoidable. It is undesirable but it is an inevitable outcome of the competition for life which drives societies forward.

Sumner also had a distinctive view of the sources of social variations generating progress. These were above all generated by **elites**, with the great middle mass of the population simply producing nothing new and merely imitating their superiors. Meanwhile, even the most advanced and civilized society has to carry the lowest social orders, those remaining ignorant, poor, and subject to disease and criminality.

PETER DICKENS

surplus value

– see **Karl Marx**.

surrogate motherhood

This is not a new phenomenon, in that women who are not the biological mothers of **children** have often taken over their **care** and mothering when circumstances have required it. But surrogacy has taken on a new meaning with the development of clinically assisted **reproduction**, because the possibility of removing eggs from one woman, fertilizing them in vitro, and implanting them in another woman who will gestate and give birth to a child to whom she is genetically unrelated, is now a routine (if not common) procedure. These clinical developments have created a new social situation in which it has become necessary to differentiate between birth mothers and genetic mothers. It is also possible that the commissioning mother is neither the birth mother, nor the genetic mother, in which case three women may be involved in the process. In the United States surrogacy has become a legitimate, for-profit activity, but in the United Kingdom egg donation and surrogacy is closely controlled and the commercial practice of surrogacy is illegal. This has arisen because there were a number of legal cases in which birth mothers refused to "give up" their babies to the commissioning parents, and also because of the fear of the exploitation of poor women. In the United Kingdom the predominant concern is with the welfare of a child born by this method, while in the United States the courts have been more concerned with enforcing contractual agreements between commissioning parents and birth mothers. The advent of surrogacy has disrupted the taken-for-granted naturalness of **motherhood** and also challenges everyday notions of lineage and inheritance.

CAROL SMART

surveys

Although the first, and most general sense of the term survey – any systematic gathering of **information** on a defined social **group** – is still technically correct, contemporary sociological surveys tend to be more precisely based on specific samples from a defined population, and to employ structured written questions, often administered verbally, via either a telephone-based or a face-to-face **interview**, designed to yield a corpus of **data** amenable to statistical analysis.

Surveys are conducted on a plethora of social issues and topics. They are used to provide descriptive **statistics** at local, regional, national, and international levels; to examine social phenomena, such as **poverty**, **work and employment**, **social stratification**, or the experience of **crime**, **discrimination**, or **racism**; and to investigate causal processes and hypotheses about social processes. The multivariate modelling methods used in econometric survey **methodologies** have, in turn, influenced the construction and analysis of sociological surveys of social phenomena.

However, as the Australian Bureau of Statistics warns, "it is not a simple process to reduce a complex social issue to a single set of numbers" (*Australian Bureau of Statistics*, 2004: np). There are a number of components that comprise survey methodology. These include sample design and selection; scope and coverage; questionnaire format and content; survey procedure; and response rate.

Sample surveys are conducted on a specified sample (usually randomly selected) from a particular population. Samples may be stratified to reflect the demographic composition of that population (for example in terms of **gender**, **race and ethnicity**, or socio-economic status). Further, the results of sample surveys are often generalized to describe that population. In order to achieve this, survey researchers use a series of techniques known as weighting. This is a process whereby the results of a sample survey are adjusted so as to infer the likely results for the total population. A weight is a **value** that indicates how many population units (or members) are represented by each sample unit (or member). Thus, if the probability of an individual being selected for a survey was 1 in 1,000, they would be assigned a weight of 1,000 (that is, they would represent 1,000 others).

A number of features of surveys may affect survey responses. Mode effects refer to the **influence** of the survey-delivery method. Survey modes include self-administered **questionnaires**, telephone interviews, and face-to-face interviews. Mixed methods are also possible (for example a self-administered postal questionnaire with a follow-up face-to-face interview). There are advantages and disadvantages of each mode. Briefly, the key disadvantages of the self-administered mode include: a lack of flexibility; little control over the response process (or who else is present during the completion of the survey form); people with lower levels of literacy may be disadvantaged; and higher rates of non-response than other modes. The advantages of this mode include: the lack of interviewer effects; suitability for surveying sensitive topics; a reduction of response- and question-order effects; and ample time for respondents to generate a considered response to the questions.

Disadvantages of the telephone interview mode include: the unknown effects of the presence of others; potential social desirability and interviewer effects; and restricted length of survey form for conversational delivery. Advantages of this mode include: greater flexibility; and the role of the interviewer in encouraging responses, and in clarifying the survey questions. Likewise, face-to-face interviews may suffer from the presence of third parties during the interview; and potential social desirability and interviewer effects. Advantages of this mode also include greater flexibility; the feasibility of longer and more complex surveys than for either self-administered or telephone-based surveys; the role of the interviewer in encouraging responses, and in clarifying the survey questions.

Increasingly, Computer Assisted Telephone Interviewing (CATI) and Computer Assisted Personal Interviewing (CAPI) are used by social researchers when conducting surveys. These techniques enable the interviewer to key in the survey respondent's answers at the time of interview, using a laptop or personal computer. Care must be taken at the design stage of the survey to ensure that the economic benefits of CATI and CAPI (in terms of time spent on data entry) are not offset by filtering or other errors in the schedule.

Survey methods, although a vital tool for social researchers, can only ever provide a partial description of complex social issues. **Harold Garfinkel** called this broad tendency towards aggregate-based research the replacement of "indexical" with "objective" expressions. They are but one tool, of many, in the sociologist's armamentarium. Further, without significant modification, surveys may be an inappropriate method for people from some developing countries, where literacy and personal record-keeping (such as date of birth) should not be assumed on the part of respondents; or where surveys may be invalidated through acquiescence **bias** – for instance, where open disagreement with an interviewer would be clearly impolite.

There are many books on how to design, conduct, and analyze surveys. Catherine Marsh's *The Survey Method* (1982) offers a classic defense of the technique against critics who object that surveys are invariably flawed and only superficially descriptive. Hanneke Houtkoop's *Interaction and the Standardised Interview: The Living Questionnaire* (2000) offers a guide to constructing and conducting face-to-face and telephone-based surveys, with attention to best practice in the phrasing of survey questions, using CAPI and CATI.

MARK RAPLEY AND SUSAN HANSEN

Sutherland, E. H. (1883–1950)

Sutherland is particularly remembered for his ideas relating to differential association which emerged from his work reported in *The Professional Thief* (1937), in which the thief, "Chic Conwell," described a **profession** which had its own techniques, codes, **social status**, **traditions**, and organization that imitated other noncriminal **groups** to a degree.

During the 1930s, Sutherland spent time at the University of Chicago working alongside others who were developing **sociological theories** of **crime** based around observations of social disorganization in **communities** (Clifford Shaw and

Henry McKay, for instance). Sutherland's own contribution to the **Chicago School** derived from his observations that, despite a context of social disorganization, the **data** collected by his colleagues sometimes revealed a certain social cohesion at the center of the criminal activity. While acknowledging that crime itself was a social construct, his attempts to explain the social cohesion at the core of social disorganization led him to reconsider the ways in which individuals learn a criminal **lifestyle**. He argued that criminal behavior is transmitted or learned through intimate relationships or associations with other people more or less disposed to crime and delinquency. The concept of differential association is thus an attempt to account for the development of criminal behavior in terms of association with particular social groups and **environments**.

Importantly, Sutherland attempted to shift the unremitting criminological gaze away from the lower or working classes and apply his theory of differential association to white-collar crime and crimes of the powerful. We can also credit Sutherland with perhaps the first integrated social psychological account of crime.

LORAINE GELSTHORPE

Swanson, Guy E. (1922–1995)

An American sociologist of religion and social psychologist, Swanson undertook his undergraduate education at the University of Pittsburgh, and received his doctoral degree from the University of Chicago in 1948. He served on the Faculty of the University of Michigan for twenty-one years, moving to the University of California, Berkeley, in 1969, where he was on the Faculty first in sociology and then in psychology. He continued to serve the University after his retirement in 1993. He made significant contributions to the sociology of **religion**. Following the theories of **Émile Durkheim**, in *The Birth of the Gods: The Origin of Primitive Beliefs* (1960) he studied the **social structure** of fifty primitive peoples to show how their social organization determines their beliefs. Similarly, in *Religion and Regime: A Sociological Account of the Reformation* (1968), he attempted to relate theological beliefs to the principal political organization of society. In particular, he showed how the experience of immanence (God's attributes in the world) was conditioned by the impact of special-interest **groups** on central government. He also wrote on *Social Change* (1971) and family life (with Daniel Miller) in *The Changing American Parent* (1958).   BRYAN S. TURNER

symbol

Associated with the notion of representation, symbols are at the heart of cultural systems and relate above all to the constitution and reproduction of meaning. The classical sociological understanding of the nature of a symbol is connected with a static, conservative view of cultural reproduction, such that our ways of representing reality to ourselves and others are presumed to have quite rigid boundaries. Contemporary discussions of symbolic structures have, however, focused more on the dynamic, shifting terrain of symbolism, in which there is emphasis on the excess or surplus of meaning within cultural systems more generally.

In *The Conflict of Interpretations* (1969 [trans. 1974]), Paul Ricoeur (1913–2005) argued that symbols draw upon a "surplus of meaning" inherent in systems of signification. Symbolism on this view connects the multiplicity of meaning to a primordial ambivalence at the core of the human condition. For Ricoeur, the potency of symbols lies in the fact that signification always outstrips itself: the meaning of everything we think is another thought, of everything we say the implication that things might be symbolized otherwise. Symbolism, then, as a surplus of meaning, interweaves both metaphor and metonymy within cultural reproduction, such that symbolic associations are intimately tied to the stimulation of new meanings. This necessarily implies that the analysis of symbols requires sociological study of how symbolic orders are interwoven with forms of legitimation and domination.

The modern emphasis on symbolic orders as tied to processes of both social **reproduction** and cultural change has received considerable analytical fine-tuning, particularly in various versions of psychoanalytic sociology, in which a particular debt to the doctrines of **Jacques Lacan** is evident. In linking the insights of **Sigmund Freud** and of **Ferdinand de Saussure**, Lacanian-inspired sociological thought has sought to unearth the functioning of the linguistic field in the symbolic determination of the subject. This has been developed through examination of the intricate connections between Oedipal identifications and projections on the one hand, and the productivities of the signifier on the other. In general, such an approach has sought to underscore the structured but unstable nature of processes of symbolism and signification in the cognitive and emotional lives of human subjects. This has been especially evident in the influential writings of

Louis **Althusser** and **Fredric Jameson**, where a revised Lacanian conceptualization of symbolic systems is tied to the production of **ideology**. For Althusser, symbolism of the ideological field serves to "hail" or "interpellate" the individual as a subject of political and **social structures**. A similar stress on the ideological role of symbolism is underlined by Jameson, but unlike Althusser he accords a greater centrality to the polyvalence of symbolic processes. Indeed, in conditions of **postmodernity**, the symbolic field of **culture** and the social is at once under- and overdetermined, which for Jameson produces a radical dispersal of desire and fragmentation of subjecthood.

ANTHONY ELLIOTT

symbolic capital
– see **social capital**.

symbolic interactionism
As a distinctive sociological perspective, symbolic interactionism emerged out of the American philosophical tradition of **pragmatism**. This approach was elaborated in the late nineteenth and early twentieth centuries in the writings of Charles S. Peirce, **William James**, and John Dewey (1859–1952). These thinkers challenged the mechanistic world-view and dualistic assumptions of classical rationalism, the philosophy that had dominated western thought since the seventeenth century.

Pragmatist philosophy entered into sociology most directly through the writings and teachings of **George Herbert Mead**, who sought to translate the insights of pragmatist thinkers into a theory and method for the **social sciences**. In doing so, Mead drew his greatest inspiration from the philosophical works of John Dewey, his friend and colleague at the University of Chicago. Building upon Dewey's seminal ideas, Mead developed a profoundly sociological account of human consciousness, selfhood, and behavior – an account that understood and explained these phenomena as products of social processes, specifically the processes of **interaction** and communication.

Mead shared his groundbreaking theories of consciousness, selfhood, and behavior in a social psychology course he taught at Chicago – a course that included graduate students in sociology as well as in philosophy. Mead's theories inspired the students in this course and his best-known book, *Mind, Self, and Society* (1934), emerged out of their transcriptions of lecture notes. One of these students, **Herbert Blumer**, became a prominent

sociologist who championed the merits and applicability of Mead's theories for sociological analysis. In the late 1960s Blumer compiled some of his own writings (which drew upon and amplified Mead's ideas) into a book entitled *Symbolic Interactionism* (1969). This book quickly became recognized as the major statement of the symbolic interactionist perspective.

Blumer originally coined the term symbolic interactionism in 1937 when writing an essay on **social psychology** for a social science textbook. In this essay Blumer emphasized how Mead's work offered the basis for a new social psychological approach that synthesized and transcended the dominant approaches of the time, behaviorism and **evolutionary theory**. Blumer referred to this, new approach as "symbolic interactionism." Because of this, Mead usually gets credited as the founder of the symbolic interactionist perspective (also known as the **Chicago School** of sociology) even though Blumer's analysis drew heavily on the ideas of other theorists, including **Robert Park**, **W. I. Thomas**, and **Ernest Burgess**, and, according to some critics, differed in important respects from Mead's writings.

While identifying Mead as the founder of interactionism, Blumer himself served as a key proponent of this perspective. Along with one of his colleagues, **Everett Hughes**, he had a major **influence** on a cohort of graduate students he taught at the University of Chicago in the 1940s and early 1950s. This cohort, which included a number of notable scholars, such as **Howard Becker**, **Erving Goffman**, and **Anselm L. Strauss**, further developed the symbolic interactionist perspective and became known as the Second Chicago School.

Like the advocates of other intellectual perspectives with some measure of popularity and longevity, symbolic interactionists regularly debate about core beliefs, theoretical interpretations, and the appropriateness of particular research methods, topics, or styles. Despite their areas of disagreement, interactionists share some common outlooks and assumptions. Central to their perspective are the following three premises articulated by Blumer:

> The first premise is that human beings act toward things on the basis of the meanings those things have for them . . . The second premise is that the meaning of such things is derived from, or arises out of, the social interaction that one has with one's fellows. The third premise is that these meanings are handled in, and modified through, an interpretive process used by the person in dealing with the things he [or she] encounters. (1969: 2)

While these premises serve as a common source of inspiration, interactionists argue over how to interpret them properly. For instance, some stress that all meaning is negotiated in interaction and that **social structures** serve primarily as a backdrop for this interaction – that is, structures are something people take into account as they create, negotiate, and act upon meanings in their ongoing interactions. Others adopt a more structuralist view, emphasizing that social structures become sedimented into interaction, imposing constraints on the creation and negotiation of meanings. Blumer's passage can be read to support either view. Beyond the implications of this passage, heated disputes exist about what presuppositions are integral to a symbolic interactionist analysis of topics such as the self, **emotion**, interaction, **power**, organization, and **collective action**. Yet, even in the heat of this debate, interactionists agree on a key point: Blumer's three premises provide the core of their theoretical perspective.

Although these premises serve as the cornerstones of the interactionist perspective, several other implicit assumptions inform and guide this perspective, providing it with its philosophical foundations.

People are unique creatures because of their ability to use **symbols**. Drawing on the insights of Mead, symbolic interactionists stress the significance of people's symbolic capacities. Because people use and rely upon symbols, they do not usually respond to stimuli in a direct or automatic way; instead, they give meanings to the stimuli they experience and then act in terms of these meanings. Their behavior is thus distinctively different from that of other organisms, who act in a more instinctive or reflex-based manner. As Blumer emphasized, things do not have intrinsic meaning. Rather, the meanings of things derive from and emerge through social interaction. Humans learn what things mean as they interact with one another. In doing so they rely heavily on **language** and the communicative processes it facilitates. Through these processes, people learn how to define and act towards the objects, events, and experiences that make up their environment. In essence, they learn to see and respond to symbolically mediated realities – realities that are socially constructed.

People become distinctively human through their interaction with others. Symbolic interactionists assume that people acquire distinctively human qualities, and become capable of distinctively human behavior, only through associating with others. According to interactionists, these uniquely human qualities and behaviors include the ability to use symbols, to think and make plans, to take the role of others, to develop a sense of **self**, and to participate in complex forms of communication and social organization. Interactionists do not believe that people are born human. They argue instead that people develop into distinctively human beings as they take part in social interaction. While acknowledging that people are born with certain kinds of biological "hardware" (for example a highly developed nervous system) that give them the potential to become fully human, interactionists stress that involvement in society is essential for realizing this potential.

People are conscious and self-reflexive beings who actively shape their own behavior. The most important capacities that people develop through their involvement in society, or social interaction, are the "mind" and the "self." As Mead observed, by developing the capacity to see and respond to themselves as objects, individuals learn to interact with themselves, or think. In thinking, people shape the meaning of objects, accepting them, rejecting them, or changing them in accord with these definitions and the acts that follow. Behavior, then, is an interplay of social stimuli and responses to those stimuli. In making this assertion, interactionists embrace a voluntaristic image of human behavior. They suggest that people exercise an important element of autonomy in their actions. At the same time, interactionists understand that a variety of social factors, such as language, **culture**, **race and ethnicity**, **social class**, and **gender**, constrain people's interpretations and behaviors. Thus, interactionists can be characterized as cautious naturalists or soft determinists; they presume that people's actions are influenced but not determined by prior events or biological and social forces.

People are purposive creatures who act in and towards situations. According to interactionists, human beings do not release their behavior, like tension in a spring, in response to biological drives, psychological needs, or social expectations. Rather, people act towards situations. In other words, people construct behavior based on the meaning they attribute to the particular situation in which they find themselves. This meaning, or definition of the situation, emerges out of ongoing interactions with others. That is, people determine what meaning to give to a situation and how to act towards it through taking account of the unfolding intentions, actions, and expressions of others. Actors derive, negotiate, and establish definitions of a situation through processes of symbolic interaction.

Human society consists of people engaging in symbolic interaction. Interactionists differ from other sociologists in their view of **society** and the relationship between society and the individual. Following Blumer, interactionists conceive of society as a fluid but structured process that consists of individuals interacting with one another. This process is grounded in individuals' abilities to assume each other's perspectives, adjust and coordinate their unfolding acts, and symbolically communicate and interpret these acts. In emphasizing that society consists of people acting and interacting symbolically, interactionists disagree with psychologistic theories that see society as existing primarily in our heads, either in the form of reward histories or socially shaped cognitions. Interactionists also depart from structuralist perspectives that reify society, suggesting that it exists independently of individuals and dictates actions through the rules, roles, statuses, or structures it imposes. While acknowledging that individuals are born into a society that frames actions through patterns of meaning and reward, interactionists stress that people actively shape **identities** and behaviors in making plans, seeking goals, and interacting with others in specific situations. They also emphasize that society and structure are human products, rooted in joint action. Hence, as **Charles Horton Cooley** noted in *Human Nature and Social Order*, "'society' and 'individual' do not denote separable phenomena" (1902: 36–7). People acquire and realize their individuality (or selfhood) through interaction and, at the same time, maintain or alter society.

The social act should be the fundamental unit of social psychological analysis. Interactionists contend that the social act, or what Blumer referred to as joint action, should be the central concern of social psychology. A social act refers to behavior that in some way takes account of others and is guided by what they do; it is formulated so that it fits together with the behavior of another person, group, or social organization. It also depends on and emerges through processes of communication and interpretation. This covers a diverse array of human action, ranging from a handshake, a kiss, a wink, and a fistfight to a lecture, a beer bash, a soccer game, and a religious revival. Whenever people orient themselves to others and their actions, regardless of whether they are trying to hurt them, help them, convert them, or destroy them, they are engaging in a social act. Individuals attempt to align and fit together their lines of behavior with others. In doing so they may be acting as individuals or as representatives of a group or organization, such as a church, university, corporation, or government. In focusing on social acts, interactionists are not limited to examining the behavior of individuals or even small groups, but also consider the social conduct of crowds, industries, **political parties**, schools, hospitals, religious **cults**, occupational groups, **social movements**, and the **mass media**. Inspired by Blumer, interactionists regard the domain of sociology – and, more generally, **social science** – as "constituted precisely by the study of joint action and the collectivities that engage in joint action" (1969: 17).

To understand people's social acts, sociologists need to use methods that enable the discernment of meanings that people attribute to these acts. As noted, interactionists emphasize the significance of the fact that people, as creatures who use symbols, act on the basis of the meanings they give to things in their world. In turn, interactionists believe it is essential to understand those worlds of meaning and to see them as the individuals or groups under investigation see them. To develop this insider's view, researchers must empathize with – or "take the role of" – the individuals or groups they are studying. They also must observe and interact with these individuals or groups in an unobtrusive way. Through adopting such an approach, researchers can gain a deeper appreciation of how these social actors define, construct, and act towards the realities that constitute their everyday worlds.

GARY ALAN FINE AND KENT SANDSTROM

symmetrical family
– see **family**.

synchrony/diachrony
– see **social change**.

syncretization
– see **hybridity**.

T

taboo

– see **sacred and profane dichotomy**.

talented tenth

A belief, developed in the nineteenth century, that society divides "naturally" into an **elite** who are innovative and imaginative and have a potential for **leadership**, and an inert mass who lacks these qualities.

The notion is elitist and pessimistic. People have all kinds of talents that are unrecognized by a society which privileges certain attributes and denigrates others. We have inherited a dualism between mind and **body** which needs to be challenged: a narrow and intellectualist notion of "talent" reinforces a disastrous underrecognition of manual skills and dexterity.

The talents that people have are the product of society, and are not simply attributes that we privately own. Reading and writing skills are hugely facilitated by a cultural background, a particular kind of **education**, parental role models, and so forth. The danger with the notion of a "talented tenth" is that it unwittingly encourages an abstract **individualism** and ignores the fact that skills derive from living in society and benefiting from relations with others.

The classical liberal view that everyone is free and equal is a premise to be concretized, not rejected. The "talented-tenth" argument assumes that the rest of society cannot govern their own lives. On the contrary, they require leadership and dynamism from "on high" to motivate them. This is not to pose an idealized order in which ultimately everyone will be able to do everything – but rather to suggest that recognizing different talents is part of a process of democratization that is ongoing and infinite in character.

JOHN HOFFMAN

Tarde, Gabriel (1843–1904)

An early advocate of social **statistics** and a founder of criminology, sociology, and **social psychology**, Tarde made many contributions that paved the way for recognition of the role of **public opinion** and **mass media and communications** in empirical research. Although Tarde was working between the schools of **F. Le Play** and **Émile Durkheim**, he enjoyed a wide public recognition (at the prestigious Collège de France and in Chicago **sociology**) but his strong emphasis on **individualism** distanced him from mainstream French sociology.

Early in his career he established himself as a criminologist and penologist, rejecting biological **determinism** of what makes a person a criminal. Among later intellectual pursuits, Tarde developed a view of **social change** as a function of the inventions of some individuals that become widely imitated (*The Laws of Imitation*, 1890 [trans. 1903]); such inventions come into conflict with established customs and **institutions** and/or with other inventions. The conflict model of Tarde, including conflict between individuals who operate with a different logic (the active innovator and the passive member), and conflict between the modern logic of individualism and the social logic of **tradition** and theology (*La Logique sociale*, 1898), put him at odds with Durkheim. Terry Clark in *Gabriel Tarde on Communication and Social Influence* (1969) provides a broad overview of the contributions of Tarde, including comparisons with Durkheim.

Tarde's discussion of **attitudes** in the formation of creative individuals overlaps with **W. I. Thomas**, his analysis of cycles in innovations and of **social stratification** offering mobility to gifted individuals ties in with **Vilfredo Pareto,** while his discussion of the role of print media in the formation of a public anticipates Benedict Anderson's seminal work on the conditions for nationalism in his *Imagined Communities* (1983) on national identity formation. Awaiting proper recognition, Tarde, as a creative but marginal figure in Paris, best bears comparison with his contemporary **Georg Simmel** in Berlin.

EDWARD TIRYAKIAN

taste

– see **Pierre Bourdieu**.

Tawney, R. H. (1880–1962)

A professor of economic history at the University of London and influential in the British Labour movement, Tawney contributed to the theory of **democracy** in his *The Acquisitive Society* (1921) and *Equality* (1931). He also made important contributions to economic history in *The Agrarian Problem in the Sixteenth Century* (1912), *Land and Labour in China* (1932), and *Studies in the Minimum Wage* (1914). Tawney is best known for his critical examination of the religious debate surrounding usury and the rise of **individualism** in his *Religion and the Rise of Capitalism* (1926), which was a critical response to **Max Weber**.   BRYAN S. TURNER

Taylorism

A term broadly applied to any management approach that aims to eliminate worker initiative in the production process, Taylorism, based by Frederick W. Taylor (1856–1915) on **scientific management**, conceives of the division of **labor** as rigid, with skills strictly associated with particular jobs, and tasks that are kept small. **Management** and production are strictly separated. Taylorism in its many empirical implementations developed from scientific management theory. Historically, Taylorism has been associated with the car industry (particularly with Ford and Fordism) but is not exclusive to or identical with it. Furthermore, it is not exclusive to capitalist **ideology**: **Vladimir Ilich Lenin** was initially critical of Taylorism, having originally favored worker control over more collective and spontaneous forms of worker agency as an important means by which the relatively backward Russian **economy** could be driven forwards. Nevertheless, a socialist variant of Taylorism was implemented in the Soviet Union under A. Gastev, the head of the Central Institute of Labor, by 1920.

Taylorist production systems have been called into question by a broad range of anti-Taylorist and neo-Taylorist movements and alternative practices. Anti-Taylorist movements, among them the program of **industrial democracy**, generally oppose Taylorist production systems on grounds of de-humanization, and work towards greater worker autonomy (for example in semi-autonomous work teams), skill enrichment, and participation in decisionmaking.

There is, however, awareness that anti-Taylorist management can be interpreted as a Janus-faced solution to Taylorist production systems because it entails work intensification. In anti-Taylorist systems, emphasis is placed on teamwork. Multifunctionality represents the core of the division of labor. These two factors preempt idle time, ensuring constant, more predictable output for employers and fewer breaks for employees. Overlap of work roles (which may or may not lead to skill enrichment as well as a fusion of low-level managerial functions with production-employee functions) and work allocation within teams have been considered as positive by management in the larger context of cost reduction independent of economies of scale, whereas labor has seen this job enlargement and reduction in personnel as threatening to its own interests. Job demarcation, which has traditionally been protective of craft or seniority status, is lifted by teamwork under the banner of greater control and shared participation by any worker in the team. Sociologists – for example **Pierre Bourdieu**, Michael Burawoy, and **Richard Sennett** – have criticized anti-Taylorism for its feature of self-disciplining of workers, arguing that self-exploitation, cheaper control at the workers' expense, and autonomy are cosmetic cover-ups of actual hierarchy.

Neo-Taylorism has come to be associated mainly with the production systems of Toyota and other Japanese companies that have proved to be highly competitive in the post-Fordist era (see **post-Fordism**). As in anti-Taylorist systems, teamwork, job enlargement, and multifunctionality, as well as financial incentives (both individual and group bonuses), play a key role. However, the principles of lean production mean that decisionmaking is strictly kept to management and the standardization of tasks (as in Taylor's theory) is central, with short-cycled and machine-paced work seen as unproblematic for human relations in production.

                                                ANN VOGEL

technological determinism

This postulates that **technology** is an important determinant of the forms of social organization that are to be found in human societies. Various technologies have undoubtedly changed constraints on human societies and their peoples, opened up new options for them, or indeed made new forms of constraint and control possible. **Karl Marx** could be characterized as a technological determinist in his observations on the ways the steam engines of the industrial revolution made the industrial capitalist possible, whereas the windmill was inevitably the technology of the feudal lord. Large-scale forms of industrial production and thus rapid wealth accumulation do depend on the ability to store, use, and control energy, and do greatly reduce a dependence on human **labor**, but the social consequences of technologies which permit this are many and variable.

Unlike financial, personal, or structural factors, which are hypothesized as having causal roles in societal development, technologies are palpable and easy to document, even when a social **group** has disappeared and has left no written records. Views on the causal potency of individual technologies are mixed. As L. Marx and M. R. Smith argue in *Does Technology Drive History? The Dilemma of Technological Determinism* (1994), "hard determinists" assign technology a degree of agency and a developmental momentum through the ways in which it leads us to understand ourselves and it. "Soft determinists," by contrast, see technology as one of many factors in a complex array of social and historical forces, and as one which has no inevitable outcome associated with it.   DAVID GOOD

technologies of the self
– see **Michel Foucault**.

technology
Because of the ubiquitous and multifaceted role that it plays in the contemporary world, technology has come to have a number of different meanings for sociologists. Since the term was first coined in the early nineteenth century, it has served as both an abstract, general concept characterizing the entire realm of material artifacts and a word used to describe specific and delimited examples of artifactual life.

At a macro-level of overarching sociological theorizing, technology has long provided one of the defining features of what some term **modernity** and others refer to as **modernization**. For most theoretically minded students of society, it is the fundamental, or determining, influence of technology over social life that is often considered to be the main difference between modern and premodern societies.

From **Karl Marx** onward, sociologists have more or less taken for granted that modern, or contemporary, societies are strongly conditioned by processes of technological change, while premodern societies or nonmodern social formations are not. According to the preferred discursive framework, technology in this sense provides a convenient, shorthand label for an entire mode of production (for theorists of a Marxian bent), form of social **differentiation** (for theorists of a Durkheimian inclination), or system of **values** (for the Weberians). It provides, we might say, the characteristic disposition, or structure, that underlies or forms a material basis for contemporary social reality.

The nature of the role that technology plays in society is, however, a topic around which there remains little theoretical consensus. We might say that theorists have disagreed as to which narrative of technological change is to be considered the most socially significant. For many, modern technology is primarily viewed as a part of economic production, according to a story-line of capitalist exploitation and capital accumulation, which places in the foreground the social activities of business **firms** and so-called entrepreneurs. This position was formulated most influentially in the writings of **Joseph Alois Schumpeter** in the first half of the twentieth century, especially perhaps his work on *Capitalism, Socialism and Society* (1941).

For others, technological change is viewed as part of a rationalization or secularization process, whereby attention is focused on the activities of bureaucratic **organizations** and so-called experts. For **Herbert Marcuse** in such works as *One-Dimensional Man* (1964), and other critical social theorists, technology was characterized as the dominant form of **rationality** in society.

For still others, technological change is seen as an autonomous process in its own right, according to a technocratic story-line by which the key actors are engineers and other human embodiments of materiality. In recent years, this position has been made popular in social constructionism, for example by Wsiebe Bijker *et al.* in *The Social Construction of Technological Systems* (1987). For the majority of social theorists, however, technology is generally discussed in an abstract or conceptual way, as principles of production on the one hand, and procedures of organization on the other.

For more empirically minded sociologists, technology is a term that is usually subjected to qualification or specification. Indeed, the notion of an abstract, all-encompassing technological system or technological rationality is seen with suspicion, or at the least with a great amount of skepticism. In many varieties of empirical sociological research, it is rejected for what is often considered to be its underlying **technological determinism**. Instead, technology is seen as something that is shaped by people in particular social settings or contexts.

What is typically of interest are the ways in which material artifacts, that is, technologies in the plural, are produced by particular actors and social **groups**, or the ways in which they are used in various locales or arenas of social **interaction**. Rather than discuss general, abstract relations between technology and society, the dominant tendency in recent decades has rather been to differentiate among technologies, and study particular cases, in relation either to the various societal sectors or branches of industry or to the variegated sites or spaces of use and application.

Most empirical sociologists of technology emphasize the importance of local contingencies, or contextual factors, in understanding what is characteristically referred to as the social shaping, or construction, of technology. Technologies, whether they be specific artifacts or more comprehensive systems or clusters of artifacts, are seen to be materializations of the interests of particular groups of people. Particularly influential has been the so-called **actor network theory**, which has been associated with Michel Callon and **Bruno Latour** in France and John Law in Britain, and the related social construction of technology, or SCOT, program, that has been promulgated by Wiebe Bijker and Trevor Pinch. According to these research approaches, technological development is investigated as specific processes of mediation and representation, in which even nonhuman objects can become agents or actors.

Another influential stream of empirical sociology has focused on user sites, or places in which specific technologies are put to use, often homes or offices. In these approaches, it is the domestication or appropriation of technology that is of interest, how artifacts are made to fit into patterns of **everyday life** or organizational routines and habits. Much of this sociology of technology has been carried out in "transdisciplinary" settings, in centers or institutes of **science and technology studies**, **cultural studies**, or **women's studies**.

As elsewhere in the **social sciences**, there is a noticeable gap between the large number of micro-level **case studies**, which have proliferated in recent years, and the more overarching theories at the macro-level that have been associated with the classical writers of the nineteenth and early twentieth centuries. In relation to technology, the micro–macro issue has been exacerbated by distinct national differences regarding the ways in which sociology of technology has been funded and institutionalized. Micro-level research has often been part of programs funded externally, either by companies or by national and local governments, as well as by international organizations.

There have been some attempts to help fill the gap by drawing on the kinds of institutional or organizational theories that have been popular in other fields of sociology. There has also developed a certain interest in the investigation of

social movements that have either fostered technological developments or opposed them, such as environmental and anti-nuclear movements. It is to be hoped that in the future the gap can continue to be bridged between the disparate case studies on the construction and use of specific technological artifacts and the broader understanding of the role that technology plays in the contemporary world.   ANDREW JAMISON

terrorism

Despite renewed efforts by official organizations and academic scholarship to define terrorism in the aftermath of September 11, 2001, there does not yet exist a single, consensual, widely shared definition. As a term of political discourse, terrorism usually implies a value judgment equivalent to moral condemnation. Although terrorism can apply to state (state terrorism) as well as non-state actors – which can act either on their own or in connection to a **state** (state-sponsored terrorism) – in the current international climate this term habitually refers to the activities of non-state transnational actors. As a concept, terrorism is usually subject to important historical reinterpretations (for example by the winners, in the context of liberation struggles). As a concrete phenomenon, it also presents itself in a variety of forms, and it involves a wide range of social behaviors. At one extreme, terrorism merges into organized **crime**, or even psychopathic behavior by an individual (for example the Shoe-bomber in the United States) or a **group** of individuals (for example the Aum Shinrikyo movement in Japan). At the other extreme, it becomes indistinguishable from guerrilla warfare and other forms of low-intensity conflict. For analytical purposes, it is useful to distinguish at least three main approaches to defining terrorism. The first focuses on the intentions of the agents perpetrating it; the second defines it in relation to the **values** and **institutions** of the society that it targets; and the third views it as a technique of **war** or direct action.

The first approach, which looks at the intentions of the agents, points to the historical origins of the word terrorism. This term initially referred to the period of the Terror (1793–4) during the French Revolution, when terrorism was a state policy designed to terrorize the enemies of the French Republic, be they domestic or foreign, individuals or collectivities. Although short-lived, this conceptualization of terrorism as a necessary evil to achieve the greater good of the nation has had numerous followers. In particular, it was reactivated in the nineteenth century by

European nationalist and anarchist groups, proponents of what became popularly known as "propaganda by deed." Of particular note were the Russian revolutionaries of Narodnaya Volya (1878–81) and the well-publicized exploits of French anarchists such as François Koeningstein, also known as Ravachol (1859–92) in the 1890s. Unlike the earlier uses of terror, however, the activities of these revolutionist and anarchist movements were not targeting the population at large but rather the political **elite**. In the early twentieth century, and again during the period of **decolonization**, such tactics became commonplace amongst many nationalist movements fighting European **imperialism**. Although terrorizing the enemy was clearly a significant part of their political and military strategy, the notion of terrorism itself became charged with negative connotations and few used it explicitly in their discourse. Notable exceptions are the advocacy of "The Philosophy of the Bomb" and the explosion of a bomb under Viceroy Irwin's special train in 1929 by the Indian nationalists of the Hindustan Socialist Republican Association, or the apology for political **violence** by Third-Worldist thinkers such as **Franz Fanon** during the Algerian war of decolonization. Generally, however, political players began to substitute the words terrorism and terrorist with positively laden terms such as liberation struggle and freedom fighter.

The second approach focuses on the actual or potential victims of terrorism. From this perspective, terrorism is the act of harming or planning to harm innocent persons (usually defined as civilians) in order to put pressure on the political elite and force it to alter its policies. To make sense of this perspective, it is crucial to be able to distinguish between those social actors who can make credible claims of exercising legitimate **violence** and those who cannot. (It is also important to determine procedurally whether those actors whose claims to **legitimacy** are well substantiated do not delegitimize themselves through their own use of violence.) One can define this legitimate violence from two main perspectives, legal and moral. In the contemporary period, states have a legal monopoly of violence over a territory – even though they can be accused of terrorism if they break existing rules and conventions – and non-state actors do not. From a moral perspective, terrorism is the epitome of illegitimate violence, destroying not only life and **property** but also breaking the **norms** and values of a given social order. After September 11, 2001, the latter became a prominent reading of terrorism and it

was popularized by the "War against Terror" launched by the United States. From this perspective, states as well as non-state actors can therefore be terrorists, but the notion of terrorism becomes harder to encapsulate as different parts of society may have different perceptions of what level of violence is justified, against whom (for example, is it acceptable to terrorize terrorists?), and so on.

The third and final approach to terrorism is the systematic and descriptive account of the means and techniques deployed in the production of acts of terrorism. This perspective is most common in the field of military science and other security-related disciplines. What characterizes terrorism from the point of view of strategy and tactics is that it is a weapon employed by a militarily weaker party against a stronger enemy. As a weapon of war, it is usually used by a few against the many. Because of its military inferiority, terrorism must create an impact on its enemy that far exceeds the actual targets that it is able to destroy (for example the Twin Towers versus the United States). Terrorist acts have therefore an exaggerated impact on how states and societies behave. At an immanent level, such impact on popular consciousness is created by the media coverage of these acts. More fundamentally, however, this outcome is a consequence of the random nature of these acts. By multiplying the number of targets that are deemed legitimate, terrorists not only force their opponents into a security race to guarantee the protection of all potential targets, but also induce the fear of attack in all corners of society, as total protection is unrealistic. One recent development in the field of terrorism that has the potential to contradict these observations is the emergence of so-called super-terrorism, particularly in the guise of nuclear terrorism. Through such technological developments it is conceivable that, in the future, terrorist **organizations** would be able to pose a serious direct military threat to states and populations.

FREDERIC VOLPI

text/textuality

What counts as a text is a matter of considerable debate in the **social sciences**. Since the impact of **poststructuralism** and **cultural studies** in the 1960s and 1970s, texts can no longer be assumed to refer simply to books. Television programs, recorded music, magazines, films, soap operas, and comics have all been studied as having the properties of texts. The study of text and textuality is bound up with concerns about the nature of meaning and discourse. Rather than assuming that meaning is stable, textual analysis has sought to demonstrate the extent to which texts can be the sites of conflict. At their most basic, texts are simply assemblages of discourse that are combined together to produce a dominant meaning. These meanings are usually thought to serve the interests of certain sections of society and can thereby seek to reinforce power relationships. Such texts are mainly produced by dominant media and cultural industries and employ identifiable social and cultural conventions to make themselves understandable to modern audiences. However, many scholars working in these fields now like to emphasize the ways in which texts can have more than one meaning. In this sense, texts might be ambiguous, internally contradictory, or be read in novel ways by certain sections of the **audience** / consumers. In this sense, texts are often thought to have a polysemic potential. By this, what is meant is that the meaning of a text depends upon the context of interpretation and the social location of the interpreter.

Intertextuality builds upon the idea of texts having meanings that are determined through their relationship to other texts. In this respect, we can broadly say that intertextuality has a horizontal and a vertical dimension. The most important aspect of horizontal intertextuality is that of genre. Genre establishes a number of categories that organize cultural production into identifiable types. For example, television employs a number of generic categories that include the news, soap operas, quiz and game shows, reality television, and so on. Vertical intertextuality, on the other hand, concerns the relationship of any text to other texts. This could include deliberate attempts to reference other works of **culture** within the text or the relationship between the text and cultural commentary or publicity material. Studying texts with this understanding requires the interpreter to look at the ways that meanings circulate between texts and other aspects of cultural experience into which they leak. In this respect, much recent work has looked at the way in which audiences often seek to produce their own texts as a response to popular or other texts. This level of intertextuality has led to the study of fanzines, websites, letters to newspapers, or even conversations in relation to a range of cultural material. It should be made clear that intertextuality is not a structureless **pluralism**, but usually involves questions of cultural **power** that inevitably structure the ways in which texts are understood. Cultural industries in capitalist societies may not be able to control the ways

in which their products are understood, but wider networks of power and **influence** will both suggest certain meanings over others and concentrate the distribution of some texts rather than others.

NICK STEVENSON

thick description
– see **ethnography**.

Third Way politics

The notion of Third Way politics derives from the writings of **Anthony Giddens** during the period since the mid-1990s (for example *The Third Way*, 1998, and *Progressive Manifesto*, 2003). The Third Way is an irenic **ideology**, which is to say that it postulates a set of principles and policies but does so without polemical intent. The Third Way is aptly named on philosophical grounds insofar as it attempts to strike a balance between liberty and **equality**, **values** that are antithetical when pushed to extremes. Its policies pivot on the notion that both increasingly global capitalist **markets** and the **welfare state** are unavoidable **institutions** in our time. Here again the Third Way tries to strike an issue-by-issue balance, in this case between laissez-faire and socialist policies.

The irenic tendency towards synthesizing extreme positions is a hallmark of Giddens's thought at large. For example, he sees **capitalism** and other modern institutional orders as replete with **risks** that simultaneously present possibilities and dangers for institutions and individuals alike. One task of state policies from the Third Way perspective is to increase the odds of positive outcomes from risks while creating programs to provide a measure of protection against the worst consequences, should there be negative outcomes. Along another line, Giddens has been proposing for many years that the global and the local are not antithetical alternatives. Rather, what matters are the ways in which local citizens and governments reconcile the structuring power of global processes with their local material needs and cultural ways of life.

The Third Way entered public life in 1997 when adopted by the British Labour Party government headed by Tony Blair (1953–). Subsequently, the term was used by Gerhard Schröder (1944–) and other European politicians and is now part of political debates in many countries around the world. The term has been used by former President Bill Clinton (1946–) in the United States, although it is not prevalent in American **politics** at large. Historically, Third Way perspectives renew the spirit of centrist politics that was influential in western Europe and the United States following World War II. Like all centrist politics, the Third Way includes an emphasis on pragmatic possibilities that does not normally evoke passionate enthusiasm. While commitments to equality and liberty keep Third Way policies oriented to moral ends, its supporters must be watchful that they do not become so mired down in short-term pragmatics that they lose sight of their moral goals. Third Way politics has long needed a philosophical redefinition of what equality and liberty can and should mean in our time. In addition, Third Way politics lacks any well-articulated conception of social **justice**. Nor has it developed many policies regarding relations between **state** and **civil society**. Giddens's forthcoming writings on equality may begin to fill in some of these gaps. But the success of the Third Way will be measured by whether it can establish centrist policies that will receive sufficient public support to keep ideological and political challenges from the left and the right at bay.

IRA COHEN

Thomas, William I. (1863–1947)

Born in Russell County, Virginia, the son of a Methodist preacher and farmer, Thomas enrolled in the University of Tennessee in 1880 and eventually became Professor of English at Oberlin College, but later became a graduate student in the first American Department of Sociology at the University of Chicago. Thomas was promoted to Associate Professor in 1900 and to a full professorship in 1910.

Thomas has been influential in modern **sociology** for two reasons. First, he developed **ethnography** as a special branch of qualitative **methodology** in his famous study, with Florian Znaniecki (1882–1958), of *The Polish Peasant in Europe and America*, which was published in five volumes between 1918 and 1920. In 1908 Helen Culver, founder of Hull House, had offered Thomas $50,000 to study problems of **migration** to the United States. Thomas decided to concentrate his research efforts on the Polish **community** in Chicago, but he also made research visits to Poland, where he met Znaniecki in 1913, to collect empirical **data**. Thomas analyzed 754 letters that had been sent to Polish families in Chicago, 8,000 documents from the archives of a Polish newspaper, documents from Polish parish histories in Chicago, and from the diaries of Polish immigrants.

Thomas left Chicago after a scandal had sullied his reputation with the local establishment, and he later taught at the New School for Social

Research and later, in 1936–7, he was appointed to a lectureship at Harvard. At the age of seventy-two he married his second wife Dorothy Swaine who later became the first female President of the American Sociological Association.

Second, Thomas is famous for the development of the so-called Thomas Theorem or "the definition of the situation" in *The Unadjusted Girl* (1923) and, with Dorothy Swaine Thomas, *The Child in America* (1928). This Theorem says that if people define situations as real, they will be real in their consequences. For example, if a **neighborhood** which is dominated by white Caucasians believes that the presence of low-status migrants would drive down house prices, they will try to resist such an influx. Their subjective "definition of the situation" (outsiders are bad for the housing **market**) has objective consequences (falling house prices and **social exclusion** of newcomers).

Thomas's sociological research and publications have had an enduring impact on the sociological study of **deviance** and on ethnographic methods.

BRYAN S. TURNER

Tilly, Charles (1929–)

The leading historical sociologist in North America, since the mid-1970s, based first at the New School for Social Research and later Columbia, Tilly has published a number of important works dealing mainly with the social history of Europe. Tilly's major theme is **social change** and its relationship with popular **politics** and state formation. A hallmark of his approach is the ability to ask large analytical questions, and to generate fresh sources of empirical **data** with which to explore them, leading to original and challenging interpretations. This broad approach has been used to tackle questions ranging from the reasons for marked contrasts in forms of European state formation, to the explanation of enduring patterns of social **inequality** across time.

His major works include *La Vendée* (1969), *The Rebellious Century* (1975), *The Contentious French* (1989), *Coercion, Capital, and European States* (1992), and *Durable Inequality* (1998). In each case, his work approaches the relationship between **social structure** and human agency as a dynamic, fluid, and complex set of processes. Tilly's approach to agency is, however, via political rather than cultural sociology. **Institutions** and organized action matter more than the meanings that individuals and collectivities give to their actions.

Tilly has also contributed to a methodological shift from heroic speculation to evidence-based **explanation** in historical sociology. This is reflected in enterprises such as the database of 8,000 English "contentious gatherings" between 1758 and 1834. His overall legacy is both multidimensional and interdisciplinary.   ROBERT HOLTON

time

Until the 1980s sociologists largely neglected the notion of "time," but some notable exceptions included **Émile Durkheim**, **Georges Gurvitch**, and **George Herbert Mead**. In *Primitive Classification* (1905 [trans. 1963]), Durkheim argued that the notion of time is relative to the type of **society**. In *Spectrum of Social Time* (1961 [trans. 1964]), Gurvitch explored the extent to which different social situations, or even different societies, can be characterized by a different rhythm or speed. In *The Philosophy of the Present* (1959), Mead presented a theory of society, central to which is the relationship between the different temporal modes (past, present, and future). In general, Martin Heidegger's *Being and Time* (1927 [trans. 1962]) influenced sociological thinking about time to a great extent.

The last couple of decades in particular have seen sociologists explore temporality in social life. In *Time and Social Theory* (1990) and *Timewatch: The Social Analysis of Time* (1995), Barbara Adam recorded these intellectual endeavors; in *Time in Contemporary Intellectual Thought* (2000), Patrick Baert compared these developments in sociology with those in other disciplines. It is important to make a distinction between the theoretical treatment of time and the empirical studies. We shall see that the most exciting new developments lie at the intersection of the two approaches.

Theoretical debates deal with time in at least three ways. One dimension refers to the importance attached to the lapse of time. Those who favor a synchronic analysis take a snapshot of society, whereas diachronic analysis studies social phenomena across time. For instance, **structuralism** attributes epistemological and ontological priority to synchronic analysis, whereas **evolutionary theory** implies a diachronic analysis. Some secondary sources erroneously conflate diachronic analysis with a study of change. The two do not necessarily go together: social order is accomplished through time, hence **Anthony Giddens**'s argument, in *The Constitution of Society* (1984), that the study of order also demands a diachronic analysis.

The second dimension of the theoretical debate deals with the relationship between change and continuity. For example, structuralism and **functionalism** explore the workings of relatively invariant structures underneath the temporal flux, whereas **Michel Foucault**'s genealogical method,

Norbert Elias's figurational **sociology**, and John Urry's use of **complexity theory** focus, all in different ways, on contingency, change, and process. Like Friedrich Nietzsche (1844–1900), Foucault was fascinated by discontinuities and contingencies in history. In *What is Sociology?* (1969), Elias deplored the tendency amongst sociologists to use static concepts and images. In *Global Complexity* (2003), Urry argued that society today is characterized by unprecedented movement, hence the need for **social theory** to reflect this development.

The third component of the theoretical debate explores the way in which the past, present, and future are related. Causal–mechanical approaches focus on how the past determines the present and future, whereas teleological perspectives conceive of the course of history as directed towards a particular goal or *telos*. Throughout the twentieth century, both views were heavily criticized. Theorists like Mead and **Niklas Luhmann** prefer instead to talk about the relative openness of the future and how the future is partly constructed and redesigned in the present. Influenced by Alfred Whitehead and Henri Bergson, Mead's *Philosophy of the Present* (1959) explores how people, once confronted with unpredictable situations, symbolically reconstruct the past and conceptualize a new future. Mead's philosophical reflections on time influenced Niklas Luhmann's **social systems theory**.

The empirical studies of time are manifold. In the last couple of decades, research on time-budgets has benefited from sophisticated techniques, which increased its reliability. Time-budget research is now a widespread methodological device, used by sociologists for a variety of purposes: for instance, to explore shifts in division of **labor** in the household, the impact of **unemployment** on people's time use, or the effects of new **technologies** in the workplace and outside. Besides time-budget research, cross-disciplinary empirical research has proved fruitful. For instance, anthropologists and sociologists have documented the different (or similar) time perceptions and perspectives of different **cultures**, classes, or ethnic **groups**. Another example is that, inspired by E. P. Thompson's *Making of the English Working Class* (1963) and Foucault's *Discipline and Punish* (1975 [trans. 1977]), historians and sociologists have studied the relationship between the creation of a disciplined work force and the implementation of a rigid time schedule.

Exciting new developments lie at the intersection between theory and empirical research. There is a considerable amount of literature on the differences between advanced societies and previous societies, and on how these differences can be expressed in temporal terms. In this context, we have to make a distinction between efforts to identify the nature of **modernity** on the one hand, and attempts to characterize contemporary society on the other.

From the outset, the **social sciences**, and **sociology** in particular, have been interested in the transition towards a modern, industrial, or advanced society. This transition can be expressed in temporal terms. Some authors, like **Max Weber** and Foucault, focus on the link between modernity, **rationalization**, and predictability. Weber pointed out that the emergence of Protestantism and rational **capitalism** was accompanied by a more methodical usage of time, and the rise of **bureaucracy** by greater predictability in the economic and political realm. In a similar fashion, Foucault showed how the shift towards a modern society was accompanied by a more rational and thorough surveillance of society; this led to greater predictability and control of people's behavior. Other authors claim that, unlike in previous eras, modern individuals are able to distance themselves from, and reflect upon, the past. The present can become a source for change. For example, in *Structural Anthropology* (1958 [trans. 1968]), **Claude Lévi-Strauss** made a distinction between "cold" and "hot" societies. Whereas the former operate in an energy-conserving fashion as if mechanical instruments, the latter resemble thermodynamic machines: they use up a huge amount of energy, need constant refilling, and are continually changing.

More recently, sociologists have reflected on the nature of *contemporary* society and its similarities with, and differences from, modernity or **industrial society**. One category of authors sees contemporary society as a radical break with modernity. For example, **Fredric Jameson** and others talk about **postmodernity**, emphasizing the fluid and transient nature of society today. In postmodern **aesthetics**, genuine novelty is regarded as impossible; we can only articulate and revamp what came before. Another category of authors emphasizes continuity with modernity. Giddens and **Ulrich Beck** refer to the present condition as "high", "late" or "second modernity." In *Consequences of Modernity* (1989), Giddens mentions "time–space distanciation": people now have technological tools at their disposal to overcome time- and space-related boundaries. People use symbolic tokens, like **money**, to transcend time and **space**. In *Risk Society* (1986 [trans. 1992]), Beck argues that

we now have to manage and control the negative, unintended effects of previous attempts to control nature. In this context, Adam notes, in *Timescapes of Modernity* (1999), that we need to go beyond the "short-termism" that characterizes current policy-making. We can no longer rely on the knowledge of the past to act effectively in the present.

PATRICK BAERT

time budgets
– see **time diary methodology**.

time diary methodology
Since Gary S. Becker's work on the allocation of **time**, "A Theory of the Allocation of Time," appeared in the *Economic Journal* in 1965, the time diary approach to the investigation of the actual disposal, or doing, of the living of everyday (economic) life asks research participants to keep a diarized record of the manner in which they used their time over generally brief periods such as a week or month. Time diaries are often supplied with pre-categorized activity codes (for example: shopping; going to the cinema; visiting friends; visiting extended family), which allow participants to record their activities readily in blocks of time – often as short as ten to fifteen minutes. Analysis of such records promises the understanding of the manner in which (everyday/social/economic) life is actually accomplished, rather than merely reported on – given a skeptical reading of the validity and reliability of interview **data**.

Time diaries have been used recently to study a disparate range of social phenomena ranging from the time-distribution spend by lone-parent families with working mothers, through the costs and benefits of educational spending in terms of teacher–pupil contact-time spend in state schools, to the comparative analysis of the work and leisure-time balance of road versus rail commuters in urban settings. Time diaries may be complemented by a range of other **methodologies** such as interview-based or post-back survey **questionnaires**, the collection of demographic data, and **participant observation**.

Time diaries suffer a range of limitations, however. As *post-hoc* records, not only are time diaries subject to the expected vagaries of attrition, sample self-selection, memory, and social desirability effects, but also time diaries appear to be prone to a range of specific over- and under-estimation effects (for example, in North American studies both hours at work and hours engaged in housework are apparently routinely over-reported). Amusingly, some researchers have noted that Americans do accurately report on the number of hours they spend watching television.

More recent developments in time diary methodology include the use of time–space diaries which attempt to capture the embodied use of time as more than an incorporeal abstraction and, rather, see humans' use of time as an essentially spatially contingent phenomenon that has, to date, been poorly captured by existing time-alone diary methods.

MARK RAPLEY AND SUSAN HANSEN

time–space distantiation
– see **Anthony Giddens**.

Titmuss, Richard (1907–1973)

Professor of Social Administration at the London School of Economics from 1950 until his premature death in 1973, Titmuss was an influential analyst of the British **welfare state**. His work emphasized the importance of linking the study of welfare to broader questions of economic policy. Titmuss extended the scope of traditional approaches to **social policy** in his examination of the three main types of welfare: social (such as social security and national insurance); fiscal (tax relief and allowances); and occupational (benefits in cash and kind through employers). In his classic essay "The Social Division of Welfare," in *Essays on "the Welfare State"* (1958), Titmuss assessed the distribution of contributions and benefits across different **social classes**, highlighting the rewards available to middle-class **groups** through the tax and occupational system. This theme was explored in essays and books such as *Problems of Social Policy* (1950), *Essays on the Welfare State* (1958), *Income Distribution and Social Change* (1962), and *Commitment to Welfare* (1968). Titmuss's approach to social policy was shaped by his work in the insurance industry, this providing the basis of his interest and expertise in social **statistics**. In 1941 he was recruited to join a team preparing a series of volumes on the history of World War II, his own volume on the organization of social services. *Problems of Social Policy* was important in shaping Titmuss's interest in the role of welfare in fostering integration and consensus within society. The idea of social policy creating opportunities for altruism was developed in *The Gift Relationship* (1970) where Titmuss examined blood donorship as a model of compassion that transcends immediate kin and community ties. This study also reflects the connections between social policy and sociology in Titmuss's work, with **Émile**

Durkheim and **Max Weber** being notable influences in his approach to understanding social **solidarity** on the one hand and the characteristics of **bureaucracy** and large-scale **organizations** on the other.

CHRIS PHILLIPSON

Tocqueville, Alexis de (1805–59)

A French political theorist, Tocqueville was also active in public as a parliamentary representative and, briefly, as Foreign Affairs Minister. *De la démocratie en Amérique* was published in two parts (1835 and 1840 [trans. 2003]). Though Tocqueville was widely recognized early on, in Europe and in the United States, as an original and profound political thinker, thanks to the success of the first part of *Democracy in America*, his contribution to **sociological theory** was acknowledged only in the mid and late twentieth century, particularly by such authors as **Raymond Aron**, **Reinhard Bendix**, and **Robert N. Bellah**. At the end of the century, the apparent universal triumph of **democracy** led some scholars to view Tocqueville's thought as a unique inspiration for a sustained consideration of that new condition. More generally, Tocqueville can be considered an inspiring forerunner or indeed a sophisticated practitioner of what currently goes under the name of comparative-historical **sociology**.

Owing to his social and economic position as a provincial aristocrat and landowner, Tocqueville was never active as an academic scholar, but as an individual of independent means who wrote (very effectively and successfully) for a broader, cultured public. He directed his attention to themes widely recognized as politically and morally, not just intellectually, significant, and although he grounded his treatment of them on serious research and reflection, he freely expounded the **values** and concerns which motivated his work. According to some critics, he relied excessively on quickly, intuitively formed assessments and evaluations of circumstances and events. Tocqueville's thinking was largely inspired by his concern about the current condition of his beloved France, but acquired a theoretical dimension through his reflections on phenomena also affecting other western countries. The most significant such phenomenon was democracy, that is the institutional affirmation of the **equality** of all individuals. This new principle denied **legitimacy** to aristocracy, that is to the social, political, and economic arrangements which for centuries had characterized European society, assigning widely different sets of **rights** and obligations, resources and liabilities to the members of various, publicly sanctioned ranks or orders.

Democracy, Tocqueville argued, was inexorably advancing throughout the western world, but at a different pace and with different effects in different parts of it. In the United States, democracy had not needed to displace previously existent aristocratic arrangements, and on this account the Americans' strong attachment to equality did not seriously threaten another social value, most dear to Tocqueville himself – freedom. Such a threat was particularly great in countries with an aristocratic past, where the democratic enthronement of equality had taken place, or had to take place, through revolution (see **revolution, theory of**).

Recent French events showed that such circumstances could lead to recurrent and violent social and political disorder, and possibly to a novel, democratic form of despotism. This respected the overwhelming attachment of the population to equality, and encouraged the resultant tendency towards social atomization and the individual's overwhelming concern with their economic security and advantage. Thus the society's political center could indefinitely increase the scope and variety of its activities, directing them to the satisfaction of that concern, and dissuading individuals from looking beyond their private circumstances and involving themselves in matters of public significance, which would remain the exclusive province of an increasingly pervasive central government.

In Tocqueville's judgment, the United States had been preserved from such a development by the concurrence of multiple, diverse factors, such as the persistence within its population of religiously inspired values, the constitutional dispersion of public **powers** through federal arrangements, the social **prestige** of law, and the freedom of the press and of association. Furthermore, Americans, without renouncing their concern with their private well-being, were often willing to associate with one another in **voluntary associations** which undertook certain public tasks instead of leaving all of them to the government. Tocqueville's reflections on this phenomenon are one of the acknowledged sources of the contemporary concept of **social capital**.

But even in the United States the institutional equilibrium between the value of equality and that of freedom was intrinsically precarious, given in particular the American tendency to moral and intellectual conformism, one aspect of what Tocqueville called "the tyranny of the majority."

On this account, later admirers have hailed him as a "prophet of the mass age."

Tocqueville's second major work, *The Old Regime and the Revolution* (1856 [trans. 1955]), expounds a bold thesis on the nature and origins of the French Revolution, denying that it constituted a sudden, wholesale break with the French past. Tocqueville considers the strengthening of French governmental **institutions** as the most significant outcome of the Revolution, but sees this as the culmination of a very long process. According to him, French absolutism had systematically deprived of political significance all autonomous social forces (beginning with the estates of the nobility, urban and regional corporate bodies, and independent tribunals) and conferred wide, unchallengeable powers upon agencies established, controlled, and activated by the monarch and his immediate collaborators. By thus depriving **civil society** of its power to counter encroachments on its autonomy, absolutism had atomized that society and rendered it incapable of acting coherently on behalf of national interests, including those entrusted to the monarchy itself and threatened, most particularly, by the disarray in the French public finances.

Whatever the merits of this thesis, in the process of arguing it Tocqueville made considerable contributions to the sociology of revolutions and other aspects of the sociological discipline. He argued, for instance, that sometimes attempts by existent regimes to improve the conditions of subaltern groups, to the very extent that they are successful, heighten those groups' awareness of their continuing condition of relative disadvantage, increasing rather than lessening their protest and mobilization. He emphasized that an openly unequal distribution of fiscal burdens has very negative effects on the ability of social **groups** to act together. He pointed out one aspect of political and social **modernization** which is what sociologists later came to call low status crystallization, that is a lack of correspondence between the rankings of an individual or group in terms, respectively, of status, of political significance, and of economic power.   GIANFRANCO POGGI

Tönnies, Ferdinand (1855–1936)

Born in Schleswig-Holstein, then under Danish control, Ferdinand Tönnies received a doctorate from the University of Tubingen in 1877. He taught intermittently at the University of Kiel from 1881 to 1933, his position unstable because his social democratic views conflicted with the conservative Prussian government. Tönnies was interested in **sociological theory**, **statistics**, applied sociology, and **crime**. He cofounded the German Society for Sociology. He is best known for his work *Gemeinschaft und Gesellschaft* (1887), translated as *Community and Society* (1957), one of the first sociological works to delineate clearly major differences between traditional and modern societies.

Gemeinschaft (**community**) consists of groups that have a strong feeling of cohesiveness. Often characteristic of rural villages, *Gemeinschaft* relations are enduring and traditional. They rarely change dramatically and involve shared **trust**, beliefs, and cooperation. In the West, *Gemeinschaft* was being replaced by *Gesellschaft* (**society**). *Gesellschaft* relationships arose in an urban and capitalist setting, characterized by **individualism** and impersonal monetary connections between people. Social ties were often instrumental and superficial, with self-interest and exploitation increasingly the norm. Tönnies based his distinction on a theory of human nature, contending that *Gemeinschaft* referred to the essential will, and *Gesellschaft* to the arbitrary will. In everyday modern life, despite the predominance of *Gesellschaft* relationships, *Gemeinschaft* ties continued to exist, exemplified in the importance of **family** and **neighborhood**.

Tönnies's distinction between *Gemeinschaft* and *Gesellschaft*, like others between **tradition** and **modernity**, has been criticized for over-generalizing differences between societies, and implying that all societies were following a similar evolutionary path (see **evolutionary theory**).

KENNETH H. TUCKER

total institution
– see **Erving Goffman**.

totalitarianism
This concept is an approach to **politics** and **society** in which the **state** is meant to know best what is good for the citizens, individually and collectively, and therefore is justified in controlling all aspects of public and private life. There are two main aspects to totalitarianism; the first is a moral and philosophical position, the second is a technical and political method. In terms of philosophical justification, totalitarianism posits the moral superiority of the collective over the individual, as well as the cognitive superiority of the state (including state officials and/or party members) over ordinary citizens – this last point being directly connected to other forms of **paternalism**. From this perspective, because the state knows best

what is required for the good of the polity, dissent from individuals or from the masses can only reflect their selfish behavioral traits and/or illustrate their limited cognitive grasp of the situation. In political and technical terms, therefore, totalitarianism requires that the state should be the sole representative of the social collective and that it should actively suppress both **pluralism** in the political society and the autonomous **institutions** of **civil society**, as these can only undermine the well-being and flourishing of the **community**.

Totalitarianism is a modern phenomenon. It can be understood as a modern form of **authoritarianism** where **technology** and **bureaucracy** give the state the means to achieve a previously unequalled degree of control and dominance over society. Earlier embodiments of authoritarianism, even in their strongest forms like absolutism, could punctually and locally claim to exercise total control in society, but it is only with the development of the bureaucratic state that such systemic forms of **social control** became possible. As **Hannah Arendt** stressed in *The Origins of Totalitarianism* (1958), totalitarian systems seek to eliminate individuality and free choice through complete politicization of the **private sphere**. In doing so, they reinforce the atomization of society and make the state the only remaining outlet for public activities.

The most common political tools of the totalitarian state fall into three main categories: **ideology**, surveillance, and repression. In the first instance, the state promotes its preferred ideology amongst the masses by strictly controlling the media and all forms of public discourse, as well as by regimenting the education system. Second, the state relies on its pervasive surveillance **networks** to monitor the everyday activities of the citizenry and ensure that they are conforming to those professed by the state ideology. Finally, the state utilizes its extensive repressive apparatus to punish dissenters, and instills fear amongst those who might be tempted to dissent.

The main political systems that have exemplified totalitarianism in the twentieth century were **fascism** and **Communism**. Although many states have been called totalitarian in recent times, totalitarianism is an extremely difficult political system to obtain in practice. True totalitarianism could be said to exist only in fictional dystopias such as George Orwell's *Nineteen Eighty-Four* (1949), which was inspired by Stalin's Soviet Union. In the modern period, most totalitarian states are in fact authoritarian regimes whose claims to organize all the relevant aspects of their subjects' life are somewhat overstated. This does not make these regimes less brutal, however, as the role of the repressive apparatus often increases when the ideological and surveillance capabilities of the would-be totalitarian state decrease.

FREDERIC VOLPI

Touraine, Alain (1925-)

A luminary of postwar French sociology, and indeed of international sociology, Touraine had an enormously productive career of research, analysis, and theorizing, and first-hand knowledge of Europe and the western hemisphere (from French-speaking Canada and the United States to Chile and Argentina). Following his early training in history, he has drawn on (and criticized) various intellectual currents, including **Marxism**, Sartrean existentialism, and Parsonian system theory, to formulate in successive decades and works a distinctive "action" approach to two major sociological fields: the question of **social change** and the question of **modernity**.

A general frame of his analysis is that the social order of modernity is neither a static nor a functional totality; it is, rather, a terrain of conflict between social forces competing for **power**, between governing **elites** and the dominated. In the **postindustrial society**, which he analyzed relatively early in *Post-Industrial Society* (1969 [trans. 1971]), control over cultural practices replaces earlier struggles by the **labor movement** for control over work practices. He founded the Center for the Study of Social Movements (now ADIS) as the École des Hautes Études en Sciences Sociales in Paris. A key unit of analysis and research for Touraine and his associates is the study of various **social movements**, from the anti-nuclear movement, to regional movements of autonomy in Europe, to the Solidarity movement in Poland, and, more recently, the feminist movement. Social movements are collective actors of change, not only as reactions against the abuses of governing power but also as (potential) cultural innovators of advanced modernity (as the labor movement had been in the nineteenth century). Touraine proposed, as a method of studying social movements called "sociological intervention," an enriched form of **participant observation** with the sociologist as a catalyst assisting collective actors to articulate, express, and pursue actively their objectives – a position he explored in *The Voice and the Eye* (1978 [trans. 1981]).

Advanced modernity is not a period of successive crises but of fundamental transformation and structural changes for which a new sociological approach is needed, to seize, in different domains, the dynamics of change. Hence Touraine's advancing concepts such as "self-production of society," subjectification (in polar tension but also complementarity with **rationalization**), and "historicity" (the adaptation of society to its environment with cultural initiatives, in contrast to **historicism** and evolutionism).

His *Critique of Modernity* (1992 [trans. 1995]) is a powerful critical interpretation of main currents that have marked the western experience, and brings into relief his views of the basic relation of the individual to society. Though highly sensitive to the role of the collective Subject as innovator of the social process, Touraine, in this and later works such as *What is Democracy?* (1997), gives primacy to the freedom and creativity of the more individual Subject (Touraine faults **George Herbert Mead**'s treatment of **socialization**). Sociology is thus an emancipatory discipline, helping actors (and not just Man but also Woman) to increase the space of **democracy**). And behind this, one may see in the action image of society of Touraine a resemblance to the perspective of Pierre-Joseph Proudhon (1809–65), who saw the historical process as a continuing battleground for social **justice**.

EDWARD TIRYAKIAN

tourism

The word tour was used in the early eighteenth century to mean "to take a turn in or about a place," or to make a circuitous journey, and by 1811 tourism referred to traveling for pleasure. The development of the railway booms in Britain in the 1830s and 1840s saw the emergence of the tourist car to accommodate railway tourists. The railways launched a new age of popular tourism. The grand tour had once been the preserve of the rich and the famous in the age of romantic travel and was associated in particular with the Italian journey of Johann Wolfgang von Goethe in 1786–8, which created the **tradition** of self-discovery through foreign travel. In the early decades of the twentieth century, the creation of annual holidays for the working class formed the basis of the holiday as an important component of popular **leisure**. In this respect, tourism illustrates the impact of **social stratification** on leisure activities. In *A Local Habitation* (1988), **Richard Hoggart** recalls how working-class **families** with working mothers would save money for public holidays that occurred around Whit Monday and Easter Monday to escape from the grind of **everyday life**.

By the 1930s trips to northern sea-side resorts such as Bridlington and Filey had become a feature of popular cultural activity. After World War II, cheap transportation and package holidays began to constitute modern tourism as a feature of **consumer society**. Whereas the working class sought leisure in popular destinations in Spain and France, tourism to more exotic and remote destinations in Asia or Africa was an aspect of status distinction and cultural capital. With **globalization** and the growing affordability of international travel, there are few areas that are any longer remote or exclusive. There has been an inevitable **McDonaldization** of tourism. The commodification of leisure now also includes sex tourism and, with the growth of regenerative medicine and the aging of the populations of the developed world, there are the beginnings of health tourism. For example, in Caribbean resorts private health corporations offer cosmetic surgery and medical treatment for degenerative diseases. Because exclusive and exotic destinations have now been heavily influenced by consumerism, the exotic has to be manufactured or invented. These developments have led some sociologists, such as John Urry in *The Tourist Gaze: Leisure and Travel in Contemporary Societies* (1990), to explore the transformation of familiar landscapes into exciting and exotic places. Tourism has become an aspect of **postmodernity** in which there are socially constructed tourist destinations. Disneyland is an aspect of this postmodern landscape. As terrestrial tourism has become overcrowded, wealthy tourists are being offered the opportunity, for example by the Russian space research agency, of travel to outer space. Space tourism is being used as a financial contribution to scientific exploration.

BRYAN S. TURNER

trade unions

These are formal **organizations** of workers that seek to represent the interests of their members through collective organization and activity, offsetting the weakness of individual employees compared with the **power** of employers and managers. A central objective of most unions is to pressure and persuade employers to improve the employment position of their members, though union agendas can embrace wider issues of power, equity, and **justice** in and beyond the workplace and address the **state** as well as employers.

Effective unionism depends upon the mobilization of power in collective organization and action (strikes or other sanctions), though that power is often translated into accommodations

with employers, while unions may also pursue their objectives through wider alliances and political campaigns. Thus, the capacity of unions to represent their members may involve agreements and even cooperative relations with employers and/or the state. However, unless such relations are based on autonomous collective organization and leverage, relationships of dependency risk compromising the unions' capacity to pursue their members' interests in conflicts with employers or the state, as analyzed by C. Offe and H. Wiesenthal in "Two Logics of Collective Action" in Offe's *Disorganised Capitalism* (1985).

In articulating the interests of workers and pursuing **collective action**, unions depend upon membership activity and **solidarity** but also seek to focus and control such activity. Thus unions combine democratic and bureaucratic features, though different participants – members, activists, officials, leaders – may have different priorities and participate in different ways in these democratic and bureaucratic processes. Furthermore, unions differ in the scope of their potential membership (some organize particular occupations, enterprises, or sectors of employment, while others open their membership more widely), and in the proportion of potential recruits who are actual members (union density).

The character, possibilities, and limits of trade unionism were widely debated from the rise of organized **labor movements** in western Europe during the nineteenth century. Founding figures included **Karl Marx, Robert Michels, Vladimir Ilich Lenin**, S. Perlman who wrote *Theory of Labour Movement* (1928), Sydney Webb (1859–1947), and Beatrice Webb (1858–1943), while P. Fosh and E. Heery, in *Trade Unions and their Members* (1990), identify pluralist, neocorporatist, Marxist, conservative, and feminist positions in recent discussions. These positions involve contrasting analyses of the employment relationship, of the interests and powers of workers and employers, and thus of the scope and limits of conflict and accommodation between workers and employers. They also differ in their accounts of unities and divisions among workers (are some groups, such as women or the unemployed, marginalized?) and in their conceptualizations of the relationship between industrial relations and the state (is the state partisan in conflicts between employers and workers?).

In addressing these questions, there is growing recognition that trade unions vary considerably, between countries, **occupations**, and sectors of the **economy**, and over time. One approach to such differences compares professional and white-collar associations with manual workers' unions. Their unionateness is assessed on such criteria as engagement in collective bargaining, strike action, and alliances with labor parties, which are seen as characteristic of manual workers' unions. However, how far such differences coincide closely with occupational hierarchies has remained contentious, as debated in contributions to R. Hyman and P. Price (eds.) *The New Working Class? White-Collar Workers and Their Organizations* (1983). Another approach argues that trade unions face persistent dilemmas in their organization and mobilization of workers, in terms of their orientation to market bargaining or class mobilization or as actors in **civil society**. Unions can then be mapped in terms of their responses to such dilemmas, to illuminate the controversies that arise within and between unions and the range of different union **traditions** found within and between societies, as in R. Hyman, *Understanding European Trade Unionism* (2001).

Contemporary **social changes**, such as the decline of traditionally unionized sectors, labor market flexibilization, and new international divisions of **labor**, have also prompted recent debates on the merits of newer forms of unionism that may depart from earlier union traditions. In particular, discussions of organizing unionism and social-movement unionism give fresh emphasis to the active mobilization of new constituencies of workers, but also recognize that unions continue to face major challenges and dilemmas.

TONY ELGER

tradition

A comprehensive treatment of this topic can be found readily available under "Tradition" in the *International Encyclopedia of the Social and Behavioral Sciences* (2001, ed. **Neil Smelser** and Paul B Bates), where there are several separate essays by R. Bauman, Edward Tiryakian, and S. Langlois. Understood generically as customary ways and beliefs handed down (usually by oral communication, **ritual**, and/or imitation) from the past for present action, tradition is an integral component of every **family**, **group**, **organization**, and nation. It is an important legacy of the past to the present, albeit on many occasions and in many historical settings, the present may reconstruct the customary past as illustrated in Eric Hobsbawm and Terence Ranger, *The Invention of Tradition* (1984). While tradition carries with it a positive evaluation in **everyday life** and in marketing (as in "prime ribs are a tradition at Simpson's"), it can also appear to be a

burden for innovation by devaluating the present. In any event, the transmission of tradition is ubiquitous if tacit in all processes of **socialization**. While an old tradition may be lost as a result of **social change** and the dispersal of members of a **community** that observed it, new traditions emerge, even unwittingly, as Sumner realized long ago, in the passage of folk ways into mores.

Sociologists have dealt with traditions, including their own, in several ways. With some ambivalence, the early sociologists noted a vast transformation in the West with a modern ethos (first grasped by the writer Charles Beaudelaire (1821–67) and sociologically analyzed by **Ferdinand Tönnies** in his classic *Gemeinschaft und Gesellschaft*, 1887 [trans. 1957]). Processes (including the rise of large urban agglomerations, rural exodus, rise of crime rates) involved in the search for and the transformation to a new social order to replace or renovate the premodern one became a rich terrain of inquiry for conservatives of the Le Play school, liberals such as **Auguste Comte** and Émile **Durkheim**, and radicals such as the Marxists. The ambivalence of sociologists and other **intellectuals** regarding tradition is brought out in the important study on *Tradition* (1981) by **Edward Shils**, who himself emphasized the functional importance of tradition in societal integration.

The theoretical analysis of tradition owes much to **Max Weber**'s seminal ideal-type discussion of traditional domination or traditionalism (well discussed by **Reinhard Bendix** in *Max Weber, An Intellectual Portrait*, 1977) as one mode of the legitimation of **power** *"legitime Herschaft"*. Arguably, Weber saw traditionalism, especially that borne by a sacred tradition, as vestigial in the **rationalization** process of **modernity**. This post-Enlightenment perspective (common to liberal and radical positions) carried over into the 1950s and 1960s in sociological and economic approaches to growth and development which saw tradition as providing non-rational obstacles to the development of new nations and to the development of a modern mentality. Illustrative here is the classical modernization study of the Middle East, Daniel Lerner's *The Passing of Traditional Society* (1958), which stressed the diversity of the Arab-Islamic world but in retrospect underestimated the unifying potency of religious traditions (for example pilgrimage to Mecca) and collective memories (of western domination).

In the current period of **globalization**, however, a more balanced view is emerging, one that stresses the multiple paths to, and modes of modernity, with a place in the sun given to tradition as a vital cog in the process of modernization (for instance **S. N. Eisenstadt**, *Japanese Civilization*, 1996). Further research will entail studying the new traditions of immigrant **communities** in different regions of the world, and the utilization of traditions to legitimate domestic and international practices in seemingly modern societies.

EDWARD TIRYAKIAN

trajectories of dying
– see **death and dying**.

transnational corporations
This term came into general use in the 1960s to refer to **firms** engaged in crossborder economic activities. The use of the term and interest in such activities were prompted by the growing penetration of western European **economies** by United-States-owned companies. This process was hard to assimilate to earlier forms of **imperialism** and **colonialism** based on relations of economic and political dependence between expanding European powers and the rest of the world. The seemingly novel operations of American multinational corporations (MNCs) led to fears that the American challenge would undermine the economic autonomy and political sovereignty of host states and create a new form of imperialism. Critics argued that MNCs induced technological dependence, destroyed local jobs, and deprived national **states** of their capacity to set interest rates, levy taxes, and plan their economies. Their defenders replied that MNCs could benefit their hosts through transferring **technology**, raising productivity, improving managerial skills, and reinvesting profits in expanding **markets**. However, with the later expansion of MNCs with their original headquarters in Europe, East Asia, Latin America, India, and China, discussion about their activities and impact has been integrated into more general debates about **globalization**.

The precursors of what are now termed MNCs originated in long-distance trade even before market forces became the dominant form of economic organization and national territorial states became the dominant form of political organization. A major expansion of MNC activities coincided with the rise of a capitalist world-system in the sixteenth century as charter companies (such as the East India Company) were granted commercial monopolies by a European **state**. MNC activities continued to expand in trade, extraction of raw materials, and indirect foreign investment in the eighteenth and nineteenth centuries, both within and beyond the borders of empires,

peaking before World War I. A further major expansion of MNC activities occurred following postwar reconstruction and the institution of a more open international economic regime after 1945. More recently still, with a further round of international deregulation and liberalization and the collapse of the Soviet bloc, further waves of MNC expansion have occurred, involving strategic alliances, joint ventures, and networked enterprises.

MNCs now comprise a mix of private, public, and hybrid economic agents that vary in size, home bases, fields of activities, and business strategies. They include merchant companies, buying cheap and selling dear; extractive enterprises; manufacturing firms; investment companies and banks; consumer service firms; and international producer service suppliers. As MNC activities have expanded, national territorial states have become less important in the economic organization and regulation of the world **market**. There is also increasing competition between **cities**, regions, and states to attract and retain MNCs, either through a deregulatory "race to the bottom," that is economic competition that results in low wages, low technology, and cheap goods produced by unskilled workers, or by providing high-tech, highly skilled, and infrastructurally well-equipped operating bases. This competition coexists with new fears that MNC activities are a threat to global economic stability and require new forms of international regulation and global governance.

BOB JESSOP

trauma
From the Greek word for "wound," trauma most commonly refers to an emotional shock that produces inescapable and enduring affects. **Sigmund Freud** introduced the concept to the **social sciences** in the 1890s, using it in connection to a theory of hysteria. More generally in the body of his writings, Freud discussed three forms of trauma in relation to the human condition: the first related to the awareness of the insignificance of the earth relative to the vastness of the universe; the second, to the awareness stemming from **evolutionary theory** that humanity was not descended from God; and third, following psychoanalytic theory, to the awareness that the ego was entirely in control.

Contemporary discussions of trauma have added a wider social focus to Freud's account, applying the concept to studies of collective memory and collective **identity**. The Holocaust, its meaning and its memory, has been the central point of reference for much of this discussion. Here the polarity between perpetrator and victim has been the defining one. As in the original Greek, trauma has been conceptualized as a wound on the soul of each, perpetrator and victim, causing great anguish, guilt, and attempts to deny or forget, setting in motion psychological processes so strong as to affect all later experience.

Sociologists have broadened the application of this concept even further, to allow discussion of national and cultural trauma in J. Alexander *et al.*, *Social and Cultural Trauma* (2004). In this publication, cultural trauma is a process whereby the formation of collective **identity** and the construction of collective memory are linked. In this sense, cultural trauma refers to a dramatic loss of identity and meaning, a tear in the social fabric, affecting a group of people. While profoundly emotional, this form of trauma does not necessarily involve the direct experience that would cause a wound, as do psychological uses of trauma. While some occurrence or event may be necessary to establish a significant cause, the meaning of this event, its trauma, requires interpretation, mediation, and representation. A significant event – a **war**, revolution, or serious attack – may tear the social fabric; what it actually means and how it can be repaired is something that is decided when various interpretations, including naming perpetrators and victims, take place.

RON EYERMAN

triangulation

This is the corroboration of research findings from the same respondents and on the same topic, by using different methods, the term triangulation being suggested by an analogy with land surveys, where a surveyor can get a fix on a position by taking a bearing on two different landmarks. The term was popularized by Norman Denzin in *The Research Act* (1970). A variant of triangulation is member validation, checking the accuracy of findings with research respondents.

The commitment to methodological rigor that is implied in triangulation is hardly controversial. More difficulty attaches to positivist claims that triangulation is a procedure for validation of findings. The main problem with triangulation-as-validation is that, for any given research topic, there will always be one best method and any supplemental method used for corroboration will be inferior for the purpose. Thus, any lack of corroboration may simply be due to the

inappropriateness of the second supplemental method, which may lack coverage or depth in comparison to the first method used.

In practice, comparison of results obtained by different methods is not a matter of straightforward juxtaposition: different methods tend to produce accounts couched at different levels of abstraction. Nevertheless, the credibility of an analysis may be extended by comparisons within a multi-method design and by respondents' endorsements of research reports. Such comparisons may act as a valuable spur to extend and deepen the analysis, but they do not provide validation.

MICK BLOOR AND FIONA WOOD

tribe(s)

These are populations asserted or assumed to be largely self-reproducing or genetically isolated, linguistically uniform, culturally uniform, self-titled, socially integrated through ties of **kinship** and **marriage**, and politically integrated under a headman, chief, or other political leader. The term tribe derives from the Latin *tribus*, which originally referred to one of the three putatively constituent patri-clans of ancient Rome, but later served as one of the designations of the ten confederations of biblical Israel.

In its modern usage, the term typically carries connotations of primitiveness (see **primitive society**). As Morton Fried points out in *The Notion of the Tribe* (1975), it enjoyed widespread favor among nineteenth-century theorists of social evolution as the designation of the earliest (and crudest) modality of collective human organization (see **evolutionary theory**). The term survived even among nonevolutionists well into the latter half of the twentieth century as a ready label for the stateless society, especially but not exclusively one of a bellicose temper. As Fried and other critics note, however, stateless societies are not structurally homogeneous. Moreover, they tend to lack in their great majority at least one of the features that the proper tribe should have. Fried himself argues that such **groups** are as a rule a derivative or secondary phenomenon that emerges "largely as a reaction to the presence of one or more states" (1975: 103). Anthropologists at present are more likely to deem what Fried thus refers to as a "secondary tribe" a politically mobilized ethnic group.

JAMES D. FAUBION

Troeltsch, Ernst (1865–1923)

A German theologian, Troeltsch developed a typology of religious thought that, while often conflated with **Max Weber**'s church–sect **ideal types**, did not have his methodological or theoretical purposes. In his two-volume treatise, *The Social Teaching of the Christian Churches* (1912 [trans. 1931]), Troeltsch identified three different and complementary ways in which Christian thought has developed over time: (1) church, a grace-endowed **institution** that is able to adjust to the world; (2) sect (see **church–sect typology**), a **voluntary association** of believers who live apart from the world and emphasize law instead of grace; and (3) mysticism, the personal, inward, and emotional experience of doctrinal ideas. Each is associated with a particular religious understanding or imagination: the church with "Christ the Redeemer" whose salvation benefits all through the church and the sacraments; the sect with "Christ the Lord," the lawgiver who will reward the elect, after their worldly pilgrimage, with the Kingdom of God; and the Christ of mysticism is the Divine, the spark that produces an inward spiritual feeling. Troeltsch argued that, from an organizational perspective, the church-type is superior because of its historical continuity and its practical adaptive and accommodative abilities to adjust to the world. His understanding of sect (quite similar to Weber's with the exception that Troeltsch tended to see sects as being comparatively small in size) has been influential among sociologists studying apocalyptic **cults** and **new religious movements** (for example B. Wilson, *Magic and the Millennium*, 1973), while his recognition of mysticism anticipated the increased attention to individualized, inner-directed religious or spiritual sensibilities associated with the cultural changes of the post-1960s era. Irrespective of type, Troeltsch argued that the Christian ethos, despite the many problems its expression encounters in **modernity**, is indispensable to creating the "charity" or "active helpfulness" that no social order can dispense with entirely.   MICHELE DILLON

trust

The concern with trust as an important phenomenon for sociology – as distinct from the earlier focus of political philosophy and psychology – emerged during the last two decades of the twentieth century. In *Trust and Power* (1979), **Niklas Luhmann** related trust to the growing complexity, uncertainty, and **risk** characterizing contemporary society. He claimed that trust is not an obsolete resource typical of traditional society, but rather it gains in importance with the development of **modernity**. In *The Logic and Limits of Trust*

(1983), Bernard Barber reviewed the manifestations of trust in various institutional and professional settings and introduced the insightful category of "fiduciary trust." In *Patrons, Clients, and Friends* (1984), **Shmuel Eisenstadt** and Louis Roniger identified trust as a core ingredient in the patron–client relations, as they appear in various guises from antiquity to modernity. In *Trust: Making and Breaking Cooperative Relations* (1988), Diego Gambetta brought together a number of authors who considered trust and distrust from various perspectives, and later in *The Sicilian Mafia* (1993) himself analyzed trust in closed, exclusive **communities**, such as the Mafia. In *Foundations of Social Theory* (1990), **James S. Coleman** provided the analysis of trust as a purely rational transaction, within the framework of **rational choice theory**. In the 1990s this avenue was pursued in a number of contributions by Russell Hardin (for example "Trusting Persons, Trusting Institutions," in R. Zeckheuser [ed.], *Strategy and Choice*, 1991, and "The Street-Level Epistemology of Trust," in *Politics and Society*, 1993). From a macro-sociological perspective, **Anthony Giddens** approached trust in *The Consequences of Modernity* (1990) as a characteristic feature of late modernity, elaborating on Luhmannian themes of complexity, uncertainty, and risk. In *Trust: Social Virtues and the Creation of Prosperity* (1995), Francis Fukuyama provided a comprehensive exposition of trust as the indispensable ingredient of viable economic systems, basing his argument on the experience of China, Japan, and other South East Asian societies. In *The Problem of Trust* (1997), Adam Seligman presented an interpretation of trust as a specifically modern phenomenon linked with the division of **labor**, **differentiation**, and pluralization of roles and the consequent indeterminacy and negotiability of role expectations. In *Trust: A Sociological Theory* (1999), Piotr Sztompka proposed a synthetic treatment of trust as a cultural resource necessary for the viable functioning of society, illustrating his argument with the vicissitudes of trust in post-communist societies of eastern Europe. In *Moral Foundations of Trust* (2003), Eric Uslaner related trust to the basic moral impulse arising in the process of **socialization.**

The importance of trust derives from some fundamental qualities of human action. In interacting with others, we must constantly form expectations about their future actions. Most often, we lack the possibility of a precise and accurate prediction or an efficient control. Facing other people, we remain in the condition of uncertainty, bafflement, and surprise. And yet, most often, we cannot refrain from acting in order to satisfy our needs, and to realize our goals. Then we have to face risks that others will turn against us.

Trusting becomes the crucial strategy to deal with an uncertain, unpredictable, and uncontrollable future. Trust consists of two main components: beliefs and commitment. When they place trust in others, people behave "as if" they know how the others will act. But trust is more than just contemplative anticipation. People must also face the future actively, by committing themselves to action with at least partly uncertain and unpredictable consequences. Thus people gamble, and make bets about the future actions and reactions of partners. As Piotr Sztompka defines it (1999), "trust is a bet about the future contingent actions of others."

We vest trust in various objects. First, there is trust in the members of our **family**, characterized by the strongest **intimacy** and closeness. Then comes the trust towards people we know personally, whom we recognize by name, and with whom we interact in face-to-face manner (our friends, neighbors, coworkers, and business partners). Here trust still involves a considerable degree of intimacy and closeness. The wider circle embraces other members of our **community**, known at most indirectly, by sight, and directly only through some individual representatives (inhabitants of our village, employees of our **firm**, professors at our university, or members of our **political party**). The widest circle includes large categories of people, with whom we believe we have something in common, but these are mostly absent others, not directly encountered, and constructed as a real collectivity only in our imagination ("imagined communities" of our compatriots, members of our ethnic **group**, our church, our **race**, our **gender**, our age cohort, our **generation**, and our profession). Here trust in concrete persons shades off imperceptibly into trust in more abstract social categories.

The next target of trust is found in **social roles**. Independent of the concrete incumbents, some roles evoke prima facie trust. Mother, friend, medical doctor, university professor, priest, judge, or notary public – these are just some examples of the trusted personal roles, or offices, endowed with public trust.

In even more abstract cases, trust is directed at **institutions** and **organizations**. The school, the university, the army, the church, the courts, the police, the banks, the stock-exchange, or the parliament, are typical targets for this type of trust. A particular variety of trust in institutions may be called procedural trust. It is trust vested in institutionalized practices or procedures. A particularly good example is trust in science as the best method for reaching the truth, or trust in democratic procedures (elections, representation, and majority vote) as the best ways to reach reasonable compromise among conflicting political interests.

The next important category of objects endowed with trust are technological systems (expert systems, or abstract systems), as described by Giddens in *Consequences of Modernity* (1990). In modern society people live surrounded by them: telecommunications, water and power systems, transportation systems, air-traffic control systems, military command **networks**, computer networks, and financial **markets**. The principles and mechanisms of their operation are opaque and cryptic for the average user. People usually take them for granted and do not even notice their pervasive presence. And everybody has learned to rely on them, to such an extent that their failure is perceived as a major crisis.

Finally, the most abstract objects of trust are the overall qualities of the social system, social order, or the regime. Trust in them engenders feelings of existential security, continuity, and stability.

The various types of trust reviewed above operate according to the same logic. Most importantly, behind all of them there looms the primordial form of trust – in people, and their actions. Appearances notwithstanding, all of the above objects of trust, even the most abstract, are reducible to human actions. We ultimately trust human actions, and only derivatively their aggregates, effects, or products.

Trusting expectations can be arranged along a sort of scale: from the least demanding to the most demanding, and, respectively, from the weakest, least risky bets, to the strongest, most risky bets of trust. First, we may expect only some instrumental qualities of actions taken by others: (1) regularity (orderliness, consistency, coherence, continuity, and persistence); (2) reasonableness (giving grounds, good justification for actions, and accepting arguments); and (3) efficiency (competence, consistency, discipline, proper performance, and effectiveness).

The second category of expectations is more demanding. We may expect some moral qualities of actions performed by others: (1) we expect them to be morally responsible (that is engaging in principled, honest, honorable conduct, following some moral rules, and showing integrity); (2) we expect them to be kind, gentle towards ourselves, and to treat us in a humane fashion; (3) we expect them to be truthful, authentic, and straightforward; and (4) we expect others to be fair and just (applying universalistic criteria, equal standards, due process, and meritocratic justice). Generally speaking, betting on the moral virtues of others is more risky than believing merely in their basic **rationality**.

We may also place the strongest bets on and expect from others what Bernard Barber (1983) called the "fiduciary" conduct, which can be defined as "duties in certain situations to place others' interests before our own." This category is exemplified by: (1) disinterestedness (that is, acting without consideration of one's own interests or even against such interests); (2) representative actions (acting on behalf of others, displaying concern for the welfare of others, or serving their interests, as depicted for example in *Life Chances* (1979) by **Ralph Dahrendorf**); and (3) benevolence and generosity (caring, helping, protecting, expressing sympathy, and being sensitive to the sufferings of others). This is the strongest, most risky bet, because the probability that most people will be disinterested is low, and that they will discharge representative duties and engage in altruistic help is even lower.

There are three grounds on which decisions to trust (to place the bets) may be based: reflected trustworthiness, personal trustfulness, and trust **culture**.

As far as trust is a relationship with others, granting trust is based on the estimate of their trustworthiness. Trust in this case may be considered as reflected trustworthiness of the partners: our perception of their reputation, performance, or appearance. The probability of well-placed trust increases with the amount and variety of true **information** about the trustee. Without such knowledge, trust is blind and the chances of a breach of trust are high.

Trust is not only a calculating relationship, it is also a psychological impulse. This point was developed by J. Q. Wilson in *The Moral Sense* (1993). Innate trustfulness may induce people to trust quite independently of any estimate of trustworthiness. This has nothing to do with knowledge about the partners of future engagements. Rather the impulse derives from the past history of diverse relationships pervaded with trust, primarily in the family and later in other **groups**, associations, or **organizations**.

People may also be encouraged to trust by the surrounding cultural rules. Normative rules may encourage trusting, and define it as proper. If the rules demanding trust are shared by a community, and perceived as given and external by each member, then they exert strong constraining pressure on actual acts of granting trust. They may significantly modify the rational estimates of trustworthiness, as well as inherent trusting impulses.

Trust culture is a system of such rules – that is, the **norms** and **values**, regulating the granting of trust as well as its reciprocation. There are normative obligations to trust and there are normative obligations to be trustworthy, credible, and reliable. One locus of both types of obligations is found in **social roles**. There are social roles which refer to trusters and include a normative imperative to trust others. This is true of the helping professions: the doctor of medicine, the defense counsel, the social worker, or the priest. There are other social roles which refer to trustees and place strong emphasis on trustworthiness (the demand for meeting trust, that is acting reliably, morally, and caringly). For example, university professors are expected to be truthful and responsible for their words, judges to be fair and just in their verdicts, and football referees to be impartial. The more general rule of *noblesse oblige* demands that those who have attained high positions in a social hierarchy and thus enjoy high esteem behave in an exemplary fashion.

All those are role-specific rules of trust. But there are also more diffuse expectations to trust, which become pervasive in some societies at some periods of time. Fukuyama (1995) makes a distinction between "high-trust cultures," among which he includes several countries of the Far East, and "low-trust cultures," among which he includes some countries of the West. Robert Putnam in *Bowling Alone* (2000) and Richard Stivers in *The Culture of Cynicism* (1994) complain about the demise of the high-trust American culture of the nineteenth century, and the emergence of the "culture of cynicism" in our time.

There are also culturally diffuse rules demanding and enforcing general trustworthiness. Mediaeval guilds, **firms** with long **traditions**, famous corporations, gold and diamond dealers, elite newspapers and journals, established publishing houses, and so forth, put great emphasis on fulfilling obligations to, and meeting the trust of, their clients. The pride of the profession, or the honor of the firm become general normative guidelines embracing various sorts of activities.

Once a trust culture emerges and becomes strongly rooted in the normative system of a society, it becomes a powerful factor influencing decisions to trust, as well as the decisions to reciprocate trust. It may become a strong stabilizing force guaranteeing persistence and continuity of trust.

PIOTR SZTOMPKA

typification

– see **life-world**.

U

underclass
– see **social class**.

underdevelopment
– see **development theory**.

understanding
– see **Verstehen**.

unemployment

A major topic of social research during periods of mass unemployment in the twentieth century, unemployment arose with the growth of dependency on waged employment. It involves exclusion from paid employment but definitions and **measurement** remain contentious. The International Labour Organization definition, widely adopted for comparative studies of countries and over time, includes people currently available for **work** who actively looked for work during the previous month. This excludes the discouraged unemployed, those not currently seeking work but who might take a job if offered. However, it includes some excluded from official counts because of ineligibility for state benefits, as eligibility is usually more restricted (and shifts with policy changes).

Sociologists often focus on the experience and consequences of unemployment, leaving economists to analyze causes. Economists distinguish between frictional unemployment, involving individual mobility of workers between jobs; structural unemployment, resulting from the decline of particular sectors or **occupations**; and cyclical unemployment, resulting from general but temporary falls in economic activity. However, consideration of the underlying processes that generate these patterns of unemployment exposes continuing controversy among economists, for example between neoliberal, neo-Keynesian, and neo-Marxist analyses of the **political economy** of contemporary **capitalism**. Thus, economic sociologists have to adjudicate between these different causal accounts, which involve implicit or explicit claims about the institutional arrangements and social class relations that help to generate different patterns and levels of unemployment in different societies and phases of capitalist development.

Early sociological accounts of the experiences and responses of the unemployed portrayed a progression from optimistic job search to pessimism, then fatalistic adaptation as unemployment lengthened. More recently the unemployed have been seen as a distinct underclass, with two contrasting versions of this diagnosis. The radical version suggests many unemployed people experience structural exclusion from secure employment, compounded by ethnic or cultural exclusion. This generates distinctive **subcultures,** alienated from mainstream society, promoting radical political dissent. The conservative variant regards much unemployment as a lifestyle choice of work avoidance, fostered by generous welfare benefits and culturally reproduced across **generations**. They argue the **state** should cut benefits and enforce "welfare-to-work" programs. However, all these approaches embrace stereotypes that have been challenged in modern research, such as that reported in D. Gallie and colleagues in *Social Change and the Experience of Unemployment* (1994).

The less skilled and poorly paid remain disproportionately vulnerable to unemployment, which usually involves further impoverishment. However, some people experience only a short period of unemployment, some face alternating periods of unemployment and insecure employment, and others suffer prolonged unemployment. Different categories of workers (by **age**, skills, **gender**, **ethnicity**, and locality) typically face different vulnerabilities and pathways through unemployment. Different household arrangements, social **networks**, and community circumstances also involve different forms of social support or susceptibility to stigmatization. Meanwhile these patterns of experience shift as the aggregate level of unemployment grows or shrinks.

Growing unemployment is less likely to involve social or cultural polarization than a shifting differentiation of labor market experiences, coupled with a wider permeation of a sense of insecurity. Thus, changing vulnerabilities to insecurity and unemployment generate overlapping patterns of experience, not a clear dividing line between employed and unemployed, challenging the adequacy of both underclass accounts. These accounts also overstate the cultural and ideological distinctiveness of the unemployed compared with the employed working class, as differences in political perspectives and work ethics are modest. The unemployed generally engage in active efforts to gain formal paid work, while informal work is poor and precarious but widely regarded as a legitimate survival strategy. Finally, limited political mobilization appears more the result of institutional obstacles than distinctive attitudes.   TONY ELGER

unionateness
– see **trade union**.

unobtrusive measures
A generic term for **methodologies** which do not disturb or disrupt subjects who are being studied, this includes the study of physical traces, archives, documents, images, and observation. Some disciplines have been closely associated with unobtrusive measures: anthropologists have employed observation, archaeologists have examined physical objects, and historians have used archives to examine **culture**. Nonetheless, unobtrusive methods have been a core method of sociological investigation; **Émile Durkheim**'s *Suicide* (1897 [trans. 1951]) is one of the more celebrated examples of a sociological analysis based on statistical archives.

Unobtrusive methods are valued because they do not require the co-operation of subjects, they can easily be repeated, they are relatively cheap to conduct, and, most importantly, can often assess actual rather than reported behavior thereby potentially improving the validity of any findings. The methods may, however, be limited by selective recording, distortions in the original documentary evidence and, crucially, ethical concerns relating to privacy, consent, and deliberate deception.

The examination and measurement of physical objects and remains can be used as an indication of human activity and cultural preferences. For example, the physical condition of a library book may be an indication of its level of popularity. Similarly, examination of the contents of a kitchen bin can indicate the types of food that a family consumes. Documentary analysis, as described in Lindsay Prior's *Using Documents in Social Research* (2003), incorporates the examination of public records, letters (personal and official), media such as newspapers, or other written works such as personal diaries. Observation is a key method of data collection within **ethnography**, but in this tradition the ethnographer generally participates in the daily life of those being studied, or is, at minimum, an added element of intrusion in the setting, if only as an observer. In contrast unobtrusive observation requires the researcher to watch and listen as a detached on-looker, perhaps with the aid of hidden cameras or videos. Covert observation, with its implications of lack of consent from those being studied, undoubtedly raises ethical concerns and can result in emotional turmoil or anxiety if subjects later discover that they have been observed.

Observational methods are particularly useful if there are methodological difficulties involved in either reliance on self-reporting or direct observation, particularly if intimate or illegal behavior is involved. For example, unobtrusive methods have been used to compare different strategies of condom provision in motels used by commercial sex workers. Condom use was assessed by fieldworkers, disguised as cleaners, searching the rooms for used condoms after the clients had left. Another unobtrusive method is the mark-recapture (or contact-recontact) method used to estimate the prevalence of hard-to-reach populations such as drug users, as an alternative to **censuses** or **surveys**. The technique capitalizes on the opportunities which individuals have to seek contact with various service providers (drug agencies, needle exchange schemes, and probation services) in order to model the dependency relationships between multiple contacts and thereby estimate the number of individuals not in contact with any service provider (the hidden population).

MICK BLOOR AND FIONA WOOD

urban ecology
An approach to the study of **cities**, **social change**, and urban life, these theories were introduced into sociology by the **Chicago School** to explain the competition between social **groups** for scarce resources such as land. The competition between groups was assumed to increase efficiency and promote a greater division of **labor**. These competitive struggles meant that distinctive social groups had adapted to their local environment, just as the competition between plants and their adaptation to the local environment in the natural world resulted in specialization. The balance

between competition and co-operation functions to allocate members of a population to urban niches. The city, like the **economy**, was seen to produce a social equilibrium.

This competitive process was also described in terms of the concentric zone theory in which the central zone of the city is occupied by banks and the service sector, while the zone of transition emerges as the central business district expands outwards. **Social classes** are distributed through various zones according to rental **values**, house prices, and the accessibility of **work**. The manual workers live in the third zone and the fourth zone houses the middle class. The fringe of the city is a commuter belt. This theory helps us to understand how migrants move into run-down areas of the city where rental costs are low and, as a result of **social mobility**, they can move eventually to better-quality housing as they join the middle class.

The urban ecology school embraced a number of prominent American sociologists, including **Robert Ezra Park**, **Ernest W. Burgess**, and Roderick D. McKenzie who published *The City* (1925). It is not clear that there is a systematic theory of the urban ecology; there appears to be rather a collection of assumptions about how cities develop over time.

Another member of the Chicago School, **Louis Wirth**, following the approach of **Georg Simmel**, wrote his famous "Urbanism as a Way of Life" (1938, *American Journal of Sociology*) in which he described the **anomie** and anonymity of city life.

Urban ecology has been criticized because its assumptions are too simple to explain the variations between cities, but its basic notions (about the central business district, transition zones, and the urban distribution of social classes) continue to influence the work of modern sociology.

BRYAN S. TURNER

urban entrepreneurialism

– see **urban managerialism**.

urban managerialism

In the 1960s, discussions of differential access to housing provision highlighted the decisionmaking role of urban managers (for example, housing managers or local government officers in the public sector and property developers or bank managers in the private sector) in influencing the **life chances** of city dwellers. This led Ray Pahl in *Whose City?* (1975) to formulate the strong thesis of urban managerialism, namely that such managers represented independent variables influencing resource allocation and class location in urban **societies**. In particular, Pahl developed the neo-Weberian argument that the bureaucratic procedures and professional **ideologies** of local state managers crosscut market relations in the constitution of patterns of urban **inequality**. This laid the basis for a liberal critique of the bureaucratic structuring of forms of local nonmarket provision, including their potential to dehumanize the urban poor.

The strong urban managerialism thesis stimulated valuable research but came under powerful criticism for its apparent claim that these managers were autonomous agents who were prime movers in the allocation of urban resources. Critics emphasized the central importance of both the national **state** and private capital in determining the policy priorities and resources with which local state managers operate. These criticisms led Pahl to reformulate his position: state managers operate within variable constellations of constraints, but still remain important mediators of some aspects of urban resource allocation. This weak version of the thesis was readily assimilated to a variety of pluralist, institutionalist, and Marxist approaches, but sympathetic critics such as Peter Saunders, in *Social Theory and the Urban Question* (1986), argued that it also risked becoming vacuous.

National and local state policies changed dramatically during the 1980s, as the **politics** of public service and collective consumption were overtaken by fiscal conservatism and privatization. In particular, urban managers gave increasing priority to the attraction of private investment, both to counteract deindustrialization and to pursue urban renewal. This led one of Pahl's neo-Marxist protagonists, David Harvey, in "From Managerialism to Entrepreneurialism: The Transformation of Urban Governance in Late Capitalism" (1989, *Geografiska Annaler*), to argue that city managers were increasingly involved in new public–private policy coalitions where the role of private capital was pivotal. Such managers formulated new entrepreneurial (see entrepreneurship) policy agendas that subordinated welfare priorities to the private regeneration and utilization of major urban spaces. This newer thesis retains significant features of Pahl's original argument: it recognizes that urban managers play an important role in the allocation of public resources, which in turn has important implications for social inequalities. However, the urban entrepreneurialism thesis suggests that such resources are currently committed in ways that are primarily responsive to the needs of private capital and usually reinforce, rather than mitigate, market inequalities.

At the same time, Harvey locates these developments within a broader analysis of capital accumulation, and also highlights their contradictory and potentially contested character. Thus, the urban entrepreneurialism thesis is compatible with the weak version of Pahl's argument, especially in suggesting that such policy priorities and coalitions may shift across time and space, but it is integrated into a more fully developed and more critical **political economy** of urban restructuring.

TONY ELGER

urban social movements
– see **social movements**.

urban way of life
– see **Louis Wirth**.

urbanization

While often defined as the increasing proportion of people living in **cities**, urbanization is best defined as the process by which cities – described as, following **Louis Wirth** in "Urbanism as a Way of Life" (1938, *American Journal of Sociology*), relatively heterogeneous, dense, and sizable settlements – emerge as concentrated control and command centers. As such, it is appropriate to talk about urbanization of **labor** as well as of different forms of capital – economic, social, cultural, or symbolic (for example, in David Harvey, *The Urbanization of Capital*, 1985). When understood as a process, the typical quantitative numbers given to indicate levels of urbanization, such as the proportion of those who live in cities, appear less defining than a measure that tells us about the concentration of different forms of capital and of labor. While we know that, sometime soon in the twenty-first century, for the first time, the majority of the world's population will live in cities, the importance of cities in **economy**, **society**, and **culture** well predates this particular benchmark. It can be argued that, since their emergence around about 7,000 to 9,000 years ago, cities have been at the center-stage of economy, society, and culture. If we understand the birth, enlargement, and multiplication of cities as the process of urbanization through which different forms of capital were concentrated, the oft-cited benchmarks such as 1851 in England, when the majority of the population became urban, must be seen against this longer historical background.

As well, what the measure of urbanization – understood as a proportion of population living in cities – cannot capture is the size and distribution of cities constituting this process. In the twentieth century, urbanization mostly took the form of megacities, defined as cities with populations of more than 10 million inhabitants, with a disproportionate number of people living in them compared to mid-size and large cities. In 2000, Tokyo (26 million), Mexico City (18.4 million), Bombay (18 million), São Paulo (17.8 million), New York (16.6 million), Lagos (13.4 million), Los Angeles (13.1 million), Calcutta (12.9 million), Shanghai (12.9 million), and Buenos Aires (12.6 million) dominated their respective **states**. This overconcentration of different forms of capital and of labor in megacities as the predominant form of urbanization raises questions about the long-term sustainability and the ecological footprint of human habitation of the world.

ENGIN ISIN

utilitarianism

This refers to a tradition in ethical theory that links rightness to happiness.

The theory was classically formulated by Jeremy Bentham (1748–1832), who argued that acts are right if they promote happiness or pleasure, and wrong if they lead to misery and pain. Bentham developed a felicity calculus so that pleasures and pains could be assessed according to their intensity, duration, and proximity. Bentham also argued that desirable policies were those that produced the greatest happiness for the greatest number.

John Stuart Mill sought to modify Bentham's theory by making a distinction between different kinds of pleasure and arguing that individuals who had experienced both higher as well as lower pleasures would always choose the former over the latter. Mill sought to link utilitarianism to development, so that individuals could change their preferences as they changed their experiences.

Two criticisms are invariably made of utilitarianism. The first is that, by basing goodness upon happiness, utilitarians reject the idea that ethics has to be based upon innate or natural rights. Critics worry that, without a conception of natural rights, Bentham's formula of the greatest happiness of the greatest number would lead to the oppression of the minority by the majority. The answer to this problem requires not the notion of god-given or natural (in the sense of timeless) rights, but a view of the individual that stresses the formation of **identity** (and thus the pursuit of pleasures) through relationships with others. This would enable rightness to be judged by the happiness of individuals as they relate to one another, so that an action can be deemed to contribute to happiness only if the act of one person increases rather than diminishes the happiness of another.

Happiness can be conceived as a right, but a right that varies according to time and place. To argue, for example, that a person has a right to good health when they are suffering from cancer ignores circumstance. Individuals have a right to whatever their society (and humanity in general) can provide to alleviate pain and suffering. Happiness cannot, in other words, ignore the constraints of time and place. Happiness, as Mill suspected, needs to be tied to development, so that what enables a person to be happy is what enables them to develop. A person who seeks happiness through alcohol or tobacco can thus be deemed misguided since the pleasures of the moment soon become pain and discomfort.

The second criticism is that happiness is seen as something purely subjective. Mill had already begun to tackle this problem, and it could be argued that a happiness that is developmental is both subjective and objective. If it were simply subjective, then happiness could be an activity that is harmful either to others or to individuals themselves. If it were purely objective, then the happiness of individuals could arise from the paternalistic insistence that insists that an individual is really experiencing pleasure when they are in pain.

JOHN HOFFMAN

utopia

– see **utopianism**.

utopianism

Utopia is a coinage by Sir Thomas More (1478–1535), in his book *Utopia* (1516), which first named and mapped out this imaginary territory. More fused two Greek words, *outopos* (nowhere) and *eutopia* (somewhere good), to make utopia, the good place that is nowhere. Not that utopia is synonymous with the fantastic or mere wishful thinking; there are other forms – Cockaygne, Schlaraffenland, the Poor Man's Heaven – that fulfill this need, just as there are golden ages and paradises galore in the literature and folktales of most societies. While these share with utopia the idea of a social order where all are free, happy, and satisfied, utopia has always been a soberer and more restrained form, with at least one foot in reality. What the story of a utopia generally tells is a story of travelers – whether in time or space – who happen upon or are transported to a totally different world where all the social, moral, and political problems of their time have been solved, and the people live a life of contentment and felicity. While the solutions adopted are usually not within the realm of the practical **politics** of the time, they are not so remote from the ideas and practices of the time as to be impossible of realization, though perhaps only at some distant date. Good examples of this would be two utopian versions of **socialism**, Edward Bellamy's *Looking Backward* (1888) and William Morris's *News from Nowhere* (1890).

Utopias are, by definition, fictions, and so their usual form, following More, has been something like the novel, though they also sometimes borrow from the dialog form of works of Plato (428–348 BC) (while the *Republic* is not a true utopia, it has certainly had an enormous influence on utopian thought). The same is true of the dystopia or anti-utopia, the analogous form that arose – as in Jonathan Swift's *Gulliver's Travels* (1726) or George Orwell's *Nineteen Eighty-Four* (1949) – to mock or attack the utopia on the grounds of its dangerous presumption and totalitarian propensities. But there has also been a genre of speculation that we can call utopian **social theory**. These are not utopias proper, that is they are not fictional accounts of ideal societies, rather they are accounts that assume that humanity is in some sense perfectible and they devise schemes for the perfection of humanity. In such a category we might include the theories of Jean-Jacques Rousseau (1712–78), **Claude Henri de Rowney, comte de Saint-Simon**, François Fournier (1772–1837), Robert Owen (1771–1858), and **Karl Marx**.

Utopianism generally has the function of criticizing existing society and proposing a radical alternative to it. In this endeavor utopian social theory can often offer a highly sophisticated analysis of the present predicament, but its solutions tend also to be very abstract and therefore less persuasive. The utopia proper, forced as it is by its form to give a more detailed portrait of the good society, is more likely to produce the necessary element of desire for change. It has often been said that Morris's glowing description of the new society in *News from Nowhere* did more to convert people to socialism than any of the works of Marx.

KRISHAN KUMAR

V

validity

– see **sampling**.

value freedom

A potentially misleading translation of the German expression *Wertfreiheit*, which conveys a statement's negative property, its not being derived from or affected by a value judgment, value freedom is perhaps the most misunderstood concept in sociological **methodology**. One reason for the confusion is that the term originated in an argument by **Max Weber** that is as subtle as it is disorganized. A second reason has to do with the fact that, besides its literal meaning, indicated above, in methodological parlance value freedom has also come to imply the proposition that empirical facts have a reality that is independent of any value-laden theory we employ. Thus, value freedom has not one but two antitheses. The first antithesis to value freedom is value judgment, a moral evaluation of a social phenomenon as good or evil, just or unjust, and so forth. The second antithesis to value freedom is methodological relativism, a doctrine which holds that facts are valid only given certain value-laden theoretical assumptions. In other words, methodological relativism maintains that facts have no value-free reality. These two antitheses complement one another in the following way: if facts depend upon value-laden theories, then any value judgments at issue in those theories cannot be refuted by empirical evidence. The principle of value freedom maintains that theories *can* be refuted by independent evidence. Social scientific theories are not in the business of making or defending value judgments. But **values** are still relevant to how theories are formed.

In his essay, "'Objectivity' in Social Science and Social Policy," in *The Methodology of the Social Sciences* (1904 [trans. 1949]), Weber sought to give value-free facts their due without denying that **social science** is always inspired by value-relevant interests. But one need not master or accept Weber's methodology at large to grasp the gist of his solution to the problem of value freedom. The following remarks summarize the principle of value freedom in generic terms, directing readers to Weber's essay for his specific approach. Return momentarily to the two antitheses of value freedom. What can go wrong if we give facts their autonomy in the absence of any value-relevant interests in the findings? To ignore values entirely can result in what **C. Wright Mills** terms abstracted **empiricism**, that is, trivial facts. For example, demographers studying mortality rates, which certainly can be a morally relevant issue, may get bogged down in disputes over fine details of statistical technique. Ultimately, arguments about technique can grow so dense that we lose sight of the moral relevance of human mortality. But what can go wrong if we give values their due without acknowledging that facts have an independent capacity to refute value-laden theories? As **Karl Popper** warned, the result can be ideological or dogmatic belief that loses touch with reality. Consider as an example the claims by a few historians that the Holocaust never occurred. In their moral judgment the Nazi regime was innocent of **crimes** against humanity. How then do they deal with the multitude of written records, photographs, and survivor reports that document the Holocaust? They challenge the validity of the evidence, accusing enemies of the Nazi regime of manufacturing some facts and tendentiously misinterpreting others because they hold an anti-Nazi point of view. Ultimately, they will admit no facts except those that support their value-laden theories. Their value judgments and the facts they will accept become a closed circle.

So, if pure empiricism uninfluenced by values can end in trivial pursuits and if unwillingness to face the facts can lead to closed-minded circular reasoning, how can we preserve both the moral relevance of social science and the openness of social science to independent facts? One of Weber's main points is of vital importance in preserving a role for values without getting carried away by dogma or **ideology**. The point to recognize is that social scientists become interested in a given problem or question on the basis of their own values. Of course, if they happen to share these values with others, then their value-relevant interests in the subject to be studied become all the more important. Notice, investigators make no hard and fast value judgment here. After they have raised a value-relevant issue, then they must follow the facts wherever they lead. To be scientific, after all, is to entertain all evidence, including evidence that Weber terms "inconvenient" to the values or ideologies we hold dear.

Frequently, the facts will turn up morally ambiguous results. Imagine that my humanitarian values judge **public policies** as good or bad depending on whether they help or hurt children in need. Therefore my values motivate my value-relevant interest in a study of policies towards children in western **welfare states**. I now collect a wide range of empirical evidence. But the **data** are morally ambiguous. On the one hand, I find empirical evidence that state subsidies secure **food**, shelter and health care for needy **children**. On the other hand I find little empirical evidence that **states** offer social support for caregivers to help nurture these children. Now I must reframe the issue in an empirically more complicated way: why do welfare states extend material aid to poor children but not social aid to their caregivers? Any empirical answer inevitably will be too complex to permit a pure judgment that state policies are good or bad based upon my original values.

The principle of value freedom stands on two assumptions, one psychological and the other philosophical. Psychologically, it assumes that moral values are central to human interest in any given issue (whether sociological or not). Philosophically, it assumes that, with very few exceptions (for example the perpetrators of the Holocaust), the empirical reality of the social world is morally too ambiguous for value judgments to be found valid on empirical grounds. Though Weber championed value freedom methodologically, Isaiah Berlin's accounts of value **pluralism** and **Karl Popper's** accounts of falsificationism offer two means (among others) to reformulate the philosophical foundations of value freedom in keeping with more recent discussions in social thought and social scientific methodology.   IRA COHEN

value neutrality
– see **value freedom**.

value relevance
– see **value freedom**.

value spheres
– see **values**.

values
Values refer to moral principles or other judgments of worth. The term is used by sociologists in a number of different ways. First, they are discussed at an epistemological and methodological level as in **Max Weber's** notion of value-relevance. Second, there is the further issue of **morality** and the good life, which is linked to debates over value-neutrality. Third, sociology is concerned to identify and analyze the values held by people in particular epochs, nations, **societies**, **subcultures**, or spheres of life. Values are regarded as deep or intense commitments embedded in taken-for-granted dispositions and can be contrasted with **attitudes**, which are thought of as more superficial and weakly held views and opinions.

Two themes can be distinguished here, one of socially differentiated value spheres and the other of degrees of homogeneity or plurality, either in general or within the spheres of life. Regarding the first, Weber noted the tendency of **modernity** to fragment social relations into different spheres of value – economics, **politics**, and science being the decisive orders within modernity, while the aesthetic, the ethical, the erotic, and the intellectual were increasingly restricted to the realms of the personal and the consolatory. Each of these spheres was subject to the processes of **rationalization** whereby beliefs and actions are slowly dominated by the need to achieve defined ends or goals by the most efficient means possible (*zweckrationalität*). **Jürgen Habermas** has extended Weber's insights, most intensively in the *Theory of Communicative Action* (1981 [trans. 1984]), by arguing that the instrumental form of rationalization, most appropriate to the value spheres of science and **technology**, has indeed made radical inroads into virtually all value spheres. This is most distorting in spheres where moral–practical and aesthetic–expressive interests and forms of reasoning should be significant. These stretch from art and literature through **education** and morality to law and politics. Distortion has meant that the liberating potential of reason within modernity has been impoverished and unduly narrowed.

The second theme concerns questions regarding the extent to which the values held in various societal groupings and spheres are homogeneous or plural and perhaps conflictual. In *The Structure of Social Action* (1937) **Talcott Parsons** distinguished between general cultural values, **norms**, and internalized values. The first two are closely linked.

Norms are the general cultural expectations (values) of how people should act when they become specified more narrowly in relation to particular action situations. The socialization process, according to Parsons, then ensures that these external expectations are internalized as values so that they become components of a person's inner life, acting as a bridge between the social system and the personality system. Parsons, like **Émile Durkheim** before him, is often criticized for overestimating the extent to which values and norms are internalized in a homogeneous manner, and for underestimating both conflict and the significance of individuals' more pragmatic submission to systems of **power** (see Abercrombie *et al.*, *The Dominant Ideology Thesis*, 1980). At the other extreme from Parsons, **Zygmunt Bauman** has argued that we now live in a postmodern age of complete uncertainty about values, although Hans Joas in *The Genesis of Values* (2000) contests this, by drawing on Ronald Inglehart's evidence of the emergence of commonly held postmaterialist values and on **Robert Bellah**'s critique of cultural **individualism** in *Habits of the Heart* (1985), to argue that there is not a lack of value-certainty but the loss of a communal **language** to reflect upon and justify the values that many continue to hold in common. There is an affinity here with the so-called **globalization** of values associated with the diffusion of the values of **democracy**, the rule of law, and human **rights** across the world, but a tension with the parallel call for greater recognition of the diversity of **cultures** and cultural values.   ROB STONES

dependent/independent variables

Variables are typically those things that we measure in any science; anything that differs between cases. At the level of the individual, common sociological variables would be **social class** or **attitudes**. But often sociologists take measures at other levels of analysis, such as the **family, subculture**, or **state**.

The division of variables into *dependent* and *independent* borrows its terminology from experimental sciences, such as biology or laboratory-based psychology. The independent variable is the one that is manipulated by the experimenter (for instance, the amount of light falling on a plant, or the level of a drug administered to a rat). The dependent variable is the one that is measured as the outcome of the experiment (such as the growth of a plant or the time the rat takes to complete a maze). If different levels of the independent variable give rise to differences in the dependent variable, then a causal link between the two variables has been demonstrated.

Sociologists are rarely in a position to manipulate the independent variable experimentally. Sociologists more often rely on naturally occurring variations in the independent variable and investigate whether that is associated with variations in the dependent variable of interest. Thus the independent variable and the dependent variable are considered to be the cause and the effect respectively. The relationship between them is typically determined by calculation of a **correlation**, or multiple **regression** if the research is considering several independent variables simultaneously, as, for example, in **multivariate analysis**.

Often in sociological analyses the relationship between two variables is more complex than a simple unidirectional one. For instance, what is the relationship between mental health and downward **social mobility**? Do individuals with mental health problems drift down into **poverty** and disadvantage? Or does the stress of poverty and low **social status** bring about mental health problems? Both may be true, and therefore the distinction into dependent and independent variables is no longer useful.

Another class of variables is mediating or moderating variables that intervene between the independent and dependent variable. For instance, is the effect of parental divorce on children's well-being caused, in part, by the poverty often associated with single-parent families? By investigating the contribution of intervening variables, one can better understand the mechanisms of a relationship.

Variables are often classified depending upon their level of measurement; are they simple categorizations, can they order cases, or are they true measures of the intervals between cases?

BRENDAN J. BURCHELL

variance

– see **statistics**.

Veblen, Thorstein (1857–1929)

An American economist and sociologist, Veblen published a series of critical works on **industrial society**, notably *The Instinct of Workmanship and the Irksomeness of Labor* (1898), *The Higher Learning in America* (1918), *The Vested Interests and the Common Man* (1919), and *The Engineers and the Price System* (1921). Veblen taught at the University of Chicago (1892–1906), Stanford University (1906–7), the University of Missouri (1911–18), and the New School for Social Research, New York (1918–26). His work criticized **capitalism** and portrayed **society** as a conflict between an acquisitive and a technocratic instinct. He is chiefly remembered today for *The Theory of the Leisure Class* (1899). Veblen argued that American society was dominated by a parasitic, predatory **social class** composed of elements from high business and industry. Their dedication to conspicuous **consumption** was presented as weakening the fabric of American society by encouraging emulation among the lower orders. Later, in *The Theory of the Business Enterprise* (1904), Veblen pointedly contrasted the decadent, spendthrift **values** of the leisure class with the prudent, industrious values held by artisans and engineers. This generated the widespread misconception that Veblen favored technocratic revolution. In fact, the poorly appreciated cultural **semiotics** and theory of **power** in industrial **civilization** that he developed in his writings suggest that display and waste are intrinsic to business **prestige** and casualize the work ethic. His work is highly critical of the form of industrial civilization, and skeptical about redemptive alternatives.

Veblen's approach submitted that the correct methodological route for the analysis of economic and social questions is through an investigation of the causal role played by socioeconomic **institutions** and **organizations**. The social and economic policies attached to this **methodology** involved restraining the excesses of the leisure class and moderating predatory **culture**. The emphasis placed on social factors precipitated resistance from orthodox economists, and the argument in favor of more state control was criticized for being tantamount to **socialism** under another name. However, with the revival of interest in questions of consumer culture and **leisure** which followed the cultural turn, the prescience and richness of Veblen's work are increasingly being recognized.

CHRIS ROJEK

verification

– see **falsification**.

Verstehen

A term of art in **hermeneutics** made prominent in the nineteenth century by Wilhelm Dilthey and other German scholars associated with the *Geisteswissenschaften* (**human sciences**). **Max Weber** incorporated this aspect of hermeneutics into his sociological method, and the term then entered the sociological lexicon. In the methodology of the *Geisteswissenschaften*, *Verstehen*, literally meaning understanding, refers to the effort to grasp

the relevant meaningful, cognitive, emotional, spiritual, and motivational qualities of the minds of individuals at historically significant moments. The term implies a line of demarcation between natural and social studies. In Dilthey's famous phrase: "we explain nature; man we must understand" (*Gessamelte Schriften V*: 144).

Weber, though an exponent of *Verstehen*, staunchly denied that it constituted a technique. We become interested in some constellation of historical events by virtue of their relevance to our cultural **values**. This interest directs us to enquire about certain states of minds of actors at a given time. *Verstehen* is thus not an attempt to grasp psychological processes at large. Instead it is a means all cultural historians use, regardless of whether or not the historians are methodologically self-conscious.

Verstehen is more oriented to historical inquiry in a second sense as well. In order to grasp the relevant states of mind of actors, a historical investigator must be knowledgeable in the ways of life and cultural conventions for framing situations typically found in indigenous cultural settings. *Verstehen* is the art of using these frames to interpret significant historical events.

IRA COHEN

victimology

This term is thought to have been coined by the American psychiatrist, Frederick Wertham, in 1949, when he called for the systematic and scientific study of victims and their relationships with offenders. But it is Hans von Hentig's *The Criminal and His Victim* (1948) that is widely regarded as the critical text in developing victim studies. Von Hentig challenged existing thinking about the victim as a passive actor and proposed a thirteen-category typology of victims that identified certain individuals as victim-prone by virtue of distinctive social and psychological characteristics (**age**, sex, or mental illness, for example). This thinking was later refined by a theorist who produced a six-stage typology of victim culpability ranging from the "completely innocent" to the "most guilty victim."

Pursuing the line of victim precipitation in sexual offenses, Menachim Amir's *Patterns of Forcible Rape* (1971) provoked strong reaction because of the attribution of blame to victims. He thought it reasonable to expect the victim to have somehow avoided the incident. Certainly, well-known judges have occasionally been known to refer to culpable negligence on the part of the victims of sexual assault because they were wearing provocative clothing. But the concepts of victim precipitation and culpability assume a level of equality in the relationship between aggressor and victim (similar physical strength, for example).

Later work in this area has concentrated on the **lifestyle** of victims and these two concepts – victim precipitation and lifestyle – have formed the core of much victimological research and thinking since the late 1980s. Ezzat Fattah's *Understanding Criminal Victimisation* (1991) outlines a number of key propositions relating to victimization: available opportunities, risk factors, the presence of motivated offenders, exposure, high-risk activities, defensive/avoidance behavior, structural/cultural proneness, dangerous times/places, dangerous behaviors. This lifestyle-exposure approach has informed some of the major victimization **surveys**; some of these are international surveys, some are carried out on an annual basis. Such surveys regularly include questions relating to routine patterns of behavior such as drinking habits or use of public transport. One criticism here, however, is that this kind of victimization survey encourages a focus on street crime rather than crime within the home (child abuse and domestic **violence**, for example) or corporate **crime**.

In essence, we can identify three main strands within victimology. First, there is a positivistic strand, which focuses on the identification of factors that contribute to patterns of nonrandom victimization and on the identification of victims who may have contributed to their own victimization. Second, there is a radical strand, which places the analysis of sexual and violent crimes in the context of wider political, economic, and social victimization. These critical perspectives are broad and accommodate victimization by the police, the victims of the correctional or criminal justice system, the victims of state violence, and the victims of oppression more generally. Here there is recognition of structural powerlessness. Third, we may identify a critical victimology which includes critical analysis of the victims' movement and constitutes an attempt to examine the wider social context in which some versions of victimology have become more dominant than others.   LORAINE GELSTHORPE

violence

The core meaning of violence is the deliberate infliction of bodily violation or harm on one individual human being by another. The forms of violence include hitting, wounding, rape, torture, and, of course, killing. Thus violence is distinguished from non-physical forms of social **power**, such as coercion or force, **ideology**, or **social control**. Violence is the most extreme expression of power, containing the ultimate potential of total power, the physical destruction of one social actor by another. Violence may be a spontaneous expression of power relations, or a planned, instrumental maximization of power.

Because of endemic **inequalities** of power, violence is a general potentiality in social relations, even if in many types of relationship this remains latent for long periods. Thus, although issues of violence may arise in all social arenas, in practice sociology has been concerned with them in a limited number of cases. The sociology of the **family** has examined the prevalence of gendered domestic violence, particularly but not only by men against women. Otherwise violence has been seen mainly as an expression of collective **social conflict**. Studies of **industrial relations** have considered violence as a result of class conflict; those of race relations and **ethnicity** have discussed racial violence; political sociology has considered the role of violence in social and political transformation, especially in revolution. The sociology of **social movements** has examined the role of violence in protest actions, although some have seen movements as by definition non-violent (non-violence as a principle has been extensively discussed in **peace studies**). Many of the forms of violence in these contexts are relatively spontaneous, for example in **strikes** or ethnic riots.

Sociologists such as **Norbert Elias** have emphasized that, through the civilizing process, many potentials for violence are constrained by social **norms**. **Karl Marx** argued that in **capitalism** the "dull compulsion" of the wage relationship had replaced the direct violence of earlier modes of production. Yet he stressed the violent nature of the "primitive accumulation" process that had given rise to this new mode, and saw a continuing potential for class relations to rupture capitalist structures, through revolutionary movements that would trigger violent resistance from ruling classes. However, in developed capitalism, **Ralph Dahrendorf** argued, there has been an institutionalization of conflict, so that class conflict is not generally expressed in violent forms and does not lead to general **social change**.

Indeed, many have argued that there is extensive pacification in modern **industrial societies**. This has been specially connected to the modern **state**, which **Max Weber** defined by its "monopoly of legitimate violence." Although others have qualified this idea, it remains seminal. **Michel Foucault** argued that **modernity** leads to comprehensive "surveillance," although he saw in this the potential for **war** and **genocide** as states directed their expanded capacity to organize society towards destruction. In *The Nation-State and Violence* (1985), **Anthony Giddens** argued that more extensive surveillance leads to the reduction of levels of violence in society. Through the control of the nation-state, violence was "extruded" from national societies and increasingly expressed only in international relations between states, in the form of war.

Thus social violence has become concentrated in special forms of social conflict, which Weber distinguished as "bloody conflict." War, genocide, armed insurrection, and counter-revolution are organized violence, in which killing and other physical harm are used instrumentally to destroy an enemy's power (in war and revolution, typically that of another armed enemy; in genocide, of a civilian social **group**). Recognizing the centrality of such organized forms, **Michael Mann**, in *The Sources of Social Power* (1986), argued that violence belongs to a special type of social power, military power, which is to be distinguished from the political power of the state. Moreover, his *Dark Side of Democracy* (2005) showed that organized political violence such as "ethnic cleansing" and genocide is often practiced by parties, militias, and other armed groups, supported by wider social constituencies, as well as by states. Thus, despite the control of violence in modern societies, the escalation of political conflict may, under certain circumstances, produce large-scale, organized violence.

Others have been skeptical of the reduction of violence because they have defined violence in a broader way. Johann Galtung, in "Violence, Peace and Peace Research" (1969, *Journal of Peace Research*), introduced the concept of "structural violence," to refer to any constraint on human potential due to economic and political structures. Unequal access to resources, to political power, to **education**, to health care, or to legal standing are forms of structural violence. It is often pointed out that more people die as a result of **poverty**, derived from global economic and social **inequalities**, than die as a result of wars and genocides. In a similar way, some scholars talk of the "violence of representation," in which ideological social categories violate the self-ascribed **identities** of individuals and social groups.

However, from a conceptual point of view, these broader usages of violence raise difficulties. Are exploitation and ideological control violent by definition, or only when they produce physically harmful results? Is mental harm no different from physical harm? Is harm that results from the unintended consequences of actions, for example in the uncoordinated operations of **markets**, no different from harm that is intentionally produced? Sociologists concerned with the forms of deliberate physical harm have tended to maintain the strict meaning of "violence," and to use other concepts such as inequality to describe what is called "structural violence." MARTIN SHAW

virtual politics

As has been true of every successful new communication medium, the internet is being used to conduct affairs of concern, especially **politics**. Although originally noncommercial in its purpose and content, political discussion has from the internet's earliest days been a central concern of many of those who have participated online. E-mailings concerning political observations and **organizations** quickly migrated to bulletin boards and Usenet groups. In turn, these forms have become complemented by websites, e-mail and list serve programs, and web logs (blogs). These forms of virtual politics have become popular and successful, and are likely to continue their evolution.

It seems clear, as J. Katz and R. Rice, in *Social Consequences of Internet Use* (2002), demonstrate, that eventually politics will be heavily virtual in its nature. The power of the internet to generate many-to-many **information** exchanges and to organize supporters is enormous. However, **progress** may be slower and remain less influential than many early observers predicted because of the limits of electronic presence and the problem of spurious attacks from opponents. Many traditional forms of politics, such as nominating conventions and/or listening to political speeches, have not met with success. This lack of success is not apparently due to limited bandwidth alone, but rather stems from the way users like to interact. On the other hand, the internet has become a vital source of political news and for following election returns for large portions of the public. Political groupings of all persuasions have been quick to grasp the communication potential of the virtual world. Ironically, many continue to believe that better communication will improve understanding and reduce political conflict. It may be that the opposite is true: namely that virtual politics will allow marginal groups to thrive, and many positions, which are highly divisive and fractionating, will continue to flow.

While numerous voting schemes have been advanced – and indeed there are many elections conducted via the internet – it appears that there is no way, using currently foreseeable **technology**, that a system of voting could be both secure and anonymous. Hence, so long as a system of secret ballot is set as a paramount requirement, online voting cannot be used.   JAMES E. KATZ

virtual reality

This describes the impression of inhabiting dimensions created by electronic media rather than material, geographically copresent spaces, and devices designed to produce this effect. Though the phrase is sometimes used interchangeably with **cyberspace**, virtual reality or VR is more specifically used to denote human-scale rather than global environments. Such environments can be roughly divided between immersive and onscreen VR. In immersive VR, a user enters a dedicated space or wears dedicated hardware, in order to experience a three-dimensional computer-generated environment. The **technology** is used in specialist training programs, in artistic productions, in entertainment venues, and in physical therapy where it may permit multiple users in a shared virtual environment. Unlike cyberspace, however, these environments are not usually networked, and require the physical presence of the participant in the same space as the technology. Onscreen VR uses three-dimensional modeling software programs to generate social and spatial environments portrayed on normal computer monitors. Unlike immersive VR, onscreen VR can be networked. Applications include scientific, technological, and medical uses in the analysis of three-dimensional models of physical forms; artistic and entertainment applications appear in motion pictures and in most commercially successful computer games.

Although the technology involved has the glamor of unfamiliarity, VR does not offer social formations fundamentally different from those available in older media. Books can offer an individual user immersion in a fantastic or unfamiliar universe. Film and television offer audiovisual fictions, the former with a more immersive, the latter with a more distributed appeal. All three have been blamed at various times for negative social consequences, especially among the young. Some observers have suggested that online gaming in virtual environments is particularly pernicious because it is very often violent, frequently sexist, and encourages unrealistic

conceptions of causality and responsibility. Others note, however, the opportunities for user agency in VR, a change from linear narratives to interactive story structures that depend in part on the choices made by players, and in part on a typical geography of "levels," transitions marked by changes to the depicted environment and the level of skill required to navigate them. Such narratives, some observers note, are more spatial than temporal, requiring navigation rather than telling.

Both immersive and onscreen VRs are widely used in aspects of social science research, notably in geographic information systems, where the ability to navigate complex datasets in visual form is highly prized. Likewise, future studies and risk analysis deploy virtual reality **modeling** as a technique for visualizing trends and crises, and for swift syntheses of changing variables. In one instance at least, that of *Sim City*, software developed for urban planning has made the crossover into the commercial field to become a commercially successful computer game. In a reverse gesture, some sociologists use the same company's *The Sims* to teach family dynamics.

Despite early fears and early "boosterism," VR has so far failed to deliver cheap, widely accessible, and convincing alternative realities. Neither feared nor yearned-for assimilation into digital environments has yet occurred. Significant technological achievements have found applications in other fields – including genome mapping, neuroscience, and cinema special effects – as well as some significant cultural achievements. But those achievements are also metaphors for an alternate future that critics and prophets alike thought would already be present. The key legacy of virtual reality is thus the concept of an alternative present.   SEAN CUBITT

visual culture

This term refers to an eclectic range of topics, linked to an interest in seeing and its connection to what Martin Jay has called "scopic regimes." Interest in the visual grew during the 1990s within sociology as part of an attempt to move beyond a focus on the linguistic features of ordering. The new concern with the visual exceeds a focus on **arts** and artifacts. Though taking inspiration from art theory and especially feminist art theory (such as Griselda Pollock's work), the concept of visual **culture** in **sociology** encompasses the visual in the gamut of social experience, from **fashion**, to science, to face-to-face communication. This perspective has been used to effect in historical sociology, as in Chandra Mukerji's work on *Landscape and Power* (1997). Models have also been taken from anthropology, where studies of visual **data** and visual systems have been de-coupled from earlier studies of **colonialism**, in particular the role of colonial photography and later, ethnographic film, and re-set in the context of systems of visual significance. In this respect, visual anthropology, visual sociology, and the analysis of visual communication merge with aspects of the sociology of the plastic arts, film, and, more recently, the virtual realm of computer media. Topics for visual sociology include physical positioning, memory work, exhibition, iconography, and the microscopy of visual perception. Simultaneously, attention within sociology has been directed to the determinants of vision itself and, in this respect, connects to philosophy and cognitive science. Main methodological perspectives within visual sociology are described by Sarah Pink in a special issue of *Visual Anthropology Review* (2004), on "Applied Visual Anthropology."   TIN DENORA

vocabularies of motives
– see **accounts**.

vocation
– see **occupations**.

voluntary associations

The **state** is not a voluntary political association. While there are procedures such as naturalization to become a member of a state, being stateless in the modern world is not an option. By contrast, voluntary associations are public associations with noncoercive and optional membership. Voluntary associations include **political parties**, professional associations, neighborhood **groups**, and **trade unions**. Voluntary associations are the building blocks of **civil society** and **associative democracy**.

Theorizing voluntary associations has a venerable **tradition** in sociology but perhaps **Émile Durkheim** was an outstanding example of a sociologist who attributed a central role to them in modern life in *The Division of Labor in Society* (1894 [trans. 1944]) and *Professional Ethics and Civic Morals* (1890 [trans. 1990]). In its very origins, sociology had already set out its problem as that of the relationship between individual and society. It was generally agreed that **modernity** came to constitute these two entities as poles around which

social relations evolved. In fact, **modernization** of social relations meant the dissolution of any intermediate associations or relations of belonging, **solidarity**, and affinity between the individual and society. For early sociologists, as much as this was a necessary process, it also created **anomie**, **alienation**, and powerlessness, especially for **Ferdinand Tönnies**, in *Community and Association* (1887 [trans. 1963]). The diagnosis was that, without intermediate associations, these would lead to dissolution of the very society itself. There is no doubt this particular interpretation of modernity owed much to the pioneering work of **Alexis de Tocqueville** and his emphasis on townships and towns in American democratic life in *Democracy in America* (1835 and 1840 [trans. 2003]). But for Durkheim, modernity, at least in Europe, had reached a stage where it was no longer reasonable to assume that face-to-face relationships would constitute the primary means by which individuals were socialized. Late in the nineteenth century, Durkheim was already aware that towns and **cities** could not remain as the fundamental milieu of democratic social life and that other intermediary associations were already emerging to respond to these needs. For Durkheim, **professions** were such intermediate associations that would constitute the secondary modes of belonging, affiliation, and solidarity in modern society.

The twentieth century has largely borne out Durkheim's anticipation: professionalization has been perhaps among the most important, enduring, and growing movements. Nevertheless, the professions were not the only intermediate associations that came to play a significant role between individual and society. The emergence of numerous other **organizations**, non- or quasi-governmental bodies, have come to affect social life so much so that they have been defined as either **social movements** or the rise of **civil society**, a social order distinct from the state but existing parallel to, if not between, individual and society. While there would be disagreement about whether to include civil society organizations or social movements within the general rubric of voluntary associations, it is useful to conceptualize them against this broader view on individual and society.

In the early twenty-first century, it would be unimaginable to conceive modern social and democratic societies without voluntary associations ranging from well-organized professions to quasi-professions, charitable organizations, foundations, **groups**, lobbies, and many other forms of belonging, solidarity, and affinities (see, for example, Don E. Eberly and Ryan Streeter, *The Soul of Civil Society: Voluntary Associations and the Public Value of Moral Habits*, 2002). The range of social issues raised, addressed, advocated, and problematized by voluntary associations is virtually endless. Children's aid societies, anti-poverty organizations, refugee rights organizations, environmental protection societies, women's rights activists, and civil rights organizations are only a few examples of this vast and vital aspect of social life in democratic states. In fact, the vitality and strength of social and democratic life cannot be measured merely by formal political **institutions** such as **voting**, but by the depth, scope, and strength of voluntary associations that prevail in any given society.   ENGIN ISIN

voting

This is a political **right** that all adults should exercise, but it does not always bring about a situation in which people can govern their own lives. Voting is therefore a necessary but not sufficient part of **democracy**.

Although all **politics** requires an element of consensus, the notion that people should consciously and specifically register their opinion arises with the liberal **tradition**. **Liberalism** argues that everyone is an individual and, being an individual, such a person should consent to government. Of course the right to vote was in practice restricted to certain categories of people well into the twentieth century, since liberals took the view historically that only individuals with **property** and **rationality** should vote. This in practice meant not only men, but men with property and the "right" **ethnicity** and **religion**. Even a celebrated liberal like **John Stuart Mill** argued that voting was for "civilized" peoples, by which he meant people of European descent. Democracy, construed as the exercise of universal suffrage, was feared by liberals until the twentieth century on the grounds that the poor, the "dependent," the female, and those of the "wrong" religion would not be able to vote sensibly and responsibly.

When the Chartists in Britain campaigned for universal male suffrage in the 1840s, they described the vote as "a knife-and-fork question" since it was clear to the poor that in itself the vote would only change their lives if used to elect governments that would make inroads into the **market**. It was not the act of voting per se that solved **social problems**: it was the policies of governments. Whereas the wealthy could educate themselves and maintain their health privately,

poor people required government provision of resources if knife-and-fork questions were to be satisfactorily addressed.

Should the act of voting be a private and secret one? Some feel that voting should be part of a public discussion process and that people should be prepared to demonstrate their opinions publicly and see how others voted. However, the secret ballot was adopted on the grounds that open voting would lead to voters being intimidated by those with social **power**, for example, workers by their employers, women by their husbands or fathers, and so on.

How frequently and on what issues should voting take place? Elitist-minded publicists favored infrequent voting while the radically minded tended to argue that voting should occur often (sometimes the demand was raised for annual parliaments). Democrats took the view that voting not only should be extended to all adults who were citizens in a society, but should be used to decide numerous issues. Voters should not merely elect representatives in a legislature, but also vote on propositions periodically put to them through referendums. Moreover, voting should occur in social as well as traditionally political contexts, so that, for example, employees should be given a vote to determine managements. Existing systems are cautious here, fearing that voters might be swayed by informal pressures, and that professionals with expertise should be appointed by those best able to judge their capacity.

Should voting be compulsory? There is a strong argument for suggesting that **rights** won after long struggles are too precious to be left to pure choice and that many more people would vote if voting for parliamentary candidates, say, was made compulsory. Clearly, such a system could be justified only if people dissatisfied with all candidates were able to vote for "none of the above." In general, however, it is felt that compulsion is inappropriate in this context (although in a number of countries voting is compulsory). It is not clear as to why people do not vote. It has been argued that nonvoting arises from satisfaction with the existing system, but this view is challenged by those who (rather more plausibly) contend that nonvoting disproportionately affects the poor and the inarticulate.

There is greater concern about the character of the electoral systems in which people vote. In Britain and the United States, the candidate with the most votes in a constituency wins and all the other votes are "wasted." This seems unfair to many, and there is considerable support for an electoral system in which there is at least an element of proportionality, so that all votes matter and parties gain representatives in proportion to the electoral strength of their members. Critics argue that such a system undermines strong government and leads to endless bargaining and deals. This argument particularly appeals to those who can win elections on a minority of votes cast. In Britain, however, it is significant that regional parliaments do have proportional voting, and it seems likely that at least elements of proportionality will be adopted in national elections as well.

Should representatives mirror their electorate? On the one hand, it is difficult to see how representatives who have significantly different social experiences from those they represent can exercise empathy and real concern. On the other hand, it is arguable that individuals have an infinity of **identities**, and to insist, say, that women representatives represent the interests of women, and that blacks represent the interests of blacks, can be naive and counterproductive.

Is there a contradiction between voting and the **state**? Anarchists argue that, if voting made a difference, it would have been abolished, and that voting is a meaningless **ritual** which gives people the illusion of **power**. It is certainly true that fear interferes with the exercise of a responsible and meaningful choice, and it could be argued that using force rather than negotiation to settle conflicts of interest prevents people from using their vote to advance their capacity to govern their own lives. Indeed, in many societies convicted lawbreakers are stripped of their right to vote.

Should voting be extended to **children**? Certainly there is a case for lowering the age of voting, and allowing boys and girls in their teens the right to vote. But democracy involves self-government, and it is important to see that voting is not an end in itself, but a way of enabling people to act in an enlightened and socially responsible way.   JOHN HOFFMAN

W

Wach, Joachim (1898–1955)

An underappreciated figure in the sociology of **religion**, Wach was born and studied in Germany, but under Nazi pressure emigrated to the United States in the mid-1930s and completed his academic career at the University of Chicago. His major work was *Sociology of Religion* (1944), which was an elaboration of his *Einführung in die Religionssoziologie* (1931). Wach believed in the universality of religious belief and argued that "communing with the deity" was as fundamental to **culture** and **society** as was recognition of our material surroundings. Influenced by **Max Weber**, Wach emphasized the importance of the historical and comparative study of religion, and especially of the need for western scholars to study eastern religions. He argued that comparative study should aim towards understanding (***Verstehen***) and not just aggregate statistical analyses.

Wach was an advocate of the intellectual **value** of the discipline of religious studies and saw it as a way of teaching students to be neither fanatical nor indifferent towards religion. He regarded the sociology of religion as providing an important bridge to theology and to making different types of religious expression more accessible to social science analysis. But, while arguing for the essentially religious nature of humans, Wach differentiated between theology and its concern with understanding its own faith or confessional **tradition** (what must I believe?), and the comparative study of religion, *Religionswissenschaft*, that seeks to establish and understand "what is there that is believed?" Unlike **Peter L. Berger**, Wach did not see religious **pluralism** as undercutting the certainty of belief; he saw it rather as potentially leading to the **reflexive** examination, preservation, and strengthening of an individual's own faith. MICHELE DILLON

Wallerstein, Immanuel (1930–)

Professor of Sociology at the State University of New York, Binghampton, Director of the Fernand Braudel Center for the Study of Economics, Historical Systems and Civilizations, and former President of the American Sociological Association, Wallerstein's early work was on Africa and **colonialism** in *The Road to Independence: Ghana and the Ivory Coast* (1964), *Africa: The Politics of Independence* (1961), *Social Change: The Colonial Situation* (1966), and *Africa: The Politics of Unity* (1967). Wallerstein became influential primarily through the development of **world-systems analysis** in his *The Modern World System: Capitalist Agriculture and the Origins of the European World Economy in the Sixteenth Century* (1974) and *The Modern World System: Mercantilism and the Consolidation of the European World Economy 1600–1750* (1980). Wallerstein criticized modernization theory and **functionalism** by showing that European **capitalism** developed by exploiting its colonial periphery. Wallerstein's theory was a modification of Marxist sociology of **social class**, demonstrating that the bourgeois class in the core states exploited the working class of the periphery. The semiperiphery included new rising powers – such as Japan and Russia – and declining old powers – such as Spain and Austria-Hungary.

Wallerstein has been a critic of American foreign policy. His political radicalism was in part a consequence of the student protests of the 1960s, which he analyzed in *University in Turmoil: The Politics of Change* (1969). His most recent publication is *The Uncertainties of Knowledge* (2004).

BRYAN S. TURNER

war

This is a type of violent **social conflict** between two or more armed powerful **organizations**, in which each aims to prevail by destroying the other's **power**, primarily through the deliberate use of armed force. As a form of social **violence**, war is distinguished first by its character as an organized contest. Although war sometimes leads to spontaneous violent acts by individuals, it centers on courses of action planned by collective social actors. War is also distinguished by the general **legitimacy** of its violence. It is the only context in which large-scale killing, in other situations highly illegitimate, has become generally legitimate in human society. Indeed in modern society, in which legitimate killing by individuals is limited to very narrow contexts of self-defense, and many **states** have abandoned the death penalty, war is almost the only context of legitimate killing of any kind.

Because violence is always an extreme form of social power, this social **institution** concerned with legitimate, organized violence is one of the most important in all societies in which it exists. A society's mode of warfare, the complex of all the social practices concerned with the organization and preparation of war, is always one of its most influential institutional clusters. Indeed the development of warfare has been associated with the emergence of many other social institutions. Thus, the **differentiation** of a warrior class has been seen as one of the first forms of **social stratification** – closely linked to the development of gender distinctions since warriors have generally, although not always, been men – and of **social class** and **social status**, since warriors often obtained greater material **wealth** and **prestige** than other members of society. The development of warfare has also been linked to the development of the **state**, as a social institution concerned first of all with the control of violence. Indeed, **Max Weber** in *Economy and Society* (1922 [trans. 1968]) classically defined the state through its monopoly of legitimate violence: the state's concern with war-making was linked to its control over other social actors and its limiting of their rights to exercise violence in their social relations. **Karl Marx** and **Friedrich Engels** in *The Communist Manifesto* (1848 [trans. 1968]) had also seen the state as constituted by "bodies of armed men"; although Marxists have often seen this kind of power as a means of **social control** within national societies, its main function has been to project power in relations between states. In *States, War and Capitalism* (1988), **Michael Mann** showed that, until the mid twentieth century, the majority of state expenditures had always been devoted to warfare.

Despite this centrality of warfare to social organization, classical **social theory**, born of the new **industrial society** of the early nineteenth century, failed to give war a central place. **Claude Henri de Rouvroy, Comte de Saint-Simon** and **Auguste Comte** saw industrial society, with its rational, scientifically based organization, as inherently peaceful, giving rise to the influential myth of pacific industrialism in modern sociology, which is discussed in **Raymond Aron**'s *War and Industrial Society* (1958). Even Marx saw **capitalism** as a mode of production characterized by relations of exploitation rather than physical violence. This issue is explored in Bernard Semmel (ed.) *Marxism and the Science of War* (1981), but warfare was not central to Marxist theory of modern society. However, later Marxists like **Vladimir Ilich Lenin** (*Imperialism*, 1916) and Rosa Luxemberg (1870–1919), (*The Accumulation of Capital* (1913 [trans. 1963]) developed a theory of "militaristic capitalism," linking war to **imperialism**. Both pacific and militaristic theories of modern society have been criticized by writers such as Mann, Martin Shaw in "Capitalism and Militarism," in *War, State and Society* (1984), and Aron, who favored more geopolitical explanations of war. Indeed, the neo-Weberian school of the late twentieth century moved away from the prevalent socioeconomic explanations of war, granting significant autonomy to warfare itself. **Theda Skocpol** has argued in *States and Social Revolutions* (1979) that international war played a significant part in activating class tensions and causing revolutions. **Anthony Giddens** (*The Nation-State and Violence*, 1985) identified warfare as one of the four primary institutional clusters of modern societies. Mann (*The Sources of Social Power*, I, 1986) claimed that military power was one of the four fundamental sources of social power, causally implicated in many fundamental **social changes**. An influential social history by William H. MacNeill (*The Pursuit of Power*, 1982) showed how the "industrialisation of warfare" had transformed the destructive power of war.

While these writers emphasized the central role of war, especially in transformations of the **state**, they gave less attention to social relations within warfare. The classic modern theorist of war, Carl von Clausewitz (1780–1831), who wrote about the same time as Comte, remains neglected in the sociological canon. His posthumous *On War* (1831 [trans. 1976]) elaborated the essential character of war as a violent clash of armed social forces, tending towards absolute destruction (although it also identified the counter-tendencies resulting from "friction"). It also proposed a primitive sociology of modern war, identifying government with the rational policy element, generals with strategic craft, and the people with war's essential violence. The latter derived from the element of popular mobilization which arose from **nationalism** and was manifested in systems of conscription and mass armies.

All of these were central to the later development of the total war, which Shaw (*Dialectics of War*, 1988) saw as a new mode of warfare, fusing popular mobilization and industrialized war to reach new levels of destruction. This in turn had transformative power in social and political relations – a recurring theme in the sociology of war from Stanislav Andreski's formulation of the "military participation ratio," according to which social change was proportional to participation levels (*Military Organization and Society*, 1968). However, as total war mutated into preparations for nuclear war, writers like Giddens argued that transformative agencies could no longer be identified within warfare, which was tending towards total social destruction.

Total warfare was also associated with the classic manifestations of militarism in social life. This is often identified in terms of **ideologies** and **cultures** that glorify military activities and **organizations**, but it has a broader meaning as the extensive influence of military organization and culture on social relations in general. Thus, although militarism is often used in a derogatory sense, it is possible to distinguish, for example, between fascist and democratic versions in which military power is evaluated quite differently. In this sense, militarism becomes a more useful analytical concept, allowing us to distinguish processes of militarization, in which military influences increase, and demilitarization, in which they contract (Shaw, *Post-Military Society*, 1991).

Total war and its associated militarism also blurred the line between combatants and civilians. Because the latter often participated in warfare – as suppliers of weapons and other material, as well as of ideological support for war – they were increasingly regarded as targets of weapons of mass destruction. However, the increasing vulnerability of many who were manifestly neither direct combatants nor even indirect contributors to war – most women, the old, and the young – meant that the civilian category became increasingly important in the analysis of war. Modern war could be seen not only as transforming all forms of social stratification – sharpening contradictions of class, **gender**, and **race and ethnicity**, for example – but also as producing a form of stratification specific to military power, the civilian–combatant division, which in turn was institutionalized in military organization and culture.

While the main period of total war saw the growth of militarism, the nuclear age saw – alongside ever more total destructiveness in military **technology** – decreasing militarism as war-preparation no longer required such high levels of mobilization and participation. The resulting changes preoccupied various kinds of sociological analysis in the last decades of the twentieth century. The subfield of *military sociology* analyzed the transformations of military institutions consequent on the "decline of mass armies" (Jacques van Doorn, *The Soldier and Social Change*,

1975), emphasizing, for example, the development of "professionalism" and even "occupationalism" (Charles Moscos and James Wood, *The Military: More Than Just a Job?* 1988). Cynthia Enloe opened up the feminist exploration of gendering in the military, asking women *Does Khaki Become You?* (1985). With the first war fought after Vietnam by a western state, namely Britain's Falklands campaign, Mann (1988) analyzed the development of "spectator-sport militarism." The 1991 Gulf War brought many studies of the role of mass media in the new western wars, such as Philip Taylor's *War and Media* (1992).

In the twenty-first century, the issues in the study of war were changing again. The end of the Cold War meant that, although the danger of nuclear war remained in a world of increasing nuclear proliferation, there was less focus on this maximal (and since 1945 hypothetical) level of war. Instead, studies focused on two parallel and intertwined trends. One set of analyses examined wars, often centered on ethnic conflict, resulting from state fragmentation in non-western countries, which in turn led to a new "convergence" of studies of war and of development (Mark Duffield, *Global Governance and the New Wars*, 2001). Mary Kaldor in *New and Old Wars* (1999) influentially claimed that these were "new wars." Other analyses focused on the new patterns of western warfare, described as "bourgeois wars" by Herfried Münkler in *New Wars* (2004). After the September 11 2001, terrorist attacks on the United States, **terrorism** (organized violence designed to create fear in civilian populations) and counter-terrorism were widely seen as taking newly global forms. The new conflicts were seen as prime examples of "asymmetric war" between opposed types of armed adversaries – states and **networks** – and also as forms of **globalization** in contemporary warfare. Hence Shaw in *The New Western Way of War* (2005) analyzed both new western and terrorist ways of war as manifestations of a "global surveillance" mode of warfare. The contribution of sociology as a discipline to the increasingly interdisciplinary study of warfare also included important reflections like Hans Joas's *War and Modernity* (2003) and Paul Hirst's *War in the Twenty-First Century* (2004). The foundations of a sociology of war were increasingly being laid, although they had yet to inform an extensive field of study within the discipline.   MARTIN SHAW

wealth

This describes a *stock* of marketable assets, usually **money** and **property**. In contrast, **income** describes a flow of resources. Wealth and income are linked, as wealth can be invested to generate income, and income can be saved to accumulate wealth. The distribution of wealth is highly unequal – much more so than the distribution of income. For example, in the United States, in 2001, 20 percent of all income went to the top-earning 1 percent of households, but these households represented 33.4 percent of net worth (or wealth). The bottom fifth of households had negative net worth – owing more than they owned. One reason for the unequal distribution of wealth is that patterns of wealth will vary over the life cycle, as people will save for old age, and average wealth is highest amongst older age **groups**. The major contributory factor to wealth **inequality**, however, is inheritance.

At any given point in time, there is a limited amount of wealth that exists. However, the totality of wealth is not fixed. Adam Smith (1723–90) (*The Wealth of Nations*, 1776) saw wealth creation as the combining of materials, **labor**, land, and **technology** so as to create a profit. The capitalist mode of production has demonstrated a considerable capacity for wealth creation. In the relatively short term, wealth can also increase (and decrease) because of market fluctuations, such as increases in house prices and booms in the stock **market**.

It has been argued that the creation of wealth, even if its distribution remains highly unequal, is nevertheless of benefit to society as a whole. The rich will reinvest, thus creating jobs, income, and more wealth. This has been described as the trickle-down effect. Others have taken a more radical view. Andrew Carnegie (1835–1919) described the millionaire as "but a trustee for the poor; intrusted for a season with a great part of the increased wealth of the community, but administering it for the community far better than it could or would have done for itself," in his article on "the Gospel of Wealth" in the *North American Review* in 1889. Thus the duty of the rich, during their lifetimes, was to benefit the **community** by "placing within its reach ladders upon which the aspiring can rise." Carnegie argued that inheritance was "most injudicious" and absolutely the worst strategy for the disposal of wealth, "Beyond providing for the wife and daughters moderate sources of income, and very moderate allowances indeed, if any, for the sons."

This view sees the creation of wealth by individuals during their lifetime as a legitimate reward for their greater abilities, but is critical of wealth acquired by inheritance, or otherwise by lack of effort, such as reductions of tax for the already wealthy. For example, Warren Buffett (1930–), a stock market investor who is one of the richest men in the United States, has been highly critical of proposals to cut tax on dividends, arguing that tax reductions should instead be directed at the lower-paid. Furthermore, Buffett does not intend to leave his wealth to his children. Nevertheless, despite these individual exceptions, the most common manner in which wealth is acquired is through inheritance, and the most certain way to become wealthy is to be born of wealthy parents.

The actual size of wealth holdings, as well as the distribution of wealth, will be much influenced by the assets that are included in wealth calculations. Wealth can include financial savings, **property**, and accumulated pension **rights**. In the United Kingdom, for the population as a whole, housing and pension rights are the most important sources of wealth. However, state pension rights (over half of the total of pension rights) do not represent marketable wealth, and some groups (lone parents, young single people, and couples with young children) have very little private pension wealth. The marketability of individual home ownership is restricted (assuming that the owner needs somewhere to live). Thus, a considerable proportion of the assets of the more moderate wealth holders is not, in fact, marketable and it may be questioned whether this constitutes "wealth." Thus a more usual measure is "marketable wealth," which does not include accrued pension rights (but does include housing).

One of the aims of neoliberal governments elected in the 1970s (particularly in Britain and the United States) was the creation of popular **capitalism** – that is, the more widespread distribution of wealth. In the United Kingdom, the sale of social housing, together with the privatization and selling off of industries such as telecommunications, gas, electricity, and water, was justified in these terms (the sale of national assets also raised considerable revenues for the government). However, aggregate **data** suggest that the development of popular capitalism does not appear to have been particularly successful.

In Britain (as in many other countries), inequalities of wealth declined between the 1920s and the 1970s, largely because of the impact of inheritance tax and taxes on dividends. In 1923, the top 1 percent owned 61 percent of marketable wealth in England and Wales, but by 1976 the top 1 percent owned 21 percent of marketable wealth in the United Kingdom. Until the 1980s, wealth distribution continued to become more equal, in some contrast with the rapid growth of income inequality that was taking place during this period. However, from the second half of the

1990s, there was a significant increase in the inequality of wealth, and by 2001 the top 1 percent owned 23 percent of marketable wealth.

It is not surprising that increases in inequalities of wealth should lag behind increases in income inequality, given that, as wealth is congealed income, it will take time for increased income inequality to show up in the wealth distribution. In addition, taxes on investment income have also fallen below those on earnings between the 1970s and the 1990s, and rates of tax on large inheritances have also fallen since the mid-1980s. Thus popular capitalism may be judged to have failed, given that wealth inequalities have increased – which is perhaps not surprising as the fiscal policies of neoliberal governments are also designed to enable the better-off to retain more of their wealth.   ROSEMARY CROMPTON

Weber, Max (1864–1920)

Max Weber is widely regarded as the greatest figure in the history of the **social sciences**, and as one of the founders of **sociology** as a discipline. His most influential works include *The Protestant Ethic and the Spirit of Capitalism* (1905 [trans. 2002]) and *Economy and Society* (1922 [trans. 1968]). His writings on the economic ethic of the world **religions** (1915–16), which deal with ancient Judaism (*Ancient Judaism*, (1921 [trans. 1952]), Buddhism and Hinduism (*The Religion of India*, 1920–1 [trans. 1958], and *The Religion of China*, 1921 [trans. 1951]), have had powerful influence on scholarship in each of these areas, as well as setting the agenda for the study of cultural influences on economic development. His writings on the modern bureaucratic state, the nature of political **authority** and **leadership**, **charisma**, and **modernity** as **rationalization** and "disenchantment" have also been influential. Moreover, Weber has had an influence in such diverse fields as international relations and political theory, in the history of law, and in philosophy and the **philosophy of the social sciences** with his methodological writings, particularly in relation to the fact–value distinction and the idea of interpretive or *verstehende* sociology.

Weber was born Karl Emil Maximilian Weber into a family of wealthy industrialists and linen merchants with international connections, who had a linen factory in Oerlinghausen, Westphalia, in what is now northwest Germany. On his mother's side there were professors as well as industrialists, of Huguenot origin. He grew up in an atmosphere not only of **wealth**, but of political **power**, intellectual distinction, and religiously motivated service. Weber's parents were, however, on the margins of wealth and power rather than at the center. Weber's father was a younger son in his family and pursued a legal and political career, which Weber himself seemed poised to follow. His most famous book, *The Protestant Ethic and the Spirit of Capitalism* (1905), contains thinly concealed elements of the business history of his family, as do passages of *Economy and Society* (1922). His mother, Helene Fallenstein, was highly educated and influenced by the socially conscious Protestant theology of the time.

Weber studied law, but also attended lectures in economics, ancient history, philosophy, and theology. He enjoyed student life, joining a fraternity, drinking beer, and playing cards. He fulfilled his obligatory military service by training in the officer corps of the army. He settled down to his legal studies after returning to Berlin in 1884, concentrated on the law and legal history, briefly clerked at a District Court, took law exams, and completed more military service. He became a doctoral student under Levin Goldschmidt (1829–97), and wrote a dissertation, "Development of the Principle of Joint Liability and the Separate Fund in the Public Trading Company from the Household and Trade Communities in the Italian Cities" (1889), based on hundreds of Italian and Spanish sources. The text traced, in the form of highly elaborated series of legal citations, a long sequence of incremental developments in the European law of commercial contracts through a variety of legal jurisdictions. Like many histories of law it recorded the small, step-by-step adjustments and extensions of the law to new circumstances and new kinds of cases over hundreds of years, in the course of which significant changes were produced in the meaning of the law itself. The puzzle that Weber wanted to solve by this incrementalist approach is the problem of the emergence of the modern law of corporations (which limits personal liability and allows fictitious persons or corporations to be liable) from the world of ancient law in which there were no corporations, and in which the only means for the accumulation of capital in support of a large-scale project, such as the shipping of goods for sale in distant **markets**, required such things as personal guarantees and hostages.

To become a professor, he needed to complete a second dissertation (*Die romische Agrargeschichte in ihrer Bedeutung für das Staars- und Privatrecht*, 1891), which used a similar incrementalist approach and an unusual set of legal documents to address a long-term transformation, in this case the decline of the Roman empire and its slave-based **economy** and the rise of serfdom. The dissertation used his knowledge of medieval land tenure law to illuminate the Roman agrarian situation. It was characteristically bold and controversial, and, though Weber later dismissed it, the argument is nevertheless interesting. Weber assumed that the Roman colonial land surveyors mapped different types of land tenure differently, so that untaxed lease rights from public land were only roughly measured, while private (taxed) lots were more precisely measured. This was not an assumption that he could substantiate in the legal sources, though it made sense. He then argued that the private lots were too small for subsistence. This meant that the poorer landowners needed to plant on public land to survive, placing them in competition for this land with the rich, who could use slaves, and that they eventually were degraded to the status of slaves. But at the same time, as a result of the shortage of slave **labor**, slaves rose in status and were given serf-like privileges, producing a convergence between the two **groups** that led to the two-tiered order based on unfree, but privileged, **labor** that characterized the European agricultural system for the next millennium.

Serfdom was only abolished in Russia in the 1860s and had been, in one form or another, central to European agriculture at the beginning of the nineteenth century. Its decline and transformation had profound consequences that were being worked out in Weber's time, and the historical debates over it had a strongly political character. He also became involved in the policy issues that arose in the course of the transformation of agriculture. Although Weber later became famous for his distinction between science and **politics**, the relation between his own activities as a scholar and as a person involved in politics were nevertheless close. The character and ultimate historical meaning of modern **capitalism** was a great theme of nineteenth-century thought, and such questions as the legal origins of private **property** were hotly debated. It is characteristic of Weber's thought that these issues appear, but in a form that is different from the usual one, often because he has converted them into an incrementalist issue in the development of the relevant **institutions**.

The *Verein für Sozialpolitik* (Association for Social Policy) was a body that tried to produce an expert consensus to guide and influence state policy. Weber joined this association, and was employed to produce a study of "The Conditions of the Agri-cultural Workers in East Elbian Regions of Germany," a topic of considerable political interest to him, as it involved the economic interests of the Prussian estates, which were reeling from the **globalization** of the wheat market, a source of worldwide economic instability as well as class conflict between the producers, who wanted protective tariffs, the workers, who opposed them, and the agricultural laborers, who were leaving and being replaced by less costly Polish labor. The success of the study enabled him to change careers. He was given a professorial appointment in economics at Freiburg in 1893, and was later appointed in economics at Heidelberg, the university with which he was to be most closely associated. Weber did not teach at Heidelberg for long. After the death of his father, with whom he had quarreled about his mother, he fell into a state of mental anguish, and quit teaching. After some recuperative traveling he returned to Heidelberg, and to an active role as an editor and author, and to the writing of *The Protestant Ethic and the Spirit of Capitalism*.

The core problem of the essay is accounting for the disruption and replacement of traditional economic life. He argued that it was in part – that part being the distinctive human type of highly self-disciplined, ascetic, rational capitalist – the indirect effect of Protestantism. The connection was complex. Reformation theology, and particularly Calvinism, altered the problem of salvation. The doctrine was a development of issues deeply rooted in the Christian **tradition**. The omniscience and omnipotence of God implies that God knows who will be saved. These persons, the Elect, believed to be a small number, are thus predestined for salvation. Weber reasoned that the doctrine of predestination was psychologically intolerable and produced deep anxiety, which had to be allayed by pastoral assurances based on some ancillary doctrines, such as the idea of callings ("Science as a Vocation," 1917 [trans. 1946] and "Politics as a Vocation," 1919 [trans. 1994]). This anxiety, however, had to be deeply concealed, as feelings of doubt were held to be a sign that one was not among the elect. Pastors, however, needed something for their flock to relieve them of the terror produced by the doctrine of predestination. Calling or vocation were originally terms that applied only to religious vocations. The Protestants, however, extended this notion to apply to worldly **occupations** (an example of the same kind of incrementalist approach as in his legal studies). Protestants taught that faithful work in a calling was a sign of election.

Weber argued that this combination of doctrines created a novel and powerful psychological sanction for conduct. To assure oneself that one was saved, one could strive to live up to the standard of doing one's daily work as though it was God's command, and (because predestination had the effect of making the idea of sin and forgiveness meaningless) to live one's life as a whole in accordance with God's particular assignment of a calling. A major element of this was asceticism, hostility to fleshly pleasures and entertainment, of which God would have disapproved. The theological premise thus had the indirect effect of producing a **personality** which, in the appropriate setting, becomes the austere, abstemious, rationalizing capitalist. These religiously motivated businessmen were economic revolutionaries, who transformed the areas of commerce and manufacturing they entered. They rationalized the workplace, invested for the long term, and sought to expand markets beyond traditional customer bases. The relation between **capitalism** and religion in this case is one of "elective affinity," as Weber put it. The two reinforced one another, with capitalism bringing religious success, and religion bringing capitalistic success.

There are many controversial features of this account, some of which result from the fact that the doctrinal element of the **ideal type** which Weber constructed, which relied heavily on Calvinism, only imperfectly corresponded to the theological doctrine of much of Protestantism in Europe, especially where Lutheran national churches existed. Nevertheless the account is deeply compelling, in part because the depictions of the believer accord so well with a character type that unquestionably did leave a profound mark on western **culture**.

Weber closed the essay with some prophetic remarks about the course of western culture, and an important analysis of the cultural situation created by the **secularization** of the "ethic." He said that the rosy blush of the Reformation's "laughing heir," the **Enlightenment**, had faded, and that the inexorable demands of the modern, rationally organized **economy**, now enforced the organization of work into callings but stripped them of their religious meaning. This process, in which **rationalization** strips the world of meaning, or disenchants it, in his phrase, was to become a major theme of his thought. The sacralization of work by the Protestants gave way as well, so that today in the United States, as he put it, even the accumulation of wealth takes on the character of **sport**. The people in the machine of capitalism

become divided beings, "specialists without spirit, sensualists without heart" (1905).

In his late lectures on economic history (*General Economic History*, 1923 [trans. [1927]), Weber restated the thesis with some different emphases, resulting from his comparative studies of religion and economics. Weber came to see the rational organization of free **labor** as especially crucial, and indeed to be the distinguishing feature of modern capitalism in contrast to booty capitalism, trade, and political capitalism, all of which were found in the ancient world. The crucial moment came when the craftsman was replaced by the worker, and the owner of the **firm** supplied tools, exacted discipline, and assumed the **risks**. This change was, Weber thought, a precondition for the mechanization of **work**, with the goal of saving labor costs and, in this sense, rationalizing labor. Rational accounting methods, rational price-setting for the purpose of profit, and a system of law with calculable results also developed at about this time, and were also necessary conditions for the development of capitalism. But the worldwide expansion and continued success of capitalism did not rest on the foundation of religious belief.

Nevertheless, he believed that in some settings the original influence of Protestantism on capitalism persisted. He traveled to the United States, where he spent several months, traveling widely, and participating (as an agricultural economist) in the scholarly meetings of the 1904 St. Louis World's Fair. His American experience was the basis of his essay "The Protestant Sects and the Spirit of Capitalism" (1905 [trans. 2002 in *From Max Weber: Essays in Sociology*]), in which he describes how church membership served to assure conformity as well as to establish the credit-worthiness of its members, preserving the strength of asceticism into Weber's own time, and accounting for the puritanism and conventionalism of American life.

Weber was an important methodological thinker. His major methodological essays were published between 1903 and 1907, including *Roscher and Knies: The Logical Problems of Historical Economics* (1903–5 [trans. 1975]), "Objectivity in Social Science and Social Policy" (1904 [trans. 1949]), "Critical Studies in the Logic of the Cultural Sciences" (1905 [trans. 1949]), and *Critique of Stammler* (1907 [trans. 1977]). In "Objectivity in Social Science and Social Policy," Weber argued that to construct a historical **explanation**, or even an object of explanation, requires conceptualization, which he examined in terms of the concept of ideal types, which he distinguished from mere classifications, which simply sorted objects into categories. He then argued that these conceptualizations have a number of problematic **properties**. One involves interests: what makes sense to us, in our historical setting, is the product of our **values**, experiences, and our own culture. History is thus a discipline that works on the small segment of the empirical that is meaningful to us, and that segment is already at least partly conceptualized.

This is a form of historical **relativism**: our concepts differ from the concepts of others, so the content of history is different. But history is also factual and causal, and to some extent, then, not subject to this sort of relativism. He speaks of the "real causal processes" (1905) which our concepts give an intelligible form to, and argues that genetic ideal types (1904) are themselves relative to a culture-bound historical interest: the calculation of probabilities is fully objective, but the selection and conceptualization of the conditions that determine action cannot be. These are inherent limitations of social science. The meaningfulness of its concepts derives from sources outside of the science itself: as he says in the "Objectivity" essay, these sciences must speak "the language of life" (*Gesammelte Aufsatze zür Wissenschaftslehre*, 1922 [trans. 1988]), a language which is itself necessarily bound to a historical moment and its values.

During the years after *The Protestant Ethic*, Weber continued to write about religion, but in order to test *The Protestant Ethic* thesis by expanding it to a general study of the relation between religion and "economic ethics," focused especially on one puzzle – the fact that a rational capitalism developed only in the West. This enlarged study had many results, and transformed the problem with which he had begun. To understand his approach in his diverse studies of the Asian religions and ancient Judaism, it is useful to begin with a much-quoted passage, written as part of the introduction to his collected studies of religion: "Not ideas, but material and ideal interests, directly govern men's conduct. Yet very frequently the 'world images' that have been created by 'ideas' have, like switchmen, determined the tracks along which action has been pushed by the dynamic of interest."

His early legal studies were implicitly about interests: contract law is a means of reconciling the interests of the contractors. And the jurisprudential theory of the time emphasized the concept of interests. His approach in his later studies was to show the interplay of interests characteristic of particular institutional forms or orders, and to identify their effects on "rationalization," both

within the sphere of religion and in other spheres. Religious ideas are the source both of interests ideal interests that include salvation as well as honor and similar "interests" that we would now regard as cultural – and of world images. But they operate in a world of other kinds of interests, including material interests, with which they can combine, or be stymied, or develop in relation to other interests in a wide variety of ways. Particular combinations of institutional forms, **feudalism**, priesthood, monarchy, **bureaucracy**, kin relations, and so forth produce characteristic interests and conflicts for religion to relate to.

The theme of rationalization is both central and puzzling. Weber identified processes of rationalization internal to each religious tradition. In the case of ancient Judaism, for example, the prophets were the rationalizers, and their prophetic messages were designed to iron out internal conflicts in the religious tradition and its world image. He noted that merchants tend to seek a kind of practical rationalization of their spheres, while the priestly class tends to seek a theoretical rationalization: these are examples of "elective affinities." But interests, especially status interests, a powerful kind of "ideal" interest, often conflict with rationalization. And fully rationalized religious **ideologies** may prove to be difficult to live with, as was the case with Calvinism.

A general question which all salvation religions must answer, and which drives rationalization, is the issue of theodicy: the problem of the relationship between destiny and merit, or, put differently, the problem of why God allows evil. The Chinese solution was to reconcile destiny and merit by recourse to popular magical practice, which in turn produced a kind of fearful **conservativism**. Ancient Judaism, in contrast, devised solutions that excluded and repudiated magic, and this carried over into Christianity and consequently into the western world-view in a way that favored the eventual development of science and **technology**. Rationalization in the religious realm, of which Reformation Protestantism is an example, can produce some peculiar historical results, because producing new coherence or consistency in religious doctrines characteristically serves to produce conduct that is discrepant with normal conduct in other "spheres" of life, as it did with the early Protestants. Thus it is a potentially powerful source of change.

The larger puzzle about rationalization is this. The West developed a series of **institutions**, notably the law, that were also unusually rational, religions that had a minimum of magic, administrative structures that were also particularly rational, and science first developed fully in the West. Yet one can see processes of rationalization in the histories of non-western **cultures**. Why did they fail to produce the same kinds of effects? And why did the distinctive mentality associated with the rationalization of **work** arise only in the West?

The answer to this question in the studies of the economic ethics of the world religions is that each of the Asian religious traditions produced an economic ethic that was inimical to the development, though not necessarily the reception, of capitalism. In the case of Chinese religion, for example, Weber shows how the Confucian religious **tradition**, together with its bureaucracy and its exam system, supported a dominant mentality that precluded the development of analogs to the western institutional structures of rational law, to western science, and to a state free of the constraints of family loyalties, and promoted values, such as piety and honor, that also had the effect of preventing their emergence.

The work we know as *Economy and Society* was the second major effort of Weber's mature years. It consists of an extensive typology of forms of **social action**, especially institutional action. Weber said that the claim to be made on behalf of the typology was its usefulness. The elaboration of the typology is an extended demonstration of the uses to which the types could be put in analyzing actual historical forms, particularly of institutional structure, and in characterizing their historical course of development as the product of the basic properties of the type, always with the caveat that these were idealizations rather than "real" types with a teleological character.

The most famous of these typologies involved beliefs legitimating **authority** and the forms that are characteristically produced by these beliefs. The categories were charismatic, traditional, and rational-legal, which were further subdivided in various ways to account for common forms of political order, such as **patrimonialism**. These were ideal types, which meant that they almost never appeared in reality in a pure form, but were typically combined with elements of other ideal types. Weber was careful to point out the attenuated charismatic element in even such things as the modern monarchy and the jury.

Traditional authority was based on unwritten rules believed to be handed down from time immemorial while rational-legal authority rested on the belief in and the validity of written rules produced according to written procedures; charis-matic authority was the authority of the extraordinary person. Weber had in mind of course such figures as Napoleon and Jesus Christ, but he found many more modest and recurrent examples in Indian gurus and medieval battle leaders. In each of these cases the obedience of their followers rested on neither written nor unwritten rules but on the direct **influence** of the exceptional individual himself.

Political authority of this kind, Weber observed, is inherently unstable. Eventually the charismatic leader must support his followers with material benefits, and this marked the beginning of the transformation of charisma into everyday authority. Charismatic regimes also face problems of succession, and the routinization of charisma through **ritual** in order to pass on charisma to successors soon becomes transformed into something akin to traditional authority, or alternatively becomes rationalized into a bureaucratic system.

Weber was self-consciously part of the **generation** that came after the unification of Germany under Bismarck, and, as an ardent nationalist, was deeply concerned about the problem of succession of leaders. Bismarck's career had shown how forceful and successful leadership produced popular acquiescence and even enthusiasm. Weber was concerned that interest-faction parties, especially parties that inevitably were bureaucratically organized, would be effective electorally, but that this would assume the predominance of party hacks rather than of figures who could act boldly as leaders. During the closing months of World War I, he published an extensive newspaper article on constitutional form, which suggested a presidential system in which the president required support in the form of a plebiscite rather than party support, and thus stood above and outside of party structures. His political thinking is striking for its brusque dismissal of the core ideas of democratic theory: the will of the people he called a "fiction," and "the Rights of Man" a rationalist fantasy. He based his defense of parliamentary government on grounds of *Realpolitik*, especially the fact that modern **states** required, in order to act politically, the mobilization of mass sentiment.

STEPHEN P. TURNER

welfare reforms

Welfare and well-being are concerned with the satisfaction of basic **human needs**. Welfare has a strong normative aspect, and there are significant conflicts about what count as basic human needs and about how to provide for human needs – whether primarily through the **market**, the **state** or the **family**. Classical sociology differentiates between three dimensions of basic needs; "to have" that refers to fundamental physiological and material needs; "to love" that is about **community**, **care**, and recognition; and "to be" about **identity** and personal development. The understanding of what counts as welfare has gradually been expanded and the concepts of welfare have become multidimensional, dynamic, and contextual. It follows that principles and **institutions** of welfare vary in and between different **welfare states**. As Nancy Fraser has argued in *Justice Interruptus* (1987), there is a "recognition/redistribution" dilemma between two forms of social **justice**. The dilemma refers to tensions between different forms of welfare **politics**: "the politics of redistribution of material needs," and "the politics of recognition and respect" that often conflicts. There is an increasing emphasis on human agency and on the individual's capability to influence their own life and society.

The evolution of welfare reform was connected to the growth of capitalist markets and to the response of the state to the demands of organized workers. Welfare reforms had different backgrounds and dynamics, and governments adopted different strategies for providing basic needs for the workers and their families, in relation to **unemployment**, health, and old **age**. The roots to welfare reforms date back to the nineteenth century. In Germany, Otto von Bismarck (1815–98) developed the social state and introduced sickness and unemployment insurance and old age pensions for workers. These conservative reforms were based upon the insurance principle and paid by both employers and workers. In the United States, Franklin D. Roosevelt (1882–1945) introduced the New Deal in the 1930s as a federal aid to combat unemployment among workers and farmers. This was a temporary relief package, which gave financial aid to the needy that was not intended to become permanent. The Nordic countries developed a more corporate model of welfare based upon negotiations between the employers and the trade union **organizations**.

Comparative scholarship has identified different welfare regimes. In Europe, political developments after World War II were followed by an expansion of the public sector and the adoption of welfare reforms in relation to unemployment, elderly care, and health care. The reforms were based upon three different principles: (1) the insurance principle, where employers and employees are the main contributors; (2) the residual principle, where the state would only provide benefits to the needy; and (3) the principle of universal social **rights**, where the state is the main provider of welfare to all citizens. In Britain, the social-liberal government inspired by the ideas of William Beveridge (1879–1963) introduced a welfare reform package after World War II based upon a principle of universal rights, including a basic right to health care and elderly care.

Political developments have contributed to create different worlds of welfare. One illustrative example is the difference between Britain and Scandinavia. Beveridge's model also inspired welfare reforms in Scandinavia based upon a principle of universal rights to health care and elderly care. From the beginning of the 1960s Britain and Scandinavia, however, developed in different directions. The Scandinavian countries, Sweden, Denmark, and Norway, developed a universal welfare state with a big public-service sector, including a public regulation of childcare. Here social rights were based upon **citizenship**, financed primarily on taxes. Britain moved towards a residual welfare state, where the market and the family are the primary welfare providers and benefits are provided according to means tests. The political development of Thatcherism and **neoliberalism** in the United Kingdom and the United States during the 1980s and 1990s has exacerbated this trend towards a residual welfare state and thus contributed to widen the gap between the social democratic Scandinavian, the continental European, and the neoliberal welfare states. One differentiating factor in welfare reforms has been the gendered distribution between wage **work** and care work and between the public and private provision of care.

The development of European integration has influenced social developments and welfare reforms in Europe. With the expansion of the European Community to include Denmark and Britain, different principles of welfare and different typologies of welfare states evolved next to the continental insurance model. European integration, **migration**, and the adoption of the Maastricht Treaty (1992) have raised new questions about the future development of **social policies** and coordination of welfare reforms in Europe, and about the double tendency towards homogenization or **differentiation** of social policies in the European Community.

Welfare and well-being are dynamic concepts that have gained new meanings and content in **postindustrial society**. In a globalized world with a growing gap between rich and poor countries, one of the main challenges is still how to satisfy basic human **rights**. Even though **poverty** worldwide is diminishing, the gap between and within different countries is at the same time widening. **Globalization** has sparked a new debate about human rights to basic resources and about the capability and responsibility of the international **community** to contribute to satisfying peoples' needs.

Globalization and migration have exacerbated the struggle about privatization of welfare and the political debate about the need for structural reform between left and right. Welfare has until recently been connected primarily to the nation-state, and it is a major challenge to rethink social **politics** from a transnational and multicultural perspective. One controversial question is whether the public sector is a barrier or a potential for economic development. Another question is what the future role of the state, market, and family should be in the restructuring of the welfare state. Finally, European integration has raised an important debate about the possibility and desirability of a transnational governance of welfare.

BIRTE SIIM

welfare rights
– see **rights**.

welfare state
This system of national welfare provision is about the satisfaction of basic **human needs**, provided through the **market**, the **state** or the **family**. The classical dimensions of welfare are related both to material needs and to recognition and respect, and the concept of welfare has increasingly become multidimensional. In western Europe, the expansion of the welfare state was connected to the growth of capitalist markets and the organization of workers, and the role of the state in the provision of welfare has been at the center of political conflicts between left and right. Welfare has been tied to the nation-state, and **globalization** has strengthened the role of the market vis-à-vis the state. This has sparked political debates about the need for structural reforms and about the future role of the welfare state in non-western countries.

The influential approach of Gösta Andersen in *The Three Worlds of Welfare Capitalism* (1990) and the power resource school have identified the driving forces and key factors in the evolution of the different welfare regimes, including benefits, labor market participation, and the general **social structure**. The main conclusion was that "politics matters," and the key factor differentiating between the social-democratic, the conservative-corporate, and the liberal models is de-commodification, that

is, to what extent the state makes individuals independent of the market forces.

Andersen's framework has become a standard reference, but it has been criticized for a normative bias in favor of the Nordic model. Feminist scholarship has criticized the neglect of the role of the family and care work in the provision of welfare. The argument is that de-commodification has a male-bias that makes it unable to explain variations in family forms and in the position of women in western societies, because individuals are already commodified as wage workers. It is also seen as a problem that the model does not include services, in the form of childcare. The high degree of "reproduction going public" in the Nordic countries is the basis for Helga Maria Hernes's concept in the *Welfare State and Women Power* (1987) of "women-friendliness," defined as states which "would not force harder choices on women than on men, or permit unjust treatment on the basis of sex." Comparative welfare research has recently become more attentive to the gender dimension, understood as the extent to which the state takes responsibility for care work.

The criticism of the three worlds of welfare has been followed by the construction of different typologies. Jane Lewis and Ilona Ostner, in *Gender and the Evolution of the European Social Policies* (1994), differentiated between strong, medium, and weak male-breadwinner models on the basis of the division between **work** and **care**, for example women's access to paid work and social benefits, family wage, and the distribution of unpaid work. They conclude that Germany and Britain both have strong male-breadwinner models, France a medium one, and the Scandinavian countries have weak male-breadwinner models.

Another approach suggests that **culture**, **norms**, and **values** play a key role in explaining variations in welfare-state models and women's position in society. The individualization of benefits is also seen as an important factor in typologies that indicates whether social **rights** are tied to the family, to the husband as head of the family, or to individuals, and whether women have benefits as citizens, employees, wives, or mothers.

There is a growing interest in new welfare typologies that can explain different forms of **inequality** related, for example to **gender**, **class**, and **ethnicity**. One example is Fiona Williams, who in "Race/ethnicity, Gender and Class in Welfare States" (1995, *Social Politics*), has developed a typology that integrates gender and welfare regimes with migration regimes. The focus is on the cross-national interaction of three key concepts: nation, work, and family. Another example is Walter Korpi, who, in his article "Faces of Inequality" (2000, *Social Politics*), developed a typology that integrates a class and a gender perspective. Mainly economic resources determine class inequality, while gender inequality ("gendered agency inequality") is determined by democratic **politics**, access to higher **education**, and labor market participation. He concludes that class inequality has been more resistant than gender inequality.

With the development towards multicultural societies, ethnicity tends to become an independent factor explaining differentiation in relation to welfare and scholars have identified different ethnicity regimes. This is followed by an academic debate about intersectionality between key categories such as gender, class, and ethnicity. Inequality has many faces and the intersection between different forms of inequality challenges existing typologies based primarily upon one form of domination. The argument is, first, that domination is contextual, and, second, that the same mechanisms cannot explain different forms of inequality, because different dimensions may be crucial for reproduction of inequality in relation to gender, class, and ethnicity, respectively.

Welfare and the welfare state are not universal but dynamic concepts that have new meanings and content in **postindustrial societies**. In a globalized world with growing immigration, one of the new challenges is to understand how different forms of inequality interact. Welfare has until recently been connected primarily to the nation-state, and the welfare state needs to be rethought from a transnational and multicultural perspective.   BIRTE SIIM

westernization

This notion has two main, and to some extent overlapping, connotations. First, the fate of the world is seen to be following the West, politically, economically, and culturally. Second, there is the connotation that this process is on the whole a healthy and progressive development, since the "West is best." In this sense, the concept of westernization is connected to **Orientalism**. Both of these ideas can be found in mainstream nineteenth-century social thought, in the writings of **Georg Wilhelm Friedrich Hegel**, **Karl Marx**, **John Stuart Mill**, **August Comte**, **Herbert Spencer**, and others. The central idea was well expressed by Marx when he said – with Britain in mind – that "the country that is more developed industrially only shows, to the less developed, the image of its own future" ("Preface" to the first edition of

volume I, *Capital*, 1867). Western-style industrialism was the future of the whole world. In the 1950s and 1960s this idea found powerful form in theories of **modernization**. Modernity was equated with its western forms; to modernize was to westernize. Such seemed to be the inevitable destiny of all the so-called "developing societies" of the Third World, those that had not yet adopted western **institutions** and practices.

For a time the western model seemed to compete with an Eastern one, the one provided by the Soviet-style **economies** and **societies** of eastern Europe (even though, being based on Marxist **ideology**, this model could as legitimately claim western origin). With the collapse of the communist regimes of eastern Europe after 1989, it has come to be widely argued that only the western model of liberal **democracy**, based on a market economy, now has any appeal in the world. In a widely discussed book *The End of History and the Last Man* (1992), the American political theorist Francis Fukuyama pronounced "the end of history," basically a restatement of the westernization philosophy that the endpoint of humanity's evolution lay in the adoption of the liberal democratic ideas and institutions of the modern West. Having seen off its ideological competitors in **Communism** and **fascism**, the West – identified with its liberal capitalist form – had won.

Such views have been contested in a number of ways. Directly opposing Fukuyama was the claim of his fellow countryman Samuel Huntington, in *The Clash of Civilizations and the Remaking of World Order* (1996), that, far from ideological conflict being over, we were faced with a future conflict over incompatible **civilizations**, in which ideologies based on the great **religions** of the world – Christianity, Islam, Hinduism, Confucianism – would compete across deep "fault lines" in the emerging world order (or disorder). In this vision, the West would be thrown increasingly on the defensive as it struggled to hold its own against the challenge of Islamic **fundamentalism** and the developing **power** of Asian giants such as China and India.

At a deeper level, westernization was challenged by a group of historians and social theorists who took issue with its whole philosophy of history as deeply "Eurocentric." Western **modernity**, they argued, was only one form of modernity, and not necessarily the one towards which the rest of the world was tending. Chinese, Indian, and Islamic civilization had all in the past made major contributions to modernity – in commerce, science, and **technology** – and could be expected to build on these in elaborating their own distinctive types of modernity in the coming years. If the future of the world was a global civilization, it would not necessarily, as many have assumed, carry a western stamp. There had been periods of non-western **globalization** before the rise of the West; the current form drew on these earlier tendencies and any emerging global order would bear the marks of non-western as much as western **culture**. As the more than 2 billion people of India and China move into an increasingly dynamic phase of economic development, it seems increasingly unlikely that western dominance – the main fact of world history for the last two to three centuries – will be the principle of the future, or that "westernization" will at all accurately describe the resulting patterns of change.

KRISHAN KUMAR

white-collar crime
– see **crime**.

Williams, Raymond (1921–1988)
A critic of **culture** and **society**, and an emblematic figure in the cultural turn and the postwar British left, Williams made decisive contributions to the study of **politics**, literature, and culture. He studied at Trinity College, Cambridge, and then worked in adult education. Between 1974 and 1983 he was Professor of Drama at Cambridge University. His approach studied culture as part of a historically structured, whole way of life and investigated the concomitant structures of feeling that operate as principles of social inclusion and exclusion in *Culture and Society* (1958) and *The Long Revolution* (1961). Writing against the grain of **empiricism** and also against the "practical criticism" of Frank Leavis (1895–1978) at Cambridge University, who had condemned the decline and standardization of culture resulting from **mass society**, Williams made a virtue of interdisciplinarity and theorizing about culture, long before either became fashionable. Among the *soi-disant* theorists of the working class and class struggle that formed the *New Reasoner* circle and, later, the *New Left Review*, Williams was comparatively rare in having impeccable proletarian origins.

Eventually, his preferred term to distinguish his approach was **cultural materialism**, by which he meant the study of all forms of signification within the actual context of their production, as in *Marxism and Literature* (1977). The approach was indebted to the neo-Marxian position, in particular with reference to the central importance of

history and **social class** in politics, culture, and communication. But Williams overhauled the Marxist engine, by breaking decisively with the base–superstructure model of vulgar **Marxism** and determining to approach local **traditions** of culture in the terms of ordinary cultural categories and representations.

Through a series of studies on **mass communications**, literature, the **city**, ecology, political revitalization, **globalization**, North–South relations, and socio-cultural forecasting, Williams tried to release the concept of culture from elitist overtones and relocate it at the heart of political, social, and cultural enquiry. His cultural materialism is inclusive, combative in that it draws attention to a selective tradition in culture, and stringent in holding that culture is one of the central resources in social, political, and economic reconstruction.

CHRIS ROJEK

Wilson, William Julius (1935–)
A professor of sociology at Harvard University since 1996, Wilson has developed a widely influential and controversial body of work on **race and ethnicity**, and urban **poverty**, in the United States. His first major book, *The Declining Significance of Race* (1978), argued that civil rights legislation of the 1960s caused **racism** to recede, but that class-based forces and economic stratification among African-Americans had created a new disadvantage for them. Fleeing poor black **neighborhoods**, middle-class blacks took with them jobs, **social capital,** and other resources that had previously stabilized black neighborhoods and **communities**. Widely disparaged by critics for prematurely dismissing racism and race-based factors in accounting for American racial **inequality**, Wilson responded a few years later with his magnum opus, *The Truly Disadvantaged* (1987). This work argued that substantial structural changes to the economic and social system of poor black neighborhoods were responsible for the plight of the African-American urban poor and producing a new kind of "social isolation." The most important of these dynamics was the "spatial mismatch" of jobs and neighborhoods, in which black urban neighborhoods were becoming increasingly "jobless ghettos" with a growing black "underclass." As a consequence of these economic shifts, Wilson argued, black youths in these areas lacked appropriate role models in the conventional **economy**. He thus reintroduced a cultural **explanation** to understanding black poverty, which generated a storm of controversy. He also argued that the lack of jobs for black men and their rising

incarceration rates led to a shortage of "marriageable" black men. This contributed to the growth of female-headed, single-parent **families** in the African-American community. These ideas – spatial mismatch of jobs and neighborhoods, the role of cultural factors, the decline of marriageable men, and, more generally, the role of neighborhood factors in shaping social and economic outcomes – generated a vast outpouring of research into urban sociology, **demography**, **race and ethnicity**, and **social stratification**, as well as becoming a central element in policy debates over the sources and consequences of urban poverty. Wilson continued to expand on these themes in later works, most notably *When Work Disappears* (1996).

JEFF MANZA

Wirth, Louis (1897–1952)

Born in Germany, Wirth studied at the University of Chicago, where he became associated with Chicago sociology during the 1930s. While mostly recognized for his classic, if not brilliant, article "Urbanism as a Way of Life," in the *American Journal of Sociology* (1938), he also produced pioneering work on the question of minorities in American **cities**. His first book, *The Ghetto* (1928), was based upon the research involving Jewish immigrants in Chicago that he undertook for his doctoral dissertation. As already apparent in *The Ghetto*, Wirth involved himself in his subjects of investigation as both researcher and activist. In his subsequent studies on Jewish immigrants and black Americans in American cities, along with his involvement with anti-discrimination committees and the civil rights movement, Wirth, as a Jewish émigré intellectual, identified with his subjects as strangers while avoiding dissolving himself into that identification. His work on minorities in "Morale and Minority Groups" (1941) and "The Problem of Minority Groups" (1945), for example, displays considerable subtlety and sophistication on the question of **identity** and difference, when the decisive, if not dominant, trend of thought was to put the question of minorities as a question of **assimilation**. With respect to minorities, Wirth argued (1945) that

> it is not the specific characteristics, therefore, whether racial or ethnic, that mark a people as a minority but the relationship of their group to some other group in society in which they live. The same characteristics may at one time and under one set of circumstances serve as marks of dominant status and at another time and under another set of circumstances symbolize identification with a minority.

Clearly, Wirth was well aware of what we would much later identify as traps of both **essentialism** and constructionism. Yet, his brilliant essay on urbanism became the defining moment of his oeuvre. While his definition of cities as relatively heterogeneous, sizable, and dense settlements drew much criticism, even from **Lewis Mumford** who otherwise appreciated and admired Wirth, the essay displays equal subtlety and sophistication to his work on minorities and shows how closely he read both **Georg Simmel** and **Max Weber**.

ENGIN ISIN

witchcraft

As the practice or the production of malign or beneficial magic, witchcraft has an enduring place in the western, and in much of the non-western, imagination of the dynamics of esoteric and exotic **powers**. Its practitioners and producers, putative or real, range from the magus and the sorcerer to the devil-worshipper and the demonically possessed. They are as ancient as Medea and as contemporary as the benign neopagans of Tanya Luhrmann's *Professions of the Witch's Craft* (1989). They might acquire their special capacities through training or inheritance or some combination of both. They might or might not be aware that they possess the capacities that a certain ordeal or process of divination or coerced confession reveals them to have exercised. Institutionalized churches can and often do incorporate magical **technologies** into their standard cultus, but they are uniformly hostile to the sorcerer or witch who asserts or represents a challenge to their ritual **authority**. The western history of the persecution of such challenges is as inseparable from the history of the Catholic inquisitions as from the structural conflicts and fractures that mark the ascendance of the bourgeoisie in the modernizing states of Europe and the Puritan colonies of North America. Hugh Trevor-Roper's *The European Witch-Craze of the Sixteenth and Seventeenth Century* (1969) and Kai Ericson's *Wayward Puritans* (1966) offer valuable sociological perspectives on the latter.

E. E. Evans-Pritchard (1902–73) put forward the seminal anthropological analysis of witchcraft in *Witchcraft, Oracles and Magic Among the Azande* (1937). He argued for two theses. The first was that the appeal to witchcraft does not amount to a confused or superstitious attempt at the proper causal **explanation** of events but instead to the deployment of a supplementary idiom that facilitates the resolution of the existential significance of events – and, in the Zande case, especially of unfortunate events. His second thesis was that the same idiom functions as an effective means of enforcement of **norms** of civility and neighborliness whose persistent violation would – in the Zande case – lead almost inevitably to accusations of witchcraft and their embarrassing and potentially even fatal aftermath. Jeanne Favret-Saada could apply Evans-Pritchard's theses with little revision in her study of the diagnostics of witchcraft among Norman **peasants**, *Deadly Words* (1977 [trans. 1980]). The contributors to Jean and John Comaroff's *Modernity and Its Malcontents* (1993) find not only that the idiom of witchcraft continues to have great currency in sub-Saharan Africa but also that it has come to supply there the primary resources for a popular critique of market **capitalism**. Yet such an idiom is not of equal service everywhere; culturally widespread, it is not culturally universal. In *Natural Symbols* (1971), **Mary Douglas** infers from comparative evidence that witches and their craft are more likely to be at the forefront of collective consciousness and concern in societies that vigilantly monitor their boundaries and the unambiguous conformity of any given individual to the **group** or groups to which he or she belongs.   JAMES D. FAUBION

Wittgenstein, Ludwig (1889–1951)

Born in Austria, Wittgenstein was preoccupied throughout his life with the nature of **language** and its relation to the world, and came to occupy a unique position in the linguistic philosophy movement that flourished during the middle part of the twentieth century. His initial "picture theory" of meaning asserted that language consists of propositions that picture the world, which he conceptualized as an arrangement of atomic facts whose logical form is mirrored in language.

Subsequently Wittgenstein came to reject this picture theory because its focus on the representational role of language excluded the innumerable other forms of language use that he evoked with his notion of **language games**. With this rejection came the recognition that language use is always part of a wider set of conventional human activities and cannot be understood apart from them. At the same time, the notion of "atomic facts" and their corresponding simple names was discarded in favor of the idea that human categories are built up of overlapping "family resemblances" – a view which has enormous influence on categorization theory.

Wittgenstein was thus a central figure in the **linguistic turn** in western philosophy. His ideas

emerged within **sociology** in the writings of Peter Winch, in *The Idea of a Social Science* (1958), and others who used his discussion of rule-following conduct to criticize excessively deterministic analyses of human action, in the movement known as **social constructionism** that developed within sociology in the late 1960s and beyond, and in the broader movement towards the study of language and discourse in the **social sciences**.

                                    JOHN HERITAGE

Wolf, Kurt H. (1912–2003)

Manuel Yellen Professor of Social Relations at Brandeis University, Wolf contributed to the study of **Georg Simmel**, the history of sociology, and the sociology of knowledge. He was born in Darmstadt, Germany, escaped to Italy in 1934, obtained his doctorate from the University of Florence in 1935, and emigrated to the United States in 1939, where he taught at the Southern Methodist University and Ohio State University. He was elected President of the International Society for the Sociology of Knowledge in 1972.

The revival of interest in Simmel was stimulated by *The Sociology of Georg Simmel* (1950), which Wolf edited and translated. He developed a unique view of **qualitative research** in his *Surrender and Catch. Experience and Inquiry Today* (1976), and *Survival and Sociology. Vindicating the Human Subject* (1991), in which he argued that the researcher should begin with immersion "surrender" in the world of the subject rather than taking an external and objective stance "catch".   BRYAN S. TURNER

women and crime

Certain trends and patterns in women's criminality compared with men's have long been observed: women commit a small share of all **crimes**; their crimes are fewer, less serious, and less likely to be repeated than men's; women form a smaller proportion of the prison population than men – although this has been changing in recent years owing to changing perceptions of women, increases in drug use, and perceptions that women are now committing more violent crimes than hitherto. These observations are shared across the world, so much so that it has frequently been argued that it is really women's conformity that we need to fathom, rather than their criminality.

While the media worldwide give attention to unusually violent or sexual crimes committed by women, and while adult women are found in all offense types, they form a numerical majority in only a small number of offenses: infanticide, offenses relating to prostitution, certain kinds of theft, and (in England and Wales) failure to pay for a television license. When women are convicted it is more likely to be for offenses involving theft and handling stolen goods, drug offenses, and fraud and forgery, than anything else.

There has been relatively little theorizing about women and crime. Rather, it is often the case that theories put forward to explain men's crime have been presented as general theories of crime and have included women without real questioning as to whether or not this is appropriate. While criminological theorizing about crime and pathways into crime has been abundant, then, **criminology** has seemingly had almost nothing to say of interest or importance about women. Whether this reflects the apparent rarity of the female offender, simple neglect, **sexism** on the part of theorists, or some other reason, it is difficult to say, but it has meant that the trajectory of theories relating to women has been unusually conservative.

Early theorists argued that the true nature of women was antithetical to crime. Reflecting dominant ideas about biological **determinism**, epitomized in **Sigmund Freud**'s widely quoted phrase "anatomy is destiny," it was thought that criminality was linked to "maleness" and "masculine traits" such as aggression and physicality. Cesare Lombroso (1835–1909), one of the most influential biological theorists, argued in *The Female Offender* (1895, cowritten with Guglielmo Ferrero) that women were less well evolved than men and that female criminality resulted from biological inferiority. A further notable strand to the biology and crime debate (in the 1960s and 1970s in particular) has revolved around menstruation and crime. Modern biological theories focus on the relation between the personality trait of sensation-seeking and the physiological/biological phenomena associated with it.

Psychological theories of women's crime also emerged in the latter half of the nineteenth century. For example, nineteenth-century **explanations** for kleptomania attributed women's shoplifting to a mental disease associated with reproductive functions. In a lecture on *The Psychology of Women* (1933), Freud attributed women's **deviance** to their inability to adjust to their biological inferiority; as a consequence, he suggested, they develop a masculinity complex. Later theories revolved around women's apparently high levels of emotional instability and poor self-image, while recent research has focused on gender differences in motivational constructs, sensation-seeking, creativity, differences in social **attitudes**, and social cognition

(those factors that affect an individual's capacity for encoding **information**, interpreting, and considering the **risks** and benefits of a particular action).

Explanations of female criminality in terms of social **differentiation** of gender roles, which emerged in the 1960s and 1970s, were heralded as a major advance on the early conservative physiological and psychological theories. References to differential opportunities for illegitimate activity, **socialization**, and expectations of behavior all point to how the social environment can limit or facilitate access to illegitimate means to achieve status or social goals. Sociological and feminist work has also included analysis of differential forms of **social control**, with greater "chaperonage" over females than males. Embedded structural factors such as **poverty** and family disruption are also thought to influence women's offending levels in the same way that they influence men's, although the "feminization of poverty" suggests that women may be particularly influenced by such factors.

In 1975 two controversial American authors, Freda Adler (*Sisters in Crime*) and Rita Simon (*Women and Crime*), argued that women's increased criminality stemmed from their liberation. The books attracted major criticism, not least because of the difficulty in measuring the impact of the women's movement and because of assumptions that women's roles had changed. Numerous feminist reviews of the relationship between women and crime followed, notably *Women, Crime and Criminology* by Carol Smart (1976) in England. A key contribution of such studies has been to highlight that our knowledge of female offenders has been beset with **myths**, muddles, and misconceptions which often reflect ideological concerns rather than objective evidence and that even self-consciously "objective" scientific approaches often reflect men's knowledge. The collective endeavors of feminist criminologists and supporters in other disciplines have offered trenchant critiques of the accumulated wisdom about female offenders and demonstrated the limitations of theories of criminality that have been developed by and applied to men in providing explanations of women's crime.

Some of the questions left unanswered by feminist critiques of crime revolve around the precise ways in which **patriarchy** might contribute to women's crime, but the concentration on **power** in feminist analyses has contributed enormously to an understanding of the gender biases built into and demonstrated by knowledge construction, legal, and criminal justice system processes.

One theme that has been consistently evident in writings about women and crime concerns gender role conditioning (whether as a result of biology, psychology, or patriarchy). Women's own accounts for their pathways into crime bear out such claims, but also emphasize the role of insurmountable social and economic difficulties which lead some women towards crime. Many female offenders indicate child sexual and violent abuse and other deprivations in early lives. Not all who are abused go on to commit crime, of course; nevertheless, women's accounts about pathways into crime, with all their contradictions, are no less valid than others.

Why some women commit crime can perhaps be approached by referring to the broad features of women's structural positions and **lifestyles** in society and then focusing on what is offending-related. Child sexual abuse and other related factors are often mentioned in this regard, although the connections between this and crime remain undertheorized. It could well be that the low self-esteem engendered by the abuse and disadvantage fosters movement towards crime simply because crime provides a way of establishing some kind of autonomy in otherwise disempowered lives, but more research is needed here.

LORAINE GELSTHORPE

women and work

Work, both paid and unpaid, has been a key concept in sociological research on **gender**. The activity of men has normally been valued more highly than the activities of women. A major theme has been the distribution between wage work, care work, and housework, which is a key factor determining the gender division of work and the reproduction of the gender hierarchy. The sexual division of work has changed radically especially since the mid-1970s, but there is at the same time a remarkable stability in the sexual division of **work** across time and place. A key question in feminist research is how to reconcile wage work with care work.

Since the industrial revolution the fundamental gender **differentiation** in paid and unpaid work is connected to the capitalist division of **labor** in production and reproduction. Women have always worked but women's position on the **labor market** was tied to responsibilities for housework and care work determined by their class position and the ability to pay others to carry out this work. The division between wage work and care work connected to the public/private divide has two aspects – one refers to a differentiation

between the **state** and the **market**, the other to the differentiation between state and **family**. As Jane Lewis and Ilona Ostner have shown in "Gender and the Evolution of European Social Policies," in S. Liebfried and P. Pierson (eds.), *European Social Policies* (1995), the male-breadwinner model was shaped by a discourse and policy premised upon men's role as the main providers and women's responsibility for children, the sick, the old, and the disabled. As a result men received higher wages than did women even if they were not providers.

The meaning of work is contested and feminist research has redefined work to include house and care work. In her *Welfare State and Women Power* (1987), Helga Hernes emphasized that care work is determined by a different logic from the state and the market. Care work is invisible and, as Kari Wærness in her essay "On the Rationality of Caring" (in A. S. Sassoon [ed.], *Women and the State*, 1987) has argued, there is a different **rationality** connected to caring for husbands who can take care of themselves and caring for dependent family members.

During the 1970s and 1980s feminist scholars debated the increasing tendency for all women, including mothers and sole mothers, to become wage workers and for the state to regulate care work. From the late 1980s there was growing interest in comparative differences in women's participation in wage work and in the organization of care work. The Anglo-American approach had a negative perception of the state and **public policies** as instruments for patriarchal control of women's work, **sexuality**, and **motherhood**. In contrast, Scandinavian research developed a positive perception of the state and "reproduction going public," inspired by the expansion of the public service sector and women's inclusion on the labor market.

European **welfare states** have since the mid-1970s moved towards a dual-breadwinner model with an increasing political emphasis on the responsibilities of all adults to engage in paid **work**. The increase in women's and decrease in men's labor market participation, as well as the changes in family structures towards an increasing individualization, has eroded the male-breadwinner model. As demonstrated by comparative gender research there are different labor market patterns. Diane Sainsbury, in *Gender and Welfare Regimes* (1999), differentiates between: (1) a male-breadwinner regime, where benefits are given solely to the male provider; (2) a separate gender roles regime, where benefits are given to both the male provider and the female caregiver; and (3) an individual earner–carer regime, where both sexes have entitlements as earners and carers, found only in Scandinavia.

In terms of the mixed **economy** of **care** there are also different patterns. In countries such as France, a general family support has given all children above three years a place in a publicly funded childcare center. In countries such as the United Kingdom, provision is likely to be a mixture of kin, market provision, public provision, and voluntary provision. Only the Nordic countries have a **tradition** for publicly funded childcare centers for under-three-year-olds.

Globalization and **migration** have created new forms of **inequality** in the division between work and care as women in the Third World increasingly migrate to the First World. Scholars have identified a care deficit in the poor countries, in the sense that women from the Third World increasingly cover the caring needs of the rich countries. They are hired to take care of children and do housework for middle- and upper-class families in the rich world, while their own children often live in poor conditions in their home countries. This has created what **Arlie Russell Hochschild** and Barbara Ehrenreich have called "global care chains" (*Global Women: Nannies, Maids and Sex Workers in the New Economy*, 2003) with the export of care from the poor to the rich world. At the same time the family work for migrant women may be dominated by poor wages and exploitative working conditions.

Globalization and migration have increased class differences among women. Scholars have identified a tendency towards a feminization of **poverty** in the global economy where women in poor countries do most of the hard work and get the least resources. Inequalities between women in the rich and poor countries and between women within many rich countries are growing. At the same time women also have common interests as wage workers in equal pay, non-discrimination hiring and firing practices, and decent working conditions. Gender interacts with other kinds of diversity and differentiation that must be taken into account in order to understand the dynamics of women's work in a globalized world. There is a growing awareness in the international system that women's work is the key to economic development in many Third World countries. Gender **equality** has become a political goal and mainstreaming has become a means to integrate a gender and ethnicity perspective in **politics** and planning. The United Nations system has strengthened women's right to basic resources, including work, **education**, and equal pay, and has developed strategies to empower women and improve their living conditions and well-being.

BIRTE SIIM

women's health
– see **health**.

women's studies

In modern **democracies** there is a close relationship between the women's movement / **feminism** and women's studies. The women's movement was a child of the American and French Revolutions that inspired demands for women's equal rights among **intellectuals** such as Mary Wollstonecraft (1759–97) and **John Stuart Mill**. The dramatic changes in relations between **work** and **family** and the integration of women in wage work after the industrial revolution were the background for studies of the women question. During the twentieth century, women's **organizations** demanded both equal civil, political, and social **rights** and special rights in relation to pregnancy and birth. In her influential book *The Sexual Contract* (1988), Carole Pateman has analyzed Wollstonecraft's dilemma – the tension between strategies based on **equality** that neglect women's experiences "as women" and strategies based upon difference that reproduce women's subordination in society.

Simone de Beauvoir's seminal book *The Second Sex* (1949 [trans. 1972]) was the first modern feminist study of the construction of women through **socialization** in the **family**, in **education**, and on the **labor market**. The opening statement, "You are not born a woman, you become a woman," is a critique of biological **essentialism** similar to the social constructivist position of postmodern feminism.

Women's studies are defined as studies "for, by and about women." The first women's study program was established in 1969/70 in the United States, inspired by the new feminist movement and developed as an interdisciplinary approach at many western universities. During the 1980s there was a growing criticism of the dominant "women-centeredness" that tended to neglect diversity among women of color. Inspired by the critique from minority women and postcolonialism, many women's studies centers changed their name to "centers for gender research" during the 1990s. This marked a change from a focus on women's common interests to a focus on men and masculinity and on the interconnection between gender, ethnicity, and sexuality.

Feminist studies included liberal feminism, radical feminism, standpoint theory, and diversity feminism, inspired by postcolonialism. Their strategies have varied from the "inclusion" of women to "reversal" and "re-conceptualizing" the discipline, and their methods range from quantitative to interpretative and deconstructive **methodology**. Since the 1990s there has been a growing critique of Anglo-American bias and the change from women's studies to gender research was followed by more contextual and situated approaches. The demobilization of the women's movement in western **democracies** has contributed to strengthening postmodernist and poststructuralist gender research at western universities. Judith Butler's book, *Gender Trouble. Feminism and the Subversion of Identity* (1990), illustrates the new tension between **deconstruction** and the normative goals of feminism.

Globalization and **migration** have been followed by a growth in the international women's movement and a public discourse about gender equality in the international **community**. Today there are women's studies and gender programs all over the world. In future, one of the challenges of women's and gender studies will be how to overcome **ethnocentrism** and develop ways to overcome the tension between the universal goals of feminism – equal respect for women and men – and the particularism of women's situation in different contexts.   BIRTE SIIM

work and employment

Paid and unpaid work of many varieties constitute defining experiences of individual **identity**, group life, and, indeed, societies as a whole. Work refers to a set of tasks that people carry out, often for a wage, to produce goods or services for others. This simple definition, however, merely scratches the surface of the myriad forms of work and employment relationships under contemporary global **capitalism**. What makes both work and employment important is that they have direct implications for nearly all subfields of sociological inquiry. From **poverty** to our access to **health care systems, consumption**, gender and race relations, **families, social psychology, social movements** – all are conditioned by the ways in which **societies** organize their systems and relations of work. At an individual and group level, particular types of jobs or **careers** shape our **lifechances**. They shape the rewards that are available to us, our experience of dignity, and the trust and loy-

alty we feel towards corporate and political leaders.

The study of work in **industrial societies** has been central to the discipline of **sociology** since its inception. **Karl Marx**, whose **influence** on sociology has been considerable, posited that the terms and social relations of **labor** are the point of departure for studying societies, historically and contemporarily. For Marx, the most essential fact about the human species is our capacity to engage self-consciously in the act of collective labor. Our species being – that which makes us distinctly human – is most fully realized when we collectively plan what we make, how we make it, how we work together with others, and how we distribute the products of our efforts. Under the capitalist mode of production, humans experience a deep-rooted **alienation** from that essence. We sell our capacity to labor to others, are subjected to systems of control that diminish our autonomy, and experience spiraling exploitation as capitalists engage in a never-ending search to cheapen the costs of production and to reduce human input to little more than a mechanical factor of production. The material and psychic injuries of capitalist social relations, according to Marx, would create irreparable class conflict, leading workers collectively to overturn **capitalism** as a mode of production. Marx's critique of capitalism remains one of the most influential perspectives in contemporary sociology.

Max Weber infused Marx's critique of capitalism with a theory of a specific process that he considered to be inevitable in modern western society: **rationalization** and its manifestation in a particular political/economic mode of **organization, bureaucracy**. Weber's **ideal-type** bureaucracy embodies many features we find in contemporary capitalist workplaces, such as division of labor, hierarchy, the proliferation of formal rules and regulations (and clearly specified rewards and punishments for adhering to or disobeying them), and the centralization of **authority** and **power**. In Weber's view, rationalization and bureaucratization provide capitalists ideal tools of control and power over the workers they employ in industrial factories.

Whereas Marx believed that marginalized and deskilled workers would develop a critical class consciousness and lead a political revolution to overturn industrial capitalist society (leading to a classless society in the form of **socialism**, then **Communism**), Weber pessimistically argued that rationalization, the consolidation of **elites**, and the silencing of the political voice of those excluded from the ranks of the powerful, would simply become more intransigent, even under socialist society. A colleague of Weber, **Robert Michels**, coined the term the iron law of oligarchy to describe this trajectory.

The insights of these classical theorists remain central to the study of work and employment in the **economy** of any advanced industrial society. Core concepts raised in their scholarly work continue to thread throughout the literature on work and labor. As industrial capitalism has been transformed into postindustrial and global capitalism, however, it has become apparent that other dimensions of work, aside from exploitation and alienation, are salient to working people. These dimensions have complicated and undermined Marx's prediction of a working-class revolution based on the premise of naked and intractable exploitation.

When we work, for example, we often derive intangible but important rewards. How we feel about our jobs can depend on nonmaterial factors such as the feeling of inherent pleasure or gratification that we derive from our work, or the worth we assign to our laboring activities. One example illustrates that how people feel about their jobs does not always follow from extrinsic factors such as wages or **prestige**. Child-care workers are amongst the lowest-paid workers in the United States and the **occupation** is not highly attractive, judging by a perpetual shortage of workers and the rates of high turnover in the field. Yet these workers often feel their work is valuable and derive intrinsic satisfaction from the occupation because they are nurturing and teaching small children, tasks that arguably constitute the very basis of social order.

Our collective work relationships and sense of membership in a **community** often counterbalance feelings of exploitation. Many people regard their job as their most important source of sociability and humanity. We receive self-validation as well as validation of our moral **values** in the course of working with others. We take pride in jobs well done. Work is often a place where a variety of personal needs are met. Co-workers celebrate birthdays, holidays, births, and weddings together; people take their work relationships beyond the factory or office door, into public spaces such as bars, political organizations, or places of recreation. **Generations** of family members have followed each other into the same factory, giving rise to cultural and oral **traditions** that become central to the definition of **family** itself. More than simply deriving job satisfaction,

then, what we do in the workplace with others constitutes our very **identity**.

Other collective activities emanate from the workplace which are constitutive of the **self** and provide opportunities for personal growth and fulfilling group **interaction**. Workers form mutually supportive "**cultures** of **solidarity**" in response to collective perceptions of injustice on the part of their employers. Randy Hodson, in *Working with Dignity* (2001), points out that workplaces are sites in which we enact **norms** and procedures of organizational **citizenship**. As organizational citizens we engage in constructive actions and relationships that improve our place of work in ways that exceed what we are required to do by managers and employers. Participating in unions and in **labor movements** is both a way to advance material and political interests and an important communal nexus in a world in which collectively oriented public life appears to be in decline. For these reasons, workplaces in contemporary capitalist society are terrains of ambiguity, of unequal power and subordination, on the one hand, and experiential gratification and positive meaning on the other.

At the beginning of the twenty-first century, work and employment form a complex kaleidoscope of experience. Paid work takes place where we most expect to find it: in factories, offices, and fields. But sociologists and other social scientists also have found that people work for pay on the streets, in their homes, in the skies, and in the bowels of the earth. Institutional and industrial context matters immeasurably. For example, knowing the job tasks any individual carries out does not reveal the full story about that individual's job, work experience, or **social status**. Exactly the same type of work can vary based on the sectoral setting; a person who assembles mother boards for computers can do so in the employ of a major core corporation, earn a living wage, enjoy job security, and receive benefits, while a different person who assembles these boards in precisely the same way might do so working as a temporary laborer for a small peripheral firm, earning low wages, and lacking job security or benefits. The first might be labeled a manufacturing worker while the second might be considered a mere assembler.

Revolutionary technological innovations have emerged in the era of **globalization** and the **transnational corporation**, innovations that facilitate the movement of **information**, knowledge, raw materials, finished products, and capital. Thus, it has become increasingly common that workers serve and produce for customers who are located literally on the other side of the planet, embedded in production systems and relations of **inequality** that have been configured at similar global remove.

Since Marx and Weber made their observations of early industrial capitalism, sociologists have introduced many new concepts and identified new forms of employment relationships. They have broadened the scope of their research to adjust to the fact that the modal form of economic organization under capitalism is far more varied and global than was the period of early capitalism on which Marx based his theory. They also have acknowledged that work cannot be viewed as one-dimensional, but must be viewed as multi-faceted, with exploitation and disenfranchisement often co-existing with pleasure, gratification, and community. Four major approaches to creating work systems have developed in industrial and postindustrial capitalist societies. An understanding of each is important, for each one holds differential implications for material well-being, power, and subjectivities. We find evidence of all these approaches today, depending on the type of work and the sector of employment and industry we study. With the globalization of production, corporations have imported these approaches to recently industrializing societies as well. The first major approach is **scientific management**, also referred to as **Taylorism** after Frederick Taylor, an engineer who lived in the United States at the turn of the twentieth century. Because he viewed autonomous workers' initiative, know-how, and social relationships as obstacles to productivity and efficiency, Taylor formulated a set of principles by which managers could rationalize and de-skill the **labor process**, undermining worker autonomy and control.

Scientific management relies on the use of time and motion studies, in which efficiency experts analyze and measure workers' movements and their tasks. They determine ways in which those tasks can be broken down into simple parts to increase efficiency, mechanisms by which the knowledge required for these tasks could be removed from workers and into the files and records of engineers and managers. Such deskilling and control can be exerted personally, through the efforts of a supervisor, or impersonally, through **technology** such as assembly lines that simplify tasks and regulate their pace or through computers that measure every key stroke and generate reports on the quality of workers' efforts. This system of control – which isolates workers and reduces their skill, autonomy, and dignity – historically has led many workers to form **trade unions** to organize collectively against employer domination. Scientific management, as an organizing principle, persists today in many work settings, primarily where costs of worker training are minimal, and employers care little about turnover and actively discourage worker attachment to the **firm**.

A second approach to the organization of work and employment is the human relations model which was influential in the United States from the late 1930s to the 1960s. Tracing its origins to American industrial psychologists Elton Mayo, Fritz Roethlisberger, and William Dickson, the human relations paradigm focuses on maximizing the creativity and loyalty of workers rather than marginalizing them, as the scientific managerial model would call for. These researchers, ironically much in the same way as Marx, theorized that what was most important to humans was their social relationships. Their goal, however, was to coopt those relationships. They also posited that workers respond positively to managerial initiatives to cultivate and acknowledge their employees' value.

Human relations theorists would design methods for taking advantage of workers' desire to be social, methods that would create workers as loyal and committed organizational participants who would view their interests as being in synch with those of managers. Such methods include soliciting workers' input, giving them opportunities to determine how to carry out their tasks, and rewarding them for their accomplishments, although human relations theorists would not, in fact, advocate that **management** yield structural power to workers. The human relations approach has appeared in different forms over the last century and is extremely pervasive in the world of management today.

A third orientation to organizing work is bureaucratic. In a bureaucratic control system, as outlined by Weber, power is embodied in the organization itself, rather than directly in supervisors or managers. As **Michel Foucault** has argued, power in modern bureaucratic institutions is ever-present and pervasive, yet invisible as it is embedded in rules, ranking schemes, and organizational structure. Bureaucratic control systems are built on hierarchy, clearly specified avenues of vertical advancement that serve to motivate workers and elicit their consent, and on centralized and impersonal power. Nearly all work organizations are bureaucratically organized to some degree but bureaucratic control is most fully developed in public-sector institutions and in the employment systems of large, monopolistic corporations. In a bureaucratic system, those working at the lowest levels are most likely to be disempowered and their work rationalized. Often, these workers lack access to formal ladders of mobility into the higher reaches of the bureaucracy. On the other hand, workers in the middle ranges of the work organization historically have had access to internal labor markets, characterized by employment stability and in which career ladders are well defined and workers are expected to move up them continuously. This type of control system has prevailed where employers wish to encourage the attachment of their workers to the firm and they do so by offering implicit guarantees in the form of upward mobility and job security.

Finally, a fourth approach to organizing work in the contemporary **economy** is decentered control. Researchers have identified this approach with many labels, including coercive autonomy, unobtrusive management, cultural control, and concertive control. The key element of this system is that power and control are located throughout the organization, in many different sites, and in the hands of **groups** other than managers. It is subtle to the participants of the work organization and, indeed, successful decentered control systems depend on workers who regulate themselves and their co-workers. As is clear, decentered control is similar to the impersonal, invisible control made possible by bureaucratic control systems.

The main organizational mechanisms which make a system of decentered control possible include worker participation schemes, team-based production methods, cultural manifestos, and organizational decentralization. Since the mid-1980s, more employers have relied on building positive corporate cultures, designing flexible work systems (**flexible specialization**) that rely on greater employee participation and self-management, and shifting responsibility down into the hands of employees, in order to create more profitable work processes. Much in the spirit of the human relations tradition, the goal behind the adoption of these new work systems is to align workers' interests with the firm, to capitalize on worker expertise and knowledge, and to increase workers' awareness that the firm's success depends on their own efforts.

In a simultaneous counter-trend that marks a clear and deleterious departure from corporate practices of the mid twentieth century, however, corporate managers increasingly are unwilling to offer security and prosperity in return for greater worker involvement. The late twentieth and early twenty-first centuries have been marked by unpredictability and insecurity for working people across the occupational spectrum. Firms have near-complete latitude to close down operations and move them overseas. There, they can find an abundant supply of cheap labor, minimal environmental and labor regulation, and generous subsidies from governments eager to attract United States and other first-world operations to their own countries. Top managers, responding to global competition and to pressure from stock market investors to improve their bottom lines, eliminate corporate divisions and lay off workers with little notice. To an increasing degree, firms outsource their operations, externalizing specific functions to other business enterprises around the world. Companies that, during the era of monopoly capitalism, offered their workforces lifelong employment, have reneged on that promise, leading to huge numbers of layoffs and the erosion of the stable employment contract.

Specifically, internal labor markets of large, bureaucratic corporations have eroded since the mid-1980s, as corporations have downsized and restructured in their pursuit of greater profits and becoming more globally competitive. Even workers who were believed to be immune to layoffs and job insecurity – white-collar professionals and managers – have been subjected to job loss, longer terms of unemployment between jobs, downward mobility, and underemployment. The studies of American sociologist Rosabeth Moss Kanter, published in Men and Women of the Corporation (1977), and employment relations specialist Paul Osterma, in Securing Prosperity (1999), show the two extremes of managerial and professional employment over the last thirty years. Workers in most advanced industrialized societies have encountered these contradictory trends. For these reasons, social theorist **Richard Sennett** and others worry that the erosion of the secure employment relationship will lead to a broader erosion of commitment to and trust in society itself.

Employment relationships are related to yet distinct from work itself, and the nature of the employment relationship has significant ramifications for individual and group well-being. Anyone can carry out the exact same work in a variety of sectors and under a variety of employment conditions. The majority of workers hold jobs in the formal sector of the economy. Workers are engaged in formal employment relationships when they receive a wage or salary from an employer in a stable economic organization and when their employment relationship is regulated by the **state**. Sometimes they have secure, ongoing employment contracts. Both full-time and part-time employment, and self employment, characterize work in the formal economy.

Workers also participate in the formal sector, yet in sporadic employment relationships, when they are paid only upon completion of a project or a batch of products produced in a home, or are hired by a temporary staffing agency to go into a firm and fulfill a temporary production need. One of the most notable trends cross-nationally at the end of the twentieth century was the growth of the contingent work force, a different temporal approach to hiring workers. The contingent category includes workers across the occupational spectrum who are employed on a short-term, unpredictable basis, such as temporary, contract, and seasonal workers. Its expansion has been fueled by employers' drive to remain competitive and profitable. The theory behind the use of contingent workers, especially temporary workers, is that employers only need to have workers on their payroll when they need them, and can release them when they do not.

Fine-tuning the size of corporate workforces in this flexible way provides some economies, such as minimizing payroll expenses and administrative costs as human resource management of temporaries is transferred to temporary help agencies. But many costs are incurred as well: new conflicts, complexities, and administrative hierarchies are necessitated by this distinct employment arrangement. For example, when company policy dictates that a certain percentage of jobs are to be staffed by temporary workers only, middle managers and supervisors often have to enter into complicated negotiations with staffing agencies over the qualifications they require of a temporary worker, the wage that will be paid, or training opportunities that temps are eligible to take advantage of. Unanticipated hierarchies can develop when co-workers are requested to direct and even train temporary workers, acting as de facto supervisors. The increased use of contingent workers has gone hand-in-hand with the corporate restructuring processes identified earlier.

People are casually employed when they work to earn **income** in the **informal economy**. In the informal economy, goods and services are rendered and compensated outside formal employment relationships and **institutions**. In nearly all societies, work in the informal economy pro- vides a significant source of income for many people who face insurmountable obstacles to finding jobs in the formal sector. **Discrimination** by employers, lack of adequate educational credentials, skills, or cultural capital, immigration status, lack of capital to start small businesses, and family responsibilities that can restrict women's abilities to participate in the formal labor force are just some of the factors determining people's decisions about whether to earn income by participating in the informal economy. Such work might take the form of preparing food in one's home and selling it on the street, doing construction or yard work as day laborers, sewing garments in sweatshops, cleaning houses, doing childcare, taking in boarders, doing laundry, and selling drugs. Since informal economic activities are not scrutinized or regulated by the state, work in this sector of the economy – sometimes referred to as the underground economy – often places workers at a considerable disadvantage with respect to income, safety, and stability. Since the 1960s feminist sociologists have highlighted the significance of unpaid work that is performed in the home. Since women are not working for an employer they are not embedded in an employment relationship per se, nor do they hold a job, technically speaking. Unpaid domestic labor is an important case of work, nevertheless. Historically, domestic labor was not considered to be productive work and was often viewed as a set of tasks quite distinct from work in the world of corporations and businesses. Work in the home was not labor as work, it was labor as love. Domestic work was not viewed as skilled or complex; rather, it was viewed as something that women carried out because they were naturally inclined towards these nurturing and relational activities. To the contrary, contemporary feminist scholars have persuasively argued that preparing **food**, tending to the health, educational, and social needs of **children** and spouses, and maintaining normative standards of living – all work that has been carried out primarily by women, even when they work for pay in the marketplace, too – form the bedrock of the production and **reproduction** of the labor force under capitalism. It is also fraught with tension because it combines the instrumentality of labor with the affectiveness of love, countervailing principles of social organization that are evoked in caring for one's family.

Feminist sociologists such as **Ann Oakley** documented the complexities in the work of maintaining households and caring for children, and traced out the value of these tasks for sustaining society as a whole. Family relations, as a nexus within which household labor is carried out, typically are relations of inequality and power between women and men, and in recent years research studies have shown that housework is a subject of contestation between husbands and wives. Thus, close examination of domestic, unpaid work raises many of the same issues one encounters when studying paid work, such as alienation, dignity, inequality, and consciousness. Increasing the complexity of analyzing domestic work is that paid domestic work, such as cleaning houses and caring for other people's children, has been commodified and organized along the same unequal relationships of employment that have characterized work in formal capitalist workplaces. Paid domestic work such as child rearing and housekeeping is vulnerable to the same tension found in unpaid domestic work, predicated on the dialectic of labor and love.

The world of work and employment has changed considerably over the last century. What are the pressing issues and questions facing scholars who do research in this field at this point in time? A major area of sociological research is the examination of ways in which work organizations are structured as vehicles of inequality in capitalist society. This literature goes beyond the simple Marxist insight that class is the only basis for inequality, to the insight that within and across classes there is significant gender and race inequality as well. Specifically, work organizations block opportunity for some groups while providing opportunities for upward mobility, status, and income to others. The study of occupational **segregation** of jobs by sex and by **race and ethnicity** has been an important topic in this area. Work organizations serve to perpetuate inequality when they have mechanisms which relegate white women and people of color to subordinate positions at work; when men and women are segregated into jobs with unequal wages, authority, and mobility; and when people of color and white women are barred from training, professional development, and leadership opportunities. White women, and men and women of color, are more likely to be found in jobs that are deskilled, marginalized, part-time, and disempowered.

Of course, many sociologists have theorized how disadvantage can be corrected. Moss Kanter, for example, argues that job ladders need to be created to link female corporate clerical workers in dead-end positions to the middle and upper reaches of managerial positions. Feminist sociologists and activists argue that comparable worth programs can rectify pay inequities between women and men that are based on unequal valuation of women's work compared with men's work.

A recent generation of scholars argue that organizations themselves are fundamentally gendered and racialized. Historically, the study of work was gender- and race-blind. Researchers often implicitly based their definition of "**career**" and the normative career worker on class-, gender-, and race-specific experiences. They defined the "typical" career worker as an unencumbered professional who could uninterruptedly pursue vertical mobility on a continuous, full-time-plus basis, ignoring the fact that this model of work conflicted with the lives of the majority of working women. Several generations of feminist scholars, however, have corrected this gender- and race-neutral model. They point out that the way jobs and careers are defined, the unnamed gendered and racialized assumptions that underlie particular organizational arrangements and policies, and the cognitive but unexamined biases that managers and employers have about who is appropriate for what type of work all play a role in maintaining gender and racial inequality in the workplace. Gendered and racialized assumptions pervade the very fabric, culture, and structure of organizations, leading many to conclude that work organizations need to be much more fundamentally restructured than just changing job ladders, mandating diversity training, or recruiting more white women and people of color into executive management positions. The recognition that work organizations are constructed around implicit biases against white women and people of color can be extended to the case of other categories of workers as well, such as the case of the disabled. National laws forbid outright sex or race **discrimination** yet sociological research has uncovered ongoing, more subtle forms of discrimination, not amenable to easy **measurement** or observation. So, too, legislation (in the United States, the Americans with Disabilities Act) prohibits employers from preventing the disabled from acquiring jobs or gaining access to promotion opportunities. Yet, in more subtle ways, work organizations hold assumptions about "able-bodied" workers that routinely present barriers to the employment and promotion of differently abled people. The central insight that workplaces are predicated on unexamined and subtle assumptions about the characteristics and abilities of workers has been a major advance in sociological studies of work and employment.

Another area of inquiry that continues to be fruitful is the study of worker participation, consent, and resistance. Building on the labor process tradition, scholars working in this area examine the specific processes through which people do their jobs, focusing on how **technology** can change, deskill, and upgrade jobs, systems of control, and worker resistance to them, and managerial **ideologies** about their workers. At heart a Marxist tradition, labor process theorists argue that workers' interests and subjectivities are shaped in the process of work and often are at odds with those of management. Thus, workers often resist managerial directives when they watch with suspicion as engineers and managers try to simplify, speed up, and rationalize their jobs, or fragment their relations with co-workers. Workers respond by fashioning their own pace and organization of work. In other words, they work on their own terms even though they are constrained by management scrutiny and **methodology**. Michael Burawoy's classic study of male machine shop workers, *Manufactured Consent* (1979), showed how the machinists accepted production quotas set for them by management but achieved their quotas in ways that allowed them to play games and to use production methods that ran counter to management's design of the production process.

The focus on resistance, consent, and subjectivity has been applied to a variety of work settings, including factories around the world, offices, restaurants, and other service-delivery organizations. This field has yielded many insights to gender and race scholars who highlight how women and people of different race and ethnic backgrounds stand their ground and reject managers' attempts to use cultural stereotypes to gain control over them. Leslie Salzinger, in *Genders in Production* (2002), points out that in the contemporary global factory, transnational managers strive to construct multiple gendered subjectivities of male and female workers in order to meet their own production and professional objectives.

The rise of the global economy and competitive pressures facing corporations in industrialized nations have engendered a proliferation of new flexible work arrangements. Researchers use different terms, such as flexible specialization and **post-Fordism**, to capture these arrangements and have shown the variety of ways in which flexible schemes are deployed in unionized blue-collar settings. A major debate in these studies has been over whether new participative production arrangements give manufacturing workers genuine flexibility and autonomy in their jobs or whether they represent a form of co-optation of workers' shop-floor power.

However, the literature on post-Fordism and flexible specialization has suffered from the adoption of a model based primarily on the experiences of white male industrial workers who are unionized. Others argue that the salient question should not be about real empowerment versus co-optation with a narrow focus on industrial settings from which most unskilled workers of color, women, and immigrant workers historically have been excluded. Instead, they argue, sociologists should shift the focus to workers who are typically left out of the debate, low-skill, low-pay workers in a variety of settings. The mechanisms and meaning of empowerment can vary for diverse groups of people, depending on their particular class, ethno-racial, gender, and occupational experiences. The subject is particularly urgent because the low-skill, low-pay employment model, often associated with the disadvantageous employment conditions of a huge retailer like Walmart, has become pervasive and is steadily corroding the union model of employment, based on a living wage and benefits.

Work and employment undoubtedly will remain among the most vibrant areas of study in the discipline of sociology. As researchers continue to study the multi-faceted impact of current trends and identify new ones, they will be well positioned to provide critical insights about stratification, identity, and the potential for **social change** at the community, state, national, and global levels.   VICKI SMITH

working class
– see **social class**.

working-class conservatism
– see **conservatism**.

world religions
– see **religion**.

world-system theory
– see **world-systems analysis**.

world-systems analysis
This approach to macro-historical questions and **social structures** arose in the 1970s as a critique of the dominant liberal consensus of **modernization** and **development theory**, framed within the context of the structural-functionalist modernization school led by Harvard's **Talcott Parsons** and

others, which took as its object of analysis nation-states developing along roughly parallel lines. As has been pointed out, this was less the objective analysis of the world it pretended to be than what William Buxton, in his *Talcott Parsons and the Capitalist Nation-State* (1985), referred to as "political sociology as a strategic vocation." World-systems analysis is associated most especially with **Immanuel Wallerstein**, who was a Professor of Sociology at Columbia University during the student revolts of 1968 over the Vietnam War and related issues, and a key part of a group of faculty supportive of the students. In contrast to the modernization school, Wallerstein argues we are all participants rather than detached observers in the world-system, something no doubt the Columbia uprising helped teach him. Moreover, in contrast with scholarly parochialism, Wallerstein calls not for a multidisciplinary but instead a unidisciplinary approach to the study of social systems. Currently at Yale, Wallerstein was for decades a Distinguished Professor of Sociology at Binghampton University (part of the State University of New York), which became for a time the center of world-systems studies. There, Wallerstein and associate Terence Hopkins founded the Fernand Braudel Center for the Study of Economies, Historical Systems and Civilizations, along with its journal *Review*. Wallerstein and his colleagues – many of whom had taken up positions at various universities – formed an associated section of the American Sociological Association, the Political Economy of the World-System (PEWS), which also holds yearly conferences and publishes an annual set of papers. Since its arrival on the scene, world-systems analysis has influenced numerous other disciplines in the United States and abroad. Indeed, the work of Wallerstein and his colleagues has played a major role in the flourishing of what **Randall Collins** calls "the golden age of historical sociology."

Wallerstein's holistic vision, inspired by socialist ideals of **equality**, fraternity, and liberty – in sharp contrast to both the brutality of "actually existing socialism" under Stalinist regimes, and global **capitalism** – poses a stark challenge to social scientific views of development as largely an internal process of modernization. While development theory, including numerous Marxist variants, largely accepted the modernization approach, this was increasingly challenged by dependency theorists, who argued that development and underdevelopment were opposite sides of the same coin. Previous to the work of Wallerstein, studies of west European and Third World economic development took place largely in isolation from each other.

Rather than focusing on ostensibly modernizing separate **states**, Wallerstein instead posited that the proper unit of analysis for the study of historical social systems was the global division of **labor**. Transgressing as it did the boundaries of territorially based states, this division of labor reflected the substantive economic interdependence between different states and regions in what was a capitalist world-economy, which became the key unit of analysis for world-system scholars. Thus, world-systems analysis, drawing on intellectual sources as diverse as the French **Annales school** with its emphasis on geoeconomic regions, the German historical school, dependency theorists, and **Marxism**, posited the study of the whole, or totalities.

A prolific author, Wallerstein is best known for the three volumes of his *The Modern World-System* (1974, 1980, and 1989). In these and a series of other works, Wallerstein brought together two largely separate areas of inquiry, European economic history and studies of the Third World. Using this material, Wallerstein argued that between roughly 1450 and 1640 there emerged a new historical social system, a capitalist world-economy, the analysis of which was the key to understanding long-term, large-scale social change. Development and underdevelopment and state formation and deformation were analyzed as part of a single historical process. Whereas modernization theorists like **Barrington Moore, Jr.**, focused on industrialization, Wallerstein instead emphasized the centrality of agricultural capitalism in the early European world-economy. Wallerstein analyzed how, in the context of the crisis of **feudalism**, the emerging states of western Europe and their capitalist classes vastly expanded through overseas conquest and colonization.

Slowly but surely, a modern world-system emerged characterized by a global division of labor, within which there were formed a tripartite relational hierarchy of core, semi-peripheral, and peripheral zones, with surplus appropriation taking place between rich and poor states in a process of uneven development. These economic zones reflected differences in productive structures, **incomes**, and state strength and had variegated modes of labor control, largely free wage labor in the core and coerced forms of labor control in the periphery. With northwestern Europe emerging as the core, the former Habsburg Empire was relegated largely to the semi-periphery, while eastern Europe and the Americas formed peripheral zones, through informal empires or formal territorial conquest respectively. Typical of Wallerstein's work is his construction of analytical concepts through comparative analysis, for example his contrast of the notion of "world-empire" with a capitalist world-economy, or of the development of England as core and Poland as periphery in what Fernard Braudel (1902–85) termed "the long sixteenth century."

In addition, Wallerstein showed how racial-ethnic and ethno-national status hierarchies – including unequal forms of **citizenship** dividing the working class while simultaneously tying it to national state-corporate **elites** and their institutional structures – formed an integral part of the global division of labor. Historical capitalism, rather than expressing the free play of market forces, is instead seen as decisively shaped by the **power** of state actors. In their endless quest to accumulate capital – preferably through super-profits – capitalists aim to distort the **market** for their own monopolistic advantage. The quest for accumulation, within the ongoing context of interstate competition and class conflict between **labor** and capital, thus forms a crucial set of keys for understanding historical change. Yet while there is movement in and out of the core, semi-periphery, and periphery, it is relatively rare, and more importantly, does not change the overall structural **inequalities** inherent in the organization of the world capitalist system.

In the world-systems perspective, the capitalist world-economy is seen as subject to cycles of expansion and contraction and related processes of hegemonic rise and decline, which reflect some of its elementary contradictions as a historical system. In addition to these cycles, there are secular trends, including expansion, commodification, proletarianization, bureaucratization, and mechanization. Wallerstein and his colleagues also incorporated into their empirical accounts a host of factors, ranging from geography to ecology and epidemiology, though these are only weakly integrated into the overall analysis. Among the topics studied by world-systems scholars and those influenced by them are processes of incorporation, whereby new locales became integrated into the world-system, and commodity chains, a concept used to analyze the production and distribution of rewards from commodity production on a world scale, be it the movement of coffee from the Third World to its consumption in the core or the role of raw cotton in the formation of the English textile industry. Crucial here is the analysis of different productive regions, state structures, and **social classes** in a global perspective.

World-systems analysis spawned an enormous literature and has been drawn upon by people using different theoretical perspectives. Among world-systems scholars there has been a proliferation of views. Giovanni Arrighi – also a leading figure in **development theory** – is one scholar in particular who stands out. In a landmark book, *The Long Twentieth Century: Money, Power and the Origins of Our Times* (1994), Arrighi offered what many believe to be the most significant study of the *longue durée* of world capitalism to date. Borrowing from Braudel's *Civilization and Capitalism* (1984), Arrighi argued that capitalism unfolded through a succession of what he called systemic cycles of accumulation (SCAs), wherein governmental and business organizations promoted material and trade expansions of the world-economy until their limits were reached, at which point capitalists shifted their investments into finance. The obverse side of this expansion of financial activity was the reciprocal stimulus of military industrialization and high finance as part of the larger restructuring of the world-system that accompanies autumns of SCAs and the hegemonic structures of which they are a part. These transitions were accompanied by organizational revolution in the strategies and structures of accumulation and the reconstitution of the global system on new and enlarged social foundations.

Unlike Wallerstein, but like Braudel, Arrighi locates the origins of capitalism not in the territorial states of Europe, but instead in the Italian city-states of the fourteenth century. He traces the early alliance of Genoese capital and Spanish power that produced the great discoveries, before going on to analyze the Dutch, British, and United States **hegemonies** and related SCAs. In earlier works, Arrighi analyzed the way in which the world **labor movement** was split as part of the polarization of the world-economy into peripheral and core locales in the late nineteenth and early twentieth centuries. In his later work, Arrighi shows that the present-day resurgence of financial capital, the troubles of United States hegemony, and the rise of a new regional economic powerhouse in East Asia are more cyclical recurrence than purely novel developments, though the question of the future is left open.

A host of other world-system scholars have produced compelling scholarship in a wide variety of areas, such as Charles Bergquist's *Labor in Latin America: Comparative Essays on Chile, Argentina, Venezuela and Columbia* (1986), to name but one example. Bruce Cumings and a host of other world-system scholars have written some of the best work on United States foreign policy and development in East Asia. The contribution of world-systems analysts and their sympathizers to the literature on development and related issues is by now vast and includes work ranging from that of Dennis O'Hearn on Ireland to Paul Farmer on Haiti and global **public health**, Bernard Magubane on South Africa, Beverly Silver on global labor movements, Maria Mies on **patriarchy**, accumulation, and women, Antonio Benitez-Rojo on the Caribbean, and Walter Mignolo on Latin America. Christopher Chase-Dunn, another leading figure in the field, developed a much more structural Marxist version of world-systems analysis, collaborated with Tom Hall on historical studies of different world-systems, and recently has set up a new Institute for Research on World-Systems at the University of California, Riverside. As for Wallerstein, he has published recent work on topics as diverse as the structures of knowledge, anti-systemic movements, and **racism**, **sexism**, and **culture** in the ideological structure of the world-system.

World-systems analysis has been greeted with celebration and criticism over the years, from both left and right. Theorists from the bringing-the-state-back-in school of comparative historical sociology and others, including **Anthony Giddens**, **Michael Mann**, **Charles Tilly**, **Theda Skocpol**, and Aristide Zolberg, have criticized world-systems' alleged economic reductionism and a neglect of the role of state **violence** and geopolitics, along with a failure to incorporate theoretically the importance of the latter into the perspective. Others, notably Robert Brenner and Maurice Zeitlin, have attacked the supposed lack of attention to class forces and relations, as well as what is perceived to be a focus on circulation rather than production.

World-systems proponents have responded to these critiques in various ways. Some have devoted more attention to military–geopolitical processes, yet in ways that retain the focus on the relationship with processes of capital accumulation. Others have pointed out the great nuance and detail about state structure and class relations in the work of Wallerstein, while admitting the lack of integration of these details at times within the overall framework of analysis. In many ways, the focus of world-systems on the global system anticipated much of the globalization literature. The perspective has expanded its frontiers, akin to the world-systemic processes it studies.

Among the challenges facing the perspective in the twenty-first century will be to deal with some of the areas of relative neglect or weaknesses in its core analytical foundations, while building on its strengths by continuing to innovate, as it seeks to understand the world and contribute to its transformation in a more egalitarian, democratic, and peaceful direction as well.   THOMAS REIFER

Wrong, Dennis Hume (1923–)

Editor of *Social Research* (1962–4) and *Contemporary Sociology* (1972–4) and Professor of Sociology at New York University, Wrong published influential studies of **demography** in *Population and Society* (1961) and *Class Fertility Trends in Western Nations* (1980), but he is best known for *Power: Its Forms, Bases and Uses* (1988). Wrong was critical of **sociology** insofar as it had neglected **Sigmund Freud**, thereby accepting what Wrong called the oversocialized concept of man – the title of a famous article in 1961 in the *American Sociological Review*. His other publications include *Skeptical Sociology* (1977) and *The Problem of Order* (1994). In his essays on *The Modern Condition* (1998), he describes himself as a "full-fledged New York intellectual," serving at times on the editorial boards of *Dissent* and *Partisan Review*.   BRYAN S. TURNER

Wuthnow, Robert (1946–)

Gerhard R. Andlinger Professor of Sociology and Director of the Center for the Study of American Religion at Princeton University, Wuthnow has undertaken research on American **religion** in *The Restructuring of American Religion* (1988) and *God and Mammon in America* (1994), and cultural analysis in *Meaning and Moral Order: Explorations in Cultural Analysis* (1987). His current research interests are concerned with the moral meanings of the American Dream and with the moral basis of society in *Acts of Compassion: Caring for Others and Helping Ourselves* (1991) and *Sharing the Journey: Support Groups and America's New Quest for Community* (1994); and the place of spirituality in contemporary American society in *After Heaven: Spirituality in America Since the 1950s* (1998). His most recent publication is *Loose Connections: Joining Together in America's Fragmented Communities* (1998). He edited the *Encyclopedia of Politics and Religion* (1998). His work has consequently contributed to the importance of the study of **culture** in **sociological theory**.   BRYAN S. TURNER

Y

Young, Michael (Lord Young of Dartington) (1915–2002)

British sociologist, political activist, policy advocate in fields of **health**, **poverty** and **education**, also involved in founding the Consumers Association, the Open University, and other distance learning initiatives, Young set up the Institute of Community Studies, in 1952, from which he conducted most of his sociological work and policy research. One of its early publications was the influential book *Family and Kinship in East London*, written with Peter Willmott, published in 1957, an ethnographic study based on observation of, and **interviews** with, members of the working-class **community** of Bethnal Green. An early contribution to the genre of **community studies** in Britain, it subsequently provided a yardstick of traditional urban working-class life. Its sequel was a study of the ways of life of former residents who relocated to the suburbs (*Family and Class in a London Suburb*, 1960). Again with Willmott, he published also the much-quoted *The Symmetrical Family: A Study of Work and Leisure in the London Region* (1975). His satirical essay *The Rise of the Meritocracy* (1958) brought him greatest publicity for its social analysis in favor of equal opportunities in **education**. During the 1980s, besides more policy reports and public campaigning, he published work on understandings of **time**, including *The Metronomic Society: Natural Rhythms and Human Timetables* (1988). Young was a prime example of a sociologist oriented to the project of improving social conditions who also engaged in political activism and organizational innovation.   ALAN WARDE

youth

At a general level, youth refers to a transitional period in the lifecycle between **childhood** and adulthood. The social definition of youth in anthropology and sociology developed against an explanation of physiological changes and maturation in young people's bodies as simply determined by nature or biology. While recognizing the interplay between biological and social dimensions, sociologists stress that the category of youth is complexly shaped within institutional settings by sociocultural, economic, and political factors. Hence, the term youth has a diverse range of meanings, both historically within a society and across different societies. The social definition of youth as an important stratified **group** experiencing shared processes of **socialization** developed within the specific conditions of urban **industrial societies**.

In the period after World War II, these conditions within western societies included increasing **wealth** across the population and the accompanying rise in disposable **income**, increasing numbers staying on in **education**, and the development of ever-expanding consumer **markets**. Youth as a distinct age group came to be variously represented as: a **social problem**, teenage rebellion, male delinquency, and a barometer of **social change**. More recently, within conditions of late **modernity**, youth and youthfulness as increasingly mobile categories emerged as defining features of consumer-based **identities** for increasing numbers of people across age cohorts in the lifecycle. With youth and **popular culture** becoming disconnected, social behavior and cultural practices of **consumption** once exclusively associated with teenagers are displayed by people in their twenties and thirties, alongside active **lifestyles** among retired people.

The idea of youth **culture** suggests that young people organizing themselves within peer-groups have a distinct way of life from that of their parents. It is suggested that the development of their own **values**, use of **language**, and distinctive leisure activities involving dress codes and musical styles result in an age-specific social **identity**. At a more popular level, a **moral panic** is created with talk of a **war** between **generations**. Earlier sociological **explanations** debated the notion of the emergence of youth culture as a means of resolving problems in the parent culture or the wider society. Functionalists, as consensus theorists, stressed the integrative function of age-specific groups in contributing to the maintenance of the wider social system. In contrast, Marxists, as conflict theorists, challenging the unitary notion of a youth culture, emphasized the need to place youth **subcultures** within the class-based social relations of capitalist society, with its underlying economic conflict of interests. So, for example, the rise of skinheads was seen not as a result of shared age-specific problems but rather as a cultural response of resistance to collective experiences of a loss of traditional working-class **community**, a community that they were attempting to recover.

During the 1960s and 1970s, sociologists and media commentators with a more specific focus on youth subcultures, such as the skinheads, created a range of youth typologies. In the United Kingdom, such spectacular types originally emphasized social-class background with later additions including **gender**, ethnic, and sexual profiles, including mods, rockers, hippies, and rastas. The 1980s witnessed a shift in research away from the world of **leisure**, accompanied by media announcements of the death of subcultures. This was a response to Britain's economic decline and resulting mass youth **unemployment**, with the transition from school to the **labor market** as the new focus. At the same time, youth culture, which had become increasingly commodified, represented a major aspect of the cultural industries within rapidly changing consumer **capitalism**. More recent academic work has argued for both giving voice to young people and recognizing the independent explanatory role of culture, rather than assuming that the latter is necessarily responding to underlying economic and social causes. Since the mid-1990s, cultural theorists have radically questioned the adequacy of the above theories in making sense of contemporary young people's lives with the diversity of lifestyles and fragmentation of musical tastes.

Within the context of global changes in youth and youth subcultures, a range of contested accounts emerge, which have continuities and discontinuities with earlier approaches. Some theorists, suggesting that we have moved from subcultures to club cultures, have focused on modern-day spectacular types, including ravers and new age travelers, with accompanying up-to-date moral panics about drug-taking folk devils. Others emphasize that postmodern youth styles are circulating globally through new **technologies**, including **cyberspace**, cable and satellite TV, and third-generation mobile telephone platforms. Within this context young people are involved in a "pick-and-mix" consumer approach, blending styles of **fashion** and music. At the same time, young people appear to be crossing social and cultural boundaries, taking up and developing cultural styles that are disconnected from their own social and cultural locations. For example, violent girl **gangs** may adopt traditional masculine youth styles and young white people are celebrating North American "black rap" cultural forms.

"Youth movements" refer to young people's involvement in a range of political, religious, or social reforms. For example, a youth movement may be seen to emerge out of youth cultures. Young people's shared **values**, beliefs, and practices may be the source of an identifiable "movement." Such movements often appear threatening to society as they may operate as a "counterculture," an alternative to the dominant or regular forms of lifestyle. Another use of youth movement refers to the process where groups of young people use conventional or democratic channels to achieve representation or get their voices heard. These might include youth councils or youth forums. Finally, youth movements may be sanctioned, run by, or promoted by the **state**, **institutions**, or religious movements. For example, the Hitler Youth Movement in twentieth-century Germany sought to cultivate particular beliefs and values in young people. Other examples might be the Scouting movement or the Young Men's/Women's Christian Association.

MAIRTIN MAC-AN-GHAILL AND CHRIS HAYWOOD

youth culture

– see **youth**.

youth movements

– see **youth**.

Z

Zola, Irving (1935–1994)

A medical sociologist, Zola was one of the founders of the interdisciplinary field of disability studies and an activist in the disability **rights** and self-help movements in the United States. His Harvard education opened the world for him but he never forgot his working-class roots, reflected in his interests in gambling, juvenile delinquency, and the downtrodden. His early experience with polio and later involvement in a serious automobile accident left him with orthopedic and neurological impairments which resulted in a **disability** affecting his mobility.

Zola's dissertation explored differential perceptions of pain and differences in behavior when seeking medical help among three diverse cultural groups in Boston: Irish Americans, Italians, and Jews. His later work highlighted the subjective experience of disability, being an embodied subject, and the universality of disability. He was Chair of the Medical Sociology Section of the American Sociological Association, founder of the *Disabilities Studies Quarterly*, which publishes articles, personal statements, book and film reviews, and news of interest to the academic disability **community**, and a key member of the disability movement responsible for the Americans with Disabilities Act of 1990 and the emergence of disability studies as a field. He was one of the moving forces in establishing the Society for Disability Studies. Zola was a scholar who contributed to **symbolic interactionism**, incorporating a critical component of **pragmatism** into his research by combining academic research and activism. He was, on the one hand, a member of the National Academy of Sciences committee on disability, organized to identify the critical research issues in need of funding, and, on the other, an activist who could be seen demonstrating on the steps of a court house about accessibility.

His principal works include "Medicine as an Institution of Social Control" (1972, *Sociological Review*) *Missing Pieces* (1982), and "Bringing our Bodies and Ourselves back in" (1991, *Journal of Health & Social Behavior*).

GARY L. ALBRECHT AND MARK SHERRY